University Casebook Series

June, 1990

ACCOUNTING AND THE LAW, Fourth Edition (1978), with Problems Pamphlet (Successor to Dohr, Phillips, Thompson & Warren)

George C. Thompson, Professor, Columbia University Graduate School of Business.

Robert Whitman, Professor of Law, University of Connecticut.

Ellis L. Phillips, Jr., Member of the New York Bar.

William C. Warren, Professor of Law Emeritus, Columbia University.

ACCOUNTING FOR LAWYERS, MATERIALS ON (1980)

David R. Herwitz, Professor of Law, Harvard University.

ADMINISTRATIVE LAW, Eighth Edition (1987), with 1989 Case Supplement and 1983 Problems Supplement (Supplement edited in association with Paul R. Verkuil, Dean and Professor of Law, Tulane University)

Walter Gellhorn, University Professor Emeritus, Columbia University.

Clark Byse, Professor of Law, Harvard University.

Peter L. Strauss, Professor of Law, Columbia University.

Todd D. Rakoff, Professor of Law, Harvard University.

Roy A. Schotland, Professor of Law, Georgetown University.

ADMIRALTY, Third Edition (1987), with Statute and Rule Supplement

Jo Desha Lucas, Professor of Law, University of Chicago.

ADVOCACY, see also Lawyering Process

AGENCY, see also Enterprise Organization

AGENCY—PARTNERSHIPS, Fourth Edition (1987)

Abridgement from Conard, Knauss & Siegel's Enterprise Organization, Fourth Edition.

AGENCY AND PARTNERSHIPS (1987)

Melvin A. Eisenberg, Professor of Law, University of California, Berkeley.

ANTITRUST: FREE ENTERPRISE AND ECONOMIC ORGANIZATION, Sixth Edition (1983), with 1983 Problems in Antitrust Supplement and 1989 Case Supplement

Louis B. Schwartz, Professor of Law, University of Pennsylvania.

John J. Flynn, Professor of Law, University of Utah.

Harry First, Professor of Law, New York University.

BANKRUPTCY, Second Edition (1989)

Robert L. Jordan, Professor of Law, University of California, Los Angeles.

William D. Warren, Professor of Law, University of California, Los Angeles.

BANKRUPTCY AND DEBTOR–CREDITOR LAW, Second Edition (1988)

Theodore Eisenberg, Professor of Law, Cornell University.

BUSINESS CRIME (1990)

Harry First, Professor of Law, New York University.

BUSINESS ORGANIZATION, see also Enterprise Organization

BUSINESS PLANNING, Temporary Second Edition (1984)

David R. Herwitz, Professor of Law, Harvard University.

BUSINESS TORTS (1972)

Milton Handler, Professor of Law Emeritus, Columbia University.

CHILDREN IN THE LEGAL SYSTEM (1983) with 1988 Supplement

Walter Wadlington, Professor of Law, University of Virginia.
Charles H. Whitebread, Professor of Law, University of Southern California.
Samuel Davis, Professor of Law, University of Georgia.

CIVIL PROCEDURE, see Procedure

CIVIL RIGHTS ACTIONS (1988), with 1989 Supplement

Peter W. Low, Professor of Law, University of Virginia.
John C. Jeffries, Jr., Professor of Law, University of Virginia.

CLINIC, see also Lawyering Process

COMMERCIAL AND DEBTOR–CREDITOR LAW: SELECTED STATUTES, 1990 EDITION

COMMERCIAL LAW, Second Edition (1987)

Robert L. Jordan, Professor of Law, University of California, Los Angeles.
William D. Warren, Professor of Law, University of California, Los Angeles.

COMMERCIAL LAW, Fourth Edition (1985)

E. Allan Farnsworth, Professor of Law, Columbia University.
John Honnold, Professor of Law, University of Pennsylvania.

COMMERCIAL PAPER, Third Edition (1984)

E. Allan Farnsworth, Professor of Law, Columbia University.

COMMERCIAL PAPER, Second Edition (1987) (Reprinted from COMMERCIAL LAW, Second Edition (1987))

Robert L. Jordan, Professor of Law, University of California, Los Angeles.
William D. Warren, Professor of Law, University of California, Los Angeles.

COMMERCIAL PAPER AND BANK DEPOSITS AND COLLECTIONS (1967), with Statutory Supplement

William D. Hawkland, Professor of Law, University of Illinois.

COMMERCIAL TRANSACTIONS—Principles and Policies (1982)

Alan Schwartz, Professor of Law, University of Southern California.
Robert E. Scott, Professor of Law, University of Virginia.

COMPARATIVE LAW, Fifth Edition (1988)

Rudolf B. Schlesinger, Professor of Law, Hastings College of the Law.
Hans W. Baade, Professor of Law, University of Texas.
Mirjan P. Damaska, Professor of Law, Yale Law School.
Peter E. Herzog, Professor of Law, Syracuse University.

COMPETITIVE PROCESS, LEGAL REGULATION OF THE, Fourth Edition (1990), with 1989 Selected Statutes Supplement

Edmund W. Kitch, Professor of Law, University of Virginia.
Harvey S. Perlman, Dean of the Law School, University of Nebraska.

CONFLICT OF LAWS, Ninth Edition (1990)

Willis L. M. Reese, Professor of Law, Columbia University.
Maurice Rosenberg, Professor of Law, Columbia University.
Peter Hay, Professor of Law, University of Illinois.

CONSTITUTIONAL LAW, Eighth Edition (1989), with 1989 Case Supplement

Edward L. Barrett, Jr., Professor of Law, University of California, Davis.
William Cohen, Professor of Law, Stanford University.
Jonathan D. Varat, Professor of Law, University of California, Los Angeles.

CONSTITUTIONAL LAW, CIVIL LIBERTY AND INDIVIDUAL RIGHTS, Second Edition (1982), with 1989 Supplement

William Cohen, Professor of Law, Stanford University.
John Kaplan, Professor of Law, Stanford University.

CONSTITUTIONAL LAW, Eleventh Edition (1985), with 1989 Supplement (Supplement edited in association with Frederick F. Schauer, Professor of Law, University of Michigan)

Gerald Gunther, Professor of Law, Stanford University.

CONSTITUTIONAL LAW, INDIVIDUAL RIGHTS IN, Fourth Edition (1986), (Reprinted from CONSTITUTIONAL LAW, Eleventh Edition), with 1989 Supplement (Supplement edited in association with Frederick F. Schauer, Professor of Law, University of Michigan)

Gerald Gunther, Professor of Law, Stanford University.

CONSUMER TRANSACTIONS (1983), with Selected Statutes and Regulations Supplement and 1987 Case Supplement

Michael M. Greenfield, Professor of Law, Washington University.

CONTRACT LAW AND ITS APPLICATION, Fourth Edition (1988)

Arthur Rosett, Professor of Law, University of California, Los Angeles.

CONTRACT LAW, STUDIES IN, Third Edition (1984)

Edward J. Murphy, Professor of Law, University of Notre Dame.
Richard E. Speidel, Professor of Law, Northwestern University.

CONTRACTS, Fifth Edition (1987)

John P. Dawson, late Professor of Law, Harvard University.
William Burnett Harvey, Professor of Law and Political Science, Boston University.
Stanley D. Henderson, Professor of Law, University of Virginia.

CONTRACTS, Fourth Edition (1988)

E. Allan Farnsworth, Professor of Law, Columbia University.
William F. Young, Professor of Law, Columbia University.

CONTRACTS, Selections on (statutory materials) (1988)

CONTRACTS, Second Edition (1978), with Statutory and Administrative Law Supplement (1978)

Ian R. Macneil, Professor of Law, Cornell University.

UNIVERSITY CASEBOOK SERIES—Continued

COPYRIGHT, PATENTS AND TRADEMARKS, see also Competitive Process; see also Selected Statutes and International Agreements

COPYRIGHT, PATENT, TRADEMARK AND RELATED STATE DOCTRINES, Third Edition (1990), with 1989 Selected Statutes Supplement and 1981 Problem Supplement

Paul Goldstein, Professor of Law, Stanford University.

COPYRIGHT, Unfair Competition, and Other Topics Bearing on the Protection of Literary, Musical, and Artistic Works, Fifth Edition (1990), with 1990 Statutory Supplement

Ralph S. Brown, Jr., Professor of Law, Yale University.
Robert C. Denicola, Professor of Law, University of Nebraska.

CORPORATE ACQUISITIONS, The Law and Finance of (1986), with 1989 Supplement

Ronald J. Gilson, Professor of Law, Stanford University.

CORPORATE FINANCE, Third Edition (1987)

Victor Brudney, Professor of Law, Harvard University.
Marvin A. Chirelstein, Professor of Law, Columbia University.

CORPORATION LAW, BASIC, Third Edition (1989), with Documentary Supplement

Detlev F. Vagts, Professor of Law, Harvard University.

CORPORATIONS, see also Enterprise Organization

CORPORATIONS, Sixth Edition—Concise (1988), with Statutory Supplement (1990)

William L. Cary, late Professor of Law, Columbia University.
Melvin Aron Eisenberg, Professor of Law, University of California, Berkeley.

CORPORATIONS, Sixth Edition—Unabridged (1988), with Statutory Supplement (1990)

William L. Cary, late Professor of Law, Columbia University.
Melvin Aron Eisenberg, Professor of Law, University of California, Berkeley.

CORPORATIONS AND BUSINESS ASSOCIATIONS—STATUTES, RULES, AND FORMS (1990)

CORPORATIONS COURSE GAME PLAN (1975)

David R. Herwitz, Professor of Law, Harvard University.

CORRECTIONS, SEE SENTENCING

CREDITORS' RIGHTS, see also Debtor-Creditor Law

CRIMINAL JUSTICE ADMINISTRATION, Third Edition (1986), with 1989 Case Supplement

Frank W. Miller, Professor of Law, Washington University.
Robert O. Dawson, Professor of Law, University of Texas.
George E. Dix, Professor of Law, University of Texas.
Raymond I. Parnas, Professor of Law, University of California, Davis.

CRIMINAL LAW, Fourth Edition (1987)

Fred E. Inbau, Professor of Law Emeritus, Northwestern University.
Andre A. Moenssens, Professor of Law, University of Richmond.
James R. Thompson, Professor of Law Emeritus, Northwestern University.

CRIMINAL LAW AND APPROACHES TO THE STUDY OF LAW (1986)

John M. Brumbaugh, Professor of Law, University of Maryland.

CRIMINAL LAW, Second Edition (1986)

Peter W. Low, Professor of Law, University of Virginia.
John C. Jeffries, Jr., Professor of Law, University of Virginia.
Richard C. Bonnie, Professor of Law, University of Virginia.

CRIMINAL LAW, Fourth Edition (1986)

Lloyd L. Weinreb, Professor of Law, Harvard University.

CRIMINAL LAW AND PROCEDURE, Seventh Edition (1989)

Ronald N. Boyce, Professor of Law, University of Utah.
Rollin M. Perkins, Professor of Law Emeritus, University of California, Hastings
College of the Law.

CRIMINAL PROCEDURE, Third Edition (1987), with 1989 Supplement

James B. Haddad, Professor of Law, Northwestern University.
James B. Zagel, Chief, Criminal Justice Division, Office of Attorney General of
Illinois.
Gary L. Starkman, Assistant U. S. Attorney, Northern District of Illinois.
William J. Bauer, Chief Judge of the U.S. Court of Appeals, Seventh Circuit.

CRIMINAL PROCESS, Fourth Edition (1987), with 1989 Supplement

Lloyd L. Weinreb, Professor of Law, Harvard University.

DAMAGES, Second Edition (1952)

Charles T. McCormick, late Professor of Law, University of Texas.
William F. Fritz, late Professor of Law, University of Texas.

DECEDENTS' ESTATES AND TRUSTS, Seventh Edition (1988)

John Ritchie, late Professor of Law, University of Virginia.
Neill H. Alford, Jr., Professor of Law, University of Virginia.
Richard W. Effland, late Professor of Law, Arizona State University.

DISPUTE RESOLUTION, Processes of (1989)

John S. Murray, President and Executive Director of The Conflict Clinic, Inc.,
George Mason University.
Alan Scott Rau, Professor of Law, University of Texas.
Edward F. Sherman, Professor of Law, University of Texas.

DOMESTIC RELATIONS, see also Family Law

DOMESTIC RELATIONS, Second Edition (1990)

Walter Wadlington, Professor of Law, University of Virginia.

EMPLOYMENT DISCRIMINATION, Second Edition (1987), with 1989 Supplement

Joel W. Friedman, Professor of Law, Tulane University.
George M. Strickler, Professor of Law, Tulane University.

EMPLOYMENT LAW (1987), with 1987 Statutory Supplement and 1989 Case Supplement

Mark A. Rothstein, Professor of Law, University of Houston.
Andria S. Knapp, Adjunct Professor of Law, University of California, Hastings
College of Law.
Lance Liebman, Professor of Law, Harvard University.

UNIVERSITY CASEBOOK SERIES—Continued

ENERGY LAW (1983) with 1986 Case Supplement

Donald N. Zillman, Professor of Law, University of Utah.
Laurence Lattman, Dean of Mines and Engineering, University of Utah.

ENTERPRISE ORGANIZATION, Fourth Edition (1987), with 1987 Corporation and Partnership Statutes, Rules and Forms Supplement

Alfred F. Conard, Professor of Law, University of Michigan.
Robert L. Knauss, Dean of the Law School, University of Houston.
Stanley Siegel, Professor of Law, University of California, Los Angeles.

ENVIRONMENTAL POLICY LAW 1985 Edition, with 1985 Problems Supplement (Supplement in association with Ronald H. Rosenberg, Professor of Law, College of William and Mary)

Thomas J. Schoenbaum, Professor of Law, University of Georgia.

EQUITY, see also Remedies

EQUITY, RESTITUTION AND DAMAGES, Second Edition (1974)

Robert Childres, late Professor of Law, Northwestern University.
William F. Johnson, Jr., Professor of Law, New York University.

ESTATE PLANNING, Second Edition (1982), with 1985 Case, Text and Documentary Supplement

David Westfall, Professor of Law, Harvard University.

ETHICS, see Legal Profession, Professional Responsibility, and Social Responsibilities

ETHICS OF LAWYERING, THE LAW AND (1990)

Geoffrey C. Hazard, Jr., Professor of Law, Yale University.
Susan P. Koniak, Professor of Law, University of Pittsburgh.

ETHICS AND PROFESSIONAL RESPONSIBILITY (1981) (Reprinted from THE LAWYERING PROCESS)

Gary Bellow, Professor of Law, Harvard University.
Bea Moulton, Legal Services Corporation.

EVIDENCE, Sixth Edition (1988 Reprint)

John Kaplan, Professor of Law, Stanford University.
Jon R. Waltz, Professor of Law, Northwestern University.

EVIDENCE, Eighth Edition (1988), with Rules, Statute and Case Supplement (1989)

Jack B. Weinstein, Chief Judge, United States District Court.
John H. Mansfield, Professor of Law, Harvard University.
Norman Abrams, Professor of Law, University of California, Los Angeles.
Margaret Berger, Professor of Law, Brooklyn Law School.

FAMILY LAW, see also Domestic Relations

FAMILY LAW Second Edition (1985), with 1988 Supplement

Judith C. Areen, Professor of Law, Georgetown University.

FAMILY LAW AND CHILDREN IN THE LEGAL SYSTEM, STATUTORY MATERIALS (1981)

Walter Wadlington, Professor of Law, University of Virginia.

UNIVERSITY CASEBOOK SERIES—Continued

FEDERAL COURTS, Eighth Edition (1988), with 1989 Supplement

Charles T. McCormick, late Professor of Law, University of Texas.
James H. Chadbourn, late Professor of Law, Harvard University.
Charles Alan Wright, Professor of Law, University of Texas, Austin.

FEDERAL COURTS AND THE FEDERAL SYSTEM, Hart and Wechsler's Third Edition (1988), with 1989 Case Supplement, and the Judicial Code and Rules of Procedure in the Federal Courts (1989)

Paul M. Bator, Professor of Law, University of Chicago.
Daniel J. Meltzer, Professor of Law, Harvard University.
Paul J. Mishkin, Professor of Law, University of California, Berkeley.
David L. Shapiro, Professor of Law, Harvard University.

FEDERAL COURTS AND THE LAW OF FEDERAL–STATE RELATIONS, Second Edition (1989), with 1989 Supplement

Peter W. Low, Professor of Law, University of Virginia.
John C. Jeffries, Jr., Professor of Law, University of Virginia.

FEDERAL PUBLIC LAND AND RESOURCES LAW, Second Edition (1987), with 1990 Case Supplement and 1990 Statutory Supplement

George C. Coggins, Professor of Law, University of Kansas.
Charles F. Wilkinson, Professor of Law, University of Oregon.

FEDERAL RULES OF CIVIL PROCEDURE and Selected Other Procedural Provisions, 1990 Edition

FEDERAL TAXATION, see Taxation

FOOD AND DRUG LAW (1980), with Statutory Supplement

Richard A. Merrill, Dean of the School of Law, University of Virginia.
Peter Barton Hutt, Esq.

FUTURE INTERESTS (1958)

Philip Mechem, late Professor of Law Emeritus, University of Pennsylvania.

FUTURE INTERESTS (1970)

Howard R. Williams, Professor of Law, Stanford University.

FUTURE INTERESTS AND ESTATE PLANNING (1961), with 1962 Supplement

W. Barton Leach, late Professor of Law, Harvard University.
James K. Logan, formerly Dean of the Law School, University of Kansas.

GOVERNMENT CONTRACTS, FEDERAL, Successor Edition (1985), with 1989 Supplement

John W. Whelan, Professor of Law, Hastings College of the Law.

GOVERNMENT REGULATION: FREE ENTERPRISE AND ECONOMIC ORGANIZATION, Sixth Edition (1985)

Louis B. Schwartz, Professor of Law, Hastings College of the Law.
John J. Flynn, Professor of Law, University of Utah.
Harry First, Professor of Law, New York University.

HEALTH CARE LAW AND POLICY (1988)

Clark C. Havighurst, Professor of Law, Duke University.

HINCKLEY, JOHN W., JR., TRIAL OF: A Case Study of the Insanity Defense (1986)

Peter W. Low, Professor of Law, University of Virginia.
John C. Jeffries, Jr., Professor of Law, University of Virginia.
Richard C. Bonnie, Professor of Law, University of Virginia.

INJUNCTIONS, Second Edition (1984)

Owen M. Fiss, Professor of Law, Yale University.
Doug Rendleman, Professor of Law, College of William and Mary.

INSTITUTIONAL INVESTORS, (1978)

David L. Ratner, Professor of Law, Cornell University.

INSURANCE, Second Edition (1985)

William F. Young, Professor of Law, Columbia University.
Eric M. Holmes, Professor of Law, University of Georgia.

INSURANCE LAW AND REGULATION (1990)

Kenneth S. Abraham, University of Virginia.

INTERNATIONAL LAW, see also Transnational Legal Problems, Transnational Business Problems, and United Nations Law

INTERNATIONAL LAW IN CONTEMPORARY PERSPECTIVE (1981), with Essay Supplement

Myres S. McDougal, Professor of Law, Yale University.
W. Michael Reisman, Professor of Law, Yale University.

INTERNATIONAL LEGAL SYSTEM, Third Edition (1988), with Documentary Supplement

Joseph Modeste Sweeney, Professor of Law, University of California, Hastings.
Covey T. Oliver, Professor of Law, University of Pennsylvania.
Noyes E. Leech, Professor of Law Emeritus, University of Pennsylvania.

INTRODUCTION TO LAW, see also Legal Method, On Law in Courts, and Dynamics of American Law

INTRODUCTION TO THE STUDY OF LAW (1970)

E. Wayne Thode, late Professor of Law, University of Utah.
Leon Lebowitz, Professor of Law, University of Texas.
Lester J. Mazor, Professor of Law, University of Utah.

JUDICIAL CODE and Rules of Procedure in the Federal Courts, Students' Edition, 1989 Revision

Daniel J. Meltzer, Professor of Law, Harvard University.
David L. Shapiro, Professor of Law, Harvard University.

JURISPRUDENCE (Temporary Edition Hardbound) (1949)

Lon L. Fuller, late Professor of Law, Harvard University.

JUVENILE, see also Children

JUVENILE JUSTICE PROCESS, Third Edition (1985)

Frank W. Miller, Professor of Law, Washington University.
Robert O. Dawson, Professor of Law, University of Texas.
George E. Dix, Professor of Law, University of Texas.
Raymond I. Parnas, Professor of Law, University of California, Davis.

LABOR LAW, Tenth Edition (1986), with 1989 Case Supplement and 1986 Statutory Supplement

Archibald Cox, Professor of Law, Harvard University.
Derek C. Bok, President, Harvard University.
Robert A. Gorman, Professor of Law, University of Pennsylvania.

LABOR LAW, Second Edition (1982), with Statutory Supplement

Clyde W. Summers, Professor of Law, University of Pennsylvania.
Harry H. Wellington, Dean of the Law School, Yale University.
Alan Hyde, Professor of Law, Rutgers University.

LAND FINANCING, Third Edition (1985)

The late Norman Penney, Professor of Law, Cornell University.
Richard F. Broude, Member of the California Bar.
Roger Cunningham, Professor of Law, University of Michigan.

LAW AND MEDICINE (1980)

Walter Wadlington, Professor of Law and Professor of Legal Medicine, University of Virginia.
Jon R. Waltz, Professor of Law, Northwestern University.
Roger B. Dworkin, Professor of Law, Indiana University, and Professor of Biomedical History, University of Washington.

LAW, LANGUAGE AND ETHICS (1972)

William R. Bishin, Professor of Law, University of Southern California.
Christopher D. Stone, Professor of Law, University of Southern California.

LAW, SCIENCE AND MEDICINE (1984), with 1989 Supplement

Judith C. Areen, Professor of Law, Georgetown University.
Patricia A. King, Professor of Law, Georgetown University.
Steven P. Goldberg, Professor of Law, Georgetown University.
Alexander M. Capron, Professor of Law, University of Southern California.

LAWYERING PROCESS (1978), with Civil Problem Supplement and Criminal Problem Supplement

Gary Bellow, Professor of Law, Harvard University.
Bea Moulton, Professor of Law, Arizona State University.

LEGAL METHOD (1980)

Harry W. Jones, Professor of Law Emeritus, Columbia University.
John M. Kernochan, Professor of Law, Columbia University.
Arthur W. Murphy, Professor of Law, Columbia University.

LEGAL METHODS (1969)

Robert N. Covington, Professor of Law, Vanderbilt University.
E. Blythe Stason, late Professor of Law, Vanderbilt University.
John W. Wade, Professor of Law, Vanderbilt University.
Elliott E. Cheatham, late Professor of Law, Vanderbilt University.
Theodore A. Smedley, Professor of Law, Vanderbilt University.

LEGAL PROFESSION, THE, Responsibility and Regulation, Second Edition (1988)

Geoffrey C. Hazard, Jr., Professor of Law, Yale University.
Deborah L. Rhode, Professor of Law, Stanford University.

UNIVERSITY CASEBOOK SERIES—Continued

LEGISLATION, Fourth Edition (1982) (by Fordham)

Horace E. Read, late Vice President, Dalhousie University.
John W. MacDonald, Professor of Law Emeritus, Cornell Law School.
Jefferson B. Fordham, Professor of Law, University of Utah.
William J. Pierce, Professor of Law, University of Michigan.

LEGISLATIVE AND ADMINISTRATIVE PROCESSES, Second Edition (1981)

Hans A. Linde, Judge, Supreme Court of Oregon.
George Bunn, Professor of Law, University of Wisconsin.
Fredericka Paff, Professor of Law, University of Wisconsin.
W. Lawrence Church, Professor of Law, University of Wisconsin.

LOCAL GOVERNMENT LAW, Second Revised Edition (1986)

Jefferson B. Fordham, Professor of Law, University of Utah.

MASS MEDIA LAW, Fourth Edition (1990)

Marc A. Franklin, Professor of Law, Stanford University.
David A. Anderson, Professor of Law, University of Texas.

MUNICIPAL CORPORATIONS, see Local Government Law

NEGOTIABLE INSTRUMENTS, see Commercial Paper

NEGOTIATION (1981) (Reprinted from THE LAWYERING PROCESS)

Gary Bellow, Professor of Law, Harvard Law School.
Bea Moulton, Legal Services Corporation.

NEW YORK PRACTICE, Fourth Edition (1978)

Herbert Peterfreund, Professor of Law, New York University.
Joseph M. McLaughlin, Dean of the Law School, Fordham University.

OIL AND GAS, Fifth Edition (1987)

Howard R. Williams, Professor of Law, Stanford University.
Richard C. Maxwell, Professor of Law, University of California, Los Angeles.
Charles J. Meyers, late Dean of the Law School, Stanford University.
Stephen F. Williams, Judge of the United States Court of Appeals.

ON LAW IN COURTS (1965)

Paul J. Mishkin, Professor of Law, University of California, Berkeley.
Clarence Morris, Professor of Law Emeritus, University of Pennsylvania.

PENSION AND EMPLOYEE BENEFIT LAW (1990)

John H. Langbein, Professor of Law, University of Chicago.
Bruce A. Wolk, Professor of Law, University of California, Davis.

PLEADING AND PROCEDURE, see Procedure, Civil

POLICE FUNCTION, Fourth Edition (1986), with 1989 Case Supplement

Reprint of Chapters 1–10 of Miller, Dawson, Dix and Parnas's CRIMINAL
JUSTICE ADMINISTRATION, Third Edition.

**PREPARING AND PRESENTING THE CASE (1981) (Reprinted from THE LAW-
YERING PROCESS)**

Gary Bellow, Professor of Law, Harvard Law School.
Bea Moulton, Legal Services Corporation.

UNIVERSITY CASEBOOK SERIES—Continued

PROCEDURE (1988), with Procedure Supplement (1989)

Robert M. Cover, late Professor of Law, Yale Law School.
Owen M. Fiss, Professor of Law, Yale Law School.
Judith Resnik, Professor of Law, University of Southern California Law Center.

PROCEDURE—CIVIL PROCEDURE, Second Edition (1974), with 1979 Supplement

The late James H. Chadbourn, Professor of Law, Harvard University.
A. Leo Levin, Professor of Law, University of Pennsylvania.
Philip Shuchman, Professor of Law, Cornell University.

PROCEDURE—CIVIL PROCEDURE, Sixth Edition (1990)

Richard H. Field, late Professor of Law, Harvard University.
Benjamin Kaplan, Professor of Law Emeritus, Harvard University.
Kevin M. Clermont, Professor of Law, Cornell University.

PROCEDURE—CIVIL PROCEDURE, Fifth Edition (1990)

Maurice Rosenberg, Professor of Law, Columbia University.
Hans Smit, Professor of Law, Columbia University.
Rochelle C. Dreyfuss, Professor of Law, New York University.

PROCEDURE—PLEADING AND PROCEDURE: State and Federal, Sixth Edition (1989)

David W. Louisell, late Professor of Law, University of California, Berkeley.
Geoffrey C. Hazard, Jr., Professor of Law, Yale University.
Colin C. Tait, Professor of Law, University of Connecticut.

PROCEDURE—FEDERAL RULES OF CIVIL PROCEDURE, 1990 Edition

PRODUCTS LIABILITY AND SAFETY, Second Edition, (1989), with 1989 Statutory Supplement

W. Page Keeton, Professor of Law, University of Texas.
David G. Owen, Professor of Law, University of South Carolina.
John E. Montgomery, Professor of Law, University of South Carolina.
Michael D. Green, Professor of Law, University of Iowa

PROFESSIONAL RESPONSIBILITY, Fourth Edition (1987), with 1990 Selected National Standards Supplement

Thomas D. Morgan, Dean of the Law School, Emory University.
Ronald D. Rotunda, Professor of Law, University of Illinois.

PROPERTY, Sixth Edition (1990)

John E. Cribbet, Professor of Law, University of Illinois.
Corwin W. Johnson, Professor of Law, University of Texas.
Roger W. Findley, Professor of Law, University of Illinois.
Ernest E. Smith, Professor of Law, University of Texas.

PROPERTY—PERSONAL (1953)

S. Kenneth Skolfield, late Professor of Law Emeritus, Boston University.

PROPERTY—PERSONAL, Third Edition (1954)

Everett Fraser, late Dean of the Law School Emeritus, University of Minnesota.
Third Edition by Charles W. Taintor, late Professor of Law, University of Pittsburgh.

PROPERTY—INTRODUCTION, TO REAL PROPERTY, Third Edition (1954)

Everett Fraser, late Dean of the Law School Emeritus, University of Minnesota.

UNIVERSITY CASEBOOK SERIES—Continued

SECURITIES REGULATION, Second Edition (1988), with Statute, Rule and Form Supplement (1988)

Larry D. Soderquist, Professor of Law, Vanderbilt University.

SECURITY INTERESTS IN PERSONAL PROPERTY, Second Edition (1987)

Douglas G. Baird, Professor of Law, University of Chicago.
Thomas H. Jackson, Professor of Law, Harvard University.

SECURITY INTERESTS IN PERSONAL PROPERTY (1985) (Reprinted from Sales and Sales Financing, Fifth Edition)

John Honnold, Professor of Law, University of Pennsylvania.

SOCIAL RESPONSIBILITIES OF LAWYERS, Case Studies (1988)

Philip B. Heymann, Professor of Law, Harvard University.
Lance Liebman, Professor of Law, Harvard University.

SOCIAL SCIENCE IN LAW, Second Edition (1990)

John Monahan, Professor of Law, University of Virginia.
Laurens Walker, Professor of Law, University of Virginia.

TAXATION, FEDERAL INCOME (1989)

Stephen B. Cohen, Professor of Law, Georgetown University

TAXATION, FEDERAL INCOME, Second Edition (1988), with 1989 Supplement

Michael J. Graetz, Professor of Law, Yale University.

TAXATION, FEDERAL INCOME, Sixth Edition (1987)

James J. Freeland, Professor of Law, University of Florida.
Stephen A. Lind, Professor of Law, University of Florida and University of California, Hastings.
Richard B. Stephens, late Professor of Law Emeritus, University of Florida.

TAXATION, FEDERAL INCOME, Successor Edition (1986), with 1989 Legislative Supplement

Stanley S. Surrey, late Professor of Law, Harvard University.
Paul R. McDaniel, Professor of Law, Boston College.
Hugh J. Ault, Professor of Law, Boston College.
Stanley A. Koppelman, Professor of Law, Boston University.

TAXATION, FEDERAL INCOME, VOLUME II, Taxation of Partnerships and Corporations, Second Edition (1980), with 1989 Legislative Supplement

Stanley S. Surrey, late Professor of Law, Harvard University.
William C. Warren, Professor of Law Emeritus, Columbia University.
Paul R. McDaniel, Professor of Law, Boston College.
Hugh J. Ault, Professor of Law, Boston College.

TAXATION, FEDERAL INCOME, OIL AND GAS, NATURAL RESOURCES TRANSACTIONS (1990)

Peter C. Maxfield, Professor of Law, University of Wyoming.
James L. Houghton, CPA, Partner, Ernst and Young.
James R. Gaar, CPA, Partner, Ernst and Young.

TAXATION, FEDERAL WEALTH TRANSFER, Successor Edition (1987)

Stanley S. Surrey, late Professor of Law, Harvard University.
Paul R. McDaniel, Professor of Law, Boston College.
Harry L. Gutman, Professor of Law, University of Pennsylvania.

TAXATION, FUNDAMENTALS OF CORPORATE, Second Edition (1987), with 1989 Supplement

Stephen A. Lind, Professor of Law, University of Florida and University of California, Hastings.
Stephen Schwarz, Professor of Law, University of California, Hastings.
Daniel J. Lathrope, Professor of Law, University of California, Hastings.
Joshua Rosenberg, Professor of Law, University of San Francisco.

TAXATION, FUNDAMENTALS OF PARTNERSHIP, Second Edition (1988)

Stephen A. Lind, Professor of Law, University of Florida and University of California, Hastings.
Stephen Schwarz, Professor of Law, University of California, Hastings.
Daniel J. Lathrope, Professor of Law, University of California, Hastings.
Joshua Rosenberg, Professor of Law, University of San Francisco.

TAXATION, PROBLEMS IN THE FEDERAL INCOME TAXATION OF PARTNERSHIPS AND CORPORATIONS, Second Edition (1986)

Norton L. Steuben, Professor of Law, University of Colorado.
William J. Turnier, Professor of Law, University of North Carolina.

TAXATION, PROBLEMS IN THE FUNDAMENTALS OF FEDERAL INCOME, Second Edition (1985)

Norton L. Steuben, Professor of Law, University of Colorado.
William J. Turnier, Professor of Law, University of North Carolina.

TORT LAW AND ALTERNATIVES, Fourth Edition (1987)

Marc A. Franklin, Professor of Law, Stanford University.
Robert L. Rabin, Professor of Law, Stanford University.

TORTS, Eighth Edition (1988)

William L. Prosser, late Professor of Law, University of California, Hastings.
John W. Wade, Professor of Law, Vanderbilt University.
Victor E. Schwartz, Adjunct Professor of Law, Georgetown University.

TORTS, Third Edition (1976)

Harry Shulman, late Dean of the Law School, Yale University.
Fleming James, Jr., Professor of Law Emeritus, Yale University.
Oscar S. Gray, Professor of Law, University of Maryland.

TRADE REGULATION, Second Edition (1983), with 1987 Supplement

Milton Handler, Professor of Law Emeritus, Columbia University.
Harlan M. Blake, Professor of Law, Columbia University.
Robert Pitofsky, Professor of Law, Georgetown University.
Harvey J. Goldschmid, Professor of Law, Columbia University.

TRADE REGULATION, see Antitrust

TRANSNATIONAL BUSINESS PROBLEMS (1986)

Detlev F. Vagts, Professor of Law, Harvard University.

TRANSNATIONAL LEGAL PROBLEMS, Third Edition (1986) with Documentary Supplement

Henry J. Steiner, Professor of Law, Harvard University.
Detlev F. Vagts, Professor of Law, Harvard University.

TRIAL, see also Evidence, Making the Record, Lawyering Process and Preparing and Presenting the Case

TRUSTS, Fifth Edition (1978)

George G. Bogert, late Professor of Law Emeritus, University of Chicago.
Dallin H. Oaks, President, Brigham Young University.

TRUSTS AND SUCCESSION (Palmer's), Fourth Edition (1983)

Richard V. Wellman, Professor of Law, University of Georgia.
Lawrence W. Waggoner, Professor of Law, University of Michigan.
Olin L. Browder, Jr., Professor of Law, University of Michigan.

UNFAIR COMPETITION, see Competitive Process and Business Torts

WATER RESOURCE MANAGEMENT, Third Edition (1988)

The late Charles J. Meyers, formerly Dean, Stanford University Law School.
A. Dan Tarlock, Professor of Law, II Chicago-Kent College of Law.
James N. Corbridge, Jr., Chancellor, University of Colorado at Boulder, and
    Professor of Law, University of Colorado School of Law.
David H. Getches, Professor of Law, University of Colorado School of Law.

WILLS AND ADMINISTRATION, Fifth Edition (1961)

Philip Mechem, late Professor of Law, University of Pennsylvania.
Thomas E. Atkinson, late Professor of Law, New York University.

WRITING AND ANALYSIS IN THE LAW (1989)

Helene S. Shapo, Professor of Law, Northwestern University
Marilyn R. Walter, Professor of Law, Brooklyn Law School
Elizabeth Fajans, Writing Specialist, Brooklyn Law School

COPYRIGHT, PATENT, TRADEMARK

AND

RELATED STATE DOCTRINES

CASES AND MATERIALS ON
THE LAW

OF

INTELLECTUAL PROPERTY

THIRD EDITION

By

PAUL GOLDSTEIN
Stella W. and Ira S. Lillick Professor of Law
Stanford University

Westbury, New York
THE FOUNDATION PRESS, INC.
1990

Library of Congress Cataloging-in-Publication Data

Goldstein, Paul, 1943–
    Copyright, patent, trademark, and related state doctrines : cases
and materials on the law of intellectual property / by Paul
Goldstein. — 3rd ed.
        p. cm. — (University casebook series)
    Kept up to date by case, problem, and statute supplements.
    ISBN 0–88277–792–0
    1. Intellectual property—United States—Cases. I. Title.
KF2978.G63 1990
346.7304'8—dc20
[347.30648]
                                                    90–3208
                                                       CIP

To
My Mother and Father

*

PREFACE

At a meeting of the American Bar Association's section on Patents, Trademarks and Copyrights, a seasoned copyright practitioner introduced his remarks with the observation that section members "are exposed to many occupational hazards. . . One of the less serious ones—but still an obstacle faced almost daily—is the fact that most people do not understand the difference between patents, trademarks and copyrights. This applies to clients, other lawyers and at times even judges. When I tell a general practitioner that I am a copyright lawyer, he immediately corrects me: 'You mean patents!' He then says: 'Well, anyway, as a patent lawyer, you can copyright a name for me can't you?' " *

Why the confusion between copyright, patent and trademark law? One reason is that these laws occupy a common ground, each seeking to stimulate investment in information through the award of property rights. The information produced, and the specific intellectual property rights that attach, are sometimes hard to separate. Adding to the confusion is the fact that state laws—principally trade secret and unfair competition law and the right of publicity—also occupy this common ground.

Because these laws occupy a common field, they invite comparison. How, and how efficiently, does each law allocate costs among producers, distributors and consumers of information? The field also invites less theoretical inquiry. A lawyer must be prepared to pick out not only a single thread of protection for a client's project (one consisting, say, of trade secret and patent protection) but possibly a more ample fabric (a combination of trade secret, patent, copyright and trademark). The lawyer must also be alert to the possibility that a client's project will infringe the intellectual property rights of others. Although the lawyer will move easily from state to federal law, the lines between—like so many other lines in a federal system, bristle with conflict—often of a constitutional dimension.

In the years since publication of the second edition, the perceived importance of intellectual property has grown dramatically—in Congress and the courts, in boardrooms and in law firms. Congress has over this period repeatedly amended the copyright, patent and trademark acts in several important respects. The new Court of Appeals for the Federal Circuit has harmonized previously disparate patent law standards and, in the process, strengthened industry confidence in the patent system. The question of protection for computer programs, virtually untouched at the time of the last edition, is today one of intellectual property law's hottest

---

* Latman, Preliminary Injunctions in Patent, Trademark and Copyright Cases, 60 Trademark Rep. 506 (1970).

topics. As intellectual property's importance to the nation's balance of trade has come into clearer focus, Congress has moved to bring U.S. law into line with international treaty requirements and has employed trade measures to ensure worldwide protection for works originating in the United States.

The third edition reflects suggestions made by many users of the second. For their good advice, I am grateful to Louis B. Altman, Margreth Barrett, Joseph P. Bauer, Glenn K. Beaton, Andrew Beckerman–Rodau, Jay Dratler, Jr., Rochelle Cooper Dreyfuss, David R. Ellis, Thomas G. Field, Jr., Theodore M. Hagelin, I. Trotter Hardy, Jr., Thomas Hemnes, Paul Horton, Roberta Rosenthal Kwall, Marshall Leaffer, David A. Lowin, J. K. Mueller, Jr., Christopher H. Munch, John J. Murphy, A. Samuel Oddi, Dale A. Oesterle, Edmund J. Sease, Harold F. See, Rena C. Seplowitz, Jeffrey G. Sheldon, Walter G. Sutcliffe and Sherman Winnick. I am also grateful to my colleagues in the intellectual property practice at Morrison & Foerster for continually challenging me with questions at the law's cutting edge.

Stanford Law School, where I completed the first and second editions of this book, continued to provide a congenial setting for work on the third. I am particularly indebted to Dean Paul Brest for his generous support, and to the staff of the Robert Crown Law Library for helping so many times in so many ways. I am also grateful to Mark W. Lerner and Karen M. Wetherell, students at the Law School, for cite-checking and proofreading the text. Mark Lerner also prepared the Index. Their work was supported by a bequest from the Claire and Michael Brown Estate. Finally, I am indebted to my secretary, Lynne Anderson, for so cheerfully and efficiently overseeing production of the manuscript.

Note on Style. The articles and many of the cases appearing in these pages have been edited. The deletion of sentences and paragraphs is indicated by ellipses. The deletion of string citations is not indicated. Most footnotes have been excised. Those that remain have not been renumbered. Parallel citation to federal, state and regional reporters and to the United States Patent Quarterly has been employed where appropriate.

P.G.

Stanford, California
April, 1990

SUMMARY OF CONTENTS

PART FOUR. INTELLECTUAL PROPERTIES IN CONCERT: COMPUTER PROGRAMS AND INDUSTRIAL DESIGN

PART FIVE. INTERNATIONAL PROTECTION: THE CONVENTIONS

TABLE OF CONTENTS

PART FOUR. INTELLECTUAL PROPERTIES IN CONCERT: COMPUTER PROGRAMS AND INDUSTRIAL DESIGN

PART FIVE. INTERNATIONAL PROTECTION OF INTELLECTUAL PROPERTY

TABLE OF CASES

Principal cases are in italic type. Non-principal cases are in roman type. References are to pages.

*

COPYRIGHT, PATENT, TRADEMARK

AND

RELATED STATE DOCTRINES

*

Part One

INTELLECTUAL PROPERTY LAW IN CONTEXT

I. THE NATURE AND FUNCTIONS OF INTELLECTUAL PROPERTY LAW

The principal object of intellectual property law in the United States is to attract private investment to the production of various forms of information. The method employed is a grant of property rights enabling individuals and businesses to appropriate to themselves the value of the information they produce. Copyright attracts investment to the production and distribution of original, expressive information by promising authors, artists, composers and their publishers exclusive rights for a limited period. Patent law uses property rights to stimulate private investment in new, useful and nonobvious technological information. Trademark law encourages businesses to invest in symbolic information about their goods and services by prohibiting competitors from using the same symbols on their own wares. Common law copyright, trade secret law and unfair competition law have historically served an auxiliary function, protecting information until it has been sufficiently developed to qualify for federal protection under the copyright, patent and trademark statutes. The more recently developed right of publicity gives individuals such as actors and sports figures the ability to capture the value of their celebrity in the marketplace.

The fact that information is intangible means that, absent property rights, a producer of information will find it difficult to appropriate the information's value in the marketplace. Much information will have little value to its producer unless she can sell it. But sale will expose the information to the public—including competitors—who, absent property rights, can freely replicate the information and sell it at a price lower than what the producer must charge to recoup her investment in producing the information. The critical point is that, unable to appropriate the value of their information, firms will be disinclined to invest in producing information. Privity requirements make contract restrictions on the use of information an unwieldy alternative to property rights.

The fact that information is intangible also means that it is indivisible: an unlimited number of users can consume it without depleting it. The hobbyist who destroys a page of printed instructions after reading them will effectively exclude anyone else from possessing that page. But destruction of the page will not diminish the ability of anyone else to use the information embodied in the instructions. The hobbyist could share the information with other hobbyists without reducing the information's use by others. Put somewhat differently, once information has been produced, its use may benefit an indeterminate number of users without imposing any additional costs on the producer. Because information can be used endlessly and by unlimited numbers of people, and because no one's use of the information will interfere with the owner's physical dominion over it, legislatures and courts tend to tolerate more extensive inroads into intellectual property than they would if land or goods were in issue.

An intellectual property solution to the problem of inappropriability—incentives—inevitably conflicts with the social benefits of indivisibility—access. Intellectual property as a solution to inappropriability implies that, to recover its investment, an information producer will use its property rights to charge consumers for access to its work. Yet indivisibility implies that, once information has been produced, its use by a prospective consumer may confer a benefit on the consumer without imposing any additional cost on the producer. If the producer charges for access to the information, consumers who are unable or unwilling to pay the price will be deprived of the information, leaving them worse off than they would be in the absence of property rights. "Put succinctly, the dilemma is that without a legal monopoly not enough information will be produced but with the legal monopoly too little of the information will be used." R. Cooter & T. Ulen, Law and Economics 135 (1988).

Intellectual property law in the United States seeks to strike a balance between the competing demands of appropriability and indivisibility. This essentially utilitarian balance leaves room for the play of other factors. One such factor is natural rights theory—the basis for protection of literary and artistic works in civil law countries—which holds that authors should receive protection for their creations, not because they need protection as an inducement for their efforts, but rather because they deserve it as an inherent natural right. Political judgments—for example, the judgment that certain uses of intellectual property in research, education and public affairs should be exempt from liability—also play a role in the design of intellectual property laws.

A. COPYRIGHT

MACAULAY, SPEECH DELIVERED IN THE HOUSE OF COMMONS, 5 FEBRUARY 1841

Macaulay, Prose and Poetry 731, 733–737 (G. Young ed. 1967).

. . . The advantages arising from a system of copyright are obvious. It is desirable that we should have a supply of good books: we cannot have such a supply unless men of letters are liberally remunerated; and the least objectionable way of remunerating them is by means of copyright. You cannot depend for literary instruction and amusement on the leisure of men occupied in the pursuits of active life. Such men may occasionally produce compositions of great merit. But you must not look to such men for works which require deep meditation and long research. Works of that kind you can expect only from persons who make literature the business of their lives. Of these persons few will be found among the rich and the noble. The rich and the noble are not impelled to intellectual exertion by necessity. They may be impelled to intellectual exertion by the desire of distinguishing themselves, or by the desire of benefiting the community. But it is generally within these walls that they seek to signalise themselves and to serve their fellow creatures. Both their ambition and their public spirit, in a country like this, naturally take a political turn. It is then on men whose profession is literature, and whose private means are not ample, that you must rely for a supply of valuable books. Such men must be remunerated for their literary labour. And there are only two ways in which they can be remunerated. One of those ways is patronage; the other is copyright.

There have been times in which men of letters looked, not to the public, but to the government, or to a few great men, for the reward of their exertions. It was thus in the time of Maecenas and Pollio at Rome, of the Medici at Florence, of Lewis the Fourteenth in France, of Lord Halifax and Lord Oxford in this country. Now, Sir, I well know that there are cases in which it is fit and graceful, nay, in which it is a sacred duty to reward the merits or to relieve the distresses of men of genius by the exercise of this species of liberality. But these cases are exceptions. I can conceive no system more fatal to the integrity and independence of literary men than one under which they should be taught to look for their daily bread to the favour of ministers and nobles. I can conceive no system more certain to turn those minds which are formed by nature to be the blessings and ornaments of our species into public scandals and pests.

We have, then, only one resource left. We must betake ourselves to copyright, be the inconveniences of copyright what they may. . . . Thus, then, stands the case. It is good that authors should be remunerated; and the least exceptionable way of remunerating them is by a monopoly. Yet monopoly is an evil. For the sake of the good we must submit to the evil; but the evil ought not to last a day longer than is necessary for the purpose of securing the good.

Now, I will not affirm, that the existing law is perfect, that it exactly hits the point at which the monopoly ought to cease; but this I confidently say, that the existing law is very much nearer that point than the law proposed by my honorable and learned friend. For consider this; the evil effects of the monopoly are proportioned to the length of its duration. But the good effects for the sake of which we bear with the evil effects are by no means proportioned to the length of its duration. A monopoly of sixty years produces twice as much evil as a monopoly of thirty years, and thrice as much evil as a monopoly of twenty years. But it is by no means the fact that a posthumous monopoly of sixty years gives to an author thrice as much pleasure and thrice as strong a motive as a posthumous monopoly of twenty years. On the contrary, the difference is so small as to be hardly perceptible.

. . . I will take an example. Dr. Johnson died fifty-six years ago. If the law were what my honorable and learned friend wishes to make it, somebody would now have the monopoly of Dr. Johnson's works. Who that somebody would be it is impossible to say; but we may venture to guess. I guess, then, that it would have been some booksell- er, who was the assign of another bookseller, who was the grandson of a third bookseller, who had bought the copyright from Black Frank, the Doctor's servant and residuary legatee, in 1785 or 1786. Now, would the knowledge that this copyright would exist in 1841 have been a source of gratification to Johnson? Would it have stimulated his exertions? Would it have once drawn him out of his bed before noon? Would it have once cheered him under a fit of the spleen? Would it have induced him to give us one more allegory, one more life of a poet, one more imitation of Juvenal? I firmly believe not. I firmly believe that a hundred years ago, when he was writing our debates for the Gentleman's Magazine, he would very much rather have had twopence to buy a plate of shin of beef at a cook's shop underground. Considered as a reward to him, the difference between a twenty years' term and a sixty years' term of posthumous copyright would have been nothing or next to nothing. But is the difference nothing to us? I can buy Rasselas for sixpence; I might have had to give five shillings for it. I can buy the Dictionary, the entire genuine Dictionary, for two guineas, perhaps for less; I might have had to give five or six guineas for it. Do I grudge this to a man like Dr. Johnson? Not at all. Show me that the prospect of this boon roused him to any vigorous effort, or sustained his spirits under depressing circumstances, and I am quite willing to pay the price of such an object, heavy as that price is. But what I do complain of is that my circumstances are to be worse, and Johnson's none the better; that I am to give five pounds for what to him was not worth a farthing.

BREYER, THE UNEASY CASE FOR COPYRIGHT: A STUDY OF COPYRIGHT IN BOOKS, PHOTOCOPIES, AND COMPUTER PROGRAMS

84 Harv.L.Rev. 281, 292–302 (1970).*

I. Would the Abolition of Copyright Protection Seriously Injure Book Production?

To abolish copyright protection would allow publishers to compete in the production and sale of an individual title. The proponents of copyright protection would argue strongly that even if such competition sometimes brings the reader books at lower prices, it may often prevent him from obtaining a book at all. A subsequent publisher could copy and sell a particular book at lower costs than those incurred by the initial publisher. If competition immediately forced that book's price down to the copier's costs, the initial publisher could not recover his fixed costs or pay the author. The fear of such a result in a world without copyright would, it is claimed, discourage publishers from publishing and authors from writing. To evaluate the importance of this economic claim for copyright protection, we must appraise the impact of possible copying on initial publishers' revenues and the possible harm that could flow from any such revenue loss.

(a) Would Competition in the Production of Individual Titles Seriously Threaten Book Publishers' Revenues?

(i) The Copying Publisher's Cost Advantage.—A copying publisher could produce a copy for considerably lower cost than an initial publisher, for the initial publisher incurs many costs that a subsequent publisher would not have to bear. The initial publisher must edit the book and he must pay various fixed manufacturing expenses, such as those of composing type into pages, making corrections, and designing plates for the jacket. A copying publisher can avoid many of these costs simply by photographing the pages of the completed book and using the photographs for printing purposes. He can also escape a portion of the selling, promotion, and overhead costs that an initial publisher must bear. And he might not pay the author a royalty.

Because a copier's cost advantage will vary considerably, depending upon the title and the number of copies that the book sells, one can more easily discuss the extent of the advantage in terms of specific dollar examples, rather than percentages. The following example is constructed to illustrate the typical extent of the cost advantage. The example shows the differing costs to the initial publisher and to a copier of producing an unillustrated 400–page college text that is expected to sell about 5000 copies.* It will be sold to booksellers for $4.80. The booksellers will retail it for $6.00. (The example is based upon average cost figures contained in the American Education Publishers' Institute Annual Survey of the textbook publishing industry for 1968. Since textbook publishers accounting for more than ninety percent of all textbooks sold provided detailed cost information for that survey, the average cost figures are reasonably representative.)

The copier's cost advantage is fairly large. To produce an edition of 5,000 copies would cost him less than two-thirds what it would cost the initial publisher. The result is that the book's initial publisher must sell 3,700 copies before he begins to earn a profit whereas a copying publisher selling the book at the same price will begin to earn a profit after selling 1,400 copies. Moreover, if the copier expects to sell 2,500 copies, he could set a price to the retailer of $3.20 instead of $4.80

---

* "*Textbooks* account for the single largest portion (about thirty-five percent) of all publishing revenues. They comprise books used in colleges and books used in elementary or high schools (known in the industry as "elhi" texts). *Tradebooks* include the novels and popular nonfiction that ordinarily spring to mind when copyright is discussed. Adult tradebooks (both hardbound and paperback) sold by booksellers account for only about ten percent of all publishing revenue. If we add in children's books, tradebooks sold through book clubs, and pulp novels, the figure rises to about twenty-seven percent." Pp. 292–293.

and still earn a small profit. And the retailer could sell the text for $4.40 instead of $6.00 while earning no less than before.

The copier's cost advantage may be larger in the case of many complicated textbooks but smaller for many bestselling tradebooks. In general, editing, illustrations, footnotes, tables, and indices raise a book's fixed manufacturing costs, increasing the copier's advantage.

Fixed Costs	First Publisher	Copier
Plant	$ 4,500	$ 900
Editorial	1,440	500
Other overhead	2,880	2,000
Selling	1,000	1,000
Promotion	700	350
Total fixed cost	$10,520	$4,750

Variable Costs		
Manufacturing	$.80 per copy	$.80 per copy
Warehouse and shipping	.16 " "	.16 " "
Royalty to author	.70 " "	.00 " "
Selling	.20 " "	.20 " "
Promotion	.14 " "	.07 " "
Publishers' total variable cost	2.00 " "	1.23 " "
Retailers' markup *	1.20 " "	1.20 " "
Total variable cost	3.20 " "	2.43 " "

A large number of sales reduces that advantage by spreading fixed costs over a large number of copies.

The copier's cost advantage today is somewhat greater than copiers enjoyed in previous generations. In the nineteenth century copiers could not photograph a book's pages and thus had to bear the heavy cost of composing type for printing; nor did they benefit much from promotional expenditures, for publishers then seem to have advertised much less than now. More importantly the copier's cost advantage may decline somewhat in the near future. With the aid of computers, printers may be able to make printing plates directly from a typed manuscript, eliminating the cost of retyping copy on, for example, a linotype machine. Computers may also lower inventory costs by making possible the printing of books "on demand."

In any event, one cannot deny the existence of a fairly large cost advantage at present. The advantage shows that copying publishers could sell books profitably at prices that will prove unremunerative for initial publishers—a fact that may lead some to copy books soon after they appear on the market. On the other hand, the cost difference does not prove by itself that copying publishers will be able to drive a book's price low enough soon enough to prevent its initial publisher from earning a profit; nor does it show by itself that several publishers will often attempt to sell the same book.

* Retailers' markup is the difference between the $6.00 price and $4.80, which the retailer pays for the book. This $4.80 figure includes the publisher's profit.

(ii) Countervailing Forces: The Initial Publisher's Advantages of Lead Time and the Threat of Retaliation.—A book's initial publisher will ordinarily enjoy several advantages that may partially offset a copier's lower production costs. For one thing, his book will reach the market first. To obtain this "lead time" in the nineteenth century an American publisher would often agree to pay a popular English novelist, such as Sir Walter Scott, substantial royalties for early proofs of a new novel. The proofs would be rushed to America before any other publisher could compete by obtaining a copy of the book's English edition. Books were sold with sufficient speed that a few days lead time could spell the difference between profit and loss. In fact, lead time was important enough that many English writers earned more from the sale of advance proofs to American publishers (despite lack of copyright protection in America) than from the copyright royalties on their English sales.

Lead time should still prove advantageous to publishers of tradebooks. Publishers expect a tradebook to begin to return a profit within a few months of publication if it is ever to do so. By the time a copier chooses a book, prints it, and distributes it to retailers, he may be six to eight weeks behind, by which time the initial publisher will have provided retailers with substantial inventories. It is unlikely that a price difference of less than a dollar will lead many retailers or customers to wait for a cheaper edition, for hardbound book customers do not seem to respond readily to price reductions. They are not willing, after all, to wait for a cheaper paperbound edition. And, if the copier tries to cut his competitor's lead by rushing publication, he will incur special costs that will cut into his price advantage. In the case of textbooks, however, lead time, while helpful, should prove less important, for college texts often take a year or more before they begin to earn a profit, and elhi texts may not begin to earn a return for two or three years.

Second, the copier will be somewhat constrained by fear of retaliation by the initial publisher. Publishers in the past protected themselves from copying by producing punitive "fighting editions," which they would sell below the copier's cost. Even if the fear of antitrust action makes the modern publisher hesitate to set a price that is lower than that of the copier, the antitrust laws should not prevent him from *meeting* the copier's price. And at equivalent prices he will benefit from marginal advantages, such as somewhat better quality reproduction, more fully developed channels of distribution, or an ability to proclaim his the "authorized" edition. When, for example, a copying publisher recently put out an $8.50 edition of a book about ancient houses, the book's original publisher responded with a new edition priced at $4.00 and, because of his better established distribution channels, drove the copier from the market.

A copying publisher, faced with the problems of "lead time" and "retaliation" is unlikely to see much profit in copying low-volume titles. It seems unlikely, for example, that a publisher thinking of copying the type of tradebook that now sells about 4,000 copies, would count on selling the 2,000 or more copies needed to earn a profit. Nor would a publisher seem likely to compete in the production of a low-volume text as long as its initial publisher is not earning unusually high profits from its sale. Indeed, pre–1958 British books, which are often in the public domain in America, are rarely copied—I should think because their market is too small to make copying attractive.

A copier is more likely to compete in the sale of those tradebooks (variously estimated at ten to fifteen percent of total tradebooks) that sell more than a few thousand copies. Yet the copier's cost advantage is smaller for such higher volume books. And with only one or a few copies we may find that price competition is not sufficiently fierce to force initial publishers to incur a loss; "duopoly" or "oligopoly" pricing may leave a profit for all publishers on books worth copying. That competition in the sale of such books is feasible is suggested by existing competition in the sale of popular government documents, such as the *Warren Report,* or of classics in the public domain, and by the fact that publishers paid popular nineteenth-century English writers substantial royalties despite the lack of copyright protection.

Nonetheless, to introduce competition and lower the return that a "best-seller" earns may make tradebook publishers less willing to run the risk of publishing books of unpredictable future popularity. Moreover, copiers are likely to compete in the production of popular texts or reference books. These books, unlike "best-selling" novels, may involve heavy fixed costs which the original publisher does not expect to recoup for two or three years or more. Such books present the strongest examples for those who fear that the threat of competition will make publishers hesitate to produce books. Yet publishers will continue to produce them as long as they can earn a reasonable profit on their sale; and copyright would be unnecessary even in this category if it proved possible to assure them this profit by developing currently underutilized marketing techniques for channeling money from reader to publisher—techniques that we shall now discuss.

NOTES

1. For a careful examination of Professor (now Judge) Breyer's uneasy case for copyright, see Tyerman, The Economic Rationale for Copyright Protection for Published Books: A Reply to Professor Breyer, 18 U.C.L.A.L.Rev. 1100 (1971). Tyerman questions whether the initial publisher will enjoy the lead time advantages claimed by Breyer. "Advances in book publishing technology have seriously diminished the time (and cost) that would be required to copy a given book." Further, "the alleged price insensitivity of book *consumers* may be largely irrelevant since to a great degree it is book *distributors* . . . who actually determine the character of the retail market for most books. Thus, if a copier could offer copies of a particular book at a price significantly below that offered by the initial publisher, many retailers would be willing to tolerate a slight delay in stocking that book in

return for the prospect of a greater profit margin on the eventual sale to the public." Pp. 1109–1111. (Emphasis in original.)

As to the fear of retaliation, Tyerman notes that "any stigma that might once have attached to book 'pirating' would probably be removed by the legislature's act of repealing copyright protection. Under these circumstances, it is unlikely that 'fighting editions' would prove to be the significant deterrent to book copying that they might have been in the nineteenth century." In his view, the important question is "how many times could a publisher sell drastically below his costs to drive out a copier and still remain financially solvent?" In a world without copyright, "there would be no safe haven in which the initial publisher could produce a book free from competition in that title and make the profits necessary to finance the production and sale of 'fighting editions' of other titles." P. 1113.

Is it relevant that, at least in the case of best-selling fiction, an important source of profit lies in the sale of subsidiary rights—rights to serialization, condensation, paperback publication and motion picture production, among others? What effect would the elimination of copyright in books have on returns from subsidiary uses?

2. The Breyer and Tyerman articles focus on copyright's effects on the *quantity* of books produced. What about copyright's effects on the *quality* of published books? Does copyright ensure the "supply of good books" promised by Macaulay? What is copyright's impact on the different kinds of writings—literary or technical—that may be embodied in books? On the production of musical works and works of visual art?

The quality of works produced under copyright is significantly connected to the rule that copyright protects expressions but not ideas—elemental plots, for example, or themes or colors. Because copyright does not protect ideas, it offers no incentive to invest in their production or dissemination; producers will instead focus on new ways of expressing old ideas. The result is a marketplace crowded with works that, though different in their expressions, are redundant in their ideas. Is this result desirable in the case of fiction, musical composition, paintings and graphics? In the case of technical works, maps and computer programs?

3. A United States Copyright Office study based on data reported in the 1977 Economic Census revealed that "2.8% of the United States Gross National Product (the sum of the values of all the goods and services sold to final consumers in this country) . . . can be attributed to 'values added' by the copyright industries." The study defined copyright industries as those whose products are copyrightable in whole or in part—among them, "book, newspaper, music and periodical publishers, motion picture companies, producers of audio and video recordings in all media, radio and television broadcasters, advertisers, producers of computer software, and semiconductor chip designers." Report of the U.S. Copyright Office to the Subcomm. on Patents, Copyrights &

Trademarks, Sen. Comm. on the Judiciary, Size of the Copyright Industries in the United States 3, 7 (Dec. 1984).

The Copyright Office study also reported that copyright royalty payments in 1977 exceeded $1.7 billion; that the United States enjoyed an $850 million positive balance of copyright trade with other countries ("[t]he strongest contributor to this surplus was, not surprisingly, the motion picture industry, followed by book and periodical publishers"); and that the copyright industries "employed 2.2 million people, or approximately 2.2% of the civilian labor force in the United States." Id. at 17.

See also Jehoram, Critical Reflections on the Economic Importance of Copyright, 20 I.I.C. 485 (1989).

B. PATENT

"TO PROMOTE THE PROGRESS OF . . . USEFUL ARTS"
Report of the President's Commission on the Patent System 1–3 (1966).

The United States patent system is an institution as old as the Nation itself. Stemming from a Constitutional mandate, patent acts were passed in 1790, 1793, and 1836. The Act of 1836 established the pattern for our present system by providing statutory criteria for the issuance of patents and requiring the Patent Office to examine applications for conformance thereto. Although the law has been amended on numerous occasions—and even rewritten twice since 1836—no basic changes have been made in its general character in the succeeding one hundred and thirty years.

However, during this period of few statutory changes, major developments have occurred in the social and economic character of the country. The United States has undergone a dramatic transformation, creating and utilizing an enormously complex technology, to emerge as the world's most productive industrial community. . . .

Agreeing that the patent system has in the past performed well its Constitutional mandate "to promote the progress of . . . useful arts," the Commission asked itself: What is the basic worth of a patent system in the context of present day conditions? The members of the Commission unanimously agreed that a patent system today is capable of continuing to provide an incentive to research, development, and innovation. They have discovered no practical substitute for the unique service it renders.

First, a patent system provides an incentive to invent by offering the possibility of reward to the inventor and to those who support him. This prospect encourages the expenditure of time and private risk capital in research and development efforts.

Second, and complementary to the first, a patent system stimulates the investment of additional capital needed for the further development and marketing of the invention. In return, the patent owner is given the right, for a limited period, to exclude others from making, using, or selling the invented product or process.

Third, by affording protection, a patent system encourages early public disclosure of technological information, some of which might otherwise be kept secret. Early disclosure reduces the likelihood of duplication of effort by others and provides a basis for further advances in the technology involved.

Fourth, a patent system promotes the beneficial exchange of products, services, and technological information across national boundaries by providing protection for industrial property of foreign nationals.

MACHLUP, AN ECONOMIC REVIEW OF THE PATENT SYSTEM

Study No. 15, Subcommittee on Patents, Trademarks and Copyrights,
Senate Committee on the Judiciary, 85th Cong., 2d Sess.
44–45, 50–52, 54–55 (1958).

Patents, by giving their owners exclusive rights to the commercial exploitation of inventions, secure to these owners profits (so-called "quasi rents") which are ultimately collected from consumers as part of the price paid for goods and services. The consumers pay; the patent owners receive. Are the consumers—the non-patent-owning people—worse off for it?

"No; they are not," says one group of economists. Patents are granted on inventions which would not have been made in the absence of a patent system; the inventions make it possible to produce more or better products than could have been produced without them; hence, whatever the consumers pay to the patent owners is only a part of the increase in real income that is engendered by the patent-induced inventions.

"Wrong," says another group of economists. Many of the inventions for which patents are granted would also be made and put to use without any patent system. The consumers could have the fruits of this technical progress without paying any toll charges. Even if *some* inventions are made and used thanks only to the incentives afforded by the patent system, consumers must pay for *all* patented inventions and, hence, lose by the bargain. Moreover, if patents result in monopolistic restrictions which hold down production and hinder the most efficient utilization of resources, it is possible that total real income is less than what it would be without the patent system. Of course, there is impressive technical progress and a substantial growth of national income under the patent system, yet perhaps less so than there would be without patents.

This is but one of the fundamental conflicts in the economics of the patent system. There is another, which is quite independent of any profits collected by the patent owners and of any monopolistic restrictions imposed on production. This second basic problem relates to the overall allocation of productive resources in a developing economy, and to the question whether at any one time the allocation to industrial research and development is deficient, excessive, or just right. . . .

Competition among rival firms which takes the form of a race between their research teams—a race, ultimately, to the patent office—may have various objectives: (a) To be the first to find a patentable solution to a problem posed by the needs and preferences of the customers—a better product—or by the technological needs and hopes of the producers—better machines, tools, processes; (b) after a competitor has found such a solution and has obtained exclusive patent rights in its exploitation, to find an alternative solution to the same problem in order to be able to compete with him in the same market—in other words, to "invent around" the competitor's patent; and (c) after having found and patented the first solution, to find and patent all possible alternative solutions, even inferior ones, in order to "block" the competitor's efforts to "invent around" the first patent.

These forms of "competitive research" were described and discussed by antipatent economists during the patent controversy of the 19th century. Concerning the first form, there was much complaint that other inventors who discovered practically simultaneously "the same utility," but were not the first in the race to the patent office, had to forego their "natural privilege of labor" and were barred from using their own inventions. The fact that there was competition in making new inventions was found to be healthy. But that he who lost the race to the patent office should be barred from using his own invention, and should have to search for a substitute invention, was found to be absurd.

What may appear absurd to a disinterested observer, or unjust and unfair to one who lost the right to use the fruit of his own labor and investment, must to an economist appear as sheer economic waste. Of course, one may regard this as an incidental expense of an otherwise beneficial institution, an unfortunate byproduct, an item of social cost, which, perhaps, is unavoidable and must be tolerated in view of the social advantages of the system as a whole. However, from merely defending the need of "inventing around a patent" as a minor item of waste, the discussion has recently proceeded to eulogize it as one of the advantages of the system, indeed as one of its "justifications."

The advantage is seen in the additional "encouragement" to research. If the competitors were given licenses under the patent of the firm that won the race, they would have to pay royalties but would not be compelled to "invent around" it. Exclusivity, however, forces some of them to search for a "substitute invention." But why should this be regarded as an advantage? The idea is probably that, if industrial research is desirable, more research is more desirable, and that it does not matter what kind of knowledge the research effort is supposed to yield. From an economic point of view, research is costly since it absorbs particularly scarce resources which could produce other valuable things. The production of the knowledge of how to do in a somewhat different way what we have already learned to do in a satisfactory way would hardly be given highest priority in a rational allocation of resources.

This same, or a still lower, evaluation must be accorded to the third form of "competitive research"—inventive effort for the purpose of obtaining patents on all possible alternatives of an existing patented invention just in order to "block" a rival from "inventing around" that patent. In this case inventive talent is wasted on a project which, even (or especially) if it succeeds exactly in achieving its objective, cannot possibly be as valuable as would be other tasks to which the talent might be assigned. When thousands of potential inventions are waiting to be made—inventions which might be of great benefit to society—how can one seriously justify the assignment of a research force to search for inventions that are not intended for use at all—but merely for satisfying a dog-in-a-manger ambition?

There is, however, another "justification" for this kind of "competitive research": it can be summarized in the colorful word "serendipity." This means "the faculty of making happy and unexpected discoveries by accident." The idea is that the research teams engaged in "inventing around patents," or in inventing to obtain patents to "block" other people's efforts to "invent around patents," might by sheer accident hit upon something really useful. In other words, the work of these research forces is justified by the possibility or probability that they might find something which they did not set out to find.

There is no doubt that these happy accidents occur again and again. But can one reasonably let an effort to produce something without social value take the credit for accidental byproducts that happen to be useful? Can one reasonably assert that research not oriented toward important objectives is more likely to yield useful results than are research efforts that are so oriented? Is it easier to find the important by seeking the unimportant? . . .

The most perplexing and disturbing confusions occur in discussions about the "value of patents." This is no wonder, what with the large number of possible meanings in the minds of the writers on the subject: they may be talking about (a) the value of patents to their owners, (b) the value of patents to society, (c) the value of the patent system to society, (d) the value of patented inventions to their users, (e) the value of patented inventions to society, (f) the value of patent-induced inventions to society. But even this is not all, because the social value of inventions may depend on the degree to which they are used, and the value of patents to their owners on the way they are exploited.

Singling out, from this long list, (b) the value of patents to society— and making quite sure that this refers neither to the social benefits of the patent system nor to the social value of the inventions, which are altogether different matters—it is worth pointing out that existing domestic patents held by domestic owners cannot be reasonably regarded as parts of the national wealth or as sources of real national income. To regard them so is as fallacious as it would be to include in national wealth such things as the right of a businessman to exclude others from using his trade name, or the right of a (domestic) creditor to collect from his (domestic) debtors, or to include such things as (domestic) money, securities, damage claims, and lottery tickets. The right of a person to keep others from doing something is no social asset and, again, somebody's right to keep others from using his invention should not be confused with the invention itself. To confuse an important invention with the patent that excludes people from using it is like confusing an important bridge with the tollgates that close it to many who might want to use it. No statistics of national wealth would ever include (domestic) "patent property." And the "destruction of patent property"—though it may affect the future performance of the economy—would leave the Nation's wealth, as it is now understood in social accounting, unimpaired. (An exception must be noted concerning foreign patent rights. One may regard domestic holdings of foreign patents as claims to future royalties and profits earned abroad and, hence, as assets; of course, foreign holdings of domestic patents, establishing foreign rights to future royalties and profits earned here, would then have to be counted among the liabilities and, therefore, as deductions from national wealth.)

NOTES

1.   Patent law, like copyright law, denies protection to abstract, fundamental ideas. "[S]urely," notes one writer, "it would be intolerable to give a patent on most of the fundamental ideas that arise from basic research." Turner, The Patent System and Competitive Policy, 44 N.Y.U.L.Rev. 450, 457 (1969). Patent law also imposes relatively high standards for protection—nonobviousness, novelty and utility. Taken together, these rules steer private research and development away from the discovery of fundamental ideas and away from inventions that make only obvious or non-novel leaps over the prior art. These twin pressures—away from fundamental discoveries and from merely incremental advances—when combined with the Patent Act's definition of protectible classes of subject matter, roughly define patent law's incentive structure.

2.   Patent law is only one of several public policy mechanisms for stimulating technological advance. The most prominent alternative—and supplement—is government subsidy. Cash from the federal government supports much of the basic research conducted in universities, government institutes and even private firms. Subsidies do not necessarily end with basic research. Government may also pay producers to implement inventions and consumers to acquire them. Agriculture and instructional technology are two fields in which consumers have been unwilling themselves to undertake the risk and expense associated with adopting new technologies. The federal government has deployed county agents and regional educational laboratories to overcome the last hurdles to innovation posed by consumer ignorance or indifference in these fields.

Subsidies may also take the form of prizes. One bill before the United States Senate would have authorized a National Science and Technology Awards Council to publish annually a list of no more than ten "most wanted scientific breakthroughs," and to award prizes ranging from $5,000 to $150,000 to the first person to meet the performance criteria established by the Council for each category. S. 1480, 94th Cong., 1st Sess., 121 Cong.Rec. 10832–34 (1975). Federal and state income tax incentives can also be used, such as by allowing investors to write off research and development costs as deductible current expenses rather than as expenditures that must be capitalized and then amortized over the life of the invention.

3. Where the federal government has supported research that the researcher later develops into a working invention, should the researcher be denied a patent on the ground that, since her research was publicly financed, its fruits should belong to the public without charge? Is it unfair or inefficient to give monopoly rewards to a private entrepreneur who has paid nothing for the basic research, and to require the public to pay for it twice—first in the tax revenues allocated to the research program, and a second time in increased prices paid for the goods produced? Some expenditure, private or public, will always be needed to put an invention into practice. This means that the public will pay a second time in any event—either through higher prices paid for private distribution or for subsidies to dissemination. Is the real question whether the private or public sector represents the more efficient vehicle for dissemination? See Leontief, On Assignment of Patent Rights on Inventions Made Under Government Research Contracts, 77 Harv. L. Rev. 492 (1964).

What effects might the prospect of—and requirements for—intellectual property protection have on the norms that traditionally govern scientific research? For a valuable analysis of this issue see Eisenberg, Proprietary Rights and the Norms of Science in Biotechnology Research, 97 Yale L.J. 177 (1987).

4. On the operation of the patent system generally, see Arrow, Economic Welfare and the Allocation of Resources for Invention, in N.B.E.R., The Rate and Direction of Inventive Activity 609 (1962); W. Nordhaus, Invention, Growth and Welfare: A Theoretical Treatment of Technological Change (1969); Plant, The Economic Theory Concerning Patents for Inventions, 1 Economica 30 (n.s.) (1934); Polanyi, Patent Reform, 11 Rev.Econ.Stud. 61 (1943); Symposium appearing in 8 Res. in L. & Econ. 3 (1986).

See also Kitch, The Nature and Function of the Patent System, 20 J. L. & Econ. 265 (1977), discussed in McFetridge & Smith, Patents, Prospects, and Economic Surplus: A Comment, 23 J. L. & Econ. 197 (1980); Beck, The Prospect Theory of the Patent System and Unproductive Competition, 5 Res. in L. & Econ. 193 (1983).

C. TRADEMARK

ECONOMIDES, THE ECONOMICS OF TRADEMARKS
78 Trademark Rep. 523, 526–531 (1988).*

The primary reasons for the existence and protection of trademarks are that (1) they facilitate and enhance consumer decisions and (2) they create incentives for firms to produce products of desirable qualities even when these are not observable before purchase. Both of these effects are a consequence of the fact that trademarks permit consumers to distinguish between goods which look identical in all features that are observable before purchase.

From an economic standpoint, the argument for trademarks is simple. In many markets, sellers have much better information as to the unobservable features of a commodity for sale than the buyers. This is known as information asymmetry. Unobservable features, valued by the consumer, may be crucial determinants of the total value of the good. Observable features can often be imitated to the smallest detail, even though huge differences remain in the unobservable features of the product. In the absence of trademarks, faced with the choice between goods which look identical, the consumer will only by chance pick the one with the desirable unobservable qualities. Further, firms would produce products with the cheapest possible unobservable qualities, because high levels of unobserved qualities would not add to a firm's ability to sell at a higher price and realize higher profits. However, if there is a way to identify the unobservable qualities, the consumer's choice becomes clear, and firms with a long horizon have an incentive to cater to a spectrum of tastes for variety and quality, even though these product features may be unobservable at the time of purchase.

The economic role of the trademark is to help the consumer identify the unobservable features of the trademarked product. This information is not provided to the consumer in an analytic form, such as an indication of size or a listing of ingredients, but rather in summary form, through a symbol which the consumer identifies with a specific combination of features. Information in analytic form is a complement to, rather than a substitute for, trademarks.

Trademarks were originally used to identify the makers of jewelry in the middle ages, but craftsmen's marks were used in pottery since ancient times. Although their original intent may have been to identify the maker for possible fraud regarding the assigned quality of the alloy, soon trademarks were utilized to identify the quality standard of particular makers. By the beginning of the twentieth century trademarks were understood not to be useful in identifying the source, but rather as identifying a quality standard. Presently the trademark typically identifies the product (the full combination of features that constitute the product), and its role of identifying the source is secondary in the minds of consumers. The consumer of NABISCO WHEAT THINS knows and cares little about source (manufacturer). Rather the consumer identifies the trademark with the features of the commodity, including crispness, sweetness or lack thereof, color, and the like. The trademark identifies both quality and variety features of the product, i.e., both features like freshness, more of which is desirable by all, and features like sweetness, over which consumers have varying preferences, some preferring little of it, and some desiring lots of it. Thus, although trademarks and trade names typically identify quality standards, often trademarks identify the full features of the product.

Moreover, the existence of trademarks allows firms to differentiate products in their unobservable features and to efficiently convey these differences to consumers. The tendency of firms to produce products that are not identical is natural in an environment where firms strive to maximize profits. The existence of trademarks allows this tendency to manifest itself with respect to unobservable characteristics of the products. The consumer is thus afforded a wider quality/variety spectrum. . . .

The degree to which a trademark is successful in conveying to the consumer unobservable features of the product before purchase depends on the underlying market conditions, the product, the frequency of purchase, the ease of information diffusion across consumers, and the ability of recall of consumers.

For products which are frequently purchased by the same consumer, trademarks function directly through the previous experience of the consumer. Consider an experience good (which the average consumer buys often). Assume further that there are certain features of the product which are unobservable at the time of purchase. A typical example of such a product is a bottle of diet COKE, the cola beverage. Information on the bottle and label give little indication of the taste. The trademark identifies the product. A consumer is typically offered a free introductory bottle, or buys the first bottle to sample it. From his experience he is then able to decide rationally as an informed consumer about his future choices between diet COKE and all other goods.

The crucial requirements for this mechanism to work are, first, that the consumer has a sufficiently good memory; second, that the consumer is able to identify the full features of the product with the trademark; and third, that the features of the product do not change between the first and subsequent consumption decisions. In the case of experience goods, the trademark has a reputation with the old customer which identifies its features. In this case, social interactions and information transfer among consumers are not necessary for the trademark to facilitate efficient choice.

For the trademark to fulfill its function all three requirements mentioned above are necessary. It can be fairly assumed that the consumer is endowed with a good memory. The second condition is likely to hold because the law protects the identification of trademarks with particular products by disallowing the use of similar symbols, words or designs on any other product in a manner likely to cause confusion. Preventing confusion is an important function of trademarks. Even in cases of no likelihood of confusion, similar trademarks have been disallowed because of the possible "dilution" of the mental association between a trademark (or trade name) and a particular product (or firm).

The last requirement is that the manufacturers do not change the features of the product between purchases. Under conditions of stability in the market, prosperity of the firm is guaranteed by its adherence to a high quality level for goods bearing its trademark or trade name. If, however, the horizon of the firm is short, it may opt to cash-in on its trade name reputation by selling lower quality goods. Events which can shorten the horizon of the firm and force it to emphasize the short run can be severe financial constraints which follow a leveraged buyout, or a dramatic fall in the demand for the product because of innovation in competing products, or a severe economic shock. . . .

In the case of experience goods where the consumer identifies the trademark with the product before purchase, it appears that there is no other mechanism which would work as efficiently. In the absence of trademarks, it could be argued that quality regulation, say through minimum quality standards, enforced through laws on fraud, could conceivably create a similar level of efficiency in the market place. Although quality minimums might be upheld through regulation, it is practically impossible to regulate variety efficiently. Given the consensus among consumers on the desirability of a quality feature, a regulatory board can set minimum quality standards. Variety features, where unanimity in the direction of preference is lacking, are very difficult and very costly to regulate. To achieve efficient regulation, estimation of the demand for each combination of variety features is needed—a very difficult task. Thus any regulatory system will most likely fail to provide the appropriate combinations of features which constitute the efficient mixture of desired varieties. . . .

For products which are consumed infrequently by the same individual, such as washing machines, refrigerators, television sets, video cassette recorders, and the like, trademarks work in an indirect way. Assume again that there are unobservable features. Lacking previous consumption, a consumer is unable to identify the trademark with the product. To be able to associate the trademark with the features of the product he has to rely on information diffused informally through friends or from evaluations disseminated centrally through magazines, radio or television. It is clear that, because of differences of interpretation as well as differences of opinion and preference across consumers, the information on which the choice will be based is most likely to be much more vague than in the case of experience goods. Most relevant information reaches the consumer in summary form. Information gathered through this process is likely to be incomplete and the consumer has little hope of more complete information on product features.

However, firms may use trade names to help the consumer identify the quality level of products. Even though the consumer is an infrequent buyer of a particular kind of electronic product, he may be a frequent buyer of the overall category of electronic products, and thus he is likely to have previous experience in the consumption of goods with the same trade name. Choosing a high quality standard in the category of electronic products, a manufacturer can use his trade name to transmit information on quality through the direct previous experience of consumers.

NOTES

1. Advertising does more than inform and persuade. Advertising sometimes becomes an element of the product or service itself. In an important article, Advertising and the Public Interest: Legal Protection of Trade Symbols, 57 Yale L.J. 1165, 1181 (1948), Professor Ralph S. Brown observed, "The buyer of an advertised good buys more than a parcel of food or fabric; he buys the pause that refreshes, the hand that has never lost its skill, the priceless ingredient that is the reputation of its maker. All these may be illusions, but they cost money to create, and if the creators can recoup their outlay, who is the poorer? Among the many illusions which advertising can fashion are those of lavishness, refinement, security, and romance. Suppose the monetary cost of compounding a perfume is trivial; of what moment is this if the ads promise, and the buyer believes, that romance, even seduction, will follow its use? The economist, whose dour lexicon defines as irrational any market behavior not dictated by a logical pecuniary calculus, may think it irrational to buy illusions; but there is a degree of that kind of irrationality even in economic man; and consuming man is full of it." *

2. For a superb treatment of trademark law's legal, intellectual and economic history, see McClure, Trademarks and Unfair Competition: A Critical History of Legal Thought, 69 Trademark Rep. 305 (1979). On the economics of trademark law generally, see Landes & Posner, Trademark Law: An Economic Perspective, 30 J.L. & Econ. 265 (1987); Backman, The Role of Trademarks in Our Competitive Economy, 58 Trademark Rep. 219 (1968).

II. THE SOURCES AND LIMITS OF INTELLECTUAL PROPERTY LAW

UNITED STATES CONSTITUTION

Article 1, Section 8

The Congress shall have power . . .

(3) To regulate Commerce with foreign Nations, and among the several States, and with the Indian Tribes . . .

(8) To promote the Progress of Science and useful Arts, by securing for limited Times to Authors and Inventors the exclusive Right to their respective Writings and Discoveries. . . .

Article 6

. . . This Constitution, and the Laws of the United States which shall be made in Pursuance thereof; and all Treaties made, or which shall be made, under the Authority of the United States, shall be the supreme Law of the Land; and the Judges in every State shall be bound thereby, any Thing in the Constitution or Laws of any State to the Contrary notwithstanding. . . .

NOTES

1. Article 1, section 8, clause 3, which describes the congressional commerce power, is the constitutional basis for federal trademark legislation. Clause 8 is the source of federal copyright and patent legislation. Courts have on occasion sought to escape the strait jacket of this traditional view, suggesting, for example, that clause 8's limitation of congressional power can be eluded by resting copyright and patent legislation on clause 3. See, e.g., Picard v. United Aircraft Corp., 128 F.2d 632, 643 n.22, 53 U.S.P.Q. 563 (2d Cir.1942). In the *Trademark Cases,* discussed at p. 201, below, the government sought unsuccessfully to avoid the requirements of clause 3 by adducing "the likeness which property in the use of trade-marks bears to that in patents and copyrights" for its argument that "the power of Congress over them might be derived from the same source"—clause 8. 100 U.S. 82, 86, 25 L.Ed. 550 (1879).

2. Colonial usage and syntax indicate that the Constitution's framers, in speaking of "Science" in clause 8, were referring to the work of authors, and by "useful Arts" meant the work of inventors. Structurally the clause is a balanced sentence—a style common to the period—and can be reworked to read:

(8) (a) To promote the Progress of Science . . . by securing for limited Times to Authors . . . the exclusive Right to their . . . Writings.

(b) To promote the Progress of . . . useful Arts, by securing for limited Times to . . . Inventors the exclusive Right to their . . . Discoveries.

See Lutz, Patents and Science: A Clarification of the Patent Clause of the U.S. Constitution, 18 Geo.Wash.L.Rev. 50 (1949).

NOTE: FEDERAL PREEMPTION OF STATE LAW

The federal copyright, patent and trademark laws strike a balance between private incentives to produce, and consumer access to, artistic, technological and commercial information. State courts and legislatures have struck their own intellectual property balance for some of this subject matter. Common law copyright, trade secret law, unfair competition law and contract law are the traditional forms of state protection for information; the right of publicity and laws against copying industrial design are among the more contemporary forms of state intellectual property law.

The subject matter and methods of federal and state intellectual property laws frequently overlap. One consequence is that, under the force of the United States Constitution's supremacy clause, federal law will sometimes preempt state law. The United States Supreme Court has addressed the possibility of preemption in no fewer than eight decisions over twenty-five years.*

In two companion decisions in 1964, *Sears, Roebuck & Co. v. Stiffel Co.,* page 103, below, and *Compco Corp. v. Day–Brite Lighting Inc.,* page 107, below, the Supreme Court held that states cannot protect subject matter that comes within Congress' copyright-patent power but fails to qualify for federal copyright or patent protection because it is not the kind of subject matter that the federal statutes protect or because it does not meet the statutes' qualitative standards. In *Sears* the district court had invalidated design and mechanical patents on Stiffel's pole lamp because the lamp did not meet the Patent Act's standard of invention; nonetheless, applying state unfair competition law, the court had enjoined *Sears* from selling its lamps because they were confusingly similar to *Stiffel's.* The Supreme Court reversed the lower court's judgment on the ground that it gave plaintiff "the equivalent of a patent monopoly on its unpatented lamp." 376 U.S. at 233, 84 S.Ct. at 789. "Just as a state cannot encroach upon the federal patent laws directly, it cannot, under some other law, such as that forbidding unfair

---

* Bonito Boats, Inc. v. Thunder Craft Boats, Inc., ___ U.S. ___, 109 S.Ct. 971, 103 L.Ed.2d 118, 9 U.S.P.Q.2d 1847 (1989); Aronson v. Quick Point Pencil Co., 440 U.S. 257, 99 S.Ct. 1096, 59 L.Ed.2d 296, 201 U.S.P.Q. 1 (1979); Kewanee Oil Co. v. Bicron Corp., 416 U.S. 470, 94 S.Ct. 1879, 40 L.Ed.2d 315, 181 U.S.P.Q. 673 (1974); Goldstein v. California, 412 U.S. 546, 93 S.Ct. 2303, 37 L.Ed.2d 163, 178 U.S.P.Q. 129 (1973), reh'g denied, 414 U.S. 883, 94 S.Ct. 27, 38 L.Ed.2d 131 (1973); Lear, Inc. v. Adkins, 395 U.S. 653, 89 S.Ct. 1902, 23 L.Ed.2d 610, 162 U.S.P.Q. 1 (1969); Brulotte v. Thys Co., 379 U.S. 29, 85 S.Ct. 176, 13 L.Ed.2d 99, 143 U.S.P.Q. 264 (1964), reh'g denied, 379 U.S. 985, 85 S.Ct. 638, 13 L.Ed.2d 579 (1965); Sears, Roebuck & Co. v. Stiffel Co., 376 U.S. 225, 84 S.Ct. 784, 11 L.Ed.2d 661, 140 U.S.P.Q. 524 (1964), reh'g denied, 376 U.S. 973, 84 S.Ct. 1131, 12 L.Ed.2d 87; Compco Corp. v. Day-Brite Lighting, Inc., 376 U.S. 234, 84 S.Ct. 779, 11 L.Ed.2d 669, 140 U.S.P.Q. 528 (1964), reh'g denied, 377 U.S. 913, 84 S.Ct. 1162, 12 L.Ed.2d 183.

competition, give protection of a kind that clashes with the objectives of the federal patent laws." Id. at 231, 84 S.Ct. at 789.

The Court's 1973 decision in *Goldstein v. California,* page 770, below, marked a partial retreat from *Sears* and *Compco.* The Court held there that a California criminal statute outlawing the piracy of recorded performances did not violate the Constitution's supremacy clause even though the copyright act in force at the time did not protect sound recordings. The following year, *Kewanee Oil Co. v. Bicron Corp.,* page 152, below, continued the retreat from *Sears* and *Compco,* holding that state trade secret law could protect secret processes that came within the Patent Act's classes of protectible subject matter but failed to meet the Act's standards for protection. In 1979 the Court held in *Aronson v. Quick Point Pencil Co.,* page 48, below, that federal patent law does not preempt state contract law enforcement of an agreement to pay royalties for the manufacture of a device for which a patent had been denied.

In 1989 the Court returned to the philosophy of *Sears* and *Compco* to hold that the Patent Act preempted a Florida statute prohibiting the duplication of certain industrial designs through a direct molding process. *Bonito Boats, Inc. v. Thunder Craft Boats, Inc.,* page 910, below. "Our decisions since *Sears* and *Compco* have made it clear that the Patent and Copyright Clauses do not, by their own force or by negative implication, deprive the States of the power to adopt rules for the promotion of intellectual creation within their own jurisdictions." 109 S.Ct. 971, 985. But, the Court added, "[a] state law that substantially interferes with the enjoyment of an unpatented utilitarian or design conception which has been freely disclosed by its author to the public at large impermissibly contravenes the ultimate goal of public disclosure and use which is the centerpiece of federal patent policy. Moreover, through the creation of patent-like rights, the States could essentially redirect inventive efforts away from the careful criteria of patentability developed by Congress over the last 200 years. We understand this to be the reasoning at the core of our decisions in *Sears* and *Compco* and we reaffirm that reasoning today." 109 S.Ct. at 980–81.

At the same time that the Supreme Court was trimming the constitutional sweep of *Sears* and *Compco,* Congress passed the 1976 Copyright Act which had potentially an even greater preemptive sweep. Section 301(a) of the 1976 Copyright Act preempts state law if three conditions are met: the state right in question is "equivalent to any of the exclusive rights within the general scope of copyright as specified by section 106" of the Act; the right is in a work of authorship that is fixed in a tangible medium of expression; and the work comes within "the subject matter of copyright as specified by sections 102 and 103" of the Act. Courts have applied section 301's preemptive formula to preempt state unfair competition and trade secret laws among others. Section 301 is discussed in detail at pages 759 to 772 below.

Part Two

STATE LAW OF INTELLECTUAL PROPERTY

I. RIGHTS IN UNDEVELOPED IDEAS

SELLERS v. AMERICAN BROADCASTING CO.

United States Court of Appeals, Eleventh Circuit, 1982.
668 F.2d 1207, 217 U.S.P.Q. 41.

JOHNSON, Circuit Judge:

Plaintiff, Larry L. Sellers, filed a three-count complaint against defendants American Broadcasting Co. (ABC) and Geraldo Rivera, alleging breach of contract, copyright infringement and misappropriation. The district court granted summary judgment in favor of the defendants and plaintiff appeals. We affirm.

In June 1978, Sellers informed Rivera, an investigative reporter occasionally employed by ABC, that he had an "exclusive story" concerning rock-and-roll singer Elvis Presley's death. Before revealing the details, however, Sellers demanded that Rivera sign an agreement guaranteeing him all copyright privileges to the story and requiring ABC to publicly credit him with uncovering the true cause of the singer's death.[1] In return, Sellers agreed to provide ABC and Rivera with the "exclusive story" and further agreed not to release the story to any other network or reporter. Upon execution of the contract, Sellers proceeded to articulate his theory. Sellers recorded the entire conversation and a transcript of the meeting has been made part of the record in this case.

According to Sellers, cortisone was prescribed for Presley during the three-year period prior to his death. Presley's personal physician and personal bodyguard replaced the cortisone with placebos. Deprivation of the cortisone caused a collapse of Presley's cardiovascular system, resulting in death. Sellers hypothesized that the physician and

---

1. The entire agreement states:

I, Larry L. Sellers, do hereby agree not to release this exclusive story to any reporter other than Geraldo Rivera or any network other than ABC until the network has first released said story within a reasonable period of time or thirty days. Once the story has been released, other media forms may be contracted by Larry Sellers.

I, Geraldo Rivera, do hereby agree to grant Larry Sellers all copy-write [sic]

privileges of the exclusive Elvis Presley story and full claim for the discovery of the story by acknowledgement in any media use made of it from this day forth.

If the story is accepted for further investigation, all expenses incurred by Larry Sellers will be reimbursed by ABC.

Should the story be proven false, this contract is hereby null and void.

the bodyguard committed the murder in order to prevent Presley from seeking the repayment of a $1.3 million loan to them to be used for the construction of a racketball center. As an alternative theory, Sellers postulated that the singer might have been suffocated by either the physician or the bodyguard.

Rivera informed the plaintiff that the story could not be used unless verified. He suggested that plaintiff investigate the matter further and contact him in the event that verification was obtained. Following the conversation with Rivera, Sellers traveled to Memphis on two occasions, apparently in an effort to obtain the needed support for his theory. During the second trip, Sellers called Mrs. Rivera and informed her that he had uncovered proof of his theory but refused to relate to her the nature of the new evidence. The phone call constituted the last time Sellers contacted either Rivera or ABC concerning the story.

More than nine months after signing the agreement with Sellers, Rivera and producer Charles Thomsen decided to do a feature story on Presley's death. After a two-month investigation, it was determined that Presley died of polypharmacy (interaction of prescription drugs) and not cardiac arrhythmia as officially listed. ABC broadcast an hour-long special concerning the information uncovered during the "Rivera–Thomsen" investigation. Geraldo Rivera appeared on the program as a correspondent. ABC also did a number of follow-up stories on Presley's death. In neither the hour-long special nor the follow-up stories did the network suggest that Presley was murdered by a withdrawal of cortisone or by suffocation.

Sellers brought suit contending that ABC and Rivera misappropriated his "exclusive story" concerning the singer's death. Sellers also asserted claims for breach of contract and copyright infringement. The district court entered summary judgment for defendants. The court determined that plaintiff's "exclusive story" consisted of the theory that Presley had been murdered by his bodyguard and his personal physician through a deprivation of cortisone. Since ABC and Rivera did not use Sellers' "exclusive story" in any of their broadcasts, the court concluded that there had not been any misappropriation or breach of the written agreement.

On appeal, Sellers contends that a dispute of material fact exists concerning the precise scope of his "exclusive story" and, accordingly, summary judgment was improvidently granted. Sellers asserts that he informed Rivera not only of the possibility that Presley might have been murdered through a deprivation of cortisone, but also that the cause of death might have been the interaction of numerous prescription drugs, that the singer's personal physician may have been grossly negligent in overprescribing drugs for Presley and that there had been a cover-up of the true cause of death. Assuming without deciding that Sellers did present these additional theories to Rivera, we nonetheless conclude that they are so vague and uncertain as to be unenforceable as a matter of law.

Under New York law,[4] a contract will not be enforced if an essential element is vague, indefinite or incomplete. A complete review of the transcribed meeting between the parties shows that at best Sellers made broad, general statements concerning the possibility of overdose, gross negligence by the personal physician and a cover-up. The transcript demonstrates that plaintiff failed to provide any substantiating details for these vague allegations. He did not make clear whether Presley's death resulted from a single drug or a combination of drugs. He made no effort to provide the name of any specific drug that had been overprescribed by the personal physician. Nor did plaintiff show that medication unnecessary for the treatment of the singer's illnesses was prescribed for Presley. Finally, references to books and newspaper articles[5] constituted the only support for these vague and uncertain statements. Sellers' theory that Presley was murdered by a withdrawal of cortisone may well have been specific enough to give rise to an enforceable agreement. The district court, however, concluded that the defendants did not utilize the cortisone-murder theory in any of their broadcasts and did not, therefore, breach the agreement. Plaintiff does not challenge this conclusion on appeal.

As to plaintiff's remaining claim, New York courts will permit recovery for the misappropriation of an idea or theory if (1) the idea is novel; (2) the idea is in a concrete form; and (3) the defendant makes use of the idea. We conclude that Sellers' theory that Presley died of an interaction of prescription drugs was neither novel, unique nor original. Plaintiff's own exhibits show that a number of newspapers had speculated that Presley's death might have been drug-related long before the meeting between Sellers and Rivera. As to Sellers' other vague theories, we conclude that they were not sufficiently concrete to give rise to a cause of action for misappropriation.[7]

For the reasons stated herein, judgment for the defendants is AFFIRMED.

OLSSON, DREAMS FOR SALE

23 Law & Contemp.Probs. 34–35, 54–55 (1958). *

Idea submission claims have been a real plague for many years, but, as an attorney writing about idea submitters and advertisers has observed, things have taken a turn for the worse in the past quarter

4. The district court concluded that New York law controlled the interpretation of the contract. Neither party disputes this conclusion.

5. We note that at least a portion of plaintiff's "exclusive story", particularly the theory that Presley died from an interaction of drugs, appeared in a number of newspaper articles prior to his discussion with Rivera. Under New York law, an idea or theory does not constitute property and will not support the right to recover in contract unless original. Thus, to the extent plaintiff's "exclusive story" was al-ready widely disseminated and in the public domain, he cannot recover in contract for the use of his theory by the defendants.

7. The only portion of plaintiff's "exclusive story" that may have been sufficiently concrete to sustain a cause of action for misappropriation was his theory that Presley died from a withdrawal of cortisone. The district court, however, found that the defendants did not use the theory in any of their broadcasts. Plaintiff does not challenge this conclusion on appeal.

century, as courts now have a tendency to allow recovery where they would not earlier have done so. Consequently, reward is being given prematurely to those who otherwise might turn their mere "ideas" into finished works, and the commercial users of ideas are exposed to danger by the law in some American jurisdictions if they depart from well-worn idea channels. The battlefield in these cases is generally that of the submitted idea for which the submitter later claims that compensation is due him as the result of a use allegedly made by the recipient of the idea.

Such a claim takes one of several guises: that the recipient expressly promised to pay the submitter if he used the idea; that he impliedly promised to pay if he used the idea; that the law imposes an obligation to pay on quasi-contractual unjust enrichment grounds if the idea is used; that the recipient took a property—the idea—belonging to the submitter and used it, thus committing a tort in the nature of a conversion; or, finally, that a fiduciary relationship was violated by the recipient.

Occasionally, the claim is made seriously that a statutory or common law copyright infringement has been committed by the recipient; but copyright lawyers, as we shall see, have had little difficulty, except for a time in opportunity-rich California, in disposing of that contention. It is sometimes claimed that the act of use constitutes unfair competition; and in this area, all lawyers have difficulty, for unfair competition has been made the bridge between law and morality, and all sorts of baggage has been trundled across it since the historic International News Service v. Associated Press case [248 U.S. 215, 39 S.Ct. 68, 63 L.Ed. 211 (1918)]. . . .

Some Statistics

Robert W. Sarnoff, president of National Broadcasting Company, recently said: "In the year now ending, NBC headquarters, its stations, its field offices, its artists, and its producers will have received some three million letters from the viewing public. In New York alone, we will have had more than 41,000 telephone calls praising or criticising our shows, and more than 100,000 telegrams." Dore Schary, one of the motion picture industry's outstanding producers, told recently on a television program that a large studio receives 20,000 stories or ideas a year, of which but twenty are made into motion pictures.

Of the three national TV networks, one, NBC, currently is receiving 30,000 to 40,000 suggestions of all types every year. These figures include everything from letter outlines to pilot films. One department alone received from 7,000 to 10,000 "approaches" a year. From 2,000 to 3,000 get some serious study. Ten thousand story submissions of all types are offered. The effect of this tremendous influx is obvious. At the present time, the idea-submission lawsuits confronting the networks probably account for sixty-five percent of all suits against them in the area of copyright, defamation, right of privacy, and unfair competition.

The extraordinary and multiple claims that result from idea protection are perhaps illustrated best by citing a case of a new program coming on the air and what happened to the network—NBC in this case—that put it on:

On March 1, 1954 the program "Home" was first presented on the NBC Television Network. Prior to its date of first broadcast, NBC had received six idea submission claims relating thereto. The six claims were entirely independent of one another, and each claimant claimed that his idea submission would form the basis of the series to be broadcast. Advance publicity about the program, the only information probably available on which each of the claims could have been based, said little more than that "Home" would be a service-type (as opposed to entertainment-type) program, like a magazine-of-the-air. But this was not the end of our trouble, for following the first broadcast of the program three more claims came in. Two of them became lawsuits. The program went off the air following its broadcast on August 9, 1957. Two of the three idea submission lawsuits concerning it are still pending. As late as July 31, 1957, a motion was noticed for an order enjoining the series three days prior to its going off the air.

The fact that the idea was old was no deterrent to the claims made regarding the "Home" program. A brief search of the exhaustive files maintained by NBC revealed that the network had received submissions of the basic "home" idea since 1929—prior to the earliest of the nine claimants' alleged submissions.

RICHTER v. WESTAB, INC., 529 F.2d 896, 902, 189 U.S.P.Q. 321, (6th Cir.1976). WEICK, J.: The law does not favor the protection of abstract ideas as the property of the originator. An idea should be free for all to use at least until someone is able to translate such idea into a sufficiently useful form that it may be patented or copyrighted. Thus competition in the use of ideas is a social good, hastening the process of invention.

When a design firm suggests that a particular product be decorated with thematic designs, this act of suggesting should not establish an exclusive right to exploit the idea. Perhaps the design firm will not be sufficiently competent to produce good designs based upon the concept. A concept is of little use until solidified into a concrete application. The idea of fashion designs is useless unless good designs are obtained. If the design firm is incapable of producing good designs the public should not be denied the benefit of the idea if another designer could produce good designs. Thus the principle denying legal protection to abstract ideas has important social interests behind it.

NOTES

1. Is the passage excerpted from Richter v. Westab correct that a "concept is of little use until solidified into concrete application"? What assumptions does this passage make about the efficient division of labor in information industries? Is it correct to assume that workers who come up with good ideas are also best placed to execute them?

That those who are well placed to execute good ideas are also capable of originating them? Does it follow from decisions like *Sellers* that a division of labor between idea origination and idea development will occur only within firms? Can contracts effectively bridge the efforts of idea originators and idea developers?

What are the likely effects of a rule that denies property protection to ideas? Will the denial of protection spur firms to originate and develop new ideas, or will firms merely take old ideas and develop them into new, concrete forms? Note that the elaboration of an idea into concrete form will not gain protection for the idea itself, but only for the specific form in which it is elaborated.

For a thoughtful analysis of organizational problems surrounding the development of ideas, and some suggestions for institutional innovation, see Udell, The Essential Nature of the Idea Brokerage Function, 57 J.Pat.Off.Soc'y 642 (1975).

2. *Professional and Amateur Submitters.* Should recovery for use of an idea ever turn on whether the submitter is an amateur or a professional? What are the respective expectations, bargaining positions and long-run interests of amateur and professional idea submitters?

The law doubtless implies a duty to compensate into the ordinary lawyer-client and doctor-patient relationships. Compensation may be characterized as for services rendered. But is it clear that these services are really anything other than submitted ideas? The overlap between services rendered and ideas submitted is well illustrated by cases involving an advertising agency's submission of a commercial slogan to its client. Some courts focus on the act of submission and permit recovery on the basis of professional services rendered, without regard to the slogan's novelty or concreteness. See, for example, How. J. Ryan Assocs., Inc. v. Century Brewing Ass'n, 185 Wash. 600, 55 P.2d 1053 (1936). Other courts ignore the service aspect, weigh the slogan's novelty and concreteness, and deny recovery if these requisites are not met. See, for example, Marcus Advertising, Inc. v. M.M. Fisher Assocs., Inc., 444 F.2d 1061, 170 U.S.P.Q. 244 (7th Cir.1971). Generally, cases in the first, services rendered, category involve established, professional advertising agencies while those in the second category involve amateur submitters. See generally, Havighurst, The Right to Compensation for an Idea, 49 Nw.U.L.Rev. 295 (1954).

3. *Company Submission Policies.* Two marketing professors at the University of Oregon have studied the treatment of unsolicited ideas in a wide variety of firms. Most firms that participated in the survey said that they will evaluate an unsolicited idea, particularly if the idea looks promising. Slightly under one-half of the respondents indicated that they require the submitter to sign a waiver before they will examine an unsolicited idea. Approximately one-half of the firms said that they ignore unsolicited ideas at least in some cases. One firm responded with unusual candor: "most of these [unsolicited ideas] are

thrown in the waste basket after we examine them. If we are interested, we proceed [to secure a waiver]."

Some companies receiving unsolicited ideas return the submitted materials together with a waiver form:

> Your letter was opened in our mail department. It apparently pertains to a new product suggestion. It is the policy of our company not to accept suggestions from outside sources without first receiving a signed copy of our disclosure form.
>
> Enclosed you will find the material you submitted as well as a copy of our policy statement on unsolicited ideas. A disclosure agreement form is also enclosed for your use if you wish to submit your idea to our company under the terms stated in the enclosed policy statement.

Other companies retain the idea while awaiting receipt of an executed waiver form:

> I do not have a technical background, and one of the obligations of my position is to insure that any information submitted such as yours is neither reviewed by me nor presented for review to anyone else in the company unless and until we have received the non-confidential disclosure agreement I have referred to above. I trust that you will sign the agreement and return it, at which point I will forward the material you sent me to the appropriate personnel for evaluation. Otherwise those materials will be returned to you by me without having been examined or reviewed by anyone. . . .

The waiver forms themselves contain a variety of conditions: that review of the idea imposes no obligation of any kind on the firm; that any review and offer to negotiate is not an admission of novelty, priority or originality; that review of the idea does not impair the firm's right to contest existing or future patents on the idea; that acceptance and review of an idea does not create a confidential relationship; and that the submitter waives all rights except those that may be acquired under patent law.

The study is reported in Hawkins & Udell, Corporate Caution and Unsolicited New Product Ideas: A Survey of Corporate Waiver Requirements, 58 J.Pat.Off.Soc'y 375 (1976).

4. *Invention Promoters.* Disillusioned by corporate rebuffs, and stymied by inhospitable legal doctrine, idea originators have turned in large numbers to professional idea brokers and invention promoters who for a fee, and sometimes part of the profits, agree to develop the idea and place it with an appropriate manufacturer. One count in 1974 revealed "about 250 idea brokers in the United States, doing about $100 million in business and servicing approximately 100,000 hopeful inventors annually." Udell, The Essential Nature of the Idea Brokerage Function, 57 J.Pat.Off.Soc'y 642, 643 (1975).

Few of these would-be inventors enjoy any success. One promoter disclosed that for every 586 of its customers only four received more income from their inventions than they paid in fees. Another indicated a success rate of two out of 3,200, and another, 3 out of 30,000. Thomas, Invention Development Services and Inventors: Recent Inroads on Caveat Inventor, 60 J.Pat.Off.Soc'y 355, n. 3 (1978). Although client cupidity doubtless contributed to this dismal record, promoter overreaching, puffing and false advertising may also have played a role. See Abrams, For Inventors: Mostly Promises, N.Y. Times, June 12, 1977, section 3 at 1, col. 5; Shaffer, Caveat Inventor: Concerns that Promise to Assist Gadgeteers are Disappointing Many, Wall Street J., Nov. 30, 1973, at 1, col. 1.

By the mid–1970's, the widespread perception of abuses sparked a fusillade of regulatory efforts. State attorneys general went after promoters for deceptive advertising practices and the unauthorized practice of law in advising on the patentability of submitted ideas. The Federal Trade Commission's investigation of the industry culminated in consent decrees or litigation with several major firms. See, generally, Udell & O'Neil, The FTC in the Matter of IRD, Inc.: An Analysis of Recent FTC Action Against Invention Promoters, 58 J.Pat.Off.Soc'y 442 (1976). State legislatures also acted. California passed a pioneer law regulating invention development contracts. The act requires developers to maintain a bond of at least $25,000 and provides for cancellation by either party within seven days of the contract's execution; clear and conspicuous disclosure of fees; and recovery of treble damages, or at least $3,000, by injured customers. Cal.Bus. & Prof.Code §§ 22370 et seq. (West Supp.1980).

For an excellent overview of practices and regulation in the invention development industry, see Thomas, Invention Development Services and Inventors: Recent Inroads on Caveat Inventor, 60 J.Pat. Off.Soc'y 355 (1978).

5. Idea submissions typically fall into one of four postures: (a) X submits her idea to Y upon Y's express solicitation; (b) X informs Y that she would like to submit an idea of possible value to Y and Y does nothing to block the submission; (c) X thrusts upon Y a full disclosure of her idea before Y has the opportunity to block the submission; (d) X makes no submission at all but charges that Y has copied her idea. As you read the materials in the next section outlining the theories on which recovery for the use of ideas can be based—express contract, implied in fact contract, quasi contract, property—consider whether one of the four theories is particularly well suited to resolve the interests at stake under each of the four postures.

A. THEORIES OF PROTECTION

LUEDDECKE v. CHEVROLET MOTOR CO.

United States Circuit Court of Appeals, Eighth Circuit, 1934.
70 F.2d 345.

WOODROUGH, Circuit Judge.

Mr. H.W. Lueddecke brought this action at law, as plaintiff, against Chevrolet Motor Company and other corporations (all referred to herein as companies), as defendants, to recover on an alleged implied contract on the part of the defendant companies to pay plaintiff the reasonable value of an idea and suggestion which he alleges he furnished to them. Demurrers were interposed to the petition and were sustained. Plaintiff having declined to plead further, the case was dismissed, and the plaintiff appeals.

The petition alleges that the plaintiff sent the following letter to the companies:

"Dear Sirs: As the proud owner of a Chevrolet Sedan, and also with the knowledge of a man who knows automobiles, I am asking you a few questions and then making you a proposition.

"Do you know that a very serious error has been made in the general location of several of the individual units or mechanisms of the Chevrolet car? Do you also know that within another year or so this very error (unless corrected) will reduce Chevrolet sales by possibly a million or even several million dollars? And again, while I, as well as many others, have had and will still have this error of your designers overcome at considerable expense, it will within a short space of time possibly cause some other low-priced car to become more popular than the Chevrolet.

"While many car owners have gone to the trouble of correcting this defect, I have found neither an owner nor a mechanic who was able to discover the cause of the defect. And, unless corrected, the defect will mean considerable annual expense to the owner of the car, for which there is really no excuse at all.

"The cost of overcoming this defect in a car should not be over 20¢ to 30¢ to you as you build the car if you take the easiest and shortest way out of the difficulty. To the owner who has purchased his car the cost will vary from $3.00 to $7.00 depending on where he lives, in city or country.

"The best way out of the difficulty, however, would necessitate a change of design as suggested above, and that can be done without great expense or without sacrificing the essential features of the design of the car.

"Now, I shall not ask you for a one-eighth royalty on $500,000 or $1,000,000 of sales, but I would like to have you make me an offer stating what such information would be worth to you—or how much you could offer and would pay for the same. Upon receipt of your reply, if your offer is satisfactory, I will give you complete information of the above mentioned changes for the Chevrolet car.

"An early reply will be appreciated.

"Yours truly,"

That reply was made as follows:

"Dear Sir: Your letter of June 27, to the Chevrolet Motor Company, regarding your suggestion to change the design of Chevrolet cars, has been forwarded to the New Devices Committee for attention.

"We have this Committee in General Motors, composed of some of our most important executives and engineers, to review all new inventions submitted direct to the Corporation or through any of its divisions or executives.

"It is against the policy of the Corporation to make any agreement for inventions until we know exactly what they are and have sufficient information to place them before the New Devices Committee for consideration.

"If you care to send us drawings and a description of your ideas, the Committee will be very glad to examine them and let you know whether or not General Motors is interested.

"We always insist, however, that everything submitted to us be protected in some way and would suggest, if you have not applied for patents, that you establish legal evidence of ownership and priority of your idea by having your original drawing signed, dated and witnessed by two or more competent persons or notarized.

"We assure you that, if we find the design of sufficient interest to warrant further investigation, some mutually satisfactory agreement will be made.

"Yours very truly,
"New Devices Committee."

That plaintiff then answered:

"Dear Sirs: I have Mr. T.O. Richards' reply (dated July 15th) to my letter of June 27th. Referring to my previous letter you will find that I said that your designers of the Chevrolet car had made a very serious blunder in the location of several of the individual units of the car. I also stated that many car owners have gone to the trouble of correcting the defect, either temporarily or permanently, at considerable expense to themselves. But I have never found either a mechanic or a car owner who knew the cause of the trouble drivers were having with their cars. Because of this fact I thought it expedient and profitable to take the matter up directly with your company.

"Now the matter that I have to present is this: You will find that the body of all Chevrolet cars that have been driven 200 miles or more is from one inch to three inches lower on the left side of the driver than on his right side. Because of this the left rear fender especially, in driving over fairly rough or wavy streets or in rounding corners to the right, will quite often strike against the tires. This has been the cause of tearing up tires or of suddenly slowing down the car—thereby making accidents likely. The experience is also annoying to the driver and occupants of the car.

"Many drivers seem to think that the springs on the left side were naturally weak and not so good; others seem to think that they struck a bad place in the road and that the springs lost their elasticity as a result. But the fact of the case is that the car is not properly balanced—right side against left side. On the left side you have the steering mechanism, the starter, the generator, and the storage battery.

This, together with a one hundred fifty pound (150#) driver, when one drives by himself, throws approximately three hundred pounds (300#) more weight on the left side than on the right side of the car.

"After I had driven my car about 2,800 miles the body was exactly two and three-quarters inches lower on the left side than on the right side. In order to level the body of the car I had an extra spring leaf put into both the front and rear springs on the left side, and that straightened the body up perfectly. My plan is that you either put in this extra spring leaf in both front and rear springs on the left side of the car when you build the car, or else you should change the location of some of the individual units—shifting those units which could be most conveniently moved to the right side of the car or motor. It is my idea that the battery should be moved from the left side to the right side. This would take about fifty pounds from the heavy side and add it to the light side. Then either or both the starter and generator should be moved to the right side of the motor—they would just about balance the weight of the steering unit and the usual excess weight of the driver over his front seat mate.

"The facts given above cannot be denied, and the remedy is simple and clear. I hope you will find them of profit to your firm. I would appreciate a reply at your earliest convenience.

"Respectfully submitted."

To which the New Devices Committee replied:

"Dear Sir: This will acknowledge your letter of July 22 regarding a system for balancing the weight of cars.

"The Committee, at its last meeting, thoroughly discussed your suggestion but decided, unfortunately, that it would not be advisable to redesign our springs in this manner at the present time. We cannot therefore, see our way clear to go into the matter with you further.

"We appreciate your interest in General Motors and regret that we cannot reply to you more favorably.

> "Yours very truly,
> "New Devices Committee."

It is then alleged in the petition that the plaintiff, by and through these letters, did sell and convey to the defendants ideas as to how to balance a Chevrolet car so that the fenders would not strike the wheels, and more particularly to balance the car so that the weight would be more evenly divided on both sides, and that he forwarded his ideas in the form that defendants had requested, and that thereafter the defendants had put into force and effect the ideas so submitted by the plaintiff, or a portion thereof, and that the defendants had, since the plaintiff's ideas were presented to them, used the same or substantial portions thereof on all Chevrolet motorcars manufactured by the defendants, and by the defendants' request that the plaintiff forward his ideas to them, and by using the same, or portions thereof, there was an implied contract on the part of the defendants to pay to the plaintiff the reasonable value of said ideas, which said reasonable value it is alleged was $2,500,000.

We are of the opinion that the demurrers were properly sustained by the trial court. In the first place we are not persuaded that the idea communicated in the letters of the plaintiff was a novel and useful idea in which plaintiff could successfully assert a property right. In the second place, the correspondence and alleged conduct of the companies controvert the claim that there was a promise to pay plaintiff for the ideas or suggestions which he transmitted, and there are no circumstances presented from which the law implies such a promise.

It appears from plaintiff's first letter to the companies that it was then known to many others besides the plaintiff that there was a defect in the Chevrolet car as it was being manufactured and sold. Plaintiff did not claim to be the discoverer of this defect in the car. He says: "I, as well as many others, have had and will still have this error of your designers to overcome at considerable expense." "Many car owners have gone to the trouble of correcting this defect." The plaintiff's second letter discloses that the defect he had in mind was that the body of the car was not held suspended in balance by the springs with sufficient strength to maintain a constant equilibrium, but that when the car was used the body would sag down on the left side. The remedy availed of by himself and others was to reinforce the springs on the side where the body sagged. This much of the idea being generally known and common property, the only other idea which the plaintiff conveyed to the defendants is in the suggestion that the defendants relocate some of the individual units contained in the body of the car with reference to the center of gravity of the car, "Shift those units which could be most conveniently moved to the right side of the car or motor." Plaintiff says: "It is my idea that the battery should be moved from the left side to the right side. This would take about fifty pounds from the heavy side and add it to the light side. Then either or both the starter and generator should be moved to the right side of the motor—they would just about balance the weight of the steering unit and the usual excess weight of the driver over his front seat mate."

From these statements it is apparent that the plaintiff did not claim to know just what shifting of individual units from one side of the car to the other would be necessary or practicable to effect the proper balance of the car in use. He recognizes cases when "one is driving by himself and thereby puts the weight of his body on one side of the car." He reflects the thought that there is a "usual excess weight of the driver over his front seat mate." In other words, that, when several passengers are riding in a car, the weight may not bear evenly on both sides of the center of gravity of the body of the vehicle. Plaintiff's suggestion really was that the companies should make experiments in redisposing some of the readily movable units mounted on the car body and in shifting them from the left to the right side of the car until a balance was effected which would turn out to be enduring in use. The plaintiff said, in effect: It is known that your car body sags lopsidedly to the left when it is being used. I suggest that you try shifting the units which can be most conveniently moved until you get a better balance.

Plaintiff did not say that he had made any such experiments himself or that he knew through experiments what the effect of the suggested shifting of units would be upon a car when the car was used. Plaintiff alleges that what the companies did after they got this letter was to shift the battery from the left side to the right side of the car and also other equipment as set out in the letter "or a portion thereof." That is, the defendants, knowing as others knew that the body of their car when the car was used sagged lopsidedly to the left, transposed fifty pounds of batteries to the opposite side and such other movable equipment as they found from experiment (or engineering calculations) sufficed to produce a more effective balance of the car body when the car was in use. The matter would be no clearer or simpler if we had to do with spring wagons or buggies rather than Chevrolet automobiles. The springs of either vehicle have to be strong enough to offset some uneven disposal of weights on the body. The mere idea of experimenting with the disposal of the weights was not novel and useful, and plaintiff had no property right therein.

In Masline v. New York, etc., R. Co., 95 Conn. 702, 112 A. 639, 641, the court stated: "An idea may undoubtedly be protected by contract. But it must be the plaintiff's idea. Upon communication to the defendant it at once did appear that the idea was not original with the plaintiff, but was a matter of common knowledge, well known to the world at large. He had thought of nothing new, and had therefore no property right to protect which would make his idea a basis of consideration for anything. His valuable information was a mere idea, worthless so far as suggesting anything new was concerned, known to every one, to the use of which the defendant had an equal right with himself."

In the second place, the letter of the New Devices Committee of the companies to the plaintiff contains no promise to pay for any mere suggestion or idea which the plaintiff might choose to send them. They said it was against the policy of the companies to make any agreement for inventions until they knew exactly what they were. They suggested that plaintiff establish legal evidence of his ownership of his ideas by having his original drawing notarized. In the first letter plaintiff said: "I, as well as many others, have had and will still have this error of your designers overcome at considerable expense." "The best way out of the difficulty would necessitate a change of design." And, therefore, the committee suggested that plaintiff send drawings and a description of his ideas, and that he establish legal evidence of ownership and priority of his ideas by having his original drawing signed or notarized, and that, if they found the design of sufficient interest to warrant further investigation, some mutually satisfactory agreement would be made.

The clear implication is that the companies did not make any agreement to pay for merely pointing out some defect in the Chevrolet car or for any mere suggestion that they perfect the car by experimentation or improvement of their own working out, but if the plaintiff should submit a design with drawings and descriptions of his ideas, then, if the design was of sufficient interest to warrant investigation, an agreement would be made. As the plaintiff did not submit any "design" or "drawings and description of his ideas" or bring himself within the committee's proposal or offer, he cannot successfully claim a contract, even if he had an idea in which he had a property right and which he could make a subject of barter and sale. The correspondence shows that the minds of the parties never met on any proposed sale of plaintiff's ideas. The law will not imply a promise on the part of any person against his own express declaration. Municipal Waterworks Co. v. City of Ft. Smith (D.C.) 216 F. 431; Landon v. Kansas City Gas Co., 300 F. 351 (D.C.); Boston Ice Co. v. Potter, 123 Mass. 28, 25 Am.Rep. 9; Earle v. Coburn, 130 Mass. 596. In the latter case it is stated: "As the law will not imply a promise, where there was an express promise, so the law will not imply a promise of any person against his own express declaration; because such declaration is repugnant to any implication of a promise."

If, in fact, the defendants did derive benefit from the plaintiff's ideas that the units on their Chevrolet car should be shifted, and if their subsequent redisposal of some of the units to the other side of the car body was in any wise inspired by the plaintiff's idea, nevertheless, they are not indebted to the plaintiff, because they did not offer to make any agreement to pay for such mere suggestion as the plaintiff made, and their correspondence did not invite such a suggestion. When plaintiff voluntarily divulged his mere idea and suggestion, whatever interest he had in it became common property, and, as such, was available to the defendants. In Bristol v. Equitable Life Assur. Soc'y [132 N.Y. 264, 267, 30 N.E. 506, 507] the court stated: "Without denying that there may be property in an idea or trade secret or system, it is obvious that its originator or proprietor must himself protect it from escape or disclosure. If it cannot be sold or negotiated or used without a disclosure, it would seem proper that some contract should guard or regulate the disclosure; otherwise, it must follow the law of ideas, and become the acquisition of whoever receives it."

The judgment is affirmed.

STANLEY v. COLUMBIA BROADCASTING SYSTEM, INC., 35 Cal.2d 653, 674–76, 221 P.2d 73, 86 U.S.P.Q. 520 (1950). TRAYNOR, J., dissenting: The policy that precludes protection of an abstract idea by copyright does not prevent its protection by contract. Even though an idea is not property subject to exclusive ownership, its disclosure may be of substantial benefit to the person to whom it is disclosed. That disclosure may therefore be consideration for a promise to pay. Unlike a copyright, a contract creates no monopoly; it is effective only between the contracting parties; it does not withdraw the idea from general circulation. Any person not a party to the contract is free to use the idea without restriction.

Even though the idea disclosed may be "widely know [sic] and generally understood," Schonwald v. F. Burkart Mfg. Co., 356 Mo. 435, 202 S.W.2d 7, 13, it may be protected by an express contract providing that it will be paid for regardless of its lack of novelty. An implied-in-fact contract differs from an express contract only in that the promise is not expressed in language but implied from the promisor's conduct. It is not a reasonable assumption, however, in the absence of an express promise, or unequivocal conduct from which one can be implied, that one would obligate himself to pay for an idea that he would otherwise be free to use. Even an express contract to pay for "valuable information" to be submitted by the plaintiff does not carry the implication of a promise to pay if it is found upon disclosure to be common knowledge. Masline v. New York, New Haven & Hartford R. Co., 95 Conn. 702, 708, 112 A. 639. If the idea is not novel, the evidence must establish that the promisor agreed expressly or impliedly to pay for the idea whether or not it was novel.

The gravamen of plaintiff's cause of action is not the unauthorized use of his idea, since ideas may be freely borrowed, but the breach of an agreement to pay for its use. If the evidence discloses that there is no express or implied-in-fact contract there can be no recovery. It is urged that even in the absence of express or implied contract recovery may be predicated upon a quasi-contract, or implied-in-law promise to pay the reasonable value of the idea if it is used. Quasi-contractual liability, however, is based, not upon any evidence of consensual agreement but in the absence of such agreement, upon the theory that the defendant would be unjustly enriched if he were allowed to use the idea without paying for it. A defendant who makes use of an abstract idea that is common property is not unjustly enriched thereby, since he has taken nothing to which the plaintiff or any other person has the right of exclusive ownership. Given the principle that abstract ideas are free, there is no more right to recovery for their use in an action in quasi-contract than in an action for infringement of copyright. It has been consistently held that an action in quasi-contract for the use of an idea is governed by the same principles that control a tort action for copyright infringement: the idea must be embodied in a concrete form attributable to plaintiff's own ingenuity, and the form as distinguished from the abstract idea must be used by the defendant. In either case the plaintiff must prove that property was taken that was his. His choice of alternative actions is analogous to that of a plaintiff whose personal property has been converted and who may elect between a tort action for the value of the converted property and an action based upon an implied-in-law contract to pay the reasonable value of its use. The plaintiff's election will govern the nature of his recovery, but it does not affect the basic elements of his cause of action.

DOWNEY v. GENERAL FOODS CORP.

Court of Appeals of New York, 1972.
31 N.Y.2d 56, 334 N.Y.S.2d 874, 286 N.E.2d 257, 175 U.S.P.Q. 374.

FULD, Chief Judge.

The plaintiff, an airline pilot, brought this action against the defendant General Foods Corporation to recover damages for the alleged misappropriation of an idea. It is his claim that he suggested that the defendant's own gelatin product, "Jell–O," be named "Wiggley" or a variation of that word, including "Mr. Wiggle," and that the product be directed towards the children's market; that, although the defendant disclaimed interest in the suggestion, it later offered its product for sale under the name "Mr. Wiggle." The defendant urges—by way of affirmative defense—that the plaintiff's "alleged 'product concept and name' was independently created and developed" by it. The plaintiff moved for partial summary judgment "on the question of liability" on 5 of its 14 causes of action and the defendant crossmoved for summary judgment dismissing the complaint. The court at Special Term denied both motions, and the Appellate Division affirmed, granting leave to appeal to this court on a certified question.

The plaintiff relies chiefly on correspondence between himself and the defendant, or, more precisely, on letters over the signature of a Miss Dunham, vice-president in charge of one of its departments. On February 15, 1965, the plaintiff wrote to the defendant, stating that he had an "excellent idea to increase the sale of your product JELL–O . . . making it available for children". Several days later, the defendant sent the plaintiff an "Idea Submitted Form" (ISF) which included a form letter and a space for explaining the idea.[2] In that form, the plaintiff suggested, in essence, that the product "be packaged & distributed to children under the name 'WIG–L–E' (meaning wiggly or wiggley) or 'WIGGLE–E' or 'WIGGLE–EEE' or 'WIGLEY.'" He explained that, although his children did not "get especially excited about the Name JELL–O, or wish to eat it", when referred to by that name, "the kids really took to it fast" when his wife "called it 'wiggle-y,'" noting that they then "associate[d] the name to the 'wiggleing' dessert." Although this is the only recorded proof of his idea, the plaintiff maintains that he sent Miss Dunham two handwritten letters in which he set forth other variations of "Wiggiley," including "Mr. Wiggley, Wiggle, Wigglee."[3]

A letter, dated March 8, 1965, over the signature of Miss Dunham, acknowledged the submission of the ISF and informed the plaintiff that

2. The form letter—signed and returned by the plaintiff—recited that "I submit this suggestion with the understanding, which is conclusively evidenced by my use and transmittal to you of this form, that this suggestion is not submitted to you in confidence, that no confidential relationship has been or will be established between us and that the use, if any, to be made of this suggestion by you and the compensation to be paid therefor, if any, if you use it, are matters resting solely in your discretion."

3. Neither of these letters was found in the defendant's files, nor did the plaintiff have the originals or exact copies.

it had no interest in promoting his suggestion. However, in July, the defendant introduced into the market a Jell–O product which it called "Mr. Wiggle." The plaintiff instituted the present action some months later. In addition to general denials, the answer contains several affirmative defenses, one of which, as indicated above, recites that the defendant independently created the product's concept and name before the plaintiff's submission to it.

In support of its position, the defendant pointed to depositions taken by the plaintiff from its employees and from employees of Young & Rubicam, the firm which did its advertising. From these it appears that the defendant first began work on a children's gelatin product in May, 1965—three months after the plaintiff had submitted his suggestion—in response to a threat by Pillsbury Company to enter the children's market with a product named "Jiggly." Those employees of the defendant in charge of the project enlisted the aid of Young & Rubicam which, solely on its own initiative, "came up with the name 'Mr. Wiggle'". In point of fact, Miss Dunham swore in her deposition that she had had no knowledge whatever of the plaintiff's idea until late in 1966, shortly before commencement of his suit; that ideas submitted by the general public were kept in a file by an assistant of hers "under lock and key"; and that no one from any other of the defendant's departments ever asked to research those files. The assistant, who had alone handled the correspondence with the plaintiff over Miss Dunham's signature—reproduced by means of a signature duplicating machine—deposed that she had no contact whatsoever with Young & Rubicam and had never discussed the name "Wiggle" or "Mr. Wiggle" with any one from that firm.

In addition to the depositions of its employees and the employees of its advertising agency, the defendant submitted documentary proof of its prior use of some form of the word "wiggle" in connection with its endeavor to sell Jell–O to children. Thus, it submitted (1) a copy of a report which Young & Rubicam furnished it in June of 1959 proposing "an advertising program directed at children as a means of securing additional sales volume"; (2) a copy of a single dimensional reproduction of a television commercial, prepared in 1959 and used thereafter by the defendant in national and local television broadcasts, which contained the phrase, "ALL THAT WIGGLES IS NOT JELL–O"; and (3) a copy of a newspaper advertisement that appeared in 1960, depicting an Indian "squaw" puppet and her "papoose" preparing Jell–O—the "top favorite in every American tepee"—and suggesting to mothers that they "[m]ake a wigglewam of Jell–O for your tribe tonight!"

The critical issue in this case turns on whether the idea suggested by the plaintiff was original or novel. An idea may be a property right. But, when one submits an idea to another, no promise to pay for its use may be implied, and no asserted agreement enforced, if the elements of novelty and originality are absent, since the property right in an idea is based upon these two elements. (See Soule v. Bon Ami Co., 201 App. Div. 794, 796, 195 N.Y.S. 574, 575, aff'd, 235 N.Y. 609, 139 N.E. 754; Bram v. Dannon Milk Prods., 33 A.D.2d 1010, 307 N.Y.S.2d 571.) The

Bram case is illustrative; in reversing Special Term and granting summary judgment dismissing the complaint, the Appellate Division made it clear that, despite the asserted existence of an agreement, the plaintiff could not recover for his idea if it was not original and had been used before (33 A.D.2d, at p. 1010, 307 N.Y.S.2d 571): "The idea submitted by the plaintiff to the defendants, the concept of depicting an infant in a highchair eating and enjoying yogurt, was lacking in novelty and had been utilized by the defendants . . . prior to its submission. Lack of novelty in an idea is fatal to any cause of action for its unlawful use. In the circumstances a question of fact as to whether there existed an oral agreement between the parties would not preclude summary judgment."

In the case before us, the record indisputably establishes, first, that the idea submitted—use of a word ("wiggley" or "wiggle") descriptive of the most obvious characteristic of Jell-O, with the prefix "Mr." added— was lacking in novelty and originality and, second, that the defendant had envisaged the idea, indeed had utilized it, years before the plaintiff submitted it. As already noted, it had made use of the word "wiggles" in a 1959 television commercial and the word "wigglewam" in a 1960 newspaper advertisement. It was but natural, then, for the defendant to employ some variation of it to combat Pillsbury's entry into the children's market with its "Jiggly." Having relied on its own previous experience, the defendant was free to make use of "Mr. Wiggle" without being obligated to compensate the plaintiff.

It is only necessary to add that, in light of the complete pretrial disclosure in this case of every one who had any possible connection with the creation of the name, the circumstance, adverted to by the courts below, that the facts surrounding the defendant's development of the name were within the knowledge of the defendant and its advertising agency does not preclude a grant of summary judgment. In the present case, it was shown beyond peradventure that there was no connection between Miss Dunham's department and the defendant's other employees or the employees of the advertising outfit who took part in the creation of "Mr. Wiggle." In exhaustive discovery proceedings—which included examinations of all parties concerned either with that name or the defendant's idea files—the plaintiff was furnished with every conceivable item of information in the defendant's possession bearing on the privacy and confidentiality of such files and on the absence of access to them by those outside of Miss Dunham's department. The hope expressed by the plaintiff that he may be able to prove that the witnesses who gave testimony in examinations before trial lied, is clearly insufficient to create an issue of fact requiring a trial or defeat the defendant's motion for summary judgment.

The order appealed from should be reversed, without costs, the question certified answered in the negative and the defendant's motion for summary judgment dismissing the complaint granted.

NOTES

1. *Property.* "In the first place we are not persuaded that the idea communicated in the letters of the plaintiff was a novel and useful idea in which plaintiff could successfully assert a property right." [*Lueddecke*, 70 F.2d at 347.]

Idea submitters rarely succeed on a property theory. Any expression of an idea that is sufficiently novel and concrete to qualify on the property ground could probably also qualify for protection under one of the more developed and traditional intellectual property systems such as trade secret or patent law. When courts invoke property doctrine in idea cases it is usually as a gentle way of telling the submitter that he will not recover in his action.

From time to time and in special circumstances, courts apply property doctrine to allow recovery. At one time, the California Supreme Court took a maverick route, actively giving property protection to ideas. So long as the idea was "novel and reduced to concrete form prior to its appropriation by the defendant," it could in the court's opinion qualify for property as well as contract protection. See, for example, Golding v. R.K.O. Pictures, Inc., 35 Cal.2d 690, 221 P.2d 95, 86 U.S.P.Q. 537 (1950); Stanley v. Columbia Broadcasting System, Inc., 35 Cal.2d 653, 221 P.2d 73, 86 U.S.P.Q. 529 (1950). The court later returned to the mainstream, substantially adopting the approach suggested by Justice Traynor in his *Stanley* dissent excerpted above. See Kurlan v. Columbia Broadcasting System, Inc., 40 Cal.2d 799, 256 P.2d 962, 97 U.S.P.Q. 556 (1953); Weitzenkorn v. Lesser, 40 Cal.2d 778, 256 P.2d 947, 97 U.S.P.Q. 545 (1953). But just three years later, in Desny v. Wilder, 46 Cal.2d 715, 299 P.2d 257, 110 U.S.P.Q. 433 (1956), the court intimated that the property ground was not completely moribund. See also, Blaustein v. Burton, 9 Cal.App.3d 161, 88 Cal.Rptr. 319, 168 U.S.P.Q. 779 (1970), which draws extensively on *Desny* and, incidentally, provides a fascinating glimpse into customs in the motion picture industry.

Can trade custom create property rights in ideas? Consider the following passage from Cole v. Phillips H. Lord, Inc., 262 App.Div. 116, 117, 120, 28 N.Y.S.2d 404, 50 U.S.P.Q. 490, 491–492 (1st Dept.1941), in which plaintiff, who had conceived and communicated to defendant production company the format for a radio series, "Racketeer and Co.," sought to recover a share of the profits from defendant's sale of the series idea under the title, "Mr. District Attorney," to a radio network:

> Plaintiff's testimony and that of the witness Titterton, who was not only disinterested but might have been partial to the defendant by reason of the fact that his employer, National Broadcasting Company, had purchased the rights to defendant's alleged creation, established that in the radio field there is a well recognized right to an original idea or combination of ideas, set forth in a formula for a program. Such program contemplates an indefinite number of broadcasts in a series. Each broadcast has a script which repre-

sents a dialogue and 'business' of that particular broadcast. The idea or the combination of ideas formulated into a program remains constant whereas, of course, the script varies in each separate broadcast.

That a property right exists with respect to a combination of ideas evolved into a program as distinguished from rights to particular scripts, finds support in defendant's own course of conduct. When it transferred any rights to Mr. District Attorney, it sold not scripts but the basic idea.

Special trade assumptions can, of course, also be construed to permit recovery on an implied contract basis. See, for example, Whitfield v. Lear, 751 F.2d 90, 224 U.S.P.Q. 540 (2d Cir.1984).

2. *Express Contract.* *"He had thought of nothing new, and had therefore no property right to protect which would make his idea a basis of consideration for anything."* [*Lueddecke,* 70 F.2d at 348, quoting from Masline v. New York, N.H. & H. R. Co., 95 Conn. 702, 112 A. 639 (1921).]

Under the facts of *Masline,* plaintiff, a brakeman and baggagemaster on defendant's line, informed defendant "that he had information of value in the operation of the defendant's road by which, if applied by the defendant, it could earn at least $100,000 a year therefrom without any expense on the part of the defendant, and that the plaintiff would furnish the defendant this information for a valuable consideration." Subsequently, plaintiff and defendant orally "agreed that, if the plaintiff would submit his proposition, and if said proposition was adopted and acted upon by the defendant, the plaintiff should receive as compensation for imparting such information," five percent of the receipts. Plaintiff then disclosed the idea that defendant sell advertising space in its cars and railway depots. Defendant promptly implemented the idea but refused to compensate plaintiff. Although the court found that, before plaintiff's disclosure, defendant had never used this type of plan, it found, too, that the idea "was not new . . . but was perfectly obvious to all men." From this, the court reasoned, the idea "could have no market value so as to form the consideration for a contract . . . and that the idea was not property nor did it constitute consideration for a promise." 112 A. at 639–640.

Should the fact that an idea is insufficiently novel and concrete to qualify as property also disqualify it as contract consideration? Could consideration have been found in plaintiff's bargained-for act of disclosure? High v. Trade Union Courier Pub. Corp., 31 Misc.2d 7, 69 N.Y.S.2d 526 (Sup.Ct.1946), states what appears to be the New York position: "While the idea disclosed may be common or even open to public knowledge, yet such disclosure, if protected by contract, is sufficient consideration for the promise to pay." 69 N.Y.S.2d 526, 529. Does the emphasis in Downey v. General Foods on proof of "novelty and originality" suggest that New York may be slipping into the *Masline* approach? See also Whitfield v. Lear, 751 F.2d 90, 224 U.S.P.Q. 540 (2d Cir.1984).

Could the *Masline* court have reached the same result by implying into the contract a condition that compensation would be paid only if the disclosed idea were concrete and novel? By finding that defendant had acted not on plaintiff's disclosure but rather on its own general knowledge and initiative?

If an idea recipient first agrees to pay for an idea after it has been disclosed to her, will the contract fail for lack of consideration? Smith v. Recrion Corp., 91 Nev. 666, 541 P.2d 663, 191 U.S.P.Q. 397 (1975), held that if the recipient subsequently promised compensation, "the promise would be unenforceable for the reason that it would have been unsupported by consideration. Past consideration is the legal equivalent of no consideration." 91 Nev. at 669, 541 P.2d at 665. Compare Desny v. Wilder, 46 Cal.2d 715, 738, 299 P.2d 257, 269, 110 U.S.P.Q. 433, 442 (1956): "where an idea has been conveyed with the expectation by the purveyor that compensation will be paid if the idea is used, there is no reason why the producer who has been the beneficiary of the conveyance of such an idea, and who finds it valuable and is profiting by it, may not then for the first time, although he is not at that time under any legal obligation so to do, promise to pay a reasonable compensation for that idea—that is, for the past service of furnishing it to him—and thus create a valid obligation."

3. *Contract Implied in Fact.* *"The correspondence shows that the minds of the parties never met on any proposed sale of plaintiff's ideas. The law will not imply a promise on the part of any person against his own express declaration."* [*Lueddecke*, 70 F.2d at 348.]

The relationship between the parties is the fact most often examined in determining whether a contract will be implied. If the submitter can show a confidential relationship with the recipient, he has gone far toward making out a case for recovery. Proof of a confidential relationship forms the basis for a series of inferences that can lead logically to the implication of a contract: disclosure of an idea within a confidential relationship indicates that the idea is disclosed in confidence; that the idea is disclosed in confidence indicates that the originator does not intend to divest his rights in it by publication, at least not without compensation; acceptance of the idea by the recipient in confidence suggests her understanding that she is not to publish or otherwise use it without the originator's consent, at least not without compensating him for the use.

Are actions for breach of confidence respecting disclosed ideas properly classified as actions for breach of an implied contract or as tort actions for breach of a confidential relationship? The distinction may be important when it comes to determining the appropriate statute of limitations. See, for example, Davies v. Krasna, 14 Cal.3d 502, 121 Cal. Rptr. 705, 535 P.2d 1161 (1975).

4. *Quasi Contract.* *"If, in fact, the defendants did derive benefit from the plaintiff's ideas . . . nevertheless, they are not indebted to the plaintiff because they did not offer to make any agreement to pay for*

such mere suggestion as the plaintiff made . . ." [*Lueddecke,* 70 F.2d at 348.]

Compare Matarese v. Moore–McCormack Lines, 158 F.2d 631, 71 U.S.P.Q. 311 (2d Cir.1946), which raised the issue "whether a corporation may be required to pay the reasonable value of the use of certain inventive ideas disclosed by an employee to an agent of the corporation in the expectation of payment where an express contract fails for want of proof of the agent's authority." 158 F.2d at 632. The court answered in the affirmative. The agent's "promise of compensation, the specific character, novelty and patentability of plaintiff's invention, the subsequent use made of it by defendants, and the lack of compensation given the plaintiff—all indicate that the application of the principle of unjust enrichment is required." 158 F.2d at 634. The court was careful to distinguish *Lueddecke:* "Courts have justly been assiduous in defeating attempts to delve into the pockets of business firms through spurious claims for compensation for the use of ideas. Thus to be rejected are attempts made by telephoning or writing vague general ideas to business corporations and then seizing upon some later general similarity between their products and the notions propounded as a basis for damages. . . ." 158 F.2d at 634. See also Werlin v. Reader's Digest Ass'n, Inc., 528 F.Supp. 451, 213 U.S.P.Q. 1041 (S.D.N.Y.1981).

5. *"Novelty" and "Concreteness".* The words "novel" and "concrete" appear in virtually all idea cases and have taken on almost talismanic significance. The terms have nonetheless gained little specific content. Presumably "novel" means the opposite of "common" or, perhaps, "old." "Concrete" is probably the antithesis of "abstract," and also implies that, to be protectible, the idea must be reduced to tangible form. Beyond this, the decisions offer nothing definitive. One reason for the lack of clarity may be that courts apply the two requirements differently depending on the plaintiff's theory of action. Courts apply the novelty and concreteness requirements least rigorously when the cause of action is for breach of an express contract, somewhat more rigorously in implied in fact contract actions, and more rigorously still in quasi-contract and property actions.

Novelty. Why did the court find that the idea in Downey v. General Foods was not novel and original? Because it did little more than reflect the tendency of defendant's product to wiggle? Because it consisted of no more than two words in common use? Because no substantial investment was needed to produce the idea? Because defendant had previously considered, but shelved, the possible use of the term? Because somebody else, somewhere, had probably coined the phrase previously?

To the extent that the term "novel" is intended to refer to a specific attribute, such as newness, how well equipped are courts to measure the attribute? Patent law uses the term "novel" in a very precise sense, and assumes that novelty will be determined through systematic searches of prior art in the Patent and Trademark Office and in the relevant technical literature. See pages 377 to 402. Are similar searches possible, or desirable, in the context of submitted ideas?

Concreteness. "The law shies away from according protection to vagueness, and must do so especially in the realm of ideas with the obvious dangers of a contrary rule." Hamilton Nat'l Bank v. Belt, 210 F.2d 706, 708, 99 U.S.P.Q. 388 (D.C.Cir.1953). Plaintiff in *Hamilton* sought to recover for the bank's use of an idea he had submitted for organizing and sponsoring radio broadcasts of student talent shows. In the court's view, "If the idea had been merely to broadcast programs of selected student talent it would have been too general and abstract and perhaps would also have lacked newness and novelty. On the other hand, had the plan been accompanied with a script for each broadcast it would have been sufficiently concrete." 210 F.2d at 709. The court observed that plaintiff's submission fell somewhere between these two poles and affirmed a judgment for plaintiff: "where the plan is for a series of broadcasts the contents of which depend upon selection of talent at different times, a detailed program cannot be presented at the preliminary stages of negotiation." 210 F.2d at 709.

A finding that the submitted idea is novel and concrete will not guarantee recovery even if the other required contract elements are found. For the submitter to recover, the court must also find that the recipient used the idea in its concrete form. Hamilton Bank probably would have escaped liability if it had used Belt's basic idea—a weekly broadcast of student talent—but had varied the trappings from those described in Belt's presentation. See Official Airlines Schedule Information Serv., Inc. v. Eastern Air Lines, Inc., 333 F.2d 672, 141 U.S.P.Q. 546 (5th Cir.1964) (affirming grant of motion to dismiss plaintiff's complaint that its idea for "Plane Facts"—an hourly, joint airline radio broadcast of flight schedule information—which had been submitted to defendant, was appropriated by defendant's hourly "Flite Facts" which broadcast information concerning defendant's flights only).

6. *Damages.* The theory of action pursued will determine the measure of damages for idea appropriations. If an express contract is proved, its terms on compensation will govern. For a factually implied contract, the measure will be what the defendant is presumed to have agreed to pay, or the reasonable value of the idea. If recovery is based on quasi contract, recovery will be measured by the defendant's unjust enrichment—its actual profit from the use of the idea. See Robbins v. Frank Cooper Assocs., 19 A.D.2d 242, 244, 241 N.Y.S.2d 259 (1st Dept. 1963), rev'd, 14 N.Y.2d 913, 252 N.Y.S.2d 318 (1964); Brunner v. Stix, Baer & Fuller Co., 352 Mo. 1225, 181 S.W.2d 643 (1944).

7. *You Can't Cheat an Honest Man.* Since rights to an idea may be lost upon the idea's unguarded communication, an idea submitter is well advised to obtain, prior to disclosure, the recipient's agreement to compensate for use of the idea. Recipients are, however, also—and more often—well advised. If they encourage the submission of ideas at all, they typically condition receipt upon a release from any obligation to pay for the ideas, whether used or not. Competing considerations of

insulation from suit and good public relations make drafting the relevant documents a particularly sensitive task. Consider how one layman botched the job:

> 43 Bock Ave. Aug. 8th 1938
> Newark, N.J., Newark, N.J.

Mr. W.C. Fields:

Dear Bill:

Enclosed find a radio script which I think suits your inimitable style of super-comedy.

To say that I rate you as the greatest of comedians is putting it mildly you old rascal you.

There isn't a greater master of mimicry, buffoonery, or what have you on the stage, radio, or screen.

When you open up your hocus pocus, hipper dipper, strong men weep and pay their income tax.

When I read in a daily paper that a medico tried to limit your liquid refreshment I knew the millenium was here.

Bill without his nourishment.

Egad! What next? Is there no Justice? Gazooks! Must an old Indian fighter turn squaw.

When Goofus, Gufus, Hoofus and Affadufus are allegedly doing comedy on the "air," your very absence and silence is "funny."

You "Old Reprobate."

When are you coming back to us over the "ether" without an operation except on our funny bone.

What's that? "Bill Cody" Fields has retired from the "Fields" of comedy.

Preposterous! Idiotic! Fantastic! Whatever you think the enclosed radio script is worth is O.K. with me "Bill."

Pardon a young man's brashness in addressing you so familiarly, but I know you'll understand.

With sincerest best wishes to you for a long life and happy days.

I remain

> Sincerely yours,
> Harry Yadkoe
> 43 Bock Ave.
> Newark, N.J.
> September 9, 1938

To which Fields replied:

Mr. Harry Yadkoe
43 Bock Ave.
Newark, N.J.

Dear Harry Yadkoe:

I liked your wheezes and your treatment, which follows along the line I have been giving our dear customers. Thanks for your gay compliments and thanks for the snake story. I shall use it in conjunction with one I have either on the radio or in a picture. I am about to embark on a new radio series and if you would like to submit a couple of scripts gratis and I am able to use them, who knows, both parties being willing, we might enter into a contract. My reason for injecting the vile word "gratis" is that we get so many letters from folks who if we even answer in the negative, immediately begin suit for plagiarism. Whilst we have never had to pay off, they sometimes become irritating no end.

> Very truly yours,
> W.C. Fields (signed)
> W.C. Fields
> c/o Beyer & MacArthur Agents
> Taft Bldg.,
> Cor. Hollywood Blvd. & Vine
> Sts., Hollywood Calif.

Plaintiff, who claimed that Fields used several of the submitted gag ideas, was awarded an $8,000 judgment for breach of an implied contract to pay for the reasonable value of the use of his material. Appropriately enough, the movie in which plaintiff's material was used was "You Can't Cheat an Honest Man." Yadkoe v. Fields, 66 Cal.App. 2d 150, 151 P.2d 906, 63 U.S.P.Q. 103 (1944).

Language more satisfactory from the viewpoint of the recipient appears in Davies v. Carnation Co., 352 F.2d 393, 147 U.S.P.Q. 350 (9th Cir.1965) and Davis v. General Foods Corp., 21 F.Supp. 445 (S.D.N.Y. 1937). For a more extensive release form, see Olsson, Dreams for Sale, 23 Law & Contemp.Probs. 34, 55–59 (1958). Reread the form letter involved in Lueddecke v. Chevrolet Motor Co., above, and consider whether, as house counsel for defendant, you would have approved its attempt at courtesy—"it would not be advisable to redesign our springs in this manner at the present time."

8. The legal theories that can be employed to recover for use of ideas are canvassed in Barrett, The "Law of Ideas" Reconsidered, 71 J.Pat. & Trademark Off. Soc'y 691 (1989); Jack, The Legal Protection of Abstract Ideas: A Remedies Approach, 18 Idea 7 (1976).

California courts have been singularly preoccupied with idea submission cases, particularly those involving ideas for motion pictures and television programs. The evolution of California's idea jurisprudence has attracted considerable commentary. See Kaplan, Implied Contract and the Law of Literary Property, 42 Calif.L.Rev. 28 (1954); Kaplan, Further Remarks on Compensation for Ideas in California, 46 Calif.L.Rev. 699 (1958); Gershon, Contractual Protection for Literary or Dramatic Material: When, Where and How Much?, 27 S.Cal.L.Rev. 290 (1954); Nimmer, The Law of Ideas, 27 S.Cal.L.Rev. 119 (1954). Comment, Television Formats—The Search for Protection, 58 Calif.L.Rev. 1169 (1970), explores the law outside, as well as within, California.

B. LIMITS OF PROTECTION: THE PLACE OF IDEAS IN THE COMPETITIVE PLAN

ARONSON v. QUICK POINT PENCIL CO.

Supreme Court of the United States, 1979.
440 U.S. 257, 99 S.Ct. 1096, 59 L.Ed.2d 296, 201 U.S.P.Q. 1.

Mr. Chief Justice BURGER delivered the opinion of the Court.

We granted certiorari to consider whether federal patent law pre-empts state contract law so as to preclude enforcement of a contract to pay royalties to a patent applicant, on sales of articles embodying the putative invention, for so long as the contracting party sells them, if a patent is not granted.

(1)

In October 1955 the petitioner Mrs. Jane Aronson filed an application, Serial No. 542677, for a patent on a new form of keyholder. Although ingenious, the design was so simple that it readily could be copied unless it was protected by patent. In June 1956, while the patent application was pending, Mrs. Aronson negotiated a contract with the respondent, Quick Point Pencil Company, for the manufacture and sale of the keyholder.

The contract was embodied in two documents. In the first, a letter from Quick Point to Mrs. Aronson, Quick Point agreed to pay Mrs. Aronson a royalty of 5% of the selling price in return for "the exclusive right to make and sell keyholders of the type shown in your application, Serial No. 542677." The letter further provided that the parties would consult one another concerning the steps to be taken "[i]n the event of any infringement."

The contract did not require Quick Point to manufacture the keyholder. Mrs. Aronson received a $750 advance on royalties and was entitled to rescind the exclusive license if Quick Point did not sell a million keyholders by the end of 1957. Quick Point retained the right to cancel the agreement whenever "the volume of sales does not meet our expectation." The duration of the agreement was not otherwise prescribed.

A contemporaneous document provided that if Mrs. Aronson's patent application was "not allowed within five (5) years, Quick Point Pencil Co. [would] pay two and one half percent (2½%) of sales . . . so long as you [Quick Point] continue to sell same."

In June 1961, when Mrs. Aronson had failed to obtain a patent on the keyholder within the five years specified in the agreement, Quick Point asserted its contractual right to reduce royalty payments to 2½% of sales. In September of that year the Board of Patent Appeals issued a final rejection of the application on the ground that the keyholder was not patentable, and Mrs. Aronson did not appeal. Quick Point continued to pay reduced royalties to her for 14 years thereafter.

The market was more receptive to the keyholder's novelty and utility than the Patent Office. By September 1975 Quick Point had made sales in excess of seven million dollars and paid Mrs. Aronson royalties totalling $203,963.84; sales were continuing to rise. However, while Quick Point was able to pre-empt the market in the earlier years and was long the only manufacturer of the Aronson keyholder, copies began to appear in the late 1960's. Quick Point's competitors, of course, were not required to pay royalties for their use of the design. Quick Point's share of the Aronson keyholder market has declined during the past decade.

(2)

In November 1975 Quick Point commenced an action in the United States District Court for a declaratory judgment, pursuant to 28 U.S. C.A. § 2201, that the royalty agreement was unenforceable. Quick Point asserted that state law which might otherwise make the contract enforceable was preempted by federal patent law. This is the only issue presented to us for decision.

Both parties moved for summary judgment on affidavits, exhibits, and stipulations of fact. The District Court concluded that the "language of the agreement is plain, clear and unequivocal and has no relation as to whether or not a patent is ever granted." Accordingly, it held that the agreement was valid, and that Quick Point was obliged to pay the agreed royalties pursuant to the contract for so long as it manufactured the keyholder.

The Court of Appeals reversed, one judge dissenting. It held that since the parties contracted with reference to a pending patent application, Mrs. Aronson was estopped from denying that patent law principles governed her contract with Quick Point. Although acknowledging that this Court had never decided the precise issue, the Court of Appeals held that our prior decisions regarding patent licenses compelled the conclusion that Quick Point's contract with Mrs. Aronson became unenforceable once she failed to obtain a patent. The court held that a continuing obligation to pay royalties would be contrary to "the strong federal policy favoring the full and free use of ideas in the public domain," Lear Inc. v. Adkins, 395 U.S. 653, 674, 89 S.Ct. 1902, 1913, 23 L.Ed.2d 610 (1969). The court also observed that if Mrs. Aronson actually had obtained a patent, Quick Point would have escaped its royalty obligations either if the patent were held to be invalid, see id., at 674, 89 S.Ct. at 1913, or upon its expiration after 17 years, see Brulotte v. Thys Co., 379 U.S. 29, 85 S.Ct. 176, 13 L.Ed.2d 99 (1964). Accordingly, it concluded that a licensee should be relieved of royalty obligations when the licensor's efforts to obtain a contemplated patent prove unsuccessful.

(3)

On this record it is clear that the parties contracted with full awareness of both the pendency of a patent application and the possibility that a patent might not issue. The clause de-escalating the royalty by half in the event no patent issued within five years makes that crystal clear. Quick Point apparently placed a significant value on exploiting the basic novelty of the device, even if no patent issued; its success demonstrates that this judgment was well founded. Assuming, *arguendo,* that the initial letter and the commitment to pay a 5% royalty was subject to federal patent law, the provision relating to the 2½% royalty was explicitly independent of federal law. The cases and principles relied on by the Court of Appeals and Quick Point do not bear on a contract that does not rely on a patent, particularly where, as here, the contracting parties agreed expressly as to alternative obligations if no patent should issue.

Commercial agreements traditionally are the domain of state law. State law is not displaced merely because the contract relates to intellectual property which may or may not be patentable; the states are free to regulate the use of such intellectual property in any manner not inconsistent with federal law. Kewanee Oil Co. v. Bicron Corp., 416 U.S. 470, 479, 94 S.Ct. 1879, 1885, 40 L.Ed.2d 315 (1974); see Goldstein v. California, 412 U.S. 546, 93 S.Ct. 2303, 37 L.Ed.2d 163 (1973). In this as in other fields, the question of whether federal law pre-empts state law "involves a consideration of whether that law 'stands as an obstacle to the accomplishment and execution of the full purposes and objectives of Congress.' Hines v. Davidowitz, 312 U.S. 52, 67 (1941)." *Kewanee Oil Co.,* supra. If it does not, state law governs.

In *Kewanee Oil Co.,* supra, 416 U.S. at 480–481, 94 S.Ct. at 1885–1886, we reviewed the purposes of the federal patent system. First, patent law seeks to foster and reward invention; second, it promotes disclosure of inventions, to stimulate further innovation and to permit the public to practice the invention once the patent expires; third, the stringent requirements for patent protection seek to assure that ideas in the public domain remain there for the free use of the public.

Enforcement of Quick Point's agreement with Mrs. Aronson is not inconsistent with any of these aims. Permitting inventors to make enforceable agreements licensing the use of their inventions in return for royalties provides an additional incentive to invention. Similarly, encouraging Mrs. Aronson to make arrangements for the manufacture of her keyholder furthers the federal policy of disclosure of inventions; these simple devices display the novel idea which they embody wherever they are seen.

Quick Point argues that enforcement of such contracts conflicts with the federal policy against withdrawing ideas from the public domain and discourages recourse to the federal patent system by allowing states to extend "perpetual protection to articles too lacking in novelty to merit any patent at all under federal constitutional standards," Sears, Roebuck & Co. v. Stiffel Co., 376 U.S. 225, 232, 84 S.Ct. 784, 789, 11 L.Ed.2d 661 (1964).

We find no merit in this contention. Enforcement of the agreement does not withdraw any idea from the public domain. The design for the keyholder was not in the public domain before Quick Point obtained its license to manufacture it. In negotiating the agreement, Mrs. Aronson disclosed the design in confidence. Had Quick Point tried to exploit the design in breach of that confidence, it would have risked legal liability. It is equally clear that the design entered the public domain as a result of the manufacture and sale of the keyholders under the contract.

Requiring Quick Point to bear the burden of royalties for the use of the design is no more inconsistent with federal patent law than any of the other costs involved in being the first to introduce a new product to the market, such as outlays for research and development and marketing and promotional expenses. For reasons which Quick Point's experience with the Aronson keyholder demonstrate, innovative entrepreneurs have usually found such costs to be well worth paying.

Finally, enforcement of this agreement does not discourage anyone from seeking a patent. Mrs. Aronson attempted to obtain a patent for over five years. It is quite true that had she succeeded, she would have received a 5% royalty only on keyholders sold during the 17–year life of the patent. Offsetting the limited terms of royalty payments, she would have received twice as much per dollar of Quick Point's sales, and both she and Quick Point could have licensed any others who produced the same keyholder. Which course would have produced the greater yield to the contracting parties is a matter of speculation; the parties resolved the uncertainties by their bargain.

(4)

No decision of this Court relating to patents justifies relieving Quick Point of its contract obligations. We have held that a state may not forbid the copying of an idea in the public domain which does not meet the requirements for federal patent protection. Compco Corp. v. Day–Brite Lighting, Inc., 376 U.S. 234, 84 S.Ct. 779, 11 L.Ed.2d 669 (1964); Sears, Roebuck & Co. v. Stiffel Co., 376 U.S. 225, 84 S.Ct. 784, 11 L.Ed.2d 661 (1964). Enforcement of Quick Point's agreement, however, does not prevent anyone from copying the keyholder. It merely requires Quick Point to pay the consideration which it promised in return for the use of a novel device which enabled it to preempt the market.

In Lear, Inc. v. Adkins, 395 U.S. 653, 89 S.Ct. 1902, 23 L.Ed.2d 610 (1969), we held that a person licensed to use a patent may challenge the validity of the patent, and that a licensee who establishes that the patent is invalid need not pay the royalties accrued under the licensing agreement subsequent to the issuance of the patent. Both holdings relied on the desirability of encouraging licensees to challenge the validity of patents, to further the strong federal policy that only inventions which meet the rigorous requirements of patentability shall be withdrawn from the public domain. Accordingly, neither the holding nor the rationale of *Lear* controls when no patent has issued, and no ideas have been withdrawn from public use.

Enforcement of the royalty agreement here is also consistent with the principles treated in Brulotte v. Thys Co., 379 U.S. 29, 85 S.Ct. 176, 13 L.Ed.2d 99 (1964). There, we held that the obligation to pay royalties in return for the use of a patented device may not extend beyond the life of the patent. The principle underlying that holding was simply that the monopoly granted *under a patent* cannot lawfully be used to "negotiate with the leverage of that monopoly." The Court emphasized that to "use that leverage to project those royalty payments beyond the life of the patent is analogous to an effort to enlarge the monopoly of a patent. . . ." Id., at 33, 85 S.Ct., at 179. Here the reduced royalty which is challenged, far from being negotiated "with the leverage" of a patent, rested on the contingency that no patent would issue within five years.

No doubt a pending patent application gives the applicant some additional bargaining power for purposes of negotiating a royalty agreement. The pending application allows the inventor to hold out the hope of an exclusive right to exploit the idea, as well as the threat that the other party will be prevented from using the idea for 17 years. However, the amount of leverage arising from a patent application depends on how likely the parties consider it to be that a valid patent will issue. Here, where no patent ever issued, the record is entirely clear that the parties assigned a substantial likelihood to that contingency, since they specifically provided for a reduced royalty in the event no patent issued within five years.

This case does not require us to draw the line between what constitutes abuse of a pending application and what does not. It is clear that whatever role the pending application played in the negotiation of the 5% royalty, it played no part in the contract to pay the 2½% royalty indefinitely.

Our holding in *Kewanee Oil Co.,* supra, puts to rest the contention that federal law pre-empts and renders unenforceable the contract made by these parties. There we held that state law forbidding the misappropriation of trade secrets was not preempted by federal patent law. We observed:

"Certainly the patent policy of encouraging invention is not disturbed by the existence of another form of incentive to invention. In this respect the two systems [patent and trade secret law] are not and never would be in conflict." Id., 416 U.S., at 484, 94 S.Ct., at 1887.

Enforcement of this royalty agreement is even less offensive to federal patent policies than state law protecting trade secrets. The most commonly accepted definition of trade secrets is restricted to confidential information which is not disclosed in the normal process of exploitation. See Restatement of Torts § 757, comment b (1939). Accordingly, the exploitation of trade secrets under state law may not satisfy the federal policy in favor of disclosure, whereas disclosure is inescapable in exploiting a device like the Aronson keyholder.

Enforcement of these contractual obligations, freely undertaken in arm's length negotiation and with no fixed reliance on a patent or a probable patent grant, will:

> "encourage invention in areas where patent law does not reach, and will prompt the independent innovator to proceed with the discovery and exploitation of his invention. Competition is fostered and the public is not deprived of the use of valuable, if not quite patentable, invention." [Footnote omitted.] Id., at 485, 94 S.Ct., at 1888.

The device which is the subject of this contract ceased to have any secrecy as soon as it was first marketed, yet when the contract was negotiated the inventiveness and novelty were sufficiently apparent to induce an experienced novelty manufacturer to agree to pay for the opportunity to be first in the market. Federal patent law is not a barrier to such a contract.

Reversed.

Mr. Justice BLACKMUN, concurring in the result.

For me, the hard question is whether this case can meaningfully be distinguished from Brulotte v. Thys Co., 379 U.S. 29, 85 S.Ct. 176, 13 L.Ed.2d 99 (1964). There the Court held a patent licensor could not use the leverage of its patent to obtain a royalty contract that extended beyond the patent's 17–year term. Here Mrs. Aronson has used the leverage of her patent application to negotiate a royalty contract which continues to be binding even though the patent application was long ago denied.

The Court asserts that her leverage played "no part" with respect to the contingent agreement to pay a reduced royalty if no patent issued within five years. Yet it may well be that Quick Point agreed to that contingency in order to obtain its other rights that depended on the success of the patent application. The parties did not apportion consideration in the neat fashion the Court adopts.

In my view, the holding in *Brulotte* reflects hostility toward extension of a patent monopoly whose term is fixed by statute, 35 U.S.C.A. § 154. Such hostility has no place here. A patent application which is later denied temporarily discourages unlicensed imitators. Its benefits and hazards are of a different magnitude from those of a granted patent that prohibits all competition for 17 years. Nothing justifies estopping a patent application licensor from entering into a contract whose term does not end if the application fails. The Court points out that enforcement of this contract does not conflict with the objectives of the patent laws. The United States, as *amicus curiae*, maintains that patent application licensing of this sort is desirable because it encourages patent applications, promotes early disclosure, and allows parties to structure their bargains efficiently.

On this basis, I concur in the Court's holding that federal patent law does not pre-empt the enforcement of Mrs. Aronson's contract with Quick Point.

NOTES

1.   Lear v. Adkins, discussed in the *Aronson* opinion, is considered at page 487, below and Brulotte v. Thys is considered at page 486, below.   Kewanee v. Bicron appears at page 152, below.   Goldstein v. California is discussed at page 770, below.   *Sears* and *Compco* appear at pages 103 and 107, below.

2.   Does *Aronson* represent a blanket endorsement of state idea protection?   What if, instead of express contract, the state law ground for recovery had been contract implied in fact?   Quasi contract?   Property?   What are the different market effects of each of these theories? Did the Court indicate a line between those state doctrines whose market effects are tolerable and those that are not?

3.   Section 301 of the Copyright Act will preempt a state law if three conditions are met: the work protected by the state law is "fixed in a tangible medium of expression;" the work comes "within the subject matter of copyright;" and the state law grants a right that is "equivalent to any of the exclusive rights within the general scope of copyright."   State law protection of ideas will characteristically escape preemption under section 301.   If the idea's creator communicated the idea orally, the work will not have been fixed in a tangible medium of expression.   Even if the idea is tangibly fixed, ideas fall outside the subject matter of copyright.   Finally, state contract rights are not equivalent to any of the rights conferred by the Copyright Act.

Section 301 is discussed in detail at pages 759 to 772, below.

II. UNFAIR COMPETITION

Unfair competition and trademark law are two threads in a single fabric. Unfair competition embraces a broad continuum of competitive conduct likely to confuse consumers as to the source of goods or services—from the appropriation of relatively nondistinctive names and symbols accompanied by acts of passing off, to the appropriation of distinctive symbols. Trademark law occupies only the last part of this continuum, protecting distinctive marks against appropriation by competitors and requiring no proof that consumers have actually been deceived.

The conduct governed by unfair competition and trademark law differs in degree rather than kind. Nonetheless, the two bodies of law are in some respects categorically distinct. Unfair competition law is entirely circumstantial. In determining whether a defendant's conduct constitutes unfair competition, courts will assess the aggregate effect of all of the elements employed in plaintiff's and defendant's marketing efforts—the nature of the product, the color, shape and size of its package, the configuration of the label, any insignia, terms and names appearing on the label, and the nature, media and content of any surrounding advertising. If a comparison of the total images created by the plaintiff and the defendant indicates that consumer confusion is likely, and if the plaintiff was the first to use the image, the court will require the defendant to modify its image to avoid confusion. The method of trademark law, by contrast, is to focus exclusively on each discrete element in the plaintiff's marketing image. If the element meets trademark's distinctiveness standards, it will be protected. If it does not, the court will disregard it. A court will enjoin the appropriation of each protected element and will give little if any weight to surrounding circumstances. The injunction will typically be absolute, even though a conditional decree or a requirement of labeling would suffice to dispel confusion.

Historically, the single most important distinction between unfair competition and trademark law was jurisdictional. Unfair competition law was principally the product of state common law and statute, while trademark law was principally the product of the federal Trademark Act. By the mid-twentieth century, state legislatures and the Congress had substantially erased the jurisdictional boundaries between unfair competition and trademark law. Most states have enacted their own trademark statutes, based on the Model State Trademark Bill promulgated by the United States Trademark Association in 1949 and revised in 1964, for the registration of marks used within their borders. Many states have enacted anti-dilution statutes giving property-like protection to distinctive symbols apart from evidence of consumer confusion as to source. At the same time, the Lanham Act, enacted in 1946, created a federal law of unfair competition that substantially parallels state unfair competition law. State antidilution laws are discussed beginning at page 76, below. The Lanham Act's unfair competition provision, section 43(a), is discussed beginning at page 343, below. Part 3, Chapter I covers the federal law of trademarks and their statutory companions—service marks, collective marks and certification marks.

Bibliographic Note. R. Callmann, The Law of Unfair Competition, Trademarks and Monopolies (L. Altman 4th ed. 1981) and J.T. McCarthy, Trademarks and Unfair Competition (2d ed. 1984) are the leading treatises on unfair competition law. State Trademark and Unfair Competition Law (1989), edited by the United States Trademark Association, compiles the trademark and unfair competition laws of all fifty states and the District of Columbia and Puerto Rico.

The history of unfair competition law is summarized in Chafee, Unfair Competition, 53 Harv.L.Rev. 1289 (1940) and is exhaustively considered in F. Schechter, The Historical Foundations of the Law Relating to Trade–Marks (1925). For a brief, comparative review, see Comment, Unfair Competition: A Comparative Study of its Role in Common and Civil Law Systems, 53 Tul.L.Rev. 164 (1978).

A. THEORY OF PROTECTION

1. PASSING OFF AND SECONDARY MEANING

WILLIAM R. WARNER & CO. v. ELI LILLY & CO.

Supreme Court of the United States, 1924.
265 U.S. 526, 44 S.Ct. 615, 68 L.Ed. 1161.

Mr. Justice SUTHERLAND delivered the opinion of the Court.

Respondent is a corporation engaged in the manufacture and sale of pharmaceutical and chemical products. In 1899 it began and has ever since continued to make and sell a liquid preparation of quinine, in combination with other substances, including yerba-santa and chocolate, under the name of Coco–Quinine.

Petitioner also is a pharmaceutical and chemical manufacturer. The Pfeiffer Chemical Company, Searle & Hereth Company and petitioner are under the same ownership and control. The first named company in 1906 began the manufacture of a liquid preparation which is substantially the same as respondent's preparation and which was put upon the market under the name of Quin–Coco. Two years later the Searle & Hereth Company engaged in the manufacture of the preparation, which ever since has been sold and distributed by petitioner.

This suit was brought in the Federal District Court for the Eastern District of Pennsylvania by respondent to enjoin petitioner from continuing to manufacture and sell the preparation if flavored or colored with chocolate; and also from using the name Quin–Coco, on the ground that it was an infringement of the name Coco–Quinine, to the use of which respondent had acquired an exclusive right. The District Court decided against respondent upon both grounds. On appeal the Court of Appeals ruled with the District Court upon the issue of infringement but reversed the decree upon that of unfair competition.

The entire record is here and both questions are open for consideration.

First. We agree with the courts below that the charge of [trademark] infringement was not sustained. The name Coco–Quinine is descriptive of the ingredients which enter into the preparation. The same is equally true of the name Quin–Coco. A name which is merely descriptive of the ingredients, qualities or characteristics of an article of trade cannot be appropriated as a trademark and the exclusive use of it afforded legal protection. The use of a similar name by another to truthfully describe his own product does not constitute a legal or moral wrong, even if its effect be to cause the public to mistake the origin or ownership of the product.

Second. The issue of unfair competition, on which the courts below differed, presents a question of more difficulty. The testimony is voluminous, more than two hundred witnesses having been examined; but, since the question with which we are now dealing is primarily one of fact, we have found it necessary to examine and consider it. Nothing is to be gained by reviewing the evidence at length, and we shall do no more than summarize the facts upon which we have reached our conclusions.

The use of chocolate as an ingredient has a three-fold effect: It imparts to the preparation a distinctive color and a distinctive flavor, and, to some extent, operates as a medium to suspend the quinine and prevent its precipitation. It has no therapeutic value; but it supplies the mixture with a quality of palatability for which there is no equally satisfactory substitute. Respondent, by laboratory experiments, first developed the idea of the addition of chocolate to the preparation for the purpose of giving it a characteristic color and an agreeable flavor. There was at the time no liquid preparation of quinine on the market containing chocolate, though there is evidence that it was sometimes so made up by druggists when called for. There is some evidence that petitioner endeavored by experiments to produce a preparation of the exact color and taste of that produced by respondent; and there is evidence in contradiction. We do not, however, regard it as important to determine upon which side lies the greater weight. Petitioner, in fact, did produce a preparation by the use of chocolate so exactly like that of respondent that they were incapable of being distinguished by ordinary sight or taste. By various trade methods an extensive and valuable market for the sale of respondent's preparation already had been established when the preparation of petitioner was put on the market. It is apparent, from a consideration of the testimony, that the efforts of petitioner to create a market for Quin–Coco were directed not so much to showing the merits of that preparation as they were to demonstrating its practical identity with Coco–Quinine, and, since it was sold at a lower price, inducing the purchasing druggist, in his own interest, to substitute, as far as he could, the former for the latter. In other words, petitioner sought to avail itself of the favorable repute which had been established for respondent's preparation in order to sell its own. Petitioner's salesmen appeared more anxious to convince the druggists with whom they were dealing that Quin–Coco was a good substitute for Coco–Quinine and was cheaper, than they were to independently demonstrate its merits. The evidence establishes by a fair preponderance that some of petitioner's salesmen suggested that, without danger of detection, prescriptions and orders for Coco–Quinine could be filled by substituting Quin–Coco. More often, however, the feasibility of such a course was brought to the mind of the druggist by pointing out the identity of the two preparations and the enhanced profit to be made by selling Quin–Coco because of its lower price. There is much conflict in the testimony; but on the whole it fairly appears that petitioner's agents induced the substitution, either in direct terms or by suggestion or insinuation. Sales to druggists are in original bottles bearing clearly distinguishing labels and there is no suggestion of deception in those transactions; but sales to the ultimate purchasers are of the product in its naked form out of the bottle; and the testimony discloses many instances of passing off by retail druggists of petitioner's preparation when respondent's preparation was called for. That no deception was practiced on the retail dealers, and that they knew exactly what they were getting is of no consequence. The wrong was in designedly enabling the dealers to palm off the preparation as that of the respondent. One who induces another to commit a fraud and furnishes the means of consummating it is equally guilty and liable for the injury.

The charge of unfair competition being established, it follows that equity will afford relief by injunction to prevent such unfair competition for the future. Several acts of unfair competition having been shown, we are warranted in concluding that petitioner is willing to continue that course of conduct, unless restrained. It remains to consider the character and extent of this relief.

Respondent has no exclusive right to the use of its formula. Chocolate is used as an ingredient not alone for the purpose of imparting a distinctive color, but for the purpose also of making the preparation peculiarly agreeable to the palate, to say nothing of its effect as a suspending medium. While it is not a medicinal element in the preparation, it serves a substantial and desirable use, which prevents it from being a mere matter of dress. It does not merely serve the incidental use of identifying the respondent's preparation, and it is doubtful whether it should be called a non-essential. The petitioner or anyone else is at liberty under the law to manufacture and market an exactly similar preparation containing chocolate and to notify the public that it is being done. But the imitator of another's goods must sell them as his own production. He cannot lawfully palm them off on the public as the goods of his competitor. The manufacturer or vendor is entitled to the reputation which his goods have acquired and the public to the means of distinguishing between them and other goods; and protection is accorded against unfair dealing whether there be a technical trademark or not. The wrong is in the sale of the goods of one manufacturer or vendor as those of another. If petitioner had been content to manufacture the preparation and let it make its own way in the field of open and fair competition, there would be nothing more to be said. It was not thus content, however, but availed itself of unfair means, either expressly or tacitly, to impose its preparation on the ultimate purchaser as and for the product of respondent.

Nevertheless, the right to which respondent is entitled is that of being protected against unfair competition, not of having the aid of a decree to create or support, or assist in creating or supporting, a monopoly of the sale of a preparation which everyone, including petitioner, is free to make and vend. The legal wrong does not consist in the mere use of chocolate as an ingredient, but in the unfair and fraudulent advantage which is taken of such use to pass off the product as that of respondent. The use dissociated from the fraud is entirely lawful, and it is against the fraud that the injunction lies. But respondent being entitled to relief, is entitled to effective relief; and any doubt in respect of the extent thereof must be resolved in its favor as the innocent producer and against the petitioner, which has shown by its conduct that it is not to be trusted. Clearly, the relief should extend far enough to enjoin petitioner, and its various agents from, directly or indirectly, representing or suggesting to its customers the feasibility or possibility of passing off Quin–Coco for Coco–Quinine. The Court of Appeals held that petitioner should be unconditionally enjoined from the use of chocolate. We think this goes too far; but, having regard to the past conduct of petitioner, the practices of some druggists to which it has led, and the right of respondent to an effective remedy, we think the decree fairly may require that the original packages sold to druggists shall not only bear labels clearly distinguishing petitioner's bottled product from the bottled product of respondent, but that these labels shall state affirmatively that the preparation is not to be sold or dispensed as Coco–Quinine or be used in filling prescriptions or orders calling for the latter. With these general suggestions, the details and form of the injunction can be more satisfactorily determined by the District Court. The decree of the Court of Appeals is reversed and the cause remanded to the District Court for further proceedings in conformity with this opinion.

Reversed.

CHARCOAL STEAK HOUSE OF CHARLOTTE, INC. v. STALEY, 263 N.C. 199, 139 S.E.2d 185, 144 U.S.P.Q. 241 (1964). SHARP, J.: Although a generic word or a geographic designation cannot become an arbitrary trademark, it may nevertheless be used deceptively by a newcomer to the field so as to amount to unfair competition, and the prohibition against any right to the exclusive use of such a word or designation has been modified by the "secondary meaning" doctrine. This was fashioned to protect the public from deception, and is but one facet of the law of unfair competition.

When a particular business has used words publici juris for so long or so exclusively or when it has promoted its product to such an extent that the words do not register their literal meaning on the public mind but are instantly associated with one enterprise, such words have attained a secondary meaning. This is to say, a secondary meaning exists when in addition to their literal, or dictionary, meaning, words connote to the public a product *from a unique source*. It has been suggested, however, that when a descriptive word or phrase has come to mean a particular entrepreneur, the term *secondary meaning* is inaccurate because, in the field in which the phrase has acquired its new meaning, its so-called secondary meaning has become its primary, or natural, meaning.

The law will afford protection against the tortious appropriation of trade names and trademarks alike. To establish a secondary meaning for either, a plaintiff must show that it has come to stand for his business in the public mind, that is, "that the primary significance of the term in the minds of the consuming public is not the product but the producer." Kellogg Co. v. Nat. Biscuit Co., 305 U.S. 111, 118, 59 S.Ct. 109, 113, 83 L.Ed. 73, 78, 39 U.S.P.Q. 296, 299. But even though generic, or descriptive, words, when used alone, have come to have a secondary meaning, "a competitor may nevertheless use them if he accompanies their use with something which will adequately show that the first person or his product is not meant." Union Oyster House v. Hi Ho Oyster House, supra, 316 Mass. at 544, 55 N.E.2d at 943, 62 U.S. P.Q. at 218.

GALT HOUSE, INC. v. HOME SUPPLY CO.

Court of Appeals of Kentucky, 1972.
483 S.W.2d 107, 174 U.S.P.Q. 268.

REED, Judge.

The plaintiff, Galt House, Inc., instituted this action to enjoin the defendants, Home Supply Company, and its principal officer and stockholder, Al J. Schneider, from operating a new hotel in Louisville, Kentucky, under the assumed trade name "Galt House." The trial judge refused to enjoin the use of the name at the plaintiff's behest. We affirm that decision for the reasons later discussed. No other issue involved in the pending litigation in the trial court is decided. We confine our consideration to the sole issue presented by this appeal.

In February 1964, the plaintiff, Galt House, Inc., incorporated under the laws of this state. In its articles of incorporation it adopted as its corporate name the term "Galt House." The articles required and specified that the minimum capital with which plaintiff would commence business would be the sum of $1,000. This amount has never been paid in. The plaintiff has no assets and no liabilities; neither does it have corporate books or records. Plaintiff's president and sole shareholder is Arch Stallard, Sr., a real estate broker in Louisville, Kentucky, who specializes in hotels and motel real estate. Mr. Stallard has on occasions since the date of the filing of plaintiff's articles of incorporation made a few sporadic inquiries concerning possible locations for a hotel and considered engaging in an enterprise by which a franchise operation would be effected. These few efforts came to naught and Mr. Stallard testified that because of illness and death in his family he had been "laying dormant."

The defendant, Home Supply Company, is a Kentucky corporation organized sometimes prior to 1950. The defendant, Al J. Schneider, is its president and controlling shareholder. Home Supply Company is active in the business of constructing and operating hotels in this state. It presently operates a hotel on the Kentucky State Fair Board property under the assumed name "Executive Inn." It is presently engaged in the construction and completion of a high-rise hotel on riverfront-development property belonging to an agency of the City of Louisville.

In April 1969, Home Supply Company, through its president Schneider, submitted to the city agency plans of a hotel bearing the name Galt House. This name had been recommended to Schneider by the then mayor of the City of Louisville, Kenneth Schmied, and the chairman of the Riverfront Development Commission, Archibald Cochran. The trial judge found from the evidence that throughout discussions leading up to the bidding, the new hotel was referred to as the Galt House and has been so referred to since. Home Supply Company was the successful bidder, was awarded the contract, and construction commenced in May 1970. A new hotel, 26 stories in height with 714 rooms, is now nearly completed and has affixed a sign bearing the name "The Galt House." The hotel already has scheduled future conventions and room reservations, although it will not open until after May 1972. In April 1971, Home Supply Company applied for and received from the Secretary of State of Kentucky a registration and service mark of the name "The Galt House."

Plaintiff filed suit in August 1971, seeking to enjoin the defendants from any use of the name Galt House. Evidence was taken in the form of depositions and written interrogatories. In February 1972, the trial judge entered a judgment that was made final for purposes of appeal; the judgment was based on findings of fact and conclusions of law set forth in two written opinions. The trial judge concluded in substance that the plaintiff did not by mere incorporation acquire property rights in the name "Galt House" and that the plaintiff had not performed sufficient acts since incorporation to acquire property rights in and to that name. Accordingly, the trial judge reasoned that the plaintiff was not entitled to injunctive relief against the defendant's use of the contested name. Plaintiff then appealed to this court and asserts several grounds on which it bases its contention that the trial court was in error in not granting it an injunction against the defendant. We shall deal with these contentions subsequently herein, but first a bit of history of the particular name that is the subject of controversy will be briefly related.

During the Nineteenth Century the Galt House Hotel was a famous hostelry in Louisville with an excellent and widely recognized reputation. In 1838 the barroom at the Galt House was the scene of a killing as a result of which an attorney and judge and his two companions were indicted for murder. They were tried and acquitted. The trial was held at Harrodsburg, Kentucky, to which venue had been transferred because of the intense public sentiment in Louisville against the defendants who were prominent citizens of Mississippi. The victims of the affray were Louisville residents. The trial itself is famous in the annals of Kentucky history.

In 1842 Charles Dickens toured America. In his account in "American Notes," he was characteristically uncomplimentary in his description of Louisville; he was impressed, however, with the Galt House. He wrote: "We slept at the Galt House; a splendid hotel; and were as handsomely lodged as though we had been in Paris, rather than hundreds of miles beyond the Alleghanies (sic)." In 1858 Charles Mackay, an English writer, passed through Louisville. In his account in "Life and Liberty in America" he remarked: ". . . we crossed in the steamer to Louisville, and once more found ourselves in a land of plenty and comfort, in a flourishing city, in an excellent hotel—the Galt House, one of the best conducted establishments in America; . . . ."

The Galt House, located on Main Street at Second Street, occupied separate buildings during its existence as a hotel. The second Galt House was destroyed by fire in January 1865 at a reported loss of $1,000,000. The third Galt House, a magnificent structure in its day, was abandoned as a hotel and ceased operations in 1920. Belknap Hardware Company thereafter occupied the site of the last Galt House.

Thus, it would appear that since 1920 there has been no use of the name Galt House in connection with or to describe a hotel. The name doubtless strikes interest when used in the presence of history buffs and among those familiar with the folklore of Louisville. Among such cognoscenti the name encourages remembrance of things past.

As found by the circuit judge, the corporation which operated the last Galt House was formed in 1911 and its formal corporate existence expired in 1961. From 1920 to 1961, however, it did not engage in the hotel business. Therefore, the name Galt House had not been used in connection with a going business for 49 years when defendants undertook to use it as the name of their new hotel in 1969.

The primary argument asserted by the plaintiff actually rests upon a premise that by mere incorporation under a corporate name it retains the right to exclude others from the use of that name so long as the corporation legally exists. In Covington Inn Corp. v. White Horse Tavern, Inc., Ky., 445 S.W.2d 135, 163 U.S.P.Q. 438 (1969), we considered the effect of KRS 271.045, a part of the corporation law of this state, and held that its provision that a corporate name shall not be the same as "nor deceptively similar to" the name of other corporations, constituted an expression by the legislature that stated a policy conforming to the common law of "unfair competition" as applied in Kentucky. Thus, when under subsection (4) of the same statute an equity action is authorized to enjoin the doing of business under a name adopted in violation of this statute, the common law of unfair competition prescribes the standards which the court applies in determining whether to enjoin.

In that same opinion we remarked that perhaps this statute could be reasonably construed to extend to an assumed name of a corporation. That is the situation in this case. The defendant Home Supply Company has undertaken to do business under the assumed trade name Galt House, which is the same as plaintiff's adopted corporate name. In Meredith v. Universal Plumbing & Construction Co., 272 Ky. 283, 114 S.W.2d 94 (1938), we held that under our corporate statutes and other statutory laws applicable to transacting business under an assumed name there was no legal impediment to a corporation using an additional trade name that was different from its adopted corporate name. The pertinent statutes read the same now as they did then. Hence, there is no legal impediment to the defendant Home Supply Company's adoption of the trade name "Galt House", unless the plaintiff by the mere act of incorporation of the same name has precluded this defendant's right to adopt and use the name.

Surely the plaintiff acquires no standing to enjoin under the accepted principles of the law of unfair competition. Under the modern extended scope of the doctrine of unfair competition, its present outer limits afford protection and relief against the unjust appropriation of, or injury to, the good will or business reputation of another, even though he is not a competitor. Plaintiff is concededly a nonuser of the contested name. Plaintiff has no customers, conducts no real or substantial business and has never held its name out to the public in connection with any going business. Therefore, by its inaction, it could not have established either a good will or reputation which the defendants could be legitimately accused of pirating as a competitor or otherwise. Therefore, if plaintiff has standing to enjoin, its status must rest upon the acquisition of a protectable right by its act of incorporation under the contested name.

In Lawyers Title Ins. Co. v. Lawyers Title Ins. Corporation, 71 App. D.C. 120, 109 F.2d 35, 43 U.S.P.Q. 166 (1939), Mr. Justice Rutledge, writing for the Circuit Court of Appeals for the District of Columbia, considered the problem. This opinion is characterized by Fletcher as a leading case. See Volume 6, Fletcher Cyc. Corp. (1968 Perm.Ed.), Sec. 2425, page 55. That case and the prior case of Waterman Co. v. Modern Pen Co., 235 U.S. 88, 45 S.Ct. 91, 59 L.Ed. 142 (1914), established clearly that mere incorporation under a particular name does not create the right to have such name protected against use by another. Mr. Justice Holmes said in Waterman:

> "While it very well may be true that the transfer of a name without a business is not enough to entitle the transferee to prevent others from using it, it still is a license that may be sufficient to put the licensee on the footing of the licensor as against the plaintiff."

The plaintiff, however, relies upon the case of Drugs Consolidated v. Drug Incorporated, 16 Del.Ch. 240, 144 A. 656 (1929). In our view the opinion in that case undertakes to prove too much. There is dictum that the corporation statutes of Delaware, which are substantially similar to the corporation statutes of Kentucky so far as the present point is concerned, assure a right to have the corporate name distinguished from other corporations of like kind subsequently created and that this right does not depend on showing of actual use, in business, of the name, but the right exists as soon as corporate existence is brought into being and as long as it continues; the specific factual findings in the opinion, however, demonstrate that the plaintiff corporation, although it was not yet actually engaged in the business of manufacturing and marketing drugs, had, nevertheless, been engaged in promoting the objects and purposes of its incorporation. Therefore, if this opinion represents a holding that a nonuser of a corporate name retains the right to pre-empt that name during the period of its formal corporate existence without ever having engaged in carrying on any of the objects and purposes of the corporation, it is contrary to the weight of authority concerning that proposition and does not, in our opinion, represent the generally accepted view.

The Drugs Consolidated opinion was cited with approval by the Mississippi Supreme Court in Meridian Yellow Cab Co. v. City Yellow Cabs, 206 Miss. 812, 41 So.2d 14 (1949). In this case, however, the plaintiff who first incorporated had actually commenced operations at the time it sought to enjoin the defendant who had later incorporated under a similar name. Although the plaintiff did not commence business until after the defendant, it, nevertheless, did actually start active operations in the taxicab business within three years of the date of its incorporation and within two months after the defendant actually operated taxicabs; whether the plaintiff was theretofore engaged in activities to promote the objects and purposes of the corporation is not mentioned. However misplaced that court's reliance on the Drugs Consolidated case may have been, its decision, which granted the plaintiff injunctive relief, does not militate against our conclusion in this case that the plaintiff's act of incorporation in a particular name pre-empts the use of that name by a subsequent user only for a reasonable period in which to allow plaintiff's business to begin. To this extent, incorporation and registration take the place of user in the case of a trade name. Pre-emption for a reasonable period of time in which to allow the business to begin is not the equivalent of a perpetual monopoly of the trade name without use in trade. . . .

The judgment from which the appeal was prosecuted is affirmed.

All concur.

NOTES

1. In its traditional design, unfair competition law protects (a) the first to use a name, brand or other symbol in connection with the sale of goods or services against (b) a competitor whose subsequent use of

the symbol (c) confuses, or is likely to confuse, consumers into believing that the first user, rather than the competitor, is the source of the goods or services. This formula seeks to accommodate the interest of competitors in choosing and investing in symbols that will capture their goodwill and the interest of consumers in being free from confusion about the source of goods and services.

Unfair competition's three operative elements—the first user's investment in goodwill, the competitor's deceptive acts, and consumer confusion as to source—are matters of degree. Each of the three reciprocates the other two. For example, the need for direct proof of consumer confusion will decrease as the distinctiveness of the first user's name or symbol, and the competitive relationship between the parties, increase.

Three typical unfair competition cases illustrate this reciprocal relationship. In one case, the first user's symbol or device has, because of its descriptiveness or brevity of use, acquired no secondary meaning—no capacity to identify the first user as a source. For the first user to prevail, it must prove that the competitor actively palmed off its goods or services as coming from the first user, and deceived consumers as to source by word or deed. The first user must also show that, as a consequence of this conduct, consumers were in fact confused as to the source of the goods or services.

In the second case, the first user's symbol or device, though descriptive or otherwise common, also possesses secondary meaning. Neither a conscious intent to deceive, nor actual deception of consumers, need be shown in this case, only the likelihood that the competitor's use of the symbol or device will deceive consumers as to source.

In the third case, the first user has adopted a distinctive, nondescriptive symbol or device that functions exclusively to identify the first user. Here courts will conclusively presume that the competitor's use of the symbol was intended to—and did—cause consumer confusion. Given the indeterminate variety of symbols and other insignia available for adoption by the competitor, courts will presume that the competitor's use of a facsimile could only have been motivated by an intent to deceive and was in fact successful in accomplishing the deception.

In any of these three situations, the symbol or device used by the competitor need not be identical to the first user's. The closer the similarity between the two, however, the greater is the probability that a court will infer deception.

2. *Nondeceptive References.* Can one who has lawfully copied a product refer to the product's trademark in his own advertising for the purpose of identifying the product he has copied? In Smith v. Chanel, Inc., 402 F.2d 562, 159 U.S.P.Q. 388 (9th Cir.1968), the court held that appellant, who advertised his less costly fragrance as an exact duplicate of plaintiff's "Chanel No. 5," could use the trademark for this purpose "and that such advertising may not be enjoined under either the Lanham Act, 15 U.S.C.A. § 1125(a), or the common law of unfair competition, so long as it does not contain misrepresentations or create

a reasonable likelihood that purchasers will be confused as to the source, identity, or sponsorship of the advertiser's product." 402 F.2d 562, 563. On remand, the district court found that defendant's fragrance was not in fact an exact duplicate of Chanel No. 5 and concluded that his advertising thus involved a misrepresentation. Chanel, Inc. v. Smith, 178 U.S.P.Q. 630, (N.D.Cal.1973), aff'd, 528 F.2d 284 (9th Cir. 1976).

3. *Injunctions.* Courts freely grant injunctive relief against unfair competition. They may enjoin a defendant from making any use of the plaintiff's trade insignia or may only require the defendant to include disclaimers indicating the true source of its goods or services.

Unfair competition injunctions are limited only by the judicial imagination. One court ordered a defendant to instruct the local telephone company to delete his confusingly similar name from future directories and to place intercepts on his present telephone number so that telephone company operators could query callers as to whether they were interested in the services of plaintiff or defendant, and relay calls accordingly. Vocational Personnel Services, Inc. v. Statistical Tabulating Corp., 305 F.Supp. 701, 163 U.S.P.Q. 55 (D.Minn.1969). Another court required the defendant not only to deliver up for destruction offending materials in its own possession, but also to recall offending materials from distributors. The court recognized that the recall provision was "an unusual, and perhaps unprecedented, remedy for a violation of New York's law of unfair competition," but concluded that it was "well within the district court's broad powers as a court of equity." Perfect Fit Industries, Inc. v. Acme Quilting Co., Inc., 646 F.2d 800, 805, 210 U.S.P.Q. 175, 179 (2d Cir.1981), cert. denied, 459 U.S. 832, 103 S.Ct. 73, 74 L.Ed.2d 71 (1982).

4. *Monetary Awards.* Courts will usually award monetary remedies for unfair competition—accounting of profits and damages—only if the defendant acted willfully or fraudulently. The formula for each remedy is relatively straightforward. The accounting measure entitles the plaintiff to all profits that the defendant earned from its unfair conduct. The defendant has the burden of apportioning its total profits between those that were consequential and those that it earned independent of its unfair competition; the defendant also bears the burden of proving deductions from profits such as manufacturing and selling costs. Under the damage measure, the plaintiff bears the burden of proving losses attributable to defendant's conduct—losses, for example, resulting from reduction in its business or prices, or from injury to its business reputation.

The general rule, that if a plaintiff is entitled to one of these two measures it is entitled to both, creates a risk of overcompensation. Where plaintiff and defendant are direct competitors, to award plaintiff the defendant's profits as well as damages for its own lost profits would give a punitive double recovery. Recognizing this, courts have in these cases allowed the accounting but confined damages to items independent of lost sales, such as price reductions and advertising outlays required to combat the defendant's activity. Where the defendant's conduct has been notably oppressive, courts may award punitive damages.

Courts have recently introduced monetary awards measured by the cost of corrective advertising that the plaintiff would have to undertake to dispel the consumer confusion created by the defendant's conduct. In the leading case, Big O Tire Dealers, Inc. v. Goodyear Tire & Rubber Co., 561 F.2d 1365, 195 U.S.P.Q. 417 (10th Cir.1977), cert. dismissed, 434 U.S. 1052, 98 S.Ct. 905, 54 L.Ed.2d 805 (1978), the court held that the plaintiff was entitled to compensatory damages to restore it to its economic position before the defendant began its competing advertising campaign. The court computed these damages by multiplying the amount ($9,690,029) that defendant had spent on its national advertising campaign by a fraction (28%) representing the proportional number of states (14 out of 50) in which plaintiff sold its goods. The court then reduced this figure by 75%, following a rule of thumb employed by the Federal Trade Commission in corrective advertising cases, on the theory that every dollar spent in misleading advertising requires no more than a 25% outlay to dispel its effects. 561 F.2d 1375–76. See also West Des Moines State Bank v. Hawkeye Bancorporation, 722 F.2d 411, 221 U.S.P.Q. 307 (8th Cir.1983).

5. *Use.* Say that plaintiff in *Galt* began operating a Galt House Hotel after the defendant announced plans for its hotel, but before the defendant opened for business. Would the court have enjoined the defendant? On a counterclaim, would it have given defendant an injunction against plaintiff? Did the court correctly weigh the fact that the name, "Galt House," possessed historic significance in Louisville? Does the fact that neither party to the action was responsible for the name's historic appeal mean that neither should have any exclusive rights in it? That neither should be allowed to use it?

Galt's principal lesson is that, to gain and maintain protection under unfair competition law, a name or other symbol must be actually used in business. Names cannot be reserved for future use. The use requirement also implies that a firm can have no exclusive rights in geographic, product or service markets that it has not yet entered. At least originally, it was thought that the use requirement correctly balanced the interests of first users, second users and consumers. Since, presumably, the first user's name or symbol did not identify it in markets it had not yet entered, the use of the name or symbol in those markets by a later user would not confuse consumers as to source nor divert trade from the first user. Indeed, one consequence of the use requirement is that the later user would gain exclusive rights to the symbol in these markets.

How can the use requirement be administered in a world of highly mobile consumers carrying the memory of symbols, goods and services from one region to another? In a world in which firms, seeking to capitalize on the symbols and goodwill associated with one line of goods or services, plan to use the same symbol in connection with different goods or services? These questions lie at the source of two doctrinal departures from unfair competition law's traditional design, the zone of expansion doctrine and dilution doctrine, considered at pages 70 and 76 below.

6. *Misrepresentations of Quality.* The interests affected by a competitor's misrepresentation about the *source* of its product closely parallel the interests affected by misrepresentations about the *quality* of the product—the misrepresentation, for example, that a zinc washboard is made of aluminum. Both misrepresentations injure consumers by inducing them to make a purchase that they would probably forego if they knew the facts. Both misrepresentations also injure the innocent producer who will lose sales to its deceitful competitor and may lose sales overall as consumers lose faith in its symbol or in its authentically described goods.

Courts have been slow to extend the common law of unfair competition, which protects against misrepresentations about source, to encompass misrepresentations about quality. The leading case, American Washboard Co. v. Saginaw Mfg. Co., 103 Fed. 281 (6th Cir.1900), held that plaintiff, which manufactured genuine aluminum washboards, did not have an unfair competition action against defendant which represented to consumers that its zinc washboards were made of aluminum. In Mosler Safe Co. v. Ely–Norris Safe Co., 273 U.S. 132, 47 S.Ct. 314, 71 L.Ed. 578 (1927), the Supreme Court suggested that an action might lie in these circumstances if the plaintiff could show that it was the only manufacturer of the genuine goods, so that any sales made by the deceitful competitor would necessarily divert sales from the manufacturer. See also Restatement of Torts § 761 (1939).

State statutes modelled on the Uniform Deceptive Trade Practices Act and on the widely-adopted Unfair Trade Practices and Consumer Protection Law have taken up the cause of the innocent producer by outlawing misrepresentations about quality along with misrepresentations about source and, in the case of the Unfair Trade Practices and Consumer Protection Law, augmenting private actions with public enforcement measures. See generally, Alexander & Coil, The Impact of New State Unfair Trade Practices Acts on the Field of Unfair Competition, 67 Trademark Rep. 625 (1977). Section 43(a) of the Lanham Act, 15 U.S.C.A. § 1125(a), effectively reverses the rule of *American Washboard* as a matter of federal law. See page 353, below.

7. Outside the basic appropriation-competition-deception formula, and actions for misrepresentation, courts have applied the term "unfair competition" to a multitude of unrelated and sometimes exotic commercial wrongs. Consider whether defendant's conduct should have been held actionable in the following situations. [Answers appear below.]

    a.   Plaintiffs are the publisher and authors of a set of physics textbooks that contain problems to be used by instructors in classroom exercises, examinations and homework assignments. Defendants publish a book with ready-made solutions to these problems. Plaintiffs seek to restrain distribution of the answer book on the ground that it will destroy the market for their textbooks.

b. In the course of setting up his own business, defendant solicits the trade of customers he serviced when he was employed by plaintiff.

c. Defendant buys bongo drums from plaintiff, removes plaintiff's trademarks and other identifying material, replaces them with defendant's own insignia, and uses the drums as a sample of its own brand of bongos. Plaintiff seeks an injunction and damages.

d. Local storekeepers in a small city, greatly disturbed by their loss of business to large mail-order houses, announce a children's show with excellent performers to be held in the local theatre. The only admission ticket required is the surrender of the family Sears, Roebuck catalogue. Sears, Roebuck seeks to have the practice enjoined.

e. Plaintiff, producer-director of a motion picture that has been licensed for television broadcast, seeks to enjoin the network licensee from inserting commercials in the broadcast in a manner that will impair the film's artistic integrity.

Answers to questions in note 7:

a. Actionable unfair competition: "The trend of the law today is to enforce higher standards of fairness and morality in trade, depending upon the character and nature thereof." Addison–Wesley Pub. Co., Inc. v. Brown, 207 F.Supp. 678, 133 U.S.P.Q. 647 (E.D.N.Y.1962).

b. Sometimes actionable, sometimes not. See generally, Hays, Unfair Competition—Another Decade, 51 Calif.L.Rev. 51 (1963).

c. Actionable depending on applicable law. "The use of its own trademark amounted to a representation that defendant and not the plaintiff stood behind the sample chattel and behind the chattels bought in reliance on the sample. This is the antithesis of palming off and the plaintiff demonstrates no actionable rights in the defendant's use of its own trademark on a product it bought to use in promoting its own products." Mastro Plastics Corp. v. Emenee Industries, Inc., 16 A.D.2d 420, 228 N.Y.S.2d 514 (1st Dept.), aff'd, 12 N.Y.2d 826, 187 N.E.2d 360 (1960). The complaint, as subsequently amended to allege a violation of Lanham Act section 43(a), 15 U.S.C.A. § 1125(a), was upheld against defendant's motion to dismiss: "The Act defines a new civil wrong and the prior dismissal of the original complaint because the common law afforded no remedy to a competitor where the wrong merely resulted in a diversion of customers without confusion or palming off is of no significance." 19 A.D.2d 600, 240 N.Y.S.2d 624 (1st Dept.1963), aff'd, 14 N.Y.2d 498, 197 N.E.2d 621 (1964).

d. Actionable—at least in an action brought by the Federal Trade Commission. Chamber of Commerce of Missoula, 5 F.T.C.D. 451 (1923). Professor Chafee, from whose lecture, Unfair Competition, 53 Harv.L. Rev. 1289 (1940), this situation is excerpted, concluded that "If Sears,

Roebuck had gone to court, it would probably have failed to get an injunction." Id. at 1307.

e. Actionable. "I think a court of equity has a duty when presented with a novel situation to fashion remedies to protect parties and litigants against new harms where it appears that there is an inadequate remedy at law, to protect against what may be an irreparable harm. I think the court has the right to protect the artistic integrity of a product, whether it be a film or a play. . . ." Stevens v. National Broadcasting Co., 148 U.S.P.Q. 755, 758 (Cal.Super.Ct.1966).

2. ZONE OF EXPANSION

THE SAMPLE, INC. v. PORRATH

Supreme Court of New York, Appellate Division, Fourth Department, 1973.
41 A.D.2d 118, 341 N.Y.S.2d 683, 178 U.S.P.Q. 365, aff'd on opinion below,
33 N.Y.2d 961, 353 N.Y.S.2d 733, 309 N.E.2d 133, 181 U.S.P.Q. 850.

GOLDMAN, Presiding Justice.

In this action appellants, The Sample, Inc. and The Sample of Buffalo, Inc., appeal from a judgment denying their application for a declaratory judgment permitting them to use the trade name "Sample" in connection with a proposed new retail outlet in the Town of Wheatfield, Niagara County, New York. The order denying appellants this requested relief granted the respondents, Theresa Porrath, Samuel Porrath, Dorothy Gellman and Samuel Gellman, copartners doing business under the firm name of The Sample Shop, a permanent injunction restraining appellants from using the name "Sample" in any business operation to be conducted within the City of Niagara Falls and the Towns of Niagara, Wheatfield, Lewiston and Porter in the County of Niagara.

The history of the business activities of the parties, their methods of operation, the territorial markets they serve and much pertinent data were fully presented to the trial court. It appears from the proof that the Buffalo based "The Sample, Inc." was established in 1929 and has advertised in Buffalo papers under the trade name "The Sample" since its founding. In its early days it specialized in the sale of women's apparel but over the years has expanded greatly the variety of merchandise offered for sale and now includes men's as well as women's clothing and in addition thereto operates other departments such as jewelry, ladies' shoes and fabrics, children's wear and many other commodities. "The Sample, Inc." opened its first branch store outside of Buffalo in the City of Lockport, Niagara County, in 1946 and now operates in nine locations in Western New York, two of which are in Niagara County. Each branch store is a separate, wholly-owned subsidiary corporation. The parent corporation had net sales in 1971 in excess of $10,600,000 with more than $1,350,000 produced by the two Niagara County stores. Over 61,500 persons hold charge accounts with "The Sample, Inc." and 7,200 of these customers live in Niagara County. Appellants have spent $2,165,461 for advertising under the name "The Sample", spending almost as much in 1971 as respondents have in the last 23 years. This advertising has appeared primarily in two large Buffalo newspapers, which have a circulation of over 25,000 in Niagara County and appellants have also advertised extensively in the Lockport Union Sun and Journal and the Tonawanda News, both of which are largely distributed throughout Niagara County.

Respondents operate two stores, the first of which was opened in 1934 in Niagara Falls under the name "Sample Dress Shop". These stores which had net sales of $678,000 in 1971 stock primarily women's apparel and do not offer for sale such items as men's wear and the various other merchandise which is sold in "The Sample, Inc." stores. Since 1948 respondents have spent a total of $311,000 in advertising, almost entirely in the Niagara Falls Gazette. The primary market of the two stores is in the City of Niagara Falls and the four towns surrounding the city.

The store which appellants desire to open would be located in the Summit Park Mall in the Town of Wheatfield in Niagara County, one and a half miles from one of respondents' stores. They propose to name it "The Sample Shop of Buffalo, Inc.". Appellants have offered to call the store by any other name, which includes the word "Sample", such as the "Bunis (family name of principal stockholders) Sample Shop", or any reasonable and distinguishing name so long as it includes the word "Sample". Appellants have demonstrated a willingness to select a name which will eliminate any conflict with respondents' "The Sample Shop".

An in-depth market survey by National Marketing Associates, Inc. was put into evidence by appellants. It indicates that women in the 18–50 years age group who live within a five mile radius of the Summit Park Mall are more likely to associate the word "Sample" with a store operated by appellants than one owned by respondents. The market data contained in the survey clearly show that a substantial majority of persons interviewed, when asked to identify a store operated under the names "The Sample" or "Sample Shops", responded by indicating the store owned by appellants.

The trial court found that respondents' name, "The Sample Shop", has "acquired a secondary meaning identifying in the minds of the public" the two stores operated by respondents in the City of Niagara Falls. It further found "that the public would be confused and deceived by plaintiffs' use of the word 'Sample'" and that there "is a likelihood of dilution of the distinctive quality of defendants' trade name by plaintiffs' use of the word 'Sample' as a part of a corporate or assumed name". The trial court concluded from its findings that appellants are not entitled to judgment declaring their right to operate the new store under the name "The Sample of Buffalo, Inc." and granted judgment to respondents restraining and enjoining appellants from the "use of the word 'Sample' as part of a corporate or assumed name". We find this determination to be against the weight of the evidence.

The preponderance of the evidence supports appellants' contention that a majority of potential customers of both parties are more likely to associate the word "Sample" with a store operated by appellants rather than one operated by respondents. The uncontradicted data of the market survey and the history of the business activities of both parties show that respondents' business name has not acquired a secondary meaning and that the greater likelihood is that appellants' name, "The Sample, Inc.", has gained such a secondary meaning in the minds of the purchasing public.

In the determination of the issue here presented, the overriding objective is to promote and protect the concept of commercial fairness. Unfair competition and trademark infringement are all unique in their particular factual patterns and each case should be decided "on its facts", and because of incompatibility there cannot be strict adherence to precedents.

The principle of commercial fairness is well enunciated by the United States Court of Appeals of the First Circuit in Food Center v. Food Fair Stores, 356 F.2d 775, 148 U.S.P.Q. 621. In that case a Massachusetts retail supermarket carried on business under the name "New England Food Fair". It sought to enjoin the defendant, the nation's fifth largest chain of grocery supermarkets operating in 15 States under the name "Food Fair", from operating under its name in the Massachusetts area. The District Court found that the plaintiff's name had acquired a secondary meaning in greater Boston and to some extent in other parts of Eastern Massachusetts. In vacating the judgment of the District Court the Circuit Court said "In attempting to apply principles and precedents to the facts of this case, we recognize at the outset that the field of protection of trade names is part of the wider domain of the law relating to unfair competition, where the overriding objective of courts and legislatures is that of commercial fairness". As in the case at bar in the use of the word "Sample", the court found that the name "Food Fair" was not of the strongest order of originality. The Federal court concerned itself, as we should, that the public be not disadvantaged by confusion of names and set forth specific recommendations as to territory and operation to avoid confusion. In the case at bar all that is required is the adoption of a name by appellants which will clearly identify appellants' store and distinguish it, in the minds of the public, from respondents' stores. This we believe is accomplished by using the word "Buffalo" in appellants' name.

Succinctly stated, the paramount question is whether the acts complained of are fair or unfair. No longer is it the law that the protection of a business name depends primarily upon whether that name has acquired a secondary meaning. If it is demonstrable and clear from the record that the acts of one charged with usurpation of another's commercial name are actually unfair, equitable principles become operative. What equity will not tolerate is the appropriation of another's business name together with the exploitation and the grasping for enjoyment of the benefits of another's labor and effort, when the latter has culminated in a special quality being attached to the particular name.

The issue of trade name infringement was not decided by the trial court because neither party had taken any action concerning the matter for many years. The court found that there were two separate and distinct market areas; that the trade name of both parties had acquired a secondary meaning in their particular area; each entity was entitled to protection in its own specialized area; the public would be confused and deceived by the appellants' use of the word "Sample" at the store at Summit Park Mall; there was a likelihood of diluting the distinctive quality of the respondents' trade name; there would be little disadvantage to the appellants if they were unable to use the word "Sample" in the name of their new store; and by using the name the appellants would be taking advantage of the goodwill associated with the word "Sample" and established by the respondents.

Secondary meaning has been defined as the trade meaning which may attach to a particular mark because its user has expended time and money in the promotion of the mark. Where a business name acquires a special significance pointing to only one business enterprise in a certain locality, it is protected from use by another in the same area. The concept of secondary meaning is that a name has become so identified with a particular business that it exclusively signifies only that one particular business. Priority of use alone is not equivalent to acquisition of that special significance which entitles a trade name to protection against infringement.

The respondents have not met the burden of establishing the existence of a secondary meaning for their trade name "The Sample Shop" and this they must do in order to restrain appellants from using that trade name. The results of the consumer attitude study conducted at the request of appellants are entitled to probative weight. This study demonstrated that many more consumers were aware of the appellants' name than that of the respondents. This awareness no doubt emanates from the considerable advertising carried on by the appellants in and by all of the media. This awareness also mitigates against a finding that the business name of respondents has acquired a secondary meaning either in the respondents' limited geographical area or within the metropolitan area constituting Buffalo and Niagara Falls in Erie and Niagara Counties.

The finding that the appellants will be taking advantage of the goodwill associated with the name "Sample" and established by the respondents is not supported by the record. The consumers in the Summit Park Mall area relate the name "Sample" to the Buffalo based retail stores more than to the Niagara Falls based stores. This identification probably stems from the advertising of the word "Sample" in connection with appellants as early as 1929.

The record fails to establish that the appellants' use of the word "Sample" would deceive the public and dilute the distinctive quality of respondents' name. The facts are that the public identifies the name

"Sample" with the appellants rather than with the respondents or at least it cannot be said on this record that the identification is more in favor of respondents than appellants.

Finally, a finding that the use of a different name would result in little disadvantage to appellants is not valid. The name associated with the Buffalo stores has acquired singular significance through substantial advertising expenditures. That the new store would be deprived of that name is of no little consequence and would be detrimental to successful operation.

There is no inkling of bad faith on the part of the appellants or of any intention to deceive and confuse the public and to identify the respondents' products with the appellants.

Of course, an injunction will issue to prevent any activity calculated to impair the value of a trade name or to deceive the public. The appellants are not attempting to trade on the goodwill of the respondents' distinctive name so that there is a misappropriation of a property right belonging to another. There may possibly be some confusion as a result of the use of appellants' name in the Summit Park Mall but we must look at the over-all picture, and it is quite clear that neither party has any manifestly superior claim to the name "Sample". The most equitable solution to this controversy is to allow the use of similar but not identical names so that both stores may use the word "Sample". By such a disposition the interests of all parties will be protected and commercial fairness will be achieved.

The judgment below should be reversed and judgment entered declaring that the appellants may operate a retail store in the Summit Park Mall, in the Town of Wheatfield, Niagara County, New York, under the name "The Sample of Buffalo, Inc.".

NOTES

1. Did the fact in *Sample* that "many more consumers were aware of the appellants' name than that of the respondents," necessarily mean that respondent's name had acquired *no* secondary meaning, even in its own limited geographical area? If so, would appellants have succeeded in an action to enjoin respondents from using the "Sample" name on their present stores? If not, would appellant's use of the "Sample" name in the Summit Park Mall necessarily produce some consumer confusion?

In Food Center, Inc. v. Food Fair Stores, Inc., relied on in *Sample,* the court observed that "as for the public, there would be confusion in areas served by both enterprises, but, at least at present, we see no evidence that it would suffer in quality of service or that the reputation of either party would suffer in the process." 356 F.2d 775, 782. What relief would, or should, be available to the parties and to the public in the event that the quality of either firm's goods and services later declined?

2. *Reverse Confusion.* What if appellant's advertising in *Sample* had been so extensive that it obliterated any goodwill that respondent had developed for its own stores, with the result that customers at respondent's stores believed the stores were part of appellant's chain? The confusion of source would be just the opposite of the sort that ordinarily occurs in unfair competition cases: instead of consumers being confused into thinking that the second user's goods and services came from the first user, they would be confused into thinking that the first user's goods and services came from the second user.

Big O Tire Dealers, Inc. v. Goodyear Tire & Rubber Co., 561 F.2d 1365, 195 U.S.P.Q. 417 (10th Cir.1977), cert. dismissed, 434 U.S. 1052, 98 S.Ct. 905, 54 L.Ed.2d 805 (1978), held that under Colorado law the first user would in these circumstances be entitled to relief against the second user on a theory of "reverse confusion." Plaintiff in *Big O* had begun selling tires under the mark "Bigfoot" in fourteen states in April, 1974. In September, 1974, over plaintiff's objections, defendant launched a national advertising campaign using the term "Bigfoot" to promote the sale of its newly-introduced tire. One result of the campaign was that customers came to plaintiff's stores to buy defendant's tires and were disappointed when they found that they could not.

The court rejected the defendant's argument that there could be no liability for unfair competition without a showing that defendant, Goodyear, intended to trade on the goodwill of plaintiff, Big O. The court relied in part on the district court's reasoning: " 'The logical consequence of accepting Goodyear's position would be the immunization from unfair competition liability of a company with a well established trade name and with the economic power to advertise extensively for a product name taken from a competitor. If the law is to limit recovery to passing off, anyone with adequate size and resources can adopt any trademark and develop a new meaning for that trademark as identification of the second user's products. The activities of Goodyear in this case are unquestionably unfair competition through an improper use of trademark and that must be actionable.' 408 F.Supp. at 1236." 561 F.2d at 1372.

3. *Zone of Expansion.* Can a firm ever have rights in a region in which it does no business? In which its name has no secondary meaning? Under the so-called zone of expansion doctrine, traditionally identified with dicta in Hanover Star Milling Co. v. Metcalf, 240 U.S. 403, 36 S.Ct. 357, 60 L.Ed. 713 (1916), a prior user can preempt the right to use its name and symbols in territories "that would probably be reached by the prior user in the natural expansion of his trade." 240 U.S. at 420, 36 S.Ct. at 363. Some cases, including *Sample,* suggest that larger, more aggressive firms will receive more commodious zones of expansion than smaller firms. Is it relevant that large retailers have been known to fail? That small firms are sometimes acquired by larger ones?

Several courts have limited the zone of expansion doctrine to situations in which the second user adopted the first user's name or symbol in bad faith—knowing of the prior use—or in which the first user's name or symbol had acquired secondary meaning in the relevant market. See Raxton Corp. v. Anania Assocs., Inc., 635 F.2d 924, 930, 208 U.S.P.Q. 769 (1st Cir.1980):

> A 'natural expansion' doctrine that penalized innocent users of a trademark simply because they occupied what for them would be a largely undiscoverable path of some remote prior user's expansion strikes us as at once unworkable, unfair, and, in the light of statutory protection available today, unnecessary. Such a doctrine would have to weigh the remote prior user's intangible and unregistered interest in future expansion as more important than the subsequent user's actual and good faith use of its name. Besides involving the obvious practical difficulties of defining the 'natural expansion path' of a business, this doctrine would also allow trademark owners to 'monopolize markets that [their] trade ha[d] never reached.' *Hanover,* 240 U.S. at 416, 36 S.Ct. at 361.

> The unfairness of this doctrine vanishes if the hypothesis of an *innocent* subsequent user is dropped, or if it is shown that the disputed trademark is known to consumers in the area of subsequent use prior to the subsequent user's adoption. In these cases it can be presumed unless demonstrated to the contrary that the subsequent user knowingly copied a mark. At the least, this suggests that the subsequent user should have been more careful to select a name free of prior rights and should be held to assume the risk of its negligence. At worst, this indicates a design to appropriate the goodwill of another.

Raxton's reference to the "statutory protection available today" was to section 22 of the Lanham Act, 15 U.S.C.A. § 1072, under which a mark's registration on the Principal Register in the Patent and Trademark Office will put subsequent users anywhere in the United States on constructive notice of the registrant's ownership of the mark, thus depriving them of a good faith defense and assuring the registrant of exclusive rights in markets not yet entered. Section 22 is discussed at pages 295 to 296 below.

---

3.   DILUTION

MEAD DATA CENTRAL, INC. v. TOYOTA MOTOR SALES, U.S.A., INC.

United States Court of Appeals, Second Circuit, 1989.
875 F.2d 1026, 10 U.S.P.Q.2d 1961.

VAN GRAAFEILAND, Circuit Judge:

Toyota Motor Sales, U.S.A., Inc. and its parent, Toyota Motor Corporation, appeal from a judgment of the United States District Court for the Southern District of New York (Edelstein, J.) enjoining them from using LEXUS as the name of their new luxury automobile and the division that manufactures it. The district court held that, under New York's antidilution statute, N.Y.Gen.Bus.Law § 368-d, Toyota's use of LEXUS is likely to dilute the distinctive quality of LEXIS, the mark used by Mead Data Central, Inc. for its computerized legal research service. On March 8, 1989, we entered an order of reversal, stating that an opinion would follow. This is the opinion.

THE STATUTE

Section 368-d of New York's General Business Law, which has counterparts in at least twenty other states, reads as follows:

> Likelihood of injury to business reputation or of dilution of the distinctive quality of a mark or trade name shall be a ground for injunctive relief in cases of infringement of a mark registered or not registered or in cases of unfair competition, notwithstanding the absence of competition between the parties or the absence of confusion as to the source of goods or services.

THE PARTIES AND THEIR MARKS

Mead and Lexis

Mead is a corporation organized under the laws of Delaware with its principal place of business in Miamisburg, Ohio. Since 1972, Mead has provided a computerized legal research service under the trademark LEXIS. Mead introduced evidence that its president in 1972 "came up with the name LEXIS based on Lex which was Latin for law and I S for information systems." In fact, however, the word "lexis" is centuries old. It is found in the language of ancient Greece, where it had the meaning of "phrase", "word", "speaking" or "diction". "Lexis" subsequently appeared in the Latin where it had a substantially similar meaning, *i.e.,* "word", "speech", or "language".

Like many other Latin words, "lexis" has been incorporated bodily into the English. It can be found today in at least sixty general dictionaries or other English word books, including Webster's Ninth New Collegiate Dictionary and Webster's New World Dictionary. Moreover, its meaning has not changed significantly from that of its Latin and Greek predecessors; *e.g.,* "Vocabulary, the total set of words in a language" (American Heritage Illustrated Encyclopedic Dictionary); "A vocabulary of a language, a particular subject, occupation, or activity" (Funk & Wagnalls Standard Dictionary). The district court's finding that "to establish that LEXIS is an English word required expert testimony at trial" is clearly erroneous. Anyone with a rudimentary knowledge of English can go to a library or bookstore and find the word in one of the above-mentioned standard dictionaries.

Moreover, the record discloses that numerous other companies had adopted "Lexis" in identifying their business or its product, *e.g.,* Lexis Ltd., Lexis Computer Systems Ltd., Lexis Language and Export Information Service, Lexis Corp., Maxwell Labs Lexis 3. In sum, we reject Mead's argument that LEXIS is a coined mark which originated in the mind of its former president and, as such, is entitled per se to the greater protection that a unique mark such as "Kodak" would receive.

Nevertheless, through its extensive sales and advertising in the field of computerized legal research, Mead has made LEXIS a strong mark in that field, and the district court so found. In particular, the district court accepted studies proffered by both parties which revealed that 76 percent of attorneys associated LEXIS with specific attributes of the service provided by Mead. However, among the general adult population, LEXIS is recognized by only one percent of those surveyed, half of this one percent being attorneys or accountants. The district court therefore concluded that LEXIS is strong only within its own market.

As appears in the Addendum to this opinion, the LEXIS mark is printed in block letters with no accompanying logo.

Toyota and Lexus

Toyota Motor Corp. has for many years manufactured automobiles, which it markets in the United States through its subsidiary Toyota Motor Sales, U.S.A. On August 24, 1987 Toyota announced a new line of luxury automobiles to be called LEXUS. The cars will be manufactured by a separate LEXUS division of Toyota, and their marketing pitch will be directed to well-educated professional consumers with annual incomes in excess of $50,000. Toyota had planned to spend $18 million to $20 million for this purpose during the first nine months of 1989.

Before adopting the completely artificial name LEXUS for its new automobile, Toyota secured expert legal advice to the effect that "there is absolutely no conflict between 'LEXIS' and 'LEXUS.'" Accordingly, when Mead subsequently objected to Toyota's use of LEXUS, Toyota rejected Mead's complaints. The district court held correctly that Toyota acted without predatory intent in adopting the LEXUS mark.

> [T]he absence of predatory intent by the junior user is a relevant factor in assessing a claim under the antidilution statute, . . . since relief under the statute is of equitable origin, ...

Sally Gee, Inc. v. Myra Hogan, Inc., 699 F.2d 621, 626 (2d Cir.1983).

However, the district court erred in concluding that Toyota's refusal to acknowledge that its use of LEXUS might harm the LEXIS mark, deprived it of the argument that it acted in good faith. If, as we now hold, Toyota's mark did not dilute Mead's, it would be anomalous indeed to hold Toyota guilty of bad faith in proceeding in reliance on its attorney's correct advice to that effect. Indeed, even if the attorney's professional advice had been wrong, it does not follow that Toyota's reliance on that advice would have constituted bad faith.

The LEXUS mark is in stylized, almost script-like lettering and is accompanied by a rakish L logo. See Addendum.

THE LAW

The brief legislative history accompanying section 368–d describes the purpose of the statute as preventing "the whittling away of an established trade-mark's selling power and value through *its* unauthorized use by others upon dissimilar products." 1954 N.Y.Legis.Ann. 49 (emphasis supplied). If we were to interpret literally the italicized word "its", we would limit statutory violations to the unauthorized use of the identical established mark. This is what Frank Schechter, the father of the dilution theory, intended when he wrote The Rational Basis of Trademark Protection, 40 Harv.L.Rev. 813 (1927). However, since the use of obvious simulations or markedly similar marks might have the same diluting effect as would an appropriation of the original mark, the concept of exact identity has been broadened to that of substantial similarity. Nevertheless, in keeping with the original intent of the statute, the similarity must be substantial before the doctrine of dilution may be applied.

Indeed, some courts have gone so far as to hold that, although violation of an antidilution statute does not require confusion of product or source, the marks in question must be sufficiently similar that confusion may be created as between the marks themselves. We need not go that far. We hold only that the marks must be "very" or "substantially" similar and that, absent such similarity, there can be no viable claim of dilution.

The district court's opinion was divided into two sections. The first section dealt with Toyota's alleged violation of the Lanham Act, and the second dealt with the alleged dilution of Mead's mark under New York's antidilution statute. The district court made several findings on the issue of similarity in its Lanham Act discussion; it made none in its discussion of section 368–d. Assuming that the district court's finding of lack of physical similarity in the former discussion was intended to carry over into the latter, we would find ourselves in complete accord with it since we would make the same finding. However, if the district court's statement in its Lanham Act discussion that "in everyday spoken English, LEXUS and LEXIS are virtually identical in pronounciation" was intended to be a finding of fact rather than a statement of opinion, we question both its accuracy and its relevance. The word LEXUS is not yet widely enough known that any definitive statement can be made concerning its pronunciation by the American public. However, the two members of this Court who concur in this opinion use "everyday spoken English", and we would not pronounce LEXUS as if it were spelled LEXIS. Although our colleague takes issue with us on this point, he does not contend that if LEXUS and LEXIS are pronounced correctly, they will sound the same. We liken LEXUS to such words as "census", "focus" and "locus", and differentiate it from such words as "axis", "aegis" and "iris".[2] If we were to

2. Similarly, we liken LEXUS to NEXUS, a nationally known shampoo, and LEXIS to NEXIS, Mead's trademark for its computerized news service. NEXXUS and NEXIS have co-existed in apparent tranquility for almost a decade.

substitute the letter "i" for the letter "u" in "census", we would not pronounce it as we now do. Likewise, if we were to substitute the letter "u" for the letter "i" in "axis", we would not pronounce it as we now do. In short, we agree with the testimony of Toyota's speech expert, who testified:

> Of course, anyone can pronounce "lexis" and "lexus" the same, either both with an unstressed I or both with an unstressed U, or schwa—or with some other sound in between. But, properly, the distinction between unstressed I and unstressed U, or schwa, is a standard one in English; the distinction is there to be made in ordinary, reasonably careful speech.

In addition, we do not believe that "everyday spoken English" is the proper test to use in deciding the issue of similarity in the instant case. . . . When Mead's speech expert was asked whether there were instances in which LEXUS and LEXIS would be pronounced differently, he replied "Yes, although a deliberate attempt must be made to do so. . . . They can be pronounced distinctly but they are not when they are used in common parlance, in everyday language or speech." We take it as a given that television and radio announcers usually are more careful and precise in their diction than is the man on the street. Moreover, it is the rare television commercial that does not contain a visual reference to the mark and product, which in the instant case would be the LEXUS automobile. We conclude that in the field of commercial advertising, which is the field subject to regulation, there is no substantial similarity between Mead's mark and Toyota's.

There are additional factors that militate against a finding of dilution in the instant case. Such a finding must be based on two elements. First, plaintiff's mark must possess a distinctive quality capable of dilution. Second, plaintiff must show a likelihood of dilution. As section 368–d expressly states, a plaintiff need not show either competition between its product or service and that of the defendant or a likelihood of confusion as to the source of the goods or services.

Distinctiveness for dilution purposes often has been equated with the strength of a mark for infringement purposes. It also has been defined as uniqueness or as having acquired a secondary meaning. Allied Maintenance Corp. v. Allied Mechanical Trades, Inc., 42 N.Y.2d at 545, 399 N.Y.S.2d 628, 369 N.E.2d 1162. A trademark has a secondary meaning if it "has become so associated in the mind of the public with that entity [Allied] or its product that it identifies the goods sold by that entity and distinguishes them from goods sold by others." Id. In sum, the statute protects a trademark's "selling power." However, the fact that a mark has selling power in a limited geographical or commercial area does not endow it with a secondary meaning for the public generally.

The strength and distinctiveness of LEXIS is limited to the market for its services—attorneys and accountants. Outside that market, LEXIS has very little selling power. Because only one percent of the general population associates LEXIS with the attributes of Mead's service, it cannot be said that LEXIS identifies that service to the general public and distinguishes it from others. Moreover, the bulk of Mead's advertising budget is devoted to reaching attorneys through professional journals.

This Court has defined dilution as either the blurring of a mark's product identification or the tarnishment of the affirmative associations a mark has come to convey. Mead does not claim that Toyota's use of LEXUS would tarnish affirmative associations engendered by LEXIS. The question that remains, therefore, is whether LEXIS is likely to be blurred by LEXUS.

Very little attention has been given to date to the distinction between the confusion necessary for a claim of infringement and the blurring necessary for a claim of dilution. Although the antidilution statute dispenses with the requirements of competition and confusion, it does not follow that every junior use of a similar mark will dilute the senior mark in the manner contemplated by the New York Legislature.

As already stated, the brief legislative history accompanying section 368–d described the purpose of the statute as preventing "the whittling away of an established trademark's selling power and value through its unauthorized use by others upon dissimilar products." The history disclosed a need for legislation to prevent such "hypothetical anomolies" as "Dupont shoes, Buick aspirin tablets, Schlitz varnish, Kodak pianos, Bulova gowns, and so forth", and cited cases involving similarly famous marks. 1954 N.Y.Legis.Ann. 49–50.

It is apparent from these references that there must be some mental association between plaintiff's and defendant's marks.

> [I]f a reasonable buyer is not at all likely to link the two uses of the trademark in his or her own mind, even subtly or subliminally, then there can be no dilution. . . . [D]ilution theory presumes *some kind of mental association* in the reasonable buyer's mind between the two party's [sic] uses of the mark.

2 J. McCarthy, Trademarks and Unfair Competition § 24.13 at 213–14 (2d ed. 1984).

This mental association may be created where the plaintiff's mark is very famous and therefore has a distinctive quality for a significant percentage of the defendant's market. However, if a mark circulates only in a limited market, it is unlikely to be associated generally with the mark for a dissimilar product circulating elsewhere. As discussed above, such distinctiveness as LEXIS possesses is limited to the narrow market of attorneys and accountants. Moreover, the process which LEXIS represents is widely disparate from the product represented by LEXUS. For the general public, LEXIS has no distinctive quality that LEXUS will dilute.

The possibility that someday LEXUS may become a famous mark in the mind of the general public has little relevance in the instant dilution analysis since it is quite apparent that the general public associates nothing with LEXIS. On the other hand, the recognized sophistication of attorneys, the principal users of the service, has substantial relevance. Because of this knowledgeable sophistication, it is unlikely that, even in the market where Mead principally operates, there will be any significant amount of blurring between the LEXIS and LEXUS marks.

For all the foregoing reasons, we hold that Toyota did not violate section 368-d. We see no need therefore to discuss Toyota's remaining arguments for reversal.

ADDENDUM

The opinion of SWEET, District Judge, concurring, is omitted.

NOTES

1. Judge Sweet, concurring in Mead v. Toyota, believed that "the majority has failed adequately to define the likelihood of dilution concept." Observing that the "tarnishing" concept "is helpful because that principle can be applied in practice," Judge Sweet noted that the "blurring" concept "offers practitioners and courts only marginally more guidance than 'likelihood of dilution.'" 875 F.2d at 1034–35. In Judge Sweet's view, "blurring sufficient to constitute dilution requires a case-by-case factual inquiry" focused on six judicially-recognized factors:

    (1) similarity of the marks

    (2) similarity of the products covered by the marks

    (3) sophistication of consumers

    (4) predatory intent

    (5) renown of the senior mark

    (6) renown of the junior mark

Only the sixth factor gave Judge Sweet any serious pause: "This case raises an issue that is likely to arise rarely in dilution law—the prospect that a junior mark may become so famous that it will overwhelm the senior mark. Dilution under this theory might occur where the senior user's advertising and marketing have established certain associations for its product among a particular consumer group, but the junior mark's subsequent renown causes the senior user's consumers to draw the associations identified with the junior user's mark. Here, for example, Toyota seeks to associate LEXUS with luxury and the carriage trade, which Mead fears may overwhelm LEXIS's association with indispensability and economy." 875 F.2d at 1038.

Nonetheless, Judge Sweet concluded that no blurring was likely to occur: "First, section 368–d protects a mark's selling power among the consuming public. Because the LEXIS mark possesses selling power only among lawyers and accountants, it is irrelevant for dilution analysis that the general public may come to associate LEXIS or LEXUS with Toyota's automobile rather than nothing at all. Second, the district court offered no evidence for its speculation that LEXUS's fame may cause Mead customers to associate 'lexis' with Toyota's cars. It seems equally plausible that no blurring will occur—because many lawyers and accountants use Mead's services regularly, their frequent association of LEXIS with those services will enable LEXIS's mark to withstand Toyota's advertising campaign." 875 F.2d at 1039–40.

Would Mead have an unfair competition action against Toyota if Toyota's widely advertised mark in fact swamped Mead's mark so that Mead customers would first think of Toyota's car when they hear the term, Lexis? See Big O Tire Dealers, Inc. v. Goodyear Tire & Rubber Co., discussed at page 75, note 2, above.

2. *Tarnishment.* Dilution doctrine's prohibition against tarnishment can be applied broadly or narrowly. Applied broadly, the prohibition encompasses any unauthorized use of a mark in any context,

commercial or noncommercial, that diminishes the mark's positive associations. Applied narrowly, the prohibition encompasses only unauthorized commercial uses of the mark in connection with shoddy goods or with goods that lack the prestige associated with the mark.

The choice between a broad and a narrow approach to tarnishment may have constitutional implications. In L.L. Bean, Inc. v. Drake Publishers, Inc., 811 F.2d 26, 1 U.S.P.Q.2d 1753 (1st Cir.1987), cert. denied, 483 U.S. 1013, 107 S.Ct. 3254, 97 L.Ed.2d 753 (1987), the court reversed the grant of an injunction against a sexual parody of plaintiff's famous catalogue that incorporated a facsimile of plaintiff's trademark. In the court's view, the Maine antidilution statute, as applied, violated the first amendment's free expression guarantees. The core of the court's concern was the application of the statute to noncommercial conduct. "Drake has not used Bean's mark to identify or market goods or services; it has used the mark solely to identify Bean as the object of its parody." Further, to deny "parodists the opportunity to poke fun at symbols and names which have become woven into the fabric of our daily life, would constitute a serious curtailment of a protected form of expression." 811 F.2d at 33, 34. Dicta throughout the opinion indicate that the court would have upheld an application of the statute limited to use of the mark in connection with the marketing of goods or services.

3. Dilution doctrine has a long common law history. Borden Ice Cream Co. v. Borden's Condensed Milk Co., 201 Fed. 510 (7th Cir.1912), reflects the early view that noncompetitive poaching is not actionable. The court denied plaintiff, a condensed milk company, an injunction against defendant's use of the name, "Borden," in connection with the sale of ice cream on the ground that plaintiff was not engaged in the ice cream business. But, soon after, the Tiffany jewelry firm, the Rolls–Royce automobile firm and the Dunhill pipe firm were respectively held entitled to injunctive relief against defendants who had used the name, "Tiffany" in connection with motion pictures, "Rolls–Royce" in connection with radio tubes, and "Dunhill" in connection with shirts. Tiffany & Co. v. Tiffany Productions, 147 Misc. 679, 264 N.Y.S. 459 (Sup.Ct. 1932), aff'd, 262 N.Y. 482, 188 N.E. 30 (1933); Wall v. Rolls–Royce of America, 4 F.2d 333 (3d Cir.1925); Alfred Dunhill of London v. Dunhill Shirt Shop, 3 F.Supp. 487 (S.D.N.Y.1929).

Common law courts typically rationalize decisions for plaintiff in dilution cases on a deception ground. Where, as in *Rolls–Royce,* there is some likelihood that consumers will believe that plaintiff manufactured defendant's goods, the deception relied on is of the usual passing off variety. Where, as in *Dunhill,* the likelihood of confusion as to source is more attenuated, confusion of sponsorship may be employed as the ground for decision. Where, as in *Tiffany,* the likelihood of confusion as to source or sponsorship is hardly colorable, courts tend to avoid the deception ground entirely and rely instead on a misappropriation ground.

Underlying all dilution decisions is the question whether one party should have rights in a product or service market it has not yet entered. How, if at all, does this question differ from the question that underlies zone of expansion cases, like *Sample,* page 70 above, in which the battleground is unoccupied geographic, rather than product or service, markets?

4. *Repackaged Goods.* Does the repackaging of goods bearing a protected mark constitute dilution? A triad of cases suggests several approaches. Clairol, Inc. v. Peekskill Thrift Drug Corp., 141 U.S.P.Q. 147 (N.Y.Sup.Ct.1964); Clairol, Inc. v. Sarann Co., 146 U.S.P.Q. 726 (Pa. Ct.Com.Pl.1965); Clairol, Inc. v. Cody's Cosmetics, Inc., 353 Mass. 385, 231 N.E.2d 912 (1967).

The facts, roughly the same in all three cases, were these: Plaintiff sold its hair coloring product, "Miss Clairol," under a dual pricing system so that the professional trade—jobbers for beauty salons—was able to buy the goods at about one-half the price charged to the retail trade—drug and cosmetic wholesalers. The products distributed through these two channels were identical, the only difference being in the method of packaging. The retail trade received individually boxed single application bottles, and the professional trade received single application bottles in six-packs. An instruction sheet containing several warnings as to the dangers of misusing the product, and advice on how to avoid them, was enclosed in each retail carton but not in the professional six-pack. Every professional carton bore the legend, "Professional Use Only." Defendants, drug and cosmetic retailers, purchased professional six-packs at the substantial discount and sold the bottles individually, without cartons, to their retail customers. To these bottles defendants attached mimeographed instruction sheets which in all three cases omitted vital information, given in Clairol's retail instruction sheet, on the methods and dangers of use.

Clairol's action to enjoin defendants from selling "Miss Clairol" in any form other than the complete Clairol retail package succeeded in New York and Pennsylvania. In the New York action, the court held that plaintiff's proof that defendant's conduct was "likely to injure plaintiff's goodwill and business reputation" was sufficient to warrant relief under the state's broad unfair competition statute, General Business Law § 368–d. Lacking the statutory authority available in New York, the Pennsylvania court rested its decision on two common law grounds. First, noting that plaintiff had not shown passing off, the court concluded that defendant's conduct nonetheless constituted unfair competition: "the consumer will attribute any unsatisfactory performance from 'Miss Clairol' to plaintiff, and not to defendant. Defendant thus used plaintiff's goodwill to make sales, but acts in a manner which can only decrease plaintiff's goodwill, thus damaging an important property interest of plaintiff." Second, the court held that "plaintiff, by placing on the bottle of 'Miss Clairol' destined for professional use the legend 'Professional Use Only,' has placed an equitable servitude or restriction on the bottle, thus preventing defendant from acting in violation of that restriction."

Clairol did not fare as well in Massachusetts. Refusing to extend unfair competition beyond its basic passing off formula, and rejecting the equitable servitude argument, the court concluded that the injury to consumers was only incidental and that the essential injury was to "an effective marketing and advertising device." Recognizing that there was some danger that consumers would suffer injury from uninstructed use, the court enjoined defendant from selling the professional bottles without a legible, printed statement containing appropriate warnings.

4. MISAPPROPRIATION

BOARD OF TRADE OF CITY OF CHICAGO v. DOW JONES & CO.

Supreme Court of Illinois, 1983.
98 Ill.2d 109, 74 Ill.Dec. 582, 456 N.E.2d 84.

GOLDENHERSH, Justice:

Defendant, Dow Jones & Company, Inc., appealed from the judgment of the circuit court of Cook County entered in favor of plaintiff, the Board of Trade of the city of Chicago, in its action for declaratory judgment. Plaintiff sought a declaration that its offering of a commodity futures contract utilizing the Dow Jones Industrial Average as the underlying commodity would not violate defendant's legal or proprietary rights. The appellate court reversed and we allowed plaintiff's petition for leave to appeal.

The opinion of the appellate court adequately sets forth the facts, and they will be restated here only to the extent necessary to discuss the issues. Defendant, a Delaware corporation with its principal office in New York City, publishes the Wall Street Journal, Barrons, a weekly business magazine, and the Asian Wall Street Journal. It also maintains the Dow Jones News Service, through which it distributes financial news to subscribers. It produces several stock market indexes, the Dow Jones Industrial Average, Transportation Average, and Utilities Average, which are computed on the basis of the current prices of stocks of certain companies selected by defendant's editorial board.

The financial news furnished by defendant is disseminated in a variety of ways. It is distributed to brokerage houses, banks, financial institutions, individual investors, and others who are interested in stock market news. This information is transmitted to teleprinters, cathode-ray-tube receivers, and other devices, such as wall displays in brokerage houses. Subscribers desiring the averages can extract them from the news service or arrange with defendant to deliver the averages directly to them by teleprinter. Through special contracts, others receive the averages through entities which are licensed by defendant to sublicense the distribution of the averages. Plaintiff has a "Subscription Agreement" under which it pays defendant for its News Service and is allowed to compute and display the Dow Jones Averages on plaintiff's trading floor on a continuous, "real time" basis.

Plaintiff is the oldest and largest commodities exchange market in the United States. It was organized in 1848, and in 1859 the General Assembly granted plaintiff a special charter which incorporated it as a not-for-pecuniary-profit organization. Over the years plaintiff has added different types of futures contracts and now offers these contracts in a variety of fields, including agricultural products, precious metals and financial instruments. All commodities exchanges in the United States are regulated by the Commodities Futures Trading Commission (CFTC), and no exchange may trade a futures contract until the CFTC approves the futures contract and designates the exchange as a contract market for that contract.

A futures contract is a contract traded on a commodities exchange which binds the parties to a particular transaction at a specified future date. A stock index futures contract is a futures contract based upon the value of a particular stock market index. Dr. James H. Lorie, stipulated by the parties to be an expert, called by plaintiff, testified that these contracts have been traded since February 1982. At the time of trial they were traded on the Kansas City Board of Trade based on the Value Line Average, on the Chicago Mercantile Exchange based on the Standard & Poor's 500 Stock Index and on the New York Futures Exchange based on the New York Stock Exchange Composite Index. He stated that their "overriding purpose is the management of risk." Unlike other futures contracts, no underlying commodity exists to be delivered at the future date, but rather the transaction is settled by the delivery of a certified promissory note in lieu of cash. He explained that the total risks of investing in the stock market are divided into two parts. One part is the "nonsystematic risk," which occurs when an individual company encounters problems such as strikes, changing consumer attitudes or other problems which would devalue that company's stock. "Nonsystematic risk" can be controlled by an investor through the use of a diversified portfolio. The other type of risk is "systematic risk," which is the risk associated with the broad general movements of the stock market as a whole. Diversification of one's stock portfolio will not provide protection against sharp declines in the stock market. He explained that there are only two ways to protect against systematic risk. The most direct way is for an investor to sell his stocks. This method is rather costly because of the transactional costs in selling and buying stocks, such as brokerage fees. Additionally, if capital gains are realized, the transactions become even more costly. The second method of protecting against systematic risk is to deal in stock market futures contracts. This method is more efficient, Professor Lorie explained, since an investor holding a hypothetical $100,000 portfolio could purchase two futures contracts in the Chicago Mercantile Exchange for one-fifteenth the cost of selling his stocks.

An investor who holds a diversified stock portfolio may "hedge" against systematic risk by entering into a stock index futures contract predicting that the market index would decline. Dr. Lorie testified that this was the most effective method of "hedging" of which he was aware.

Plaintiff, desiring to be designated as a contract market for stock index futures contracts, devoted more than two years to developing its own index to be used as the basis for its stock index futures contract. During the greater part of this period, the Securities and Exchange Commission (SEC) and the CFTC were in a dispute concerning which agency had jurisdiction to regulate stock index futures contracts. In December 1981, the two Federal agencies agreed on the scope of their respective jurisdiction and on recommendations to Congress for regulatory legislation. They agreed that the CFTC would regulate trading in stock market index contracts and that such trading would be permitted only if the contracts were based on widely known and well-established stock market indexes. This jurisdictional agreement effectively precluded CFTC approval of a contract based on the index developed by plaintiff.

On February 26, 1982, plaintiff submitted an application to the CFTC asking that it be designated as a contract market for Chicago Board of Trade Portfolio Futures Contracts. The application proposed the use of three indexes, the stock market index, transport index, and the electric index portfolio contracts. It was explained:

> Each index covers a significant portion of the overall stock market. The stock market index covers industrial firms, the Transport Index covers air, rail, and trucking firms, and the Gas and Electric Index covers utility companies. This division is similar to the way other major market indices divide the stock market.

No mention of the Dow Jones name appeared in the application, but the stocks used in each of the indexes were identical to those used in the Dow Jones averages. In a draft proposal to the CFTC for trading "CBT indexes," the Dow Jones averages stock lists were cut out of the Wall Street Journal and pasted into the proposals. The CFTC advised plaintiff that the CBT indexes were not just similar to, but were identical to the Dow Jones averages and that this should be explicitly stated in its application. On May 7, 1982, plaintiff amended its application to state that the CBT indexes were identical to Dow Jones averages and that when Dow Jones changed a component stock or revised the divisor, plaintiff would make the same change so that the CBT indexes would remain identical to the Dow Jones averages. Plaintiff also added a disclaimer to the application disclaiming any association with Dow Jones. On May 13, the CFTC approved plaintiff's use of the stock market index portfolio contract, but did not rule concerning the use of the transportation or utility index portfolio contracts.

The circuit court held that the burden of producing evidence and the burden of persuading the trier of fact fell upon defendant and found that defendant had a "property right and valuable interest in the Dow Jones averages" but that plaintiff's use of the averages in the manner proposed did not violate those rights. The order, however, required that there be imprinted upon the CBT index contract a disclaimer disavowing any association with or sponsorship by defendant, Dow Jones. The appellate court reversed, holding that plaintiff had the burden of production and persuasion, and that plaintiff's use of the averages constituted commercial misappropriation "of the Dow Jones index and averages.". . . .

Plaintiff argues that the appellate court's holding erroneously expands the tort of misappropriation and that its decision contravenes public policy. Citing Capitol Records, Inc. v. Spies (1970), 130 Ill.App.2d 429, 264 N.E.2d 874, Metropolitan Opera Association v. Wagner–Nichols Recorder Corp. (199 Misc. 786, 101 N.Y.S.2d 483, aff'd (1951), 279 A.D. 632, 107 N.Y.S.2d 795, Standard & Poor's Corp. v. Commodity Exchange, Inc. (2d Cir.1982), 683 F.2d 704, and International News Service v. Associated Press (1918), 248 U.S. 215, 39 S.Ct. 68, 63 L.Ed. 211, plaintiff argues that competitive injury is a fundamental prerequisite essential to a finding of misappropriation. It argues that the facts of this case are analogous to National Football League v. Governor of Delaware (D.Del.1977), 435 F.Supp. 1372, and Loeb v. Turner (Tex.Civ. App.1953), 257 S.W.2d 800, in which the courts refused to find misappropriation because, *inter alia,* the parties were not in competition with each other. It argues that it has done nothing immoral or unethical but has merely created a "new product" which is "outside the primary market which the producer of the original product originally set out to satisfy * * *." Finally, plaintiff argues that the appellate court's decision is against public policy in that it grants what amounts to a common law patent monopoly to defendant which permits it to exclude others from using its product for any purpose "regardless of whether the producer is being injured or intends to exploit the product itself."

Defendant responds that the tort of misappropriation should be flexible so that, by carefully tailoring their misappropriation to avoid the strict rules of the tort, "enterprising pirates" cannot avoid the application of the doctrine. Citing Sims v. Mack Truck Corp. (3d Cir. 1979), 608 F.2d 87, 95, cert. denied, (1980), 445 U.S. 930, 100 S.Ct. 1319, 63 L.Ed.2d 764, defendant argues that under the doctrine of misappropriation direct competition is not essential to tort liability. Defendant argues that plaintiff seeks to exploit defendant's reputation for accuracy and impartiality without compensating it for its good will. Finally, in response to plaintiff's argument that the appellate court's opinion is against public policy, defendant argues that the appellate court's opinion is consistent with public policy in that it maintains the incentive for the creation of intellectual property. Defendant argues that if its rights in the averages are not protected, there will be a diminished incentive for it to continue to provide the averages. Defendant points out that it does not seek to monopolize the production of stock indexes and that plaintiff is free to develop its own, but that it desires to protect its rights in the averages which it created and continues to produce.

None of the many cases cited by the parties presents facts sufficiently similar to serve as definitive authority for the decision of the issue presented here. The rationales applied in developing a basis for the tort of misappropriation appear to be as diverse as the factual situations out of which the issues in those cases arose.

The doctrine of misappropriation as a form of unfair competition was first enunciated by the Supreme Court in International News Service v. Associated Press (1918), 248 U.S. 215, 39 S.Ct. 68, 63 L.Ed. 211. In that case, INS was copying news stories from bulletin boards of members of AP and transmitting the fresh news contained on those bulletin boards to its own members. Thus, INS could obtain information collected by AP at great expense and transmit this information to its midwestern and west coast members, who could then print the news at the same time as the competing AP members or, in some instances, earlier. In affirming the decree enjoining the practice the majority opinion suggested that without the revenues derived from this exclusive, timely presentation of the news, AP or other news services would not have sufficient incentive to continue performing their services.

The tort of misappropriation was recognized in Illinois for the first time in Capitol Records, Inc. v. Spies (1970), 130 Ill.App.2d 429, 264 N.E.2d 874. There the defendant purchased records and magnetic tapes sold by the plaintiff and recorded them on magnetic tapes. He then sold these re-recordings to his customers. A disclaimer was placed on the cassette tapes disclaiming any relationship between the defendant and plaintiff or the recorded artists. Defendant was able to sell his product at a lesser price than plaintiff since he avoided the costs of contracting with the performers, producing the master recordings, paying royalty fees, and advertising. Relying on the rationale of Schulenburg v. Signatrol, Inc., (1964), 50 Ill.App.2d 402, 411–12, 200 N.E.2d 615, affirmed in part and reversed in part (1965), 33 Ill.2d 379, 212 N.E.2d 865, the court reasoned that the manner of competition was "unfair" since the defendant was able to compete on equal terms by avoiding those costs normally associated with producing such recordings. Underlying the court's reasoning is the premise that the plaintiff's pecuniary reward for producing its intangible product would be severely reduced if other competitors could avoid production costs by merely waiting until a record became popular and then recording the work for resale.

Competing with the policy that protection should be afforded one who expends labor and money to develop products is the concept that freedom to imitate and duplicate is vital to our free market economy. Indeed, when the doctrine of misappropriation was first enunciated, Justice Brandeis recognized this competing policy:

> He who follows the pioneer into a new market, or who engages in the manufacture of an article newly introduced by another, seeks profits due largely to the labor and expense of the first adventurer; but the law sanctions, indeed encourages, the pursuit. (International News Service v. Associated Press (1918), 248 U.S. 215, 259, 39 S.Ct. 68, 79, 63 L.Ed. 211, 229 (Brandeis, J., dissenting).)

Similarly, Professor Rahl reasons:

> Substantial similarity of alternatives can come about in only one of two ways—by independent development or by imitation.

While there are many instances of simultaneous independent innovation, our economy would still be in the Dark Ages if this were the only circumstance under which competing alternatives could be offered. Imitation is inherent in any system of competition and it is imperative for an economy in which there is rapid technological advance. Rahl, The Right to "Appropriate" Trade Values, 23 Ohio St.L.J. 56, 72 (1962).

In balancing the factors that should determine which of the competing concepts should prevail, it appears unlikely that an adverse decision will cause defendant to cease to produce its averages or that the revenue it currently receives for the distribution of those averages will be materially affected. Defendant correctly asserts that it will lose its right to prospective licensing revenues in the event that in the future it elects to have its name associated with stock index futures contracts, but reliance upon the existence of a property right based upon the ability to license the product to prospective markets which were not originally contemplated by the creator of the product is somewhat "circular." Williams & Wilkins Co. v. United States (1973) 203 Ct.Cl. 74, 487 F.2d 1345, 1357 n. 19.

Alternatively, holding that plaintiff's use of defendant's indexes in the manner proposed is a misappropriation may stimulate the creation of new indexes perhaps better suited to the purpose of "hedging" against the "systematic" risk present in the stock market.

Whether protection against appropriation is necessary to foster creativity depends in part upon the expectations of that sector of the business community which deals with the particular intangible. If the creator of an intangible product expects to be able to control the licensing or distribution of the intangible in order to profit from his effort, and similarly those who would purchase the product expect and are willing to pay for the use of the intangible, a better argument can be made in favor of granting protection. The record shows that the plaintiff sought to develop its own index prior to the CFTC's requirement that the contracts be based on well-known, well-established indexes. It then offered defendant 10 cents per transaction, which it estimated would be somewhere between $1 million and $2 million per year, for the use of its name and averages. While there appears to be some dispute as to whether this offer of payment was primarily for the use of defendant's name or for the use of the averages, the offer of money is relevant to the extent that it acknowledges the value of the association of defendant's name and good will with the averages it produces.

To hold that defendant has a proprietary interest in its indexes and averages which vests it with the exclusive right to license their use for trading in stock index futures contracts would not preclude plaintiff and others from marketing stock index futures contracts. The extent of defendant's monopoly would be limited, for as defendant points out, there are an infinite number of stock market indexes which could be devised. As one commentator notes, the effect of granting a "monopoly" at the base of the production pyramid is much less objectionable than granting a monopoly at the top of the pyramid:

Social cost assumes more manageable size and so less significance near the base of the pyramid. Exclusive rights in a special kind of typewriter key are far less objectionable than a monopoly in the lever, because far less is swept into the monopolist's control. Developments In the Law: Competitive Torts, 77 Harv.L.Rev. 888, 938 (1964).

We conclude that the possibility of any detriment to the public which might result from our holding that defendant's indexes and averages may not be used without its consent in the manner proposed by plaintiff are outweighed by the resultant encouragement to develop new indexes specifically designed for the purpose of hedging against the "systematic" risk present in the stock market.

We have considered plaintiff's contention that defendant has failed to prove that the proposed use of the averages would cause it injury. The publication of the indexes involves valuable assets of defendant, its good will and its reputation for integrity and accuracy. Despite the fact that plaintiff's proposed use is not in competition with the use defendant presently makes of them, defendant is entitled to protection against their misappropriation. . . .

For the reasons stated, the judgment of the appellate court is affirmed.

Judgment affirmed.

The opinion of SIMON, J., dissenting is omitted.

NOTE

Many courts require a competitive relationship between the plaintiff and defendant for a misappropriation action to lie. In United States Golf Ass'n v. St. Andrews Sys., Data–Max, Inc., 749 F.2d 1028, 224 U.S.P.Q. 646 (3d Cir.1984), the court held that defendant's use of plaintiff U.S.G.A.'s handicapping formula in its computer program providing instant handicaps did not constitute misappropriation because plaintiff and defendant were not in direct competition: "The competition in this case is indirect. The U.S.G.A. is not in the business of selling handicaps to golfers, but is primarily interested in the promotion of the game of golf, and in its own position as the governing body of amateur golf."

In Standard & Poor's Corp. v. Commodity Exchange, Inc., 683 F.2d 704, 216 U.S.P.Q. 841 (2d Cir.1982), which involved facts similar to those in Board of Trade v. Dow Jones, the court rested its decision for plaintiff in part on the fact that plaintiff had licensed its popular stock index to another commodities exchange and thus was effectively in competition with the defendant commodity exchange. Does the simple expedient of entering into a licensing arrangement break the "circular" reasoning that Justice Goldenhersh rejected in Board of Trade v. Dow Jones? If an existing license can be used to bootstrap a property right, should not the prospect of a licensing arrangement also support a property right? If neither a licensing arrangement nor the prospect of one will create the required competitive relationship, would the competition requirement be met if the plaintiff directly entered the market itself? What relevant difference is there between a firm's decision to enter a market itself and its decision to enter the market through a licensed agent?

Apart from the historical fact that misappropriation is rooted in unfair competition law, what reason is there for the competition requirement? Justice Goldenhersh may have touched on the reason in his reference to "the ability to license the product to prospective markets *which were not originally contemplated by the creator of the product.*" (Emphasis added.) Only if, at the outset of its investment, a firm contemplated reaping rewards from a particular market is it likely that the firm proportioned its investment to these prospective returns; after the event, the firm should receive a property right to secure these expectations.

See generally, Baird, Common Law Intellectual Property and the Legacy of International News Service v. Associated Press, 50 U.Chi.L. Rev. 411 (1983).

B. LIMITS OF PROTECTION

---

1. PERSONAL INTERESTS: RIGHTS IN NAMES

DAVID B. FINDLAY, INC. v. FINDLAY
Court of Appeals of New York, 1966.
18 N.Y.2d 12, 271 N.Y.S.2d 652, 218 N.E.2d 531, 150 U.S.P.Q. 223,
modified, 18 N.Y.2d 676, 219 N.E.2d 872, cert. denied,
385 U.S. 930, 87 S.Ct. 289, 17 L.Ed.2d 212.

KEATING, J. When should a man's right to use his own name in his business be limited? This is the question before us.

The individual plaintiff David B. Findlay ("David") and the individual defendant Walstein C. Findlay ("Wally") are brothers. The Findlay art business was founded in 1870 by their grandfather in Kansas City. Their father continued and expanded the business with a Chicago branch managed by Wally and a New York branch established and managed by David on East 57th Street. In 1936 the Kansas City gallery was closed and in 1938, after a dispute, the brothers separated. By agreement David, as president of Findlay Galleries, Inc., and owner of nearly all of the stock of the original Missouri corporation, sold to Wally individually the Chicago gallery and allowed Wally to use the name "Findlay Galleries, Inc." in the conduct of his business in Chicago. Wally organized an Illinois corporation under the name "Findlay Galleries, Inc." in 1938 and has since operated his Chicago gallery. He also opened, in 1961, a Palm Beach, Florida, gallery.

David, since the separation, has operated his gallery on East 57th Street in Manhattan. For many years he has conducted his business on the second floor of 11–13 East 57th Street.

In October, 1963, Wally purchased the premises at 17 East 57th Street and informed David of his plans to open an art gallery. David objected to Wally's use of the name "Findlay" on 57th Street and by letter announced he would "resist any appropriation by you in New York of the name Findlay in connection with a gallery . . . any funds spent by you to establish a gallery at 17 East 57th Street under the name Findlay Galleries, Inc. (or any variation thereof using the name Findlay) are spent at your peril." David also, in self-defense and in an effort to survive, rented additional space at 15 East 57th Street so as to have a street level entrance.

David's objections and pleas seemed to have some effect on Wally. As renovation on the building was carried on from October, 1963 to September, 1964, a large sign proclaimed the coming opening of "W.C.F. Galleries, Inc." There was also a display and listing in the New York Telephone directory under the same name and similar advertisements in other publications. However, in September, 1964 the sign was suddenly changed to announce the imminent opening of "Wally Findlay Galleries" affiliated with "Findlay Galleries, Inc." David immediately sought an injunction. Wally went ahead with his opening and erected a sidewalk canopy from the curb to the building displaying the name "Wally Findlay Galleries."

The trial court made very detailed findings and, based on them, enjoined defendant from using the names "Wally Findlay Galleries," "Findlay Galleries" and any other designation including the name "Findlay" in the conduct of an art gallery on East 57th Street. The Appellate Division has affirmed on the trial court's findings and we find evidence to sustain them.

The trial court concluded that if injunctive relief were not granted, plaintiff would continue to be damaged by confusion and diversion and would suffer great and irreparable loss in his business and in his name and reputation. In his quarter of a century on East 57th Street David has established a valuable good will and reputation as an art dealer. Through hard work, business ability and expenditure of large sums of money, David has reached the level where a significant portion of his business comes from people who have been referred to him by others and told to go to "Findlay's on 57th St."

The effect of Wally's new gallery, with its long canopy, can only be that those looking for "Findlay's on 57th St." will be easily confused and find their way into Wally's rather than David's gallery. Though Wally perhaps did not deliberately set out to exploit David's good will and reputation, the trial court found, and we agree, that such a result would follow if Wally were permitted to operate a gallery under the name "Wally Findlay Galleries" next door to David.

There were numerous instances of people telephoning or asking at David's for personnel of Wally's or for art work exhibited at Wally's. Many regular customers congratulated David on the opening of "his" new gallery next door. Moreover, advertisements frequently appeared on the same pages of the local press for "Findlay Galleries", "Findlay's", or "Wally Findlay Galleries" thus making it very difficult to tell whose advertisement it was. Even the art editors and reporters referred to Wally as "Findlay Galleries"—the name used for many years by David—or as "the new Findlay Gallery."

It is apparent that confusion has and must result from Wally's opening next to David. This is compounded by the fact that both brothers have for years specialized in French impressionist and post-impressionist painters. Therefore, quite naturally, both brothers have in the past dealt in the works of such famous deceased painters as Modigliani, Degas, Renoir, Gauguin, Bonnard, Braque, Monet and many others.

Although someone seeking a Renoir from David is unlikely to purchase a Degas from Wally, it is likely that with respect to some of the lesser-known impressionists such diversion might happen. More important, someone wishing to own a nude by Modigliani, a dancer by Degas or a portrait of a girl by Renoir would not necessarily have a particular painting in mind and would likely purchase any of these species, whether it be in Wally's or David's. The items sold by the two brothers are not unique, nonsubstitutional works.

Moreover, art, particularly modern art, is sold only to those who see it. Works of art are sold to those who cross the threshold of the art gallery and the more people you get into your gallery, the more art you will sell. To this end David has worked hard to develop the name "Findlay's on 57th St." and bring in customers. Many people who have the finances to purchase art do not necessarily have the knowledge to distinguish between the works of all the various painters represented by galleries such as Wally's or David's. For this reason they rely on the reputation of the gallery. David has spent over 25 years in developing satisfied customers who will tell others to go to "Findlay's on 57th St." This good will brings in customers who look for a work of art that suits their fancy and if Wally were to continue to use the name Findlay, it is inevitable that some would walk into Wally's by mistake and would have their tastes satisfied there, to David's great harm.

The so-called "sacred right" theory that every man may employ his own name in his business is not unlimited. Moreover, fraud or deliberate intention to deceive or mislead the public are not necessary ingredients to a cause of action.

The present trend of the law is to enjoin the use even of a family name when such use tends or threatens to produce confusion in the public mind. Whether this confusion should be satisfied by misplaced phone calls or confusing advertisements alone we do not decide because there has been a finding that diversion, as well as confusion, will exist if Wally is not enjoined. Thus it is clear that the "confusion" with which we are dealing includes impairment of good will of a business.

In Meneely v. Meneely (62 N.Y. 427) this court noted that one can use his own name provided he does not resort to any artifice or contrivance for the purpose of producing the impression that the establishments are identical, or do anything calculated to mislead the public.

Thirty-five years later, we noted that, as a general principle of law, one's name is his property and he is entitled to its use. However, it was equally a principle of law that no man can sell his goods as those of another. "He may not through unfairness, artifice, misrepresentation or fraud injure the business of another or induce the public to believe his product is the product of that other." (World's Dispensary Medical Ass'n v. Pierce, 203 N.Y. 419, 424, 96 N.E. 738, 740.)

Ryan & Son v. Lancaster Homes (15 N.Y.2d 812, 257 N.Y.S.2d 934, 205 N.E.2d 859, aff'g 22 A.D.2d 186, 254 N.Y.S.2d 473) is distinguishable from the present case because there was lacking in *Ryan* the crucial finding that in the absence of relief plaintiff would be damaged by confusion and diversion. There was no real competition between the two businesses. Again, unlike the instant case where "Findlay's on 57th St." is synonymous in New York City with quality art galleries, "Homes by Ryan" had not become a trade name with a secondary meaning. The court reviewed the law and cited the rule in *Meneely*. "This rule has been qualified, as we have said, only to the extent that use of a family name will be restricted where such use tends or threatens to induce confusion in the public mind". (22 A.D.2d, p. 190, 254 N.Y.S.2d, p. 477.)

In the present case Wally knew that David had conducted his business and built a reputation under the names "Findlay Galleries" and "Findlay's on 57th St." and that many years of effort and expenses had gone into promoting the name of "Findlay" in the art business on 57th Street. He also knew that people would come into his gallery looking for "Findlay Galleries" and even instructed his employees on this matter before he opened. Nonetheless he opened his gallery next door to David dealing in substantially similar works and using the name Findlay. The bona fides of Wally's intentions do not change the applicable principles. The objective facts of this unfair competition and injury to plaintiff's business are determinative, not the defendant's subjective state of mind. Wally's conduct constituted unfair competition and an unfair trade practice, and it is most inequitable to permit Wally to profit from his brother's many years of effort in promoting the name of "Findlay" on 57th Street. Wally should use any name other than "Findlay" in the operation of his business next door to his brother.

In framing its injunction the trial court went no farther than was necessary to avoid the harm threatened. It prevented the use of the name Findlay but limited this to the particular area in which its use would cause confusion and diversion—East 57th Street. It resolved the conflict with as little injury as possible to Wally. The proof showed and the trial court found that many, if not most of the leading art galleries, are now located on Madison Avenue and in the area of the 60's, 70's and 80's in New York City. Wally could probably have found an appropriate place for his New York gallery other than at 17 East 57th

Street and can now either find such another location or remain where he is under some name such as "W.C.F. Galleries."

The decision in this case is in accord with the directions of our court: "The defendant has the right to use his name. The plaintiff has the right to have the defendant use it in such a way as will not injure his business or mislead the public. Where there is such a conflict of rights, it is the duty of the court so to regulate the use of his name by the defendant that, due protection to the plaintiff being afforded, there will be as little injury to him as possible." (World's Dispensary Med. Ass'n v. Pierce, supra, 203 N.Y. p. 425, 96 N.E. p. 740.)

The order of the Appellate Division should be affirmed, with costs.

The opinion of BURKE, J., dissenting, is omitted.

SULLIVAN v. ED SULLIVAN RADIO & T.V., INC.

Supreme Court of New York, Appellate Division, First Department, 1956.
1 A.D.2d 609, 152 N.Y.S.2d 227, 110 U.S.P.Q. 106.

COX, Justice.

In this proceeding, in which plaintiff moved for an injunction pendente lite, the facts are not in dispute. Appellant Ed Sullivan, who has been nationally known for over twenty years through his widely syndicated newspaper column, appearing in thirty-five newspapers throughout the country, including the Buffalo Courier–Express, is likewise known nationally in a much wider field as a radio and television personality presented weekly before an audience estimated at over 50 million people on the TV program, "The Ed Sullivan Show." This program is presented regularly in Buffalo through the facilities of Station WBEN–TV. Appellant also has been the subject of many articles and comments in magazines and newspapers, on radio and television. He has, in the past, endorsed particular brands of television sets and, in the future, expects to continue making such endorsements.

Respondent Ed Sullivan Radio & TV, Inc., engaged in the business of selling and repairing radio and television sets in Buffalo, N.Y., was incorporated in the state of New York on March 3, 1955, its three incorporators being Edward J. Sullivan, Robert J. Bender and Brunon V. Boroszewski. Edward J. Sullivan is the president and principal stockholder. This corporation took over the business formerly owned by this same Edward J. Sullivan individually and which was operated by him for some time prior to March 3, 1955, as a side line and on a part-time basis under the name "Ed Sullivan Radio & TV."

The question before us is whether or not a corporation of which the individual named Edward J. Sullivan is an incorporator, engaged in one phase of the radio and television field, may select the diminutive "Ed" for use in connection with the surname "Sullivan" of one of its incorporators as a part of its corporate title, when it is undisputed that the name "Ed Sullivan" is automatically identified by the general public with appellant *alone*, insofar as radio and television are concerned.

It is quite clear that, at the present time at least, there is no direct competition between appellant and respondent. However, both operate in the same general field and this court has consistently held that it is not essential for parties to be in competition with each other in order to sustain an injunction, . . . and injunctions have issued against the use of similar names in business even in the absence of a threat of confusion as to the source or sponsorship of the goods or services.

Although the courts usually will not interfere with the right of a person to use his own name in business, the present trend of the law is to enjoin the use even of a family name where such use tends or threatens to induce confusion in the public mind. . . .

Respondent herein makes use of no words in its corporate name which would indicate that it is engaged solely or exclusively in the business of selling and repairing radio and television sets. Since, therefore, it participates in the field in which appellant Ed Sullivan is broadly and generally known, to the degree of national prominence, respondent's use of its present title tends to identify appellant with the business of respondent. Moreover, appellant voices no objection to use of the name "Sullivan" as such nor even "E.J. Sullivan," nor the full name "Edward J. Sullivan," since he feels that such forms of the name would not induce or result in any confusion in the public mind. The objection here stems from the use of the diminutive form "Ed" in conjunction with the surname "Sullivan" in the combined name "Ed Sullivan" which appellant has continuously used throughout his entire career. In this regard it is to be noted that our courts have, on a number of occasions, enjoined the use even of variants of a name where such use threatened confusion in the public mind.

Although, in fact, but one isolated store in Buffalo is involved at the present time, nevertheless the state of facts may so change as to encompass a situation wherein there may be a series or a chain of similar stores throughout the country, in which case indeed, unless appellant had taken this present, prompt action, he might at a later date encounter great difficulty in obtaining an injunction because of his own laches. Also, at this stage the corporate enterprise would suffer minimal inconvenience in dropping the diminutive prefix, a situation which might not hold true at some future time.

Moreover, the significance of corporate identity is not to be lightly disregarded. Even on casual analysis there appears to be no present obstacle to interfere with or prevent the future sale or disposition by defendant's president, Edward J. Sullivan, of his interest in the business, thereby opening the door to others either to continue the business or by corporate amendment to extend the purposes and activities to more direct and active competition with the plaintiff.

The order appealed from should be reversed and a temporary injunction granted. Settle order.

NOTES

1. In principle, unfair competition cases involving personal names are no different than cases involving other sorts of commercial insignia. If her name is common and has no secondary meaning, the plaintiff, must show that defendant's use of the name is part of an active scheme of passing off and that consumers have actually been confused. If plaintiff's name has attracted some secondary meaning, she need show only likelihood of confusion. If the name is particularly distinctive, and secondary meaning is particularly strong, consumer deception will be presumed and relief granted even absent proof that confusion is likely.

The often asserted difference between personal name and other unfair competition cases stems from the view that "A man's name is his own property, and he has the same right to its use and enjoyment as he has to that of any other species of property." The view was hardly more than dicta in the case that introduced it into the United States, Brown Chem. Co. v. Meyer, 139 U.S. 540, 544, 11 S.Ct. 625, 627, 35 L.Ed. 247 (1891). The name involved there, "Brown," was common—as indicated by the name of the opinion's author, Mr. Justice Brown. Since the name had captured scant secondary meaning, and no confusion or fraud had been proved, the decision permitting defendant's use of the name can be easily rationalized in terms of general unfair competition doctrine. Compare Brown Sheet Iron & Steel Co. v. Brown Steel Tank Co., 198 Minn. 276, 269 N.W. 633 (1936), which recognized that free use of even a common name like Brown may be curtailed if, as to one user, it has gained secondary meaning.

Should the fact that the personal name employed by the defendant is not his name—or, in the case of a corporation, is not the name of a founder—bar him from its use, or should it only constitute some evidence of his intent to palm off his goods or services as those of plaintiff whose name it is? Of plaintiff whose name also it is not?

2. Many personal name cases are, like *Findlay*, precipitated by a family dispute. In Edison v. Thomas A. Edison, Jr. Chem. Co., 128 Fed. 957 (D.Del.1904), Thomas A. Edison filed a complaint that sounded more in parental dismay than in unfair competition, seeking to restrain his son, Thomas A. Edison, Jr., from using his name in competing fields of invention:

> That your orator has a son named Thomas A. Edison, Jr., who is now about thirty years of age; that your orator's said son was employed by your orator in your orator's various interests for a short time; that since that time your orator's said son has had no regular occupation, but as your orator is informed and believes, partially supports himself by trading on his name and by selling the use of his name to various unprincipled persons, who use the said name for the purpose of defrauding the public; that your orator's said son while he was in your orator's employ made no

practical inventions, and your orator is satisfied that he has made no invention since that time.

The court refused an injunction. Since defendant's advertisements referred to plaintiff only for the purpose of identifying its founder as his son, the court concluded that "There is nothing in any of them to confuse or confound, in the mind of any such [ordinarily intelligent and prudent] person, the complainant either with his son, Thomas A. Edison, Jr., or the defendant [corporation] with respect to the production and sale of the device." Id. at 961.

Greater success for plaintiff in actions between feuding relatives was attained in Friend v. H.A. Friend & Co., Inc., 416 F.2d 526, 163 U.S. P.Q. 159 (9th Cir.), cert. denied, 397 U.S. 914, 90 S.Ct. 916, 25 L.Ed.2d 94 (1970), and Lyon v. Lyon, 246 Cal.App.2d 519, 54 Cal.Rptr. 829, 152 U.S. P.Q. 719 (1966). Should family cases, like *Findlay* and *Edison,* be decided on principles different from those governing nonfamily cases, like *Brown* and *Sullivan?*

3. When a founder leaves the company that bears her name, can she, in competing with her former firm, publicize herself and her earlier track record? In Levitt Corp. v. Levitt, 593 F.2d 463, 201 U.S. P.Q. 513 (2d Cir.1979), the Second Circuit Court of Appeals concluded that cases of this sort should be treated differently from garden variety cases like *Sullivan.* "Where, as here, however, the infringing party has previously sold his business, including use of his name and its goodwill to the plaintiff, sweeping injunctive relief is more tolerable." 593 F.2d at 468.

Defendant was the founder of Levitt & Sons, a major builder of residential communities best known for its "Levittown" tract developments in New York and Pennsylvania. After fifty years at the helm of Levitt & Sons, defendant merged the business into a wholly-owned subsidiary of ITT Corporation, the predecessor in interest to plaintiff. The new company succeeded to and continued to exploit Levitt & Sons' goodwill, trademarks and trade names, including "Levitt" and "Levittown." In November, 1975, as part of his arrangement with ITT and the successor owners of Levitt & Sons, defendant covenanted not to compete with Levitt & Sons until June, 1977. The agreement provided that, although defendant could enter the industry after that time, he did not "have any right to use the name 'Levitt' as a corporate title, trademark or trade name in the construction business. He did retain the right to use his own name publicly as a corporate officer or director of a business enterprise, but only to the extent that such use would not be likely to create confusion with the corporate title, trademarks, or trade names of Levitt & Sons, Inc." 593 F.2d at 466.

In February, 1978, after the covenant not to compete had expired, defendant issued a press release stating that plaintiff's acquisition of Levitt Corporation was "totally confusing the general public and the business community," and that the question being posed by all is "who and what is the real Levitt." The press release announced that Mr. Levitt would soon reveal plans to build "a new Levittown in the United

States." Subsequently, defendant placed advertisements in the *Washington Post* and the *New York Times* for "Levittown Florida," and referring to "Levitt and Sons" and to "Levitt's Engineering and Planning Department." "Most significantly, William Levitt identified himself as the founder of the company that had built the Levittowns of New York, New Jersey, and elsewhere." 593 F.2d at 466.

Agreeing with the district court that defendant Levitt had infringed the trademarks of the Levitt Corporation, and that his use of his name in conjunction with the marks had caused substantial confusion between the two enterprises, the court of appeals affirmed the district court's order enjoining defendant from using the term "Levittown" in connection with his Florida project and requiring defendant not only to remove the "Levittown" name from all advertising, maps, streets, government application forms and other documents, but also, upon plaintiff's request, to issue corrective advertising explaining the lawsuit in order to restore the plaintiffs to the position they held before Mr. Levitt invaded the Florida market.

Since defendant Levitt's skill in planning, site selection and construction doubtless played an important role in the success of his former company, should he, at the least, have been allowed to identify himself with its past ventures? The court also affirmed a part of the district court decree that permanently enjoined Levitt from publicizing his prior connection with Levitt & Sons "to avoid the likelihood of confusion that would arise if the defendants should invoke the names of earlier Levitt projects in reciting the highlights of his career." 593 F.2d at 467. The circuit court concluded that "under these circumstances, a disclaimer of any *current* relationship between Mr. Levitt and the corporation will not protect the plaintiff's rights, for the effect of such a statement would be to inform the public that the achievements to which Levitt Corporation justly lays claim really are attributable to the efforts of someone else, now in business for himself." 593 F.2d at 470 n.12.

What does a company acquire when it buys goodwill? If defendant had labelled his original company with a coined name, like "Strathmore," rather than with his own name, do you think that the court would have allowed him to refer to his former association with the company by that name? Was the decision in *Levitt* properly sensitive to the expectations and interests of housing consumers?

2. ECONOMIC INTERESTS: THE PLACE OF UNFAIR COMPETITION IN THE COMPETITIVE PLAN

CRESCENT TOOL CO. v. KILBORN & BISHOP CO.

Circuit Court of Appeals, Second Circuit, 1917.
247 Fed. 299.

LEARNED HAND, District Judge. The cases of so-called "nonfunctional" unfair competition, starting with the "coffee mill case," Enterprise Mfg. Co. v. Landers, Frary & Clark, 131 Fed. 240, 65 C.C.A.

587, are only instances of the doctrine of "secondary" meaning. All of them presuppose that the appearance of the article, like its descriptive title in true cases of "secondary" meaning, has become associated in the public mind with the first comer as manufacturer or source, and, if a second comer imitates the article exactly, that the public will believe his goods have come from the first, and will buy, in part, at least, because of that deception. Therefore it is apparent that it is an absolute condition to any relief whatever that the plaintiff in such cases show that the appearance of his wares has in fact come to mean that some particular person—the plaintiff may not be individually known—makes them, and that the public cares who does make them, and not merely for their appearance and structure. It will not be enough only to show how pleasing they are, because all the features of beauty or utility which commend them to the public are by hypothesis already in the public domain. The defendant has as much right to copy the "nonfunctional" features of the article as any others, so long as they have not become associated with the plaintiff as manufacturer or source. The critical question of fact at the outset always is whether the public is moved in any degree to buy the article because of its source and what are the features by which it distinguishes that source. Unless the plaintiff can answer this question he can take no step forward; no degree of imitation of details is actionable in its absence.

In the case at bar * it nowhere appears that before 1910, when the defendant began to make its wrenches, the general appearance of the

* "This is an appeal from a temporary injunction granted by the District Court for Connecticut on the 25th day of January, 1917, restraining the defendant pendente lite from manufacturing and selling its adjustable wrenches. The facts as set forth in the affidavits are substantially as follows:

"The plaintiff is a New York corporation, organized in 1907 for the purpose of manufacturing tools, and has since that time been engaged in the manufacture among other things of pliers and wrenches. In December, 1908, it put upon the market an adjustable wrench, and has widely advertised the same from that time to the present. The wrench, on account of its appearance and new and original shape, pleased the public, and its sales grew rapidly from year to year, so that it became known to the jobbing trade and retailers and consumers as the 'Crescent' type of wrench. Its main structural features were all old in detail. It was adjustable to bolts and nuts of different sizes somewhat after the manner of a monkey wrench, but it was nevertheless quite different mechanically from a monkey wrench. It had a straight handle of web and rib construction, spreading slightly from the neck to the end, with a hole in the end of the web by which it could be hung up. No adjusta-

ble wrench of precisely the same character had ever appeared upon the market. There had, however, been adjustable wrenches, some with straight handles, some with web and rib curved handles, and there had been other tools with straight web and rib handles, somewhat broader at the end than at the neck. Plaintiff's name is plainly printed upon the web of the handle in raised letters.

"The defendant is a Connecticut corporation, organized in 1896 and engaged in the manufacture of wrenches and other hardware for some 18 years past. Some time in 1910 it began the manufacture of an adjustable wrench, which it called its 'K & B 22½° adjustable.' This is substantially a direct facsimile of the plaintiff's wrench, with the exception that the defendant's name appears upon the web in place of the plaintiff's as follows: 'The Kilborn & Bishop Company, New Haven, Connecticut, U.S.A.,' in distinct raised letters. The defendant made no effort to imitate the boxes or packages of the plaintiff's wrench, nor did it use the word 'Crescent' in any way in its sale; but it did begin selling the goods in general competition with the plaintiff's wrenches until the order issued herein.

"There is evidence in the correspondence between the plaintiff and its customers plaintiff's wrench had come to indicate to the public any one maker as its source, or that the wrench had been sold in any part because of its source, as distinct from its utility or neat appearance. It is not enough to show that the wrench became popular under the name "Crescent"; the plaintiff must prove that before 1910 the public had already established the habit of buying it, not solely because they wanted that kind of wrench, but because they also wanted a Crescent, and thought all such wrenches were Crescents.

Upon the trial the plaintiff may, however, be able to establish this, and it is only fair to indicate broadly the considerations which will then determine the scope of his relief. In such cases neither side has an absolute right, because their mutual rights conflict. Thus the plaintiff has the right not to lose his customers through false representations that those are his wares which in fact are not, but he may not monopolize any design or pattern, however trifling. The defendant, on the other hand, may copy the plaintiff's goods slavishly down to the minutest detail; but he may not represent himself as the plaintiff in their sale. When the appearance of the goods has in fact come to represent a given person as their source, and that person is in fact the plaintiff, it is impossible to make these rights absolute; compromise is essential, exactly as it is with the right to use the common language in cases of "secondary" meaning. We can only say that the court must require such changes in appearance as will effectively distinguish the defendant's wares with the least expense to him; in no event may the plaintiff suppress the defendant's sale altogether. The proper meaning of the phrase "nonfunctional," is only this: That in such cases the injunction is usually confined to nonessential elements, since these are usually enough to distinguish the goods, and are the least burdensome for the defendant to change. Whether changes in them are in all conceivable cases the limit of the plaintiff's right is a matter not before us. If a case should arise in which no effective distinction was possible without change in functional elements, it would demand consideration; but the District Court may well find an escape here from that predicament. Certainly the precise extent and kind of relief must in the first instance be a matter for the discretion of that court.

Order reversed, and motion denied.

SEARS, ROEBUCK & CO. v. STIFFEL CO.

Supreme Court of the United States, 1964.
376 U.S. 225, 84 S.Ct. 784, 11 L.Ed.2d 661, 140 U.S.P.Q. 524.

Mr. Justice BLACK delivered the opinion of the Court.

The question in this case is whether a State's unfair competition law can, consistently with the federal patent laws, impose liability for or prohibit the copying of an article which is protected by neither a

that confusion has arisen between the plaintiff's wrenches and the defendant's, customers having supposed that the Kilborn & Bishop wrench was a Crescent, but there was no evidence that the defendant in any way facilitated this confusion." 247 F. 299–300.

federal patent nor a copyright. The respondent, Stiffel Company, secured design and mechanical patents on a "pole lamp"—a vertical tube having lamp fixtures along the outside, the tube being made so that it will stand upright between the floor and ceiling of a room. Pole lamps proved a decided commercial success, and soon after Stiffel brought them on the market Sears, Roebuck & Company put on the market a substantially identical lamp, which it sold more cheaply, Sears' retail price being about the same as Stiffel's wholesale price. Stiffel then brought this action against Sears in the United States District Court for the Northern District of Illinois, claiming in its first count that by copying its design Sears had infringed Stiffel's patents and in its second count that by selling copies of Stiffel's lamp Sears had caused confusion in the trade as to the source of the lamps and had thereby engaged in unfair competition under Illinois law. There was evidence that identifying tags were not attached to the Sears lamps although labels appeared on the cartons in which they were delivered to customers, that customers had asked Stiffel whether its lamps differed from Sears', and that in two cases customers who had bought Stiffel lamps had complained to Stiffel on learning that Sears was selling substantially identical lamps at a much lower price.

The District Court, after holding the patents invalid for want of invention, went on to find as a fact that Sears' lamp was "a substantially exact copy" of Stiffel's and that the two lamps were so much alike, both in appearance and in functional details, "that confusion between them is likely, and some confusion has already occurred." On these findings the court held Sears guilty of unfair competition, enjoined Sears "from unfairly competing with [Stiffel] by selling or attempting to sell pole lamps identical to or confusingly similar to" Stiffel's lamp, and ordered an accounting to fix profits and damages resulting from Sears' "unfair competition."

The Court of Appeals affirmed. That court held that, to make out a case of unfair competition under Illinois law, there was no need to show that Sears had been "palming off" its lamps as Stiffel lamps; Stiffel had only to prove that there was a "likelihood of confusion as to the source of the products"—that the two articles were sufficiently identical that customers could not tell who had made a particular one. Impressed by the "remarkable sameness of appearance" of the lamps, the Court of Appeals upheld the trial court's findings of likelihood of confusion and some actual confusion, findings which the appellate court construed to mean confusion "as to the source of the lamps." The Court of Appeals thought this enough under Illinois law to sustain the trial court's holding of unfair competition, and thus held Sears liable under Illinois law for doing no more than copying and marketing an unpatented article. We granted certiorari to consider whether this use of a State's law of unfair competition is compatible with the federal patent law.

Before the Constitution was adopted, some States had granted patents either by special act or by general statute, but when the Constitution was adopted provision for a federal patent law was made one of the enumerated powers of Congress because, as Madison put it in The Federalist No. 43, the States "cannot separately make effectual provision" for either patents or copyrights. That constitutional provision is Art. I, § 8, cl. 8, which empowers Congress "To promote the Progress of Science and useful Arts, by securing for limited Times to Authors and Inventors the exclusive Right to their respective Writings and Discoveries." Pursuant to this constitutional authority, Congress in 1790 enacted the first federal patent and copyright law, and ever since that time has fixed the conditions upon which patents and copyright shall be granted. These laws, like other laws of the United States enacted pursuant to constitutional authority, are the supreme law of the land. When state law touches upon the area of these federal statutes, it is "familiar doctrine" that the federal policy "may not be set at naught, or its benefits denied" by the state law. Sola Elec. Co. v. Jefferson Elec. Co., 317 U.S. 172, 173, 176, 63 S.Ct. 172, 173, 87 L.Ed. 165 (1942). This is true, of course, even if the state law is enacted in the exercise of otherwise undoubted state power.

The grant of a patent is the grant of a statutory monopoly; indeed, the grant of patents in England was an explicit exception to the statute of James I prohibiting monopolies. Patents are not given as favors, as was the case of monopolies given by the Tudor monarchs, but are meant to encourage invention by rewarding the inventor with the right, limited to a term of years fixed by the patent, to exclude others from the use of his invention. During that period of time no one may make, use, or sell the patented product without the patentee's authority. But in rewarding useful invention, the "rights and welfare of the community must be fairly dealt with and effectually guarded." Kendall v. Winsor, 21 How. 322, 329, 16 L.Ed. 165 (1859). To that end the prerequisites to obtaining a patent are strictly observed, and when the patent has issued the limitations on its exercise are equally strictly enforced. To begin with, a genuine "invention" or "discovery" must be demonstrated "lest in the constant demand for new appliances the heavy hand of tribute be laid on each slight technological advance in an art." Cuno Engineering Corp. v. Automatic Devices Corp., 314 U.S. 84, 92, 62 S.Ct. 37, 41, 86 L.Ed. 58 (1941). Once the patent issues, it is strictly construed, it cannot be used to secure any monopoly beyond that contained in the patent, the patentee's control over the product when it leaves his hands is sharply limited, and the patent monopoly may not be used in disregard of the antitrust laws. Finally, and especially relevant here, when the patent expires the monopoly created by it expires, too, and the right to make the article—including the right to make it in precisely the shape it carried when patented—passes to the public.

Thus the patent system is one in which uniform federal standards are carefully used to promote invention while at the same time preserving free competition. Obviously a State could not, consistently with the Supremacy Clause of the Constitution, extend the life of a patent beyond its expiration date or give a patent on an article which lacked the level of invention required for federal patents. To do either would run counter to the policy of Congress of granting patents only to true inventions, and then only for a limited time. Just as a State cannot encroach upon the federal patent laws directly, it cannot, under some other law, such as that forbidding unfair competition, give protection of a kind that clashes with the objectives of the federal patent laws.

In the present case the "pole lamp" sold by Stiffel has been held not to be entitled to the protection of either a mechanical or a design patent. An unpatentable article, like an article on which the patent has expired, is in the public domain and may be made and sold by whoever chooses to do so. What Sears did was to copy Stiffel's design and to sell lamps almost identical to those sold by Stiffel. This it had every right to do under the federal patent laws. That Stiffel originated the pole lamp and made it popular is immaterial. "Sharing in the goodwill of an article unprotected by patent or trade-mark is the exercise of a right possessed by all—and in the free exercise of which the consuming public is deeply interested." Kellogg Co. v. National Biscuit Co., 305 U.S., at 122, 59 S.Ct. at 115. To allow a State by use of its law of unfair competition to prevent the copying of an article which represents too slight an advance to be patented would be to permit the State to block off from the public something which federal law has said belongs to the public. The result would be that while federal law grants only 14 or 17 years' protection to genuine inventions, States could allow perpetual protection to articles too lacking in novelty to merit any patent at all under federal constitutional standards. This would be too great an encroachment on the federal patent system to be tolerated.

Sears has been held liable here for unfair competition because of a finding of likelihood of confusion based only on the fact that Sears' lamp was copied from Stiffel's unpatented lamp and that consequently the two looked exactly alike. Of course there could be "confusion" as to who had manufactured these nearly identical articles. But mere inability of the public to tell two identical articles apart is not enough to support an injunction against copying or an award of damages for copying that which the federal patent laws permit to be copied. Doubtless a State may, in appropriate circumstances, require that goods, whether patented or unpatented, be labeled or that other precautionary steps be taken to prevent customers from being misled as to the source, just as it may protect businesses in the use of their trademarks, labels, or distinctive dress in the packaging of goods so as to prevent others, by imitating such markings, from misleading purchasers as to the source of the goods. But because of the federal patent laws a State may not, when the article is unpatented and uncopyrighted, prohibit the copying of the article itself or award damages for such copying. The judgment below did both and in so doing gave Stiffel the equivalent of a patent monopoly on its unpatented lamp. That was error, and Sears is entitled to a judgment in its favor.

Reversed.

COMPCO CORP. v. DAY–BRITE LIGHTING, INC.

Supreme Court of the United States, 1964.
376 U.S. 234, 84 S.Ct. 779, 11 L.Ed.2d 669, 140 U.S.P.Q. 531.

Mr. Justice BLACK delivered the opinion of the Court.

As in Sears, Roebuck & Co. v. Stiffel Co., ante, . . . the question here is whether the use of a state unfair competition law to give relief against the copying of an unpatented industrial design conflicts with the federal patent laws. Both Compco and Day–Brite are manufacturers of fluorescent lighting fixtures of a kind widely used in offices and stores. Day–Brite in 1955 secured from the Patent Office a design patent on a reflector having cross-ribs claimed to give both strength and attractiveness to the fixture. Day–Brite also sought, but was refused, a mechanical patent on the same device. After Day–Brite had begun selling its fixture, Compco's predecessor began making and selling fixtures very similar to Day–Brite's. This action was then brought by Day–Brite. One count alleged that Compco had infringed Day–Brite's design patent; a second count charged that the public and the trade had come to associate this particular design with Day–Brite, that Compco had copied Day–Brite's distinctive design so as to confuse and deceive purchasers into thinking Compco's fixtures were actually Day–Brite's, and that by doing this Compco had unfairly competed with Day–Brite. The complaint prayed for both an accounting and an injunction.

The District Court held the design patent invalid; but as to the second count, while the court did not find that Compco had engaged in any deceptive or fraudulent practices, it did hold that Compco had been guilty of unfair competition under Illinois law. The court found that the overall appearance of Compco's fixture was "the same, to the eye of the ordinary observer, as the overall appearance" of Day–Brite's reflector, which embodied the design of the invalidated patent; that the appearance of Day–Brite's design had "the capacity to identify [Day–Brite] in the trade and does in fact so identify [it] to the trade"; that the concurrent sale of the two products was "likely to cause confusion in the trade"; and that "[a]ctual confusion has occurred." On these findings the court adjudged Compco guilty of unfair competition in the sale of its fixtures, ordered Compco to account to Day–Brite for damages, and enjoined Compco "from unfairly competing with plaintiff by the sale or attempted sale of reflectors identical to, or confusingly similar to" those made by Day–Brite. The Court of Appeals held there was substantial evidence in the record to support the District Court's finding of likely confusion and that this finding was sufficient to support a holding of unfair competition under Illinois law. Although the District Court had not made such a finding, the appellate court observed that "several choices of ribbing were apparently available to meet the functional needs of the product," yet Compco "chose precisely the same design used by the plaintiff and followed it so closely as to make confusion likely." 311 F.2d, at 30. A design which identifies its maker to the trade, the Court of Appeals held, is a "protectable" right under Illinois law, even though the design is unpatentable. We granted certiorari.

To support its findings of likelihood of confusion and actual confusion, the trial court was able to refer to only one circumstance in the record. A plant manager who had installed some of Compco's fixtures later asked Day–Brite to service the fixtures, thinking they had been made by Day–Brite. There was no testimony given by a purchaser or by anyone else that any customer had ever been misled, deceived, or "confused," that is, that anyone had ever bought a Compco fixture thinking it was a Day–Brite fixture. All the record shows, as to the one instance cited by the trial court, is that both Compco and Day–Brite fixtures had been installed in the same plant, that three years later some repairs were needed, and that the manager viewing the Compco fixtures—hung at least 15 feet above the floor and arranged end to end in a continuous line so that identifying marks were hidden—thought they were Day–Brite fixtures and asked Day–Brite to service them. Not only is this incident suggestive only of confusion *after* a purchase had been made, but also there is considerable evidence of the care taken by Compco to prevent customer confusion, including clearly labeling both the fixtures and the containers in which they were shipped and not selling through manufacturers' representatives who handled competing lines.

Notwithstanding the thinness of the evidence to support findings of likely and actual confusion among purchasers, we do not find it necessary in this case to determine whether there is "clear error" in these findings. They, like those in Sears, Roebuck & Co. v. Stiffel Co., supra, were based wholly on the fact that selling an article which is an exact copy of another unpatented article is likely to produce and did in this case produce confusion as to the source of the article. Even accepting the findings, we hold that the order for an accounting for damages and the injunction are in conflict with the federal patent laws. Today we have held in Sears, Roebuck & Co. v. Stiffel Co., supra, that when an article is unprotected by a patent or a copyright, state law may not forbid others to copy that article. To forbid copying would interfere with the federal policy, found in Art. I, § 8, cl. 8, of the Constitution and in the implementing federal statutes, of allowing free access to copy whatever the federal patent and copyright laws leave in the public domain. Here Day–Brite's fixture has been held not to be entitled to a design or mechanical patent. Under the federal patent laws it is, therefore, in the public domain and can be copied in every detail by whoever pleases. It is true that the trial court found that the configuration of Day–Brite's fixture identified Day–Brite to the trade because the arrangement of the ribbing had, like a trademark, acquired a "secondary meaning" by which that particular design was associated with Day–Brite. But if the design is not entitled to a design patent or other federal statutory protection, then it can be copied at will.

As we have said in Sears, while the federal patent laws prevent a State from prohibiting the copying and selling of unpatented articles, they do not stand in the way of state law, statutory or decisional, which requires those who make and sell copies to take precautions to identify their products as their own. A State of course has power to impose liability upon those who, knowing that the public is relying upon an original manufacturer's reputation for quality and integrity, deceive the public by palming off their copies as the original. That an article copied from an unpatented article could be made in some other way, that the design is "nonfunctional" and not essential to the use of either article, that the configuration of the article copied may have a "secondary meaning" which identifies the maker to the trade, or that there may be "confusion" among purchasers as to which article is which or as to who is the maker, may be relevant evidence in applying a State's law requiring such precautions as labeling; however, and regardless of the copier's motives, neither these facts nor any others can furnish a basis for imposing liability for or prohibiting the actual acts of copying and selling. And of course a State cannot hold a copier accountable in damages for failure to label or otherwise to identify his goods unless his failure is in violation of valid state statutory or decisional law requiring the copier to label or take other precautions to prevent confusion of customers as to the source of the goods.

Since the judgment below forbids the sale of a copy of an unpatented article and orders an accounting for damages for such copying, it cannot stand.

Reversed.

Mr. Justice HARLAN, concurring in the result.

In one respect I would give the States more leeway in unfair competition "copying" cases than the Court's opinions would allow. If copying is found, other than by an inference arising from the mere act of copying, to have been undertaken with the dominant purpose and effect of palming off one's goods as those of another or of confusing customers as to the source of such goods, I see no reason why the State may not impose reasonable restrictions on the future "copying" itself. Vindication of the paramount federal interest at stake does not require a State to tolerate such specifically oriented predatory business practices. Apart from this, I am in accord with the opinions of the Court, and concur in both judgments since neither case presents the point on which I find myself in disagreement.

NOTES

1. How wide a preemptive swath did *Sears* and *Compco* intend to cut? The decisions recognized that states might prohibit the imitation of trade insignia in order to prevent consumer deception as to source of goods. Would the Court require a showing of actual confusion before enjoining the competitor's use? Would likelihood of confusion suffice? What if the action was brought on a dilution or zone of expansion theory, and plaintiff could show no consumer confusion?

Is there any logic to the distinction between goods or articles on the one hand, and packages or marks on the other? Can you think of situations in which the trademark *is* the article? In National Football

League Properties, Inc. v. Consumer Enterprises, Inc., 26 Ill.App.3d 814, 327 N.E.2d 242, 185 U.S.P.Q. 550 (1st Dist.1975), cert. denied, 423 U.S. 1018, 96 S.Ct. 454, 46 L.Ed.2d 390, 188 U.S.P.Q. 96, plaintiff, the exclusive licensing agent for the name and symbol of each club in the National Football League, obtained an injunction against defendant's unauthorized manufacture and sale of emblems duplicating club marks. Defendant unsuccessfully argued that it was "selling the emblem designs as merely decorative products," that the emblems were not "performing the trademark function of source identification," and that, under *Sears* and *Compco,* states cannot "prohibit the copying of unpatented and uncopyrighted" articles. 327 N.E.2d at 246. While the court could have rested its decision on *Sears'* exemption of trademarks, it chose instead to hold that a trademark could not be considered an "article" within the terms of *Sears* and *Compco.*

What force, if any, is left to *Sears* and *Compco* after the Court's decisions in *Aronson,* page 48, above, Kewanee v. Bicron, page 152, below, and Goldstein v. California, discussed at page 770? If these decisions reduced the sweep of *Sears* and *Compco,* did Bonito Boats v. Thunder Craft Boats, page 910, below, widen it?

2. How would you have counselled plaintiff in *Crescent Tool* to market its wrench so that it would have been able to capture the goodwill that accrued to the wrench? Some courts equate functionality with strictly utilitarian aspects, following the Restatement definition that a feature of goods is functional if "it affects their purpose, action or performance, or the facility or economy of processing, handling or using them." Restatement of Torts § 742 (1938). Other courts have expanded functionality to include any feature, including aesthetic appeal, affecting consumer choice. See Zippo Mfg. Co. v. Rogers Imports, Inc., 216 F.Supp. 670, 137 U.S.P.Q. 413 (S.D.N.Y.1963). See also Inwood Laboratories, Inc. v. Ives Laboratories, Inc., 456 U.S. 844, 851 n. 10, 102 S.Ct. 2182, 2187 n.10, 72 L.Ed.2d 606, 214 U.S.P.Q. 1 (1982) ("In general terms, a product feature is functional if it is essential to the use or purpose of the article or if it affects the cost or quality of the article.").

What, if anything, did *Sears* and *Compco* add to *Crescent?* The rule allowing simulation of an article's functional features, but not its distinctive nonfunctional features, accommodates state law to federal competitive interests. "If any portion of the goods or their packages are functional, then, in determining whether protection should be extended, the functional features are properly judged only by Federal patent law standards, such as novelty and nonobviousness, and not by a State's law of unfair competition. If protection is given to such functional aspects under a State's unfair competition law the State, in effect, would be granting a perpetual monopoly, whereas the protection available under the federal patent laws is only a limited monopoly. But where the feature, or more aptly design, is a mere arbitrary embellishment, imitation may be forbidden where the requisite showing of secondary meaning is made." Duo–Tint Bulb & Battery Co., Inc. v. Moline Supply Co., 46 Ill.App.3d 145, 151, 4 Ill.Dec. 685, 360 N.E.2d 798 (3d Dist.1977).

Careful readers of *Sears* and *Compco* thought that the Court had obliterated the functional-nonfunctional distinction by banning all state prohibitions of product simulation. See, for example, the essay by Brown, in Symposium, Product Simulation: A Right or a Wrong? 64 Colum.L.Rev. 1178, 1220–1221 (1964). Reread the next-to-last paragraph in Justice Black's *Compco* opinion to see if you agree. The Eighth Circuit Court of Appeals has characterized this crucial passage as dictum. "The law of trademark and the issues of functionality and secondary meaning were not before the Court. The issue before the Court was whether state law could extend the effective term of patent protection granted by the federal statutes." Truck Equipment Serv. Co. v. Fruehauf Corp., 536 F.2d 1210, 1214, 191 U.S.P.Q. 79 (8th Cir. 1976), cert. denied, 429 U.S. 861, 97 S.Ct. 164, 50 L.Ed.2d 139, 191 U.S. P.Q. 588.

3. *Trade Dress.* If *Sears* made any one thing clear, it is that states are free to regulate unfair competition when it takes the form of copying distinctive trade dress—"Doubtless a State may . . . protect businesses in the use of their trademarks, labels, or distinctive dress in the packaging of goods so as to prevent others, by imitating such markings, from misleading purchasers as to the source of goods." In many cases, however, the difference between a product's trade dress and the product itself may be neither apparent nor real. Several courts have relied on this abstract distinction to avoid the preemptive effect of *Sears* and *Compco.*

In Samson Cordage Works v. Puritan Cordage Mills, 243 F.Supp. 1, 145 U.S.P.Q. 602 (W.D.Ky.1964), the court ruled on defendant's post-*Sears* motion to set aside a contempt judgment that had been entered two months before *Sears:* "The injunction involved here was not directed against defendant's copying of complainant's product itself. As this Court noted in its conclusions of law, relief would have been denied if complainant had merely sought to prevent defendant from copying its sash cord. Injunctive relief was granted originally because it was shown that the spiral pattern of spots embedded in the surface of the sash cord had been adopted by the complainant as a distinctive trade dress to indicate source, and that such spot pattern had acquired a secondary meaning. Having established the fact that a secondary meaning attached to the spiral spot pattern when it appeared on the sash cord, the complainant was entitled to protection in the exclusive use of its trade dress.

"The fact that the spot pattern of necessity becomes an integral part of the product itself makes this a borderline case between copying of a product's design and the copying of a product's trade dress. After a full adjudication of that issue between the parties here, it is not for this Court to say now that the injunction prohibits the copying of an unpatented article. The product involved is sash cord, and the defendant can make sash cord which is identical in physical qualities and has the same configuration as that produced by complainant. What defendant may not do under the injunction is decorate its cord with a spiral

spot pattern in imitation of the markings on complainant's product."
243 F.Supp. at 7–8.

4. *Preemption From Other Sources.* The Constitution's copyright-patent clause is not the only source of federal preemption of state law. Section 39(b) of the Lanham Act, 15 U.S.C.A. § 1121(b), prohibits states from requiring the alteration of a federally registered mark or requiring that "additional trademarks, service marks, trade names, or corporate names that may be associated with or incorporated into the registered mark be displayed in the mark in a manner differing from the display of such additional trademarks, service marks, trade names, or corporate names contemplated by the registered mark as exhibited in the certificate of registration issued by the United States Patent and Trademark Office." The provision, added in 1982, was specifically aimed at preventing state regulatory agencies from requiring a national real estate brokerage franchisor to display its mark along with the name of local franchisees in formats that departed from the format for which the franchisor had obtained federal registration. See J.T. McCarthy, Trademarks and Unfair Competition § 22.2 (2d ed. 1984).

Somewhat farther afield, the Washington Supreme Court has held that the exercise of federal regulatory authority over the names of national banks overrides state unfair competition law, so that a court could not prohibit a federally-regulated bank from using a name, approved by the Comptroller of the Currency, that was confusingly similar to a name earlier adopted by a savings and loan association in the state. Pioneer First Federal Savings & Loan Assoc. v. Pioneer Nat'l Bank, 98 Wash.2d 853, 659 P.2d 481 (1983). But see First Nat'l Bank of Lander v. First Wyo. Sav. & Loan Ass'n, 592 P.2d 697, 205 U.S.P.Q. 866 (Wyo.1979).

5. *Preemption Under Copyright Act Section 301.* Section 301 of the Copyright Act will preempt state unfair competition law if three conditions are met: the protected work is fixed in a tangible medium of expression; the work comes within the subject matter of copyright as described in sections 102 and 103 of the Copyright Act; and the right granted is equivalent to one or more of the exclusive rights granted by section 106 of the Copyright Act. The tangible fixation requirement will usually be met in all forms of unfair competition actions, but the conditions respecting subject matter and equivalent rights will only sometimes be met. Section 301 is discussed in detail beginning at page 759, below. See generally Abrams, Copyright, Misappropriation, and Preemption: Constitutional and Statutory Limits of State Law Protection 1983 Sup.Ct.Rev. 509.

6. One reason that firms have sought to use state unfair competition law to protect product designs like those involved in *Sears* and *Compco* is that federal law does not offer full protection for industrial design. Protection of industrial design under copyright, patent and trademark law is considered in Part Four, below.

III. TRADE SECRETS

A. THEORY OF PROTECTION

FOREST LABORATORIES, INC. v. FORMULATIONS, INC.

United States District Court of Wisconsin, 1969.
299 F.Supp. 202, 161 U.S.P.Q. 622, rev'd in part,
452 F.2d 621, 171 U.S.P.Q. 731 (7th Cir.).

GORDON, District Judge.

This is an action for improper use and disclosure of what are alleged to be the plaintiff's trade secrets. Jurisdiction is based on diversity of citizenship, and state law is to be used to determine the substantive issues. In addition, the defendant, Pillsbury, has counterclaimed for a declaratory judgment of invalidity of the plaintiff's patent. . . .

I. The Trade Secret Cause of Action

It is alleged that Pillsbury has illegally used and divulged the plaintiff's trade secrets for packaging effervescent sweetener tablets. Originally the allegations included a claim that Pillsbury had also violated trade secrets for the manufacture of such sweeteners, but the plaintiff abandoned that attack and proceeded at trial only with respect to the packaging techniques.

The plaintiff is a manufacturer and packager of food and drug items. It claims to have developed a successful process for packaging effervescent sweetener tablets so that their shelf life is lengthy. The production and sale of effervescent sweetener tablets is limited to a small group of companies; of the approximately 1000 tablet manufacturers in the United States, only a few produce this type of tablet.

Tidy House Corporation, the defendant's predecessor, had been interested in marketing an effervescent sweetener tablet. Prior to 1957, Tidy House had engaged several firms to manufacture tablets for this purpose. However, Tidy House experienced difficulties with each of these sources of supply, and in 1958 Tidy House learned that the plaintiff manufactured such tablets. In December, 1958, Tidy House sent its technical director, Mr. Egan, and his co-employee, Mr. Steinhauser, to observe the plaintiff's operation in New York. During that visit Mr. Lowey, the president of the plaintiff, claims to have disclosed to Mr. Egan what are alleged to be Forest Laboratories' trade secrets for packaging. Shortly thereafter, the plaintiff began to supply Tidy House with tablets in bulk; Tidy House packaged the tablets for the consumer.

In 1960, the Tidy House assets were purchased by the Pillsbury Company, and the plaintiff continued to supply the tablets to what became known as the Tidy House division of Pillsbury. This relationship continued until January, 1964, when Pillsbury engaged Formulations, Inc. as a new source of supply. Subsequently, the plaintiff brought this action, alleging that Pillsbury was using its confidential packaging secrets. In addition, the plaintiff charges that the defendant improperly disclosed such secrets to Mankato, Inc., a contract packager hired by Pillsbury in 1965.

The applicable law on trade secrets was set down in Abbott Laboratories v. Norse Chemical Corp., 33 Wis.2d 445, 147 N.W.2d 529, 152 U.S. P.Q. 640 (1967). The court determined that the Restatement of Torts correctly states the Wisconsin law. In particular, the Abbott court ruled that there were two essential elements to a cause of action for misappropriation of trade secrets: there must be an actual trade secret and there must likewise be a breach of confidence. Each factor will be discussed in turn.

A. Are These "Trade Secrets?"

A trade secret is defined by the Restatement as

> Any formula, pattern, device or compilation of information which is used in one's business, and which gives him an opportunity to obtain an advantage over competitors who do not know or use it. It may be a . . . process of . . . treating or preserving materials . . . Restatement of Torts, § 757, comment (b).

The Restatement and Abbott set forth six factors to be considered in determining whether given information qualifies as a trade secret. These six factors are: (1) the extent to which the information is known outside of his business; (2) the extent to which it is known by employees and others involved in his business; (3) the extent of measures taken by him to guard the secrecy of the information; (4) the value of the information to him and to his competitors; (5) the amount of effort or money expended by him in developing the information; (6) the ease or difficulty with which the information could be properly acquired or duplicated by others.

The plaintiff contended at the trial that its packaging procedure consists of the following steps: (a) the entire packaging operation must take place in a room in which the relative humidity is maintained at 40% or less; (b) before packaging, the tablets are to be tempered in a room having 40% or less relative humidity for a period of between 24 to 48 hours; (c) before packaging, the bottles into which the tablets are to be packaged are to be tempered in a room having 40% or less relative humidity for a period of between 24 to 48 hours; (d) before packaging, the bottle caps are to be tempered in a room having 40% or less relative humidity for a period of between 24 to 48 hours; (e) before packaging, the cotton used to stuff the bottles is to be tempered in a room having 40% or less relative humidity for between 24 to 48 hours; (f) the bottles should not be washed; (g) an air space should remain in the bottles after the caps are applied.

The purpose of the foregoing procedure is to make certain that the tablets and the materials are dry and that they are in a state of equilibrium with each other. By using these techniques, the plaintiff asserts that it was able to produce and package a tablet with a high degree of stability. In contrast, the testimony shows that prior to the plaintiff's association with Tidy House, the latter had had difficulties with its prior suppliers whose products on occasion exploded on store shelves or otherwise proved unstable.

Pillsbury denies that the recited techniques constitute trade secrets. To determine that issue, we will consider seriatim, the six Abbott factors listed above.

(1) Pillsbury asserts that each step in the packaging procedure was well known in the trade, and that it cannot, therefore, qualify as secret material.

Pillsbury's expert witness, Dr. Wurster, a professor of pharmacy at the University of Wisconsin, testified that in his opinion these procedures were "just common knowledge." Professor Wurster prepared a compilation of textbook materials that he claimed set forth the procedures claimed by the plaintiff as trade secrets. (Def. exh. 1) This compilation makes references to the fact that effervescent tablets must be handled and packaged under controlled humidity conditions. Several of the articles refer to specific humidity levels; the references vary between 25% and 50%. The literature in evidence also contains admonitions that moisture must be kept out of the entire procedure. In addition, there was testimony that when Tidy House first became interested in effervescent tablets, it had been advised by The DuPont Corporation that operations would have to be conducted under low (40%) humidity conditions to eliminate moisture.

The foregoing supports my conclusion that the industry was quite well aware of point (a) listed in the plaintiff's procedure: that packaging operations must be conducted under controlled humidity (40%) conditions. I am also convinced that steps (f) and (g), which relate to washing of the bottles and an air space above the cotton, likewise cannot be claimed to be trade secrets. There was testimony that others in the industry refrained from the practice of washing the bottles. Competitive products introduced into evidence clearly show that other producers utilize an air space above the cotton.

While Dr. Wurster thought that all of the plaintiff's procedures were well known, nothing that he said or compiled persuades me that the tempering steps, numbered (b), (c), (d) and (e) were known in the industry. On the contrary, the plaintiff's witness, Mr. Reamer, a fully qualified expert in the field, testified that the tempering steps were "new, intriguing. I think it's a break-through . . ." It was also his opinion that the defendant's compilation of literature did not set forth these procedures.

Mr. Lowey testified that when he first became interested in effervescent tablets, he found that the literature on the subject did not teach him enough to package a stable tablet. It was only through trial and error, he averred, that he arrived at this process. As already noted, few firms engaged in packaging effervescent tablets, and those that did so often produced an inferior tablet. If proper techniques for packaging were broadly known, there would be little reason for this difficulty, unless the flaws stemmed from defective manufacturing practices.

The defendant asserts, however, that the tablet tempering stage [step (b)] is in the public domain because it is disclosed in the plaintiff's patent in suit. The argument is that under such circumstances plaintiff cannot claim this step as a secret. The patent discloses the tablet tempering step. The general rule is that the issuance of a patent which clearly discloses all essentials of a process destroys any secrecy that previously attached to that process. However, if there is a wrongful use or disclosure prior to the issuance of the patent, the wrongdoer will not be absolved from liability for his wrong committed during that prior period.

There is a decision in this circuit which holds that the wrongdoer may be permanently enjoined from use or disclosure even though the subsequently issued patent has made the information public. Shellmar Products Co. v. Allen–Qualley Co., 87 F.2d 104, 32 U.S.P.Q. 24 (7th Cir. 1936). That rule has been severely criticized in other circuits. See, e.g., Conmar Products Corp. v. Universal Slide Fastener Co., Inc., 172 F.2d 150, 80 U.S.P.Q. 108 (2d Cir.1949). On the other hand, once the plaintiff has [been] issued a patent setting out the process, some courts hold that the disclosure in the patent precludes liability for use of the information subsequent to issue. Schreyer v. Casco Products Corp., 190 F.2d 921, 90 U.S.P.Q. 271 (2d Cir.1951); Tempo Instrument, Inc. v. Logitek, Inc., 229 F.Supp. 1, 142 U.S.P.Q. 76 (N.Y.1964). The Shellmar case is often cited for the opposite conclusion.

In our case the confidential disclosure allegedly occurred in 1958; the improper use occurred in 1964 after Pillsbury discontinued purchases from Forest Laboratories. The patent was issued in March, 1965. There was an allegedly improper disclosure to Mankato, Inc. in May, 1965.

Since jurisdiction in this case is based upon diversity, Wisconsin law controls. However, the Wisconsin supreme court has not decided the instant question. In my opinion, the better rule is that which holds an improper use of a trade secret prior to the issuance of the patent to be an actionable wrong. This rule is in accord with the Restatement, which makes breach of faith an essence of the wrong. The plaintiff is not in a position to complain of a disclosure of the information occurring after his patent has issued. When the patent was issued, he dedicated his information to the public in return for a monopoly. To permit him to have both a monopoly and a cause of action for subsequent disclosure is inequitable. The plaintiff, in effect, has changed his position. Whereas he had previously kept this information secret (the sine qua non of a trade secret), he has now decided that it shall no longer be his knowledge alone. The key element of secrecy is gone.

Therefore, Pillsbury cannot be held liable for any disclosure after March, 1965.

The improper adoption of steps (b) through (e), which were not well known in the industry, are actionable; on the other hand, steps (a), (f) and (g) were sufficiently well-known so that they cannot be called trade secrets.

(2) With reference to the second Abbott factor, the evidence discloses that only a handful of the plaintiff's employees knew of his packaging operations, and they were all bound by secrecy agreements.

(3) Mr. Lowey testified that all of his employees who deal with packaging were bound by secrecy agreements. There was also testimony that packaging information was closely guarded in the trade. (Tr. 46–47).

(4) The information would be of significant value to the plaintiff. Since technical problems prevent more than a few companies from packaging effervescent tablets, one who has the ability to do so is in an advantageous position.

(5) Mr. Lowey testified that he spent a long time developing and testing the process before he was able to devise a packaging procedure that insured stability. No exact time period was mentioned, however. There is no evidence as to the amount of money expended to develop the process. There is evidence that other firms in the industry hesitated to enter this particular field unless they had two years to test the stability of the product.

(6) This process is not so ingenious that it could not be duplicated by others; but invention is not the keynote of a trade secret under the liberal test of the Restatement. All that is needed is some procedure which gives an advantage over a competitor who does not have it. Restatement of Torts, § 757, comment (b).

My conclusion is that the tempering portions of the packaging process must be classified as a trade secret. The Restatement test is not overly stringent. Even though a given procedure seems simple by hindsight, that is not conclusive. A trade secret requires some process or method which is not obvious or generally known in the trade, and which gives the innovator a substantial advantage over a competitor. I find that the plaintiff has established the tempering process in connection with packaging as a trade secret.

B. Was There a Confidential Relationship?

The second issue presented is whether *these* trade secrets were given by Mr. Lowey to the defendant under circumstances which reveal that a confidential relationship existed between them.

At the outset, Pillsbury argues that even if a confidential relationship as to these secrets was established with Tidy House, Pillsbury would not be bound unless it had actual notice of these facts. It bases its argument on § 758, Restatement of Torts. That section deals with situations in which a distinct third party receives confidential information without being aware of its secret nature; but that section does not apply to the situation at hand. In this case, Pillsbury purchased all the assets of Tidy House, which thereafter became known as the Tidy House division of the Pillsbury Company. Most employees remained the same. In my opinion, Pillsbury, as successor, was bound by any confidential disclosure made to Tidy House. If Tidy House had notice that these secrets were confidentially disclosed, that knowledge does not end when the Tidy House personnel become Pillsbury employees. It does not matter, therefore, whether any member of the Pillsbury management actually received notice that the packaging information was a confidential trade secret.

The testimony on whether this information was given to Tidy House in confidence is contradictory. It is my conclusion, however, that the plaintiff has established that there was a confidential disclosure to Tidy House employees in 1958.

When early arrangements were made with Tidy House, which was looking for a new supplier of effervescent sweetener tablets, Mr. Lowey sent the plaintiff's manufacturing formula to Mr. Sherrard, Tidy House's purchasing agent. The letter which conveyed this information said that the formula was to be kept confidential. The letter also stated that "we agree with you that details on packaging, etc. should be taken up later." In December, 1956, Mr. Egan, the Tidy House technical director, and Mr. Steinhauser, Mr. Egan's associate, were authorized by Mr. Tieszin, the Tidy House Executive Vice President, to visit the plaintiff's facilities in New York. During that meeting, Mr. Lowey told Mr. Egan that Forest Laboratories did not want to package the tablets for the consumer because of a lack of space. Mr. Egan testified that he asked Mr. Lowey to give him "some advice as to the conditions under which this packaging should be carried on" because Tidy House had not previously packaged tablets. Both Mr. Lowey and Mr. Egan testified that Mr. Lowey agreed to furnish the packaging techniques in confidence; both men also testified that all of the trade secrets were communicated orally to Mr. Egan, who took notes at such meeting.

Mr. Egan testified that he then returned to Tidy House and both orally and in writing informed Mr. Sherrard, Mr. Tieszin, Mr. Williams, and "maybe" Mr. Rapp, the Tidy House President, that what he had learned at the meeting had been received in confidence.

Mr. Egan's written memo was never introduced into evidence, but Mr. Sherrard corroborated Mr. Egan's testimony by stating that although he did not remember seeing any memorandum, he did learn that the disclosure of packaging techniques to Mr. Egan had been made in confidence. Further, Mr. Egan's statement that he also informed Mr. Tieszin is uncontradicted.

Mr. Steinhauser, who accompanied Mr. Egan on the trip, testified that Mr. Lowey never cautioned Mr. Egan or himself that they were hearing confidential information. However, Mr. Steinhauser stated that the information disclosed was confidential on a "moral" basis. Mr. Rapp testified that neither Mr. Egan nor Mr. Steinhauser told him that any information given to them was to be kept in confidence, however, he also testified that he was never aware that *any* confidential relationship existed with the plaintiff and it is quite clear that a confidential relationship existed at least as to certain manufacturing information. Mr. Williams and Mr. McCarron also did not remember any statement that a confidential relationship existed.

Although the foregoing proof is conflicting, I believe that the record establishes that a confidential relationship as to packaging information arose in 1958 between the plaintiff and Tidy House. Mr. Sherrard's testimony corroborates the testimony of the participants—Mr. Lowey and Mr. Egan. It is uncontradicted that Mr. Egan also reported this information to Mr. Tieszin. The contrary negative assertions of Messrs. Rapp, Williams, and McCarron do not convince me otherwise.

I have concluded that a confidential relationship as to "packaging information" was established in 1958, but Pillsbury argues that *tempering* secrets were not disclosed at that time. Both Mr. Egan and Mr. Lowey testified that such data was supplied, and they both detailed what those secrets were. I believe that tempering information was discussed at the meeting between Mr. Lowey and Mr. Egan; such conclusion is not reversed by Mr. Steinhauser's statement that he only remembers a discussion of manufacturing techniques. Pillsbury points out that Mr. Egan had testified at a deposition taken some months before the trial that the tablet tempering secrets were disclosed by Mr. Lowey during 1960 when Pillsbury's packaging facilities were being conducted at its Omaha facility and not at the 1958 meeting. Mr. Egan explained this discrepancy by saying that his recollection had been refreshed. I find that the disclosure of the tablet tempering secrets was made in 1958, and thereafter Tidy House was under an agreement of confidence.

The defendant asserts that Mr. Lowey never formally reasserted after the 1958 meeting that the packaging techniques were trade secrets. While this may be true, the parties appear to have clearly *understood* that this was the case. Mr. Steinhauser, who met with Mr. Lowey in 1961, stated that while no specific admonition of secrecy was made at that time, "We had confidence in Mr. Lowey and I thought he had confidence in us and that is pretty much the way I recall it being handled." Mr. Boand, a Tidy House employee, also made a similar statement. Mr. Lowey testified that since a confidential relationship had been established in 1958, and since he was dealing with Tidy House employees or people who were under contract with them, he felt no need to reiterate what was already an established fact. I do not believe that Mr. Lowey was careless in his dealings with the defendant.

The Restatement provides as follows:

> The question is simply whether in the circumstances B knows or should know that the information is [the plaintiff's] trade secret and that its disclosure is made in confidence. Restatement of Torts, § 757, comment on cl. (b) at 14.

In regard to the tempering of materials, both Mr. Lowey and Mr. Egan stated that these steps were also disclosed in the meeting held in 1958. The defendant challenges this position and urges that the steps relating to the tempering of materials did not arise from Mr. Lowey but, instead, were the result of suggestions made by Mr. Pasternak of Magna, Inc. The latter company was hired in 1962 by Pillsbury to handle packaging.

The practice of tempering materials was utilized in 1962, but there was no reference to such procedures in the set of specifications which were composed when Pillsbury resumed its own packaging.

I conclude that the plaintiff has failed to satisfy its burden of proving that the tempering techniques as to materials (as distinguished from tablets) were its confidential trade secrets. While there are inconsistencies on both sides of the question, it is the plaintiff's burden to establish its case; in my opinion, it has failed on this point.

To entitle the plaintiff to recovery, it is only necessary that "some secret information relating to one or more essentials" belonging to the plaintiff has been misappropriated. Engelhard Industries, Inc. v. Research Instrumental Corp., 324 F.2d 347, 139 U.S.P.Q. 179 (9th Cir. 1963). In my opinion, the information regarding the *tablet* tempering step constitutes essential and confidential information belonging to the plaintiff. Therefore, if it was misappropriated, the defendant will be liable to the plaintiff.

As already noted, however, since the plaintiff's patent was issued in March, 1965, that is the cut-off date for any wrongdoing by the defendant. This court need not, therefore, examine the alleged improper disclosure to Mankato in May, 1965.

C. Was There a Breach of Confidence by the Defendant?

The plaintiff has alleged a wrongful use of the tablet tempering information by the defendant subsequent to the time that Pillsbury dropped Forest Laboratories as its supplier in January, 1964. Pillsbury, on the other hand, insists that it made no use of this information after that time. I think the record fairly establishes that Pillsbury made use of the tablet tempering procedure after the plaintiff was dismissed as supplier of the tablets.

Pillsbury's confidential manufacturing specifications for these tablets, dated March 19, 1964, disclosed the following notation:

"Temper tablets 11805 in unopened supplier's containers for a minimum period of 48 hours. During tempering, handling and packaging of tablets maintain environmental:

a. R.H. at 40%

b. Temperature of 70° F."

Dr. Stein of Pillsbury testified that the purpose of this type of requirement was "to allow the temperature of the tablets to equilibrate with the temperature of the room."

The defendant argues that this specification is different from the plaintiff's trade secret because the former specifies tempering in an "unopened" container. Mr. Dienat, the defendant's witness, testified that experiments showed that it would take much longer for tablets to equilibrate in a closed container than in a container open to the air. Other witnesses testified that the tablets would still equilibrate.

In my opinion, the question of how long it would take the tablets to equilibrate is not controlling. An improper use need not be in exactly the same form as that contemplated by the plaintiff. Restatement of Torts, § 767, comment (b), p. 9. The only purpose of the tablet tempering procedure was to place the tablets in an ambient condition; that the defendant's method of utilizing this information may have been somewhat inefficient does not detract from the fact that the tablet tempering procedure was the plaintiff's secret and that it was improperly used by Pillsbury.

While the plaintiff has requested an injunction to prevent further use of the trade secret by the defendant, it is my opinion that such an injunction should not issue where, as here, the trade secret process has now been made public by the declarations made in the plaintiff's patent. Damages will suffice to compensate the plaintiff for its injury.

III. Conclusion

The plaintiff has established that the tablet tempering process was its trade secret; that it was given to the defendant in confidence, and that the defendant violated that confidence by using that process after Forest Laboratories was discharged as the tablet supplier. The other elements of the trade secret cause of action have not been established. The plaintiff is entitled to damages, but not to injunctive relief.

In addition, the court declines to exercise its jurisdiction to declare the rights of the parties in regard to the plaintiff's patent.

NOTES

1. On appeal, the district court's decision in *Forest Laboratories* and in a subsequent phase of the litigation, 320 F.Supp. 211, 168 U.S. P.Q. 97 (E.D.Wis.1970), was affirmed in part and reversed in part. Forest Laboratories, Inc. v. Pillsbury Co., 452 F.2d 621, 171 U.S.P.Q. 731 (7th Cir.1971). Note 7, below, discusses the part reversed.

Although the circuit court agreed with the district court that Pillsbury was liable, it disagreed with the lower court's reasoning. Adverting to the "well settled rule" that "a corporation which purchases the assets of another corporation does not, by reason of succeeding to the ownership of property, assume the obligations of the transferor corporation," the court rejected the district court's conclusion that "as Tidy House's successor, Pillsbury was bound by the confidential disclosure to Tidy House." "Moreover," the circuit court reasoned, "the knowledge of Tidy House's employees cannot properly be imputed to Pillsbury just because they went to work for Pillsbury."

The court then turned to Restatement, Torts, § 758, upon which Pillsbury had based its argument below:

Section 758(b) of the Restatement states:

'One who learns another's trade secret from a third person without notice that it is secret and that the third person's disclosure is a breach of his duty to the other, or who learns the secret through a mistake without notice of the secrecy and the mistake,

. . .

'(b) is liable to the other for a disclosure or use of the secret after the receipt of such notice unless prior thereto he has in good faith paid value for the secret or has so changed his position that to subject him to liability would be inequitable.'

"Thus under Sec. 758(b) of the Restatement of Torts, Pillsbury would be liable for its use of the secret after receipt of the notice unless prior thereto it had in good faith paid value for the secret. To satisfy this exception, Pillsbury argues that it purchased the trade secret when it acquired Tidy House's assets, and that Mr. Egan's communications did not occur until well after the acquisition. However, the record does not show that Pillsbury paid anything specifically for the trade secret. For all that appears on the record, Pillsbury's purchase of Tidy House assets at most involved only the purchase of its packaging facilities as part of the existing marketing structure, which included plaintiff as supplier. Nothing has been brought to our attention which would show that Pillsbury actually gave value for Tidy House's tempering expertise with a view toward independently exploiting that know-how for its intrinsic value." 452 F.2d at 627.

2. The Restatement of Torts, Second (1979) dropped sections 757 and 758, dealing with trade secrets, along with several other provisions on interference with business relations. The first Restatement had included these topics "despite the fact that the fields of Unfair Competition and Trade Regulation were rapidly developing into independent bodies of law with diminishing reliance upon the traditional principles of Tort law. In the more than 40 years since that decision was initially made, the influence of Tort law has continued to decrease, so that it is now largely of historical interest." For this reason, "the Council formally reached the decision that these chapters no longer belong in the Restatement of Torts, and they are omitted from this Second Restatement." Restatement of Torts, Second, Division 9, Introductory Note, at 1–2.

The Restatesmen's decision will probably have little effect on the administration of trade secret law in the courts. *Forest Laboratories* typifies the many decisions that explicitly rely on the Restatement rules. Because the rules have become so deeply embedded in judicial decisions, the force of *stare decisis* will doubtless ensure their long life.

The Uniform Trade Secrets Act, approved by the National Conference of Commissioners on Uniform State Laws in 1979 and amended in 1985, follows the Restatement approach in many respects but differs in others, including a broader definition of trade secret subject matter and more flexible provisions for injunctive and monetary relief. At last count, the Uniform Trade Secrets Act has been enacted in one form or another in sixteen states.

3. *Subject Matter.* Comment (b) to Restatement of Torts section 757 defines a trade secret as "a process or device for continuous use in the operation of the business," including information related to "the sale of goods or to other operations in the business, such as a code for determining discounts, rebates or other concessions in a price list or catalogue, or a list of specialized customers, or a method of bookkeeping or other office management." Comment (b) excludes protection for information that relates only to "single or ephemeral events in the conduct of the business, as, for example, the amount or other terms of a secret bid for a contract or the salary of certain employees, or the security investments made or contemplated, or the date fixed for the announcement of a new policy or for bringing out a new model or the like." *

Unlike the Restatement, the Uniform Trade Secrets Act protects isolated and ephemeral data such as the amount of a secret bid made by a firm or the salary of a key employee. The Uniform Act also extends protection to negative information—information about research paths or marketing programs that, after some experimentation, have proved unproductive or unprofitable and thus not worth pursuing further. Uniform Trade Secrets Act § 1 comment, 14 U.L.A. 543 (1985).

Computer programs may be subject to trade secret protection. See page 844, below.

4. *Secrecy.* Secrecy is the pivotal standard of trade secret protection. Courts sometimes apply two additional requirements. One, imposed by section 757 of the Restatement of Torts, is that the information must be "used in one's business." A second requirement, imposed expressly by the Uniform Trade Secrets Act and implicitly by the Restatement, is that the information derive "independent economic value, actual or potential, from not being generally known to, and not being readily ascertainable by proper means by, other persons who can obtain economic value from its disclosure or use. . . ." Uniform Trade Secrets Act § 1(4)(i), 14 U.L.A. 542 (1985).

How heavy must the cloak of secrecy be for subject matter to qualify as a trade secret? The law does not require absolute secrecy; if information were completely secret no one other than its creator would know it and there would rarely be a need for the law to intervene. The test, rather, is one of reasonableness in the steps taken to cabin the information in issue. The answer to the "question whether a plaintiff has taken 'all proper and reasonable steps' depends on the circumstances of each case considering the nature of the information sought to be protected as well *as the conduct of the parties.*" USM Corp. v.

Marson Fastener Corp., 379 Mass. 90, 393 N.E.2d 895, 902, 204 U.S.P.Q. 233 (1979) (emphasis the court's).

The Massachusetts Supreme Court ruled in *Marson* that plaintiff's safeguards, though by no means foolproof, were adequate. Plaintiff, "USM required supervisory, technical, and research personnel, including the defendant Lahnston, to sign nondisclosure agreements." While these agreements did not itemize the information that USM considered secret, "such specificity is not required to put employees on notice that their work involves access to trade secrets and confidential information." Nor was it fatal "that the blueprints and parts drawings were not labeled 'confidential' or 'secret' or that USM had not expressly informed its employees that these parts drawings were considered secret by USM." Finally, although USM conducted escorted tours for employees' families and its distributors, the company's plant security precautions "were sufficient to exclude the general public from the production areas of USM's plants, thereby denying access to USM's factory equipment." 393 N.E.2d at 901.

The *Marson* court contrasted the facts before it with those it had faced several years earlier in J.T. Healy & Son, Inc. v. James A. Murphy & Son, Inc., 357 Mass. 728, 260 N.E.2d 723, 166 U.S.P.Q. 443 (1970): "Applying this standard, we denied trade secret protection in *Healy* because the plaintiff had made a conscious policy decision to do nothing to safeguard the confidentiality of its manufacturing processes. In *Healy,* the employees were never informed that any of the manufacturing processes were considered secret; employees were not required to sign nondisclosure agreements; the plant was not partitioned into sections; and employees engaged in other work could plainly see the two 'secret processes' in operation. The plaintiff in *Healy,* other than excluding the general public from the manufacturing plant, took no security precautions whatever." 393 N.E.2d at 902.

For an overview of the practical security measures that a firm can employ to protect its trade secrets, together with a program of legal protection, see Arnold & McGuire, Law and Practice of Corporate Information Security, 57 J.Pat.Off.Soc'y (pts. 1 & 2) 169, 237 (1975).

5. *Novelty.* Courts divide on whether a protectible trade secret must possess some degree of novelty. *Forest Laboratories* takes the Restatement position that novelty is unnecessary: "All that is needed is some procedure which gives an advantage over a competitor who does not have it." 299 F.Supp. at 208. The contrary view, requiring a degree of novelty, is represented by Sarkes Tarzian, Inc. v. Audio Devices, Inc., 166 F.Supp. 250, 119 U.S.P.Q. 20 (S.D.Cal.1958), aff'd, 283 F.2d 695, 127 U.S.P.Q. 410 (9th Cir.1960), cert. denied, 365 U.S. 869, 81 S.Ct. 903, 5 L.Ed.2d 859, 129 U.S.P.Q. 410 (1961): "While they need not amount to invention, in the patent law sense, they must, at least, amount to discovery." 166 F.Supp. at 265.

The division is in fact only nominal. Novelty is a function of secrecy, and all courts require the subject information to be secret. The evidence typically adduced to defeat novelty in *Sarkes* jurisdictions is widespread knowledge in the trade of the claimed or closely similar information—precisely the evidence used in both *Sarkes* and *Forest* jurisdictions to disprove secrecy.

6. *Injunctions.* What should be the length and breadth of a trade secret injunction? The conflict between the *Shellmar* and *Conmar* rules, reviewed in *Forest Laboratories,* centers on the appropriate length of the injunctive decree. *Shellmar's* injunction was perpetual, permanently restraining the defendant from using the trade secret, even after secrecy was lost through the issuance of a patent. Some courts will issue a perpetual injunction as a punitive measure to deter particularly egregious conduct. See Valco Cincinnati, Inc. v. N & D Machining Serv., 24 Ohio St.3d 41, 492 N.E.2d 814 (1986).

Conmar, following the majority rule, held that a trade secret should be protected only so long as it remains secret. Under this rule, a court will dissolve a trade secret injunction once the protected information becomes generally known. Alternatively the court can pre-set the injunction's length by estimating the time that it would take a competitor to reverse engineer the product or process. To this period most courts will add a "head start" period measured by the lead time over competitors that the defendant otherwise would have gained as a result of its improper appropriation. See K–2 Ski Co. v. Head Ski Co., 506 F.2d 471, 183 U.S.P.Q. 724 (9th Cir.1974); Uniform Trade Secrets Act § 2(a), 14 U.L.A. 544 (1980).

The proper breadth of trade secret injunctions raises distinct questions. As an abstract proposition, the appropriator should be enjoined from using or disclosing only information that she obtained improperly. While this goal is sometimes reached, courts often find that to frame so discerning a decree is impractical or ineffectual. In Head Ski Co. v. Kam Ski Co., 158 F.Supp. 919, 116 U.S.P.Q. 242 (D.Md.1958), plaintiff had employed defendants to assist it in the development of an improved ski. At about the time plaintiff's skis began to enjoy commercial success, defendants left plaintiff's employ to start their own ski manufacturing enterprise. Although "the defendants could not have produced their ski at all, but for the knowledge gleaned from their employment by plaintiff," the court also found that defendants' product incorporated their own "innovation of importance" and "an important independent contribution." Regardless, the court held that "a broad injunction appears to be necessary to protect plaintiff from unlawful use of its trade secrets by defendants . . . (whose) entire operation has been built upon plaintiff's techniques, methods, materials and design. In such a case injunction against manufacture of the product is appropriate." 158 F.Supp. 923–24.

Head Ski skirted a difficult problem. It is hard to determine in any case how much of a secret came from the claimant and how much from independent sources. Particularly in the employment context, separating the employee's contributions from the secret itself is usually an impracticable task. The problem is deepened by the fact that an undiscriminating decree may entirely bar the appropriator from competing with the claimant. See Note, Injunctions to Protect Trade Secrets—The Goodrich and DuPont Cases, 51 Va.L.Rev. 917 (1965). In the circumstances, would it be appropriate for a court to award damages or an accounting but withhold injunctive relief on the ground of undue hardship to the appropriator? Courts in patent cases sometimes refuse injunctions on the basis of disproportionate harm to the infringer. See page 503, below.

Questions of both duration and breadth are carefully examined in Winston Research Corp. v. Minnesota Mining & Mfg. Co., 350 F.2d 134, 146 U.S.P.Q. 422 (9th Cir.1965). See also, Note, Trade Secrets: How Long Should an Injunction Last?, 26 UCLA L.Rev. 203 (1978); Berryhill, Trade Secret Litigation: Injunctions and Other Equitable Remedies, 48 Colo.L.Rev. 189 (1977). Trade secrets and the employment relationship are considered further beginning at page 137, below.

7. *Monetary Awards.* In Forest Laboratories, Inc. v. Pillsbury Co., 452 F.2d 621, 171 U.S.P.Q. 731 (7th Cir.1971), the court of appeals approved the lower court's award of $75,000 damages assessed on a reasonable royalty basis—"What the parties would have agreed upon, if both were reasonably trying to reach an agreement." 452 F.2d at 627. At the same time, the court overturned the district court's award of $15,000 attorneys' fees. "Just as the Ninth Circuit found no general federal rule or policy favoring an award of attorneys' fees to prevailing defendants in trade secret cases, Monolith Portland Midwest Co. v. Kaiser Aluminum & Chem. Corp., 407 F.2d 288, 298, 160 U.S.P.Q. 577, 584 (9th Cir.1969), we find none favoring an award to prevailing plaintiffs. Wisconsin law is to the same effect. . . . In the absence of any overriding federal policy to the contrary, Wisconsin law should be followed." 452 F.2d at 628.

Courts frequently measure monetary recovery by the claimant's lost profits or by the infringer's unlawfully gained profits. While the claimant is not entitled to a double recovery, he is " 'entitled to the profit he would have made had his secret not been unlawfully used, but not less than the monetary gain which the defendant reaped from his improper acts.' 2 R. Callmann, Unfair Competition, Trademarks and Monopolies § 59.3 at 496 (3d ed. 1968). Once the plaintiffs demonstrate that the defendants have made profits from sales of products incorporating the misappropriated trade secrets, the burden shifts to the defendants to demonstrate the portion of their profits which is not attributable to the trade secrets." Jet Spray Cooler, Inc. v. Crampton, 377 Mass. 159, 174, 385 N.E.2d 1349, 1358–59 n.14, 203 U.S.P.Q. 363 (1979). *Jet Spray* held that defendants had not sustained this burden, but allowed the corporate defendant to deduct from gross profits the bad debts it had incurred on sales of the infringing products and reasonable salaries and consultant fees it had paid to the individual defendants.

The Uniform Trade Secrets Act allows a successful trade secret plaintiff to recover damages measured by "both the actual loss caused by misappropriation and the unjust enrichment caused by misappropriation that is not taken into account in computing actual loss." If the misappropriation is "willful and malicious," the "court may award exemplary damages in an amount not exceeding twice any award" made under the damages and profits provisions and reasonable attorney's fees. Reasonable attorney's fees may also be awarded if "(i) a claim of misappropriation is made in bad faith, or (ii) a motion to terminate an injunction is made or resisted in bad faith." Uniform Trade Secrets Act §§ 3, 4, 14 U.L.A. 546–48 (1980).

Should monetary awards, like injunctive decrees, be measured by the trade secret's probable life? Justice Kaplan, concurring in *Jet Spray,* noted "the feeling that the damages allowed are excessive. They are made so by being cast over a period of eleven years. The court indicates . . . that the 'secret' was a simple one, a result of ordinary mechanical skill, and intimates some doubt that it could survive as a protectible entity on October 1, 1975. I suspect that it had perished in that sense sometime before; that is to say, in the ordinary course of events the secret in substance would have become known and available at an earlier date, even if the defendants had not appropriated it and the plaintiffs had tried to keep it to themselves. This, however, was a matter of proof, and the trouble was, and is, that the record is virtually barren of the relevant facts and inferences." 385 N.E.2d at 1364.

Can a trade secret claimant recover the cost of security measures taken to rebuff defendant's forays? Observing that such damages "might well, under different circumstances be proper," the court of appeals in Telex Corp. v. International Business Machines Corp., 510 F.2d 894, 184 U.S.P.Q. 521 (10th Cir.1975), overturned the trial court's $3,000,000 award to IBM for "increased extraordinary security costs— additional guards, television cameras, sensors, locks, safes, computer-controlled access system and the like." The court of appeals failed to see "how the increased security costs were the proximate result of Telex's hiring of IBM employees. Telex was not climbing fences or breaking down doors in its appropriation of IBM trade secrets. Telex's methods were more subtle, involving the luring of IBM employees who brought with them the trade secrets in question." 510 F.2d at 933.

E. I. DUPONT deNEMOURS & CO. v. CHRISTOPHER

United States Court of Appeals, Fifth Circuit, 1970.
431 F.2d 1012, 166 U.S.P.Q. 421, cert. denied, 400 U.S. 1024, 91 S.Ct. 581, 27 L.Ed.2d 637, reh'g denied, 401 U.S. 967, 91 S.Ct. 968, 28 L.Ed.2d 250.

GOLDBERG, Circuit Judge:

This is a case of industrial espionage in which an airplane is the cloak and a camera the dagger. The defendants-appellants, Rolfe and Gary Christopher, are photographers in Beaumont, Texas. The Christophers were hired by an unknown third party to take aerial photographs of new construction at the Beaumont plant of E.I. DuPont deNemours & Company, Inc. Sixteen photographs of the DuPont facility were taken from the air on March 19, 1969, and these photographs were later developed and delivered to the third party.

DuPont employees apparently noticed the airplane on March 19 and immediately began an investigation to determine why the craft was circling over the plant. By that afternoon the investigation had disclosed that the craft was involved in a photographic expedition and that the Christophers were the photographers. DuPont contacted the Christophers that same afternoon and asked them to reveal the name of the person or corporation requesting the photographs. The Christophers refused to disclose this information, giving as their reason the client's desire to remain anonymous.

Having reached a dead end in the investigation, DuPont subsequently filed suit against the Christophers, alleging that the Christophers had wrongfully obtained photographs revealing DuPont's trade secrets which they then sold to the undisclosed third party. DuPont contended that it had developed a highly secret but unpatented process for producing methanol, a process which gave DuPont a competitive advantage over other producers. This process, DuPont alleged, was a trade secret developed after much expensive and time-consuming research, and a secret which the company had taken special precautions to safeguard. The area photographed by the Christophers was the plant designed to produce methanol by this secret process, and because the plant was still under construction parts of the process were exposed to view from directly above the construction area. Photographs of that area, DuPont alleged, would enable a skilled person to deduce the secret process for making methanol. DuPont thus contended that the Christophers had wrongfully appropriated DuPont trade secrets by taking the photographs and delivering them to the undisclosed third party. In its suit DuPont asked for damages to cover the loss it had already sustained as a result of the wrongful disclosure of the trade secret and sought temporary and permanent injunctions prohibiting any further circulation of the photographs already taken and prohibiting any additional photographing of the methanol plant.

The Christophers answered with motions to dismiss for lack of jurisdiction and failure to state a claim upon which relief could be granted. Depositions were taken during which the Christophers again refused to disclose the name of the person to whom they had delivered the photographs. DuPont then filed a motion to compel an answer to this question and all related questions.

On June 5, 1969, the trial court held a hearing on all pending motions and an additional motion by the Christophers for summary judgment. The court denied the Christophers' motions to dismiss for want of jurisdiction and failure to state a claim and also denied their motion for summary judgment. The court granted DuPont's motion to compel the Christophers to divulge the name of their client. Having made these rulings, the court then granted the Christophers' motion for an interlocutory appeal under 28 U.S.C.A. § 1292(b) to allow the Christophers to obtain immediate appellate review of the court's finding that DuPont had stated a claim upon which relief could be granted. Agreeing with the trial court's determination that DuPont had stated a valid claim, we affirm the decision of that court.

This is a case of first impression, for the Texas courts have not faced this precise factual issue, and sitting as a diversity court we must sensitize our *Erie* antennae to divine what the Texas courts would do if such a situation were presented to them. The only question involved in this interlocutory appeal is whether DuPont has asserted a claim upon which relief can be granted. The Christophers argued both at trial and before this court that they committed no "actionable wrong" in photographing the DuPont facility and passing these photographs on to their client because they conducted all of their activities in public airspace, violated no government aviation standard, did not breach any confidential relation, and did not engage in any fraudulent or illegal conduct. In short, the Christophers argue that for an appropriation of trade secrets to be wrongful there must be a trespass, other illegal conduct, or breach of a confidential relationship. We disagree.

It is true, as the Christophers assert, that the previous trade secret cases have contained one or more of these elements. However, we do not think that the Texas courts would limit the trade secret protection exclusively to these elements. On the contrary, in Hyde Corporation v. Huffines, 1958, 158 Tex. 566, 314 S.W.2d 763, the Texas Supreme Court specifically adopted the rule found in the Restatement of Torts which provides:

> One who discloses or uses another's trade secret, without a privilege to do so, is liable to the other if
>
> (a) he discovered the secret by improper means, or
>
> (b) his disclosure or use constitutes a breach of confidence reposed in him by the other in disclosing the secret to him. . . .

Restatement of Torts § 757 (1939).

Thus, although the previous cases have dealt with a breach of a confidential relationship, a trespass, or other illegal conduct, the rule is much broader than the cases heretofore encountered. Not limiting itself to specific wrongs, Texas adopted subsection (a) of the Restatement which recognizes a cause of action for the discovery of a trade secret by any "improper" means.

The defendants, however, read Furr's Inc. v. United Specialty Advertising Co., Tex.Civ.App.1960, 338 S.W.2d 762, writ ref'd n.r.e., as limiting the Texas rule to breach of a confidential relationship. The court in Furr's did make the statement that

> The use of someone else's idea is not automatically a violation of the law. It must be something that meets the requirements of a 'trade secret' *and has been obtained through a breach of confidence* in order to entitle the injured party to damages and/or injunction. 338 S.W.2d at 766 (emphasis added).

We think, however, that the exclusive rule which defendants have extracted from this statement is unwarranted. In the first place, in Furr's the court specifically found that there was no trade secret involved because the entire advertising scheme claimed to be the trade secret had been completely divulged to the public. Secondly, the court found that the plaintiff in the course of selling the scheme to the defendant had voluntarily divulged the entire scheme. Thus the court was dealing only with a possible breach of confidence concerning a properly discovered secret; there was never a question of any impropriety in the discovery or any other improper conduct on the part of the defendant. The court merely held that under those circumstances the defendant had not acted improperly if no breach of confidence occurred. We do not read Furr's as limiting the trade secret protection to a breach of confidential relationship when the facts of the case do raise the issue of some other wrongful conduct on the part of one discovering the trade secrets of another. If breach of confidence were meant to encompass the entire panoply of commercial improprieties, subsection (a) of the Restatement would be either surplusage or persiflage, an interpretation abhorrent to the traditional precision of the Restatement. We therefore find meaning in subsection (a) and think that the Texas Supreme Court clearly indicated by its adoption that there is a cause of action for the discovery of a trade secret by any "improper means."

The question remaining, therefore, is whether aerial photography of plant construction is an improper means of obtaining another's trade secret. We conclude that it is and that the Texas courts would so hold. The Supreme Court of that state has declared that "the undoubted tendency of the law has been to recognize and enforce higher standards of commercial morality in the business world." Hyde Corporation v. Huffines, supra, 314 S.W.2d at 773. That court has quoted with approval articles indicating that the *proper* means of gaining possession of a competitor's secret process is "through inspection and analysis" of the product in order to create a duplicate. K & G Tool & Service Co. v. G & G Fishing Tool Service, 1958, 158 Tex. 594, 314 S.W.2d 782, 783, 788. Later another Texas court explained:

> The means by which the discovery is made may be obvious, and the experimentation leading from known factors to presently unknown results may be simple and lying in the public domain. But these facts do not destroy the value of the discovery and will not advantage a competitor who by unfair means obtains the knowledge *without paying the price expended by the discoverer.* Brown v. Fowler, Tex.Civ.App.1958, 316 S.W.2d 111, 114, writ ref'd n.r.e. (emphasis added).

We think, therefore, that the Texas rule is clear. One may use his competitor's secret process if he discovers the process by reverse engineering applied to the finished product; one may use a competitor's process if he discovers it by his own independent research; but one may not avoid these labors by taking the process from the discoverer without his permission at a time when he is taking reasonable precautions to maintain its secrecy. To obtain knowledge of a process without spending the time and money to discover it independently is *improper* unless the holder voluntarily discloses it or fails to take reasonable precautions to ensure its secrecy.

In the instant case the Christophers deliberately flew over the DuPont plant to get pictures of a process which DuPont had attempted to keep secret. The Christophers delivered their pictures to a third party who was certainly aware of the means by which they had been acquired and who may be planning to use the information contained therein to manufacture methanol by the DuPont process. The third party has a right to use this process only if he obtains this knowledge through his own research efforts, but thus far all information indicates that the third party has gained this knowledge solely by taking it from DuPont at a time when DuPont was making reasonable efforts to preserve its secrecy. In such a situation DuPont has a valid cause of action to prohibit the Christophers from improperly discovering its trade secret and to prohibit the undisclosed third party from using the improperly obtained information.

We note that this view is in perfect accord with the position taken by the authors of the Restatement. In commenting on improper means of discovery the savants of the Restatement said:

> f. *Improper means of discovery.* The discovery of another's trade secret by improper means subjects the actor to liability independently of the harm to the interest in the secret. Thus, if one uses physical force to take a secret formula from another's pocket, or breaks into another's office to steal the formula, his conduct is wrongful and subjects him to liability apart from the rule stated in this Section. Such conduct is also an improper means of procuring the secret under this rule. But means may be improper under this rule even though they do not cause any other harm than that to the interest in the trade secret. Examples of such means are fraudulent misrepresentations to induce disclosure, tapping of telephone wires, eavesdropping or other espionage. A complete catalogue of improper means is not possible. In general they are means which fall below the generally accepted standards of commercial morality and reasonable conduct. Restatement of Torts § 757, comment f at 10 (1939).

In taking this position we realize that industrial espionage of the sort here perpetrated has become a popular sport in some segments of our industrial community. However, our devotion to free wheeling industrial competition must not force us into accepting the law of the jungle as the standard of morality expected in our commercial relations. Our tolerance of the espionage game must cease when the protections required to prevent another's spying cost so much that the spirit of inventiveness is dampened. Commercial privacy must be protected from espionage which could not have been reasonably anticipated or prevented. We do not mean to imply, however, that everything not in plain view is within the protected vale, nor that all information obtained through every extra optical extension is forbidden. Indeed, for our industrial competition to remain healthy there must be breathing room for observing a competing industrialist. A competitor can and must shop his competition for pricing and examine his products for quality, components, and methods of manufacture.

Perhaps ordinary fences and roofs must be built to shut out incursive eyes, but we need not require the discoverer of a trade secret to guard against the unanticipated, the undetectable, or the unpreventable methods of espionage now available.

In the instant case DuPont was in the midst of constructing a plant. Although after construction the finished plant would have protected much of the process from view, during the period of construction the trade secret was exposed to view from the air. To require DuPont to put a roof over the unfinished plant to guard its secret would impose an enormous expense to prevent nothing more than a school boy's trick. We introduce here no new or radical ethic since our ethos has never given moral sanction to piracy. The market place must not deviate far from our mores. We should not require a person or corporation to take unreasonable precautions to prevent another from doing that which he ought not do in the first place. Reasonable precautions against predatory eyes we may require, but an impenetrable fortress is an unreasonable requirement, and we are not disposed to burden industrial inventors with such a duty in order to protect the fruits of their efforts. "Improper" will always be a word of many nuances, determined by time, place, and circumstances. We therefore need not proclaim a catalogue of commercial improprieties. Clearly, however, one of its commandments does say "thou shall not appropriate a trade secret through deviousness under circumstances in which countervailing defenses are not reasonably available."

Having concluded that aerial photography, from whatever altitude, is an improper method of discovering the trade secrets exposed during construction of the DuPont plant, we need not worry about whether the flight pattern chosen by the Christophers violated any federal aviation regulations. Regardless of whether the flight was legal or illegal in that sense, the espionage was an improper means of discovering DuPont's trade secret.

The decision of the trial court is affirmed and the case remanded to that court for proceedings on the merits.

NOTES

1. *Reverse Engineering.* Individuals who are not in a confidential relationship with the trade secret owner and who have not appropriated the secret improperly are free to replicate and use the secret subject matter. This freedom extends to "reverse engineering," a technique by which the product of a secret formula or process is analyzed, first to retrace the steps essential to its creation and then to recreate the formula or process itself.

The line between unlawful appropriation and lawful reverse engineering is not always clear. The question whether the defendant crossed the line will arise any time the defendant used secondary information to obtain the secret information. Did the court draw the line correctly in *DuPont?* Would the court have reached a different result if, instead of hiring a pilot to fly over DuPont's unfinished factory, the competitor had read classified advertisements in local newspapers and in trade journals to determine the kinds of employees DuPont was hiring, and had followed trucks making deliveries to the construction site to determine that nature of supplies DuPont was using?

Consider whether the court drew the line correctly in Chicago Lock Co. v. Fanberg, 676 F.2d 400, 216 U.S.P.Q. 289 (9th Cir.1982). Plaintiff there manufactured tubular locks, each with its own serial number, and maintained all of the serial numbers in secrecy. If a lock owner lost her key, she could either obtain a duplicate from the plaintiff or have a locksmith pick the lock and grind a duplicate key. Having once picked the lock, locksmiths often recorded the key code along with the serial number of the customer's lock in order to avoid having to pick the lock again. Defendant published a manual listing key codes and accompanying serial numbers for plaintiff's locks that it had received from locksmiths.

In plaintiff's suit for improper appropriation of its trade secret in the key codes, the court held that the defendant's conduct did not constitute "improper means" under Restatement section 757. Accepting for purposes of decision that the plaintiff had a trade secret in the serial numbers and accompanying key codes, the court observed that if the defendants had bought and examined the locks on their own, their reverse engineering and publication of the key codes would not have constituted an "improper means." Although the individual locksmiths may have been under a duty to their customers not to disclose their codes, neither the lock owners nor the locksmiths had any duty to the plaintiff. Defendants, "therefore, cannot be said to have procured the individual locksmiths to breach a duty of nondisclosure they owed to the [plaintiff] Company, for the locksmiths owed no such duty." 676 F.2d at 405.

2. *Litigation Hazards.* It is the wise trade secret claimant who does not rush into suit. "In such cases the greatest disadvantage of bringing suit is that plaintiff will have to disclose his trade secrets to defendant in the process of attempting to prove that defendant is using them. Although protective orders would be available to plaintiff to protect his disclosures in the course of litigation, they may not offer the degree of assurance plaintiff would like.

"A court, in entering a protective order, is faced with a seemingly unavoidable dilemma. If the order limits disclosure to the parties' counsel, it may well be impossible for the lawyers properly to prepare their cases, since they lack the technical background in the industry necessary to compare the processes involved. On the other hand, if a party's trade secrets are revealed to his opponent's technical staff, it may be virtually impossible to prevent their later use.

"Disclosures made in the course of litigation will have independent significance only in the event that plaintiff loses on his basic claim. In that event, plaintiff begins with one strike against him if he later tries to hold defendant liable for violation of the protective order. If defendant imposes a normal degree of industrial security, he may be able to use plaintiff's secrets without plaintiff ever becoming aware of it. Even assuming that plaintiff finds out about defendant's subsequent use, he will have difficulty proving that such use is due only to the disclosure under the protective order; a court, moreover, is less likely to foreclose defendant from use of a process because he may have learned it in the course of being unsuccessfully sued than if defendant's use is traceable to the wrongdoing of an ex-employee of plaintiff. In addition, defendant may, in the course of defending himself, discover a number of references in the literature or patents from which plaintiff's process can be put together, and it may be difficult to prove that the later use is necessarily due to plaintiff's disclosure rather than to defendant's search of sources in the public domain." Doyle & Joslyn, The Role of Counsel in Litigation Involving Technologically Complex Trade Secrets, 6 B.C.Ind. & Com.L.Rev. 743, 744 (1965).*

Trade secrets may be exposed to discovery in contexts other than trade secret infringement cases. Products liability actions are one recurrent context. See, for example, Smith v. BIC Corp., 869 F.2d 194, 10 U.S.P.Q.2d 1052 (3d Cir.1989). Trade secret owners do not always succeed in obtaining protective orders in these contexts. See, for example, Farnum v. G.D. Searle & Co., 339 N.W.2d 384 (Iowa 1983).

3. *Freedom of Information Act.* Local, state and federal administrative agencies routinely mark trade secrets for safe handling, often waiving their disclosure requirements or providing that they will maintain trade secrets submitted to them in confidence. At the same time, the Freedom of Information Act, 5 U.S.C.A. § 552 (1988), and counterpart state statutes subject trade secret submissions to the risk of exposure. Courts have not been entirely successful in striking a steady balance between the interests of submitters who want to keep their information secret and members of the public—including competitors—who desire access to the information.

The Freedom of Information Act provides at least two possible exemptions for trade secrets. Section 552(b)(4) specifically exempts "trade secrets and commercial or financial information obtained from a person and privileged or confidential" from disclosure. The United States Supreme Court has held that the exemption is permissive rather than mandatory, and that an agency could in its discretion disclose information that fell within section 552(b)(4)'s exemption. Chrysler Corp. v. Brown, 441 U.S. 281, 293, 99 S.Ct. 1705, 1713, 60 L.Ed.2d 208 (1979).

The second possible exemption for trade secrets is section 552(b)(3)'s exemption of matters that are specifically exempted from disclosure by another statute, "provided that such statute (A) requires that the matters be withheld from the public in such manner as to leave no discretion on the issue, or (B) establishes particular criteria for withholding or refers to particular types of matters to be withheld." This provision, taken together with the Trade Secrets Act, 18 U.S.C.A. § 1905 (1988), making it a crime for a federal official to disclose confidential information without authority of law, may provide an alternative basis for exempting trade secrets from disclosure under the Freedom of Information Act.

Before the *Chrysler* decision, many courts held that the Freedom of Information Act and the Trade Secrets Act gave submitters a private cause of action to enjoin an agency's proposed disclosure of their secret information in a so-called reverse FOIA suit. *Chrysler* held that neither statute created a private cause of action and that trade secret submitters must proceed instead under the Administrative Procedure Act's provision for judicial review of administration action. 441 U.S. at 316–18, 99 S.Ct. at 1725–26.

For an exhaustive analysis of the intersections between trade secret protection and the Freedom of Information Act, see M. Jager, Trade Secrets Law, ch. 12 (1988). See also Note, Protecting Confidential Business Information from Federal Agency Disclosure After Chrysler Corp. v. Brown, 80 Colum.L.Rev. 109 (1980).

4. *"Takings."* Does a federal statute that authorizes the administrative disclosure of trade secrets constitute a taking of property under the Fifth Amendment to the United States Constitution? In Ruckelshaus v. Monsanto Co., 467 U.S. 986, 104 S.Ct. 2862, 81 L.Ed.2d 815 (1984), the United States Supreme Court reviewed the constitutionality of several provisions of the Federal Insecticide, Fungicide, and Rodenticide Act (FIFRA) authorizing the Environmental Protection Agency to publicly disclose certain data submitted by applicants for pesticide registration. The Court held that plaintiff, Monsanto had a property right in data that it had submitted to the EPA "protected by the Takings Clause of the Fifth Amendment" to the extent that the data were protectible as a trade secret under the applicable state law. The Court further held that whether Monsanto's property had in fact been taken turned on whether, at the time Monsanto submitted its data to the government, the company had a "reasonable investment-backed expectation" that the information would be kept secret. The answer to this question in turn depended on the specific version of FIFRA that was in force at the time Monsanto submitted its data.

The Court held that in the case of submissions made after October 1, 1978, the effective date of the 1978 FIFRA amendments expanding the EPA's right to disclose submitted information, "Monsanto could not have had a reasonable, investment-backed expectation that EPA would keep the data confidential beyond the limits prescribed in the amended statute itself. Monsanto was on notice of the manner in which EPA was authorized to use and disclose any data turned over to it by an applicant for registration." 467 U.S. at 1006, 104 S.Ct. at 2874. Similarly, no taking had occurred in connection with submissions made before October 22, 1972, the effective date of the 1972 FIFRA amendments, when FIFRA "was silent with respect to EPA's authorized use and disclosure of data submitted to it in connection with an application for registration;" during this period, too, there was "no basis for a reasonable investment-backed expectation that data submitted to EPA would remain confidential." 467 U.S. at 1009, 104 S.Ct. at 2876.

The Court held that the "situation may be different, however, with respect to data submitted by Monsanto to EPA during the period from October 22, 1972, through September 30, 1978. Under the statutory scheme then in effect, a submitter was given an opportunity to protect its trade secrets from disclosure by designating them as trade secrets at the time of submission. When Monsanto provided data to EPA during this period, it was with the understanding, embodied in FIFRA, that EPA was free to use any of the submitted data that were not trade secrets in considering the application of another, provided that EPA required the subsequent applicant to pay 'reasonable compensation' to the original submitter. But the statute also gave Monsanto explicit assurance that EPA was prohibited from disclosing publicly, or considering in connection with the application of another, any data submitted by an applicant if both the applicant and EPA determined the data to constitute trade secrets. Thus, with respect to trade secrets submitted under the statutory regime in force between the time of the adoption of the 1972 amendments and the adoption of the 1978 amendments, the Federal Government had explicitly guaranteed to Monsanto and other registration applicants an extensive measure of confidentiality and exclusive use. This explicit governmental guarantee formed the basis of a reasonable investment-backed expection." 467 U.S. at 1010–11, 104 S.Ct. at 2877.

See Gelfand, "Taking" Informational Property Through Discovery, 66 Wash. U.L.Q. 703 (1988).

5. *Bibliographic Note.* The standard treatises on the law of trade secrets in the United States are M. Jager, Trade Secrets Law (1988) and R. Milgrim, Milgrim on Trade Secrets (1989). A. Turner, The Law of Trade Secrets (1962), describes United States law in a chapter-by-chapter comparison with English law. See also Dratler, Trade Secrets in the United States and Japan: A Comparison and Prognosis, 14 Yale J. Int'l L. 68 (1989). An introduction to relevant continental law considerations appears in Ladas, Legal Protection of Know–How, 54 Trademark Rep. 160 (1964) and Comment, Misappropriation of Trade Secrets, 53 Tul.L.Rev. 215 (1978).

B. LIMITS OF PROTECTION

1. PERSONAL INTERESTS: RESTRAINTS ON POST–EMPLOYMENT COMPETITION

WEXLER v. GREENBERG

Supreme Court of Pennsylvania, 1960.
399 Pa. 569, 160 A.2d 430, 125 U.S.P.Q. 471.

COHEN, Justice.

Appellees, trading as Buckingham Wax Company, filed a complaint in equity to enjoin Brite Products Co., Inc., and its officers, Greenberg, Dickler and Ford, appellants, from disclosing and using certain formulas and processes pertaining to the manufacture of certain sanitation and maintenance chemicals, allegedly trade secrets. After holding lengthy hearings, the Chancellor concluded that the four formulas involved are trade secrets which appellant Greenberg disclosed in contravention of his duty of nondisclosure arising from his confidential relationship with Buckingham. He decreed that appellants, jointly and severally, be enjoined permanently from disclosing the formulas or processes or any substantially similar formulas and from making or selling the resulting products. He also ordered an accounting for losses. After the dismissal by the court en banc of appellants' exceptions to the Chancellor's findings of fact and conclusions of law, the Chancellor's decree was made final and this appeal followed.

Buckingham Wax Company is engaged in the manufacture, compounding and blending of sanitation and maintenance chemicals. In March, 1949, appellant Greenberg, a qualified chemist in the sanitation and maintenance field entered the employ of Buckingham as its chief chemist and continued there until April 28, 1957. In the performance of his duties, Greenberg consumed half of his working time in Buckingham's laboratory where he would analyze and duplicate competitors' products and then use the resulting information to develop various new formulas. He would change or modify these formulas for color, odor or viscosity in order that greater commercial use could be made of Buckingham's products. The remainder of his time was spent in ordering necessary materials and interviewing chemical salesmen concerning new, better or cheaper ingredients for the multitude of products produced by Buckingham so that costs could be lowered and quality increased. As a result of his activities Greenberg was not only familiar with Buckingham's formulas, he was also fully conversant with the costs of the products and the most efficient method of producing them.

Appellant Brite Products Co., Inc., is a Pennsylvania corporation organized on or about August 1, 1956, when it succeeded to the business, formerly operated by appellant Dickler, known as "Gem Shine Sales Co." From October, 1952, to August, 1956, Dickler and Brite, in unbroken succession, did most of their purchasing from Buckingham;

and from August, 1956, until August 20, 1957, the date of Brite's last order, Brite exclusively purchased Buckingham's manufactured products. These products were in turn distributed by Brite to its customers, mostly industrial users, marked with labels which identified said products as products of Brite. Brite's purchases of sanitation and maintenance products from Buckingham amounted annually to approximately $35,000.00.

Dickler, president of Brite, met Greenberg in 1952 as a result of his business transactions with Buckingham, and had contact with Greenberg over the years in connection with the special products which were being made by Buckingham, first for Gem Shine Sales Co. and then for Brite. In June, 1957, Greenberg first approached Dickler in reference to employment; and negotiations began for Greenberg to associate himself with Brite. An agreement between them was reached whereby Greenberg became a director, the treasurer and chief chemist of Brite and, as a further consideration, received 25% of Brite's outstanding and issued capital stock. In August, 1957, Greenberg left Buckingham and went to work for Brite. At no time during Greenberg's employment with Buckingham did there exist between them a written or oral contract of employment or any restrictive agreement.

Prior to Greenberg's association with Brite, the corporation's business consisted solely of selling a complete line of maintenance and sanitation chemicals, including liquid soap cleaners, wax base cleaners, disinfectants and floor finishes. Upon Greenberg's arrival, however, the corporation purchased equipment and machinery and, under the guidance and supervision of Greenberg, embarked on a full-scale program for the manufacture of a cleaner, floor finish and disinfectant, products previously purchased from Buckingham. The formulas in issue in this litigation are the formulas for each of these respective products. The appellants dispute the Chancellor's findings as to the identity of their formulas with those of Buckingham, but there was evidence that a spectrophometer [sic] examination of the respective products of the parties revealed that the formulas used in making these products are substantially identical. Appellants cannot deny that they thought the products sufficiently similar as to continue delivery of their own products to their customers in the same cans and drums and with the same labels attached which they had previously used in distributing the products manufactured by Buckingham, and to continue using the identical promotional advertising material. Appellees' formulas had been developed during the tenure of Greenberg as chief chemist and are unquestionably known to him.

The Chancellor found that Greenberg did not develop the formulas for Brite's products after he left Buckingham, but rather that he had appropriated them by carrying over the knowledge of them which he had acquired in Buckingham's employ. The Chancellor went on to find that the formulas constituted trade secrets and that their appropriation was in violation of the duty that Greenberg owed to Buckingham by virtue of his employment and the trust reposed in him. Accordingly, the relief outlined above was ordered.

We are initially concerned with the fact that the final formulations claimed to be trade secrets were not disclosed to Greenberg by the appellees during his service or because of his position. Rather, the fact is that these formulas had been developed by Greenberg himself, while in the pursuit of his duties as Buckingham's chief chemist, or under Greenberg's direct supervision. We are thus faced with the problem of determining the extent to which a former employer, without the aid of any express covenant, can restrict his ex-employee, a highly skilled chemist, in the uses to which this employee can put his knowledge of formulas and methods he himself developed during the course of his former employment because this employer claims these same formulas, as against the rest of the world, as his trade secrets. This problem becomes particularly significant when one recognizes that Greenberg's situation is not uncommon. In this era of electronic, chemical, missile and atomic development, many skilled technicians and expert employees are currently in the process of developing potential trade secrets. Competition for personnel of this caliber is exceptionally keen, and the interchange of employment is commonplace. One has but to reach for his daily newspaper to appreciate the current market for such skilled employees. We must therefore be particularly mindful of any effect our decision in this case might have in disrupting this pattern of employee mobility, both in view of possible restraints upon an individual in the pursuit of his livelihood and the harm to the public in general in forestalling, to any extent, widespread technological advances.

The principles outlining this area of the law are clear. A court of equity will protect an employer from the unlicensed disclosure or use of his trade secrets by an ex-employee provided the employee entered into an enforceable covenant so restricting his use or was bound to secrecy by virtue of a confidential relationship existing between the employer and employee, Pittsburgh Cut Wire Co. v. Sufrin, 1944, 350 Pa. 31, 38 A.2d 33. Where, however, an employer has no legally protectable trade secret, an employee's "aptitude, his skill, his dexterity, his manual and mental ability, and such other subjective knowledge as he obtains while in the course of his employment, are not the property of his employer and the right to use and expand these powers remains his property unless curtailed through some restrictive covenant entered into with the employer." Id., 350 Pa. at page 35, 38 A.2d at page 34. The employer thus has the burden of showing two things: (1) a legally protectable trade secret; and (2) a legal basis, either a covenant or a confidential relationship, upon which to predicate relief.

Since we are primarily concerned with the fact that Buckingham is seeking to enjoin Greenberg from using formulas he developed without the aid of an agreement, we shall assume for the purpose of this appeal that the appellees have met their burden of proving that the formulas in issue are trade secrets. The sole issue for us to decide, therefore, is whether or not a confidential relationship existed between Greenberg and Buckingham binding Greenberg to a duty of nondisclosure.

The usual situation involving misappropriation of trade secrets in violation of a confidential relationship is one in which an employer *discloses to his employee* a pre-existing trade secret (one already developed or formulated) so that the employee may duly perform his work. In such a case, the trust and confidence upon which legal relief is predicated stems from the instance of the employer's *turning over to the employee* the pre-existing trade secret. It is then that a pledge of secrecy is impliedly extracted from the employee, a pledge which he carries with him even beyond the ties of his employment relationship. Since it is conceptually impossible, however, to elicit an implied pledge of secrecy from the sole act of an employee turning over to his employer a trade secret which he, the employee, has developed, as occurred in the present case, the appellees must show a different manner in which the present circumstances support the permanent cloak of confidence cast upon Greenberg by the Chancellor. The only avenue open to the appellees is to show that the nature of the employment relationship itself gave rise to a duty of nondisclosure.

The burden the appellees must thus meet brings to the fore a problem of accommodating competing policies in our law: the right of a businessman to be protected against unfair competition stemming from the usurpation of his trade secrets and the right of an individual to the unhampered pursuit of the occupations and livelihoods for which he is best suited. There are cogent socio-economic arguments in favor of either position. Society as a whole greatly benefits from technological improvements. Without some means of post-employment protection to assure that valuable developments or improvements are exclusively those of the employer, the businessman could not afford to subsidize research or improve current methods. In addition, it must be recognized that modern economic growth and development has pushed the business venture beyond the size of the one-man firm, forcing the businessman to a much greater degree to entrust confidential business information relating to technological development to appropriate employees. While recognizing the utility in the dispersion of responsibilities in larger firms, the optimum amount of "entrusting" will not occur unless the risk of loss to the businessman through a breach of trust can be held to a minimum.

On the other hand, any form of post-employment restraint reduces the economic mobility of employees and limits their personal freedom to pursue a preferred course of livelihood. The employee's bargaining position is weakened because he is potentially shackled by the acquisition of alleged trade secrets; and thus, paradoxically, he is restrained, because of his increased expertise, from advancing further in the industry in which he is most productive. Moreover, as previously mentioned, society suffers because competition is diminished by slackening the dissemination of ideas, processes and methods.

Were we to measure the sentiment of the law by the weight of both English and American decisions in order to determine whether it favors protecting a businessman from certain forms of competition or protecting an individual in his unrestricted pursuit of a livelihood, the balance would heavily favor the latter. Indeed, even where the individual has to some extent assumed the risk of future restriction by express covenant, this Court will carefully scrutinize the covenant for reasonableness "in the light of the need of the employer for protection and the hardship of the restriction upon the employes." Morgan's Home Equipment Corp. v. Martucci, 1957, 390 Pa. 618, 631, 136 A.2d 838, 846. It follows that no less stringent an examination of the relationship should be necessary where the employer has not seen fit to protect himself by binding agreement.

Coming to the case before us, in support of their position appellees cite mostly decisions involving the disclosure of pre-existing secrets to establish that a binding confidential relationship existed between Greenberg and Buckingham. As we have previously noted, the pre-existence itself gives rise to the implied pledge of confidence; these cases are thus inapposite here. In Extrin Foods, Inc. v. Leighton, 1952, 202 Misc. 592, 115 N.Y.S.2d 429, also cited by appellees, the New York Court found sufficient circumstances to give rise to an implied agreement not to reveal the trade secrets that the defendant developed during his employment. The employee therein, a chemist, was assigned a specific task for which he was given valuable leading information, including pre-existing trade secrets, careful supervision and license to enter into research and experimentation so as to attain the theretofore unobtainable goal which Extrin had been seeking. A similar situation may be found in Wireless Specialty Apparatus Co. v. Mica Condenser Co., Ltd., 1921, 239 Mass. 158, 131 N.E. 307, 16 A.L.R. 1170, where defendant engineers were enjoined from disclosing trade secrets they had developed while employed by the Wireless company. There, the company, in order to remain in business after the close of the war, had assigned its six engineers, including the defendants, to the specific research project of developing a method of manufacturing magneto condensers (the trade secret in issue) and had committed them to six months of extensive research and experimentation solely towards this end under the general supervision of its chief engineer.

As decisions of sister jurisdictions, these two cases, of course, are not binding upon this Court. Nevertheless, they are good examples of the kind of employment relationships in which a Court will find that a confidential relationship exists. Upon our examination of the record here, however, we find that the instant circumstances fall far short of such a relationship. The Chancellor's finding that Greenberg, while in the employ of Buckingham, never engaged in research nor conducted any experiments nor created or invented any formula was undisputed. There is nothing in the record to indicate that the formulas in issue were specific projects of great concern and concentration by Buckingham; instead it appears they were merely the result of Greenberg's routine work of changing and modifying formulas derived from competitors. Since there was no experimentation or research, the developments by change and modification were fruits of Greenberg's own skill as a chemist without any appreciable assistance by way of information or great expense or supervision by Buckingham, outside of the normal expenses of his job. Nor can we find anything that would indicate to Greenberg that these particular results were the goal which Buckingham expected him to find for its exclusive use. The Chancellor's finding that Greenberg knew at all times that it would be prejudicial and harmful to Buckingham for the formulas to be disclosed merely shows that Greenberg knew the value of his finds and the harmful effects that competition by similar products could bring. His knowledge, by itself, however, cannot support a finding that he was never to compete.

Accordingly, we hold that appellant Greenberg has violated no trust or confidential relationship in disclosing or using formulas which he developed or were developed subject to his supervision. Rather, we hold that this information forms part of the technical knowledge and skill he has acquired by virtue of his employment with Buckingham and which he has an unqualified privilege to use.

Having found Greenberg was privileged to disclose and use the formulas in issue, the case against the other appellants must also fall. With regard to appellants Brite, Dickler and Ford, the formulas here may be said to be trade secrets. Ownership of a trade secret, however, does not give the owner a monopoly in its use, but merely a proprietary right which equity protects against usurpation by unfair means. Former customers are legally entitled to compete with their suppliers, even if they use identical goods, as long as they do so properly. From the legal standpoint these appellants have done nothing improper. Greenberg approached Dickler here with a proposition; Dickler did not entice him away. Even so, what appellants wanted and needed was a qualified chemist in the maintenance and sanitation field; and who was better than the chemist of their supplier if they could properly get him. They sought not Buckingham's trade secrets, but Greenberg's expertise. Since we have found that Greenberg divulged only information which he had a privilege to divulge, no legal wrong has been committed. To hold that Greenberg had a privilege to divulge this information but that the other appellants committed a wrong in receiving it would be to render the privilege illusory.

Decree reversed, at appellees' costs.

REED, ROBERTS ASSOCIATES, INC. v. STRAUMAN

Court of Appeals of New York, 1976.
40 N.Y.2d 303, 386 N.Y.S.2d 677, 353 N.E.2d 590.

WACHTLER, Judge.

These cross appeals involve the efficacy of an employment contract provision barring an employee from either directly or indirectly competing with, or soliciting clients of, his former employer. This restrictive covenant is not a proper subject for specific enforcement since the services of the employee were not unique or extraordinary and the employer failed to establish a studied copying of a customer list.

Reed, Roberts Associates, Inc., with over 6,000 customers being served through some 21 offices scattered throughout the nation and with gross sales of almost $4 million, is one of the top three companies in its field. The lion's share of its business involves supplying advice and guidance to employers with respect to their obligations under State unemployment laws. The object of this service is to minimize the tax liability and administrative expenses involved in complying with these laws. Other services performed by Reed, Roberts include consultation regarding workmen's compensation, disability benefits and pension plans. This action was commenced by Reed, Roberts to prevent a former employee from competing against them and soliciting their customers.

When John Strauman was hired by Reed, Roberts in November, 1962 he signed a restrictive covenant which read in pertinent part: "I do therefore consent that at no time shall I either directly or indirectly solicit any of your clients, and I do further agree that for a period of three years from the date of termination of my employment that I will not either directly or indirectly be engaged in, nor in any manner whatsoever become interested directly or indirectly, either as employee, owner, partner, agent, stockholder, director or officer of a corporation or otherwise, in any business of the type and character engaged in by your company within the geographical limits of the City of New York and the counties of Nassau, Suffolk and Westchester."

Strauman's first position as an employee of Reed, Roberts was technical man-auditor. Since he had four years' experience in the field by virtue of having previously worked for a major competitor, Strauman became a valuable employee and over the next 10 years received three important promotions rising to senior vice-president in charge of operations. Throughout his tenure with Reed, Roberts, Strauman was instrumental in devising most of the forms utilized by the company in rendering its service and in setting up its computer system. On becoming vice-president he was given increased responsibility with regard to internal affairs including the formulation of company policy. Importantly, however, he was not responsible for sales or obtaining new customers. The record indicates that while the business forms used by Reed, Roberts were unique to that service industry, they were not much different from those used by other companies.

After 11 years with Reed, Roberts, Strauman decided to strike off on his own and formed a company called Curator Associates, Inc. This company was in direct competition with his former employer and was even located in the same municipality. Although Reed, Roberts alleges that Curator has been soliciting its customers, Curator sustained losses of some $38,000 with gross sales of only $1,100 during its first year of operations. Nevertheless, fearful of competition from the former employee, Reed, Roberts commenced this action seeking to enforce the post-termination covenant not to compete signed by Strauman in 1962. Specifically Reed, Roberts seeks to enjoin Strauman and Curator from engaging in the business of unemployment tax control within the metropolitan area for a period of three years and to enjoin them from soliciting any of Reed, Roberts' customers permanently.

The trial court granted this relief in part. The court refused to prohibit defendants from engaging in a competitive enterprise finding that there were no trade secrets involved here and that although Strauman was a key employee his services were not so unique or extraordinary as to warrant restraining his attempt to compete with his former employer. Nevertheless the court believed that it would be unjust and unfair for Strauman to utilize his knowledge of Reed, Roberts' internal operations to solicit its clients and permanently enjoined defendants from doing so. The Appellate Division affirmed, without opinion. We believe the order of the Appellate Division should be modified to the extent of reversing so much thereof as grants a permanent injunction against the defendants.

Generally negative covenants restricting competition are enforceable only to the extent that they satisfy the overriding requirement of reasonableness. Yet the formulation of reasonableness may vary with the context and type of restriction imposed. For example, where a business is sold, anticompetition covenants will be enforceable, if reasonable in time, scope and extent. These covenants are designed to protect the goodwill integral to the business from usurpation by the former owner while at the same time allowing an owner to profit from the goodwill which he may have spent years creating. However, where an anticompetition covenant given by an employee to his employer is involved a stricter standard of reasonableness will be applied.

In this context a restrictive covenant will only be subject to specific enforcement to the extent that it is reasonable in time and area, necessary to protect the employer's legitimate interests, not harmful to the general public and not unreasonably burdensome to the employee. Undoubtedly judicial disfavor of these covenants is provoked by "powerful considerations of public policy which militate against sanctioning the loss of a man's livelihood" (Purchasing Assoc. v. Weitz, 13 N.Y.2d p. 272, 246 N.Y.S.2d p. 604, 196 N.E.2d p. 247). Indeed, our economy is premised on the competition engendered by the uninhibited flow of services, talent and ideas. Therefore, no restrictions should fetter an employee's right to apply to his own best advantage the skills and knowledge acquired by the overall experience of his previous employment. This includes those techniques which are but "skillful variations of general processes known to the particular trade" (Restatement, Agency 2d, § 396, Comment b).

Of course, the courts must also recognize the legitimate interest an employer has in safeguarding that which has made his business successful and to protect himself against deliberate surreptitious commercial piracy. Thus restrictive covenants will be enforceable to the extent necessary to prevent the disclosure or use of trade secrets or confidential customer information. In addition injunctive relief may be available where an employee's services are unique or extraordinary and the covenant is reasonable. This latter principle has been interpreted to reach agreements between members of the learned professions.

With these principles in mind we consider first the issue of solicitation of customers in the case at bar. The courts below found, and Reed, Roberts does not dispute, that there were no trade secrets involved here. The thrust of Reed, Roberts' argument is that by virtue of Strauman's position in charge of internal administration he was privy to sensitive and confidential customer information which he should not be permitted to convert to his own use. The law enunciated in Leo Silfen, Inc. v. Cream, 29 N.Y.2d 387, 328 N.Y.S.2d 423, 278 N.E.2d 636 is dispositive. There, as here, the plaintiff failed to sustain its allegation that the defendant had pirated the actual customer list. Rather Silfen argued that in light of the funds expended to compile the list it would be unfair to allow the defendant to solicit the clients of his former employer. We held that where the employee engaged in no wrongful conduct and the names and addresses of potential customers were readily discoverable through public sources, an injunction would not lie. Similarly here there was no finding that Strauman acted wrongfully by either pilfering or memorizing the customer list. More important, by Reed, Roberts' own admission every company with employees is a prospective customer and the solicitation of customers was usually done through the use of nationally known publications such as Dun and Bradstreet's Million Dollar Directory where even the name of the person to contact regarding these services is readily available. It strains credulity to characterize this type of information as confidential. Consequently, the trial court's determination that Strauman and Curator should be permanently enjoined from soliciting Reed, Roberts' customers as of the date of his termination was erroneous.

Apparently, the employer is more concerned about Strauman's knowledge of the intricacies of their business operation. However, absent any wrongdoing, we cannot agree that Strauman should be prohibited from utilizing his knowledge and talents in this area. A contrary holding would make those in charge of operations or specialists in certain aspects of an enterprise virtual hostages of their employers. Where the knowledge does not qualify for protection as a trade secret and there has been no conspiracy or breach of trust resulting in commercial piracy we see no reason to inhibit the employee's ability to realize his potential both professionally and financially by availing himself of opportunity. Therefore, despite Strauman's excellence or value to Reed, Roberts the trial court's finding that his services were not extraordinary or unique is controlling and properly resulted in a denial of the injunction against operating a competing business.

Accordingly, the order of the Appellate Division should be modified in accordance with this opinion.

NOTES

1. *Covenants Not to Compete and Trade Secrets Compared.* In their attempts to restrain departing employees from using or disclosing information developed in the course of their employment, employers commonly take either or both of two precautions: (a) at the outset of

employment, obtaining the employee's covenant not to engage in post-employment competition, and (b) upon departure, seeking to enjoin the employee's disclosure or use of trade secrets imparted by the employer. While the covenant not to compete might appear to be a broader, more effective precaution than trade secret protection, the two measures in fact have very similar effects.

Covenants Not to Compete. Courts construe covenants not to compete narrowly. Presumptively invalid, these covenants are generally enforced only upon proof that they are reasonably necessary to the employer's business security. The covenant must reasonably delimit the breadth of its subject matter and the period and geographic area in which the former employee cannot compete. Courts roughly measure "reasonable" breadth by the range of the employer's trade secrets along with some interstitial, otherwise unprotectible, technical information. In determining whether a covenant's duration is reasonable, courts often employ the same measure that they use in determining how long a trade secret injunction may run: the time that it would take a competitor to arrive independently at the former employer's protected methods. See, for example, Allis Chalmers Mfg. Co. v. Continental Aviation & Eng'g Corp., 255 F.Supp. 645, 655, 151 U.S.P.Q. 25 (E.D. Mich.1966).

Trade Secrets. The effects of a trade secret injunction will characteristically exceed the bounds of the injunctive decree. Trade secrets commonly have value only in the industry in which the former employer is engaged so that an injunction against their use is in effect an injunction against their use in competition. See, for example, Head Ski Co. v. Kam Ski Co., 158 F.Supp. 919, 116 U.S.P.Q. 242 (D.Md.1958), discussed at page 125, above. Since the departing employee carries a potential trade secret lawsuit with her, she may encounter difficulty getting a job with a competitor of her former employer—unless, of course, the competitor was responsible for luring her away in the first place.

There are at least two important differences between the scope of an enforceable covenant not to compete and the scope of protection that trade secret law would offer in the same circumstances. For purposes of sustaining the covenant not to compete, the employer need only show that the employee is in a position to use its trade secrets. To receive a trade secret injunction the employer must prove that the employee is in fact using the trade secrets. Further, in the trade secret action the employer bears the heavy burden of demonstrating that the particular information being used by the employee constitutes a trade secret and is not just part of the employee's general knowledge and skills.

2. *Shop Rights.* Absent an express contract between employer and employee allocating rights to inventions made by the employee in the course of his employment, all rights to the inventions belong to the employee. Two important exceptions virtually swallow this general rule. First, if the employee was specifically hired to engage in research and development, courts will imply an agreement that rights to his

inventions belong to the employer. See Solomons v. United States, 137 U.S. 342, 11 S.Ct. 88, 34 L.Ed. 667 (1890) ("If one is employed to devise or perfect an instrument, or a means for accomplishing a prescribed result, he cannot, after successfully accomplishing the work for which he was employed, plead title thereto as against his employer. That which he has been employed and paid to accomplish becomes, when accomplished, the property of his employer." 137 U.S. at 346, 11 S.Ct. at 89).

Second, if the employee was not hired specifically for research and development but made the invention during working hours, or with the use of his employer's equipment or materials, the employer obtains a "shop right," essentially an irrevocable, nonexclusive license to practice the invention. See, for example, Kinkade v. New York Shipbuilding Corp., 21 N.J. 362, 122 A.2d 360 (1956); United States v. Dubilier Condenser Corp., 289 U.S. 178, 188–89, 53 S.Ct. 554, 557–58, 77 L.Ed. 1114 (1933) ("Since the servant uses his master's time, facilities and materials to attain a concrete result, the latter is in equity entitled to use that which embodies his own property and to duplicate it as often as he may find occasion to employ similar appliances in his business. But the employer in such a case has no equity to demand a conveyance of the invention, which is the original conception of the employee alone, in which the employer had no part.").

Judged against this background, was the decision in Wexler v. Greenberg correct? For a contrary result on similar facts, see Basic Chemicals, Inc. v. Benson, 251 N.W.2d 220, 195 U.S.P.Q. 197 (Iowa 1977). Would *Wexler* be more acceptable if the court had ruled that the formulas Greenberg devised while working for Buckingham did not qualify for protection as trade secrets? Does it follow from *Wexler* that in a subsequent action Greenberg would be entitled to an injunction against Buckingham's continued use of the formulas that Greenberg had developed while in its employ?

3. *Customer Lists.* In principle, an employer's customer lists can qualify as trade secrets and a departing employee can be enjoined from using them in her new business. See Restatement of Torts § 757 comment b (1939). In practice, former employers often fail in their efforts to protect customer lists, largely because these lists frequently fall short of the standards imposed on trade secret subject matter.

Ruesch v. Ruesch Int'l Monetary Servs., 479 A.2d 295 (D.C.App. 1984) is typical. Plaintiff there failed to obtain an order requiring the defendant, a former employee, to return a card file containing between 800 and 1000 client names and to refrain from soliciting these clients. In the court's view, virtually all of the Restatement's six trade secret factors weighed against the plaintiff: the names and addresses of clients were widely known because they came primarily from mailing lists and other publicly available sources; the card file was accessible to other employees; the client list by itself had little value to the plaintiff because it embodied no marketing data indicating a particular client's interests; any expenditures by plaintiff in compiling the file were

merely incidental to its normal marketing efforts; and "anyone knowledgeable in the business could compile such a list from commonly
available sources."   479 A.2d at 297–99.

Restatement of Agency, Second, § 396 (1958) takes a different
approach to customer lists. After termination of an agency relationship, the agent has no duty not to compete with the principal, but does
have a duty "not to use or to disclose to third persons, on his own
account or on account of others, in competition with the principal or to
his injury, trade secrets, written lists of names, or other similar
confidential matters given to him only for the principal's use or
acquired by the agent in violation of duty. The agent is entitled to use
general information concerning the method of business of the principal
and the names of the customers retained in his memory, if not acquired
in violation of his duty as agent." What reasons are there for the
"memory rule," prohibiting the former employee from taking copies of
customer lists with him, but allowing him to use any customer information that he can remember? What is the status of information that the
employee has deliberately committed to memory?

4.   Why is there so little litigation over the use of trade secrets by
departing employees? Against the vast number of defections that occur
each year, the number of reported cases is very small; there is no
evidence that this number would be significantly increased by the
addition of settled cases. Compare the decision for a former employer
in B.F. Goodrich Co. v. Wohlgemuth, 117 Ohio App. 493, 192 N.E.2d 99,
137 U.S.P.Q. (1963), with its follow-up coverage, Brooks, Annals of
Business, The New Yorker, Jan. 11, 1964, at 37, suggesting that,
litigation notwithstanding, the highly skilled employee in fact enjoys
considerable freedom in competitive employ.

One reason for the dearth of litigation is doubtless the difficulty of
proving that the employer's information qualifies as a trade secret, that
the trade secret is hers, and that the departing employee is in fact
using it. Even if the former employer had extracted a covenant against
postemployment competition from all of her technical employees, she
may be reluctant to take the risk that a court reviewing the covenant
will hold it invalid. Litigation may also expose other information that
the former employer wishes to keep secret, including information about
the trade secrets that she may have pirated from her competitors.

For background on law and practice in the area, see S. Lieberstein,
Who Owns What is in Your Head? (1979); R. Spanner, Who Owns
Innovation? The Rights and Obligations of Employers and Employees
(1984).

5. *History.* Rules governing trade secrets and related postemployment restraints originated in commercial settings that differ in important respects from those that prevail today. The modern action for
employee appropriation of trade secrets traces to Roman law's *actio
servi corrupti.* Under the general action for corruption of a slave, the
slave owner received double damages against a third person who
maliciously enticed his slave to commit a wrong. Applied at the

instance of a master against a business competitor, the *actio* compensated for the loss of business secrets divulged by the slave to the competitor at the latter's instigation. Damages included the diminution in the value of the slave and all other provable direct and indirect harm. See Schiller, Trade Secrets and the Roman Law: The Actio Servi Corrupti, 30 Colum.L.Rev. 837 (1930).

The fifteenth- and sixteenth-century cases, often cited as marking the common law's early distaste for postemployment restraints as departures from principles of economic freedom, should be viewed against the background of the craft guilds that were economically predominant at the time. Because the cases involved restraints imposed by masters upon apprentices to prolong their period of noncompetitive—and often wageless—service, it has been argued that the decisions striking down the restraints should be narrowly interpreted as endorsements of the guild customs which established a limited indenture period. "If the early cases represent, in fact, the courts' attempt to assist the guilds and legislative bodies in shoring up the crumbling values of the medieval economic system, they cannot fairly be described as indicative of an attitude of economic liberalism." Blake, Employee Agreements Not To Compete, 73 Harv.L.Rev. 625, 632 (1960).

2. ECONOMIC INTERESTS: THE PLACE OF TRADE SECRETS IN THE COMPETITIVE PLAN

TABOR v. HOFFMAN

Court of Appeals of New York, Second Division, 1889.
118 N.Y. 30, 23 N.E. 12.

Appeal from a judgment of the general term of the supreme court in the fifth judicial department, affirming a judgment in favor of the plaintiff entered upon the decision of a special term.

The object of this action was to restrain the defendant from using certain patterns alleged to have been surreptitiously copied from patterns belonging to the plaintiff that had not been made public. The trial court found that the plaintiff, having invented a pump known as "Tabor's Rotary Pump," made a complete set of patterns to manufacture the same; that he necessarily spent much time, labor, and money in making and perfecting such patterns, which were always in his exclusive possession; that from time to time he made improvements upon the pump, and incorporated the same in the patterns, which were never thrown on the market nor given to the public; that one Francis Walz surreptitiously made for the defendant a duplicate set of said patterns from measurements taken from the patterns of the plaintiff, without his knowledge or consent, while they were in possession of said Walz to be repaired; that before the commencement of this action the defendant, with knowledge of all these facts and without the consent of the plaintiff, had commenced to make, and since then has made, pumps from said patterns, thus obtained; that plaintiff has established a large and profitable trade in said pumps, which "will be injured, and the plaintiff damaged, if the defendant is permitted" to continue to manufacture from said patterns. The trial court further found, upon the request of the defendant, "that a competent pattern-maker can make a set of patterns from measurements taken from the pump itself, without the aid of plaintiff's patterns," but refused to find, upon the like request, that this could be done "with little more expense and trouble than from measurements taken from plaintiff's said patterns." It appeared from the evidence that the finished pump "does not comply with the patterns," because it is made of brass and iron, which expand unequally in the finished casting, and also contract unequally when cooling during the process of casting; that some of the patterns are subdivided into sections, which greatly facilitates measurements and drawings, as each section can be laid flat upon the wood or paper; and that it would take longer to make a set of patterns from the pump than it would to copy the perfected patterns themselves. The special term, by its final decree, restrained the defendant "from manufacturing any more pumps from the set of patterns made by Francis Walz from measurements taken from the plaintiff's patterns . . . and from selling, disposing of, or using in any manner said patterns."

VANN, J., (after stating the facts as above.) It is conceded by the appellant that, independent of copyright or letters patent, an inventor or author has, by the common law, an exclusive property in his invention or composition, until by publication it becomes the property of the general public. This concession seems to be well founded, and to be sustained by authority. As the plaintiff had placed the perfected pump upon the market, without obtaining the protection of the patent laws, he thereby published that invention to the world, and no longer had any exclusive property therein. But the completed pump was not his only invention, for he had also discovered means, or machines in the form of patterns, which greatly aided, if they were not indispensable, in the manufacture of the pumps. This discovery he had not intentionally published, but had kept it secret, unless, by disclosing the invention of the pump, he had also disclosed the invention of the patterns by which the pump was made. The precise question, therefore, presented by this appeal, as it appears to us, is whether there is a secret in the patterns that yet remains a secret, although the pump has been given to the world. The pump consists of many different pieces, the most of which are made by running melted brass or iron in a mould. The mould is formed by the use of patterns, which exceed in number the separate parts of the pump, as some of them are divided into several sections. The different pieces out of which the pump is made are not of the same size as the corresponding patterns, owing to the shrinkage of the metal in cooling. In constructing patterns it is necessary to make allowances, not only for the shrinkage, which is greater in brass than in iron, but also for the expansion of the completed casting under different conditions of heat and cold, so that the different parts of the pump will properly fit together and adapt themselves, by nicely balanced expansion and contraction, to pumping either hot or cold liquids. If the patterns were of the same size as the corresponding portions of the pump, the castings made therefrom would neither fit together, nor, if fitted, work properly when pumping fluids varying in temperature. The size of the patterns cannot be discovered by merely using the different sections of the pump, but various changes must be made, and those changes can only be ascertained by a series of experiments, involving the expenditure of both time and money. Are not the size and shape of the patterns, therefore, a secret which the plaintiff has not published, and in which he still has an exclusive property? Can it be truthfully said that this secret can be learned from the pump, when experiments must be added to what can be learned from the pump before a pattern of the proper size can be made? As more could be learned by measuring the patterns than could be learned by measuring the component parts of the pump, was there not a secret that belonged to the discoverer, until he abandoned it by publication, or it was fairly discovered by another? If a valuable medicine, not protected by patent, is put upon the market, any one may, if he can by chemical analysis and a series of experiments, or by any other use of the medicine itself, aided by his own resources only, discover the ingredients and their proportions. If he thus finds out the secret of the proprietor, he may use it to any extent that he desires without danger of interference by the courts. But, because this discovery may be possible by fair means, it would not justify a discovery by unfair means, such as the bribery of a clerk who, in the course of his employment, had aided in compounding the medicine, and had thus become familiar with the formula. The courts have frequently restrained persons who have learned a secret formula for compounding medicines, beverages, and the like, while in the employment of the proprietor, from using it themselves, or imparting it to others to his injury; thus, in effect, holding, as was said by the learned general term, "that the sale of the compounded article to the world was not a publication of the formula or device used in its manufacture." Hammer v. Barnes [26 How.Pr. 174].

The fact that one secret can be discovered more easily than another does not affect the principle. Even if resort to the patterns of the plaintiff was more of a convenience than a necessity, still, if there was a secret, it belonged to him, and the defendant had no right to obtain it by unfair means, or to use it after it was thus obtained. We think that the patterns were a secret device that was not disclosed by the publication of the pump, and that the plaintiff was entitled to the preventive remedies of the court. While the defendant could lawfully copy the pump, because it had been published to the world, he could not lawfully copy the patterns, because they had not been published, but were still, in every sense, the property of the plaintiff, who owned not only the material substance, but also the discovery which they embodied. The judgment should be affirmed, with costs.

FOLLETT, C.J., (dissenting.) An inventor of a new and useful improvement has a right to its exclusive enjoyment, which right he may protect by a patent or by concealment. The plaintiff's patent had expired, and all of the parts of the pump represented by the patterns had been for a long time on sale in the form of a completed pump. The patent on the original invention having expired, and the plaintiff having voluntarily made the subsequent improvements public by selling the improved article, he lost his right to their exclusive use. The plaintiff's counsel concedes this, but says that while patterns could be made from the several parts of the pump, from which pumps like those made and sold by the plaintiff could be produced, it was more difficult to make patterns from sections of the pump than from the patterns. This was so found by the court, and cannot be gainsaid. The invention was not the patterns, but the idea represented by them, to which the plaintiff had lost his exclusive right. Neither the defendant nor the man who made the patterns sustained any relation by contract with the plaintiff. They were neither the servants nor partners of the plaintiff, and they owed him no duty not owed by the whole world. The act, at most, was a trespass, and the plaintiff made no case for equitable relief. It is neither asserted nor found that the defendant is unable to respond in damages. The cases cited to sustain the judgment arose out of the relation of master and servant, or between partners, and in all of them the idea had not been disclosed to the public, but had been kept secret by the inventor. The judgment should be reversed, and a new trial granted, with costs to abide the event.

KEWANEE OIL CO. v. BICRON CORP.

Supreme Court of the United States, 1974.
416 U.S. 470, 94 S.Ct. 1879, 40 L.Ed.2d 315, 181 U.S.P.Q. 673.

Mr. Chief Justice BURGER delivered the opinion of the Court.

We granted certiorari to resolve a question on which there is a conflict in the courts of appeals: whether state trade secret protection is pre-empted by operation of the federal patent law. In the instant case the Court of Appeals for the Sixth Circuit held that there was preemption. The Courts of Appeals for the Second, Fourth, Fifth, and Ninth Circuits have reached the opposite conclusion.

I

Harshaw Chemical Co., an unincorporated division of petitioner, is a leading manufacturer of a type of synthetic crystal which is useful in the detection of ionizing radiation. In 1949 Harshaw commenced research into the growth of this type crystal and was able to produce one less than two inches in diameter. By 1966, as the result of expenditures in excess of $1 million, Harshaw was able to grow a 17-inch crystal, something no one else had done previously. Harshaw had developed many processes, procedures, and manufacturing techniques in the purification of raw materials and the growth and encapsulation of the crystals which enabled it to accomplish this feat. Some of these processes Harshaw considers to be trade secrets.

The individual respondents are former employees of Harshaw who formed or later joined respondent Bicron. While at Harshaw the individual respondents executed, as a condition of employment, at least one agreement each, requiring them not to disclose confidential information or trade secrets obtained as employees of Harshaw. Bicron was formed in August 1969 to compete with Harshaw in the production of the crystals and by April 1970, had grown a 17–inch crystal.

Petitioner brought this diversity action in United States District Court for the Northern District of Ohio seeking injunctive relief and damages for the misappropriation of trade secrets. The District Court, applying Ohio trade secret law, granted a permanent injunction against the disclosure or use by respondents of 20 of the 40 claimed trade secrets until such time as the trade secrets had been released to the public, had otherwise generally become available to the public, or had been obtained by respondents from sources having the legal right to convey the information.

The Court of Appeals for the Sixth Circuit held that the findings of fact by the District Court were not clearly erroneous, and that it was evident from the record that the individual respondents appropriated to the benefit of Bicron secret information on processes obtained while they were employees at Harshaw. Further, the Court of Appeals held that the District Court properly applied Ohio law relating to trade secrets. Nevertheless, the Court of Appeals reversed the District Court, finding Ohio's trade secret law to be in conflict with the patent laws of the United States. The Court of Appeals reasoned that Ohio could not grant monopoly protection to processes and manufacturing techniques that were appropriate subjects for consideration under 35 U.S.C.A. § 101 for a federal patent but which had been in commercial use for over one year and so were no longer eligible for patent protection under 35 U.S.C.A. § 102(b).

We hold that Ohio's law of trade secrets is not preempted by the patent laws of the United States, and, accordingly, we reverse.

II

Ohio has adopted the widely relied-upon definition of a trade secret found at Restatement of Torts § 757, comment *b* (1939). According to the Restatement,

> [a] trade secret may consist of any formula, pattern, device or compilation of information which is used in one's business, and which gives him an opportunity to obtain an advantage over competitors who do not know or use it. It may be a formula for a chemical compound, a process of manufacturing, treating or preserving materials, a pattern for a machine or other device, or a list of customers.

The subject of a trade secret must be secret, and must not be of public knowledge or of a general knowledge in the trade or business. This necessary element of secrecy is not lost, however, if the holder of the trade secret reveals the trade secret to another "in confidence, and under an implied obligation not to use or disclose it." Cincinnati Bell Foundry Co. v. Dodds, 10 Ohio Dec. Reprint 154, 156, 19 Weekly L.Bull. 84 (Super.Ct.1887). These others may include those of the holder's "employees to whom it is necessary to confide it, in order to apply it to the uses for which it is intended." National Tube Co. v. Eastern Tube Co., [3 Ohio C.C.R. (n.s.) 459, (1902)] 462. Often the recipient of confidential knowledge of the subject of a trade secret is a licensee of its holder.

The protection accorded the trade secret holder is against the disclosure or unauthorized use of the trade secret by those to whom the secret has been confided under the express or implied restriction of nondisclosure or nonuse. The law also protects the holder of a trade secret against disclosure or use when the knowledge is gained, not by the owner's volition, but by some "improper means," Restatement of Torts § 757(a), which may include theft, wiretapping, or even aerial reconnaissance. A trade secret law, however, does not offer protection against discovery by fair and honest means, such as by independent invention, accidental disclosure, or by so-called reverse engineering, that is by starting with the known product and working backward to divine the process which aided in its development or manufacture.

Novelty, in the patent law sense, is not required for a trade secret. "Quite clearly discovery is something less than invention." A.O. Smith Corp. v. Petroleum Iron Works Co., 73 F.2d 531, 538 (C.A.6 1934); modified to increase scope of injunction, 74 F.2d 934 (1935). However, some novelty will be required if merely because that which does not possess novelty is usually known; secrecy, in the context of trade secrets, thus implies at least minimal novelty.

The subject matter of a patent is limited to a "process, machine, manufacture, or composition of matter, or . . . improvement thereof," 35 U.S.C.A. § 101, which fulfills the three conditions of novelty and utility as articulated and defined in 35 U.S.C.A. §§ 101 and 102, and nonobviousness, as set out in 35 U.S.C.A. § 103. If an invention meets the rigorous statutory tests for the issuance of a patent, the patent is granted, for a period of 17 years, giving what has been described as the "right of exclusion," R. Ellis, Patent Assignments and Licenses § 4, p. 7 (2d ed. 1943). This protection goes not only to copying the subject matter, which is forbidden under the Copyright Act, but also to independent creation.

III

The first issue we deal with is whether the States are forbidden to act at all in the area of protection of the kinds of intellectual property which may make up the subject matter of trade secrets.

Article I, § 8, cl. 8, of the Constitution grants to the Congress the power

[t]o promote the Progress of Science and useful Arts, by securing for limited Times to Authors and Inventors the exclusive Right to their respective Writings and Discoveries. . . .

In the 1972 Term, in Goldstein v. California, 412 U.S. 546, 93 S.Ct. 2303, 37 L.Ed.2d 163 (1973), we held that the cl. 8 grant of power to

Congress was not exclusive and that, at least in the case of writings, the States were not prohibited from encouraging and protecting the efforts of those within their borders by appropriate legislation. The States could, therefore, protect against the unauthorized rerecording for sale of performances fixed on records or tapes, even though those performances qualified as "writings" in the constitutional sense and Congress was empowered to legislate regarding such performances and could preempt the area if it chose to do so. This determination was premised on the great diversity of interests in our Nation—the essentially nonuniform character of the appreciation of intellectual achievements in the various States. Evidence for this came from patents granted by the States in the 18th century.

Just as the States may exercise regulatory power over writings so may the States regulate with respect to discoveries. States may hold diverse viewpoints in protecting intellectual property relating to invention as they do in protecting the intellectual property relating to the subject matter of copyright. The only limitation on the States is that in regulating the area of patents and copyrights they do not conflict with the operation of the laws in this area passed by Congress, and it is to that more difficult question we now turn.

IV

The question of whether the trade secret law of Ohio is void under the Supremacy Clause involves a consideration of whether that law "stands as an obstacle to the accomplishment and execution of the full purposes and objectives of Congress." Hines v. Davidowitz, 312 U.S. 52, 67, 61 S.Ct. 399, 404, 85 L.Ed. 581 (1941). We stated in Sears, Roebuck & Co. v. Stiffel Co., 376 U.S. 225, 229, 84 S.Ct. 784, 11 L.Ed.2d 661 (1964), that when state law touches upon the area of federal statutes enacted pursuant to constitutional authority, "it is 'familiar doctrine' that the federal policy 'may not be set at naught, or its benefits denied' by the state law. Sola Elec. Co. v. Jefferson Elec. Co., 317 U.S. 173, 176, 63 S.Ct. 172, 173, 87 L.Ed. 165 (1942). This is true, of course, even if the state law is enacted in the exercise of otherwise undoubted state power."

The laws which the Court of Appeals in this case held to be in conflict with the Ohio law of trade secrets were the patent laws passed by the Congress in the unchallenged exercise of its clear power under Art. I, § 8, cl. 8, of the Constitution. The patent law does not explicitly endorse or forbid the operation of trade secret law. However, as we have noted, if the scheme of protection developed by Ohio respecting trade secrets "clashes with the objectives of the federal patent laws," Sears, Roebuck & Co. v. Stiffel Co., supra, 376 U.S., at 231, 84 S.Ct., at 789 then the state law must fall. To determine whether the Ohio law "clashes" with the federal law it is helpful to examine the objectives of both the patent and trade secret laws.

The stated objective of the Constitution in granting the power to Congress to legislate in the area of intellectual property is to "promote the Progress of Science and useful Arts." The patent laws promote this progress by offering a right of exclusion for a limited period as an incentive to inventors to risk the often enormous costs in terms of time, research, and development. The productive effort thereby fostered will have a positive effect on society through the introduction of new products and processes of manufacture into the economy, and the emanations by way of increased employment and better lives for our citizens. In return for the right of exclusion—this "reward for inventions," Universal Oil Co. v. Globe Co., 322 U.S. 471, 484, 64 S.Ct. 1110, 1116, 88 L.Ed. 1399 (1944)—the patent laws impose upon the inventor a requirement of disclosure. To insure adequate and full disclosure so that upon the expiration of the 17–year period "the knowledge of the invention enures to the people, who are thus enabled without restriction to practice it and profit by its use," United States v. Dubilier Condenser Corp., 289 U.S. 178, 187, 53 S.Ct. 554, 77 L.Ed. 1114 (1933), the patent laws require that the patent application shall include a full and clear description of the invention and "of the manner and process of making and using it" so that any person skilled in the art may make and use the invention. 35 U.S.C.A. § 112. When a patent is granted and the information contained in it is circulated to the general public and those especially skilled in the trade, such additions to the general store of knowledge are of such importance to the public weal that the Federal Government is willing to pay the high price of 17 years of exclusive use for its disclosure, which disclosure, it is assumed, will stimulate ideas and the eventual development of further significant advances in the art. The Court has also articulated another policy of the patent law: that which is in the public domain cannot be removed therefrom by action of the States.

> [F]ederal law requires that all ideas in general circulation be dedicated to the common good unless they are protected by a valid patent. Lear, Inc. v. Adkins, 395 U.S., at 668, 89 S.Ct., at 1910.

The maintenance of standards of commercial ethics and the encouragement of invention are the broadly stated policies behind trade secret law. "The necessity of good faith and honest, fair dealing, is the very life and spirit of the commercial world." National Tube Co. v. Eastern Tube Co., 3 Ohio Cir.Ct.R. (n.s.), at 462. In A.O. Smith Corp. v. Petroleum Iron Works Co., 73 F.2d, at 539, the Court emphasized that even though a discovery may not be patentable, that does not

> destroy the value of the discovery to one who makes it, or advantage the competitor who by unfair means, or as the beneficiary of a broken faith, obtains the desired knowledge without himself paying the price in labor, money, or machines expended by the discoverer.

In Wexler v. Greenberg, 399 Pa. 569, 578–579, 160 A.2d 430, 434–435 (1960), the Pennsylvania Supreme Court noted the importance of trade secret protection to the subsidization of research and development and to increased economic efficiency within large companies through the dispersion of responsibilities for creative developments.

Having now in mind the objectives of both the patent and trade secret law, we turn to an examination of the interaction of these systems of protection of intellectual property—one established by the Congress and the other by a State—to determine whether and under what circumstances the latter might constitute "too great an encroachment on the federal patent system to be tolerated." Sears, Roebuck & Co. v. Stiffel Co., 376 U.S., at 232, 84 S.Ct., at 789.

As we noted earlier, trade secret law protects items which would not be proper subjects for consideration for patent protection under 35 U.S.C.A. § 101. As in the case of the recordings in Goldstein v. California, Congress, with respect to nonpatentable subject matter, "has drawn no balance; rather, it has left the area unattended, and no reason exists why the State should not be free to act." Goldstein v. California, supra, 412 U.S., at 570, 93 S.Ct., at 2316 (footnote omitted).

Since no patent is available for a discovery, however useful, novel, and nonobvious, unless it falls within one of the express categories of patentable subject matter of 35 U.S.C.A. § 101, the holder of such a discovery would have no reason to apply for a patent whether trade secret protection existed or not. Abolition of trade secret protection would, therefore, not result in increased disclosure to the public of discoveries in the area of nonpatentable subject matter. Also, it is hard to see how the public would be benefited by disclosure of customer lists or advertising campaigns; in fact, keeping such items secret encourages businesses to initiate new and individualized plans of operation, and constructive competition results. This, in turn, leads to a greater variety of business methods than would otherwise be the case if privately developed marketing and other data were passed illicitly among firms involved in the same enterprise.

Congress has spoken in the area of those discoveries which fall within one of the categories of patentable subject matter of 35 U.S.C.A. § 101 and which are, therefore, of a nature that would be subject to consideration for a patent. Processes, machines, manufactures, compositions of matter, and improvements thereof, which meet the tests of utility, novelty, and nonobviousness are entitled to be patented, but those which do not, are not. The question remains whether those items which are proper subjects for consideration for a patent may also have available the alternative protection accorded by trade secret law.

Certainly the patent policy of encouraging invention is not disturbed by the existence of another form of incentive to invention. In this respect the two systems are not and never would be in conflict. Similarly, the policy that matter once in the public domain must remain in the public domain is not incompatible with the existence of trade secret protection. By definition a trade secret has not been placed in the public domain.

The more difficult objective of the patent law to reconcile with trade secret law is that of disclosure, the *quid pro quo* of the right to exclude. We are helped in this stage of the analysis by Judge Henry Friendly's opinion in Painton & Co. v. Bourns, Inc., 442 F.2d 216 (C.A.2

1971). There the Court of Appeals thought it useful, in determining whether inventors will refrain because of the existence of trade secret law from applying for patents, thereby depriving the public from learning of the invention, to distinguish between three categories of trade secrets:

> (1) the trade secret believed by its owner to constitute a validly patentable invention; (2) the trade secret known to its owner not to be so patentable; and (3) the trade secret whose valid patentability is considered dubious. Id., at 224.

Trade secret protection in each of these categories would run against breaches of confidence—the employee and licensee situations—and theft and other forms of industrial espionage.

As to the trade secret known not to meet the standards of patentability, very little in the way of disclosure would be accomplished by abolishing trade secret protection. With trade secrets of nonpatentable subject matter, the patent alternative would not reasonably be available to the inventor. "There can be no public interest in stimulating developers of such [unpatentable] know-how to flood an overburdened Patent Office with applications [for] what they do not consider patentable." Ibid. The mere filing of applications doomed to be turned down by the Patent Office will bring forth no new public knowledge or enlightenment, since under federal statute and regulation patent applications and abandoned patent applications are held by the Patent Office in confidence and are not open to public inspection. 35 U.S.C.A. § 122; 37 C.F.R. § 1.14(b).

Even as the extension of trade secret protection to patentable subject matter that the owner knows will not meet the standards of patentability will not conflict with the patent policy of disclosure, it will have a decidedly beneficial effect on society. Trade secret law will encourage invention in areas where patent law does not reach, and will prompt the independent innovator to proceed with the discovery and exploitation of his invention. Competition is fostered and the public is not deprived of the use of valuable, if not quite patentable, invention.

Even if trade secret protection against the faithless employee were abolished, inventive and exploitive effort in the area of patentable subject matter that did not meet the standards of patentability would continue, although at a reduced level. Alternatively with the effort that remained, however, would come an increase in the amount of self-help that innovative companies would employ. Knowledge would be widely dispersed among the employees of those still active in research. Security precautions necessarily would be increased, and salaries and fringe benefits of those few officers or employees who had to know the whole of the secret invention would be fixed in an amount thought sufficient to assure their loyalty. Smaller companies would be placed at a distinct economic disadvantage, since the costs of this kind of self-help could be great, and the cost to the public of the use of this invention would be increased. The innovative entrepreneur with limited resources would tend to confine his research efforts to himself and those few he felt he could trust without the ultimate assurance of legal protection against breaches of confidence. As a result, organized scientific and technological research could become fragmented, and society, as a whole, would suffer.

Another problem that would arise if state trade secret protection were precluded is in the area of licensing others to exploit secret processes. The holder of a trade secret would not likely share his secret with a manufacturer who cannot be placed under binding legal obligation to pay a license fee or to protect the secret. The result would be to hoard rather than disseminate knowledge. Instead, then, of licensing others to use his invention and making the most efficient use of existing manufacturing and marketing structures within the industry, the trade secret holder would tend either to limit his utilization of the invention, thereby depriving the public of the maximum benefit of its use, or engage in the time-consuming and economically wasteful enterprise of constructing duplicative manufacturing and marketing mechanisms for the exploitation of the invention. The detrimental misallocation of resources and economic waste that would thus take place if trade secret protection were abolished with respect to employees or licensees cannot be justified by reference to any policy that the federal patent law seeks to advance.

Nothing in the patent law requires that States refrain from action to prevent industrial espionage. In addition to the increased costs for protection from burglary, wiretapping, bribery, and the other means used to misappropriate trade secrets, there is the inevitable cost to the basic decency of society when one firm steals from another. A most fundamental human right, that of privacy, is threatened when industrial espionage is condoned or is made profitable; the state interest in denying profit to such illegal ventures is unchallengeable.

The next category of patentable subject matter to deal with is the invention whose holder has a legitimate doubt as to its patentability. The risk of eventual patent invalidity by the courts and the costs associated with that risk may well impel some with a good-faith doubt as to patentability not to take the trouble to seek to obtain and defend patent protection for their discoveries, regardless of the existence of trade secret protection. Trade secret protection would assist those inventors in the more efficient exploitation of their discoveries and not conflict with the patent law. In most cases of genuine doubt as to patent validity the potential rewards of patent protection are so far superior to those accruing to holders of trade secrets, that the holders of such inventions will seek patent protection, ignoring the trade secret route. For those inventors "on the line" as to whether to seek patent protection, the abolition of trade secret protection might encourage some to apply for a patent who otherwise would not have done so. For some of those so encouraged, no patent will be granted and the result

will have been an unnecessary postponement in the divulging of the trade secret to persons willing to pay for it. If [the patent does issue], it may well be invalid, yet many will prefer to pay a modest royalty than to contest it, even though *Lear* allows them to accept a license and pursue the contest without paying royalties while the fight goes on. The result in such a case would be unjustified royalty payments from many who would prefer not to pay them rather than agreed fees from one or a few who are entirely willing to do so. Painton & Co. v. Bourns, Inc., 442 F.2d, at 225.

The point is that those who might be encouraged to file for patents by the absence of trade secret law will include inventors possessing the chaff as well as the wheat. Some of the chaff—the nonpatentable discoveries—will be thrown out by the Patent Office, but in the meantime society will have been deprived of use of those discoveries through trade secret-protected licensing. Some of the chaff may not be thrown out. This Court has noted the difference between the standards used by the Patent Office and the courts to determine patentability. In Lear, Inc. v. Adkins, 395 U.S. 653, 89 S.Ct. 1902, 23 L.Ed.2d 610 (1969), the Court thought that an invalid patent was so serious a threat to the free use of ideas already in the public domain that the Court permitted licensees of the patent holder to challenge the validity of the patent. Better had the invalid patent never been issued. More of those patents would likely issue if trade secret law were abolished. Eliminating trade secret law for the doubtfully patentable invention is thus likely to have deleterious effects on society and patent policy which we cannot say are balanced out by the speculative gain which might result from the encouragement of some inventors with doubtfully patentable inventions which deserve patent protection to come forward and apply for patents. There is no conflict, then, between trade secret law and the patent law policy of disclosure, at least insofar as the first two categories of patentable subject matter are concerned.

The final category of patentable subject matter to deal with is the clearly patentable invention, i.e., that invention which the owner believes to meet the standards of patentability. It is here that the federal interest in disclosure is at its peak; these inventions, novel, useful and nonobvious, are " 'the things which are worth to the public the embarrassment of an exclusive patent.' " Graham v. John Deere Co., supra, at 9, 86 S.Ct., at 689 (quoting Thomas Jefferson). The interest of the public is that the bargain of 17 years of exclusive use in return for disclosure be accepted. If a State, through a system of protection, were to cause a substantial risk that holders of patentable inventions would not seek patents, but rather would rely on the state protection, we would be compelled to hold that such a system could not constitutionally continue to exist. In the case of trade secret law no reasonable risk of deterrence from patent application by those who can reasonably expect to be granted patents exists.

Trade secret law provides far weaker protection in many respects than the patent law. While trade secret law does not forbid the discovery of the trade secret by fair and honest means, e.g., independent creation or reverse engineering, patent law operates "against the world," forbidding any use of the invention for whatever purpose for a significant length of time. The holder of a trade secret also takes a substantial risk that the secret will be passed on to his competitors, by theft or by breach of a confidential relationship, in a manner not easily susceptible of discovery or proof. Where patent law acts as a barrier, trade secret law functions relatively as a sieve. The possibility that an inventor who believes his invention meets the standards of patentability will sit back, rely on trade secret law, and after one year of use forfeit any right to patent protection, 35 U.S.C.A. § 102(b), is remote indeed.

Nor does society face much risk that scientific or technological progress will be impeded by the rare inventor with a patentable invention who chooses trade secret protection over patent protection. The ripeness-of-time concept of invention, developed from the study of the many independent multiple discoveries in history, predicts that if a particular individual had not made a particular discovery others would have, and in probably a relatively short period of time. If something is to be discovered at all very likely it will be discovered by more than one person. Even were an inventor to keep his discovery completely to himself, something that neither the patent nor trade secret laws forbid, there is a high probability that it will be soon independently developed. If the invention, though still a trade secret, is put into public use, the competition is alerted to the existence of the inventor's solution to the problem and may be encouraged to make an extra effort to independently find the solution thus known to be possible. The inventor faces pressures not only from private industry, but from the skilled scientists who work in our universities and our other great publicly supported centers of learning and research.

We conclude that the extension of trade secret protection to clearly patentable inventions does not conflict with the patent policy of disclosure. Perhaps because trade secret law does not produce any positive effects in the area of clearly patentable inventions, as opposed to the beneficial effects resulting from trade secret protection in the areas of the doubtfully patentable and the clearly unpatentable inventions, it has been suggested that partial pre-emption may be appropriate, and that courts should refuse to apply trade secret protection to inventions which the holder should have patented, and which would have been, thereby, disclosed. However, since there is no real possibility that trade secret law will conflict with the federal policy favoring disclosure of clearly patentable inventions partial pre-emption is inappropriate. Partial pre-emption, furthermore, could well create serious problems for state courts in the administration of trade secret law. As a preliminary matter in trade secret actions, state courts would be obliged to distinguish between what a reasonable inventor would and would not correctly consider to be clearly patentable, with the holder of the trade secret arguing that the invention was not patentable and the misappropriator of the trade secret arguing its undoubted novelty, utility, and nonobviousness. Federal courts have a difficult enough time trying to determine whether an invention, narrowed by the patent application procedure and fixed in the specifications which describe the invention for which the patent has been granted, is patentable. Although state courts in some circumstances must join federal courts in judging whether an issued patent is valid, Lear, Inc. v. Adkins, supra, it would be undesirable to impose the almost impossible burden on state courts to determine the patentability—in fact and in the mind of a reasonable inventor—of a discovery which has not been patented and remains entirely uncircumscribed by expert analysis in the administrative process. Neither complete nor partial pre-emption of state trade secret law is justified.

Our conclusion that patent law does not pre-empt trade secret law is in accord with prior cases of this Court. Trade secret law and patent law have co-existed in this country for over one hundred years. Each has its particular role to play, and the operation of one does not take away from the need for the other. Trade secret law encourages the development and exploitation of those items of lesser or different invention than might be accorded protection under the patent laws, but which items still have an important part to play in the technological and scientific advancement of the Nation. Trade secret law promotes the sharing of knowledge, and the efficient operation of industry; it permits the individual inventor to reap the rewards of his labor by contracting with a company large enough to develop and exploit it. Congress, by its silence over these many years, has seen the wisdom of allowing the States to enforce trade secret protection. Until Congress takes affirmative action to the contrary, States should be free to grant protection to trade secrets.

Since we hold that Ohio trade secret law is not pre-empted by the federal patent law, the judgment of the Court of Appeals for the Sixth Circuit is reversed, and the case is remanded to the Court of Appeals with directions to reinstate the judgment of the District Court.

It is so ordered.

Mr. Justice POWELL took no part in the decision of this case.

Mr. Justice MARSHALL, concurring in the result.

Unlike the Court, I do not believe that the possibility that an inventor with a patentable invention will rely on state trade secret law rather than apply for a patent is "remote indeed." State trade secret law provides substantial protection to the inventor who intends to use or sell the invention himself rather than license it to others, protection which in its unlimited duration is clearly superior to the 17–year monopoly afforded by the patent laws. I have no doubt that the existence of trade secret protection provides in some instances a substantial disincentive to entrance into the patent system, and thus deprives society of the benefits of public disclosure of the invention which it is the policy of the patent laws to encourage. This case may well be such an instance.

But my view of sound policy in this area does not dispose of this case. Rather, the question presented in this case is whether Congress, in enacting the patent laws, intended merely to offer inventors a limited monopoly in exchange for disclosure of their invention, or instead to exert pressure on inventors to enter into this exchange by withdrawing any alternative possibility of legal protection for their inventions. I am persuaded that the former is the case. State trade secret laws and the federal patent laws have co-existed for many, many years. During this time, Congress has repeatedly demonstrated its full awareness of the existence of the trade secret system, without any indication of disapproval. Indeed, Congress has in a number of instances given explicit federal protection to trade secret information provided to federal agencies. Because of this, I conclude that there is "neither such actual conflict between the two schemes of regulation that both cannot stand in the same area, nor evidence of a congressional design to pre-empt the field." Florida Lime Avocado Growers v. Paul, 373 U.S. 132, 141, 83 S.Ct. 1210, 1217, 10 L.Ed.2d 248 (1963). I therefore concur in the result reached by the majority of the Court.

Mr. Justice DOUGLAS, with whom Mr. Justice BRENNAN concurs, dissenting.

Today's decision is at war with the philosophy of Sears, Roebuck & Co. v. Stiffel Co., 376 U.S. 225, 84 S.Ct. 784, 11 L.Ed.2d 661, and Compco Corp. v. Day–Brite Lighting, Inc., 376 U.S. 234, 84 S.Ct. 779, 11 L.Ed.2d 669. Those cases involved patents—one of a pole lamp and one of fluorescent lighting fixtures each of which was declared invalid. The lower courts held, however, that though the patents were invalid the sale of identical or confusingly similar products to the products of the patentees violated state unfair competition laws. We held that when an article is unprotected by a patent, state law may not forbid others to copy it, because every article not covered by a valid patent is in the public domain. Congress in the patent laws decided that where no patent existed, free competition should prevail; that where a patent is rightfully issued, the right to exclude others should obtain for no longer than 17 years, and that the States may not "under some other law, such as that forbidding unfair competition, give protection of a kind that clashes with the objectives of the federal patent laws," 376 U.S., at 231, 84 S.Ct., at 789.

The product involved in this suit, sodium iodide synthetic crystals, was a product that could be patented but was not. Harshaw the inventor apparently contributed greatly to the technology in that field by developing processes, procedures, and techniques that produced much larger crystals than any competitor. These processes, procedures, and techniques were also patentable; but no patent was sought. Rather Harshaw sought to protect its trade secrets by contracts with its employees. And the District Court found that, as a result of those secrecy precautions, "not sufficient disclosure occurred so as to place the claimed trade secrets in the public domain"; and those findings were sustained by the Court of Appeals.

The District Court issued a permanent injunction against respondents, ex-employees, restraining them from using the processes used by Harshaw. By a patent which would require full disclosure Harshaw could have obtained a 17–year monopoly against the world. By the District Court's injunction, which the Court approves and reinstates,

Harshaw gets a permanent injunction running into perpetuity against respondents. In *Sears,* as in the present case, an injunction against the unfair competitor issued. We said: "To allow a State by use of its law of unfair competition to prevent the copying of an article which represents too slight an advance to be patented would be to permit the State to block off from the public something which federal law has said belongs to the public. The result would be that while federal law grants only 14 or 17 years' protection to genuine inventions, see 35 U.S. C.A. §§ 154, 173, States could allow perpetual protection to articles too lacking in novelty to merit any patent at all under federal constitutional standards. This would be too great an encroachment on the federal patent system to be tolerated." 376 U.S., at 231–232, 84 S.Ct., at 789.

The conflict with the patent laws is obvious. The decision of Congress to adopt a patent system was based on the idea that there will be much more innovation if discoveries are disclosed and patented than there will be when everyone works in secret. Society thus fosters a free exchange of technological information at the cost of a limited 17–year monopoly.

A trade secret, unlike a patent, has no property dimension. That was the view of the Court of Appeals, 478 F.2d 1074, 1081; and its decision is supported by what Mr. Justice Holmes said in Du Pont de Nemours Powder Co. v. Masland, 244 U.S. 100, 102, 37 S.Ct. 575, 576, 61 L.Ed. 1016:

> The word property as applied to trade-marks and trade secrets is an unanalyzed expression of certain secondary consequences of the primary fact that the law makes some rudimentary requirements of good faith. Whether the plaintiffs have any valuable secret or not the defendant knows the facts, whatever they are, through a special confidence that he accepted. The property may be denied but the confidence cannot be. Therefore the starting point for the present matter is not property or due process of law, but that the defendant stood in confidential relations with the plaintiffs, or one of them. These have given place to hostility, and the first thing to be made sure of is that the defendant shall not fraudulently abuse the trust reposed in him. It is the usual incident of confidential relations. If there is any disadvantage in the fact that he knew the plaintiffs' secrets he must take the burden with the good.

A suit to redress theft of a trade secret is grounded in tort damages for breach of a contract—a historic remedy. Damages for breach of a confidential relation are not pre-empted by this patent law, but an injunction against use is pre-empted because the patent law states the only monopoly over trade secrets that is enforceable by specific performance; and that monopoly exacts as a price full disclosure. A trade secret can be protected only by being kept secret. Damages for breach of a contract are one thing; an injunction barring disclosure does service for the protection accorded valid patents and is therefore pre-empted.

From the findings of fact of the lower courts, the process involved in this litigation was unique, such a great discovery as to make its patentability a virtual certainty. Yet the Court's opinion reflects a vigorous activist antipatent philosophy. My objection is not because it is activist. This is a problem that involves no neutral principle. The Constitution in Art. I, § 8, cl. 8, expresses the activist policy which Congress has enforced by statutes. It is that constitutional policy which we should enforce, not our individual notions of the public good.

I would affirm the judgment below.

NOTES

1. How extensively did *Kewanee* undermine *Sears* and *Compco*, pages 103, 107 above? Did *Kewanee* validate only trade secret causes of action that rest on contract or confidence grounds? Would the *Kewanee* Court have approved state law decisions like DuPont v. Christopher, page 127, that rest trade secret protection on a property rationale? Or do *Sears* and *Compco* continue to control cases in this class?

This and other lines of inquiry are developed in Goldstein, Kewanee Oil Co. v. Bicron Corp.: Notes on a Closing Circle, 1974 Sup. Ct.Rev. 81. For a different view, see Stern, A Reexamination of State Trade Secret Law after Kewanee, 42 Geo.Wash.L.Rev. 927 (1974).

2. *Trade Secrets and Patents.* A trade secret holder has some freedom to choose which aspects of her discovery to lodge in a patent and which to withhold as a trade secret. She cannot, however, withhold facts that are necessary to the public's understanding of the patented subject matter. Van Products Co. v. General Welding & Fabricating Co., 419 Pa. 248, 213 A.2d 769, 147 U.S.P.Q. 221 (1965), indicates the extent to which a patentee can maintain the veil of secrecy. Plaintiff there had received a patent on an air drier apparatus and had retained as a trade secret the formula for the chemical desiccant that was crucial to its operation. "Of course, the idea and the practical functioning of such a deliquescent desiccant could not be a secret, in itself, since the product was advertised, described, and sold on the open market. Its remarkable characteristics, vaunted in sales literature, were the exact factor which made the Van drier desirable (i.e., it was a desiccant which did not require regeneration). Therefore, it was only the composition which was secret, and remained so. . . ." 419 Pa. at 268–69, 213 A.2d at 780.

3. In Warner–Lambert Pharmaceutical Co., Inc. v. John J. Reynolds, Inc., 178 F.Supp. 655, 123 U.S.P.Q. 431 (S.D.N.Y.1959), aff'd, 280 F.2d 197, 126 U.S.P.Q. 3 (2d Cir.1960), plaintiff unsuccessfully sought a declaratory judgment relieving it of royalty obligations for the manufacture of Listerine, the formula of which had been sold to plaintiff's predecessor by defendant's predecessor in 1881. The unpatented formula subsequently became public knowledge. Plaintiff argued that for this reason it should pay no tithe for what others were using free. Finding in the 1881, and subsequent, contracts no express or implied

limitation on the royalty obligation, the court ruled that the plaintiff must abide by the royalty schedule so long as it used the formula.

What flaws, if any, can you find in the court's reasoning on the policy ground: "In the patent and copyright cases the parties are dealing with a fixed statutory term and the monopoly granted by that term. This monopoly, created by Congress, is designed to preserve exclusivity in the grantee during the statutory term and to release the patented or copyrighted material to the general public for general use thereafter. This is the public policy of the statutes in reference to which such contracts are made and it is against this background that the parties to patent and copyright license agreements contract. Here, however, there is no such public policy. The parties are free to contract with respect to a secret formula or trade secret in any manner which they determine for their own best interests. A secret formula or trade secret may remain secret indefinitely. It may be discovered by someone else almost immediately after the agreement is entered into. Whoever discovers it for himself by legitimate means is entitled to its use. But that does not mean that one who acquires a secret formula or a trade secret through a valid and binding contract is then enabled to escape from an obligation to which he bound himself simply because the secret is discovered by a third party or by the general public." 178 F.Supp. 665.

Can *Warner–Lambert* be reconciled with cases like *Reed, Roberts,* page 142, that trim down or void excessive covenants against post-employment competition? With cases like *Conmar,* page 125, that confine injunctions to the time it would take to reverse engineer the trade secret in suit? What are *Kewanee's* implications for the continued vitality of *Warner–Lambert?* Note that the injunction approved in *Kewanee* was to last only "until such time as the trade secrets had been released to the public, had otherwise generally become available to the public or had been obtained by [defendants] from sources having the legal right to convey the information." Does *Aronson,* p. 48, above, offer a complete vindication of *Warner–Lambert?*

Recall that *Kewanee* and *Conmar* involved trade secret appropriations, while *Aronson* and *Warner–Lambert* involved negotiated licenses. Licensees can, between themselves, estimate the life and value of a secret and then settle on any mutually agreeable schedule for repaying its value—a continuing royalty, for example, or a lump sum representing the secret's continuing worth discounted to present value. Little reason exists for a court to intervene and rewrite the payment schedule. Where, however, a trade secret has been appropriated, and no voluntary bargain struck, courts do their best to approximate what the parties would have estimated as the secret's value. The natural starting point is for the court to estimate the secret's probable life, the same starting point as is used in fashioning trade secret injunctions.

Altman, A Quick Point Regarding Perpetual Trade Secret Royalty Liability, 13 J.Marshall L.Rev. 127 (1979), offers some penetrating insights into these and connected issues.

4. *Trade Secrets in the Patent and Trademark Office.* The inventor who has doubts about the patentability of his invention faces a hard choice. To rely on trade secret law means that protection will be limited by the realities of reverse engineering, faithless employees and the difficulties of enforcement. To pursue a patent, however, entails not only the possibility of added expense without reward but, even if a patent issues, the risk that it may later be invalidated, by which point the secret information will have become public. The Patent Act partially reduces the difficulty of this choice by requiring the Patent and Trademark Office to hold all patent applications in confidence so that trade secret protection is maintained even after the application is filed. Rejection of the application will not destroy the inventor's interest. 35 U.S.C. § 122.

The Court of Customs and Patent Appeals—the predecessor of the present Court of Appeals for the Federal Circuit—applied its rules of practice to maintain the secrecy on appeal of a patent application rejected by the Patent and Trademark Office. In Application of Sarkar, 575 F.2d 870, 197 U.S.P.Q. 788 (C.C.P.A.1978), the court, recognizing the public's interest in access to court records and proceedings, nonetheless ordered that the record be sealed, and that the proceedings be conducted *in camera.* "We are guided in our determination by the opinion of the Supreme Court in *Kewanee* . . . that, wherever possible, trade secret law and patent law should be administered in such manner that the former will not deter an inventor from seeking the benefit of the latter, because the public is *most* benefited by the early disclosure of the invention in consideration of the patent grant." 575 F.2d at 872 (emphasis in original). See Note, Preservation of Trade Secret Protection During a Patent Application Appeal, 15 Wake Forest L.Rev. 559 (1979).

Although section 122 has secured applications against requests made under the Freedom of Information Act, it has not proved to be a complete guard against public prying. See Irons & Sears v. Dann, 606 F.2d 1215, 202 U.S.P.Q. 798 (D.C.Cir.1979), cert. denied, 444 U.S. 1075, 100 S.Ct. 1021, 62 L.Ed.2d 757, 204 U.S.P.Q. 1060 (1980).

5. Section 301 of the Copyright Act will preempt state trade secret law if three conditions are met: the subject matter of trade secret protection is fixed in a tangible medium of expression; the subject matter comes within the subject matter of copyright as defined by sections 102 and 103 of the Copyright Act; and the right granted by trade secret law is equivalent to one or more of the rights granted by section 106 of the Copyright Act. The first requirement, fixation in a tangible medium of expression, is easily applied; it will exempt from preemption state protection of a trade secret that has never been reduced to writing and has only been communicated orally by its owner. Section 301's second and third requirements—that the trade secret come within the subject matter of copyright and that the right granted be equivalent to copyright—are more problematic. They are considered in detail beginning at page 759, below.

IV. COMMON LAW COPYRIGHT

From the first federal copyright act, passed in 1790, until the 1976 Copyright Act, Congress carved out an important place for state common law copyright. Common law copyright protection attached automatically from the moment of a work's creation, and essentially, conferred a right of first publication. Short of publication, common law copyright could last forever. Upon publication, common law protection ceased and the work became eligible for protection under the federal statute. Publication would invest federal statutory copyright only if the statutorily required copyright notice appeared on all publicly distributed copies. If copyright notice did not appear on publicly distributed copies the work would fall into the public domain.

Over the years, friction between the state and federal copyright systems grew as publication became an increasingly artificial concept. An adequate mechanism in the eighteenth and nineteenth centuries when works were typically distributed in printed copies, publication took on different forms as courts shaped the rule to meet the demands of newer media. Did broadcast of a work over radio or television constitute publication, divesting common law copyright? Did the sale and distribution of phonograph records publish the musical compositions embodied in the records? Solicitude for author's rights generally led to a negative answer—and to the complaint that, as a vehicle for perpetual protection, common law copyright affronted the constitutional injunction of protection only for "limited times."

One of the major changes wrought by the 1976 Copyright Act was to make federal protection attach not from the moment of a work's publication, but rather from the moment of the work's first fixation in tangible form. This change implied that common law copyright was no longer needed to protect a tangibly fixed work before publication. Section 301 of the 1976 Act makes this implication explicit by abolishing common law copyright for most purposes: "On and after January 1, 1978, all legal or equitable rights that are equivalent to any of the exclusive rights within the general scope of copyright as specified by section 106 in works of authorship that are fixed in a tangible medium of expression and come within the subject matter of copyright as specified by sections 102 and 103, whether created before or after that date and whether published or unpublished, are governed exclusively by this title. Thereafter, no person is entitled to any such right or equivalent right in any such work under the common law or statutes of any State." Section 301 is discussed at pages 759 to 772 below.

The 1976 Act narrowed, but did not completely eliminate common law copyright. Since the Act protects only works fixed in a "tangible medium of expression," it leaves protection of unfixed works to the common law. The House Report on the 1976 Act gives several examples of unfixed works that remain subject to state protection: choreography that has never been filmed or notated, an extemporaneous speech, conversations, live broadcasts, "and a dramatic sketch or musical composition improvised or developed from memory and without being recorded or written down." The Act defines "fixed" to exclude a work's incorporation in media that are not "sufficiently permanent or stable" to permit the work "to be perceived, reproduced, or otherwise communicated for a period of more than transitory duration." Consequently states can protect works that are only "projected briefly on a screen, shown electronically on a television or other cathode ray tube, or captured momentarily in the 'memory' of a computer." A work will not be "fixed" under the Act unless it was embodied in a copy or phonorecord "by or under the authority of the author." State law could, for example, protect a performance of a musical composition that has only been recorded by a member of the audience without the performer's permission. H.R.Rep. No. 94–1476, 94th Cong., 2d Sess. 131 (1976).

Publication has continued importance under the 1976 Act. The Act protects anonymous and pseudonymous works and works made for hire for seventy-five years from the work's first publication or one hundred years from its creation, whichever expires first. See page 689, below. Publication also has retrospective significance. Publication of a work before the effective date of the 1976 Copyright Act—January 1, 1978—without the copyright notice required by the predecessor 1909 Copyright Act, placed the work in the public domain. The work will not be protected under the 1976 Act since the Act excludes protection for any work that was in the public domain on its effective date.

For a detailed discussion of common law copyright, see P. Goldstein, Copyright §§ 15.4 et seq. (1989). The role of publication in copyright law is considered at page 542, below. The 1976 Copyright Act's preemption of common law copyright and other state doctrines is considered at page 759, below.

V. RIGHT OF PUBLICITY

A. THEORY OF PROTECTION

CARSON v. HERE'S JOHNNY PORTABLE TOILETS, INC.

United States Court of Appeals, Sixth Circuit, 1983.
698 F.2d 831, 218 U.S.P.Q. 1.

BAILEY BROWN, Senior Circuit Judge.

This case involves claims of unfair competition and invasion of the right of privacy and the right of publicity arising from appellee's adoption of a phrase generally associated with a popular entertainer.

Appellant, John W. Carson (Carson), is the host and star of "The Tonight Show," a well-known television program broadcast five nights a week by the National Broadcasting Company. Carson also appears as an entertainer in night clubs and theaters around the country. From the time he began hosting "The Tonight Show" in 1962, he has been introduced on the show each night with the phrase "Here's Johnny." This method of introduction was first used for Carson in 1957 when he hosted a daily television program for the American Broadcasting Company. The phrase "Here's Johnny" is generally associated with Carson by a substantial segment of the television viewing public. In 1967, Carson first authorized use of this phrase by an outside business venture, permitting it to be used by a chain of restaurants called "Here's Johnny Restaurants."

Appellant Johnny Carson Apparel, Inc. (Apparel), formed in 1970, manufactures and markets men's clothing to retail stores. Carson, the president of Apparel and owner of 20% of its stock, has licensed Apparel to use his name and picture, which appear on virtually all of Apparel's products and promotional material. Apparel has also used, with Carson's consent, the phrase "Here's Johnny" on labels for clothing and in advertising campaigns. In 1977, Apparel granted a license to Marcy Laboratories to use "Here's Johnny" as the name of a line of men's toiletries. The phrase "Here's Johnny" has never been registered by appellants as a trademark or service mark.

Appellee, Here's Johnny Portable Toilets, Inc., is a Michigan corporation engaged in the business of renting and selling "Here's Johnny" portable toilets. Appellee's founder was aware at the time he formed the corporation that "Here's Johnny" was the introductory slogan for Carson on "The Tonight Show." He indicated that he coupled the phrase with a second one, "The World's Foremost Commodian," to make "a good play on a phrase."

Shortly after appellee went into business in 1976, appellants brought this action alleging unfair competition, trademark infringement under federal and state law, and invasion of privacy and publicity rights. They sought damages and an injunction prohibiting appellee's further use of the phrase "Here's Johnny" as a corporate name or in connection with the sale or rental of its portable toilets.

After a bench trial, the district court issued a memorandum opinion and order which served as its findings of fact and conclusions of law. The court ordered the dismissal of the appellants' complaint. On the unfair competition claim, the court concluded that the appellants had failed to satisfy the "likelihood of confusion" test. On the right of privacy and right of publicity theories, the court held that these rights extend only to a "name or likeness," and "Here's Johnny" did not qualify.

I.

Appellants' first claim alleges unfair competition from appellee's business activities in violation of § 43(a) of the Lanham Act, 15 U.S.C. § 1125(a) (1976), and of Michigan common law. The district court correctly noted that the test for equitable relief under both § 43(a) and Michigan common law is the "likelihood of confusion" standard. Frisch's Restaurants, Inc. v. Elby's Big Boy of Steubenville, Inc., 670 F.2d 642 (6th Cir.), cert. denied, 459 U.S. 916, 103 S.Ct. 231, 74 L.Ed.2d 182 (1982).

In *Frisch's Restaurants* we approved the balancing of several factors in determining whether a likelihood of confusion exists among consumers of goods involved in a § 43(a) action. In that case we examined eight factors:

1. strength of the plaintiff's mark;
2. relatedness of the goods;
3. similarity of the marks;
4. evidence of actual confusion;
5. marketing channels used;
6. likely degree of purchaser care;
7. defendant's intent in selecting the mark;
8. likelihood of expansion of the product lines.

670 F.2d at 648. The district court applied a similar analysis. Under the two-step process adopted in *Frisch's Restaurants*, these eight foundational factors are factual and subject to a clearly erroneous standard of review, while the weighing of these findings on the ultimate issue of the likelihood of confusion is a question of law.

The district court first found that "Here's Johnny" was not such a strong mark that its use for other goods should be entirely foreclosed. Although the appellee had intended to capitalize on the phrase popularized by Carson, the court concluded that appellee had not intended to deceive the public into believing Carson was connected with the product. The court noted that there was little evidence of actual confusion and no evidence that appellee's use of the phrase had damaged appellants. For these reasons, the court determined that appellee's use of the phrase "Here's Johnny" did not present a likelihood of confusion, mistake, or deception.

Our review of the record indicates that none of the district court's findings is clearly erroneous. Moreover, on the basis of these findings, we agree with the district court that the appellants have failed to establish a likelihood of confusion. The general concept underlying the likelihood of confusion is that the public believe that "the mark's owner *sponsored or otherwise approved* the use of the trademark." Warner Bros., Inc. v. Gay Toys, Inc., 658 F.2d 76, 79 (2d Cir.1981) (emphasis added) (quoting Dallas Cowboys Cheerleaders, Inc. v. Pussycat Cinema, Ltd., 604 F.2d 200, 205 (2d Cir.1979)).

The facts as found by the district court do not implicate such likelihood of confusion, and we affirm the district court on this issue.

II.

The appellants also claim that the appellee's use of the phrase "Here's Johnny" violates the common law right of privacy and right of publicity.[1] The confusion in this area of the law requires a brief analysis of the relationship between these two rights.

In an influential article, Dean Prosser delineated four distinct types of the right of privacy: (1) intrusion upon one's seclusion or solitude, (2) public disclosure of embarrassing private facts, (3) publicity which places one in a false light, and (4) appropriation of one's name or likeness for the defendant's advantage. Prosser, *Privacy*, 48 Calif.L. Rev. 383, 389 (1960). This fourth type has become known as the "right of publicity." Henceforth we will refer to Prosser's last, or fourth, category as the "right of publicity."

Dean Prosser's analysis has been a source of some confusion in the law. His first three types of the right of privacy generally protect the right "to be let alone," while the right of publicity protects the celebrity's pecuniary interest in the commercial exploitation of his identity. Thus, the right of privacy and the right of publicity protect fundamentally different interests and must be analyzed separately.

We do not believe that Carson's claim that his right of privacy has been invaded is supported by the law or the facts. Apparently, the gist of this claim is that Carson is embarrassed by and considers it odious to be associated with the appellee's product. Clearly, the association does not appeal to Carson's sense of humor. But the facts here presented do not, it appears to us, amount to an invasion of any of the interests protected by the right of privacy. In any event, our disposition of the claim of an invasion of the right of publicity makes it unnecessary for us to accept or reject the claim of an invasion of the right of privacy.

The right of publicity has developed to protect the commercial interest of celebrities in their identities. The theory of the right is that

1. Michigan law, which governs these claims, has not yet clearly addressed the right of publicity. But the general recognition of the right, see W. Prosser, Handbook of the Law of Torts § 117, at 805 (4th ed. 1971), suggests to us that the Michigan courts would adopt the right. Michigan has recognized a right of privacy.

a celebrity's identity can be valuable in the promotion of products, and the celebrity has an interest that may be protected from the unauthorized commercial exploitation of that identity. In Memphis Development Foundation v. Factors Etc., Inc., 616 F.2d 956 (6th Cir.), cert. denied, 449 U.S. 953, 101 S.Ct. 358, 66 L.Ed.2d 217 (1980), we stated: "The famous have an exclusive legal right during life to control and profit from the commercial use of their name and personality." Id. at 957.

The district court dismissed appellants' claim based on the right of publicity because appellee does not use Carson's name or likeness. It held that it "would not be prudent to allow recovery for a right of publicity claim which does not more specifically identify Johnny Carson." We believe that, on the contrary, the district court's conception of the right of publicity is too narrow. The right of publicity, as we have stated, is that a celebrity has a protected pecuniary interest in the commercial exploitation of his identity. If the celebrity's identity is commercially exploited, there has been an invasion of his right whether or not his "name or likeness" is used. Carson's identity may be exploited even if his name, John W. Carson, or his picture is not used.

In Motschenbacher v. R.J. Reynolds Tobacco Co., 498 F.2d 821 (9th Cir.1974), the court held that the unauthorized use of a picture of a distinctive race car of a well known professional race car driver, whose name or likeness were not used, violated his right of publicity. In this connection, the court said:

> We turn now to the question of 'identifiability.' Clearly, if the district court correctly determined as a matter of law that plaintiff is not identifiable in the commercial, then in no sense has plaintiff's identity been misappropriated nor his interest violated.

> Having viewed a film of the commercial, we agree with the district court that the 'likeness' of plaintiff is itself unrecognizable; however, the court's further conclusion of law to the effect that the driver is not identifiable as plaintiff is erroneous in that it wholly fails to attribute proper significance to the distinctive decorations appearing on the car. As pointed out earlier, these markings were not only peculiar to the plaintiff's cars but they caused some persons to think the car in question was plaintiff's and to infer that the person driving the car was the plaintiff.

Id. at 826–827 (footnote omitted).

In Ali v. Playgirl, Inc., 447 F.Supp. 723 (S.D.N.Y.1978), Muhammad Ali, former heavyweight champion, sued Playgirl magazine under the New York "right of privacy" statute and also alleged a violation of his common law right of publicity. The magazine published a drawing of a nude, black male sitting on a stool in a corner of a boxing ring with hands taped and arms outstretched on the ropes. The district court concluded that Ali's right of publicity was invaded because the drawing sufficiently identified him in spite of the fact that the drawing was captioned "Mystery Man." The district court found that the identification of Ali was made certain because of an accompanying verse that identified the figure as "The Greatest." The district court took judicial notice of the fact that "Ali has regularly claimed that appellation for himself." Id. at 727.

In Hirsch v. S.C. Johnson & Son, Inc., 90 Wis.2d 379, 280 N.W.2d 129 (1979), the court held that use by defendant of the name "Crazylegs" on a shaving gel for women violated plaintiff's right of publicity. Plaintiff, Elroy Hirsch, a famous football player, had been known by this nickname. The court said:

> The fact that the name, 'Crazylegs,' used by Johnson, was a nickname rather than Hirsch's actual name does not preclude a cause of action. All that is required is that the name clearly identify the wronged person. In the instant case, it is not disputed at this juncture of the case that the nickname identified the plaintiff Hirsch. It is argued that there were others who were known by the same name. This, however, does not vitiate the existence of a cause of action. It may, however, if sufficient proof were adduced, affect the quantum of damages should the jury impose liability or it might preclude liability altogether. Prosser points out 'that a stage or other fictitious name can be so identified with the plaintiff that he is entitled to protection against its use.' 49 Cal.L.Rev., supra at 404. He writes that it would be absurd to say that Samuel L. Clemens would have a cause of action if that name had been used in advertising, but he would not have one for the use of 'Mark Twain.' If a fictitious name is used in a context which tends to indicate that the name is that of the plaintiff, the factual case for identity is strengthened.

280 N.W.2d at 137.

In this case, Earl Braxton, president and owner of Here's Johnny Portable Toilets, Inc., admitted that he knew that the phrase "Here's Johnny" had been used for years to introduce Carson. Moreover, in the opening statement in the district court, appellee's counsel stated:

> Now, we've stipulated in this case that the public tends to associate the words 'Johnny Carson', the words 'Here's Johnny' with plaintiff, John Carson and, Mr. Braxton, in his deposition, admitted that he knew that and probably absent that identification, he would not have chosen it.

That the "Here's Johnny" name was selected by Braxton because of its identification with Carson was the clear inference from Braxton's testimony irrespective of such admission in the opening statement.

We therefore conclude that, applying the correct legal standards, appellants are entitled to judgment. The proof showed without question that appellee had appropriated Carson's identity in connection with its corporate name and its product. . . .

The judgment of the district court is vacated and the case remanded for further proceedings consistent with this opinion.

CORNELIA G. KENNEDY, Circuit Judge, dissenting.

I respectfully dissent from that part of the majority's opinion which holds that appellee's use of the phrase "Here's Johnny" violates appellant Johnny Carson's common law right of publicity. While I agree that an individual's identity may be impermissibly exploited, I do not believe that the common law right of publicity may be extended beyond an individual's name, likeness, achievements, identifying characteristics or actual performances, to include phrases or other things which are merely associated with the individual, as is the phrase "Here's Johnny." The majority's extension of the right of publicity to include phrases or other things which are merely associated with the individual permits a popular entertainer or public figure, by associating himself or herself with a common phrase, to remove those words from the public domain.

The phrase "Here's Johnny" is merely associated with Johnny Carson, the host and star of "The Tonight Show" broadcast by the National Broadcasting Company. Since 1962, the opening format of "The Tonight Show," after the theme music is played, is to introduce Johnny Carson with the phrase "Here's Johnny." The words are spoken by an announcer, generally Ed McMahon, in a drawn out and distinctive manner. Immediately after the phrase "Here's Johnny" is spoken, Johnny Carson appears to begin the program. This method of introduction was first used by Johnny Carson in 1957 when he hosted a daily television show for the American Broadcasting Company. This case is not transformed into a "name" case simply because the diminutive form of John W. Carson's given name and the first name of his full stage name, Johnny Carson, appears in it. The first name is so common, in light of the millions of persons named John, Johnny or Jonathan that no doubt inhabit this world, that, alone, it is meaningless or ambiguous at best in identifying Johnny Carson, the celebrity. In addition, the phrase containing Johnny Carson's first stage name was certainly selected for its value as a double entendre. Appellee manufactures portable toilets. The value of the phrase to appellee's product is in the risqué meaning of "john" as a toilet or bathroom. For this reason, too, this is not a "name" case.

Appellee has stipulated that the phrase "Here's Johnny" is associated with Johnny Carson and that absent this association, he would not have chosen to use it for his product and corporation, Here's Johnny Portable Toilets, Inc. I do not consider it relevant that appellee intentionally chose to incorporate into the name of his corporation and product a phrase that is merely associated with Johnny Carson. What is not protected by law is not taken from public use. Research reveals no case in which the right of publicity has been extended to phrases or other things which are merely associated with an individual and are not part of his name, likeness, achievements, identifying characteristics or actual performances. Both the policies behind the right of publicity and countervailing interests and considerations indicate that such an extension should not be made.

I. Policies Behind Right of Publicity

The three primary policy considerations behind the right of publicity are succinctly stated in Hoffman, Limitations on the Right of Publicity, 28 Bull. Copr. Soc'y, 111, 116–22 (1980). First, "the right of publicity vindicates the economic interests of celebrities, enabling those whose achievements have imbued their identities with pecuniary value to profit from their fame." Id. 116. Second, the right of publicity fosters "the production of intellectual and creative works by providing the financial incentive for individuals to expend the time and resources necessary to produce them." Limitations on the Right of Publicity, supra, 118. Third, "[t]he right of publicity serves both individual and societal interests by preventing what our legal tradition regards as wrongful conduct: unjust enrichment and deceptive trade practices." Limitations on the Right of Publicity, supra, 118.

None of the above-mentioned policy arguments supports the extension of the right of publicity to phrases or other things which are merely associated with an individual. First, the majority is awarding Johnny Carson a windfall, rather than vindicating his economic interests, by protecting the phrase "Here's Johnny" which is merely associated with him. In *Zacchini*, the Supreme Court stated that a mechanism to vindicate an individual's economic rights is indicated where the appropriated thing is "the product of . . . [the individual's] own talents and energy, the end result of much time, effort and expense." *Zacchini*, supra, 433 U.S. at 575, 97 S.Ct. at 2857. There is nothing in the record to suggest that "Here's Johnny" has any nexus to Johnny Carson other than being the introduction to his personal appearances. The phrase is not part of an identity that he created. In its content "Here's Johnny" is a very simple and common introduction. The content of the phrase neither originated with Johnny Carson nor is it confined to the world of entertainment. The phrase is not said by Johnny Carson, but said of him. Its association with him is derived, in large part, by the context in which it is said—generally by Ed McMahon in a drawn out and distinctive voice after the theme music to "The Tonight Show" is played, and immediately prior to Johnny Carson's own entrance. Appellee's use of the content "Here's Johnny," in light of its value as a double entendre, written on its product and corporate name, and therefore outside of the context in which it is associated with Johnny Carson, does little to rob Johnny Carson of something which is unique to him or a product of his own efforts.

The second policy goal of fostering the production of creative and intellectual works is not met by the majority's rule because in awarding publicity rights in a phrase neither created by him nor performed by him, economic reward and protection is divorced from personal incentive to produce on the part of the protected and benefited individual. Johnny Carson is simply reaping the rewards of the time, effort and work product of others.

Third, the majority's extension of the right of publicity to include the phrase "Here's Johnny" which is merely associated with Johnny Carson is not needed to provide alternatives to existing legal avenues for redressing wrongful conduct. The existence of a cause of action under section 43(a) of the Lanham Act, 15 U.S.C.A. § 1125(a) (1976) and Michigan common law does much to undercut the need for policing against unfair competition through an additional legal remedy such as the right of publicity. The majority has concluded, and I concur, that the District Court was warranted in finding that there was not a reasonable likelihood that members of the public would be confused by appellee's use of the "Here's Johnny" trademark on a product as dissimilar to those licensed by Johnny Carson as portable toilets. In this case, this eliminates the argument of wrongdoing. Moreover, the majority's extension of the right of publicity to phrases and other things merely associated with an individual is not conditioned upon wrongdoing and would apply with equal force in the case of an unknowing user. With respect to unjust enrichment, because a celebrity such as Johnny Carson is himself enriched by phrases and other things associated with him in which he has made no personal investment of time, money or effort, another user of such a phrase or thing may be enriched somewhat by such use, but this enrichment is not at Johnny Carson's expense. The policies behind the right of publicity are not furthered by the majority's holding in this case.

II.　Countervailing Interests and Considerations

The right of publicity, whether tied to name, likeness, achievements, identifying characteristics or actual performances, etc. conflicts with the economic and expressive interests of others. Society's interests in free enterprise and free expression must be balanced against the interests of an individual seeking protection in the right of publicity where the right is being expanded beyond established limits. In addition, the right to publicity may be subject to federal preemption where it conflicts with the provisions of the Copyright Act of 1976.

A.　Federal Policy: Monopolies

Protection under the right of publicity creates a common law monopoly that removes items, words and acts from the public domain. That federal policy favors free enterprise was recently reaffirmed by the Supreme Court in National Society of Professional Engineers v. United States, 435 U.S. 679, 98 S.Ct. 1355, 55 L.Ed.2d 637 (1978), in which the Supreme Court indicated that outside of the "rule of reason," only those anticompetitive restraints expressly authorized by Congress would be permitted to stand. Concern for the impact of adopting an overbroad approach to the right of publicity was also indicated in this Court's decision in Memphis Development Foundation v. Factors Etc., Inc., 616 F.2d 956 (6th Cir.), cert. denied, 449 U.S. 953, 101 S.Ct. 358, 66 L.Ed.2d 217 (1980). In *Memphis Development*, this Court held that the right of publicity does not survive a celebrity's death under Tennessee law. In so holding, this Court recognized that commercial and competitive interests are potentially compromised by an expansive approach to the right of publicity. This Court was concerned that an extension of the right of publicity to the exclusive control of the celebrity's heirs might compromise the efficiency, productivity and fairness of our economic system without enlarging the stock or quality of the goods, services, artistic creativity, information, invention or entertainment available and detract from the equal distribution of economic opportunity available in a free market system. *Memphis Development* recognized that the grant of a right of publicity is tantamount to the grant of a monopoly, in that case, for the life of the celebrity. The majority's grant to Johnny Carson of a publicity right in the phrase "Here's Johnny" takes this phrase away from the public domain, giving him a common law monopoly for it, without extracting from Johnny Carson a personal contribution for the public's benefit.

Protection under the right of publicity confers a monopoly on the protected individual that is potentially broader, offers fewer protections and potentially competes with federal statutory monopolies. As an essential part of three federal monopoly rights, copyright, trademark and patents, notice to the public is required in the form of filing with the appropriate governmental office and use of an appropriate mark. This apprises members of the public of the nature and extent of what is being removed from the public domain and subject to claims of infringement. The right of publicity provides limited notice to the public of the extent of the monopoly right to be asserted, if one is to be asserted at all. As the right of privacy is expanded beyond protections of name, likeness and actual performances, which provide relatively objective notice to the public of the extent of an individual's rights, to more subjective attributes such as achievements and identifying characteristics, the public's ability to be on notice of a common law monopoly right, if one is even asserted by a given famous individual, is severely diminished. Protecting phrases and other things merely associated with an individual provides virtually no notice to the public at all of what is claimed to be protected. By ensuring the invocation of the adjudicative process whenever the commercial use of a phrase or other associated thing is considered to have been wrongfully appropriated, the public is left to act at their peril. The result is a chilling effect on commercial innovation and opportunity.

Also unlike the federal statutory monopolies, this common law monopoly right offers no protections against the monopoly existing for an indefinite time or even in perpetuity.

B. Federal Policy: Free Expression and Use of Intellectual Property

The first amendment protects the freedom of speech, including commercial speech. U.S. Const. amend. I; Goldfarb v. Virginia State Bar, 421 U.S. 773, 95 S.Ct. 2004, 44 L.Ed.2d 572 reh'g denied, 423 U.S. 886, 96 S.Ct. 162, 46 L.Ed.2d 118 (1975). Strong federal policy permits the free use of intellectual property, words and ideas that are in general circulation and not protected by a valid copyright, patent or trademark. The federal copyright statute only protects original works that fix the author's particular expression of an idea or concept in a tangible form. State statutory or common law protection against activities violating rights that are not equivalent to those granted under copyright law or protection of subject matter which is not copyrightable, including works that are not fixed in any tangible form of expression, are not preempted. 17 U.S.C.A. § 301(b) (1977). Apart from the technical arguments regarding preemption, if federal law and policy does not protect phrases such as "Here's Johnny," which is certainly not an original combination of words, state law should not protect them either under a right of publicity for want of a sufficient interest justifying protection. See U.S. Const., art. I, § 8 (purpose of copyright and patent laws is to "promote the Progress of Science and the useful Arts"); *Zacchini,* supra, 433 U.S. at 575, 576–77, 97 S.Ct. at 2857, 2858 (purpose of right of publicity is to promote production of works that benefit the public that are product of individual's own talents and energy). In addition, because copyright does not restrain the use of a mere idea or concept but only protects particular tangible expressions of an idea or concept, it has been held not to run afoul of first amendment challenges. The protected tangible expressions are asserted to not run afoul of first amendment challenges because the notice requirements and limited duration of copyright protection balances the interest of individuals seeking protection under the copyright clause and the first amendment. Because the phrase "Here's Johnny" is more akin to an idea or concept of introducing an individual than an original protectable fixed expression of that idea and because the right of publicity in this instance is not complemented by saving notice or duration requirements, phrases such as "Here's Johnny" should not be entitled to protection under the right of publicity as a matter of policy and concern for the first amendment.

Apart from the possibility of outright federal preemption, public policy requires that the public's interest in free enterprise and free expression take precedence over any interest Johnny Carson may have in a phrase associated with his person.

III. Case Law

The common law right of publicity has been held to protect various aspects of an individual's identity from commercial exploitation: name, likeness, achievements, identifying characteristics, actual performances, and fictitious characters created by a performer. Research reveals no case which has extended the right of publicity to phrases and other things which are merely associated with an individual.

The three cases cited by the majority in reaching their conclusion that the right of privacy should be extended to encompass phrases and other things merely associated with an individual and one other case merit further comment. Hirsch v. S.C. Johnson & Son, Inc., 90 Wis.2d

379, 280 N.W.2d 129 (1979), Ali v. Playgirl, Inc., 447 F.Supp. 723 (S.D. N.Y.1978), and Motschenbacher v. R.J. Reynolds Tobacco Co., 498 F.2d 821 (9th Cir.1974), are factually and legally distinguishable from the case on appeal. *Hirsch* simply stands for the principle accepted by the commentators, if not by the courts, that the right of publicity extends not only to an individual's name but to a nickname or stage name as well. *Hirsch* required that the name clearly identify the wronged person. *Hirsch* goes on to state that if a fictitious name is used, context may be sufficient to link the fictitious name with the complaining individual, and therefore give rise to protection under a right of publicity. In the *Hirsch* case, context supplied the missing link which is not present here. Hirsch, a/k/a "Crazylegs," was a famous football player and all around athlete. He is described as the superstar of the era. He made a number of commercials and advertisements during his career and a movie was produced on his life. His unique running style, which was described by the *Hirsch* court as looking something like a whirling egg-beater, earned him his nickname. The defendant in *Hirsch*, S.C. Johnson & Son, marketed a moisturizing shaving gel for women under the name of "Crazylegs." The context linking this product to Hirsch was Johnson's first promotion of its product at a running event for women, the use of a cheer in a television commercial similar to the "Crazylegs" cheer initiated at a college where Hirsch became athletic director, and the fact that the product was for women's legs. Based on this evidence of "context," the Wisconsin appellate court found a question of fact for the jury as to whether "Crazylegs" identified Hirsch. In this case, not only is the majority not dealing with a nickname or a stage name, but there is not a scintilla of evidence to support the context requirement of *Hirsch*. Appellee has only used the content of the "Here's Johnny" phrase on its product and its corporate name as transfigured by the double meaning of "John."

    In *Ali*, Muhammad Ali sought protection under the right of publicity for the unauthorized use of his picture in Playgirl Magazine. *Ali* is a "likeness" case reinforced by the context in which the likeness occurs and further bolstered by a phrase, "the Greatest," commonly stated by Ali regarding himself. The essence of the case, and the unauthorized act from which Ali claims protection, is a drawing of a nude black man seated in the corner of a boxing ring with both hands taped and outstretched resting on the ropes on either side. The *Ali* court found that even a cursory inspection of the picture suggests that the facial characteristics of the man are those of Ali. The court stated: "The cheekbones, broad nose and wideset brown eyes, together with the distinctive smile and close cropped black hair are recognizable as the features of . . . [Ali]." *Ali* supra, 726. Augmenting this likeness and reinforcing its identification with Ali was the context in which the likeness appeared—a boxing ring. The court found that identification of the individual depicted as Ali was further implied by the accompanying phrase "the Greatest." Based on these facts, the court had no difficulty concluding that the drawing was Ali's portrait or picture. To the extent the majority uses the phrase "the Greatest" to support its position that the right of publicity encompasses phrases or other things which are merely associated with an individual, they misstate the law of *Ali.* Once again, *Ali* is clearly a "likeness" case. To the extent the likeness was not a photographic one free from all ambiguity, identification with Muhammad Ali was reinforced by context and a phrase "the Greatest" stated by Ali about himself. The result in that case is so dependent on the identifying features in the drawing and the boxing context in which the man is portrayed that the phrase "the Greatest" may not be severed from this whole and the legal propositions developed by the *Ali* court in response to the whole applied to the phrase alone. To be analogous, a likeness of Johnny Carson would be required in addition to the words "Here's Johnny" suggesting the context of "The Tonight Show" or the *Ali* court would have to have enjoined all others from using the phrase "the Greatest." In short, *Ali* does not support the majority's holding.

Motschenbacher, the third case cited by the majority, is an "identifying characteristics" case. Motschenbacher, a professional driver of racing cars who is internationally known, sought protection in the right of publicity for the unauthorized use of a photograph of his racing car, slightly altered, in a televised cigarette commercial. Although he was in fact driving the car at the time it was photographed, his facial features are not visible in the commercial. The Ninth Circuit found as a matter of California law, that the right of publicity extended to protect the unauthorized use of photographs of Motschenbacher's racing car as one of his identifying characteristics. Identifying characteristics, such as Motschenbacher's racing car, are not synonymous with phrases or other things which are merely associated with an individual. In *Motschenbacher,* the Ninth Circuit determined that the car driver had "consistently 'individualized' his cars to set them apart from those of other drivers and to make them more readily identifiable as his own." Since 1966, each car had a distinctive narrow white pinstripe appearing on no other car. This decoration has always been in the same place on the car bodies, which have uniformly been red. In addition, his racing number "11" has always been against an oval background in contrast to the circular white background used by other drivers. In the commercial, the photo of Motschenbacher's car was altered so that the number "11" was changed to "71," a spoiler with the name "Winston" was added, and other advertisements removed. The remainder of the individualized decorations remained the same. Despite these alterations, the Ninth Circuit determined that car possessed identifying characteristics *peculiar* to Motschenbacher. This case is factually and legally distinguishable from the case on appeal. Motschenbacher's racing car was not merely associated with him but was the vehicle, literally and figuratively, by which he achieved his fame. The identifying characteristics, in the form of several decorations peculiar to his car, were the product of his personal time, energy, effort and expense and as such are inextricably interwoven with him as his individual work product, rather than being merely associated with him. Furthermore, the number and combination of the peculiar decorations on his cars results in a set of identifying characteristics, which although inanimate, are unique enough to resist duplication other than by intentional copying. This uniqueness provides notice to the public of what is claimed as part of his publicity right, as does an individual's name, likeness or actual performance, and narrowly limits the scope of his monopoly. In contrast to *Motschenbacher,* Johnny Carson's fame as a comedian and talk show host is severable from the phrase with which he is associated, "Here's Johnny." This phrase is not Johnny Carson's "thumbprint"; it is not his work product; it is not original; it is a common, simple combination of a direct object, a contracted verb and a common first name; divorced from context, it is two dimensional and ambiguous. It can hardly be said to be a symbol or synthesis, *i.e.,* a tangible "expression" of the "idea," of Johnny Carson the comedian and talk show host, as Motschenbacher's racing car was the tangible expression of the man.

Finally, Lombardo v. Doyle, Dane & Bernbach, Inc., 58 A.D.2d 620, 396 N.Y.S.2d 661 (App.Div.1977), which although not cited by the majority is discussed by a number of the commentators with the cases cited by the majority, does not go so far as to extend the right of publicity to phrases or things which are merely associated with an individual. In *Lombardo,* an advertising agency and foreign automobile manufacturer entered into negotiations with the band leader, Guy Lombardo, for the purpose of producing a television commercial designed to depict Lombardo and his orchestra in New Year's Eve party hats, playing "Auld Lang Syne" while models of cars rotated in the foreground. After negotiations between the parties fell through, the agency and manufacturer proceeded with the commercial. An actor was employed to lead a band playing "Auld Lang Syne" in the same musical beat as developed by Lombardo, using the same gestures as Lombardo employed in conducting his band. Lombardo then instituted suit claiming that the agency and manufacturer had used a "likeness and representation" of himself without his consent, violating his statutory right to privacy under New York law and his common law right to be free from the misappropriation of his cultivated public persona as "Mr. New Year's Eve." The *Lombardo* court found no statutory violation but did find a cause of action to be stated under Lombardo's common law theory. *Lombardo* appears to be in part a "likeness" case based on impersonation reinforced by context, and in part an "identifying characteristics" case like *Motschenbacher.* The "likeness" aspect comes from the actor portraying a band leader, Lombardo's profession and vehicle for his fame, while using the same gestures employed by Lombardo and a musical beat linked to him. As in *Ali,* likeness is reinforced by context—the trappings of New Year's Eve, balloons, party hats and the band playing "Auld Lang Syne." Like *Motschenbacher,* Lombardo's gestures while conducting are part of his "thumbprint" and his musical beat and rendition of "Auld Lang Syne" on New Year's Eve are probably inseverable from his fame. *Lombardo,* however, is a less compelling case for finding a right of privacy than *Motschenbacher* and has similarities to the case on appeal. Unlike the several individualized decorations on Motschenbacher's car, only the conducting gestures and musical beat are unique to Lombardo. The very elements that he urged tied him to his persona as "Mr. New Year's Eve" are not peculiar to him but are shared with numerous band leaders on New Year's Eve—balloons, party hats and "Auld Lang Syne." The commonness of these crucial alleged "identifying characteristics" undercuts the value of their combination by Lombardo. In *Motschenbacher,* the combination of several individualized decorations peculiar to Motschenbacher resulted in relatively clear notice to the public of what the extent of Motschenbacher's monopoly right was and resulted in this monopoly right being very narrow; it protected only the unauthorized use of photographs or depictions of a particular set of identical cars. In contrast, in *Lombardo,* the net result of the court's opinion would seem to be that Lombardo has a monopoly right enforceable against anyone who wishes to duplicate a band leader playing "Auld Lang Syne" amid the trappings of a New Year's Eve party. The *Lombardo* court did not explore the anticompetitive or free expression ramifications of its decision. As with the holiday New Year's Eve, the song "Auld Lang Syne" and party trappings such as balloons and party hats in *Lombardo,* the phrase "Here's Johnny" is very common and hardly peculiar to a particular individual. Unlike the combination of common and unique (gestures and musical beat) elements in *Lombardo,* the phrase "Here's Johnny" as used here does not exist in combination with other elements, with the exception of the pun, the "Great Commodian," an indirect reference to Johnny Carson, to narrow the monopoly right proposed or apprise the public of what is claimed. Unlike the situation in *Motschenbacher* and *Lombardo,* the phrase contains nothing personal to Carson in the sense of being caused by him or a product of his time, effort and energies. Therefore, while questioning the merits of extending the right of privacy as far as the court did in *Lombardo,* primarily for the court's lack of policy analysis concerning anticompetitive consequences and first amendment problems, I believe that *Lombardo* is distinguishable.

Accordingly, neither policy nor case law supports the extension of the right of publicity to encompass phrases and other things merely associated with an individual as in this case. I would affirm the judgment of the District Court on this basis as well.

NOTES

1. Celebrity often provides its own abundant rewards in the form of fees and salaries. It is the rare celebrity who would curb his activities if he were denied property rights in his persona. Does this suggest that unjust enrichment is the only true rationale for the right of publicity and that there is little room for the other rationales noted in Judge Kennedy's dissenting opinion? Even if celebrities do not need a property incentive to invest in developing their public personas, can the right of publicity be justified by the needs of their licensees? Would the operators of the "Here's Johnny" restaurant chain have

been willing to invest in promoting that name without a licensed property right from the entertainer?

The celebrity who receives the economic reward generated by the right of publicity will not always be the individual who invested in creating the protected persona. Judge Kennedy observed in a footnote to her *Carson* dissent that "Ed McMahon arguably has a competing publicity interest" in the "Here's Johnny" phrase "because it is said by him in a distinctive and drawn out manner as his introduction to entertainers who appear on 'The Tonight Show,' including Johnny Carson." 698 F.2d at 839 n. 5. Who should be entitled to publicity rights in the motion picture character, Count Dracula—the actor, Bela Lugosi, whose likeness as the Count was exploited by licensees, or the motion picture producer who helped shape, promote and give content to the Count's appearance? See Lugosi v. Universal Pictures, 25 Cal.3d 813, 160 Cal.Rptr. 323, 603 P.2d 425, 205 U.S.P.Q. 1090 (1979).

The authoritative treatise on the right of publicity is J.T. McCarthy, The Rights of Publicity and Privacy (1987).

2. In one form or another, the right of publicity has been adopted by common law, statute or both in close to half the states. See P. Goldstein, Copyright § 15.17 (1989). The right of publicity overlaps other bodies of tort and intellectual property law—the right of privacy, unfair competition and trademark law, and statutory and common law copyright. If Carson had been able to show that the defendant's use of the phrase, "Here's Johnny" placed the entertainer in a false light, he might have prevailed on a privacy theory. Had he been able to show that the phrase had acquired a secondary meaning, he might have prevailed on an unfair competition or trademark theory. Had the phrase been more expressively elaborated, it might have qualified for protection under a statutory or common law copyright theory.

3. *Right of Publicity in Voice.* The common law and statutory right of publicity traditionally encompass an individual's name and likeness. Some states protect other elements of an individual's persona. California's statute, for example, protects an individual's "name, voice, signature, photograph, or likeness" Cal.Civ.Code §§ 990(a), 3344(a) (West Supp.1989). Nebraska's statute protects against commercial exploitation of "a natural person, name, picture, portrait, or personality." Neb.Rev.Stat. § 20–202 (1987).

Early decisions held that the right of publicity did not protect against imitations of a celebrity's voice, and that a plaintiff in these circumstances could recover only on an unfair competition theory. In Lahr v. Adell Chem. Co., 300 F.2d 256, 132 U.S.P.Q. 662 (1st Cir.1962), plaintiff Bert Lahr complained that "defendant Adell Chemical Company, in advertising its product 'Lestoil' on television, used as a commercial a cartoon film of a duck and, without the plaintiff's consent 'as the voice of the aforesaid duck, an actor who specialized in imitating the vocal sounds of the plaintiff.'" Reading New York's privacy statute literally, to cover only a "name, portrait or picture," the court concluded that plaintiff might instead recover on his unfair competition count.

"Plaintiff's complaint is that defendant is 'stealing his thunder' in the direct sense; that defendant's commercial had greater value because his audience believed it was listening to him. . . . It could well be found that defendant's conduct saturated plaintiff's audience to the point of curtailing his market." 300 F.2d at 257–59. See also Sinatra v. Goodyear Tire and Rubber Co., 435 F.2d 711, 168 U.S.P.Q. 12 (9th Cir. 1970), cert. denied, 402 U.S. 906, 91 S.Ct. 1376, 28 L.Ed.2d 646, 169 U.S. P.Q. 321 (1971).

More recently, one court has held that the right of publicity extends to "sound-alikes." In Midler v. Ford Motor Co., 849 F.2d 460, 7 U.S.P.Q.2d 1398 (9th Cir.1988), the defendant, having been rebuffed in its efforts to get popular singer, Bette Midler, to perform in one of its commercials a song that she had popularized, obtained the services of another singer, Ula Hedwig, whose performance of the song sounded like a Midler performance. The court ruled that Midler could recover on a common law, rather than statutory, right of publicity theory. While holding that California's publicity statute, which protects against the unauthorized use of an individual's voice, did not help Midler—the "voice they used was Hedwig's, not hers"—the court concluded that "when a distinctive voice of a professional singer is widely known and is deliberately imitated in order to sell a product, the sellers have appropriated what is not theirs and have committed a tort in California." 849 F.2d at 463. Do you agree with the court that the defendant did not use the plaintiff's voice?

4. *Identifiability.* A defendant will violate the right to publicity only if it appropriates those elements that identify the plaintiff to the public. In one case a court held that a woodcarver named T.J. Hooker had no cause of action against the producer of a television series, "T.J. Hooker," featuring a fictional policeman, T.J. Hooker, as its star. The "facts and circumstances alleged by plaintiff provide no basis upon which it can be found that the name 'T.J. Hooker,' as used in the defendants' fictional television series, in any way refers to the real T.J. Hooker." T.J. Hooker v. Columbia Pictures Indus., 551 F.Supp. 1060, 1062 (N.D.Ill.1982). Similarly, the *Carson* court observed that the defendant would not have violated Carson's right of publicity if it had used plaintiff's name, "such as 'J. William Carson Portable Toilet' or the 'John William Carson Portable Toilet' or the 'J.W. Carson Portable Toilet.' The reason is that, though literally using appellant's 'name,' the appellee would not have appropriated Carson's identity as a celebrity." 698 F.2d at 837.

The identifiability requirement may raise thorny questions in cases involving celebrity "look-alikes." Will an individual's resemblance to a celebrity enable her to cash in on the value of the celebrity's identity or disable her from making any commercial use of her own identity? In Onassis v. Christian Dior–New York, Inc., 122 Misc.2d 603, 472 N.Y.S.2d 254 (Sup.Ct.1984), the court enjoined defendant's magazine advertisement portraying a model who bore a striking resemblance to the public figure, Jacqueline Kennedy Onassis. Allen v. National Video, Inc., 610 F.Supp. 612, 226 U.S.P.Q. 483 (S.D.N.Y.1985), involving a claim by Woody Allen against defendant's use of a "look-alike" in advertisements for its video rental chain, distinguished *Onassis:*

> When as in *Onassis,* the look-alike seems indistinguishable from the real person and the context of the advertisement clearly implies that he or she is the real celebrity, a court may hold as a matter of law that the look-alike's face is a 'portrait or picture' of plaintiff. *Onassis* presented an unusual factual setting, in which the mixture of fantasy and reality suggested almost unavoidably the actual presence of the real-life celebrity. In order for the court to reach the same conclusion in the present case, it must conclude on the undisputed facts that the photograph in question similarly creates, as a matter of law, the illusion of Woody Allen's actual presence in the advertisement.

610 F.Supp. at 623–24.

5. *Remedies.* Statutes and common law offer coercive and monetary relief for violations of the right to publicity. Courts grant permanent injunctions freely on the premise that publicity interests are unique and that the computation of damages will be problematic. One court, applying the New York statute, held that once a plaintiff establishes a violation she "may have an absolute right to injunction, regardless of the relative damage to the parties." Onassis v. Christian Dior–New York, Inc., 122 Misc.2d 603, 607, 472 N.Y.S.2d 254, 258 (Sup. Ct.1984). Some statutes authorize courts to impound offending materials and, if the plaintiff prevails on the merits, to destroy or make other reasonable disposition of the offending materials and of articles used to produce the materials. See Tenn.Code Ann. § 47–25–1106(b), (c) (1988).

Courts will measure damages for right of publicity violations by a reasonable royalty or market value. Courts may also award any profits earned by the infringer from its unauthorized use of the plaintiff's persona. In many states a plaintiff can recover exemplary damages if he can show that the defendant acted knowingly. Statutes in some states authorize the award of attorney's fees to prevailing plaintiffs, and in other states make attorney's fees awardable to any prevailing party, plaintiff or defendant. Compare Wis.Stat.Ann. § 895.50(1)(c) (West 1983) with Cal.Civ.Code §§ 990(a), 3344(a) (West Supp.1988).

B. LIMITS OF PROTECTION

ZACCHINI v. SCRIPPS–HOWARD BROADCASTING CO.

Supreme Court of the United States, 1977.
433 U.S. 562, 97 S.Ct. 2849, 53 L.Ed.2d 965, 205 U.S.P.Q. 741.

Mr. Justice WHITE delivered the opinion of the Court.

Petitioner, Hugo Zacchini, is an entertainer. He performs a "human cannonball" act in which he is shot from a cannon into a net some 200 feet away. Each performance occupies some 15 seconds. In August and September 1972, petitioner was engaged to perform his act on a regular basis at the Geauga County Fair in Burton, Ohio. He performed in a fenced area, surrounded by grandstands, at the fair grounds. Members of the public attending the fair were not charged a separate admission fee to observe his act.

On August 30, a freelance reporter for Scripps–Howard Broadcasting Co., the operator of a television broadcasting station and respondent in this case, attended the fair. He carried a small movie camera. Petitioner noticed the reporter and asked him not to film the performance. The reporter did not do so on that day; but on the instructions of the producer of respondent's daily newscast, he returned the following day and videotaped the entire act. This film clip, approximately 15 seconds in length, was shown on the 11 o'clock news program that night, together with favorable commentary.

Petitioner then brought this action for damages, alleging that he is "engaged in the entertainment business," that the act he performs is one "invented by his father and . . . performed only by his family for the last fifty years," that respondent "showed and commercialized the film of his act without his consent," and that such conduct was an "unlawful appropriation of plaintiff's professional property." Respondent answered and moved for summary judgment, which was granted by the trial court.

The Court of Appeals of Ohio reversed. The majority held that petitioner's complaint stated a cause of action for conversion and for infringement of a common-law copyright, and one judge concurred in the judgment on the ground that the complaint stated a cause of action for appropriation of petitioner's "right of publicity" in the film of his act. All three judges agreed that the First Amendment did not privilege the press to show the entire performance on a news program without compensating petitioner for any financial injury he could prove at trial.

Like the concurring judge in the Court of Appeals, the Supreme Court of Ohio rested petitioner's cause of action under state law on his "right to publicity value of his performance." 47 Ohio St.2d 224, 351 N.E.2d 454, 455 (1976). The opinion syllabus, to which we are to look for the rule of law used to decide the case, declared first that one may not use for his own benefit the name or likeness of another, whether or not the use or benefit is a commercial one, and second that respondent would be liable for the appropriation, over petitioner's objection and in the absence of license or privilege, of petitioner's right to the publicity value of his performance. The court nevertheless gave judgment for respondent because, in the words of the syllabus:

> A TV station has a privilege to report in its newscasts matters of legitimate public interest which would otherwise be protected by an individual's right of publicity, unless the actual intent of the TV station was to appropriate the benefit of the publicity for some non-privileged private use, or unless the actual intent was to injure the individual.

We granted certiorari, to consider an issue unresolved by this Court: whether the First and Fourteenth Amendments immunized respondent from damages for its alleged infringement of petitioner's state-law "right of publicity." Insofar as the Ohio Supreme Court held that the First and Fourteenth Amendments of the United States Constitution required judgment for respondent, we reverse the judgment of that court. . . .

The Ohio Supreme Court held that respondent is constitutionally privileged to include in its newscasts matters of public interest that would otherwise be protected by the right of publicity, absent an intent to injure or to appropriate for some nonprivileged purpose. If under this standard respondent had merely reported that petitioner was performing at the fair and described or commented on his act, with or without showing his picture on television, we would have a very different case. But petitioner is not contending that his appearance at the fair and his performance could not be reported by the press as newsworthy items. His complaint is that respondent filmed his entire act and displayed that film on television for the public to see and enjoy. This, he claimed, was an appropriation of his professional property. The Ohio Supreme Court agreed that petitioner had "a right of publicity" that gave him "personal control over commercial display and exploitation of his personality and the exercise of his talents." This right of "exclusive control over the publicity given to his performances" was said to be such a "valuable part of the benefit which may be attained by his talents and efforts" that it was entitled to legal protection. It was also observed, or at least expressly assumed, that petitioner had not abandoned his rights by performing under the circumstances present at the Geauga County Fair Grounds.

The Ohio Supreme Court nevertheless held that the challenged invasion was privileged, saying that the press "must be accorded broad latitude in its choice of how much it presents of each story or incident, and of the emphasis to be given to such presentation. No fixed standard which would bar the press from reporting or depicting either an entire occurrence or an entire discrete part of a public performance can be formulated which would not unduly restrict the 'breathing room' in reporting which freedom of the press requires." 47 Ohio St.2d, at 235, 351 N.E.2d, at 461. Under this view, respondent was thus constitutionally free to film and display petitioner's entire act.

The Ohio Supreme Court relied heavily on Time, Inc. v. Hill, 385 U.S. 374, 87 S.Ct. 534, 17 L.Ed.2d 456 (1967), but that case does not mandate a media privilege to televise a performer's entire act without his consent. Involved in Time, Inc. v. Hill was a claim under the New York "Right to Privacy" statute that Life Magazine, in the course of reviewing a new play, had connected the play with a long-past incident involving petitioner and his family and had falsely described their experience and conduct at that time. The complaint sought damages for humiliation and suffering flowing from these nondefamatory falsehoods that allegedly invaded Hill's privacy. The Court held, however, that the opening of a new play linked to an actual incident was a matter of public interest and that Hill could not recover without showing that the Life report was knowingly false or was published with reckless disregard for the truth—the same rigorous standard that had been applied in New York Times Co. v. Sullivan, 376 U.S. 254, 84 S.Ct. 710, 11 L.Ed.2d 686 (1964).

Time, Inc. v. Hill, which was hotly contested and decided by a divided Court, involved an entirely different tort from the "right of publicity" recognized by the Ohio Supreme Court. As the opinion reveals in Time, Inc. v. Hill, the Court was steeped in the literature of privacy law and was aware of the developing distinctions and nuances in this branch of the law. The Court, for example, cited W. Prosser, Law of Torts 831–832 (3d ed. 1964), and the same author's well-known article, Privacy, 48 Calif.L.Rev. 383 (1960), both of which divided privacy into four distinct branches. The Court was aware that it was adjudicating a "false light" privacy case involving a matter of public interest, not a case involving "intrusion," 385 U.S., at 384–385, n. 9, 87 S.Ct., at 539, "appropriation" of a name or likeness for the purposes of trade, id., at 381, 87 S.Ct., at 538, or "private details" about a non-newsworthy person or event, id., at 383 n. 7, 87 S.Ct. at 539. It is also abundantly clear that Time, Inc. v. Hill did not involve a performer, a person with a name having commercial value, or any claim to a "right of publicity." This discrete kind of "appropriation" case was plainly identified in the literature cited by the Court and had been adjudicated in the reported cases.

The differences between these two torts are important. First, the State's interests in providing a cause of action in each instance are different. "The interest protected" in permitting recovery for placing the plaintiff in a false light "is clearly that of reputation, with the same overtones of mental distress as in defamation." Prosser, supra, 48 Calif.L.Rev., at 400. By contrast, the State's interest in permitting a "right of publicity" is in protecting the proprietary interest of the individual in his act in part to encourage such entertainment. As we later note, the State's interest is closely analogous to the goals of patent and copyright law, focusing on the right of the individual to reap the reward of his endeavors and having little to do with protecting feelings or reputation. Second, the two torts differ in the degree to which they intrude on dissemination of information to the public. In "false light" cases the only way to protect the interests involved is to attempt to minimize publication of the damaging matter, while in "right of publicity" cases the only question is who gets to do the publishing. An entertainer such as petitioner usually has no objection to the widespread publication of his act as long as he gets the commercial benefit of such publication. Indeed, in the present case petitioner did not seek to enjoin the broadcast of his act; he simply sought compensation for the broadcast in the form of damages.

Nor does it appear that our later cases, such as Rosenbloom v. Metromedia, Inc., 403 U.S. 29, 91 S.Ct. 1811, 29 L.Ed.2d 296 (1971); Gertz v. Robert Welch, Inc., 418 U.S. 323, 94 S.Ct. 2997, 41 L.Ed.2d 789 (1974); and Time, Inc. v. Firestone, 424 U.S. 448, 96 S.Ct. 958, 47 L.Ed. 2d 154 (1976), require or furnish substantial support for the Ohio court's privilege ruling. These cases, like *New York Times,* emphasize the protection extended to the press by the First Amendment in defamation cases, particularly when suit is brought by a public official or a public figure. None of them involve an alleged appropriation by the press of a right of publicity existing under state law.

Moreover, Time, Inc. v. Hill, *New York Times, Metromedia, Gertz,* and *Firestone* all involved the reporting of events; in none of them was there an attempt to broadcast or publish an entire act for which the performer ordinarily gets paid. It is evident, and there is no claim here to the contrary, that petitioner's state-law right of publicity would not serve to prevent respondent from reporting the newsworthy facts about petitioner's act. Wherever the line in particular situations is to be drawn between media reports that are protected and those that are not, we are quite sure that the First and Fourteenth Amendments do not immunize the media when they broadcast a performer's entire act without his consent. The Constitution no more prevents a State from requiring respondent to compensate petitioner for broadcasting his act on television than it would privilege respondent to film and broadcast a copyrighted dramatic work without liability to the copyright owner, or to film and broadcast a prize fight, or a baseball game, where the promoters or the participants had other plans for publicizing the event. There are ample reasons for reaching this conclusion.

The broadcast of a film of petitioner's entire act poses a substantial threat to the economic value of that performance. As the Ohio court recognized, this act is the product of petitioner's own talents and energy, the end result of much time, effort, and expense. Much of its economic value lies in the "right of exclusive control over the publicity given to his performance"; if the public can see the act free on television, it will be less willing to pay to see it at the fair. The effect of a public broadcast of the performance is similar to preventing petitioner from charging an admission fee. "The rationale for [protecting the right of publicity] is the straightforward one of preventing unjust enrichment by the theft of good will. No social purpose is served by having the defendant get free some aspect of the plaintiff that would have market value and for which he would normally pay." Kalven, Privacy in Tort Law—Were Warren and Brandeis Wrong?, 31 Law & Contemp.Prob. 326, 331 (1966). Moreover, the broadcast of petitioner's entire performance, unlike the unauthorized use of another's name for purposes of trade or the incidental use of a name or picture by the press, goes to the heart of petitioner's ability to earn a living as an entertainer. Thus, in this case, Ohio has recognized what may be the strongest case for a "right of publicity"—involving, not the appropriation of an entertainer's reputation to enhance the attractiveness of a commercial product, but the appropriation of the very activity by which the entertainer acquired his reputation in the first place.

Of course, Ohio's decision to protect petitioner's right of publicity here rests on more than a desire to compensate the performer for the time and effort invested in his act; the protection provides an economic incentive for him to make the investment required to produce a performance of interest to the public. This same consideration underlies the patent and copyright laws long enforced by this Court. As the Court stated in Mazer v. Stein, 347 U.S. 201, 219, 74 S.Ct. 460, 471, 98 L.Ed. 630 (1954):

> The economic philosophy behind the clause empowering Congress to grant patents and copyrights is the conviction that encouragement of individual effort by personal gain is the best way to advance public welfare through the talents of authors and inventors in 'Science and useful Arts.' Sacrificial days devoted to such creative activities deserve rewards commensurate with the services rendered.

These laws perhaps regard the "reward to the owner [as] a secondary consideration," United States v. Paramount Pictures, 334 U.S. 131, 158, 68 S.Ct. 915, 929, 92 L.Ed. 1260 (1948), but they were "intended definitely to grant valuable, enforceable rights" in order to afford greater encouragement to the production of works of benefit to the public. Washingtonian Publishing Co. v. Pearson, 306 U.S. 30, 36, 59 S.Ct. 397, 400, 83 L.Ed. 470 (1939). The Constitution does not prevent Ohio from making a similar choice here in deciding to protect the entertainer's incentive in order to encourage the production of this type of work.

There is no doubt that entertainment, as well as news, enjoys First Amendment protection. It is also true that entertainment itself can be important news. But it is important to note that neither the public nor respondent will be deprived of the benefit of petitioner's performance as long as his commercial stake in his act is appropriately recognized. Petitioner does not seek to enjoin the broadcast of his performance; he simply wants to be paid for it. Nor do we think that a state-law damages remedy against respondent would represent a species of liability without fault contrary to the letter or spirit of Gertz v. Robert Welch, Inc., 418 U.S. 323, 94 S.Ct. 2997, 41 L.Ed.2d 789 (1974). Respondent knew that petitioner objected to televising his act but nevertheless displayed the entire film.

We conclude that although the State of Ohio may as a matter of its own law privilege the press in the circumstances of this case, the First and Fourteenth Amendments do not require it to do so.

Reversed.

Mr. Justice POWELL, with whom Mr. Justice BRENNAN and Mr. Justice MARSHALL join, dissenting.

Disclaiming any attempt to do more than decide the narrow case before us, the Court reverses the decision of the Supreme Court of Ohio based on repeated incantation of a single formula: "a performer's entire act." The holding today is summed up in one sentence:

> Wherever the line in particular situations is to be drawn between media reports that are protected and those that are not, we are quite sure that the First and Fourteenth Amendments do not immunize the media when they broadcast a performer's entire act without his consent.

I doubt that this formula provides a standard clear enough even for resolution of this case. In any event, I am not persuaded that the Court's opinion is appropriately sensitive to the First Amendment values at stake, and I therefore dissent.

Although the Court would draw no distinction, I do not view respondent's action as comparable to unauthorized commercial broadcasts of sporting events, theatrical performances, and the like where the broadcaster keeps the profits. There is no suggestion here that respondent made any such use of the film. Instead, it simply reported on what petitioner concedes to be a newsworthy event, in a way hardly surprising for a television station—by means of film coverage. The report was part of an ordinary daily news program, consuming a total of 15 seconds. It is a routine example of the press' fulfilling the informing function so vital to our system.

The Court's holding that the station's ordinary news report may give rise to substantial liability has disturbing implications, for the decision could lead to a degree of media self-censorship. Hereafter, whenever a television news editor is unsure whether certain film footage received from a camera crew might be held to portray an "entire act," he may decline coverage—even of clearly newsworthy events—or confine the broadcast to watered-down verbal reporting, perhaps with an occasional still picture. The public is then the loser. This is hardly the kind of news reportage that the First Amendment is meant to foster.

In my view the First Amendment commands a different analytical starting point from the one selected by the Court. Rather than begin with a quantitative analysis of the performer's behavior—is this or is this not his entire act?—we should direct initial attention to the actions of the news media: what use did the station make of the film footage? When a film is used, as here, for a routine portion of a regular news program, I would hold that the First Amendment protects the station from a "right of publicity" or "appropriation" suit, absent a strong showing by the plaintiff that the news broadcast was a subterfuge or cover for private or commercial exploitation.

I emphasize that this is a "reappropriation" suit, rather than one of the other varieties of "right of privacy" tort suits identified by Dean Prosser in his classic article. Prosser, Privacy, 48 Calif.L.Rev. 383 (1960). In those other causes of action the competing interests are considerably different. The plaintiff generally seeks to avoid any sort of public exposure, and the existence of constitutional privilege is therefore less likely to turn on whether the publication occurred in a news broadcast or in some other fashion. In a suit like the one before us, however, the plaintiff does not complain about the fact of exposure to the public, but rather about its timing or manner. He welcomes some publicity, but seeks to retain control over means and manner as a way to maximize for himself the monetary benefits that flow from such publication. But having made the matter public—having chosen, in essence, to make it newsworthy—he cannot, consistent with the First Amendment, complain of routine news reportage.

Since the film clip here was undeniably treated as news and since there is no claim that the use was subterfuge, respondent's actions were constitutionally privileged. I would affirm.

The opinion of Mr. Justice Stevens, dissenting, is omitted.

NOTES

1. Right of publicity statutes commonly forestall constitutional issues of the sort raised in *Zacchini* by prohibiting only unauthorized uses for trade or advertising purposes and by excusing uses made in connection with news and public affairs accounts. Compare N.Y.Civ. Rights Law § 51 (McKinney 1976) with Cal.Civ.Code § 3344(d) (West Supp.1989).

The New York Court of Appeals explored these nonconstitutional limitations in Stephano v. News Group Publications, 64 N.Y.2d 174, 485 N.Y.S.2d 220, 474 N.E.2d 580 (1984). The court held there that it did not constitute a trade or advertising purpose for defendant's magazine to publish a photograph of plaintiff modelling a jacket in a news feature about the jacket. Noting that the New York statute nowhere defines trade or advertising purposes, the court added that "courts have consistently held, from the time of its enactment, that these terms should not be construed to apply to publications concerning newsworthy events or matters of public interest."

In the *Stephano* court's view, the newsworthiness exception applies not only to reports of political happenings and social trends, but also to news stories and articles of consumer interest. Further, the "fact that the defendant may have included this item in its column solely or primarily to increase the circulation of its magazine and therefore its profits, as the Appellate Division suggested, does not mean that the defendant has used the plaintiff's picture for trade purposes within the meaning of the statute. Indeed, most publications seek to increase their circulation and also their profits. It is the content of the article and not the defendant's motive or primary motive to increase circulation which determines whether it is a newsworthy item, as opposed to a trade usage, under the Civil Rights Law." 64 N.Y.2d at 184–85.

2. The *Zacchini* Court displayed a striking indifference to the impact of the Constitution's supremacy clause on the right of publicity. Should the Court have held that the state right of publicity was preempted under the principles announced in *Sears* and *Compco*, pages 103, 107, above? *Zacchini* did not involve the garden variety subject matter of publicity lawsuits—an individual's name or likeness—but rather a relatively lengthy and elaborate act. Indeed the intermediate state court held that the act qualified for protection on a common law copyright theory. 47 Ohio St.2d 224, 351 N.E.2d 454, 193 U.S.P.Q. 734 (1976). Did this fact make the state claim more or less susceptible to federal preemption than the typical right of publicity claim?

3. Section 301 of the 1976 Copyright Act will preempt a state right of publicity that meets all of three conditions: the subject matter of protection is fixed in a tangible medium of expression; the subject matter comes within the subject matter of copyright under sections 102 and 103 of the Copyright Act; and the state right is equivalent to one or more of the rights granted by section 106 of the Copyright Act.

The right of publicity will only rarely be preempted under section 301. Characteristically, the subject matter of the right of publicity will not be fixed in a tangible medium of expression; specifically, there is a distinction between the subject matter of the right of publicity—an individual's unfixed name or likeness—and the medium in which that persona is tangibly fixed—a photograph or other depiction of the individual's name or likeness. Second, names and likenesses will usually lie outside the subject matter of copyright because they are unprotectible "ideas" rather than protectible expressions. Third, the requirements of identifiability and commercial purpose will often distinguish the right of publicity from the rights extended by copyright.

On section 301 generally, see pages 759 to 772 below.

Part Three

FEDERAL LAW OF INTELLECTUAL PROPERTY

NOTE: JURISDICTION AND COURTS

See Statute Supplement 28 U.S.C.A. §§ 1295, 1338, 1400

A. STATE AND FEDERAL JURISDICTION

Section 1338 of the Judicial Code defines the jurisdiction of federal district courts over federal intellectual property actions and over certain state law claims connected to federal intellectual property actions. Section 1338(a) gives federal district courts original jurisdiction over "any civil action arising under any Act of Congress relating to patents, plant variety protection, copyrights and trade-marks." District court jurisdiction is exclusive in patent, copyright and plant variety protection cases. District courts share their jurisdiction with state courts in trademark cases. Section 1338(b) gives federal district courts pendent jurisdiction over state unfair competition claims if the claim is "joined with a substantial and related claim under the copyright, patent, plant variety protection or trade-mark laws."

1. *Section 1338(a): "Arising Under" Jurisdiction*

a. *When does an action arise under an act relating to copyrights, patents or trademarks?* In a much-cited passage, Judge Henry Friendly suggested that "an action 'arises under' the Copyright Act if and only if the complaint is for a remedy expressly granted by the Act, e.g., a suit for infringement or for the statutory royalties for record reproduction, or asserts a claim requiring construction of the Act . . . or, at the very least and perhaps more doubtfully, presents a case where a distinctive policy of the Act requires that federal principles control the disposition of the claim." T.B. Harms Co. v. Eliscu, 339 F.2d 823, 828, 144 U.S.P.Q. 46 (2d Cir.1964), cert. denied, 381 U.S. 915, 85 S.Ct. 1534, 14 L.Ed.2d 435, 145 U.S.P.Q. 743 (1965). Similarly, federal district courts have original jurisdiction over patent and trademark infringement actions, actions requiring construction of the Patent or Trademark Act and, possibly, actions implicating a distinctive policy of the Patent or Trademark Act.

Does an action to foreclose a copyright mortgage "arise under any act of Congress 'relating to patents, copyrights and trade-marks' simply because . . . [17 U.S.C.A. § 28] provides that a copyright may be mortgaged?" Republic Pictures Corp. v. Security–First Nat'l Bank of Los Angeles, 197 F.2d 767, 769, 94 U.S.P.Q. 291 (9th Cir.1952), answered that it did not. Finding little help in the dictionary definition of "relate" and in the legislative history of section 28, Judge Goodrich considered the question from "a wider aspect": "It is not just because a right has its origin in federal law that a federal court has jurisdiction over matters which grow from that right. A large number of land titles in this country originate with a grant from the United States of America. Yet no one would now seriously claim that federal courts had authority to hear and decide litigation involving disputes among persons claiming the land because of the original grant by the United States." 197 F.2d at 769.

b. *The Well–Pleaded Complaint.* In deciding whether an action arises under the Patent, Copyright or Trademark Acts, courts will honor the well-pleaded complaint. If the complaint discloses the elements required for an infringement action or reflects a claim requiring construction of the federal statute or implicating the policies of the statute, federal jurisdiction will lie under section 1338(a). If the complaint fails to allege any of these elements, federal jurisdiction will not lie. The fact that the defendant interposes a state law defense to a well-pleaded federal cause of action will not defeat federal jurisdiction. Nor will it defeat federal jurisdiction if the copyright owner, in an otherwise well-pleaded complaint, refers to a state law defense by way of anticipatory replication. Similarly, a complaint that discloses only state law grounds for recovery cannot bootstrap federal jurisdiction by anticipating possible defenses resting on federal law. Christianson v. Colt Industries Operating Corp., 486 U.S. 800, 108 S.Ct. 2166, 100 L.Ed. 2d 811, 7 U.S.P.Q.2d 1109 (1988).

Christianson added a fine point to the rule of the well-pleaded complaint: "Nor is it necessarily sufficient that a well-pleaded claim alleges a single theory under which resolution of a patent-law question is essential. If on the face of a well-pleaded complaint there are . . . reasons completely unrelated to the provisions and purposes of [the patent laws] why the [plaintiff] may or may not be entitled to the relief it seeks, then the claim does not 'arise under' those laws. Thus, a claim supported by alternative theories in the complaint may not form the basis for § 1338 jurisdiction unless patent law is essential to each of those theories." 486 U.S. at 810, 108 S.Ct. at 2174.

In some cases the well-pleaded complaint rule enables the plaintiff to control the forum—federal or state—for its action. For example, a patent licensor whose licensee has broken their agreement, can "declare the license forfeited for breach of a condition subsequent and sue for infringement. If it is correct as to its right to declare such a forfeiture unilaterally (a question of state law) federal jurisdiction of the infringement suit exists. But where the licensor stands on the license agreement and seeks contract remedies, even an allegation of infringement will not create federal jurisdiction, for the existence of the license precludes the possibility of infringement." Milprint, Inc. v. Curwood, Inc., 562 F.2d 418, 420, 196 U.S.P.Q. 147 (7th Cir.1977).

2. *Section 1338(b): Pendent Jurisdiction*

Many actions that section 1338(a) allocates between federal and state fora can be more conveniently decided in a single case in a single forum. Section 1338(b), which provides for pendent jurisdiction over state claims, imposes three jurisdictional requirements for a state claim to be resolved by a federal court: (1) the claim must be for "unfair competition;" (2) the federal claim to which it is attached must be "substantial;" and (3) the federal claim to which it is attached must be "related." Courts generally treat pendent jurisdiction as discretionary, and appellate courts only rarely reverse district court dismissals of pendent state claims. See Verdegaal Bros. v. Union Oil Co., 750 F.2d 947, 224 U.S.P.Q. 249 (Fed.Cir.1984).

a. *"Unfair Competition."* Courts construe the term "unfair competition" broadly to embrace not only common law passing off and misappropriation but also a wide variety of commercial misconduct such as appropriation of trade secrets and bad faith attempts to convince a competitor's customers that the competitor's product infringes a valid patent. See General Foods Corp. v. Struthers Scientific & Int'l Corp., 297 F.Supp. 271, 161 U.S.P.Q. 250 (D.Del.1969); Denys Fisher (Spirograph) Ltd. v. Louis Marx & Co., 306 F.Supp. 956, 164 U.S.P.Q. 314 (N.D.W.Va.1969).

b. *"Substantial."* Courts read the term "substantial" pragmatically. For example, in Walters v. Shari Music Publishing Corp., 193 F.Supp. 307, 129 U.S.P.Q. 145 (S.D.N.Y.1961), the court observed that "it is entirely proper for a federal court to proceed with the determination of the state claim when, in the course of trial, and after the expenditure of considerable judicial effort, the supporting federal claim is found to be wanting in merit. However, there is a considerable difference between a federal claim which fails during trial and one which has been dismissed on pretrial motion. In the later situation— the one presented in this case—there has been no substantial commitment of federal judicial resources to the state claim at the time the federal claim is rejected. Since a federal court should not be eager to offer its facilities for the trial of a case which has lost its federal character, the appropriate course, as indicated by Judge Magruder in Strachman v. Palmer, 1 Cir., 1949, 177 F.2d 427, 433, 12 A.L.R.2d 687, is to dismiss the action without prejudice." 193 F.Supp. at 308.

c. *"Related."* The most problematic of the three requirements for pendent jurisdiction is the requirement that the attached federal claim be "related." The Reviser's Notes on section 1338(b) shed some light. "Subsection (b) is added and is intended to avoid 'piecemeal' litigation to enforce common-law and statutory copyright, patent, and trade-mark rights by specifically permitting such enforcement in a single civil action in the district court. While this is the rule under Federal decisions, this section would enact it as statutory authority. The problem is discussed at length in Hurn v. Oursler, 289 U.S. 238, 53 S.Ct. 586, 77 L.Ed. 1148 (1933), and in Musher Foundation v. Alba Trading Co., 127 F.2d 9 (2d Cir.1942) (majority and dissenting opinions)."

Hurn v. Oursler had put the proposition on a nice, conceptual basis. "The distinction to be observed is between a case where two distinct grounds in support of a single cause of action are alleged, one only of which presents a federal question, and a case where two separate and distinct causes of action are alleged, one only of which is federal in character. In the former, where the federal question averred is not plainly wanting in substance, the federal court, even though the federal ground be not established, may nevertheless retain and dispose of the case upon the non-federal *ground;* in the latter it may not do so upon the non-federal *cause of action.*" 289 U.S. at 246, 53 S.Ct. at 589–90 (emphasis the Court's).

Musher v. Alba Trading read *Hurn* to hold that "a non-federal claim, over which the United States Court had no jurisdiction because of an absence of diverse citizenship, might be joined with a federal claim if the non-federal count differed from the federal count only because it asserted a different ground for recovery upon substantially the same state of facts," and ruled that the two claims before the court—one for patent infringement, the other for passing off—were insufficiently related to warrant the exercise of federal jurisdiction over the second. 127 F.2d at 10. To Judge Clark, dissenting, it seemed clear that "the rule is wholly illusory unless we grant a reasonable and practical content to the yardstick and require for our unitary cause only a substantial amount of overlapping testimony, rather than complete identity of the facts." 127 F.2d at 11.

Courts have since interpreted section 1338(b)'s relatedness requirement more expansively than even the most liberal reading of *Hurn* would warrant and, possibly, more expansively than Congress intended when it adopted the measure. For example, one court held that it had pendent jurisdiction over claims for passing off, trade secret appropriation and interference with contractual relations joined to a federal claim for copyright infringement of a sales manual. Although the facts and issues underlying the state and federal claims differed, "the facts of the transactions alleged by the plaintiffs are likely to be so interwoven that a joinder of claims would serve the convenience of the parties, and judicial economy." American Foresight, Inc. v. Fine Arts Sterling Silver, Inc., 268 F.Supp. 656, 662, 152 U.S.P.Q. 576 (E.D.Pa.1967).

d. *Applicable Law.* Having taken pendent jurisdiction, what substantive law should a federal court apply in resolving the state claim? State law—the obvious answer since Erie v. Tomkins—is also the generally accepted answer. In an extensive footnote to his opinion for the court in Maternally Yours, Inc. v. Your Maternity Shop, Inc., 234 F.2d 538, 540–41 n.1, 110 U.S.P.Q. 462 (2d Cir.1956), Judge Waterman reasoned that "despite repeated statements implying the contrary, it is the *source* of the right sued upon, and not the ground on which federal jurisdiction over the case is founded, which determines the governing law. . . . Thus, the *Erie* doctrine applies, whatever the ground for federal jurisdiction, to any issue or claim which has its source in state law." (Emphasis the court's).

B. COURT OF APPEALS FOR THE FEDERAL CIRCUIT

The Federal Courts Improvement Act of 1982, P.L. 97–164, 96 Stat. 25 (April 2, 1982), created a thirteenth court of appeals, the United

States Court of Appeals for the Federal Circuit (CAFC). The CAFC, an Article III court with twelve judges appointed by the President with the advice and consent of the Senate, merges the former Court of Customs and Patent Appeals and the Court of Claims. The court's initial membership consisted of the five sitting judges of the Court of Customs and Patent Appeals and the seven sitting judges of the Court of Claims. In its first decided case, the CAFC adopted the precedents of the Court of Customs and Patent Appeals and the Court of Claims as its own. South Corp. v. United States, 690 F.2d 1368, 1370, 215 U.S.P.Q. 657 (Fed.Cir.1982). Unlike the twelve other circuit courts, whose jurisdiction is defined by region, the CAFC's jurisdiction is defined by subject matter.

The Federal Courts Improvement Act gives the CAFC exclusive jurisdiction over appeals from district court decisions in patent and plant variety protection cases. 28 U.S.C.A. § 1295(a)(1). The Act also vests in the CAFC the Court of Customs and Patent Appeals' former jurisdiction over appeals from the Board of Patent Appeals and Interferences of the Patent and Trademark Office involving patent applications and interferences. 28 U.S.C.A. § 1295(a)(4)(A). Sections 1295(a) (4)(A) and 1295(a)(4)(C) contemplate two avenues for review of Board decisions. Under section 1295(a)(4)(A) a party can appeal a Board decision directly to the CAFC. Alternatively, a party can proceed by civil action against the Commissioner of Patents and Trademarks in federal district court. See 35 U.S.C.A. §§ 145, 146. Section 1295(a)(4) (C) gives the CAFC exclusive jurisdiction over appeals from the district courts in these cases.

The principal reason Congress created the CAFC was to eliminate a persistent disparity in patent law standards among courts of appeals deciding patent cases coming to them from the district courts in their region. Today, district court decisions in patent infringement and declaratory judgment actions are the major source of patent issues coming before the CAFC. The CAFC also takes appeals from the United States Claims Court, some of whose decisions involve patent and copyright claims against the United States government; appeals from the International Trade Commission relating to unfair trade practices in the import trade, including patent infringement; and appeals from decisions of the Commissioner of Patents and Trademarks or the Trademark Trial and Appeal Board involving trademark registration applications and other proceedings.

For an excellent analysis of the work of the CAFC, see Dreyfuss, The Federal Circuit: A Case Study in Specialized Courts, 64 N.Y.U. L.Rev. 1 (1989). On the CAFC, generally, see R. Harmon, Patents and the Federal Circuit (1988); Adams, The Court of Appeals for the Federal Circuit: More than a National Patent Court, 49 Mo.L.Rev. 43 (1984).

I. TRADEMARK LAW

Merchants have used marks for centuries to indicate the ownership or source of goods. Some Greek vases of the fifth and sixth centuries B.C. have been found that bear their potter's mark. In the Middle Ages, merchants affixed distinctive marks to their goods before shipment to identify them in the event of shipwreck or piracy. Although such early practices may represent the beginnings of a tradition, these were essentially proprietary marks, intended to indicate ownership, and differed from modern trademarks intended to indicate the source of goods.

Guild practices requiring craftsmen to affix production marks to their goods lie closer to the source of modern trademarks. "Every craft, of course, either had its own ordinances concerning such marks or administered statutory or municipal regulations of a similar nature. All of these regulations, whatever their source, made use of the production mark compulsory. Their expressed purpose was to facilitate the tracing of 'false' or defective wares and the punishment of the offending craftsman. The compulsory production mark likewise assisted the gild authorities in preventing those outside the gild from selling their products within the area of the gild monopoly." Over time, in certain trades, these marks became "asset marks—that is to say they became valuable symbols of individual good-will." This was particularly so in the case of durable goods, and goods transported great distances, "especially in the clothing and cutlery trades." F. Schechter, The Historical Foundations of the Law Relating to Trade-Marks 47 (1925).

Systematic legal protection of trademarks began to take shape in the early years of the nineteenth century. The starting point was the common law of deceit, from which courts in both England and the United States gradually evolved a distinct tort of passing off. An action for passing off would lie if the plaintiff could prove that the defendant had used plaintiff's mark to deceive consumers into thinking that plaintiff was the source of defendant's goods. Intent to deceive was the gravamen of the action for passing off and remains so today in unfair competition cases in which the plaintiff's symbol is descriptive or otherwise weak. In cases where plaintiff's symbol was arbitrary or otherwise highly distinctive, courts came to insist less on proof of fraudulent intent; the fact that defendant had copied a distinctive mark was itself evidence of intent to deceive. Courts eventually categorized disputes over distinctive symbols as trademark infringement cases rather than unfair competition cases and conclusively removed any requirement that fraudulent intent be proved. See page 55 above.

The first United States trademark statute, Act of July 8, 1870, ch. 230, 16 Stat. 198, created few substantive rights, providing instead for the registration of marks protected under common law. Congress amended the Act in 1876 to add criminal penalties for infringing or counterfeiting registered marks. Act of August 14, 1876, ch. 274, 19 Stat. 141. In 1879 the United States Supreme Court ruled that the Act of 1870, as amended, was unconstitutional. Trade–Mark Cases, 100 U.S. 82, 25 L.Ed. 550 (1879).

Justice Miller, writing for the Court in the Trade–Mark Cases, began by rejecting the claim that Article I, § 8, cl. 8, the copyright-patent clause, gave Congress the necessary authority. "The ordinary trademark has no necessary relation to invention or discovery. The trademark recognized by the common law is generally the growth of a considerable period of use, rather than a sudden invention. It is often the result of accident rather than design, and when under the act of Congress it is sought to establish it by registration, neither originality, invention, discovery, science, nor art is in any way essential to the right conferred by that act. If we should endeavor to classify it under the head of writings of authors, the objections are equally strong. . . . The writings which are to be protected are the *fruits of intellectual labor*, embodied in the form of books, prints, engravings and the like. The trade-mark may be, and generally is, the adoption of something already in existence as the distinctive symbol of the party using it." 100 U.S. at 94 (emphasis the Court's).

Justice Miller also rejected the argument that the Act could be rested on the commerce clause. When "Congress undertakes to enact a law, which can only be valid as a regulation of commerce, it is reasonable to expect to find on the face of the law, or from its essential nature, that it is a regulation of commerce with foreign nations, or among the several States, or with the Indian tribes. If not so limited, it is in excess of the power of Congress. If its main purpose be to establish a regulation applicable to all trade, to commerce at all points, especially if it be that it is designed to govern the commerce wholly between the citizens of the same State, it is obviously the exercise of a power not confided to Congress." Because the Act stated no such jurisdictional limits, the Court could not sustain it under the commerce power. 100 U.S. at 96–97.

Despite the care that Justice Miller took to narrow the Court's holding, and to signal to Congress that it could repair the constitutional flaw by expressly limiting the Act to objects covered by the commerce clause, it soon became evident that federal trademark protection had started off on the wrong foot. Until passage of the Lanham Act, nearly three-quarters of a century later, Congress and the courts took few steps toward an enlarged federal role. Congress' first response to the Court's decision, the Act of March 3, 1881, 21 Stat. 502, expressly conditioned federal registration on the mark's use in foreign commerce or in commerce with the Indian tribes. Registration of marks used in interstate commerce came only with passage of the comprehensive Act of Feb. 20, 1905, ch. 592, 33 Stat. 724. Influenced in part by the Trademark Cases, and in part by dicta in American Steel Foundries v. Robertson, 269 U.S. 372, 46 S.Ct. 160, 70 L.Ed. 317 (1926) and American Trading Co. v. Heacock Co., 285 U.S. 247, 52 S.Ct. 387, 76 L.Ed. 740, 12

U.S.P.Q. 453 (1932), courts as late as 1932 assumed that "Congress has been given no power to legislate on the substantive law of trademarks," and that congressional authority is limited to providing "a federally controlled place of registration and to deny registration therein, where confusion would likely result to the trade from the trademark use of such registered marks." A. Leschen & Sons Rope Co. v. American Steel and Wire Co., 55 F.2d 455, 459, 12 U.S.P.Q. 272 (C.C.P.A.1932).

The Lanham Act, signed into law on July 5, 1946, was the first major step toward substantive federal trademark legislation in the United States. The efforts at revision began in 1924, with the introduction of S. 2679. First spearheaded by Representative Albert Vestal, the revision effort was later taken over by Representative Fritz Lanham. Since 1946, the Lanham Act, which is the trademark statute now in force, has been amended several times. The 1962 "housekeeping" amendments, Act of October 9, 1962, P.L. 87–772, 76 Stat. 769, also contain some substance. See page 340, below. The 1975 amendments, Act of January 2, 1975, P.L. 93–600, § 3, 88 Stat.1955, provided, among other things, for the award of attorneys' fees in exceptional cases.

The Trademark Law Revision Act of 1988 has materially altered the premises and provisions of the Lanham Act. Among other changes, the 1988 Act alters trademark law's traditional use requirement; strengthens the evidentiary effect of a registration certificate; reduces the term of trademark registration; and widens the compass of section 43(a), 15 U.S.C.A. § 1125(a). The Act traces to the work of the United States Trademark Association and its specially-chartered Trademark Review Commission. Although the Act differs in important respects from the Commission's recommendations, it reflects their impress. See United States Trademark Association Trademark Review Commission Report and Recommendations to USTA President and Board of Directors, 77 Trademark Rep. 375 (1987). For a detailed overview of the 1988 amendments, see Hellwig, The Trademark Law Revision Act of 1988: The 100th Congress Leaves Its Mark, 79 Trademark Rep. 287 (1989). The entire May–June, 1989 issue of the Trademark Reporter is devoted to the 1988 amendments.

For a superb study of the evolution of trademark law from its earliest origins, see F. Schechter, The Historical Foundations of the Law Relating to Trade–Marks (1925). See also, Burrell, Two Hundred Years of English Trademark Law, and Pattishall, Two Hundred Years of American Trademark Law, in American Bar Association, Two Hundred Years of English and American Patent, Trademark and Copyright Law 35, 51 (1977); Diamond, The Historical Development of Trademarks, 65 Trademark Rep. 265 (1975); McClure, Trademarks and Unfair Competition: A Critical History of Legal Thought, 69 Trademark Rep. 305 (1979); Paster, Trademarks—Their Early History, 59 Trademark Rep. 551 (1969).

General reference works on trademark law and practice include R. Callmann, The Law of Unfair Competition, Trademarks, and Monopolies (L. Altman, 4th ed. 1981); J. Gilson, Trademark Protection and

Practice (1974); J.T. McCarthy, Trademarks and Unfair Competition (2d ed. 1984).

The Trademark Reporter, published bimonthly by the United States Trademark Association, is an excellent source of articles on topics of current importance.

A. REQUIREMENTS FOR PROTECTION

1. USE AND USE IN COMMERCE

See Statute Supplement 15 U.S.C.A. §§ 1051, 1055, 1057, 1060.

Until the Trademark Law Revision Act of 1988, which came into effect on November 16, 1989, trademark ownership and registration in the United States turned on the mark's use in connection with goods or services in the marketplace. No ownership or rights attached to a mark until it was used in commerce. Use was also a condition precedent to an application to register the mark in the Patent and Trademark Office. Simply, a firm could not select a mark for a new but unmarketed product and reserve the mark until it was ready to market the product.

The Revision Act substantially altered the use requirement by allowing trademark registration applications to be made upon a showing of a bona fide intention to use the mark. The change brings United States trademark law into line with the laws of most other countries. Some countries have long allowed registration based on the applicant's intent to use the mark; use in these countries is only a condition subsequent to the mark's continued validity. Other countries permit registration without a showing even of an intent to use the mark. See II S. Ladas, Patents, Trademarks, and Related Rights § 567 (1975).

The principal argument against a use requirement is that it requires a firm to invest sometimes substantial sums in marketing its goods or services before the firm has any assurance that the mark will meet the other conditions, such as distinctiveness, required for registration. The requirement also gave a distinct advantage to foreign applicants who, under Lanham Act § 44, 15 U.S.C.A. § 1126, did not have to allege use. See page 215, note 4, below. One argument for retaining a use requirement is that it prevents firms from warehousing marks; under this view, warehousing is bad because it precludes newcomers to the marketplace from using the warehoused marks, and confers no benefit on consumers who have had no opportunity to identify the warehoused mark with a source of goods or services. The use requirement also keeps deadwood off the trademark registers. The Revision Act strikes a balance between these competing claims.

The 1988 amendments introduce a new distinction into the Lanham Act's provisions on trademark application, registration and use. The distinction is between applications based on use of a mark and applications based only on an intent to use the mark.

Applications Based on Use. As amended, the Lanham Act general-ly treats applications based on use in the same way that it treated them before the 1988 amendments. Examiners in the Patent and Trademark Office will review the application for compliance with statutory formali-ties and will determine whether registration of the mark is barred on any of the grounds specified in section 2 of the Lanham Act, 15 U.S.C.A. § 1052. If the mark qualifies for registration, the examiner will approve its publication in the Official Gazette for purposes of opposi-tion. See page 281, below. If no one successfully opposes the applica-tion, the Patent and Trademark Office will then register the mark. 15 U.S.C.A. § 1063(b)(1).

Applications Based on Intent to Use. Under the 1988 amendments, the Patent and Trademark Office subjects intent to use applications to the same initial steps as applications based on use—comparison with possibly conflicting marks and publication for opposition. The differ-ence lies in the steps that follow the opposition period. If no one successfully opposes the application, the Patent and Trademark Office will issue a "notice of allowance." Following the notice of allowance, it will register the mark if, within six months, the applicant files "a verified statement that the mark is in use in commerce. . . ." 15 U.S.C.A. § 1051(d)(1). Section 1051(d)(2) gives the intent to use appli-cant a second six-month waiting period as a matter of course and, "upon a showing of good cause," the Office may further extend the time for filing a statement of use for periods aggregating not more than 24 months. This three-year waiting period, when taken together with the twelve months or more that may elapse between the filing date and the date of allowance, effectively gives the intent to use applicant more than four years to reserve its mark.

What does an applicant gain by filing an intent to use application? Under section 1057(c), once a mark is registered on the Principal Register the filing of the application to register the mark "shall constitute constructive use of the mark, conferring a right of priority, nationwide in effect, on or in connection with the goods or services specified in the registration. . . ." The constructive use priority effectively gives the successful applicant the same rights it would have received had it actually used the mark throughout the United States on the date it filed its application—specifically the right to bar the mark's use by all later applicants or users. The priority does not, however, obtain against certain foreign applicants or against anyone who used the mark or applied for registration before the registrant's filing date.

The Trademark Review Commission, whose proposals formed the basis for the 1988 amendments, gives an example of the priority conferred by the intent to use provisions:

> P files an intent-to-use application on June 1, 1988 to register the mark BRAVO for cheese. D commences use of the mark BRAVO for yogurt November 1, 1988. P begins shipping BRAVO cheese in commercial quantities to its brokers and retail accounts in several states on February 1, 1989. In an injunction action by P against D,

P prevails, provided: (a) P's application is allowed, (b) P files a declaration of use within six months after Notice of Allowance or during an extension thereof, (c) a principal register registration issues to P, and (d) P proves that the public in D's locale is likely to be confused by D's use of BRAVO on yogurt.

United States Trademark Association, Trademark Review Commission Report and Recommendations to USTA President and Board of Directors, 77 Trademark Rep. 398–99 (1987).* D could in this case have protected itself by searching the Patent and Trademark Office records before adopting the Bravo mark for its yogurt.

Token Use. The same considerations that led to passage of the intent to use provisions in 1988 contributed before 1988 to the Patent and Trademark Office's toleration of token uses—spare, contrived uses of a mark made for the single purpose of obtaining registration. See Blue Bell, Inc. v. Farah Mfg. Co., below. The 1988 Revision Act abolished token use registrations across the board by defining "use in commerce" to mean "the bona fide use of a mark in the ordinary course of trade, and not made merely to reserve a right in a mark." 15 U.S. C.A. § 1127. In reporting the bill that became the Revision Act, Senator DeConcini stated that the amended definition of "use in commerce" was intended "to assure that the commercial sham of 'token use'—which becomes unnecessary under the intent-to-use application system we designed—would actually be eliminated. In doing so, however, Congress' intent that the revised definition still encompass genuine, but less traditional, trademark uses must be made clear. For example, such uses as clinical shipments of a new drug awaiting FDA approval, test marketing, or infrequent sales of large or expensive or seasonal products, reflect legitimate trademark uses in the normal course of trade and are not to be excluded by the House language." 134 Cong. Rec. 16,973 (Oct. 20, 1988).

For a detailed discussion of the intent to use provisions, see Leeds, Intent to Use—Its Time Has Come, 79 Trademark Reporter 269 (1989).

BLUE BELL, INC. v. FARAH MFG. CO.
United States Court of Appeals, Fifth Circuit, 1975.
508 F.2d 1260, 185 U.S.P.Q. 1.

GEWIN, Circuit Judge.

In the spring and summer of 1973 two prominent manufacturers of men's clothing created identical trademarks for goods substantially identical in appearance. Though the record offers no indication of bad faith in the design and adoption of the labels, both Farah Manufacturing Company (Farah) and Blue Bell, Inc. (Blue Bell) devised the mark "Time Out" for new lines of men's slacks and shirts. Both parties market their goods on a national scale, so they agree that joint utilization of the same trademark would confuse the buying public.

Thus, the only question presented for our review is which party established prior use of the mark in trade. A response to that seemingly innocuous inquiry, however, requires us to define the chameleonic term "use" as it has developed in trademark law.

After a full development of the facts in the district court both parties moved for summary judgment. The motion of Farah was granted and that of Blue Bell denied. It is not claimed that summary judgment procedure was inappropriate; the controversy presented relates to the application of the proper legal principles to undisputed facts. A permanent injunction was granted in favor of Farah but no damages were awarded, and Blue Bell was allowed to fill all orders for garments bearing the Time Out label received by it as of the close of business on December 5, 1973. For the reasons hereinafter stated we affirm.

Farah conceived of the Time Out mark on May 16, after screening several possible titles for its new stretch menswear. Two days later the firm adopted an hourglass logo and authorized an extensive advertising campaign bearing the new insignia. Farah presented its fall line of clothing, including Time Out slacks, to sales personnel on June 5. In the meantime, patent counsel had given clearance for use of the mark after scrutiny of current federal registrations then on file. One of Farah's top executives demonstrated samples of the Time Out garments to large customers in Washington, D.C. and New York, though labels were not attached to the slacks at that time. Tags containing the new design were completed June 27. With favorable evaluations of marketing potential from all sides, Farah sent one pair of slacks bearing the Time Out mark to each of its twelve regional sales managers on July 3. Sales personnel paid for the pants, and the garments became their property in case of loss.

Following the July 3 shipment, regional managers showed the goods to customers the following week. Farah received several orders and production began. Further shipments of sample garments were mailed to the rest of the sales force on July 11 and 14. Merchandising efforts were fully operative by the end of the month. The first shipments to customers, however, occurred in September.

Blue Bell, on the other hand, was concerned with creating an entire new division of men's clothing, as an avenue to reaching the "upstairs" market. Though initially to be housed at the Hicks–Ponder plant in El Paso, the new division would eventually enjoy separate headquarters. On June 18 Blue Bell management arrived at the name Time Out to identify both its new division and its new line of men's sportswear. Like Farah, it received clearance for use of the mark from counsel. Like Farah, it inaugurated an advertising campaign. Unlike Farah, however, Blue Bell did not ship a dozen marked articles of the new line to its sales personnel. Instead, Blue Bell authorized the manufacture of several hundred labels bearing the words Time Out and its logo shaped like a referee's hands forming a T. When the labels were completed on June 29, the head of the embryonic division flew them to El Paso. He instructed shipping personnel to affix the new Time Out labels to slacks that already bore the "Mr. Hicks" trademark. The new tags, of varying sizes and colors, were randomly attached to the left hip pocket button of slacks and the left hip pocket of jeans. Thus, although no change occurred in the design or manufacture of the pants, on July 5 several hundred pair left El Paso with two tags.

Blue Bell made intermittent shipments of the doubly-labeled slacks thereafter, though the out-of-state customers who received the goods had ordered clothing of the Mr. Hicks variety. Production of the new Time Out merchandise began in the latter part of August, and Blue Bell held a sales meeting to present its fall designs from September 4–6. Sales personnel solicited numerous orders, though shipments of the garments were not scheduled until October.

By the end of October Farah had received orders for 204,403 items of Time Out sportswear, representing a retail sales value of over $2,750,000. Blue Bell had received orders for 154,200 garments valued at over $900,000. Both parties had commenced extensive advertising campaigns for their respective Time Out sportswear.

Soon after discovering the similarity of their marks, Blue Bell sued Farah for common law trademark infringement and unfair competition, seeking to enjoin use of the Time Out trademark on men's clothing. Farah counterclaimed for similar injunctive relief. The district court found that Farah's July 3 shipment and sale constituted a valid use in trade, while Blue Bell's July 5 shipment was a mere "token" use insufficient at law to create trademark rights. While we affirm the result reached by the trial court as to Farah's priority of use, the legal grounds upon which we base our decision are somewhat different from those undergirding the district court's judgment.

Federal jurisdiction is predicated upon diversity of citizenship, since neither party has registered the mark pursuant to the Lanham Act. Given the operative facts surrounding manufacture and shipment from El Paso, the parties agree the Texas law of trademarks controls. In 1967 the state legislature enacted a Trademark Statute.[5] Section 16.02 of the Act explains that a mark is "used" when it is affixed to the goods and "the goods are sold, displayed for sale, or otherwise publicly distributed." Thus the question whether Blue Bell or Farah established priority of trademark use depends upon interpretation of the cited provision. Unfortunately, there are no Texas cases construing § 16.02. This court must therefore determine what principles the highest state court would utilize in deciding such a question. In view of the statute's stated purpose to preserve common law rights, we conclude the Texas Supreme Court would apply the statutory provision in light of general principles of trademark law.

A trademark is a symbol (word, name, device or combination thereof) adopted and used by a merchant to identify his goods and distinguish them from articles produced by others. Ownership of a

5. Vernon's Tex.Code, Ann., Bus. & Comm. §§ 16.01–16.28 (1968).

mark requires a combination of both appropriation and use in trade. Thus, neither conception of the mark, nor advertising alone establishes trademark rights at common law. Rather, ownership of a trademark accrues when goods bearing the mark are placed on the market.

The exclusive right to a trademark belongs to one who first uses it in connection with specified goods. Such use need not have gained wide public recognition, and even a single use in trade may sustain trademark rights if followed by continuous commercial utilization.

The initial question presented for review is whether Farah's sale and shipment of slacks to twelve regional managers constitutes a valid first use of the Time Out mark. Blue Bell claims the July 3 sale was merely an internal transaction insufficiently public to secure trademark ownership. After consideration of pertinent authorities, we agree.

Secret, undisclosed internal shipments are generally inadequate to support the denomination "use." Trademark claims based upon shipments from a producer's plant to its sales office, and vice versa, have often been disallowed. Though none of the cited cases dealt with *sales* to intra-corporate personnel, we perceive that fact to be a distinction without a difference. The sales were not made to customers, but served as an accounting device to charge the salesmen with their cost in case of loss. The fact that some sales managers actively solicited accounts bolsters the good faith of Farah's intended use, but does not meet our essential objection: that the "sales" were not made to the public.

The primary, perhaps singular purpose of a trademark is to provide a means for the consumer to separate or distinguish one manufacturer's goods from those of another. Personnel within a corporation can identify an item by style number or other unique code. A trademark aids the public in selecting particular goods. As stated by the First Circuit:

> But to hold that a sale or sales are the sine qua non of a use sufficient to amount to an appropriation would be to read an unwarranted limitation into the statute, for so construed registration would have to be denied to any manufacturer who adopted a mark to distinguish or identify his product, and perhaps applied it thereon for years, if he should in practice lease his goods rather than sell them, as many manufacturers of machinery do. It seems to us that although evidence of sales is highly persuasive, the question of use adequate to establish appropriation remains one to be decided on the facts of each case, and that evidence showing, first, adoption, and, second, *use in a way sufficiently public to identify or distinguish the marked goods in an appropriate segment of the public mind as those of the adopter of the mark,* is competent to establish ownership. . . .

New England Duplicating Co. v. Mendes, 190 F.2d 415, 418, 90 U.S.P.Q. 151, 153 (1st Cir.1951) (Emphasis added). Similarly, the Trademark Trial and Appeal Board has reasoned:

To acquire trademark rights there has to be an 'open' use, that is to say, a use has to be made to the relevant class of purchasers or prospective purchasers since a trademark is intended to identify goods and distinguish those goods from those manufactured or sold by others. There was no such 'open' use, rather the use can be said to be an 'internal' use, which cannot give rise to trademark rights.

Sterling Drug, Inc. v. Knoll A.G. Chemische Fabriken, supra at 631.

Farah nonetheless contends that a recent decision of the Board so undermines all prior cases relating to internal use that they should be ignored. In Standard Pressed Steel Co. v. Midwest Chrome Process Co., 183 U.S.P.Q. 758 (T.T.A.B.1974), the agency held that internal shipment of marked goods from a producer's manufacturing plant to its sales office constitutes a valid "use in commerce" for registration purposes.

An axiom of trademark law has been that the right to register a mark is conditioned upon its actual use in trade. Theoretically, then, common law use in trade should precede the use in commerce upon which Lanham Act registration is predicated. Arguably, since only a trademark owner can apply for registration, any activity adequate to create registrable rights must perforce also create trademark rights. A close examination of the Board's decision, however, dispels so mechanical a view. The tribunal took meticulous care to point out that its conclusion related solely to registration use rather than ownership use.

It has been recognized and especially so in the last few years that, in view of the expenditures involved in introducing a new product on the market generally and the attendant risk involved therein prior to the screening process involved in resorting to the federal registration system and in the absence of an "intent to use" statute, a token sale or a single shipment in commerce *may be sufficient to support an application to register a trademark* in the Patent Office notwithstanding that the evidence may not show what disposition was made of the product so shipped. That is, the fact that a sale or a shipment of goods bearing a trademark was *designed primarily to lay a foundation for the filing of an application for registration* does not, per se, invalidate any such application or subsequent registration issued thereon.

. . .

Inasmuch as it is our belief that a most liberal policy should be followed in a situation of this kind [*in which dispute as to priority of use and ownership of a mark is not involved*], applicant's initial shipment of fasteners, although an intra-company transaction in that it was to a company sales representative, was a bona fide shipment. . . .

Standard Pressed Steel Co. v. Midwest Chrome Process Co., supra at 764–65 (Emphasis added).

Priority of use and ownership of the Time Out mark are the only issues before this court. The language fashioned by the Board clearly indicates a desire to leave the common law of trademark ownership intact. The decision may demonstrate a reversal of the presumption that ownership rights precede registration rights, but it does not affect our analysis of common law use in trade. Farah had undertaken substantial preliminary steps toward marketing the Time Out garments, but it did not establish ownership of the mark by means of the July 3 shipment to its sales managers. The gist of trademark rights is actual use in trade. Though technically a "sale", the July 3 shipment was not "publicly distributed" within the purview of the Texas statute.

Blue Bell's July 5 shipment similarly failed to satisfy the prerequisites of a bona fide use in trade. Elementary tenets of trademark law require that labels or designs be affixed to the merchandise actually intended to bear the mark in commercial transactions. Furthermore, courts have recognized that the usefulness of a mark derives not only from its capacity to identify a certain manufacturer, but also from its ability to differentiate between different classes of goods produced by a single manufacturer. Here customers had ordered slacks of the Mr. Hicks species, and Mr. Hicks was the fanciful mark distinguishing these slacks from all others. Blue Bell intended to use the Time Out mark on an entirely new line of men's sportswear, unique in style and cut, though none of the garments had yet been produced.

While goods may be identified by more than one trademark, the use of each mark must be bona fide. Mere adoption of a mark without bona fide use, in an attempt to reserve it for the future, will not create trademark rights. In the instant case Blue Bell's attachment of a secondary label to an older line of goods manifests a bad faith attempt to reserve a mark. We cannot countenance such activities as a valid use in trade. Blue Bell therefore did not acquire trademark rights by virtue of its July 5 shipment.

We thus hold that neither Farah's July 3 shipment nor Blue Bell's July 5 shipment sufficed to create rights in the Time Out mark. Based on a desire to secure ownership of the mark and superiority over a competitor, both claims of alleged use were chronologically premature. Essentially, they took a time out to litigate their differences too early in the game. The question thus becomes whether we should continue to stop the clock for a remand or make a final call from the appellate bench. While a remand to the district court for further factual development would not be improper in these circumstances, we believe the interests of judicial economy and the parties' desire to terminate the litigation demand that we decide, if possible, which manufacturer first used the mark in trade.

Careful examination of the record discloses that Farah shipped its first order of Time Out clothing to customers in September of 1973. Blue Bell, approximately one month behind its competitor at other relevant stages of development, did not mail its Time Out garments until at least October. Though sales to customers are not the sine qua non of trademark use, they are determinative in the instant case. These sales constituted the first point at which the public had a chance to associate Time Out with a particular line of sportswear. Therefore,

Farah established priority of trademark use; it is entitled to a decree permanently enjoining Blue Bell from utilization of the Time Out trademark on men's garments.

The judgment of the trial court is affirmed.

MANHATTAN INDUSTRIES, INC. v. SWEATER BEE BY BANFF, LTD.

United States Court of Appeals, Second Circuit, 1980.
627 F.2d 628, 207 U.S.P.Q. 89.

LUMBARD, Circuit Judge:

Sweater Bee by Banff, Ltd. and Robert Belsky (collectively "Sweater Bee") appeal from a judgment entered on April 11, 1980, in the Southern District of New York, Broderick, J., permanently enjoining it from further use of the trademark "Kimberly" on the women's apparel it manufactures and markets. Sweater Bee argues that the district court erred in finding that the appellees—Manhattan Industries, Inc., Bayard Shirt Corporation and Don Sophisticates, Inc.—have acquired the right of ownership in the "Kimberly" mark. We conclude that the district court's findings of fact are supported by the record, but we remand for the fashioning of an order allowing both appellants and appellees to use the "Kimberly" mark with such distinctions as the district court finds appropriate.

The "Kimberly" mark was owned as a registered trademark and used to identify high quality women's clothing by General Mills, Inc., until May 7, 1979. On that day, General Mills formally abandoned the mark.[1] In response to rumors circulating within the trade in March and April 1979 that General Mills intended to discontinue using the mark, executives at Don Sophisticates and at Sweater Bee sought to acquire this valuable mark directly from General Mills, but neither succeeded because General Mills, for reasons unimportant here, decided to abandon rather than sell the mark.[2]

Upon the mark's abandonment, a free-for-all ensued. The district court found that Don Sophisticates began shipping merchandise with labels bearing a "Kimberly" mark on May 9.[3] Even before May 9, Don Sophisticates had displayed to customers "Kimberly" clothing which it had purchased from a supplier in anticipation of General Mills' discontinuance of the mark. From May 7 until October, when the complaint was filed, Don Sophisticates shipped over $10,000 worth of merchandise bearing the "Kimberly" mark.

---

1. General Mills signed Surrenders of Cancellation of its "Kimberly" marks on May 3. The letter transmitting the surrenders to the United States Patent and Trademark Office was dated May 7.

2. Although the record does not show General Mills' reason for abandoning the mark, counsel suggested at oral argument, in answer to the court's question, that the abandonment might have been for tax purposes.

3. The evidence shows that Don Sophisticates had begun shipping merchandise with labels bearing a "Kimberly" mark on May 7, making one shipment on that day, five on May 8, and one more on both May 10 and 14. These shipments went to five states. We consider it immaterial in this case whether Don Sophisticates began its shipments on May 7 or 9.

Sweater Bee began shipping merchandise with labels bearing a "Kimberly" mark on May 10, the day the mark's abandonment was reported in the trade newspaper, *Women's Wear Daily*. Sweater Bee's four shipments on that day went to four states and since then Sweater Bee has shipped over $130,000 worth of merchandise with labels bearing a "Kimberly" mark. Bayard Shirt entered the race on May 11. By an assignment executed on June 29, Bayard Shirt and its parent company, Manhattan Industries, received all of Don Sophisticates' rights to the mark. By mid-September, Bayard Shirt had shipped over $45,000 worth of merchandise with labels bearing a "Kimberly" mark, and had spent over $9,000 in advertising and promoting its "Kimberly" line. Don Sophisticates, Sweater Bee and Bayard Shirt all applied to the United States Patent and Trademark Office for the registration of the mark.

Appellees brought this action under the Lanham Act, 15 U.S.C. § 1125(a), claiming the trademark right to the mark by virtue of prior and continuous use and seeking, in addition to an injunction against Sweater Bee's further use of the mark, an accounting of profits derived from the alleged infringement, damages, and costs. Sweater Bee counterclaimed on similar grounds and sought similar relief. Both parties claimed an exclusive, nationwide right to use the mark. The district court, after receiving the parties' affidavits and documents and hearing arguments, concluded that Don Sophisticates, and by assignment Bayard Shirt and Manhattan Industries, had acquired the sole right to the mark by virtue of its prior use. However, in light of the evenly balanced equities, the district court denied appellees' request for an accounting, damages, and costs. Pending this expedited appeal, we stayed the district court's order that Sweater Bee destroy its "Kimberly" labels.

The record supports the district court's findings of fact whether we apply the clearly erroneous standard or review *de novo* the affidavits and documents which wholly comprise the evidence in the record. When General Mills abandoned its mark, Don Sophisticates and Sweater Bee "were equally free to attempt to capture the mark to their own use." Sutton Cosmetics (P.R.) v. Lander Co., 455 F.2d 285, 288 (2d Cir. 1972). Don Sophisticates won the race, for it was the first to ship merchandise with labels bearing a "Kimberly" mark after the abandonment, and it did so with the intent of acquiring the mark. Accordingly, Don Sophisticates would ordinarily have "the right to use the mark unadorned," id., and Bayard Shirt and Manhattan Industries, as its assignees, would receive that right, id. However, in light of the significant shipments and investment by Sweater Bee, we do not believe that Don Sophisticates' slight priority in time justifies awarding to the appellees the exclusive, nationwide right to the "Kimberly" mark. We have previously stated that "the concept of priority in the law of trademarks is applied 'not in its calendar sense' but on the basis of 'the equities involved.'" Chandon Champagne Corp. v. San Marino Wine Corp., 335 F.2d 531, 534 (2d Cir.1964). Given the evenly balanced equities in this case, it would be inequitable to allow only the appellees to use the "Kimberly" mark. Sweater Bee has proved "that it entered the market sufficiently early to be equally entitled with [appellees] to the use of the ['Kimberly'] mark. In such case, to protect the public, each company [will] have to differentiate its product from that of the other company and perhaps also from the original ['Kimberly'] mark." P. Daussa Corp. v. Sutton Cosmetics (P.R.) Inc., 462 F.2d 134, 136 (2d Cir.1972).

One of the purposes of the Lanham Act is to prevent confusion among the public as to the source of goods. We have recognized, however, that the likelihood of confusion may decrease as the sophistication of the relevant purchasers increases. "The greater the value of an article the more careful the typical consumer can be expected to be; the average purchaser of an automobile will no doubt devote more attention to examining the different products and determining their manufacturer or source than will the average purchaser of a ball of twine." McGregor–Doniger, Inc. v. Drizzle Inc., 599 F.2d at 1137. No doubt the parties can create and present to the district court sufficiently distinct labels bearing the "Kimberly" mark so that the purchasers of high quality women's clothing can distinguish appellees' "Kimberly" goods from appellant's. We therefore remand to the district court for the fashioning of an appropriate order not inconsistent with this opinion.

Reversed and remanded.

NOTES

1. *Blue Bell's* discussion of *Standard Pressed Steel* highlights the two different use standards that courts employed before the Trademark Law Revision Act of 1988. For purposes of ownership and priority under state law, courts generally required substantial use in connection with goods or services in the marketplace and assigned ownership to the first firm that made such a use. By contrast, for purposes of federal registration, courts frequently held that a token, noncommercial use of the mark in commerce sufficed even though it was evident that the token use was made exclusively for the purpose of obtaining registration.

What is the effect of having two different standards of use—one for ownership and priority, the other for registration? If Blue Bell had made sufficient use of the mark to obtain registration, followed several months later by a *bona fide* commercial use establishing priority, what would it have gained from the earlier registration? How would Blue Bell have fared in an infringement action against Farah? Might Blue Bell have exposed itself to statutory liability by applying for early registration? Lanham Act § 38, 15 U.S.C.A. § 1120 provides that "[a]ny person who shall procure registration in the Patent and Trademark Office of a mark by false or fraudulent declaration or representation, oral or in writing, or by any false means, shall be liable in a civil action by any person injured thereby for any damages sustained in consequence thereof." See Blue Bell, Inc. v. Jaymar–Ruby, Inc., 497 F.2d 433, 182 U.S.P.Q. 65 (2d Cir.1974).

2. *Bona Fide Use.* What is a bona fide use sufficient to establish trademark ownership and priority? Anthony L. Fletcher has identified several factors that courts weigh in favor of finding a genuine commercial use. In order of importance they are: (1) quantity and continuity of sale ("the question, of course, is how much is enough? Perhaps the answer is that he who needs to ask the question has not enough."); (2) consumer purchases ("such sales would seem to be a *sine qua non* of real use"); (3) business of mark owner; (4) quality control; (5) a distinguishing mark ("Blue Bell's trouble was that it slapped Time Out labels at random on slacks known, listed, ordered and sold as Mr. Hicks slacks."); (6) intent; (7) profit or loss ("plainly, this consideration is little more than a makeweight; there are plenty of *bona fide* marks whose products are sold at a loss"); (8) advertising; and (9) test market. Fletcher, "Time Out," "Snob," "Wipeout," and "Chicken of the Sea": The Death Knell of "Token Use"? 65 Trademark Rep. 336, 346–348 (1975).*

3. *Use in Commerce.* The Lanham Act defines commerce broadly, to mean "all commerce which may lawfully be regulated by Congress." 15 U.S.C.A. § 1127. Nonetheless, courts have construed the term more narrowly than contemporary constitutional doctrine would permit. As late as 1957, the Court of Customs and Patent Appeals ruled that a Philadelphia restaurant could not obtain service mark registration for its name because it "failed to establish that the services for which registration is sought are rendered in commerce which may lawfully be regulated by Congress within the meaning of the Trademark Act of 1946." Application of Bookbinder's Restaurant, Inc., 240 F.2d 365, 368, 112 U.S.P.Q. 326, 328 (1957). The applicant argued to no avail that its customers traveled to the restaurant in interstate commerce.

Judicial and administrative attitudes began to change in the mid-1960's. In Application of Gastown, Inc., 326 F.2d 780, 140 U.S.P.Q. 216 (1964), the Court of Customs and Patent Appeals allowed registration of a service mark used in a filling station situated on an interstate highway. Although the applicant was situated in only one state, its services to interstate travelers were in commerce. The court ruled that use in commerce includes use in intrastate commerce that directly affects interstate commerce.

Gastown involved a service mark. Thirteen years elapsed before trademarks received similarly liberal treatment. In Application of Silenus Wines, Inc., 557 F.2d 806, 194 U.S.P.Q. 261 (1977), the Court of Customs and Patent Appeals held that applicant, a wine importer, could register a mark affixed to wine it imported from France and sold only in Massachusetts. Recognizing that the applicant's importation "is not itself a 'use in commerce'," the court drew on the *Gastown* rationale to conclude "that intrastate sale of goods by the party who caused those goods to move in regulatable commerce, directly affects that commerce and is itself regulatable. Clearly, intrastate sale of imported wines by the importer sufficiently affects commerce with foreign nations to qualify those intrastate sales for the Trademark Act definition of 'commerce'." 557 F.2d at 809.

For a thoughtful review of *Silenus* and its background, see Calhoun, Use in Commerce After Silenus: What Does It Mean? 70 Trademark Rep. 47 (1980).

4. *Foreign Registrations.* One purpose of the intent to use provisions introduced by the 1988 amendments to the Lanham Act was to level the playing field for domestic and foreign trademark applicants. Other countries allow registration without use. By treaty, and under Lanham Act § 44, 15 U.S.C.A. § 1126, the United States is committed to honor these foreign registrations. As a result, first users in the United States can lose out to later users elsewhere.

SCM Corp. v. Langis Foods Ltd., 539 F.2d 196, 190 U.S.P.Q. 288 (D.C.Cir.1976), illustrates the problem. On March 28, 1969 defendant, a Canadian corporation, filed applications to register three trademarks in Canada. On May 15, 1969 defendant began to use these marks in Canada. On the same day—doubtless by coincidence—plaintiff's predecessor in interest, a United States corporation, began to use the identical mark in the United States. On June 18, 1969, plaintiff applied for registration in the United States. On September 19, 1969, defendant applied for registration in the United States, claiming priority on the basis of its Canadian applications. Registration issued to the defendant. Plaintiff petitioned for cancellation on the ground that it was the mark's first user in the United States. The Trademark Trial and Appeal Board ruled for the defendant. The District Court for the District of Columbia ruled for the plaintiff.

The Court of Appeals reversed. "Our holding in this case is that section 44(d) of the Trademark Act of 1946, which implements Article 4 of the Paris Union Treaty, accorded to appellant Langis a 'right to priority' for the six months following the filing of its Canadian application for registration, that is to say, from March 28, 1969 to September 27, 1969; and that an intervening use in the United States during that period cannot invalidate Langis's right to registration in this country pursuant to an application filed on September 19, 1969." 539 F.2d at 201. The court left open the question whether the defendant would have prevailed if it had made no use of the mark anywhere prior to its United States application. In Crocker National Bank v. Canadian Imperial Bank of Commerce, 223 U.S.P.Q. 909 (1984), the Trademark Trial and Appeal Board ruled that foreign applicants can register without proof of use anywhere.

The 1988 amendments to the Lanham Act reduced the disparate treatment of domestic and foreign applicants in two ways. First, the amendments enable United States nationals to apply for registration on the basis of an intent to use their marks in trade. Second, under

Lanham Act § 44(e), foreign applicants must state their bona fide intention to use their mark in commerce. 15 U.S.C.A. § 1126(d)(2). To be sure, section 44(e) provides that "use in commerce shall not be required prior to registration;" but the applicant must, as a practical matter use the mark within two years of its registration or face a presumption that it has abandoned the mark. See Lanham Act § 45, 15 U.S.C.A. § 1127 (definition of "abandoned.").

For a review of practice under Canada's intent to use provisions, see Bereskin, Intent–to–Use in Canada After Three Decades, 79 Trademark Rep. 379 (1989) ("Today, intent-to-use applications are very popular in Canada, accounting for more than half of all applications filed.").

5. *Affixation.* Trademark law has historically required that a trademark be affixed to the goods with which it is used in order to qualify for registration. Before the 1988 amendments, the Lanham Act required the mark to be "placed in any manner on the goods or their containers or the displays associated therewith or on the tags or labels affixed thereto." The 1988 amendments added: "or if the nature of the goods makes such placement impracticable, then on documents associated with the goods or their sale. . . ." 15 U.S.C.A. § 1127 (definition of "use in commerce").

The affixation requirement traces to the early practice of attaching or embedding marks in the goods whose source they were intended to identify. The law developed around the assumption that marks could be effective only in connection with the goods to which they were affixed. But what of marks for services? Since trademark law made affixation to goods necessary to a mark's inception and continued validity, logic dictated that there could be no valid trademark if there were no goods to which the mark could be affixed. Since services characteristically involve no goods, it followed that service marks could not be protected as trademarks and could only be protected, if at all, under unfair competition law. Congress finally eluded this logic by ignoring it. The Lanham Act puts service marks on a par with trademarks and treats use or display of the mark in the sale or advertising of services as the equivalent of affixation. See generally, Treece, Developments in the Law of Trademarks and Service Marks— Contributions of the Common Law, The Federal Act, State Statutes and the Restatement of Torts, 58 Calif.L.Rev. 885 (1970).

NOTE: TRADEMARK ABANDONMENT

Courts and the Congress apply two distinct tests for trademark abandonment. One test treats trademark abandonment as the obverse of trademark use. Just as use of a mark in connection with goods or services is required to obtain rights in the mark, so the mark's non-use in connection with goods or services forms the basis for loss of rights. The test for abandonment by non-use is whether the mark's use has been discontinued with the intention not to resume use. The second test treats trademark abandonment as the obverse of distinctiveness and secondary meaning. Just as rights will attach to a mark only if the mark indicates the source of goods or services to consumers, so rights will be lost when the mark loses its capacity to indicate source.

These two tests of trademark abandonment sometimes overlap. For example, if a firm stops using a mark for a long period, the mark will probably lose its capacity to indicate source to consumers, and a court will hold the mark to have been abandoned both because of its non-use and because of its inability to indicate source. But the two tests may also diverge. For example, there was no question in *Sweater Bee* but that General Mills had formally abandoned the "Kimberly" mark through nonuse. But, in observing that the parties might have to differentiate their product from General Mills' original Kimberly product, the court acknowledged the mark's continued identification of General Mills as the source of the product.

Abandonment by Non–Use. Section 45 of the Lanham Act, 15 U.S. C.A. § 1127, as amended by the 1988 Trademark Law Revision Act, provides that a mark shall be deemed to be abandoned "[w]hen its use has been discontinued with intent not to resume such use. Intent not to resume may be inferred from circumstances. Non-use for two consecutive years shall be prima facie evidence of abandonment. 'Use' of a mark means the bona fide use of that mark made in the ordinary course of trade, and not made merely to reserve a right in a mark." The last sentence of this provision, added by the 1988 amendments, means that token use of a mark will be insufficient to forestall a finding of abandonment.

Silverman v. CBS Inc., 870 F.2d 40 (2d Cir.1989) exemplifies the test for abandonment by non-use. Defendant there had acquired rights in the scripts and radio programs of the "Amos 'n' Andy Show" in 1948 and had subsequently broadcast the show, first on radio and then on television, through 1966 when it took the program off the air in response to complaints by civil rights organizations that the programs were demeaning to Blacks. By the time the question of abandonment came before the district court, the "Amos 'n' Andy" marks had not been used for twenty-one years. The district court ruled that the marks had not been abandoned because CBS had offered a reasonable explanation for its decision to keep the program off the air and because the company claimed an intention to resume use at some indefinite point in the future.

The court of appeals reversed. The court rejected the district court's interpretation of the statutory phrase, "intent not to resume," to mean an intent never to resume use, and held instead that the phrase means "intent not to resume use within the reasonably foreseeable future." According to the court, "[a] proprietor who temporarily suspends use of a mark can rebut the presumption of abandonment by showing reasonable grounds for the suspension and plans to resume use in the reasonably foreseeable future when the conditions requiring suspension abate." In the court's view, "this standard is sufficient to protect against the forfeiture of marks by proprietors who are temporarily unable to continue using them, while it also prevents warehousing of marks, which impedes commerce and competition."   870 F.2d at 46–47.

The *Silverman* court distinguished two earlier decisions in which it had found no abandonment. "In Saratoga Vichy Spring Co. v. Lehman, [625 F.2d 1037 (2d Cir.1980)], we rejected a claim of abandonment based on seven years of non-use where the initial decision to cease use resulted from a decision of the state legislature and the state, which was the trademark owner, continuously sought to sell the mark along with the mineral water business to which it applied. Similarly, in Defiance Button Machine Co. v. C & C Metal Products Corp., 759 F.2d 1053 (2d Cir.), cert. denied, 474 U.S. 844, 106 S.Ct. 131, 88 L.Ed.2d 108 (1985), we rejected an abandonment claim where, during a brief period of non-use, the proprietor tried to sell the mark, its associated goodwill, and some other assets and, upon failing to find a buyer, became a subsidiary of a company in its original line of trade and prepared to resume its business. In both cases, the proprietor of the mark had an intention to exploit the mark in the reasonably foreseeable future by resuming its use or permitting its use by others."   870 F.2d at 47.

Abandonment Through Loss of Distinctiveness.   Section 45 of the Lanham Act also defines abandonment to include the situation where "any course of conduct of the owner, including acts of omission as well as commission, causes the mark to become the generic name for the goods or services on or in connection with which it is used or otherwise to lose its significance as a mark. . . ."   For example, if the term, "Thermos," originally used to identify the source of a particular brand of vacuum bottle, comes in common parlance to describe the vacuum bottle itself, the mark will be held to have been abandoned under this provision. See King–Seeley Thermos Co. v. Aladdin Industries, Inc., page 224, below. Other instances of abandonment through loss of capacity to indicate source include the trademark owner's licensing of the mark without adequate control over the quality of goods or services purveyed by the licensee, see Dawn Donut Co. v. Hart's Food Stores, Inc., page 287, below; assignment of the mark without a contemporaneous transfer of the goodwill associated with the mark, see page 297, below; and, possibly, the failure to sue infringers who are making confusingly similar uses of the mark. See Uncas Mfg. Co. v. Clark & Coombs Co., 309 F.2d 818, 820, 135 U.S.P.Q. 282 (1st Cir.1962).

Consequences of Abandonment.   A finding of abandonment implies that the mark is in the public domain and that the mark's owner no longer has any rights in the mark. Does abandonment also imply that anyone is free to adopt the mark as her own? The answer turns on the rationale behind the finding of abandonment. If the trademark owner accompanies its cessation of use with a formal declaration of abandonment, as in *Sweater Bee,* any other firm can adopt the mark as its own. The question remains, however, whether the second comer *should* be allowed to use the mark since the mark will, for a time, identify the abandoning owner as the source of the second comer's goods or services, with consequent consumer confusion as to source. When the mark has been abandoned by non-use for two years or longer, or by uncontrolled licensing or assignment without associated goodwill, problems of consumer confusion are less likely to arise and the second comer has a better claim to making the mark its own. Where, however, the owner has abandoned the mark by allowing it to become generic, as in the *Thermos* case, no one firm should be entitled to make the mark its own since, by definition, the mark is incapable of indicating source.

2. DISTINCTIVENESS

a. COMMON LAW THEORY

DELAWARE & HUDSON CANAL CO. v. CLARK

Supreme Court of the United States, 1871.
80 U.S. 311, 20 L.Ed. 581.

Mr. Justice STRONG delivered the opinion of the court.

The first and leading question presented by this case is whether the complainants have an exclusive right to the use of the words "Lackawanna coal," as a distinctive name or trade-mark for the coal mined by them and transported over their railroad and canal to market.

The averments of the bill are supported by no inconsiderable evidence. The complainants were undoubtedly, if not the first, among the first producers of coal from the Lackawanna Valley, and the coal sent to market by them has been generally known and designated as Lackawanna coal. Whether the name "Lackawanna coal" was devised or adopted by them as a trade-mark before it came into common use is not so clearly established. On the contrary the evidence shows that long before the complainants commenced their operations, and long before they had any existence as a corporation, the region of country in which their mines were situated was called "The Lackawanna Valley"; that it is a region of large dimensions, extending along the Lackawanna River to its junction with the Susquehanna, embracing within its limits great bodies of coal lands, upon a portion of which are the mines of the complainants, and upon other portions of which are the mines of The Pennsylvania Coal Company, those of The Delaware, Lackawanna, and Western Railroad Company, and those of other smaller operators. The word "Lackawanna," then, was not devised by the complainants. They found it a settled and known appellative of the district in which their coal deposits and those of others were situated. At the time when they began to use it, it was a recognized description of the region, and of course of the earths and minerals in the region.

The bill alleges, however, not only that the complainants devised, adopted, and appropriated the word, as a name or trade-mark for their coal, but that it had never before been used, or applied in combination with the word "coal," as a name or trade-mark for any kind of coal, and it is the combination of the word Lackawanna with the word coal that constitutes the trade-mark to the exclusive use of which they assert a right.

It may be observed there is no averment that the other coal of the Lackawanna Valley differs at all in character or quality from that mined on the complainants' lands. On the contrary, the bill alleges that it cannot easily be distinguished therefrom by inspection. The bill is therefore an attempt to secure to the complainants the exclusive use of the name "Lackawanna coal," as applied, not to any manufacture of theirs, but to that portion of the coal of the Lackawanna Valley which they mine and send to market, differing neither in nature or quality from all other coal of the same region.

Undoubtedly words or devices may be adopted as trademarks which are not original inventions of him who adopts them, and courts of equity will protect him against any fraudulent appropriation or imitation of them by others. Property in a trade-mark, or rather in the use of a trade-mark or name, has very little analogy to that which exists in copyrights, or in patents for inventions. Words in common use, with some exceptions, may be adopted, if, at the time of their adoption, they were not employed to designate the same, or like articles of production. The office of a trade-mark is to point out distinctively the origin, or ownership of the article to which it is affixed; or, in other words, to give notice who was the producer. This may, in many cases, be done by a name, a mark, or a device well known, but not previously applied to the same article.

But though it is not necessary that the word adopted as a trade-name should be a new creation, never before known or used, there are some limits to the right of selection. This will be manifest when it is considered that in all cases where rights to the exclusive use of a trade-mark are invaded, it is invariably held that the essence of the wrong consists in the sale of the goods of one manufacturer or vendor as those of another; and that it is only when this false representation is directly or indirectly made that the party who appeals to a court of equity can have relief. This is the doctrine of all the authorities. Hence the trade-mark must either by itself, or by association, point distinctively to the origin or ownership of the article to which it is applied. The reason of this is that unless it does, neither can he who first adopted it be injured by any appropriation or imitation of it by others, nor can the public be deceived. The first appropriator of a name or device pointing to his ownership, or which, by being associated with articles of trade, has acquired an understood reference to the originator, or manufacturer of the articles, is injured whenever another adopts the same name or device for similar articles, because such adoption is in effect representing falsely that the productions of the latter are those of the former. Thus the custom and advantages to which the enterprise and skill of the first appropriator had given him a just right are abstracted for another's use, and this is done by deceiving the public, by inducing the public to purchase the goods and manufactures of one person supposing them to be those of another. The trade-mark must therefore be distinctive in its original signification, pointing to the origin of the article, or it must have become such by association. And there are two rules which are not to be overlooked. No one can claim protection for the exclusive use of a trade-mark or trade-name which would practically give him a monopoly in the sale of any goods other than those produced or made by himself. If he could, the public would be injured rather than protected, for competition would be destroyed. Nor can a generic name, or a name merely descriptive of an article of trade, of its qualities, ingredients, or characteristics, be employed as a trade-mark and the exclusive use of it be entitled to legal protection. As we said in the well-considered case of The Amoskeag Manufacturing Company v. Spear, "the owner of an original trade-mark has an undoubted right to be protected in the exclusive use of all the marks, forms, or symbols, that were appropriated as designating the true origin or ownership of the article or fabric to which they are affixed; but he has no right to the exclusive use of any words, letters, figures, or symbols, which have no relation to the origin or ownership of the goods, but are only meant to indicate their names or quality. He has no right to appropriate a sign or a symbol, which, from the nature of the fact it is used to signify, others may employ with equal truth, and therefore have an equal right to employ for the same purpose."

And it is obvious that the same reasons which forbid the exclusive appropriation of generic names or of those merely descriptive of the article manufactured and which can be employed with truth by other manufacturers, apply with equal force to the appropriation of geographical names, designating districts of country. Their nature is such that they cannot point to the origin (personal origin) or ownership of the articles of trade to which they may be applied. They point only at the place of production, not to the producer, and could they be appropriated exclusively, the appropriation would result in mischievous monopolies. Could such phrases, as "Pennsylvania wheat," "Kentucky hemp," "Virginia tobacco," or "Sea Island cotton," be protected as trade-marks; could any one prevent all others from using them, or from selling articles produced in the districts they describe under those appellations, it would greatly embarrass trade, and secure exclusive rights to individuals in that which is the common right of many. It can be permitted only when the reasons that lie at the foundation of the protection given to trade-marks are entirely overlooked. It cannot be said that there is any attempt to deceive the public when one sells as Kentucky hemp, or as Lehigh coal, that which in truth is such, or that there is any attempt to appropriate the enterprise or business reputation of another who may have previously sold his goods with the same description. It is not selling one man's goods as and for those of another. Nothing is more common than that a manufacturer sends his products to market, designating them by the name of the place where they were made. But we think no case can be found in which other producers of similar products in the same place, have been restrained from the use of the same name in describing their goods. . . .

It must then be considered as sound doctrine that no one can apply the name of a district of country to a well-known article of commerce, and obtain thereby such an exclusive right to the application as to prevent others inhabiting the district or dealing in similar articles coming from the district, from truthfully using the same designation. It is only when the adoption or imitation of what is claimed to be a trade-mark amounts to a false representation, express or implied, designed or incidental, that there is any title to relief against it. True it may be that the use by a second producer, in describing truthfully his product, of a name or a combination of words already in use by another, may have the effect of causing the public to mistake as to the origin or ownership of the product, but if it is just as true in its application to his goods as it is to those of another who first applied it, and who therefore claims an exclusive right to use it, there is no legal or moral wrong done. Purchasers may be mistaken, but they are not deceived by false representations, and equity will not enjoin against telling the truth.

These principles, founded alike on reason and authority, are decisive of the present case, and they relieve us from the consideration of much that was pressed upon us in the argument. The defendant has advertised for sale and he is selling coal not obtained from the plaintiffs, not mined or brought to market by them, but coal which he purchased from the Pennsylvania Coal Company, or from the Delaware, Lackawanna, and Western Railroad Company. He has advertised and sold it as Lackawanna coal. It is in fact coal from the Lackawanna region. It is of the same quality and of the same general appearance as that mined by the complainants. It is taken from the same veins or strata. It is truly described by the term Lackawanna coal, as is the coal of plaintiffs. The description does not point to its origin or ownership, nor indicate in the slightest degree the person, natural or artificial, who mined the coal or brought it to market. All the coal taken from that region is known and has been known for years by the trade, and rated in public statistics as Lackawanna coal. True the Delaware, Lackawanna, and Western Railroad Company have sometimes called their coal Scranton coal, and sometimes Scranton coal from the Lackawanna, and the Pennsylvania Coal Company have called theirs Pittston coal, thus referring to the parts of the region in which they mine. But the generic name, the comprehensive name for it all is Lackawanna coal. In all the coal regions there are numerous collieries, owned and operated by different proprietors, yet the product is truly and rightfully described as Schuylkill, Lehigh, or Lackawanna coal, according to the region from which it comes. We are therefore of opinion that the defendant has invaded no right to which the plaintiffs can maintain a claim. By advertising and selling coal brought from the Lackawanna Valley as Lackawanna coal, he has made no false representation, and we see no evidence that he has attempted to sell his coal as and for the coal of the plaintiffs. If the public are led into mistake, it is by the truth, not by any false pretense. If the complainants' sales are diminished, it is because they are not the only producers of Lackawanna coal, and not because of any fraud of the defendant. The decree of the Circuit Court dismissing the bill must, therefore, be Affirmed.

NOTE

Trademark law's distinctiveness requirement serves two related purposes. One is to ensure that a mark identifies a single source for goods or services, thus securing consumer expectations respecting source. Second, by denying protection to descriptive terms, the requirement ensures that competitors will be free to use these terms in describing their own goods or services. The distinctiveness requirement curbs the natural tendency of firms to select marks that not only have the capacity to indicate source but that also, through their descriptive elements, may capture a greater market share for goods or services than would be obtained by indication of source alone.

Distinctiveness occupies a spectrum. At one end of the spectrum are generic or common descriptive terms that are generally used as the names or descriptions of the goods or services to which the trademark is applied. "Soap" or "Hand Soap" for a bar of soap are two examples. These terms cannot become trademarks under any circumstances. Next on the spectrum are merely descriptive terms that describe a characteristic or ingredient of an article or service. These terms can become valid trademarks by acquiring secondary meaning—the capacity to identify the goods with a single source. "100% Pure Soap" is a possible example. A suggestive term only suggests an ingredient or characteristic of goods or services, and requires the consumer to use his imagination to determine the nature of the goods. "Ivory Soap" is an example. Suggestive terms can be protected without proof of secondary meaning. Finally, there are arbitrary or fanciful terms that are so far removed from the quality of goods or services that they not only receive the same protection as suggestive marks, but are also invulnerable to attack as being merely descriptive rather than suggestive. "Camay Soap" is an example. See Miller Brewing Co. v. G. Heileman Brewing Co., 561 F.2d 75, 195 U.S.P.Q. 281 (7th Cir.1977), cert. denied, 434 U.S. 1025, 98 S.Ct. 751, 54 L.Ed.2d 772 (1978).

Geographic terms occupy a comparable spectrum of distinctiveness. Where, as in Canal Co. v. Clark, the geographic term is synonymous with the quality of goods, courts will treat it as a generic or common descriptive term that is not entitled to protection. If the geographic term does not describe the quality of the goods to which it is applied, courts will treat it as geographically descriptive—not because it describes a characteristic or ingredient of the goods, but because firms frequently use geographic names to describe the source of a good's manufacture. Like merely descriptive terms, courts will protect these geographic terms if they acquire secondary meaning. "Thus if a manufacturer located in Chicago were to display the name CHICAGO on his shirts, for example, it has been the law for over a century that he could prevent another's subsequent use only if he could establish 'secondary meaning' in the term." In re Nantucket, Inc., 677 F.2d 95, 102–103, 213 U.S.P.Q. 889 (C.C.P.A.1982) (Nies, J., concurring). Where the geographic term only suggests a quality of the goods with which it is used, or is entirely fanciful or arbitrary as applied to the goods, courts will protect it even absent proof of secondary meaning. Professor McCarthy gives as examples, "NORTH POLE for bananas; SALEM for cigarettes; ATLANTIC for magazines; ENGLISH LEATHER for men's after-shave lotion; or ARCTIC for ice cream." J.T. McCarthy, Trademarks and Unfair Competition § 14:3 (2d ed. 1984).

b. STATUTORY VARIATIONS ON THE COMMON LAW THEME

See Statute Supplement 15 U.S.C.A. § 1052.

(i.) *"TRADEMARK BY WHICH THE GOODS OF THE APPLICANT MAY BE DISTINGUISHED FROM THE GOODS OF OTHERS"*

KING–SEELEY THERMOS CO. v. ALADDIN INDUSTRIES, INC.

United States Court of Appeals, Second Circuit, 1963.
321 F.2d 577, 138 U.S.P.Q. 349.

LEONARD P. MOORE, Circuit Judge.

This action by [sic] brought by appellant King–Seeley Thermos Co. (King–Seeley) to enjoin the defendant, Aladdin Industries, Incorporated from threatened infringement of eight trademark registrations for the word "Thermos" owned by appellant. Defendant answered, acknowledging its intention to sell its vacuum-insulated containers as "thermos bottles," asserted that the term "thermos" or "thermos bottle" is a generic term in the English language, asked that plaintiff's registrations of its trademark "Thermos" be cancelled and that it be adjudicated that plaintiff have no trademark rights in the word "thermos" on its vacuum bottles. The trial court held that plaintiff's registrations were valid but that the word "thermos" had become "a generic descriptive word in the English language . . . as a synonym for 'vacuum insulated' container." 207 F.Supp. 9.

The facts are set out at great length in the comprehensive and well-reasoned opinion of the district court and will not be detailed here. In that opinion, the court reviewed King–Seeley's corporate history and its use of the trademark "Thermos." He found that from 1907 to 1923, King–Seeley undertook advertising and educational campaigns that tended to make "thermos" a generic term descriptive of the product rather than of its origin. This consequence flowed from the corporation's attempt to popularize "Thermos bottle" as the name of that product without including any of the generic terms then used, such as "Thermos vacuum-insulated bottle." The court found that by 1923 the word "thermos" had acquired firm roots as a descriptive or generic word.

At about 1923, because of the suggestion in an opinion of a district court that "Thermos" might be a descriptive word, King–Seeley adopted the use of the word "vacuum" or "vacuum bottle" with the word "Thermos." Although "Thermos" was generally recognized in the trade as a trademark, the corporation did police the trade and notified those using "thermos" in a descriptive sense that it was a trademark. It failed, however, to take affirmative action to seek out generic uses by non-trade publications and protested only those which happened to come to its attention. Between 1923 and the early 1950's the generic use of "thermos" had grown to a marked extent in non-trade publications and by the end of this period there was wide-spread use by the unorganized public of "thermos" as a synonym for "vacuum insulated." The court concluded that King–Seeley had failed to use due diligence to rescue "Thermos" from becoming a descriptive or generic term.

Between 1954 and 1957, plaintiff showed awareness of the wide-spread generic use of "thermos" and of the need to educate the public to the word's trademark significance. It diversified its products to include those not directly related to containers designed to keep their contents hot or cold. It changed its name from the American Thermos Bottle Company to The American Thermos Products Company and intensified its policing activities of trade and non-trade publications. The court found, however, that the generic use of "thermos" had become so firmly impressed as a part of the everyday language of the American public that plaintiff's extraordinary efforts commencing in the mid–1950's came too late to keep "thermos" from falling into the public domain. The court also held that appellant's trademarks are valid and because there is an appreciable, though minority, segment of the consumer public which knows and recognizes plaintiff's trademarks, it imposed certain restrictions and limitations on the use of the word "thermos" by defendant.

We affirm the district court's decision that the major significance of the word "thermos" is generic. No useful purpose would be served by repeating here what is fully documented in the opinion of the court below.

Appellant's primary protest on appeal is directed at the district court's finding that

> The word 'thermos' became a part of the public domain because of the plaintiff's wide dissemination of the word 'thermos' used as a synonym for 'vacuum-insulated' and as an adjectival-noun, 'thermos', through its educational and advertising campaigns and because of the plaintiff's lack of reasonable diligence in asserting and protecting its trademark rights in the word 'Thermos' among the members of the unorganized public, exclusive of those in the trade, from 1907 to the date of this action. 207 F.Supp. at 14.

We are not convinced that the trademark's loss of distinctiveness was the result of some failure on plaintiff's part. Substantial efforts to preserve the trademark significance of the word were made by plaintiff, especially with respect to members of the trade. However, there was little they could do to prevent the public from using "thermos" in a generic rather than a trademark sense. And whether the appropriation by the public was due to highly successful educational and advertising campaigns or to lack of diligence in policing or not is of no consequence; the fact is that the word "thermos" had entered the public domain beyond recall. Even as early as 1910 plaintiff itself asserted that "Thermos had become a household word."

Judge Anderson found that although a substantial majority of the public knows and used the word "thermos", only a small minority of the public knows that this word has trademark significance. He wrote at 207 F.Supp. 21–22:

> The results of the survey [conducted at the behest of the defendant] were that about 75% of adults in the United States who were familiar with containers that keep the contents hot or cold, call such a container a 'thermos'; about 12% of the adult American public know that 'thermos' has a trade-mark significance, and about 11% use the term 'vacuum bottle'. This is generally corroborative of the court's conclusions drawn from the other evidence, except that such other evidence indicated that a somewhat larger minority than 12% was aware of the trade-mark meaning of 'thermos'; and a somewhat larger minority than 11% used the descriptive term 'vacuum' bottle or other container.

The record amply supports these findings.

Appellant argues that the court below misapplied the doctrine of the Aspirin and Cellophane cases. Its primary contention is that in those cases, there was no generic name, such as vacuum bottle, that was suitable for use by the general public. As a result, to protect the use of the only word that identified the product in the mind of the public would give the owners of the trademark an unfair competitive advantage. The rule of those cases, however, does not rest on this factor. Judge Learned Hand stated the sole issue in Aspirin to be: "What do the buyers understand by the word for whose use the parties are contending? If they understand by it only the kind of goods sold, then, I take it, it makes no difference whatever what efforts the plaintiff has made to get them to understand more." 272 F. at 509. Of course, it is obvious that the fact that there was no suitable descriptive word for either aspirin or cellophane made it difficult, if not impossible, for the original manufacturers to prevent their trademark from becoming generic. But the test is not what is available as an alternative to the public, but what the public's understanding is of the word that it uses. What has happened here is that the public had become accustomed to calling vacuum bottles by the word "thermos." If a buyer walked into a retail store asking for a thermos bottle, meaning any vacuum bottle and not specifically plaintiff's product, the fact that the appellation "vacuum bottle" was available to him is of no significance. The two terms had become synonymous; in fact, defendant's survey showed that the public was far more inclined to use the word "thermos" to describe a container that keeps its contents hot or cold than the phrase "vacuum bottle."

Appellant asserts that the courts in a number of cases have upheld the continued exclusive use of a dual functioning trademark, which both identifies the class of product as well as its source. As this court recently indicated:

a mark is not generic merely because it has *some* significance to the public as an indication of the nature or class of an article. . . . In order to become generic the *principal* significance of the word must be its indication of the nature or class of an article, rather than an indication of its origin.

Feathercombs, Inc. v. Solo Products Corp., 306 F.2d 251, 256 (2 Cir.), cert. denied, 371 U.S. 910, 83 S.Ct. 253, 9 L.Ed.2d 170. But see Marks v. Polaroid Corp., supra, 129 F.Supp. at 270 ("a defendant alleging invalidity of a trademark for genericness must show that to the consuming public as a whole the word has lost all its trademark significance").

Since in this case, the primary significance to the public of the word "thermos" is its indication of the nature and class of an article rather than as an indication of its source, whatever duality of meaning the word still holds for a minority of the public is of little consequence except as a consideration in the framing of a decree. Since the great majority of those members of the public who use the word "thermos" are not aware of any trademark significance, there is not enough dual use to support King–Seeley's claims to monopoly of the word as a trademark.

No doubt, the Aspirin and Cellophane doctrine can be a harsh one for it places a penalty on the manufacturer who has made skillful use of advertising and has popularized his product. However, King–Seeley has enjoyed a commercial monopoly of the word "thermos" for over fifty years. During that period, despite its efforts to protect the trademark, the public has virtually expropriated it as its own. The word having become part of the public domain, it would be unfair to unduly restrict the right of a competitor of King–Seeley to use the word.

The court below, mindful of the fact that some members of the public and a substantial portion of the trade still recognize and use the word "thermos" as a trademark, framed an eminently fair decree designed to afford King–Seeley as much future protection as was possible. The decree provides that defendant must invariably precede the use of the word "thermos" by the possessive of the name "Aladdin"; that the defendant must confine its use of "thermos" to the lower-case "t"; and that it may never use the words "original" or "genuine" in describing its product. In addition, plaintiff is entitled to retain the exclusive right to all of its present forms of the trademark "Thermos" without change. These conditions provide a sound and proper balancing of the competitive disadvantage to defendants arising out of plaintiff's exclusive use of the word "thermos" and the risk that those who recognize "Thermos" as a trademark will be deceived.

The courts should be ever alert, as the district court said, "to eliminate confusion and the possibility of deceit." The purchasing public is entitled to know the source of the article it desires to purchase. It is not within our province to speculate whether the dire predictions made by appellant in forceful appellate argument will come to pass. Certain it is that the district court made every endeavor in its judgment to give as much protection to plaintiff as possible. The use by defendant of the now generic word "thermos" was substantially curtailed. Plaintiff's trademark "thermos" was protected in every style of printing except the lower case "thermos" and then the use of the word must be preceded by the possessive of defendant's name "Aladdin" or the possessive of "Aladdin" plus one of defendant's brand names. Any doubt about plaintiff's position in the field is removed by the prohibition against the use by defendant in labeling, advertising or publication of the words "genuine" or "original" in referring to the word "thermos". Furthermore, the district court has given both parties the opportunity to apply to it for such orders and directions as may be warranted in the light of changed circumstances and for the enforcement of compliance or for the punishment of violations. In our opinion the trial court has reached a most equitable solution which gives appropriate consideration to the law and the facts.

Affirmed.

NOTES

1. The *Thermos* court was premature in its optimism about the security to be afforded by the trial court decree. Although Judge Anderson's careful resolution no doubt gave "appropriate consideration to the law and the facts," it did not staunch the further erosion of plaintiff's mark. In 1968 the district court denied Aladdin's petition to modify the injunction, 289 F.Supp. 155, 159 U.S.P.Q. 604 (1968). On Aladdin's appeal, the court of appeals vacated the order of denial, 418 F.2d 31, 163 U.S.P.Q. 65 (2d Cir.1969).

Judge Anderson, who by now had ascended to the court of appeals, was designated to consider the petition on the remand to the district court. Recognizing that "it is unrealistic to assume that the situation has remained unchanged since 1962," and that "more than eight years of widespread use of the word 'thermos' as a generic term must, to a considerable degree, have brought home to the unorganized public, including the approximately 11% who in 1962 recognized and relied upon King–Seeley's trademarks, that there were both the trade name use and the generic use," he held that Aladdin was entitled to a modification of the decree, "which will, first, afford to it, in its advertising material, trade literature and press releases, the use of the word 'thermos' with an initial capital 'T' where such initial capitalization is required by the generally accepted and authoritatively approved rules of grammar, and second, eliminate the requirement that the use of lower case 'thermos,' in its advertising material, trade literature and press releases, be preceded by the possessive of 'Aladdin' or by the possessive of 'Aladdin' with one of Aladdin's brand names provided any such use makes clear that it emanates from Aladdin." 320 F.Supp. 1156, 1159, 166 U.S.P.Q. 381, 383 (D.Conn.1970).

In Bayer v. United Drug Co., 272 Fed. 505 (2d Cir.1921), Judge Learned Hand took a different approach to arresting the erosion of a mark that had generic connotations. Hand found that for physicians,

Once a trademark, not always a trademark.

They were once proud trademarks, now they're just names. They failed to take precautions that would have helped them have a long and prosperous life.

We need your help to stay out of there. Whenever you use our name, please use it as a proper adjective in conjunction with our products and services: e.g., Xerox copiers or Xerox financial services. And never as a

verb: "to Xerox" in place of "to copy," or as a noun: "Xeroxes" in place of "copies."

With your help and a precaution or two on our part, it's "Once the Xerox trademark, always the Xerox trademark."

Team Xerox. We document the world.

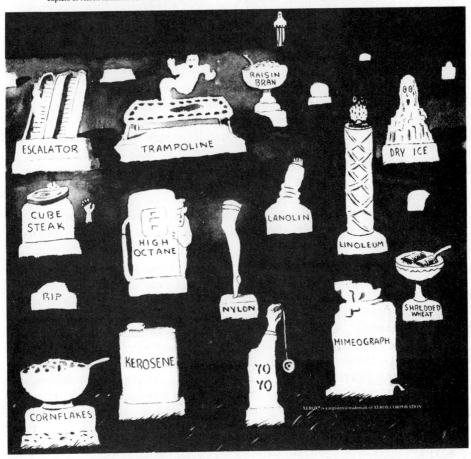

manufacturing chemists, and probably retail druggists, the term "Aspirin" had always functioned as a trademark and signified the plaintiff, while, for the general consuming public, the term had become generic, describing acetylsalicylic acid. Hand entered a bifurcated decree enjoining defendant's use of the term in its sales to manufacturing chemists, physicians and retail druggists but permitting its unfettered use in direct sales to the general public. Given the typical ungainliness of names assigned on the basis of a product's chemical formula, could you, as counsel to a pharmaceutical concern, devise a program that would assure your client full trademark protection in both markets, professional and nonprofessional, identified by Judge Hand? See Weigel, Generic Names versus Trademarks, 52 Trademark Rep. 768 (1962) for one approach.

2. It is a standard bromide of trademark law that a mark's distinctiveness turns on a showing "that the primary significance of the term in the minds of the consuming public is not the product but the producer." Kellogg Co. v. National Biscuit Co., 305 U.S. 111, 118, 39 U.S.P.Q. 296 (1938). The test should be taken with a grain of salt. Few consumers care to know the name of the company that produced the cereal they had for breakfast. Doubtless, few even care to know that the same anonymous company that produced the last box of cereal also produced the one they are about to buy—so long as the quality of the product is the same.

At least one court has read the distinctiveness test literally—with disastrous results. In Anti–Monopoly, Inc. v. General Mills Fun Group, Inc., 684 F.2d 1316, 216 U.S.P.Q. 588 (9th Cir.1982), cert. denied, 459 U.S. 1227, 103 S.Ct. 1234, 75 L.Ed.2d 468 (1983), the court held that the word, "Monopoly" as applied to the popular board game had become generic because consumers associated the word with a product—the board game—rather than with its producer—Parker Brothers. A consumer survey introduced at trial had asked consumers to pick between two alternatives to describe their motivation in purchasing the Monopoly game: "Sixty-five percent chose: 'I want a "Monopoly" game primarily because I am interested in playing "Monopoly," I don't much care who makes it.' Thirty-two percent chose: 'I would like Parker Brothers' "Monopoly" game primarily because I like Parker Brothers' products.'" In the court's view, the overwhelming choice of the first alternative indicated that the primary significance of the term to consumers was the product, not the producer. 684 F.2d 1324–26.

Congress moved quickly to reverse the Anti–Monopoly result. The Trademark Clarification Act of 1984, P.L. 98–620, § 102, 98 Stat. 3335 (1984), amended section 14(c) of the Lanham Act, 15 U.S.C.A. § 1064(c), dealing with cancellation of registrations, to provide that "[t]he primary significance of the registered mark to the relevant public rather than purchaser motivation shall be the test for determining whether the registered mark has become the common descriptive name of goods or services in connection with which it has been used." The Act also amended section 45's definition of "trademark" to read "[t]he term 'trademark' includes any word, name, symbol, or device or any combination thereof adopted and used by a manufacturer or merchant to identify and distinguish his goods, including a unique product, from those manufactured or sold by others and to indicate the source of the goods, even if that source is unknown." P.L. 98–620, § 103(1).

3. *Preventing Genericide.* What practical steps can a trademark owner take to prevent its mark from falling victim to genericide? What practical steps, in addition to those already undertaken, could King–Seeley have taken to protect its "Thermos" mark?

What legal steps can a trademark owner take to prevent its mark from becoming generic? Competitors' use of the mark on similar goods and services clearly falls within the ambit of trademark infringement. But what rights does the trademark owner have against individuals who use the term descriptively in conversation? What rights might it have against publishers of trade and popular journals and dictionaries that refer to the mark in its descriptive sense? In Selchow & Righter Co. v. McGraw–Hill Book Co., 580 F.2d 25, 198 U.S.P.Q. 577 (2d Cir. 1978), plaintiff, registrant of the mark "Scrabble" for use in connection with games, scoring devices, score pads and accessories, obtained a preliminary injunction against defendant's distribution of "The Complete Scrabble Dictionary." The court of appeals agreed with the district court that, because publication of defendant's book "might render the 'SCRABBLE' trademark generic," plaintiff had sufficiently demonstrated the possibility of irreparable injury. 580 F.2d 27.

See generally, Robb, Trademark Misuse in Dictionaries: Inadequacy of Existing Legal Action and a Suggested Cure, 65 Marq.L.Rev. 179 (1981); Treece & Stephenson, Another Look at Descriptive and Generic Terms in American Trademark Law, 29 Sw.L.Rev. 547 (1975).

4. In May, 1978 the Federal Trade Commission filed a petition under Lanham Act § 14, 15 U.S.C.A. § 1064, seeking cancellation of the trademark, "Formica," on the ground that the term had become generic as applied to "laminated sheets of wood, fabric, or paper impregnated with synthetic resin and consolidated under heat and pressure, for use on table tops, furniture and wall panelling." Petition for Cancellation, F.T.C. v. Formica Corp., 200 U.S.P.Q. 182, 185 (T.T.A.B. May 31, 1978). The move produced a small furor among advertisers and the trademark bar. One result of the ensuing congressional inquiry was that Congress cut off funds for the F.T.C. suit. On June 13, 1980, the Trademark Trial and Appeal Board dismissed the action with prejudice. 209 U.S. P.Q. 255 (1980).

For a superb review and analysis of the *Formica* petition and the ensuing judicial and legislative developments, see Comment, Section 14 of the Lanham Act—F.T.C. Authority to Challenge Generic Trademarks, 48 Fordham L.Rev. 437 (1980).

5. *Bibliographic Note.* Generic marks have provoked a lively debate in the literature. See Folsom & Teply, Trademarked Generic Words, 89 Yale L.J. 1323 (1980); Swann, An Economic Approach to Genericness: A Reply to Folsom and Teply, 70 Trademark Rep. 243 (1980); Folsom & Teply, Surveying "Genericness" in Trademark Litiga-

tion, 78 Trademark Rep. 1 (1988); Swann & Palladino, Surveying "Genericness": A Critique of Folsom and Teply, 78 Trademark Rep. 179 (1988); Folsom & Teply, A Reply to Swann and Palladino's Critique of Folsom and Teply's Model Survey, 78 Trademark Rep. 197 (1988); Oddi, Assessing "Genericness": Another View, 78 Trademark Rep. (1988).

See also, Burgunder, An Economic Approach to Trademark Genericism, 23 Am.Bus.L.J. 391 (1985).

6. *Expired Patents.* Should a trademark used in connection with patented subject matter fall into the public domain upon expiration of the patent? In Kellogg Co. v. National Biscuit Co., 305 U.S. 111, 59 S.Ct. 109, 83 L.Ed. 73, 39 U.S.P.Q. 296 (1938), the Court drew on broad dicta in Singer Mfg. Co. v. June Mfg. Co., 163 U.S. 169, 16 S.Ct. 1002, 41 L.Ed. 118 (1896), for an affirmative answer: "Since during the life of the patent 'Shredded Wheat' was the general designation of the patented product, there passed to the public on the expiration of the patent, not only the right to make the article as it was made during the patent period, but also the right to apply thereto the name by which it had become known." 305 U.S. at 118, 59 S.Ct. at 113.

The *Singer* Court did not in fact rule that, as a matter of law, trademarks used with patented subject matter fall into the public domain upon the patent's expiration. The Court held only that previous patent protection is one of several facts to be considered in the determination whether a mark has become generic. The Court viewed the case as raising two essentially factual questions—"first, were the sewing machines made by the Singer Company so, in whole or in part, protected by patents as to cause the name 'Singer' to become, during the existence of the monopoly, the generic designation of such machines . . . second, irrespective of the question of patent, was the name 'Singer' by the consent and acquiescence of Singer himself and that of the Singer Company, voluntarily used as a generic designation of the class and character of machines manufactured by I.M. Singer & Co. or the Singer Manufacturing Company so that in consequence of this voluntary action the name became the generic designation of the machines. . . ."

The Court's answer to the first question merged with its resolution of the second. The Court noted that, from "the beginning every machine had conspicuously marked on it the name of the manufacturer, 'I.M. Singer & Co.' or the 'Singer Mfg. Co.'; only occasionally was the word 'Singer' alone attached to any of the machines;" and that, at about the time the patents expired, "the trade-mark was affixed to the machines, and the name of the manufacturer, except as indicated by the trade-mark, disappeared, and was regularly supplanted by the word 'Singer' alone." The Court concluded: "This coincidence between the expiration of the patents and the appearance of the trade-mark on the machines and the use of the word 'Singer' alone tends to create a strong implication that the company, with the knowledge that the patents, which covered their machines, were about to expire substituted the trade-mark for the plain designation of the source of manufacture theretofore continuously used and added the word 'Singer' which had become the designation by which the public knew the machine, as a distinctive and separate mark, in order thereby to retain in the possession of the company the real fruits of the monopoly when that monopoly had passed away." 163 U.S. at 181, 16 S.Ct. at 1006. After an extensive review of this and other facts, the Court decided that the mark "Singer" had become generic. It also ruled, however, that defendant was not at complete liberty and must accompany uses of the mark on its products with a clear indication that it, not Singer, was their source. For the suggestion that the "Singer" mark itself has been substantially resurrected, see Singer Mfg. Co. v. Redlich, 109 F.Supp. 623, 96 U.S.P.Q. 85 (S.D.Cal.1952).

(ii.) *"DECEPTIVE . . . MATTER"*

IN RE BUDGE MANUFACTURING CO.

United States Court of Appeals, Federal Circuit, 1988.
857 F.2d 773, 8 U.S.P.Q.2d 1259.

NIES, Circuit Judge.

Budge Manufacturing Co., Inc., appeals from the final decision of the United States Trademark Trial and Appeal Board refusing registration of LOVEE LAMB for "automotive seat covers," application Serial No. 507,974 filed November 9, 1984. The basis for rejection is that the term LAMB is deceptive matter within the meaning of section 2(a) of the Lanham Act, 15 U.S.C. § 1052(a) (1982), as applied to Budge's goods which are made wholly from synthetic fibers. We affirm.

Opinion

Section 2(a) of the Lanham Act bars registration of a mark which: "Consists of or comprises . . . deceptive . . . matter. . . ." As stated in In re Automatic Radio Mfg. Co., 404 F.2d 1391, 1396, 160 USPQ 233, 236 (CCPA 1969): "The proscription [of section 2(a)] is not against misdescriptive terms unless they are also deceptive." Thus, that a mark or part of a mark may be inapt or misdescriptive as applied to an applicant's goods does not make it "deceptive." Id. (AUTOMATIC RADIO not a deceptive mark for air conditioners, ignition systems, and antennas). Recognizing that premise, the Trademark Trial and Appeal Board has sought to articulate a standard by which "deceptive matter" under section 2(a) can be judged. In this case, the board applied the three-part test which was stated in In re Shapely, Inc., 231 USPQ 72, 73 (TTAB 1986): (1) whether the term is misdescriptive as applied to the goods, (2) if so, whether anyone would be likely to believe the misrepresentation, and (3) whether the misrepresentation would materially affect a potential purchaser's decision to buy the goods.

Budge argues that the board was bound to follow the standard articulated in In re Simmons, Inc., 192 USPQ 331 (TTAB 1976). Per Budge, *Simmons* sets forth a different standard in that it requires as a minimum that "the mark convey some information, upon which an intended customer may reasonably rely, concerning something about the character, quality, function, composition or use of the goods to induce the purchase thereof, but which information, in fact, is misleadingly false." Id. at 332.

The standard applied by the board for determining deceptive matter in section 2(a) cases has not been uniformly articulated in some material respects. For example, in at least one opinion an *intent* to mislead was required to establish section 2(a) deceptiveness. See Steinberg Bros., Inc. v. Middletown Rubber Corp., 137 USPQ 319, 321 (TTAB 1963). However, while phrased differently, we discern no material difference between the standard set forth in *Shapely* and that in *Simmons*. Budge points to no substantive difference and, indeed, merely quarrels over the different result here from that in *Simmons*. Thus, we need not address the question of the extent to which panels of the board are required to follow prior decisions of other board panels.

What is more significant, in any event, is that this court is bound only by its own precedent, none of which Budge discusses. Although we will give deference in appropriate circumstances to a board's decision on a question of law, we are, of course, not bound by such rulings. Where the issue relates to deceptive misdescriptiveness within the meaning of 2(a), we are in general agreement with the standard set out by the board in *Shapely*, with the following amplification in part drawn from *Simmons:*

(1) Is the term misdescriptive of the character, quality, function, composition or use of the goods?

(2) If so, are prospective purchasers likely to believe that the misdescription actually describes the goods?

(3) If so, is the misdescription likely to affect the decision to purchase?

In *ex parte* prosecution, the burden is initially on the Patent and Trademark Office (PTO) to put forth sufficient evidence that the mark for which registration is sought meets the above criteria of unregistrability. Mindful that the PTO has limited facilities for acquiring evidence—it cannot, for example, be expected to conduct a survey of the marketplace or obtain consumer affidavits—we conclude that the evidence of record here is sufficient to establish a *prima facie* case of deceptiveness. That evidence shows with respect to the three-pronged test:

(1) Budge admits that its seat covers are not made from lamb or sheep products. Thus, the term LAMB is misdescriptive of its goods.

(2) Seat covers for various vehicles can be and are made from natural lambskin and sheepskin. Applicant itself makes automobile seat covers of natural sheepskin. Lambskin is defined, inter alia, as fine-grade sheepskin. See Webster's Third New International Dictionary 639 (unabr. 1976). The board's factual inference

is reasonable that purchasers are likely to believe automobile seat covers denominated by the term LAMB or SHEEP are actually made from natural sheep or lamb skins.

(3) Evidence of record shows that natural sheepskin and lambskin is more expensive than simulated skins and that natural and synthetic skins have different characteristics. Thus, the misrepresentation is likely to affect the decision to purchase.

Faced with this *prima facie* case against registration, Budge had the burden to come forward with countering evidence to overcome the rejection. It wholly failed to do so.

Budge argues that its use of LAMB as part of its mark is not misdescriptive when considered in connection with the text in its advertising, which states that the cover is of "simulated sheepskin." Some, but not all, of Budge's specimen labels also have this text. This evidence is unpersuasive. In R. Neumann & Co. v. Overseas Shipments, Inc., 326 F.2d 786, 51 CCPA 946, 140 USPQ 276 (1964), a similar argument was made that the mark DURAHYDE on shoes was not deceptive as an indication of leather because of tags affixed to the shoes proclaiming the legend "Outwears leather." In discounting the evidence, the court stated: "The legends constitute advertisement material separate and apart from any trademark significance." Id. at 790, 51 CCPA at 951, 140 USPQ at 279. To the same effect is In re Bonide Chemical Co., 46 F.2d 705, 18 CCPA 909, 8 USPQ 297 (1931). There the court held, with respect to a clarifying statement made in advertising circulars, which the applicant urged negated the deceptive nature of the mark, "This argument is beside the issue. It is the word of the mark, not the statement of an advertising circular which appellant seeks to register. . . ." Id. at 708, 18 CCPA at 913, 8 USPQ at 300.

Thus, we conclude that the board properly discounted Budge's advertising and labeling which indicate the actual fabric content. Misdescriptiveness of a term may be negated by its meaning in the context of the whole mark inasmuch as the combination is seen together and makes a unitary impression. A.F. Gallun & Sons Corp. v. Aristocrat Leather Prods., Inc., 135 USPQ 459, 460 (TTAB 1962) (COPY CALF not misdescriptive, but rather suggests *imitation* of calf skin). The same is not true with respect to explanatory statements in advertising or on labels which purchasers may or may not note and which may or may not always be provided. The statutory provision bars registration of *a mark* comprising deceptive matter. Congress has said that the advantages of registration may not be extended to a mark which deceives the public. Thus, the mark standing alone must pass muster, for that is what the applicant seeks to register, not extraneous explanatory statements.

Budge next argues that no reasonable purchaser would expect to purchase lambskin automobile seat covers because none made of lambskin are on the market. Only sheepskin automobile seat covers are being made, per Budge. Not only was no evidence submitted on the point Budge seeks to make, only statements of Budge's attorney, but also the argument is without substance. The board properly equated sheepskin and lambskin based on the dictionary definition which indicates that the terms may be used interchangeably. In addition, while Budge would discount the evidence presented that bicycle and airline seat coverings are made of lambskin, we conclude that it does support the board's finding that there is nothing incongruous about automobile seat covers being made from lambskin. We also agree with the board's conclusion that any differences between sheepskin and lambskin would not be readily apparent to potential purchasers of automobile seat covers. The board's finding here that purchasers are likely to believe the misrepresentation is not clearly erroneous.

To overturn the board's finding that misdescribing synthetic fabric as "lamb" would affect a purchaser's decision to purchase the item, Budge merely reiterates its argument that its advertising negates the possibility of misdescriptiveness. We find that argument no more persuasive in this context than previously and, in any event, wholly unresponsive to this issue.

Finally, we note the evidence of Budge's extensive sales since 1974 under the mark. However, it is too well established for argument that a mark which includes deceptive matter is barred from registration and cannot acquire distinctiveness.

Conclusion

None of the facts found by the board have been shown to be clearly erroneous nor has the board erred as a matter of law. Accordingly, we affirm the board's decision that Budge's mark LOVEE LAMB for automobile seat covers made from synthetic fibers is deceptive within the meaning of 15 U.S.C. § 1052(a) and is, thus, barred from registration.

AFFIRMED.

The opinion of NICHOLS, Senior Circuit Judge, concurring, is omitted.

(iii.) CONFUSING SIMILARITY TO PRIOR MARKS

IN RE N.A.D., INC.

United States Court of Appeals, Federal Circuit, 1985.
754 F.2d 996, 224 U.S.P.Q. 969.

RICH, Circuit Judge.

This appeal is from the February 29, 1984 decision of the United States Patent and Trademark Office (PTO) Trademark Trial and Appeal Board (board), 221 USPQ 1115, affirming the PTO Trademark Attorney's refusal to register a trademark by reason of 15 U.S.C. § 1052(d), section 2(d) of the Trademark Act of 1946. We reverse.

The mark sought to be registered is NARKOMED. The goods named in the application are "anesthesia machines for use in surgery." Application to register was filed May 7, 1980, alleging first use April 3,

1972. The rejection is predicated on two prior registrations: (1) Reg.
No. 982,657, April 23, 1974, or [sic] NARCO MEDICAL SERVICES for
"rental and leasing of hospital and surgical equipment and consultation
services relating to the operation of such equipment." This service
mark registration issued to Air–Shields, Inc. and on April 26, 1978 was
assigned to Narco Scientific Industries, Inc. (2) Reg. No. 1,036,695,
March 30, 1976, of NARCO and design (see board opinion for illustration) for a long list of specialized medical equipment including, as most
relevant here, "apparatus for administration of anesthesia." This
registration issued to Narco Scientific Industries, Inc. which changed its
name to Narco Scientific, Inc. The board opinion contains the full list
of goods named in the registration.

The examining attorney and the board were both of the view that
registration must be refused under § 2(d)[1] because, in their commonly
held opinions, on which they had no doubts, "confusion between the
applicant's mark and the cited registered marks is likely," to quote
from the board's opinion. Applicant's arguments relying on differences
in the marks, sophistication of purchasers of the equipment or services,
and the high prices thereof were summarily dismissed as "not persuasive." As to registration (2), supra, there is no question that identical
goods are named by both applicant and registrant. As to the services
in registration (1), they are clearly closely related to applicant's goods,
all being in the medical equipment field.

As this court and its predecessor, the Court of Customs and Patent
Appeals, have often said, each likelihood-of-confusion trademark case
must be determined on its own facts. Beside that, however, the salient
feature of this case is an argument, which has several times been fully
dealt with in earlier cases, based on agreements between appellant and
the owner of the prior registrations relied on to support the rejection
containing a consent to the use and registration of NARKOMED by
appellant.

The agreements containing the consent to use and register came
about as follows. Applicant-appellant, N.A.D., Inc., which also does
business as North American Drager, is a Pennsylvania corporation the
majority of the stock of which is owned by Draegerwerk AG, of
Luebeck, Federal Republic of Germany. Draegerwerk AG brought
cancellation proceedings to cancel the two reference registrations herein, now both owned by Narco Scientific, Inc. These cancellations were
inter partes proceedings extending over several years in which competitors in a relatively restricted field were involved, the disputes involving
many marks other than NARKOMED. By written settlement agreements, Draegerwerk AG and N.A.D. undertook to abandon certain
pending trademark registration applications and to discontinue the use

---

1. "No trademark by which the goods of
the applicant may be distinguished from
the goods of others shall be refused registration on the principal register on account
of its nature unless it—

    *   *   *   *   *

(d) Consists of or comprises a mark
which so resembles a mark registered in
the Patent and Trademark Office . . . as
to be likely, when applied to the goods of
the applicant, to cause confusion, or to
cause mistake, or to deceive. . . ."

of four different NARKO– marks, provision being made for a phasing-out period. Money changed hands. In the course of it all, the other party, Narco Scientific Inc., owner of the two references, expressly acknowledged N.A.D.'s right "to the use and registration of the trademark NARKOMED . . . for use in the sale of hospital and medical equipment." The first agreement so providing was in November 1975 and the second one, reaffirming that provision, was in September 1979. While we are uninformed as to all the details of the disputes and negotiations, these competitors clearly thought out their commercial interests with care. We think it highly unlikely that they would have deliberately created a situation in which the sources of their respective products would be confused by their customers. As was said by our predecessor court in In re E.I. duPont de Nemours & Co., 476 F.2d 1357, 1362, 177 USPQ 563, 568 (CCPA 1973), "It can be safely taken as fundamental that reputable businessmen-users of valuable trademarks have no interest in *causing* public confusion."

The Examining Attorney, while citing *DuPont* and saying that "great weight is to be accorded consent agreements," interpreted that case, erroneously, as allowing registration only "where the goods of the respective parties were disparate, and the markets and trade channels were different." She held that "Notwithstanding an agreement between the parties, the likelihood of confusion cannot be avoided." She concluded that "refusal of registration is appropriate notwithstanding the consent agreement." In affirming, the board refused to give any weight to the contractual consent to use and to register, saying:

> An *appropriate* consent agreement can tip the scales in favor of an applicant *if there is doubt* as to the likelihood of confusion. * * * In light of the *fact* that no doubt exists [in the board's mind] and the parties have failed to *specify how* customer confusion can be avoided, we do not find that the consent agreement is an appropriate basis upon which to base registration. [Emphasis ours.]

. . . Consents come in different forms and under circumstances in infinite variety. They are, however, but one factor to be taken into account with all of the other relevant circumstances bearing on the likelihood of confusion referred to in § 2(d). The board spent much of its opinion analyzing and dissecting the *marks* in arriving at its opinion that *they* are "confusingly similar," and then finding it "axiomatic that confusion is likely when confusingly similar marks are used to identify closely related goods and services." We have never found anything axiomatic about the application of § 2(d) to fact situations, especially when consent agreements are involved. All aspects of the fact situation must be appraised and the situation judged as a whole.

In the present case, we start with the marks. They are not identical, as the marks have been in some other cases such as *DuPont* [476 F.2d 1357 (CCPA 1973)], *United,* [508 F.2d 1341 (CCPA 1975)] and *Loew's* [197 U.S.P.Q. 183 (TTAB 1977)]. Appellant's mark is NARKOMED; the reference marks are NARCO and NARCO MEDI-

CAL SERVICES. An alert purchaser could readily distinguish them. We turn next to the goods. With reference to NARCO, there is identity; with reference to NARCO MEDICAL SERVICES there is not. The most that can be said is that appellant's anesthesia machines and Narco Scientific's rental and leasing services are both in the medical field. A most important factor, in our view, is the specific nature of appellant's goods. The record shows the machines to be elaborate, sizeable, complex pieces of technical apparatus of the kind which would be purchased only in consultation with an anesthesiologist or someone with equivalent technical knowledge. In other words, only very sophisticated purchasers are here involved who would buy with great care and unquestionably know the source of the goods. There would be no likelihood of confusing source merely by reason of the similarity between NARCO and NARKOMED. Cf. In re General Electric Co., 304 F.2d 688, 134 USPQ 190 (CCPA 1962) (VULCAN and VULKENE for commercial electrical wire held readily distinguishable). Another factor is the cost of appellant's apparatus. Though not of record, it would obviously be considerable—definitely not in the class of the cigarettes and smokers pipes involved in *Loew's*.

Taking all of the above facts into account, it is not at all surprising that the owner of the reference marks was willing to consent to the use and registration by N.A.D. Inc. of NARKOMED for "hospital and medical equipment." This consent, moreover, having been given by a competitor well acquainted with the realities of the business suffices to persuade us, when taken together with all of the other facts, that the board and the Examining Attorney were simply wrong in their opinions that there would be a likelihood of confusion, and we so hold. "A mere *assumption* that confusion is likely will rarely prevail against uncontroverted evidence from those on the firing line that it is not." *DuPont*, supra, 476 F.2d at 1363, 177 USPQ at 568.

The decision of the board affirming the refusal to register is *reversed*.

REVERSED.

(iv.) *"MERELY DESCRIPTIVE OR DECEPTIVELY MISDESCRIPTIVE"*

IN RE SUN OIL CO.

United States Court of Customs and Patent Appeals, 1970.
426 F.2d 401, 165 U.S.P.Q. 718.

ALMOND, Judge.

Sun Oil Company brings this appeal from the decision of the Trademark Trial and Appeal Board, affirming the examiner's refusal to allow appellant's application to register "Custom-Blended" for gasoline on the ground that the mark is merely descriptive of applicant's goods within the meaning of section 2(e)(1) of the Trademark Act of 1946 (15 U.S.C.A. § 1052(e)(1)) and because the evidence submitted has not clearly established a secondary meaning, denoting that the mark has become distinctive of appellant's goods, within section 2(f) of the Act (15 U.S.C.A. § 1052(f)).

The application seeking registration on the Principal Register alleges use since 1956. The mark is displayed on special pumps, called "blending pumps," at appellant's service stations. The application is designated a continuation of an earlier application filed July 13, 1961, in which registration on the Principal Register was sought for the same mark for gasoline and refused by the Trademark Trial and Appeal Board on the ground that the mark was merely a descriptive connotation to purchasers of applicant's goods.

In his Answer, the examiner predicated refusal of registration on the ground that Custom–Blended is merely descriptive of appellant's goods within the meaning of section 2(e)(1) because it is so highly descriptive of appellant's blended gasoline that it is incapable of becoming distinctive as claimed. It was the examiner's opinion that the term Custom–Blended merely informs purchasers that various grades of gasoline from appellant's blending pumps are custom blended for them; that the word "custom" is commonly used to indicate things made to order; that it has very little trademark significance when used in connection with blended gasoline; that appellant is not entitled to exclusive appropriation of this term, which so aptly describes custom-blended gasoline; and that the conclusion derived from surveys conducted by appellant is that purchasers who are acquainted with appellant's Blue Sunoco gasoline know that such gasoline is custom blended.

In affirming refusal of registration, the board stated that granted that the generic terms for appellant's blended gasolines are pump-blended and multiple-grade gasolines, there is no question that " 'Custom–Blended' has a merely descriptive significance in that it will immediately indicate to patrons of applicant's service stations that the various grades of gasoline dispensed thereat are custom blended to their needs and requirements;" that in view thereof and the decision on applicant's prior application, it was incumbent upon applicant to show that the facts and circumstances since that decision have changed in that " 'Custom–Blended' now serves as an indication of origin of applicant's gasoline to the general public;" that the case, therefore, turned upon the sufficiency of applicant's evidence in that regard; that "the only definite conclusion that can be drawn from the surveys is that purchasers who are acquainted with applicant's 'Sunoco' gasoline know that such gasoline is custom blended;" that this manifestly does not support applicant's assertion that Custom–Blended has acquired a secondary meaning as an indication of origin for gasoline, and that upon the record presented Custom–Blended does not possess anything "other than a descriptive significance to purchasers of gasoline."

We have given a synoptic analysis of the board's able, well-considered and exhaustive opinion without reiterating essential facts of record. These facts are detailed in their essence and relevancy and supportive of the board's conclusions so clearly and aptly enunciated in its decision. We, therefore, incorporate herein by reference the opinion of the board and affirm its refusal of registration. The decision of the Trademark Trial and Appeal Board is, accordingly, affirmed.

RICH, Acting Chief Judge, concurring.

I agree with the result reached by the majority which is supported by an opinion largely relying on and incorporating by reference the opinion of the board. While I do not disagree with anything said in the majority's opinion, I do not accord the survey evidence, by which it was attempted to show "secondary meaning," the significance apparently accorded it by the board. The examiner accorded it none. I do not agree with the board's statement that "This case turns upon the sufficiency of applicant's evidence" of "secondary meaning."

The examiner in this case was of the view, as the board reported, that Custom–Blended "is *so highly* descriptive of applicant's blended gasoline that it is *incapable* of becoming distinctive as claimed." (My emphasis.) If that is so, registration must be refused under 15 U.S.C.A. § 1052(e)(1) no matter what evidence of alleged "secondary meaning" is adduced; in other words, under the facts of this case the law proscribes the possibility of a de jure "secondary meaning," notwithstanding the existence of 15 U.S.C.A. § 1052(f) and a de facto "secondary meaning."

In my opinion, Custom–Blended is so highly descriptive that it cannot, under the law, be accorded trademark rights even though at some times, or to some people, or in some places, it has a de facto secondary meaning. My view was expressed by the examiner. I think that conclusively disposes of the matter. While I see no objection to pointing out to appellant that its evidence has not established "secondary meaning," I am unwilling to lead appellant or others to think that the fault was in the quantity or quality of its evidence rather than in the descriptiveness of the words sought to be registered. Appellant should not be encouraged to try again to prove "secondary meaning." The only particular in which I do not fully agree with the examiner is that he said the word "custom" in Custom–Blended "has very little trademark significance." I think it has none.

Appellant has argued that the descriptive term for its gasoline is "pump-blended." I do not question that that is a descriptive—or as appellant calls it "generic"—term; but a product may have more than one generically descriptive name. Because one merchandiser has latched onto one of the descriptive terms does not mean it can force its competitors to limit themselves to the use of the others, which appellant, it seems to me, is trying to do here. *All* of the generic names for a product belong in the public domain. The product itself, for example, is called gasoline in the United States but petrol in England. Clearly both of those names must remain free of proprietary claims, in either country. So it is, in my view, with respect to pump-blended and custom-blended. The examiner stated the factual basis for this view in pointing out that "custom," as in custom-built, custom-service, custom-cut, custom-made, custom-tailored, custom-work, etc., merely indicates that it is done according to the customer's desire. That is exactly how appellant's gasolines are pump-blended—to give the customer what he asks for. I can think of no descriptive term which is more apt.

FISHER, District Judge, dissenting.

Under the doctrine of "secondary meaning," a trademark, though originally descriptive of a type of product, is nonetheless entitled to registration if the mark has, by association with a business, come primarily to identify its user, rather than the product, to that part of the public interested in contracting with the trademark user. Whether a descriptive mark has acquired secondary meaning depends upon the particular facts of each case.

Briefly, it has been shown that appellant has used the mark in question for its gasoline exclusively and continuously over a period of some twelve years. There is evidence of extensive advertising of and sales of large volumes of gasoline under that mark during this period. Surveys of record suggest that in at least two areas where there are other marketers of multi-grade, pump-blended gasoline, the term Custom-Blended is associated in the public mind with this appellant in a preponderance which can only be accounted for by recognition of origin. There is no evidence which would imply that the mark is of such a descriptive nature that granting trademark rights therein to the user would deprive others of their right to normal use of the language.

In light of these facts, it is respectfully submitted that the decision of the Trademark Trial and Appeal Board should be reversed and registration granted on the basis that the mark Custom-Blended has acquired secondary meaning within Section 2(f) of the Act (15 U.S.C.A. § 1052(f)).

(v.) *"PRIMARILY GEOGRAPHICALLY DESCRIPTIVE OR DECEPTIVELY MISDESCRIPTIVE"*

IN RE LOEW'S THEATRES, INC.

United States Court of Appeals, Federal Circuit, 1985.
769 F.2d 764, 226 U.S.P.Q. 865.

NIES, Circuit Judge.

This appeal is from the decision of the Trademark Trial and Appeal Board sustaining a refusal to register the mark DURANGO for chewing tobacco. The board held that the subject mark was unregistrable under § 2(e)(2) of the Lanham Act (15 U.S.C. § 1052(e)(2)), which bars registration of a mark which is "primarily geographically deceptively misdescriptive" of the goods to which it is applied. We affirm.

I.

Background

The subject of this appeal is Application Serial No. 341,663, filed on December 14, 1981, in the U.S. Patent and Trademark Office (PTO) by Loew's Theatres, Inc., doing business through its Lorillard Division (hereinafter LTI) for the mark DURANGO for chewing tobacco, claiming use since on or before September 9, 1981. Registration was initially refused on the Principal Register on the grounds that the mark appeared to be either primarily geographically descriptive or deceptively misdescriptive of the goods and was, thus, barred from registration on the Principal Register pursuant to § 2(e) of the Lanham Act. In support of this rejection, the examiner relied on information in the Columbia Lippincott Gazetteer of the World, Columbia University Press (1952). The examiner concluded that because the reference disclosed that tobacco was a crop of the Durango, Mexico area, it would be reasonable for the purchasing public to expect chewing tobacco bearing the name DURANGO to have its origin in that area. He advised that additional evidence of registrability could be filed.

LTI sought to overcome this rejection by argument that: (1) LTI's existing Registration No. 923,094 for the mark DURANGOS for cigars on the Principal Register entitled it to registration of the subject mark, and (2) the evidence on which the examiner relied was insufficient to indicate that the purchasing public would make a goods/place association between tobacco and the Durango, Mexico area.

The examining attorney adhered to his rejection and buttressed the record with respect to the geographic significance of the name Durango by reference to the geographical names section of Webster's New Collegiate Dictionary, G. & C. Merriam Company, Springfield, Massachusetts (1979). In view of the substantial population of the state and city of Durango in Mexico, he concluded that Durango could not be deemed a "minor, obscure, or remote" geographic place name. Further, the examining attorney believed that the evidence of tobacco production in Durango established a *prima facie* case that there would be a goods/place association by the public, as required for a rejection under § 2(e), citing In re Nantucket, Inc., 677 F.2d 95, 213 USPQ 889 (CCPA 1982). While acknowledging LTI's ownership of the registration for DURANGOS cigars, the examining attorney deemed such evidence insufficient to establish distinctiveness of the mark sought to be registered. He noted the continued absence of any evidence concerning the length and manner of LTI's use of the mark, the nature and extent of advertising, or any other efforts by LTI which would tend to establish that the mark had acquired distinctiveness and thereby entitle LTI to a registration in accordance with § 2(f) (15 U.S.C. § 1052(f)). Finally, he stated that, since LTI's goods did not come from the place named, the mark was being refused registration as primarily geographically deceptively misdescriptive.

Appellant did not controvert the statement concerning origin of the goods nor submit any additional evidence tending to establish secondary meaning in the mark sought to be registered. Instead, appeal was taken to the Trademark Trial and Appeal Board (board). In a thorough opinion reported at 223 USPQ 513 (1984), adhered to on reconsideration, the board upheld the examining attorney's refusal of registration. This appeal, pursuant to 15 U.S.C. § 1071, followed.

II.

Issues

1. Did the PTO establish a *prima facie* case that the mark DURANGO is primarily geographically deceptively misdescriptive for chewing tobacco within the meaning of § 2(e)?

Since we conclude that a *prima facie* case was proved, the following issue must also be addressed.

2. Is registration, nevertheless, mandated by LTI's ownership of Registration No. 923,094 for the mark DURANGOS for cigars?

III.

Analysis

A.

Under § 2(e)(2) of the Lanham Act, a mark may not be registered on the Principal Register if the mark "when applied to the goods of the applicant is . . . primarily geographically deceptively misdescriptive." This provision of the statute was extensively analyzed in the precedential decision In re Nantucket, Inc., 677 F.2d 95, 213 USPQ 889 (CCPA 1982). That case concerned the registrability on the Principal Register of the mark NANTUCKET for shirts not originating in Nantucket, Massachusetts. The PTO had argued to the court in the *Nantucket* case that a *prima facie* case of unregistrability was shown simply by proof that the mark was the name of a geographic place known generally to the public. The court rejected this argument, holding that in order to make a valid rejection under § 2(e), the PTO not only had to establish that the mark was the name of a generally known geographic place, but also that the public would be likely to believe that the goods for which the mark is sought to be registered originate in that place. The latter requirement was held to follow from the statutory language that the descriptiveness or deceptive misdescriptiveness of the mark must be determined as "applied to the goods of the applicant." In this respect the statute reflects the common law principle that a geographic term, used in a fictitious, arbitrary, or fanciful manner, is protectable like any other nondescriptive term. Usage in such manner is not "primarily" as a geographic designation.

While the above cited precedent requires a goods/place association to support a refusal to register under § 2(e)(2), it does not follow that such association embraces only instances where the place is well-known or noted for the goods, a position which the *Nantucket* applicant, as well as LTI, have urged. The court, in *Nantucket*, did not adopt that position. Rather, our precedent continues to hold that to establish a "primarily geographically deceptively misdescriptive" bar, the PTO must show only a reasonable basis for concluding that the public is likely to believe the mark identifies the place from which the goods originate and that the goods do not come from there.[6]

B.

In support of its finding that more than a *de minimus* segment of the public would reasonably associate chewing tobacco with the city and/or state of Durango, Mexico, the PTO relies on the evidence of record which shows that tobacco is a crop produced and marketed in that area. This finding may only be overturned if clearly erroneous.

LTI attacks the sufficiency of the evidence of record on several grounds:

1. The Gazetteer relied upon by the PTO shows that Durango is also the name of towns in Colorado and in Spain. Therefore, per appellant, Durango would not be associated with Mexico's tobacco region of that name.

2. The PTO produced no evidence that the public would actually make the asserted association.

Contrary to LTI's position, we conclude that the PTO made a *prima facie* showing of a goods/place association between tobacco and the geographic name Durango. Durango (Mexico) is not an obscure place name to the Mexican population of this country nor to reasonably informed non-Mexicans. The cited Gazetteer shows tobacco to be one in a short list of principal crops of the region. No more can be expected from the PTO in the way of proof. The PTO does not have means to conduct a marketing survey as LTI would require. The practicalities of the limited resources available to the PTO are routinely taken into account in reviewing its administrative action. Accordingly, it was suggested in the *Nantucket* decision that precisely the type of evidence utilized here would establish a *prima facie* case by the PTO. 677 F.2d at 106, 213 USPQ at 898 (Nies, J., concurring). The trademark examining attorney, in prosecuting the subject application, followed those suggestions which have been specifically endorsed by the board in this and other cases. We affirm that a *prima facie* case can be established by the type of evidence of record here where the question concerns the registrability of a geographic name.

Finally, it does not detract from the *prima facie* case made by the PTO that there are a few other uses of Durango as a geographic name, such as Durango, Colorado. The PTO's burden is simply to establish that there is a reasonable predicate for its conclusion that the public would be likely to make the particular goods/place association on which it relies. That there is more than one place bearing the name or that one place is better known than another is not dispositive. The issue is not the fame or exclusivity of the place name, but the likelihood that a particular place will be associated with particular goods. Thus, the mark DURANGO for skis might also be barred (without proof of

---

6. In contrast, if the place is noted for the particular goods, a mark for such goods which do not originate there is likely to be deceptive under § 2(a) and not registrable under any circumstances.

secondary meaning) if it were shown that Durango, Colorado, is a ski resort.

We conclude that, on the record here, the findings underlying the *prima facie* case that DURANGO for tobacco falls within the proscription of § 2(e)(2) are not clearly erroneous.

C.

In rejecting the subject application, the trademark examining attorney followed a two-step examination process, first, determining whether the mark applied for came within the bar of § 2(e) and, second, evaluating whether the applicant had overcome it with evidence of distinctiveness in accordance with § 2(f).

LTI argues that, as the owner of an "incontestible" registration for virtually the identical mark for closely related goods, i.e., DURANGOS for cigars, registration of the subject mark is mandated. . . .

The basic flaw in LTI's analysis is that each application for registration of a mark for particular goods must be separately evaluated. Nothing in the statute provides a right *ipso facto* to register a mark for additional goods when items are added to a company's line or substituted for other goods covered by a registration. Nor do the PTO rules afford any greater rights. Under Rule 2.41(b), in appropriate cases, a prior registration on the Principal Register for the same mark "may" be accepted as "evidence" of distinctiveness, but the same rule reserves to the PTO discretion to require additional proof. The examining attorney and the board considered LTI's registration but were unpersuaded as to the sufficiency of this proof alone in view of the absence of any evidence concerning the extent of actual usage. LTI was unable or unwilling to supply *any* additional evidence to support a claim of distinctiveness.

The issue of acquired distinctiveness is a question of fact. We can not say that a requirement for some additional evidence was unduly burdensome or unreasonable or that the finding that distinctiveness was not established is clearly erroneous.

IV.

The trademark examining attorney acted entirely in accordance with the statute, the PTO rules, and precedent of this court in his refusal to register DURANGO for chewing tobacco on the record of this case. For the foregoing reasons, the decision of the Trademark Trial and Appeal Board upholding the rejection under § 2(e)(2) is *affirmed.*

AFFIRMED.

NOTES

1. *"Primarily Merely a Surname."* In addition to barring registration of marks that are merely descriptive or deceptively misdescriptive and of marks that are primarily geographically descriptive or deceptively misdescriptive, without proof of secondary meaning, Lanham Act

§ 2(e), 15 U.S.C.A. § 1052(e), bars the registration of marks that consist of "primarily merely a surname" absent proof of secondary meaning. One reason for the bar is that a competitor having the same surname as an applicant should not be disabled from using her name in trade. Compare pages 93 to 101, above.

Courts have generally relied on Assistant Commissioner Daphne Leeds' formulation of the "primarily merely a surname" test in Ex Parte Rivera Watch Corp., 106 U.S.P.Q. 145, 149 (1955):

> A trademark is a trademark only if it is used in trade. When it is used in trade it must have some impact upon the purchasing public, and it is that impact or impression which should be evaluated in determining whether or not the primary significance of a word when applied to a product is a surname significance. If it is, *and it is only that,* then it is primarily merely a surname. 'Reeves', 'Higgins', and 'Wayne' are thus primarily merely surnames. If the mark has well known meanings as a word in the language and the purchasing public, upon seeing it on the goods, may not attribute surname significance to it, it is not primarily merely a surname. 'King', 'Cotton,' and 'Boatman' fall in this category.

See Application of Harris–Intertype Corp., 518 F.2d 629, 186 U.S.P.Q. 238 (C.C.P.A.1975); Application of Kahan & Weisz Jewelry Mfg. Corp., 508 F.2d 831, 184 U.S.P.Q. 421 (C.C.P.A.1975). See generally, Fowler, When are Surnames Registrable?, 70 Trademark Rep. 66 (1980).

2. *Secondary Meaning.* A mark that fails to qualify under Lanham Act section 2(e) may nonetheless be registered on the Principal Register if it "has become distinctive of the applicant's goods in commerce." Lanham Act § 2(f), 15 U.S.C.A. § 1052(f). Acquisition of secondary meaning is the fact to be proved, and any evidence is admissible if it tends to show that the mark signifies a single source to consumers. Applicants sometimes offer consumer survey evidence to prove that secondary meaning has attached to a term. Section 2(f) also provides that the Commissioner may accept proof of five years' "substantially exclusive and continuous" use of the mark by the applicant as prima facie evidence that the mark has become distinctive.

See generally, Lunsford, The Mechanics of Proof of Secondary Meaning, 60 Trademark Rep. 263 (1970). For an interesting, contextual approach to the treatment of secondary meaning marks, see Garner, A Display Theory of Trademarks, 25 Geo.Wash.L.Rev. 53 (1956).

3. *Supplemental Register.* A mark that fails to meet the requirements of Lanham Act sections 2(e) or 2(f) may be registered on the Supplemental Register if, among other things, it is "capable of distinguishing applicant's goods or services." The Supplemental Register is open not only to nondistinctive marks, but also to types of commercial insignia—labels, packages, configurations of goods, phrases and slogans, for example—that may be barred from the Principal Register. As might be expected, the Lanham Act gives marks registered on the

Supplemental Register substantially fewer rights than it gives to marks registered on the Principal Register. See p. 279, below.

4. *Concurrent Registration.* The Trademark Law Revision Act of 1988 amended the proviso of Lanham Act section 2(d), 15 U.S.C.A. § 1052(d), dealing with concurrent registrations by adding that "[u]se prior to the filing date of any pending application or a registration shall not be required when the owner of such application or registration consents to the grant of a concurrent registration to the applicant." According to the Senate report on the Act, the purpose of the amendment was "to modify existing language which prohibits institution of a concurrent use proceeding at the Patent and Trademark Office if the junior user initiated use of the mark after the filing date of the senior user's application or its registration, even if the parties enter into an agreement establishing their respective rights. This provision is counterproductive because it often forces parties, who would otherwise be able to reach an amicable settlement, into litigation.

"As amended, the proviso will permit the Commissioner to institute a concurrent use proceeding if the owner of the earlier filed application or registration consents to the issuance of a concurrent use registration to the other party. In adopting this amendment, however, the committee does not intend to alter two important aspects of the law governing the issuance of concurrent use registrations: The Commissioner will still be required to determine that confusion or deception is not likely to result from issuance of the concurrent use registration and he will be able to impose conditions relating to the mode or place of use of the marks to prevent such confusion or deception." S.Rep. No. 100–515, 100th Cong., 2d Sess. 27 (1988).

5. *Suggestive Marks.* A firm that wants a mark to serve an advertising function by suggesting the qualities of its goods or services must chart a sometimes treacherous course between making the mark accurately suggestive—and thus descriptive—or inaccurately suggestive—and thus deceptively misdescriptive or deceptive.

Two Supreme Court cases provide common law guides to navigation between descriptive and deceptive marks. In Worden v. California Fig Syrup Co., 187 U.S. 516, 23 S.Ct. 161, 47 L.Ed. 282 (1903), the Court ruled that plaintiff, which marketed a laxative under the name, "Syrup of Figs" was not entitled to relief against defendant's use of the term, "Fig Syrup" for its laxative. "If this preparation is in fact a syrup of figs, the words are clearly descriptive, and not the proper subject of a trade mark." 187 U.S. at 533, 23 S.Ct. at 166. Since the plaintiff's compound in fact contained only minimal amounts of fig syrup, the Court concluded that use of the term tended to deceive consumers as to the nature of its product. By contrast, in The Coca–Cola Co. v. The Koke Co. of America, 254 U.S. 143, 41 S.Ct. 113, 65 L.Ed. 189 (1920), the Court ruled that, although plaintiff's product contained only trace amounts of coca leaf and cola nut derivative, "[w]e are dealing here with a popular drink not with a medicine. . . . Coca–Cola probably means to most persons the plaintiff's familiar product to be had everywhere rather than a compound of particular substances." *

6. *"Deceptive" and "Deceptively Misdescriptive" Marks.* The consequences of a mark's nonregistrability because it is "deceptive" under section 2(a) differ dramatically from the consequences of a mark's nonregistrability because it is "deceptively misdescriptive" under section 2(e). Deceptively misdescriptive marks can be registered upon proof of secondary meaning under section 2(f). Deceptive marks can never be registered. Despite this difference in consequence, the statute nowhere defines the distinction between "deceptive" and "deceptively misdescriptive." The scant legislative history suggests only that both disqualifications were intended to serve the same purpose. Hearings on H.R. 5461 before the Subcomm. on Trademarks of the House Comm. on Patents, 77th Cong. 1st Sess. 84–87 (1941).

In explicating the indicia of deceptive marks in *Budge Manufacturing,* Judge Nies also indicated the hallmarks of deceptively misdescriptive marks. Under *Budge,* a mark is deceptive (1) if it misdescribes the goods to which it is attached; (2) if consumers are likely to believe that the misdescription accurately describes the goods; and (3) if the misdescription is likely to be material to a consumer's decision to purchase the goods. If the mark has the first two characteristics, but not the third, it is only deceptively misdescriptive. See Gold Seal Co. v. Weeks, 129 F.Supp. 928, 105 U.S.P.Q. 407 (D.D.C.1955), aff'd, 230 F.2d 832, 108 U.S.P.Q. 400 (D.C.Cir.1956). This approach effectively distinguishes between lies that injure consumers by distorting their purchase decisions and lies that have no economic consequence.

The distinction between "deceptive" geographic marks—disqualified from protection under section 2(a)—and "primarily geographically deceptively misdescriptive" marks—entitled to protection under section 2(f)—parallels the distinction between deceptive and deceptively misdescriptive marks. *Loew's Theatres* held that a mark is primarily geographically deceptively misdescriptive if the goods to which it is attached do not come from the place indicated and if the public is likely to believe that the goods do in fact come from that place. But, as Judge Nies added in footnote 6 to her opinion, "if the place is noted for the particular goods, a mark for such goods which do not originate there is likely to be deceptive under § 2(a) and not registrable under any circumstances." As in the distinction between deceptively misdescriptive marks and deceptive marks, the difference is between lies that have no direct effect on consumer choice and lies that motivate consumer purchases by playing on associations between product quality and place of manufacture.

---

* "Before 1900 the beginning of the good will was more or less helped by the presence of cocaine, a drug that, like alcohol or caffeine or opium, may be described as a deadly poison or as a valuable item of the pharmacopoeia according to the rhetorical purposes in view. The amount seems to have been very small, but it may have been enough to begin a bad habit and after the Food and Drug Act of June 30, 1906, c. 3915, 34 Stat. 768, if not earlier, long before this suit was brought, it was eliminated from the plaintiff's compound." 254 U.S. at 145–146, 41 S.Ct. at 113–114.

7. *Scandalous Matter.* In In re McGinley, 660 F.2d 481, 211 U.S. P.Q. 668 (C.C.P.A.1981), the Court of Customs and Patent Appeals affirmed a decision rejecting an application to register a mark consisting of "a photograph of a nude man and woman kissing and embracing in a manner appearing to expose the male genitalia" for use in connection with a "Newsletter Devoted to Social and Interpersonal Relationship Topics" and "Social Club Services." In concluding that the mark was scandalous under Lanham Act section 2(a), 15 U.S.C.A. § 1052(a), the court relied on dictionary definitions of the term, such as "[g]iving offense to the conscience or moral feelings; exciting reprobation, calling out condemnation," and observed that whether a mark is scandalous "is to be ascertained from the standpoint of not necessarily a majority, but a substantial composite of the general public." 660 F.2d at 485–86.

Does the United States Constitution constrain the test for scandalous subject matter? *McGinley* discounted any First Amendment constraints with the observation that refusal to register a mark does not affect the right to use it. "No conduct is proscribed, and no tangible form of expression is suppressed." Further, in the court's view, "the term 'scandalous' is sufficiently precise to satisfy due process requirements." The court noted "the similarity of the issue in this case to such issues as likelihood of confusion and descriptiveness for purposes of sections 2(d) and (e) of the Lanham Act, and that, although 'each case involving a trademark (or service mark) stands on its own facts,' such terms are not considered 'void for vagueness.' Nor does the fact that decisions of the board and the courts on the issue of likelihood of confusion are often subjective detract from their validity." 660 F.2d at 484–85.

Judge Rich, joined by Judge Baldwin, dissented on a factual ground: "Like the majority and the members of the board, I have seen every version of the picture contained in the certified record and briefs and I do not find use of this picture on the goods or services named in the application to present a 'scandalous' mark. I agree that the heterosexual couple are nude, that they are kissing, that they are embracing in that sense (the man has his arm around the woman's neck and the woman is holding the man's head in her hand), but, amazingly, on the crucial matter the majority equivocates in the phrase 'appearing to expose the male genitalia.' Either it does or it doesn't and I find it doesn't. Therefore, I find the record does not support a fact I believe the majority thinks is controlling but I speculate since I do not really know why the majority holds the mark to be scandalous." 660 F.2d at 487.

3. STATUTORY SUBJECT MATTER

See Statute Supplement 15 U.S.C.A. §§ 1053, 1054, 1064(e), 1091–1096.

a. TYPES OF MARKS

(i.) *TRADEMARKS AND SERVICE MARKS*

IN RE CARSON

Trademark Trial and Appeal Board, 1977.
197 U.S.P.Q. 554.

RICE, Member.

An application has been filed by John W. Carson to register "JOHNNY CARSON" for entertainment services, namely, the rendering of entertainment to the general public by way of personal performances at shows such as by monologues, comedy routines and the hosting of guest appearances of others, use since 1952 being asserted.

Registration has been refused on the ground that the specimens filed show use of the designation "JOHNNY CARSON" only to identify the individual who performs or will perform the services claimed rather than as a mark used to identify and distinguish services rendered by applicant. That is, it is the Examiner's position that "JOHNNY CARSON" is not being used as a service mark. During the prosecution of the application, applicant submitted additional specimens showing, inter alia, use of the designation "THE JOHNNY CARSON SHOW" in a service mark manner. On the basis thereof, the Examiner advised applicant that its application would be allowed if applicant amended its mark to read "THE JOHNNY CARSON SHOW" and submitted a disclaimer of the word "Show", but applicant was unwilling to amend its mark in this fashion.

Applicant has appealed.

Applicant contends that his mark identifies both a service and an individual simultaneously, and hence is capable of registration as a service mark; that in the past marks which constitute the names of individuals have been passed to publication when use in the manner of a trademark or service mark has been demonstrated; that the fact that applicant is a well-known television and show business personality should not preclude him from registering the designation "JOHNNY CARSON" as a service mark; that the question presented herein is whether the specimens filed evidence service mark use of applicant's mark; that among the specimens of record are advertisements for one of applicant's concerts, which advertisements contain a picture of applicant as well as the name and address of the agency to which orders for tickets were to be mailed; that these specimens clearly meet the criteria set forth in In re Ames, 160 U.S.P.Q. 214 (T.T. & A. Bd., 1968); that other specimens submitted by applicant show use of the designation "THE JOHNNY CARSON SHOW" as a service mark; that the word "show" appearing therein is a generic description of the services rendered by applicant and thus, under the decision of In re Servel, Inc., 85 U.S.P.Q. 257 (C.C.P.A.1950), need not be included in the drawing of applicant's mark; that consumers would recognize the words "JOHNNY CARSON" as such; that no clarity of distinctiveness is gained by the addition of the word "show"; and that these specimens showing use of the mark "THE JOHNNY CARSON SHOW" are hence further evidence of applicant's use of "JOHNNY CARSON" as a service mark.

As indicated by the Board in In re Lee Trevino Enterprises, Inc., 182 U.S.P.Q. 253 (T.T. & A. Bd., 1974), the name of an individual may function not only to identify the individual but also as a trademark or service mark to identify goods sold or services rendered by the individual, or by an authorized corporation, in commerce. Accordingly, such a name may be registered provided that the specimens filed with the application evidence use of the name not just to identify the individual but rather to identify goods sold or services rendered by the applicant in commerce.

Thus the question to be determined herein is whether any of the various specimens of use made of record by applicant during the prosecution of its application show use of the designation "JOHNNY CARSON" to identify the entertainment services for which registration is sought.

The specimens which were originally filed with applicant's application consist of copies of a page from a newspaper whereon appears a picture of applicant together with the words: "JOHNNY CARSON is in the Congo Room at Del Webb's Hotel Sahara with Bette Midler." Inasmuch as these specimens contain no reference whatsoever to any services to be performed by applicant, they do not in our opinion show use of the name "JOHNNY CARSON" as a service mark.

However, applicant has also submitted a large number of additional specimens. The most pertinent of these are a group of advertisements characterized by use of the designation "JOHNNY CARSON" in connection with the words "IN CONCERT", such as an advertisement which appeared in the September 12, 1971 issue of The New York Times and which includes, inter alia, a picture of applicant and the words "IN CONCERT" to the left of and slightly above the designation "JOHNNY CARSON" in large letters, together with information as to place and times of performances and as to where and for how much tickets may be purchased; and another advertisement which appeared in the September 13, 1971 issue of Newsday and which similarly includes, inter alia, a picture of applicant and the words "IN CONCERT" directly below the designation "JOHNNY CARSON" in large letters, together with phone numbers for ticket purchases and information as to time and place of performance. These specimens, unlike those originally filed with applicant's application, demonstrate use of the name "JOHNNY CARSON" presented in a technical service mark manner in close association with a clear reference (i.e., "IN CONCERT") to entertainment services to be performed by him, together with information as to how members of the public may avail themselves of such services. In view thereof, we believe that these specimens are sufficient to establish that the designation "JOHNNY CARSON" is used by applicant not only as a name to identify himself but also as a service mark to identify services rendered by him in commerce. To hold otherwise would be to discriminate against applicant simply because he is an individual. Our conclusion is supported by certain supplemental specimens (which may or may not have been in use as of the filing date of this application) of record, such as the advertisements showing use of the phrase "THE JOHNNY CARSON SHOW" together with ticket information, which advertisements are illustrative of another way in which the mark "JOHNNY CARSON" is used; and advertisements showing use of the designation "JOHNNY CARSON" in close association with the phrase "3 BIG PERFORMANCES AT THE MUSIC HALL!", together with ticket information.

While it might appear at first blush that our conclusion herein is inconsistent with that reached in the case of In re Lee Trevino Enterprises, Inc., supra, each such case must, as indicated above, be decided on the basis of the specimens made of record therein. In the Trevino case, it was the opinion of the Board that those specimens which contained a reference to the services for which registration was sought did not show use of the designation "LEE TREVINO" set off in a service mark manner, but rather only as part of a textual reference to Lee Trevino as an individual; other specimens referred to services not listed in the identification of goods set forth in the application there involved; and the remainder neither referred to applicant's services nor had use of "LEE TREVINO" set off in a service mark manner.

Decision

The refusal to register is reversed.

EX PARTE HANDMACHER–VOGEL, INC.

Commissioner of Patents, 1953.
98 U.S.P.Q. 413.

LEEDS, Assistant Commissioner.

Application has been filed to register as a service mark on the principal register the word "Weathervane" superimposed upon a representation of a weathervane and enclosed within a circle formed of the words "Women's Open Golf Tournament," for the service of "conducting golf tournaments" in Class 107, Education and Entertainment. The words "Women's Open Golf Tournament" are disclaimed. Use is claimed since February, 1950. Registration was refused on the ground that the mark does not meet the statutory requirement of a service mark because the service claimed is a vehicle or medium employed by the applicant to advertise and promote the sale of its goods. Applicant has appealed from this refusal.

Handmacher–Vogel, Inc., the applicant herein, is a manufacturer and distributor of women's wearing apparel. It owns Registration No. 554,949, comprising the word "Weathervane," coupled with the representation of a weathervane, for women's suits; Registration No. 553,814, comprising the word "Weathervane," coupled with the word "Golfer" and a representation of a weathervane, for shirts, women's jackets and women's hats; and Registration No. 339,318, comprising the word "Weathervane" alone for piece goods made wholly or partially of cellulose derivatives. The word "Weathervane" has been used by applicant and its predecessor since 1936 in the piece goods field, and by applicant since 1941 in the women's apparel field.

The various papers, documents and exhibits filed in this case show that during the year 1950 Handmacher–Vogel, Inc., commenced conducting golf tournaments in four different places located in different States, and has, since that time, used the "Weathervane" mark involved here to identify such tournaments. In connection with the tournaments, the mark is used on entry blanks furnished by applicant to participants, on tickets sold, on information cards and score cards distributed by applicant, on advertising posters, and in newspaper advertising paid for by applicant. These papers, documents and exhibits are sufficient to support the claim of use of the mark in connection with services rendered in commerce which may lawfully be regulated by Congress.

Tickets to the tournaments are sold to the public, entry fees are charged the entrants, and prizes are awarded to both participating professional and amateur players.

Numerous press clippings have been filed, and these clippings show a widespread press coverage of the sporting events identified as "Weathervane Women's Open golf tournament," "Weathervane Cross Country golf tournament" and "Women's Weathervane golf tournament." They also indicate participation by some of the nation's outstanding golfers, namely, Babe D. Zaharias, Betsy Rawls, Patty Berg, Louise Suggs, Betty Jameson, and Marlene and Alice Bauer. Prizes in the 1951 tournaments totalled $17,000. In other words, the tournaments conducted by applicant are of more than passing interest and importance as sporting events.

The original rejection states in part:

> While the examiner does not take the position that a manufacturer or merchant may not also render services or that the same mark may not be used both as a trade mark and a service mark, it is his view that all services which constitute operations involved in the designing, production, sale, sales promotion, advertising or build-up of good-will of one's own goods do not constitute services within the purview of the Act.

As a broad and general statement this may be a substantially correct interpretation of the law.

The examiner has taken a narrow view of the statutory provisions dealing with registration of service marks, and has apparently given little or no weight to any evidence submitted other than the specimens filed with the application. These specimens are mailing pieces designed for distribution to retail outlets selling women's apparel manufactured by applicant. They contain such statements as: "This greatest of women's sporting events will make the immensely popular Weathervane line even more popular"; "Schedule tie-in ads now. Plan your Weathervane windows now. Plan to cash in on this event that means big volume for your store"; and "Each year you will benefit by the tremendous advertising and promotional value of this great event." After quoting from the specimens, he concluded:

> . . . it is believed that the service claimed by the applicant is merely a means of advertising and promoting the sale of its goods; and as such is not considered a service within the meaning of the Statute.

This position was retained in final rejection. It is not clear just what the examiner's position would have been had the golf tournaments been instituted first in point of time and as a subsequent venture, the applicant decided to go into the manufacturing of women's apparel.

In the Examiner's Statement filed on appeal, the following appears:

> While the applicant may be rendering a service in conducting these tournaments, this service *is rendered primarily as a means of promoting the sale of these goods* [women's apparel] and comes within the scope of the decisions cited. . . . (Emphasis Added)

There is no evidence to support such a statement; but, on the contrary, the evidence indicates that in this case the services are entertainment services completely unrelated to the designing, production, sale, sales promotion or advertising of the applicant's goods sold under the "Weathervane" mark. None of such goods are designed, produced, advertised, promoted, sold or offered for sale at the tournaments. It cannot be said to be a sales promotion program directed to purchasers of such goods. The goods are nowhere mentioned in the press releases, on entry blanks, on tickets, on score cards, in advertising of the tournaments, or in announcements or information bulletins. If additional good-will attaches to the trade mark as a result of the services performed, it is not seen how this can have any bearing on the question of whether or not a bona fide service is being performed. Careful consideration of all the evidence submitted convinces me that the applicant here is performing a bona fide service unconnected with the manufacture and sale of its goods, and that any effect which the conducting of the golf tournaments under the "Weathervane" mark may have upon the sale of women's apparel under the same mark is remote and incidental.

A mark used by a person on or in connection with services normally expected of him and rendered merely as an accessory to and solely in furtherance of the sale, offering for sale, or distribution of his goods is not a service mark within the purview of the Act; but a manufacturer, seller or distributor of goods who supplies a bona fide service or services over and above those normally expected and only incidentally related to the furtherance of such manufacture, sale or distribution is entitled to have the registrability of his mark judged by the standards ordinarily applied in determining registrability—whether the mark used to identify the service is the same as or different from that used to identify the goods.

The examiner cited and relied on six cases, namely: Ex parte Pacific Coast Aggregates, Inc., 91 U.S.P.Q. 210; Ex parte Tampax, Inc., 91 U.S.P.Q. 215; Ex parte Radio Corporation of America, 92 U.S.P.Q. 247 (affirmed C.C.P.A. 98 U.S.P.Q. 157); Ex parte The Elwell–Parker Electric Company, 93 U.S.P.Q. 229; Ex parte The Arco Company, 96 U.S.P.Q. 171; and Ex parte The Procter & Gamble Company, 97 U.S. P.Q. 78. The first five cases are readily distinguishable from the present case, and in view of the pendency of an appeal in the last mentioned case, comment is withheld. In each of the five cases the mark was used on or in connection with services rendered merely as an accessory to and solely in furtherance of the sale of the applicant's goods. In the first case, the claimed "service" consisted of preparing the applicant's concrete for sale. In the second the claimed "service" consisted of an advertisement containing a list of the physical characteristics of the applicant's goods and featuring some of those descriptions in the form of a slogan. In the third case the claimed "service" comprised the mere playing of the applicant's own phonograph records with an invitation to the public to purchase them. In the fourth the claimed "service" was the rendering of advice as to the use of applicant's industrial equipment. In the fifth case the claimed "service" was the mixing of applicant's paints and rendering advice as to color matching in using applicant's paints. None of these cases is controlling under the facts and circumstances of the present case.

The decision of the Examiner of Trade Marks is reversed.

(ii.) CERTIFICATION MARKS AND COLLECTIVE MARKS

IN RE FLORIDA CITRUS COMM'N
Trademark Trial and Appeal Board, 1968.
160 U.S.P.Q. 495.

LEFKOWITZ, Member.

An application has been filed by the Florida Citrus Commission to register the following as a certification mark for oranges and orally ingestible products which are made from oranges, use of the mark as a certification mark since on or before March 23, 1964 being alleged.

[C3047]

It is alleged in the application that:

> The certification mark is used by persons authorized by Applicant to certify that the goods bearing the mark are oranges grown within the State of Florida or are products which (1) are made from oranges grown within the State of Florida and (2) meet the Applicant's standards of identity.

Applicant is the owner of two subsisting registrations covering the designation "O.J.", per se, and the identical composite mark for which registration is sought herein as a service mark for services described as:

> Creation and promotion of standards for, and the promotion of consumer purchases of, orange juice, canned orange juice, chilled orange juice, and frozen concentrated orange juice, made from oranges grown within the State of Florida.

The application contains the statement that "Applicant is not engaged in the production or marketing of any goods to which the mark is applied as a certification mark."

Registration has been refused on the ground that it is the practice of the Patent Office not to register the same mark both as a service mark and as a certification mark in view of Section 14(e)(2) of the Act of 1946 which provides for the filing of a petition to cancel at any time in the case of a certification mark on the ground that the registrant engages in the production or marketing of any goods or services to which the certification mark is applied.

Applicant has appealed.

According to the record, applicant, The Florida Citrus Commission, is a corporate body organized under the Florida Statutes, as amended. It is an arm or branch of the State of Florida charged with taxing, and using the proceeds of such taxation to control, regulate, and promote the production of citrus products in Florida, and to administer various aspects of the Florida Citrus Code which relate to such things as the size of oranges and grapefruits, their solid to acid ratio, their juice content and color, the size of boxes in which they are shipped, and the markings, grading, and other indicia thereon. In like manner, it promulgates standards for the solid and acid contents, color, and taste of canned orange juice and canned grapefruit juice, canned blended juices, and frozen concentrates of orange juice. These activities are financed by a special tax on each box of citrus fruit grown in Florida. The enforcement of these standards is but one facet of the Florida Citrus Commission's activities. Part of the above-mentioned tax money is, pursuant to the Statutes, used to:

> Conduct a campaign for commodity advertising, publicity, and sales promotion to increase the consumption of citrus fruits. . . .

That same section of the Statute also directs the Commission to:

> Decide upon some distinctive and suggestive trade name and to promote its use in all ways to advertise Florida citrus fruits.

Applicant, assertedly, pursuant to these statutory defined obligations, created the mark which is the subject of the instant application. The first use of the mark was on September 5, 1963 as a service mark to identify the Commission's regulating functions, and to identify certain advertising and promotion of Florida citrus fruit and citrus products. Applicant formally filed an application for registration thereof on September 10, 1963 submitting specimens reflecting usage of the mark on stationery employed by the Commission in the performance of its statutory duties and consumer advertising directed to promote the citrus products of Florida in general. This application matured in Registration No. 767,305 on March 24, 1964.

After the service mark had been used by the Commission for about six months, the Commission began to authorize, under its supervision and control, Florida citrus producers to use the identical trademark as a trademark on citrus fruit and fruit products produced by them to identify their Florida origin. The subject application was filed on November 13, 1964 accompanied by specimens showing use of the mark on a carton of orange juice distributed, in this instance, by Manhan Indian River Juices, Inc. There is no question but that the Florida Citrus Commission itself has, at no time, ever sold any citrus products of any sort under any mark much less the mark in question; and that the only use which the Commission itself has made of the mark is to employ it in connection with the services it renders to the Florida citrus industry and in the consumer advertising of the industry which it serves.

It is the examiner's position that the provisions of Section 14(e)(2) providing for the cancellation of a certification mark at any time on the ground that the registrant "engages in the production or marketing of any goods or services to which the certification mark is applied" prohibits the issuance of a registration for a certification mark to any applicant who engages in the production or marketing of any goods or any services under a mark identical to the certification mark.

The thrust of applicant's position is twofold, namely, that:

(A) The insertion of the language proscribing 'the production or marketing of any goods or services to which the certification mark is applied' in Section 14(e)(2) of the Statute indicates a legislative intent that any question arising thereunder can and should only be considered in an inter partes case, and

(B) The language of Section 14(e)(2) was inserted in the Statute for the specific purpose of prohibiting the owner of a certification mark from actively engaging in the production or marketing of those same goods or same services to which the mark is applied as a certification mark.

It is applicant's argument that the language of Section 14(e)(2) was originally proposed in the form of a qualification of Section 4 and was intended to be considered by the Patent Office during the ex parte prosecution of an application for registration of a certification mark. The Congress, however, did not accept this proposal and instead inserted the language in Section 14 in such a way that the question of whether or not the owner of a registration "engages in the production or marketing of any goods or services to which the certification mark is applied" can only be decided in an inter partes proceeding.

The legislative history of the Lanham Act does reveal, as indicated by applicant, that there was an attempt to incorporate the language of Section 14(e)(2) as a subsection of Section 4, but the Congress chose to include it only as a part of Section 14(e)(2). . . .

While the language in Section 4 relating to the proscriptions concerning the use of a certification mark and a collective mark is somewhat vague and ambiguous and leaves much to be desired in the way of statutory language, it nevertheless appears therefrom that there is a prohibition against the registration of a certification mark where the use of the mark by the registrant or owner falsely suggests that he makes the goods or performs the services on or in connection with which the certification mark is used. This prohibition appears on its face not to be as broad in scope as the language in Section 14(e)(2) providing for the cancellation of a certification mark at any time where the registrant engages in the production or marketing of *any goods or services* to which the certification mark is applied. If applicant's theory, which concedes the broad character of Section 14(e)(2), is to be followed, the prohibition in Section 4 would be applied in ex parte proceedings and the prohibition set forth in Section 14(e)(2) in inter partes proceedings. The application of this "dual standard" is manifestly not feasible for it would give rise to situations where a registration of a certification mark would be subject to the filing of a petition to cancel under Section 14(e)(2) immediately after it is issued. Under these circumstances, it is of paramount interest to owners of certification marks that a single standard be used to determine both the right to register a certification mark and the right to maintain a certification mark registration. That is, the interpretation of Section 4 should be consonant with that of Section 14(e)(2) for to do otherwise would be to create a situation which the Congress and framers of the Statute surely did not intend.

We recognize that in view of the language in Section 4 referring *to the making or selling of the goods or services on or in connection with which such mark is used* and the language in Section 14(e)(2) precluding the production or marketing of *any goods or services to which the certification mark is applied,* a reasonable interpretation may be that the only proscription in both sections is against the owner of the mark from using the mark in connection with the production or marketing of the specific goods or services in connection with which the mark is being used by others as a certification mark. But, the language in these sections is likewise susceptible of the examiner's interpretation, namely, that in view of the specific function of a certification mark, the owner of a certification mark cannot apply the identical mark to any goods or services that it produces or sells. . . .

Applicant's position on this point is that the legislative history of the Lanham Act indicates that the only purpose of the language incorporated in Sections 4 and 14(e)(2) was to prevent the registration of a certification mark for a specified product by a party who sells that product, and was in no way directed to barring such a registration by a party who actually uses the mark as a non-certification mark (service mark or trademark) on different products or services; that applicant is not engaged in the conduct sought to be precluded because it is not engaged in the production or marketing of any of the goods for which registration is sought as a certification mark; and that therefore applicant's ownership of a registration of the identical mark for services cannot preclude applicant from the registration sought herein. Applicant also urges that, in any event, the mere act of registration of the mark as a trademark or service mark as distinguished from proof of actual use of the certification mark in commerce in connection with the marketing or production of goods or services should not be deemed a bar under Section 4 or 14(e)(2) to the registration thereof as a certification mark.

A reading of the legislature hearings leading to the enactment of the Lanham Act reveals an intent to preclude the owner of a certification mark from producing or selling goods or services in connection with which the certification mark is to be used. That is, to prevent a party from certifying his own goods or services. It also appears therefrom that there was a continuing deep concern on the part of the framers of the Statute over the possible use of the certification mark as a weapon to create a monopoly in a particular field and to perpetuate a fraud upon the purchasing public; and that they attempted through the proscriptive language in Sections 4 and 14(e)(2) to preclude the possibility of such fraudulent misuse occurring through the sanction of a Federal registration. These persons recognized, as we must do in determining which of the two possible constructions is to be applied, in a situation involving the registration of a certification mark, the particular or peculiar nature, character, and function of such a mark. A certification mark is a special creature created for a purpose uniquely different from that of an ordinary service mark or trademark as evidenced, inter alia, by the fact that Section 4 provides that a separate register be provided for such marks. It is a mark owned by one person and used by one or more parties on or in connection with their goods or services to certify quality, regional or other origin, and the like. As a consequence of the certification feature of the mark, it is a device which persons generally look for and many times are governed by in making their purchases. It is not unreasonable to assume that purchasers familiar with the use of a mark in connection with goods or services to certify quality, accuracy, or other characteristics of such goods or services will, upon encountering the identical mark on or in association with other goods or services, mistakenly attribute to it the same certification function as that to which they have been previously exposed. To permit the indiscriminate use of a certification mark with different goods or services will only lead to the dilution and impairment of the purpose and function of a certification mark as well as to practices wholly inconsistent with the public desirability of safeguarding the consuming public from confusion and damage not of its own making.

This is not intended to imply any devious intention on the part of applicant, the Florida Citrus Commission, in authorizing the use of its mark as a certification mark in the citrus fruit field and in using the identical mark itself as a service mark for services which it performs; but the standard to be applied in construing a portion of a Statute must necessarily have a general rather than a specific application. In order to effectuate the Congressional intent to maintain the true character of a certification mark and the unique function that it plays in the marketplace, it is our opinion that the owner of a certification mark cannot use the identical mark as a service mark or a trademark on or in connection with any goods or services that it markets or performs. A certification mark should be used only to certify. Any such other use is proscribed by both Section 4 and by Section 14(e)(2), the former as an ex parte bar to registration, and the latter as an inter partes ground for cancellation of an existing registration of a certification mark. . . .

Decision

The refusal of registration is affirmed.

LEACH, Member, dissenting.

The legislative hearings alluded to in the majority opinion do not in any way support the conclusion of my colleagues that a mark used as a certification mark for goods or services cannot be used by the owner thereof as a trademark or service mark for different goods or services.

Furthermore, I do not agree with my colleagues that there is any such ambiguity in the language of Sections 4 and 14 of the Act, insofar as it pertains to the issue hereof, as would necessitate resorting to the legislative hearings thereon to ascertain the intentions of the framers thereof. On the contrary, it is implicit therefrom that the only proscription against the registration of a mark as a certification mark is that the applicant not be engaged in the marketing of the specific goods or services in connection with which the mark is used as a certification mark.

In the present case, applicant is not engaged in the marketing of the goods for which it is seeking registration of its mark as a certification mark, and I would therefore reverse the examiner's refusal of registration.

BREITENFELD, COLLECTIVE MARKS—SHOULD THEY BE ABOLISHED?
47 Trademark Rep. 1, 3–6, 9, 14–15 (1957).*

Assistant Commissioner of Patents Leeds said in 1947: "Certification marks are now in our law and some administrative difficulties may have to be overcome before the distinction between collective marks and certification marks is clearly defined."

The Trademark Act of 1946 has been in effect for over nine years, and it seems that there is still confusion surrounding these marks. The fact is that the indistinction got off to a good start long before the Lanham Act, when collective marks first appeared in the law in 1938, by amendment to the 1905 Act. In commenting upon these 1938 collective marks, Dr. Derenberg said in 1948: "Most of the marks registered as collective marks under the (1938) amendment would appear to come within the definition of a certification mark rather than a collective mark under the new Act."

The lack of any clear distinction between collective and certification marks was apparent even while the Lanham Act was still in the process of being enacted. In an early form in which the House passed the Act, collective marks and certification marks were defined together in a single definition; and the later separation of the definitions did little to distinguish the marks clearly. Confusion has continued and, in addition, the separate definitions have given rise to other perplexing questions. . . .

In her book, Mrs. Leeds distinguished between collective and certification marks with an illustration of the use of the name INDIAN RIVER for fruit. She pointed out that if the mark is used to indicate that the fruit comes from a certain region, it is a certification mark, whereas, if it is used by members of an association "to distinguish the fruit of the members, and not to certify regional origin, it is a 'collective mark'." This seems clear enough, but when organizations require that certain standards be met before membership is granted, or that members can be drawn only from a certain region, then membership itself may certify quality, regional origin, etc. In such cases it is clear that if Mrs. Leeds' criterion is used, the mark may be both a collective *and* a certification mark. . . .

To illustrate still more dramatically the lack of real distinction between the marks appearing on the two registers, the reader is invited to check his collective-certification mark I.Q. by indicating in the boxes on the left of the following list of marks, which, in his opinion, are certification marks, and which are collective marks.

Certifica- tion	Collec- tive	
1. ☐	☐	No. 568,413, granted to International Association of Clothing Designers, for Men's and Boys' clothing—namely, suits, overcoats, topcoats and sport coats; "The . . . mark is used upon the goods to indicate that the clothing is designed by a member of the association."

	Certification	Collective
2.	☐	☐

No. 589,240, granted to Douglas Fir Plywood Association, for Plywood; "The . . . mark is used in connection with the goods to indicate that the plywood meets standards promulgated by the applicant."

3.	☐	☐

No. 567,487, granted to Prefinished Wallpanel Council, for Prefinished wall panels; "The . . . mark is used upon the goods to indicate the quality and commercial standard of the goods and that the manufacturer of the goods is a member of the Prefinished Wall-panel Council."

4.	☐	☐

No. 577,817, granted to The Irish Linen Guild, for Irish linen piece goods; "The . . . mark is used in connection with the goods to indicate membership in the association, source and origin, genuineness, and high quality of the goods."

5.	☐	☐

No. 529,630, granted to Paint Research Associates, Inc., for Ready-mixed paints, etc.; "The . . . mark is used upon the goods to indicate the quality of same."

6.	☐	☐

No. 589,483, granted to The Missouri Farmers Association, Inc., for Vegetable seeds, lawn seeds and field crop seeds; "The . . . mark is used in connection with the goods to indicate that they comply with certain requirements as to excellence and quality, which compliance with said requirements is maintained through inspection and supervision by duly authorized representatives of the Missouri Farmers Association, Inc."

7.	☐	☐

No. 515,204, granted to National Sanitary Supply Association, for Sanitary and janitor supplies— namely, cleaning compounds and cleaning chemicals; soaps; soap powders; liquid soaps; "The . . . mark is used upon the goods to indicate the mode of manufacture and quality of such goods and to indicate membership in the association."

8.	☐	☐

No. 569,909, granted to Brazil Nut Association, for Brazil nuts; "The . . . mark is used in connection with the goods to indicate origin of the product sold."

9.	☐	☐

No. 543,809, granted to The Journeymen Barbers, Hairdressers and Cosmetologists' International Union of America, for Cutting of hair, shampooing of hair, shaving, application of facial treatments; ". . . to indicate that all persons employed therein are members of the union."

Certifica- Collec-
   tion   tive

10.   ☐   ☐   No. 541,207, granted to Toy Manufacturers of the U.S.A., Inc., for Toys and playthings, etc.; "The . . . mark is used in connection with the goods to indicate that the members using the mark are domestic U.S. manufacturers and distributors of toys and that the toys are American made."

If you studied the marks carefully and came to the conclusion that they are all certification marks except number 9, you are intelligent but mistaken. If you judged the even numbered registrations to be *collective* marks and the odd numbered registrations to be *certification* marks you were right; but the chances are that you peeked at this paragraph before making your choices.

It has been said that the essential difference between the two types of marks is that "collective marks indicate no more than mere association, while certification marks constitute a representation *with respect to the goods themselves* by someone other than the producer. The collective mark is a 'lodge button'; the certification mark is a 'guarantee'." . . .

The difference between a mark which "identifies" the goods or services of members of an organization and one which "certifies" that the labor on the goods or services was performed by the members of the organization is not only difficult to ascertain, but a distinction that seems wholly unnecessary. The elimination of one of these classifications seems advisable, therefore, and it is suggested that it be stricken from the definition of a *collective* mark. This would leave, in the section defining collective marks, only the reference to membership marks. Obviously, "membership" has reference to a "collection" of persons, and the obfuscating term "collective" is therefore redundant and could be eliminated entirely. A new definition is suggested for marks to be included on the newly-established "Collective Membership Register" (a more suitable name for which might well be the shorter, easier term: "Membership Register"):

The term 'membership mark' means a mark used by the members of a cooperative, an association, or other collective group or organization to indicate membership in a union, an association or other organization.

This is believed to be a clean-cut statement of the membership "lodge-button" function of what is now known as a collective mark. It states what seems to have become Patent Office practice i.e., to classify *membership* registrations in one group (collective) and marks referring to *work done by members* in another (certification). . . .

The fourth ground for cancellation of a certification mark refers to the discriminate refusal of a registrant to certify the goods or services of a person who establishes standards or conditions that the mark certifies, but whom the registrant doesn't wish to take into camp. Of course this is a real shortcoming of certification marks, not suffered by collective marks. In fact, it was cited by Derenberg in 1949, as being one of the causes for the limited number of applications to register marks as certification marks. Dr. Derenberg contended, at that time, that because of this restriction

> . . . it would seem to be better business policy not to register such marks as certification marks, but wherever possible, as trademarks or service marks used by related companies.

As it happens, it appears that since then many registrants have registered such marks not only as trademarks or service marks but, in many instances, as collective marks.

However, is it sensible to maintain in existence a special register entitled "Collective Marks" merely to serve as a convenient alternative for those who own certification marks and are reluctant to register them as such? It would be preferable to amend the law to remove the cause of such reluctance; and if there is no legitimate need for collective marks they should be done away with.

NOTE

The Trademark Law Revision Act of 1988 amended the Lanham Act's definitional provisions, section 45, 15 U.S.C.A. § 1127, to expand the class whose use of a mark will qualify the mark as a trademark or service mark. Before the amendments, the definition of "trademark" contemplated use "by a manufacturer or merchant;" the definition now requires only use by "a person." The amended definition of "service mark" dropped the requirement of use "in the sale or advertising of services." These changes brought marks used by licensees, brokers and distributors within the definition of trademarks and service marks. The amendments also accommodated the Act's new intent to use provisions by encompassing both marks "used by a person" and marks "which a person has a bona fide intention to use in commerce. . . ."

In addition to conforming the definitions of "certification mark" and "collective mark" to the new intent to use provisions, the 1988 amendments sharpened the distinction between the two types of marks by inserting the phrase, "in the case of certification marks," immediately after the word "except" in section 1054's provision that registered collective marks and certification marks "shall be entitled to the protection provided in this chapter in the case of trade-marks, except *in the case of certification marks* when used so as to represent falsely that the owner or user thereof makes or sells the goods or performs the services on or in connection with which such mark is used." According to the Senate Report on the Act, the change "clarifies the difference between collective and certification marks, the former of which, by definition, can be used to represent that their owners (that is, unions, associations or other organizations) make or sell the goods or perform the services on or in connection with which the mark is used." S.Rep. No. 100–515, p. 28 (1988).

b. CONTENT

IN RE OWENS–CORNING FIBERGLAS CORP.

United States Court of Appeals, Federal Circuit, 1985.
774 F.2d 1116, 227 U.S.P.Q. 417.

PAULINE NEWMAN, Circuit Judge.

Owens–Corning Fiberglas Corporation (OCF) appeals from the decision of the United States Patent and Trademark Office's Trademark Trial and Appeal Board (the Board) affirming the examining attorney's denial of registration of the color "pink" as a trademark for fibrous glass residential insulation. We reverse.

I.

Alleging use in commerce since 1956, OCF applied on January 25, 1980, application Serial No. 247,707, for registration on the Principal Register of the color "pink" as uniformly applied to OCF's fibrous glass residential insulation. The Board held that the overall color of goods is capable of functioning as a trademark, but affirmed the examiner's denial of registration on the ground that OCF had not adequately demonstrated that the color "pink" is distinctive of OCF's goods.

The Board's conclusion that there is no inherent bar to trademark registration of the color of goods, when the color is an overall color rather than in the form of a design, is in harmony with modern trademark theory and jurisprudence. Prior to passage of the Trademark Act of 1946, 15 U.S.C. § 1051 et seq. (the Lanham Act), color alone could not be registered as a trademark. In 1906 the Supreme Court wrote:

> Whether mere color can constitute a valid trade-mark may admit of doubt. Doubtless it may, if it be impressed in a particular design, as a circle, square, triangle, a cross, or a star. But the authorities do not go farther than this.

A. Leschen & Sons Rope Co. v. Broderick & Bascom Rope Co., 201 U.S. 166, 171, 26 S.Ct. 425, 426, 50 L.Ed. 710 (1906). The Patent Office and the courts followed this view. For example, applications were rejected to register the color violet for gasoline, In re General Petroleum Corp. of California, 49 F.2d 966, 9 USPQ 511 (CCPA 1931); and a blue-and-aluminum color for oil well reamers, In re Security Engineering Co., Inc., 113 F.2d 494, 46 USPQ 219 (CCPA 1940).

Despite the prohibition on registration during this early period some courts accorded owners of color marks protection against unfair competition upon a showing of secondary meaning in the mark. In Clifton Mfg. Co. v. Crawford–Austin Mfg. Co., 12 S.W.2d 1098 (Tex.Civ. App.1929), for example, the defendant was enjoined from copying plaintiff's distinctive reddish-brown coloring for tents, tarpaulins, and wagon covers; and in Yellow Cab Transit Co. v. Louisville Taxicab & Transfer Co., 147 F.2d 407, 64 USPQ 348 (6th Cir.1945), the color yellow for taxicab services received protection on principles of unfair competition.

The principal purpose of the Lanham Act was the modernization of trademark law, to facilitate commerce and to protect the consumer. As noted by the Supreme Court in Park 'N Fly, Inc. v. Dollar Park and Fly, Inc., 469 U.S. 189, 105 S.Ct. 658, 664, 83 L.Ed.2d 582, 224 USPQ 327, 331 (1985):

> The Lanham Act provides national protection of trademarks in order to secure to the owner of the mark the good will of his business and to protect the ability of consumers to distinguish among competing producers.

Section 45 of the Act defines "trademark" to include "any word, name, symbol, or device or any combination thereof adopted and used by a manufacturer or merchant to identify his goods and distinguish them from those manufactured or sold by others." This was a departure from the past, as prior statutes only permitted registration of "technical" common law trademarks.

The preamble of section 2 of the Lanham Act states that "[n]o trademark . . . shall be refused registration on the principal register on account of its nature", unless one or more specific exceptions to registrability set forth in that section apply. Color is not such an exception. . . .

Under the Lanham Act trademark registration became available to many types of previously excluded indicia. Change was gradual and evolutionary, as the Patent and Trademark Office and the courts were presented with new concepts. Registration has been granted, for example, for containers; product configurations; and packaging, even if subject to design patent protection; for tabs having a particular location on a garment; slogans; sounds; ornamental labels; and goods which take the form of the mark itself. The jurisprudence under the Lanham Act developed in accordance with the statutory principle that if a mark is capable of being or becoming distinctive of applicant's goods in commerce, then it is capable of serving as a trademark.

Color marks, as other indicia, were no longer barred from registration. As for all marks, compliance with the legal requirements for registration depends on the particular mark and its circumstances of use. In determining registrability of color marks, courts have considered factors such as the nature of the goods, how the color is used, the number of colors or color combinations available, the number of competitors, and customary marketing practices. In the case of Campbell Soup Co. v. Armour & Co., 175 F.2d 795, 798, 81 USPQ 430, 432 (3d Cir.), cert. denied, 338 U.S. 847, 70 S.Ct. 88, 94 L.Ed. 518, 83 USPQ 543 (1949), the court refused to protect the red and white colors of Campbell's labels on the ground that if Campbell were to "monopolize red in all of its shades" competition would be affected in an industry where colored labels were customary.

The court in *Campbell Soup* referred to the color depletion theory: that there are a limited number of colors in the palette, and that it is not wise policy to foster further limitation by permitting trademark registrants to deplete the reservoir. This theory is not faulted for appropriate application, but following passage of the Lanham Act courts have declined to perpetuate its per se prohibition which is in conflict with the liberating purposes of the Act.

Note the following examples where, in determining registrability of trademarks based on color, the Lanham Act has been applied with exercise of judgment, as Congress intended. In In re Hehr Mfg. Co., 279 F.2d 526, 126 USPQ 381 (CCPA 1960), the court allowed registration of a square red label for use on automobile trailer windows wherein the only distinctiveness of the label was its color. In In re Data Packaging Corp., 453 F.2d 1300, 172 USPQ 396 (CCPA 1972), the court allowed registration of a mark consisting of a colored band applied to a computer tape reel of contrasting color. In Plastilite Corp. v. Kassnar Imports, 508 F.2d 824, 184 USPQ 348 (CCPA 1975), registration was denied to a combination of yellow and orange colors for fishing floats, on the basis that the color scheme lacked distinctiveness. In In re Shaw, 184 USPQ 253 (TTAB 1974), the Board denied trademark registration for green suede book covers on the ground of lack of distinctiveness. The standard for registrability was that the color be arbitrarily applied to the goods, in a distinctive way. Contrary to an absolute prohibition on registrability of color marks, administrative and judicial implementation of the statute illustrates that each case is decided upon its facts.

As with utilitarian features in general, when the color applied to goods serves a primarily utilitarian purpose it is not subject to protection as a trademark. See, e.g., In re Pollak Steel Co., 314 F.2d 566, 136 USPQ 651 (CCPA 1963) (registration of reflective fence post coating refused despite de facto secondary meaning), and Sylvania Electric Products, Inc. v. Dura Electric Lamp Co., 247 F.2d 730, 114 USPQ 434 (3d Cir.1957) (blue dot on flashbulb not a valid trademark because functional, whether or not a de facto secondary meaning had been acquired). In William R. Warner & Co. v. Eli Lilly & Co., 265 U.S. 526, 44 S.Ct. 615, 68 L.Ed. 1161 (1924), the Supreme Court refused to authorize exclusive rights in the brown color of a quinine preparation which was due to the presence of chocolate as a masking agent and suspension medium. The Court carefully distinguished that situation from one where the ingredient was "non-essential", "a mere matter of dress", or one where it "merely serve[s] the incidental use of identifying the respondent's preparation". 265 U.S. at 531, 44 S.Ct. at 617. In Deere & Co. v. Farmhand, Inc., 560 F.Supp. 85, 217 USPQ 252 (S.D.Iowa 1982), aff'd, 721 F.2d 253 (8th Cir.1983), the court refused to enforce the color "John Deere green" as a common law trademark for front end loaders on the bases that the color green was "aesthetically functional" in that purchasers wanted their farm equipment to match, and that secondary meaning had not been established. Such conditions limit an applicant's right to register a color for its goods, in order to prevent the appropriation of functional product features from the public domain. We thus consider whether the color "pink" may be so characterized.

The Supreme Court has stated "a product feature is functional if it is essential to the use or purpose of the article or if it affects the cost or quality of the article." Inwood Laboratories, Inc. v. Ives Laboratories, Inc., 456 U.S. 844, 850 n. 10, 102 S.Ct. 2182, 2187 n. 10, 72 L.Ed.2d 606, 214 USPQ 1, 4 n. 10 (1983). In In re Morton–Norwich Products, Inc., 671 F.2d 1332, 1340–41, 213 USPQ 9, 15–16 (CCPA 1982), the court looked at the following factors to determine functionality: (1) whether a particular design yields a utilitarian advantage, (2) whether alternative designs are available in order to avoid hindering competition, and (3) whether the design achieves economies in manufacture or use.

No argument has been raised that the color "pink" for OCF's fibrous glass residential insulation violates any of these factors, or that alternative, equally arbitrary designs are not available to other producers of fibrous glass insulation. To the contrary, when the arbitrary color arrangement distinguishes the goods from other sources of the same product, as in In re AFA Corp., 196 USPQ 772 (TTAB 1977), or where a variety of color designs has been utilized by other producers, courts have viewed this as evidence that such design features are primarily non-functional in nature . . .

We agree with the Board that the color "pink" has no utilitarian purpose, does not deprive competitors of any reasonable right or competitive need, and is not barred from registration on the basis of functionality.

The Board also correctly observed that even if the "pink" color is considered to be ornamental, this does not prevent it from acting as a trademark. Courts have noted that the "line distinguishing between mere ornamentation and ornamentation which is merely an incidental quality of a trademark is not always clearly ascertainable, the application of legal principles to fit one situation or the other requires proper reflection upon the impression likely to govern the ordinary purchaser in the marketplace." In re Swift & Co., 223 F.2d 950, 954, 106 USPQ 286, 288 (CCPA 1955). . . .

We conclude that OCF's use of the color "pink" performs no non-trademark function, and is consistent with the commercial and public purposes of trademarks. A pink color mark registered for fibrous glass insulation does not confer a "monopoly" or act as a barrier to entry in the market. It has no relationship to production of fibrous glass insulation. It serves the classical trademark function of indicating the origin of the goods, and thereby protects the public, as discussed in the legislative history of the Lanham Act . . .

II.

The Board, having established the potential trademark character of the color "pink" for fibrous glass residential insulation, nonetheless refused registration on the ground that OCF had not met its burden of proving "that pink functions as a trademark for that insulation." In re Owens–Corning Fiberglas Corp., 221 USPQ at 1199.

OCF argues that the color "pink" has become distinctive of its insulation by virtue of exclusive and continuous use since 1956, and has acquired a secondary meaning in the marketplace. OCF had taken the position before the examiner and the Board that its mark was registrable under section 2(f) of the Lanham Act (15 U.S.C. § 1052(f)), and had submitted extensive evidence in support of acquired distinctiveness. . . .

OCF submitted extensive affidavit and documentary evidence. Joseph Doherty, OCF's Vice President of Marketing Communications, averred that OCF has advertised the "pink" color mark as applied to fibrous glass residential insulation since 1956; that OCF spent approximately $42,421,000 on consumer advertising for its "pink" insulation in the media of television, radio, newspapers, and consumer magazines during the period of 1972 through 1981, with an estimated expenditure of $11,400,000 in 1981 alone; and that additional sums were spent on brochures, displays, and other promotional items that highlighted the "pink" color as applied to applicant's insulation.

The Board found OCF's totality of evidence insufficient because it "does not indicate to what extent that advertising has emphasized 'pink' as a mark" and because it does not provide any "indication of the extent to which the sample advertising materials of record (which emphasize the 'pink' mark) have been used." In re Owens–Corning Fiberglas Corp., 221 USPQ at 1199. We have reviewed the showing in light of the Board's criticisms. . . .

OCF submitted to the Examiner and to the Board its network television advertising schedule for the period August 17, 1980 through March 30, 1981. This schedule shows that OCF purchased nearly two hundred separate blocks of network time during broadcasts of major sporting events such as the Super Bowl, the Rose Bowl, the U.S. Tennis Open, and the World Series; prime time network series including "Sixty Minutes", "M*A*S*H*", and "Magnum, P.I."; and network showing of theatrical movies; all to advertise its "pink" insulation. The breadth of this exposure was not challenged by the Board, unlike the submissions in In re Soccer Sport Supply Co., 507 F.2d at 1403, 184 USPQ at 348, where "the evidence fail[ed] to disclose information from which the number of people exposed to the design could be estimated".

The record contains detailed storyboards for two different commercials aired during this time period featuring the "Pink Panther", a pink cartoon character promoting the use of "pink" Owens–Corning Fiberglas insulation. The narration for these commercials discusses how homeowners can cut the high cost of fuel if they would only "[a]dd another layer of pink" in their attics. The scenes emphasize the distinctive "pink" color of OCF's product and reinforce the image with the slogan "Put your house in the pink" . . .

In addition, the record contains consumer survey evidence. This survey was conducted to enable OCF to evaluate an advertising program, but its data are pertinent to the issue. In June 1980 male homeowners were asked the question "To the best of your knowledge, what manufacturer makes pink insulation?". Forty-one percent responded with applicant's name and 14% responded with the name of some other insulation manufacturer. A similar survey in January 1981, after the first Pink Panther television commercial blitz, showed that applicant's recognition rate had increased to 50%.

The Board held that this evidence was not convincing because it did not "establish that those respondents associate pink insulation with a single source." In re Owens–Corning Fiberglas Corp., 221 USPQ at 1198. The Solicitor further criticized the survey on the basis that the way the question was presented inhibited plural responses from persons who might have believed that more than one manufacturer makes "pink" insulation. We do not agree that such criticism requires outright rejection of survey data showing that 50% of the respondents named OCF, the only manufacturer to color its insulation pink. Whether or not this survey alone is conclusive, the results show a syndetic relationship between the color "pink" and Owens–Corning Fiberglas in the minds of a significant part of the purchasing public.

By their nature color marks carry a difficult burden in demonstrating distinctiveness and trademark character. Each case must be considered on its merits. OCF's evidence shows advertising expenditures exceeding $42,000,000; in *Hehr* the advertising expenditures that were deemed adequate to show secondary meaning were about $112,000. Consumer recognition in 1981 as to the source of "pink" insulation was 50%, a percentage considerably greater than that held sufficient in many cases. We conclude that the Board placed an inappropriately heavy evidentiary burden on OCF. As stated in In re Hollywood Brands, Inc., 214 F.2d 139, 141, 102 USPQ 294, 296 (CCPA 1954), there is nothing in the statute "which expressly or impliedly imposes an unreasonable burden of proof upon an applicant for registration thereunder, nor is it within our province to read such rigid provisions into it."

On the totality of the evidence, the Board's finding that the color "pink" does not function as a trademark for OCF's fibrous glass residential insulation is clearly erroneous.

The requirements of the statute having been met, OCF is entitled to register its mark under 15 U.S.C. § 1052(f).

REVERSED.

BISSELL, Circuit Judge, dissenting.

I respectfully dissent.

I

I adhere to the view that "the law is well-settled today that the overall color of a product . . . cannot be a trade identity designation, nor is it entitled to registration." 3 R. Callman, The Law of Unfair Competition Trademarks and Monopolies § 18.13 (4th ed. 1983). That was the law long before the 1946 Lanham Act, it continued to be the law after the Act, and it ought to be the law in this case.[1]

A

More than two decades before the Lanham Act the Supreme Court applied that rule of law in denying trademark protection to the color of a beverage, announcing that "the coloring matter is free to all who can make it if no extrinsic deceiving element is present." Coca–Cola Co. v. Koke Co., 254 U.S. 143, 147, 41 S.Ct. 113, 114, 65 L.Ed. 189 (1920). . . .

B

After the Act, all the regional circuit courts that confronted the issue continued to recognize the validity of the rule.

Similarly, the Court of Customs and Patent Appeals has applied the rule. Before the Act the court held that "a mark is not registrable if color alone is its distinguishing characteristic." In re Canada Dry Ginger Ale, 86 F.2d 830, 833 (CCPA 1936). After the Act, the court continued to recognize the validity of the rule as it had been expressed in other federal courts. . . .

The development of the jurisprudence under the Lanham Act distills into this rule: "A color, per se, is not capable of appropriation *as a trademark*." 1 J. McCarthy, Trademarks and Unfair Competition § 7:16 (2d ed. 1984) (emphasis added).

C

The Act does not require the result the majority reaches, nor is there any persuasive reason for this court to discard decades of jurisprudence in order to extend trademark protection to color per se. There are at least four reasons for this court not to discard this established jurisprudence.

First, the majority's result ignores the principle of comity. Unlike our exclusive jurisdiction over patent law, this court's jurisdiction over trademark law is shared with the regional circuits. While the decisions of the regional circuits are certainly not binding precedent on this court, they are entitled to at least a modicum of respect and deference. This deference is especially due where there is such a unanimity among circuit courts which have primary responsibility for determining infringement and equal responsibility with this court for determining registrability of a mark under 15 U.S.C. § 1071(b)(1) (1982).[3] . . .

---

1. The only issue which the parties treated as present in this case was the establishment of secondary meaning. Accordingly, I believe that the issue of registrability of color per se remains open in an opposition proceeding or in litigation respecting this application or a resulting registration.

3. Moreover, there is no point in granting a registration which will not be recognized by the regional circuits (nor, for that matter, by this circuit which must follow the law of a regional circuit on questions of trademark infringement).

Second, there is no need to create such a division in the law. The current interpretation of the Act adequately protects the use of color as an *element* of a trademark.

Even though color itself alone cannot be protected as a trademark, this court and the regional circuit courts, consistent with the rule expressed in *Decca Records* [51 F.Supp. 493 (S.D.N.Y.1943)], have permitted registration of a trademark which used color in a particular design or in an arbitrary or distinctive design.

Unfortunately for Owens–Corning, the *Decca Records* rule cuts against it in this case. Color uniformly applied to a product is *not* a design because it has not been used in connection or combination with or impressed in some definite arbitrary symbol or design. This is the crucial distinction between this case and the *In re Todd Co.* and *Vuitton et Fils* cases cited by the majority.

Third, there is a reason not to change the law on the factual setting of this case. Changing the law based on the peculiar factual circumstances of this case might create a barrier to otherwise lawful competition in the home insulation trade. Since Owens–Corning on the record before us appears to be the only manufacturer in the trade applying a color to its product and since the majority disparages the color depletion doctrine, the majority finds no public policy reasons for refusal of registration. However, by reason of the dominance of Owens–Corning in the field (its advertising claims a 75 percent market share), pink insulation has become virtually synonymous with home insulation. Thus, new entrants may be unable to effectively compete if barred from making pink insulation. Indeed, the record reveals that Owens–Corning dominates the field to such an extent that "some shoppers will no longer buy fiberglass insulation unless it is pink." Cf. Deere & Co. v. Farmhand, Inc., 560 F.Supp. 85, 98 (S.D.Iowa 1982) (green farm equipment; protecting "John Deere green" would hinder competition), aff'd, 721 F.2d 254 (8th Cir.1983). . . .

The final reason for the general rule that denies to one the appropriation of a particular color is that infringement actions could soon denigrate into questions of shade confusion. As one trial court stated concerning its discussion with counsel regarding the practical difficulty of enjoining the use of "John Deere green": "The practical problems identified in this discussion lend credence to the 'shade confusion' rationale for denying protection of color under the Lanham Act." *Deere & Co.*, 560 F.Supp. at 97 n. 20. Considering that registrations are printed only in black and white, 37 C.F.R. § 2.52(e), and have only code linings for color (pink and red being the same), registration will add only greater imprecision.

There are such sound reasons against altering the rule that I am convinced this rule should continue to be applied. Since color per se does not have trademark significance and does not fall into the realm of registrable matter as contemplated by the Act, I would affirm the result that Owens–Corning is not entitled to register its asserted mark.

II

Alternatively, even if color itself could be capable of trademark significance, I would affirm based on the Board's finding that Owens–Corning failed to prove secondary meaning. That finding is not clearly erroneous.

Owens–Corning relied on affidavit evidence to establish the acquired distinctiveness of its asserted mark. The Board carefully considered the evidence and concluded that the proof was insufficient; the Board found that pink did not function as a trademark for the insulation. I agree with the majority that color marks carry a difficult burden and that each case must be considered on its own merits. I do not agree that the Board placed too heavy a burden on Owens–Corning. . . .

The Board's evaluation of the evidence leading to its finding that Owens–Corning failed to establish that pink insulation is associated with a single source does not evoke a "definite and firm conviction that a mistake has been made." United States v. United States Gypsum Co., 333 U.S. 364, 365, 68 S.Ct. 525, 92 L.Ed. 746 (1948). Accordingly, its finding cannot be regarded as clearly erroneous and must be affirmed.

NOTES

1. Patent and Trademark Office decisions on trademark registration and judicial decisions on trademark infringement aim to serve the same general purposes—encouraging firms to invest in symbols that will identify them as the source of goods or services; leaving competitors free to invest in equally effective symbols; and securing consumer expectations about consistency of product quality. But registration decisions and infringement decisions differ in their method. A Patent and Trademark Office decision to publish a mark for opposition is *ex parte* and essentially abstract. A judicial decision that one mark is confusingly similar to another is *inter partes* and contextual.

The differences between these two methods helps to explain the differences between the majority and dissenting opinions in *Owens–Corning.* Judge Newman's opinion for the court viewed the registrability of color trademarks primarily through the prism of *ex parte* Patent and Trademark Office decisions. In the court's view, the only questions were whether color is capable of indicating source and whether the color in issue did in fact indicate source. Judge Bissell, by contrast, viewed the question from the perspective of *inter partes* infringement decisions. Underlying his dissenting opinion is the view that, even if a registration issued, the trademark would enjoy little deserved power in the marketplace. As one of only a limited number of colors, the mark would be weak and consequently entitled to only a narrow range of protection against competing colors.

The division between the majority and dissenting opinions in *Owens–Corning* reveals some of the most profound questions about the virtues and vices of the trademark registration system. One virtue of registration is that, buttressed by the presumption of validity that attaches to registered marks, it gives the trademark owner some degree of certainty that its mark will withstand attack in the marketplace. Registration also promises the relatively robust remedies given for trademark infringement. Both features encourage investment in promoting a registered mark. Should weak marks that only barely qualify for registration enjoy the same *in terrorem* effect in the marketplace as far stronger marks? Or should these marks be denied registration so that they pose the far less intimidating threat of unfair competition litigation in which relief may only require the competitor to label its goods to dispel consumer confusion?

See generally, Burgunder, Trademark Registration of Product Colors: Issues and Answers, 26 Santa Clara L.Rev. 581 (1986).

2. *Location on Goods.* In In re Kotzin, 47 C.C.P.A. 852, 276 F.2d 411, 125 U.S.P.Q. 347 (1960), the Court of Customs and Patent Appeals affirmed a refusal to register a mark consisting of "a woven rectangular tag distinctively located by being vertically disposed and having one longitudinal edge inserted beneath and permanently attached by a seam or pleat across the waistband of the trousers. . . ." The assistant commissioner had given as the ground for refusal that the "distinctive location of a label is not a word, name, symbol or device adopted and used by one manufacturer or merchant to identify his goods and distinguish them from those of others. The location of a label is not and cannot be a trademark under the statutory definition." 118 U.S. P.Q. 465.

The court affirmed on the facts, not the law. As a matter of law, the court believed "that anything recognized as a trademark prior to the 1946 Act would still be so considered, notwithstanding § 45," and "we do not see why the mark sought to be registered could not be considered to be either a symbol or device or a combination thereof." As a matter of fact, it found that because the tag "is, as the specimen shows, more accurately described as a label, bearing a word trademark, descriptive indications of origin, and descriptions of the goods, we do not believe that the purchasing public would regard the described location of this label as an indication of the origin of the goods," and that the evidence of secondary meaning was, on the record, insufficient to support registration under Section 2(f).

Kotzin set the stage for a case in which the primary purpose of the specifically positioned tag was not to bear a word mark and in which the tag had attracted considerable secondary meaning. The case was In re Levi Strauss & Co., 165 U.S.P.Q. 348 (T.T.A.B.1970), and the tag was the familiar rectangular bit of fabric affixed to applicant's garments at the hip pocket. The factual deficiencies of *Kotzin* were missing. Along with supporting letters, affidavits and results of reaction tests showing secondary meaning, "the advertisements illustrative of applicant's promotions of its goods show the garments displayed in such a fashion that the Tab is apparent to the reader and the Tab as so illustrated is without color and no mark or other indicia appears thereon, or if so, is illegible." To the examiner's argument "that applicant cannot obtain a registration (1) for a colorless tab or all tabs regardless of color (2) because of a particular location on its apparel," the Board answered that, (1) applicant had already obtained registration for red tabs, white tabs and black tabs similarly located and "purchasers do recognize that applicant's Tab, notwithstanding differences in color, indicates origin with applicant," and (2) "we do not see why a particular 'Tab' particularly located on particular goods cannot indicate origin."

In Levi Strauss & Co. v. Blue Bell, Inc., 632 F.2d 817, 208 U.S.P.Q. 713 (9th Cir.1980), the court held that defendant's use of a tab on the right rear pocket of its pants infringed plaintiff's registered mark. Subsequently, in Levi Strauss & Co. v. Blue Bell, Inc., 778 F.2d 1352, 228 U.S.P.Q. 346, (9th Cir.1985), the court held that the earlier decision did not collaterally estop the defendant from claiming that its placement of a tab on its shirts did not infringe plaintiff's registered mark. "The district court correctly recognized that secondary meaning inhered in the tab as applied to the pants market, but it did not err in finding no secondary meaning in the tab as applied to the shirt market. Because the tab is a location specific mark, the court could not properly have made findings concerning trademark rights in a pocket tab on garments generally." 778 F.2d at 1359.

3. *Ingredients.* Two inconsistent lines of authority survived passage of the Lanham Act. One line of cases suggested that terms that are used only in connection with ingredients or components of products cannot be registered. The other line of cases indicated that they could be. Assistant Commissioner Leeds set out to resolve the conflict in Winthrop–Stearns, Inc. v. Milner Products Co., 106 U.S.P.Q. 382 (Comm'r.1955), which involved a refusal to register "KoCal" for a brightening agent in applicant's "Pine–Sol" detergent on the ground that it was "not a trademark use within the meaning of the statute."

After reviewing the cases, Assistant Commissioner Leeds determined that the second line of authority represented the correct view. "The question is one of fact. If the mark is used to identify a component—e.g., an ingredient, an added substance, a finish, or a part—and distinguishes such component from those of others, and if it is properly used on or in connection with the goods, or on displays associated with the goods, and the goods are sold or transported in commerce, it is registrable even though it may have originally been an 'advertising gimmick' to aid the sales promotion. As stated, the question is a fact question, namely does the mark, as used, identify and distinguish the goods for which registration is sought?" The assistant commissioner concluded that the record indicated "that applicant's mark was adopted and is used to identify and distinguish a whitening and brightening agent used as an ingredient in a detergent. If the application is amended so to identify the goods, the registration should issue." 106 U.S.P.Q. at 384–85.

Can a fragrance ever qualify for registration as a trademark? See Hawes, Fragrances as Trademarks, 79 Trademark Rep. 134 (1989).

4. *Corporate and Firm Names.* Courts today generally treat the registrability of firm names used in connection with goods as a question of fact. For example, in In re Walker Process Equipment, Inc., 233 F.2d 329, 110 U.S.P.Q. 41 (1956), the court affirmed the examiner's decision refusing registration on the Principal Register of the words, "Walker Process Equipment, Inc.," which applicant used on its goods in conjunction with the trademark, "Proquip," and the firm's address, "Aurora, Ill. U.S.A." From the fact that "Proquip," "which is unquestionably a trademark," constituted the most prominent feature of the label, the court drew the "natural inference . . . that the remaining words on the label are not to be considered a trademark." Further, the court concluded that the addition of the company's address indicated that the firm name was being used for the purpose of distinguishing the applicant from other producers rather than for the purpose of distinguishing applicant as the source of goods.

In light of the distinction between the function of a firm name—to identify a producer—and the function of a trademark—to identify goods with a producer—should the governing principles differ when applicant seeks to register its firm name as a service mark rather than as a trademark? Compare Ex parte Great American Ins. Co., 111 U.S.P.Q. 163 (Comm'r.1956) with In re Amex Holding Corp., 163 U.S.P.Q. 558 (Comm'r.1969).

5. *Slogans.* Slogan trademarks gained entry to the Principal Register only after considerable rough going in the Patent Office in the early years of the Lanham Act's administration. The ground commonly given for refusing registration was that the slogan constituted "an advertising feature used in connection with the actual trademarks used by applicant upon the goods." Ex parte William Skinner & Sons, 82 U.S.P.Q. 315, 318 (Comm'r.1949).

The question of the registrability of slogans was eventually settled in the affirmative in American Enka Corp. v. Marzall, 92 U.S.P.Q. 111 (D.D.C.1952). The court there held that plaintiff's slogan, "The Fate of a Fabric Hangs by a Thread," was registrable. The court reasoned that "certain combinations of words, albeit that they are also slogans, may properly function as trademarks." That this last terse statement represents the sum of the court's reasoning on the matter may, in retrospect, not be surprising. Is it not self evident that a slogan is just "a combination" of "word[s]" within the terms of section 45? Or is this too simplistic a reading of section 45?

Because slogans are characteristically less concise than word or symbol marks, they inevitably invite the charge of descriptiveness—a charge frequently repelled on the ground that the slogan is only suggestive. In Lincoln Park Van Lines, 149 U.S.P.Q. 313 (1966), the Trademark Trial and Appeal Board reversed the examiner's refusal to register "From Maine's Cool Breeze to the Florida Keys" as a mark for applicant's moving and storage services conducted along the entire east coast. Alluding to applicant's assertion that "its mark is poetical or allegorical," the board concluded, "[t]rue the mark comprises bad poetry but nevertheless it is suggestive in connotation rather than descriptive." If the slogan is overly suggestive it may be attacked as puffery—an objection apparently drawn from a pre-Lanham Act case, Burmel Handkerchief Corp. v. Cluett, Peabody & Co., 127 F.2d 318, 53 U.S.P.Q. 369 (1942).

6. *Packages, Buildings, Industrial Design.* Color, location, names and slogans are clearly the stuff of which Principal Register marks are made—"any word, name symbol, or device or any combination thereof." The statutory case for registering packages and buildings is less clear. In Ex parte Minnesota Mining & Mfg. Co., 92 U.S.P.Q. 74 (1952), the Patent Office examiner-in-chief, affirming an examiner's refusal to register applicant's sleigh-shaped container for cellophane adhesive tape, noted that "the word 'device' appearing in the definition of a trademark cannot aid applicant. The word 'device,' which also appears in the older definitions, is not used as referring to a mechanical or structural device but is used in the sense of one of the definitions of the word: 'an artistic figure or design used as a heraldic bearing or as an emblem, badge, trademark, or the like,' rather than in one of the other meanings of the word." 92 U.S.P.Q. at 76.

Ex parte Haig & Haig Ltd., 118 U.S.P.Q. 229 (Comm'r 1958), marked the first faltering break from the position that packages are not registrable. Assistant Commissioner Leeds posed the issue obliquely: "The fundamental question, then, is not whether or not containers are registrable on the Principal Register, but it is whether or not what is presented" (applicant's well-known and distinctive pinch bottle for its Scotch whiskey) "is a trademark—a symbol or device—identifying applicant's goods and distinguishing them from those of others. This is really a question of fact and not of law. . . ." Observing that "customers of today order applicant's whiskey as 'Pinch' and 'Pinch bottle,'" and that applicant had registered the word, "Pinch," Leeds concluded that because "there is no way of identifying or asking for such brand of product other than by describing the contour or conformation of the container . . . the contour or conformation of the container may be a trademark—a symbol or device—which distinguishes the applicant's goods, and it may be registrable on the Principal Register." 118 U.S.P.Q. at 230–31.

The assistant commissioner's decision was a *tour de force* that necessarily turned on the peculiar facts of the case. Taken literally, the decision offered little to encourage the use of package designs to designate source. It was, however, the spirit, not the holding, of *Haig & Haig* that prevailed. Two years later, the well-known Coca–Cola bottle configuration was registered on the Principal Register. See Lunsford, The Protection of Packages and Containers, 56 Trademark Rep. 567 (1966). The registrability of packages on the Principal Register is today unquestioned.

If a container's design can be registered as a trademark if it indicates the source of the goods it contains, can the design of a structure be registered as a service mark if it indicates the source of the services it houses? The trend has been to allow the registration of buildings as marks so long as the applicant can overcome problems of distinctiveness and functionality. See Fotomat Corp. v. Cochran, 437 F.Supp. 1231, 194 U.S.P.Q. 128 (D.Kan.1977); Fotomat Corp. v. Photo Drive–Thru, Inc., 425 F.Supp. 693, 193 U.S.P.Q. 342 (D.N.J.1977). See generally, Fletcher, Buildings as Trademarks, 69 Trademark Rep. 229 (1979).

Industrial design—the configuration of a chair, for example, or a lamp—may also indicate source. The registrability of such designs is considered in Part Four, below, in the context of protection of industrial design generally.

7. *Product Depictions.* Can a two-dimensional depiction of a product be registered as a trademark for the product? In In re DC Comics, Inc., 689 F.2d 1042, 215 U.S.P.Q. 394 (C.C.P.A.1982), the Court of Customs and Patent Appeals held that it could. The Court reversed a decision of the Trademark Trial and Appeal Board which, asserting that the marks were descriptive, had denied registration for drawings of Superman, Batman and Joker for toy dolls resembling these fictional characters. Writing for the court, Judge Baldwin observed, "Whatever information a drawing of Superman or Batman or Joker might convey to the average prospective purchaser regarding a doll resembling one of the related fictional characters is wholly dependent on appellant's efforts to associate each character in the public's awareness with numerous attributes, including a single source of sponsorship. While a drawing of Superman on a box may tell a would-be buyer something about the actual appearance of a doll within, this information-conveying aspect of the drawing does not . . . conclusively eliminate its possible trademark role." 689 F.2d at 1044.

NOTE: THE SUPPLEMENTAL REGISTER

See Statute Supplement, 15 U.S.C.A. §§ 1091–1096.

The Supplemental Register embraces a wider range of subject matter than the Principal Register and is less insistent about the subject matter's distinctiveness. Lanham Act section 23, 15 U.S.C.A. § 1091, allows any "trade-mark, symbol, label, package, configuration of goods, name, word, slogan, phrase, surname, geographical name, numeral or device or any combination of the foregoing" to be registered on the Supplemental Register and requires only that the mark be "*capable* of distinguishing applicant's goods or services." (Emphasis added.) Section 27 of the Lanham Act, 15 U.S.C.A. § 1095, provided that a mark's registration on the Supplemental Register would not preclude registration on the Principal Register. The 1988 amendments to the Lanham Act added, "[r]egistration of a mark on the supplemental register shall not constitute an admission that the mark has not acquired distinctiveness."

By design, the Supplemental Register encompasses virtually all subject matter that is protectible under state unfair competition law. The intention in creating the Register was to continue the register established by the Trademark Act of 1920 and to "provide a quick and simple registration to protect American traders abroad." Hearings on S. 4811 before Sen.Comm. on Patents, 69th Cong., 2d Sess. 13 (1927) (statement of Edward S. Rogers). "In many foreign countries, the only way one can get trademark protection is by registration. That is generally so in Latin America. Moreover, in order to get protection there—and protection depends on registration—a foreigner must produce a certificate of registration from his home land, and one purpose of the supplemental register is to provide protection in foreign countries." Hearings on H.R. 4744 Before the Subcomm. on Trademarks of the House Comm. on Patents, 76th Cong., 1st Sess. 127 (1939) (testimony of Edward S. Rogers).

As other countries drop the requirement that United States nationals seeking their protection show that they have a United States registration, the importance of the Supplemental Register's original objective has declined. Yet, the Supplemental Register has continuing importance domestically, offering an array of rights and remedies unavailable under state unfair competition law. Registration on the Supplemental Register ensures access to federal courts without a showing of diversity jurisdiction, amount in controversy or pendent jurisdiction. Marks on the Supplemental Register are subject neither to opposition nor to interferences; cancellation offers the only channel for attack.

Because the requirements for registration on the Supplemental Register are less exacting than those for registration on the Principal Register, it is no surprise that marks on the Supplemental Register enjoy a narrower range of rights. Among the benefits that do *not* attach to Supplemental Register registrations are the presumptions of validity, ownership and exclusive right to use that attach to registrations on the Principal Register, and constructive notice of the registrant's claim of ownership of the mark. Registrations on the Supplemental Register cannot be deposited with the Secretary of the Treasury or otherwise employed to bar the importation of goods bearing infringing marks. Supplemental Register applications do not qualify for intent to use status under 15 U.S.C.A. § 1051(b). Finally, the right to use the registered subject matter cannot become incontestable.

B. ADMINISTRATIVE PROCEDURES

See Statute Supplement 15 U.S.C.A. §§ 1051, 1056–1059, 1062–1064, 1066–1071, 1112, 1113, 1123.

Before investing heavily in a mark, a prospective trademark owner will typically conduct a trademark search to determine whether its use of the mark will infringe the trademark rights of anyone else and whether the mark will qualify for federal registration. The search, often performed by a professional search service, will be as wide and deep as the occasion warrants. At the least, the searcher will check the Patent and Trademark Office's application and registration files. If the company intends to mount a substantial merchandising program, it will probably also search application and registration files in each of the states as well as trade journals and telephone directories.

Even the most thorough search cannot ensure that the mark will be free of infringement claims or attacks on registration based on prior, undocumented common law uses. The National Broadcasting Company reportedly invested about $750,000 to develop an "N" logo, only to discover that, eight months earlier, the Nebraska Educational Television Network had begun using a virtually identical symbol which it had developed for less than $100. According to news reports, NBC gave the educational network $500,000 in new equipment and $25,000 cash in exchange for clear rights to the mark. Washington Post, Another Suit at NBC, Mar. 26, 1976, at B10, col. 1; Washington Post, At NBC, All's Well That N's Well, July 19, 1985, at B1, col. 1.

A. Examination

The first of the several administrative checkpoints confronting a Principal Register applicant is the trademark examiner's review of the application. The initial procedures will be the same whether the application is a use application under 15 U.S.C.A. § 1051(a) or an intent to use application under 15 U.S.C.A. § 1051(b). After reviewing the application for compliance with the statutory formalities, the examiner will determine whether registration is barred on any of the grounds specified in section 2 of the Lanham Act, 15 U.S.C.A. § 1052. The examiner will search prior registrations and pending applications to determine whether the mark is confusingly similar to any other mark previously used and not abandoned. He may consult trade periodicals to determine whether the mark has a descriptive connotation in the industry in which it is used.

If the examiner concludes that the mark qualifies for registration on the Principal Register, he will approve it for publication in the *Official Gazette.* If no one successfully files an opposition within thirty days of the mark's publication in the *Gazette,* a registration will issue in the case of a use application, and a notice of allowance will issue in the case of an intent to use application. 15 U.S.C.A. § 1063(b). If the examiner rejects the application, the applicant can amend the application to meet the examiner's objections or, if she disagrees with the examiner, can file a response rebutting the grounds for rejection. If these efforts fail and the mark is finally rejected, the applicant can appeal to the Trademark Trial and Appeal Board. 15 U.S.C.A. § 1070.

The *ex parte* proceeding before the trademark examiner is a relatively inexpensive way to screen trademark registration applications for the most obvious, easily discovered objections. For the comparatively few applications that require more extensive scrutiny, the system relies on *inter partes* actions between the applicant and potentially injured competitors to weed out marks that do not qualify for registration. The examiner's approval for publication in the *Official Gazette* sets the stage for the first three forms of *inter partes* proceedings— oppositions, concurrent use proceedings and interference proceedings.

B. *Inter Partes* Proceedings

1. *Oppositions.* Opposition proceedings, conducted by the Trademark Trial and Appeal Board under 15 U.S.C.A. § 1067, give competitors and other potentially injured parties the opportunity to object to registration of a mark. To be heard, the opposer must file its opposition within thirty days of the mark's publication in the *Official Gazette*. To prevail, the opposer must demonstrate that it is likely to be damaged by the mark's registration and that the mark is not entitled to registration under the terms of the Act. The opposer's claimed damage may be that the mark is a descriptive term and that its registration will jeopardize the opposer's freedom to use the term descriptively in its own business. The opposer may allege that the applicant's mark is confusingly similar to the opposer's mark. Having established standing through proof of prospective damage, the opposer can assert any of the available statutory grounds for denying registration—most typically, one or more of the section 2 bars.

2. *Concurrent Use Proceedings.* If the applicant's trademark search revealed an earlier, localized use of the same or a similar mark by someone else, the applicant could initiate a concurrent use proceeding to limit its registration to territories not yet occupied by the earlier user. Section 2(d) provides that the Commissioner may issue concurrent registrations upon determining that "confusion, mistake or deception is not likely to result from the continued use by more than one person of the same or similar marks under conditions and limitations as to the mode or place of use of the marks or the goods in connection with which such marks are used." A concurrent use application will first be reviewed *ex parte* by a trademark examiner. Rules of Practice in Trademark Cases, 37 C.F.R. § 2.99(a) (1988). After notice to the adverse parties named in the application, an *inter partes* proceeding before the Trademark Trial and Appeal Board may ensue. 15 U.S.C.A. § 1067.

3. *Interferences.* Lanham Act section 16, 15 U.S.C.A. § 1066, provides for interference proceedings to determine priority of use any time "application is made for the registration of a mark which so resembles a mark previously registered by another, or for the registration of which another has previously made application, as to be likely when used on or in connection with the goods or services of the applicant to cause confusion or mistake or to deceive." Since March 1, 1972, amendments to the Trademark Rules have substantially confined interference proceedings "to rare cases in which a party might be able to prove that he would suffer irrevocable harm if his only recourse was to file an opposition or a petition for cancellation." These amendments were expected "virtually to eliminate interferences in trademark cases." 36 Fed.Reg. 18002–03 (1971).

4. *Cancellation.* Many marks published for opposition in the *Official Gazette* will pass unnoticed by those most interested in opposing their registration. Fairness to competitors, and deference to the public's interest in freedom from confusion, require that interested parties be given some later opportunity to object to registration. But fairness to registrants and the public's interest in encouraging investment in trademarks, also requires a secure foundation for the registrant's investment. Lanham Act § 14, 15 U.S.C.A. § 1064, balances these interests by authorizing cancellation of Principal Register registrations upon petition "by any person who believes that he is or will be damaged by the registration of a mark on the principal register. . . ." Registrations may be cancelled within five years of the date of registration on any ground that would have barred registration initially. After five years, the grounds for cancellation become more limited. See Note: Incontestability and Immunity from Cancellation, page 284, below. Like opposition and concurrent use proceedings, cancellation applications are heard by the Trademark Trial and Appeal Board under 15 U.S.C.A. § 1067.

C. Renewal

Even after the Trademark Law Revision Act of 1988, trademark rights essentially turn on use. The duration of trademark protection is consequently indeterminate, lasting as long as the trademark owner uses its mark commercially. To terminate the owner's exclusive rights at some fixed and arbitrary point, after which competitors could use the mark freely, would expose consumers to the very deception, confusion and mistake that the Trademark Act aims to prevent. Unlike the Patent and Copyright Acts, which impose fixed terms, the Lanham Act provides that certificates of registration shall remain in force for ten years, renewable indefinitely for successive ten year terms. 15 U.S.C.A. §§ 1058, 1059. The ten year term is the product of the 1988 amendments; the Lanham Act previously prescribed a twenty year renewable term.

The Lanham Act imposes two checkpoints to ensure that marks that are no longer in use will drop from the Principal Register. The first checkpoint comes six years after the mark's registration. Under 15 U.S.C.A. § 1058(a), the registration of any mark "shall be cancelled by the Commissioner at the end of six years following its date, unless within one year next preceding the expiration of such six years the registrant shall file in the Patent and Trademark Office an affidavit setting forth those goods or services recited in the registration on or in connection with which the mark is in use in commerce and attaching to the affidavit a specimen or facsimile showing current use of the mark, or showing that any nonuse is due to special circumstances which excuse such nonuse and is not due to any intention to abandon the mark."

The next checkpoint is periodic, coming at the end of each ten-year period. Under 15 U.S.C.A. § 1059, registrations can be renewed for successive ten year periods upon "payment of the prescribed fee and the filing of a verified application therefor, setting forth those goods or services recited in the registration on or in connection with which the mark is still in use in commerce and having attached thereto, a specimen or facsimile showing current use of the mark, or showing that any nonuse is due to special circumstances which excuse such nonuse and it is not due to any intention to abandon the mark."

D. Appeals

The Trademark Trial and Appeal Board hears appeals from *ex parte* trademark examiner decisions refusing registration. The Board is also the initial forum for *inter partes* proceedings—oppositions, concurrent use, interferences and cancellations. The Commissioner of Patents and Trademarks hears appeals from trademark examiner decisions rejecting a registrant's section 8 affidavit, 15 U.S.C.A. § 1058, or application for renewal under section 1059. A trademark applicant or registrant who loses in an *ex parte* or *inter partes* proceeding before the Board, or before the Commissioner on a section 8 affidavit or registration renewal, may appeal to the Court of Appeals for the Federal Circuit under 15 U.S.C.A. § 1071(a) or seek *de novo* review through a civil action in a United States district court under 15 U.S.C.A. § 1071(b). Recourse from an adverse decision of the Court of Appeals for the Federal Circuit is to the United States Supreme Court under 28 U.S.C.A. § 1254. Recourse from an adverse district court decision is to the regional circuit court of appeals, under 15 U.S.C.A. § 1121, and then to the Supreme Court under 28 U.S.C.A. § 1254.

NOTE: INCONTESTABILITY AND IMMUNITY FROM CANCELLATION

The proponents of the Lanham Act's incontestability provisions had originally hoped for a strong, unified standard that would govern both cancellation proceedings and infringement actions. One early bill had provided that a mark's registration could not be cancelled or attacked in an infringement action after five years on the Principal Register. H.R. 9041, 75th Cong., 3d Sess., §§ 13, 14 (1938). The provisions that finally emerged from the push and tug of legislative compromise are far more limited and fragmented. They include the incontestability provisions of sections 15 and 33(b), 15 U.S.C.A. §§ 1065, 1115(b), and the cancellation provisions of section 14, 15 U.S.C.A. § 1064, which substantially parallel the incontestability provisions.

Sections 14, 15 and 33(b) rest on the premise that, to encourage investment in trademarks, time and use must be allowed to heal many original defects in a mark. Each section focuses its curative power on a different context. Section 14 applies when the registrant is defending its mark against a petition to cancel. Section 15, which establishes the registrant's incontestable right to use, applies when the registrant is defending an infringement action brought to enjoin it from using the mark. Section 33(b) applies when the registrant seeks to prevent someone else from using a confusingly similar mark. Several early cases rejected this last, offensive use of incontestability. See, for example, John Morrell & Co. v. Reliable Packing Co., 295 F.2d 314, 131 U.S.P.Q. 155 (7th Cir.1961); Tillamook County Creamery Ass'n v. Tillamook Cheese & Dairy Ass'n, 345 F.2d 158, 145 U.S.P.Q. 244 (9th Cir.1965), cert. denied, 382 U.S. 903, 86 S.Ct. 239, 15 L.Ed.2d 157, 147 U.S.P.Q. 541. In 1985 the United States Supreme Court resolved any doubt about the offensive use of incontestability by holding that "the holder of a registered mark may rely on incontestability to enjoin infringement." Park 'N Fly, Inc. v. Dollar Park and Fly, Inc., 469 U.S. 189, 205, 224 U.S.P.Q. 327, 334 (1985).

Section 14. Although section 14 is sometimes called an incontestability provision, only section 15 and 33(b) in fact use that term expressly. Section 14 approximates incontestability by providing that, after five years on the Principal Register, a mark will generally be immune from attack in a cancellation proceeding. Among the grounds left open for attack after the five year period are fraudulent registration, abandonment, the mark's having become the "generic name for the goods or services, or a portion thereof, for which it is registered," and any of the grounds that would bar registration under section 2(a), (b) or (c). Thus, after five years, a registered mark cannot be cancelled simply because it lacks distinctiveness or is confusingly similar to other marks.

Section 15. Section 15 provides that a registrant's right to use its mark in commerce "shall be incontestable" if the mark has been used for five consecutive years after its registration and the registrant files an affidavit to that effect. Under section 15, a party can defeat incontestability on the same grounds that, under section 14, would require cancellation after five years' registration. Section 15 also provides that a registration will not become incontestable if use of the mark "infringes a valid right acquired under the law of any State or Territory by use of a mark or trade name continuing from a date prior to the date of registration" of the registered mark. Further, "no incontestable right shall be acquired in a mark which is the generic name for the goods or services or a portion thereof, for which it is registered."

Section 33(b). Section 33(a) of the Lanham Act provides that any registration of a mark on the Principal Register "shall be admissible in evidence and shall be prima facie evidence of the validity of the registered mark and of the registration of the mark, of the registrant's ownership of the mark, and of the registrant's exclusive right to use the registered mark in commerce. . . ." 15 U.S.C.A. § 1115(a). Section 33(b) gives substantially greater evidential weight to incontestable marks by making them "conclusive evidence," rather than merely prima facie evidence, of validity, ownership and exclusive right to use. For example, in the *Park 'N Fly* case, the Supreme Court held that it is no defense to an action for infringement of an incontestable mark that the mark is merely descriptive under the terms of section 2(e), 15 U.S.C.A. 1052(e). Among other grounds, section 33(b) deprives the registration certificate of conclusive effect if the registration or incontestable right was obtained fraudulently or if the mark has been abandoned or used to violate federal antitrust laws. 15 U.S.C.A. § 1115(b).

The 1988 amendments to the Lanham Act resolved a conflict among the circuits by adding as a defense to incontestability that "equitable principles, including laches, estoppel, and acquiescence, are applicable." § 33(b)(8). The 1988 amendments also removed any question whether a registrant can prevail in an infringement action on the basis of incontestability alone. As amended, section 33(b) provides that "conclusive evidence of the right to use the registered mark shall be subject to proof of infringement as defined in section 1114 of this title."

See generally Wallen & MacDermott, Federal Registration and Incontestability, 79 Trademark Rep. 373 (1989); Naresh, Incontestability and Rights in Descriptive Trademarks, 53 U.Chi.L.Rev. 953 (1986); Fletcher, Incontestability and Constructive Notice: A Quarter Century of Adjudication, 63 Trademark Rep. 71 (1973).

C. RIGHTS AND REMEDIES

1. RIGHTS

See Statute Supplement 15 U.S.C.A. §§ 1057(b), 1060, 1065, 1072, 1115.

a. GEOGRAPHIC BOUNDARIES

UNITED DRUG CO. v. THEODORE RECTANUS CO., 248 U.S. 90, 96–98, 100, 39 S.Ct. 48–50, 63 L.Ed. 141 (1918). Mr. Justice PITNEY: The entire argument for the petitioner is summed up in the contention that whenever the first user of a trade-mark has been reasonably diligent in extending the territory of his trade, and as a result of such extension has in good faith come into competition with a later user of the same mark who in equal good faith has extended his trade locally before invasion of his field by the first user, so that finally it comes to pass that the rival traders are offering competitive merchandise in a common market under the same trade-mark, the later user should be enjoined at the suit of the prior adopter, even though the latter be the last to enter the competitive field and the former have already established a trade there. Its application to the case is based upon the hypothesis that the record shows that Mrs. Regis and her firm, during the entire period of limited and local trade in her medicine under the Rex mark, were making efforts to extend their trade so far as they were able to do with the means at their disposal. There is little in the record to support this hypothesis; but, waiving this, we will pass upon the principal contention.

. . . Undoubtedly, the general rule is that, as between conflicting claimants to the right to use the same mark, priority of appropriation determines the question. But the reason is that purchasers have come to understand the mark as indicating the origin of the wares, so that its use by a second producer amounts to an attempt to sell his goods as those of his competitor. The reason for the rule does not extend to a case where the same trade-mark happens to be employed simultaneously by two manufacturers in different markets separate and remote from each other, so that the mark means one thing in one market, an entirely different thing in another. It would be a perversion of the rule of priority to give it such an application in our broadly extended country that an innocent party who had in good faith employed a trademark in one State, and by the use of it had built up a trade there, being the first appropriator in that jurisdiction, might afterwards be prevented from using it, with consequent injury to his trade and good-will, at the instance of one who theretofore had employed the same mark but only in other and remote jurisdictions, upon the ground that its first employment happened to antedate that of the first-mentioned trader.

DAWN DONUT CO. v. HART'S FOOD STORES, INC.

United States Court of Appeals, Second Circuit, 1959.
267 F.2d 358, 121 U.S.P.Q. 430.

LUMBARD, Circuit Judge.

The principal question is whether the plaintiff, a wholesale distributor of doughnuts and other baked goods under its federally registered trademarks "Dawn" and "Dawn Donut," is entitled under the provisions of the Lanham Trademark Act to enjoin the defendant from using the mark "Dawn" in connection with the retail sale of doughnuts and baked goods entirely within a six county area of New York State surrounding the city of Rochester. The primary difficulty arises from the fact that although plaintiff licenses purchasers of its mixes to use its trademarks in connection with the retail sales of food products made from the mixes, it has not licensed or otherwise exploited the mark at the retail level in defendant's market area for some thirty years.

We hold that because no likelihood of public confusion arises from the concurrent use of the mark in connection with retail sales of doughnuts and other baked goods in separate trading areas, and because there is no present likelihood that plaintiff will expand its retail use of the mark into defendant's market area, plaintiff is not now entitled to any relief under the Lanham Act, 15 U.S.C.A. § 1114. Accordingly, we affirm the district court's dismissal of plaintiff's complaint.

This is not to say that the defendant has acquired any permanent right to use the mark in its trading area. On the contrary, we hold that because of the effect of the constructive notice provision of the Lanham Act, should the plaintiff expand its retail activities into the six county area, upon a proper application and showing to the district court, it may enjoin defendant's use of the mark.

With respect to defendant's counterclaim to cancel plaintiff's registration on the ground that its method of licensing its trademarks violates the Lanham Act, a majority of the court holds that the district court's dismissal of defendant's counterclaim should be affirmed. They conclude that the district court's finding that the plaintiff exercised the degree of control over the nature and quality of the products sold by its licensees required by the Act was not clearly erroneous, particularly in view of the fact that the defendant had the burden of proving its claim for cancellation. I dissent from this conclusion because neither the finding of the trial judge nor the undisputed evidence in the record indicates the extent of supervision and control actually exercised by the plaintiff.

We are presented here with cross-appeals from a judgment entered by the District Court for the Western District of New York dismissing both plaintiff's complaint for infringement of its federally registered trademarks and defendant's counterclaim to cancel plaintiff's federal registrations.

Plaintiff, Dawn Donut Co., Inc., of Jackson, Michigan since June 1, 1922 has continuously used the trademark "Dawn" upon 25 to 100 pound bags of doughnut mix which it sells to bakers in various states, including New York, and since 1935 it has similarly marketed a line of sweet dough mixes for use in the baking of coffee cakes, cinnamon rolls and oven goods in general under that mark. In 1950 cake mixes were added to the company's line of products. Dawn's sales representatives call upon bakers to solicit orders for mixes and the orders obtained are filled by shipment to the purchaser either directly from plaintiff's Jackson, Michigan plant, where the mixes are manufactured, or from a local warehouse within the customer's state. For some years plaintiff maintained a warehouse in Jamestown, New York, from which shipments were made, but sometime prior to the commencement of this suit in 1954 it discontinued this warehouse and has since then shipped its mixes to its New York customers directly from Michigan.

Plaintiff furnishes certain buyers of its mixes, principally those who agree to become exclusive Dawn Donut Shops, with advertising and packaging material bearing the trademark "Dawn" and permits these bakers to sell goods made from the mixes to the consuming public under that trademark. These display materials are supplied either as a courtesy or at a moderate price apparently to stimulate and promote the sale of plaintiff's mixes.

The district court found that with the exception of one Dawn Donut Shop operated in the city of Rochester, New York during 1926–27, plaintiff's licensing of its mark in connection with the retail sale of doughnuts in the state of New York has been confined to areas not less than 60 miles from defendant's trading area. The court also found that for the past eighteen years plaintiff's present New York state representative has, without interruption, made regular calls upon bakers in the city of Rochester, N.Y., and in neighboring towns and cities, soliciting orders for plaintiff's mixes and that throughout this period orders have been filled and shipments made of plaintiff's mixes from Jackson, Michigan into the city of Rochester. But it does not appear that any of these purchasers of plaintiff's mixes employed the plaintiff's mark in connection with retail sales.

The defendant, Hart Food Stores, Inc., owns and operates a retail grocery chain within the New York counties of Monroe, Wayne, Livingston, Genesee, Ontario and Wyoming. The products of defendant's bakery, Starhart Bakeries, Inc., a New York corporation of which it is the sole stockholder, are distributed through these stores, thus confining the distribution of defendant's product to an area within a 45 mile radius of Rochester. Its advertising of doughnuts and other baked products over television and radio and in newspapers is also limited to this area. Defendant's bakery corporation was formed on April 13, 1951 and first used the imprint "Dawn" in packaging its products on August 30, 1951. The district court found that the defendant adopted the mark "Dawn" without any actual knowledge of plaintiff's use or federal registration of the mark, selecting it largely because of a slogan "Baked at midnight, delivered at Dawn" which was originated by defendant's president and used by defendant in its bakery operations from 1929 to 1935. Defendant's president testified, however, that no investigation was made prior to the adoption of the mark to see if anyone else was employing it. Plaintiff's marks were registered federally in 1927, and their registration was renewed in 1947. Therefore by virtue of the Lanham Act, 15 U.S.C.A. § 1072, the defendant had constructive notice of plaintiff's marks as of July 5, 1947, the effective date of the Act.

Defendant does not contest the similarity of the marks. Its principal contention is that because plaintiff has failed to exploit the mark "Dawn" for some thirty years at the retail level in the Rochester trading area, plaintiff should not be accorded the exclusive right to use the mark in this area. We reject this contention as inconsistent with the scope of protection afforded a federal registrant by the Lanham Act.

Prior to the passage of the Lanham Act courts generally held that the owner of a registered trademark could not sustain an action for infringement against another who, without knowledge of the registration, used the mark in a different trading area from that exploited by the registrant so that public confusion was unlikely. By being the first to adopt a mark in an area without knowledge of its prior registration, a junior user of a mark could gain the right to exploit the mark exclusively in that market.

But the Lanham Act, 15 U.S.C.A. § 1072, provides that registration of a trademark on the principal register is constructive notice of the registrant's claim of ownership. Thus, by eliminating the defense of good faith and lack of knowledge, § 1072 affords nationwide protection to registered marks, regardless of the areas in which the registrant actually uses the mark.

That such is the purpose of Congress is further evidenced by 15 U.S.C.A. § 1115(a) and (b) which make the certificate of registration evidence of the registrant's "exclusive right to use the mark in commerce." "Commerce" is defined in 15 U.S.C.A. § 1127 to include all the commerce which may lawfully be regulated by Congress. These two provisions of the Lanham Act make it plain that the fact that the defendant employed the mark "Dawn," without actual knowledge of plaintiff's registration, at the retail level in a limited geographical area of New York state before the plaintiff used the mark in that market, does not entitle it either to exclude the plaintiff from using the mark in that area or to use the mark concurrently once the plaintiff licenses the mark or otherwise exploits it in connection with retail sales in the area.

Plaintiff's failure to license its trademarks in defendant's trading area during the thirty odd years that have elapsed since it licensed them to a Rochester baker does not work an abandonment of the rights in that area. We hold that 15 U.S.C.A. § 1127, which provides for abandonment in certain cases of nonuse, applies only when the registrant fails to use his mark within the meaning of § 1127, anywhere in the nation. Since the Lanham Act affords a registrant nationwide protection, a contrary holding would create an insoluble problem of measuring the geographical extent of the abandonment. Even prior to the passage of the Lanham Act, when trademark protection flowed from state law and therefore depended on use within the state, no case, as far as we have been able to ascertain, held that a trademark owner abandoned his rights within only part of a state because of his failure to use the mark in that part of the state.

Accordingly, since plaintiff has used its trademark continuously at the retail level, it has not abandoned its federal registration rights even in defendant's trading area. . . .

Accordingly, we turn to the question of whether on this record plaintiff has made a sufficient showing to warrant the issuance of an injunction against the defendant's use of the mark "Dawn" in a trading area in which the plaintiff has for thirty years failed to employ its registered mark.

The Lanham Act, 15 U.S.C.A. § 1114, sets out the standard for awarding a registrant relief against the unauthorized use of his mark by another. It provides that the registrant may enjoin only that concurrent use which creates a likelihood of public confusion as to the origin of the products in connection with which the marks are used. Therefore if the use of the marks by the registrant and the unauthorized user are confined to two sufficiently distinct and geographically separate markets, with no likelihood that the registrant will expand his use into defendant's market, so that no public confusion is possible, then the registrant is not entitled to enjoin the junior user's use of the mark.

As long as plaintiff and defendant confine their use of the mark "Dawn" in connection with the retail sale of baked goods to their present separate trading areas it is clear that no public confusion is likely.

The district court took note of what it deemed common knowledge, that "retail purchasers of baked goods, because of the perishable nature of such goods, usually make such purchases reasonably close to their homes, say within about 25 miles, and retail purchases of such goods beyond that distance are for all practical considerations negligible." No objection is made to this finding and nothing appears in the record which contradicts it as applied to this case.

Moreover, we note that it took plaintiff three years to learn of defendant's use of the mark and bring this suit, even though the plaintiff was doing some wholesale business in the Rochester area. This is a strong indication that no confusion arose or is likely to arise either from concurrent use of the marks at the retail level in geographically separate trading areas or from its concurrent use at different market levels, viz. retail and wholesale in the same area.

The decisive question then is whether plaintiff's use of the mark "Dawn" at the retail level is likely to be confined to its current area of use or whether in the normal course of its business, it is likely to expand the retail use of the mark into defendant's trading area. If such expansion were probable, then the concurrent use of the marks would give rise to the conclusion that there was a likelihood of confusion.

The district court found that in view of the plaintiff's inactivity for about thirty years in exploiting its trademarks in defendant's trading area at the retail level either by advertising directed at retail purchasers or by retail sales through authorized licensed users, there was no reasonable expectation that plaintiff would extend its retail operations into defendant's trading area. There is ample evidence in the record to support this conclusion and we cannot say that it is clearly erroneous.

We note not only that plaintiff has failed to license its mark at the retail level in defendant's trading area for a substantial period of time, but also that the trend of plaintiff's business manifests a striking decrease in the number of licensees employing its mark at the retail level in New York state and throughout the country. In the 1922–1930 period plaintiff had 75 to 80 licensees across the country with 11 located in New York. At the time of the trial plaintiff listed only 16 active licensees not one of which was located in New York.

The normal likelihood that plaintiff's wholesale operations in the Rochester area would expand to the retail level is fully rebutted and overcome by the decisive fact that plaintiff has in fact not licensed or otherwise exploited its mark at retail in the area for some thirty years.

Accordingly, because plaintiff and defendant use the mark in connection with retail sales in distinct and separate markets and because there is no present prospect that plaintiff will expand its use of the mark at the retail level into defendant's trading area, we conclude that there is no likelihood of public confusion arising from the concurrent use of the marks and therefore the issuance of an injunction is not warranted. A fortiori plaintiff is not entitled to any accounting or damages. However, because of the effect we have attributed to the constructive notice provision of the Lanham Act, the plaintiff may later, upon a proper showing of an intent to use the mark at the retail level in defendant's market area, be entitled to enjoin defendant's use of the mark. . . .

We are all agreed that the Lanham Act places an affirmative duty upon a licensor of a registered trademark to take reasonable measures to detect and prevent misleading uses of his mark by his licensees or suffer cancellation of his federal registration. The Act, 15 U.S.C.A. § 1064, provides that a trademark registration may be cancelled because the trademark has been "abandoned." And "abandoned" is defined in 15 U.S.C.A. § 1127 to include any act or omission by the registrant which causes the trademark to lose its significance as an indication of origin.

Prior to the passage of the Lanham Act many courts took the position that the licensing of a trademark separately from the business in connection with which it had been used worked an abandonment. The theory of these cases was that:

> A trademark is intended to identify the goods of the owner and to safeguard his good will. The designation if employed by a person other than the one whose business it serves to identify would be misleading. Consequently a right to the use of a trademark or a trade name cannot be transferred in gross. American Broadcasting Co. v. Wahl Co., [121 F.2d 412, 413].

Other courts were somewhat more liberal and held that a trademark could be licensed separately from the business in connection with which it had been used provided that the licensor retained control over the quality of the goods produced by the licensee. But even in the duPont case the court was careful to point out that naked licensing, viz. the grant of licenses without the retention of control, was invalid. E.I. duPont de Nemours & Co. v. Celanese Corporation of America, [35 C.C. P.A. 1061, 167 F.2d 484, 489.]

The Lanham Act clearly carries forward the view of these latter cases that controlled licensing does not work an abandonment of the licensor's registration, while a system of naked licensing does. 15 U.S. C.A. § 1055 provides:

> Where a registered mark or a mark sought to be registered is or may be used legitimately by related companies, such use shall inure to the benefit of the registrant or applicant for registration, and such use shall not affect the validity of such mark or of its registration, provided such mark is not used in such manner as to deceive the public.

And 15 U.S.C.A. § 1127 defines "related company" to mean "any person who legitimately controls or is controlled by the registrant or applicant for registration in respect to the nature and quality of the goods or services in connection with which the mark is used."

Without the requirement of control, the right of a trademark owner to license his mark separately from the business in connection with which it has been used would create the danger that products bearing the same trademark might be of diverse qualities. If the licensor is not compelled to take some reasonable steps to prevent misuses of his trademark in the hands of others the public will be deprived of its most effective protection against misleading uses of a trademark. The public is hardly in a position to uncover deceptive uses of a trademark before they occur and will be at best slow to detect them after they happen. Thus, unless the licensor exercises supervision and control over the operations of its licensees the risk that the public will be unwittingly deceived will be increased and this is precisely what the Act is in part designed to prevent. Clearly the only effective way to protect the public where a trademark is used by licensees is to place on the licensor the affirmative duty of policing in a reasonable manner the activities of his licensees.

The critical question on these facts therefore is whether the plaintiff sufficiently policed and inspected its licensees' operations to guarantee the quality of the products they sold under its trademarks to the public. The trial court found that: "By reason of its contracts with its licensees, plaintiff exercised legitimate control over the nature and quality of the food products on which plaintiff's licensees used the trademark 'Dawn.' Plaintiff and its licensees are related companies within the meaning of Section 45 of the Trademark Act of 1946." It is the position of the majority of this court that the trial judge has the same leeway in determining what constitutes a reasonable degree of supervision and control over licensees under the facts and circumstances of the particular case as he has on other questions of fact; and particularly because it is the defendant who has the burden of proof on this issue they hold the lower court's finding not clearly erroneous.

I dissent from the conclusion of the majority that the district court's findings are not clearly erroneous because (1) while it is true that the trial judge must be given some discretion in determining what constitutes reasonable supervision of licensees under the Lanham Act, it is also true that an appellate court ought not to accept the conclusions of the district court unless they are supported by findings of sufficient facts. It seems to me that the only findings of the district judge regarding supervision are in such general and conclusory terms as to be meaningless. In the absence of supporting findings or of undisputed evidence in the record indicating the kind of supervision and inspection the plaintiff actually made of its licensees, it is impossible for us to pass upon whether there was such supervision as to satisfy the statute. There was evidence before the district court in the matter of supervision, and more detailed findings thereon should have been made.

Plaintiff's licensees fall into two classes: (1) those bakers with whom it made written contracts providing that the baker purchase exclusively plaintiff's mixes and requiring him to adhere to plaintiff's directions in using the mixes; and (2) those bakers whom plaintiff permitted to sell at retail under the "Dawn" label doughnuts and other baked goods made from its mixes although there was no written agreement governing the quality of the foods sold under the Dawn mark.

The contracts that plaintiff did conclude, although they provided that the purchaser use the mix as directed and without adulteration, failed to provide for any system of inspection and control. Without such a system plaintiff could not know whether these bakers were adhering to its standards in using the mix or indeed whether they were selling only products made from Dawn mixes under the trademark "Dawn."

The absence, however, of an express contract right to inspect and supervise a licensee's operations does not mean that the plaintiff's method of licensing failed to comply with the requirements of the Lanham Act. Plaintiff may in fact have exercised control in spite of the absence of any express grant by licensees of the right to inspect and supervise.

The question then, with respect to both plaintiff's contract and non-contract licensees, is whether the plaintiff in fact exercised sufficient control.

Here the only evidence in the record relating to the actual supervision of licensees by plaintiff consists of the testimony of two of plaintiff's local sales representatives that they regularly visited their particular customers and the further testimony of one of them, Jesse Cohn, the plaintiff's New York representative, that "in many cases" he did have an opportunity to inspect and observe the operations of his customers. The record does not indicate whether plaintiff's other sales representatives made any similar efforts to observe the operations of licensees.

Moreover, Cohn's testimony fails to make clear the nature of the inspection he made or how often he made one. His testimony indicates that his opportunity to observe a licensee's operations was limited to "those cases where I am able to get into the shop" and even casts some doubt on whether he actually had sufficient technical knowledge in the use of plaintiff's mix to make an adequate inspection of a licensee's operations.

The fact that it was Cohn who failed to report the defendant's use of the mark "Dawn" to the plaintiff casts still further doubt about the extent of the supervision Cohn exercised over the operations of plaintiff's New York licensees.

Thus I do not believe that we can fairly determine on this record whether plaintiff subjected its licensees to periodic and thorough inspections by trained personnel or whether its policing consisted only of chance, cursory examinations of licensees' operations by technically untrained salesmen. The latter system of inspection hardly constitutes a sufficient program of supervision to satisfy the requirements of the Act.

Therefore it is appropriate to remand the counterclaim for more extensive findings on the relevant issues rather than hazard a determination on this incomplete and uncertain record. I would direct the district court to order the cancellation of plaintiff's registrations if it should find that the plaintiff did not adequately police the operations of its licensees.

But unless the district court finds some evidence of misuse of the mark by plaintiff in its sales of mixes to bakers at the wholesale level, the cancellation of plaintiff's registration should be limited to the use of the mark in connection with sale of the finished food products to the consuming public. Such a limited cancellation is within the power of the court. Section 1119 of 15 U.S.C.A. specifically provides that "In any action involving a registered mark the court may . . . order cancellation of registrations in whole or in part, . . ." Moreover, partial cancellation is consistent with § 1051(a)(1) of 15 U.S.C.A., governing the initial registration of trademarks which requires the applicant to specify "the goods in connection with which the mark is used and the manner in which the mark is used in connection with such goods. . . ."

The district court's denial of an injunction restraining defendant's use of the mark "Dawn" on baked and fried goods and its dismissal of defendant's counterclaim are affirmed.

NOTES

1. There is probably no more intricate task in trademark law than coordinating the rights accruing to senior and junior users under common law and under section 22's constructive notice provisions. It is clear under the common law that, until a mark is registered, each user has rights in the territory it has occupied. But, to what extent will registration freeze the rights of one and expand the rights of the other? Say that *A* first used the mark, "Rex," in connection with its shampoo in 1951. It applied for registration on the Principal Register in 1954 and the registration issued in 1956. *A*'s distribution of the shampoo has at all times been restricted to three states, New York, New Jersey, and Connecticut. *B* first used the mark, "Rex," in connection with its shampoo in 1949 and applied for registration on the Principal Register in 1959. *B*'s distribution of its goods has at all times been restricted to three states, California, Oregon and Washington. Now, *B*'s 1959 application has become the basis for a concurrent use proceeding under section 2, 15 U.S.C.A. § 1052(d). What are the respective territorial rights of the parties?

In 1970, the Court of Customs and Patent Appeals definitively outlined the substantive rules governing concurrent use. In re Beatrice Foods Co., 429 F.2d 466, 166 U.S.P.Q. 431 (C.C.P.A.1970). *Beatrice Foods* stated that, as a general rule, in concurrent use proceedings between two applicants, the senior user is entitled to a registration covering the entire United States, less the area in which the junior user has established territorial rights. But, the court noted, territorial rights need not to be coextensive with territorial use. The court confirmed and elaborated the *Beatrice Foods* analysis in Weiner King, Inc. v. The Weiner King Corp., 615 F.2d 512, 522–23 n. 6, 204 U.S.P.Q. 820 (C.C.P.A.1980): "While it is clear that appropriation of a mark with knowledge that it is being used by another is not in good faith, it does not follow that a later user who has adopted in good faith *must* forego any further expansion after learning of the prior user. We believe that, even under the common law, such an issue depends on such factors as natural area of expansion, the possibility of encroachment on the area of the other party, and other equitable considerations."

See generally, Lefkowitz, A Concurrent Use Registration as a Reflection of Established Territorial Rights; Fact or Fiction, 65 Trademark Rep. 71 (1975); Kaul, Concurrent Use and Registration of Trademarks, 62 Trademark Rep. 581 (1972); Schwartz, Concurrent Registration Under the Lanham Trademark Act of 1946: What is the Impact on Section 2(d) of Section 22?, 55 Trademark Rep. 413 (1965).

2. *Constructive Notice and Constructive Use.* The 1988 amendments to the Lanham Act complicated the allocation of territorial rights by introducing the concept of constructive use arising from the filing of an intent to use application. See page 204, above. Constructive *notice* under section 22, 15 U.S.C.A. § 1072, has two consequences: it prevents a junior user who begins her use after the date of the senior user's registration from acquiring any right to use the mark; and it confines the rights of any senior, unregistered user to the territory that the user occupied at the time of the registration. Constructive *use* prevents a junior user from acquiring any right to use the mark after the filing date of an intent to use application; it does not, however, freeze the rights of any senior unregistered user.

3. Say that *A* first used the mark, "Rex," in connection with its shampoo in 1961, limiting its distribution at the time to east coast states. In 1968, *A* obtained registration for the mark on the Principal Register. In 1969, *B* first used the mark "Rex" in connection with its shampoo, limiting its trade to west coast states. *A* has not yet marketed its shampoo on the west coast. Should *A* be entitled to an injunction against *B*? Sterling Brewing, Inc. v. Cold Spring Brewing Corp., 100 F.Supp. 412, 90 U.S.P.Q. 242 (D.Mass.1951), the first case to apply section 22 to this fact situation, held that the injunction should issue at once even though "the plaintiff's zone of potential expansion of business cannot reasonably be expected to extend [into defendant's territory]." 100 F.Supp. 412, 415.

Which decision, *Dawn* or *Sterling,* provides the better solution? As a practical matter, *Dawn* converts the question whether the junior user should stop using the senior user's mark from a legal question to a business judgment. In arriving at its business decision, the junior user will, of course, speculate as to whether and when the senior user will enter. What other factors should it weigh? If the junior user decides to risk the senior user's entry into its market, and proceeds to invest heavily in the continued use and promotion of its mark, how will consumers be affected when the senior user enters the junior user's market and obtains an injunction against the junior user's continued use of the mark?

See generally, Fletcher, The Chextra Case and Other Spawn of Dawn Donut, 66 Trademark Rep. 285 (1976); Alexander & Coil, Geographic Rights in Trademarks and Service Marks, 68 Trademark Rep. 101 (1978).

4. *Trademark Assignments and Licenses.* It is a hoary maxim that a trademark cannot be assigned in gross—that is, apart from the assignor's business, assets or goodwill. Section 10 of the Lanham Act, 15 U.S.C.A. § 1061, provides, "[a] registered mark or a mark for which application to register has been filed shall be assignable with the goodwill of the business in which the mark is used, or with that part of the goodwill of the business connected with the use of and symbolized by the mark." While transfers in gross are sometimes held to constitute abandonment, it is probably better on principle to treat the naked transfer as merely depriving the assignee of the priority created by the assignor's earlier use. A court may also hold that a mark has been abandoned if its owner licenses others to use the mark but fails to control the quality of goods or services that the licensees sell under the mark. As indicated by *Dawn Donut*, courts have been less than rigorous in requiring vigilant quality control programs.

The premise underlying the abandonment rules for both assignments and licenses is that a mark symbolizes a particular level of quality to consumers and that transfers of the mark without the economic factors responsible for that quality may undermine consumer expectations. Do these abandonment rules make sense? What business incentives do assignees and licensees have to depart from the quality symbolized by the mark they are acquiring? What business incentives do trademark owners who do not assign or license their marks have to maintain the quality of goods and services symbolized by the mark?

The rule against assignments in gross has its detractors. An early version of the bill that eventually became the Lanham Act provided, "[a] registered trade-mark shall be assignable either with or without the goodwill of the business." H.R. 9041, 75th Cong., 3d Sess. (1938). Most countries today permit the assignment of trademarks without accompanying goodwill. II S. Ladas, Patents, Trademarks, and Related Rights § 617 (1975).

On abandonment generally, see p. 216, above.

b.   PRODUCT BOUNDARIES: DILUTION

SCARVES BY VERA, INC. v. TODO IMPORTS LTD.

United States Court of Appeals, Second Circuit, 1976.
544 F.2d 1167, 192 U.S.P.Q. 289.

LUMBARD, Circuit Judge.

This appeal raises the familiar problem of determining under what circumstances a trademark owner may protect his trademark against use on products other than those to which the owner has applied it. Specifically, we must decide whether plaintiff, who uses the trademark

"VERA" on a well-known line of women's scarves, apparel, and linens, is entitled to prevent defendant's use of the same mark on cosmetics and fragrances.

Appeal is from a judgment entered on August 28, 1975 after a two day bench trial in the Southern District of New York, Robert L. Carter, District Judge, dismissing plaintiff's action for trademark infringement and unfair competition. Plaintiff had been seeking injunctive relief, damages and an accounting.

For the reasons stated below we hold that the defendant infringed plaintiff's trademark, and that the plaintiff is entitled to injunctive relief. Accordingly, we reverse and remand.

Plaintiff Scarves by Vera, Inc. is a well known and highly successful fashion designer. Plaintiff designs and manufactures a line of women's signature scarves, medium-high fashion women's sportswear, and a variety of dining room, bedroom and bathroom linens. Defendant Todo Imports Ltd. is a New York corporation which, since 1970, has been the exclusive distributor in New York of certain cosmetics and toiletries manufactured by Vera Perfumeria y Cosmetica, S.A. of Barcelona, Spain (Vera S.A.).

On July 7, 1971, plaintiff commenced this action for trademark infringement and unfair competition under the Lanham Act of 1946, 15 U.S.C.A. § 1051 et seq., and under state law. Jurisdiction was based on 15 U.S.C.A. § 1121 and 28 U.S.C.A. § 1338.

In its complaint, plaintiff alleged its ownership of the registered trademark "VERA" on scarves, women's sportswear, and a large variety of linens. Plaintiff claimed that the defendant had infringed its trademark by using the mark "VERA" on cosmetics and toiletries manufactured in Spain by Vera, S.A. and distributed in the United States by the defendant. Plaintiff sought injunctive relief, damages and an accounting. Vera, S.A. was not named as a defendant and has not sought to intervene in this action.

The evidence adduced during the two day trial in October 1974 presented no substantial dispute as to the historical facts. In 1945 Mrs. Vera Neumann, her husband and a partner formed Scarves by Vera, a partnership which was plaintiff's predecessor. Plaintiff soon gained wide success as one of the first designers of high-fashion signature scarves. From the outset, plaintiff made scarves, women's blouses and some linen goods. Subsequently, plaintiff expanded into a wide variety of women's sportswear, including dresses, belts and sweaters, and a line of designer home accessory items, such as sheets, towels, table linens and place settings. The fabrics or facings of all these goods contained colorful patterns created by Mrs. Neumann, who is a well known artist.

Plaintiff's goods were sold under the trademark "VERA." Plaintiff is the owner of two registrations for the mark "VERA" in the United States Patent and Trademark Office. The first, covering scarves, neckties, blouses, shawls and kerchiefs, was filed on August 12, 1958 and issued on August 11, 1959. The second, covering the same items, plus a broad range of women's sportswear, apartment accessories and linens, was filed on September 2, 1969 and issued on August 11, 1970.

Plaintiff sells its goods in some 8,000 medium-to high-fashion department stores, boutiques and specialty shops across the nation. A representative sample of plaintiff's principal retail outlets includes Bergdorf Goodman, Bonwit Teller, Saks Fifth Avenue, Bloomingdale's, Macy's and Gimbel's.

Plaintiff introduced extensive evidence of its considerable success and wide recognition in the fashion-conscious consumer market. Plaintiff's sales rose from $10.5 million in 1966 to over $21 million in 1972, before falling to $18 million in 1973 due to the general economic downturn.

Plaintiff has spent more than $3 million since 1966 in advertising and promoting its products under the "VERA" trademark. Since 1970 plaintiff has spent $300 to $500 thousand dollars annually. In addition, the plaintiff's licensees and retailers have also contributed to the advertising pool pursuant to cooperative advertising arrangements.

The plaintiff also produced examples of its advertisements and an impressive volume of articles which had appeared in publications including the New York Times, The New Yorker, Vogue, Town & Country, Harper's Bazaar, and Mademoiselle. These articles, written by independent journalists about plaintiff's growth and products and discussing plaintiff along with such names as Blass, Cardin, Pucci, and St. Laurent, were evidence that plaintiff was recognized as a leader in the fashion industry. The plaintiff also called three experts on the fashion industry who testified that plaintiff was recognized among the top "name" designers, although plaintiff's apparel was slightly lower fashion than that of the other designers mentioned above.

Defendant is the exclusive distributor in New York State of products manufactured by Vera, S.A. in Spain pursuant to a written agreement dated June 1, 1970. Vera, S.A. was founded in the 1930s by its present owner, Abelardo Vera Martinez. Vera, S.A. obtained International Registration No. 134,216 in 1948 for the mark "VERA" for toiletries and cosmetics, and renewed that registration in 1968. However, the only registration which Vera, S.A. has in the United States is for the trademark "SIGLO DE ORO." Vera, S.A.'s United States trademark for "SIGLO DE ORO" was registered in 1967; the name "Vera (Espana)" appears on that registration in small type in the corner of the certificate to identify the manufacturer, rather than as part of the trademark. On May 6, 1971, Vera, S.A. filed a United States application for registration of the mark "VERA" for toiletries and cosmetics, including nail lacquer, lipstick, face powder, cologne, perfume, after-shave lotion, deodorants and soap. On May 29, 1973, Vera, S.A.'s application was published for opposition. Plaintiff filed an opposition, and proceedings have since been suspended pending termination of this action.

Vera, S.A. began exporting small amounts of perfumes and cosmetics from Spain into the United States in 1962. Soaps and other toiletries were later included. From 1962 to 1964 these items were handled by local distributors, and from 1964 to 1970 by Sara Feldschtein (now doing business as Vera Cosmetics, Ltd.).

Defendant introduced no evidence that Vera, S.A. ever sold its goods in the United States under the mark "VERA," with the exception of a single line of men's cologne sold after 1970. In its answer, defendant pleaded as an affirmative defense that "the notation 'Vera,' except in the case of cologne for men . . . was used to indicate the manufacturer and not the product" and that its products were "identified by such trademarks as 'SIGLO DE ORO,' 'ISABEL MARIA,' '74,' 'ISABELINA' " etc.

Although the defendant called one of Vera, S.A.'s officers from Spain to testify, defendant introduced no evidence regarding any labels used on its products before 1970 and no proof that the name "VERA" appeared prominently on those products, which were all sold under other trademarks. The only documentary evidence introduced by defendant—invoices, shipping records, and customs documents—indicated that "Vera" was used merely to identify the manufacturer, and was not used as a significant part of the marks under which Vera, S.A.'s items were sold. After mid or late 1970, defendant began to display the name "VERA" more prominently on its items, although all of these goods except for men's cologne were still sold under other trademarks.

Prior to 1971, Vera, S.A.'s sales in the United States were negligible. Its goods were sold primarily through Spanish language newspapers. Vera, S.A.'s records showed only seven sales to five customers between 1962 and 1964 amounting to $3,823.79. Between 1965 and 1970, Vera, S.A.'s sales in this country totalled no more than $25,000, ranging from $5,872.02 in 1965, to $1,211.98 in 1968 and $8,573.70 in 1970.

After 1970, when Vera, S.A. began distributing its products through defendant and began using the name "VERA" more prominently on its packaging, sales increased dramatically. Defendant's sales of Vera, S.A.'s products reached $100,000 annually by 1974. Defendant has greatly expanded the geographical market in which these items are sold. Defendant's products are now sold in New York through such stores as Gimbel's and Bloomingdale's—the very stores in which plaintiff's lines are sold—and advertised in prominent publications such as The New Yorker, The Daily News and The New York Post.

Plaintiff proved that most of the top designers also marketed their own lines of perfumes, cosmetics and toiletries, including such designers as Bill Blass, Cardin, Christian Dior, Lanvin, Norell, Patou, Pucci, Gucci, Hattie Carnegie, Chanel, Yves St. Laurent and Faberge.

In 1969 plaintiff considered selling its own line of cosmetics and fragrances. Columbia Broadcasting System first approached plaintiff to propose a joint venture, but plaintiff was advised to go into the field with a firm that had had experience. Plaintiff then approached Max Factor, but Max Factor had just come out with a new line of its own cosmetics and perfumes and was unwilling to make further investment at the time, even though it thought favorably of plaintiff's idea. Finally, plaintiff approached Estee Lauder, which did not want to put another line of cosmetics under a women's name on the market. Plaintiff took no further steps on the proposal.

Plaintiff noticed one of defendant's advertisements for sales representatives in the July 29, 1970 issue of Women's Wear Daily. The advertisement mentioned that defendant planned to introduce a line of toiletries from "VERA/BARCELONA SPAIN." By letter dated August 3, 1970, plaintiff warned defendant that it would bring suit if defendant began marketing its products under the name "VERA." Defendant did not respond, but instead began marketing its toiletries with prominent use of the name "VERA." On June 10, 1971 plaintiff again protested, and, after its second protest was ignored, commenced this action on July 7, 1971.

Judge Carter, in his opinion dated July 9, 1975, held that plaintiff was not entitled to injunctive relief against defendant's use of the name "VERA." He found the difference between plaintiff's mark "VERA" in script and defendant's use in block letters insignificant. Despite plaintiff's success in the market, its large expenditures on advertising and the other evidence of plaintiff's wide recognition, the district court found plaintiff's mark to be weak because it was a common name and because a number of third parties had registrations which included the same name. The court noted that although plaintiff might argue that its mark has acquired secondary meaning with respect to scarves, the contention was "dubious" and, even if conceded, would "not establish plaintiff's right to bar use of the mark in other fields since there is . . . no right to a mark in gross." The court found no evidence that defendant intended to palm its products off as plaintiff's. The court also noted that although plaintiff "may not be barred by laches," the fact that Vera, S.A. had been importing its products into the United States since 1962 "with the mark Vera on them . . . does help underscore the fact that both parties have been operating in their respective fields for a long time without knowledge of each other . . . which further erodes any argument to the likelihood of confusion." The district court rejected plaintiff's claim that it was likely to enter the cosmetics and fragrance field "as other couturiers have done," and reasoned that the public would probably not identify defendant's products with plaintiff in view of the fact that plaintiff was not like the well-known and well-established figures in high fashion who use their names on cosmetics and fragrances.

The essential question here is whether plaintiff is entitled to protection of its trademark "VERA" against defendant's use of the name on cosmetics, perfumes and toiletries. We answer this question in the affirmative.

The trademark laws protect three interests which are present here: first, the senior user's interest in being able to enter a related field at some future time; second, his interest in protecting the good reputation associated with his mark from the possibility of being tarnished by inferior merchandise of the junior user; and third, the public's interest in not being misled by confusingly similar marks—a factor which may weigh in the senior user's favor where the defendant has not developed the mark himself.

We have heretofore protected the trademark owner's rights against use on related, non-competing products—a result in accord with the realities of mass media salesmanship and the purchasing behavior of consumers. See, e.g., Yale Electric Corp. v. Robertson, 26 F.2d 972 (2 Cir.1928) (flashlights v. locks); L.E. Waterman Co. v. Gordon, 72 F.2d 272, (2 Cir.1934) (mechanical pens and pencils v. razor blades); S.C. Johnson & Son, Inc. v. Johnson, 116 F.2d 427, (2 Cir.1940) (waxes and floor cleaners v. fabric cleaners); Triangle Publications, Inc. v. Rohrlich, 167 F.2d 969, (2 Cir.1948) (magazines v. girdles); Pure Foods, Inc. v. Minute Maid Corp., 214 F.2d 792, (5 Cir.1954) (juices v. meats); Safeway Stores, Inc. v. Safeway Properties, Inc., 307 F.2d 495 (2 Cir. 1962) (groceries v. real estate); Communications Satellite Corp. v. Comcet, Inc., 429 F.2d 1245, (4 Cir.1970) (communications services v. computers); Alfred Dunhill of London, Inc. v. Kasser Distillers Products Corp., 350 F.Supp. 1341, (E.D.Pa.1972), aff'd, 480 F.2d 917 (3 Cir.1973) (pipes and tobacco v. Scotch whiskey). Even when we have rejected infringement claims with respect to non-competing goods, we have carefully limited our holdings.

Absent equities in the junior user's favor, he should be enjoined from using a similar trademark whenever the non-competitive products are sufficiently related that customers are likely to confuse the source of origin.

We turn now to the grounds for the district court's holding that defendant's use of the mark "VERA" did not infringe plaintiff's trademark.

As the district court pointed out, a trademark owner's right to relief where the products are non-competitive depends upon a number of variables including the strength of his mark; the degree of similarity between the two marks; the proximity of the products; the likelihood that the prior owner will bridge the gap; actual confusion; the defendant's good faith in adopting his mark; the quality of defendant's product and the sophistication of the buyers.

Plaintiff claims that the district court improperly concluded that "VERA" was a weak mark merely because it was a common name and because of third party registrations; that the district court erred in finding that Vera, S.A. had been importing its products into the United States under the "VERA" mark since 1962; that the district court erroneously concluded that plaintiff's and defendant's products were so unrelated that consumers were not likely to be misled; and that the district court erred in concluding that there was no reasonable probability that plaintiff would enter the cosmetics, fragrances and toiletries market. We agree with all of these claims except the last, as to which we need express no opinion.

Plaintiff's "VERA" trademark clearly is a strong mark. Plaintiff's sales figures, its advertising expenditures and the many articles written about plaintiff clearly established that plaintiff's "VERA" trademark was highly successful and widely recognized in the medium-high fashion market. Our conclusion that "VERA" is a strong mark is not affected by the fact that Vera is a common name. We need not decide whether such a name might provide a weaker mark in other circumstances, since we think plaintiff has clearly established secondary meaning entitling it to broad protection of the "VERA" mark. Moreover, even when the mark in question is the name of the junior user, his right to use the name on his products may be limited, and he may be compelled to add some distinguishing words to reduce the possibility of confusion.

In holding that plaintiff's trademark was weakened by third-party registrations, the district court relied upon the following registered marks: "Vera" for foods; "Vera Smart" for women's full fashion hosiery; "Vera Stewart" for cosmetics; "Vera Sharp" for cheeses; "Medicamentie Vera" for a medical publication; "Vera Cruz" for textile products; and "Vera Horn" for women's apparel. We think the district court erred in giving such weight to these registrations.

The significance of third-party trademarks depends wholly upon their usage. Defendant introduced no evidence that these trademarks were actually used by third parties, that they were well promoted or that they were recognized by consumers. As the Court pointed out in Lilly Pulitzer, Inc. v. Lilli Ann Corp., 376 F.2d 324, 325, 153 U.S.P.Q. 406, 407 (C.C.P.A.1967), "the existence of these registrations is not evidence of what happens in the market place or that customers are familiar with their use." Compare Triumph Hosiery Mills, Inc. v. Triumph International Corp., supra, 308 F.2d at 199, 135 U.S.P.Q. at 48 n. 2 (207 registrations under same name). Moreover, all but one of the third-party registrations cited by the district court contained combinations of words, rather than the word "Vera" alone, and several were registered for entirely unrelated products, such as foods or a medical publication. The record does not contain any evidence to support the claim that plaintiff's trademark was weakened by uses of similar marks by third parties.

Likewise, we think the district court erred in attaching any significance to the fact that Vera, S.A. has been importing toiletries into the United States since 1962. There is no evidence in the record to support the district court's finding that Vera, S.A. had imported its products continuously since 1962 "under the mark Vera" or that "VERA" was part of Vera, S.A.'s trademark registered in the United States. Vera, S.A.'s only trademark registered in the United States is for "SIGLO DE ORO." On that registration the phrase "Vera (Espana)," rather than the name "Vera" alone, appears in small type, in the corner of the certificate merely to identify the manufacturer, not as part of the trademark.

Moreover, the significance of Vera, S.A.'s imports since 1962 depends upon its usage of the name "VERA." Defendant introduced no evidence that Vera, S.A. had ever sold its goods under the "VERA" trademark, with the exception of a single line of men's cologne sold after 1970. In its answer, defendant pleaded that the word Vera was merely used to identify the manufacturer and "not the product", and that its products were identified by other trademarks. Defendant introduced no copies of labels used on Vera, S.A.'s products prior to 1970, and no evidence that "Vera" was a prominent part of the name under which those products were sold before that date. Moreover, prior to 1970, Vera, S.A.'s sales in the United States were negligible, and it was not until 1970 or so that defendant began selling its products in some of the same stores in which plaintiff sold its goods.

On this record, we think the district court erred in concluding that Vera, S.A.'s sales in this country since 1962 negate any inference of confusion between plaintiff's and defendant's products. Moreover, the defendant has not introduced any evidence of longstanding sales under a similar mark that would in any way affect the equities of this case.

Finally, the district court found that the plaintiff was not likely to enter the cosmetics, perfume or toiletries market and that that market was unrelated to the apparel market in which plaintiff sold its goods. We have no need to decide whether there is a substantial likelihood that plaintiff will enter the cosmetics and fragrances market, although we cannot agree with defendant that this likelihood is small simply because the firms which plaintiff approached in 1969 were themselves unwilling to go through with the joint venture at that time.

Rather, we hold that defendant's products were by their nature so closely related to plaintiff's own products that plaintiff was entitled to protection against defendant's use of the mark "VERA" on its products. As Judge Learned Hand wrote in his frequently quoted opinion in Yale Electric Corp. v. Robertson, supra, 26 F.2d at 974, "it has come to be recognized that, unless the borrower's use is so foreign to the owner's as to insure against any identification of the two, it is unlawful."

We think the record clearly establishes that defendant's use of the name "VERA" on its products is likely to confuse customers. Plaintiff proved that many, if not most, of the leading designers sell perfumes and cosmetics under their own trademarks. The many newspaper articles which plaintiff introduced, as well as the testimony of plaintiff's expert witnesses, clearly established that plaintiff's recognition is equivalent to that of designers who had expanded into the cosmetics and fragrances fields. Like these other designers, plaintiff appeals to the name-conscious customer. Although plaintiff is not a couturier and sells medium fashion apparel, plaintiff's reputation as a "name" designer would, in all likelihood, lead many customers to think that cosmetics and fragrances sold under the "VERA" trademark were manufactured by plaintiff. Plaintiff's trademark is strong in the market in which it sells its goods. Moreover, defendant has recently expanded its marketing of cosmetics and fragrances, and is now selling those products in the very same stores in which plaintiff's lines are sold.

A trademark owner need not prove that a junior user's conduct will mislead all customers, but only that it is likely to mislead many customers. Moreover, as we have held on numerous occasions, "a showing of actual confusion is not necessary and in fact is very difficult to demonstrate" with reliable proof. W.E. Bassett Co. v. Revlon, Inc., 435 F.2d at 662.

We think that plaintiff, who has expended large sums in promoting its "VERA" trademark, and who has gained wide recognition in the market through its efforts is entitled to relief which will protect its good name against misassociation with defendant's products.

We direct the district court to enter appropriate injunctive relief protecting the plaintiff against any prominent display of the word "VERA" on defendant's cosmetics, toiletries and fragrances. Since Vera is also the name of Vera, S.A.'s founder, defendant should be allowed to use that name in small type, but only in conjunction with other words which prevent any likelihood of confusion (e.g., "Vera y Cosmetica, S.A.").

An award of damages and an accounting "is not an automatic concomitant of the grant of injunctive relief," Grotrian, Helfferich, Schulz, Th. Steinweg Nachf. v. Steinway & Sons, 523 F.2d 1331, 1344, 186 U.S.P.Q. 436, 446–447 (2 Cir.1975), and we do not think the plaintiff is entitled to such an award here. Although plaintiff promptly objected to defendant's first prominent use of the name "VERA", defendant's goods were non-competitive with plaintiffs, and so defendant's profits could not have come from diverting plaintiff's customers. Moreover, the district court's finding that defendant acted in good faith is not clearly erroneous, since Vera is also the surname of Vera, S.A.'s founder, since defendant might have believed that defendant's products were not sufficiently related to plaintiffs to infringe plaintiff's mark, and since Vera, S.A. sells its products in many countries other than the United States, thus reducing the likelihood that it adopted the "Vera" display solely to profit from plaintiff's good reputation.

Reversed and remanded with instructions to grant relief in accordance with this opinion.

NOTES

1. To what extent have the constructive notice doctrine, applied in *Dawn Donut,* and the dilution doctrine, applied in *Scarves by Vera,* moved trademark rights away from their original dependence on trademark use? Can the two doctrines be reconciled with the rule that long nonuse constitutes abandonment? See p. 217, above. Would a statutory rule of partial abandonment be appropriate when a trademark owner fails to enter a geographic, product or service market? Under such a rule, a first user could be given a specified period within which to exploit its mark in all markets. After that period, it would forfeit any prospect of exclusive rights in unoccupied markets.

Can you reconcile Judge Lumbard's conclusions that an immediate injunction was proper in *Scarves by Vera* but improper in *Dawn Donut?* Is the difference between the two cases simply that the parties were more proximate—and that consumers were more likely to be confused—in *Scarves by Vera* than in *Dawn Donut?* Or is there a relevant difference between business expectations that focus on future geographic markets and business expectations that focus on future product or service markets? Should the effect of constructive notice ever be extended beyond the realm of geographic priority into the realm of product and service priority? Consider, for example, whether it would be appropriate for the Lanham Act to provide that once a mark is registered for use in connection with one class of goods no one can subsequently adopt the mark for any other class of goods.

Schechter, The Rational Basis of Trademark Protection, 40 Harv.L. Rev. 813 (1927) is the seminal article on trademark dilution. Its thesis has been criticized in Brown, Advertising and the Public Interest: Legal Protection of Trade Symbols, 57 Yale L.J. 1165 (1948) and Middleton, Some Reflections on Dilution, 42 Trademark Rep. 175 (1952). The Middleton article also appraises the Lanham Act's impact upon dilution doctrine, as do Deering, Trademarks on Noncompetitive Products, 36 Or.L.Rev. 1 (1956) and Note, Dilution: Trademark Infringement or Will–O'–The Wisp?, 77 Harv.L.Rev. 520 (1964). See also, Pattishall, The Dilution Rationale for Trademark—Trade Identity Protection, Its Progress and Prospects, 71 Nw.U.L.Rev. 618 (1976).

2. *Dilution, Confusion and the Constitution.* Does the United States Constitution limit dilution doctrine? In San Francisco Arts & Athletics, Inc. v. United States Olympic Comm., 483 U.S. 522, 107 S.Ct. 2971, 97 L.Ed.2d 427, 3 U.S.P.Q.2d 1145 (1987), the United States Supreme Court held that section 110 of the Amateur Sports Act, 36 U.S.C.A. § 380, granted the United States Olympic Committee the exclusive right to prohibit certain commercial and promotional uses of the word, "Olympic," and of certain other Olympic symbols, apart from any showing that unauthorized use would confuse consumers. The defendant, which had used the term "Olympic" in promoting its "Gay Olympic Games," argued that, in eliminating the confusion requirement and withholding the normal statutory defenses, the Act violated the First Amendment. The Court rejected this argument and the argument that, because the term, "Olympic" had become generic, the First Amendment prohibited its statutory protection.

The Court observed: "Although the Lanham Act protects only against confusing uses, Congress' judgment respecting a certain word is not so limited. Congress reasonably could conclude that most commercial uses of the Olympic words and symbols are likely to be confusing. It also could determine that unauthorized uses, even if not confusing, nevertheless may harm the USOC by lessening the distinctiveness and thus the commercial value of the marks. . . . Even though this protection may exceed the traditional rights of a trademark owner in certain circumstances, the application of the Act to this commercial speech is not broader than necessary to protect the legitimate congres-

sional interest and therefore does not violate the First Amendment."
483 U.S. at 539–540, 107 S.Ct. at 2982–2983.

Justice Brennan, joined by Justice Marshall, dissented. "Trademark protection has been carefully confined to the realm of commercial speech by two important limitations in the Lanham Act. First, the danger of substantial regulation of noncommercial speech is diminished by denying enforcement of a trademark against uses of words that are not likely to cause confusion, to cause mistake, or to deceive. . . . The fair use defense also prevents the award of a trademark from regulating a substantial amount of noncommercial speech. The Lanham Act allows 'the use of the name, term, or device . . . which is descriptive of and used fairly and in good faith only to describe to users the goods or services of such party.' Again, a wide array of noncommercial speech may be characterized as merely descriptive of the goods or services of a party, and thus not intended to propose a commercial transaction. For example, the SFAA's description of its community services appears to be regulated by § 110, although the main purpose of such speech may be to educate the public about the social and political views of the SFAA. Congress' failure to incorporate this important defense in § 110(a)(4) confers an unprecedented right on the USOC." 483 U.S. at 564–565, 107 S.Ct. at 2995–2996. The fair use defense is discussed in note 4 below.

See generally, Kravitz, Trademarks, Speech and the Gay Olympics Case, 69 B.U.L.Rev. 131 (1989).

3. *Families of Marks.* "If the owner of the trademark Servo seeks to prevent the registration of Servotorque, or Servospeed, for related products in the field of servomechanisms, is his position any stronger if he also owns Servoscope, Servosync, Servoflight, Servotherm, Servoflex and Servoboard? The Court of Customs and Patent Appeals said No. [Servo Corp. of America v. Electro–Devices, Inc., 289 F.2d 955, 129 U.S. P.Q. 352 (1961); Servo Corp. of America v. Kelsey–Hayes Co., 289 F.2d 957, 129 U.S.P.Q. 354 (1961).]

"Can the owner of the trademarks Clean–Master, Sweep–Master, Dust–Master, and Dirt–Master for carpet sweepers prevail in an opposition against Squeez–Master for sponge mops? The Trademark Trial and Appeal Board said No. [Bissell, Inc. v. Easy Day Mfg. Co., 130 U.S. P.Q. 485 (1961).]

"On the other hand, the owner of the trademarks Fritos, Chilitos, Fritatos, Ta–Tos, Chee–Tos, Corntos, and Tos successfully opposed the registration of Prontos. [The Frito Co. v. Buckeye Foods, Inc., 130 U.S. P.Q. 347 (T.T.A.B.1961).]

"Each of these cases involved the problem of a 'family of trademarks.' This is a term applied to a group of trademarks, owned by one company, in which the same syllable or syllables recur. Eastman Kodak Company, for example, owns not only the well-known trademarks Kodak, Kodacraft, Kodafix, Kodaflat, Kodagraph, Kodaguide, Kodaline, Kodamatic, but numerous others starting with the characteristic prefix Koda, thus creating a 'family' of Koda trademarks." Breitenfeld, When Is a "Family of Trademarks" Effective? 52 Trademark Rep. 351 (1962).*

The Patent and Trademark Office is reluctant to find rights in families of trademarks. The few cases in which it has sustained a family constellation reflect the view that the family should surround a strong mark; a sprinkling of related uses of the mark, such as in slogans or in the firm name, may help. As to the recommended number of progeny, the more the better. For example, in Dan River Mills, Inc. v. Danfra Ltd., 120 U.S.P.Q. 126 (T.T.A.B.1959), Dan River Mills successfully deployed its family of marks, used in connection with textiles, in opposing the proposed registration of "Danfra" for men's clothes. At the time, Dan River owned about 30 marks—"Dan Master," "Dantwill," "Danshrunk" and "Dantone" among them—and used the parent mark in such other settings as the slogan, "It's a Dan River Fabric."

4. *Fair Use.* Competitors are free to use the descriptive elements of a registered mark in a non-trademark sense. For example, in Zatarains, Inc. v. Oak Grove Smokehouse, Inc., 698 F.2d 786, 217 U.S. P.Q. 988 (5th Cir.1983), the court held that defendants' use of the term "Fish Fry" on packages of its coating mix for fried foods was a noninfringing "fair use" of plaintiff's mark, "Fish–Fri," used in connection with a coating mix for fried foods. Upholding the lower court's finding that "Fish–Fri" is a descriptive term that had acquired secondary meaning, the court observed that "only that penumbra or fringe of secondary meaning is given legal protection. Zatarain's has no legal claim to an exclusive right in the original, descriptive sense of the term; therefore, Oak Grove and Visko's are still free to use the words 'fish fry' in their ordinary, descriptive sense, so long as such use will not tend to confuse customers as to the source of the goods." 698 F.2d 796.

Section 33(b)(4) of the Lanham Act, 15 U.S.C.A. § 1115(b)(4), allows as a defense to incontestability that "the use of the name, term, or device charged to be an infringement is a use, otherwise than as a mark, of the party's individual name in his own business, or of the individual name of anyone in privity with such party, or of a term or device which is descriptive of and used fairly and in good faith only to describe the goods or services of such party, or their geographic origin. . . . ."

5. *Collateral Use.* Can merchants refer to the goods they sell by the trademark of the manufacturer? Before giving the easy and obvious answer, remember that there is a large market for secondhand, repaired, and reconstructed goods, and that the conditions of this market may complicate the question of collateral trademark use.

In Prestonettes, Inc. v. Coty, 264 U.S. 359, 44 S.Ct. 350, 68 L.Ed. 731 (1924), Coty sought to "restrain alleged unlawful uses of the plaintiff's registered trademarks, 'Coty' and 'L'Origan' upon toilet powders and perfumes. The defendant purchases the genuine powder, subjects it to pressure, adds a binder to give it coherence and sells the compact in a metal case. It buys the genuine perfume in bottles and sells it in smaller bottles." The district court would have permitted a truthful allusion to Coty—a label on the compacts, for example, reading, "Prestonettes, Inc., not connected with Coty, states that the compact of face powder herein was independently compounded by it from Coty's—(giving the name) loose powder and its own binder. Loose powder—per cent, Binder—per cent," with "every word to be in letters of the same size, color, type and general distinctiveness."

The circuit court concluded that the district court's decree did not sufficiently protect Coty and absolutely enjoined any use of its marks: "to permit the plaintiff's name and trade-mark to be used on other than his original packages should be forbidden, as the value of his name and trade-mark would be endangered through the deterioration of his product due to the action of unauthorized and unsupervised persons in changing the perfumes from the receptacles in which they were originally placed into others which may be wholly unfit even though the perfumes remain unadulterated." 285 Fed. 501, 513 (2d Cir.1922).

The Supreme Court, in an opinion by Mr. Justice Holmes, reversed and ordered the district court decree reinstated. Since "[t]he plaintiff could not complain of its [defendant's] stating the nature of the component parts and the source from which they were derived if it did not use the trademark in doing so," the fact that its trademark was involved added nothing to plaintiff's rights. "When the mark is used in a way that does not deceive the public we see no such sanctity in the word as to prevent its being used to tell the truth. It is not taboo." As to the possible deterioration in the product's quality and consequent injury to the manufacturer's reputation, Justice Holmes concluded, "it might be a misfortune to the plaintiff, but the plaintiff would have no cause of action, as the defendant was exercising the rights of ownership and only telling the truth." 264 U.S. 359, 368, 44 S.Ct. 350, 351.

Twenty-three years later, in Champion Spark Plug Co. v. Sanders, 331 U.S. 125, 67 S.Ct. 1136, 91 L.Ed. 1386, 73 U.S.P.Q. 133 (1947), involving defendant's repair, reconditioning, and sale of spark plugs bearing the mark of their original manufacturer, the Court affirmed an order permitting collateral use of the plaintiff's mark so long as the plugs also bore the word "Repaired" or "Used." Recognizing that, unlike *Prestonettes,* the case involved questions of unfair competition as well as trademark infringement, the court nonetheless followed the *Prestonettes* reasoning and result. In dicta, however, it cautioned that "[c]ases may be imagined where the reconditioning or repair would be so extensive or basic that it would be a misnomer to call the article by its original name, even though the words 'used' or 'repaired' were added."

6. *Parody and Satire.* Will a satirical purpose excuse an otherwise infringing use of a trademark? In Reddy Communications, Inc. v. Environmental Action Foundation, 477 F.Supp. 936, 203 U.S.P.Q. 144

(D.D.C.1979), the court dismissed an infringement action brought by the owner of the service mark, "Reddy Kilowatt"—a cartoon figure licensed for advertising use by investor-owned public utilities—against defendant's use of caricatures of Reddy Kilowatt in newsletters and magazines criticizing the electric power industry. The gist of plaintiff's argument was that "by casting Reddy in a negative light as the 'villainous utility company' in its publications," defendant had "reduced Reddy's attractiveness to investor utilities as a public relations tool for promotion of the utility industry."

Recognizing that the defendant had indeed imitated the "Reddy" mark, the court nonetheless concluded that "EAF's use of Reddy is merely incidental to the sale of its publications." *"[W]ithin the context of its publications,* . . . EAF's caricatures are dissimilar from Reddy in connotation and overall impression . . . the EAF publications are obtained by careful, sophisticated purchasers who will view the EAF caricatures not in isolation but in conjunction with the surrounding text; and . . . the surrounding text and other identifying indicia adequately signal to the reader the critical use being made of Reddy by an opponent of the electric utility industry." 477 F.Supp. at 945–46, 948 (emphasis the court's).

Other courts have enjoined satirical trademark uses on the ostensible ground that satiric purpose cannot excuse consumer confusion. But these decisions also reflect a solicitude for well-established marks and disdain for the form of satire employed. See, e.g., Mutual of Omaha Insurance Co. v. Novak, 836 F.2d 397, 5 U.S.P.Q.2d 1314 (8th Cir.1987) (permanent injunction granted against defendant's modified version of plaintiff's Indian head logo and use of the words "Mutant of Omaha" and "Nuclear Holocaust Insurance"), cert. denied, 109 S.Ct. 326 (1988); General Electric Co. v. Alumpa Coal Co., 205 U.S.P.Q. 1036 (D.Mass. 1979) (preliminary injunction granted against defendant's marketing of T-shirts and briefs bearing plaintiff's distinctive monogram and the words, "Genital Electric"); Coca–Cola Co. v. Gemini Rising, Inc., 346 F.Supp. 1183, 175 U.S.P.Q. 56 (E.D.N.Y.1972) (preliminary injunction granted against distributors of a "blown-up reproduction of plaintiff's familiar 'Coca–Cola' trademark and distinctive format except for the substitution of the script letters 'ine' for '–Cola,' so that poster reads 'Enjoy Cocaine.' ").

Compare a case noted by Professor Derenberg in which "the owner of the famous '4711' trademark for *eau de cologne* got an injunction in Cologne, Germany, against a manure collector who used his telephone number, 4711, painted in 20–inch high numerals across both sides of his horse-drawn fertilizer wagon." Derenberg, The Problem of Trademark Dilution and the Anti-dilution Statutes, 44 Calif.L.Rev. 439, 448 n. 49 (1956). See generally, Denicola, Trademarks as Speech: Constitutional Implications of the Emerging Rationales for the Protection of Trade Symbols, 1982 Wis.L.Rev. 158; Tasker, Parody or Satire as a Defense to Trademark Infringement, 77 Trademark Rep. 216 (1987); Note, Trademark Parody: A Fair Use and First Amendment Analysis, 72 Va.L.Rev. 1079 (1986).

2. REMEDIES

See Statute Supplement 15 U.S.C.A. §§ 1111, 1114, 1116–1121, 1124.

MALTINA CORP. v. CAWY BOTTLING CO.

United States Court of Appeals, Fifth Circuit, 1980.
613 F.2d 582, 205 U.S.P.Q. 489.

JOHNSON, Circuit Judge:

I. The Facts

Cawy Bottling Company (Cawy), defendant below, appeals from the judgment of the district court in favor of the plaintiffs Maltina Corporation and Julio Blanco–Herrera in their trademark infringement action. The district court enjoined Cawy from further infringement, awarded the plaintiffs $35,000 actual damages, and ordered the defendant to account for $55,050 of gross profit earned from the sale of infringing products.

Julio Blanco–Herrera fled to this country from Cuba in late 1960 after that country nationalized the company of which he was president and, along with his family, majority stockholder. Before that year, this company was one of the largest breweries and beverage distributors in Cuba. Among its products was malta, a dark, non-alcoholic carbonated beverage brewed similar to beer. The Cuban company distributed malta under the trademarks "Malta Cristal" and "Cristal" in Cuba and in the United States. The Cuban company had registered the marks both in Cuba and the United States. When Blanco–Herrera arrived in the United States, he formed the Maltina Corporation and assigned the "Cristal" trademark to it. He attempted to produce and distribute "Cristal" in this country, but despite his efforts Maltina Corporation was never able to obtain sufficient financial backing to produce more than $356 worth of "Cristal".

Cawy Bottling, however, had an altogether different experience in producing malta. At the outset, it attempted to register the "Cristal" trademark so that it might be utilized in marketing the product. This attempt was rejected by the Patent Office because of plaintiffs' prior registration. After this attempted registration and with the knowledge of the plaintiffs' ownership of the trademark, Cawy began producing and distributing malta under the "Cristal" label in February 1968.

In 1970 the plaintiffs sued Cawy under 15 U.S.C.A. § 1117 for trademark infringement and unfair competition. They sought an injunction against further use of their mark, damages, and an accounting. The district court dismissed the suit on the ground that Cuba's confiscation of the assets of Blanco–Herrera's Cuban corporation made Blanco–Herrera's assignment of the "Cristal" mark to the Maltina Corporation invalid. This Court reversed, holding Cuba's confiscation decree did not extend to the "Cristal" mark registered by the United States Patent

Office, Maltina Corp. v. Cawy Bottling Co., 462 F.2d 1021, 174 U.S.P.Q. 74 (5th Cir.), cert. denied, 409 U.S. 1060, 176 U.S.P.Q. 33 (1972). On remand, the district court determined that the plaintiffs had a valid trademark. Cawy appealed, and we affirmed, Maltina Corp. v. Cawy Bottling Co., 491 F.2d 1391 (1974) (per curiam).

At trial on the merits, from which this appeal is taken, the district court determined that Cawy had infringed the plaintiffs' mark and assigned the case to a magistrate for determination of what recovery was appropriate under 15 U.S.C.A. Section 1117. Before holding a hearing the magistrate wrote a memorandum to the district court stating that he thought that the plaintiffs were entitled to an injunction but not to an accounting for defendant's profits.

After holding the hearing, however, the magistrate changed his recommendation. He noted that Cawy designed its "Cristal" label to resemble the label used by Maltina's predecessor in Cuba. He found that Cawy intended to exploit the reputation and good will of the "Cristal" mark and to deceive and mislead the Latin community into believing that the "Cristal" once sold in Cuba was now being sold in the United States. The magistrate further found that Cawy wilfully infringed the plaintiffs' mark and had been unjustly enriched to the detriment of plaintiffs' reputation and good will. He recommended that Cawy account to the plaintiffs for the profit it earned from the infringement, and he directed Cawy to report its sales of "Cristal" and associated costs to the plaintiffs for determination of its profits. The magistrate also found Cawy's infringement damaged the reputation and good will of the plaintiffs in the amount of $35,000. He recommended that Cawy compensate plaintiffs in that amount.

The district court, after a complete and independent review of the record, adopted the magistrate's recommendations as its order. As more fully discussed below, the district court eventually found Cawy liable to the plaintiffs for its gross profits from the sale of "Cristal", $55,050. The court entered judgment against Cawy for $55,050 gross profits plus $35,000 damages and enjoined Cawy from any further infringement of the plaintiffs' mark.

Cawy presents three arguments on appeal. First, it argues that an accounting was inappropriate. Second, that if an accounting was appropriate, the district court erred in awarding to the plaintiff Cawy's entire gross profits from the sales of "Cristal". Third, Cawy argues that the award of $35,000 actual damages cannot stand in the absence of any evidence to support it. We accept this final contention but reject the first two. Cawy does not complain on appeal of the district court's enjoining it from further infringement of the plaintiffs' mark.

II. Was an Accounting Appropriate?

Section 1117, 15 U.S.C.A. entitles a markholder to recover, subject to the principles of equity, the profits earned by a defendant from infringement of the mark. The courts have expressed two views of the circumstances in which an accounting is proper under 15 U.S.C.A. Section 1117. Some courts view the award of an accounting as simply a means of compensating a markholder for lost or diverted sales. Other courts view an accounting not as compensation for lost or diverted sales, but as redress for the defendant's unjust enrichment and as a deterrent to further infringement. See Maier Brewing Co. v. Fleischmann Distilling Corp., 390 F.2d 117, 121, 157 U.S.P.Q. 76, 78–79 (9th Cir.) cert. denied, 391 U.S. 966, 157 U.S.P.Q. 720 (1968). In this case, the plaintiffs never sold any appreciable amount of "Cristal" in the United States so they cannot claim that Cawy diverted any of their sales. Accordingly, we must decide whether diversion of sales is a prerequisite to an award of an accounting. We hold that it is not.

In Maier Brewing the Ninth Circuit awarded an accounting to a plaintiff who was not in direct competition with a defendant and who, accordingly, had not suffered any diversion of sales from the defendant's infringement. The court noted that the defendant had wilfully and deliberately infringed. It reasoned that awarding an accounting would further Congress' purpose in enacting 15 U.S.C.A. Section 1117 of making infringement unprofitable. This Court is in accord with this reasoning. See also Monsanto Chemical Co. v. Perfect Fit Products Manufacturing Co., 349 F.2d 389, 146 U.S.P.Q. 512 (2nd Cir.1965) (holding that a trademark holder was entitled to an accounting to protect the public from infringement). The Fifth Circuit has not addressed the issue whether an accounting only compensates for diverted sales or whether an accounting serves the broader functions of remedying an infringer's unjust enrichment and deterring future infringement. A recent opinion by this Court, however, recognizes that a trademark is a protected property right. Boston Professional Hockey Association v. Dallas Cap and Emblem Manufacturing, Inc., 597 F.2d 71, 75, 202 U.S.P.Q. 536, 539 (5th Cir.1979). This recognition of a trademark as property is consistent with the view that an accounting is proper even if the defendant and plaintiff are not in direct competition, and the defendants' infringement has not diverted sales from the plaintiff. The Ninth Circuit in Maier Brewing noted that the infringer had used the mark-holder's property to make a profit and that an accounting would force the infringer to disgorge its unjust enrichment. 390 F.2d at 121, 157 U.S.P.Q. at 78–79. Here, the only valuable property Blanco–Herrera had when he arrived in this country was his right to the "Cristal" mark. Cawy used this property, and an accounting is necessary to partially remedy its unjust enrichment.

The district court relied, in part, on W.E. Bassett Co. v. Revlon, Inc., 435 F.2d 656, 168 U.S.P.Q. 1 (2nd Cir.1970), in ordering an accounting. That case held that an accounting should be granted "if the defendant is unjustly enriched, if the plaintiff sustained damages from the infringement, or if an accounting is necessary to deter a willful infringer from doing so again." Id. at 664, 168 U.S.P.Q. at 7. Revlon sold a cuticle trimmer embossed with a "Cuti–Trim" mark "in the teeth of the Patent Office's refusal to register" that mark. Id. at 662, 168 U.S.P.Q. at 5. This was willful infringement that an accounting would deter in the future. In the instant case, the district court found that Cawy's "infringement was willful and that such infringement resulted in [Cawy] being unjustly enriched . . . ." Cawy used the

"Cristal" mark after the Patent Office refused to register it. This clearly and explicitly supports the finding of willful infringement. An injunction alone will not adequately deter future infringement. In short, we find the district court properly ordered Cawy to account to the plaintiffs for the profits it earned from its willful infringement. This accounting serves two purposes: remedying unjust enrichment and deterring future infringement.

III. Did the District Court Err in Requiring Cawy to Account for Its Entire Gross Profit from the Sale of "Cristal"?

The district court ordered Cawy to account to the plaintiffs for $55,050, the entire gross profit (total revenue less cost of goods sold) from the sale of "Cristal". The district court did not allow Cawy to deduct overhead and other expenses. These expenses would have produced a net loss from the sale of "Cristal" and, if allowed, would have enabled Cawy to escape liability to the plaintiffs for its infringement.

Under 15 U.S.C.A. Section 1117, the plaintiff has the burden of showing the amount of the defendant's sales of the infringing product. The defendant has the burden of showing all elements of cost and other deductions. In this case, the court ordered Cawy to report its total sales of "Cristal" and associated costs to the plaintiffs. If the plaintiffs objected to Cawy's estimate of its net profits from "Cristal", they were to file their objection with the court. The record on appeal reflects that Cawy submitted three exhibits showing its net loss on "Cristal" sales. These exhibits are set out in the appendix. The plaintiffs filed their objections to Cawy's figures with the court. They accepted Cawy's estimate of gross revenues from the sale of "Cristal" and the cost of goods sold. Thus, they met the burden of proving the amount of sales of the infringing product. The plaintiffs, however, did not accept other deductions claimed by Cawy. Cawy claimed deductions for *"Expenses Specifically Identified with Malta Cristal"*, as set out in Exhibit 2. Plaintiffs objected to these claimed deductions because Cawy did not show they were actually spent on "Cristal". Cawy also claimed deductions for general overhead, apportioned to "Cristal" on the basis of the ratio of "Cristal" sales to Cawy's total sales. Exhibit 3 displays these claimed overhead deductions. The plaintiffs objected to the overhead deductions because the infringing product constituted only a small percentage of the defendant's business.

Cawy responded to the plaintiffs' objections by asserting that it did have "specific and detailed figures and corroborating sales slips, invoices and the like to support" its claims of expenses attributable to "Cristal". Cawy failed, however, to submit any of this corroboration to the district court.

The district court, after noting that Cawy had the burden of establishing deductions from gross profits, disallowed Cawy's claims of expenses specifically attributable to "Cristal" as set forth in Exhibit 2. The court stated that it could not determine whether the advertising, sales, commissions, legal fees, telephone, and other expenses claimed by Cawy related to "Cristal" sales or to the sales of other products. It then held that Cawy failed to sustain its burden of proof with respect to those claimed expenses. We cannot say that the district court erred in its holding. The record on appeal, like the record before the district court, simply affords no support for the contention that the claimed *"Expenses Specifically Identified with Malta Cristal"* actually related to "Cristal" sales. Furthermore, Cawy's claims of deductions of legal fees, as the district court noted, would not be allowable in any case. While we cannot tell whether these fees related to this suit, if they did, they would not be deductible.

The district court also disallowed Cawy's deductions of a proportionate part of its overhead expenses as set forth in Exhibit 3. Quoting from Société Anonyme v. Western Distilling Co., 46 F. 921 (C.C.E.D.Mo. 1891), the district court noted: "It appears that 'the unlawful venture increased the gross profits without swelling the gross expenses'." It then held that Cawy failed to sustain its burden of showing the propriety of allowing deductions for overhead. Again, we must agree with the district court that Cawy failed to meet its burden of showing its expenses in the absence from the record on appeal of any evidence that Cawy's production of "Cristal" actually increased its overhead expenses. Furthermore, we note that a proportionate share of overhead is not deductible when the sales of an infringing product constitute only a small percentage of total sales. See S.C. Johnson & Son, Inc. v. Drop Dead Co., 144 U.S.P.Q. 257 (S.D.Cal.1965) (disallowing overhead deduction when infringing sales were only 6% of total sales). Here, on the average, infringing sales constituted just over 6% of total sales. Accordingly, we think it unlikely, especially in the absence of any evidence to the contrary, that Cawy's production of "Cristal" increased its overhead expenses.

The district court properly ordered Cawy to account for its entire gross profit from the sale of "Cristal". Cawy failed to meet its burden of showing that the overhead and other expenses that it claimed in Exhibits 2 and 3 actually related to the production of "Cristal".

IV. Did the District Court Err in Awarding the Plaintiffs $35,000 as Actual Damages for Cawy's Infringement?

The district court awarded the plaintiffs $35,000 as actual damages from Cawy's infringement. The record, however, is wholly devoid of support for this figure. Accordingly, we must reverse as to this element.

The plaintiffs have never been able to get sufficient financial backing to produce more than a very small amount of "Cristal" in the United States. That inability makes proof of actual damages from Cawy's infringement unlikely. In any event, the plaintiffs have had an opportunity to show their damages and have failed to do so. This Court concludes that plaintiffs should not have another opportunity to show their damages just as Cawy should not have another opportunity to prove its expenses.

In the ten years since the plaintiffs filed their original petition, this case has been before us three times. All litigation must end. We remand only for entry of judgment in accordance with this opinion.

Affirmed in part, reversed in part, and remanded for entry of judgment.

APPENDIX

DEFENDANT'S EXHIBIT 1

NET LOSS ON SALES OF MALTA CRISTAL

	1969	1970	1971	1972	1973	1974	1975	TOTAL
Revenues from sales of Malta Cristal	$ 40,032	$ 41,708	$ 83,861	$ 60,119	$ 31,099	$ 14,666	—	$271,482
Less cost of goods sold—Malta	31,883	34,059	67,285	46,438	25,209	11,558	—	216,432
GROSS PROFIT	8,149	7,646	16,576	13,681	5,890	3,108	—	55,050
Less expenses:								
per exhibit 2	8,165	6,479	10,175	17,870	17,007	9,353	500	69,549
per exhibit 3	6,683	4,250	7,859	6,448	3,199	1,762	—	30,201
TOTAL EXPENSES	14,848	10,729	18,034	24,318	20,206	11,115	500	99,750
NET LOSS( )	$ (6,699)	$ (3,083)	$ (1,458)	$ (10,637)	$ (14,316)	$ (8,007)	$ (500)	$ (44,700)

CAWY BOTTLING CO., INC.

(s) Vincent Cossio

DEFENDANT'S EXHIBIT 2

EXPENSES SPECIFICALLY IDENTIFIED WITH MALTA CRISTAL

	1969	1970	1971	1972	1973	1974	1975	TOTAL
Advertising	$ 2,277	$ 1,723	$ 4,299	$ 13,080	$ 13,124	$ 6,510	—	$ 41,013
Sales commissions	3,137	3,172	5,505	4,116	1,732	752	—	18,414
Legal fees	2,130	1,500	200	483	1,988	709	—	7,010
Telephone and Telegraph	43	84	171	191	163	13	—	665
Other	578	—	—	—	—	1,369	500	2,447
	$ 8,165	$ 6,479	$ 10,175	$ 17,870	$ 17,007	$ 9,353	$ 500	$ 69,549

DEFENDANT'S EXHIBIT 3

EXPENSES RELATED TO MALTA CRISTAL ALLOCATED BASED ON SALES RATIO

	1969	1970	1971	1972	1973	1974	1975	TOTAL
Malta Cristal cases sold	15,139	15,439	30,451	21,471	10,849	5,238	0	98,287
Total number of cases sold	176,458	228,000	276,424	288,500	296,590	314,485	0	1,580,457
Ratio of Malta's cases to total cases sold	8.58%	6.77%	10.91%	7.44%	3.66%	1.67%	—	6.22%

EXPENSES RELATED TO MALTA:

		1969	1970	1971	1972	1973	1974	TOTAL
1.	Repairs and maintenance	$ 1,323	$ 524	$ 762	$ 1,256	$ 663	$ 1,091	$ 5,619
2.	Rent	6,864	6,864	7,938	—	—	—	21,666
3.	Building depreciation	—	—	—	3,073	3,073	3,073	9,219
3.	Interest—mostly building	—	—	—	11,958	14,408	13,758	40,124
4.	Taxes other than payroll	4,932	8,065	5,645	12,456	11,964	10,791	53,853
5.	Payroll taxes	7,718	6,282	8,582	6,624	6,859	6,787	42,852
6.	Trucks' expenses	7,238	6,301	12,502	13,083	9,482	8,668	57,274
7.	Utilities	1,620	—	509	—	—	—	2,129
5.	Indirect labor	23,156	9,360	9,360	11,305	12,480	12,450	78,111
5.	Officers salaries	17,500	13,000	13,000	13,000	31,750	—	101,250
8.	Office expenses	403	665	—	1,046	767	1,503	4,384
9.	Sales promotion	808	95	275	1,513	—	82	2,773
10.	Insurance	3,536	5,031	6,967	6,566	8,722	8,265	39,087
11.	Uniforms	916	926	1,119	1,129	1,180	1,483	6,753
11.	Traveling	—	2,613	2,255	324	820	2,938	8,950
11.	Accounting fees	165	970	800	1,485	—	2,875	6,295
11.	Miscellaneous	1,714	2,088	2,320	1,843	3,980	—	11,945
	TOTAL EXPENSES	77,893	62,784	72,034	86,661	87,398	105,514	492,281
	MALTA TO TOTAL RATIO	8.58%	6.77%	10.91%	7.44%	3.66%	1.67%	
		$ 6,683	$ 4,250	$ 7,859	$ 6,448	$ 3,199	$ 1,762	$ 30,201

NOTES

1. Characterizing trademark rights as property rights may, as noted in *Maltina,* be "consistent with the view that an accounting is proper even if the defendant and plaintiff are not in direct competition." But does property status compel the accounting remedy? *Maltina* may obscure the real question—whether the trademark owner should be given profits earned in markets it has not yet entered. Will the answer to this question differ depending on whether the market not yet entered is a geographic market, as in *Maltina,* or a product or service market, as in dilution cases? Should the answer to the question be affected by the relative availability of injunctive relief? Reconsider the discussion of *Dawn Donut,* p. 287 above.

2. *Monetary Relief.* Because the remedies of damages and profits are intertwined, and because each alone serves at least two functions, the array of monetary awards available to the successful trademark owner is far richer than might appear from the face of section 35. Damages can be measured by

   (1) loss of sales and profits caused by the infringer's use of the owner's mark; or

   (2) consequent economic injury to the trademark owner's reputation and goodwill.

Profits earned by the infringer through its use of the mark can be treated

   (1) as presumptively equivalent to the profits lost by the trademark owner and, thus, awarded on a compensatory basis; or

   (2) under the approach taken in *Maltina,* as unjust enrichment.

Type (1) profit awards are the intended equivalent of type (1) damage awards, the difference lying in the critical shift of the burden of proof from owner to infringer. The assumption implicit in this shift, that the owner's sales have been diverted by the infringer's, is warranted only when the parties are in competition. Type (2) profit awards, because they rest on an unjust enrichment rationale, do not require competition between the parties. To bar double recovery, an award of type (1) profits will preclude an award of type (1) damages but will not preclude an award of type (2) damages. Is an award of type (1) damages inconsistent with an award of type (2) profits? Restatement, Restitution § 136, Comment a (1937), explores the general principles that underlie these distinctions.

Monetary awards generally are considered in Koelemay, Monetary Relief for Trademark Infringement Under the Lanham Act, 72 Trademark Rep. 458 (1982).

3. *Marking.* Under section 29, 15 U.S.C.A. § 1111, the owner of a registered mark can recover damages and profits only if it can show that the infringer knew of the registration or that notice of the registration, such as the familiar ®, accompanied displays of the mark.

If the registrant intentionally employs a false or misleading notice, its unclean hands will bar injunctive relief. See, for example, Fox–

Stanley Photo Products, Inc. v. Otaguro, 339 F.Supp. 1293, 174 U.S.P.Q. 257 (D.Mass.1972). Is it false marking if the notice of registration is located under a composite mark, one part of which is registered and one part of which is not? Compare Straus v. Notaseme Hosiery Co., 240 U.S. 179, 36 S.Ct. 288, 60 L.Ed. 590 (1916), with Coca–Cola Co. v. Victor Syrup Corp., 42 C.C.P.A. 751, 218 F.2d 596, 104 U.S.P.Q. 275 (1954).

4. *Attorney's Fees.* In Fleischmann Distilling Corp. v. Maier Brewing Co., 386 U.S. 714, 87 S.Ct. 1404, 18 L.Ed.2d 475, 153 U.S.P.Q. 432 (1967), the Supreme Court ruled that a prevailing trademark owner is not entitled to recover attorney's fees, even from a deliberate infringer. Justice Stewart dissented. "Until this case, every federal court that has faced the issue has upheld judicial power to award counsel fees in trademark infringement cases. In order to overrule that unbroken line of authority, I would have to be satisfied that Congress has made any such declaration."

Congress soon made its intentions clear. P.L. 93–600, 88 Stat. 1955 (1975), provides in part that "the court in exceptional cases may award reasonable attorney fees to the prevailing party." 15 U.S.C.A. § 1117. The rationale for the remedy was that "effective enforcement of trademark rights is left to the trademark owners and they should, in the interest of preventing purchaser confusion, be encouraged to enforce trademark rights." The revisors recognized that "section 35 of the present Trademark Act provides for awarding treble damages in appropriate circumstances in order to encourage the enforcement of trademark rights. The availability of treble damages, however, cannot be regarded as a substitute for the recovery of attorney fees. In suits brought primarily to obtain an injunction, attorney fees may be more important than treble damages. Frequently, in a flagrant infringement where the infringement action is brought promptly, the measurable damages are nominal." Sen.Rep. No. 93–1400, (93d Cong.2d Sess.).

5. *Injunctive Relief.* Injunctions granted in unfair competition actions are typically shaped to meet the particular circumstances of the case. See page 66 above. Trademark injunctions, by contrast, are characteristically granted absolutely or not at all, with scant attention given to the possibilities in between. The reason for the difference lies in trademark law's exclusive focus on marks and its disregard for contextual factors such as format, usage, typographic style and other overt elements of passing off. In appropriate circumstances, however, such as where the registered mark is weak, a court may only require the defendant to label its goods to disclaim an association with the plaintiff. See, e.g., Springs Mills, Inc. v. Ultracashmere House, Ltd., 724 F.2d 352, 261 U.S.P.Q. 577 (2d Cir.1983). See also Jacoby & Raskopf, Disclaimers in Trademark Infringement Litigation: More Trouble Than They are Worth? 76 Trademark Rep. 35 (1986). See generally, Latman, Preliminary Injunctions in Patent, Trademark and Copyright Cases, 60 Trademark Rep. 506 (1970); Dorr & Duft, Trademark Preliminary Injunctive Relief, 62 J.Pat.Off.Soc'y. 3 (1980).

6. *Compulsory Licensing.* Congress and the courts sometimes compel copyright and patent owners to license their works in order to forestall or dissipate monopoly effects. Should trademarks be subjected to compulsory licensing in similar circumstances?

In Borden, Inc., 92 F.T.C. 669 (1976), a Federal Trade Commission administrative law judge found that Borden's trademark, "ReaLemon," used in connection with reconstituted lemon juice, was a significant barrier to the entry of new products, and ordered Borden to license the mark for ten years to any firm desiring to enter the reconstituted lemon juice market. Acknowledging that the Commission had never before ordered trademark licensing, the judge ruled that it "is not essentially different from a requirement of compulsory licensing of a patent." 92 F.T.C. 775.

The decision drew heavy fire. The United States Trademark Association filed an *amicus* brief with the F.T.C. arguing that compulsory licensing "could have an adverse impact upon the interests of the public in the use of trademarks and upon the integrity of trademarks." According to the Association, compulsory trademark licensing disserves the public interest because "it permits more than one business to use a single trademark on goods, causing the trademark to fail in its essential purpose and producing public injury by impairing consumers' freedom of choice, whether or not all goods sold under the trademark are of equal quality." The private value of the ReaLemon mark would be impaired to "the extent that its proprietor's right to the exclusive use thereof is abrogated for ten years. And, at the end of that term, it may be so diluted or sullied by the acts of competitor-licensees as to be worthless."

On November 7, 1978 the F.T.C. voted against ordering compulsory licensing of the ReaLemon mark. Recognizing that "an order requiring licensing or suspension of a trademark may be ordered as a means of dissipating illegally used or acquired monopoly power," a majority of the Commission was "mindful that the remedy is a severe one, and should be imposed only where less drastic means appear unlikely to suffice." In the judgment of the majority "an order that simply prohibits Borden from pricing to exclude or minimize new entry should be sufficient to dissipate its unlawfully maintained monopoly position, which is the only permissible object of relief in this case." 92 F.T.C. at 807–08. The case was eventually settled. Borden, Inc. v. Federal Trade Commission, 711 F.2d 758 (6th Cir.1983).

See generally McCarthy, Compulsory Licensing of a Trademark: Remedy or Penalty? 67 Trademark Rep. 197 (1977); Palladino, Compulsory Licensing of a Trademark, 26 Buffalo L.Rev. 457 (1977); Ball, Government Versus Trademarks: Today—Pharmaceuticals, ReaLemon and Formica—Tomorrow? 68 Trademark Rep. 471 (1978); Keating, FTC Authority to Order Compulsory Trademark Licensing: Is "ReaLemon" Really Real Lemon?, 85 Dick.L.Rev. 191 (1981). On the economics of compulsory licensing for trademarks, see Scherer, The Posnerian Harvest: Separating Wheat from Chaff, 86 Yale L.J. 974, 998–1000 (1977).

7. *Counterfeiting Remedies.* Counterfeit goods—for example, fake Rolex watches bearing a facsimile of the Rolex trademark—pose special problems for trademark relief. Injunctive decrees have little effect, and monetary awards promise scant recovery, against offshore manufacturers and fly-by-night distributors. The real need is for substantial deterrents.

The Trademark Counterfeiting Act of 1984, P.L. 98–473, 98 Stat. 2178, substantially bolstered the Lanham Act's provisions for civil relief and also introduced criminal sanctions against traffic in counterfeit goods or services. Amendments to the Lanham Act mandate awards of attorney's fees and treble damages against counterfeiters and authorize *ex parte* orders to seize counterfeit goods. See 15 U.S.C.A. §§ 1116(d), 1117(b). Section 1118 provides for destruction of infringing articles. The Act also amended Title 18 to provide that individuals who intentionally traffic, or attempt to traffic, in goods or services and knowingly use a counterfeit mark on or in connection with the goods or services may be fined not more than $250,000 or imprisoned not more than five years, or both. For the same offense, companies may be fined not more than $1,000,000. Individual repeat offenders may be fined not more than $1,000,000 or imprisoned not more than fifteen years or both; companies that are repeat offenders may be fined not more than $5,000,000. 18 U.S.C.A. § 2320 (1989).

D. INFRINGEMENT

See Statute Supplement 15 U.S.C.A. §§ 1114, 1119, 1121.

PIKLE–RITE CO. v. CHICAGO PICKLE CO.

United States Dist. Court, Northern Dist. Illinois, 1959.
171 F.Supp. 671, 121 U.S.P.Q. 128.

JULIUS J. HOFFMAN, District Judge.

This is an action for trade-mark infringement and unfair competition in which the plaintiff seeks an injunction, an accounting and treble damages.

The plaintiff is an Illinois corporation having its principal office and place of business in Pulaski, Wisconsin. The defendant is an Illinois corporation having its principal office and place of business in Chicago. In 1932, plaintiff's predecessor, John A. Wood, established the business of preparing and selling bottled pickles and related products. In 1942, this business was taken over by Pikle–Rite Company, an unincorporated business entity which was incorporated in 1948. Since 1932, plaintiff and its predecessors have owned and used the trademark "Polka" to designate different varieties of pickles which are sold primarily in self-service grocery stores in Illinois, Wisconsin, Iowa, Michigan, Minnesota, Indiana and Ohio. Since 1934, the name "Polka" has been registered as a trade-mark under the laws of Illinois. On August 7, 1956, plaintiff was granted a federal trade-mark registration on the name "Polka." As registered, the name is preceded and followed by a pair of musical notes. The name "Polka," as applied to pickle products, is fanciful, arbitrary, non-descriptive and non-generic, and is a valid trade-mark.

Representative labels under which plaintiff markets some of its "Polka"–brand pickle products are as follows:

Although the plaintiff prepares and bottles other vegetables, its "Polka"–brand pickle products are its principal items of business. The plaintiff has advertised its "Polka"–brand products through the media of television, radio, newspapers, window posters, shelf posters and gifts such as pencils, lazy susans and plastic aprons. However, the evidence discloses no comprehensive advertising expenditures.

For the period January 1953 through June 1957, the total amount of sales of "Polka"–brand products was $311,184.11. The yearly amount of sales of these products was as follows:

1953	$ 49,014.75
1954	45,230.58
1955	68,461.56
1956	100,037.32
1957	48,439.90
(through June)	

There is no evidence on the question whether the pickle business as a whole was substantially better in 1956 than it was in 1955. Nor is there any evidence on the question whether the plaintiff expanded its business or its advertising in 1956.

In December 1956, defendant began to distribute pickles in bottles which bore the brand-name "Pol–Pak." Defendant's label is as follows:

The defendant markets its products through self-service grocery stores. However, the evidence does not disclose whether the defendant utilizes this method exclusively or even primarily.

With reference to infringement, the basic issue in this case is whether the defendant's use of the name "Pol–Pak" on its products ". . . is likely to cause confusion or mistake or to deceive purchasers as to the source of origin of such goods." 15 U.S.C.A. § 1114(1)(a). For the reasons which follow, I am of the opinion that the defendant's brand-name "Pol–Pak" is confusingly similar to the plaintiff's trademark "Polka," and the plaintiff is entitled to injunctive relief. However, I am also of the opinion that the plaintiff is not entitled to an accounting and damages.

There is no dispute between the parties as to the law which is applicable to the instant case. In Northam Warren Corp. v. Universal Cosmetic Co., 7 Cir., 1927, 18 F.2d 774, at page 775, the law of infringement was stated as follows:

> Whether there is an infringement of a trade-mark does not depend upon the use of identical words, nor on the question as to whether they are so similar that a person looking at one would be deceived into the belief that it was the other; but it is sufficient if one adopts a trade-name or a trade-mark so like another in form, spelling, or sound that one, *with a not very definite or clear recollection as to the real trade-mark, is likely to become confused or misled.* . . . (Emphasis added.) . . .

In determining whether the likelihood of confusion exists, it should be noted that:

> The ascertainment of probability of confusion because of similarity of trade names presents a problem not solvable by a precise

rule or measure. Rather is it a matter of varying human reactions to situations incapable of exact appraisement. We are to determine, as was the District Judge, the purchasing public's state of mind when confronted by somewhat similar trade names singly presented. Is the similarity of name or dress such as to delude the public or will the prospective buyer readily differentiate between the two names? We can only contemplate, speculate, and weigh the probabilities of deception arising from the similarities and conclude as our, and the District Judge's, reactions persuade us. Colburn v. Puritan Mills, 7 Cir., 1939, 108 F.2d 377, at page 378.

Although the question presented by the instant case cannot be solved by precise rule or measure, certain factors are relevant. Whether infringement exists is not to be determined solely by a side-by-side comparison of the names in question. Although it is proper to consider the names as a whole, the names should not be examined with a microscope to detect minute differences. To constitute infringement, it is not necessary that the defendant appropriate the whole of plaintiff's mark, and the imitation need only be slight if it attaches to the salient feature of plaintiff's mark. The court should also consider the form, spelling and sound of the marks in question; whether the products involved are the same or similar, whether the products are sold to the same prospective customers, and whether the conditions under which the products are purchased are the same or similar.

In the instant case, there is no evidence that any purchaser was, in fact, confused or misled by the defendant's use of the name of "Pol–Pak." However, it was not necessary for the plaintiff to prove actual confusion. The statutory test is likelihood of confusion.

I am of the opinion that the defendant's use of the name "Pol–Pak" gives rise to the likelihood of confusing similarity. The salient part of defendant's brand-name, i.e., "Pol," constitutes three-fifths of plaintiff's trade-mark. Common experience teaches that an individual will more readily remember the first part of a name than some other part. Further, to the extent that the defendant's pickles are sold in self-service grocery stores, the parties utilize the same or similar commercial channels, the prospective purchaser is the same, and the conditions under which the products are purchased are the same or similar. The names "Polka" and "Pol–Pak" are not more dissimilar than the names "Cutex" and "Cuticlean" which were held to be confusingly similar in Northam Warren Corp. v. Universal Cosmetic Co., 7 Cir., 1927, 18 F.2d 774. The Northam case also refutes defendant's contention that the name "Pol" is but an abbreviation for the descriptive word, "Polish," and is, therefore, not infringing. In the Northam case, the designation "Cuti" was an abbreviation for the descriptive or generic word, "cuticle," but the court held that "Cuticlean" infringed "Cutex."

The defendant contends that a side-by-side comparison of the *labels* in question discloses no confusing similarity. However, as noted above, infringement is not to be determined solely by such comparison. The reason for this rule is that the ultimate purchaser is seldom presented with the opportunity of making such comparison. Further, it is to be doubted that the labels, apart from the marks in question, should be considered. It has been asserted as a general rule that differences in labels should not be considered in determining whether defendant's brand-name infringes plaintiff's trade-mark. 1 Nims, Unfair Competition and Trade Marks, § 221k, p. 716 et seq. However, Nims cites, as a case contrary to the general rule, John Morrell & Co. v. Doyle, 7 Cir., 1938, 97 F.2d 232, certiorari denied 1938, 305 U.S. 643, 59 S.Ct. 146, 83 L.Ed. 415. In the Morrell case, the plaintiff sold dog food under the trade-mark "Red Heart" which comprised those words superimposed upon a red heart. The defendant sold dog and cat food under the brand-name "Strong Heart" which name was accompanied by the picture of a famous dog, Strongheart. In holding that the plaintiff's trade-mark was not infringed, the court considered and emphasized the picture of the dog, and the court expressly declined to consider the name "Strong Heart" in vacuo. In spite of this fact, I am of the opinion that the Morrell case does not derogate from the general rule. The rationale of that decision is that, with regard to the defendant's label,

> . . . the characteristic feature, the thing which appeals to the eye and which, no doubt, makes the lasting impression upon a person's memory, is not Strongheart or Heart, but the picture of a dog. Assuming that persons who are interested in dog foods are dog fanciers, what could make such an appeal or create such a lasting impression as an imposing picture of a dog and especially if it be the picture of a dog of fame such as the record here indicates to be the case?

Thus, the court merely held that the essence of defendant's brand-name was a picture and not a name. In the instant case, the salient part of defendant's label is the brand-name "Pol–Pak"; the picture of a pickle is without significance. Further, to the extent that the representation of Polish dancers is a salient part of plaintiff's label, the representation reinforces the trade-mark "Polka." It does not derogate from the mark as the picture of the dog derogated from the brand-name "Strong Heart." In addition, it should be noted that the plaintiff has advertised the name "Polka" apart from the representation of Polish dancers.

Even in an economy in which diverse methods of advertising are employed, the spoken word is of great importance. A prospective purchaser may learn of plaintiff's "Polka"-brand products from her neighbor; she may hear radio advertisements; she may hear and see television advertisements and the memory of the spoken word may exist long after the memory of the image has faded. Further, the law does not presume that the prospective purchaser will have the opportunity to make a side-by-side comparison of different products and brand-names. As stated in Colburn v. Puritan Mills, 7 Cir., 1939, 108 F.2d 377, at page 378:

> We are to determine, as was the District Judge, the purchasing public's state of mind when confronted by somewhat similar trade names *singly presented.* (Emphasis added.)

Also, it must be borne in mind that we are dealing neither with an unusual product which requires discriminating purchase nor with a purchasing public which is discriminating. To the contrary, it has been asserted that the average purchaser undergoes, while in a super-market, an experience not unlike that of hypnosis. Packard, The Hidden Persuaders, pp. 91–2 (Cardinal Edition, 1958). Under such circumstances, it is not unduly harsh to restrain the defendant's use of the name "Pol–Pak." The defendant, in selecting a name for its product, could have drawn upon the entire range of its imagination. It chose not to do so and, instead, selected a name which is likely to confuse prospective purchasers of plaintiff's products. I conclude that the defendant's use of the name "Pol–Pak" should be enjoined.

Consideration will next be given to the territorial scope of the injunction. On this issue, a division of authority exists. In 87 C.J.S. Trade–Marks, etc. § 211d, p. 597, it is stated:

> The wrongful appropriation of plaintiff's trade-mark will be enjoined wherever it is used by him, including those places where he might do so in the course of normal business expansion. On the other hand, it has been held that injunctive relief should be limited to states in which plaintiff has established a market for the articles bearing his trade-mark. . . .

On the facts of the instant case, it is impossible to determine whether it may reasonably be anticipated that the plaintiff will expand its business. Accordingly, I am of the opinion that the injunction should be limited to those states in which plaintiff has established a market for its "Polka"-brand products.

The above discussion, although limited to the claim of trade-mark infringement, applies with equal vigor to plaintiff's claim of unfair competition, and as to both of these claims, I am of the opinion that plaintiff is entitled to no relief other than an injunction. In Square D. Co. v. Sorenson, 7 Cir., 1955, 224 F.2d 61, at pages 65–66, it was stated:

> Plaintiffs failed to prove fraud or a palming off by defendants of any article to persons who believed they were buying plaintiff's product. While the absence of fraud or palming off does not undermine a finding of unfair competition, the character of the conduct giving rise to the unfair competition is relevant to the remedy which should be afforded. An accounting will not be ordered merely because there has been an infringement. As under the trade mark act of 1905, under the present act an accounting has been denied where an injunction will satisfy the equities of the case.

In the instant case, the evidence is insufficient to warrant the conclusion that the defendant was guilty of fraud, palming off or intentional infringement, and I conclude that an injunction will satisfy the equities of the case. The defendant will bear the costs of this action. The plaintiff is directed to submit a judgment order in conformity with the views herein expressed on or before January 21, 1959.

McGREGOR–DONIGER, INC. v. DRIZZLE, INC.

United States Court of Appeals, Second Circuit, 1979.
599 F.2d 1126, 202 U.S.P.Q. 81.

MESKILL, Circuit Judge.

McGregor–Doniger Inc. ("McGregor"), a New York corporation founded in 1921, is a manufacturer of apparel for both men and women. Since 1947 McGregor has sold golf jackets under the trademark Drizzler, and in 1965 the company registered this mark for use in connection with golf jackets. Although McGregor had in the past used the word Drizzler in connection with other types of apparel, by 1965 the company had ceased using the mark in connection with any goods other than golf jackets. McGregor owns a variety of other trademarks, such as Brolly Dolly and Bernhard Altmann, which have been used in connection with goods other than golf jackets. Drizzler jackets sell for about $25 to $50.

Drizzle Inc. ("Drizzle"), a New York corporation established in 1969, sells only women's coats. Drizzle's coats, which are manufactured for Drizzle by various contractors, have been sold under the unregistered trademark Drizzle since the founding of the company. It appears from the record that Drizzle has to date employed no other trademark. Drizzle coats range in price from about $100 to $900.

In 1974 McGregor's management first became aware of the Drizzle company and of its use of the Drizzle mark in connection with the sale of women's coats. In January of 1975 McGregor notified Drizzle that if use of the Drizzle trademark on Drizzle's goods continued, legal proceedings would be instituted. The warning went unheeded and in March of 1975 McGregor brought suit against Drizzle in the United States District Court for the Southern District of New York, alleging trademark infringement, 15 U.S.C.A. § 1114, false designation of origin, 15 U.S.C.A. § 1125(a), and, in a pendent claim, common law unfair competition. McGregor sought an injunction barring Drizzle's further use of Drizzle as a trademark, an accounting for profits, damages, and other relief.

After a two-day bench trial, Judge Morris E. Lasker dismissed McGregor's complaint. 446 F.Supp. 160, 199 U.S.P.Q. 466 (S.D.N.Y. 1978). On appeal, McGregor challenges both the factual findings of the trial court and the trial court's interpretation of the legal significance of the facts found. Although the trial court's statement of the applicable principles needs modification, we conclude that reversal is not warranted.

Discussion

We are once again called upon to decide when a trademark owner will be protected against the use of its mark, or one very similar, on products other than those to which the owner has applied it. As we have observed before, the question "does not become easier of solution with the years." Polaroid Corp. v. Polarad Electronics Corp., 287 F.2d

492, 495, 128 U.S.P.Q. 411, 412–413 (2d Cir.), cert. denied, 368 U.S. 820, 82 S.Ct. 36, 7 L.Ed.2d 25, 131 U.S.P.Q. 499 (1961).

The crucial issue in these cases is "whether there is any likelihood that an appreciable number of ordinarily prudent purchasers are likely to be misled, or indeed simply confused, as to the source of the goods in question." Mushroom Makers, Inc. v. R.G. Barry Corp., 580 F.2d 44, 47, 199 U.S.P.Q. 65, 66–67 (2d Cir.1978), cert. denied, 439 U.S. 1116, 99 S.Ct. 1022, 59 L.Ed.2d 75, 200 U.S.P.Q. 832 (U.S. Jan. 15, 1979), 3 R. Callmann, The Law of Unfair Competition, Trademarks and Monopolies § 84, at 929 (3d ed. 1969) (hereinafter Callmann). In assessing the likelihood of such confusion we consider the factors laid out in the now classic Polaroid formula:

> Where the products are different, the prior owner's chance of success is a function of many variables: the strength of his mark, the degree of similarity between the two marks, the proximity of the products, the likelihood that the prior owner will bridge the gap, actual confusion, and the reciprocal of defendant's good faith in adopting its own mark, the quality of defendant's product, and the sophistication of the buyers. Even this extensive catalogue does not exhaust the possibilities—the court may have to take still other variables into account.

Polaroid Corp. v. Polarad Electronics Corp., supra, 287 F.2d at 495, 128 U.S.P.Q. at 412–413, citing Restatement of Torts §§ 729, 730, 731. The parties agree that Judge Lasker was correct in giving consideration to each of the factors mentioned in Polaroid before reaching a decision on the ultimate question of likelihood of confusion.

1. Strength of the Mark

The most complex issue raised by McGregor concerns the trial court's attempt to gauge the strength of the Drizzler mark. Our prior opinions and those of the district courts of this Circuit have left litigants and judges uncertain as to the appropriate way to demonstrate and determine the strength of a mark. In the hope of providing some guidance to bench and bar, we set out in some detail our view of this issue.

The term "strength" as applied to trademarks refers to the distinctiveness of the mark, or more precisely, its tendency to identify the goods sold under the mark as emanating from a particular, although possibly anonymous, source. The Restatement of Torts uses the term "distinctiveness" in place of the term "strength." § 731(f) and Comment e at 602. The strength or distinctiveness of a mark determines both the ease with which it may be established as a valid trademark and the degree of protection it will be accorded.

In an effort to liberate this aspect of trademark law from the "welter of adjectives" which had tended to obscure its contours, we recently reviewed the four categories into which terms are classified for trademark purposes. Abercrombie & Fitch Co. v. Hunting World, Inc., 537 F.2d 4, 9, 189 U.S.P.Q. 759, 764 (2d Cir.1976). Arranged in ascending order of strength, these categories are: (1) generic, (2) descriptive, (3) suggestive, and (4) arbitrary or fanciful. A generic term can never become a valid trademark and cannot be registered. A descriptive term can be registered as a mark only if it has "become distinctive of the applicant's goods in commerce," 15 U.S.C.A. § 1052(f), that is, in the unfortunate parlance of the cases, only if it has acquired "secondary meaning." Suggestive marks, falling between the merely descriptive and the arbitrary or fanciful, are entitled to registration without proof of secondary meaning, as are fully arbitrary or fanciful terms. 537 F.2d at 9–11, 189 U.S.P.Q. at 764–765. The boundaries between these categories are not fixed.

> [A] term that is in one category for a particular product may be in quite a different one for another, because a term may shift from one category to another in light of differences in usage through time, because a term may have one meaning to one group of users and a different one to others, and because the same term may be put to different uses with respect to a single product.

Abercrombie & Fitch Co. v. Hunting World, Inc., supra, 537 F.2d at 9, 189 U.S.P.Q. at 764.

Thus, while these categories can be useful for analytical purposes, the strength of a mark depends ultimately on its distinctiveness, or its "origin-indicating" quality, in the eyes of the purchasing public. Two familiar examples suffice to illustrate this principle. A coined term, initially suggestive or even fanciful, can lose its full trademark status if it comes to signify to the public the generic name of an article rather than the source of a particular brand of that article. In contrast, a descriptive mark that is not distinctive on its face may acquire secondary meaning so as to identify the source of the goods and thus claim status as a valid mark deserving of registration and protection against infringement. In Judge Lasker's words, "strength may derive from the intrinsic quality of a mark or from its public history." 446 F.Supp. at 162, 199 U.S.P.Q. at 467.

The many cases announcing that a mark found to be suggestive, arbitrary or fanciful (i.e., more than merely descriptive) is entitled to protection without proof of secondary meaning are correct as far as they go, for any term that is more than descriptive can be established as a valid mark which others may not infringe. Where the products involved are competitive and the marks quite similar, for example, the senior user of a more-than-descriptive mark need not prove secondary meaning. And where the marks involved are virtually identical, even if the products are non-competitive, a senior user of a more-than-descriptive mark can carry its burden on the "strength of the mark" component of the Polaroid formula without proving secondary meaning. But these cases do not require us to hold that Judge Lasker erred in considering evidence of secondary meaning in determining whether McGregor is entitled to protection against the use, on non-competitive goods, of a mark similar to its own. The cases agree that it is appropriate to consider all factors bearing on the likelihood of confusion. We view evidence concerning the origin-indicating significance of a mark in the marketplace as relevant to and probative of the strength of a mark and hence useful in assessing the likelihood of confusion.

Consideration of evidence of secondary meaning will almost always work in favor of the senior user. Its mark, if registered, is presumptively distinctive. Proof of secondary meaning, acquired perhaps through successful advertising, can only enhance the strength of its mark and thus enlarge the scope of the protection to which it is entitled. On the other hand, the owner of a distinctive mark need not introduce evidence of secondary meaning in order to gain protection for its mark against the confusing similarity of others. Thus, for example, the relatively small size of a senior user's advertising budget or sales volume will not diminish the strength of its valid mark, and the scope of protection accorded to that mark will not be narrowed because of such evidence. Only if the junior user carries the burden of affirmatively demonstrating that a term is generic is the senior user stripped of protection.

McGregor claims that the district court erred in requiring proof of secondary meaning. We agree with McGregor's contention that the decision of the Patent and Trademark Office to register a mark without requiring proof of secondary meaning affords a rebuttable presumption that the mark is more than merely descriptive. The trial court did in fact find the term Drizzler more than merely descriptive, although apparently only barely over the "suggestive" line. As a suggestive term, the Drizzler mark would be entitled to protection, regardless of proof of secondary meaning, *if* McGregor could prove that confusion of origin was likely to result from the use of a similar mark on non-competing goods. To the extent the district court held proof of secondary meaning *necessary*, it was in error. However, it was *not* error for the court to consider evidence bearing on the strength of the mark in determining the likelihood of consumer confusion and thus the scope of protection to which the Drizzler mark was entitled. Trademark strength is "an amorphous concept with little shape or substance when divorced from the mark's commercial context," E.I. DuPont de Nemours & Co. v. Yoshida Internat'l, Inc., supra, 393 F.Supp. at 512, 185 U.S.P.Q. at 604–605. We see no advantage to be derived from barring judicial consideration of the realities that give content to the concept of trademark strength.

2. Similarity of the Marks

"To the degree that the determination of 'likelihood of confusion' rests upon a comparison of the marks themselves, the appellate court is in as good a position as the trial judge to decide the issue." Miss Universe, Inc. v. Patricelli, 408 F.2d 506, 509, 161 U.S.P.Q. 129, 130–131 (2d Cir.1969). There are two principles especially important to performing this task.

First, even close similarity between two marks is not dispositive of the issue of likelihood of confusion. "Similarity in and of itself is not the acid test. Whether the similarity is likely to provoke confusion is the crucial question." Callmann § 82.1(a), at 601–02 (footnote omitted). For this reason cases involving the alteration, addition or elimination of only a single letter from the old mark to the new reach divergent results. Second, in assessing the similarity of two marks, it is the effect upon prospective purchasers that is important. Restatement of Torts § 728, Comment b at 591.

The district court quite correctly took into consideration all the factors that could reasonably be expected to be perceived by and remembered by potential purchasers. "[T]he setting in which a designation is used affects its appearance and colors the impression conveyed by it." Id. § 729, Comment b at 593. Thus while observing that the typewritten and aural similarity of the two marks "approaches identity," the district judge noted that the contexts in which the respective marks are generally presented reduces the impact of this similarity. The court observed that the label in each Drizzler jacket prominently features the McGregor name, which is printed in striking plaid letters. In addition, although there was testimony that retail stores on occasion in independent advertisements omit the McGregor logo, the evidence showed that McGregor always emphasizes the company name in its own advertising of Drizzler jackets. The fact that a trademark is always used in conjunction with a company name may be considered by the trial court as bearing on the likelihood of confusion.

The law does not require that trademarks be carefully analyzed and dissected by the purchasing public. "[I]t is sufficient if the *impression* which the infringing product makes upon the consumer is such that he is likely to believe the product is from the same source as the one he knows under the trade-mark." Stix Products, Inc. v. United Merchants & Mfrs., Inc., 295 F.Supp. 479, 494, 160 U.S.P.Q. 777, 789–790 (S.D.N.Y.1968) (footnote omitted; emphasis added). The court below properly focused on the general impression conveyed by the two marks. If Drizzle had chosen consistently to present its mark in red plaid lettering or to advertise its coats as the McGregor Drizzle line, we would be compelled to conclude that the similarity between the Drizzler mark and the Drizzle mark, *as generally presented to the public,* had been heightened and that the likelihood of confusion had been enhanced. Conversely, the fact that only one mark generally appears in close conjunction with the red plaid McGregor name increases the likelihood that the public, even when viewing the marks individually, will not confuse the two. The likelihood of confusion is further reduced by Drizzle's use of its mark to identify itself as the producer of the products advertised by it rather than as the name of a particular jacket or line of jackets, in contrast to McGregor's practice.

The district court's reasoning is sound. The differing methods of presentation of the two marks were properly examined. We agree with Judge Lasker's appraisal that they reduce to some degree the potential for confusion inherent in the close similarity between the two marks.

3. and 4. Product Proximity and Quality of Defendant's Product

The district court concluded on the basis of differences in appearance, style, function, fashion appeal, advertising orientation, and price that the competitive distance between Drizzler jackets and Drizzle coats is "significant." This conclusion is too amply supported by the evidence to be characterized as clearly erroneous.

McGregor does not claim that Drizzler jackets and Drizzle coats are directly competitive. Customers shopping for an inexpensive golf jacket are not likely to become confused by the similarity of the marks and mistakenly purchase a fashionable and expensive woman's coat. Thus the degree of proximity between the two products is relevant here primarily insofar as it bears on the likelihood that customers may be confused as to the *source* of the products, rather than as to the products themselves, and the concern is not direct diversion of purchasers but indirect harm through loss of goodwill or tarnishment of reputation. It is evident that customers would be more likely to assume that Drizzler golf jackets and Drizzle golf jackets come from the same source than they would be likely to assume that Drizzler golf jackets and Drizzle steam shovels come from the same source. Drizzle coats for women fall between the two extremes. In locating the appropriate place for Drizzle coats on this continuum, the district court considered many of the factors that are generally viewed as relevant.

> The impression that noncompeting goods are from the same origin may be conveyed by such differing considerations as the physical attributes or essential characteristics of the goods, with specific reference to their form, composition, texture or quality, the service or function for which they are intended, the manner in which they are advertised, displayed or sold, the place where they are sold, or the class of customers for whom they are designed and to whom they are sold.

Callmann § 82.2(c), at 807.

Looking at these very factors, the district judge found:

> Beyond the fact that they might both be crudely classified as outerwear, the 'Drizzler' and defendant's products have nothing in common. McGregor's garment is a relatively inexpensive, lightweight, waistlength jacket—a windbreaker. . . . As is apparent from advertisements for the jacket, it is intended for casual wear, particularly in connection with sports activities. Moreover, although the Drizzler can be worn by either men or women, sales are pitched primarily to the former. . . . Furthermore, a Drizzler is ordinarily sold in the men's department of stores which carry both men's and women's garments. . . .
>
> Unlike McGregor's products, the coats manufactured by Drizzle are distinctly and exclusively tailored for women. They are generally full length raincoats and capes. Although it is true that Drizzle manufactures a style that might be called a jacket . . . it is longer than the Drizzler and entirely different in appearance.

Drizzle's garments are within the medium to high fashion range. . . . The price range of Drizzle's line, running from approximately $100 to $900 . . . reflects the coats' position in the fashion hierarchy.

446 F.Supp. at 164, 199 U.S.P.Q. at 469.

In Blue Bell, Inc. v. Jaymar–Ruby, Inc., 497 F.2d 433, 182 U.S.P.Q. 65 (2d Cir.1974), we recognized that due to diversification in the garment business, men's apparel and women's apparel had in certain cases been regarded as sufficiently related to justify the denial of registration to similar marks. However, in Blue Bell we characterized the proximity between men's sportswear and women's sportswear as only "moderate" and held that the likelihood of confusion was reduced by the rather "detailed purchasing process" appropriate to the goods in question. 497 F.2d at 435–36, 182 U.S.P.Q. 66–67. We know of no case holding that, as a matter of law, the competitive distance between men's apparel and women's apparel cannot be demonstrated to be significant on the basis of the many factors relevant to such a determination. The district court's finding on this issue, based on the proper indicia and supported by the evidence, should not be disturbed.

The high quality of Drizzle's coats is not contested by McGregor.

5. Bridging the Gap

In assessing the likelihood of confusion, the district court was required to consider the likelihood that Drizzler would "bridge the gap," that is, the likelihood that McGregor would enter the women's coat market under the Drizzler banner. McGregor presented no evidence that such a step was being considered. Clearly the absence of any present intention or plan indicates that such expansion is less, rather than more, probable. Also of probative value is the fact that McGregor has for many years marketed its women's apparel under names bearing no similarity to Drizzler—such as Brolly Dolly. On the other hand, the absence of a present intent to bridge the gap is not determinative. In a given case, sufficient likelihood of confusion may be established although likelihood of bridging the gap is not demonstrated. Because consumer confusion is the key, the assumptions of the typical consumer, whether or not they match reality, must be taken into account.

The district court's finding that it is unlikely that Drizzler will bridge the gap is not clearly erroneous. Nor does the evidence presented below regarding McGregor's own history of trademark use, as well as industry custom, compel the conclusion that, despite the improbability that McGregor will move into the women's coat market under the Drizzler trademark, consumers will assume otherwise.

6. Actual Confusion

McGregor's claim that the district court erred in considering the absence of proof of *actual* consumer confusion in assessing the *likeli-*

hood of confusion is without merit. Actual confusion is one of several factors to be considered in making such a determination. Although we have recognized the difficulty of establishing confusion on the part of retail customers, the district judge quite properly noted that not a single instance of consumer confusion had actually been demonstrated. While a plaintiff need not prove actual confusion in order to prevail, "it is certainly proper for the trial judge to infer from the absence of actual confusion that there was also no likelihood of confusion." Affiliated Hosp. Prod., Inc. v. Merdel Game Mfg. Co., 513 F.2d 1183, 1188, 185 U.S.P.Q. 321, 324 (2d Cir.1975).

Finally, the district court was not required, as McGregor urges, to find actual *consumer* confusion on the basis of the testimony of one McGregor employee that she had been momentarily confused by a Drizzle advertisement. The weighing of evidence, particularly where credibility judgments must be made, is for the trial judge. His determination regarding actual confusion is not clearly erroneous.

7. Good Faith

McGregor contends that the district court improperly placed the burden of proof on the good faith issue on McGregor rather than on Drizzle. However, assuming without deciding that McGregor is correct in its view of the proper placement of the burden of proof, there is simply no indication in Judge Lasker's opinion that this burden was in fact placed on McGregor.

We recently held that adoption of the mark Mushroom for women's sportswear despite actual and constructive notice of another company's prior registration of the mark Mushrooms for women's shoes was not necessarily indicative of bad faith, because the presumption of an exclusive right to use a registered mark extends only so far as the goods or services noted in the registration certificate. Mushroom Makers, Inc. v. R.G. Barry Corp., supra, 580 F.2d at 48, 199 U.S.P.Q. at 67–68. Here, as in Mushroom Makers, the district court was entitled to consider and to credit the uncontradicted testimony of Drizzle's witnesses that the Drizzle mark was selected without knowledge of McGregor's prior use of the Drizzler mark. "Normally, the alleged infringer's intent is an issue for district court determination," Grotrian, Helfferich, Schulz, Etc. v. Steinway & Sons, supra, 523 F.2d at 1338 n. 14, 186 U.S. P.Q. at 441–442 n. 14, and findings as to such intent will be upset only if clearly erroneous.

8. Sophistication of Buyers

McGregor asserts that the trial court erroneously considered only the typical "sophisticated" purchaser of Drizzle's coats, to the exclusion of the casual or unsophisticated purchaser. We do not read the decision below in this manner.

The relevant cases not only authorize but instruct the trial courts, in making a determination as to likelihood of confusion, to consider the level of sophistication of the relevant purchasers. "The general impression of the ordinary purchaser, buying under the normally prevalent conditions of the market and giving the attention such purchasers usually give in buying that class of goods, is the touchstone." Callmann § 81.2, at 577. As we observed recently in Taylor Wine Co. v. Bully Hill Vineyards, Inc., 569 F.2d 731, 733, 196 U.S.P.Q. 593, 593–594 (2d Cir.1978), "every product has its own separate threshold for confusion of origin." The greater the value of an article the more careful the typical consumer can be expected to be; the average purchaser of an automobile will no doubt devote more attention to examining different products and determining their manufacturer or source than will the average purchaser of a ball of twine. The degree of reliance by consumers on labels and trademarks will also vary from product to product. It is easy to see that such differences in purchasing patterns affect the likelihood that confusion will result from the use of similar marks on noncompeting goods from different sources.

In some cases, of course, as where the products are identical and the marks are identical, the sophistication of buyers cannot be relied on to prevent confusion. For example, in Omega Importing Corp. v. Petri-Kine Camera Co., 451 F.2d 1190, 1195, 171 U.S.P.Q. 769, 772–773 (2d Cir.1971), we held that even though the ordinary purchaser would be expected to make "more than a casual inspection" before buying an expensive camera, such inspection would be of doubtful value because the cameras from each of two different sources were both labelled "Exakta." In the instant case, however, where both the products involved and the marks involved are distinguishable, the care exercised by typical consumers is likely to reduce confusion.

In Omega we noted that where a buyer market was composed of both discriminating and relatively unknowledgeable buyers, a court must consider the probability of confusion on the part of the latter as well as the former. However, it is also true that the crucial issue is confusion on the part of an "appreciable number" of consumers. Mushroom Makers, Inc. v. R.G. Barry Corp., supra, 580 F.2d at 47, 199 U.S.P.Q. at 66–67. At a certain point, confusion "will be too slight to bring the case above the rule of de minimis." Triumph Hosiery Mills v. Triumph Internat'l Corp., supra, 308 F.2d at 199, 135 U.S.P.Q. at 47–48. "The remote possibility of occasional confusion in those who observe less than ordinary care under the circumstances does not concern us." Modular Cinemas of America, Inc. v. Mini Cinemas Corp., supra, 348 F.Supp. at 582, 175 U.S.P.Q. at 358–359. " 'The purchasing public must be credited with at least a modicum of intelligence. . . .' " Carnation Co. v. California Growers Wineries, 97 F.2d 80, 81, 37 U.S.P.Q. 735, 735–736 (C.C.P.A.1938).

McGregor offered no evidence establishing that any significant number of Drizzle purchasers are casual or unsophisticated. The district court was entitled to rely on the evidence indicating that the relevant purchasing group in fact tends to be sophisticated and knowledgeable about women's apparel. We cannot classify his findings in this regard as clearly erroneous.

Conclusion

In trademark infringement cases involving non-competing goods, it is rare that we are "overwhelmed by the sudden blinding light of the justness of one party's cause." King Research, Inc. v. Shulton, Inc., supra, 454 F.2d at 69, 172 U.S.P.Q. at 323. Most often our affirmances in such cases rest on the more modest conclusion that the trial judge was not wrong in reaching the result appealed from. It is on this basis that we affirm the district judge's decision. Judge Lasker applied the correct legal standard (likelihood of confusion) and the correct criteria (those enumerated in Polaroid) in reaching his result. Moreover, he quite properly regarded no single factor as determinative. Although the two marks at issue are concededly quite similar, the court below found that the Drizzler mark is only moderately strong, that the competitive distance between the products is significant, that there was no intention to bridge the gap, that no actual confusion has occurred, and that Drizzle adopted its mark in good faith. Thus the court's conclusion that likelihood of confusion had not been proved by McGregor is amply supported by its findings, none of which is clearly erroneous. And we do not believe that the error in analysis discussed in our opinion today compels reversal of the result reached by the district court.

Because McGregor has failed to establish a likelihood of confusion, the balance of interests of necessity tips in Drizzle's favor. Because the goods are concededly not competitive, McGregor's sales of Drizzler jackets cannot be expected to suffer. Where non-competitive goods are involved the trademark laws protect the senior user's interest in an untarnished reputation and his interest in being able to enter a related field at some future time. Because consumer confusion as to source is unlikely, McGregor's reputation cannot be expected to be harmed. Because of the improbability that McGregor will enter the women's coat field under the Drizzler name, its right to expand into other fields has not been unduly restricted. Thus we see no injury to McGregor resulting from denial of the relief requested. On the other hand, if forced to give up its mark Drizzle could be expected to be harmed by loss of the goodwill that has been associated with the Drizzle name since 1969.

As we noted in Chandon Champagne Corp. v. San Marino Wine Corp., 335 F.2d 531, 536, 142 U.S.P.Q. 239, 243 (2d Cir.1964):

> Although this court was the leader in granting relief to a trademark owner when there had been and was no likelihood of actual diversion [i.e., in cases involving non-competitive products], we have likewise emphasized that, in such cases, 'against these legitimate interests of the senior user are to be weighed the legitimate interests of the innocent second user' and that we must balance 'the *conflicting interests* both parties have in the unimpaired continuation of their trade mark use.' Avon Shoe Co. v. David Crystal, Inc. [supra, 279 F.2d at 613, 125 U.S.P.Q. at 612–613].

Following this approach, this Court has frequently supplemented its consideration of the Polaroid factors by balancing the conflicting interests of the parties involved. Particularly when viewed in light of a balancing of the interests involved, the decision below warrants affirmance.

SEARS, ROEBUCK & CO. v. ALLSTATE DRIVING SCHOOL, 301 F.Supp. 4, 163 U.S.P.Q. 335 (E.D.N.Y.1969). ZAVATT, J.: . . . Prior to the trial of this case, and in preparation for it, plaintiffs engaged a market analyst to conduct a telephone survey in order to try to establish that the public is likely to be confused as to the origin of defendant's services. They had hoped that the survey would indicate that a large number of persons responding to it were actually confused, and that therefore, the court would draw the inference that there was a strong likelihood of confusion as to the origin of defendant's services. The results of the survey were offered through the testimony of Albert Sindlinger, President of Sindlinger & Co., located in Philadelphia, Pennsylvania. Mr. Sindlinger supervised the preparation of the survey questionnaire, and the tabulation of the results. Two interviewers and one supervisor testified. All but three of the remaining interviewers were available in court to testify. The parties stipulated that these people would give the same answers to the questions posed as those who did testify.

999 telephone interviews were tabulated over a two week period by 24 women who were part-time employees of Sindlinger & Co. Every telephone call was placed from Philadelphia to a Suffolk County residential subscriber chosen by a random selection procedure devised by Sindlinger. These employees, all but two of whom were high school graduates, worked approximately 20 hours per week at the rate of $1.60 per hour (the minimum wage). They were not skilled or experienced public opinion researchers. They had received preliminary "training" for a three day period. It consisted of listening to telephone calls made by other Sindlinger employees for other surveys. They were able to listen only to the questions posed by the interviewers; they could not overhear the responses to those questions. They received no special instructions regarding the manner of asking questions, or of recording responses. The nature of the tabulating process required that short responses be recorded. Therefore, summaries of actual answers were recorded where the answers were too long to record verbatim. Supervisors could have monitored any interview they chose to, but they generally did so only when a particular interviewer requested assistance. Since many other surveys were being conducted by Sindlinger & Co. during this period, the supervisors could not be sure that any interviews were monitored in this particular survey.

The answers which were recorded by the interviewers were coded and tabulated according to Sindlinger's instructions. The report containing the computer tabulation of the responses was received in evidence. The defendant, after initially objecting to its admissibility at the trial, now concedes that it was properly admitted, but argues that very little weight ought to be attributed to the findings. The report indicates that 37.6% of the respondents were of the opinion that Sears owns or operates the Allstate Driving School, and that an additional 12.2% thought that Allstate Insurance owns or operates the Allstate Driving School. Other responses such as "Allstate Company" and "Allstate" are inconclusive as far as plaintiffs seek to interpret them as further evidence of confusion. Finally, 39.1% responded that they did not have an opinion as to the ownership or operation of the Allstate Driving School. The results are much more impressive when restricted to those respondents who had an opinion (60.1% of the total sample). Of these 61.8% indicated that in their opinion Sears owns or operates the Allstate Driving School, and 20.1% indicated Allstate Insurance. Thus, 49.8% of the total sample (which includes those who "didn't know") were of the opinion that one of the plaintiffs owns or operates the Allstate Driving School, while 81.9% of those who had an opinion indicated that one of the plaintiffs owns or operates the Allstate Driving School. This survey is not of sufficient weight to persuade the court, in the light of all the other evidence in the case, that the ordinary prospective purchaser is likely to be confused as to the origin of defendant's services. There are several inadequacies in the design and execution of the survey which lead the court to give it little weight. Only some of the more serious are analyzed here.

The women who conducted the telephone interviews were low paid, part time employees of Sindlinger & Co. rather than professional public opinion researchers. Their brief training period did not even include their observation of a single complete interview. That is, they heard only the questions asked and they observed the recording of the responses, but they never heard the responses personally. Since the accuracy of a survey such as this depends heavily on the good judgment of the interviewers, this training deficiency is particularly relevant when weighing the results. Unforeseen circumstances may arise which must be solved quickly by the interviewer without the assistance of a supervisor. Recording errors may occur not only through inadvertent error, but also when an interviewer exercises poor judgment in interpreting a response. See H.C. Barksdale, The Use of Survey Research Findings as Legal Evidence 28, 33 (1957). The evidence in this case indicates that the interviewers were indeed often called upon to interpret and summarize responses so that they could later be coded for computer tabulation.

For example, in answer to the question "In your opinion—who owns or operates the Allstate Driving School?" 3.5% responded with "Allstate Company" and 4.4% with "Allstate." While these responses were accurately recorded, there is certainly a danger that many of the other responses which should have been tabulated in these categories (and thus less helpful to plaintiffs) were coded as "Allstate Insurance Co." The danger is amplified by the fact that the term "Allstate" has a secondary meaning widely known to the general public and hence probably to the interviewers and, therefore, interviewers exercising poor judgment might have improperly recorded the response "Allstate

Company" or "Allstate" as "Allstate Insurance Co." It would appear obvious that if professionals were not to be used then at the very least it would have been wiser to provide interviewer trainees with the opportunity to overhear a sampling of responses so that they might have gained useful experience in interpretation and recording.

The questionnaire itself raises serious problems. Question 19 is the key to the study ("In your opinion—who owns or operates the Allstate Driving School?"). However, the sequence in which the questions were asked, and the content of the other questions, necessarily had an impact on the nature of the responses. One of the dangers inherent in an ex parte solicitation of public opinion was noted in National Biscuit Co. v. Princeton Mining Co., 137 U.S.P.Q. 250:

> It is of course recognized that proof of a substantial amount of actual confusion of marks as an incident to bona fide purchases of goods under the normal circumstances and conditions surrounding the sale thereof constitutes the best evidence of continued confusion of the marks. On the other hand, a survey, such as that of opposer, intended to demonstrate the same thing, and not conducted in the presence of other persons who might be vitally concerned therewith, might frequently be carried out in such a manner, whether designedly or not, as practically to insure the desired results, and it ordinarily would be impossible to ascertain from the recollections of the persons participating therein what factors of conversation, expression or the like may have been responsible for the results obtained. 137 U.S.P.Q. at 253.

The Fifth Circuit in Sears, Roebuck & Co. v. All States Life Insurance Co., supra, went so far as to say that:

> [I]t is not truly illustrative of what the public thinks to permit one party to propound questions [in a survey] chosen on its behalf, however fairly attempted, with no opportunity given to the other party to test the answers given by the persons interviewed. 246 F.2d at 172, 114 U.S.P.Q. at 26.

Two examples of suggestion readily come to mind. There are several introductory questions (4 through 10) included in the survey ostensibly for "interest value," that is, to maintain the interviewee's interest so that he or she will respond later to the key question. Question 6 asks "What does the name Coldspot mean to you?" Those who respond to this question without naming Sears (the manufacturer and retailer for Coldspot appliances) are then asked specifically "Where would you go to buy a Coldspot product?" The only correct answer to this inquiry would be Sears. At this very early stage of the questioning, therefore, the name Sears was brought to the attention of a large number of the respondents. In fact, almost 45% of those who completed interviews identified the trade name "Coldspot" with Sears.

The second example of suggestion appears by way of a series of questions which, when considered together, might be characterized as leading. Before any mention is made of the Allstate Driving School interviewers asked, "What does the name Allstate mean to you?";

"Have you ever bought any Allstate products?"; "What . . . and where did you buy it?"; "Do you recall seeing the name Allstate mentioned recently in any advertisement anywhere?"; "What do you recall being advertised?". As this court has found, "Allstate" has developed a secondary meaning, and is widely known by consumers in the automotive related field to be a brand name for automobile accessories and insurance. Suffice to say, as might be expected, a large number of respondents associated "Allstate" with either or both plaintiffs, and had themselves purchased various "Allstate" products. Of course, that plaintiff's trademark is widely known does not by itself indicate a likelihood of confusion. With this preliminary build-up accomplished, however, the questions begin to probe in the area of driving schools. Question 14(a) asks, "Can you name any driving schools that are located within the Suffolk County area?" If the response to this question did not include the Allstate Driving School, the respondent was asked, "Have you ever heard of the Allstate Driving School?" (only 9.3% said that they had heard of the school and only 1.4% [fourteen persons] knew its correct location). Eventually the clincher is asked: "In your opinion—who owns or operates the Allstate Driving School?" It is not surprising that after Sears and its "Allstate" products were repeatedly brought to the attention of the respondents, who by this time were thinking of the plaintiffs, a large number were of the opinion that one or both of the plaintiffs owns or operates the Allstate Driving School.

One of the dangers inherent in a consumer reaction test is that it is not administered in the context of the market place. Respondents to such a test do not consider those factors which are relevant to the particular purchasing decision at hand. They must give their opinion in a vacuum without regard to the type of advertising or manner of marketing used in connection with the goods and services involved. For example, the respondents to the survey in this case were unaware that the defendant advertised only in the Suffolk County classified telephone directory; that the school was operated from the owner's home, which was located in a residential area; that only one automobile was used for instruction. This danger is emphasized when they have been indoctrinated to think in terms of famous brand names in general (see questions 4 to 9) and "Allstate" in particular, before being asked the $64 question, and where the survey is the only evidence of confusion. In no case which has come to the attention of the court, in which surveys were used to support a finding of a substantial likelihood of confusion, was the particular survey the only evidence relating to that issue. Concrete instances of actual confusion by purchasers were introduced to buttress the findings of the survey.

It is important to bear in mind that the relevant group with which we are concerned is the prospective purchaser of plaintiffs' or defendant's products and services. It is their confusion that would be noteworthy. In face of this legal imperative, the survey questionnaire does not inquire whether or not those interviewed had driver's licenses, or owned automobiles, or were considering taking lessons, etc. [They were asked whether they had already taken lessons.] In addition, it is arguable that the universe selected by Sindlinger for this survey, the entire County of Suffolk, was too large. Since 80% of defendant's business comes from within the 8 to 10 mile radius of the school, a more accurate sampling of prospective purchasers would have confined itself to this geographic area.

NOTES

1. Despite frequent exhortations that marks should be viewed in their entirety, courts in infringement cases will usually first dissect the mark to separate its distinctive and protectible components from those that are nondistinctive. Against this background, the court will then evaluate plaintiff's and defendant's marks in their entirety to determine the likelihood of confusion.

Flintkote Co. v. Tizer, 158 F.Supp. 699, 701, 115 U.S.P.Q. 3, 4 (E.D. Pa.1957), aff'd, 266 F.2d 849, 121 U.S.P.Q. 284 (3d Cir.1959) is typical. "As to the alleged infringement of Tile–Tex by Tile–Tone, we start with the fact that the word 'tile' is wholly descriptive, could not by itself qualify as a trademark, and can be freely used by anyone. When it is used as one part of a trademark, the combination may be registrable, but when it comes to the question of infringement, while the entire mark must be considered as a whole, the descriptive word cannot constitute the dominant part of it. Whatever confusion may be caused by the fact that the same descriptive word appears in the two marks must be discounted. Conversely, infringement cannot be found if the nondescriptive parts of the two marks are distinctive enough to prevent confusion." Would a similarly careful dissection of the two marks in *Pikle–Rite* have led to a different result in that case? Might Chicago Pickle have availed itself of the fair use defense, discussed at page 308 above?

2. Trademark's common law design, transformed in many respects by the Lanham Act, was further altered by "housekeeping" amendments to the Act, P.L. 87–772, 76 Stat. 769, passed in 1962. One of these amendments went beyond housekeeping to strike the last twelve words from section 32's prescription, "is likely to cause confusion, or to cause mistake, or deceive *purchasers as to the source of origin of such goods or services.*" (Emphasis added.)

The amendment's implications were briefly explored in Syntex Laboratories, Inc. v. Norwich Pharmacal Co., 437 F.2d 566, 169 U.S.P.Q. 1 (2d Cir.1971). Defendant there argued that, in finding that its unregistered mark "Vagestrol" for a vaginal suppository product, infringed plaintiff's registered mark "Vagitrol" for a vaginal cream product, the trial court erred in choosing a test for infringement that looked to confusion of the products themselves by physicians and pharmacists instead of to confusion among ordinary prudent purchasers as to the "source of origin." Noting that the amendment of section 32 evidenced Congress's "clear purpose to outlaw the use of trademarks which are likely to cause confusion, mistake or deception of any kind, not merely of purchasers nor simply as to source of origin," Judge Lumbard concluded that, "in a case such as the one at Bar where *product* confusion could have dire effects upon public health, looking to such confusion, in addition to source-of-origin confusion, in determining whether there has been trademark infringement is entirely in accord with public policy, as well as with the Lanham Act." 437 F.2d 566, 568–569 (emphasis in original).

The special facts of *Syntex* doubtless justified the decision reached. But are "purchasers" and "source of origin" to be disregarded in garden variety infringement cases?

3. *What Proportion of the Consuming Public Must Be Likely to Be Confused?* In the simpler, not distant past plaintiffs proved likelihood of confusion by convincing the trier of fact that *it* would be likely to be confused by the defendant's use of the plaintiff's mark. Since the parties addressed only the fact-trier's perceptions, there was no need to quantify the measure alluded to in *McGregor–Doniger*—whether "an appreciable number of ordinarily prudent purchasers are likely to be misled, or indeed simply confused, as to the source of goods in question." With the advent and widespread use of consumer surveys, however, the numbers game has become all-important.

Henri's Food Products Co. v. Kraft, Inc., 717 F.2d 352, 220 U.S.P.Q. 386 (7th Cir.1983), was a declaratory judgment action. The court of appeals held that the district court had properly weighed survey evidence that only 7.6% of survey respondents had confused the source of plaintiff's "Yogowhip" salad dressing with defendant's "Miracle Whip" salad dressing against a finding of infringement. "Kraft has pointed to no case in which a 7.6% figure constituted likelihood of confusion." 717 F.2d at 358. Judge Coffey, dissenting in part, objected that the relevant cases "are concerned with the existence of *some* 'confusion' rather than a specific amount of confusion. Indeed the underlying purpose of trademark law is to *prevent* confusion. The survey evidence unquestionably proves that *some* 'confusion' exists in the minds of consumers. This 'confusion' is sufficient to establish the likelihood the public will be moved in some degree to purchase 'Yogowhip' due to the misperception it is manufactured by Kraft." 717 F.2d at 365.

Techniques for the design and conduct of surveys are considered in Evans & Gunn, Trademark Surveys, 79 Trademark Rep. 1 (1989); Sorensen, Survey Research Execution in Trademark Litigation: Does Practice Make Perfection?, 73 Trademark Rep. 349 (1983); Boal, Techniques for Ascertaining Likelihood of Confusion and the Meaning of Advertising Communications, 73 Trademark Rep. 405 (1983); The Structure and Uses of Survey Evidence in Trademark Cases, 67 Trademark Rep. 97 (1977).

4. *Similarity.* In the usual trademark infringement case, the registered mark and the mark alleged to infringe will be in the same symbolic format—word v. word or picture v. picture. The only question

will be whether the defendant's word or picture is sufficiently similar to the registered word or picture to support a finding of infringement.

Can a word mark infringe a picture mark? In Mobil Oil Corp. v. Pegasus Petroleum Corp., 818 F.2d 254, 2 U.S.P.Q.2d 1677 (2d Cir.1987), the court held that defendant's use of the term, "Pegasus" in connection with its oil trading activities infringed plaintiff's registered trademark of a flying horse—representing Pegasus, the winged horse of Greek mythology—in connection with its petroleum business. Agreeing "that words and their pictorial representations should not be equated as a matter of law," the court concluded that "a district court may make such a determination as a factual matter" and upheld the district court's determination "that the word 'Pegasus' evokes the symbol of the flying red horse and that the flying horse is associated in the mind with Mobil. In other words, the symbol of the flying horse and its name 'Pegasus' are synonymous." 818 F.2d at 257.

5. *Contributory Infringement.* Trademark infringement is sometimes dispersed, with scores of small merchants, rather than a single large firm, committing the infringement. In these circumstances trademark owners will often find it too costly to pursue infringers individually, and will instead rely on a contributory infringement theory to proceed against the single firm that facilitated the individual direct infringements.

Inwood Laboratories, Inc. v. Ives Laboratories, Inc., 456 U.S. 844, 102 S.Ct. 2182, 72 L.Ed.2d 606, 214 U.S.P.Q. 1 (1982), explored the question of liability for contributory trademark infringement. Following expiration of plaintiff's patent on the drug, Cyclospasmol, competing drug manufacturers had produced, and sold to pharmacists, a generic equivalent that copied the appearance of plaintiff's capsules. When pharmacists began repackaging and mislabelling the generic products as Cyclospasmol, plaintiff sued the generic drug manufacturers on the theory that their use of look-alike capsules and distribution of catalogs comparing the prices of the generic drug with Cyclospasmol induced pharmacists to substitute and mislabel the generic drug as Cyclospasmol.

The district court held for the defendant and the circuit court held for the plaintiff. The Supreme Court reversed the circuit court decision on the ground that the court had failed to apply the Federal Rules' "clearly erroneous" standard in reviewing the district court decision. The Court's statement of the test for contributory trademark infringement, though *dicta,* will doubtless be influential: "As the lower courts correctly discerned, liability for trademark infringement can extend beyond those who actually mislabel goods with the mark of another. Even if a manufacturer does not directly control others in the chain of distribution, it can be held responsible for their infringing activities under certain circumstances. Thus, if a manufacturer or distributor intentionally induces another to infringe a trademark, or if it continues to supply its product to one whom it knows or has reason to know is engaging in trademark infringement, the manufacturer or distributor is contributorily responsible for any harm done as a result of the deceit." 456 U.S. at 853–854, 102 S.Ct. at 2188.

Justice White, joined by Justice Marshall, concurred in the reversal "because I believe the Court of Appeals has watered down to an impermissible extent the standard for finding a violation of § 32 of the Lanham Act, 15 U.S.C. § 1114," and because the Court's majority opinion acquiesced in this new standard. The test to which Justice White objected was that:

> By using capsules of identical color, size, and shape, together with a catalog describing their appearance and listing comparable prices of CYCLOSPASMOL and generic cyclandelate, appellees *could reasonably anticipate* that their generic drug product would by a substantial number of druggists be substituted illegally. . . . This amounted to a suggestion, at least by implication, that the druggists take advantage of the opportunity to engage in such misconduct. 638 F.2d at 543 (emphasis added).

In Justice White's view, "[t]he mere fact that a generic drug company can anticipate that some illegal substitution will occur to some unspecified extent, and by some unknown pharmacists, should not by itself be a predicate for contributory liability." 456 U.S. at 859–860, 102 S.Ct. at 2191.

See Germain, The Supreme Court's Opinion in the *Inwood* Case: Declination of Duty, 70 Kentucky L.J. 731 (1981–82).

E. FEDERAL UNFAIR COMPETITION LAW: LANHAM ACT § 43(a)

See Statute Supplement 15 U.S.C.A. § 1125.

CAN–AM ENGINEERING CO. v. HENDERSON GLASS, INC.

United States Court of Appeals, Sixth Circuit, 1987.
814 F.2d 253, 2 U.S.P.Q.2d 1197.

RALPH B. GUY, Jr., Circuit Judge.

Plaintiff brought an action pursuant to § 43(a) of the Lanham Act, 15 U.S.C. § 1125(a). This action followed the unauthorized use of a photograph of plaintiff's product on one of defendant's advertising price lists. Plaintiff claimed injuries flowing from false designation of origin and false description or representation. After a bench trial, the district court found in favor of the defendant. Upon a consideration of plaintiff's claims of error and a full review of the record, we affirm.

I.

The facts are not in dispute and can be briefly summarized. Automobile wire wheel covers are a frequently stolen item and consequently are the subject of a large volume of insurance claims. As a result of this, a brisk business is done in furnishing after-market wire wheel covers for replacements.[1] Both Can–Am and Henderson sell after-market wire wheel covers principally to insurance replacement companies. Can–Am just started in the after-market wheel cover business in 1982 when it conceived a product and produced an advertising brochure to promote the product. In the fall of 1982 a Can–Am sales representative called on Henderson Glass soliciting business and left a copy of Can–Am's sales brochure. Henderson purchased no product from Can–Am but rather bought from Norris Industries, a competitor.

In December of 1983, Henderson decided to run a special on General Motor's (GM) OEM wheel covers. The advertising director of Henderson was instructed to put together on a rush basis a flyer listing the prices for the GM wheel covers. The decision was made to depict wheel covers on the flyer, but no picture of the GM wheel covers was available in Henderson's files, and so they used the wheel cover picture from Can–Am's advertising brochure which Henderson had in its files. Since the Can–Am wheel cover had a distinctive logo in the center of its also distinctive seven-sided wheel cover hub, a GM decal was pasted over the logo prior to copying. Somehow the decal fell off, leaving a glue residue and a distorted logo which was neither that of Can–Am nor GM. The seven-sided hub was clearly visible, however.

When completed, the price list flyer was mailed by Henderson to the insurance companies and other agencies on its mailing list (1,273 copies) and distributed to Henderson's 16 branch stores (1,757 copies). Very shortly after this distribution, Henderson received a telephone call from Can–Am's attorney complaining of the use of its wheel cover in the Henderson flyer. Henderson immediately called back all of the flyer copies sent to its branch managers. Since it was not feasible to try and retrieve all of the copies sent out to Henderson's mailing list customers, Henderson sent out a new price list flyer which contained a retraction in the place where the wheel cover picture previously appeared. The retraction read:

"NOTICE:

JANUARY VERSION OF THIS AD IMPROPERLY INCLUDED (IN THIS SPACE) A PHOTOGRAPH OF A WIRE COVER BY CAN–AM ENGINEERING CO. THIS AD PERTAINS ONLY TO G.M. ACCESSORY PACKAGES, WIRE WHEEL COVERS AND TO OEM REPLACEMENT COVERS. WE DO NOT OFFER THE WHEEL COVER BY CAN–AM ENGINEERING CO. SHOWN IN THE PREVIOUS AD."

Despite these efforts on the part of Henderson, Can–Am filed suit. Immediately after suit was entered, Henderson agreed to a voluntary consent order that it would not use any photos of Can–Am's products. The suit continued, however, with Can–Am seeking only money damages.

---

1. After-market wire wheel covers are used as replacements for wire wheel covers originally sold by automobile manufactur- ers with a new automobile and are generally cheaper than original equipment manufacturer's (OEM) wire wheel covers.

. . . Although the parties each offer their own version of the issues presented on appeal, they can all be consolidated and summarized by the general inquiry as to whether the Lanham Act, 15 U.S.C. § 1125(a), affords any basis for relief under the facts presented here.

Section 43(a) of the Lanham Act, which governs plaintiff's claim, provides in pertinent part:

§ 1125. False designations of origin and false descriptions forbidden

(a) Any person who shall affix, apply, or annex, or use in connection with any goods or services, or any container or containers for goods, a false designation of origin, or any false description or representation, including words or other symbols tending falsely to describe or represent the same, and shall cause such goods or services to enter into commerce, and any person who shall with knowledge of the falsity of such designation of origin or description or representation cause or procure the same to be transported or used in commerce or deliver the same to any carrier to be transported or used, shall be liable to a civil action by any person doing business in the locality falsely indicated as that of origin or in the region in which said locality is situated, or by any person who believes that he is or is likely to be damaged by the use of any such false description or representation.

Based upon this section of the Lanham Act, it is plaintiff's contentions that its wheel hub with its heptagonal configuration is distinctive and that defendant's use of a photograph of this wheel cover constitutes either a false designation of origin or a false representation. Although the statutory language of § 43(a) is brief and seemingly unambiguous, judicial gloss of considerable significance has been placed on this section.

Section 43(a) contains two separate prohibitions: one against false designation of origin and one against false representation or description. In false designation of origin cases, a plaintiff can only succeed in an action for money damages if he can show that the product features allegedly copied are nonfunctional *and* have acquired secondary meaning in the market place. Vibrant Sales Inc. v. New Body Boutique, Inc., 652 F.2d 299 (2nd Cir.1981), cert. denied, 455 U.S. 909, 102 S.Ct. 1257, 71 L.Ed.2d 448 (1982). Although plaintiff's seven-sided wheel hub is nonfunctional, as a brand new product it has acquired no secondary meaning. Consequently, plaintiff has no Lanham Act action for false designation of origin. Plaintiff is thus left with its false representation or false description argument.

It is not open to question that "one who uses a photograph of his competitor's unpatented and untrademarked product to advertise his own wares *may* be guilty of false representation if the product pictured is not identical to one he is prepared to deliver." *Vibrant*, 652 F.2d at 304 (emphasis added). In stating this proposition of law the *Vibrant* court cited to what they referred to as the "seminal decision" in

L'Aiglon Apparel, Inc. v. Lana Lobell, Inc., 214 F.2d 649 (3rd Cir.1954). In L'Aiglon, the court summarized the operative facts as follows:

> The present complaint alleges that plaintiff created and alone sold to the retail trade throughout the country a certain distinctively styled dress. To advertise this dress plaintiff published pictures of it, together with its price, $17.95, in advertisements in leading newspapers and in some two million individual mailing pieces distributed through retailers. In this way the picture and price of this dress became associated in the minds of many readers and identified as plaintiff's $17.95 dress.
>
> It is further alleged that, at about the same time, defendant was offering for sale through mail order and otherwise in interstate commerce a dress which in fact was much inferior to plaintiff's in quality and notably different in appearance. In this connection defendant published under its name in a magazine of national circulation a display advertisement worded and designed to promote the mail order sale of its dress at a stated price of $6.95, but showing as the most prominent feature of the advertisement an actual photographic reproduction of plaintiff's dress, thus fraudulently represented as the article defendant was selling for $6.95.

Id. at 650.

The difference between the egregriousness of the *L'Aiglon* facts and those presented here can only be characterized as global. Unlike the plaintiff in *L'Aiglon,* Can–Am had no market identity for anyone to trade on. Second, the product being offered by Henderson was General Motor's OEM wheel covers which are of equal if not greater quality than the after-market product of Can–Am. It simply defies logic and reason to suggest that one would try to market an established product like a GM wheel cover by depicting a product no one knew or had ever heard of. The whole purpose of the Henderson flyer was to let prospective purchasers know that there was an attractive sale price on an established product. It would have been counter-productive to display a different product not generally known.

Last, and perhaps most important, is that we are dealing here with the aftermath of a mistake in judgment and a short-cut taken by the advertising director of Henderson. We are *not* dealing with any attempted misappropriation of the product or goodwill of a competitor. Henderson wanted a picture to dress up its ad and Can–Am's photo which gave the feeling of wheel covers in motion apparently filled the bill. Plaintiff confuses the intentional use of the photo with the kind of intent to misrepresent which is the cornerstone of a money damage action. We note in this regard the swift and effective remedial action Henderson undertook immediately upon being notified of its error. Under such circumstances we find no false representation which is actionable under the Lanham Act.

Since the district court found no liability it did not consider the issue of damages. Contrary to plaintiff's assertion, however, it did make a damage finding when it concluded that since there was no evidence to prove "that the public was actually deceived" there could be no damages. We would add to this finding of the district court by indicating that "a plaintiff who establishes false advertising in violation of § 43(a) of the Lanham Act will be entitled to only such damages as were caused by the violation." Burndy Corp. v. Teledyne Industries, Inc., 748 F.2d 767, 771 (2nd Cir.1984). "Although a court may engage in some degree of speculation in computing the *amount* of damages . . . causation must first be established." Id. at 771.

Plaintiff's product was so new that it had no meaningful sales records to indicate it had been damaged by the action of Henderson. Although Can–Am attempted to show one or two slow months contemporaneous with the release of the Henderson flyer, this may well be due to GM's OEM product being offered at an attractive price in competition with Can–Am's after-market product. If anything, Can–Am received more free publicity for its new product out of this whole episode than anything they had done on their own prior to this time.

IV.

Can–Am raises a number of other issues relating to secondary meaning, some of which ask this court to extend Lanham Act jurisdiction into new areas. Since we find no Lanham Act coverage on these specific facts we find it unnecessary to consider these other arguments. We note in passing, however, that were we inclined to consider blazing new Lanham Act trails we certainly would not use this fragile fact situation as a vehicle.

Although we find this to be ill-conceived "pound of flesh" litigation, we do note that Can–Am does have one legitimate complaint. Henderson did use one of Can–Am's photos which Can–Am had spent good money on developing. We pass no judgment on whether there is some other cause of action, state or federal, of which plaintiff may avail itself in this regard. We limit our holding here to finding, as did the district court, no cause of action under the Lanham Act for these facts.

AFFIRMED.

JOHNSON & JOHNSON v. CARTER–WALLACE, INC.

United States Court of Appeals, Second Circuit, 1980.
631 F.2d 186, 208 U.S.P.Q. 169.

MANSFIELD, Circuit Judge.

Johnson & Johnson ("Johnson"), manufacturer of Johnson's Baby Oil and Johnson's Baby Lotion, appeals from a judgment of the United States District Court for the Southern District of New York, entered by Judge Constance Baker Motley, dismissing at the end of the plaintiff's case during a non-jury trial its suit for injunctive relief brought under § 43(a) of the Lanham Act, 15 U.S.C. § 1125(a), against Carter–Wallace ("Carter"), the manufacturer of NAIR, a leading depilatory product. Because we believe Johnson's showing on the required elements of its false advertising claim was sufficient to withstand a motion to dismiss, we reverse and remand for further proceedings.

Johnson's claim arises out of Carter's use of baby oil in NAIR and its advertising campaign regarding that inclusion. In 1977, Carter added baby oil to its NAIR lotion and initiated a successful advertising campaign emphasizing this fact. NAIR is sold in a pink plastic bottle with the word "NAIR" written in large, pink letters. A bright turquoise-blue banner, open at both ends, contains the words "with baby oil." In addition to its packaging of NAIR, Carter's television advertisements emphasize that NAIR contains baby oil.

Alleging (1) that Carter is making false claims for NAIR with baby oil and (2) that it is packaging and advertising NAIR so as to give consumers the false impression that NAIR is a Johnson & Johnson product, plaintiff filed the instant suit for injunctive relief under § 43(a) of the Lanham Act, 15 U.S.C. § 1125(a), and under New York's common law of unfair competition. Section 43(a) of the Lanham Act provides for two separate causes of action: one is for "false designation of origin," the other for a "false description or representation, including words or symbols tending falsely to describe or represent" the product. Johnson's false representation claim alleges that Carter's "NAIR with baby oil" campaign falsely represents to consumers that the baby oil in NAIR has moisturizing and softening effect on the skin of the user. While recognizing that Carter's advertising makes no explicit claims for its product, Johnson alleges that this claim is implicit in the manner in which NAIR has been marketed. It contends that these false claims have unfairly dissuaded consumers from using its products in favor of NAIR with baby oil.

Johnson's application for a temporary restraining order was denied by the district court, as was its motion for a preliminary injunction. The motion for a preliminary injunction was denied in an unreported memorandum order dated August 15, 1979, in which the district court found that plaintiff had failed to make the requisite showing for either its false designation of origin claim or its false advertising claim.

The bench trial of the suit was conducted from March 31, 1980 to April 7, 1980. Pursuant to Rule 65(a) of the Federal Rules of Civil Procedure, the parties relied upon previous testimony and evidence presented at the preliminary injunction hearing. Although plaintiff offered no new evidence on its false designation of origin claim, it did present new testimony and evidence on the false advertising claim. At the close of plaintiff's case, the trial court granted defendant's motion to dismiss the action. Plaintiff appeals from the dismissal of its false advertising claim under § 43(a). The propriety of the dismissal of its false designation of origin claim is not raised on appeal.

In dismissing Johnson's false advertising claim, the trial court did not reach either the question of whether Carter advertises or implies in its advertising that baby oil as an ingredient in NAIR has a moisturizing and softening effect, or the issue of whether such a claim is false. Instead, its dismissal was "granted on the ground that [Johnson] failed

to carry its burden of proving damage or the likelihood of damage."
Just what that burden is and what evidence will satisfy it, are the
central issues in this appeal.

Discussion

Prior to the enactment of § 43(a) of the Lanham Act, false advertising claims were governed by the common law of trade disparagement.
Under the common law, liability was generally confined to "palming-
off" cases where the deceit related to the origin of the product. In
these cases the offending product was foisted upon an unwary consumer
by deceiving him into the belief that he was buying the plaintiff's
product (normally an item with a reputation for quality). Other
instances of false advertising were safe from actions by competitors due
to the difficulty of satisfying the requirement of proof of actual damage
caused by the false claims. In an open market it is normally impossible
to prove that a customer, who was induced by the defendant through
the use of false claims to purchase the product, would have bought from
the plaintiff if the defendant had been truthful.

The passage of § 43(a) represented a departure from the common
law action for trade disparagement and from the need to prove actual
damages as a prerequisite for injunctive relief. This departure marked
the creation of a "new statutory tort" intended to secure a market-place
free from deceitful marketing practices. L'Aiglon Apparel v. Lana
Lobell, Inc., 214 F.2d 649, 651, 102 USPQ 94, 96 (3d Cir.1954). The new
tort, as subsequently interpreted by the courts, differs from the common law action for trade disparagement in two important respects: (1)
it does not require proof of intent to deceive, and (2) it entitles a broad
range of commercial parties to relief.

The broadening of the scope of liability results from a provision in
§ 43(a) allowing suit to be brought "by any person who believes that he
is or is likely to be damaged by the use of any false description or
representation." 15 U.S.C. § 1125(a). Whether this clause is viewed as
a matter of standing to sue, or as an element of the substantive claim
for relief, certain bounds are well established. On the one hand,
despite the use of the word "believes," something more than a plaintiff's mere subjective belief that he is injured or likely to be damaged is
required before he will be entitled even to injunctive relief. On the
other hand, as the district court in this case recognized, a plaintiff
seeking an injunction, as opposed to money damages, need not quantify
the losses actually borne. What showing of damage in between those
two extremes will satisfy the statute is the subject of the instant
dispute.

Johnson claims, in effect, that once it is shown that the plaintiff's
and the defendant's products compete in a relevant market and that
the defendant's ads are false, a likelihood of damage sufficient to satisfy
the statute should be *presumed* and an injunction should issue "as a

matter of course." [3] The district court, in contrast, drew the line as follows: "Of course, J&J [Johnson] need not quantify its injury in order to obtain injunctive relief. But J&J must at least prove the existence of some injury caused by Carter." The court had said that "J&J has failed to prove that its loss of sales was in any way *caused* by NAIR's allegedly false advertising."

Both the case law and the policy behind § 43(a) indicate that the district court's construction of the statute placed too high a burden on the plaintiff in this case. To require a plaintiff to "prove the existence of some injury caused by" the defendant, is to demand proof of actual loss and specific evidence of causation. Perhaps a competitor in an open market could meet this standard with proof short of quantified sales loss, but it is not required to do so. The statute demands only proof providing a reasonable basis for the belief that the plaintiff is likely to be damaged as a result of the false advertising. The correct standard is whether it is likely that Carter's advertising has caused or will cause a loss of Johnson sales, not whether Johnson has come forward with specific evidence that Carter's ads actually resulted in some definite loss of sales. Contrary to Johnson's argument, however, the likelihood of injury and causation will not be presumed, but must be demonstrated. If such a showing is made, the plaintiff will have established a reasonable belief that he is likely to be damaged within the meaning of § 43(a) and will be entitled to injunctive relief, as distinguished from damages, which would require more proof. We believe that the evidence offered by Johnson, though not overwhelming, is sufficient to prove a likelihood of damage from loss of sales.

Initially, we find that Johnson has shown that it and Carter are competitors in a relevant market. Although Johnson's Baby Oil and Lotion do not compete with NAIR in the narrower depilatory market, they do compete in the broader hair removal market. NAIR is used for hair removal by depilation. Johnson's Baby Lotion has been promoted as a substitute for shaving cream and is used for removal of hair by shaving. Also, both of Johnson's products are used as skin moisturizers after shaving or after the use of depilatories. Such indirect competitors may avail themselves of the protection of § 43(a); the competition need not be direct. Moreover, Carter's advertising campaign itself, by its emphasis on baby oil, directly links the depilation and the moisturizer markets. Johnson's stake in the shaving market gives it a "reasonable interest to be protected against the alleged false advertising." 1 R. Callman, Unfair Competition, Trademarks and Monopolies, § 18.2(b) at 625 (3rd ed. 1967).

To prove a likelihood of injury Johnson must also show a logical causal connection between the alleged false advertising and its own sales position. This it has done with specific evidence. It has shown that large numbers of consumers in fact use its baby lotion for shaving

---

3. Specially, Johnson alleges that it has suffered a loss in sales of Baby Lotion and Baby Oil and also a tarnishment of the reputation of these products due to Carter's alleged false advertising. The district court rejected Johnson's tarnishment theory of damage and we believe that this rejection was not clearly erroneous.

and its baby oil as an after-shave and after-depilation moisturizer. Carter's "NAIR with baby oil" campaign affects both markets. First, NAIR's share of the hair removal market has increased since its baby oil advertising began. For each new depilatory user, a corresponding decline in the use of shaving products such as oils and lotions appears probable. Second, the use of baby oil after depilation is likely to be reduced if, as Johnson contends, Carter's advertising conveys to consumers the idea that NAIR's baby oil has a moisturizing and softening effect and leads the consumer to believe that use of a second, post-depilation, moisturizer is unnecessary. Of course, if Carter's ads are truthful, then its gains at Johnson's expense are well earned. If false, however, the damage to Johnson is unfair.

Johnson's case is supported by more than just the above logic. First, sales of its baby oil have in fact declined. Second, a consumer witness testified at trial that she switched from use of baby oil by shaving to NAIR because it was advertised as containing baby oil. Third, Johnson introduced surveys indicating that some people, after viewing NAIR ads, thought they would not have to use baby oil if they used NAIR. Together, Johnson's evidence was enough to prove a likelihood of competitive injury resulting from the NAIR advertising.

That much of the decline in Johnson's Baby Oil sales may be due to competition from lower priced baby oils, does not save Carter. In Donsco Inc. v. Casper Corp., 587 F.2d 602, 607, 199 USPQ 705, 708–709 (3d Cir.1978), for example, the court found that "the decline in Donsco's [the plaintiff's] sales is largely attributable to increased competition from lower-priced competitors and to Donsco's slow delivery of its [product]." Although it refused to award damages, it upheld the grant of an injunction. Further, the possibility that the total pecuniary harm to Johnson might be relatively slight does not bar injunctive relief.

Finally, Johnson's inability to point to a definite amount of sales lost *to Carter* (a failure which would bar monetary relief) does not preclude injunctive relief. Likelihood of competitive injury sufficient to warrant a § 43(a) injunction has been found in the absence of proof of actual sales diversion in numerous cases. See American Home Products Corp. v. Johnson & Johnson, 436 F.Supp. 785, 196 USPQ 484 (S.D. N.Y.1977), affd., 577 F.2d 160, 198 USPQ 132 (2d Cir.1978); Quabaug Rubber Co. v. Fabiano Shoe Co., Inc., 567 F.2d 154, 15 USPQ 689 (1st Cir.1977); Potato Chip Institute, supra; Parkway Baking Co., supra; American Brands, Inc. v. R.J. Reynolds Tobacco Co., 413 F.Supp. 1352 (S.D.N.Y.1976); Ames Publishing Co., supra; Mutation Mink Breeders Assn. v. Lou Nierenberg Corp., 23 F.R.D. 155, 120 USPQ 270 (S.D.N.Y. 1959). Although the overall likelihood of harm to the plaintiff from the defendant's ads in some of these cases was perhaps greater than here, e.g., American Home Products Corp., supra (defendant's false advertising disparaged plaintiff's product); Quabaug Rubber Co., supra ("palming off" of shoe soles by defendant to create impression they were made by plaintiff); American Brands, Inc., supra (suit by cigarette manufacturer based on defendant's claim that its cigarettes had "the lowest tar of all cigarettes"), there was little or even no evidence of all actual sales losses to the defendant. Moreover, in other of the above cases granting injunctive relief despite the absence of proof of any specific loss attributable to the false advertising, the likelihood of damage was no greater than it is in this case. See, e.g., Ames Publishing Co., supra, 372 F.Supp. at 12, 182 USPQ at 53; Potato Chip Institute, supra, 333 F.Supp. at 179, 171 USPQ at 542–543; Mutation Mink, supra, 23 F.R.D. at 161, 120 USPQ at 272–273 ("The plaintiffs did not monopolize the industry and proof of actual diversion of trade was, therefore, in all practical respects, impossible. * * * [T]he 'likely to be damaged' provision of § 43(a) obviates the necessity of proving actual diversion of trade.")

Neither Mutation Mink nor Potato Chip Institute can be discounted as "palming-off" cases. The advertising claims made by the defendants in those two cases tended to create the impression that their products were either genuine mink or genuine potato chips, respectively. But these are both generic terms. False generic description of a product is very different from a false designation of origin which trades on a particular competitor's goodwill, as in Quabaug Rubber. Conveying a false impression that the product is a certain generic item is no more likely to divert trade than conveying a false impression that additional use of a generic product is unnecessary. The latter deceit is the type alleged by Johnson.

Sound policy reasons exist for not requiring proof of actual loss as a prerequisite to § 43(a) injunctive relief. Failure to prove actual damages in an injunction suit, as distinguished from an action for damages, poses no likelihood of a windfall for the plaintiff. The complaining competitor gains no more than that to which it is already entitled—a market free of false advertising.

While proof of actual diversion of sales is not required for a § 43(a) injunction to issue, proof that the advertising complained of is in fact false is essential. This issue, though briefed by parties in this case, is not before the court at this time. The district court did not reach the question for purposes of determining whether permanent relief should issue. Since the action was dismissed at the close of the plaintiff's case, Carter was afforded no opportunity to introduce additional evidence answering the plaintiff on this point. Johnson, having shown that it is likely to be damaged by Carter's advertising, must prove that the NAIR advertising was false before being entitled to injunctive relief under the Lanham Act. Should the district court find that the defendant's advertising conveys a false message, irreparable injury for the purpose of injunctive relief would be present for the very reason that in an open market it is impossible to measure the exact amount of Johnson's damages.

Accordingly, this cause is reversed and remanded for further proceedings in conformity with this opinion. We retain jurisdiction.

NOTES

1. For several years after its enactment, courts applied section 43(a) sparingly. Not until 1954 did a court authoritatively declare that section 43(a) created a federal cause of action against misrepresentations about product quality. L'Aiglon Apparel, Inc. v. Lana Lobell, Inc., 214 F.2d 649, 102 U.S.P.Q. 94 (3d Cir.1954). The Lanham Act had been law for a decade before a federal circuit court suggested that section 43(a) also proscribed common law trademark violations. Joshua Meier Co. v. Albany Novelty Mfg. Co., 236 F.2d 144, 111 U.S.P.Q. 197 (2d Cir. 1956). Subsequently, Federal–Mogul–Bower Bearings, Inc. v. Azoff, 313 F.2d 405, 136 U.S.P.Q. 500 (6th Cir.1963), held that section 43(a) encompassed common law passing off. The 1988 amendments to the Lanham Act clarified section 43(a)'s embrace of actions for misrepresentation, common law trademark infringement and passing off.

For the view that Congress did not originally intend section 43(a) to cover common law trademark infringement and passing off, see Germain, Unfair Trade Practices Under Section 43(a) of the Lanham Act: You've Come A Long Way, Baby—Too Far, Maybe?, 49 Ind.L.J. 84, 109–112 (1973). See generally, Bauer, A Federal Law of Unfair Competition: What Should be the Reach of Section 43(a) of the Lanham Act?, 31 UCLA L.Rev. 671 (1984). On the impact of the 1988 Trademark Law Revision Act on section 43(a), see Driscoll, The "New" 43(a), 79 Trademark Rep. 238 (1989).

2. *Defendant Misrepresents Quality of Its Own Goods or Services.* Early cases under section 43(a) involved defendants' blatant misrepresentations about the quality of their goods. See, e.g., Crossbow, Inc. v. Dan–Dee Imports, Inc., 266 F.Supp. 335, 153 U.S.P.Q. 163 (S.D.N.Y. 1967) (defendant liable for removing plaintiff's trademark and other identifying insignia from plaintiff's product, replacing them with its own, and using the mislabeled product as a demonstration model for its own inferior imitation); Mutation Mink Breeders Ass'n v. Lou Nierenberg Corp., 23 F.R.D. 155, 120 U.S.P.Q. 270 (S.D.N.Y.1959) (defendant enjoined from using the word "mink" on its "fake-fur" fabrics); Consumers Union of U.S., Inc. v. Theodore Hamm Brewing Co., 314 F.Supp. 697, 166 U.S.P.Q. 48 (D.C.Conn.1970) (defendant enjoined from misrepresenting the rating its product had received from the Consumers Union).

More recent cases have tested section 43(a)'s capacity to control subtler misrepresentations, most notably in connection with artists' contributions to sound recordings and motion pictures. See, e.g., Smith v. Montoro, 648 F.2d 602, 221 U.S.P.Q. 775 (9th Cir.1981) (film distributor's removal of actor's name from film credits and substitution of name of another actor constituted "express reverse passing off"—the mislabelling of plaintiff's product as defendant's); Lamothe v. Atlantic Recording Corp., 847 F.2d 1403, 7 U.S.P.Q.2d 1249 (9th Cir.1988) (section 43(a) provides relief to co-authors whose names have been omitted from record album and sheet music of co-authored compositions).

3. *Defendant Misrepresents Quality of Plaintiff's Goods or Services.* Before the 1988 amendments to the Lanham Act, disparagement was not actionable under section 43(a) because it misrepresented the quality of plaintiff's product, not defendant's. See Bernard Food Industries v. Dietene Co., 415 F.2d 1279, 163 U.S.P.Q. 264 (7th Cir.1969), cert. denied, 397 U.S. 912, 90 S.Ct. 911, 25 L.Ed.2d 92, 164 U.S.P.Q. 481 (1970). If, however, the criticism of plaintiff's product falsely implied that the defendant's product was better, an action could lie. See American Home Products Corp. v. Johnson & Johnson, 577 F.2d 160, 198 U.S.P.Q. 132 (2d Cir.1978).

Several courts chafed under this limitation. Recognizing its obligation to follow *Dietene* as the law in its circuit, one district court observed that "it would seem that in comparison advertising, a false statement by the defendant about plaintiff's product would have the same detrimental effect as a false statement about defendant's product. I.e., it would tend to mislead the buying public concerning the relative merits and qualities of the products, thereby inducing the purchase of a possibly inferior product." Skil Corp. v. Rockwell Int'l Corp., 375 F.Supp. 777, 782 n. 10, 183 U.S.P.Q. 157 (N.D.Ill.1974).

The 1988 amendments to the Lanham Act made disparagement actionable under section 43(a). As amended, section 43(a) imposes liability on any person who uses a "false or misleading description of fact, or false or misleading representation of fact, which . . . (2) in commercial advertising or promotion, misrepresents the nature, characteristics, qualities, or geographic origin of his or her *or another person's* goods, services, or commercial activities." (Emphasis added.) According to Senator DeConcini, Congress intended the requirement that the misrepresentation be made in "commercial advertising or promotion" to "eliminate any possibility that the section might be applied to political speech." 134 Cong.Rec. S 16,973 (daily ed. Oct. 20, 1988). In Congressman Kastenmeier's view, "consumer reporting, editorial comment, political advertising, and other constitutionally protected material is not covered by this provision." 134 Cong.Rec. H 10419 (daily ed. Oct. 19, 1988).

4. *Passing Off.* Section 43(a) has not only federalized the common law tort of passing off; it has also expanded the tort's reach beyond traditional common law doctrine. The most prominent area of expansion is trade dress simulation. See, for example, Fuddruckers, Inc. v. Doc's B.R. Others, Inc., 826 F.2d 837, 4 U.S.P.Q.2d 1026 (9th Cir.1987), holding that a restaurant's decor, layout and style of service could constitute protectible trade dress under section 43(a), entitling plaintiff to protection against a restaurant simulating its protected ambience.

Hartford House, Ltd. v. Hallmark Cards, Inc., 846 F.2d 1268, 6 U.S. P.Q.2d 2038 (10th Cir.1988), cert. denied, 109 S.Ct. 260, 102 L.Ed.2d 248, holding that plaintiff was entitled to protection against defendant's imitation of its greeting cards, may be a high watermark for trade dress protection under section 43(a). The protected trade dress embodied, among other elements, a two-fold card containing poetry on the first and third pages, a deckle edge on the right side of the first page, a rough-edge stripe of color on the outside of the deckle edge of the first page, hand-lettered calligraphy with the first letter of the words often enlarged, and an illustration that wrapped around the card and spread over three pages, including the back of the card.

The problem in *Hartford House* was that the claimed trade dress in fact constituted the product itself and was, in that limited sense, "functional." Nonetheless, the court held that the district court's fact findings were not clearly erroneous: " '[a]n emotional non-occasion greeting card can be folded, colored, shaped, cut, edged, and designed in infinite ways and still function to send its message.' In light of the available alternatives, the district court further concluded that allowing Blue Mountain to exclude others from using its trade dress 'will not hinder competition nor will it interfere with the rights of others to compete.' Consequently, the district court found that the overall appearance, i.e., trade dress, of Blue Mountain's cards was nonfunctional. In the district court's words: 'Paper, verse and ink are functional features of a greeting card. The design and amalgamation of those features in a uniform fashion with other features, however, has produced the non-functional Blue Mountain "look".' " 846 F.2d at 1274.

Section 43(a)'s expanded protection against trade dress imitation and product simulation came at a time when courts, under the preemptive compulsion of *Sears* and *Compco,* pages 103, 107, above, and Copyright Act section 301, section 759, below, were trimming back state unfair competition law in the area. Because *Sears* and *Compco* were decided under the Constitution's Supremacy Clause, they do not control federal law unfair competition actions. Section 301(d) expressly excludes federal laws from the Copyright Act's preemptive thrust.

Section 43(a)'s role in protecting industrial design is considered beginning at page 895, below.

5. Courts will not find in section 43(a) a salve for every conceivable competitive injury. In Societe Comptoir De L'Industrie Cotonniere Etablissements Boussac v. Alexander's Dept. Stores, 299 F.2d 33, 132 U.S.P.Q. 475 (2d Cir.1962), the Second Circuit Court of Appeals held that defendant should not be enjoined from truthfully advertising that its inexpensive dresses were copies of original Dior designs. "The Lanham Act does not prohibit a commercial rival's truthfully denominating his goods a copy of a design in the public domain, though he uses the name of the designer to do so." 299 F.2d 33, 36. Section 43(a) also gave the Girl Scouts of America no aid in its attempt to enjoin the distribution of a poster depicting "a smiling girl dressed in the well-known green uniform of the Junior Girl Scouts, with her hands clasped above her protruding, clearly pregnant abdomen. The caveat 'be prepared' appears next to her hands." With the terse observation that "plaintiff has failed utterly to establish the requisite element of customer confusion," the court dismissed the claim that defendant had violated section 43(a) by using plaintiff's marks and insignia to designate falsely the paternity of its poster. Girl Scouts of the United States of

America v. Personality Posters Mfg. Co., 304 F.Supp. 1228, 1230–1231, 163 U.S.P.Q. 505 (S.D.N.Y.1969).

Alfred Dunhill, Ltd. v. Interstate Cigar Co., Inc., 364 F.Supp. 366, 177 U.S.P.Q. 346 (S.D.N.Y.1973), rev'd, 499 F.2d 232, 183 U.S.P.Q. 193 (2d Cir.1974), raised a more subtle question about section 43(a)'s scope. Does the language "affix, apply, or annex or use" cover acts of omission as well as commission? The lower court answered that it does, and enjoined defendant from distributing damaged tobacco, bearing plaintiff's trademark, purchased from plaintiff's agent at salvage prices. In the court's judgment, "sales of damaged tobacco in tins bearing trademarks associated with high quality tobacco without adequate warnings to customers that the goods are damaged, involve false representations of their quality." 364 F.Supp. 366, 372. The court of appeals reversed, holding that the district court's result "cannot be reached through an interpretation of the statutory language or legislative or judicial history of the Lanham Act." The court also noted that Dunhill's problem was in part of its own making. "If Dunhill had wished to distinguish the salvaged tobacco from that sold through its normal channels of distribution, it should have done so while the allegedly damaged tobacco was still under its control and before it was released into the salvage markets. From the beginning Dunhill was in the best position to effect the relabeling." 499 F.2d 232, 237–238.

6. *Standing.* Courts have read section 43(a)'s prescription, "any person who believes that he is or is likely to be damaged" broadly and have rejected claims that only competitors have standing to sue under the provision. See, e.g., Thorn v. Reliance Van Co., 736 F.2d 929, 222 U.S.P.Q. 775 (3d Cir.1984).

Courts divide on whether consumers have standing to sue under section 43(a). In Colligan v. Activities Club of New York, Ltd., 442 F.2d 686, 170 U.S.P.Q. 113 (2d Cir.1971), cert. denied, 404 U.S. 1004, 92 S.Ct. 559, 30 L.Ed.2d 557, 172 U.S.P.Q. 97, disappointed ski weekenders sought monetary and injunctive relief—the latter on behalf of "all high school students within the New York metropolitan area who are likely to be deceived and thereby injured by defendants' similarly deceptive practices in the future"—against defendant which, they alleged, had deceived and damaged them by "use of false descriptions and representations of the nature, sponsorship, and licensing of their interstate ski tour service." 442 F.2d at 687. The court of appeals affirmed the district court's dismissal of the complaint. "Congress' purpose in enacting section 43(a) was to create a special and limited unfair competition remedy, virtually without regard for the interests of consumers generally and almost certainly without any consideration of consumer rights of action in particular. The Act's purpose, as defined in § 45, is exclusively to protect the interests of a purely commercial class against unscrupulous commercial conduct." 442 F.2d at 692.

Arnesen v. The Raymond Lee Organization, Inc., 333 F.Supp. 116, 172 U.S.P.Q. 1 (C.D.Cal.1971), looked to another part of section 45's statement of purpose and concluded that section 43(a) does give standing to consumers. "The liability clause of section 43(a) is clear on its face; it applies to any person who is or is likely to be damaged. Defendant would have us construe against the plain language of the statute. Since the liability clause also mentions 'any person doing business' it would be plausible to apply the *ejusdem generis* rules and thus construe the subsequent use of the words 'any person' to mean any person doing business or any competitor. If the purpose of the Lanham Act were solely to protect competitors this construction would be sound. However, the plain language of the intent section, 15 U.S.C.A. § 1127, makes actionable, *inter alia,* the deceptive and misleading use of marks and descriptions. Since that same section defines 'persons' as both natural and juristic persons, this Court cannot conclude that competitors were the only persons protected by the Act." 333 F.Supp. at 120. Class action status was later denied. 59 F.R.D. 145, 179 U.S.P.Q. 210 (C.D.Cal.1973).

After some legislative to and fro, Congress, in passing the Trademark Law Revision Act of 1988, left the question of consumer standing unresolved. See Thompson, Consumer Standing Under Section 43(a): More Legislative History, More Confusion, 79 Trademark Rep. 341 (1989).

7. *Remedies.* The original language of Lanham Act section 35, 15 U.S.C.A. § 1117, literally limited recovery of profits, damages, costs and attorney fees to prevailing parties who had registered their marks in the Patent and Trademark Office. Nonetheless, courts generally granted profits, damages and, in some cases, attorney's fees to prevailing plaintiffs under section 43(a). See, e.g., Metric & Multistandard Components Corp. v. Metric's, Inc., 635 F.2d 710, 716, 209 U.S.P.Q. 97 (8th Cir. 1980). Following the recommendations of the Trademark Review Commission, the 1988 amendments to the Lanham Act made damages, profits, attorney's fees, costs and destruction of infringing goods available to prevailing plaintiffs in actions under section 43(a).

II. PATENT LAW

The first known system for awarding patents for inventions in the useful arts dates to Venice in the mid-fifteenth century. The Venetian system, codified into a general patent statute in 1474, sought to spur the introduction of new technologies and industries by awarding patentees the exclusive right to practice their art for a specified period, generally ranging from ten to fifty years. Some patents issued to technologies that had been imported into Venice from other regions and that had been invented by someone other than the individual seeking the patent. Other patented inventions originated with the patentee. Bruce Bugbee writes of a 1460 patent "issued to one Jacobus 'in reward of his pertinent thoughts and labors' as the 'first inventor and builder' of a water-raising mechanism. Evidently a true patent of invention, it carried a term of protection measured by the life of the grantee. Each imitator constructing such a device in Venetian territory without the 'express license' of Jacobus was to be fined 1,000 gold ducats and the infringing machines were to be 'thoroughly destroyed.' " B. Bugbee, Genesis of American Patent and Copyright Law 21 (1967).

Early English patent practice followed the Venetian model, awarding durationally limited monopolies to importers of already established crafts and industries as well as to originators of new devices. The system was generally ratified by the Statute of Monopolies, 21 Jac. 1 c. 3 (1624), probably the major document in the history of English patent law. The Statute, which prohibited monopolies "for the sole buying, selling, making, working, or using of anything within this Realm," was enacted in response to the Crown's overly generous grants of monopolies to court favorites to manufacture such common items as vinegar and starch. The Statute did, however, allow the Crown to grant patents for fourteen years or less "to the true and first inventor or inventors" for "the sole working or making of any manner of new manufactures within this realm" provided "they be not contrary to the law nor mischievous to the state, by raising prices of commodities at home, or hurt of trade, or generally inconvenient."

The American colonies and, after the Revolution, the state legislatures, generally followed England's ad hoc system, awarding patents through private acts passed in response to individual petitions. The first federal patent law, Act of April 10, 1790, ch. 7, 1 Stat. 109–110, was a general, rather than a private act, authorizing patents for "any useful art, manufacture, engine, machine, or device, or any improvement therein not before known or used." Upon a showing that the claimed invention was "sufficiently useful and important," a patent board composed of the Secretary of State, the Secretary of War and the Attorney General was to grant a patent for a term of up to fourteen years. The burden of examining patent applications soon proved too heavy for these busy civil servants, and a new patent law, Act of February 21, 1793, ch. 11, 1 Stat. 318, substituted the simple act of registration for the previous examination system. The new act also eliminated the requirement that the invention be "sufficiently useful and important." The Act of July 4, 1836, ch. 357, 5 Stat. 117, reinstated the examination system and inventiveness requirement and also fixed the patent term at fourteen years with a seven year renewal period.

To the chagrin of many observers today, the 1836 Act continues to provide the basic structure and principles of United States patent law. The Act's last major revision, in the Act of July 19, 1952, 66 Stat. 792, left the basic system virtually unchanged. Congress has, in the years since, significantly amended several features of the 1952 Act.

The Court of Appeals for the Federal Circuit, created by the Federal Courts Improvement Act of 1982, has significantly changed contemporary patent law and practice. Congress created the CAFC to eliminate a persistent disparity in patent law standards among courts of appeals deciding cases coming to them from the district courts in their region. The Act withdrew the patent jurisdiction of the twelve regional courts of appeals and vested exclusive jurisdiction over these appeals in the CAFC. The CAFC has not only eliminated intramural conflict and forum shopping. The court has also buttressed the patent grant itself, giving new force to the statutory presumption of validity, easing the standards of patentability and strengthening the procedural and remedial relief available to patent owners. The jurisdiction of the CAFC is discussed at pages 198 to 199, above.

B. Bugbee, Genesis of American Patent and Copyright Law (1967) thoughtfully chronicles the history of United States patent, as well as copyright, law from its early European roots. Summary reviews of the English and American history appear in a special number of the Journal of the Patent Office Society celebrating the centennial of the 1836 Act, 18 J.P.O.S. No. 7 (1936), and in American Bar Association, Two–Hundred Years of English and American Patent, Trademark and Copyright Law, 3, 21 (1976). Developments since 1952 are closely reviewed in Scott & Unkovic, Patent Law Reform: A Legislative Perspective of an Extended Gestation, 16 Wm. & Mary L.Rev. 937 (1975).

Professor Donald Chisum's fine work, Patents (1989), is the leading treatise. R. Harmon, Patents and the Federal Circuit (1988); E. Lipscomb, Walker on Patents (1984); and P. Rosenberg, Patent Law Fundamentals (1989), are also valuable. The American Intellectual Property Law Association Quarterly Journal and the Journal of the Patent and Trademark Office Society regularly publish topical papers.

A. REQUIREMENTS FOR PROTECTION

---

1. STATUTORY STANDARDS

See Statute Supplement 35 U.S.C.A. §§ 100–104, 111, 112, 116–118; 256.

a. SECTION 103: NONOBVIOUSNESS

GRAHAM v. JOHN DEERE CO.

Supreme Court of the United States, 1966.
383 U.S. 1, 86 S.Ct. 684, 15 L.Ed.2d 545, 148 U.S.P.Q. 459.

Mr. Justice CLARK delivered the opinion of the Court.

After a lapse of 15 years, the Court again focuses its attention on the patentability of inventions under the standard of Art. I, § 8, cl. 8, of the Constitution and under the conditions prescribed by the laws of the United States. Since our last expression on patent validity, A. & P. Tea Co. v. Supermarket Corp., 340 U.S. 147, 71 S.Ct. 127, 95 L.Ed. 162 (1950), the Congress has for the first time expressly added a third statutory dimension to the two requirements of novelty and utility that had been the sole statutory test since the Patent Act of 1793. This is the test of obviousness, i.e., whether "the subject matter sought to be patented and the prior art are such that the subject matter as a whole would have been obvious at the time the invention was made to a person having ordinary skill in the art to which said subject matter pertains. Patentability shall not be negatived by the manner in which the invention was made." § 103 of the Patent Act of 1952, 35 U.S.C.A. § 103.

The questions, involved in each of the companion cases before us, are what effect the 1952 Act had upon traditional statutory and judicial tests of patentability and what definitive tests are now required. We have concluded that the 1952 Act was intended to codify judicial precedents embracing the principle long ago announced by this Court in Hotchkiss v. Greenwood, 52 U.S. (11 How.) 248, 13 L.Ed. 683 (1851), and that, while the clear language of § 103 places emphasis on an inquiry into obviousness, the general level of innovation necessary to sustain patentability remains the same. . . .

II.

At the outset it must be remembered that the federal patent power stems from a specific constitutional provision which authorizes the Congress "To promote the Progress of . . . useful Arts, by securing for limited Times to . . . Inventors the exclusive Right to their . . . Discoveries." Art. I, § 8, cl. 8. The clause is both a grant of power and a limitation. This qualified authority, unlike the power often exercised in the sixteenth and seventeenth centuries by the English Crown, is limited to the promotion of advances in the "useful arts." It was written against the backdrop of the practices—eventually curtailed by the Statute of Monopolies—of the Crown in granting monopolies to court favorites in goods or businesses which had long before been enjoyed by the public. The Congress in the exercise of the patent power may not overreach the restraints imposed by the stated constitutional purpose. Nor may it enlarge the patent monopoly without regard to the innovation, advancement or social benefit gained thereby.

Moreover, Congress may not authorize the issuance of patents whose effects are to remove existent knowledge from the public domain, or to restrict free access to materials already available. Innovation, advancement, and things which add to the sum of useful knowledge are inherent requisites in a patent system which by constitutional command must "promote the Progress of . . . useful Arts." This is the *standard* expressed in the Constitution and it may not be ignored. And it is in this light that patent validity "requires reference to a standard written into the Constitution." A. & P. Tea Co. v. Supermarket Corp., *supra*, at 154 (concurring opinion).

Within the limits of the constitutional grant, the Congress may, of course, implement the stated purpose of the Framers by selecting the policy which in its judgment best effectuates the constitutional aim. This is but a corollary to the grant to Congress of any Article I power. Within the scope established by the Constitution, Congress may set out conditions and tests for patentability. It is the duty of the Commissioner of Patents and of the courts in the administration of the patent system to give effect to the constitutional standard by appropriate application, in each case, of the statutory scheme of the Congress.

Congress quickly responded to the bidding of the Constitution by enacting the Patent Act of 1790 during the second session of the First Congress. It created an agency in the Department of State headed by the Secretary of State, the Secretary of the Department of War and the Attorney General, any two of whom could issue a patent for a period not exceeding 14 years to any petitioner that "hath . . . invented or discovered any useful art, manufacture, . . . or device, or any improvement therein not before known or used" if the board found that "the invention or discovery [was] sufficiently useful and important. . . ." 1 Stat. 110. This group, whose members administered the patent system along with their other public duties, was known by its own designation as "Commissioners for the Promotion of Useful Arts."

Thomas Jefferson, who as Secretary of State was a member of the group, was its moving spirit and might well be called the "first administrator of our patent system." See Federico, Operation of the Patent Act of 1790, 18 J.Pat.Off.Soc. 237, 238 (1936). He was not only an administrator of the patent system under the 1790 Act, but was also the author of the 1793 Patent Act. In addition, Jefferson was himself an inventor of great note. His unpatented improvements on plows, to mention but one line of his inventions, won acclaim and recognition on both sides of the Atlantic. Because of his active interest and influence in the early development of the patent system, Jefferson's views on the general nature of the limited patent monopoly under the Constitution, as well as his conclusions as to conditions for patentability under the statutory scheme, are worthy of note.

Jefferson, like other Americans, had an instinctive aversion to monopolies. It was a monopoly on tea that sparked the Revolution and Jefferson certainly did not favor an equivalent form of monopoly under the new government. His abhorrence of monopoly extended initially to patents as well. From France, he wrote to Madison (July 1788) urging a Bill of Rights provision restricting monopoly, and as against the argument that limited monopoly might serve to incite "ingenuity," he argued forcefully that "the benefit even of limited monopolies is too doubtful to be opposed to that of their general suppression," V Writings of Thomas Jefferson, at 47 (Ford ed., 1895).

His views ripened, however, and in another letter to Madison (Aug. 1789) after the drafting of the Bill of Rights, Jefferson stated that he would have been pleased by an express provision in this form:

> "Art 9. Monopolies may be allowed to persons for their own productions in literature & their own inventions in the arts, for a term not exceeding _____ years but for no longer term & no other purpose." Id., at 113.

. . . He rejected a natural-rights theory in intellectual property rights and clearly recognized the social and economic rationale of the patent system. The patent monopoly was not designed to secure to the inventor his natural right in his discoveries. Rather, it was a reward, an inducement, to bring forth new knowledge. The grant of an exclusive right to an invention was the creation of society—at odds with the inherent free nature of disclosed ideas—and was not to be freely given. Only inventions and discoveries which furthered human knowledge, and were new and useful, justified the special inducement of a limited private monopoly. Jefferson did not believe in granting patents for small details, obvious improvements, or frivolous devices. His writings evidence his insistence upon a high level of patentability.

As a member of the patent board for several years, Jefferson saw clearly the difficulty in "drawing a line between the things which are worth to the public the embarrassment of an exclusive patent, and those which are not." The board on which he served sought to draw such a line and formulated several rules which are preserved in Jefferson's correspondence. Despite the board's efforts, Jefferson saw "with what slow progress a system of general rules could be matured." Because of the "abundance" of cases and the fact that the investigations occupied "more time of the members of the board than they could spare from higher duties, the whole was turned over to the judiciary, to be matured into a system, under which every one might know when his actions were safe and lawful." . . . . Apparently Congress agreed with Jefferson and the board that the courts should develop additional conditions for patentability. Although the Patent Act was amended, revised or codified some 50 times between 1790 and 1950, Congress steered clear of a statutory set of requirements other than the bare novelty and utility tests reformulated in Jefferson's draft of the 1793 Patent Act.

III.

The difficulty of formulating conditions for patentability was heightened by the generality of the constitutional grant and the statutes implementing it, together with the underlying policy of the patent system that "the things which are worth to the public the embarrassment of an exclusive patent," as Jefferson put it, must outweigh the restrictive effect of the limited patent monopoly. The inherent problem was to develop some means of weeding out those inventions which would not be disclosed or devised but for the inducement of a patent.

This Court formulated a general condition of patentability in 1851 in Hotchkiss v. Greenwood, 11 How. 248. The patent involved a mere substitution of materials—porcelain or clay for wood or metal in doorknobs—and the Court condemned it, holding:

> [U]nless more ingenuity and skill . . . were required . . . than were possessed by an ordinary mechanic acquainted with the business, there was an absence of that degree of skill and ingenuity which constitute essential elements of every invention. In other words, the improvement is the work of the skilful mechanic, not that of the inventor. At p. 267.

Hotchkiss, by positing the condition that a patentable invention evidence more ingenuity and skill than that possessed by an ordinary mechanic acquainted with the business, merely distinguished between new and useful innovations that were capable of sustaining a patent and those that were not. The Hotchkiss test laid the cornerstone of the judicial evolution suggested by Jefferson and left to the courts by Congress. The language in the case, and in those which followed, gave birth to "invention" as a word of legal art signifying patentable inventions. Yet, as this Court has observed, "[t]he truth is the word ['invention'] cannot be defined in such manner as to afford any substantial aid in determining whether a particular device involves an exercise of the inventive faculty or not." McClain v. Ortmayer, 141 U.S. 419, 427, 12 S.Ct. 76, 78, 35 L.Ed. 800 (1891); A. & P. Tea Co. v. Supermarket Corp., supra, at 151. Its use as a label brought about a large variety of opinions as to its meaning both in the Patent Office, in the courts, and at the bar. The Hotchkiss formulation, however, lies not in any label, but in its functional approach to questions of patentability. In practice, Hotchkiss has required a comparison between the subject matter of the patent, or patent application, and the background skill of the calling. It has been from this comparison that patentability was in each case determined.

IV.

The 1952 Patent Act

The Act sets out the conditions of patentability in three sections. An analysis of the structure of these three sections indicates that patentability is dependent upon three explicit conditions: novelty and utility as articulated and defined in § 101 and § 102, and nonobviousness, the new statutory formulation, as set out in § 103. The first two sections, which trace closely the 1874 codification, express the "new and useful" tests which have always existed in the statutory scheme and, for our purposes here, need no clarification. The pivotal section around which the present controversy centers is § 103. It provides:

§ 103. *Conditions for patentability; non-obvious subject matter*

A patent may not be obtained though the invention is not identically disclosed or described as set forth in section 102 of this title, if the differences between the subject matter sought to be patented and the prior art are such that the subject matter as a whole would have been obvious at the time the invention was made to a person having ordinary skill in the art to which said subject matter pertains. Patentability shall not be negatived by the manner in which the invention was made.

The section is cast in relatively unambiguous terms. Patentability is to depend, in addition to novelty and utility, upon the "non-obvious" nature of the "subject matter sought to be patented" to a person having ordinary skill in the pertinent art.

The first sentence of this section is strongly reminiscent of the language in Hotchkiss. Both formulations place emphasis on the pertinent art existing at the time the invention was made and both are implicitly tied to advances in that art. The major distinction is that Congress has emphasized "nonobviousness" as the operative test of the section, rather than the less definite "invention" language of Hotchkiss that Congress thought had led to "a large variety" of expressions in decisions and writings. . . .

It is undisputed that this section was, for the first time, a statutory expression of an additional requirement for patentability, originally expressed in Hotchkiss. It also seems apparent that Congress intended by the last sentence of § 103 to abolish the test it believed this Court announced in the controversial phrase "flash of creative genius," used in Cuno Corp. v. Automatic Devices Corp., 314 U.S. 84, 62 S.Ct. 37, 86 L.Ed. 58 (1941).

It is contended, however, by some of the parties and by several of the *amici* that the first sentence of § 103 was intended to sweep away judicial precedents and to lower the level of patentability. Others contend that the Congress intended to codify the essential purpose reflected in existing judicial precedents—the rejection of insignificant variations and innovations of a commonplace sort—and also to focus inquiries under § 103 upon nonobviousness, rather than upon "invention," as a means of achieving more stability and predictability in determining patentability and validity.

The Reviser's Note to this section, with apparent reference to Hotchkiss, recognizes that judicial requirements as to "lack of patentable novelty [have] been followed since at least as early as 1850." The note indicates that the section was inserted because it "may have some stabilizing effect, and also to serve as a basis for the addition at a later time of some criteria which may be worked out." To this same effect are the reports of both Houses, supra, which state that the first sentence of the section "paraphrases language which has often been used in decisions of the courts, and the section is added to the statute for uniformity and definiteness."

We believe that this legislative history, as well as other sources, shows that the revision was not intended by Congress to change the general level of patentable invention. We conclude that the section was intended merely as a codification of judicial precedents embracing the Hotchkiss condition, with congressional directions that inquiries into the obviousness of the subject matter sought to be patented are a prerequisite to patentability.

V.

Approached in this light, the § 103 additional condition, when followed realistically, will permit a more practical test of patentability. The emphasis on nonobviousness is one of inquiry, not quality, and, as such, comports with the constitutional strictures.

While the ultimate question of patent validity is one of law, the § 103 condition, which is but one of three conditions, each of which must be satisfied, lends itself to several basic factual inquiries. Under § 103, the scope and content of the prior art are to be determined; differences between the prior art and the claims at issue are to be ascertained; and the level of ordinary skill in the pertinent art resolved. Against this background, the obviousness or nonobviousness of the subject matter is determined. Such secondary considerations as commercial success, long felt but unsolved needs, failure of others, etc., might be utilized to give light to the circumstances surrounding the origin of the subject matter sought to be patented. As indicia of obviousness or nonobviousness, these inquiries may have relevancy.

This is not to say, however, that there will not be difficulties in applying the nonobviousness test. What is obvious is not a question upon which there is likely to be uniformity of thought in every given factual context. The difficulties, however, are comparable to those encountered daily by the courts in such frames of reference as negligence and scienter, and should be amenable to a case-by-case development. We believe that strict observance of the requirements laid down here will result in that uniformity and definiteness which Congress called for in the 1952 Act.

While we have focused attention on the appropriate standard to be applied by the courts, it must be remembered that the primary responsibility for sifting out unpatentable material lies in the Patent Office. To await litigation is—for all practical purposes—to debilitate the patent system. We have observed a notorious difference between the standards applied by the Patent Office and by the courts. While many reasons can be adduced to explain the discrepancy, one may well be the free rein often exercised by Examiners in their use of the concept of "invention." In this connection we note that the Patent Office is confronted with a most difficult task. Almost 100,000 applications for patents are filed each year. Of these, about 50,000 are granted and the backlog now runs well over 200,000. 1965 Annual Report of the

Commissioner of Patents 13–14. This is itself a compelling reason for the Commissioner to strictly adhere to the 1952 Act as interpreted here. This would, we believe, not only expedite disposition but bring about a closer concurrence between administrative and judicial precedent.

Although we conclude here that the inquiry which the Patent Office and the courts must make as to patentability must be beamed with greater intensity on the requirements of § 103, it bears repeating that we find no change in the general strictness with which the overall test is to be applied. We have been urged to find in § 103 a relaxed standard, supposedly a congressional reaction to the "increased standard" applied by this Court in its decisions over the last 20 or 30 years. The standard has remained invariable in this Court. Technology, however, has advanced—and with remarkable rapidity in the last 50 years. Moreover, the ambit of applicable art in given fields of science has widened by disciplines unheard of a half century ago. It is but an evenhanded application to require that those persons granted the benefit of a patent monopoly be charged with an awareness of these changed conditions. The same is true of the less technical, but still useful arts. He who seeks to build a better mousetrap today has a long path to tread before reaching the Patent Office.

We now turn to the application of the conditions found necessary for patentability to the cases involved here:

A.   The Patent in Issue in No. 11, Graham v. John Deere Co.

This patent, No. 2,627,798 (hereinafter called the '798 patent) relates to a spring clamp which permits plow shanks to be pushed upward when they hit obstructions in the soil, and then springs the shanks back into normal position when the obstruction is passed over. The device, which we show diagrammatically in the accompanying sketches (Appendix, Fig. 1), is fixed to the plow frame as a unit. The mechanism around which the controversy centers is basically a hinge. The top half of it, known as the upper plate (marked 1 in the sketches), is a heavy metal piece clamped to the plow frame (2) and is stationary relative to the plow frame. The lower half of the hinge, known as the hinge plate (3), is connected to the rear of the upper plate by a hinge pin (4) and rotates downward with respect to it. The shank (5), which is bolted to the forward end of the hinge plate (at 6), runs beneath the plate and parallel to it for about nine inches, passes through a stirrup (7), and then continues backward for several feet curving down toward the ground. The chisel (8), which does the actual plowing, is attached to the rear end of the shank. As the plow frame is pulled forward, the chisel rips through the soil, thereby plowing it. In the normal position, the hinge plate and the shank are kept tight against the upper plate by a spring (9), which is atop the upper plate. A rod (10) runs through the center of the spring, extending down through holes in both plates and the shank. Its upper end is bolted to the top of the spring while its lower end is hooked against the underside of the shank.

When the chisel hits a rock or other obstruction in the soil, the obstruction forces the chisel and the rear portion of the shank to move upward. The shank is pivoted (at 11) against the rear of the hinge plate and pries open the hinge against the closing tendency of the spring. (See sketch labeled "Open Position," Appendix, Fig. 1.) This closing tendency is caused by the fact that, as the hinge is opened, the connecting rod is pulled downward and the spring is compressed. When the obstruction is passed over, the upward force on the chisel disappears and the spring pulls the shank and hinge plate back into their original position. The lower, rear portion of the hinge plate is constructed in the form of a stirrup (7) which brackets the shank, passing around and beneath it. The shank fits loosely into the stirrup (permitting a slight up and down play). The stirrup is designed to prevent the shank from recoiling away from the hinge plate, and thus prevents excessive strain on the shank near its bolted connection. The stirrup also girds the shank, preventing it from fish-tailing from side to side.

In practical use, a number of spring-hinge-shank combinations are clamped to a plow frame, forming a set of ground-working chisels capable of withstanding the shock of rocks and other obstructions in the soil without breaking the shanks.

Background of the Patent

Chisel plows, as they are called, were developed for plowing in areas where the ground is relatively free from rocks or stones. Originally, the shanks were rigidly attached to the plow frames. When such plows were used in the rocky, glacial soils of some of the Northern States, they were found to have serious defects. As the chisels hit buried rocks, a vibratory motion was set up and tremendous forces were transmitted to the shank near its connection to the frame. The shanks would break. Graham, one of the petitioners, sought to meet that problem, and in 1950 obtained a patent, U.S. No. 2,493,811 (hereinafter '811), on a spring clamp which solved some of the difficulties. Graham and his companies manufactured and sold the '811 clamps. In 1950, Graham modified the '811 structure and filed for a patent. That patent, the one in issue, was granted in 1953. This suit against competing plow manufacturers resulted from charges by petitioners that several of respondents' devices infringed the '798 patent.

The Prior Art

Five prior patents indicating the state of the art were cited by the Patent Office in the prosecution of the '798 application. Four of these patents, 10 other United States patents and two prior-use spring-clamp arrangements not of record in the '798 file wrapper were relied upon by respondents as revealing the prior art. The District Court and the Court of Appeals found that the prior art "as a whole in one form or another contains all of the mechanical elements of the '798 Patent." One of the prior-use clamp devices not before the Patent Examiner— Glencoe—was found to have "all of the elements."

We confine our discussion to the prior patent of Graham, '811, and to the Glencoe clamp device, both among the references asserted by respondents. The Graham '811 and '798 patent devices are similar in all elements, save two: (1) the stirrup and the bolted connection of the shank to the hinge plate do not appear in '811; and (2) the position of the shank is reversed, being placed in patent '811 above the hinge plate, sandwiched between it and the upper plate. The shank is held in place by the spring rod which is hooked against the bottom of the hinge plate passing through a slot in the shank. Other differences are of no consequence to our examination. In practice the '811 patent arrangement permitted the shank to wobble or fish-tail because it was not rigidly fixed to the hinge plate; moreover, as the hinge plate was below the shank, the latter caused wear on the upper plate, a member difficult to repair or replace.

Graham's '798 patent application contained 12 claims. All were rejected as not distinguished from the Graham '811 patent. The inverted position of the shank was specifically rejected as was the bolting of the shank to the hinge plate. The Patent Office examiner found these to be "matters of design well within the expected skill of the art and devoid of invention." Graham withdrew the original claims and substituted the two new ones which are substantially those in issue here. His contention was that wear was reduced in patent '798 between the shank and the heel or rear of the upper plate. He also emphasized several new features, the relevant one here being that the bolt used to connect the hinge plate and shank maintained the upper face of the shank in continuing and constant contact with the underface of the hinge plate.

Graham did not urge before the Patent Office the greater "flexing" qualities of the '798 patent arrangement which he so heavily relied on in the courts. The sole element in patent '798 which petitioners argue before us is the interchanging of the shank and hinge plate and the consequences flowing from this arrangement. The contention is that this arrangement—which petitioners claim is not disclosed in the prior art—permits the shank to flex under stress for its *entire* length. As we have sketched (see sketch, "Graham '798 Patent" in Appendix, Fig. 2), when the chisel hits an obstruction the resultant force (A) pushes the rear of the shank upward and the shank pivots against the rear of the hinge plate at (C). The natural tendency is for that portion of the shank between the pivot point and the bolted connection (i.e., between C and D) to bow downward and away from the hinge plate. The maximum distance (B) that the shank moves away from the plate is slight—for emphasis, greatly exaggerated in the sketches. This is so because of the strength of the shank and the short—nine inches or so—length of that portion of the shank between (C) and (D). On the contrary, in patent '811 (see sketch, "Graham '811 Patent" in Appendix, Fig. 2), the pivot point is the upper plate at point (c); and while the tendency for the shank to bow between points (c) and (d) is the same as in '798, the shank is restricted because of the underlying hinge plate and cannot flex as freely. In practical effect, the shank flexes only between points (a) and (c), and not along the entire length of the shank, as in '798. Petitioners say that this difference in flex, though small, effectively absorbs the tremendous forces of the shock of obstructions whereas prior art arrangements failed.

The Obviousness of the Differences

We cannot agree with petitioners. We assume that the prior art does not disclose such an arrangement as petitioners claim in patent '798. Still we do not believe that the argument on which petitioners' contention is bottomed supports the validity of the patent. The tendency of the shank to flex is the same in all cases. If free-flexing, as petitioners now argue, is the crucial difference above the prior art, then it appears evident that the desired result would be obtainable by not boxing the shank within the confines of the hinge. The only other effective place available in the arrangement was to attach it below the hinge plate and run it through a stirrup or bracket that would not disturb its flexing qualities. Certainly a person having ordinary skill in the prior art, given the fact that the flex in the shank could be utilized more effectively if allowed to run the entire length of the shank, would immediately see that the thing to do was what Graham did, i.e., invert the shank and the hinge plate.

Petitioners' argument basing validity on the free-flex theory raised for the first time on appeal is reminiscent of Lincoln Engineering Co. v. Stewart–Warner Corp., 303 U.S. 545, 58 S.Ct. 662, 82 L.Ed. 1008 (1938), where the Court called such an effort "an afterthought. No such function . . . is hinted at in the specifications of the patent. If this were so vital an element in the functioning of the apparatus it is strange that all mention of it was omitted." At p. 550. No "flexing" argument was raised in the Patent Office. Indeed, the trial judge specifically found that "flexing is not a claim of the patent in suit . . ." and would not permit interrogation as to flexing in the accused devices. Moreover, the clear testimony of petitioners' experts shows that the flexing advantages flowing from the '798 arrangement are not, in fact, a significant feature in the patent.

We find no nonobvious facets in the '798 arrangement. The wear and repair claims were sufficient to overcome the patent examiner's original conclusions as to the validity of the patent. However, some of the prior art, notably Glencoe, was not before him. There the hinge plate is below the shank but, as the courts below found, all of the elements in the '798 patent are present in the Glencoe structure. Furthermore, even though the position of the shank and hinge plate appears reversed in Glencoe, the mechanical operation is identical. The shank there pivots about the underside of the stirrup, which in Glencoe is *above* the shank. In other words, the stirrup in Glencoe serves exactly the same function as the heel of the hinge plate in '798. The mere shifting of the wear point to the heel of the '798 hinge plate from the stirrup of Glencoe—itself a part of the hinge plate—presents no operative mechanical distinctions, much less nonobvious differences.

. . .

The judgment of the Court of Appeals in No. 11 is affirmed.

APPENDIX TO OPINION OF THE COURT

Figure 1.—GRAHAM '798 PATENT

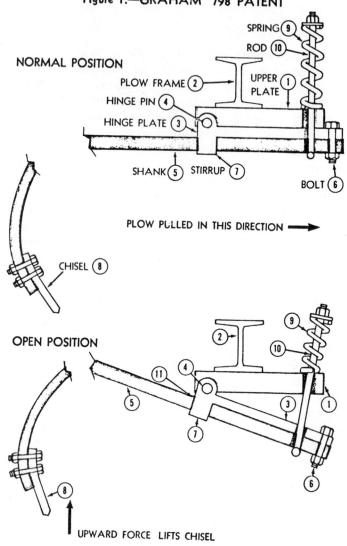

Figure 2.—FLEX COMPARISON

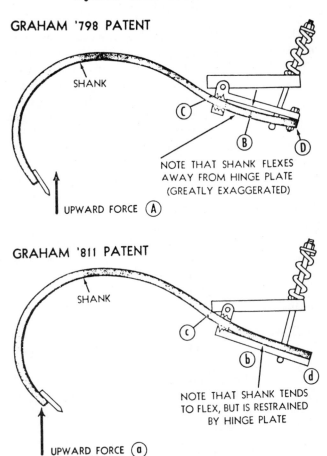

GRAHAM '798 PATENT

SHANK

(C)

(B) (D)

NOTE THAT SHANK FLEXES
AWAY FROM HINGE PLATE
(GREATLY EXAGGERATED)

UPWARD FORCE (A)

GRAHAM '811 PATENT

SHANK

(c)

(b) (d)

NOTE THAT SHANK TENDS
TO FLEX, BUT IS RESTRAINED
BY HINGE PLATE

UPWARD FORCE (a)

NOTES

1. *Section 103 and the CAFC.* In the decades before Congress created the Court of Appeals for the Federal Circuit, the regional circuits divided over how, and how high, to set patent law's standard of invention. By choosing the right circuit for suit, the adroit forum shopper could save a patent that might fall in other circuits. An agile infringer, seeking a declaratory judgment of invalidity, could pick a less hospitable circuit. One study of patentability decisions during this period revealed that "the Fourth and Fifth Circuits have been the places to sue on a borderline patent. They held approximately 40% valid and infringed in that period [1945–1957]. The First, Third, Sixth, Seventh, Ninth and Tenth Circuits are fairly close together at 19% plus or minus 2.4%. And finally, the Second and Eighth Circuits held approximately 6% of the patents coming before them valid, the Second Circuit being the lowest with 4.8%." Cooch, The Standard of Invention in the Courts, in Dynamics of the Patent System, 34, 56, 59 (W. Ball ed. 1960).

Supreme Court decisions abetted the disarray by constantly re-phrasing the standard of invention:

> Back in the late 'twenties you can see the courts were holding from 35% to 40% of all the litigated patents valid and infringed. Fol-lowing this period, the trend is downward, and in 1937 and 1938 came the TNEC hearings which had a definitely anti-patent flavor. In 1941 the *Cuno* case was decided, with its 'flash of genius' test, and in the following year, 1942, only 10% of the litigated patents were upheld. Then things tended to improve a little bit up to the point where *Graver v. Linde* case [sic] was decided. . . . [T]hat was the only case in which either Mr. Justice Douglas or Mr. Justice Black ever voted to uphold a patent. Right after that the curve climbs back almost to 30%, but the gain was short-lived. In the following year came the *A & P* case and *Crest v. Trager* (the infant feeding device). The curve then drops back down to 7%, the lowest point at any time during the thirty year period. The new Patent Act was passed in 1952, and presumably as a result the curve has shot up, wavering at first, but in 1956 it reached 33%, and in 1957 through September 9th, 30%, which seems to me quite encouraging.

Discussion following presentation of paper by Cooch, The Standard of Invention in the Courts, in Dynamics of the Patent System, 34, 56 (W. Ball ed. 1960). See Note, The Impact of the Supreme Court Section 103 Cases on the Standard of Patentability in the Lower Federal Courts, 35 Geo.Wash.L.Rev. 818, 826 (1967). See also, Note, The Standard of Patentability—Judicial Interpretation of Section 103 of the Patent Act, 63 Colum.L.Rev. 306 (1963).

By taking over the jurisdiction of the regional courts of appeals in patent cases, the CAFC has eliminated intramural conflicts involving section 103's nonobviousness test. The CAFC has also put its own gloss on the nonobviousness standard—one that is generally favorable to patent applicants and patent owners. The court has effectively equated the secondary tests of invention, such as commercial success, with the three statutory tests described in *Deere*. The court has also rejected the rigorous nonobviousness test earlier applied to so-called combination patents and has characterized nonobviousness as a question of law, not fact. Notes 2, 3 and 4, below describe these three developments.

2. *Secondary Tests of Nonobviousness.* In *Deere* the Supreme Court prescribed three inquiries into nonobviousness: "the scope and content of the prior art are to be determined; differences between the prior art and the claims at issue are to be ascertained; and the level of ordinary skill in the pertinent art resolved." The Court added, "[s]uch secondary considerations as commercial success, long felt but unsolved needs, failure of others, etc., might be utilized to give light to the circumstances surrounding the origin of the subject matter sought to be patented. As indicia of obviousness or nonobviousness, these inquiries may have relevancy." 383 U.S. at 17–18.

Commercial success is the most frequently employed subtest of nonobviousness. The subtest predicates that commercial success is a competitive goal, and that if the successful invention had been obvious to competitors they would have developed it first. Professor Edmund Kitch has traced the chain of inferences that underlies this subtest: "First, that the commercial success is due to the innovation. Second, that if an improvement has in fact become commercially successful, it is likely that this potential commercial success was perceived before its development. Third, the potential commercial success having been perceived, it is likely that efforts were made to develop the improvement. Fourth, the efforts having been made by men of skill in the art, they failed because the patentee was the first to reduce his development to practice." Kitch, Graham v. John Deere Co.: New Standards for Patents, 1966 Sup.Ct.Rev. 293, 332.

Courts also admit proof of industry acquiescence in patentability and long-felt demand for the invention as evidence of nonobviousness. The theory behind commercial acquiescence is that when competitors—who have the greatest interest in attacking a patent—take a license or try to invent around the patent, it is evidence that they consider the patent claims to be valid. The theory behind long-felt demand is that firms characteristically seek to correct defects that increase production costs or decrease product quality; if a corrective method or apparatus had been obvious to workers ordinarily skilled in the industry, they would have adopted it earlier. Other subtests of nonobviousness include the failure of others to make the invention, research and development in directions diverging from the patentee's unexpected results, and the accused infringer's admission of nonobviousness. See Harris, The Emerging Primacy of "Secondary Considerations" as Validity Ammunition: Has the Federal Circuit Gone Too Far? 71 J.Pat. & Trademark Off. Soc'y 185, 191–192 (1989).

Courts recognize that facts other than nonobviousness sometimes explain commercial success, industry acquiescence or satisfaction of long felt demand. A patent owner must show that commercial success stems from the quality of the invention and not from such extrinsic factors as market position and advertising efforts. Pentec, Inc. v. Graphic Controls Corp., 776 F.2d 309, 227 U.S.P.Q. 766 (Fed.Cir.1985). Proof of long felt demand may be undercut by proof that the invention was made possible only by a recent advance in the art. Allen v. Standard Crankshaft and Hydraulic Co., 323 F.2d 29, 139 U.S.P.Q. 20 (4th Cir.1963). Proof of industry acquiescence may collapse before the fact that "[t]o take a license, calling for small royalty payments, frequently involves less expense than prolonged litigation. . . ." Kleinman v. Kobler, 230 F.2d 913, 914, 108 U.S.P.Q. 301 (2d Cir.1956), cert. denied, 352 U.S. 830, 77 S.Ct. 44, 1 L.Ed.2d 51.

The Court of Appeals for the Federal Circuit has placed secondary considerations alongside the three factual inquiries prescribed in *Deere*. See Uniroyal, Inc. v. Rudkin–Wiley Corp., 837 F.2d 1044, 5 U.S.P.Q.2d 1434 (Fed.Cir.), cert. denied, ___ U.S. ___, 109 S.Ct. 75, 102 L.Ed.2d 51 (1988). Where earlier courts admitted secondary proofs only if the patent owner could directly connect them to the patented invention, the CAFC has allowed these proofs as a matter of course. See Stratoflex, Inc. v. Aeroquip Corp., 713 F.2d 1530, 218 U.S.P.Q. 871 (Fed.Cir.1983). Where earlier courts required a direct connection between commercial success and nonobviousness, the CAFC requires only a "nexus." See Windsurfing Int'l, Inc., v. AMF, Inc., 782 F.2d 995, 228 U.S.P.Q. 562 (Fed.Cir.), cert. denied, 477 U.S. 905, 106 S.Ct. 3275, 91 L.Ed.2d 565 (1986). See generally, Merges, Commercial Success and Patent Standards: Economic Perspectives on Innovation, 76 Cal.L.Rev. 803 (1988).

3. *"Combination" Patents.* The United States Supreme Court historically held mechanical inventions combining old elements—"combination" patents—to a more stringent standard than other inventions. For example, in Sakraida v. Ag Pro, Inc., 425 U.S. 273, 96 S.Ct. 1532, 47 L.Ed.2d 784 189 U.S.P.Q. 449 (1976), reh'g denied, 426 U.S. 955, 96 S.Ct. 3182, 49 L.Ed.2d 1194 (1976), the Court held that the trial court had correctly invalidated a patent for a water flush system combining several old elements into a mechanism for removing cow manure from dairy barn floors: "the combination of these old elements to produce an abrupt release of water directly on the barn floor from storage tanks or pools" cannot "properly be characterized as synergistic, that is, 'result[ing] in an effect greater than the sum of the several effects taken separately.' Anderson's–Black Rock v. Pavement Co., 396 U.S. 57, 61 (1969). Rather, this patent simply arranges old elements with each performing the same function it had been known to perform, although perhaps producing a more striking result than in previous combinations. Such combinations are not patentable under standards appropriate for a combination patent." 425 U.S. at 282, 96 S.Ct. at 1537.

The Court of Appeals for the Federal Circuit has rejected "synergism" as a requirement of invention. It has also rejected the notion of a separate category for "combination patents." "Reference to 'combination' patents is, moreover, meaningless. Virtually *all* patents are 'combination patents,' if by that label one intends to describe patents having claims to inventions formed of a combination of elements. It is difficult to visualize, at least in the mechanical-structural arts, a 'non-combination' invention, i.e., an invention consisting of a *single* element. Such inventions, if they exist, are rare indeed." Stratoflex, Inc. v. Aeroquip Corp., 713 F.2d 1530, 1540, 218 U.S.P.Q. 871 (Fed.Cir.1983) (emphasis in original). For the suggestion that the CAFC may be slipping into a more rigorous test of nonobviousness for mechanical combinations, see Klein, Comment: Is the Federal Circuit Adopting the Supreme Court's Obviousness Standard for Inventions Combining Old Elements?, 71 J.Pat. & Trademark Off. Soc'y 460 (1989).

4. *Is Nonobviousness a Question of Law or Fact?* The answer to this question has great consequence, both at the trial and appellate levels. At the trial level, the answer will control the allocation of responsibility between judge and jury. On appeal, it will control the scope of review and the applicability of the "clearly erroneous" standard of Federal Rules of Civil Procedure, Rule 52(a).

Deere established the principle that "the ultimate question of patent validity is one of law. . . ." 383 U.S. at 475. In Dennison Mfg. Co. v. Panduit Corp., 475 U.S. 809, (1986), the Supreme Court remanded to the CAFC for consideration of the "complex issue of the degree to which the obviousness determination is one of fact." The CAFC responded:

A § 103 determination involves fact and law. There may be these facts: what a prior art patent as a whole discloses; what it in fact disclosed to workers in the art; what differences exist between the entire prior art, or a whole prior art structure, and the whole claimed invention; what the differences enabled the claimed subject matter as a whole to achieve; that others for years sought and failed to arrive at the claimed invention; that one of those others copied it; that the invention met on its merits with outstanding commercial success.

With the involved facts determined, the decisionmaker confronts a ghost, i.e., 'a person having ordinary skill in the art,' not unlike the 'reasonable man' and other ghosts in the law. To reach a proper conclusion under § 103, the decisionmaker must step backward in time and into the shoes worn by that 'person' when the invention was unknown and just before it was made. In light of *all* the evidence, the decisionmaker must then determine whether the patent challenger has convincingly established that the claimed invention as a whole would have been obvious at *that* time to *that* person. The answer to that question partakes more of the nature of law than of fact, for it is an ultimate conclusion based on a foundation formed of all the probative facts. If itself a fact, it would be part of its own foundation.

Panduit Corp. v. Dennison Mfg. Co., 810 F.2d 1561, 1566, 1 U.S.P.Q.2d 1593 (Fed.Cir.), cert. denied, 481 U.S. 1052, 107 S.Ct. 2187, 95 L.Ed.2d 843 (1987) (emphasis the court's). See generally, Hofer, The Obviousness Issue: The Jury Takes Over!, 71 J.Pat. & Trademark Off. Soc'y 107 (1989).

5. *The Problem of Hindsight.* Hindsight offers 20/20 vision. There is a natural inclination to view a completed, working invention from hindsight and to ignore the inchoate state of the art that existed when the invention was made. The Court of Appeals for the Federal Circuit has repeatedly warned against the dangers of hindsight. See, e.g., Loctite Corp. v. Ultraseal Ltd., 781 F.2d 861, 872, 228 U.S.P.Q. 90 (Fed.Cir.1985) ("In patent cases, the need for express Graham [v. John Deere] findings takes on an especially significant role because of an occasional tendency of district courts to depart from the *Graham* test, and from the statutory standard of unobviousness that it helps determine, to the tempting but forbidden zone of hindsight. Thus, we must be convinced from the opinion that the district court actually applied *Graham* and must be presented with enough express and necessarily implied findings to know the basis of the trial court's opinion.").

6. *"Person Having Ordinary Skill in the Art. . . ."* Section 103 views nonobviousness from the perspective of a person having ordinary skill in the art to which the subject matter in issue pertains. Essentially this person is the counterpart of tort law's "reasonable person." The Court of Appeals for the Federal Circuit elaborated the reasonable person standard in Standard Oil Co. v. American Cyanamid Co., 774 F.2d 448, 454, 227 U.S.P.Q. 293 (Fed.Cir.1985): "The issue of obviousness is determined entirely with reference to a *hypothetical* 'person having ordinary skill in the art.' It is only that hypothetical person who is presumed to be aware of all the pertinent prior art. The actual inventor's skill is irrelevant to the inquiry, and this is for a very important reason. The statutory emphasis is on a person of *ordinary* skill. Inventors, as a class, according to the concepts underlying the Constitution and the statutes that have created the patent system, possess something—call it what you will—which sets them apart from the workers of *ordinary* skill, and one should not go about determining obviousness under § 103 by inquiring into what *patentees* (i.e., inventors) would have known or would likely have done, faced with the revelations of references." (Emphasis the court's).

7. *Expert Testimony.* Courts, and the Patent and Trademark Office, often rely on expert testimony in determining the scope of prior art and the level of skill of a person ordinarily skilled in the art. A court unconvinced by either party's witnesses may appoint an independent expert. See, e.g., Reeves Bros., Inc. v. United States Laminating Corp., 282 F.Supp. 118, 157 U.S.P.Q. 235 (E.D.N.Y.1968), aff'd, 417 F.2d 869, 163 U.S.P.Q. 577 (2d Cir.1969). There is good reason for courts to rely on expert testimony when the relevant art is technical and complex. Is there even greater reason to defer to expertise in cases involving easily comprehensible subject matter, where the tendency is to equate an invention's apparent simplicity with its obviousness?

8. *The Economics of Nonobviousness.* In an important article, Professor Robert P. Merges has argued that CAFC decisions encouraging the use of secondary considerations to prove nonobviousness have effectively reduced the level of invention required by section 103. "By relying on this objective evidence of patentability, as the Federal Circuit calls it, the court threatens to transform patents into rewards for such nontechnical achievements as superior distribution systems, marketing decisions, and service networks. In so doing, it has begun to undermine the patent system's traditional emphasis on rewarding invention." Merges, Commercial Success and Patent Standards: Economic Perspectives on Innovation, 76 Cal.L.Rev. 803, 806 (1988).

To what extent should economic analysis inform the nonobviousness standard? Judge Richard Posner, concurring and dissenting in Roberts v. Sears, Roebuck & Co., 723 F.2d 1324, 1344, 221 U.S.P.Q. 504 (7th Cir.1983), acknowledged "that many lawyers and judges find the language of economics repulsive. Yet the policies that have given shape to the patent statute are quintessentially economic, and the language of economics is therefore the natural language in which to articulate the test for obviousness." 723 F.2d at 1347. In Posner's view, the statutory term, " 'obvious' . . . identifies the cases in which patent protection is not necessary to induce invention and would therefore visit the costs of monopoly on the consuming public with no offsetting gains." Consequently, "if a court thinks an invention for which a patent is being sought would have been made as soon or almost as soon as it was made even if there were no patent laws, then it must pronounce the invention obvious and the patent invalid." 723 F.2d at 1346.

9. *The Nonobviousness Standard in the Patent and Trademark Office.* Was *Deere* correct to criticize the Patent Office for applying a more liberal invention standard than the one announced by the Court? Very few issued patents will ever enjoy commercial success. Fewer still will find their validity tested in litigation. Can you think of a more efficient system than one in which the Patent and Trademark Office makes a comparatively quick pass at investigating the prior art and postpones closer, more costly, inquiry to infringement actions involving the relatively few patents that turn out to have commercial significance?

Difference in standards may also stem from the different proofs available to the Patent and Trademark Office and to the courts. Patent and Trademark Office proceedings usually measure nonobviousness directly. The examiner compares the claimed subject matter with the prior art to determine whether the subject matter would have been obvious to a worker ordinarily skilled in the art. Evidence of secondary considerations such as commercial success will often be unavailable. By the time the patent reaches the courts in the context of an infringement or declaratory judgment action, evidence bearing on commercial success and the other secondary considerations is more likely to have materialized. Failure to meet these subtests may lead a court to invalidate the patent.

Does the invalidation of patents coming into the courts indicate a flaw in the patent system? Or does it suggest that the two tribunals are effectively serving different functions—the Patent and Trademark Office to grant patents on the basis of prior art appraisals, and courts to weed out subject matter that more highly-focussed factfindings—and subsequently-occurring events—prove to have been obvious?

b. SECTION 102: NOVELTY AND THE STATUTORY BARS

APPLICATION OF BORST

United States Court of Customs and Patent Appeals, 1965.
52 C.C.P.A. 1398, 345 F.2d 851, 145 U.S.P.Q. 554, cert. denied, 382 U.S. 973,
86 S.Ct. 537, 15 L.Ed.2d 465, 148 U.S.P.Q. 771.

SMITH, Judge.

The invention for which appellant seeks a patent comprises means for safely and effectively controlling a relatively large neutron output by varying a small and easily controlled neutron input source. . . .

Appellant asserts that the claimed invention affords a revolutionary approach to the safety problem in the nuclear reactor art. As the amplifier is said to be inherently safe from divergent nuclear chain reaction, the intricate systems needed to monitor and control the operation of conventional neutron amplifiers to prevent an explosion are unnecessary.

The single reference relied upon by the Patent Office in rejecting the appealed claims is an Atomic Energy Commission document entitled "KAPL–M–RWS–1, A Stable Fission Pile with High Speed Control." The document is in the form of an unpublished memorandum authored by one Samsel, and will hereinafter be referred to as "Samsel." Samsel is dated February 14, 1947 and was classified as a secret document by the Commission until March 9, 1957, when it was declassified. In essence, Samsel sets forth and discusses the problems present in the control of a nuclear reactor, the concept of use of successive fuel stages to effect such control, and a description of the arrangement, composition and relative proportions of materials required to obtain the sought-for results. Samsel is prefaced by a statement that it was made to record an idea, and it nowhere indicates that the idea had been tested in an operating reactor.

The Patent Office does not invoke Samsel as a publication (which it apparently was not, at any pertinent date). Rather, the contention is that Samsel constitutes evidence of prior knowledge within the meaning of 35 U.S.C.A. § 102(a).

While there seems to be some disagreement on the part of the solicitor, we think the most reasonable interpretation of the examiner's rejection, and one which is concurred in by the board and by appellant, is that claims 27, 30, 31 and 32 are fully met by Samsel and thus the subject matter defined therein is unpatentable because it was known by another in this country prior to appellant's invention thereof. As to claims 28, 29 and 33, even though not fully met by Samsel, they are said to be obvious within the meaning of 35 U.S.C.A. § 103 in view of the prior knowledge evidenced by Samsel.

Our own independent consideration of Samsel has convinced us that it contains adequate enabling disclosure of the invention of claims 27 and 30–32, and appellant does not appear to contend otherwise. Rather, appellant contends that Samsel is not available as evidence of prior knowledge under sections 102(a) and 103. Appellant also argues that, even if Samsel is available, the subject matter of claims 28, 29 and 33 is not obvious in view thereof. We agree with this characterization of the essential issues presented on this appeal, and will treat them in the order stated above.

In the case of In re Schlittler, 234 F.2d 882, 43 C.C.P.A. 986, this court was presented with the following situation: A manuscript containing an anticipatory disclosure of the appellants' claimed invention had been submitted to The Journal of the American Chemical Society and was later published. The date to which the appellants' application was entitled for purposes of constructive reduction to practice was earlier than the publication date of the Journal article, and therefore the Patent Office did not contend that the "printed publication" portion of section 102(a) was applicable. However, the manuscript bore a notation that it had been received by the publisher on a date prior to the effective filing date of the appellants' application. On the basis of this notation the Patent Office argued that the article constituted sufficient evidence of prior knowledge under section 102(a).

After an exhaustive review of the authorities, and of the legislative history of the Patent Act of 1952, this court rejected the contention of the Patent Office, and concluded that such a document was not proper evidence of prior knowledge. In reversing, the court stated (234 F.2d at 886, 433 C.C.P.A. at 992):

> In our opinion, one of the essential elements of the word 'known' as used in 35 U.S.C.A. § 102(a) is knowledge of an invention which has been completed by reduction to practice, actual or constructive, and is not satisfied by disclosure of a conception only.

And therefore, since the Journal article, "at best, could be evidence of nothing more than conception and disclosure of the invention," the

> . . . placing of the Nystrom article in the hands of the publishers did not constitute either prima facie or conclusive evidence of knowledge or use by others in this country of the invention disclosed by the article, within the meaning of Title 35, § 102(a) of the United States Code, since the knowledge was of a conception only and not of a reduction to practice.

Another aspect of the court's discussion in Schlittler involved the well-established principle that "prior knowledge of a patented invention would not invalidate a claim of the patent unless such knowledge was available to the public." After reaffirming that principle, the court went on to state:

> Obviously, in view of the above authorities, the mere placing of a manuscript in the hands of a publisher does not necessarily make it available to the public within the meaning of said authorities.

However, the court did not go on to determine whether the Journal article was in fact available to the public, since such determination was deemed unnecessary for disposition of the case, under the court's theory.

We shall consider first the public availability aspect of the Schlittler case. Although that portion of the Schlittler opinion is clearly dictum, we think it just as clearly represents the settled law. The knowledge contemplated by section 102(a) must be accessible to the public.

In the instant case, Samsel was clearly not publicly available during the period it was under secrecy classification by the Atomic Energy Commission. We note that the date of declassification, however, was prior to appellant's filing date, and it is perhaps arguable that Samsel became accessible to the public upon declassification. But we do not find it necessary to decide that difficult question, for there is a statutory provision which is, we think, dispositive of the question of publicity. Section 155 of the Atomic Energy Act of 1954 (42 U.S.C.A. § 2185) provides:

> In connection with applications for patents covered by this subchapter, the fact that the invention or discovery was known or used before shall be a bar to the patenting of such invention or discovery even though such prior knowledge or use was under secrecy within the atomic energy program of the United States.

We think the meaning and intent of this provision is so clear as to admit of no dispute: With respect to subject matter covered by the patent provisions of the Atomic Energy Act, prior knowledge or use under section 102(a) *need not* be accessible to the public. Therefore, Samsel is available as evidence of prior knowledge insofar as the requirement for publicity is concerned.

The remaining consideration regarding the status of Samsel as evidence of prior knowledge directly calls into question the correctness of the unequivocal holding in Schlittler that the knowledge must be of a reduction to practice, either actual or constructive. After much deliberation, we have concluded that such a requirement is illogical and anomalous, and to the extent Schlittler is inconsistent with the decision in this case, it is hereby expressly overruled.

The mere fact that a disclosure is contained in a patent or application and thus "constructively" reduced to practice, or that it is found in a printed publication, does not make the disclosure itself any more meaningful to those skilled in the art (and thus, ultimately, to the public). Rather, the criterion should be whether the disclosure is *sufficient to enable one skilled in the art to reduce the disclosed invention to practice.* In other words, the disclosure must be such as will give possession of the invention to the person of ordinary skill. Even the act of publication or the fiction of constructive reduction to practice will not suffice if the disclosure does not meet this standard.

Where, as is true of Samsel, the disclosure constituting evidence of prior knowledge contains, in the words of the Board of Appeals, "a description of the invention fully commensurate with the present patent application," we hold that the disclosure need not be of an invention reduced to practice, either actually or constructively. We therefore affirm the rejection of claims 27, 30, 31 and 32. . . . Modified.

NOTE, NOVELTY AND REDUCTION TO PRACTICE: PATENT CONFUSION

75 Yale L.J. 1194–96, 1198–1201 (1966).*

The rewards of a patent monopoly are reserved for contributions which may significantly increase existing knowledge. Under the present law an applicant must show not only that his device was an "invention" and had "utility," but also that it meets the requirement of "novelty." The prerequisite of novelty reflects a basic policy of the law to reward only those inventors who first place the device in the public domain. If knowledge of the subject sought to be patented has already been made available to the public, then a patent grant would not only serve no useful purpose, but would injure the public by removing existing knowledge from the public domain.

The novelty requirement is spelled out in Section 102(a) of the Patent Act of 1952: a patent will be barred for lack of novelty if the invention had previously been described in a prior patent or printed publication, or if it had been "known or used by others." While prior patents and printed publications are relatively clear categories, the "known or used by others" obstacle is ill-defined; read expansively, it would bar *any* invention which had previously been thought of— however vaguely—by someone else. To prevent yesterday's science-fiction from becoming today's patent bar, courts have long read the statutory language restrictively. An invention was not "known or used" unless it had been *actually reduced to practice,* by building a working and tested embodiment, *or constructively reduced to practice,* by filing a detailed patent application, which later ripened into a patent. And it was not known or used "by others" unless the inventor had made knowledge of his device available to the public.

This interpretation has been upset by a recent decision of the Court of Customs and Patent Appeals, In re Borst, which may severely tighten the requirement of novelty. . . .

The potential impact of *Borst* is its effect on the old rules for determining when a prior description would bar a patent. Before *Borst,* a mere description of an idea or conception could defeat a claim of novelty only if it were included in a "printed publication" or a patent. These descriptions, and no others, were thought likely to bring knowledge of the invention to the public. And unless the public knew of the earlier discovery, the subsequent invention would be considered novel.

The "printed publication" clause has consistently been interpreted in light of this purpose—to bar a patent only if the earlier invention were known to society. At the time the statute was enacted, the printing press was the only device for inexpensive reproduction of documents. As techniques have grown, courts have broadened the definition of "printing" to include typewritten and mimeographed documents deposited in public libraries. Provision for dissemination of the knowledge is supplied by the "publication" requirement, under which a printed document will not bar a patent unless it has been made available to the public. In Badowski v. United States [164 F.Supp. 252 (1958)], for example, the government challenged a patent by unearthing a Russian document describing the device. The court found that the document had been obtained in 1958 only after "months of diplomatic endeavor by defendant's embassy in Moscow." There was no evidence that it had ever been accessible to the public in any country prior to the 1942 patent application; nor had the document been contained in any library anywhere, even at the time of litigation. Consequently, the document was held not to be a prior publication, and the patent was granted. Similarly, private reports, confidential papers, and documents intended for distribution solely within an organization have all failed the publication test. On the other hand, even a single copy of a typed thesis meets the publication test if it has been deposited in a public library.

What *Borst* may do is to add another bar to novelty: a memorandum describing an idea but which falls short of the requirements for printed publication. Unless construed with care, the new bar to novelty may prove a troublesome category.

First, *Borst* weakens the dissemination requirement for written descriptions. Unpublished memoranda necessarily fall short of the level of distribution demanded of publications, and yet the court left unclear exactly what lesser requirement *Borst*-type disclosures must meet. If no significant dissemination is required, severe damage may be done to patent policy. Inventors may be discouraged from investing in an idea if an obscure prior disclosure may lurk as a threat to patentability. Moreover, there is no reasonable basis for denying the second inventor a patent where the first invention was effectively kept from public knowledge.

Second, *Borst*-type disclosures may be used to avoid the goals of the printed publication rule. Publishing involves effort; costs are high, access to scientific journals limited, and libraries restrictive in what they will allow deposited. *Borst* may tempt inventors to use the easier method of protecting their discoveries from being patented by a later inventor at the expense of the greater exchange of information provided by publications.

A more serious defect is that the *Borst*-type disclosure avoids the time limit which patent law imposes on printed publications. Under § 102(b), an inventor loses his patent rights if he does not file an application within one year of publication, public use or sale or patenting of the device. *Borst*-type disclosures, being none of these, do not fall within the one year rule. The decision may thus defeat the policy of this section by enabling inventors to enjoy the pre-patent fruits of discovery with the security that a later inventor cannot gain a patent, but without effectively bringing their ideas before the public.

Finally, *Borst*-type disclosures contain no assurances that the device is of any worth—assurances which other methods of barring patents all possess. An actual reduction to practice proves an invention works. Constructive reductions—the filing of patent applications—are not likely to be based on mere conjecture. Not only do filing and attorney fees exert a sobering effect, but the Commissioner of Patents may require a working model of an invention whose operativeness appears doubtful. Printing expenses, or the scrutiny of publishers and editors, help assure that purely frivolous claims are not likely to be found in printed publications. Moreover, the scientific community is likely to judge irresponsible representations harshly; the risk of reputation helps insure that discoveries revealed in publication are of practical benefit. . . .

UMC ELECTRONICS CO. v. UNITED STATES

United States Court of Appeals, Federal Circuit, 1987.
816 F.2d 647, cert. denied, 484 U.S. 1025, 108 S.Ct. 748, 98 L.Ed.2d 761 (1988).

NIES, Circuit Judge.

UMC Electronics Company brought this action, pursuant to 28 U.S.C. § 1498(a), to recover compensation for use of its patented invention by the United States. UMC is the owner of Patent No. 3,643,513, issued February 22, 1972, by assignment from the inventor Preston Weaver. The United States Claims Court upheld the validity of all claims (1–4) but dismissed the complaint on the ground of no infringement or, more accurately, no use of the patented invention by the United States. Both parties appeal. We reverse the Claims Court's holding that the patented invention was not on sale within the meaning of 35 U.S.C. § 102(b). Accordingly, we affirm the judgment in favor of the government, but on different grounds.

I

Background

The claimed invention is an aviation counting accelerometer (ACA), a device for sensing and for recording the number of times an aircraft has been subjected to predetermined levels of acceleration. The sensor component is mounted on the aircraft in a direction to measure acceleration loading and is connected electrically to the recorder component. Records produced by an ACA can indicate an aircraft's remaining useful life and show the need for structural inspection, overhaul, or rotation to less demanding service.

The patent application which became the patent in this suit ('513) was filed on August 1, 1968. Under 35 U.S.C. § 102(b) the commercial exploitation and the state of development of the invention one year before the filing of the application for the subject invention are critical to resolution of the on-sale issue.

Prior to the late 1960's when UMC first entered this field, the U.S. Navy had procured ACA's from Maxson Electronics Company and from Giannini Controls Corporation. The Navy was dissatisfied with these ACA's because they sometimes recorded data that defied common sense, failed to count accelerations, or counted accelerations that never occurred. In 1966 the Navy contacted Preston Weaver, an employee of UMC, told him of the problems with existing ACA's and informed him of the Navy's interest in buying improved devices. Weaver designed an accelerometer, model UMC–A, and in late 1966, UMC was awarded a contract to supply the Navy with approximately 1600 units.

In early 1967, UMC concluded that its model UMC–A would not meet the Navy's performance specification required by its contract.

Like the Maxson and Giannini ACA's, the UMC–A accelerometer utilized, as part of its sensor, an electromechanical transducer to mechanically generate signals that indicate levels of acceleration. Like the Maxson and Giannini devices, the UMC–A device sometimes counted and sometimes did not count the same acceleration load. The problem lay in the inherent frequency of the mass-spring system in the transducer. The devices could not distinguish between acceleration due to inflight maneuvers, which determines actual stress, and acceleration from other sources, e.g., windgusts or weapons release.

To prevent UMC from losing the ACA contract, Weaver began work to improve the sensor portion of an ACA and conceived his invention which uses an analog transducer in the sensor. An analog transducer electrically generates a varying signal (in contrast to the mechanically produced signal of prior devices) which can be filtered electronically to selectively remove the effects of superimposed vibrations. The Claims Court found that in April–May of 1967 Weaver built and tested an engineering prototype of his ACA containing a commercial analog transducer, a filter, a timing circuit and a voltage sensor that measured one load level. UMC sought to modify the existing contract for ACA's to substitute an analog transducer for the electromechanical transducer specified in the contract, but was unsuccessful in negotiating a modification.

In late May, 1967, the Navy issued new specifications and in July, 1967, requested proposals from contractors to deliver ACA's built to the new specification (Mil–A–22145B). Technically, the request for proposals called separately for a certain number of sensor components of an ACA system and a certain number of recorders, the two units being compatible in combination. UMC responded to the request on July 27, 1967, the final date for making a proposal, with an offer to supply $1,668,743 worth of its improved ACA (hereinafter model UMC–B). UMC represented as part of its proposal that the sensor portion "has been constructed and tested in conjunction with voltage sensing and time controlled circuitry." In response to a Navy inquiry, on August 2, 1967, after the critical date, UMC submitted a technical proposal which described the model UMC–B in detail and included test results and schematic drawings. On August 9, 1967, UMC gave a demonstration of its device to the Navy at the UMC facility.

In early 1968 the Navy canceled the request to which the above submission of UMC was directed, and in July 1968, it issued another. The latter request eventually led to a contract with Systron–Donner Corporation, which company has been providing the Navy with ACA's utilizing analog transducers since 1970.

In June, 1980, UMC filed the instant action against the United States seeking compensation (after attempting for a number of years to obtain compensation directly from the Navy) by reason of the Navy's alleged use of its invention in the Systron–Donner ACA's. The Claims Court upheld the validity of the patent claims, which were challenged by the government on a number of grounds, but found that the

Systron–Donner ACA's did not fall within the scope of the claims. Both parties appeal: UMC asking for reversal of the Claims Court's finding of no infringement; the government seeking to have the claims in suit held invalid. Since we conclude that the Claims Court erred as a matter of law in holding that the claims of the '513 patent were not invalid under section 102(b), we need discuss only that issue in detail.

II

The Claims Court Decision

The Claims Court analyzed the on-sale bar under the following three-part test set out in In re Corcoran, 640 F.2d 1331, 1333–34, 208 USPQ 867, 870 (CCPA 1981), taken from Timely Prods. Corp. v. Arron, 523 F.2d 288, 302, 187 USPQ 257, 267–68 (2d Cir.1975):

(1) The complete invention claimed must have been embodied in or obvious in view of the thing offered for sale. . . . Complete readability of the claim on the thing offered is not required because whatever is published (or on sale) more than one year prior to the filing of a patent application becomes part of the prior art over which the claim must be patentable. . . .

(2) The invention must have been tested sufficiently to verify that it is operable and commercially marketable. This is simply another way of expressing the principle that an invention cannot be offered for sale until it is completed, which requires not merely its conception but its reduction to practice. . . .

(3) Finally, the sale must be primarily for profit rather than for experimental purposes. . . . [Citations omitted.]

Proceeding through the *Timely Products* requirements in reverse order, the Claims Court first noted that UMC had admitted that its offer to the Navy was for profit, not for experimentation. The court then found that the invention of the '513 patent had been reduced to practice before the critical date by Weaver's tests of the engineering prototype of the ACA in April–May, 1967, because Weaver admitted that as a result of those tests he was satisfied that his invention would serve its intended purpose. However, the court found the first requirement that the complete invention must be embodied in the thing offered for sale was not met because the engineering prototype did not include all elements of the claims. The court found that the evidence established that the inventor had not built a physical embodiment of the invention including all limitations of the claims before the critical date.

The court then construed the decision of this court in Barmag Barmer Maschinenfabrik AG v. Murata Mach., Ltd., 731 F.2d 831, 221 USPQ 561 (Fed.Cir.1984). It interpreted *Barmag* as making an exception to the physical embodiment requirement where "commercial benefits outside the allowed time have been great." Because UMC "never produced its ACA," the court found it "reaped no commercial benefits."

Based on those findings, the court held that the invention of the '513 patent was not on sale within the meaning of section 102(b).

The court also held that the invention would not have been obvious from the prototype, which the court considered to be the thing offered for sale. This was error in the court's analysis, the *prototype* not being the thing offered for sale. The subject matter of the offer for sale is admittedly the claimed invention.

The government maintains that, properly interpreted, all three *Timely Products* requirements had been met, namely, (1) there was an offer to sell model UMC–B accelerometers which embodied the invention of the claims, (2) the invention had been reduced to practice, and (3) the offer to sell was for profit, not experimentation. Thus, per the government, the Claims Court erred as a matter of law in not holding the claims barred under section 102(b). UMC counters that because the inventor never built a physical embodiment containing all elements of the claims, the Claims Court erred in finding a reduction to practice of the invention, but that the court's error was cancelled out by its separate requirement for a physical embodiment.

III

As an initial matter, UMC is correct in pointing out the inconsistency between the Claims Court's conclusion that the claimed invention was "reduced to practice" before the critical date and its separate finding that no physical embodiment of the invention existed at that time. It is not sufficient for a reduction to practice that Weaver built and tested only a part of the later-claimed model UMC–B accelerometer. Under our precedent there cannot be a reduction to practice of the invention here without a physical embodiment which includes all limitations of the claim. Because the court found and the parties do not dispute that there was no physical embodiment containing all limitations of the claimed invention before the critical date, we conclude that the Claims Court erred in holding that there had been a reduction to practice.

The clarification of that issue, however, does not resolve the precise dispute here. Per the government, UMC's substantial attempted commercial exploitation of the claimed invention contravenes the policies of the on-sale bar despite the absence of a complete embodiment and, thus, raises an on-sale bar under section 102(b). For this proposition the government relies on the decision of this court in *Barmag*. On the other hand, UMC maintains that, as a matter of law, there is no on-sale bar unless the claimed invention had been reduced to practice before the critical date, and urges that we here reject the contrary suggestion in *Barmag*. Thus, we address first the issue whether reduction to practice of the claimed invention before the critical date is required to invoke the on-sale bar, and conclude, for reasons that follow, that reduction to practice is not always a requirement of the on-sale bar.[5]

5. The public use bar of section 102(b) implicates different considerations and nothing said here should be construed to encompass that part of the statute.

This leads to the issue whether there is an on-sale bar in this case. On the undisputed facts, we hold that the invention of the '513 patent was on sale within the meaning of section 102(b).

IV

Whether a reduction to practice is a requirement of the on-sale bar of 35 U.S.C. § 102(b) requires a review of our precedent. However, the issue has been directly addressed by this court or its predecessors in only two cases, *Barmag* and General Electric Co. v. United States, 654 F.2d 55, 60–61, 211 USPQ 867, 872–73 (Ct.Cl.1981) (en banc), although the issue has surfaced in others. In General Electric Co. v. United States, 654 F.2d at 61–64, 211 USPQ at 873–75, the Court of Claims, one of this court's predecessors, analyzed an on-sale bar issue by focusing on the policies underlying the bar to determine whether application of the bar would further those policies. Those policies were stated to be:

> First, there is a policy against removing inventions from the public which the public has justifiably come to believe are freely available to all as a consequence of prolonged sales activity. Next, there is a policy favoring prompt and widespread disclosure of new inventions to the public. The inventor is forced to file promptly or risk possible forfeiture of his invention [patent] rights due to prior sales. A third policy is to prevent the inventor from commercially exploiting the exclusivity of his invention substantially beyond the statutorily authorized 17–year period. The on-sale bar forces the inventor to choose between seeking patent protection promptly following sales activity or taking his chances with his competitors without the benefit of patent protection. The fourth and final identifiable policy is to give the inventor a reasonable amount of time following sales activity (set by statute as 1 year) to determine whether a patent is a worthwhile investment. This benefits the public because it tends to minimize the filing of inventions [sic] of only marginal public interest.

654 F.2d at 61, 211 USPQ at 873. On the facts of that case, the court held that the policies were violated and that there was a reduction to practice before the critical date. The latter holding obviated the need to agree or disagree with a detailed analysis of the trial judge, who had concluded that reduction to practice was not "indispensable in every case."

In *Barmag*, the court went out of its way to reserve the question whether a physical embodiment should be a requirement of the on-sale bar in all cases. Without a physical embodiment, as stated above, there can be no reduction to practice.

Contrary to the Claims Court's interpretation, *Barmag* did not suggest that an embodiment might not be required only in instances where there had been actual sales of goods. An *offer* to sell a later-claimed invention may be sufficient to invoke the bar whether the offer is accepted or rejected. . . .

The case law of other courts regarding the on-sale bar is not uniform. Some courts have rejected any rigid rules for the operation of the statutory bar, focusing, as much of our precedent does, on the policies of the statute. Chief Judge Wright's comments in Philco Corp. v. Admiral Corp., 199 F.Supp. 797, 815, 131 USPQ 413, 428–29 (D.Del. 1961), are as apt today as when made in 1961:

> The cases dealing with § 102(b) of the Patent Act are in a state of confusion resulting in part from an attempt to establish hard and fast rules of law based upon overly refined legal distinctions. The area sought to be governed by these rules, however, encompasses an infinite variety of factual situations which, when viewed in terms of the policies underlying § 102(b), present an infinite variety of legal problems wholly unsuited to mechanically-applied, technical rules.

The regional circuits that have considered the question have given lip service to a requirement of reduction to practice as part of the on-sale bar. However, when faced with a specific factual situation which appeared to fall within the intent of the statutory bar but did not technically satisfy the requirements for reduction to practice, these courts have stepped back from a rigid application of that requirement. In such cases, in an attempt to shoehorn the reduction to practice concept into the on-sale bar analysis, the courts looked to see whether the invention was "sufficiently" reduced to practice for purposes of the bar. In this case, the government appears to urge such a position.

Adoption of a "sufficiently" reduced-to-practice requirement is in fact an abandonment of reduction to practice as that term is used in other contexts. This court observed in *Barmag*, 731 F.2d at 838 n. 6, 221 USPQ at 567 n. 6, that our case law does not support a variegated definition of reduction to practice. At this point, we point out that "reduction to practice" is a term of art which developed in connection with interference practice to determine priority of invention between rival claimants. In that context Judge Rich has said: "There are no degrees of reduction to practice; either one has or has not occurred." Wolter v. Belicka, 409 F.2d 255, 262, 161 USPQ 335, 340 (CCPA 1969) (Rich, J., dissenting). It can only cause confusion in interference law, with its special technical considerations, and in operation of the on-sale bar, which is guided by entirely different policies, to adopt modifiers in connection with "reduction to practice," whatever the context.

Moreover, since reduction to practice is a term of art under this court's precedent, any specific ruling in one context on whether there is or is not a "reduction to practice" necessarily carries over into the other. For example, a holding here, like the trial court's, that there can be a reduction to practice without an embodiment containing all elements of the claim would have a major unintended impact on interference law. Conversely, by invoking reduction to practice as developed in interference law, an inventor might be able to escape the on-sale bar simply through deft claim draftsmanship.[9]

---

9. Weaver could have claimed "an aircraft with an accelerometer . . . ." instead of "an accelerometer. . . ." In that instance, the *claimed invention* would not

Finally, a major flaw in reduction to practice as a *per se* requirement of the on-sale bar in all cases is disclosed by a close analysis of *Timely Products,* the leading case which purports to adopt that requirement. A significant development with respect to the scope of section 102(b) occurred in a series of decisions beginning with those of another of our predecessors, the Court of Customs and Patent Appeals, when it recognized the operation of the bar in conjunction with the obviousness determination under section 103. In In re Foster, 343 F.2d at 988, 145 USPQ at 173, that court held:

> [S]ince the purpose of the statute has always been to require filing of the application within the prescribed period after the time the public came into possession of the invention, we cannot see that it makes any difference *how* it came into such possession, whether by a public use, a sale, a single patent or publication or by combinations of one or more of the foregoing. In considering this principle, *we assume,* of course, that by these means *the invention has become obvious* to that segment of the "public" having ordinary skill in the art. Once this has happened, the purpose of the law is to give the inventor only a year within which to file and this would seem to be liberal treatment.

Implicit in the operation of a sections 102(b)/103 bar is the *absence* of reduction to practice of the *claimed invention* as a requirement for the bar to operate. The invention, i.e., as claimed with all elements, is not the subject of the sale. If it were, section 103 would not be involved. With respect to non-claimed subject matter of the sale in a sections 102(b)/103 situation, it is meaningless to speak of "reduction to practice" of what was sold. "Reduction to practice" relates only to the precise invention expressed *in a claim.* Thus, the second requirement of *Timely Products,* reduction to practice of the *claimed invention,* is inherently inconsistent with the first requirement under which the bar is applicable if the claimed invention is merely "obvious in view of the thing offered for sale."

In view of all the above considerations, we conclude that reduction to practice of the claimed invention has not been and should not be made an absolute requirement of the on-sale bar.

We hasten to add, however, that we do not intend to sanction attacks on patents on the ground that the inventor or another offered for sale, before the critical date, the mere concept of the invention. Nor should inventors be forced to rush into the Patent and Trademark Office prematurely. On the other hand, we reject UMC's position that as a matter of law no on-sale bar is possible unless the claimed invention has been reduced to practice in the interference sense.

We do not reject "reduction to practice" as an important analytical tool in an on-sale analysis. A holding that there has or has not been a reduction to practice of the claimed invention before the critical date may well determine whether the claimed invention was in fact the

have been reduced to practice even if
Weaver had built and tested the entire
ACA.

subject of the sale or offer to sell or whether a sale was primarily for an experimental purpose. A holding that there is a reduction to practice of the claimed invention "may, of course, lighten the burden of the party asserting the bar." *General Electric,* 206 USPQ at 271. Thus, we simply say here that the on-sale bar does not necessarily turn on whether there was or was not a reduction to practice of the claimed invention. All of the circumstances surrounding the sale or offer to sell, including the stage of development of the invention and the nature of the invention, must be considered and weighed against the policies underlying section 102(b).

The above conclusion does not lend itself to formulation into a set of precise requirements such as that attempted by the *Timely Products* court. However, we point out certain critical considerations in the on-sale determination and the respective burdens of proof which have already been established in our precedent. Thus, without question, the challenger has the burden of proving that there was a definite sale or offer to sell more than one year before the application for the subject patent, and that the subject matter of the sale or offer to sell fully anticipated the claimed invention or would have rendered the claimed invention obvious by its addition to the prior art. If these facts are established, the patent owner is called upon to come forward with an explanation of the circumstances surrounding what would otherwise appear to be commercialization outside the grace period. The possibilities of such circumstances cannot possibly be enumerated. If the inventor had merely a conception or was working towards development of that conception, it can be said there is not yet any "invention" which could be placed on sale. A sale made because the purchaser was participating in experimental testing creates no on-sale bar.

V

The issue of whether an invention is on sale is a question of law. Because the Claims Court's factual findings are not disputed, and the issue may be resolved by application of the proper rule of law to those findings, we need not remand.

UMC made a definite offer to sell its later patented UMC–B accelerometer to the Navy more than one year prior to the date of the application for the patent in suit. In its bid, UMC specified a price of $404.00 for each sensor component of the ACA and $271.00 for the compatible recorder component. The total contract price was in excess of $1.6 million. This written offer which revealed use of the analog transducer in the ACA was supplied on July 27, 1967. UMC admits that the offer it made was for profit, not to conduct experiments.

UMC's activities evidence, at least *prima facie,* an attempt to commercialize the invention of the '513 patent by bidding on a large government contract more than one year prior to the filing of the underlying application and thereby to expand the grace period in contravention of the policies underlying the statute.

Countering the *prima facie* case, UMC offers only the purely technical objection that no complete embodiment of the invention existed at the time of the sale. In this case, that circumstance is unavailing when we look at the realities of the development of this invention. While UMC asserts that its improved ACA required further "development," as evidenced by its seeking a waiver of the liquidated damages provision in the RFP, that fact might weigh in UMC's favor if UMC had sought by convincing evidence to prove that the primary purpose of the sale was for experimental work. However, the contract was not a research and development contract, and UMC admits that the offer it made was for profit, not to conduct experimental work.

We do not attempt here to formulate a standard for determining when something less than a complete embodiment of the invention will suffice under the on-sale bar. However, the development of the subject invention was far beyond a mere conception. Much of the invention was embodied in tangible form. The prior art devices embodied each element of the claimed invention, save one, and that portion was available and had been sufficiently tested to demonstrate to the satisfaction of the inventor that the invention as ultimately claimed would work for its intended purpose. Thus, we conclude from the unchallenged facts with respect to the commercial activities of UMC, coupled with the extent to which the invention was developed, the substantial embodiment of the invention, the testing which was sufficient to satisfy the inventor that his later claimed invention would work, and the nature of the inventor's contribution to the art, that the claimed invention was on sale within the meaning of section 102(b).

Accordingly, we hold all claims of the '513 patent invalid. That issue being determinative of the case, we vacate the remainder of the Claims Court opinion.

Affirmed on different grounds.

Vacated-in-part.

[The opinion of EDWARD S. SMITH, Circuit Judge, dissenting, is omitted.]

PAULIK v. RIZKALLA

United States Court of Appeals, Federal Circuit, 1985.
760 F.2d 1270, 226 U.S.P.Q. 224.

PAULINE NEWMAN, Circuit Judge.

This appeal is from the decision of the United States Patent and Trademark Office Board of Patent Interferences (Board), awarding priority of invention to the senior party Nabil Rizkalla and Charles N. Winnick (Rizkalla), on the ground that the junior party and de facto first inventors Frank E. Paulik and Robert G. Schultz (Paulik) had suppressed or concealed the invention within the meaning of 35 U.S.C. § 102(g). We vacate this decision and remand to the Board.

I.

Rizkalla's patent application has the effective filing date of March 10, 1975, its parent application. Paulik's patent application was filed on June 30, 1975. The interference count is for a catalytic process for producing alkylidene diesters such as ethylidene diacetate, which is useful to prepare vinyl acetate and acetic acid. Paulik presented deposition testimony and exhibits in support of his claim to priority; Rizkalla chose to rely solely on his filing date.

The Board held and Rizkalla does not dispute that Paulik reduced the invention of the count to practice in November 1970 and again in April 1971. On about November 20, 1970 Paulik submitted a "Preliminary Disclosure of Invention" to the Patent Department of his assignee, the Monsanto Company. The disclosure was assigned a priority designation of "B", which Paulik states meant that the case would "be taken up in the ordinary course for review and filing."

Despite occasional prodding from the inventors, and periodic review by the patent staff and by company management, this disclosure had a lower priority than other patent work. Evidence of the demands of other projects on related technology was offered to justify the patent staff's delay in acting on this invention, along with evidence that the inventors and assignee continued to be interested in the technology and that the invention disclosure was retained in active status.

In January or February of 1975 the assignee's patent solicitor started to work toward the filing of the patent application; drafts of the application were prepared, and additional laboratory experiments were requested by the patent solicitor and were duly carried out by an inventor. The evidentiary sufficiency of these activities was challenged by Rizkalla, but the Board made no findings thereon, on the basis that these activities were not pertinent to the determination of priority. The Board held that "even if Paulik demonstrated continuous activity from prior to the Rizkalla effective filing date to his filing date . . . such would have no bearing on the question of priority in this case", and cited 35 U.S.C. § 102(g)[1] as authority for the statement that "[w]hile diligence during the above noted period may be relied upon by one alleging prior conception and subsequent reduction to practice, it is of no significance in the case of the party who is not the last to reduce to practice". The Board thus denied Paulik the opportunity to antedate Rizkalla, for the reason that Paulik was not only the first to conceive but he was also the first to reduce to practice.

The Board then held that Paulik's four-year delay from reduction to practice to his filing date was prima facie suppression or conceal-

---

1. 35 U.S.C. § 102(g) provides: A person shall be entitled to a patent unless . . . (g) before the applicant's invention thereof the invention was made in this country by another who had not abandoned, suppressed, or concealed it. In determining priority of invention there shall be considered not only the respective dates of conception and reduction to practice of the invention, but also the reasonable diligence of one who was first to conceive and last to reduce to practice, from a time prior to conception by the other.

ment under the first clause of section 102(g), that since Paulik had reduced the invention to practice in 1971 and 1972 he was barred by the second clause of section 102(g) from proving reasonable diligence leading to his 1975 filing, and that in any event the intervening activities were insufficient to excuse the delay. The Board refused to consider Paulik's evidence of renewed patent-related activity.

II.

The Board's decision converted the case law's estoppel against reliance on Paulik's early work for priority purposes, into a forfeiture encompassing Paulik's later work, even if the later work commenced before the earliest activity of Rizkalla. According to this decision, once the inference of suppression or concealment is established, this inference cannot be overcome by the junior party to an interference. There is no statutory or judicial precedent that requires this result, and there is sound reason to reject it.

United States patent law embraces the principle that the patent right is granted to the first inventor rather than the first to file a patent application. The law does not inquire as to the fits and starts by which an invention is made. The historic jurisprudence from which 35 U.S.C. § 102(g) flowed reminds us that "the mere lapse of time" will not prevent the inventor from receiving a patent. Mason v. Hepburn, 13 App.D.C. 86, 91, 1898 C.D. 510, 513 (1898). The sole exception to this principle resides in section 102(g) and the exigencies of the priority contest.

There is no impediment in the law to holding that a long period of inactivity need not be a fatal forfeiture, if the first inventor resumes work on the invention before the second inventor enters the field. We deem this result to be a fairer implementation of national patent policy, while in full accord with the letter and spirit of section 102(g).

The Board misapplied the rule that the first inventor does not have to show activity following reduction to practice to mean that the first inventor will not be allowed to show such activity. Such a showing may serve either of two purposes: to rebut an inference of abandonment, suppression, or concealment; or as evidence of renewed activity with respect to the invention. Otherwise, if an inventor were to set an invention aside for "too long" and later resume work and diligently develop and seek to patent it, according to the Board he would always be worse off than if he never did the early work, even as against a much later entrant.

Such a restrictive rule would merely add to the burden of those charged with the nation's technological growth. Invention is not a neat process. The value of early work may not be recognized or, for many reasons, it may not become practically useful, until months or years later. Following the Board's decision, any "too long" delay would constitute a forfeiture fatal in a priority contest, even if terminated by extensive and productive work done long before the newcomer entered the field.

We do not suggest that the first inventor should be entitled to rely for priority purposes on his early reduction to practice if the intervening inactivity lasts "too long," as that principle has evolved in a century of judicial analysis. Precedent did not deal with the facts at bar. There is no authority that would estop Paulik from relying on his resumed activities in order to pre-date Rizkalla's earliest date. We hold that such resumed activity must be considered as evidence of priority of invention. Should Paulik demonstrate that he had renewed activity on the invention and that he proceeded diligently to filing his patent application, starting before the earliest date to which Rizkalla is entitled—all in accordance with established principles of interference practice—we hold that Paulik is not prejudiced by the fact that he had reduced the invention to practice some years earlier.

III.

This appeal presents a question not previously treated by this court or, indeed, in the historical jurisprudence on suppression or concealment. We take this opportunity to clarify an apparent misperception of certain opinions of our predecessor court which the Board has cited in support of its holding.

There is over a hundred years of judicial precedent on the issue of suppression or concealment due to prolonged delay in filing. From the earliest decisions, a distinction has been drawn between deliberate suppression or concealment of an invention, and the legal inference of suppression or concealment based on "too long" a delay in filing the patent application. Both types of situations were considered by the courts before the 1952 Patent Act, and both are encompassed in 35 U.S.C. § 102(g). The result is consistent over this entire period—loss of the first inventor's priority as against an intervening second inventor— and has consistently been based on equitable principles and public policy as applied to the facts of each case. . . .

IV.

The decisions applying section 102(g) balanced the law and policy favoring the first person to make an invention, against equitable considerations when more than one person had made the same invention: in each case where the court deprived the de facto first inventor of the right to the patent, the second inventor had entered the field during a period of either inactivity or deliberate concealment by the first inventor. Often the first inventor had been spurred to file a patent application by news of the second inventor's activities. Although "spurring" is not necessary to a finding of suppression or concealment, the courts' frequent references to spurring indicate their concern with this equitable factor.

Some decisions used the word "forfeiture" to describe the first inventor's loss of priority; but none interpreted section 102(g) as requiring an absolute forfeiture rather than requiring a balance of equities. In *Brokaw v. Vogel,* for example, the court said "the *Mason v.*

Hepburn principle is not a forfeiture in the true sense; rather it is a rule according to which the patent right goes to the most deserving. Realistically, it is a forfeiture by the de facto first inventor of the right to rely on his earlier reduction to practice." 429 F.2d at 480, 57 C.C. P.A. at 1302, 166 USPQ at 431. In *Young v. Dworkin* Judge Rich wrote "I cannot agree with the board that the question in this case is whether Young 'forfeited his *right to a patent*'. But for Dworkin's conflicting claim, Young forfeited nothing and would get a patent. All he *forfeited* . . . was the right to rely on his prior actual reduction to practice in a priority dispute." 489 F.2d at 1286, 180 USPQ at 395–96 (emphasis in original).

In no case where the first inventor had waited "too long" did he end his period of inactivity before the second inventor appeared. We affirm the long-standing rule that too long a delay may bar the first inventor from reliance on an early reduction to practice in a priority contest. But we hold that the first inventor will not be barred from relying on later, resumed activity antedating an opponent's entry into the field, merely because the work done before the delay occurred was sufficient to amount to a reduction to practice.

This result furthers the basic purpose of the patent system. The exclusive right, constitutionally derived, was for the national purpose of advancing the useful arts—the process today called technological innovation. As implemented by the patent statute, the grant of the right to exclude carries the obligation to disclose the workings of the invention, thereby adding to the store of knowledge without diminishing the patent-supported incentive to innovate.

But the obligation to disclose is not the principal reason for a patent system; indeed, it is a rare invention that cannot be deciphered more readily from its commercial embodiment than from the printed patent. The reason for the patent system is to encourage innovation and its fruits: new jobs and new industries, new consumer goods and trade benefits. We must keep this purpose in plain view as we consider the consequences of interpretations of the patent law such as in the Board's decision.

A foreseeable consequence of the Board's ruling is to discourage inventors and their supporters from working on projects that had been "too long" set aside, because of the impossibility of relying, in a priority contest, on either their original work or their renewed work. This curious result is neither fair nor in the public interest. We do not see that the public interest is served by placing so severe a sanction on failure to file premature patent applications on immature inventions of unknown value. In reversing the Board's decision we do not hold that such inventions are necessarily entitled to the benefits of their earliest dates in a priority contest; we hold only that they are not barred from entitlement to their dates of renewed activity. . . .

VI.

Having established the principle that Paulik, although not entitled to rely on his early work, is entitled to rely on his renewed activity, we vacate the decision of the Board and, in the interest of justice, remand to the PTO for new interference proceedings in accordance with this principle.

VACATED AND REMANDED.

[The opinions of Rich, J., concurring, Markey, C.J., providing additional views; and Friedman, dissenting, are omitted.]

NOTES

1. The path through section 102 is tortuous and strewn with snares. The basic principle, that patents should not protect subject matter that fails to increase society's store of technological information, offers a rough-and-ready guide through the thicket: If the subject matter sought to be patented is disclosed by any other source, a patent will be denied because it serves no socially useful purpose.

Section 102's complexity lies not in its deviation from this principle, but in its use of several distinctions to enforce the principle. Consider, for example, the distinctions that underlie this synthesis of section 102: An inventor cannot obtain a patent for his subject matter if it has been known or used in this country by others before he invented it, or if it has been patented or described in a printed publication in this or a foreign country more than one year before he applied for a patent, or if it has been in public use or on sale in this country for more than one year before the date of his patent application.

2. *The Novelty Requirement and the Statutory Bars.* Section 102 distinguishes between the acts of an applicant seeking patent protection and the acts of others. A comparison of subsections (a) and (b) reveals a difference not only in operative point of time, but also in the range of persons whose conduct is relevant. Knowledge or use under subsection (a) must be "by others," while public use or sale in (b) is not so limited. Simply, under section 102(b) the incautious inventor may discover that he has barred his own claim. Although this bar looks like the novelty bar, its motive is different. "It is well settled that the policy consideration behind the 'public use' rule is to stimulate a seasonable disclosure of new inventions within the framework of the patent laws." Atlas v. Eastern Air Lines, Inc., 311 F.2d 156, 136 U.S.P.Q. 4 (1st Cir.1962). An analogous motive underlies subsections (d), (e) and, in part, subsection (g).

3. There is some overlap between the terms that subsections 102(a) and (b) employ to itemize and distinguish among the various anticipating sources—"known," "used," "patented," "described in a printed publication," "public use" and "sale." For example, although a patent can anticipate even if it is not printed, a patent once printed

also constitutes a printed publication. When, as in some countries, an invention's complete specifications are published before the patent is granted, it is the printed publication rather than the patent that poses the earlier bar. Since for a sale to anticipate under section 102(b) it can be neither secret nor conditional, some "knowledge" or "use" of the invention will be implicit in the transaction. See generally, Note, New Guidelines for Applying the On Sale Bar to Patentability, 24 Stan. L. Rev. 730 (1972).

Two requirements are common to all these sources of prior art. First, the anticipating source must place the claimed subject matter within public reach. Second, the source must disclose the subject matter for which patent protection is sought with sufficient clarity to instruct those skilled in the relevant art to recreate it—a requirement explicated in *Borst*.

Several of section 102's distinctions are rehearsed in section 102(g). Subsection (g)'s bar is, for example, limited to prior inventions made in "this country" by "another." Also, the term, "abandoned" holds the same consequence for the prior inventor under section 102(g) as it does for the applicant inventor under section 102(c). Unlike its companion subsections, however, section 102(g) does double service. It forms the basis for determining which of two or more applicants claiming priority for the same invention is to receive a patent. The role of these determinations, rendered in the first instance in the Patent and Trademark Office in the course of interference proceedings, is noted at p. 467, below.

4. *Anticipation.* Section 102 bars a patent only if the prior art is identical to—"anticipates"—the invention for which a patent is sought. The identity requirement distinguishes section 102 from section 103, where prior art—though nonidentical—may make an invention obvious and unpatentable. Unlike section 103, section 102 requires a single prior art reference to disclose every element of the invention for which the patent is sought. See, e.g., Structural Rubber Products Co. v. Park Rubber Co., 749 F.2d 707, 715–716, 223 U.S.P.Q. 1264, 1270–71 (Fed.Cir. 1984) ("This court has repeatedly stated that the defense of lack of novelty (i.e., 'anticipation') can only be established by a single prior art reference which discloses each and every element of the claimed invention. . . . While the teaching in the prior reference need not be *ipsissimis verbis,* nevertheless, there must be a teaching with respect to the entirety of the claimed invention.")

Can a product or process produced accidentally or unwittingly anticipate a later, advertent and conscious invention of the same subject matter? In Tilghman v. Proctor, 102 U.S. 707, 26 L.Ed. 279 (1880), the United States Supreme Court held that an earlier, accidental formation of fat acid would not defeat a patent on a process for separating fats into fat acids and glycerine: "We do not regard the accidental formation of fat acid in Perkins's steam cylinder from the tallow introduced to lubricate the piston (if the scum which rose on the water issuing from the ejection pipe was fat acid) as of any consequence in this inquiry. What the process was by which it was generated or formed was never fully understood. Those engaged in the art of making candles, or in any other art in which fat acids are desirable, certainly never derived the least hint from this accidental phenomenon in regard to any practicable process for manufacturing such acids." 102 U.S. at 711.

5. *Printed Publication.* What is a "printed publication"? In a long and thoughtful essay, Gerald Rose concludes that the law on the subject is "a muddled mess." Rose samples some holdings on what is and is not a printed publication:

"(a) a handwritten manuscript in a public library is *not.*

(b) a single typewritten thesis in a college library *is.*

(c) a scientific paper delivered orally to an audience is *not.*

(d) a scientific paper submitted for refereeing before publication *is.*

(e) an article in a Russian library was *not.*

(f) an instruction sheet distributed on one island in Japan *is.*

(g) a microfilm in the Library of Congress *is* or *is not,* depending on whether it is properly indexed.

(h) a trade circular that is thrown away *is.*"

Rose, Do You Have a "Printed Publication?" If Not, Do You Have Evidence of Prior "Knowledge or Use?" 61 J.Pat. Off. Soc'y 643, 644 (1979). See also Rothschild & White, Printed Publication: What is it Now? 70 J.Pat. & Trademark Off. Soc'y 42 (1988).

The golden thread running through the cases is that the term, "printed publication," embodies section 102's general requirement that prior art be publicly accessible. The fact that a reference is both printed and published is strong evidence of its public availability. Indeed, one case has held that "once it has been established that the item has been both printed and published, it is not necessary to further show that any given number of people actually saw it or that any specific number of copies have been circulated. The law sets up a *conclusive presumption* to the effect that the public has knowledge of the publication when a single printed copy is proved to have been so published." In re Tenney, 45 C.C.P.A. 894, 254 F.2d 619, 626–627, 117 U.S.P.Q. 348 (1958) (emphasis the court's). See also, In re Hall, 781 F.2d 897, 228 U.S.P.Q. 453 (Fed.Cir.1986).

When, if at all, did publication occur under the following facts: On April 30, 1959, a printer delivered a report disclosing the claimed subject matter to *J*, a research laboratory's technical editor. On May 5, 1959, *J* mailed these copies to individuals on a distribution list. *J*, testifies "that if counsel had come to his office on April 30, and requested a copy of the report, he would 'very likely' have been given one." Both parties concede that if the report was published more than one year before May 3, 1960, the patent would be invalid under section 102(b). See University of Illinois Foundation v. Blonder–Tongue Laboratories, Inc., 422 F.2d 769, 164 U.S.P.Q. 545 (7th Cir.1970), vacated, 402 U.S. 313, 91 S.Ct. 1434, 28 L.Ed.2d 788, 167 U.S.P.Q. 321. Would the invention have been "known" under section 102(a)?

6. Was section 102(b) applied too strictly in Egbert v. Lippmann, 104 U.S. 333, 26 L.Ed. 755 (1881)? Defendant, charged with infringement, argued that the inventor had publicly used the subject matter in suit—corset springs—more than two years (the grace period then in effect) before he filed his patent application. Evidently, eleven years before filing, the inventor had presented his fiancee with a pair of the corset springs. During this period she was the only person to use them and, by their nature, they were not exposed to public view.

The Court, concerned that the inventor had "slept on his rights for eleven years," decided that the facts supported a finding of public use. To be public, the Court declared, a use need not be of more than one device, nor by more than one person. The decisive fact was that the inventor had given the device to his fiancee without at the same time restricting its use. Justice Miller indulged some refreshing realism in his dissent: "It may well be imagined that a prohibition to the party so permitted against exposing her use of the steel spring to public observation would have been supposed to be a piece of irony." 104 U.S. at 339.

7. *Anticipating Events that Occur Abroad.* Section 102 distinguishes between anticipating events that occur in the United States and those that occur abroad. Two questions frequently arise in determining whether a foreign patent or printed publication anticipates: Does the foreign document, regardless of its characterization under local law, in fact constitute a patent or a printed publication? If so, to what extent does the patent or publication disclose the subject matter in question?

Carter Products Inc. v. Colgate–Palmolive Co., 130 F.Supp. 557, 104 U.S.P.Q. 314 (D.Md.1955), aff'd, 230 F.2d 855, 108 U.S.P.Q. 383 (4th Cir. 1956), raised and answered both questions. Defendant claimed that, over a year before the patent in suit was applied for, an Argentine patent had been granted on identical subject matter. The Argentine patent, defendant argued, also constituted a printed publication so that section 102(b) barred a patent on not one, but two grounds.

Reasoning from the undisputed premise "that what was publicly known or used in the foreign country is not a bar to a United States patent unless such was either patented or described in a printed publication in the foreign country," the court rejected both contentions. First, "since the Argentine patent is a typewritten document, it could not qualify as printed." Second, the court found it "necessary to determine what was in fact 'patented' by the Argentine patent." Resting its conclusion upon the testimony of two experts in Argentine law and upon a statement in the patent itself, the court ruled that the scope of the patent was limited to its claim, which in no way taught the subject matter in question: "the three composition examples set forth in the Argentine patent, upon which defendants rely . . . bear no relationship to the claimed subject matter of the Argentine patent, and also are unrelated to anything else in the patent specification." The court was alternatively disposed to ignore Argentine law entirely and impose the United States domestic rule of patent construction: "That nothing is to be treated as patented except what is actually claimed therein is well settled under our decisions."

See generally, Chisum, Foreign Activity: Its Effect on Patentability Under United States Law, 11 Int'l.Rev.Indus.Prop. & Copyright L. 26 (1980).

8. *Experimental Use.* Experimental use of an invention does not constitute public use or sale for purposes of section 102(b). Courts exclude time devoted to the invention's development and refinement from section 102's prior use period. The experimental use exception is narrow. Courts exclude the time taken for tests of an invention's utility and practical value, but include the time taken by tests of the invention's marketability and commercial value.

In re Smith, 714 F.2d 1127, 218 U.S.P.Q. 976 (Fed.Cir.1983), illustrates the distinction between experimentation and marketing tests. The applicant in *Smith* had invented a vacuumable carpet and room deodorizer. The applicant's assignee had given 76 St. Louis consumers two different prototypes of the composition to use in their homes for two weeks without legal restriction. The court rejected the applicant's assertion that the testing activities constituted an "integral part of their research and development process" and emphasized the importance of objective evidence of experimentation—evidence, for example, that the inventor inspected the invention regularly, that the inventor retained control over the invention, and that "the commercial exploitation was merely incidental to the primary purpose of experimentation." 714 F.2d at 1135.

> Contrary to appellants' contention that the St. Louis test was needed to obtain scientific data on their invention's operation and usefulness, such data could have been easily obtained in their own facilities. The operability and other properties of the claimed invention could have been verified without the assistance of 'typical housewives' (consumers). Instead, there was a more dominant purpose behind the St. Louis test, *viz.* to determine whether potential consumers would buy the product and how much they would pay for it—commercial exploitation.

Further, "the procedures used by the appellants suggest that the test was designed primarily to determine how well the product would sell, not to isolate systematically technical problems which remained in the product. Appellants did not control the actual testing of the composition. For example, the testing of the composition in the instant case was not conducted in the presence of appellants. Nor were restrictions placed on the consumers as to the use of the product." 714 F.2d at 1135–36.

9. *Conception and Reduction to Practice.* To qualify for protection, patent subject matter must have been "conceived" and "reduced to practice." The distinction between conception and reduction to prac-

tice is central to section 102's operation. Section 102(g) employs the distinction to determine priority of invention as between competing inventors. It assigns priority not to the first inventor who completed the invention—conceived and reduced it to practice—but rather to the first who conceived it. Reduction to practice comes into play only in the requirement that priority may be defeated if the first inventor to conceive was not reasonably diligent in reducing his conception to practice. The distinction is also implicit in subsections 102(a) and (b). For anticipating subject matter to have been patented, used or known, it must have been reduced to practice. Knowledge or use of a conception alone will not anticipate.

The measure of conception is simple enough. It requires that there exist at the threshold of the invention some idea of a useful result to be achieved and some specific method for achieving that result. Reduction to practice, which requires that the conception be embodied in readily utilizable form, has received three different formulations. The first, original formula identifies reduction with that moment at which the invention is first made to work in the environment in which it is to be used rather than in some experimental setting. Under this rule, a voting machine intended for use in public elections is not reduced to practice by its use in the election of a corporate board of directors. Ocumpaugh v. Norton, 25 App.D.C. 90 (D.C.Cir.1905).

The Telephone Cases, 126 U.S. 1, 8 S.Ct. 778, 31 L.Ed. 863 (1888), involving two of Alexander Bell's patents, established the first broad exception to the orthodox formula. The Court there decided that it was inconsequential that, at the time the patent in dispute issued to him, Bell had not reduced his device to actual practice, nor even demonstrated that it could transmit intelligible sounds. Actual reduction was unnecessary, the Court held, since Bell had in the specifications of his patent application described the device with sufficient accuracy to instruct a worker ordinarily skilled in the art to construct a manifestly operative device. The Court viewed reduction to practice as a function of two statutory objectives—that patented subject matter be operative, and that it be placed in a form capable of teaching the public how to recreate it. The first objective could be met under the statutory test of utility, for which proof of operativeness short of reduction will suffice. The second could be met by the detailed and precise disclosure required for the patent application. From this the Court concluded that the filing of a patent application should operate as a constructive reduction to practice of the underlying invention.

Borst, decided almost a century later, invoked the same statutory objectives to derive the third formulation of reduction to practice.

See Moldovanyi, Reduction to Practice By Computer Simulation . . . Is It Ever Possible? 65 J.Pat.Off.Soc'y 497 (1983).

10. *First-to-Invent v. First-to-File.* Section 102's foundation stone is the principle that a patent belongs to the first person who invented the claimed subject matter and not to the first person who filed a patent application for it. This principle, which dates to the 1836

Patent Act, predicates that the patent system should reward the first, true inventor rather than a later inventor who wins the race to the Patent and Trademark Office.

The only remarkable feature of the first-to-invent principle is its uniqueness. Apart from the Philippines, the United States is the only country in the world to follow a first-to-invent system. All other countries with patent laws have a first-to-file system. Systematic efforts to introduce a first-to-file rule in the United States date to the 1966 report of the President's Commission on the Patent System, To Promote the Progress of Useful Arts in an Age of Exploding Technology.

Among the arguments in favor of a first-to-file system are: it will eliminate costly interference proceedings in which, as a general rule, the first party to file will prevail in any event; patent practice in the United States already approximates a first-to-file system since inventors file promptly in order to obtain priority under the first-to-file systems of other countries; and a first-to-file system would eliminate the uncertainty associated with the determination of who in fact first invented the subject matter in issue.

Among the arguments against a first-to-file system are: most interference proceedings are settled and, in those that are not, the first party to invent prevails in a substantial number of cases; early filing to obtain priority in other countries has been true only of large multinational corporations with international interests; and a first-to-invent system protects against theft of patents by later "inventors" who devote their resources not to invention but to early filing.

Practical politics—specifically international politics—may prove to be more important than reasoned argument in resolving the first-to-file debate. A draft treaty on the harmonization of patent laws, prepared under the auspices of the World Intellectual Property Organization, would require all adhering countries to maintain a first-to-file system. The United States has indicated its willingness to adhere to the proposed treaty, but on conditions. Among the conditions are that the treaty provide for a grace period, like the one currently provided under the United States Patent Act, allowing an inventor to publish her invention before filing a patent application.

On the pros and cons of a first-to-file system, see Dunner, First to File: Should Our Interference System Be Abolished?, 68 J.Pat. & Trade. Off.Soc'y 561 (1986); Banner & McDonnell, First-to-File, Mandatory Reexamination, and Mandatory "Exceptional Circumstance": Ideas for Better? Or Worse?, 69 J.Pat. & Trademark Off. Soc'y 595 (1987).

c. SECTIONS 102 AND 103 IN CONCERT: WHAT IS PRIOR ART?

HAZELTINE RESEARCH, INC. v. BRENNER

Supreme Court of the United States, 1965.
382 U.S. 252, 86 S.Ct. 335, 15 L.Ed.2d 304, 147 U.S.P.Q. 429.

Mr. Justice BLACK delivered the opinion of the Court.

The sole question presented here is whether an application for patent pending in the Patent Office at the time a second application is filed constitutes part of the "prior art" as that term is used in 35 U.S. C.A. § 103, which reads in part:

> A patent may not be obtained . . . if the differences between the subject matter sought to be patented and the prior art are such that the subject matter as a whole would have been obvious at the time the invention was made to a person having ordinary skill in the art. . . .

The question arose in this way. On December 23, 1957, petitioner Robert Regis filed an application for a patent on a new and useful improvement on a microwave switch. On June 24, 1959, the Patent Examiner denied Regis' application on the ground that the invention was not one which was new or unobvious in light of the prior art and thus did not meet the standards set forth in § 103. The Examiner said that the invention was unpatentable because of the joint effect of the disclosures made by patents previously issued, one to Carlson (No. 2,491,644) and one to Wallace (No. 2,822,526). The Carlson patent had been issued on December 20, 1949, over eight years prior to Regis' application, and that patent is admittedly a part of the prior art insofar as Regis' invention is concerned. The Wallace patent, however, was pending in the Patent Office when the Regis application was filed. The Wallace application had been pending since March 24, 1954, nearly three years and nine months before Regis filed his application and the Wallace patent was issued on February 4, 1958, 43 days after Regis filed his application.[1]

After the Patent Examiner refused to issue the patent, Regis appealed to the Patent Office Board of Appeals on the ground that the Wallace patent could not be properly considered a part of the prior art because it had been a "co-pending patent" and its disclosures were secret and not known to the public. The Board of Appeals rejected this argument and affirmed the decision of the Patent Examiner. Regis and Hazeltine, which had an interest as assignee, then instituted the present action in the District Court pursuant to 35 U.S.C.A. § 145 to compel the Commissioner to issue the patent. The District Court agreed with the Patent Office that the co-pending Wallace application was a part of the prior art and directed that the complaint be dis-

---

1. It is not disputed that Regis' alleged invention, as well as his application, was made after Wallace's application was filed. There is, therefore, no question of priority of invention before us.

missed. On appeal the Court of Appeals affirmed per curiam. We granted certiorari to decide the question of whether a co-pending application is included in the prior art, as that term is used in 35 U.S. C.A. § 103.

Petitioners' primary contention is that the term "prior art," as used in § 103, really means only art previously publicly known. In support of this position they refer to a statement in the legislative history which indicates that prior art means "what was known before as described in section 102." [2] They contend that the use of the word "known" indicates that Congress intended prior art to include only inventions or discoveries which were already publicly known at the time an invention was made.

If petitioners are correct in their interpretation of "prior art," then the Wallace invention, which was not publicly known at the time the Regis application was filed, would not be prior art with regard to Regis' invention. This is true because at the time Regis filed his application the Wallace invention, although pending in the Patent Office, had never been made public and the Patent Office was forbidden by statute from disclosing to the public, except in special circumstances, anything contained in the application.

The Commissioner, relying chiefly on Alexander Milburn Co. v. Davis–Bournonville Co., 270 U.S. 390, 46 S.Ct. 324, 70 L.Ed. 651, contends that when a patent is issued, the disclosures contained in the patent become a part of the prior art as of the time the application was filed, not, as petitioners contend, at the time the patent is issued. In that case a patent was held invalid because, at the time it was applied for, there was already pending an application which completely and adequately described the invention. In holding that the issuance of a patent based on the first application barred the valid issuance of a patent based on the second application, Mr. Justice Holmes, speaking for the Court, said, "The delays of the patent office ought not to cut down the effect of what has been done. . . . [The first applicant] had taken steps that would make it public as soon as the Patent Office did its work, although, of course, amendments might be required of him before the end could be reached. We see no reason in the words or policy of the law for allowing [the second applicant] to profit by the delay. . . ." At p. 401, 46 S.Ct. at p. 325.

In its revision of the patent laws in 1952, Congress showed its approval of the holding in *Milburn* by adopting 35 U.S.C.A. § 102(e) which provides that a person shall be entitled to a patent unless "(e) the invention was described in a patent granted on an application for patent by another filed in the United States before the invention thereof by the applicant for patent." Petitioners suggest, however, that the question in this case is not answered by mere reference to § 102(e), because in *Milburn*, which gave rise to that section, the co-pending applications described the same identical invention. But here the Regis

2. H.R.Rep. No. 1923, 82d Cong., 2d Sess., p. 7 (1952).

invention is not precisely the same as that contained in the Wallace patent, but is only made obvious by the Wallace patent in light of the Carlson patent. We agree with the Commissioner that this distinction is without significance here. While we think petitioners' argument with regard to § 102(e) is interesting, it provides no reason to depart from the plain holding and reasoning in the *Milburn* case. The basic reasoning upon which the Court decided the *Milburn* case applies equally well here. When Wallace filed his application, he had done what he could to add his disclosures to the prior art. The rest was up to the Patent Office. Had the Patent Office acted faster, had it issued Wallace's patent two months earlier, there would have been no question here. As Justice Holmes said in *Milburn*, "The delays of the patent office ought not to cut down the effect of what has been done." P. 401, 46 S.Ct. at p. 325.

To adopt the result contended for by petitioners would create an area where patents are awarded for unpatentable advances in the art. We see no reason to read into § 103 a restricted definition of "prior art" which would lower standards of patentability to such an extent that there might exist two patents where the Congress has plainly directed that there should be only one.

Affirmed.

APPLICATION OF FOSTER, 343 F.2d 980, 987–990, 145 U.S.P.Q. 166 (C.C.P.A.), cert. denied, 383 U.S. 966, 86 S.Ct. 1270, 16 L.Ed.2d 307, 149 U.S.P.Q. 906 (1965). ALMOND, J.: Sections 101, 102 and 103, generally speaking, deal with two different matters: (1) the factors to be considered in determining whether a patentable invention has been *made*, i.e., novelty, utility, unobviousness, and the categories of patentable subject matter; and (2) "loss of right to patent" as stated in the heading of section 102, even though an otherwise patentable invention has been made. On the subject of loss of right, appellant's brief contains a helpful review of the development of the statutory law since 1793. It says:

> In 1897 the patent laws were amended to make the . . . two-year bar period apply to all public uses, publications and patents *regardless of the source* from which they emanated. The change was a consequence, primarily, of greatly improved communications within the country which had rendered inventors easily able to acquire knowledge of the public acts of others within their own fields. It was reasoned that any inventor who *delayed in filing* a patent application for more than two years after a public disclosure of the invention would obtain *an undeserved reward in derogation of the rights of the public* if he were granted a patent.

> In 1939, in recognition of further improvements in communications, Congress reduced the two-year bar period to one year. . . .

> That 1939 Act was carried over unchanged in the 1952 recodification of the patent laws as 35 U.S.C.A. § 102(b). . . .

Manifestly, Section 102(b) from its earliest beginnings has been and was intended to be directed toward the encouragement of *diligence* in the filing of patent applications and the protection of the public from monopolies on subject matter which had already been fully disclosed to it.

These statements are in accord with our understanding of the history and purposes of section 102(b). It presents a sort of statute of limitations, formerly two years, now one year, within which an inventor, even though he has made a patentable invention, must act on penalty of loss of his right to patent. What starts the period running is clearly the availability of the invention *to the public* through the categories of disclosure enumerated in 102(b), which include "a printed publication" anywhere describing the invention. There appears to be no dispute about the operation of this statute in "complete anticipation" situations but *the contention seems to be that 102(b) has no applicability where the invention is not completely disclosed in a single patent or publication,* that is to say where the rejection involves the addition to the disclosure of the reference of the ordinary skill of the art or the disclosure of another reference which indicates what those of ordinary skill in the art are presumed to know, *and to have known for more than a year before the application was filed.* Upon a complete reexamination of this matter we are convinced that the contention is contrary to the policy consideration which motivated the enactment by Congress of a statutory bar. On logic and principle we think this contention is unsound, and we also believe it is contrary to the patent law as it has actually existed since at least 1898.

First, as to principle, since the purpose of the statute has always been to require filing of the application within the prescribed period after the time the public came into possession of the invention, we cannot see that it makes any difference *how* it came into such possession, whether by a public use, a sale, a single patent or publication, or by combinations of one or more of the foregoing. In considering this principle *we assume,* of course, that by these means *the invention has become obvious* to that segment of the "public" having ordinary skill in the art. Once this has happened, the purpose of the law is to give the inventor only a year within which to file and this would seem to be liberal treatment. Whenever an applicant undertakes, under Rule 131,[8] to swear back of a reference having an effective date more than a

---

8. "*131. Affidavit of prior invention to overcome cited patent or publication.* (a) When any claim of an application is rejected on reference to a domestic patent which substantially shows or describes but does not claim the rejected invention, or on reference to a foreign patent or to a printed publication, and the applicant shall make oath to facts showing a completion of the invention in this country before the filing date of the application on which the domestic patent issued, or before the date of the foreign patent, or before the date of the printed publication, then the patent or publication cited shall not bar the grant of a patent to the applicant, *unless the date of such patent or printed publication be more than one year prior to the date on which the application was filed in this country.*" [Emphasis ours.]

The italicized clause at the end of the foregoing paragraph or its equivalent has been present in the rule and its predecessor Rule 75 since January 1, 1898, when the rule was amended to include:

. . . unless the date of such patent or printed publication is more than two years prior to the date on which application was filed in this country.

[Opinion of court, 343 F.2d 980, 987 n. 8.]

year before his filing date, he is automatically conceding that he made his invention more than a year before he filed. If the reference contains enough disclosure to make his invention obvious, the principle of the statute would seem to require denial of a patent to him. The same is true where a combination of two publications or patents makes the invention obvious and they both have dates more than a year before the filing date.

As to dealing with the express language of 102(b), for example, "described in a printed publication," technically, we see no reason to so read the words of the statute as to preclude the use of more than one reference; nor do we find in the context anything to show that "a printed publication" cannot include two or more printed publications. We do not have two publications here, but we did in Palmquist [319 F.2d 547, 138 U.S.P.Q. 234 (1963)] and it is a common situation.

As to what the law has been, more particularly what it was prior to 1953, when the new patent act and its section 103 became effective, there is a paucity of direct precedents on the precise problem. We think there is a reason for this. Under the old law (R.S. § 4886, where 102(b) finds its origin) patents were refused or invalidated on references dated more than a year before the filing date because the invention was anticipated or, if they were not, then *because there was no "invention,"* the latter rejection being based either on (a) a single nonanticipatory reference plus the skill of the art *or (b) on a plurality of references.* There was no need to seek out the precise statutory basis because it was R.S. § 4886 in any event, read in the light of the Supreme Court's interpretation of the law that there must always be "invention." This issue was determined on the disclosures of the references relied on and if they had dates more than one year before the filing date, it was assumed they could be relied on to establish a "statutory bar." There was an express prohibition in Rule 131 and in its predecessor Rule 75 against antedating a reference having a date more than a year prior to the filing date and there was no basis on which to contest it. . . .

It would seem that the practical operation of the prior law was that references having effective dates more than a year before applicant's filing date were always considered to be effective as references, regardless of the applicant's date of invention, and that rejections were then predicated thereon for "lack of invention" without making the distinction which we now seem to see as implicit in sections 102 and 103, "anticipation" or no novelty situations under 102 and "obviousness" situations under 103. But on further reflection, we now feel bound to point out that of equal importance is the question of *loss of right* predicated on a one-year *time-bar* which, it seems clear to us, has never been limited to "anticipation" situations, involving only a single reference, but has included as well "no invention" (now "obviousness") situations. It follows that where the time-bar is involved, *the actual date of invention becomes irrelevant* and that it is not in accordance with either the letter or the principle of the law, or its past interpretation over a very long period, to permit an applicant to dispose of a reference having a date more than one year prior to his filing date by proving his actual date of invention.

Such a result was permitted by our decision in Palmquist and to the extent that it permitted a reference, having a publication date more than one year prior to the United States filing date to which the applicant was entitled, to be disposed of by proof of a date of invention earlier than the date of the reference, that decision is hereby overruled.

We wish to make it clear that this ruling is predicated on our construction of section 102(b) and has no effect on the statements in Palmquist respecting the determination of obviousness under section 103 when a statutory time-bar is not involved. The existence of unobviousness under that section, as a necessary prerequisite to patentability, we reiterate, must be determined as of "the time the invention was made" without utilizing after-acquired knowledge.

NOTES

1. Section 103's opening clause—"A patent may not be obtained though the invention is not identically disclosed or described as set forth in section 102 of this title"—implicates section 102 in section 103's design. *Hazeltine* rolled section 103 forward to include references that first arise or become public after the date of invention. *Foster* allowed a wider range of references to bar patentability under section 102(b) than the "complete anticipation" measure of section 102(a). To what extent do the two decisions obliterate the distinctions between sections 102 and 103? Consider Judge Giles Rich's crystallization of the assumptions that underlie sections 102 and 103:

> The anatomy of section 102 is fairly clear. As forecast in its heading, it deals with the two questions of 'novelty and loss of right.' It also deals with originality in subsection (f) which says that one who 'did not himself invent the subject matter' (i.e., he did not originate it) has no right to a patent on it. Subsections (c) on abandonment and (d) on first patenting the invention abroad, before the date of the U.S. application, on an application filed more than a year before filing in the U.S., are loss of right provisions and in no way relate to 'prior art'. Of course, (c), (d), and (f) have no relation to section 103 and no relevancy to what is 'prior art' under section 103. Only the remaining portions of section 102 deal with 'prior art.' Three of them, (a), (e), and (g), deal with events prior to applicant's *invention* date and the other, (b), with events more than one year prior to the U.S. *application* date. These are the 'prior art' subsections.

In re Bass, 474 F.2d 1276, 1290, 177 U.S.P.Q. 178 (C.C.P.A.1973).

See generally, Walterscheid, The Ever Evolving Meaning of Prior Art (Part I), 64 J.Pat.Off.Soc'y 457 (1982) (continued in succeeding numbers of the Journal).

2. Judge Arthur Smith, who wrote for a unanimous court in *Palmquist,* dissented in *Foster* which overruled it. In Judge Smith's

view, neither section 102 nor section 103 expressly addressed the issue raised by *Foster* and *Palmquist,* and the court reached too far to repair the legislative oversight. According to Smith, "the majority decision amounts to an interpretation of section 102(b) as though it contained the following italicized words: "

> A person shall be entitled to a patent unless— . . . (b) the invention was patented or described in a printed publication in this or a foreign country *or* in public use or on sale in this country or *unless the invention became obvious* more than one year prior to the date of the application for patent in the United States. . . .

Further, "the majority must also intend to rewrite section 103 so that the phrase 'at the time the invention was made' now is to be limited by a proviso which reduces this time to a period of one year prior to the filing of the application." 343 F.2d at 980, 996–997.

In Judge Smith's view, the majority decision also contradicted sound patent policy. "In overruling *Palmquist,* the majority gives lip service to the truism that 'section 103 per se has nothing whatever to do' with the issue of loss of right to patent, but then proceeds to decide the case as one of obviousness using Binder [the defeating reference] as *prior art* under section 103, which it most emphatically is not, since it *did not exist* 'at the time the invention was made.' . . . Today's decision destroys any meaningful differences that may have existed in the past between sections 102(a) and (b) and section 103. . . . Most disturbing of all is the fact that from this day forward obviousness under section 103 will be tested, *not as of the time the invention was made,* but *as of one year prior to the filing date of the application."* 343 F.2d at 980, 998–999 (emphasis in original).

   3. Does a prior invention under section 102(g) constitute prior art for purposes of section 103? Sutter Products Co. v. Pettibone Mulliken Corp., 428 F.2d 639, 646, 166 U.S.P.Q. 100 (7th Cir.1970), answered that it does. Noting a parallel to the situation in *Hazeltine,* which involved section 102(e), the court concluded that "the considerations expressed are equally applicable to prior inventions under section 102(g)." Section 102(f) may also be used to prove obviousness. See Dale Elecs., Inc. v. R.C.L. Elecs., 488 F.2d 382, 180 U.S.P.Q. 225 (1st Cir.1973).

   4. The Patent Law Amendments Act of 1984 added a last sentence to section 103: "Subject matter developed by another person, which qualifies as prior art only under subsection (f) or (g) of section 102 of this title, shall not preclude patentability under this section where the subject matter and the claimed invention were, at the time the invention was made, owned by the same person or subject to an obligation of assignment to the same person." P.L. 98–622, § 103, 98 Stat. 3384. The purpose of the amendment was to change existing case law, including In re Bass "and its progeny," and to provide "material benefit to university and corporate research laboratories where the free exchange of ideas and concepts may have been hampered by the current state of the law with respect to what constitutes 'prior art.'" Remarks

of Robert W. Kastenmeier, 129 Cong.Rec. E5777, E5778 (daily ed. Nov. 18, 1983, part II).

d. UTILITY

LOWELL v. LEWIS, 15 Fed.Cas. 1018 (No. 8568) (C.C.D.Mass.1817). STORY, Circuit Justice (charging jury): The present action is brought by the plaintiff for a supposed infringement of a patent-right, granted, in 1813, to Mr. Jacob Perkins (from whom the plaintiff claims by assignment) for a new and useful improvement in the construction of pumps. The defendant asserts, in the first place, that the invention is neither new nor useful; and, in the next place, that the pumps used by him are not of the same construction as those of Mr. Perkins, but are of a new invention of a Mr. Baker, under whom the defendant claims by assignment. . . .

To entitle the plaintiff to a verdict, he must establish, that his machine is a new and useful invention; and of these facts his patent is to be considered merely prima facie evidence of a very slight nature. He must, in the first place, establish it to be a useful invention; for the law will not allow the plaintiff to recover, if the invention be of a mischievous or injurious tendency. The defendant, however, has asserted a much more broad and sweeping doctrine; and one, which I feel myself called upon to negative in the most explicit manner. He contends that it is necessary for the plaintiff to prove that his invention is of general utility; so that in fact, for the ordinary purposes of life, it must supersede the pumps in common use. In short, that it must be, for the public, a better pump than the common pump; and that unless the plaintiff can establish this position, the law will not give him the benefit of a patent, even though in some peculiar cases his invention might be applied with advantage. I do not so understand the law. The patent act (Act Feb. 21, 1793, c. 11 [1 Stat. 31]) uses the phrase "useful invention" mere incidentally; it occurs only in the first section, and there it seems merely descriptive of the subject matter of the application, or of the conviction of the applicant. The language is, "when any person or persons shall allege, that he or they have invented any new and useful art, machine," &c., he or they may, on pursuing the directions of the act, obtain a patent. Neither the oath required by the second section, nor the special matter of defence allowed to be given in evidence by the sixth section of the act, contains any such qualification or reference to general utility, to establish the validity of the patent. Nor is it alluded to in the tenth section as a cause, for which the patent may be vacated. To be sure, all the matters of defence or of objection to the patent are not enumerated in these sections. But if such an one as that now contended for had been intended, it is scarcely possible to account for its omission. In my judgement the argument is utterly without foundation. All that the law requires is, that the invention should not be frivolous or injurious to the well-being, good policy, or sound morals of society. The word "useful," therefore, is incorporated into the act in contradistinction to mischievous or immoral. For instance, a new invention to poison people, or to promote debauchery, or to facilitate private assassination, is not a patentable invention. But if the invention steers wide of these objections, whether it be more or less useful is a circumstance very material to the interests of the patentee, but of no importance to the public. If it be not extensively useful, it will silently sink into contempt and disregard. There is no pretence, that Mr. Perkins' pump is a mischievous invention; and if it has been used injuriously to the patentee by the defendant, it certainly does not lie in his mouth to contest its general utility. Indeed the defendant asserts, that Baker's pump is useful in a very eminent degree, and, if it be substantially the same as Perkins', there is an end of the objection; if it be not substantially the same, then the plaintiff must fail in his action. So that, in either view, the abstract question seems hardly of any importance in this cause.

BRENNER v. MANSON

Supreme Court of the United States, 1966.
383 U.S. 519, 86 S.Ct. 1033, 16 L.Ed.2d 69, 148 U.S.P.Q. 689.

Mr. Justice FORTAS delivered the opinion of the Court.

. . . Our starting point is the proposition, neither disputed nor disputable, that one may patent only that which is "useful." In Graham v. John Deere Co., 383 U.S. 1, at 5–10, 86 S.Ct. 684, at 687–690, 148 U.S.P.Q. 459, we have reviewed the history of the requisites of patentability, and it need not be repeated here. Suffice it to say that the concept of utility has maintained a central place in all of our patent legislation, beginning with the first patent law in 1790 and culminating in the present law's provision that

> Whoever invents or discovers any new and useful process, machine, manufacture, or composition of matter, or any new and useful improvement thereof, may obtain a patent therefor, subject to the conditions and requirements of this title.

As is so often the case, however, a simple, everyday word can be pregnant with ambiguity when applied to the facts of life. That this is so is demonstrated by the present conflict between the Patent Office and the C.C.P.A. over how the test is to be applied to a chemical process which yields an already known product whose utility—other than as a possible object of scientific inquiry—has not yet been evidenced. It was not long ago that agency and court seemed of one mind on the question. In Application of Bremner, 182 F.2d 216, 217, 37 C.C.P.A. (Pat.) 1032, 1034, 86 U.S.P.Q. 74, 75, the court affirmed rejection by the Patent Office of both process and product claims. It noted that "no use for the products claimed to be developed by the processes had been shown in the specification." It held that "It was never intended that a patent be granted upon a product, or a process producing a product, unless such product be useful." Nor was this new doctrine in the court.

The Patent Office has remained steadfast in this view. The C.C.P.A. however, has moved sharply away from Bremner. The trend began in Application of Nelson, 280 F.2d 172, 47 C.C.P.A. (Pat.), 1031,

126 U.S.P.Q. 242. There, the court reversed the Patent Office's rejection of a claim on a process yielding chemical intermediates "useful to chemists doing research on steroids," despite the absence of evidence that any of the steroids thus ultimately produced were themselves "useful." The trend has accelerated, culminating in the present case where the court held it sufficient that a process produces the result intended and is not "detrimental to the public interest." 333 F.2d, at 238, 52 C.C.P.A., at 745, 142 U.S.P.Q. at 38.

It is not remarkable that differences arise as to how the test of usefulness is to be applied to chemical processes. Even if we knew precisely what Congress meant in 1790 when it devised the "new and useful" phraseology and in subsequent re-enactments of the test, we should have difficulty in applying it in the context of contemporary chemistry where research is as comprehensive as man's grasp and where little or nothing is wholly beyond the pale of "utility"—if that word is given its broadest reach.

Respondent does not—at least, in the first instance—rest upon the extreme proposition, advanced by the court below, that a novel chemical process is patentable so long as it yields the intended product and so long as the product is not itself "detrimental." Nor does he commit the outcome of his claim to the slightly more conventional proposition that any process is "useful" within the meaning of § 101 if it produces a compound whose potential usefulness is under investigation by serious scientific researchers, although he urges this position too as an alternative basis for affirming the decision of the C.C.P.A. Rather, he begins with the much more orthodox argument that his process has a specific utility which would entitle him to a declaration of interference even under the Patent Office's reading of § 101. The claim is that the supporting affidavits filed pursuant to Rule 204(b), by reference to Ringold's 1956 article, reveal that an adjacent homologue of the steroid yielded by his process has been demonstrated to have tumor-inhibiting effects in mice, and that this discloses the requisite utility. We do not accept any of these theories as an adequate basis for overriding the determination of the Patent Office that the "utility" requirement has not been met.

Even on the assumption that the process would be patentable were respondent to show that the steroid produced had a tumor-inhibiting effect in mice, we would not overrule the Patent Office finding that respondent has not made such a showing. The Patent Office held that, despite the reference to the adjacent homologue, respondent's papers did not disclose a sufficient likelihood that the steroid yielded by his process would have similar tumor-inhibiting characteristics. Indeed, respondent himself recognized that the presumption that adjacent homologues have the same utility has been challenged in the steroid field because of "a greater known unpredictability of compounds in that field." In these circumstances and in this technical area, we would not overturn the finding of the Primary Examiner, affirmed by the Board of Appeals and not challenged by the C.C.P.A.

The second and third points of respondent's argument present issues of much importance. Is a chemical process "useful" within the meaning of § 101 either (1) because it works—i.e., produces the intended product? or (2) because the compound yielded belongs to a class of compounds now the subject of serious scientific investigation? These contentions present the basic problem for our adjudication. Since we find no specific assistance in the legislative materials underlying § 101, we are remitted to an analysis of the problem in light of the general intent of Congress, the purposes of the patent system, and the implications of a decision one way or the other.

In support of his plea that we attenuate the requirement of "utility," respondent relies upon Justice Story's well-known statement that a "useful" invention is one "which may be applied to a beneficial use in society, in contradistinction to an invention injurious to the morals, health, or good order of society, or frivolous and insignificant"—and upon the assertion that to do so would encourage inventors of new processes to publicize the event for the benefit of the entire scientific community, thus widening the search for uses and increasing the fund of scientific knowledge. Justice Story's language sheds little light on our subject. Narrowly read, it does no more than compel us to decide whether the invention in question is "frivolous and insignificant"—a query no easier of application than the one built into the statute. Read more broadly, so as to allow the patenting of any invention not positively harmful to society, it places such a special meaning on the word "useful" that we cannot accept it in the absence of evidence that Congress so intended. There are, after all, many things in this world which may not be considered "useful" but which, nevertheless, are totally without a capacity for harm.

It is true, of course, that one of the purposes of the patent system is to encourage dissemination of information concerning discoveries and inventions. And it may be that inability to patent a process to some extent discourages disclosure and leads to greater secrecy than would otherwise be the case. The inventor of the process, or the corporate organization by which he is employed, has some incentive to keep the invention secret while uses for the product are searched out. However, in light of the highly developed art of drafting patent claims so that they disclose as little useful information as possible—while broadening the scope of the claim as widely as possible—the argument based upon the virtue of disclosure must be warily evaluated. Moreover, the pressure for secrecy is easily exaggerated, for if the inventor of a process cannot himself ascertain a "use" for that which his process yields, he has every incentive to make his invention known to those able to do so. Finally, how likely is disclosure of a patented process to spur research by others into the uses to which the product may be put? To the extent that the patentee has power to enforce his patent, there is little incentive for others to undertake a search for uses.

Whatever weight is attached to the value of encouraging disclosure and of inhibiting secrecy, we believe a more compelling consideration is that a process patent in the chemical field, which has not been developed and pointed to the degree of specific utility, creates a monopoly of knowledge which should be granted only if clearly commanded by the statute. Until the process claim has been reduced to production of a product shown to be useful, the metes and bounds of that monopoly are not capable of precise delineation. It may engross a vast, unknown, and perhaps unknowable area. Such a patent may confer power to block off whole areas of scientific development, without compensating benefit to the public. The basic quid pro quo contemplated by the Constitution and the Congress for granting a patent monopoly is the benefit derived by the public from an invention with substantial utility. Unless and until a process is refined and developed to this point— where specific benefit exists in currently available form—there is insufficient justification for permitting an applicant to engross what may prove to be a broad field.

These arguments for and against the patentability of a process which either has no known use or is useful only in the sense that it may be an object of scientific research would apply equally to the patenting of the product produced by the process. Respondent appears to concede that with respect to a product, as opposed to a process, Congress has struck the balance on the side of nonpatentability unless "utility" is shown. Indeed, the decisions of the C.C.P.A. are in accord with the view that a product may not be patented absent a showing of utility greater than any adduced in the present case. We find absolutely no warrant for the proposition that although Congress intended that no patent be granted on a chemical compound whose sole "utility" consists of its potential role as an object of use-testing, a different set of rules was meant to apply to the process which yielded the unpatentable product. That proposition seems to us little more than an attempt to evade the impact of the rules which concededly govern patentability of the product itself.

This is not to say that we mean to disparage the importance of contributions to the fund of scientific information short of the invention of something "useful," or that we are blind to the prospect that what now seems without "use" may tomorrow command the grateful attention of the public. But a patent is not a hunting license. It is not a reward for the search, but compensation for its successful conclusion. "[A] patent system must be related to the world of commerce rather than to the realm of philosophy. . . ."

The judgment of the C.C.P.A. is reversed.

Mr. Justice DOUGLAS, while acquiescing in Part I of the Court's opinion, dissents on the merits of the controversy for substantially the reasons stated by Mr. Justice HARLAN.

Mr. Justice HARLAN, concurring in part and dissenting in part.

While I join the Court's opinion on the issue of certiorari jurisdiction, I cannot agree with its resolution of the important question of patentability.

Respondent has contended that a workable chemical process, which is both new and sufficiently nonobvious to satisfy the patent statute, is by its existence alone a contribution to chemistry and "useful" as the statute employs that term. Certainly this reading of "useful" in the statute is within the scope of the constitutional grant, which states only that "[t]o promote the Progress of Science and useful Arts," the exclusive right to "Writings and Discoveries" may be secured for limited times to those who produce them. Art. I, § 8. Yet the patent statute is somewhat differently worded and is on its face open both to respondent's construction and to the contrary reading given it by the Court. In the absence of legislative history on this issue, we are thrown back on policy and practice. Because I believe that the Court's policy arguments are not convincing and that past practice favors the respondent, I would reject the narrow definition of "useful" and uphold the judgment of the Court of Customs and Patent Appeals (hereafter C.C. P.A.).

The Court's opinion sets out about half a dozen reasons in support of its interpretation. Several of these arguments seem to me to have almost no force. For instance, it is suggested that "[u]ntil the process claim has been reduced to production of a product shown to be useful, the metes and bounds of that monopoly are not capable of precise delineation" and "[i]t may engross a vast, unknown, and perhaps unknowable area." I fail to see the relevance of these assertions; process claims are not disallowed because the products they produce may be of "vast" importance nor, in any event, does advance knowledge of a specific product use provide much safeguard on this score or fix "metes and bounds" precisely since a hundred more uses may be found after a patent is granted and greatly enhance its value.

The further argument that an established product use is part of "[t]he basic quid pro quo" for the patent or is the requisite "successful conclusion" of the inventor's search appears to beg the very question whether the process is "useful" simply because it facilitates further research into possible product uses. The same infirmity seems to inhere in the Court's argument that chemical products lacking immediate utility cannot be distinguished for present purposes from the processes which create them, that respondent appears to concede and the C.C.P.A. holds that the products are nonpatentable, and that therefore the processes are nonpatentable. Assuming that the two classes cannot be distinguished, a point not adequately considered in the briefs, and assuming further that the C.C.P.A. has firmly held such products nonpatentable this permits us to conclude only that the C.C. P.A. is wrong either as to the products or as to the processes and affords no basis for deciding whether both or neither should be patentable absent a specific product use.

More to the point, I think, are the Court's remaining, prudential arguments against patentability: namely that disclosure induced by allowing a patent is partly undercut by patent-application drafting techniques, that disclosure may occur without granting a patent, and that a patent will discourage others from inventing uses for the product. How far opaque drafting may lessen the public benefits resulting from the issuance of a patent is not shown by any evidence in this case but, more important, the argument operates against all patents and gives no reason for singling out the class involved here. The thought that these inventions may be more likely than most to be disclosed even if patents are not allowed may have more force; but while empirical study of the industry might reveal that chemical researchers would behave in this fashion, the abstractly logical choice for them seems to me to maintain secrecy until a product use can be discovered. As to discouraging the search by others for product uses, there is no doubt this risk exists but the price paid for any patent is that research on other uses or improvements may be hampered because the original patentee will reap much of the reward. From the standpoint of the public interest the Constitution seems to have resolved that choice in favor of patentability.

What I find most troubling about the result reached by the Court is the impact it may have on chemical research. Chemistry is a highly interrelated field and a tangible benefit for society may be the outcome of a number of different discoveries, one discovery building upon the next. To encourage one chemist or research facility to invent and disseminate new processes and products may be vital to progress, although the product or process be without "utility" as the Court defines the term, because that discovery permits someone else to take a further but perhaps less difficult step leading to a commercially useful item. In my view, our awareness in this age of the importance of achieving and publicizing basic research should lead this Court to resolve uncertainties in its favor and uphold the respondent's position in this case.

This position is strengthened, I think, by what appears to have been the practice of the Patent Office during most of this century. While available proof is not conclusive, the commentators seem to be in agreement that until Application of Bremner, 182 F.2d 216, 37 C.C.P.A. (Pat.) 1032, 86 U.S.P.Q. 74, in 1950, chemical patent applications were commonly granted although no resulting end use was stated or the statement was in extremely broad terms. Taking this to be true, Bremner represented a deviation from established practice which the C.C.P.A. has now sought to remedy in part only to find that the Patent Office does not want to return to the beaten track. If usefulness was typically regarded as inherent during a long and prolific period of chemical research and development in this country, surely this is added reason why the Court's result should not be adopted until Congress expressly mandates it, presumably on the basis of empirical data which this Court does not possess.

Fully recognizing that there is ample room for disagreement on this problem when, as here, it is reviewed in the abstract, I believe the decision below should be affirmed.

NOTES

1. Principles of early English patent law underlie the measure of utility that Justice Story adopted in Lowell v. Lewis. A year later,

Story returned to these principles in the course of a more extensive commentary, 16 U.S. 302 (1818), to observe that, in sanctioning letters patent, the Statute of Monopolies, 21 Jac. I ch. III (1623), expressly required that "they be not contrary to the law, nor mischievous to the state, by raising prices of commodities at home, or hurt of trade, or generally inconvenient. . . ."

Whether or not Justice Story's inference was correct, his test of utility took hold in American patent jurisprudence. Rickard v. Du Bon, 103 Fed. 868 (2d Cir.1900), is typical. Defendant, accused of infringing plaintiff's patented process for flecking the leaves of tobacco plants, countered that the patent was invalid for lack of utility. Conceding that the process effectively achieved its avowed purpose, defendant argued that the purpose itself was fraudulent. The many consumers who believed that cigars with spotted leaf wrappers are better than those with unspotted wrappers were deceived into thinking that the wrappers treated by plaintiff's process belonged to the better class.* Ruling for the defendant, the court agreed with the trial judge that "the patent was void for want of utility, 'except to deceive.'"

Under the *Rickard* test, utility will be found if the subject matter in question can be put to some beneficial use. Thus, had plaintiff succeeded in proving his claim that his treatment also improved the burning quality of the leaf, the court probably would have upheld the patent. Consider the utility, under this test, of narcotic compounds that are generally dangerous but also possess some therapeutic capacity, or of a safecracking device that can be applied to surgical advantage. Is it a proper function of patent law to discriminate among permitted and proscribed areas of conduct?

See generally, Mirabel, "Practical Utility" Is a Useless Concept, 36 Am.U.L.Rev. 811 (1987); Meyer, Utility Requirement in the Statute, 49 J.Pat.Off.Soc'y 533 (1967).

2. *Operability.* "Operability," in the patent lexicon, is quite different from "utility." Operability's function is to assist in determinations of actual reduction to practice. Recall from the earlier discussion of novelty that invention consists of conception and reduction to practice, and that reduction to practice is demonstrated either actually, through completion of a working model of the invention, or constructively, through the filing of a patent application. Operability is the hallmark of actual reduction to practice.

Even if an invention is inoperative as disclosed, it will be considered operative if it can be made operative by procedures that would naturally occur to a worker ordinarily skilled in the relevant art. Bennett v. Halahan, Aronsen & Lyon, 285 F.2d 807, 128 U.S.P.Q. 398 (C.C.P.A.1961). Also, an invention is considered operative if it substan-

---

* Caveat cigar smokers: "The notion has long prevailed with a numerous class of smokers that cigars having spotted wrappers are superior to those without them. This notion is a pure delusion. It originated and has been propagated by the coinci-dence that much choice tobacco is spotted, being raised in localities where this characteristic is imparted by natural causes, although without improving or impairing the quality of the leaf." 103 Fed. at 869.

tially achieves its avowed purpose. Hildreth v. Mastoras, 257 U.S. 27, 42 S.Ct. 20, 66 L.Ed. 112 (1921). Excluded from the benefits of both these rules is the invention that, unless it is perfect, is no good at all. In McKenzie v. Cummings, 24 App.D.C. 137 (D.C.Cir.1904), for example, the court ruled that a vote-registering machine that failed to properly register one of every hundred votes cast was inoperative. Distinguishing Coffee v. Guerrant, 3 App.D.C. 497 (D.C.Cir.1894), in which the operability of a tobacco-stemming device with 70% efficiency was sustained, the court held that, "[i]n order to be operative at all, absolute accuracy is here required."

Although an invention's operability may be saved under either of these two meliorative rules, some positive evidence of operability may be required. Proof of commercial success, typically associated with section 103's nonobviousness requisite, is frequently adduced. See, e.g., Raytheon Co. v. Roper Corp., 724 F.2d 951, 220 U.S.P.Q. 592 (Fed.Cir. 1983), cert. denied, 469 U.S. 835, 105 S.Ct. 127, 83 L.Ed.2d 69, 225 U.S. P.Q. 232 (1984). If the invention obviously contradicts established physical laws, as in the case of a perpetual motion machine, or if absolute accuracy is critical, the Commissioner may avail himself of the authority provided by section 114 to require that the applicant furnish a working model of the subject matter. For affirmance of the Commissioner's request in the case of some particularly outlandish claims, see Upton v. Ladd, 227 F.Supp. 261, 140 U.S.P.Q. 646 (D.D.C.1964). See generally, Ederer, On Operability as an Aspect of Patent Law, 42 J.Pat. Off.Soc'y 398 (1960).

3. *Pharmaceuticals.* In a footnote, *Manson* raised but did not decide the question of the proper utility test to be applied to pharmaceuticals. 383 U.S. 519, 531 n. 17, 86 S.Ct. 1033, 1040. One line of decisions, dating from the early 1900's, engrafted on the general utility requisite a specific requirement that a drug's fitness for human use be convincingly proved. Proof of successful tests on laboratory animals was considered insufficient to establish utility. "While the granting of a patent does not legally constitute a certificate that the medicine to which it relates is a good medicine and will cure the disease or successfully make the test which it was intended to do, nevertheless, the granting of such a patent gives a kind of official imprimatur to the medicine in question on which as a moral matter some members of the public are likely to rely." Isenstead v. Watson, 157 F.Supp. 7, 115 U.S. P.Q. 408 (D.D.C.1957).

The modern trend, inaugurated by In re Krimmel, 292 F.2d 948, 130 U.S.P.Q. 215 (C.C.P.A.1961), has been to liberalize the utility test for pharmaceuticals. The applicant in *Krimmel* sought a patent for an eye medicine that he had successfully tested on rabbits. The examiner, affirmed by the Board of Appeals, ruled that absent a showing of successful tests on humans, utility had not been proved. The Court of Customs and Patent Appeals reversed, holding that applicant had proved some usefulness for his medicine—to cure eye disease in rabbits—and that this was sufficient to meet the statutory test. The court took another liberalizing step the following year when, in In re Hartop,

311 F.2d 249, 135 U.S.P.Q. 419 (C.C.P.A.1962), it held that although the applicant specifically asserted that his medicine had utility for humans, but had only demonstrated its safety and effectiveness on animals, "appellants' claimed solutions have been shown to be useful within the meaning of U.S.C.A. § 101. . . . We think that a sufficient probability of safety in human therapy has been demonstrated in the case at bar to set aside the requirements of 35 U.S.C.A. § 101 that appellants' invention be useful."

In re Anthony, 414 F.2d 1383, 162 U.S.P.Q. 594 (C.C.P.A.1969), expanded on the rationale underlying *Krimmel* and *Hartop:* "Congress has given the responsibility to the FDA, not to the Patent Office, to determine in the first instance whether drugs are sufficiently safe for use that they can be introduced in the commercial market, under the conditions prescribed, recommended, or suggested in the proposed labeling thereof. . . ." The court emphasized that although 21 U.S.C.A. § 372(d) authorized the Secretary of Health, Education and Welfare to furnish the Commissioner of Patents with FDA data respecting drugs for which a patent was sought, this information had only persuasive, and not binding, effect on the issue of utility.

e. INVENTORSHIP

For a valid patent to issue, the claimed invention must have originated with the applicant or applicants. See 35 U.S.C.A. § 102(f). The inventor may of course draw his ideas from other sources and may arrange for others to assemble his invention, all without losing his claim of originality. But, for the patent to be valid, the named inventor or inventors must themselves have conceived the specific invention claimed. In International Carrier–Call & Television Corp. v. Radio Corp. of America, 142 F.2d 493, 61 U.S.P.Q. 392 (2d Cir.1944), the court ruled that a patentee who had merely asked an engineer to build an intercom that would perform more efficiently than an already existing device, was too far removed from the resulting subject matter to be considered its inventor. As a consequence, his patent was invalid. "An employer who seeks to patent the fruits of his employees' labors must go further than merely to express a purpose to be realized. . . . It is one thing for an employer to suggest improvements of a device with sufficient elaboration to enable a person skilled in the art to make a machine embodying the employer's conception; it is another to suggest merely a desired result without any disclosure of the means by which it is to be attained." 142 F.2d at 493, 496.

The requirement that the patent application accurately identify the inventor or inventors becomes particularly problematic in modern research and development departments where joint, rather than individual, invention is the rule. An invention may be the product of many hands and minds, from the research director, who first suggested and guided the idea, to product engineers and technicians who executed it. And what of the patent attorney who, in advising on prior art, may have suggested important, patentable alterations in the invention?

Because some products and processes are developed over long periods, workers may have left or joined the research team at all stages of development. These and other realities of large scale research and development create a substantial risk that the patent application will be underinclusive, omitting some inventors, or overinclusive, naming some noninventors.

Judicial decisions offer only the broadest guidelines for determining when a contributor to an invention will be considered a co-inventor. Worden v. Fisher, 11 Fed. 505, (C.C.E.D.Mich.1882) made what has become the classic statement of criteria for joint inventorship:

> To constitute two persons joint inventors it is not necessary that exactly the same idea should have occurred to each at the same time, and that they should work out together the embodiment of this idea in a perfected machine. Such a coincidence of ideas would scarcely ever occur to two persons at the same time. If an idea is suggested to one, and he even goes so far as to construct a machine embodying this idea, but it is not a completed and working machine, and another person takes hold of it, and by their joint labors, one suggesting one thing and the other another, a perfect machine is made, a joint patent may properly issue to them. If, upon the other hand, one person invents a distinct part of a machine, and another person invents another distinct and independent part of the same machine, then each should obtain a patent for his own invention.

After reviewing *Worden* and many later decisions, John Tresansky arrived at the following restatement: "Joint inventorship exists where parties working in a cooperative effort to solve a problem make a mental contribution to the final conception of the solution. All of the parties need not have participated in each contribution nor need the contribution of each party have occurred simultaneously while working proximately with the others. The contributions of each need not be equal either qualitatively or quantitatively. The contributors need not personally have performed the actual reduction to practice of the inventive concept." Tresansky, Joint Inventorship, 7 APLA Q.J. 96, 108–109 (1979).* The Patent Law Amendments Act of 1984 amended section 116 to provide: "Inventors may apply for a patent jointly even though (1) they did not physically work together or at the same time, (2) each did not make the same type or amount of contribution, or (3) each did not make a contribution to the subject matter of every claim of the patent." Pub.L. No. 98–622, § 104(a), 98 Stat. 3384–85.

The hazards of misjoinder and nonjoinder are significantly reduced by the fact that courts are generally slow to invalidate patents on these essentially technical grounds and, further, attach a presumption of correctness to the patentee's identification of inventors. See, e.g., General Motors Corp. v. Toyota Motor Co., 667 F.2d 504, 212 U.S.P.Q. 659 (6th Cir.1981), cert. denied, 456 U.S. 937, 102 S.Ct. 1994, 72 L.Ed.2d

---

* Reprinted with permission of A.P.L.A.
Quarterly Journal.

457, 215 U.S.P.Q. 95 (1982). Also, sections 116 and 256 respectively create procedures for correcting the identification of inventors in applications and in patents. The provisions require a showing that the misjoinder or nonjoinder was the result of a mistake made without intent to deceive. "Sections 116 and 256 evidence realization on the part of Congress that because of the haziness of the boundaries of co-inventorship status and the realities of work in large research labs, misjoinder is bound to be common and should be easily correctable at any time with no loss of benefit under the law." Mueller Brass Co. v. Reading Indus., 352 F.Supp. 1357, 1379, 176 U.S.P.Q. 361 (E.D.Pa.1972), aff'd without opinion, 487 F.2d 1395, 180 U.S.P.Q. 547 (3d Cir.1973).

What if the patent fails to name any of the true inventors? The Act contains no provisions comparable to sections 116 or 256 for correcting the misidentification of an invention's sole inventor—from *A* named as the inventor, to *B* who was in fact the inventor. In a much-discussed decision, the District of Columbia Court of Appeals read section 116 broadly and relied on section 251's reissue provisions to allow correction of a wrongly named sole inventor in a pending application and in an issued patent. A.F. Stoddard & Co., Ltd. v. Dann, 564 F.2d 556, 195 U.S.P.Q. 97 (1977). "Congress having provided [in section 116] for the correction of innocent error in stating the inventive entity when the application is filed, whether that entity be singular or plural, we see no rational reason to discriminate against the correction of the same innocent error involving sole inventors and their assignees, or to impute that intent to Congress." 564 F.2d 556, 566.

See Meiklejohn, Misjoinder, Non–Joinder and Whatever—Stoddard v. Dann, 60 J.Pat. Off. Soc'y 487 (1978); Welch, Stoddard v. Dann—Fundamental Principles from A to C, 61 J.Pat. Off. Soc'y 185 (1979). Articles on several joint inventorship topics are collected at 7 A.P.L.A. Q.J. No. 2 (1979).

f. ENABLING DISCLOSURE

W.L. GORE & ASSOCIATES v. GARLOCK, INC.

United States Court of Appeals, Federal Circuit, 1983.
721 F.2d 1540, 220 U.S.P.Q. 303, cert. denied, 469 U.S. 851, 105 S.Ct. 172, 83 L.Ed.2d 107 (1984).

MARKEY, Chief Judge.

Appeal from a judgment of the District Court for the Northern District of Ohio holding U.S. Patents 3,953,566 ('566) and 4,187,390 ('390) invalid. We affirm in part, reverse in part, and remand for a determination of the infringement issue.

Background

Tape of unsintered polytetrafluorethylene (PTFE) (known by the trademark TEFLON of E.I. du Pont de Nemours, Inc.) had been stretched in small increments. W.L. Gore & Associates, Inc. (Gore), assignee of the patents in suit, experienced a tape breakage problem in the operation of its "401" tape stretching machine. Dr. Robert Gore, Vice President of Gore, developed the invention disclosed and claimed in the '566 and '390 patents in the course of his effort to solve that problem. The 401 machine was disclosed and claimed in Gore's U.S. Patent 3,664,915 ('915) and was the invention of Wilbert L. Gore, Dr. Gore's father. PTFE tape had been sold as thread seal tape, i.e., tape used to keep pipe joints from leaking. The '915 patent, the application for which was filed on October 3, 1969, makes no reference to stretch rate, at 10% per second or otherwise, or to matrix tensile strength in excess of 7,300 psi.

Dr. Gore experimented with heating and stretching of highly crystalline PTFE rods. Despite slow, careful stretching, the rods broke when stretched a relatively small amount. Conventional wisdom in the art taught that breakage could be avoided only by slowing the stretch rate or by decreasing the crystallinity. In late October, 1969, Dr. Gore discovered, contrary to that teaching, that stretching the rods as fast as possible enabled him to stretch them to more than ten times their original length with no breakage. Further, though the rod was thus greatly lengthened, its diameter remained virtually unchanged throughout its length. The rapid stretching also transformed the hard, shiny rods into rods of a soft, flexible material.

Gore developed several PTFE products by rapidly stretching highly crystalline PTFE, including: (1) porous film for filters and laminates; (2) fabric laminates of PTFE film bonded to fabric to produce a remarkable material having the contradictory properties of impermeability to liquid water and permeability to water vapor, the material being used to make "breathable" rainwear and filters; (3) porous yarn for weaving or braiding into other products, like space suits and pump packing; (4) tubes used as replacements for human arteries and veins; and (5) insulation for high performance electric cables.

On May 21, 1970, Gore filed the patent application that resulted in the patents in suit. The '566 patent has 24 claims directed to processes for stretching highly crystalline, unsintered, PTFE. The processes, *inter alia,* include the steps of stretching PTFE at a rate above 10% per second and at a temperature between about 35°C and the crystalline melt point of PTFE. The '390 patent has 77 claims directed to various products obtained by processes of the '566 patent. . . .

(c) § 112 and the '566 and '390 patents

The patents in suit resulted from a single application and thus have substantially identical specifications. The holding of invalidity on the basis of § 112 is common to both patents.

The district court found that the patents did not disclose sufficient information to enable a person of ordinary skill in the art to make and use the invention, as required by § 112, first paragraph, and that certain claim language was indefinite, presumably in light of § 112, second paragraph, because: (1) there was no definition in the specification of "stretch rate", different formulae for computing stretch rate having been developed and presented at trial; (2) there was no way taught in the specification to calculate the minimum rate of stretch above 35°C; (3) the phrase "matrix tensile strength" is indefinite; and (4) the phrase "specific gravity of the solid polymer" is indefinite.

The findings rest on a misinterpretation of § 112, its function and purpose. The district court considered whether certain terms would have been enabling to the public and looked to formula developments and publications occurring well after Dr. Gore's filing date in reaching its conclusions under § 112. Patents, however, are written to enable those skilled in the art to practice the invention, not the public, and § 112 speaks as of the application filing date, not as of the time of trial. There was no evidence and no finding that those skilled in the art would have found the specification non-enabling or the claim language indefinite on May 21, 1970, when the application which resulted in issuance of Dr. Gore's patents was filed. Indeed, the expert quoted by the district court and whose testimony was primarily relied upon respecting formulae, was still in school at that time.

There is uncontradicted evidence in the record that at the time the application was filed "stretch rate" meant to those skilled in the art the percent of stretch divided by the time of stretching, and that the latter was measurable, for example, with a stopwatch. Concern for the absence from the specification of a formula for calculating stretch rate is therefore misplaced, and the post-filing date development of varying formulae, including Dr. Gore's later addition of a formula in his corresponding Japanese patent, is irrelevant.

Section 112 requires that the inventor set forth the best mode of practicing the invention known to him at the time the application was filed. Calculating stretch rate at that time was accomplished by actually measuring the time required to stretch the PTFE material. That was the only mode then used by the inventor, and it worked. The record establishes that calculation by that mode would have been employed by those of ordinary skill in the art at the time the application was filed. As indicated, Dr. Gore's disclosure must be examined for § 112 compliance in light of knowledge extant in the art on his application filing date.

The district court, though discussing enablement, spoke also of indefiniteness of "stretch rate", a matter having to do with § 112, second paragraph, and relevant in assessment of infringement. The use of "stretching . . . at a rate exceeding about 10% per second" in the claims is not indefinite. Infringement is clearly assessable through use of a stopwatch. No witness said that could not be done. As above indicated, subsequently developed and therefore irrelevant formulae cannot be used to render non-enabling or indefinite that which was enabling and definite at the time the application was filed.

Similarly, absence from the specification of a method for calculating the minimum rate of stretch above 35°C does not render the specification non-enabling. The specification discloses that "[t]he lower limit of expansion rates interact with temperature in a roughly logarithmic fashion, being much higher at higher temperatures." Calculation of minimum stretch rate above 35°C is nowhere in the claims, and it is the *claimed* invention for which enablement is required. The claims require stretching at a rate greater than 10% per second at temperatures between 35°C and the crystalline melt point of unsintered PTFE. That the minimum rate of stretch may increase with temperature does not render non-enabling Dr. Gore's specification, particularly in the absence of convincing evidence that those skilled in the art would have found it non-enabling at the time the application was filed.

The district court invalidated both patents for indefiniteness because of its view that some "trial and error" would be needed to determine the "lower limits" of stretch rate above 10% per second at various temperatures above 35°C. That was error. Assuming some experimentation were needed, a patent is not invalid because of a need for experimentation. A patent is invalid only when those skilled in the art are required to engage in *undue* experimentation to practice the invention. There was no evidence and the court made no finding that undue experimentation was required.

Moreover, the finding here rested on confusion of the role of the specification with that of the claims. The court found that the specification's failure to state the lower limit of stretch rate (albeit above 10% per second) at each degree of temperature above 35°C (a requirement for at least hundreds of entries in the specification) did not "distinguish processes performed above the 'lower limit' from those performed below the 'lower limit'". The claims of the '390 patent say nothing of processes and lower limits. Distinguishing what infringes from what doesn't is the role of the claims, not of the specification. It is clear that the specification is enabling and that the claims of both patents are precise within the requirements of the law.

The finding that "matrix tensile strength" is indefinite, like the other findings under § 112, appears to rest on a confusion concerning the roles of the claims and the specification. While finding "matrix tensile strength" in the claims indefinite, the district court at the same time recognized that the specification itself disclosed how to compute matrix tensile strength, in stating "to compute matrix tensile strength of a porous specimen, one divides the maximum force required to break the sample by the cross sectional area of the porous sample, and then multiplies this quantity by the ratio of the specific gravity of the solid polymer divided by the specific gravity of the porous specimen." Further, the specification provided the actual matrix tensile strength in several examples. It is well settled that a patent applicant may be his own lexicographer. In light of the disclosure of its calculation in the specification, we cannot agree that "matrix tensile strength" is either indefinite or non-enabling.

Nor does absence from the specification of a definition for "specific gravity of the solid polymer", a part of the computation of matrix tensile strength, render that computation indefinite. It is undisputed that in the many examples in the application the specific gravity values used for unsintered and sintered PTFE were 2.3 and 2.2, respectively. There was no testimony that those values were not known to persons of ordinary skill in the art or could not be calculated or measured. There is simply no support for the conclusion that "specific gravity of the solid polymer" is indefinite or that absence of its definition renders the specification non-enabling.

We conclude that Garlock has failed to prove that at the time the application was filed, the specification was not enabling or that the claims were indefinite within the meaning of § 112. . . .

Decision

The holdings of invalidity of claim 1 of the '566 patent under § 102(a) and of claim 17 of the '566 patent under § 103, the determination that Gore did not commit fraud on the PTO, and the denial of attorney fees, are affirmed; the holdings that all claims of the '566 patent are invalid under § 102(b), that claims 3 and 19 of the '566 patent are invalid under § 103, and that all claims of the '566 patent are invalid under § 112, are reversed. The holdings that claims 1, 9, 12, 14, 18, 35, 36, 43, 67, and 77 of the '390 patent are invalid under §§ 102 and 103, and that all claims of the '390 patent are invalid under § 112, are reversed. The case is remanded for determination of the infringement issue.

AFFIRMED IN PART, REVERSED IN PART, AND REMANDED.

[The opinion of Davis, J., concurring in part and dissenting in part, is omitted.]

NOTE

Section 112's requirement of an enabling disclosure dates to the first United States patent act, Act of Apr. 10, 1790, ch. 7, § 2, 1 Stat. 109. The requirement reflects the bargain struck by the patent system generally: society grants exclusive property rights in an invention in return for disclosure of information sufficient for practicing the invention upon the patent's expiration.

The enablement requirement is distinct from the "best mode" requirement that also appears in section 112. The enablement requirement is objective; the best mode requirement is subjective. Where the enablement requirement calls for an objective description of the invention and the method for making or using it, the best mode requirement requires the inventor only to disclose what she contemplates as the best mode for carrying out the invention. Best mode does not mean an objectively optimal mode, nor even a better mode contemplated by someone else. For a patent to be denied or invalidated for failure to disclose the best mode, it must be shown that the inventor concealed a better mode than the one disclosed. See, e.g., Hybritech, Inc. v. Monoclonal Antibodies, Inc., 802 F.2d 1367, 231 U.S.P.Q. 81 (Fed.Cir. 1986), cert. denied, 480 U.S. 947, 107 S.Ct. 1606, 94 L.Ed.2d 792 (1987).

See generally, Herbert, Failure to Disclose the "Best Mode": What the Public Doesn't Know Will Hurt Them, 64 J.Pat.Off.Soc'y 12 (1982).

2. STATUTORY SUBJECT MATTER

See Statute Supplement 35 U.S.C.A. §§ 100, 101, 161–164.

Utility patents, considered immediately below, are the usual grist of the patent law mill. Utility patents may be granted for "any new and useful process, machine, manufacture, or composition of matter, or any new and useful improvement thereof. . . ." 35 U.S.C.A. § 101. The Patent Act also authorizes patents for plants and patents for designs. Plant patents are considered beginning at page 437, below. Design patents are considered in connection with legal protection for industrial design, beginning at page 857 below. Patent protection for computer programs is considered in connection with legal protection for computer programs, beginning at page 827 below.

a. UTILITY PATENTS

DIAMOND v. CHAKRABARTY

Supreme Court of the United States, 1980.
447 U.S. 303, 100 S.Ct. 2204, 65 L.Ed.2d 144, 206 U.S.P.Q. 193.

Mr. Chief Justice BURGER delivered the opinion of the Court.

We granted certiorari to determine whether a live, human-made micro-organism is patentable subject matter under 35 U.S.C.A. § 101.

I.

In 1972, respondent Chakrabarty, a microbiologist, filed a patent application, assigned to the General Electric Company. The application asserted 36 claims related to Chakrabarty's invention of "a bacterium from the genus Pseudomonas containing therein at least two stable energy-generating plasmids, each of said plasmids providing a separate hydrocarbon degradative pathway." [1] This human-made, genetically engineered bacterium is capable of breaking down multiple components of crude oil. Because of this property, which is possessed by no naturally occurring bacteria, Chakrabarty's invention is believed to have significant value for the treatment of oil spills. [2]

1. Plasmids are hereditary units physically separate from the chromosomes of the cell. In prior research, Chakrabarty and an associate discovered that plasmids control the oil degradation abilities of certain bacteria. In particular, the two researchers discovered plasmids capable of degrading camphor and octane, two components of crude oil. In the work represented by the patent application at issue here, Chakrabarty discovered a process by which four different plasmids, capable of degrading four different oil components, could be transferred to and maintained stably in a single Pseudomonas bacteria, which itself has no capacity for degrading oil.

2. At present, biological control of oil spills requires the use of a mixture of naturally occurring bacteria, each capable of degrading one component of the oil complex. In this way, oil is decomposed into simpler substances which can serve as food for aquatic life. However, for various reasons, only a portion of any such mixed culture survives to attack the oil spill. By breaking down multiple components of oil, Chakrabarty's micro-organism promises more efficient and rapid oil-spill control.

Chakrabarty's patent claims were of three types: first, process claims for the method of producing the bacteria; second, claims for an inoculum comprised of a carrier material floating on water, such as straw, and the new bacteria; and third, claims to the bacteria themselves. The patent examiner allowed the claims falling into the first two categories, but rejected claims for the bacteria. His decision rested on two grounds: (1) that micro-organisms are "products of nature," and (2) that as living things they are not patentable subject matter under 35 U.S.C.A. § 101.

Chakrabarty appealed the rejection of these claims to the Patent Office Board of Appeals, and the Board affirmed the Examiner on the second ground.[3] Relying on the legislative history of the 1930 Plant Patent Act, in which Congress extended patent protection to certain asexually reproduced plants, the Board concluded that § 101 was not intended to cover living things such as these laboratory created micro-organisms.

The Court of Customs and Patent Appeals, by a divided vote, reversed on the authority of its prior decision in In re Bergy, 563 F.2d 1031, 195 U.S.P.Q. 344 (1978), which held that "the fact that microorganisms . . . are alive . . . [is] without legal significance" for purposes of the patent law. Subsequently, we granted the Government's petition for certiorari in Bergy, vacated the judgment, and remanded the case "for further consideration in light of Parker v. Flook, 437 U.S. 584 [98 S.Ct. 2522, 57 L.Ed.2d 451], 198 U.S.P.Q. 193." 438 U.S. 902, 98 S.Ct. 3119, 57 L.Ed.2d 1145, 198 U.S.P.Q. 257 (1978). The Court of Customs and Patent Appeals then vacated its judgment in Chakrabarty and consolidated the case with Bergy for reconsideration. After re-examining both cases in the light of our holding in Flook, that court, with one dissent, reaffirmed its earlier judgments.

The Government again sought certiorari, and we granted the writ as to both Bergy and Chakrabarty. Since then, Bergy has been dismissed as moot, leaving only Chakrabarty for decision.

II.

The Constitution grants Congress broad power to legislate to "promote the Progress of Science and the useful Arts, by securing for limited times to authors and inventors the exclusive right to their respective writings and discoveries." Art. I, § 8. The patent laws promote this progress by offering inventors exclusive rights for a limited period as an incentive for their inventiveness and research efforts. Kewanee Oil Co. v. Bicron Corp., 416 U.S. 470, 480–481, 94 S.Ct. 1879, 1885–1886, 40 L.Ed.2d 315, 181 U.S.P.Q. 673, 678 (1974); Universal Oil Co. v. Globe Co., 322 U.S. 471, 484, 64 S.Ct. 1110, 1116, 88 L.Ed. 1399, 61 U.S.P.Q. 382, 388 (1944). The authority of Congress is exercised in the hope that "[t]he productive effort thereby fostered will

---

3. The Board concluded that the new bacteria were not "products of nature," because Pseudomonas bacteria containing two or more different energy-generating plasmids are not naturally occurring.

have a positive effect on society through the introduction of new products and processes of manufacture into the economy, and the emanations by way of increased employment and better lives for our citizens." Kewanee, supra, at 480, 94 S.Ct., at 1885–86, 181 U.S.P.Q. at 678.

The question before us in this case is a narrow one of statutory interpretation requiring us to construe 35 U.S.C.A. § 101, which provides:

> Whoever invents or discovers any new and useful process, machine, manufacture, or composition of matter, or any new and useful improvement thereof, may obtain a patent therefor, subject to the conditions and requirements of this title.

Specifically, we must determine whether respondent's micro-organism constitutes a "manufacture" or "composition of matter" within the meaning of the statute.

III.

In cases of statutory construction we begin, of course, with the language of the statute. And "unless otherwise defined, words will be interpreted as taking their ordinary, contemporary, common meaning." Perrin v. United States, 444 U.S. 37, 100 S.Ct. 311, 314, 62 L.Ed.2d 199 (1979). We have also cautioned that courts "should not read into the patent laws limitations and conditions which the legislature has not expressed." United States v. Dubilier Condenser Corp., 289 U.S. 178, 199, 53 S.Ct. 554, 561, 77 L.Ed. 1114, 17 U.S.P.Q. 154, 162 (1933).

Guided by these canons of construction, this Court has read the term "manufacture" in § 101 in accordance with its dictionary definition to mean "the production of articles for use from raw materials prepared by giving to these materials new forms, qualities, properties, or combinations whether by hand labor or by machinery." American Fruit Growers, Inc. v. Brogdex Co., 283 U.S. 1, 11, 51 S.Ct. 328, 330, 75 L.Ed. 801, 8 U.S.P.Q. 131, 133 (1931). Similarly, "composition of matter" has been construed consistent with its common usage to include "all compositions of two or more substances and . . . all composite articles, whether they be the results of chemical union, or of mechanical mixture, or whether they be gases, fluids, powders, or solids." Shell Dev. Co. v. Watson, 149 F.Supp. 279, 280, 113 U.S.P.Q. 265, 266 (D.C.1957). In choosing such expansive terms as "manufacture" and "composition of matter," modified by the comprehensive "any," Congress plainly contemplated that the patent laws would be given wide scope.

The relevant legislative history also supports a broad construction. The Patent Act of 1793, authored by Thomas Jefferson, defined statutory subject matter as "any new and useful art, machine, manufacture, or composition of matter, or any new or useful improvement [thereof]." Act of Feb. 21, 1793, ch. 11, § 1, 1 Stat. 318. The Act embodied Jefferson's philosophy that "ingenuity should receive a liberal encouragement." V Writings of Thomas Jefferson, at 75–76. See Graham v.

John Deere Co., 383 U.S. 1, 7–10, 86 S.Ct. 684, 688–690, 15 L.Ed.2d 545, 148 U.S.P.Q. 459, 462–464 (1966). Subsequent patent statutes in 1836, 1870 and 1874 employed this same broad language. In 1952, when the patent laws were recodified, Congress replaced the word "art" with "process," but otherwise left Jefferson's language intact. The Committee Reports accompanying the 1952 act inform us that Congress intended statutory subject matter to "include anything under the sun that is made by man." S.Rep.No.1979, 82d Cong., 2d Sess., 5 (1952); H.R.Rep. No.1923, 82d Cong., 2d Sess., 6 (1952).

This is not to suggest that § 101 has no limits or that it embraces every discovery. The laws of nature, physical phenomena, and abstract ideas have been held not patentable. See Parker v. Flook, 437 U.S. 584, 98 S.Ct. 2522, 57 L.Ed.2d 451, 198 U.S.P.Q. 193 (1978); Gottschalk v. Benson, 409 U.S. 63, 67, 93 S.Ct. 253, 255, 34 L.Ed.2d 273, 175 U.S.P.Q. 673, 674–675 (1973); Funk Seed Co. v. Kalo Co., 333 U.S. 127, 130, 68 S.Ct. 440, 441, 92 L.Ed. 588, 76 U.S.P.Q. 280, 281 (1948); O'Reilly v. Morse, 15 How. 61, 112–121, 14 L.Ed. 601 (1853); Le Roy v. Tatham, 14 How. 155, 175, 14 L.Ed. 367 (1852). Thus, a new mineral discovered in the earth or a new plant found in the wild is not patentable subject matter. Likewise, Einstein could not patent his celebrated law that $E = mc^2$; nor could Newton have patented the law of gravity. Such discoveries are "manifestations of . . . nature, free to all men and reserved exclusively to none." Funk, supra, at 130, 76 U.S.P.Q. at 281.

Judged in this light, respondent's micro-organism plainly qualifies as patentable subject matter. His claim is not to a hitherto unknown natural phenomenon, but to a nonnaturally occurring manufacture or composition of matter—a product of human ingenuity "having a distinctive name, character [and] use." Hartranft v. Wiegmann, 121 U.S. 609, 615, 7 S.Ct. 1240, 1243, 30 L.Ed. 1012 (1887). The point is underscored dramatically by comparison of the invention here with that in Funk. There, the patentee had discovered that there existed in nature certain species of root-nodule bacteria which did not exert a mutually inhibitive effect on each other. He used that discovery to produce a mixed culture capable of inoculating the seeds of leguminous plants. Concluding that the patentee had discovered "only some of the handiwork of nature," the Court ruled the product nonpatentable:

> Each of the species of root-nodule bacteria contained in the package infects the same group of leguminous plants which it always infected. No species acquires a different use. The combination of the six species produces no new bacteria, no change in the six bacteria, and no enlargement of the range of their utility. Each species has the same effect it always had. The bacteria perform in their natural way. Their use in combination does not improve in any way their natural functioning. They serve the same ends nature originally provided and act quite independently of any effort by the patentee. 333 U.S., at 127, 68 S.Ct., at 442, 76 U.S. P.Q. at 280.

Here, by contrast, the patentee has produced a new bacterium with markedly different characteristics from any found in nature and one having the potential for significant utility. His discovery is not nature's handiwork, but his own; accordingly it is patentable subject matter under § 101.

IV.

Two contrary arguments are advanced, neither of which we find persuasive.

A.

The Government's first argument rests on the enactment of the 1930 Plant Patent Act, which afforded patent protection to certain asexually reproduced plants, and the 1970 Plant Variety Protection Act, which authorized patents for certain sexually reproduced plants but excluded bacteria from its protection. In the Government's view, the passage of these Acts evidences congressional understanding that the terms "manufacture" or "composition of matter" do not include living things; if they did, the Government argues, neither Act would have been necessary.

We reject this argument. Prior to 1930, two factors were thought to remove plants from patent protection. The first was the belief that plants, even those artificially bred, were products of nature for purposes of the patent law. This position appears to have derived from the decision of the Patent Office in Ex parte Latimer, 1889 C.D. 123, in which a patent claim for fiber found in the needle of the Pinus australis was rejected. The Commissioner reasoned that a contrary result would permit "patents [to] be obtained upon the trees of the forests and the plants of the earth, which of course would be unreasonable and impossible." Id., at 126. The Latimer case, it seems, came to "set[ ] forth the general stand taken in these matters" that plants were natural products not subject to patent protection. H. Thorne, Relation of Patent Law to Natural Products, 6 J.Pat.Off.Soc. 23, 24 (1923). The second obstacle to patent protection for plants was the fact that plants were thought not amenable to the "written description" requirement of the patent law. Because new plants may differ from old only in color or perfume, differentiation by written description was often impossible.

In enacting the Plant Patent Act, Congress addressed both of these concerns. It explained at length its belief that the work of the plant breeder "in aid of nature" was patentable invention. S.Rep. No. 315, 71st Cong., 2d Sess., 6–8 (1930); H.R.Rep. No. 1129, 71st Cong., 2d Sess., 7–9 (1930). And it relaxed the written description requirement in favor of "a description . . . as complete as is reasonably possible." 35 U.S. C.A. § 162. No Committee or Member of Congress, however, expressed the broader view, now urged by the Government, that the terms "manufacture" or "composition of matter" exclude living things. The sole support for that position in the legislative history of the 1930 Act is found in the conclusory statement of Secretary of Agriculture Hyde, in a letter to the Chairmen of the House and Senate committees considering the 1930 Act, that "the patent laws . . . at the present time are understood to cover only inventions or discoveries in the field of inanimate nature." See S.Rep. No. 315, supra, at Appendix A; H.R. Rep. No. 1129, supra, at Appendix A. Secretary Hyde's opinion, however, is not entitled to controlling weight. His views were solicited on the administration of the new law and not on the scope of patentable subject matter—an area beyond his competence. Moreover, there is language in the House and Senate Committee reports suggesting that to the extent Congress considered the matter it found the Secretary's dichotomy unpersuasive. The reports observe:

> There is a clear and logical distinction *between the discovery of a new variety of plant and of certain inanimate things,* such for example, as a new and useful natural mineral. The mineral is created wholly by nature unassisted by man. . . . On the other hand, a plant discovery resulting from cultivation is unique, isolated, and is not repeated by nature, nor can it be reproduced by nature unaided by man. . . . S.Rep. No. 315, supra, at 6; H.R. Rep. No. 1129, supra, at 7 (emphasis added).

Congress thus recognized that the relevant distinction was not between living and inanimate things, but between products of nature, whether living or not, and human-made inventions. Here respondent's microorganism is the result of human ingenuity and research. Hence, the passage of the Plant Patent Act affords the Government no support.

Nor does the passage of the 1970 Plant Variety Protection Act support the Government's position. As the Government acknowledges, sexually reproduced plants were not included under the 1930 Act because new varieties could not be reproduced true-to-type through seedlings. Brief for United States 27, n. 31. By 1970, however, it was generally recognized that true-to-type reproduction was possible and that plant patent protection was therefore appropriate. The 1970 Act extended that protection. There is nothing in its language or history to suggest that it was enacted because § 101 did not include living things.

In particular, we find nothing in the exclusion of bacteria from plant variety protection to support the Government's position. The legislative history gives no reason for this exclusion. As the Court of Customs and Patent Appeals suggested, it may simply reflect congressional agreement with the result reached by that court in deciding In re Arzberger, 112 F.2d 834, 46 U.S.P.Q. 32 (1940), which held that bacteria were not plants for the purposes of the 1930 Act. Or it may reflect the fact that prior to 1970 the Patent Office had issued patents for bacteria under § 101.[9] In any event, absent some clear indication that Congress "focused on [the] issues . . . directly related to the one presently before the Court," SEC v. Sloan, 436 U.S. 103, 120–121, 98 S.Ct. 1702,

---

9. In 1873, the Patent Office granted Louis Pasteur a patent on "yeast, free from organic germs of disease, as an article of manufacture." And in 1967 and 1968, immediately prior to the passage of the Plant Variety Protection Act, that office granted two patents which, as the Government concedes, state claims for living micro-organisms. The Reply Brief of United States, at 3, and n.2.

1713, 56 L.Ed.2d 148 (1978), there is no basis for reading into its actions an intent to modify the plain meaning of the words found in § 101.

B.

The Government's second argument is that micro-organisms cannot qualify as patentable subject matter until Congress expressly authorizes such protection. Its position rests on the fact that genetic technology was unforeseen when Congress enacted § 101. From this it is argued that resolution of the patentability of inventions such as respondent's should be left to Congress. The legislative process, the Government argues, is best equipped to weigh the competing economic, social, and scientific considerations involved, and to determine whether living organisms produced by genetic engineering should receive patent protection. In support of this position, the Government relies on our recent holding in Parker v. Flook, 437 U.S. 584, 98 S.Ct. 2522, 57 L.Ed. 2d 451, 198 U.S.P.Q. 193 (1978), and the statement that the judiciary "must proceed cautiously when . . . asked to extend patent rights into areas wholly unforeseen by Congress." Id., at 596.

It is, of course, correct that Congress, not the courts, must define the limits of patentability; but it is equally true that once Congress has spoken it is "the province and duty of the judicial department to say what the law is." Marbury v. Madison, 1 Cranch 137, 177, 2 L.Ed. 60 (1803). Congress has performed its constitutional role in defining patentable subject matter in § 101; we perform ours in construing the language Congress has employed. In so doing, our obligation is to take statutes as we find them, guided, if ambiguity appears, by the legislative history and statutory purpose. Here, we perceive no ambiguity. The subject matter provisions of the patent law have been cast in broad terms to fulfill the constitutional and statutory goal of promoting "the Progress of Science and the useful Arts" with all that means for the social and economic benefits envisioned by Jefferson. Broad general language is not necessarily ambiguous when congressional objectives require broad terms.

Nothing in Flook is to the contrary. That case applied our prior precedents to determine that a "claim for an improved method of calculation, even when tied to a specific end use, is unpatentable subject matter under § 101." 437 U.S., at 595, n. 18, 98 S.Ct., at 2528, n. 18, 198 U.S.P.Q. at 199, n. 18. The Court carefully scrutinized the claim at issue to determine whether it was precluded from patent protection under "the principles underlying the prohibition against patents for 'ideas' or phenomena of nature." Id., at 593, 98 S.Ct., at 2527, 198 U.S.P.Q. at 198–199. We have done that here. Flook did not announce a new principle that inventions in areas not contemplated by Congress when the patent laws were enacted are unpatentable per se.

To read that concept into Flook would frustrate the purposes of the patent law. This Court frequently has observed that a statute is not to be confined to the "particular application[s] . . . contemplated by the legislators." Barr v. United States, 324 U.S. 83, 90, 65 S.Ct. 522, 525,

89 L.Ed. 765 (1945). This is especially true in the field of patent law. A rule that unanticipated inventions are without protection would conflict with the core concept of the patent law that anticipation undermines patentability. Mr. Justice Douglas reminded that the inventions most benefiting mankind are those that "push back the frontiers of chemistry, physics, and the like." A. & P. Tea Co. v. Supermarket Corp., 340 U.S. 147, 154, 71 S.Ct. 127, 131, 95 L.Ed. 162, 87 U.S.P.Q. 303, 306–307 (1950) (concurring opinion). Congress employed broad general language in drafting § 101 precisely because such inventions are often unforeseeable.[10]

To buttress its argument, the Government, with the support of amicus, points to grave risks that may be generated by research endeavors such as respondent's. The briefs present a gruesome parade of horribles. Scientists, among them Nobel laureates, are quoted suggesting that genetic research may pose a serious threat to the human race, or, at the very least, that the dangers are far too substantial to permit such research to proceed apace at this time. We are told that genetic research and related technological developments may spread pollution and disease, that it may result in a loss of genetic diversity, and that its practice may tend to depreciate the value of human life. These arguments are forcefully, even passionately presented; they remind us that, at times, human ingenuity seems unable to control fully the forces it creates—that, with Hamlet, it is sometimes better "to bear those ills we have than fly to others that we know not of."

It is argued that this Court should weigh these potential hazards in considering whether respondent's invention is patentable subject matter under § 101. We disagree. The grant or denial of patents on microorganisms is not likely to put an end to genetic research or to its attendant risks. The large amount of research that has already occurred when no researcher had sure knowledge that patent protection would be available suggests that legislative or judicial fiat as to patentability will not deter the scientific mind from probing into the unknown any more than Canute could command the tides. Whether respondent's claims are patentable may determine whether research efforts are accelerated by the hope of reward or slowed by want of incentives, but that is all.

What is more important is that we are without competence to entertain these arguments—either to brush them aside as fantasies generated by fear of the unknown, or to act on them. The choice we are urged to make is a matter of high policy for resolution within the legislative process after the kind of investigation, examination, and study that legislative bodies can provide and courts cannot. That process involves the balancing of competing values and interests, which

---

10. Even an abbreviated list of patented inventions underscores the point: telegraph (Morse, No. 1647); telephone (Bell, No. 174,465); electric lamp (Edison, No. 223,898); airplane (the Wrights, No. 821,393); transistor (Bardeen & Brattain, No. 2,524,035); neutronic reactor (Fermi & Szilard, No. 2,708,656); laser (Schawlow & Townes, No. 2,929,922). See generally Revolutionary Ideas, Patents & Progress in America, Office of Patents (1976).

in our democratic system is the business of elected representatives. Whatever their validity, the contentions now pressed on us should be addressed to the political branches of the government, the Congress and the Executive, and not to the courts.

We have emphasized in the recent past that "[o]ur individual appraisal of the wisdom or unwisdom of a particular [legislative] course . . . is to be put aside in the process of interpreting a statute." TVA v. Hill, 437 U.S. 153, 194, 98 S.Ct. 2279, 2302, 57 L.Ed.2d 117 (1978). Our task, rather, is the narrow one of determining what Congress meant by the words it used in the statute; once that is done our powers are exhausted. Congress is free to amend § 101 so as to exclude from patent protection organisms produced by genetic engineering. Compare 42 U.S.C.A. § 2181, exempting from patent protection inventions "useful solely in the utilization of special nuclear material or atomic energy in an atomic weapon." Or it may choose to craft a statute specifically designed for such living things. But, until Congress takes such action, this Court must construe the language of § 101 as it is. The language of that section fairly embraces respondent's invention.

Accordingly, the judgment of the Court of Customs and Patent Appeals is affirmed.

Affirmed.

Mr. Justice BRENNAN, with whom Mr. Justice WHITE, Mr. Justice MARSHALL, and Mr. Justice POWELL join, dissenting.

I agree with the Court that the question before us is a narrow one. Neither the future of scientific research, nor even the ability of respondent Chakrabarty to reap some monopoly profits from his pioneering work, is at stake. Patents on the processes by which he has produced and employed the new living organism are not contested. The only question we need decide is whether Congress, exercising its authority under Art. I, § 8, of the Constitution, intended that he be able to secure a monopoly on the living organism itself, no matter how produced or how used. Because I believe the Court has misread the applicable legislation, I dissent.

The patent laws attempt to reconcile this Nation's deepseated antipathy to monopolies with the need to encourage progress. Given the complexity and legislative nature of this delicate task, we must be careful to extend patent protection no further than Congress has provided. In particular, were there an absence of legislative direction, the courts should leave to Congress the decisions whether and how far to extend the patent privilege into areas where the common understanding has been that patents are not available.

In this case, however, we do not confront a complete legislative vacuum. The sweeping language of the Patent Act of 1793, as re-enacted in 1952, is not the last pronouncement Congress has made in this area. In 1930 Congress enacted the Plant Patent Act affording patent protection to developers of certain asexually reproduced plants. In 1970 Congress enacted the Plant Variety Protection Act to extend protection to certain new plant varieties capable of sexual reproduction.

Thus, we are not dealing—as the Court would have it—with the routine problem of "unanticipated inventions." In these two Acts Congress has addressed the general problem of patenting animate inventions and has chosen carefully limited language granting protection to some kinds of discoveries, but specifically excluding others. These Acts strongly evidence a congressional limitation that excludes bacteria from patentability.

First, the Acts evidence Congress' understanding, at least since 1930, that § 101 does not include living organisms. If newly developed living organisms not naturally occurring had been patentable under § 101, the plants included in the scope of the 1930 and 1970 Acts could have been patented without new legislation. Those plants, like the bacteria involved in this case, were new varieties not naturally occurring. Although the Court rejects this line of argument, it does not explain why the Acts were necessary unless to correct a pre-existing situation. I cannot share the Court's implicit assumption that Congress was engaged in either idle exercises or mere correction of the public record when it enacted the 1930 and 1970 Acts. And Congress certainly thought it was doing something significant. The committee reports contain expansive prose about the previously unavailable benefits to be derived from extending patent protection to plants. Because Congress thought it had to legislate in order to make agricultural "human-made inventions" patentable and because the legislation Congress enacted is limited, it follows that Congress never meant to make patentable items outside the scope of the legislation.

Second, the 1970 Act clearly indicates that Congress has included bacteria within the focus of its legislative concern, but not within the scope of patent protection. Congress specifically excluded bacteria from the coverage of the 1970 Act. 7 U.S.C.A. § 2402(a). The Court's attempts to supply explanations for this explicit exclusion ring hollow. It is true that there is no mention in the legislative history of the exclusion, but that does not give us license to invent reasons. The fact is that Congress, assuming that animate objects as to which it had not specifically legislated could not be patented, excluded bacteria from the set of patentable organisms.

The Court protests that its holding today is dictated by the broad language of § 101, which "cannot be confined to the 'particular application[s] . . . . contemplated by the legislators.'" But as I have shown, the Court's decision does not follow the unavoidable implications of the statute. Rather, it extends the patent system to cover living material even though Congress plainly has legislated in the belief that § 101 does not encompass living organisms. It is the role of Congress, not this Court, to broaden or narrow the reach of the patent laws. This is especially true where, as here, the composition sought to be patented uniquely implicates matters of public concern.

NOTES

1. *Natural Principles.* Why should patent law refuse protection to newly discovered natural principles? The reason commonly given is that, as technological building blocks, natural principles are too important to be subjected to private control. What dangers, if any, would in fact attend private control of basic principles? What effect, if any, does the absence of patent protection have on private incentives to invest in the research required to discover important and far-reaching principles? Can firm size, industry structure and public subsidies safely be relied upon to produce the needed level and direction of investment in such basic research?

2. *Chakrabarty* attracted considerable commentary even before the Supreme Court's decision. See, for example, the wide-ranging symposium in 7 APLA Q.J. 175 et seq. (1979). See also Guttag, The Patentability of Microorganisms: Statutory Subject Matter and Other Living Things, 13 U.Rich.L.Rev. 247 (1979); Note, Patentability of Living Organisms Under 35 U.S.C.A. § 101, 91 Harv.L.Rev. 1357 (1978).

For some philosophical reflections on *Chakrabarty* see Kass, Patenting Life, 63 J.Pat.Off. Soc'y 571 (1981); Smith, The Promise of Abundant Life: Patenting a Magnificent Obsession, 8 J.Contemp.L. 85 (1982).

3. *Patenting Animals.* The evolution of life forms as patentable subject matter since *Chakrabarty* has been rapid and increasingly controversial. In 1987 the Board of Patent Appeals and Interferences held that certain man-made, non-naturally occurring polyploid oysters were patentable subject matter. In re Allen, 2 U.S.P.Q.2d 1425 (1987). Four days later the Commissioner of Patents and Trademarks announced the Office's intention to treat "nonnaturally occurring non-human multicellular organisms, including animals, [as] patentable subject matter." The Patent and Trademark Office later agreed to an eight-month moratorium on animal patents at the request of Robert Kastenmeier, Chairman of the House Subcommittee on Courts, Civil Liberties and the Administration of Justice. 36 Pat., Trademark & Copyr.J. 272 (1988). On April 12, 1988, after the voluntary moratorium had expired, the Patent and Trademark Office issued its first animal patent. The patent was for a mouse, developed by researchers at Harvard University, that had been genetically altered to facilitate cancer research, U.S. Patent No. 4,736,866.

Moral and economic arguments dominate the debate over animal patents. In the view of the General Secretary of the National Council of Churches, "[t]he gift of life from God, in all its forms and species, should not be regarded solely as if it were a chemical product, subject to genetic alteration and patentable for economic benefit. . . ." The National Farmers Union said "it favors a moratorium on patenting animals until the impact on the farm animal gene pool can be assessed and royalty obligations understood. The Humane Society of America worries that animals will suffer as a result of human genes being spliced into their genetic code for experimental and possibly for commercial purposes." Crawford, Religious Groups Join Animal Patent Battle, 237 Science 480 (1987).

See generally, Adler, Controlling the Application of Biotechnology: A Critical Analysis of the Proposed Moratorium on Animal Patenting, 1 Harv.J.Law and Tech. 1 (1988).

4. *"New Use" Patents.* The 1952 amendments to the Patent Act replaced the term "art" with "process" and defined "process" to mean "process, art or method, and includes a new use of a known process, machine, manufacture, composition of matter, or material." 35 U.S. C.A. § 101(b). The definition confirmed a line of decisions that had allowed process patents for new uses of old products, such as the use of the old and well-known compound, DDT, in insects sprays. Ex parte Muller, 81 U.S.P.Q. 261 (Pat.Off.Bd.App.1947). The new definition also dispelled the lingering question left by a much earlier decision, Morton v. New York Eye Infirmary, 17 F.Cas. 879 (C.C.S.D.N.Y.1862) (No. 9865), which held that plaintiffs, who had discovered the anesthetic qualities of the old compound, ether, were not entitled to a patent on the process of using ether as an anesthetic in surgery.

The claimed invention in a "new use" patent will often combine an old process and an old product to produce a new result. Does this suggest that "new use" applicants face higher hurdles under sections 102 and 103 than applicants whose subject matter involves entirely new processes or products?

As a practical matter, what range of protection do "new use" patents give? Since the patent owner will typically have no rights in the old product, it can bring a direct infringement action only against those who use the old product according to the method described in the patent. How much success is the patent owner likely to enjoy in bringing a contributory infringement action against the manufacturer of the old product that is used to infringe the process patent? See page 484 below.

b. PLANT PATENTS

YODER BROS., INC. v. CALIFORNIA–FLORIDA PLANT CORP.

United States Court of Appeals, Fifth Circuit, 1976.
537 F.2d 1347, 193 U.S.P.Q. 264, cert. denied, 429 U.S. 1094, 97 S.Ct. 1108,
51 L.Ed.2d 540, 200 U.S.P.Q. 128 (1977).

GOLDBERG, Circuit Judge:

In this clash between two giants of the chrysanthemum business, we confront a myriad of antitrust and plant patent issues. Yoder Brothers (Yoder), plaintiff in the district court, sued, alleging infringement of twenty-one chrysanthemum plant patents by California–Florida Plant Corp. (CFPC) and California–Florida Plant Corp. of Florida (CFPCF) (sometimes referred to collectively as Cal–Florida). CFPC and CFPCF denied the infringement and filed antitrust counterclaims under sections 1 and 2 of the Sherman Act. As to seven of the chrysanthemum plant patents, the lower court directed verdicts for Yoder that the patents were valid and infringed and awarded treble damages. The court also ruled for Yoder on Cal–Florida's section 2 claim. CFPC and CFPCF, however, prevailed in their anti-trust counterclaim under section 1 and received treble damages for Yoder's derelictions.

Because many of the issues in this case turn on the particular nature of the ornamental plant industry and the specific characteristics of chrysanthemums, we shall describe the background facts in some detail before discussing the many complex legal issues presented on this appeal. Following our description of the facts, we shall briefly sketch the procedural history of the case. Finally, we shall consider the antitrust claims and the issues relating to the plant patent law.

I. General Background

A. *The Chrysanthemum Industry*

Chrysanthemums, in their natural state, blossom only during the fall. This is because they are photoperiodic in nature, meaning that their growth is affected by the relative lengths of lightness and darkness in the day. When the days are long, the chrysanthemum plant remains in a vegetative state. As the nights become longer, the initiation process of the chrysanthemum bud begins. Thus, in early August, when the nights achieve a duration of nine and one-half continuous dark hours, the chrysanthemum plant in its natural state will begin the process of developing a flower. During the fall and early winter months, the mature flower appears.

Yoder began doing business in the 1930's as a simple greenhouse operator, specializing in tomatoes. Soon thereafter, because the fall tomato crop was less profitable than the spring crop, it decided to replace the fall crop with chrysanthemums. In 1939 or 1940, Yoder employees began research into out-of-season flowering of chrysanthemums. By applying black cloth shades over the chrysanthemums when dark hours were needed and applying artificial light when light hours were needed, it became possible to flower chrysanthemums on a year-round basis. Yet this breakthrough was not without its problems. For example, the use of black cloth shades resulted in an abnormally high temperature build-up around the plants, which in turn retarded bud initiation. Similarly, when the finishing temperatures were too warm, the chrysanthemums would not hold their color. In an effort to adjust for these conditions and to improve the quality of the chrysanthemum generally, Yoder initiated a breeding program in the early 1940's. One of the most important goals of the breeding program was the development of new varieties for consumers.

Although the ornamental plant industry encompasses many different kinds of flowers, including azaleas, carnations, roses, african violets, geraniums, snapdragons, and others, chrysanthemums are one of the most popular of the genre. According to the United States Department of Agriculture, in 1971 approximately 2,134 growers in twenty-three states sold nearly 145 million blooms from about 129 million standard variety chrysanthemum plants, 34.5 million blooms from 136 million pompon chrysanthemum plants, and 17.5 million potted chrysanthemum plants. At the time of the trial there were over 475 different varieties of chrysanthemums available. The total wholesale value of growers' sales in the twenty-three states that year was approximately 83.5 million dollars.

Chrysanthemums have been subject to intensive breeding efforts over the past thirty years; each individual specimen is a genetically unique complex organism. Several definitions of the term "variety" of chrysanthemum were offered at trial. Mr. Duffett, Yoder's head breeder, defined a variety as a group of individual plants which, on the basis of observation by skilled floriculturists and according to reasonable commercial tolerances, display identical characteristics under similar environments. Cal–Florida defined variety in its complaint as "a subspecies or class of chrysanthemums distinguishable from other subspecies or classes of chrysanthemums by distinct characteristics, such as color, hue, shape and size of petal or blossom or any of them."

New varieties of chrysanthemums are developed in two major ways: by sexual reproduction and by mutagenic techniques. Sexual reproduction, the result of self or cross pollination, produces a genetically unique seedling, the characteristics of which are impossible to predict. Mutagenic techniques simply accelerate the natural rate of mutation in the chrysanthemum plant itself. A mutation was defined by Mr. Duffett as "a change in the number of chromosomes or a change in the chromosome position or a specific change in the genes within those chromosomes." Technically, only those mutations that first express themselves as bud variations are properly called "sports"; however, the word is used loosely in the industry as a general synonym for mutation, and we will so use it. Two types of sports can appear: spontaneous sports and radiation sports. The cells of all living things occasionally mutate, and spontaneous sports are simply the result of that process. Radiation sports, on the other hand, are induced artificially, through exposure to such things as gamma radiation from radioactive cobalt and X-rays. These techniques do nothing that could not occur in nature apart from speeding up the natural mutation process. Although most of the mutations induced by radiation are not commercially usable plants, a skilled breeder will select for further development those that display such desirable characteristics as fast response time, temperature tolerance, durability, size, and vigor.

After a breeder has successfully isolated a new variety, the only way he can preserve his creation is by means of asexual reproduction. In the case of chrysanthemums, the most common technique of asexual reproduction is the taking of cuttings from a stock plant. Cuttings, as defined in the Cal–Florida complaint, are "sections or parts of chrysanthemum plants which may be grown into mature plants for sale as cut flowers and/or potted plants or from which additional cuttings may be harvested." According to Yoder's suggested definition, cuttings are simply immature chrysanthemum plants. Since a cutting is genetically identical to the parent plant, it will develop into a plant whose characteristics match the parent's exactly, so long as the same environmental conditions obtain. A central fact of life in the chrysanthemum industry is the ease with which cuttings can be taken from parent plants: from one chrysanthemum, it is theoretically possible to develop an infinitely large stock, by taking cuttings, maturing some into flowered plants, taking more cuttings, and so on.

Over the years since Yoder first entered the chrysanthemum business, the industry has become internally specialized. At the first functional level are the breeders, who create new varieties of chrysanthemums. Breeding is an expensive, complex procedure. The breeder must possess the skill and discrimination to spot potential new varieties and recognize whether they possess desirable traits; facilities for elaborate testing and development must be available. Because chrysanthemums mutate rapidly, a breeder must always be on the lookout for new changes.

At the next level in the industry are the propagator-distributors. The propagator-distributors build up mother stock from sources such as breeders, retail florists, or their existing flowers, and reproduce cuttings from that mother stock. In a sense they are simply mass producers of cuttings. They do not develop cuttings to the mature flower stage (except for purposes of their own testing). Next are the growers, who develop cuttings purchased from propagator-distributors into mature plants either for cut flowers or potted plants. Combining the function of propagator-distributors and growers are the self-propagators. Cal–Florida defined a "self-propagator" as "a person who either buys or establishes stock and takes cuttings for the sole purpose of producing cut flowers and/or potted plants for resale or own use." In other words, the self-propagators are vertically integrated into one step. Finally, the growers (or self-propagators) sell their products to retail florists, who in turn sell to ultimate consumers.

[The court's description of the procedural history of the case and its discussion and resolution of the antitrust issues are omitted.]

IV. Plant Patents

A. Introduction

With the antitrust issues decided, we return to the problem that initially gave rise to this lawsuit—Yoder's allegation that Cal–Florida was infringing its plant patents and its consequent demand for damages. Cal–Florida responded with the predictable assertions of patent invalidity and noninfringement, among others. As discussed above, the only issues before this Court concern the seven patents that the district court ruled valid and infringed as a matter of law: [30] Red Torch, Gold Marble, Morocco, Promenade, Southern Gold, Mountain Snow, and Mountain Sun. After considerable thought, we have decided that the

---

30. An eighth plant patent, Deep Conquest, was found valid and infringed by the jury. Cal–Florida's only point regarding that patent goes to the court's trebling of the damages for infringement. See Part IV. E., infra.

district court correctly ruled that Cal–Florida failed to rebut the statutory presumption of validity with sufficient relevant evidence. Nevertheless, we hold that the court should not have trebled the damages found for the infringement, in light of the difficulty and novelty of the issues presented and the good faith defense of invalidity.

B. Constitutional and Statutory Background

Article I, section 8, clause 8 of the Constitution provides that Congress shall have the power:

> To promote the Progress of Science and useful Arts, by securing for limited Times to Authors and Inventors the exclusive Right to their respective Writings and Discoveries; . . .

Although the first legislation implementing this provision for mechanical inventions was passed in 1790 by the first Congress, 1 Stat. 109, Congress did not include plants within the clause's protection until 1930. Act of May 23, 1930, 46 Stat. 376. In its present form, the principal statute allowing patents on plants reads:

> Whoever invents or discovers and asexually reproduces any distinct and new variety of plant, including cultivated sports, mutants, hybrids, and newly found seedlings, other than a tuber-propagated plant or a plant found in an uncultivated state, may obtain a patent therefor, subject to the conditions and requirements of this title.
>
> The provisions of this title relating to patents for inventions shall apply to patents for plants, except as otherwise provided.

35 U.S.C.A. § 161. Since section 161 makes the general patent law applicable to plant patents except as otherwise provided, we take as our starting point the general requisites for patentability, and then apply them as well as we can to plants.

Normally, the three requirements for patentability are novelty, utility, and nonobviousness. For plant patents, the requirement of distinctness replaces that of utility, and the additional requirement of asexual reproduction is introduced.

The concept of novelty refers to novelty of conception, rather than novelty of use; no single prior art structure can exist in which all of the elements serve substantially the same function. In Beckman Instruments, Inc. v. Chemtronics, Inc., 5 Cir., 439 F.2d 1369, 1375, cert. denied, 1970, 400 U.S. 956, 91 S.Ct. 353–54, 27 L.Ed.2d 264, this Court said:

> [S]ection 102, which pertains to novelty, requires that the patentee be the original inventor of the object claimed in his patent, and also that the invention not have been known or used by others before his discovery of it. . . . Furthermore the prior art is to be considered as covering all uses to which it could have been put.

As applied to plants, the Patent Office Board of Appeals held that a "new" plant had to be one that literally had not existed before, rather than one that had existed in nature but was newly found, such as an exotic plant from a remote part of the earth.[34] Ex parte Foster, 90 U.S. P.Q. 16 (1951). In Application of Greer, Ct.Cust. & Pat.App. 1973, 484 F.2d 488, the court indicated that the Board believed that novelty was to be determined by a detailed comparison with other known varieties.

The legislative history of the Plant Patent Act is of considerable assistance in defining "distinctness." The Senate Report said:

> [I]n order for the new variety to be distinct it must have characteristics clearly distinguishable from those of existing varieties and it is immaterial whether in the judgment of the Patent Office the new characteristics are inferior or superior to those of existing varieties. Experience has shown the absurdity of many views held as to the value of new varieties at the time of their creation.

> The characteristics that may distinguish a new variety would include, among others, those of habit; immunity from disease; or soil conditions; color of flower, leaf, fruit or stems; flavor; productivity, including ever-bearing qualities in case of fruits; storage qualities; perfume; form; and ease of asexual reproduction. Within any one of the above or other classes of characteristics the differences which would suffice to make the variety a distinct variety, will necessarily be differences of degree.

S.Rep. 315, 71st Cong., 2d Sess. (1930). (Emphasis omitted.) A definition of "distinctness" as the aggregate of the plant's distinguishing characteristics seems to us a sensible and workable one.

The third requirement, nonobviousness, is the hardest to apply to plants, though we are bound to do so to the best of our ability. The traditional three part test for obviousness, as set out in *John Deere,* inquires as to (1) the scope and content of the prior art, (2) the differences between the prior art and the claims at issue, and (3) the level of ordinary skill in the prior art. 383 U.S. at 17, 86 S.Ct. at 694, 15 L.Ed.2d at 556. Secondary characteristics such as commercial success, long felt but unsolved needs, and failure of others can be used to illuminate the circumstances surrounding the subject matter sought to be patented.

The Supreme Court has viewed the obviousness requirement of section 103 as Congress's articulation of the constitutional standard of invention. Dann v. Johnston, 425 U.S. at 225, 96 S.Ct. at 1397, 47 L.Ed. 2d at 698. In *Dann,* the Court commented that

> [a]s a judicial test, 'invention'—i.e., 'an exercise of the inventive faculty,' . . .—has long been regarded as an absolute prerequisite to patentability.

---

34. In order for a plant to have "existed" before in nature, we think that it must have been capable of reproducing itself. Thus, we have concluded that the mere fact that a sport of a plant had appeared in the past would not be sufficient to preclude the patentability of the plant on novelty grounds, since each sport is a one-time phenomenon absent human intervention. See in this connection the discussion on validity, at IV. C., infra.

425 U.S. at 225, 96 S.Ct. at 1397, 47 L.Ed.2d at 697–98. An "invention" is characterized by a degree of skill and ingenuity greater than that possessed by an ordinary mechanic acquainted with the business. The obviousness requirement appears to presume that if the gap between the prior art and the claimed improvement is small, then an ordinary mechanic skilled in the art would have been able to create the improvement, thus leading to the conclusion that the improvement was obvious and a patentable invention not present. Section 103 requires the determination of obviousness *vel non* to be made with reference to the time the invention was made. Obviousness, like the general question of patent validity, is ultimately a question of law, though factual inquiries are often necessary to its resolution.

Rephrasing the *John Deere* tests for the plant world, we might ask about (1) the characteristics of prior plants of the same general type, both patented and nonpatented, and (2) the differences between the prior plants and the claims at issue. We see no meaningful way to apply the third criterion to plants—i.e. the level of ordinary skill in the prior art. Criteria one and two are reminiscent of the "distinctness" requirement already in the Plant Patent Act. Thus, if we are to give obviousness an independent meaning, it must refer to something other than observable characteristics.

We think that the most promising approach toward the obviousness requirement for plant patents is reference to the underlying constitutional standard that it codifies—namely, invention.

The general thrust of the "invention" requirement is to ensure that minor improvements will not be granted the protection of a seventeen year monopoly by the state. In the case of plants, to develop or discover a new variety that retains the desirable qualities of the parent stock and adds significant improvements, and to preserve the new specimen by asexually reproducing it constitutes no small feat.

This Court's case dealing with the patent on the chemical compound commonly known as the drug "Darvon," Eli Lilly & Co. v. Generix Drug Sales, Inc., 5 Cir.1972, 460 F.2d 1096, provides some insight into the problem of how to apply the "invention" requirement to a new and esoteric subject matter. The court first noted that

> [a]nalogical reasoning is necessarily restricted in many chemical patent cases because of the necessity for physiological experimentation before any use can be determined.
>
> . . .
>
> In fact, such lack of predictability of useful result from the making of even the slightest variation in the atomic structure or spatial arrangement of a complex molecule . . . deprives the instant claims of obviousness and anticipation of most of their vitality. . . .

460 F.2d at 1101. The court resolved the apparent dilemma by looking to the therapeutic value of the new drug instead of to its chemical composition:

[R]eason compels us to agree that novelty, usefulness and non-obviousness inhere in the true discovery that a chemical compound exhibits a new needed medicinal capability, even though it be closely related in structure to a known or patented drug.

460 F.2d at 1103.

The same kind of shift in focus would lead us to a more productive inquiry for plant patents. If the plant is a source of food, the ultimate question might be its nutritive content or its prolificacy. A medicinal plant might be judged by its increased or changed therapeutic value. Similarly, an ornamental plant would be judged by its increased beauty and desirability in relation to the other plants of its type, its usefulness in the industry, and how much of an improvement it represents over prior ornamental plants, taking all of its characteristics together.

Before reaching the issues on appeal, we make a final comment about the requirement of asexual reproduction. It has been described as the "very essence" of the patent. Langrock, Plant Patents—Biological Necessities in Infringement Suits, 41 J.Pat.Off.Soc. 787 (1959). Asexual reproduction is literally the only way that a breeder can be sure he has reproduced a plant identical in every respect to the parent. It is quite possible that infringement of a plant patent would occur only if stock obtained from one of the patented plants is used, given the extreme unlikelihood that any other plant could actually infringe. If the alleged infringer could somehow prove that he had developed the plant in question independently, then he would not be liable in damages or subject to an injunction for infringement. This example illustrates the extreme extent to which asexual reproduction is the heart of the present plant patent system: the whole key to the "invention" of a new plant is the discovery of new traits *plus* the foresight and appreciation to take the step of asexual reproduction.

C.   Yoder's Plant Patents—Validity

During the trial, Cal–Florida offered as evidence certain documents showing that growers had found mutations on the Mandalay variety that were the same as the patented variety Glowing Mandalay—i.e. evidence that the sport Glowing Mandalay had recurred. Although Glowing Mandalay is no longer in the case, Cal–Florida later proffered similar evidence with respect to Gold Marble, Promenade, and Red Torch, which are three of the patents whose validity is challenged on appeal. Gold Marble, Promenade, and Red Torch are all sport patents, meaning that they first appeared as a sport of another plant, in contrast to seedling patents, which develop from seeds. Of the remaining four challenged patents, two were sport patents and two were seedling patents. Cal–Florida never proffered any sport recurrence evidence as to the other two sport patents, Mountain Sun and Southern Gold, nor did it offer any specific evidence attacking the seedling patents, Morocco and Mountain Snow. Since we find that the district court's ruling on the sport recurrence evidence did not preclude Cal–Florida from introducing other types of evidence to attack the validity of the patents, and since no sport recurrence evidence was introduced as to Mountain Sun and Southern Gold, we find no warrant on appeal to disturb the ruling that Mountain Sun, Southern Gold, Morocco, and Mountain Snow were valid and infringed. Plant patents, like others, enjoy a statutory presumption of validity that was not rebutted as to those four.

At the time the court rejected the sport return evidence for Glowing Mandalay, it made a ruling designed to apply to the rest of the trial with respect to that kind of evidence. That ruling is the focus of Cal–Florida's cross appeal on the plant patent validity point. Because of its importance, we set out the pertinent parts in some detail here:

> [I]t seems clear that it was the Congressional intent that a person who discovered an asexually reproduced variety of a new and distinct plant was entitled to a patent.

> It was not contemplated, apparently, that he invent, in the term that is used, or in the significance of that term, as we understand it, traditional concept of inventing a machine. . . .

> . . .

> In any event, the issue presented here is a rather narrow one and it has some practical overtones.

> I am frank to confess that I think Mr. Foster's [Yoder's counsel] presentation here . . . is very persuasive. In all probability, this will be, or may be, the ultimate result of this trial. It may not be, after we have listened to the testimony, of course, of Mr. Boone's [Cal–Florida's counsel] other witnesses who are coming in to testify on the genetics of this thing, but on this one narrow limited issue, it would seem that the plaintiffs [Yoder] were entitled to prevail.

> . . .

> Therefore, the objection to the introduction of the various letters and documents from . . . the growers and plant propagators around the country, which were forwarded to Yoder Brothers over the years, is sustained.

Cal–Florida construes the above-quoted ruling as an all-encompassing holding that the constitutional standard of invention does not apply to plant patents. It further claims that since the ruling was admittedly intended to apply to the entire trial, it was precluded from offering evidence on the issues of newness, distinctness, and obviousness by the court's action. In fact, it never even tried to introduce the expected expert genetics testimony, although it did make a formal offer of more sport return evidence at a later time in the trial.

Yoder disputes the breadth of the ruling and its effect on any other evidence Cal–Florida might have offered, and notes that the court's actual ruling on the issues of newness and distinctness did not come until some two weeks later. With regard to the ruling on the admissibility of the evidence, Yoder argues that the documents would not have shown lack of distinctness, since the fact that a sport with particular traits recurs says nothing about what those traits are and how they differ from other plants. Furthermore, Yoder argues that the documents would not have shown obviousness, because if sport recurrence were evidence of obviousness, then almost no mutations would be patentable, and that would be contrary to Congress' intent.

We do not construe the district court's evidentiary ruling as anything more than that; in our opinion, it simply held that the sport recurrence evidence was not relevant to any of the patent validity issues. We therefore confine our remarks accordingly.

The only possible probative value of the sport recurrence evidence would be to show that a sport of that particular size, shape, color, or other trait is predictable from a given variety of parent plant. Thus, we must first determine whether Congress intended predictability to negate the possibility of "invention." Next, if Congress considered that factor irrelevant, we must decide if the Constitution is offended by permitting patents on the kinds of sports that recur.

Both the language of the statute and its legislative history persuade us that Congress did not intend to exclude the kind of mutation that might recur from the Act's protection. Instead, both Senate Report 315, 71st Cong., 2d Sess. (1930), on the original bill, and Senate Report 1937, 83d Cong., 2d Sess. (1954), on the 1954 amendment, speak generally about sports and mutations. The 1954 amendment was added to clarify Congress' intention that seedlings should be patentable, but in the process of describing the bill, the report states:

> The enactment of this legislation will remove any doubt that the legislative intent of the Congress clearly means that sports, mutants, hybrids, and seedlings, discovered by persons engaged in agriculture or horticulture, should be patentable. . . .

S.Rep. 1937, supra.

Although we are willing to assume for purposes of this argument that some mutations may appear that would have been genetically impossible before—i.e. that a fundamental change in the biochemical structure of the chromosome may take place—by far the majority of mutations and sports of chrysanthemums are predictable to some extent for those skilled in the field. For example, the testimony at trial indicated that a yellow sport could be expected from a white chrysanthemum. Indeed, part of the skill required of a chrysanthemum breeder is to know what to look for and to take steps immediately to preserve it by asexual reproduction if the desired trait appears. Given that fact, we think that the purpose of the Plant Patent Act would be frustrated by a requirement that only those rare, never-before-seen, if not genetically impossible sports or mutations would be patentable. That purpose was "to afford agriculture, so far as practicable, the same opportunity to participate in the benefits of the patent system as has been given industry, and thus assist in placing agriculture on a basis of economic equality with industry." S.Rep. 315, supra. To make it significantly more difficult to obtain a plant patent than another type of patent would frustrate that purpose.

We therefore find that Congress did not intend to exclude the kind of sport that recurs frequently from the Plant Patent Act. That being the case, the district court correctly ruled that the evidence proffered by Cal–Florida was irrelevant, as a matter of statutory law.

The only way that the Constitution would be offended by permitting patents on recurring sports would be if such leniency indicated that no "invention" was present. We do not think that sport recurrence would negate invention, however. An infinite number of a certain sized sport could appear on a plant, but until someone recognized its uniqueness and difference and found that the traits could be preserved by asexual reproduction in commercial quantities, no patentable plant would exist. An objective judgment of the value of the sport's new and different characteristics—i.e. nutritive value, ornamental value, hardiness, longevity, etc.—would not depend in any way on whether a similar sport had appeared in the past, or whether that particular sport was predictable. We therefore find no reason to disturb our approval of the district court's evidentiary ruling based on the constitutional standard of invention. As that standard applies to plant patents, the proffered evidence was irrelevant.

Viewing the evidence offered on the patent validity question as a whole, we find that Cal–Florida failed to rebut the statutory presumption of validity as to Gold Marble, Promenade, and Red Torch, as well as the other four discussed above. Thus, the lower court's finding of validity must be affirmed on this record.

D. *Patent Infringement*

On cross appeal, Cal–Florida asserts that the absence of flowering plants grown from the cuttings it had admittedly taken from Yoder's patented plants was fatal to Yoder's infringement counts. This is because the patent claim in each instance describes a mature flowering plant, and it is Cal–Florida's position that only another mature flowering plant could directly infringe. Yoder retorts that the Plant Patent Act provides that

> [i]n the case of a plant patent the grant shall be of the right to exclude others from asexually reproducing the plant or selling or using the plant so reproduced.

35 U.S.C.A. § 163. The district court ruled that the act of asexual reproduction was complete at the time the cutting was taken. Finally, the pretrial stipulations established that Cal–Florida had taken plant material, or cuttings, from Yoder's patented plants.

We agree with Yoder that it was not necessary to prove that the cuttings actually matured into flowered plants to show infringement. Under such a rule, it would be virtually impossible for a propagator-distributor directly to infringe a patent, despite the vital role he plays in dissemination of plant material. Furthermore, we think section 163 is plain in its statement that a patentee may exclude others from asexually reproducing, selling or using the plant. The negative inference to be drawn from this is that commission of one of those acts would constitute infringement. We therefore affirm the finding of infringement. . . .

V. Conclusion

In light of our ruling on the price differential theory of damages we reverse and remand the antitrust claims for retrial of damages. We affirm the district court's ruling of patent validity and infringement; and finally, we direct that the patent damage award be reduced to actual damages.

Affirmed in part, reversed and remanded in part.

NOTES

1.   *Yoder* is discussed in Jeffery, The Patentability and Infringement of Sport Varieties: Chaos or Clarity, 59 J.Pat.Off.Soc'y 645 (1977). See generally, Magnuson, A Short Discussion of Various Aspects of Plant Patents, 30 J.Pat.Off.Soc'y 493 (1948); Note, 61 Mich.L.Rev. 997 (1963).

2.   A bare handful of judicial decisions have defined the scope and thrust of the plant patent provisions. Legislative history has been particularly influential. In answering the question, "what is meant by 'invented or discovered' and by 'new variety of plant' in the statute," The Board of Appeals in Ex parte Foster, 90 U.S.P.Q. 16 (1951), turned to the legislative history to determine whether "these words mean that the plant must be new in fact in the sense that the plant did not exist before," or whether "they include what is old and has existed before but what has been merely newly found." "The bill which resulted in the Act was Senate Bill 4015 introduced March 24, 1930, by Senator Townsend, superseding a previous bill, S. 3530 February 11, 1930. This bill defined the added class of patentable subject matter in the words in italics in the following quotation from the bill: 'Any person . . . *who has invented or discovered and asexually reproduced (1) any distinct and new variety of plant or (2) any distinct and newly found variety of plant, other than a tuberpropagated plant,* . . . *may* . . . obtain a patent therefore.' Two classes of plants were thus specified in the bill, one, distinct and new varieties of plants, and two, distinct and newly found varieties of plants, and a clear distinction made between new plants and newly found plants.

"The Senate Committee on Patents reported the bill favorably, with amendments, Senate Report No. 315, 71st Congress, April 3, 1930. One of the amendments consisted in striking out from the bill the words 'or (2) any distinct and newly found variety of plant,' thus eliminating newly found plants from the scope of the bill. In explanation of this amendment the Senate Committee Report (page 1) states that it 'eliminates from the scope of the bill patents for varieties of plants which exist in an uncultivated or wild state, but are newly found by plant explorers or others.' " 90 U.S.P.Q. 17–18.

3. *Statutory Bars.* Will the depiction of an applicant's roses in a printed publication more than one year before he files patent applications on them defeat patentability under section 102(b)? Judge Smith, writing for the Court of Customs and Patent Appeals in Application of LeGrice, 301 F.2d 929, 133 U.S.P.Q. 365 (1962), concluded that it would not.

Smith acknowledged that "Congress, by enacting no exception to 35 U.S.C.A. § 102(b) with respect to patents for plants, intended that it be interpreted the same for plant patents as it has been interpreted in relation to patents for other inventions." 301 F.2d 929, 933. Yet, because of the special nature of plant subject matter, application of section 102 required special consideration. "Appellant in his brief points out 'The description of a plant in a plant patent or in a printed publication at best can only recite, as historical facts, that at one time a certain plant existed, was discovered in a certain manner, and was asexually reproduced. This information may be interesting history, but cannot enable others to reproduce the plant. . . . Prior public use and sale of a plant are the avenues by which a plant enters the public domain.'" 301 F.2d 929, 935.

According to Smith, "In the case of manufactured articles, processes and chemical compositions, a different situation prevails. Written descriptions and drawings and publications can often enable others to manufacture the article, practice the process or produce the chemical composition. Thus, with respect to publications in these fields, there is a valid basis in public policy for 35 U.S.C.A. § 102(b) which bars the granting of patents on inventions 'described in a printed publication in this or a foreign country . . . more than one year prior to the date of the application for patent in the United States.'" Id.

. . . "The Board of Appeals stated in its decision below that 'it is no more absurd to use a disclosure which is not enabling as a bar than it is to grant a patent on such a disclosure; the disclosure in the specifications of these applications are admittedly just as unenabling as the disclosures of the publications.' The answer to this apparent anomaly lies in 35 U.S.C.A. § 162 in which Congress 'otherwise provided' by specifically allowing for such a description in plant patent applications. *No such allowance has been made in 35 U.S.C.A. § 102(b) with reference to the sufficiency of the description of new plant varieties in printed publications.*

"Another answer to this apparent 'anomaly' is implicit in 35 U.S.C.A. § 163. The plant patent grant differs from that given with respect to other inventions. Infringers must be shown to have asexually reproduced or sold or used the plant on which the patent was granted. This section implicitly recognizes there is no possibility of producing the plant *from a disclosure* as 35 U.S.C.A. § 112 contemplates. Therefore, there is no requirement for any how-to-make disclosure in the application for a plant patent." 301 F.2d 929, 944 (emphasis the court's).

4. *Plant Variety Protection Act.* The plant patent provisions authorize protection only for asexually reproduced plant varieties. The Plant Variety Protection Act, enacted December 24, 1970, Pub.L. No. 91–577, 84 Stat. 1542, and amended on December 22, 1980, Pub.L. No. 96–574, 94 Stat. 3350, offers protection for new varieties of plants that reproduce sexually, through seeds. A certificate of plant variety protection will issue if the applicant's variety meets the statutory requirements of distinctness, uniformity and stability, and passes several novelty and other statutory bars comparable to those imposed by section 102 of the Patent Act. §§ 41, 42. Protection lasts for a period of eighteen years from the date the certificate is issued. §§ 83, 123–125. The Act is administered by the Plant Variety Protection Office in the United States Department of Agriculture.

Among the reasons given for enacting the Plant Variety Protection Act was that "it will allow our Government Agricultural experiment stations to increase their efforts on needed basic research." Also, according to the House Report, "the new law will definitely stimulate plant breeding. Experience in England provides a good case history. Prior to the enactment of its Plant Varieties and Seeds Act 1964, little plant breeding was done in England by private companies, and not much was done by government agencies. Since the new law came into effect, there has been a great upsurge of plant breeding, and a once moribund seed industry is now showing signs of great new vitality." H.R.Rep. No. 91–1605, 91st Cong., 2d Sess. (1970).

In In re Hibberd, 227 U.S.P.Q. 443 (1985), the Patent and Trademark Office relied on *Chakrabarty,* p. 426, above, to hold that utility patent protection could encompass seeds. Because utility patents offer greater protection than plant variety protection certificates, seed developers can be expected to migrate to utility patents. See Lesser, Patenting Seeds in the United States of America: What to Expect, 25 Indust.Prop. 360 (1986).

B. ADMINISTRATIVE PROCEDURES

See Statute Supplement 35 U.S.C.A. §§ 1–14, 21–26, 31–33, 41–42, 111–122, 131–135, 141–146, 151–154, 251–256.

This section narrates the application, prosecution and grant to Baxter I. Scoggin, Jr., of Patent No. 2,870,943 for a pump-type liquid sprayer with hold-down cap. The section also introduces the litigation, culminating in Calmar, Inc. v. Cook Chem. Co., 383 U.S. 1, 26, 86 S.Ct. 684, 698, 15 L.Ed.2d 545, 148 U.S.P.Q. 459 (1966), that subsequently enmeshed the Scoggin patent.

For introductory reading, see Roberts, A Reappraisal of the American System of Patent Examining, 48 J.Pat.Off.Soc'y 156 (1966); Frost, Patent Office Performance in Perspective, 54 Mich.L.Rev. 591 (1956); Woodward, A Reconsideration of the Patent System as a Problem of Administrative Law, 55 Harv.L.Rev. 950 (1942).

1. APPLICATION

Once a preliminary search of the art has been completed, and a decision reached to file a patent application, the application is assembled for submission to the United States Patent and Trademark Office. Typically, the application consists of a signed oath or declaration, power of attorney, an executed assignment if one has been made, filing fee, receipt postcard, transmittal letter, an information disclosure statement and the claims, specification and drawings.

a. CLAIMS

"Having thus described the invention what is claimed as new and desired to be secured by Letters Patent is:

"1. In a closure assembly for an open-top container having a perforated cap over said open top thereof mounting a spray unit including a barrel provided with a tubular extension passing coaxially upwardly through the perforation in said cap, a plunger reciprocally carried by the barrel and normally extending therebeyond and a spray head on the upper end of the plunger above said extension, the combination with said spray unit of an annular retainer telescoped over and secured to the extension above said cap and provided with external, circumferentially disposed screw threads and an annular, continuous segment at the upper part of the retainer above said screw threads, and a cup-shaped hold-down member housing the head and holding the plunger depressed at substantially the innermost path of travel thereof within the barrel, said member being provided with internal screw threads complementally engaging said screw threads on the retainer and having an internal, circumferentially extending, continuous shoulder disposed to engage said segment around the entire periphery thereof and thereby present a liquid-tight seal located between the spray head and said threads on the retainer and said member respectively, said shoulder being spaced from the lower annular peripheral edge of the member a distance at least slightly less than the distance from that portion of said segment normally engaged by said shoulder, to the proximal upper surface of the cap whereby said lower edge of the member is maintained out of contacting relationship with the cap when the member is on the retainer in a position with said shoulder in tight sealing engagement with the segment.

"2. A closure assembly as set forth in claim 1 wherein one of the normally interengaged surfaces of the shoulder and segment respectively is substantially conical to present an inclined annular face coaxial with the member and said retainer and of sufficient diameter at the largest end thereof to cause the seal effected between the shoulder and said segment to become tighter as the shoulder slides on said segment during shifting of the member toward the cap.

"3. A closure assembly as set forth in claim 2 wherein said retainer is provided with a continuous, annular rib integral with the normally upper edge thereof and defining said segment, said rib having an outwardly facing, inclined surface presenting said conical face of greatest external diameter at the zone of juncture of the rib with the retainer, said member having a pair of inner, coaxial, longitudinally spaced, cylindrical surfaces, the innermost cylindrical surface having a smaller diameter than the outermost cylindrical surface and presenting said shoulder therebetween lying in a plane perpendicular to the axes of said cylindrical surfaces, the diameter of said innermost cylindrical surface of the member being intermediate the diameters of opposed external end margins of said rib.

"4. A closure assembly as set forth in claim 3 wherein the member and retainer are constructed of materials having different coefficients of hardness whereby one of the interengaged faces of the rib and said shoulder respectively is deformed as the member is shifted toward the cap to thereby produce a more effective seal therebetween."

———

Like a legal description of real property, each claim of a patent describes the boundaries of the patent owner's property. Note, for example, that in claim 1, which is presented as a one-sentence paragraph, each of the comma-separated clauses following the words, "the combination with said spray unit of" cooperatively defines an essential structural element of the invention—a "retainer." By use of more specific language and additional structural elements, each of the four claims successively confines the invention's boundaries. Thus if, because of its breadth, claim 1 is declared invalid as anticipated by the prior art, claim 2 may succeed by reason of its narrower construction. Note that claim 1 is complete in itself and, for this reason, is characterized as an "independent claim." Claims 2–4, on the other hand, are written in "dependent" form, with claim 2 including the elements of claim 1, claim 3 including the elements of claims 1 and 2, and claim 4 including the elements of claims 1, 2, and 3.

b.   SPECIFICATION

The language of the specification is the dictionary, or exegesis, for the claims. Both drawings and specification must support the claims. The format followed in the Scoggin specification was: title; statement of the field of invention [col. 1, lines 15–18]; background description of the prior art, setting forth the problem to be solved [col. 1, lines 19–35]; series of objects to which the claims should respond [col. 1, lines 36–57]; brief description of the drawings [col. 1, lines 58–72]; and, using reference numerals for the correspondingly labelled drawing elements, a detailed description of a preferred embodiment of the invention's construction and operation. Under the practice preferred by the Patent and Trademark Office, the format employs subtitle headings to identify these sections:

2,870,943

PUMP-TYPE LIQUID SPRAYER HAVING
HOLD-DOWN CAP

Baxter I. Scoggin, Jr., Kansas City, Mo., assignor, by
mesne assignments, to Cook Chemical Company, Kansas City, Mo., a corporation of Missouri

Application March 4, 1957, Serial No. 643,711

4 Claims. (Cl 222–182)

This invention relates to improvements in structures for dispensing liquids wherein is provided a spray-type hand pump within a container for the liquid through use of the closure cap of such container.

It is common practice, as exemplified for example by Patent No. 2,362,080, issued November 7, 1944, to dispense various types of liquids such as insecticides, through use of a finger-manipulated spray pump normally sold as a component part of the container itself. The pump includes a vertically reciprocable plunger extending upwardly beyond the top of the cap within which the pump is mounted and provided with a spray head or nozzle structure capable of emitting a fine mist-like spray when the plunger is depressed by engagement with a finger-receiving saddle forming a part of the spray head.

Difficulties have been experienced in the field by virtue of the inherent nature of such structure since accidental actuation of the plunger causes dispensing of the fluid and oftentimes the material is used in part by store employees prior to sale because of the ready accessibility to the pump itself.

It is the most important object of the present invention, therefore, to provide structure for rendering the pump inoperable during shipment and while in storage, as well as on the shelves of the retail dealer.

Another important object of the present invention is to provide structure capable of carrying out the functions above set forth which is also adapted to enclose the head of the plunger and thereby protect the same, as well as handlers of the merchandise by virtue of the fact that the said plunger is completely enclosed and held at the innermost end of its reciprocable path of travel.

A further object of the instant invention is to provide a hold-down cap that may be quickly and easily applied and removed by virtue of a releasable attachment to a part of the entire unit such as by use of screw-threaded interengagement therewith.

A further object of this invention is to provide improvements of the aforementioned character that advantageously employs a part of the unit which has a secondary function of attaching the barrel of the spray pump to the closure cap of the container.

Other objects include important details of construction to be made clear or become apparent as the following specification progresses, reference being had to the accompanying drawing, wherein:

Figure 1 is a fragmentary, elevational view of a liquid container showing a pump-type sprayer as a part thereof and including the novel hold-down cap of the instant invention, parts being in section for clearness.

Figure 2 is a fragmentary, vertical, cross-sectional view through the container and its cap showing the pump assembly in its operable position with the hold-down cap removed; and

Figure 3 is an exploded perspective view showing the hold-down cap and certain parts of the sprayer with which the same is operably associated.

Pump-type sprayer 10 for liquid container 12 is attached to cap 14 for retention thereby when cap 14 is removed from threaded neck 16 of container 12, and if desired, there may be provided sufficient clearance between cup-shaped retainer 18 and annular outturned flange 20 to permit rotation of cap 14 relative to sprayer 10.

Both cap or closure 14 and retainer 18 are received by a cylindrical extension 22 of frusto-conical barrel 24, forming a part of the sprayer 10, extension 22 being integral with flange 20 at the innermost edge of the latter. Flange 20 is integral with barrel 24 near the larger, uppermost edge of the latter and is held against the under side of gasket 38 in the cap 14 when the sprayer 10 is operably associated with container 12.

Retainer 18 is provided with a central opening 25 which receives tubular plunger 26 and has a cavity 27 that accommodates the enlarged extension 22 as is clear in Fig. 2. Retainer 18 is fitted tightly over the extension 22 and maintains the retainer in place with flange 20 against gasket 38 as above set forth.

Reduced end 28 of barrel 24 receives a tube 30 that extends to the bottom of container 12, it being understood that the sprayer 10 is internally constructed in a suitable manner as, for example, in accordance with teachings of the aforementioned patent to pump liquid from the container 12 into the tube 30 and thence through nozzle 32 forming a part of a spray head 34 secured to the uppermost end of plunger 26. The enlarged head 34 is normally depressed by one finger as the operator grasps the container 12 as is well understood in this art.

Cap 14 has a clearance opening therein, as best shown in Fig. 2, for the extension 22 of barrel 24 and when the cap 14 is in screw-threaded engagement with neck 16, the gasket 38 which surrounds barrel 24, is clamped tightly between flange 20 and the under side of the top of cap 14.

A hold-down member broadly designated by the numeral 40, is provided to hold the plunger 26 at the lowermost end of its path of travel within the barrel 24 in the manner illustrated by Fig. 1, it being understood as by reference to said patent, that a spring (not shown) within the barrel 24, yieldably biases the plunger 26 upwardly to the position shown in Fig. 2. The hold-down member 40 is preferably in the nature of a hollow cap so that the same not only encloses or houses the upper end of plunger 26, i. e. spray head 34, but releasably attaches to the retainer 18 and also houses the latter.

A cylindrical bore 42 within the hold-down cap 40 receives the head 34 as seen in Fig. 1, and enlargement of the bore 42 adjacent the lowermost open end of the cap 40 is provided with internal screw threads 44 that mesh with external screw threads 46 on the retainer 18, thereby releasably attaching the cap 40 to the retainer 18.

An enlarged, annular boss 48 on the cap 40 is provided with a ribbed, outermost surface to facilitate mounting and removal of the cap 40 relative to retainer 18. A downwardly-facing shoulder 50 within the cap 40 engages the upper surface of retainer 18, thereby preventing engagement between cap 40 and closure 14 to prevent forcing of the retainer 18 from its tight press-fit engagement with extension 22. As illustrated, the screw threads 46 on the retainer 18 are in the nature of a pair of substantially semi-circular, spirally arranged sections 52 and 54, permitting molding of the retainer 18 with its screw threads 46 as a single unitary part.

In addition to the seal provided between shoulder 50 and the top surface of retainer 18, there is established an additional annular seal between annular rib 56 and the annular surface of cap 40 immediately adjacent to shoulder 50. This seal is clearly illustrated in Figure 1. The cross-sectional contour of rib 56 is as shown in Fig. 2 to present an upwardly and inwardly inclined annular face which snugly fits against the "corner," or line of juncture between shoulder 50 and the adjacent annular inner face of cap 40.

The interfitting surfaces between extension 22 and retainer 18 are as illustrated in Fig. 2. There is an annular notch formed in extension 22 at the outer extremity thereof and this notch 58 receives a similarly formed, continuous annular projection 60 formed integrally with retainer 18 and at a point where elements 58 and 60 will interlock when the parts are in assembled condition.

Thus, any accidental leakage or seepage from container 12 through the parts after they are assembled is obviated.

The material from which retainer 18 is produced is soft enough to be slightly compressed when shoulder 50 and the corner adjacent thereto, rides along the upwardly and inwardly inclined outer face of rib 56 when cap 40 is moved to position.

c. Drawings

Jan. 27, 1959   B. I. SCOGGIN, JR   2,870,943

PUMP—TYPE LIQUID SPRAYER HAVING HOLD—DOWN CAP

Filed March 4, 1957

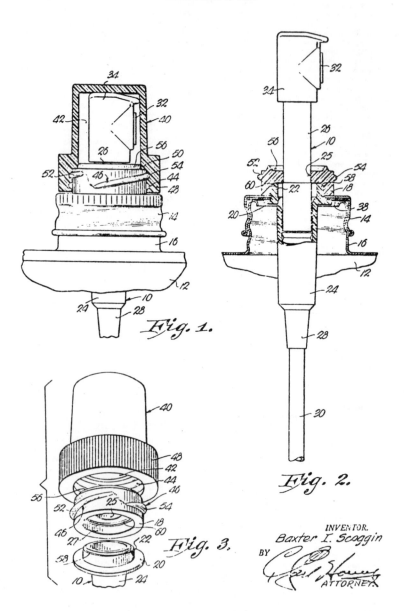

Fig. 1.

Fig. 2.

Fig. 3.

INVENTOR.
Baxter I. Scoggin
BY
ATTORNEY.

2. PROSECUTION

The claims, specification and drawings set out above are taken not from Scoggin's original application, filed March 4, 1957, but from a strikingly different document—the patent that finally issued. The Patent Office positions and the argument and negotiation that produced the differences—a small change in the specification and a complete revision of the claims—typify the basic format of the patent prosecution.

a. *First Office Action.* Scoggin received the first Office Action on November 5, 1957. In this action, the examiner pointed out a minor discrepancy between the specification and drawings and rejected claims 1–11; apparently inadvertently, he overlooked claims 12–15. The examiner gave two grounds for rejecting claims 1–11: they were (1) vague and indefinite; and (2) "substantially met by Lohse"—Patent No. 2,119,884 issued to F.W. Lohse, June 7, 1938.

Scoggin's first amendment, filed April 30, 1958, corrected the specification, cancelled claims 1–15, added new claims 16 and 17, and attempted to demonstrate that the new claims were distinguishable over Lohse. The new claims and the arguments in support of their allowability stressed a leakproof sealing feature of the hold-down cap, a feature not defined in the original claims and only peripherally alluded to in the specification.

b. *Second Office Action.* The examiner initiated this action on October 1, 1958, widening his prior art references to include two patents, Slade and Nilson, covering threaded container caps without a spray head. Specifically, the examiner rejected claims 16 and 17 as unpatentable over a combination of prior art—Lohse in view of either Slade or Nilson. Scoggin responded with a second amendment cancelling claims 16 and 17 and adding narrower new claims, 18–24; he also offered detailed arguments to distinguish the new claims from the cited art.

Subsequently, Scoggin's attorney and the examiner met for a personal interview in the course of which the examiner cited two new patents in combination with Lohse—Darley and Mellon.

At the interview, attorney and examiner finally agreed on the claim limitations necessary to define the invention over the new combination of prior art. Shortly afterward, Scoggin submitted a third, supplementary amendment cancelling claims 18–24 and adding new claims, 25–28. Apart from being more definite in three areas, claim 25 was similar to claim 18 and claims 26–28 were identical to claims 19–21. Claims 22–24 were dropped.

c. *Notice of Allowance.* The notice, dated November 20, 1958, allowed claims 25–28, which became claims 1–4 of the issued patent. Upon payment of the requisite fee, Patent No. 2,870,943 issued January 27, 1959. The application's pending period, slightly under two years, was shorter than usual.

LOHSE PATENT 2,119,884
(Prior art 1938)

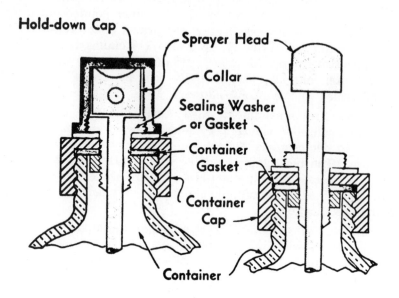

July 22, 1958   W. J. SLADE   2,844,290

DETERGENT CAN

Filed July 27, 1955

FIG.1.

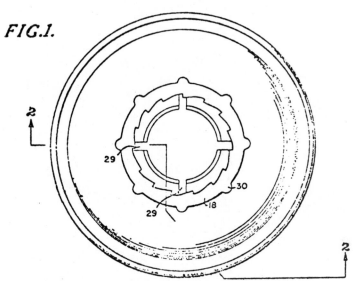

FIG.2.

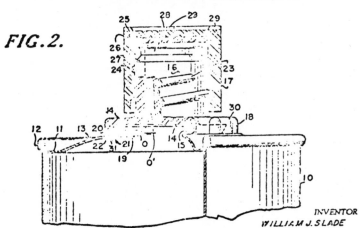

INVENTOR

WILLIAM J. SLADE

BY *Cushman, Darby & Cushman*

ATTORNEYS

May 24, 1938.   O. G. NILSON   2,118,222

COMBINED CAP AND SPOUT FOR LIQUID-DISPENSING CONTAINERS

Filed Feb. 17, 1936   2 Sheets—Sheet 1

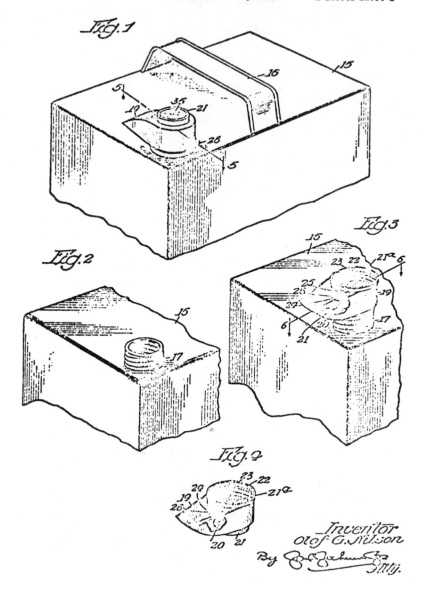

Inventor
Olof G. Nilson
By
Atty.

May 24, 1938.   O. G. NILSON   2,118,222

COMBINED CAP AND SPOUT FOR LIQUID DISPENSING CONTAINERS

Filed Feb. 17, 1936   2 Sheets-Sheet 2

Inventor
Olof G. Nilson

Atty

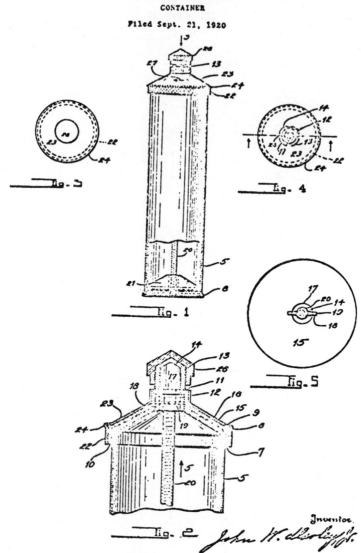

Mar. 6, 1923.

J. W. DARLEY, JR

CONTAINER

Filed Sept. 21, 1920

1,447,712

Fig. 3

Fig. 4

Fig. 1

Fig. 5

Fig. 2

Inventor

John W. Darley Jr.

FIG. 5. MELLON PATENT 2,586,687
(Prior art 1952)

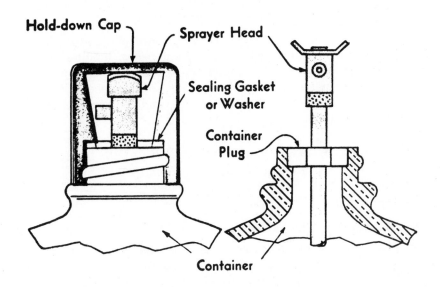

Hold-down Cap

Sprayer Head

Sealing Gasket or Washer

Container Plug

Container

3. JUDICIAL REVIEW

"By 1956 Scoggin had perfected the shipper-sprayer in suit and a patent was granted in 1959 to Cook Chemical as his assignee. In the interim Cook Chemical began to use Scoggin's device and also marketed it to the trade. The device was well received and soon became widely used. In the meanwhile, Calmar employed two engineers, Corsette and Cooprider, to perfect a shipper-sprayer and by 1958 it began to market its SS–40, a device very much similar to Scoggin's. When the Scoggin patent issued, Cook Chemical charged Calmar's SS–40 with infringement and this suit followed." Calmar, Inc. v. Cook Chem. Co., 383 U.S. 1, 28–29, 86 S.Ct. 684, 699, 700, 15 L.Ed.2d 545 (1966).

Upon being charged with infringement, Calmar, on April 27, 1959, instituted a declaratory judgment action against Cook Chemical in Cook's home district, the Western District of Missouri. The complaint asked the court to declare Scoggin's patent invalid and not infringed by Calmar. On October 5, 1960, the Colgate–Palmolive Company, a customer of Calmar, and user-seller of the Calmar device, brought a similar action in the same court. In its answers to both complaints, Cook admitted jurisdiction and the existence of a justiciable controversy, and counterclaimed for a declaration of the validity of the patent and a finding that it was infringed by Calmar's device. The actions were consolidated for trial on the issues of validity and infringement only.

The court's judgment, rendered July 31, 1963, decreed that (1) Cook was owner of the patent; (2) claims 1 and 2 were valid; (3) Calmar had infringed claims 1 and 2 by manufacture and sale, and Colgate had infringed claims 1 and 2 by use and sale; (4) plaintiffs' request for relief was dismissed; (5) plaintiffs were permanently enjoined from making, using or selling the accused device; (6) defendant was entitled to damages and an accounting and (7) defendant could move for an accounting and attorney's fees under 35 U.S.C.A. § 285.

Calmar and Colgate appealed to the Court of Appeals for the Eighth Circuit, which affirmed the judgment below, holding claims 1 and 2 valid and infringed. On certiorari to the court of appeals, the Supreme Court considered the *Calmar* and *Colgate* cases along with Graham v. John Deere Co., page 360, above, and rendered its decision on February 21, 1966.

CALMAR, INC. v. COOK CHEM. CO.

Supreme Court of the United States, 1966.
383 U.S. 1, 26, 86 S.Ct. 684, 698, 15 L.Ed.2d 545, 148 U.S.P.Q. 459.

CLARK, J.

The Opinions of the District Court and the Court of Appeals

At the outset it is well to point up that the parties have always disagreed as to the scope and definition of the invention claimed in the patent in suit. Cook Chemical contends that the invention encompasses a unique combination of admittedly old elements and that patentability is found in the result produced. Its expert testified that the invention was "the first commercially successful, inexpensive integrated shipping closure pump unit which permitted automated assembly with a container of household insecticide or similar liquids to produce a practical, ready-to-use package which could be shipped without external leakage and which was so organized that the pump unit with its hold-down cap could be itself assembled and sealed and then later assembled and sealed on the container without breaking the first seal." Cook Chemical stresses the long-felt need in the industry for such a device; the inability of others to produce it; and its commercial success—all of which, contends Cook, evidences the nonobvious nature of the device at the time it was developed. On the other hand, Calmar says that the differences between Scoggin's shipper-sprayer and the prior art relate only to the design of the overcap and that the differences are so inconsequential that the device as a whole would have been obvious at the time of its invention to a person having ordinary skill in the art.

Both courts accepted Cook Chemical's contentions. While the exact basis of the District Court's holding is uncertain, the court did find the subject matter of the patent new, useful and nonobvious. It concluded that Scoggin "had produced a sealed and protected sprayer unit which the manufacturer need only screw onto the top of its container in much the same fashion as a simple metal cap." 220 F.Supp., at 418. Its decision seems to be bottomed on the finding that the Scoggin sprayer solved the long-standing problem that had confronted the industry. The Court of Appeals also found validity in the "novel 'marriage' of the sprayer with the insecticide container" which took years in discovery and in "the immediate commercial success" which it enjoyed. While finding that the individual elements of the invention were "not novel per se" the court found "nothing in the prior art suggesting Scoggin's unique combination of these old features . . . as would solve the . . . problems which for years beset the insecticide industry." It concluded that "the . . . [device] meets the exacting standard required for a combination of old elements to rise to the level of patentable invention by fulfilling the long-felt need with an economical, efficient, utilitarian apparatus which achieved novel results and immediate commercial success." 336 F.2d, at 114.

The Prior Art

Only two of the five prior art patents cited by the Patent Office Examiner in the prosecution of Scoggin's application are necessary to our discussion, i.e., Lohse U.S. Patent No. 2,119,884 (1938) and Mellon U.S. Patent No. 2,586,687 (1952). Others are cited by Calmar that were not before the Examiner, but of these our purposes require discussion of only the Livingstone U.S. Patent No. 2,715,480 (1953). Simplified drawings of each of these patents are reproduced in the Appendix, Figs. 4–6, for comparison and description.

The Lohse patent (Fig. 4) is a shipper-sprayer designed to perform the same function as Scoggin's device. The differences, recognized by the District Court, are found in the overcap seal which in Lohse is formed by the skirt of the overcap engaging a washer or gasket which rests upon the upper surface of the container cap. The court emphasized that in Lohse "[t]here are no seals above the threads and below the sprayer head." 220 F.Supp., at 419.

The Mellon patent (Fig. 5), however, discloses the idea of effecting a seal above the threads of the overcap. Mellon's device, likewise a shipper-sprayer, differs from Scoggin's in that its overcap screws directly on the container, and a gasket, rather than a rib, is used to effect the seal.

Finally, Livingstone (Fig. 6) shows a seal above the threads accomplished without the use of a gasket or washer. Although Livingstone's arrangement was designed to cover and protect pouring spouts, his sealing feature is strikingly similar to Scoggin's. Livingstone uses a tongue and groove technique in which the tongue, located on the upper surface of the collar, fits into a groove on the inside of the overcap. Scoggin employed the rib and shoulder seal in the identical position and with less efficiency because the Livingstone technique is inherently a more stable structure, forming an interlock that withstands distortion of the overcap when subjected to rough handling. Indeed, Cook Chemical has now incorporated the Livingstone closure into its own shipper-sprayers as had Calmar in its SS–40.

The Invalidity of the Patent

Let us first return to the fundamental disagreement between the parties. Cook Chemical, as we noted at the outset, urges that the invention must be viewed as the overall combination, or—putting it in the language of the statute—that we must consider the subject matter sought to be patented taken as a whole. With this position, taken in the abstract, there is, of course, no quibble. But the history of the prosecution of the Scoggin application in the Patent Office reveals a substantial divergence in respondent's present position.

As originally submitted, the Scoggin application contained 15 claims which in very broad terms claimed the entire combination of spray pump and overcap. No mention of, or claim for, the sealing features was made. All 15 claims were rejected by the Examiner because (1) the applicant was vague and indefinite as to what the invention was, and (2) the claims were met by Lohse. Scoggin canceled these claims and submitted new ones. Upon a further series of rejections and new submissions, the Patent Office Examiner, after an office interview, at last relented. It is crystal clear that after the first rejection, Scoggin relied entirely upon the sealing arrangement as the exclusive patentable difference in his combination. It is likewise clear that it was on that feature that the Examiner allowed the claims. In fact, in a letter accompanying the final submission of claims, Scoggin, through his attorney, stated that "agreement was reached between the Honorable Examiner and applicant's attorney relative to *limitations* which must be in the claims in order to define novelty over the previously applied disclosure of Lohse when considered in view of the newly cited patents of Mellon and Darley, Jr." (Italics added.)

Moreover, those limitations were specifically spelled out as (1) the use of a rib seal and (2) an overcap whose lower edge did not contact the container cap. Mellon was distinguished, as was the Darley patent on the basis that although it disclosed a hold-down cap with a seal located above the threads, it did not disclose a rib seal disposed in such position as to cause the lower peripheral edge of the overcap "to be maintained out of contacting relationship with [the container] cap . . . when . . . [the overcap] was screwed [on] tightly. . . ." Scoggin maintained that the "obvious modification" of Lohse in view of Mellon would be merely to place the Lohse gasket above the threads with the lower edge of the overcap remaining in tight contact with the container cap or neck of the container itself. In other words, the Scoggin invention was limited to the use of a rib—rather than a washer or gasket—and the existence of a slight space between the overcap and the container cap.

It is, of course, well settled that an invention is construed not only in the light of the claims, but also with reference to the file wrapper or prosecution history in the Patent Office. Claims as allowed must be read and interpreted with reference to rejected ones and to the state of the prior art; and claims that have been narrowed in order to obtain the issuance of a patent by distinguishing the prior art cannot be sustained to cover that which was previously by limitation eliminated from the patent.

Here, the patentee obtained his patent only by accepting the limitations imposed by the Examiner. The claims were carefully drafted to reflect these limitations and Cook Chemical is not now free to assert a broader view of Scoggin's invention. The subject matter as a whole reduces, then, to the distinguishing features clearly incorporated into the claims. We now turn to those features.

As to the space between the skirt of the overcap and the container cap, the District Court found:

> Certainly without a space so described, there could be no inner seal within the cap, but such a space is not new or novel, but it is necessary to the formation of the seal within the hold-down cap.
>
> *To me this language is descriptive of an element of the patent but not a part of the invention.* It is too simple, really, to require much discussion. In this device the hold-down cap was intended to perform two functions—to hold down the sprayer head and to form a solid tight seal between the shoulder and the collar below. In assembling the element it is necessary to provide this space in order to form the seal. 220 F.Supp. at 420. (Italics added.)

The court correctly viewed the significance of that feature. We are at a loss to explain the Examiner's allowance on the basis of such a distinction. Scoggin was able to convince the Examiner that Mellon's cap contacted the bottle neck while his did not. Although the drawings included in the Mellon application show that the cap might touch the neck of the bottle when fully screwed down, there is nothing—absolutely nothing—which indicates that the cap was designed at any time to *engage* the bottle neck. It is palpably evident that Mellon embodies a seal formed by a gasket compressed between the cap and the bottle neck. It follows that the cap in Mellon will not seal if it does not bear down on the gasket and this would be impractical, if not impossible, under the construction urged by Scoggin before the Examiner. Moreover, the space so strongly asserted by Cook Chemical appears quite plainly on the Livingstone device, a reference not cited by the Examiner.

The substitution of a rib built into a collar likewise presents no patentable difference above the prior art. It was fully disclosed and dedicated to the public in the Livingstone patent. Cook Chemical argues, however, that Livingstone is not in the *pertinent* prior art because it relates to liquid containers having pouring spouts rather than pump sprayers. Apart from the fact that respondent made no such objection to similar references cited by the Examiner, so restricted a view of the applicable prior art is not justified. The problems confronting Scoggin and the insecticide industry were not insecticide problems; they were mechanical closure problems. Closure devices in such a closely related art as pouring spouts for liquid containers are at the very least pertinent references.

Cook Chemical insists, however, that the development of a workable shipper-sprayer eluded Calmar, who had long and unsuccessfully sought to solve the problem. And, further, that the long-felt need in the industry for a device such as Scoggin's together with its wide commercial success supports its patentability. These legal inferences or subtests do focus attention on economic and motivational rather than technical issues and are, therefore, more susceptible of judicial treatment than are the highly technical facts often present in patent litigation. Such inquiries may lend a helping hand to the judiciary which, as Mr. Justice Frankfurter observed, is most ill-fitted to discharge the technological duties cast upon it by patent legislation. Marconi Wireless Co. v. United States, 320 U.S. 1, 60, 63 S.Ct. 1393, 87 L.Ed. 1731 (1943). They may also serve to "guard against slipping into use of hindsight," Monroe Auto Equipment Co. v. Heckethorn Mfg. & Supply Co., 332 F.2d 406, 412 (1964), and to resist the temptation to read into the prior art the teachings of the invention in issue.

However, these factors do not, in the circumstances of this case, tip the scales of patentability. The Scoggin invention, as limited by the Patent Office and accepted by Scoggin, rests upon exceedingly small and quite nontechnical mechanical differences in a device which was old in the art. At the latest, those differences were rendered apparent in 1953 by the appearance of the Livingstone patent, and unsuccessful attempts to reach a solution to the problems confronting Scoggin made before that time became wholly irrelevant. It is also irrelevant that no one apparently chose to avail himself of knowledge stored in the Patent Office and readily available by the simple expedient of conducting a patent search—a prudent and nowadays common preliminary to well organized research. To us, the limited claims of the Scoggin patent are clearly evident from the prior art as it stood at the time of the invention.

We conclude that the claims in issue in the Scoggin patent must fall as not meeting the test of § 103, since the differences between them and the pertinent prior art would have been obvious to a person reasonably skilled in that art.

The judgment of the Court of Appeals in No. 11 is affirmed. The judgment of the Court of Appeals in Nos. 37 and 43 is reversed and the cases remanded to the District Court for disposition not inconsistent with this opinion.

It is so ordered.

NOTES

1. *Reissue and Reexamination.* There are two avenues for modifying issued patents. Section 251 of the Patent Act provides for patent reissue: "Whenever any patent is, through error without any deceptive intention, deemed wholly or partly inoperative or invalid, by reason of a defective specification or drawing, or by reason of the patentee claiming more or less than he had a right to claim in the patent, the Commissioner shall, on the surrender of such patent and the payment of the fee required by law, reissue the patent for the invention disclosed in the original patent, and in accordance with a new amended application, for the unexpired part of the term of the original patent. No new matter shall be introduced into the application for reissue." On reissue, see Dunner & Lipsey, The New Reissue Practice, 61 J.Pat.Off.Soc'y

68 (1979); Silverman, To Err is Human—Patent Reissues and the Doctrine of Intervening Rights, 48 J.Pat.Off.Soc'y 696, 727 (1966).

Chapter 30 the Patent Act, added by Pub.L. No. 96–517, 94 Stat. 3015 (1980), provides in part that "[a]ny person at any time may file a request for reexamination by the Office of any claim of a patent on the basis of any prior art. . . ." 35 U.S.C.A. § 302. On signing Public Law 96–517, President Jimmy Carter observed:

> The patent reexamination procedures established by this legisla-
> tion constitute the most significant improvement in our patent
> laws in more than a century. Under these procedures, during the
> life of an issued patent any interested person—for example, a
> patent owner, a potential licensee, or a competitor—may obtain a
> prompt and relatively inexpensive reevaluation of its validity by
> the Patent and Trademark Office. Patent reexamination will
> make it possible to focus extra attention on the most commercially
> significant patents. This legislation will improve the reliability of
> reexamined patents, thereby reducing the costs and uncertainties
> of testing patent validity in the courts. The provisions of this
> legislation will result in less cost to the public for patent reexami-
> nation.

Public Papers of Presidents of the United States, Jimmy Carter 2803 (Dec. 12, 1980). See Adamo, Patent Reexamination, 58 Chi.Kent L.Rev. 59 (1981).

What interests would be served by a system that postponed *all* examination of claimed subject matter to a point sometime after a patent issues? See McKie, Is Deferred Examination of Patent Applications Desirable in the United States? 55 J.Pat.Off.Soc'y 691 (1973). See also, Lowin, Reexamination "Catch 22," 14 AIPLA Q.J. 218 (1986).

2. *Statutory Invention Registrations.* The Patent Law Amend-ments of 1984, Pub.L. No. 98–622, 98 Stat. 3383, introduced statutory invention registrations into the patent system, effectively enabling inventors to obtain defensive patent protection. "Under current law, there is no simple, practical method by which an inventor can protect his ability to exploit the invention without obtaining a patent. The new procedure created by section 102 [35 U.S.C.A. § 157] would confer on an inventor the same rights that a patent provides to prevent others from patenting the invention. However, it would not permit the holder to exclude others from making, using or selling the invention. . . . Due to the fact that a SIR does not grant an exclusive right to an inventor, it would not be necessary to subject a SIR to the lengthy examination process required for the granting of a patent. Such an examination would only be necessary if the SIR was subjected to an interference proceeding to determine priority of invention. In all other instances, the Patent and Trademark Office would only review the application for adherence to formal printing and payment requirements and to ensure that the requirements of 35 U.S.C. § 112 were satisfied." Statement of Rep. Robert Kastenmeier, 130 Cong.Rec.H.10526 (daily ed. Oct. 1, 1984).

See Gholz & Pope, The Impact of Statutory Invention Registrations on Interference Practice, 67 J.Pat. & Trademark Off.Soc'y 645 (1985).

NOTE: FRAUD AND INEQUITABLE CONDUCT IN THE PATENT AND TRADEMARK OFFICE

A patent is a contract between the patentee and society: society gives the patentee a durationally limited property right in return for the patentee's enabling disclosure of her invention. With rights come duties. In her "contract negotiations" with the Patent and Trademark Office, the patent applicant has a duty not to induce the patent grant through fraudulent misrepresentations. This duty dates to the first patent act, Act of Apr. 10, 1790, ch. 7, § 5, 1 Stat. 109, 111, which gave private parties standing to seek repeal of a patent "obtained surreptitiously by, or upon false suggestion. . . . ." Today, fraud or inequitable conduct may lead the Patent and Trademark Office to strike a patent application from its files or prompt the government to cancel the patent. Antitrust liability may also ensue. Probably most important, fraud or inequitable conduct in the Patent and Trademark Office may give an accused infringer the defense that the patent is invalid or unenforceable. See D. Chisum, Patents § 19.03[6] (1989).

Patent fraud or inequitable conduct characteristically involves nondisclosure of pertinent information such as relevant prior art. In FMC Corp. v. Manitowoc Co., 835 F.2d 1411, 5 U.S.P.Q.2d 1112 (Fed.Cir.1987), Chief Judge Howard Markey described the "clear and convincing proof" that a party must offer to support a claim of inequitable nondisclosure: "(1) prior art or information that is material; (2) knowledge chargeable to applicant of that prior art or information and of its materiality; and (3) failure of the applicant to disclose the art or information resulting from an intent to mislead the PTO. That proof may be rebutted by a showing that: (a) the prior art or information was not material (e.g., because it is less pertinent than or merely cumulative with prior art or information cited to or by the PTO); (b) if the prior art or information was material, a showing that applicant did not know of that art or information; (c) if applicant did know of that art or information, a showing that applicant did not know of its materiality; (d) a showing that applicant's failure to disclose art or information did not result from an intent to mislead the PTO." 835 F.2d at 1415.

Kingsdown Medical Consultants, Ltd. v. Hollister Inc., 863 F.2d 867, 9 U.S.P.Q.2d 1384 (Fed.Cir.1988), cert. denied, 109 S.Ct. 2068, 104 L.Ed.2d 633 (1989), clarified the role of gross negligence in proof of intent to mislead the Patent and Trademark Office. Recognizing that "[s]ome of our opinions have suggested that a finding of gross negligence compels a finding of an intent to deceive" and that "[o]thers have indicated that gross negligence alone does not mandate a finding of intent to deceive," the court, en banc, adopted "the view that a finding that particular conduct amounts to 'gross negligence' does not of itself justify an inference of intent to deceive; the involved conduct, viewed in light of all the evidence, including evidence indicative of good faith, must indicate sufficient culpability to require a finding of intent to deceive." 863 F.2d at 876.

Judicial decisions on fraud and inequitable conduct have been unpredictable. One reason is that the standard is so fact-specific. Another reason is that courts often weigh the two relevant elements—intent and materiality—together, sometimes allowing strong proof of materiality to offset a weak showing of intent. The elements themselves have fluctuated widely. The intent requirement has wavered between objective and subjective measures. Materiality has fluctuated between a "but for" test and an "influence" test—whether it is likely that a reasonable examiner would have considered the information withheld to be important to the decision to grant a patent.

In an absolute sense, fraud and inequitable conduct are bad. But making them a defense in patent infringement actions can be costly. Professor Donald Chisum has observed that the defense injects "an element of moral turpitude into an area of law where it is especially important that attention be focused on the technical and economic facts." Chisum, Patent Law and the Presumption of Moral Regularity: A Critical Review of Recent Federal Circuit Decisions on Inequitable Conduct and Willful Infringement, 69 J.Pat. & Trademark Off.Soc'y 27, 28 (1987). An overly sensitive standard for fraud and inequitable conduct will lead applicants and their attorneys to search for and disclose information that offers no independent benefit to them or society. An uncertain standard will only magnify these expenditures.

See generally, Adamo & Ducatman, The Status of the Rules of Prohibited Conduct Before the Office: "Violation of the Duty of Disclosure" Out of "Inequitable Conduct" by "Fraud," 68 J.Pat. & Trademark Off.Soc'y 193 (1986); Pretty, Inequitable Conduct in the PTO—Is the "Plague" Entering Remission?, 71 J.Pat. & Trademark Off.Soc'y 46 (1989).

C. RIGHTS AND REMEDIES

See Statute Supplement 35 U.S.C.A. §§ 154, 261–262, 271–272, 283–287, 292.

1. RIGHTS

PAPER CONVERTING MACHINE CO. v. MAGNA-GRAPHICS CORP.

United States Court of Appeals, Federal Circuit, 1984.
745 F.2d 11, 223 U.S.P.Q. 591.

NICHOLS, Senior Circuit Judge.

This appeal is from a judgment of the United States District Court for the Eastern District of Wisconsin (Reynolds, C.J.) entered on December 1, 1983, and awarding plaintiff Paper Converting Machine Company (Paper Converting) $893,064 as compensation for defendant Magna-

Graphics Corporation's (Magna–Graphics) willful infringement of United States Patent No. Re. 28,353. We *affirm-in-part and vacate-in-part.*

I

Although the technology involved here is complex, the end product is one familiar to most Americans. The patented invention relates to a machine used to manufacture rolls of densely wound ("hard-wound") industrial toilet tissue and paper toweling. The machine, commonly known as an automatic rewinder, unwinds a paper web continuously under high tension at speeds up to 2,000 feet per minute from a large-diameter paper roll—known as the parent roll or bedroll—and simultaneously rewinds it onto paperboard cores to form individual consumer products.

Before the advent of automatic rewinders, toilet tissue and paper towel producers used "stop-start" rewinders. With these machines, the entire rewinding operation had to cease after a retail-sized "log" was finished so that a worker could place a new mandrel (the shaft for carrying the paperboard core) in the path of the paper web. In an effort to increase production, automatic rewinders were introduced in the early 1950's. These machines automatically moved a new mandrel into the path of the paper web while the machine was still winding the paper web onto another mandrel, and could operate at a steady pace at speeds up to about 1,200 feet per minute.

In 1962, Nystrand, Bradley, and Spencer invented the first successful "sequential" automatic rewinder, a machine which not only overcame previous speed limitations, but also could handle two-ply tissue. This rewinder simultaneously cut the paper web and impaled it on pins against the parent roll. Then, after a new mandrel was automatically moved into place, a "pusher" would move the paper web away from the parent roll and against a glue-covered paperboard core to begin winding a new paper log.

On April 20, 1965, United States Patent No. 3,179,348 (the '348 patent) issued, giving to Paper Converting (to whom rights in the invention had been assigned) patent protection for machines incorporating the sequential rewinding approach. On September 1, 1972, Paper Converting applied to have the claims of the '348 patent narrowed by reissue, and on March 4, 1975, United States Patent No. Re. 28,353 (the '353 patent) issued on this application. The '353 patent, like the original '348 patent on which it is based, received an expiration date of April 20, 1982. Claim 1 of the '353 patent defines the improvement in the web-winding apparatus as an improvement comprising:

(C) means for transversely severing said web to provide a free leading edge on said web for approaching a mandrel on which said web is to be wound in said path, and

(D) pin means extensibly mounted on said roll for maintaining a web portion spaced from said edge in contact with said roll, and pusher means extensibly mounted on said roll to urge said maintained web portion against an adjacent mandrel.

Paper Converting achieved widespread commercial success with its patented automatic rewinder. Although there are not many domestic producers of toilet tissue and paper toweling, Paper Converting has sold more than 500 machines embodying the invention.

In 1979, Paper Converting brought the present action against Magna–Graphics for infringement of the '353 patent. After a trial concerning only issues of liability, the district court held the '353 patent valid and found it willfully infringed. It awarded treble damages, finding that Magna–Graphics had acted without the advice of counsel as to the change it made in its machines to avoid infringement. The Seventh Circuit affirmed. The parties commendably raise no issues here which the Seventh Circuit has already decided as to Magna–Graphics' liability.

When the district court held the accounting for damages (after the Seventh Circuit had affirmed it on the liability portion of the case), it found that Magna–Graphics had made two sales of infringing rewinders and associated equipment: one to the Fort Howard Paper Company (Fort Howard) under circumstances to be described, and one to the Scott Paper Company (Scott). The court awarded to Paper Converting $112,163 for Magna–Graphics' sale to Scott, and $145,583 for Magna–Graphics' sale to Fort Howard. The court then trebled these damages, and added $119,826 as prejudgment interest on the untrebled award. This appeal is from the judgment awarding damages.

II

Magna–Graphics asserts reversible error in virtually every element of the district court's "accounting" or award of damages. In particular, Magna–Graphics contends that the district court erred in (1) finding the sale, substantial manufacture, and delivery of the Fort Howard rewinder to be an infringement, (2) basing the damages award on Paper Converting's lost profits, (3) adopting an incremental income theory when determining Paper Converting's lost profits, (4) computing Paper Converting's lost profits based on the value of the entire rewinder line as opposed to the patented rewinder alone, and (5) awarding prejudgment interest to Paper Converting. Despite Magna–Graphics' many arguments, however, we are not persuaded that the district court made any reversible error in its lengthy and detailed analysis of its accounting.

III

A

Magna–Graphics first argues that it should bear no liability whatsoever for its manufacture, sale, or delivery of the Fort Howard rewinder because that machine was never *completed* during the life of the '353 patent. We disagree.

In early 1980 Fort Howard became interested in purchasing a new high-speed rewinder line. Both Paper Converting and Magna–Graphics offered bids. Because Magna–Graphics offered to provide an entire rewinder line for about 10 percent less than did Paper Converting, it won the contract. Delivery would have been before the '353 patent expired. Magna–Graphics began to build the contracted for machinery, but before it completed the rewinder, on February 26, 1981, the federal district court in Wisconsin determined that a similar Magna–Graphics' rewinder built for and sold to Scott infringed the '353 patent. The court enjoined Magna–Graphics from any future infringing activity.

Because at the time of the federal injunction the rewinder intended for Fort Howard was only 80 percent complete, Magna–Graphics sought a legal way to fulfill its contract with Fort Howard rather than abandon its machine. First, Magna–Graphics tried to change the construction of the rewinder so as to avoid infringement. It submitted to Paper Converting's counsel three drawings illustrating three proposed changes, and asked for an opinion as to whether the changes would avoid infringement. Paper Converting's counsel replied, however, that until a fully built and operating machine could be viewed, no opinion could be given. Magna–Graphics, believing such a course of action unfeasible because of the large risks in designing, engineering, and building a machine without knowing whether it would be considered an infringement, instead negotiated with Fort Howard to delay the final assembly and delivery of an otherwise infringing rewinder until after the '353 patent expired in April 1982.

Magna–Graphics thereafter continued to construct the Fort Howard machine, all the while staying in close consultation with its counsel. After finishing substantially all of the machine, Magna–Graphics tested it to ensure that its moving parts would function as intended at a rate of 1,600 feet of paper per minute. Although Magna–Graphics normally *fully* tested machines at its plant before shipment, to avoid infringement in this instance, Magna–Graphics ran its tests in two stages over a period of several weeks in July and August of 1981.

To understand Magna–Graphics' testing procedure, it is necessary to understand the automatic transfer operation of the patented machine. First, from within a 72–inch long "cutoff" roll, a 72–inch blade ejects to sever the continuous web of paper which is wound around the bedroll. Then, pins attached to the bedroll hold the severed edge of the web while pushers, also attached to the bedroll, transfer the edge of the web towards the mandrel (the roll on which the paperboard core is mounted).

In the first stage of its test, Magna–Graphics checked the bedroll to determine whether the pushers actuated properly. It installed on the bedroll two pusher pads instead of the thirty pads normally used in an operating machine. It greased the pads and operated the bedroll to determine whether the pads, when unlatched, would contact the core on the mandrel. (Magna–Graphics greased the pads so as to provide a visual indication that they had touched the core.) During this stage of tests, no cutoff blades or pins were installed.

In the second stage of the test, Magna–Graphics checked the cutoff roll to determine whether the cutting blade actuated as intended. It tested the knife actuating mechanism by installing into the cutoff roll a short 4–inch section of cutter blade rather than the 72–inch blade normally used. After taping a 4–inch wide piece of paper to the outer surface of the cutoff roll, Magna–Graphics operated the cutoff roll to determine whether the latch mechanism would eject the blade to cut the paper. During *this* phase of the testing, no pins or pusher pads were installed. At no time during the tests were the pins, pushers, and blade installed and operated together.

To further its scheme to avoid patent infringement, Magna–Graphics negotiated special shipment and assembly details with Fort Howard. Under the advice of counsel, Fort Howard and Magna–Graphics agreed that the rewinder's cutoff and transfer mechanism would not be finally assembled until April 22, 1982, two days after the expiration of the '353 patent. With this agreement in hand, Magna–Graphics shipped the basic rewinder machine to Fort Howard on September 17, 1981, and separately shipped the cutoff roll and bedroll on October 23, 1981. The rewinder machine was not assembled or installed at the Fort Howard plant until April 26, 1982.

B

With this case we are once again confronted with a situation which tests the temporal limits of the American patent grant. See Roche Products, Inc. v. Bolar Pharmaceutical Co., 733 F.2d 858, 221 USPQ 937 (Fed.Cir.1984). We must decide here the extent to which a competitor of a patentee can *manufacture* and test during the life of a patent a machine intended solely for post-patent use. Magna–Graphics asserts that no law prohibits it from soliciting orders for, *substantially* manufacturing, testing, or even delivering machinery which, if *completely* assembled during the patent term, would infringe. We notice, but Magna–Graphics adds that it is totally irrelevant, that Paper Converting has lost, during the term of its patent, a contract for the patented machine which it would have received but for the competitor's acts.

Clearly, any federal right which Paper Converting has to suppress Magna–Graphics' patent-term activities, or to receive damages for those activities, must be derived from its patent grant, and thus from the patent statutes. "Care should be taken not to extend by judicial construction the rights and privileges which it was the purpose of Congress to bestow." Bauer v. O'Donnell, 229 U.S. 1, 10, 33 S.Ct. 616, 617, 57 L.Ed. 1041 (1913). The Supreme Court, in Brown v. Duchesne, 60 U.S. (19 How.) 183, 195, 15 L.Ed. 595 (1856), stated that:

> [T]he right of property which a patentee has in his invention, and his right to its exclusive use, is derived altogether from these statutory provisions; * * * an inventor has no right of property in his invention, upon which he can maintain a suit, unless he obtains a patent for it, according to the acts of Congress; and

* * * his rights are to be regulated and measured by these laws, and cannot go beyond them.

The disjunctive language of the patent grant gives a patentee the "right to exclude others from making, using or selling" a patented invention during the 17 years of the patent's existence. 35 U.S.C. § 154. Congress has never deemed it necessary to define any of this triad of excludable activities, however, leaving instead the meaning of "make," "use," and "sell" for judicial interpretation. Nevertheless, by the terms of the patent grant, *no* activity other than the unauthorized making, using, or selling of the claimed invention can constitute direct infringement of a patent, *no matter* how great the adverse impact of that activity on the economic value of a patent. Judge Learned Hand stated, in Van Kannell Revolving Door Co. v. Revolving Door & Fixture Co., 293 F. 261, 262 (S.D.N.Y.1920), that irrespective of where the equities may lie:

> [A] patent confers an exclusive right upon the patentee, limited in those terms. He may prevent any one from making, selling, or using a structure embodying the invention, but the monopoly goes no further than that. It restrains every one from the conduct so described, and it does not restrain him from anything else. If, therefore, any one says to a possible customer of a patentee, 'I will make the article myself; don't buy of the patentee,' while he may be doing the patentee a wrong, and while equity will forbid his carrying out his promise, the promise itself is not part of the conduct which the patent forbids; it is not a 'subtraction' from the monopoly. If it injures the plaintiff, though never performed, perhaps it is a wrong, like a slander upon his title, but certainly it is not an infringement of the patent.

Here, the dispositive issue is whether Magna–Graphics engaged in the making, use, or sale of something which the law recognizes as embodying an invention protected by a patent. Magna–Graphics relies on Deepsouth Packing Co. v. Laitram Corp., 406 U.S. 518, 92 S.Ct. 1700, 32 L.Ed.2d 273, 173 USPQ 769 (1972). That case dealt with a "combination patent" covering machinery for shrimp deveining. The only active issue was whether certain export sales were properly prohibited in the district court's injunction and whether damages should include compensation for past infringement by these exports. The infringer had put in effect a practice of selling the machines disassembled for export, but with the subassemblies so far advanced, and with such instructions, that the foreign consignee could put them together on receipt in operable condition with an hour's work. The Supreme Court's five to four holding that these exports did not infringe was interwoven of three strands of thought: (1) that the patent laws must be construed strictly because they create a "monopoly" in the patentee; (2) that a "combination patent" is not infringed until its elements are brought together into an "operable assembly;" and (3) that an attempt to enforce the patent against a machine assembled abroad was an attempt to give it extraterritorial application and to invade improperly the sovereignty of the country where the final assembly and the intended use occurred.

Magna–Graphics' effort to apply *Deepsouth* as precedential runs into the obvious difficulty that the element of extraterritoriality is absent here, yet it obviously was of paramount importance to the *Deepsouth* Court. We must be cautious in extending five to four decisions by analogy. The analysis of *where* infringement occurs is applicable, Magna–Graphics says, to determining *when* an infringement occurs, whether before or after a patent expires. We have not found any case that has so held, and are not cited to any. It does not at all necessarily follow, for the *Deepsouth* analysis is made to avert a result, extraterritoriality, that would not occur whatever analysis was made in the instant case.

Although in *Deepsouth* the Court at times used broad language in reaching its decision, it is clear that *Deepsouth* was intended to be narrowly construed as applicable only to the issue of the extraterritorial effect of the American patent law. The Court so implied not only in *Deepsouth* ("[A]t stake here is the right of American companies to compete with an American patent holder *in foreign markets. Our patent system makes no claim to extraterritorial effect, * * *" 406 U.S. at 531, 92 S.Ct. at 1708, 173 USPQ at 774 (emphasis added)), but in a subsequent decision as well ("The question under consideration [in *Deepsouth*] was whether a patent is infringed when unpatented elements are assembled into the combination *outside the United States.*" Dawson Chemical Co. v. Rohm & Haas Co., 448 U.S. 176, 216, 100 S.Ct. 2601, 2623, 65 L.Ed.2d 696, 206 USPQ 385, 405 (1980) (emphasis added).). Moreover, in Decca Limited v. United States, 544 F.2d 1070 (Ct.Cl.1976), the Court of Claims considered the worldwide system of electronic navigation aids called "Omega," which employs as a means of fixing the locations of ships and planes "master" and "slave" transmission stations, and receivers making computer printouts on board the ships and planes to be guided. The government relied on *Deepsouth* to establish that the involved patent, if enforced against it, would be given an extraterritorial application. The Court of Claims held that the application was not extraterritorial and therefore *Deepsouth* was not implicated. The Court of Claims viewed *Deepsouth* as simply and wholly a decision against extraterritorial application of United States patent laws.

While there is thus a horror of giving extraterritorial effect to United States patent protection, there is no corresponding horror of a valid United States patent giving economic benefits not cut off entirely on patent expiration. Thus, we hold that the expansive language used in *Deepsouth* is not controlling in the present case. The facts in *Deepsouth* are *not* the facts here. Because no other precedent controls our decision here, however, we nevertheless look to *Deepsouth* and elsewhere for guidance on the issue of whether what Magna–Graphics did is an infringement of the '353 patent. . . .

Whether Magna–Graphics' rewinder infringed the '353 patent is a question of fact which the Federal Rules leave to the district court to decide. The question is not always so simply decided as the dissent makes it out to be. In particular, where it is necessary to decide whether a complex mechanical contraption infringes a claim in a patent, the district court is often faced with a difficult chore. To require that in all situations the district court must decide a complicated factual issue within the narrow confines of a simple bright-line test makes the district judge's function nothing more than that of a master assigned to set out simple facts.

The dissent's argument is based on the utopian belief that a copier "should be able to look to the patent claims and know whether his [or her] activity infringes or not." Although this may be a desirable goal for the patent laws, it is *not* the law as it exists. In particular, the doctrine of equivalents has been judicially created to ensure that a patentee can receive full protection for his or her patented ideas by making it difficult for a copier to maneuver around a patent's claims. In view of this doctrine, a copier rarely knows whether his product "infringes" a patent or not until a district court passes on the issue. We see no difference in putting a copier into the same position here.

It is undisputed that Magna–Graphics intended to finesse Paper Converting out of the sale of a machine on which Paper Converting held a valid patent during the life of that patent. Given the amount of testing performed here, coupled with the sale and delivery during the patent-term of a "completed" machine (completed by being ready for assembly and with no useful noninfringing purpose), we are not persuaded that the district court committed clear error in finding that the Magna–Graphics' machine infringed the '353 patent.

To reach a contrary result would emasculate the congressional intent to prevent the making of a patented item during the patent's full term of 17 years. If without fear of liability a competitor can assemble a patented item past the point of testing, the last year of the patent becomes worthless whenever it deals with a long lead-time article. Nothing would prohibit the unscrupulous competitor from aggressively marketing its own product and constructing it to all but the final screws and bolts, as Magna–Graphics did here. We rejected any reduction to the patent-term in *Roche;* we cannot allow the inconsistency in the patent law which would exist if we permitted it here. Magna–Graphics built and tested a patented machine, albeit in a less than preferred fashion. Because an "operable assembly" of components was tested, this case is distinguishable from Interdent Corp. v. United States, 531 F.2d 547, 552 (Ct.Cl.1976) (omission of a claimed element from the patented combination avoids infringement) and Decca Ltd. v. United States, 640 F.2d 1156, 1168, 209 USPQ 52, 61 (Ct.Cl.1980) (infringement does not occur until the combination has been constructed and available for use). Where, as here, significant, unpatented assemblies of elements are tested during the patent term, enabling the infringer to deliver the patented combination in parts to the buyer, without testing the entire combination together as was the infringer's usual practice, testing the assemblies can be held to be in essence testing the patented combination and, hence, infringement.

That the machine was not operated in its optimum mode is inconsequential: imperfect practice of an invention does not avoid infringement. We affirm the district court's finding that "[d]uring the testing of the Fort Howard machine in July and August 1981, Magna–Graphics completed an operable assembly of the infringing rewinder."

[The court's discussion of monetary relief, omitted here, is reprinted beginning at page 490, below.]

V

The judgment of the district court awarding damages and prejudgment interest for Paper Converting's lost profits on two automatic rewinder lines is affirmed. The trebling of damages on the Fort Howard machine is vacated, and remanded for a determination of willfulness. Each party is to bear its own costs of this appeal.

Affirmed in Part and Vacated in Part.

NIES, Circuit Judge, dissenting-in-part.

I dissent from the majority's holding that Magna–Graphics' activities in connection with the Fort Howard machine constitute direct infringement of any claim of Paper Converting's patent. The majority's conclusion necessitates giving a meaning to "patented invention" contrary to the definition set forth by the Supreme Court in Deepsouth Packing Co. v. Laitram Corp., 406 U.S. 518, 92 S.Ct. 1700, 32 L.Ed.2d 273, 173 USPQ 769 (1972).

The analysis must begin with the statutory language of 35 U.S.C. § 271(a):

> Except as otherwise provided in this title, whoever without authority makes, uses or sells any *patented invention,* within the United States during the term of the patent therefor, infringes the patent. [Emphasis added.]

The majority holds that *incomplete assembly* of the patented invention is making, *testing of subassemblies* is using, and *a sale of an unassembled machine* is selling the *patented invention* within the meaning of the above section. The majority reasons that a contrary result would emasculate the congressional intent to prevent the making of a patented item during the patent's full term of 17 years. It could be said with equal validity that, given the lead time necessary to make the invention here, the majority effectively extends the patentee's right of exclusivity beyond the statutory 17 years.

I do not see in *Deepsouth* that the Supreme Court's only concern was the extraterritorial operation of our patent laws. The activities of Deepsouth under attack were all performed in the United States and were found not to result in direct or contributory infringement of the patent. That the activities of final assembly occurred abroad merely precluded a holding that Deepsouth's activities constituted contributory infringement. Contributory infringement cannot arise without a direct infringement. The situation in *Deepsouth* is exactly comparable to the one at hand. That the activities of final assembly occurred after the patent expired precludes holding Magna–Graphics to be a contributory infringer, there being no direct infringement by another to which the charge can be appended.

Thus, we are back to the dispositive direct infringement issue in *Deepsouth,* which is the same as the issue here. What is the meaning of "patented invention" in 35 U.S.C. § 271(a)? The alleged infringer, in each case, made and sold something, but was it the "patented invention"?   . . . .

It is not surprising that Magna–Graphics' counsel read *Deepsouth* as permitting the course of conduct condemned here. The majority opinion is no less than a reversal of *Deepsouth.* Regardless of the reasonableness of the alternative interpretation of § 271(a) given by the majority, we are bound by the Supreme Court's decision. No greater prerogative to modify it accrues to us from a 5–4 vote than from a unanimous decision. Change must be left to Congress, or the Court itself. In *Deepsouth* the extension of patent protection which had been urged was viewed as a matter for a legislative directive:

> In sum: the case and statutory law resolves this case against the respondent. When so many courts have so often held what appears so evident—a combination patent can be infringed only by combination—we are not prepared to break the mold and begin anew. And were the matter not so resolved, we would still insist on a clear congressional indication of intent to extend the patent privilege before we could recognize the monopoly here claimed. Such an indication is lacking.

406 U.S. at 532, 92 S.Ct. at 1708, 173 USPQ at 774.

Such indication is still lacking. We cannot assume that the present Court would find reason to depart from *Deepsouth* in the face of congressional inaction over the twelve years since the decision was handed down.

Indeed, the *Deepsouth* decision is not without redeeming virtue. This is one of the few areas of patent law where a bright line can be, and has been, drawn. That consideration in itself has merit. A competitor should be able to look to the patent claims and know whether his activity infringes or not. Here, the majority provides no guidance to industry or the district courts. One cannot tell from the opinion whether testing and sales activity must also accompany substantial assembly, as it appears to hold, or whether simply substantially making the device preparatory to selling after the patent expires would be sufficient. Given the disjunctive language of the statute, no basis appears for "summing up" partial making with the testing of partial assemblies and with sales made by the alleged infringer. Those activities do not, in some nebulous way, supply the missing physical elements of the "patented invention."

The determinative factor in *Deepsouth* was that the alleged infringer had never made, used or sold the "patented invention." Its activities fell short of direct infringement because the court rejected the view that direct infringement required anything less than "the operable assembly of the whole and not the manufacture of its parts." In this case as well, no operable assembly of the whole was ever made by Magna–Graphics. If the patented invention was not made, *a fortiori,* it could not have been used or sold. Thus, there is no direct infringement.

As a final matter, a decision of non-infringement here would not create an "inconsistency" with the decision in Roche Products, Inc. v. Bolar Pharmaceutical Co., 733 F.2d 858, 221 USPQ 937 (Fed.Cir.1984). In *Roche,* the patented invention had been made, albeit not by the alleged infringer, Bolar. The only issue was whether Bolar's testing of the patented invention for FDA purposes was "use" within § 271(a). The *Roche* decision lends no support to the proposition that testing of components of a patented invention constitutes infringement.

I would, accordingly, reverse.

WILBUR–ELLIS CO. v. KUTHER

Supreme Court of the United States, 1964.
377 U.S. 422, 84 S.Ct. 1561, 12 L.Ed.2d 419, 141 U.S.P.Q. 703.

Mr. Justice DOUGLAS delivered the opinion of the Court.

Respondent is the owner of a combination patent covering a fish-canning machine. A number of machines covered by the patent were manufactured and sold under his authorization. Among them were the four machines in suit, petitioner Wilbur–Ellis Company being the second-hand purchaser. Respondent received out of the original purchase price a royalty of $1,500 per machine. As originally constructed each of these machines packed fish into "1–pound" cans: 3 inches in diameter and 4$\frac{1}{16}$ inches high. Three of the machines when acquired by Wilbur–Ellis were corroded, rusted, and inoperative; and all required cleaning and sandblasting to make them usable. Wilbur–Ellis retained petitioner Leuschner to put the machines in condition so they would operate and to resize six of the 35 elements that made up the patented combination. The resizing was for the purpose of enabling the machines to pack fish into "5–ounce" cans: 2$\frac{1}{8}$ inches in diameter and 3$\frac{1}{2}$ inches long. One of the six elements was so corroded that it could be rendered operable only by grinding it down to a size suitable for use with the smaller "5–ounce" can.

This suit for infringement followed; and both the District Court and the Court of Appeals, held for respondent. The case is here on certiorari.

We put to one side the case where the discovery or invention resided in or embraced either the size or locational characteristics of the replaced elements of a combination patent or the size of the commodity on which the machine operated. The claims of the patent before us do not reach that far. We also put to one side the case where replacement was made of a patented component of a combination patent. We deal here with a patent that covered only a combination of unpatented components.

The question in terms of patent law precedents is whether what was done to these machines, the original manufacture and sale of which had been licensed by the patentee, amounted to "repair," in which event there was no infringement, or "reconstruction," in which event there was. The idea of "reconstruction" in this context has the special connotation of those acts which would impinge on the patentee's right *"to exclude others from making,"* 35 U.S.C.A. § 154, the article. As stated in Wilson v. Simpson, 9 How. 109, 123, 13 L.Ed. 66, ". . . when the material of the combination ceases to exist, in whatever way that may occur, the right to renew it depends upon the right to make the invention. If the right to make does not exist, there is no right to rebuild the combination." On the other hand, "When the wearing or injury is partial, then repair is restoration, and not reconstruction." Ibid. Replacing worn-out cutting knives in a planing machine was held to be "repair," not "reconstruction," in Wilson v. Simpson, supra. Our latest case was Aro Mfg. Co. v. Convertible Top Replacement Co., 365 U.S. 336, 81 S.Ct. 599, 5 L.Ed.2d 592, which a majority of the Court construe as holding that it was not infringement to replace the worn-out fabric of a patented convertible automobile top, whose original manufacture and sale had been licensed by the patentee. See No. 75, Aro Mfg. Co. v. Convertible Top Replacement Co., 376 U.S. 476, 84 S.Ct. 1526, decided this day. . . .

Whatever view may be taken of the holding in the first Aro case, the majority believe that it governs the present one. These four machines were not spent; they had years of usefulness remaining though they needed cleaning and repair. Had they been renovated and put to use on the "1–pound" cans, there could be no question but that they were "repaired," not "reconstructed," within the meaning of the cases. When six of the 35 elements of the combination patent were resized or relocated, no invasion of the patent resulted, for as we have said the size of cans serviced by the machine was no part of the invention; nor were characteristics of size, location, shape and construction of the six elements in question patented. Petitioners in adapting the old machines to a related use were doing more than repair in the customary sense; but what they did was kin to repair for it bore on the useful capacity of the old combination, on which the royalty had been paid. We could not call it "reconstruction" without saying that the patentee's right "to exclude others from making" the patented machine, 35 U.S.C.A. § 154, had been infringed. Yet adaptation for use of the machine on a "5–ounce" can is within the patent rights purchased, since size was not an invention.

The adaptation made in the six nonpatented elements improved the usefulness of these machines. That does not, however, make the adaptation "reconstruction" within the meaning of the cases. We are asked in substance to treat the case as if petitioners had a license for use of the machines on "1–pound" cans only. But the sales here were outright, without restriction. Adams v. Burke, 17 Wall. 453, 456, 21 L.Ed. 700, therefore controls:

. . . when the patentee, or the person having his rights, sells a machine or instrument whose sole value is in its use, he receives the consideration for its use and he parts with the right to restrict that use.

Reversed.

Mr. Justice HARLAN would affirm the judgment substantially for the reasons given in the majority opinion in the Court of Appeals.

NOTES

1. At the time the United States Supreme Court decided Deepsouth Packing v. Laitram, discussed in *Magna–Graphics,* and Wilbur–Ellis v. Kuther, it had set a singularly high standard of invention for "combination" patents. By contrast, the Court of Appeals for the Federal Circuit, which decided *Magna–Graphics,* believed that "[v]irtually *all* patents are combination patents" and had rejected a special standard of invention for these inventions. See Stratoflex, Inc. v. Aeroquip Corp., p. 374, above. Is there a connection between the Supreme Court's patentability standard for combinations and its infringement standard for combination patents? Between the CAFC's undifferentiated standards for patentability and infringement?

2. *Repair or Reconstruction?* Aro Mfg. Co., Inc. v. Convertible Top Replacement Co., Inc., 365 U.S. 336, 81 S.Ct. 599, 5 L.Ed.2d 592, 128 U.S.P.Q. 354 (1961), mentioned in *Wilbur–Ellis,* held that replacement of the fabric in a convertible automobile top constituted repair, rather than reconstruction, of the entire top assembly so that the unauthorized manufacture and sale of replacement fabrics did not directly or contributorily infringe the combination patent covering the top assembly. Writing for the Court, Justice Whittaker stated the question for decision to be "whether the owner of a combination patent, comprised entirely of unpatented elements, has a patent monopoly on the manufacture, sale or use of the several unpatented components of the patented combination." By framing the issue in terms of the distinction between unpatented and patented components, rather than between repair and reconstruction, Justice Whittaker anticipated the decision in the case; replacement of any part of a combination, no matter how significant, can never be reconstruction. "The decisions of this Court require the conclusion that reconstruction of a patented entity, comprised of unpatented elements, is limited to such a true reconstruction of the entity as to 'in fact make a new article' . . . after the entity, viewed as a whole, has become spent."

Justice Brennan, concurring, and Justice Harlan, dissenting, disagreed with Justice Whittaker's test. According to Justice Harlan, "none of the past cases in this Court or in the lower federal courts remotely suggests that 'reconstruction' can be found only in a situation where the patented combination has been rebuilt de novo from the ground up." Because the two lower courts "adverted to all the relevant standards," Justice Harlan thought it best to defer to their decisions.

Justice Brennan perceived "circumstances in which the replacement of a singly unpatented component of a patented combination short of a second creation of the patent entity may constitute 'reconstruction.'" Brennan interpreted the precedents to require that the determination in any case "be based upon the consideration of a number of factors. . . . Appropriately to be considered are the life of the part replaced in relation to the useful life of the whole combination, the importance of the replaced element to the inventive concept, the cost of the component relative to the cost of the combination, the common sense understanding and intention of the patent owner and the buyer of the combination as to its perishable components, whether the purchased component replaces a worn-out part or is bought for some other purpose, and other pertinent factors." Although the district and circuit courts below had considered such factors, Justice Brennan concurred in the reversal because, under his own analysis, the replacement of tops constituted repair.

See Farley, Infringement Questions Stemming From the Repair or Reconstruction of Patented Combinations, 68 J.Pat. & Trademark Off. Soc'y 149 (1986).

3. *Experimental Use.* In two cases decided on circuit in 1813, Justice Joseph Story carved out an experimental use exception from patent infringement. Whittemore v. Cutter, 29 F.Cas. 1120 (C.C.D. Mass.1813) (No. 17,600); Sawin v. Guild, 21 F.Cas. 554 (C.C.D.Mass. 1813) (No. 12,391). Accused infringers have asserted the experimental use exception in relatively few cases since, and courts have applied the exception sparingly.

One writer has concluded that "[i]n order to qualify for the experimental use exception to patent infringement, the infringing activity must fall within one of two classes of activities introduced by Justice Story in *Sawin:* (1) ascertain the verity and exactness of the specification, and (2) philosophical experiment. If the infringing activity falls within one of these categories, then it must be determined if the experimentor infringed the patent for profit. . . . The cases support the position that the experimental use exception applies to testing a patented invention for adaptation to the experimentor's business provided that the experimental use does not result in a 'use for profit.' As determined in the cases involving private parties, 'use for profit' means to make or attempt to make a monetary profit while infringing the patented invention." Hantman, Experimental Use as an Exception to Patent Infringement, 67 J.Pat. & Trademark Off. Soc'y 617, 644 (1985). See also Bee, Experimental Use as an Act of Patent Infringement, 39 J.Pat.Off.Soc'y 357 (1957).

Roche Products, Inc. v. Bolar Pharmaceutical Co., 733 F.2d 858, 221 U.S.P.Q. 937 (Fed.Cir.), cert. denied, 469 U.S. 856, 105 S.Ct. 183, 83 L.Ed.2d 117 (1984), held that, because defendant's testing and investigation of a patented drug to obtain Food and Drug Administration approval was done "solely for business reasons," it did not qualify for the experimental use exception. Congress overturned *Bolar* by adding section 271(e)(1) to the Patent Act:

> It shall not be an act of infringement to make, use, or sell a patented invention (other than a new animal drug or veterinary biological product (as those terms are used in the Federal Food, Drug, and Cosmetic Act and the Act of March 4, 1913) which is primarily manufactured using recombinant DNA, recombinant RNA, hybridoma technology, or other processes involving site specific genetic manipulation techniques) solely for uses reasonably related to the development and submission of information under a Federal law which regulates the manufacture, use, or sale of drugs or veterinary biological products.

The Court of Appeals for the Federal Circuit has read this provision to encompass medical devices as well as pharmaceuticals. Eli Lilly & Co. v. Medtronic, Inc., 872 F.2d 402, 10 U.S.P.Q.2d 1304 (Fed.Cir.1989), cert. granted, 110 S.Ct. 232, 107 L.Ed.2d 183 (1989).

4. *Liability in the United States for Acts Abroad.* Deepsouth Packing v. Laitram, discussed in *Magna–Graphics,* illustrates one strategy that competitors have used to circumvent United States patent law—shipping domestically manufactured components of a patented invention for final assembly abroad. Another strategy has been to make a product abroad through a process patented in the United States and then to import the finished—unpatented—product into the United States. Amendments to the United States Patent Act in 1984 and 1988, respectively, substantially curtailed both strategies.

Section 271(f), added by the Patent Law Amendments Act of 1984, Pub.L. No. 98–622, § 101(a) 98 Stat. 3383, plugged the *Deepsouth* loophole by providing in part that "[w]hoever without authority supplies or causes to be supplied in or from the United States all or a substantial portion of the components of a patented invention, where such components are uncombined in whole or in part, in such manner as to actively induce the combination of such components outside of the United States in a manner that would infringe the patent if such combination occurred within the United States, shall be liable as an infringer." 35 U.S.C.A. 271(f)(1).

Section 271(g) of the Patent Act, added by the Omnibus Trade and Competitiveness Act of 1988, Pub.L. No. 100–418, § 9003, 102 Stat. 1563–1564, enlarges the scope of patent rights by providing in part: "[w]hoever without authority imports into the United States or sells or uses within the United States a product which is made by a process patented in the United States shall be liable as an infringer, if the importation, sale, or use of the product occurs during the term of such process patent." Section 295 buttresses the new right by creating a presumption that a product was made by a patented process where the court finds "(1) that a substantial likelihood exists that the product was made by the patented process, and (2) that the plaintiff has made a reasonable effort to determine the process actually used in the production of the product and was unable to so determine. . . ."

5. *Inducement of Infringement.* Section 271(b) imposes liability on anyone who actively induces direct infringement. Among the acts that may be proscribed are distribution of brochures advertising the sale of infringing equipment or instructing in the use of a patented process, purchase of articles made by an infringing process, indemnification of an infringer, and encouragement of a licensee to breach its patent license agreement.

Consider the advantages that section 271(b) may give patent owners in the following situations:

> The direct infringer is judgment proof and the contributory infringer is solvent; the direct infringer's liability is limited by its corporate form and certain corporate officers can be treated as contributory infringers. See Timely Products Corp. v. Arron, 303 F.Supp. 713, 163 U.S.P.Q. 663 (D.C.Conn.1969).

> Acts of contributory, but not direct, infringement have occurred in the district most convenient for suit under the patent venue statute. See Watsco, Inc. v. Henry Valve Co., 232 F.Supp. 38, 142 U.S. P.Q. 219 (S.D.N.Y.1964).

> A contributory infringer, but not a direct infringer, exhibits the animus necessary to recovery of treble or otherwise increased damages.

Miller, Some Views on the Law of Patent Infringement by Inducement, 53 J.Pat.Off.Soc'y 86, 139 (1971), is a comprehensive survey of the subject.

6. *Contributory Infringement and Patent Misuse.* A patent owner will sometimes condition a customer's use of its patented product—a refrigerator for example—on the customer's purchase from the patent owner of an unpatented product—dry ice—used with the patented product. If the customer instead purchases its dry ice from a third party, this would breach the agreement with the patent owner, giving it an action for patent infringement against the customer. The third party supplier, who facilitated the infringement, would be liable for contributory infringement. Yet, courts have long recognized that for the patent owner to use the threat of a contributory infringement action to monopolize the market for an unpatented product may constitute patent misuse because it gives the patent owner greater market power than its patent warrants.

Section 271(c) of the Patent Act employs the concept of "staple" articles to draw the line between contributory infringement and patent misuse. The provision includes the supply of only certain types of articles within the scope of contributory infringement:

> Whoever sells a component of a patented machine, manufacture, combination or composition, or a material or apparatus for use in practicing a patented process, constituting a material part of the invention, knowing the same to be especially made or especially adapted for use in an infringement of such patent, and not a staple

article or commodity of commerce suitable for substantial noninfringing use, shall be liable as a contributory infringer.

Section 271(d) provides: "No patent owner otherwise entitled to relief for infringement or contributory infringement of a patent shall be denied relief or deemed guilty of misuse or illegal extension of the patent right by reason of his having done one or more of the following: (1) derived revenue from acts which if performed by another without his consent would constitute contributory infringement of the patent. . . ."

What of nonstaple articles? In Dawson Chem. Co. v. Rohm & Haas Co., 448 U.S. 176, 100 S.Ct. 2601, 65 L.Ed.2d 696, 206 U.S.P.Q. 385 (1980), Rohm & Haas owned a patent on a process for applying an unpatented herbicide, propanil. Rohm & Haas impliedly licensed farmers who purchased the herbicide from it to practice the patented process but refused to give defendants, chemical manufacturers, a license to practice the patented process so that they could sell the herbicide to farmers. The defendants conceded that propanil was a nonstaple article and that their manufacture and sale of the herbicide, including instructions for its use, contributorily infringed the process patent. However, they argued that plaintiff's practices constituted patent misuse.

The United States Supreme Court held that the plaintiff's conduct did not constitute patent misuse:

> In our view, the provisions of § 271(d) effectively confer upon the patentee, as a lawful adjunct of his patent rights, a limited power to exclude others from competition in nonstaple goods. A patentee may sell a nonstaple article himself while enjoining others from marketing that same good without his authorization. By doing so, he is able to eliminate competitors and thereby to control the market for that product. Moreover, his power to demand royalties from others for the privilege of selling the nonstaple item itself implies that the patentee may control the market for the nonstaple good; otherwise, his 'right' to sell licenses for the marketing of the nonstaple good would be meaningless, since no one would be willing to pay him for a superfluous authorization.

> Rohm & Haas' conduct is not dissimilar in either nature or effect from the conduct that is thus clearly embraced within § 271(d). It sells propanil; it authorizes others to use propanil; and it sues contributory infringers. These are all protected activities. Rohm & Haas does *not* license others to sell propanil, but nothing on the face of the statute requires it to do so. To be sure, the sum effect of Rohm & Haas' action is to suppress competition in the market for an unpatented commodity. But as we have observed, in this its conduct is no different from that which the statute expressly protects.

448 U.S. at 201–02. The Court read section 271's legislative history to support the conclusion that "Congress granted to patent holders a statutory right to control nonstaple goods that are capable only of

infringing use in a patented invention, and that are essential to that invention's advance over prior art." 448 U.S. at 213.

Justice White, joined by Justices Brennan, Marshall and Stevens, dissented. According to Justice White, the Supreme Court had for decades "denied relief from contributory infringement to patent holders who attempt to extend their patent monopolies to unpatented materials used in connection with patented inventions. The Court now refuses to apply this 'patent misuse' principle in the very area in which such attempts to restrain competition are most likely to be successful." 448 U.S. at 223. In White's view, the Court misread section 271(d). "The plain language of section 271(d) indicates that respondent's conduct is not immunized from application of the patent misuse doctrine. . . . Section 271(d) does not define conduct that constitutes patent misuse; rather it simply outlines certain conduct that is not patent misuse." 448 U.S. at 232–34.

Courts have divided on whether conduct that does not rise to the level of an antitrust violation can constitute patent misuse. Compare USM Corp. v. SPS Technologies, Inc., 694 F.2d 505, 512, 216 U.S.P.Q. 959 (7th Cir.1982) (". . . apart from the conventional applications of the doctrine we have found no cases where standards different from those of antitrust law were actually applied to yield different results.") with Senza–Gel Corp. v. Seiffhart, 803 F.2d 661, 668, 231 U.S.P.Q. 363 (Fed.Cir.1986) (". . . [an] act may constitute patent misuse without rising to the level of an antitrust violation.") In 1988 the Senate passed a bill that would have provided that it is not misuse for a patent owner to engage in "licensing practices, actions or inactions relating to his or her patent, unless such practices or actions or inactions, in view of the circumstances in which such practices or actions or inactions are employed, violate the antitrust laws." S.Rep. No. 100–492, 100th Cong., 2d Sess. 17–18 (Aug. 25, 1988). A subsequent compromise with the House resulted in Pub.L. No. 100–703, 102 Stat. 4674 (1988), adding subsections (4) and (5) to section 271(d).

See generally, Oddi, Contributory Infringement/Patent Misuse: Metaphysics and Metamorphosis, 44 U.Pitt.L.Rev. 73 (1982); Bennett, Patent Misuse: Must an Alleged Infringer Prove an Antitrust Violation?, 17 AIPLA Q.J. 1 (1989).

7. In Brulotte v. Thys Co., 379 U.S. 29, 85 S.Ct. 176, 13 L.Ed.2d 99, 143 U.S.P.Q. 264 (1964), defendants, hop farmers, had bought from plaintiff, patent owner, hop picking machines that incorporated several of plaintiff's patented devices. Under the purchase agreement, the buyers were to pay royalties based upon the quantities of crops harvested over a seventeen-year period. The contract period exceeded the life of all of the patents. Alleging patent misuse, defendants refused to pay royalties accruing both before and after expiration of the patents' statutory term.

The Supreme Court, in an opinion by Justice Douglas, ruled that defendants could not be held for royalties accruing after the expiration of the last of the patents. The defect in the seventeen-year license,

Douglas wrote, was that it extended the patent monopoly beyond the point required by the Constitution's "limited times" provision, and by negative implication from the patent statute, to be free from monopoly restraint. Reasoning that if contractual devices of this sort were tolerated, "the free market visualized for the post-expiration period would be subject to monopoly influences that have no proper place there," the Court struck down the contract rule applied by the state courts as "unlawful *per se*." 379 U.S. at 29, 32–33, 85 S.Ct. 176, 179–80.

To what extent did the Supreme Court's 1979 decision in Aronson v. Quick Point, page 48, above, limit *Brulotte?*

8. *Licensee Estoppel.* Can a patent licensee defend an action for nonpayment of royalties by asserting that the licensed patent is invalid? Courts have long held that licensees are privileged to stop paying royalties if a third party proves that the patent is invalid. But, where the licensee itself sought to challenge validity, the doctrine of licensee estoppel traditionally barred the defense. Automatic Radio Mfg. Co. v. Hazeltine Research, Inc., 339 U.S. 827, 70 S.Ct. 894, 94 L.Ed. 1312, 85 U.S.P.Q. 378 (1950). In Adkins v. Lear, Inc., 67 Cal.2d 882, 891, 64 Cal. Rptr. 545, 435 P.2d 321, 156 U.S.P.Q. 258 (1967), the California Supreme Court recognized that "one of the oldest doctrines in the field of patent law establishes that so long as a licensee is operating under a license agreement he is estopped to deny the validity of his licensor's patent in a suit for royalties under the agreement. The theory underlying this doctrine is that a licensee should not be permitted to enjoy the benefit afforded by the agreement while simultaneously urging that the patent which forms the basis of the agreement is void."

The Supreme Court granted certiorari in Lear v. Adkins to "reconsider the validity of the *Hazeltine* rule in the light of our recent decisions emphasizing the strong federal policy favoring free competition in ideas which do not merit patent protection, Sears, Roebuck v. Stiffel Co., 376 U.S. 225 (1964); Compco Corp. v. Day–Brite Lighting, Inc., 376 U.S. 234 (1964)." 395 U.S. 653, 89 S.Ct. 1902, 23 L.Ed.2d 610, 162 U.S.P.Q. 1 (1969). The first part of Justice Harlan's opinion for the Court traced *Hazeltine's* "clouded history" to conclude that "the uncertain status of licensee estoppel in the case law is a product of judicial efforts to accommodate the competing demands of the common law of contracts and the federal law of patents. On the one hand, the law of contracts forbids a purchaser to repudiate his promises simply because he later becomes dissatisfied with the bargain he has made. On the other hand, federal law requires that all ideas in general circulation be dedicated to the common good unless they are protected by a valid patent. When faced with this basic conflict in policy, both this Court and courts throughout the land have naturally sought to develop an intermediate position which somehow would remain responsive to the radically different concerns of the two different worlds of contract and patent. The result has been a failure. Rather than creative compromise, there has been a chaos of conflicting case law, proceeding on inconsistent premises." 395 U.S. at 653, 668.

It was the practical marketplace effects of licensee estoppel that convinced the Court to overrule *Hazeltine.* "A patent, in the last analysis, simply represents a legal conclusion reached by the Patent Office. Moreover, the legal conclusion is predicated on factors as to which reasonable men can differ widely. Yet the Patent Office is often obliged to reach its decision in an ex parte proceeding, without the aid of the arguments which could be advanced by parties interested in proving patent invalidity. Consequently, it does not seem to us to be unfair to require a patentee to defend the Patent Office's judgment when his licensee places the question in issue, especially since the licensor's case is buttressed by the presumption of validity which attaches to his patent. Thus, although licensee estoppel may be consistent with the letter of contractual doctrine, we cannot say that it is compelled by the spirit of contract law, which seeks to balance the claims of promisor and promisee in accord with the requirements of good faith.

"Surely the equities of the licensor do not weigh very heavily when they are balanced against the important public interest in permitting full and free competition in the use of ideas which are in reality a part of the public domain. Licensees may often be the only individuals with enough economic incentive to challenge the patentability of an inventor's discovery. If they are muzzled, the public may continually be required to pay tribute to would-be monopolists without need or justification. We think it plain that the technical requirements of contract doctrine must give way before the demands of the public interest in the typical situation involving the negotiation of a license after a patent has issued." 395 U.S. at 653, 670–671.

Can a patent assignor, later sued by its assignee for patent infringement, defend on the ground that the patent is invalid? The doctrine of assignor estoppel has not suffered the fate of licensee estoppel. In Diamond Scientific Co. v. Ambico, Inc., 848 F.2d 1220, 6 U.S.P.Q.2d 2028 (Fed.Cir.), cert. dismissed, 109 S.Ct. 28, 101 L.Ed.2d 978 (1988), the Court of Appeals for the Federal Circuit held that the doctrine estopped an inventor from challenging the validity of a patent that he had earlier assigned to his former employer. "We are, of course, not unmindful of the general public policy disfavoring the repression of competition by the enforcement of worthless patents. Yet despite the public policy encouraging people to challenge potentially invalid patents, there are still circumstances in which the equities of the contractual relationships between the parties should deprive one party (as well as others in privity with it) of the right to bring that challenge." 848 F.2d at 1225. See Ubell, Assignor Estoppel: A Wrong Turn From *Lear,* 71 J.Pat. & Trademark Off. Soc'y 26 (1989).

See generally, Dreyfuss, Dethroning *Lear:* Licensee Estoppel and the Incentive to Innovate, 72 Va.L.Rev. 677 (1986); McCarthy, "Unmuzzling" the Patent Licensee: Chaos in the Wake of Lear v. Adkins, 45 Geo.Wash.L.Rev. 429 (1977); Rooklidge, Licensee Validity Challenges and the Obligation to Pay Accrued Royalties: Lear v. Adkins Revisited,

68 J.Pat. & Trademark Off. Soc'y 506 (1986), 69 J.Pat. & Trademark Off. Soc'y 5, 63 (1987).

9. *Suppression of Patents.* There is no stronger belief in patent folklore than the belief that patentees sometimes use the patent grant to suppress their inventions for reasons that are mercenary at best, evil at worst. Justice William Douglas invoked this suspicion in his dissenting opinion in Special Equipment Co. v. Coe, 324 U.S. 370, 380, 65 S.Ct. 741, 89 L.Ed. 1006, 64 U.S.P.Q. 525 (1945):

> It is difficult to see how that use [suppression] of patents can be reconciled with the purpose of the Constitution 'to promote the Progress of Science and the useful Arts.' Can the suppression of patents which arrests the progress of technology be said to promote that progress? It is likewise difficult to see how suppression of patents can be reconciled with the provision of the statute which authorizes a grant of the 'exclusive right to make, use, and vend the invention or discovery.' Rev.Stat. § 4884, 35 U.S.C.A. § 40. How may the words 'to make, use, and vend' be read to mean 'not to make, not to use, and not to vend'? Take the case of an invention or discovery which unlocks the doors of science and reveals the secrets of a dread disease. Is it possible that a patentee could be permitted to suppress that invention for seventeen years (the term of the letters patent) and withhold from humanity the benefits of the cure? But there is no difference in principle between that case and any case where a patent is suppressed because of some immediate advantage to the patentee.

324 U.S. at 383. What motives do patent owners have to patent but not market their inventions? How likely is it that the owner of a patent on an invention that "unlocks the doors of science and reveals the secrets of a dread disease" will "withhold from humanity the benefits of the cure" rather than cash in on the value of the discovery?

Many countries remedy patent suppression through compulsory licensing regimes. These systems generally provide that if a patent owner fails to exploit an invention within a specified period, anyone may, upon payment of a predetermined reasonable royalty, take a license under the patent. One observer has noted that there are very few applications for these compulsory licenses; this "does not mean, however, that the system has no effect, but rather that the prospective licensee and patentee usually try to reach an agreement directly rather than through official channels, with the patentee of course realizing that compulsory licensing is available if agreement is not reached." Goldsmith, Patent Protection for United States Inventions in the Principal European Countries—Existing Systems, 6 B.C.Comm. & Indus.L. Rev. 533, 535 (1965). See also, Tanabe, Compulsory Licensing in Japanese Patent Law, 8 Int'l Rev.Indus.Prop. & Copyright L. 42 (1977).

10. *Patent Term.* The first patent act, Act of April 10, 1790, ch. 7, 1 Stat. 109, prescribed a fourteen-year term, copying the term employed in the English Statute of Monopolies of 1623, 21 Jac. 1, ch. 3. The English term had been based on the seven-year apprenticeship period

universally practiced by the mid-sixteenth century. Underlying the fourteen-year term was the theory that an invention should come into general use only after the artisan-inventor had the opportunity to instruct two consecutive sets of apprentices in the subject matter.

The Act of July 4, 1836, ch. 357, 5 Stat. 117, supplemented the fourteen-year term with a seven-year renewal period. It was a Senate attempt to repeal this renewal period, and a House effort to retain it, that in 1861 led to enactment of the present seventeen-year term. To accommodate the House position with the Senate's, the Conference Committee roughly split the difference and reported out a provision changing the term to seventeen years and dropping the renewal period.

How efficient is a single term, uniformly applicable to all types of subject matter? Custom-tailored terms, varying in length from three to twenty years, were common under early colonial patent practice. Consider one economist's view of the present system: "[A] moment's consideration suggests that patents of uniform duration unduly reward some inventions and inadequately compensate others. Surely, all inventions cannot be exploited in exactly the same length of time nor can the monetary profitability, if any, of patent monopolies of uniform length be equated to the social contribution of the inventions covered." White, Why a Seventeen Year Patent?, 38 J.Pat.Off.Soc'y 839, 842 (1956).

Section 156 of the Patent Act, added in 1984 and amended in 1988, extends the patent term for certain human and animal drugs and other federally regulated products to compensate for the time lost in federal regulatory review of the drugs. Pub.L. No. 98–417, § 201(a), 98 Stat. 1598 (1984); Pub.L. 100–670, § 201(a), 102 Stat. 3984 (1988). See two articles by Lourie, Patent Term Restoration, 66 J.Pat.Off.Soc'y 526 (1984); A Review of Recent Patent Term Extension Data, 71 J.Pat. & Trademark Off.Soc'y 171 (1989).

2. REMEDIES

PAPER CONVERTING MACHINE CO. v. MAGNA–GRAPHICS CORP.

United States Court of Appeals, Federal Circuit, 1984.
745 F.2d 11, 223 U.S.P.Q. 591.

NICHOLS, Senior Circuit Judge.

This appeal is from a judgment of the United States District Court for the Eastern District of Wisconsin (Reynolds, C.J.), 576 F.Supp. 967, entered on December 1, 1983, and awarding plaintiff Paper Converting Machine Company (Paper Converting) $893,064 as compensation for defendant Magna–Graphics Corporation's (Magna–Graphics) willful infringement of United States Patent No. Re. 28,353. We *affirm-in-part and vacate-in-part.*

[The court's discussion of liability, omitted here, is reprinted beginning at page 469, above.]

Although Magna–Graphics does not raise the issue, we nevertheless find bothersome the district court's summary award of treble damages as to the Fort Howard machine. At the *liability* phase of this action, the district court found that Magna–Graphics willfully infringed, 211 USPQ at 798:

> Defendant made and sold the accused [Scott] machine with full knowledge of plaintiff's patent and without having obtained an opinion of counsel relative to infringement as to changes made only to avoid the patent with no corresponding change in function. Defendant is therefore an intentional infringer * * *.

When the district court made this finding, Magna–Graphics had not yet completed the Fort Howard machine and obviously the court did not have it in mind. On the basis of the record before us, it appears that if Magna–Graphics had immediately ceased production of the machine intended for Fort Howard, the district court would not have awarded damages to Paper Converting for that machine.

Magna–Graphics completed the Fort Howard machine, however, *after* the district court issued its injunction and *before* the '353 patent expired. Thus, when the district court determined during the accounting stage of this action that the Fort Howard machine infringed, it should have made new findings as to the willfulness of Magna–Graphics' *post-injunction* activities. In particular, if Magna–Graphics' continued manufacture of the Fort Howard machine *was* willful infringement, it was done in contempt of the district court's order.

Our review of the record appears to indicate that there are several factual differences between Magna–Graphics' activities leading to the construction of the Scott machine and its activities leading to the construction of the Fort Howard machine. Magna–Graphics, for example, consulted its counsel several times before performing any post-injunction activities towards the completion of the Fort Howard machine. Its attorneys apparently believed that by carefully planning the construction schedule, Magna–Graphics could complete the machine without infringing the '353 patent. Each calculated step Magna–Graphics took, it meticulously documented for the inevitable day in court.

We do not pretend that we ourselves should act as fact-finders and determine willfulness of infringement. An increase in damages for willfulness, however, is generally inappropriate when the infringer mounts a good faith and substantial challenge to the existence of infringement. We need explicit findings with which we can review the district court's decision. Since no such findings were made here, we vacate that part of the lower court's judgment awarding trebled damages for the infringing manufacture of the Fort Howard machine. We remand for a determination of Magna–Graphics' willfulness in infringing the '353 patent after the district court issued its injunction against infringement on February 26, 1981. Finally, we hasten to add, if Magna–Graphics continued infringement *was* willful, it was done in contempt of the district court's decree, and the district court may therefore consider appropriate remedies other than the mere trebling of damages.

IV

After the district court has determined the quantity of infringing articles, it must choose a methodology with which to compute damages. Magna–Graphics argues here, in effect, that although it has been adjudged a willful infringer, the district court should have chosen the accounting method which provides for the least amount of damages. We disagree.

Congress established in 35 U.S.C. § 284 the requirement of a damage award for patent infringement:

> Upon finding for the claimant the court shall award the claimant damages adequate to compensate for the infringement but in no event less than a reasonable royalty for the use made of the invention and costs as fixed by the court.

Section 284 does not instruct a court on how to compute damages: the only congressional intent expressed ensures that a claimant receive *adequate* damages, *not less than* a reasonable royalty. The size of an award is left to the trial court's sound discretion. Thus, our review is limited to a determination of whether the trial court has abused its discretion in choosing a method with which to compute an award. Simply because different accounting methods lead to different results does not make an award at the higher end of a spectrum "more than adequate." The burden is on the infringer to persuade us that the amount of the award, or the choice of accounting method, constitutes an abuse of the trial court's discretion. Magna–Graphics has not met its burden here.

A

Whenever determining the quantum of a damage award adequate to compensate a patent holder for infringement, the district court may consider the profits the patent holder lost as a result of the infringement. In particular, the award of lost profits is proper when it can be demonstrated that "but for" the infringement, the patent holder would have made the sales. To justify a damage award equal to lost profits, the patent holder can present affirmative evidence of the demand for his patented product in the marketplace, the absence of acceptable noninfringing substitutes, his production and marketing capacity to meet the demand, and computations on the loss of profits. A patent holder can most commonly show these elements when the parties involved in the action are the only suppliers.

The patent holder does not need to negate *all* possibilities that a purchaser might have bought a different product or might have foregone the purchase altogether. The "but for" rule only requires the patentee to provide proof to a reasonable probability that the sale would have been made but for the infringement.

Magna–Graphics places in issue here only the magnitude of demand for the patented product. Indeed, Magna–Graphics concedes that Paper Converting has the requisite production and marketing capacity (the sales of the two additional machines would have constituted but a minor portion of Paper Converting's total capacity) and that there is a total absence of acceptable noninfringing high-speed machines. Magna–Graphics contends, in effect, that because of Paper Converting's high prices, Scott and Fort Howard would have foregone their purchase of new rewinders altogether if Magna–Graphics had not submitted its low bid. Magna–Graphics argues, therefore, that the district court failed to give proper consideration to price differentials.

"Determining the weight and credibility of the evidence," however, "is the special province of the trier of fact." Inwood Laboratories, Inc. v. Ives Laboratories, Inc., 456 U.S. 844, 856, 102 S.Ct. 2182, 2189, 72 L.Ed.2d 606, 214 USPQ 1 (1982). Here, the district court thought more persuasive the long history and continuous volume of Paper Converting's sales than Magna–Graphics' price-related data and testimony. The simple assertion that a fact-finding is clearly erroneous never makes it so; where, as here, merely the weight given to one subfactor is termed "clearly erroneous," the appellant faces a Sisyphean task to leave us with a "definite and firm conviction that the trial judge has committed a mistake." Seattle Box Co. v. Industrial Crating & Packing, Inc., 731 F.2d 818, 823, 221 USPQ 568, 572 (Fed.Cir.1984). Magna–Graphics has not persuaded us here. We affirm the district judge's award of lost profits here.

B

Magna–Graphics next argues that the district court relied on improper or inaccurate figures to determine Paper Converting's lost profits, and that the district court erred in using an incremental income method for computing lost profits. We disagree.

The incremental income approach to the computation of lost profits is well established in the law relating to patent damages. The approach recognizes that it does not cost as much to produce unit $N + 1$ if the first N (or fewer) units produced already have paid the fixed costs. Thus fixed costs—those costs which do not vary with increases in production, such as management salaries, property taxes, and insurance—are excluded when determining profits.

After it has chosen an accounting method, the district court is free to use its discretion in choosing the charts or figures from which to determine the amount of damages. A computation of damages, of course, is not always amenable to a precise determination. "In such case, while the damages may not be determined by mere speculation or guess, it will be enough if the evidence show the extent of the damages as a matter of just and reasonable inference, although the result be only approximate." Story Parchment Co. v. Paterson Parchment Paper Co., 282 U.S. 555, 563, 51 S.Ct. 248, 250, 75 L.Ed. 544 (1931).

In the district court's exhaustive analysis here, it found Paper Converting's figures reasonable and not utterly without basis; it concluded that a 61.8 percent cost rate generates a "reasonably fair estimate" of Paper Converting's total lost profits. Magna–Graphics is not entitled to any higher level of certainty: fundamental principles of justice require us to throw the risk of any uncertainty upon the wrongdoer instead of upon the injured party. We affirm the method of computing the damage award here.

C

Magna–Graphics next assigns error to the district court's award of lost profits as to the entire rewinder line rather than to the rewinder itself. Again, we affirm.

The "entire market value rule" allows for the recovery of damages based on the value of an entire apparatus containing several features, even though only one feature is patented. In Leesona Corp. v. United States, 599 F.2d 958, 974, 202 USPQ 424, 439 (Ct.Cl.1981), our predecessor court stated that under the entire market value rule:

> [I]t is not the physical joinder or separation of the contested items that determines their inclusion in or exclusion from the compensation base, so much as their financial and marketing dependence on the patented item under standard marketing procedures for the goods in question.

The present case differs from the usual one in which the patented and unpatented components are part of a *single* machine. Here, the mechanism for the high speed manufacture of paper rolls comprises several components, only one of which incorporates the invention claimed in the '353 patent. The auxiliary equipment includes an "unwind stand" which supports the large roll of paper which is supplied to the rewinder for cutting and rewinding, a "core loader" which supplies paperboard cores to the rewinder, an "embosser" which when located between the unwind stand and the rewinder embosses the paper and provides a special textured surface, and a "tail sealer" which seals the paper's trailing end (the tail) to the consumer-sized roll.

None of the auxiliary units here are integral parts of the rewinder; rather, they each have separate usage. Paper Converting therefore obviously cannot prevent the manufacture or sale of these auxiliary units. This fact, however, does not control our decision. The deciding factor, rather, is whether "[n]ormally the patentee (or its licensee) can anticipate sale of such unpatented components as well as of the patented" ones. Tektronix, Inc. v. United States, 552 F.2d 343, 351, 193 USPQ 385, 393 (Ct.Cl.1977). If in all reasonable probability the patent owner would have made the sales which the infringer has made, what the patent owner in reasonable probability would have netted from the sales denied to him is the measure of his loss, and the infringer is liable for that.

The district court found that Paper Converting adduced sufficient evidence at trial to sustain its burden of showing that if Magna–

Graphics had not infringed the '353 patent, Paper Converting would have sold its entire rewinder line to Scott and Fort Howard. Substantial evidence showed, for instance, that the entire industry routinely purchased a complete rewinder line from the seller of the rewinder machine so as to ensure a single source of responsibility. Fort Howard and Scott exemplify this industry practice: *every* time Paper Converting sold a highspeed automatic rewinder to either of them, they purchased the *entire* rewinder line including auxiliary equipment. Moreover, in the two infringing sales which Magna–Graphics made, both Fort Howard and Scott again purchased the *entire* rewinder line including auxiliary equipment. Indeed, of Paper Converting's 572 rewinder sales, only *nine* involved rewinders alone.

Whether a patentee could anticipate additional income from the auxiliary parts is a question of fact which we cannot and will not disturb unless *clearly* erroneous. Fed.R.Civ.P. 52(a). The evidence amply supports the district court's finding that Paper Converting would have made these sales but for Magna–Graphics' infringing sales. We affirm.

D

Not allowing a single item of the damage award to go unchallenged, Magna–Graphics argues that the district court erred in awarding prejudgment interest on the untrebled portion of the award "in view of the fact that the court already had trebled plaintiff's damages." The frivolity of this argument is readily apparent in view of General Motors Corp. v. Devex Corp., 461 U.S. 648, 655, 103 S.Ct. 2058, 2062, 76 L.Ed.2d 211, 217 USPQ 1185, 1188 (1983) and our own decisions. Prejudgment interest should *ordinarily* be awarded absent some justification for withholding such award, it is to compensate for the delay a patentee experiences in obtaining money he would have received sooner if no infringement had occurred. On the other hand, damages are trebled as punishment. There is no conflict in the award of both.

V

The judgment of the district court awarding damages and prejudgment interest for Paper Converting's lost profits on two automatic rewinder lines is affirmed. The trebling of damages on the Fort Howard machine is vacated, and remanded for a determination of willfulness. Each party is to bear its own costs of this appeal.

Affirmed in part and vacated in part.

HANSON v. ALPINE VALLEY SKI AREA, INC.

United States Court of Appeals, Federal Circuit, 1983.
718 F.2d 1075, 219 U.S.P.Q. 679.

FRIEDMAN, Circuit Judge.

This is an appeal from a judgment of the United States District Court for the Eastern District of Michigan adopting the report of the

United States Magistrate determining the damages in a patent infringement case. We affirm.

I.

The patent involved in this case was issued to the appellee Hanson in 1961. It covers a method and apparatus for making snow used in winter sports. Prior to Hanson's invention, snow was made by mixing water and compressed air, and ejecting the combination under high pressure from a nozzle. The water froze and, by combining with water in the air, produced snow crystals. This method required a considerable amount of energy to compress the air, and the nozzles frequently froze.

Hanson's patent disclosed a new method of making snow. As the magistrate explained, rather than relying on compressed air,

> [t]he Hanson process discharges water into a hub mounted in the center of a spinning propeller. The water is then fragmented into droplets by the propeller blades generating spontaneous ice nuclei.
> * * * The efficiency of the [Hanson] snowmaking system [as opposed to the prior art method] is based upon the turbulence of the air created by the airstream which increased cooling capacity.

The magistrate found that "the airless snowmaking method of the Hanson patent is at least five to seven times as energy efficient as the prior art compressed air method * * *."

In 1969, Hanson licensed his patent to Snow Machines International, which subsequently assigned the license to Snow Machines Incorporated (both referred to as "SMI"), for a royalty of 2½ percent of sales and 2½ percent of the stock of SMI. Since 1969, about 1,500 SMI machines have been manufactured and sold, and SMI paid total royalties of approximately $26,000. The magistrate found that "[w]ithin the short span of twelve years, the airless snowmaking process had developed substantially and presently accounts for almost one half of all artificially produced snow." The Hanson patent expired in 1978.

Hanson filed the present suit in February 1973. He alleged that appellant Alpine Valley Ski Area, Inc. ("Alpine") had infringed his patent through the use of three snowmaking machines manufactured by Hedco, Inc. Hedco defended the suit for Alpine.

After a trial without a jury, the district court held that the Hanson patent was valid, that Alpine had infringed the patent by its use of the Hedco machines, and that Hanson was entitled to an accounting for damages. The court found that Alpine "has used the Hedco H–2d, Mark II and Mark III machines to produce snow" (finding 54). The court of appeals affirmed the determinations of validity and infringement. Hanson v. Alpine Valley Ski Area, 611 F.2d 156, 204 USPQ 803 (6th Cir.1979).

The district court referred the issue of damages to the United States Magistrate as a special master. After a trial, the magistrate recommended that Hanson be awarded damages of $12,250 for the infringement. In its review of the magistrate's report, the district court "considered the objections and arguments of counsel, and independently examined the legal basis for the Magistrate's conclusions and recommendation[s]." The court concluded that "the Magistrate correctly decided this matter" and adopted the magistrate's report as the opinion of the court.

The magistrate found that Alpine had used the three Hedco machines to produce snow and that Alpine had operated one of the machines during the 1972–73 and 1973–74 seasons and the two other machines during one season. He held that the evidence did not provide any basis for determining either the profits Alpine made or the profits Hanson lost through the infringement, and that damages therefore had to be determined on the basis of a reasonable royalty for the patent. In making that determination, the magistrate applied the "willing licensee-willing licensor rule. That is, at what royalty rate would a licensee accept a license and a licensor grant a license if both parties genuinely wish to execute a license in an arm's length transaction."

The magistrate accepted the testimony of Hanson's witness, Sidney Alpert, whom he characterized as "a highly regarded expert in the field of negotiating patent licenses," that "the royalty rate and licenses granted under the Hanson patent must be uniform." The magistrate stated that "[p]erhaps, if Defendant had proffered its own expert in licensing and negotiating patents to refute the testimony elicited from Plaintiff's expert, the Court would not be so inclined to accept these elements impelling a uniform license," but that "[o]n the record before this Court the credible testimony of Plaintiff's expert stands as the sole guidance germane to the question of licensing distinctions for manufacturers and users. The Court is limited to consideration of the record presented and as such Defendant's analysis falls."

Applying the pertinent factors for determining a reasonably royalty set forth in Georgia–Pacific Corp. v. United States Plywood Corp., 318 F.Supp. 1116, 166 USPQ 235 (S.D.N.Y.1970), modified and aff'd sub nom., Georgia–Pacific Corp. v. United States Plywood–Champion Papers, 446 F.2d 295, 170 USPQ 369 (2d Cir.), cert. denied, 404 U.S. 870, 171 USPQ 322 (1971), the magistrate concluded that

> the reasonable royalty in this case must be based upon a portion of the annual cost savings attributable to use of the Hanson patent. Expert testimony on this record indicates that one-third of the cost savings would be deemed acceptable to both parties in an arm's length license negotiation. Furthermore, based upon energy costs at the time of infringement in 1972–73, the airless snowmaking method of the Hanson patent generates a dollar savings of $75.00 per gallon (of water used to make snow) per minute. That is, under the Hanson method, the cost of producing snow using one gallon of water for one minute is $75.00 less than the cost of producing snow under the compressed air method using one gallon of water for one minute. Thus the cost savings for the Hanson method is a function of any machine's capacity to make snow.

The magistrate concluded that a reasonable royalty would be one-third of the $75 savings per gallon of water that the Hanson method produced over the earlier compressed air method. Multiplying the $25 per gallon by the snowmaking capacity of the three Hedco machines Alpine used and the four years of use involved, the magistrate determined that Hanson was entitled to royalties of $3,000, $1,750, and $7,500 for each of the Hedco machines used, or a total of $12,250.

II.

The award of damages for patent infringement is governed by 35 U.S.C. § 284 (1976). . . .

There are two methods by which damages may be calculated under this statute. If the record permits the determination of actual damages, namely, the profits the patentee lost from the infringement, that determination accurately measures the patentee's loss. If actual damages cannot be ascertained, then a reasonable royalty must be determined. Panduit Corp. v. Stahlin Bros. Fibre Works, 575 F.2d 1152, 1157, 197 USPQ 726, 736 (6th Cir.1978).

The reasonable royalty may be based upon an established royalty, if there is one, or if not upon a hypothetical royalty resulting from arm's length negotiations between a willing licensor and a willing licensee. As the Court of Claims stated with respect to the statute applicable to determining damages in infringement suits against the United States (28 U.S.C. § 1498 (1976)): "Where an established royalty rate for the patented inventions is shown to exist, the rate will usually be adopted as the best measure of reasonable and entire compensation." Tektronix, Inc. v. United States, 552 F.2d 343, 347, 193 USPQ 385, 390 (Ct.Cl.1977), cert. denied, 439 U.S. 1048 (1978).

A. The magistrate held that

[t]he proofs offered in the case at hand do not suggest any basis for establishing profits experienced by the infringing Defendant in the use of the process patent nor do they establish a loss of income or loss of profit suffered by the patentee on any tangible basis by virtue of the nature of the interest the patentee has.

We have no basis for rejecting that factual determination.

B. The magistrate also ruled that the record did not show an established royalty. Alpine argues that Hanson's license to SMI at a 2½ percent royalty shows an established royalty. In rejecting this contention, the magistrate correctly pointed out that under the license SMI

paid Hanson 2.5% of the selling price and a 2.5% interest in a predecessor corporation SMI a New York corporation. Thus in granting this license Hanson speculated on the value of his interest in SMI as a corporate entity. The worth of that investment and the extent to which it enhanced the royalty is unknown. Such speculation hampers a finding of an established royalty * * *

Moreover, as the magistrate stated, "a single licensing agreement does not generally demonstrate uniformity nor acquiescence in the reasonableness of the royalty rate." For a royalty to be "established," it "must be paid by such a number of persons as to indicate a general acquiescence in its reasonableness by those who have occasion to use the invention." Rude v. Westcott, 130 U.S. 152, 165 (1889).

Finally, we cannot say that the magistrate erred in refusing to consider certain offers to license the Hanson patent at a 2½ percent royalty as showing an established rate. The magistrate excluded evidence of those proposals because they were offers in compromise made in contemplation of infringement litigation and therefore inadmissible under Rule 408 of the Federal Rules of Evidence.

The fact that licenses were offered at a particular rate does not show that that rate was the "established" rate, since the latter requires actual licenses, not mere offers to license. (We discuss below the exclusionary ruling insofar as the excluded evidence related to the magistrate's determination of a reasonable royalty under the willing licensor-willing licensee rule.) Moreover, since the offers were made after the infringement had begun and litigation was threatened or probable, their terms "should not be considered evidence of an 'established royalty,' " since "[l]icense fees negotiated in the face of a threat of high litigation costs 'may be strongly influenced by a desire to avoid full litigation * * *' " Panduit, 575 F.2d at 1164, n. 11, 197 USPQ at 736, n. 11.

C. Since there was no established royalty for licensing the Hanson patent, the magistrate necessarily had to use "a willing-buyer/willing-seller concept, in which a suppositious meeting between the patent owner and the prospective [user] of the infringing [method] is held to negotiate a license agreement." Tektronix, 552 F.2d at 349, 193 USPQ at 391. "The key element in setting a reasonable royalty * * * is the necessity for return to the date when the infringement began." Panduit, 575 F.2d at 1158, 197 USPQ at 731. The infringement in the present case began in 1972. As 35 U.S.C. § 284 states, expert testimony may be considered "as an aid to the determination * * * of what royalty would be reasonable under the circumstances."

Each party presented two witnesses. Hanson's witnesses were James L. Dilworth, an expert in snowmaking and the use of snowmaking machines, who had experience in designing and operating various types of snowmaking systems at a number of resorts; and Sidney Alpert, an expert in the negotiation of licenses for a broad range of patents. Alpine's witnesses were Joseph F. Kosik, a 50–percent shareholder and the operator of Alpine's resort in Michigan, who described the use of snowmaking machinery there; and Joseph J. Kohler, an expert who was the president and general manager of a ski resort in New York and who presented a study showing that use of the Hanson process at his resort would not have produced any savings over the cost of using the compressed air method. The magistrate credited the testimony of Hanson's experts, which Alpine's witnesses did not refute.

That testimony formed the factual bases for the magistrate's determination of a reasonable royalty.

Dilworth described the relative costs of using the Hanson and the compressed air methods of making snow. He concluded that by installing a Hanson method apparatus, a hypothetical but apparently representative ski resort would have saved in 1972 (the year infringement began) $75 per gallon per minute of the machine's rated capacity over the cost of a compressed air system.

Alpert described a hypothetical license negotiation between Hanson and Alpine in 1972. He explained that, acting for Hanson, he would "need to set up a uniform standardized approach that will go across all potential licensees, all users of the patented method independent of the machine they use * * *." The magistrate summarized Alpert's testimony on the need for a uniform license as follows:

> [T]he royalty rate and licenses granted under the Hanson patent must be uniform, and the distinctions between manufacturer and user disregarded for purposes of negotiating licenses. Various factors coerce Hanson in this case to adhere to a reasonable licensing policy throughout the multitude of potential licensors [sic]. Integrity of Hanson as a licensor, exposure to antitrust violations, and lack of controls by Hanson over both manufacturers and users were elements cited by the expert as dictating a pervasive licensing pattern and for disregarding the distinctions between manufacturers and users.

Alpert further stated that the licensor would have insisted on a uniform license based on the gallons-per-minute rated capacity of the Hanson-method machines, and would have refused to grant a license based on actual use or other criteria relating to the situation of the particular licensee.

The magistrate's acceptance of Alpert's analysis and approach was fully justified by the record before him. As he pointed out, only Hanson introduced expert testimony regarding the basis upon which a willing licensor and a willing licensee would have negotiated a license of the Hanson patent in 1972, and the magistrate found this evidence credible and convincing. The magistrate pointed out that if Alpine had presented "its own expert in licensing and negotiating patents," he might have viewed the case differently, but that "[o]n the record before this court the credible testimony of Plaintiff's expert stands as the sole guidance germane to the question of licensing distinctions for manufacturers and users."

On the basis of our review of the record in this case, we cannot reject as clearly erroneous the magistrate's factual conclusions (a) that Hanson would have required uniform terms in all his licenses and would not have varied those terms to reflect the situation of a particular licensee, and (b) that a reasonable royalty would have been based upon one-third of the estimated cost savings resulting from use of the Hanson method instead of the compressed air method of making snow, calculated on the basis of savings of $75 per machine multiplied by the snowmaking capacity of the machine times the number of years used. To the contrary, these conclusions are fully supported by the record, and we affirm them.

D. Alpine challenges the magistrate's determination of a reasonable royalty on a number of grounds. Most of these contentions founder upon the magistrate's factual determination, which we have upheld, that the royalty rate would have been uniform for all licensees. They also are subject to the additional infirmities discussed below.

1. Alpine contends that because it acquired the Hedco machines for experimental purposes and did not use them much, the royalty should have been based upon actual use rather than upon estimated savings reflecting the snowmaking capacity of the machines.

Apart from the fact that this theory is inconsistent with the magistrate's determination that Hanson would have granted licenses only at a uniform rate and not based on actual use, the record contains substantial evidence that actual use of the snowmaking machinery would not have been the basis upon which a willing licensor and a willing licensee would have established the royalty. As Alpert noted, it would have been extremely difficult to monitor actual use. Apparently no complete or accurate records were kept of the actual use of the Hedco machines at Alpine's resort.

Equally or more important, a royalty based upon actual use would have been inconsistent with the function snowmaking equipment serves at a ski resort and the reasonable needs and expectations of both the licensor and the licensee. A resort has snowmaking machinery to enable it to function at times when there is no or insufficient natural snow. As the magistrate stated, the resort hopes that "natural snow will always be sufficient and that artificial snow will never be needed." He noted that the "machines insure the business can function without natural snow" and that Hanson's "expert likened the machine to an insurance policy." The magistrate justifiably concluded that in these circumstances "[t]he number of hours a machine is used is irrelevant; the desire is never to use the machine. The machine's utility simply does not depend upon its hours of operation."

A royalty based on actual use would produce unsatisfactory results here for both the licensor and the licensee. If there were extensive snow during the season, there would be little use of the machine and the patentee would receive an inadequate return for the value of his invention. On the other hand, if there were little or no snow, the licensee would have to pay exceptionally large royalties.

We have no basis for rejecting the magistrate's factual conclusion that in the circumstances the parties to the licensing negotiations would have agreed upon a royalty rate that would insure a fair and reasonable return to the patentee and avoid the payment of excessive royalties by the licensee, without regard to the size of the snowfall. The royalty rate the magistrate used, based upon the expert evidence, would have accomplished that objective. . . .

6.   During the trial, the magistrate excluded evidence Alpine proffered that in 1972 Hanson offered to three manufacturers of snowmaking machinery (including Hedco), whose machines Hanson believed infringed his patent, licenses at a royalty of 2½ percent of the selling price of the machines.   The magistrate excluded this evidence under Rule 408 of the Federal Rules of Evidence, which states that "[e]vidence of (1) furnishing or offering or promising to furnish, or (2) accepting or offering or promising to accept, a valuable consideration in compromising or attempting to compromise a claim which was disputed as to either validity or amount, is not admissible to prove liability for or invalidity of the claim or its amount.   Evidence of conduct or statements made in compromise negotiations is likewise not admissible." With respect to one of the license offers, the magistrate also questioned the relevance of the evidence, since the offer was made to a manufacturer, not to a user.

The parties dispute whether this evidence of offers to license at a specified royalty, made to alleged infringers before any infringement litigation against them had been instituted, was inadmissible under Rule 408.   We find it unnecessary to resolve the question.   Even assuming arguendo that the magistrate erred in holding the evidence inadmissible, we cannot say that the exclusion was prejudicial.

The uncontested expert testimony, which the magistrate accepted and upon which he based his findings that we have held are not clearly erroneous, was that in pre-infringement negotiations between a willing licensor and a willing licensee the royalty would have been based upon the snowmaking capacity of the machine and the estimated savings from use of the machine, and not upon the actual use of the machine. The royalty rate in the license offers was not based on estimated savings.   It was based upon the licensee's use of the patented process in the machines the licensee would make, calculated as a percentage of the selling price of each machine.

The fact that Hanson offered to license manufacturers based upon a percentage of the selling price of the machines they made is not inconsistent with and does not undermine the magistrate's conclusion that any license Hanson would have granted a willing user would have been based upon the formula the magistrate employed and not upon actual use of the machine.   There is nothing in the record to indicate or even suggest that, in view of the considerations involving a ski resort's use of snowmaking machinery described above, Hanson would have been willing to license a user on the basis of a percentage of the manufacturer's selling price of the machine.   We accordingly conclude that if the magistrate had considered those offers, they would not have changed his decision.   Any error in the exclusion of the evidence therefore was harmless.

III.

Alpine contends that Hanson is precluded from recovering for the infringing use, prior to the filing of the complaint, of two of the Hedco machines because Hanson did not prove that Hanson's licensee SMI had marked the machines it sold, as 35 U.S.C. § 287 (1976) allegedly required. That section provides that if the patentee or persons making or selling any patented product fail to mark the article as patented, the patentee may recover damages only for infringement committed after the infringer was notified of the infringement, and that the filing of an infringement action constitutes such notice.

The magistrate rejected the contention on two grounds: (1) it was untimely raised, since Alpine had not presented it in any pretrial pleadings, and (2) the patent is a process patent, to which section 287 does not apply. We agree with the latter ground of decision, and therefore do not reach the former ruling.

Alpine states that the Hanson patent also includes apparatus claims. The only claims that were found infringed in this case, however, were claims 1, 2, and 6 of the Hanson patent, which are drawn to "[t]he method of forming, distributing and depositing snow upon a surface * * *." In affirming the district court's finding of infringement in this case, the court of appeals stated in the first sentence of its opinion that "the patent alleged to be infringed is [for] a process for making snow for winter sports." 611 F.2d at 157, 204 USPQ at 803–04. It is "settled in the case law that the notice requirement of this statute does not apply where the patent is directed to a process or method." Bandag, Inc. v. Gerrard Tire Co., 704 F.2d 1578, 1581, 217 USPQ 977, 979 (Fed.Cir.1983).

IV.

Our decision is a narrow one. We hold that on the record in this case, the findings of the magistrate are not clearly erroneous, and his determination of a reasonable royalty based upon those findings has not been shown to be legally erroneous. On this basis, the judgment of the district court is affirmed.

Affirmed.

DAVIS, Circuit Judge, concurring.

I join in the court's opinion and add, for myself, that I believe, *first*, that the excluded licenses were admissible (see the court's opinion and my separate opinion in Deere & Co. v. International Harvester Co., 710 F.2d 1551, 218 USPQ 481 (Fed.Cir.1983)); but, *second*, that the licenses to the manufacturers were sufficiently different from licenses to a user that the magistrate could and should have considered them of little probative value in this instance.

NOTES

1. *Permanent Injunctions.* Courts will grant a prevailing patent owner an injunction for the remainder of the patent's life almost as a matter of course; they will, however, withhold injunctive relief on such traditional equitable grounds as laches, estoppel or disproportionate harm to the public interest. Courts will—though less frequently—deny

injunctive relief where the disproportionate harm is only to the infringer; the infringer may, for example, have innocently and substantially invested in the equipment necessary to manufacture the patented subject matter. See Electric Smelting & Aluminum Co. v. Carborundum Co., 189 Fed. 710 (C.C.W.D.Pa.1900), rev'd on other grounds, 203 Fed. 976 (3d Cir.1913), cert. denied, 231 U.S. 754 (1913). See also Nerney v. New York, N.H. & H.R. Co., 83 F.2d 409, 29 U.S.P.Q. 456 (2d Cir.1936).

2. *Preliminary Injunctions.* For many years, courts in patent cases dispensed preliminary relief sparingly. Apart from requiring the patent owner to show that it would be irreparably harmed unless it received a preliminary injunction, courts required the patent owner to establish title, validity and infringement to an extent variously described as "beyond question" or "without reasonable doubt." One reason for these rigorous standards was judicial skepticism about the validity of patents issued *ex parte* in the Patent and Trademark Office. Another reason was the fear that "[t]he granting of temporary injunctive relief on the basis of incomplete facts may often settle the ultimate issues immediately and cause irreparable injury to the enjoined party. If a temporary injunction is unwarranted, a few years will probably elapse before final determination that the injunction was improvidently granted. By this time, the alleged infringer's loss of competitive advantage over the patentee may be incapable of repair by money damages." Note, Injunctive Relief in Patent Infringement Suits, 112 U.Pa.L.Rev. 1025 (1964).

The Court of Appeals for the Federal Circuit has loosened the requirements for preliminary relief in patent cases. "The burden upon the movant should be no different in a patent case than for other kinds of intellectual property, where, generally, only a 'clear showing' is required. Requiring a 'final adjudication,' 'full trial,' or proof 'beyond question' would support the issuance of a permanent injunction and nothing would remain to establish the liability of the accused infringer. That is not the situation before us. We are dealing with a provisional remedy which provides equitable *preliminary* relief. Thus, when a patentee 'clearly shows' that his patent is valid and infringed, a court may, after a balance of all of the competing equities, preliminarily enjoin another from violating the rights secured by the patent." Atlas Powder Co. v. Ireco Chemicals, 773 F.2d 1230, 1233, 227 U.S.P.Q. 289 (Fed.Cir.1985). See also Smith Int'l, Inc. v. Hughes Tool Co., 718 F.2d 1573, 219 U.S.P.Q. 686 (Fed.Cir.), cert. denied, 464 U.S. 996, 104 S.Ct. 493, 78 L.Ed.2d 689 (1983).

See generally, Duft, Patent Preliminary Injunctions and the United States Court of Appeals for the Federal Circuit, 65 J.Pat.Off. Soc'y 131 (1983).

3. *Damages.* Before 1946, when Congress amended the Patent Act's damages provision to substantially its present form, a successful patent claimant could choose between the amount of damages she suffered and the amount of profits earned by the infringer. To discover

which was greater, the patent owner could request judicial determination of both amounts. The high cost of determining an infringer's profits eventually led Congress to drop infringer's profits as an alternative measure of recovery. However, evidence of an infringer's profits continues to be relevant in computing the patent owner's damages—either as a factor in determining a reasonable royalty or as a surrogate for the patent owner's lost profits. See Kori Corp. v. Wilco Marsh Buggies & Draglines, Inc., 761 F.2d 649, 225 U.S.P.Q. 985 (Fed.Cir.), cert. denied, 474 U.S. 902, 106 S.Ct. 230, 88 L.Ed.2d 229 (1985).

Courts originally awarded a reasonable royalty out of reluctance to award only nominal damages in cases where the successful claimant could prove neither actual damages nor infringer's profits. Congress introduced the reasonable royalty measure into the statute in 1922. Under the present act, a reasonable royalty represents the floor of recovery. Courts will sometimes assess a reasonable royalty for those aspects of an infringement that are not compensated by other damage measures. For example, in Broadview Chem. Corp. v. Loctite Corp., 311 F.Supp. 447, 164 U.S.P.Q. 419 (D.Conn.1970), the court applied the lost profit measure to sales in the United States—where defendant was the plaintiff's sole competitor—but applied the reasonable royalty measure to the more competitive foreign market.

On patent damages, see Baker, Patent Damages—Quantifying the Award, 69 J.Pat. & Trademark Off.Soc'y 121 (1987); Conley, An Economic Approach to Patent Damages, 15 AIPLA Q.J. 354 (1987); Frank & Wagner, Computing Lost Profits and Reasonable Royalties, 15 AIPLA Q.J. 391 (1987); Skenyon & Porcelli, Patent Damages, 70 J.Pat. & Trademark Off.Soc'y 762 (1988).

4. *Increased Damages; Attorney Fees.* Section 284 of the Patent Act authorizes courts to treble patent infringement damages. Section 285 authorizes courts, "in exceptional cases," to award reasonable attorney fees to the prevailing party.

Willful infringement is the principal ground for giving prevailing patent owners increased damages and attorney fees. In determining whether an infringer's conduct was willful, the Court of Appeals for the Federal Circuit has given particular weight to whether the infringer had obtained a lawyer's opinion before undertaking its manufacture, use or sale of the patented invention. See, e.g., Underwater Devices, Inc. v. Morrison–Knudsen Co., 717 F.2d 1380, 1389, 219 U.S.P.Q. 569 (Fed.Cir.1983) ("Where . . . a potential infringer has actual notice of another's patent rights, he has an affirmative duty to exercise due care to determine whether or not he is infringing. Such an affirmative duty includes, *inter alia,* the duty to seek and obtain competent legal advice from counsel *before* the initiation of any possible infringing activity.")

Congress intended attorney fee awards to deter not only willful infringers but vexatious patent owners as well. A prevailing defendant may, for example, recover attorney fees where the patent owner litigated in bad faith or engaged in fraud or other inequitable conduct in the Patent and Trademark Office. See Rohm & Haas Co. v. Crystal Chem.

Co., 736 F.2d 688, 222 U.S.P.Q. 97 (Fed.Cir.), cert. denied, 469 U.S. 851, 105 S.Ct. 172, 83 L.Ed.2d 107 (1984). Proof that a defeated opponent acted unconscionably is not always a sufficient basis for recovery, and not every successful party is a "prevailing" party. In one case, a court set aside an award of $500,000 attorney's fees to claimant, Union Carbide, on the ground that it was not the prevailing party. "After years of litigation it prevailed only on four claims, under the doctrine of equivalents, out of a total of twenty-nine claims. It lost all process claims. It can hardly be said that Union Carbide was the prevailing party and Lincoln the losing party." Union Carbide Corp. v. Graver Tank & Mfg. Co., 345 F.2d 409, 145 U.S.P.Q. 240, 242 (7th Cir.1965).

5. *Marking.* As indicated in *Alpine Valley,* a patent owner can recover damages only from the time the infringer had notice of the subsisting patent. Notice is typically given by the mark, "Patented" or "Pat.," along with the patent number, placed on articles manufactured or sold under the patent. In the absence of marking, the patent owner can give the requisite notice directly—orally or in writing—and, at the latest, by beginning an infringement action.

Section 292 of the Patent Act proscribes counterfeit marking and false marking. The purpose of the counterfeit marking provision is to protect the public against deception about the source of goods. The purpose of the false marking provisions is to keep the marketplace free of unwarranted monopoly effects. Section 292's predecessors provided exclusively for a *qui tam* action. The section now makes false and counterfeit marking an ordinary federal criminal offense and retains the *qui tam* action as a supplementary sanction. Informer-plaintiffs are rarely disinterested. In Brose v. Sears, Roebuck & Co., 455 F.2d 763, 172 U.S.P.Q. 454 (5th Cir.1972), an appeal from dismissal of a *qui tam* action, the court observed that, "[a]s is true in nearly all of the relatively few *qui tam* informer actions brought in the past one and a quarter century this one is used as a weapon in the arsenal of patent litigation. . . ."

D. INFRINGEMENT

See Statute Supplement 35 U.S.C.A. §§ 281–282, 288, 290, 293.

CREWS, PATENT CLAIMS AND INFRINGEMENT
Dynamics of the Patent System 128, 133 (W.Ball Ed.1960).[*]

In the subject of patent claims and infringement we all know that what you do is take the copy of the patent and the copy of the accused device and you read the claims and if the claims read, there is infringement, and if the claims do not read there is not infringement. There is a little more to it than that. The little more I think, reminds me somewhat of the law of evidence. You take a course in evidence in law school and you spend the first five minutes learning the rules of

---

[*] Copyright 1960 by Villanova University.

evidence and the next two years trying to learn the exceptions to the hearsay rule. And it is really the exceptions to the rule of simply reading the claims on the device that we are concerned with in considering the question of patent claims and infringement. . . .

So in any and every question of infringement, the prior art makes a difference and must be looked at. What difference it makes depends upon the difference between the patent, the prior art and the patent, the difference between the patent and the accused structure and the difference between the prior art and the accused structure. All must be considered and it is impossible to have any sound opinion on the question of whether or not a claim of a patent is infringed, in my opinion, unless all are considered. Of course, what that means as a practical matter, is that since you never know all the prior art, you never know when another patent will turn up; it may be a little closer than anything you know of; you can do the best you can with what you have, but like so many questions of patent law, we have to advise our clients that it is a field of uncertainty. It depends so much on subjective analysis and subjective appraisal, that you cannot advise with great confidence that any patent is valid or invalid or is infringed or is not infringed.

EIBEL PROCESS CO. v. MINNESOTA & ONTARIO PAPER CO., 261 U.S. 45, 43 S.Ct. 322, 67 L.Ed. 523 (1923). TAFT, C.J.: In administering the patent law the court first looks into the art to find what the real merit of the alleged discovery or invention is and whether it has advanced the art substantially. If it has done so, then the court is liberal in its construction of the patent to secure to the inventor the reward he deserves. If what he has done works only a slight step forward and that which he says is a discovery is on the border line between mere mechanical change and real invention, then his patent, if sustained, will be given a narrow scope and infringement will be found only in approximate copies of the new device. It is this differing attitude of the courts toward genuine discoveries and slight improvements that reconciles the sometimes apparently conflicting instances of construing specifications and the finding of equivalents in alleged infringements. In the case before us, for the reasons we have already reviewed, we think that Eibel made a very useful discovery which has substantially advanced the art. His was not a pioneer patent, creating a new art; but a patent which is only an improvement on an old machine may be very meritorious and entitled to liberal treatment. Indeed, when one notes the crude working of machines of famous pioneer inventions and discoveries, and compares them with the modern machines and processes exemplifying the principle of the pioneer discovery, one hesitates in the division of credit between the original inventor and the improvers; and certainly finds no reason to withhold from the really meritorious improver, the application of the rule *"ut res magis valeat quam pereat,"* which has been sustained in so many cases in this Court.

GRAVER TANK & MFG. CO. v. LINDE AIR PRODUCTS CO.

Supreme Court of the United States, 1950.
339 U.S. 605, 70 S.Ct. 854, 94 L.Ed. 1097, 85 U.S.P.Q. 328.

Mr. Justice JACKSON delivered the opinion of the Court.

Linde Air Products Co., owner of the Jones patent for an electric welding process and for fluxes to be used therewith, brought an action for infringement against Lincoln and the two Graver companies. The trial court held four flux claims valid and infringed and certain other flux claims and all process claims invalid. 75 U.S.P.Q. 231. The Court of Appeals affirmed findings of validity and infringement as to the four flux claims but reversed the trial court and held valid the process claims and the remaining contested flux claims. 167 F.2d 531. We granted certiorari, 335 U.S. 810, 69 S.Ct. 50, 93 L.Ed. 366, and reversed the judgment of the Court of Appeals insofar as it reversed that of the trial court, and reinstated the District Court decree. 336 U.S. 271, 69 S.Ct. 535, 93 L.Ed. 672. Rehearing was granted, limited to the question of infringement of the four valid flux claims and to the applicability of the doctrine of equivalents to findings of fact in this case.

At the outset it should be noted that the single issue before us is whether the trial court's holding that the four flux claims have been infringed will be sustained. Any issue as to the validity of these claims was unanimously determined by the previous decision in this Court and attack on their validity cannot be renewed now by reason of limitation on grant of rehearing. The disclosure, the claims, and the prior art have been adequately described in our former opinion and in the opinions of the courts below.

In determining whether an accused device or composition infringes a valid patent, resort must be had in the first instance to the words of the claim. If accused matter falls clearly within the claim, infringement is made out and that is the end of it.

But courts have also recognized that to permit imitation of a patented invention which does not copy every literal detail would be to convert the protection of the patent grant into a hollow and useless thing. Such a limitation would leave room for—indeed encourage—the unscrupulous copyist to make unimportant and insubstantial changes and substitutions in the patent which, though adding nothing, would be enough to take the copied matter outside the claim, and hence outside the reach of law. One who seeks to pirate an invention, like one who seeks to pirate a copyrighted book or play, may be expected to introduce minor variations to conceal and shelter the piracy. Outright and forthright duplication is a dull and very rare type of infringement. To prohibit no other would place the inventor at the mercy of verbalism and would be subordinating substance to form. It would deprive him of the benefit of his invention and would foster concealment rather than disclosure of inventions, which is one of the primary purposes of the patent system.

The doctrine of equivalents evolved in response to this experience. The essence of the doctrine is that one may not practice a fraud on a patent. Originating almost a century ago in the case of Winans v. Denmead, 15 How. 330, it has been consistently applied by this Court and the lower federal courts, and continues today ready and available for utilization when the proper circumstances for its application arise. "To temper unsparing logic and prevent an infringer from stealing the benefit of an invention" a patentee may invoke this doctrine to proceed against the producer of a device "if it performs substantially the same function in substantially the same way to obtain the same result." Sanitary Refrigerator Co. v. Winters, 280 U.S. 30, 42, 50 S.Ct. 9, 13, 74 L.Ed. 147. The theory on which it is founded is that "if two devices do the same work in substantially the same way, and accomplish substantially the same result, they are the same, even though they differ in name, form, or shape." Machine Co. v. Murphy, 97 U.S. 120, 125, 24 L.Ed. 935. The doctrine operates not only in favor of the patentee of a pioneer or primary invention, but also for the patentee of a secondary invention consisting of a combination of old ingredients which produce new and useful results, although the area of equivalence may vary under the circumstances. The wholesome realism of this doctrine is not always applied in favor of a patentee but is sometimes used against him. Thus, where a device is so far changed in principle from a patented article that it performs the same or a similar function in a substantially different way, but nevertheless falls within the literal words of the claim, the doctrine of equivalents may be used to restrict the claim and defeat the patentee's action for infringement. In its early development, the doctrine was usually applied in cases involving devices where there was equivalence in mechanical components. Subsequently, however, the same principles were also applied to compositions, where there was equivalence between chemical ingredients. Today the doctrine is applied to mechanical or chemical equivalents in compositions or devices.

What constitutes equivalency must be determined against the context of the patent, the prior art, and the particular circumstances of the case. Equivalence, in the patent law, is not the prisoner of a formula and is not an absolute to be considered in a vacuum. It does not require complete identity for every purpose and in every respect. In determining equivalents, things equal to the same thing may not be equal to each other and, by the same token, things for most purposes different may sometimes be equivalents. Consideration must be given to the purpose for which an ingredient is used in a patent, the qualities it has when combined with the other ingredients, and the function which it is intended to perform. An important factor is whether persons reasonably skilled in the art would have known of the interchangeability of an ingredient not contained in the patent with one that was.

A finding of equivalence is a determination of fact. Proof can be made in any form: through testimony of experts or others versed in the technology; by documents, including texts and treatises; and, of course, by the disclosures of the prior art. Like any other issue of fact, final determination requires a balancing of credibility, persuasiveness and weight of evidence. It is to be decided by the trial court and that court's decision, under general principles of appellate review, should not be disturbed unless clearly erroneous. Particularly is this so in a field where so much depends upon familiarity with specific scientific problems and principles not usually contained in the general store-house of knowledge and experience.

In the case before us, we have two electric welding compositions or fluxes: the patented composition, Unionmelt Grade 20, and the accused composition, Lincolnweld 660. The patent under which Unionmelt is made claims essentially a combination of alkaline earth metal silicate and calcium fluoride; Unionmelt actually contains, however, silicates of calcium and magnesium, two alkaline earth metal silicates. Lincolnweld's composition is similar to Unionmelt's, except that it substitutes silicates of calcium and manganese—the latter not an alkaline earth metal—for silicates of calcium and magnesium. In all other respects, the two compositions are alike. The mechanical methods in which these compositions are employed are similar. They are identical in operation and produce the same kind and quality of weld.

The question which thus emerges is whether the substitution of the manganese which is not an alkaline earth metal for the magnesium which is, under the circumstances of this case, and in view of the technology and the prior art, is a change of such substance as to make the doctrine of equivalents inapplicable; or conversely, whether under the circumstances the change was so insubstantial that the trial court's invocation of the doctrine of equivalents was justified.

Without attempting to be all-inclusive, we note the following evidence in the record: Chemists familiar with the two fluxes testified that manganese and magnesium were similar in many of their reactions. There is testimony by a metallurgist that alkaline earth metals are often found in manganese ores in their natural state and that they serve the same purpose in the fluxes, and a chemist testified that "in the sense of the patent" manganese could be included as an alkaline earth metal. Much of this testimony was corroborated by reference to recognized texts on inorganic chemistry. Particularly important, in addition, were the disclosures of the prior art, also contained in the record. The Miller patent, No. 1,754,566, which preceded the patent in suit, taught the use of manganese silicate in welding fluxes. Manganese was similarly disclosed in the Armor patent, No. 1,467,825, which also described a welding composition. And the record contains no evidence of any kind to show that Lincolnweld was developed as the result of independent research or experiments.

It is not for this Court to even essay an independent evaluation of this evidence. This is the function of the trial court. And, as we have heretofore observed, "To no type of case is this . . . more appropriately applicable than to the one before us, where the evidence is largely the testimony of experts as to which a trial court may be enlightened by scientific demonstrations. This trial occupied some three weeks, during which, as the record shows, the trial judge visited laboratories with counsel and experts to observe actual demonstrations of welding as taught by the patent and of the welding accused of infringing it, and of various stages of the prior art. He viewed motion pictures of various welding operations and tests and heard many experts and other witnesses." 336 U.S. 271, 274–275, 69 S.Ct. 535, 537, 93 L.Ed. 672.

The trial judge found on the evidence before him that the Lincolnweld flux and the composition of the patent in suit are substantially identical in operation and in result. He found also that Lincolnweld is in all respects equivalent to Unionmelt for welding purposes. And he concluded that "for all practical purposes, manganese silicate can be efficiently and effectually substituted for calcium and magnesium silicates as the major constituent of the welding composition." These conclusions are adequately supported by the record; certainly they are not clearly erroneous.

It is difficult to conceive of a case more appropriate for application of the doctrine of equivalents. The disclosures of the prior art made clear that manganese silicate was a useful ingredient in welding compositions. Specialists familiar with the problems of welding compositions understood that manganese was equivalent to and could be substituted for magnesium in the composition of the patented flux and their observations were confirmed by the literature of chemistry. Without some explanation or indication that Lincolnweld was developed by independent research, the trial court could properly infer that the accused flux is the result of imitation rather than experimentation or invention. Though infringement was not literal, the changes which avoid literal infringement are colorable only. We conclude that the trial court's judgment of infringement respecting the four flux claims was proper, and we adhere to our prior decision on this aspect of the case.

Affirmed.

Mr. Justice BLACK, with whom Mr. Justice DOUGLAS concurs, dissenting.

I heartily agree with the Court that "fraud" is bad, "piracy" is evil, and "stealing" is reprehensible. But in this case, where petitioners are not charged with any such malevolence, these lofty principles do not justify the Court's sterilization of Acts of Congress and prior decisions, none of which are even mentioned in today's opinion.

The only patent claims involved here describe respondent's product as a flux "containing a major proportion of alkaline earth metal silicate." The trial court found that petitioners used a flux "composed principally of manganese silicate." Finding also that "manganese is not an alkaline earth metal," the trial court admitted that petitioners' flux did not "literally infringe" respondent's patent. Nevertheless it invoked the judicial "doctrine of equivalents" to broaden the claim for "alkaline earth metals" so as to embrace "manganese." On the ground that "the fact that manganese is a proper substitute . . . is fully disclosed in the specification" of respondent's patent, it concluded that "no determination need be made whether it is a known chemical fact *outside* the teachings of the patent that manganese is an equivalent. . . ." Since today's affirmance unquestioningly follows the findings of the trial court, this Court necessarily relies on what the specifications revealed. In so doing, it violates a direct mandate of Congress without even discussing that mandate.

R.S. § 4888, as amended, 35 U.S.C.A. § 33, provides that an applicant "shall particularly point out and distinctly claim the part, improvement, or combination which he claims as his invention or discovery." We have held in this very case that this statute precludes invoking the specifications to alter a claim free from ambiguous language, since "it is the claim which measures the grant to the patentee." Graver Mfg. Co. v. Linde Co., 336 U.S. 271, 277, 69 S.Ct. 535, 538, 93 L.Ed. 672. What is not specifically claimed is dedicated to the public. For the function of claims under R.S. § 4888, as we have frequently reiterated, is to exclude from the patent monopoly field all that is not specifically claimed, whatever may appear in the specifications. Today the Court tacitly rejects those cases. It departs from the underlying principle which, as the Court pointed out in White v. Dunbar, 119 U.S. 47, 51, 7 S.Ct. 72, 74, 30 L.Ed. 303, forbids treating a patent claim "like a nose of wax which may be turned and twisted in any direction, by merely referring to the specification, so as to make it include something more than, or something different from what its words express. . . . The claim is a statutory requirement, prescribed for the very purpose of making the patentee define precisely what his invention is; and it is unjust to the public, as well as an evasion of the law, to construe it in a manner different from the plain import of its terms." Giving this patentee the benefit of a grant that it did not precisely claim is no less "unjust to the public" and no less an evasion of R.S. § 4888 merely because done in the name of the "doctrine of equivalents."

In seeking to justify its emasculation of R.S. § 4888 by parading potential hardships which literal enforcement might conceivably impose on patentees who had for some reason failed to claim complete protection for their discoveries, the Court fails even to mention the program for alleviation of such hardships which Congress itself has provided. 35 U.S.C.A. § 64 authorizes reissue of patents where a patent is "wholly or partly inoperative" due to certain errors arising from "inadvertence, accident, or mistake" of the patentee. And while the section does not expressly permit a patentee to expand his claim, this Court has reluctantly interpreted it to justify doing so. Miller v. Brass Co., 104 U.S. 350, 353–354, 26 L.Ed. 783. That interpretation, however, was accompanied by a warning that "Reissues for the enlargement of claims should be the exception and not the rule." Id. at 355. And Congress was careful to hedge the privilege of reissue by exacting conditions. It also entrusted the Patent Office, not the courts, with initial authority to determine whether expansion of a claim was justified, and barred suits for retroactive infringement based on such expansion. Like the Court's opinion, this congressional plan adequately protects patentees from "fraud," "piracy," and "stealing." Unlike the Court's opinion, it also protects businessmen from retroactive infringement suits and judicial expansion of a monopoly sphere beyond that which a patent expressly authorizes. The plan is just, fair, and reasonable. In effect it is nullified by this decision undercutting what the Court has heretofore recognized as wise safeguards. One need not be a prophet to suggest that today's rhapsody on the virtue of the "doctrine of equivalents" will, in direct contravention of the Miller case, supra, make enlargement of patent claims the "rule" rather than the "exception."

Whatever the merits of the "doctrine of equivalents" where differences between the claims of a patent and the allegedly infringing product are de minimis, colorable only, and without substance, that doctrine should have no application to the facts of this case. For the differences between respondent's welding substance and petitioners' claimed flux were not nearly so slight. The claims relied upon here did not involve any mechanical structure or process where invention lay in the construction or method rather than in the materials used. Rather they were based wholly on using particular materials for a particular purpose. Respondent's assignors experimented with several metallic silicates, including that of manganese. According to the specifications (if these are to be considered) they concluded that while several were "more or less efficacious in our process, we prefer to use silicates of the alkaline earth metals." Several of their claims which this Court found too broad to be valid encompassed manganese silicate; the only claims found valid did not. Yet today the Court disregards that crucial deficiency, holding those claims infringed by a composition of which 88.49% by weight is manganese silicate.

In view of the intense study and experimentation of respondent's assignors with manganese silicate, it would be frivolous to contend that failure specifically to include that substance in a precise claim was unintentional. Nor does respondent attempt to give that or any other explanation for its omission. But the similar use of manganese in prior expired patents, referred to in the Court's opinion, raises far more than a suspicion that its elimination from the valid claims stemmed from fear that its inclusion by name might result in denial or subsequent invalidation of respondent's patent.

Under these circumstances I think petitioners had a right to act on the belief that this Court would follow the plain mandates of Congress that a patent's precise claims mark its monopoly boundaries, and that expansion of those claims to include manganese could be obtained only in a statutory reissue proceeding. The Court's ruling today sets the stage for more patent "fraud" and "piracy" against business than could be expected from faithful observance of the congressionally enacted plan to protect business against judicial expansion of precise patent claims. Hereafter a manufacturer cannot rely on what the language of a patent claims. He must be able, at the peril of heavy infringement damages, to forecast how far a court relatively unversed in a particular technological field will expand the claim's language after considering the testimony of technical experts in that field. To burden business enterprise on the assumption that men possess such a prescience bodes ill for the kind of competitive economy that is our professed goal.

The way specific problems are approached naturally has much to do with the decisions reached. A host of prior cases, to some of which I have referred, have treated the 17-year monopoly authorized by valid patents as a narrow exception to our competitive enterprise system. For that reason, they have emphasized the importance of leaving business men free to utilize all knowledge not preempted by the precise language of a patent claim. E.g., Sontag Stores Co. v. Nut Co., 310 U.S. 281, and cases there cited. In the Sontag case Mr. Justice McReynolds, speaking for a unanimous Court, said in part: "In the case under consideration the patentee might have included in the application for the original patent, claims broad enough to embrace petitioner's accused machine, but did not. This 'gave the public to understand' that whatever was not claimed 'did not come within his patent and might rightfully be made by anyone.'" Id. at 293.

The Court's contrary approach today causes it to retreat from this sound principle. The damages retroactively assessed against petitioners for what was authorized until today are but the initial installment on the cost of that retreat.

Mr. Justice DOUGLAS, dissenting.

The Court applies the doctrine of equivalents in a way which subverts the constitutional and statutory scheme for the grant and use of patents.

The claims of the patent are limited to a flux "containing a major proportion of alkaline earth metal silicate." Manganese silicate, the flux which is held to infringe, is not an alkaline earth metal silicate. It was disclosed in the application and then excluded from the claims. It therefore became public property. It was, to be sure, mentioned in the specifications. But the measure of the grant is to be found in the claims, not in the specifications. The specifications can be used to limit but never to expand the claim.

The Court now allows the doctrine of equivalents to erase those time-honored rules. Moreover, a doctrine which is said to protect against practicing "a fraud on a patent" is used to extend a patent to a composition which could not be patented. For manganese silicate had been covered by prior patents, now expired. Thus we end with a strange anomaly: a monopoly is obtained on an unpatented and unpatentable article.

TOWNSEND ENGINEERING CO. v. HITEC CO.

United States Court of Appeals, Federal Circuit, 1987.
829 F.2d 1086, 4 U.S.P.Q.2d 1136.

FRIEDMAN, Circuit Judge.

This is an appeal from a judgment of the United States District Court for the Northern District of Illinois granting summary judgment for the defendant in a patent infringement suit. The court found that there was no infringement, either literal or under the doctrine of equivalents. We affirm.

I

The invention the patent (No. 3,694,853) (the '853 patent) discloses is a sausage-stuffing machine. This case involves the "looper horn" claimed in the '853 patent, which loops stuffed sausages on hooks for further processing.

The appellant Townsend Engineering Company (Townsend) obtained the '853 patent by assignment from its inventor, Charles Austin Greider. Townsend also owned an earlier and now expired U.S. Patent (No. 3,191,222) (the '222 patent), on a sausage-stuffing machine, issued to its chief executive officer, Ray T. Townsend.

Encasing machines made according to the '222 patent had difficulty handling delicate casing material because of the shape of the machines' looper horn. In his specification in the '853 patent, Greider explained that he could avoid the tearing problems encountered in machines manufactured under the '222 patent by changing the shape and geometry of the looper horn:

> The horn extension shown in U.S.Pat. No. 3,191,222 is helical or spiral in shape whereas the horn extension of the present invention is substantially straight and disposed at an angle with respect to the rotational axis of the bearing means (horn base 202) which supports the horn extension.

The application for the '853 patent originally included 27 claims. Claim 27 of the application, which as amended is now claim 5 of the '853 patent, the claim covering the looper horn, is the only claim relevant in this appeal. In pertinent part, claim 27 set forth

> an elongated tube-like horn extension having first and second ends and a longitudinal base [sic: bore] extending there-through for slidably receiving said casing, said first end of said horn extension being adapted to receive said casing; bearing means on said support having an axis of rotation and rotatably supporting said first end of said horn extension, the longitudinal axis of said horn extension being substantially straight and forming an angle with respect to said axis of rotation of said bearing means. . . .

In the first Office Action, the patent examiner rejected claim 27 as anticipated by the looper horn of the '222 patent. In response, Greider cancelled claim 27 and substituted claim 30, which ultimately became claim 5 of the '853 patent. The most significant differences between claim 30 and claim 27 relate to the shape and length of the looper horn. The relevant portion of claim 30 is reproduced below, with underlining and brackets showing the language added to and deleted from claim 27:

> an elongated tube-like horn extension having first and second <u>end portions</u> [ends] and a [longitudinal] bore extending therethrough <u>and therebetween</u> for slidably receiving said casing [, said first end

of said horn extension being adapted to receive said casing], <u>said second end portion having a length substantially greater than the length of said first end portion,</u>

bearing means on said support having an axis of rotation and rotatably supporting said first end <u>portion</u> of said horn extension, <u>said second end portion having a</u> [the] longitudinal axis [of said horn extension] <u>which is</u> [being] substantially straight <u>and which is angularly disposed</u> [and forming an angle] <u>with respect to the longitudinal axis of said first end portion and angularly disposed</u> with respect to said axes of rotation of said bearing means. . . .

In the remarks explaining the substitution of claim 30 for claim 27, Greider noted that the looper horn of the application differed from that in the '222 patent because the latter was both curved and rotating:

> In the specification, [Greider] recognized that looping horns such as the one disclosed in the ['222 patent] have been previously used for looping link casings but it was specifically stated at page 18 of the specification that previous horns have not been adapted to handle delicate casings satisfactorily. The horn extension shown in the ['222] patent is helical or spiral in shape whereas the horn extension of the present invention is substantially straight and disposed at an angle with respect to the rotational axis of the bearing means which supports the horn extension. The result of the device described in claim 30 is that the casings are gently swung back and forth for looping over the hooks of the conveyor. This action is gentler and less likely to cause tearing of the casing than the action obtained from the previous helical horn.

With these changes, claim 30 was issued as claim 5 of the '853 patent.

Townsend filed the present suit against appellee HiTec Co., Ltd. (HiTec), alleging that HiTec's "Auto Wienker" sausage-stuffing machine infringed claim 5 of the '853 patent. The patented and accused looper horns are illustrated below:

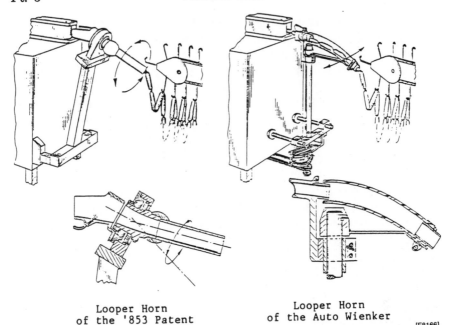

Looper Horn
of the '853 Patent

Looper Horn
of the Auto Wienker

[F8166]

HiTec moved for summary judgment of non-infringement, asserting that the Auto Wienker did not infringe either literally or under the doctrine of equivalents. The district court granted the motion and dismissed the complaint. The court ruled that in order to infringe claim 5 literally, HiTec's looper horn had to:

> consist of two parts, one part of which is (1) substantially longer than the other part and (2) substantially straight. In addition the horn must be rotated by a bearing means that supports the shorter part of the horn. Finally the longer part of the horn must be set off at an angle from the shorter part.

Townsend Eng'g Co. v. HiTec Co., 1 USPQ2d 1987, 1989 (N.D.Ill.1986).

The district court noted that unlike the two-part, substantially straight horn claimed in the '853 patent, the Auto Wienker's horn was "a one-piece continuously curved plastic tube. . . ." Id. at 1989–90. Because it found that "even a cursory examination of the Auto Wienker horn establishes it does not truly have *any* of those crucial properties of the [looper horn disclosed in the '853 patent]," the court determined that there was no literal infringement. Id. at 1989 (emphasis in original).

The court also rejected Townsend's contention that the accused device infringed under the doctrine of equivalents. The court held that Townsend was barred by the doctrine of prosecution history estoppel from reading claim 5 to cover a looper horn like that embodied in the '222 patent:

> [Claim 5 of the '853 patent] was amended after an initial rejection by the patent examiner. That amendment was necessary to distinguish Claim 5 from material already embraced by the ['222] Patent and therefore found to have been anticipated under 35

U.S.C. § 102. Because the looper horn in the [′222] Patent was curved or spiral, Greider was forced to add the limitation that his own looper horn comprises two parts, one of which is longer than and angularly disposed to the shorter part. Indeed, Greider's attorney emphasized the newlynarrowed description of the looper horn in the argument that accompanied amended Claim 5.

In light of that prosecution history, Townsend is estopped from using the doctrine of equivalents to avoid the specific words of limitation Greider chose to add to Claim 5 to obtain issuance of his patent. . . .

Accordingly Townsend cannot argue the curved single-piece Auto Wienker looper horn (an embodiment abandoned in Claim 5 as amended) is the functional equivalent of the substantially straight two-piece Greider looper horn. . . .

Id. at 1990–91.

II

Although infringement, either literal or under the doctrine of equivalents, is a question of fact " '[s]ummary judgment is as appropriate in a patent case as in any other' where no genuine issue of material fact is present and the movant is entitled to judgment as a matter of law." Brenner v. United States, 773 F.2d 306, 307, 227 USPQ 159, 160 (Fed.Cir.1985) (quoting Barmag Barmer Maschinenfabrik AG v. Murata Mach., Ltd., 731 F.2d 831, 835, 221 USPQ 561, 564 (Fed.Cir.1984)). Thus, the granting of summary judgment will be upheld "where the claims do not 'read on' the accused structure" to establish literal infringement "and a prosecution history estoppel makes clear that no actual infringement under the doctrine of equivalents can be found." Id., Builders Concrete, Inc. v. Bremerton Concrete Prods. Co., 757 F.2d 255, 225 USPQ 240 (Fed.Cir.1985).

Townsend contends that there are disputed issues of material fact relating to both literal infringement and infringement by equivalents that precluded the grant of summary judgment, and that in any event the district court erred in holding that the doctrine of prosecution history estoppel bars Townsend from invoking the doctrine of equivalents. To establish the existence of disputed issues of material fact, Townsend relies mainly upon the affidavit of its chief executive officer, Mr. Townsend, which it asserts established the existence of nine disputed issues of material fact. Townsend further asserts that in granting summary judgment the district court ignored the Townsend affidavit and improperly resolved factual issues that could be determined only after a trial.

We have concluded, however, that the district court correctly held that there are no disputed issues of material fact and that on the undisputed facts HiTec was entitled to judgment as a matter of law. The Townsend affidavit largely consists of Mr. Townsend's opinion about the meaning and application of various phrases and provisions of claim 5, and does not create factual disputes that precluded the grant of summary judgment.

A. *Literal Infringement.* The district court correctly determined that there were no genuine issues of material fact regarding literal infringement by the accused device. "Literal infringement requires that the accused device embody every element of the claim." *Builders Concrete,* 757 F.2d at 257, 225 USPQ at 241. Claim 5 of the '853 patent is drawn to a two-part horn, and literally requires that (1) one part of the horn must be substantially longer than the other part, and (2) that this longer portion must be substantially straight. In addition, the horn must be rotatable by a bearing means that supports the shorter part of the horn. Furthermore, the longer part of the horn must "be angularly disposed with respect to" the shorter part of the horn.

The district court correctly determined that the accused device differs markedly from the horn claimed in the '853 patent. Unlike the two-part device claimed in the '853 patent, the accused device consists of a single piece of plastic tubing. While the patented device rotates, the accused device oscillates between two points. Furthermore, although the patented device has two portions, one of which is "substantially straight," the accused device consists of a single piece that is continuously curved along its entire length.

Because the accused device does not embody every element of claim 5 of the '853 patent, the district court correctly granted HiTec's motion for summary judgment on the literal infringement issue.

B. *Doctrine of Equivalents.* The district court also correctly determined that there were no genuine issues of material fact regarding infringement under the doctrine of equivalents. Under that doctrine, an accused product that does not literally infringe a structural claim may infringe "if it performs substantially the same function in substantially the same way to obtain the same result." *Graver Tank,* 339 U.S. at 608, 70 S.Ct. at 856, 85 USPQ at 330 (quoting Sanitary Refrigerator Co. v. Winters, 280 U.S. 30, 42, 50 S.Ct. 9, 13, 74 L.Ed. 147 (1929)), Hughes Aircraft Co. v. United States, 717 F.2d 1351, 1361, 219 USPQ 473, 480 (Fed.Cir.1983).

The doctrine of equivalents, however, is limited by prosecution history estoppel, which "limits a patentee's reliance on the doctrine of equivalents by preventing him from contending later in an infringement action that his claims should be interpreted as if limitations added by amendment were not present. . . ." *Thomas & Betts Corp. v. Litton Sys., Inc.,* 720 F.2d 1572, 1579, 220 USPQ 1, 6 (Fed.Cir.1983).

Prosecution history estoppel applies both "to claim amendments to overcome rejections based on prior art, and to arguments submitted to obtain the patent." *Hughes Aircraft,* 717 F.2d at 1362, 219 USPQ at 481. When claim 5 of the accused device was originally submitted, the patent examiner rejected it as having been anticipated by the '222 patent. Because the '222 patent disclosed a one-part spiral or helical looper horn, the patentee added the limitations that its own horn consists of two "portions," one of which is "substantially straight" and which has a length "substantially greater" than the other portion. The patentee also added the limitation that the second end portion of its horn is angularly disposed to the first end portion.

In the remarks explaining the substitution of claim 30 for claim 27, the patentee emphasized the difference in length between the first and second end portions of the looper horn:

> The claim describes that the second end portion has a length substantially greater than the length of the first end portion.

The patentee also pointed out that the second end portion of the looper horn was substantially straight:

> The horn extension shown in the ['222] patent is helical or spiral in shape whereas the horn extension of the present invention is substantially straight. . . .

Contrary to Townsend's contention, these amendments were not limited to avoiding the " 'helical or spiral' nature" of the horn of the '222 patent, but imposed broader limitations upon the claim.

Having added limitations to avoid the device disclosed in the prior art, Townsend is barred by prosecution history estoppel from interpreting his claim as broadly as the claim originally filed. The accused device, like the prior art embodied in the '222 patent, is a one-piece looper horn that curves over its entire length. Townsend amended its claim to make clear that its looper horn (1) had first and second end portions, (2) that the second end portion was substantially longer than the first end portion, (3) that the second end portion was substantially straight, and (4) that the second end portion was angularly disposed with respect to the first end portion. Townsend is now precluded from contending that the accused device—which has none of the characteristics added by the amendments—is equivalent to the invention claimed in the '853 patent.

For this reason the district court cannot be faulted, as Townsend would do, for failing to make the three-part analysis that defines the doctrine of equivalents.

C. Townsend makes a number of creative, but unpersuasive, arguments in support of its contention that there were factual issues that precluded summary judgment on the prosecution history estoppel issue.

First, Townsend asserts that the HiTec horn, like the horn disclosed in the '853 patent, consists of two pieces. Townsend argues that it is theoretically possible to divide the HiTec horn into two "portions" based on the horn's inner diameter.

As the district court recognized, however, Townsend's attempt to divide the HiTec looper horn into two portions based on the horn's inner diameter ignores the basic structure of the HiTec horn. The district court, after viewing the HiTec horn, correctly determined that

> [e]ven if this Court buys Townsend's statements that one section of the HiTec horn gradually becomes wider while a longer portion is

consistently of the same diameter, that does not alter the nature of the Auto Wienker as a single piece of plastic tubing.

Id.

Townsend further asserts that the accused device, like the device claimed in claim 5 of the '853 patent, contains a "second portion" that is "substantially straight." In support of this contention, Townsend presents a number of illustrations of the accused and the patented devices viewed from above. As the district court correctly noted, however, "even a Hula–Hoop is 'substantially straight' when viewed from a point in its own plane." Id. at 1990 n. 5. The district court properly refused to adopt this artificial interpretation of the structure of the two devices.

Even assuming *arguendo* that the HiTec horn could be divided into two portions, and that a small portion of the horn could be viewed as "substantially straight," Townsend's argument still is fatally flawed. Even under Townsend's analysis, the "substantially straight portion" of the HiTec horn does not have a length substantially longer than the horn's other portion. Moreover, even if the HiTec horn were viewed as consisting of two portions, those portions are not "angularly disposed" but instead meet to form a continuous curve.

Contrary to Townsend's assertions, therefore, the accused device does not contain the limitations that were added to the patented device to avoid the prior art. The district court properly determined that there were no genuine issues of material fact regarding infringement under the doctrine of equivalents, and that HiTec was entitled to judgment on the equivalents issue as a matter of law.

CONCLUSION

The judgment of the district court granting HiTec's motion for summary judgment and dismissing the suit is affirmed.

AFFIRMED.

CREWS, PATENT CLAIMS AND INFRINGEMENT
Dynamics of the Patent System 128, 139–140 (W.Ball Ed.1960).*

In other words, if you go to the Patent Office and are required to restrict your claim by the prior art, and you come out with a narrower claim than when you went in and then you try to interpret it to be infringed by a device you are accusing, you cannot, of course, give it in the court the interpretation that you had to read out of it in order to get it allowed by the Patent Office. But suppose the Patent Office does not make you amend your claim. Then when the prior art is shown under this decision, the District Court, or the courts, will do exactly what the Patent Office would have done if this particular prior art had been cited during the prosecution. Since the Patent Office would not have allowed the claim, the courts said, we will hold that the claim cannot be read on the accused device, and it is not infringed. In other words, you have a doctrine of file wrapper estoppel, but does the doctrine of file wrapper estoppel mean anything? What difference does it make whether your claim is limited by the Patent Office by reason of the prior art that is cited there, when if you get into the courts and the same prior art is cited against you, the court says this claim must be held to be limited in exactly the same manner in which we think it would have been limited if this art had been cited in the Patent Office. The doctrine of file wrapper estoppel does not seem to have any significance when looked at in that light. And yet in actual practice, the doctrine is a doctrine of tremendous importance. If you have two alleged infringing devices in one case, you have limited your claims in the Patent Office in order to assert a limitation and you are now trying to read it out. Your chances of success in court are practically nil. However, if you do not have that limitation and that art was not cited by the Patent Office, your chances of success in court are, in my opinion, very much greater.

NOTES

1. Does the label, "patent," possess more than jurisdictional consequence? What interests are served by a system that makes no threshold distinction between "weak," "intermediate" and "strong" patents, leaving these and finer qualitative distinctions to judicial decisions on infringement? In one case in which the court avoided a decision on a patent's validity by finding that, if valid, the patent had not been infringed, Judge Jerome Frank concurred, contending that, "we should also hold the patent invalid." Weak patents like the one in suit, he argued, may constitute "vicious Zombis;" the majority decision left the patentee "free to sue others as alleged infringers, putting them to the expense—notoriously great in patent suits—of defending themselves." Aero Spark Plug Co., Inc. v. B.G. Corp., 130 F.2d 290, 54 U.S.P.Q. 348 (2d Cir.1942).

2. *Doctrine of Equivalents: History.* At least at the time of its origin, in Winans v. Denmead, 15 How. 330, 56 U.S. 330, 14 L.Ed. 717 (1853), elastic application of the doctrine of equivalents was clearly proper: "The doctrine of equivalents is an inheritance from that period during which the patent statutes required the patent claim merely to 'specify and point out' the invention protected. At that time, claims were usually of the 'as shown and described' variety, importing into the claim the text of the specification and the drawing. 'Interpretation' of patent claims was then the rule; the courts were called upon to determine the actual extent of the invention, and it is obvious that the doctrine of equivalents was then continually necessary as a routine rule of the patent law. Today, patent applicants are required to 'particularly point out and distinctly claim' their inventions and patent claims are now recognized as definitions of the scope of the patent—word fences which exclude the public from the patented invention but also leave open that public domain which the patent may not protect. So long as a claim of a modern patent is not ambiguous, that claim is certainly the

measure of the patentee's monopoly under all normal situations, and it now appears futile to contend that the claim may be expanded by the doctrine of equivalents or any other doctrine every time that the claim fails to encompass that which is used by a potential infringer." Note, The Doctrine of Equivalents Revalued, 19 Geo.Wash.L.Rev. 491–492 (1951).

One conclusion to be drawn from this historical analysis is that, under present practice, the doctrine of equivalents should be available only in cases of ambiguous claims and, then, only as an interpretive tool. Aside from whether the application in *Graver* was historically correct, it was probably excessive in terms of the range of equivalents commonly applied. Can you reconcile *Graver's* expansionist views with the antimonopoly bias of the court's contemporaneous decisions on the standard of patentability? See p. 371, above.

3. *Doctrine of Equivalents: Policy.* The doctrine of equivalents mediates between two views of desirable investment behavior. On one side is the view that if competitors are to invest confidently in producing noninfringing products, they must be able to rely on the metes and bounds set out in a patent's claims. On the other side is the view that if competitors are to be discouraged from investing in only small, artful changes, the patent owner's scope of protection should exceed its literal claims. Adherents to the first view favor a narrow range of equivalents; adherents to the second view favor a more generous range of equivalents.

Like the Supreme Court in *Graver*, the Court of Appeals for the Federal Circuit has divided on the proper scope of equivalents. In Pennwalt Corp. v. Durand–Wayland, Inc., 833 F.2d 931, 4 U.S.P.Q.2d 1737 (Fed.Cir.1987), cert. denied, 485 U.S. 961, 108 S.Ct. 1226, 99 L.Ed. 2d 426 (1988), the court applied the doctrine of equivalents "element-by-element" and held that, to infringe, the defendant's product had to embody an equivalent of each element of the claimed invention. The dissenting judges took an "invention as a whole" approach, requiring the patent owner to prove only that, considered in their entirety, the patented invention and the accused product are equivalent. Judge Bennett, writing for the dissenters, objected that "the same features which defeat the possibility of literal infringement are now being used to preclude possible application of the doctrine of equivalents." 833 F.2d at 947.

In an exhaustive and searching analysis of *Pennwalt*, Professors Martin Adelman and Gary Francione conclude that "[a]lthough both the majority and the dissent obviously thought that the debate was important, the crucial issue involved in the doctrine of equivalents is not the question that the court answered, but the one that it did not: What is an equivalent? The Federal Circuit seems prepared to allow the doctrine of equivalents to play a major role as a factual issue to be decided in every case, but the court has yet to address the meaning of this fundamental concept." Adelman & Francione, The Doctrine of

Equivalents in Patent Law: Questions that *Pennwalt* Did Not Answer, 137 U.Pa.L.Rev. 673 (1989).

4. The general tests of infringement announced in *Graver* represent only part of the picture. Specific tests, oriented to the particular type of subject matter in suit, also play a role. Because patent claims for compositions of matter can be distinctly characterized in terms of the ingredients' nature and proportions, infringement consists of replication of the ingredients in substantially the same proportions. For a process patent, it is the series of steps comprising the process that is central; replication of every step in substantially the same operative order constitutes infringement. In the case of a machine or device, it is substantial similarity in the means, mode and results of operation that infringes.

5. *"Reverse Doctrine of Equivalents."* *Graver* observed that the doctrine of equivalents "is not always applied in favor of a patentee but is sometimes used against him. Thus, where a device is so far changed in principle from a patented article that it performs the same or a similar function in a substantially different way, but nevertheless falls within the literal words of the claim, the doctrine of equivalents may be used to restrict the claim and defeat the patentee's action for infringement." 339 U.S. 608–09.

In Mead Digital Systems, Inc. v. A.B. Dick Co., 723 F.2d 455, 221 U.S.P.Q. 1035 (6th Cir.1983) the court applied the doctrine of equivalents as a "two-edged sword" and held that an ink jet printer designed to print letters did not infringe a patent on a printer designed to record waveforms of electrical signals. In the court's view, the accused printer "is a more sophisticated device, embodying inventive insights not part of the Sweet patent." Although the accused device relied on Sweet's "fundamental concept of ink jet charging and deflection," the device incorporated other concepts as well, including "the coordination of multiple jets, interception for creating an apparent discontinuity in the image, and a charging and deflection system whereby the final picture is not characteristic of the charging signals." 723 F.2d at 464.

The court rejected *Graver's* assertion that "[i]f accused matter falls clearly within the claim, infringement is made out and that is the end of it." According to the court, "[t]his so-called doctrine of 'literal infringement' continues to live in the cases despite repeated pronouncements that infringement is not a mere matter of words. . . . Courts, however unfortunately, continue to pay lip service to the doctrine of literal infringement as though it were the rule in *Shelley's Case.* Perhaps we are embarrassed to expose the 'wholesale realism' which controls many infringement cases, and we choose instead to present the facade of precision and certainty which attends the doctrine of literal infringement." 723 F.2d at 462.

6. *Prosecution History Estoppel.* Three possible rationales underlie the doctrine of prosecution history estoppel—earlier called "file wrapper estoppel"—applied in *Townsend Engineering.* One is a common law estoppel theory. Because competitors may circuminvent in

reliance on the recorded prosecution history in the Patent and Trademark Office, the patent owner should be estopped from reclaiming later what it gave up earlier. The difference from common law estoppel is that an accused infringer does not have to prove reliance to invoke the estoppel. Second is an abandonment rationale: the patent applicant abandoned for all time the scope of claims that it gave up in the Patent and Trademark Office. Third is an exhaustion of administrative remedies rationale. "If an inventor adopts a narrow definition in the Patent and Trademark Office in order to obtain a patent and then relies upon a broader definition in an infringement suit, he *pro tanto* circumvents the administrative procedures and expertise of the Office." D. Chisum, Patents § 18.05[1] (1989).

The fact that prosecution history estoppel is not a true common law estoppel may have procedural consequence. In General Instrument Corp. v. Hughes Aircraft Co., 399 F.2d 373, 158 U.S.P.Q. 498 (1st Cir. 1968), the patent owner prevailed in the district court on a finding that the accused composition fell within its claims under the doctrine of equivalents. On appeal, the defendant asserted the doctrine of file wrapper estoppel for the first time. Agreeing that file wrapper estoppel applied, the court of appeals reversed. "Were this doctrine only that of 'estoppel' and nothing more, we would be inclined to treat this as a defense which, not having been asserted below, is deemed waived. But this doctrine is more. 'It is a rule of patent construction consistently observed that a claim in a patent as allowed must be read and interpreted with reference to claims that have been cancelled or rejected, and the claims allowed cannot by construction be read to cover what was thus eliminated from the patent.' Schriber–Schroth v. Cleveland Trust Co., 311 U.S. 211, 220–221, 47 U.S.P.Q. 345, 348–349 (1940)." 399 F.2d at 385.

7. Subsequent developments in the protracted *Graver* litigation illustrate the close relationship between the doctrine of equivalents and prosecution history estoppel. Union Carbide & Carbon Corp. v. Graver Tank & Mfg. Co., Inc., 196 F.2d 103, 93 U.S.P.Q. 137 (7th Cir.1952), involved review of a judgment holding Graver in contempt for marketing a new flux series in violation of the injunction that had issued under the Supreme Court's mandate in the principal case. Union Carbide—Linde's parent—had argued in the contempt proceeding that Graver's new series, no less than its old, infringed flux claims, 18, 20, 22, 23. Specifically, it charged that the fraction of silicates in Graver's compositions—between 24% and 41% by plaintiff's count—was substantially equivalent to the "major proportion of silicates" protected by plaintiff's patent claims.

The court of appeals ruled that, by its concessions in the Patent Office, plaintiff was estopped from maintaining that a fraction of less than 50% is equivalent to a "major proportion". "We suspect, however, that plaintiff's failure previously to advance its present definition of 'a major proportion' was due to the realization that such a concession would place in serious question the validity of the claims." In argument to the examiner, plaintiff had distinguished an anticipating reference on the ground that it contained only a "minor proportion of silicates"—between 20% and 33%. Reversing the judgment below, the court of appeals noted: "The question arises, however, as to the validity of its [the doctrine of equivalents'] application where the doctrine of estoppel is properly invoked. While we find no case where this question has been discussed, we think it obvious that there are instances where both doctrines cannot be given effect because of their inconsistency." 196 F.2d at 108.

8. *Collateral Estoppel.* Can a patent owner who has once suffered a finding of invalidity relitigate the patent's validity in another action against another infringer? Until 1971, the answer was that, under the mutuality of estoppel doctrine, he could. That year, the Supreme Court decided Blonder–Tongue Laboratories, Inc. v. University of Illinois Foundation, 402 U.S. 313, 91 S.Ct. 1434, 28 L.Ed.2d 788, 169 U.S.P.Q. 513, overturning Triplett v. Lowell, 297 U.S. 638, 56 S.Ct. 645, 80 L.Ed. 949, 29 U.S.P.Q. 1 (1936) "to the extent it forecloses a plea of estoppel by one facing a charge of infringement of a patent that has once been declared invalid." 402 U.S. 313, 350, 91 S.Ct. 1434, 1453, 1454.

The Court's decision drew in part on the contemporary erosion of the mutuality of estoppel doctrine in other fields. Also, in the Court's opinion, the doctrine's cost—to plaintiffs, defendants and courts facing recurrent litigation over the same issue—far outweighed its benefits. "Some courts have frankly stated that patent litigation can present issues so complex that legal minds, without appropriate grounding in science and technology, may have difficulty in reaching decision. . . . Assuming a patent case so difficult as to provoke a frank admission of judicial uncertainty, one might ask what reason there is to expect that a second District Judge or Court of Appeals would be able to decide the issue more accurately." Finally, "when these judicial developments are considered in the light of our consistent view—last presented in Lear, Inc. v. Adkins—that the holder of a patent should not be insulated from the assertion of defenses and thus allowed to exact royalties for the use of an idea that is not in fact patentable or that is beyond the scope of the patent monopoly granted, it is apparent that the uncritical acceptance of the principle of mutuality of estoppel expressed in Triplett v. Lowell is today out of place." 402 U.S. 313, 349–350, 91 S.Ct. 1434, 1453, 1454.

The Court ruled that an alleged infringer's plea of estoppel would not entirely bar the patent owner from a second hearing. "Rather the patentee-plaintiff must be permitted to demonstrate, if he can, that he did not have a 'fair opportunity procedurally, substantively and evidentially to pursue his claim the first time.'" The Court gave some examples of the facts to be found in determining whether the patent owner had enjoyed a fair opportunity: "If the issue is nonobviousness, appropriate inquiries would be whether the first validity determination purported to employ the standards announced in Graham v. John Deere Co., whether the opinions filed by the District Court and the reviewing court, if any, indicate that the prior case was one of those relatively rare instances where the courts wholly failed to grasp the technical subject matter and issues in suit; and whether without fault of his own, the patentee was deprived of crucial evidence or witnesses in the first litigation."

Will an initial determination of a patent's *validity* bar nonparticipants in the litigation from subsequently asserting the patent's invalidity? Or is comity the only constraint? See Boutell v. Volk, 449 F.2d 673, 171 U.S.P.Q. 668 (10th Cir.1971); Columbia Broadcasting System, Inc. v. Zenith Radio Corp., 391 F.Supp. 780, 185 U.S.P.Q. 662 (N.D.Ill. 1975). ("A prior finding of validity should be given as much weight as possible consistent with the dictates of due process. Without violating due process, a court can require a defendant to prove that a factual or legal error occurred in the previous adjudication of validity or that the previous litigation was incomplete in some material aspect.") 391 F.Supp. 386. See Kidwell, Comity, Patent Validity and The Search for Symmetry: Son of Blonder–Tongue, 57 J.Pat.Off.Soc'y 473 (1975).

Kahn, Blonder–Tongue and the Shape of Future Patent Litigation, 53 J.Pat.Off.Soc'y 581 (1971), canvasses the Court's opinion for difficult questions left unanswered. On the decision generally, see Smith, The Collateral Estoppel Effect of a Prior Judgment of Patent Invalidity: Blonder–Tongue Revisited, (pts. 1, 2, 3) 55 J.Pat.Off.Soc'y 285, 363, 436 (1973), and Halpern, Blonder–Tongue: A Discussion and Analysis, (pts. 1, 2) 53 J.Pat.Off.Soc'y 761 (1971), 54 J.Pat.Off.Soc'y 5 (1972).

III. COPYRIGHT LAW

Copyright law began in England with the printing press. Within a decade after William Caxton founded his press at Westminster in 1476, the Crown sought to control the new art through royal grants of patents for printing. In 1557 control was largely transferred to the printers themselves with the formation of the Stationers' Company to prosecute printers who published seditious matter or who infringed others' licensed works. Through a series of Star Chamber decrees, royal proclamations and legislation, censorship and the regulation of piracy became inseparable. As Benjamin Kaplan observed, "copyright has the look of being gradually secreted in the interstices of the censorship." B. Kaplan, An Unhurried View of Copyright 4 (1967).

As censorship declined at the end of the seventeenth century, the Stationers petitioned Parliament for aid. The response was the Statute of Anne, 8 Ann., c. 19 (1709), the first English copyright act. The Statute established a copyright term of 14 years from the date of publication, renewable once, and provided for fines and forfeiture of infringing copies. The Stationers' role under the statute was limited to registering titles and accepting deposits of copyrighted works.

The English copyright system was adopted in the American colonies. On May 2, 1783, the Continental Congress passed a resolution urging "the several States . . . to secure to the authors or publishers of any new books . . . the copy right of such books. . . ." See U.S. Copyright Office, Copyright Enactments, Bull. No. 3, p. 1 (1973). All states but Delaware complied, most with laws modeled on the Statute of Anne. The first federal copyright law, the Act of May 31, 1790, was also closely patterned after the English statute. Congress gradually expanded the Act's original subject matter—charts and books—as new economic interests and technologies pressed for recognition. Prints were added in the Act of 1802, musical compositions in the Act of 1831, photographs and negatives in the Act of 1865, paintings, drawings, chromos, and statuary in the Act of 1870, and motion pictures in the Act of 1912, the last expansion of coverage until sound recordings were added in 1971.

Despite these expansions in coverage, the Copyright Act remained in many ways wedded to the technology of Caxton's printing press. Efforts to revise the 1909 Act began in 1955 when Congress voted funds to support research into the issues to be resolved by a new law. The research effort culminated in a 1961 Report of the Register of Copyrights on the General Revision of the U.S. Copyright Law, 87th Cong., 1st Sess. The Report provided the impetus for the First Draft General Revision Bill, H.R. 11947 and S. 3008, 88th Cong., 2d Sess., introduced in 1964. Revisions, hearings, more revisions and more hearings followed. On February 19, 1976, the Senate passed a much worn and traveled revision bill, S. 22. On September 22, 1976 the House passed a slightly different version. Both houses adopted a conference report ironing out the differences on September 30, 1976. On October 19, 1976, President Ford signed the bill into law. The law, Pub.L. No. 94–553, came into effect for most purposes on January 1, 1978.

After more than a century outside the oldest and most important international copyright convention, the United States adhered to the Berne Convention for the Protection of Literary and Artistic Works, effective March 1, 1989. The Berne Convention Implementation Act of 1988, Pub.L. No. 100–568, 102 Stat. 2853 (Oct. 31, 1988), conformed United States law to the Convention's requirements. The Act's most dramatic feature was to eliminate the requirement that copyright notice be affixed to publicly-distributed copies and phonorecords as a condition of copyright protection; after the Act's effective date, copyright notice is optional rather than mandatory.

On the early history of copyright, see L. Patterson, Copyright in Historical Perspective (1968); B. Bugbee, Genesis of American Patent and Copyright Law (1967); R. Bowker, Copyright: Its History and Its Law (1912). The efforts to revise the 1909 Copyright Act stimulated some good writing on copyright law and policy. Thirty-five studies initiated by the Copyright Office, and reprinted in Studies on Copyright (Arthur Fisher Memorial Ed. 1963), examine a variety of topics within the reform context. See also Copyright Law Revision, Report of the Register of Copyrights on the General Revision of the U.S. Copyright Law, 87th Cong., 1st Sess. (1961); Supplementary Report of the Register of Copyrights on the General Revision of the U.S. Copyright Law: 1965 Revision Bill; and Second Supplementary Report of the Register of Copyrights on the General Revision of the U.S. Copyright Law (1975). H.R.Rep. No. 94–1476, 94th Cong., 2d Sess. (1976) and House Conf.Rep. No. 94–1733, 94th Cong., 2d Sess. (1976), are the authoritative legislative sources interpreting the 1976 Act. Debate on the floor of the House of Representatives appears at pp. H–10872 through H–10911 of the Congressional Record, Vol. 122, # 144 (Daily ed., September 22, 1976).

P. Goldstein, Copyright (1989) and M. Nimmer & D. Nimmer, Nimmer on Copyright (1989) are multivolume reference works. N. Boorstyn, Copyright Law (1981) and W. Patry, Latman's The Copyright Law (6th ed. 1986) are one-volume works. M. Leaffer, Understanding Copyright Law (1989) is an excellent student text.

The Journal of the Copyright Society of the U.S.A. regularly publishes articles on copyright law as well as summaries of judicial, legislative and administrative developments in the United States and abroad. The Nathan Burkan Memorial Competition has greatly enriched copyright literature; the competition's sponsor, The American Society of Composers, Authors and Publishers, annually publishes award-winning student papers in the competition.

A. REQUIREMENTS FOR PROTECTION

1. FORMALITIES

See Statute Supplement 17 U.S.C.A. §§ 401–412, 601, 701–710.

a. NOTICE

Until March 1, 1989, the effective date of the Berne Implementation Act, successive United States copyright acts required copyright notice to appear on publicly-distributed copies of a work as a condition to the work's protection. Apart from special circumstances, if the required notice did not appear, the work fell into the public domain.

Over the course of the twentieth century, Congress and the courts gradually relaxed the notice requirement. The 1909 Copyright Act liberalized the requirement imposed by predecessor acts, and judicial decisions under the 1909 Act loosened it still more. The 1976 Act further eased the notice requirement, principally by loosening the earlier rules on form, content and position, and by carving out more generous excuses for errors or omissions. Finally, the Berne Implementation Act entirely eliminated the notice requirement in order to bring United States copyright law into compliance with the Berne Convention for the Protection of Literary and Artistic Works, to which the United States adhered, effective March 1, 1989.

Although copyright notice as a condition to protection has now disappeared from the Copyright Act, it will continue to be important in copyright litigation for many years to come. The reason is that the Berne amendments operate prospectively, eliminating the notice requirement only for copies or phonorecords disseminated after the amendments' effective date. Any work published before the amendments' effective date without the then-required notice fell into the public domain unless the error or omission was excused by the terms of the statute.

The retrospective determination whether a work has fallen into the public domain because of noncompliance with the notice formality requires an archeological dig into whether the work was published before or after the effective date of the 1976 Act, January 1, 1978. If the copies or phonorecords were publicly distributed on or after January 1, 1978, but before the effective date of the Berne amendments, the 1976 Act's notice rules will govern. If the work was published before January 1, 1978, the 1909 Act's rules will govern. As a result, a work published before January 1, 1978 without the notice required by the 1909 Act will be in the public domain today unless the terms of the 1909 Act excused the error or omission; it will make no difference that the notice would have met the 1976 Act's less stringent requirements or that the 1976 Act would have excused the error or omission.

HASBRO BRADLEY, INC. v. SPARKLE TOYS, INC.

United States Court of Appeals, Second Circuit, 1985.
780 F.2d 189, 228 U.S.P.Q. 423.

FRIENDLY, Circuit Judge:

The companies involved in this copyright case in the District Court for the Southern District of New York are Takara Co., Ltd. ("Takara"), a Japanese company that designed the toys here in question; plaintiff Hasbro Bradley, Inc. ("Hasbro"), a large American toy manufacturer and seller that acquired Takara's rights to United States copyrights for the toys; and defendant Sparkle Toys, Inc. ("Sparkle"), a smaller American toy manufacturer and seller that copied the toys in Asia from models manufactured by Takara which did not carry the copyright notice required by § 401 of the Copyright Act of 1976 (the "Act"), 17 U.S.C. § 101 et seq., and by Article III(1) of the Revised Universal Copyright Convention (U.C.C.), 25 U.S.T. 1341 (1971), to which the United States and Japan are parties. The appeal, by Sparkle, is from an order of Judge Broderick entered April 29, 1985, granting Hasbro a preliminary injunction prohibiting Sparkle from "distributing, selling, marketing, promoting, advertising, imitating or exploiting, in this country, its toys, formerly denoted 'Trans Robot,' which are in violation of plaintiff's registered copyrights in the sculptural embodiments of its 'Topspin' and 'Twin Twist' toys."

"Topspin" and "Twin Twist" (the "toys") are part of Hasbro's "The Transformers" series of changeable robotic action figures. The sculptural expressions of the toys are original designs of Takara, which manufactures "The Transformers" for Hasbro. Takara authored the designs in the summer of 1983 and by the end of November had completed molds for manufacturing the toys. These molds did not contain a copyright notice. Takara avers that the omission was due to the facts that Japanese law does not recognize copyright in toy products and that Takara was unaware that American law does recognize copyright in such works but requires notice, even on copies of the work distributed outside the United States, for copyright protection to be claimed inside the United States. Production of the unmarked toys began in December 1983 and ended in February 1984. Between January and March, approximately 213,000 of the unmarked toys were sold; thereafter, sales were minor and were made only to remove inventory. Whether the unmarked toys were sold only in Asia or some of them were sold as well in the United States is in dispute.

Hasbro was shown the toys by Takara in June 1984 and decided to adopt them into "The Transformers" series. In the course of modifying the toys to meet Hasbro's specifications, Takara designed new molds that contained a copyright notice; at the same time, it added a copyright notice to its old molds. Takara avers that after August 1984 no toys using molds that did not contain a copyright notice were manufactured for sale anywhere in the world. Hasbro has widely distributed the toys in the United States, beginning in January 1985.

Sparkle does not dispute that all of the toys sold in this country by Hasbro have born copyright notice.

Sometime in June 1984, Takara orally granted Hasbro the exclusive right to import and sell the toys in the United States and assigned to Hasbro the United States copyrights in the designs of the toys, including the right to apply for copyright registration. A written confirmation of assignment was executed as of November 12, 1984. Hasbro applied to register copyrights in the United States in both sculptural expressions of each toy on November 29, 1984, listing Takara as the "author" and itself as the "copyright claimant" by virtue of the assignment from Takara. Certificates of registration were granted effective December 3, 1984.

Discussion

The settled law of this circuit is that a preliminary injunction may be granted only upon a showing of "(a) irreparable harm and (b) either (1) likelihood of success on the merits or (2) sufficiently serious questions going to the merits to make them a fair ground for litigation and a balance of hardships tipping decidedly toward the party requesting the preliminary relief." Jackson Dairy, Inc. v. H.P. Hood & Sons, 596 F.2d 70, 72 (2 Cir.1979). Irreparable harm may ordinarily be presumed from copyright infringement. A prima facie case of copyright infringement consists of proof that the plaintiff owns a valid copyright and the defendant has engaged in unauthorized copying. Novelty Textile Mills, Inc. v. Joan Fabrics Corp., 558 F.2d 1090, 1092 (2 Cir.1977); 3 Nimmer on Copyright § 13.01 (1985) [hereafter *Nimmer*]. Since Sparkle admits to unauthorized copying, the only issue before us in reviewing the grant of the preliminary injunction is whether Hasbro's copyrights for the toys are valid. Under § 410(c) of the Act, Hasbro's certificates of copyright registration are prima facie evidence that the copyrights are valid, shifting to Sparkle the burden of proving the contrary. Sparkle attempts to meet this burden with various lines of argument, all stemming from the fact that the toys were initially sold by Takara without copyright notice. We hold that the efforts fail on the facts of this case, although we reject some of the arguments made by Hasbro in seeking to counter them.

Sparkle's most basic position is that sale of the unmarked toys by Takara in Japan injected the designs into the public domain. If the designs were truly in the public domain, Hasbro could have enjoyed no copyrights in the toys, and Sparkle's copying would have been permissible. Sparkle's argument, however, ignores the scheme for the protection of copyrightable works set up by the Act and the U.C.C. If the toys, though not initially qualifying for copyright protection, subsequently did, Sparkle's position loses its glow.

There is no dispute that the toys here at issue were originally designed by Takara in June 1983. Although the toys enjoyed no copyright protection under Japanese law,[3] they fell within the class of "pictorial, graphic, and sculptural works" covered by § 102(a)(5) of the Act. Since the toys were authored by a Japanese national and first "published" (i.e. sold) in Japan, they enjoyed copyright protection under United States law from the moment they were created by virtue of both § 104(b) of the Act and Article II(1) of the U.C.C.

As previously stated, there is also no dispute that before the assignment of Takara's copyrights to Hasbro approximately 213,000 of the toys were sold, mostly in Japan, without copyright notice. This omission of notice from toys sold by Takara or with its authority outside the United States violated § 401(a) of the Act, which requires:

> Whenever a work protected under this title is published in the United States *or elsewhere* by authority of the copyright owner, a notice of copyright as provided by this section shall be placed on all publicly distributed copies from which the work can be visually perceived, either directly or with the aid of a machine or device. (Emphasis added.)

This does not mean, however, that the Takara designs were immediately thrust into the public domain. The Act explicitly provides in § 405(a) that the omission of notice from copies of a protected work may be excused or cured under certain circumstances, in which case the copyright is valid from the moment the work was created, just as if no omission had occurred. The House Report accompanying the Act stated with respect to § 405(a) that "[u]nder the general scheme of the bill, statutory copyright protection is secured automatically when a work is created, and is not lost when the work is published, even if the copyright notice is omitted entirely." H.Rep. No. 1476, 94th Cong., 2d Sess. 147 [hereafter *House Report*], *reprinted in* 1976 U.S.Code Cong. & Ad.News 5659, 5763. In the opinion of the committee that authored the report, the excuse and cure provisions of § 405(a) represented "a major change in the theoretical framework of American copyright law." Id. at 146, *reprinted in* 1976 U.S.Code Cong. & Ad.News at 5762.[6]

It is not contended that the omission of notice from the toys could have been excused under either subsections (1) or (3) of § 405(a); rather, reliance is placed on subsection (2). In effect, § 405(a)(2) allows a person who publishes a copyrightable work without notice to hold a kind of incipient copyright in the work for five years thereafter: if the omission is cured in that time through registration and the exercise of "a reasonable effort . . . to add notice to all copies . . . that are distributed to the public in the United States after the omission has been discovered," the copyright is perfected and valid retroactively for

3. See 4 Z. Kitagawa, Doing Business in Japan § 8.02[5][c] (1985) ("[M]odels devised for the purpose of mass-producing practical goods are subject to the Design Act rather than the Copyright Act.").

6. Section 21 of the Copyright Act of 1909, Pub.L. No. 60–349, 35 Stat. 1075 (codified as amended at 17 U.S.C. (1976)), had relieved against failure to affix the notice of copyright required by § 10 only where the copyright proprietor had sought to comply with the notice provisions and the omission from a particular copy or copies was by accident or a mistake. Even in such cases damages could not be recovered against an innocent infringer who had been misled by the omission of the notice.

the entire period after cure; if the omission is not cured in that time, the incipient copyright never achieves enforceability. The *quid pro quo* in the Act for persons who have been misled by the omission of copyright notice before the cure is the more liberal provision of § 405(b), as compared with § 21 of the 1909 Act, regarding innocent infringers, of which more hereafter.

There is no dispute that Takara had not cured the omission of notice from the toys under § 405(a)(2) before assigning to Hasbro in June 1984 "the entire right, title and interest to any copyrights on the DESIGNS for the United States of America." Takara's copyrights thus were merely incipient—though subject to cure—at the time of the assignment. It is axiomatic that an assignee of a copyright can take no more than his assignor has to give. See Bong v. Alfred S. Campbell Art Co., 214 U.S. 236, 245–47, 29 S.Ct. 628, 629–30, 53 L.Ed. 979 (1909) (if a foreign author is ineligible to claim copyright under United States law, his assignee may claim no greater rights, even if the assignee would otherwise be eligible to claim copyright in the United States were he the author).

In view of this, we reject Hasbro's argument that the omission of notice by Takara is irrelevant in assessing the validity of Hasbro's copyrights. Hasbro relies on the language of § 401(a), see supra, pointing out that this requires notice only with respect to works published "by authority of the copyright owner." According to Hasbro, since it—not Takara—is the copyright owner in the United States, and since all of the toys sold by its authority in the United States and elsewhere have displayed proper copyright notice, it cannot be in violation of the notice requirement. The fallacy with this argument is that it starts by assuming the very point here in dispute: that Hasbro is the owner of valid copyrights in the United States. Our discussion of *Bong* shows that Hasbro's copyrights initially had only such validity as Takara's. For purposes of determining the validity in the United States of Takara's copyrights at the time of assignment, Takara is the relevant "copyright owner" under § 401(a). As shown above, Takara's violation of the notice requirement left Hasbro with only an incipient copyright, subject to cure.

The issue thus becomes whether Hasbro has cured Takara's omission of notice under § 405(a)(2). There is no question that Hasbro, as Takara's assignee, is permitted to effect cure through its own efforts. The "copyright claimant" entitled under the Act to register a copyright in the United States may be either the author of the work or his assignee, and any registration is of the work *per se* and redounds to the benefit of the assignor as well as the assignee. Not disputing this, Sparkle argues that Hasbro cannot effect cure under § 405(a)(2) because Takara's omission of notice was deliberate.

On its face, § 405(a)(2) is not restricted to unintentional omissions. Its language permits cure if registration is made "within five years after *the publication without notice*"—not, as Sparkle would read it, "the [unintentional] publication without notice." The difference between the broad language of § 405(a) and the more limited language of § 21 of the 1909 Act, see supra note 6, shows that Congress no longer wished to deal only with omissions of notice due to accident or mistake. Moreover, the legislative history of the 1976 Act affords ample demonstration that Congress intended to bring deliberate omissions within the ambit of § 405(a)(2). The House Report comments with respect to § 405(a) that "[u]nder the proposed law a work published without any copyright notice will still be subject to statutory protection for at least 5 years, whether the omission was partial or total, *unintentional or deliberate." House Report,* supra, at 147 (emphasis added), *reprinted in* 1976 U.S.Code Cong. & Ad.News at 5763. Professor Nimmer adds:

> In explaining the same statutory text [§ 405], the Register of Copyrights stated: ". . . it was urged that, to make the validity of a copyright turn on the question of whether the omission of notice was 'deliberate' or 'unintentional' would involve impossible problems of proof and would result in uncertainty and injustice. After considering these arguments we concluded that questions involving the subjective state of mind of one or more persons and their ignorance or knowledge of the law should be avoided if at all possible . . . we decided that the bill should drop any distinction between 'deliberate' and 'inadvertent' or 'unintentional' omission and, subject to certain conditions, should preserve the copyright in all cases." Reg.Supp.Rep., p. 105.

2 *Nimmer,* supra, § 7.13[B][3], at 7–96 n. 43.

Against this, Sparkle relies on Judge Sand's opinion in Beacon Looms, Inc. v. S. Lichtenberg & Co., 552 F.Supp. 1305 (S.D.N.Y.1982), and on Professor Nimmer's approval of the reasoning of that opinion, see 2 *Nimmer,* supra, § 7.13[B][3].

The result in *Beacon Looms* depended almost entirely on the language in § 405(a)(2) that reasonable efforts to affix notice need begin only "after the omission has been discovered." Judge Sand reasoned that since "one cannot 'discover' an omission that has been deliberate," 552 F.Supp. at 1310, to permit the cure of deliberate omissions would do violence to the unambiguous "plain meaning" of the statute. See contra O'Neill Developments, Inc. v. Galen Kilburn, Inc., 524 F.Supp. 710 (N.D.Ga.1981) (deliberate omissions curable under § 405(a)(2); reasonable efforts requirement applies to "copies published after 'discovery' of the fact that the existence of a copyright has become an issue."). In view of this supposedly plain meaning, Judge Sand felt compelled to ignore the legislative history outlined above.

With due respect, we cannot agree with *Beacon Looms.* The operative language of the statute in this context comes at the beginning of § 405(a), covers all three methods of cure, and is not restricted in any way. The language relied on by Judge Sand, which comes at the end of § 405(a)(2), is relevant only with respect to unmarked copies that have been publicly distributed in the United States. More important, the premise of the argument—namely, that a deliberate omission cannot be "discovered"—is unsound. As discussed above, an assignee or licensee may effect cure under § 405(a)(2) on behalf of itself and its assignor or licensor. In such a situation—the very one presented in this case—no violence is done to the statutory language by saying that the omission, though deliberate on the part of the assignor or licensor, was "discovered" by the person later attempting to cure it. Similarly, a deliberate omission at a lower level of a corporate hierarchy might well be "discovered," in realistic terms, by someone at a higher level. Instances like these at least indicate that the "discovered" language does not reveal a plain intent to exclude all deliberate omissions.

The meaning that § 405(a)(2) does not apply to intentional omissions thus seems to us anything but "plain." At most, the "discovered" language introduces an ambiguity. It thus becomes appropriate to look at the legislative history, and this demonstrates that intentional as well as unintentional omissions were intended to be made curable. While there may be some difficulties in determining what constitutes "a reasonable effort to add notice to all copies . . . that are distributed to the public in the United States after the omission has been discovered" in cases where the omission was intentional and the person attempting to cure is the same person who omitted notice, as argued in *Beacon Looms,* 552 F.Supp. at 1310–11, and 2 *Nimmer,* supra, § 7.13B3, at 7–96, these difficulties are by no means insuperable and constitute no sufficient reason for disregarding the declared legislative intent. We therefore conclude that the omission of notice from the toys, even if deliberate on Takara's part, was subject to cure under § 405(a)(2), and we pass on to the question whether Hasbro in fact effectuated cure.

Apart from Sparkle's contention that Hasbro committed fraud on the Copyright Office, see infra, there is no dispute that Hasbro validly registered its copyrights in the Takara designs within five years of publication of the unmarked toys, thus satisfying one of the two requirements for cure under § 405(a)(2). Sparkle admits also that Hasbro has affixed notice to all of the toys since sold under its authority in the United States and elsewhere. It argues, however, that Hasbro did not make "a reasonable effort" to affix notice to toys from the unmarked batch initially produced by Takara and thus failed to satisfy the second requirement of § 405(a)(2). Hasbro asserts that this was unnecessary: that its obligations under § 405(a)(2) are limited to unmarked toys distributed to the public in the United States by its own authority as the "copyright owner" and, insofar as we have previously concluded that this phrase includes Takara, to unmarked toys so distributed by Takara before the assignment.

We are not prepared to endorse this. The introductory words to § 405(a) indeed speak of copies "publicly distributed by authority of the copyright owner." However, as we have held above, the sales of unmarked toys by Takara in Japan before the assignment of the copyright fall within this phrase. In the absence of any prohibition on resale of these toys in the United States, the purchasers were free to sell them here. To be sure, the requirement of § 405(a)(2) to add notice is limited to copies "that are distributed to the public in the United

States," but it seems significant that Congress did not here repeat the words "by authority of the copyright owner."

We are content, however, to leave undecided the question whether Hasbro would be obligated under § 405(a)(2) to make a reasonable effort to affix notice even with respect to unmarked toys distributed in the United States by persons other than itself or Takara. At this juncture, Sparkle has yet to produce credible evidence that any of the unmarked toys have been publicly distributed in the United States *at all*, let alone evidence of who distributed them. Whether any unmarked toys were introduced into the United States and, if so, who introduced them and what efforts to mark them would be reasonable are questions that can be resolved at trial when Hasbro seeks a permanent injunction.

Sparkle further alleges that Hasbro failed to advise the Copyright Office of the prior sales of the unmarked toys by Takara when applying for registration and argues that this constituted fraud on the Copyright Office, thereby invalidating Hasbro's copyrights. But Sparkle did not respond in brief or at argument to Hasbro's contention, which is supported by the record, that the Copyright Office was informed of the sales of the unmarked toys when registration was made. Sparkle likewise has not shown that Hasbro was even obligated under the Act to give the Copyright Office this information. The legislative history of § 405(a) suggests that no such obligation exists: "[S]ince the reasons for the omission have no bearing on the validity of copyright [under § 405(a)(2)], there would be no need for the [registration] application to refer to them." *House Report,* supra, at 147, *reprinted in* 1976 U.S.Code Cong. & Ad.News at 5763. Finally, this point was not raised in the district court, and we see no reason to permit Sparkle to raise it here for the first time.

Turning finally to Sparkle's claim that it should have been recognized as an innocent infringer under § 405(b), we think the record did not contain sufficient information for the district judge to have decided this issue, and he properly declined to do so. However, it should be promptly dealt with, either on an application by Hasbro for a permanent injunction or on one by Sparkle for a declaration of its rights.

Affirmed.

NOTES

1. *Berne Amendments.* Doubtless the most dramatic feature of the Berne amendments to the 1976 Copyright Act is to make the affixation of copyright notice optional rather than mandatory. Copyright owners nonetheless have good reason to affix copyright notice to copies or phonorecords of their works. Affixation of notice may affect the copyright owner's monetary recovery for infringement. New subsections 401(d) and 402(d) provide as a general rule that if notice appears on the published copy or phonorecord to which the infringer had access, a court shall give no weight to a defense that innocent infringement mitigates actual or statutory damages.

The validity of copyright in works published on or after January 1, 1978, but before the effective date of the Berne amendments, turns on compliance with the requirements of the 1976 Copyright Act. The validity of copyright in works published before January 1, 1978 turns on compliance with the requirements of the 1909 Copyright Act. Consequently, it may be important in any case to consult the requirements of either the 1909 Act or the pre-Berne 1976 Act governing the content and position of copyright notice and the respective acts' provisions excusing faulty or omitted notice. The notes that follow discuss the rules under both acts.

2. *Content: Name of Copyright Owner.* In addition to an indication of copyright—"the symbol © . . . or the word 'Copyright,' or the abbreviation 'Copr.' "—and the year of the work's first publication, the 1976 Copyright Act provides that copyright notice shall include "the name of the owner of copyright in the work, or an abbreviation by which the name can be recognized, or a generally known alternative designation of the owner."

In Herbert Rosenthal Jewelry Corp. v. Grossbardt, 436 F.2d 315, 168 U.S.P.Q. 193 (2d Cir.1970), decided under the 1909 Act, the only notice appearing on plaintiff's jewelled bee pin consisted of the letters, "HR," within a diamond and an encircled "C" imprinted on the back of a wing. Noting that "there have been numerous holdings that the use of a well-advertised or widely known trademark or trade name on the copyrighted article itself will suffice," Judge Friendly conceded that "[o]n the specific question whether mere initials can constitute an acceptable substitute . . . the decisions are not so clear." 436 F.2d at 318. The court finally rested its decision for plaintiff on "HR" 's trademark status. "[W]e stress the evidence that Rosenthal has used HR as a trade name or mark since 1945, that it applied for trademark registration on June 1, 1962 and received it on Jan. 29, 1963 (barely three months after the first bee was sold)." 436 F.2d at 318.

Grossbardt stopped short of a possibly more extensive holding. "We thus have no occasion to consider the correctness of the statement in Dan Kasoff, Inc. v. Novelty Jewelry Co., 309 F.2d 745, 135 U.S.P.Q. 234 (2d Cir.1962), that an infringer aware of the existence of copyright is in no position to assert insufficiency of the notice." 436 F.2d 315, 319. Judge Friendly underscored his reservations about *Kasoff* a year later in Puddu v. Buonamici Statuary, Inc., 450 F.2d 401, 171 U.S.P.Q. 709 (2d Cir.1971). "Although Professor Nimmer states that even illegible notices may be good 'as against infringers who managed to decipher them or who should have been put on inquiry by the illegible printing, or who had actual notice of the plaintiff's copyright,' Nimmer, Copyright § 90.4, only three of the seven decisions cited can be said to support this proposition." 450 F.2d at 405.

By permitting use of a recognizable "abbreviation" or "a generally known alternative designation of the owner," Congress evidently intended to follow 1909 Act decisions like *Grossbardt* permitting use of the copyright owner's initials, trademark or other identifying insignia.

What is the consequence of including the wrong name in a copyright notice? See 1976 Act § 406.

3. *Content: Date.* Section 401(b)(2), which generally requires copyright notice to include the year of the work's first publication, also provides that "[t]he year date may be omitted where a pictorial, graphic, or sculptural work, with accompanying text matter, if any, is reproduced in or on greeting cards, postcards, stationery, jewelry, dolls, toys, or any useful articles. . . ." Congress probably intended this exemption, which is narrower than the 1909 Act's more general exemption for pictorial, graphic and sculptural works, to accommodate the interest of novelty producers in having their merchandise appear fresh rather than dated.

What is the consequence of including the wrong date in a copyright notice? See 1976 Act § 406.

4. *Position of Notice.* Section 20 of the 1909 Copyright Act specified the position of copyright notice for three classes of works—books or other printed publications, periodicals and musical works. For example, notice on books and other printed publications had to appear on the "title page or the page immediately following." Mislocation forfeited copyright.

Some courts were relentless in their insistence on punctilio. In Booth v. Haggard, 184 F.2d 470, 87 U.S.P.Q. 141 (8th Cir.1950), the court concluded that the cover of plaintiff's book, bearing the phrase "1948–1949, Kossuth County, Iowa TAM Service," was the book's title page and not page 3, which contained a full page of printed text bearing, at the top, the words "The 1948–1949 Rural TAM For Kossuth County, Iowa." The copyright notice, "Copyright 1948, R.C. Booth Enterprises, Harlan, Iowa," appeared at the bottom of page 3. The court held that plaintiff's notice was deficient because it did not appear on the title page or the page immediately following.

Outside section 20's requirements for books, periodicals and musical works, courts used a reasonableness standard to determine whether the location of copyright notice satisfied the statute. Sections 401(c) and 402(c) of the 1976 Act adopt this measure for all classes of works, requiring notice to be affixed to copies or placed on phonorecords so that they "give reasonable notice of the claim of copyright." Section 401(c) further provides that "[t]he Register of Copyrights shall prescribe by regulation, as examples, specific methods of affixation and positions of the notice on various types of works that will satisfy this requirement, but these specifications shall not be considered exhaustive." See 37 C.F.R. § 201.20 (1989).

5. *What Is a Copy?* What constitutes a "copy" for purposes of section 401(a)'s requirement that copyright notice be placed "on all publicly distributed copies from which the work can be visually perceived, either directly or with the aid of a machine or device"? Answers, easy in the case of a novel or motion picture, are more difficult for other types of subject matter. For example, in the case of a strip of wrapping paper bearing twelve reproductions, arranged side by side, of

a holly, mistletoe and spruce sprig cluster, what constitutes the copy—each of the twelve paintings or each strip of wrapping paper? In DeJonge & Co. v. Breuker & Kessler Co., 235 U.S. 33, 35 S.Ct. 6, 59 L.Ed. 113 (1914), in which plaintiff had affixed one copyright notice per strip, Justice Holmes agreed with the courts below that "the notice must be repeated on each of the twelve squares, although they did not present themselves as separate squares on the continuous strip." Holmes answered the assertion that "it is overtechnical to require a repetition of the notice upon every square in a single sheet that makes a harmonious whole," with the observation that "[t]his argument tacitly assumes that we can look to such larger unity as the sheet possesses. . . . The protected object does not gain more extensive privileges by being repeated several times upon one sheet of paper, as any one would recognize if it were the Gioconda. The appellant is claiming the same rights as if this work were one of the masterpieces of the world, and he must take them with the same limitations that would apply to a portrait, a holy family, or a scene of war." 235 U.S. at 36–37.

Contemporary decisions have generally departed from the DeJonge approach and held that a copy consists of any commercially discrete unit. The fabric design considered in H.M. Kolbe Co., Inc. v. Armgus Textile Co., 315 F.2d 70, 137 U.S.P.Q. 9 (2d Cir.1963), consisted of a checkerboard pattern created by the repetition of clusters of purple roses. Plaintiff printed a copyright notice on the selvage down one side of the fabric at sixteen-inch intervals. Rejecting defendant's argument "that the statute required one notice for each rose square of Kolbe's design," the court held that "the 'work' or 'reproduction of a work of art' which Kolbe sought to copyright was not merely the single rose square from which its textile design was created. It was rather the composite design itself, which depends for its aesthetic effect upon both the rose figure and the manner in which the reproductions of that figure are arranged in relation to each other upon the fabric." 315 F.2d at 72. The court distinguished DeJonge in a footnote: "Because the component picture rather than the total design was the copyrighted 'work,' the Supreme Court held that each reproduction of the picture within the design required a notice of copyright."

The Kolbe court recognized, however, that this did not completely dispose of the defendant's argument. "Because of the continuous nature of the composition design printed on Kolbe's fabric there are conceptual difficulties inherent in determining the limits of the protected 'work,' and the number of 'copies' thereof contained in a bolt of the printed fabric." The court rested its eventual determination, that notice at 16–inch intervals was sufficient, upon two practical grounds. First, the basic pattern, formed by a single revolution of the roller that embodied the master pattern, was sixteen inches in length. Second, "textiles are normally sold by the bolt at wholesale, in units of a yard at retail. By repeating its notice of copyright every 16 inches on the length of its printed fabric, therefore, Kolbe affixed at least one statutory notice to each smallest commercial unit by which its product is normally sold." 315 F.2d at 72–73.

6. *Excused Errors and Omissions.* The 1909 Copyright Act excused faulty or omitted copyright notices on narrow grounds. Section 21 of the Act provided that "[w]here the copyright proprietor has sought to comply with the provisions of this title with respect to notice, the omission by accident or mistake of the prescribed notice from a particular copy or copies" would not invalidate the copyright. In National Comics Publications, Inc. v. Fawcett Publications, Inc., 191 F.2d 594, 90 U.S.P.Q. 274 (2d Cir.1951), Judge Learned Hand suggested that a work would not lose copyright if the notice was omitted in violation of an agreement that conditioned the licensee's publication of the work on proper affixation of notice. According to Hand, publication in these circumstances would not forfeit copyright because it would not be authorized.

The 1976 Copyright Act substantially broadened the excuses for faulty or omitted notice. Section 405(a)(1) parallels section 21 of the 1909 Act by saving copyright if "the notice has been omitted from no more than a relatively small number of copies or phonorecords distributed to the public." The House Report states that the phrase, "relatively small number," is "intended to be less restrictive than the phrase 'a particular copy or copies' now in section 21 of the present law." H.R. Rep. No. 1476, 94th Cong., 2d Sess. 147 (1976). Unlike section 21, section 405(a)(1) does not require the omission to be by accident or mistake.

Section 405(a)(2), explicated in *Sparkle Toys*, allows a five-year *locus poenitentiae* for publication without notice if two requirements are met: the work is registered in the interim and a reasonable effort is made to place notice on copies publicly distributed in the United States after discovery of the omission. What constitutes "reasonable effort"? One court has held that it requires that "an expenditure of time and money over and above that required in the normal course of business will be made." Videotronics, Inc. v. Bend Electronics, 586 F.Supp. 478, 483, 223 U.S.P.Q. 936 (D.Nev.1984). Where 900,000 copies of a work had been distributed without notice, it was not a "reasonable effort" for the copyright owner to send distributors 50,000 notice labels and offer to send additional labels if needed. Beacon Looms, Inc. v. S. Lichtenberg & Co., 552 F.Supp. 1305, 220 U.S.P.Q. 960 (S.D.N.Y.1982).

What if notice is omitted without the authority of the copyright owner? Section 405(a)(3) embodies Learned Hand's suggestion in *National Comics* that a licensee's omission will have no effect if it violates an agreement requiring the licensee to affix notice. Section 405(a)(3)'s requirements are more rigorous than Hand's because they require a "writing" and because the condition must be "express." They are less rigorous since the party at fault need not be a licensee. Section 405(c) provides that the copyright's validity will be unaffected if notice, having once been affixed, is later removed without the owner's consent.

Under sections 401(a) and 402(a), for the notice requirement to apply, the work must be published "by authority of the copyright owner." Can the owner's "authority" rest on an oral or implied—

rather than a written and express—condition that notice be affixed? If so, is section 405(a)(3) surplusage?

NOTE: PUBLICATION

Publication has played an important role in United States copyright law, from the first Copyright Act, Act of May 31, 1790, to the present. The evolving statutory and judicial definition of publication, as well as the changing consequences of publication, reflect an effort to accommodate copyright law to new technologies and to the increasingly important arena of international copyright.

1. *Consequences of Publication.*

a. *1909 Act.* Until the 1976 Copyright Act, which came into effect on January 1, 1978, publication marked the dividing line between state and federal copyright protection. State common law copyright protected a work until its publication. As a rule, federal statutory copyright protected the work from the moment of publication through the expiration of a fixed twenty-eight year term, with a renewal option for a second twenty-eight year term. (The exception to the rule was section 12 of the 1909 Act which allowed the registration of certain unpublished works.) If a work was published without the notice required by the 1909 Act—and if the Act did not excuse the faulty or omitted notice—the work fell into the public domain.

b. *1976 Act.* The 1976 Copyright Act removed publication as the dividing line between state and federal protection. Protection under the 1976 Act begins not with a work's publication but, rather, with its first fixation in a tangible medium of expression. It nonetheless remains important to determine when a work was published. If a work was published without the required copyright notice before the effective date of the Berne Convention Implementation Act of 1988, March 1, 1989—and if one of the Act's curative provisions did not save the copyright—the work fell into the public domain; if, however, the work was published after the amendments' effective date, a faulty or omitted copyright notice will not affect the validity of copyright.

Publication also retains some importance in measuring the copyright term under the 1976 Act. Unlike earlier acts, which measured the term of protection from the date of publication, the 1976 Act measures the statutory term for most purposes by the life of the author plus fifty years. But the Act measures the term of protection for anonymous and pseudonymous works and works made for hire by seventy-five years from the date of the work's first publication or one hundred years from its creation, whichever expires first. Date of publication may even become important in determining the duration of copyright in works governed by the life plus fifty term. Seventy-five years after a work's first publication, or one hundred years after its creation, a prospective user of the work will generally be entitled to a presumption that the author has been dead for at least fifty years. 1976 Copyright Act § 302(e).

2. *When is a Work "Published"?*

a. *1909 Act.* In determining whether a work was published before the effective date of the 1976 Act, courts generally distinguish between *divestitive* publication—publication that forfeited common law copyright—and *investitive* publication—publication that, if made with the statutorily required notice, obtained statutory copyright for the work.

Investitive Publication. For a work to be investitively published under the 1909 Act, the copyright owner, or someone acting under his authority, had to distribute one or more copies of the work. Investitive publication generally required less extensive acts of dissemination than divestitive publication. "[C]ourts apply different tests of publication depending on whether plaintiff is claiming protection because he did not publish and hence has a common law claim of infringement—in which case the distribution must be quite large to constitute 'publication'—or whether he is claiming under the copyright statute—in which case the requirements for publication are quite narrow. In each case the courts appear so to treat the concept of 'publication' as to prevent piracy." American Visuals Corp. v. Holland, 239 F.2d 740, 744, 111 U.S.P.Q. 288 (2d Cir.1956).

Divestitive Publication. As a general rule, divestitive publication occurred under the 1909 Act when the copyright owner distributed copies of her work to the general public. The distribution, if not to the general public, could still be divestitive if the copyright owner imposed no express or implied restrictions on further distribution or copying. As a general rule, the distribution of copies to a limited class of persons and for a limited purpose did not divest common law copyright under the 1909 Act; the limited distribution had to be "to a definitely selected group and for a limited purpose, and without the right of diffusion, reproduction, distribution or sale. . . ." White v. Kimmell, 193 F.2d 744, 746–47, 92 U.S.P.Q. 400 (9th Cir.), cert. denied, 343 U.S. 957, 72 S.Ct. 1052, 96 L.Ed. 1357 (1952).

A work's dissemination other than through the distribution of copies did not divest common law copyright under the 1909 Act. For example, the display of a painting in a public gallery did not divest common law copyright in the work. American Tobacco Co. v. Werckmeister, 207 U.S. 284, 28 S.Ct. 72, 52 L.Ed. 208 (1907). One court held that it was not divestitive publication for civil rights leader, Martin Luther King, Jr. to deliver his famous address, "I Have a Dream," to a live audience of 200,000. King v. Mister Maestro, Inc., 224 F.Supp. 101 (S.D.N.Y.1963).

Public distribution of phonorecords raised hard questions under the 1909 Act. Because they did not visually reflect the musical compositions they embodied, phonograph records were not considered to be "copies" for purposes of the 1909 Act's notice requirements. The owner of common law copyright in a musical composition could secure statutory copyright by publishing sheet music bearing the statutory notice, but did not have to affix copyright notice to subsequently distributed phonorecords to maintain statutory protection. What if the common law copyright owner first disseminated his work not through the medium of sheet music but rather through the medium of phonorecords? Courts divided on whether the public distribution of phonorecords divested common law copyright in works embodied in the phonorecords. Compare Shapiro, Bernstein & Co. v. Miracle Record Co., 91 F.Supp. 473, 85 U.S.P.Q. 39 (N.D.Ill.1950), with Rosette v. Rainbo Record Mfg. Corp., 354 F.Supp. 1183, 177 U.S.P.Q. 631 (S.D.N.Y. 1973), aff'd, 546 F.2d 461, 192 U.S.P.Q. 673 (2d Cir.1976).

b. *1976 Act.* Section 101 of the 1976 Act defines "publication" as "the distribution of copies or phonorecords of a work to the public by sale or other transfer of ownership, or by rental, lease, or lending. The offering to distribute copies or phonorecords to a group of persons for purposes of further distribution, public performance, or public display, constitutes publication. A public performance or display of a work does not of itself constitute publication."

This definition of publication effectively combines the definitions of investitive and divestitive publication that evolved under the 1909 Act. "Distribution" implies that copies or phonorecords have changed hands; as under the 1909 Act, it also implies physical transfer to more than one person, although not necessarily to the public at large. While section 101 does not expressly require the distribution to be authorized by the copyright owner, it doubtless incorporates the 1909 Act's rule that unauthorized distribution does not constitute publication.

The 1976 Act also embodies the earlier rule that dissemination to a limited group for a limited purpose does not constitute publication. According to the House Report, the "public" generally consists of "persons under no explicit or implicit restrictions with respect to disclosure of [a work's] contents." H.R.Rep. No. 1476, 94th Cong., 2d Sess., 138 (1976). Section 101's statement that "public performance or display of a work does not of itself constitute publication" evidently overturns the rule that public performance or display of a work may constitute publication if the copyright owner imposes no conditions on the public's freedom to copy the work. According to the House Report, "under the definition of 'publication' in section 101, there would no longer be any basis for holding, as a few court decisions have done in the past, that the public display of a work of art under some conditions (e.g., without restriction against its reproduction) would constitute publication of the work." Id. at 144.

b. REGISTRATION AND DEPOSIT

B. KAPLAN, THE REGISTRATION OF COPYRIGHT

Study No. 17, Subcommittee on Patents, Trademarks, and Copyrights,
Senate Committee on the Judiciary, 86th Cong., 2d Sess. 35–36, 41
(Comm.Print 1960).

1. Record Material

The chief record material flowing into the Copyright Office in consequence of the various provisions of the act consists of applications for original registration and works (or substitutes) deposited therewith; applications for renewal of copyright; assignments and related documents; notices of use and notices of intention to use. The records of the Copyright Office are built fundamentally upon this submitted material. Library of Congress collections are fed from the deposited copies. . . .

3. Examination of Applications and Deposits

When applications are received in the Copyright Office, the Examining Division scrutinizes them together with the accompanying deposited copies. The check is for compliance with law, but the examiner does not and cannot investigate at large; he generally confines himself to the application and the deposited copies; occasionally, when put on inquiry by this internal examination, he may go elsewhere to relevant records of the Copyright Office. He is certainly not expected to check whether the work duplicates a previously copyrighted work or a work in the public domain. He checks for adequacy of the notice of copyright; agreement in dates, names, etc., between the application and the deposited copies; propriety of the "class" in which copyright is claimed; evident copyrightability of the work, and some other matters. The various forms of letters sent to claimants calling attention to errors spotted by the examiners, and usually soliciting corrections by the claimants, are revealing of the kind of examination that is conducted, as is section 202.2 of the Copyright Office regulations, listing common defects in the notice.

The Register has stated that an examiner is expected to deal with about 40 registrations per day. With respect to perhaps 15 percent of the applications correspondence with the claimant becomes necessary. As to rejections, the Register's annual report for fiscal 1957 says:

> Approximately 3 percent of the applications filed during the fiscal year were rejected. . . . Most rejections were in connection with published works lacking notice of copyright, uncopyrightable items, and works other than books, periodicals, or musical compositions, although many renewal applications had to be rejected because of untimely filing (p 2).

Reasons are given for rejections and claimants are permitted to present arguments in writing and orally. There is no formally established procedure by which a claimant or other interested party can secure review of a decision within the Copyright Office; but apparently informal "appeal" lies to the Chief or Assistant Chief of the Examining Division, with final resort to the Register. The policy of the Office, as we have seen, is to be liberal in registering claims.

Assignments and related instruments appearing on their face to relate to copyrights and to be properly executed are not checked but are immediately recorded. Renewal applications are checked and in ordinary cases will not be registered unless original registration has been accomplished.

When a claimant files his application and makes deposit he is in effect submitting himself to an official determination of whether he has complied with the law. The check carried out by the Examining Division is a means of enforcing both formal and substantive requirements including provisions or standards governing notice, copyrightability, manufacturing, import, etc. As a practical matter this check is perhaps the chief official instrument of law enforcement. Were it not for administrative surveillance "at the source," a considerable number of works belonging in the public domain would circulate with notice of copyright inhibiting access to the works. In many cases the check serves to advise or warn claimants about legal requirements with which they are then quite willing to comply. The fact that applications are officially examined puts a certain pressure on claimants to examine and attempt to comply with the law before attempting registration.

Administrative examination of claims to copyright is however far from complete. It is necessarily limited in the great majority of cases to a check of obvious points arising on the claimants' ex parte submissions. Invalid claims may slip by; and when they do, they carry a kind of official imprimatur which may itself operate unjustly in creating a preserve that is practically effective although legally unjustified.

The Copyright Office policy of registering doubtful claims can be objected to on the ground that it fosters "monopolies" which are in last analysis illegal. On the other side, objection has been voiced to any administrative decisions of invalidity. As these decisions are not conclusive on the courts, it has been argued that the Office should abandon the whole effort to examine claims and register all claims as such, so that the contentions of interested parties regarding particular works will be disclosed of record, giving users and others a better basis for deciding how they should act.

ORIGINAL APPALACHIAN ARTWORKS, INC. v. THE TOY LOFT, INC., 684 F.2d 821, 215 U.S.P.Q. 745 (11th Cir.1982), KRAVITCH, J.: Lawson's third defense is that Roberts is guilty of fraud and unclean hands in failing to supply certain relevant information on the copyright application. Specifically, Lawson cites Roberts' failure to list Ms. Morehead as a co-author and his failure to complete item six on the copyright application headed "Compilation or Derivative Work" as the fraudulent omissions which make OAA's copyright unenforceable.

In Russ Berrie & Co., Inc. v. Jerry Elsner Co., 482 F.Supp. 980, 205 USPQ 320 (S.D.N.Y.1980), the court found that the copyright holder had intentionally failed to inform the copyright office that his copyrighted stuffed gorilla was based on a pre-existing Japanese gorilla, and held that "the knowing failure to advise the copyright office of facts which might have occasioned a rejection of the application constitutes reason for holding the copyright invalid." Id. at 988. Similar situations occurred in Vogue Ring Creations, Inc. v. Hardman, 410 F.Supp. 609, 190 USPQ 329 (D.R.I.1976) (unexplained omission of pre-existing work coupled with other misleading conduct made copyright unenforceable); and Ross Products, Inc. v. New York Merchandise Co., 242 F.Supp. 878, 146 USPQ 107 (S.D.N.Y.1965) (failure to indicate prior publication of work in Japan raised issue of whether omission was purposeful thus invalidating copyright).

While these cases establish that omissions or misrepresentations in a copyright application can render the registration invalid, a common element among them has been intentional or purposeful concealment of relevant information. Where this element of "scienter" is lacking, courts generally have upheld the copyright. See Advisers, Inc. v. Wiesen–Hart, Inc., 238 F.2d 706, 708, 111 USPQ 318, 319 (6th Cir.1956) ("innocent misstatement * * * in the affidavit and certificate of registration, unaccompanied by fraud" does not invalidate copyright); Ross Products, supra, 242 F.Supp. at 879, 146 USPQ at 108 (cases overlooking omissions or misstatements emphasize "that the errors involved were honest, innocent and not intended to be misleading"). See also Mitchell Brothers Film Group v. Cinema Adult Theater, 604 F.2d 852, 863, 203 USPQ 1041, 1050 (5th Cir.1979) (doctrine of unclean hands does not bar relief unless defendant can show he has personally been injured by plaintiff's conduct).

The evidence in this case fails to show the scienter element necessary for Lawson to assert his claim successfully. Roberts explained that his omission of Morehead as a co-author was due to Morehead's leaving the doll operation in February 1978 and indicating she wanted nothing further to do with the company. Given that Roberts freely admitted he and Morehead had collaborated on the dolls, and that several newspaper and magazine articles during 1977 indicated that the dolls were the joint product of Roberts and Morehead, we find it impossible to ascribe to this omission an intent to mislead. As to item 6, the pre-existing works, the undisputed evidence showed that Roberts and Allen completed this item initially in some detail, even indicating that the dolls were derived in part from viewing other artists' soft-sculpture work. Although item 6 was left blank in the application that finally was filed with the copyright office, the sole reason for this omission was that after speaking to copyright office personnel, Roberts and Allen thought that the information was unnecessary. Accordingly, we reject Lawson's assertion that OAA's copyright is unenforceable due to fraud on the Copyright Office.

FORM TX
UNITED STATES COPYRIGHT OFFICE

REGISTRATION NUMBER

_____

TX _____ TXU _____
EFFECTIVE DATE OF REGISTRATION

_____

Month   Day   Year

DO NOT WRITE ABOVE THIS LINE. IF YOU NEED MORE SPACE, USE A SEPARATE CONTINUATION SHEET.

1

TITLE OF THIS WORK ▼

PREVIOUS OR ALTERNATIVE TITLES ▼

PUBLICATION AS A CONTRIBUTION   If this work was published as a contribution to a periodical, serial, or collection, give information about the collective work in which the contribution appeared.   **Title of Collective Work ▼**

If published in a periodical or serial give: **Volume ▼**   **Number ▼**   **Issue Date ▼**   **On Pages ▼**

2
a

NAME OF AUTHOR ▼

DATES OF BIRTH AND DEATH
Year Born ▼   Year Died ▼

Was this contribution to the work a   "work made for hire"?
☐ Yes
☐ No

AUTHOR'S NATIONALITY OR DOMICILE
Name of Country
OR { Citizen of ▶ _____
{ Domiciled in ▶ _____

WAS THIS AUTHOR'S CONTRIBUTION TO THE WORK
Anonymous?   ☐ Yes ☐ No
Pseudonymous? ☐ Yes ☐ No
If the answer to either of these questions is "Yes," see detailed instructions.

NATURE OF AUTHORSHIP   Briefly describe nature of the material created by this author in which copyright is claimed. ▼

NOTE
Under the law, the "author" of a "work made for hire" is generally the employer, not the employee (see instructions). For any part of this work that was "made for hire" check "Yes" in the space provided, give the employer (or other person for whom the work was prepared) as "Author" of that part, and leave the space for dates of birth and death blank.

b

NAME OF AUTHOR ▼

DATES OF BIRTH AND DEATH
Year Born ▼   Year Died ▼

Was this contribution to the work a   "work made for hire"?
☐ Yes
☐ No

AUTHOR'S NATIONALITY OR DOMICILE
Name of country
OR { Citizen of ▶ _____
{ Domiciled in ▶ _____

WAS THIS AUTHOR'S CONTRIBUTION TO THE WORK
Anonymous?   ☐ Yes ☐ No
Pseudonymous? ☐ Yes ☐ No
If the answer to either of these questions is "Yes," see detailed instructions.

NATURE OF AUTHORSHIP   Briefly describe nature of the material created by this author in which copyright is claimed. ▼

c

NAME OF AUTHOR ▼

DATES OF BIRTH AND DEATH
Year Born ▼   Year Died ▼

Was this contribution to the work a   "work made for hire"?
☐ Yes
☐ No

AUTHOR'S NATIONALITY OR DOMICILE
Name of Country
OR { Citizen of ▶ _____
{ Domiciled in ▶ _____

WAS THIS AUTHOR'S CONTRIBUTION TO THE WORK
Anonymous?   ☐ Yes ☐ No
Pseudonymous? ☐ Yes ☐ No
If the answer to either of these questions is "Yes," see detailed instructions.

NATURE OF AUTHORSHIP   Briefly describe nature of the material created by this author in which copyright is claimed. ▼

3

YEAR IN WHICH CREATION OF THIS WORK WAS COMPLETED This information must be given in all cases.
◀ Year

DATE AND NATION OF FIRST PUBLICATION OF THIS PARTICULAR WORK
Complete this information ONLY if this work has been published.
Month ▶ _____ Day ▶ _____ Year ▶ _____
◀ Nation

4

Instructions for completing this space

COPYRIGHT CLAIMANT(S) Name and address must be given even if the claimant is the same as the author given in space 2.▼

TRANSFER If the claimant(s) named here in space 4 are different from the author(s) named in space 2, give a brief statement of how the claimant(s) obtained ownership of the copyright.▼

APPLICATION RECEIVED

ONE DEPOSIT RECEIVED

TWO DEPOSITS RECEIVED

REMITTANCE NUMBER AND DATE

DO NOT WRITE HERE
OFFICE USE ONLY

MORE ON BACK ▶ • Complete all applicable spaces (numbers 5-11) on the reverse side of this page.
• See detailed instructions.   • Sign the form at line 10.

DO NOT WRITE HERE

Page 1 of _____ pages

EXAMINED BY	FORM TX
CHECKED BY	
☐ CORRESPONDENCE Yes	FOR COPYRIGHT OFFICE USE ONLY
☐ DEPOSIT ACCOUNT FUNDS USED	

DO NOT WRITE ABOVE THIS LINE. IF YOU NEED MORE SPACE, USE A SEPARATE CONTINUATION SHEET.

5

PREVIOUS REGISTRATION Has registration for this work, or for an earlier version of this work, already been made in the Copyright Office?
☐ Yes ☐ No If your answer is "Yes," why is another registration being sought? (Check appropriate box) ▼
☐ This is the first published edition of a work previously registered in unpublished form.
☐ This is the first application submitted by this author as copyright claimant.
☐ This is a changed version of the work, as shown by space 6 on this application.
If your answer is "Yes," give: **Previous Registration Number** ▼   **Year of Registration** ▼

6

DERIVATIVE WORK OR COMPILATION Complete both space 6a & 6b for a derivative work; complete only 6b for a compilation.
a. Preexisting Material Identify any preexisting work or works that this work is based on or incorporates. ▼

See instructions before completing this space.

b. Material Added to This Work Give a brief, general statement of the material that has been added to this work and in which copyright is claimed. ▼

7

MANUFACTURERS AND LOCATIONS If this is a published work consisting preponderantly of nondramatic literary material in English, the law may require that the copies be manufactured in the United States or Canada for full protection. If so, the names of the manufacturers who performed certain processes, and the places where these processes were performed **must** be given. See instructions for details.
Names of Manufacturers ▼   **Places of Manufacture** ▼

8

REPRODUCTION FOR USE OF BLIND OR PHYSICALLY HANDICAPPED INDIVIDUALS A signature on this form at space 10, and a check in one of the boxes here in space 8, constitutes a non-exclusive grant of permission to the Library of Congress to reproduce and distribute solely for the blind and physically handicapped and under the conditions and limitations prescribed by the regulations of the Copyright Office: (1) copies of the work identified in space 1 of this application in Braille (or similar tactile symbols); or (2) phonorecords embodying a fixation of a reading of that work; or (3) both.
   a ☐ Copies and Phonorecords   b ☐ Copies Only   c ☐ Phonorecords Only   *See instructions.*

9

DEPOSIT ACCOUNT If the registration fee is to be charged to a Deposit Account established in the Copyright Office, give name and number of Account.
Name ▼   **Account Number** ▼

CORRESPONDENCE Give name and address to which correspondence about this application should be sent. Name/Address/Apt/City/State/Zip ▼

Be sure to give your daytime phone ◄ number.

Area Code & Telephone Number ▶

10

CERTIFICATION* I, the undersigned, hereby certify that I am the
Check one ▶
☐ author
☐ other copyright claimant
☐ owner of exclusive right(s)
☐ authorized agent of _____
Name of author or other copyright claimant, or owner of exclusive right(s) ▲

of the work identified in this application and that the statements made by me in this application are correct to the best of my knowledge.

Typed or printed name and date ▼ If this is a published work, this date must be the same as or later than the date of publication given in space 3.
_____ date ▶ _____

✍ **Handwritten signature (X)** ▼

11

MAIL CERTIFI-CATE TO
Name ▼
Number/Street/Apartment Number ▼
City/State/ZIP ▼

Certificate will be mailed in window envelope

Have you:
• Completed all necessary spaces?
• Signed your application in space 10?
• Enclosed check or money order for $10 payable to *Register of Copyrights?*
• Enclosed your deposit material with the application and fee?
MAIL TO: Register of Copyrights, Library of Congress, Washington, D.C. 20559

* 17 U.S.C. § 506(e): Any person who knowingly makes a false representation of a material fact in the application for copyright registration provided for by section 409, or in any written statement filed in connection with the application, shall be fined not more than $2,500.

☆ U.S. GOVERNMENT PRINTING OFFICE: 1983: 381-278/507   Sept. 1983—600,000

NOTES

1. *Reasons to Register.* Registration is not a condition of copyright protection, and a copyright owner may obtain registration for her work at any time during the copyright term. The 1976 Copyright Act offers several incentives to prompt registration. Section 405(a)(2) allows registration to cure errors or omissions in copyright notice only if "registration for the work has been made before or is made within five years after the publication without notice." Section 410(c) limits the

automatic prima facie effect of registration certificates to registrations made "before or within five years after first publication of the work." As a general rule, section 412 provides that no award of statutory damages or attorney's fees can be made for "(1) any infringement of copyright in an unpublished work commenced before the effective date of its registration; or (2) any infringement of copyright commenced after first publication of the work and before the effective date of its registration, unless such registration is made within three months after the first publication of the work."

2. *Registration as a Condition to Suit.* Before the effective date of the Berne Implementation Act, March 1, 1989, section 411(a) of the 1976 Act generally required copyright owners to obtain registration in order to file a copyright infringement action. As amended, section 411(a) retains this requirement for works originating in the United States, but eliminates the requirement for works originating in other countries belonging to the Berne Convention. The amendments' exemption for works originating in other Berne member countries is a compromise between the Senate bill—which viewed registration as a formal condition of protection proscribed by the Berne Convention— and the House bill—which did not view registration as a condition to protection, and would have retained the requirement for both domestic and foreign works. See Joint Explanatory Statement on House–Senate Compromise Incorporated in Senate Amendment to H.R. 4262, 134 Cong.Rec. H10095 (daily ed. Oct. 12, 1988).

3. *Classification.* Application Form TX, reproduced above, covers nondramatic literary works such as fiction, nonfiction, poetry, directories, catalogs, advertising copy and periodicals. The Register of Copyrights has prescribed three other classes of works for purposes of copyright registration. Class PA covers works "prepared for the purpose of being performed directly before an audience or indirectly by means of a device or process," including musical works, dramatic works, choreographic works, and motion pictures and other audiovisual works. Class VA encompasses pictorial, graphic and sculptural works such as photographs, maps, advertisements, and works of fine, graphic and applied arts. Class SR covers "all published and unpublished sound recordings fixed on and after February 15, 1972." 37 C.F.R. § 202.3(b) (1989).

4. *Deposit.* Deposit of copies or phonorecords of a copyrighted work in the Copyright Office is not a condition to copyright protection. However, deposit is mandatory. Failure to deposit copies or phonorecords within three months after receiving a written demand for deposit from the Register of Copyrights will expose the person obligated to make the deposit to fines and charges. 1976 Act § 407(d). Section 407's purpose is to supply the Library of Congress with copies and phonorecords for its collections.

5. *"Secure Tests."* The Copyright Office's "secure test" regulations attempt to reconcile the registration and deposit provisions with interests in closeting some copyrighted information—such as questions

repeatedly used in standardized tests—from public view. "In the case of tests, and answer material for tests, published separately from other literary works, the deposit of one complete copy will suffice in lieu of two copies. In the case of any secure test the Copyright Office will return the deposit to the applicant promptly after examination: Provided, That sufficient portions, description, or the like are retained so as to constitute a sufficient archival record of the deposit." 37 C.F.R. 202.20(c)(2)(vi) (1989). The Regulations define "secure test" in part as "a non-marketed test administered under supervision at specified centers on specific dates, all copies of which are accounted for and either destroyed or returned to restricted locked storage following each administration." 37 C.F.R. § 202.20(b)(4) (1989).

In National Conference of Bar Examiners v. Multistate Legal Studies, Inc., 692 F.2d 478, 216 U.S.P.Q. 279 (7th Cir.1982), cert. denied, 464 U.S. 814, 104 S.Ct. 69, 78 L.Ed.2d 83 (1983), the copyright owner of the multistate portion of state bar examinations sued a bar review program for reconstructing and reproducing questions from its exam. The defendant answered that the secure test regulations, under which the plaintiff had obtained its copyright registration, exceeded the Register's statutory authority and that, if the statute authorized the regulation, it violated the Constitution's copyright clause, art. 1, § 8, cl. 8.

The court rejected both arguments. Against the argument that section 704(d) requires the Library of Congress to retain the entire deposit of an unpublished work during the copyright term, and that section 408(b) requires a deposit to include "in the case of unpublished works, one complete copy or phonorecord," the court cited section 408(c)(1)'s provision that "[t]he Register of Copyrights is authorized to specify by regulation the administrative classes into which works are to be placed for purposes of deposit and registration, and the nature of the copies or phonorecords to be deposited in the various classes specified. The regulations may require or permit, for particular classes, the deposit of identifying material instead of copies or phonorecords, the deposit of only one copy or phonorecord where two would normally be required, or a single registration for a group of related works." 692 F.2d at 483.

The court also rejected defendant's argument "that the regulation serves to conceal the deposited material from public view and thus defeats the purpose of copyright registration as mandated by art. I, § 8 cl. 8, of the United States Constitution. . . ." Against the claim that "actual copies are necessary to provide a public record that delineates the scope of the copyright monopoly," the court concluded that "the statutory scheme of the Copyright Act demonstrates that the deposit provisions are not for the purposes of disclosure." 692 F.2d at 484–86.

6. *The Register's Authority.* Several judicial decisions have sketched in the Register's authority over registration. Bouvé v. Twentieth Century–Fox Film Corp., 122 F.2d 51, 50 U.S.P.Q. 338 (D.C.Cir. 1941), described the Register's role: "It seems obvious . . . that the Act establishes a wide range of selection within which discretion must

be exercised by the Register in determining what he has no power to accept. The formula which he must apply is a more difficult one than that of the Recorder of Deeds, upon which appellee relies by way of analogy. Nor would there seem to be any doubt that the Register may refuse to issue a certificate of registration until the required fee is paid, and until other formal requisites of the Act have been satisfied." 122 F.2d at 53–54. The Register's discretion is bounded, however, and decisions refusing registration must explain the statutory basis for refusal. See Atari Games Corp. v. Oman, 888 F.2d 878, 12 U.S.P.Q.2d 1791 (D.C.Cir.1989).

Under the 1909 Copyright Act, a copyright owner could not bring an infringement action until it had registered its claim to copyright. If the Register refused registration, an infringement suit had to await the copyright owner's success in a direct action against the Register. Vacheron & Constantin–Le Coultre Watches, Inc. v. Benrus Watch Co., 260 F.2d 637, 119 U.S.P.Q. 189 (2d Cir.1958). Section 411(a) of the 1976 Act reversed the *Vacheron* rule, and allows the applicant to institute an infringement action if the "deposit, application and fee required for registration have been delivered to the Copyright Office in proper form and registration has been refused." The copyright owner must give notice of the action and a copy of the complaint to the Register, who is allowed to intervene.

Copyright owners, particularly in fast-paced industries like newspaper and magazine publishing, sometimes need an injunction within days of publication and cannot abide the delay that registration entails. Does section 411(a) enable them to bring an infringement action without registration? Compare sections 410(d) and 411(b).

2. STATUTORY SUBJECT MATTER

See Statute Supplement 17 U.S.C.A. §§ 101–105.

COPYRIGHT LAW REVISION, H.R. REP. NO. 94–1476
94th Cong., 2d Sess. 51–58 (1976).

Section 102. General Subject Matter of Copyright

"Original Works of Authorship"

The two fundamental criteria of copyright protection—originality and fixation in tangible form—are restated in the first sentence of this cornerstone provision. The phrase "original works of authorship," which is purposely left undefined, is intended to incorporate without change the standard of originality established by the courts under the present copyright statute. This standard does not include requirements of novelty, ingenuity, or esthetic merit, and there is no intention to enlarge the standard of copyright protection to require them.

In using the phrase "original works of authorship," rather than "all the writings of an author" now in section 4 of the statute, the committee's purpose is to avoid exhausting the constitutional power of

Congress to legislate in this field, and to eliminate the uncertainties arising from the latter phrase. Since the present statutory language is substantially the same as the empowering language of the Constitution, a recurring question has been whether the statutory and the constitutional provisions are coextensive. If so, the courts would be faced with the alternative of holding copyrightable something that Congress clearly did not intend to protect, or of holding constitutionally incapable of copyright something that Congress might one day want to protect. To avoid these equally undesirable results, the courts have indicated that "all the writings of an author" under the present statute is narrower in scope than the "writings" of "authors" referred to in the Constitution. The bill avoids this dilemma by using a different phrase—"original works of authorship"—in characterizing the general subject matter of statutory copyright protection.

The history of copyright law has been one of gradual expansion in the types of works accorded protection, and the subject matter affected by this expansion has fallen into two general categories. In the first, scientific discoveries and technological developments have made possible new forms of creative expression that never existed before. In some of these cases the new expressive forms—electronic music, filmstrips, and computer programs, for example—could be regarded as an extension of copyrightable subject matter Congress had already intended to protect, and were thus considered copyrightable from the outset without the need of new legislation. In other cases, such as photographs, sound recordings, and motion pictures, statutory enactment was deemed necessary to give them full recognition as copyrightable works.

Authors are continually finding new ways of expressing themselves, but it is impossible to foresee the forms that these new expressive methods will take. The bill does not intend either to freeze the scope of copyrightable subject matter at the present stage of communications technology or to allow unlimited expansion into areas completely outside the present congressional intent. Section 102 implies neither that that subject matter is unlimited nor that new forms of expression within that general area of subject matter would necessarily be unprotected.

The historic expansion of copyright has also applied to forms of expression which, although in existence for generations or centuries, have only gradually come to be recognized as creative and worthy of protection. The first copyright statute in this country, enacted in 1790, designated only "maps, charts, and books"; major forms of expression such as music, drama, and works of art achieved specific statutory recognition only in later enactments. Although the coverage of the present statute is very broad, and would be broadened further by the explicit recognition of all forms of choreography, there are unquestionably other areas of existing subject matter that this bill does not propose to protect but that future Congresses may want to.

Fixation in Tangible Form

As a basic condition of copyright protection, the bill perpetuates the existing requirement that a work be fixed in a "tangible medium of expression," and adds that this medium may be one "now known or later developed," and that the fixation is sufficient if the work "can be perceived, reproduced, or otherwise communicated, either directly or with the aid of a machine or device." This broad language is intended to avoid the artificial and largely unjustifiable distinctions, derived from cases such as White–Smith Publishing Co. v. Apollo Co., 209 U.S. 1, 28 S.Ct. 319, 52 L.Ed. 655 (1908), under which statutory copyrightability in certain cases has been made to depend upon the form or medium in which the work is fixed. Under the bill it makes no difference what the form, manner, or medium of fixation may be— whether it is in words, numbers, notes, sounds, pictures, or any other graphic or symbolic indicia, whether embodied in a physical object in written, printed, photographic, sculptural, punched, magnetic, or any other stable form, and whether it is capable of perception directly or by means of any machine or device "now known or later developed."

Under the bill, the concept of fixation is important since it not only determines whether the provisions of the statute apply to a work, but it also represents the dividing line between common law and statutory protection. As will be noted in more detail in connection with section 301, an unfixed work of authorship, such as an improvisation or an unrecorded choreographic work, performance, or broadcast, would continue to be subject to protection under State common law or statute, but would not be eligible for Federal statutory protection under section 102.

The bill seeks to resolve, through the definition of "fixation" in section 101, the status of live broadcasts—sports, news coverage, live performances of music, etc.—that are reaching the public in unfixed form but that are simultaneously being recorded. When a football game is being covered by four television cameras, with a director guiding the activities of the four cameramen and choosing which of their electronic images are sent out to the public and in what order, there is little doubt that what the cameramen and the director are doing constitutes "authorship." The further question to be considered is whether there has been a fixation. If the images and sounds to be broadcast are first recorded (on a video tape, film, etc.) and then transmitted, the recorded work would be considered a "motion picture" subject to statutory protection against unauthorized reproduction or retransmission of the broadcast. If the program content is transmitted live to the public while being recorded at the same time, the case would be treated the same; the copyright owner would not be forced to rely on common law rather than statutory rights in proceeding against an infringing user of the live broadcast.

Thus, assuming it is copyrightable—as a "motion picture" or "sound recording," for example—the content of a live transmission should be regarded as fixed and should be accorded statutory protection if it is being recorded simultaneously with its transmission. On the other hand, the definition of "fixation" would exclude from the concept purely evanescent or transient reproductions such as those projected briefly on a screen, shown electronically on a television or other cathode ray tube, or captured momentarily in the "memory" of a computer.

Under the first sentence of the definition of "fixed" in section 101, a work would be considered "fixed in a tangible medium of expression" if there has been an authorized embodiment in a copy or phonorecord and if that embodiment "is sufficiently permanent or stable" to permit the work "to be perceived, reproduced, or otherwise communicated for a period of more than transitory duration." The second sentence makes clear that, in the case of "a work consisting of sounds, images, or both, that are being transmitted," the work is regarded as "fixed" if a fixation is being made at the same time as the transmission.

Under this definition "copies" and "phonorecords" together will comprise all of the material objects in which copyrightable works are capable of being fixed. The definitions of these terms in section 101, together with their usage in section 102 and throughout the bill, reflect a fundamental distinction between the "original work" which is the product of "authorship" and the multitude of material objects in which it can be embodied. Thus, in the sense of the bill, a "book" is not a work of authorship, but is a particular kind of "copy." Instead, the author may write a "literary work," which in turn can be embodied in a wide range of "copies" and "phonorecords," including books, periodicals, computer punch cards, microfilm, tape recordings, and so forth. It is possible to have an "original work of authorship" without having a "copy" or "phonorecord" embodying it, and it is also possible to have a "copy" or "phonorecord" embodying something that does not qualify as an "original work of authorship." The two essential elements—original work and tangible object—must merge through fixation in order to produce subject matter copyrightable under the statute.

Categories of Copyrightable Works

The second sentence of section 102 lists seven broad categories which the concept of "works of authorship" is said to "include." The use of the word "include," as defined in section 101, makes clear that the listing is "illustrative and not limitative," and that the seven categories do not necessarily exhaust the scope of "original works of authorship" that the bill is intended to protect. Rather, the list sets out the general area of copyrightable subject matter, but with sufficient flexibility to free the courts from rigid or outmoded concepts of the scope of particular categories. The items are also overlapping in the sense that a work falling within one class may encompass works coming within some or all of the other categories. In the aggregate, the list covers all classes of works now specified in section 5 of title 17; in addition, it specifically enumerates "pantomimes and choreographic works".

Of the seven items listed, four are defined in section 101. The three undefined categories—"musical works," "dramatic works," and "pantomimes and choreographic works"—have fairly settled meanings. There is no need, for example, to specify the copyrightability of electronic or concrete music in the statute since the form of a work would no longer be of any importance, nor is it necessary to specify that "choreographic works" do not include social dance steps and simple routines.

The four items defined in section 101 are "literary works," "pictorial, graphic, and sculptural works," "motion pictures and audiovisual works," and "sound recordings." In each of these cases, definitions are needed not only because the meaning of the term itself is unsettled but also because the distinction between "work" and "material object" requires clarification. The term "literary works" does not connote any criterion of literary merit or qualitative value: it includes catalogs, directories, and similar factual reference, or instructional works and compilations of data. It also includes computer data bases, and computer programs to the extent that they incorporate authorship in the programmer's expression of original ideas, as distinguished from the ideas themselves.

Correspondingly, the definition of "pictorial, graphic, and sculptural works" carries with it no implied criterion of artistic taste, aesthetic value, or intrinsic quality. The term is intended to comprise not only "works of art" in the traditional sense but also works of graphic art and illustration, art reproductions, plans and drawings, photographs and reproductions of them, maps, charts, globes, and other cartographic works, works of these kinds intended for use in advertising and commerce, and works of "applied art." There is no intention whatever to narrow the scope of the subject matter now characterized in section 5(k) as "prints or labels used for articles of merchandise." However, since this terminology suggests the material object in which a work is embodied rather than the work itself, the bill does not mention this category separately.

In accordance with the Supreme Court's decision in Mazer v. Stein, 347 U.S. 201, 74 S.Ct. 460, 98 L.Ed. 630 (1954), works of "applied art" encompass all original pictorial, graphic, and sculptural works that are intended to be or have been embodied in useful articles, regardless of factors such as mass production, commercial exploitation, and the potential availability of design patent protection. The scope of exclusive rights in these works is given special treatment in section 113, to be discussed below.

The Committee has added language to the definition of "pictorial, graphic, and sculptural works" in an effort to make clearer the distinction between works of applied art protectable under the bill and industrial designs not subject to copyright protection. The declaration that "pictorial, graphic, and sculptural works" include "works of artistic craftsmanship insofar as their form but not their mechanical or utilitarian aspects are concerned" is classic language: it is drawn from Copyright Office regulations promulgated in the 1940's and expressly endorsed by the Supreme Court in the *Mazer* case.

The second part of the amendment states that "the design of a useful article . . . shall be considered a pictorial, graphic, or sculptural work only if, and only to the extent that, such design incorporates pictorial, graphic, or sculptural features that can be identified separately from, and are capable of existing independently of, the utilitarian aspects of the article." A "useful article" is defined as "an article having an intrinsic utilitarian function that is not merely to portray the appearance of the article or to convey information." This part of the amendment is an adaptation of language added to the Copyright Office Regulations in the mid–1950's in an effort to implement the Supreme Court's decision in the *Mazer* case.

In adopting this amendatory language, the Committee is seeking to draw as clear a line as possible between copyrightable works of applied art and uncopyrighted works of industrial design. A two-dimensional painting, drawing, or graphic work is still capable of being identified as such when it is printed on or applied to utilitarian articles such as textile fabrics, wallpaper, containers, and the like. The same is true when a statue or carving is used to embellish an industrial product or, as in the *Mazer* case, is incorporated into a product without losing its ability to exist independently as a work of art. On the other hand, although the shape of an industrial product may be aesthetically satisfying and valuable, the Committee's intention is not to offer it copyright protection under the bill. . . .

Enactment of Public Law 92–140 in 1971 marked the first recognition in American copyright law of sound recordings as copyrightable works. As defined in section 101, copyrightable "sound recordings" are original works of authorship comprising an aggregate of musical, spoken, or other sounds that have been fixed in tangible form. The copyrightable work comprises the aggregation of sounds and not the tangible medium of fixation. Thus, "sound recordings" as copyrightable subject matter are distinguished from "phonorecords," the latter being physical objects in which sounds are fixed. They are also distinguished from any copyrighted literary, dramatic, or musical works that may be reproduced on a "phonorecord."

As a class of subject matter, sound recordings are clearly within the scope of the "writings of an author" capable of protection under the Constitution, and the extension of limited statutory protection to them was too long delayed. Aside from cases in which sounds are fixed by some purely mechanical means without originality of any kind, the copyright protection that would prevent the reproduction and distribution of unauthorized phonorecords of sound recordings is clearly justified.

The copyrightable elements in a sound recording will usually, though not always, involve "authorship" both on the part of the performers whose performance is captured and on the part of the record producer responsible for setting up the recording session, capturing and electronically processing the sounds, and compiling and editing them to make the final sound recording. There may, however, be cases where the record producer's contribution is so minimal that the performance is the only copyrightable element in the work, and there may be cases (for example, recordings of birdcalls, sounds of racing cars, et cetera) where only the record producer's contribution is copyrightable.

Sound tracks of motion pictures, long a nebulous area in American copyright law, are specifically included in the definition of "motion pictures," and excluded in the definition of "sound recordings." To be a "motion picture," as defined, requires three elements: (1) a series of images, (2) the capability of showing the images in certain successive order, and (3) an impression of motion when the images are thus shown. Coupled with the basic requirements of original authorship and fixation in tangible form, this definition encompasses a wide range of cinematographic works embodied in films, tapes, video disks, and other media. However, it would not include: (1) unauthorized fixations of live performances or telecasts, (2) live telecasts that are not fixed simultaneously with their transmission, or (3) filmstrips and slide sets which, although consisting of a series of images intended to be shown in succession, are not capable of conveying an impression of motion.

On the other hand, the bill equates audiovisual materials such as filmstrips, slide sets, and sets of transparencies with "motion pictures" rather than with "pictorial, graphic, and sculptural works." Their sequential showing is closer to a "performance" than to a "display," and the definition of "audiovisual works," which applies also to "motion pictures," embraces works consisting of a series of related images that are by their nature, intended for showing by means of projectors or other devices.

Nature of Copyright

Copyright does not preclude others from using the ideas or information revealed by the author's work. It pertains to the literary, musical, graphic, or artistic form in which the author expressed intellectual concepts. Section 102(b) makes clear that copyright protection does not extend to any idea, procedure, process, system, method of operation, concept, principle, or discovery, regardless of the form in which it is described, explained, illustrated, or embodied in such work.

Some concern has been expressed lest copyright in computer programs should extend protection to the methodology or processes adopted by the programmer, rather than merely to the "writing" expressing his ideas. Section 102(b) is intended, among other things, to make clear that the expression adopted by the programmer is the copyrightable element in a computer program, and that the actual processes or methods embodied in the program are not within the scope of the copyright law.

Section 102(b) in no way enlarges or contracts the scope of copyright protection under the present law. Its purpose is to restate, in the context of the new single Federal system of copyright, that the basic dichotomy between expression and idea remains unchanged.

Section 103. Compilations and Derivative Works

Section 103 complements section 102: A compilation or derivative work is copyrightable if it represents an "original work of authorship" and falls within one or more of the categories listed in section 102. Read together, the two sections make plain that the criteria of copyrightable subject matter stated in section 102 apply with full force to works that are entirely original and to those containing preexisting material. Section 103(b) is also intended to define, more sharply and clearly than does section 7 of the present law, the important interrelationship and correlation between protection of preexisting and of "new" material in a particular work. The most important point here is one that is commonly misunderstood today: copyright in a "new version" covers only the material added by the later author, and has no effect one way or the other on the copyright or public domain status of the preexisting material.

Between them the terms "compilations" and "derivative works" which are defined in section 101, comprehend every copyrightable work that employs preexisting material or data of any kind. There is necessarily some overlapping between the two, but they basically represent different concepts. A "compilation" results from a process of selecting, bringing together, organizing, and arranging previously existing material of all kinds, regardless of whether the individual items in the material have been or ever could have been subject to copyright. A "derivative work," on the other hand, requires a process of recasting, transforming, or adapting "one or more preexisting works"; the "preexisting work" must come within the general subject matter of copyright set forth in section 102, regardless of whether it is or was ever copyrighted.

The second part of the sentence that makes up section 103(a) deals with the status of a compilation or derivative work unlawfully employing preexisting copyrighted material. In providing that protection does not extend to "any part of the work in which such material has been used unlawfully," the bill prevents an infringer from benefiting, through copyright protection, from committing an unlawful act, but preserves protection for those parts of the work that do not employ the preexisting work. Thus, an unauthorized translation of a novel could not be copyrighted at all, but the owner of copyright in an anthology of poetry could sue someone who infringed the whole anthology, even though the infringer proves that publication of one of the poems was unauthorized. Under this provision, copyright could be obtained as long as the use of the preexisting work was not "unlawful," even though the consent of the copyright owner had not been obtained. For instance, the unauthorized reproduction of a work might be "lawful" under the doctrine of fair use or an applicable foreign law, and if so the work incorporating it could be copyrighted.

NOTES

1. Copyright in computer programs is considered beginning at page 773, below. Copyright in industrial design is considered beginning at page 870, below.

2. *Characters.* Copyrightable characters may emerge from literary works, dramatic works, pictorial works and audiovisual works. To be protected, fictional characters must possess the same degree of original expression required of other copyright subject matter. Learned Hand stated the test for copyright in characters in Nichols v. Universal Pictures Corp., 45 F.2d 119, 121 (2d Cir.1930):

> If Twelfth Night were copyrighted, it is quite possible that a second comer might so closely imitate Sir Toby Belch or Malvolio as to infringe, but it would not be enough that for one of his characters he cast a riotous knight who kept wassail to the discomfort of the household, or a vain and foppish steward who became amorous of his mistress. These would be no more than Shakespeare's 'ideas' in the play, as little capable of monopoly as Einstein's Doctrine of Relativity, or Darwin's theory of the Origin of Species. It follows that the less developed the characters, the less they can be copyrighted; that is the penalty an author must bear for marking them too indistinctly.

What doctrines other than copyright offer shelter to characters? In Columbia Broadcasting System, Inc. v. DeCosta, 377 F.2d 315, 153 U.S.P.Q. 649 (1st Cir.), cert. denied, 389 U.S. 1007, 88 S.Ct. 565, 19 L.Ed. 2d 603 (1967), the court, following *Sears* and *Compco,* pp. 103 and 107, above, held that character protection under state law misappropriation doctrine was preempted. Would section 301 of the Copyright Act require a similar result today? See p. 759, below. Do the more traditional unfair competition doctrines of passing off and dilution offer protection without the risk of preemption? See DeCosta v. Columbia Broadcasting System, Inc., 520 F.2d 499, 186 U.S.P.Q. 305 (1st Cir.1975), cert. denied, 423 U.S. 1073, 96 S.Ct. 856, 47 L.Ed.2d 83 (1976). What of federal trademark law? See Frederick Warne & Co. v. Book Sales, Inc., 481 F.Supp. 1191, 1196, 205 U.S.P.Q. 444 (S.D.N.Y.1979) ("The fact that a copyrightable character or design has fallen into the public domain should not preclude protection under the trademark laws so long as it is shown to have acquired independent trademark significance, identifying in some way the source or sponsorship of the goods.")

See generally, Kurtz, The Independent Legal Lives of Fictional Characters, 1986 Wis.L.Rev. 429; Brylawski, Protection of Characters— Sam Spade Revisited, 22 Bull. Copyright Soc'y 77 (1974); Umbreit, A Consideration of Copyright, 87 U.Pa.L.Rev. 932 (1939); Zissu, Whither Character Rights: Some Observations, 29 J. Copyright Soc'y 121 (1981).

3. *Labels.* When Congress was considering the bill that ultimately became the Print and Label Law, 18 Stat. 79 (1874), the Librarian of

Congress managed to fob off responsibility for registration of labels on the Patent Office, apparently because "he regarded [them] as beneath the dignity of literature proper." Howell, The Copyright Law 27 (3d Ed.1952). The Patent Office's Trademark Division handled copyright for labels and prints until 1940 when Congress transferred jurisdiction to the Register of Copyrights, 53 Stat. 1142 (1939).

Copyright protection for labels often intersects unfair competition and trademark protection. In keeping these two areas separate, courts sometimes follow the test for copyrightability stated in Higgins v. Keuffel, 140 U.S. 428, 11 S.Ct. 731, 35 L.Ed. 470 (1891): "To be entitled to a copyright the article must have by itself some value as a composition, at least to the extent of serving some purpose other than as a mere advertisement or designation of the subject to which it is attached." 140 U.S. at 431, 11 S.Ct. at 732.

In Alberto–Culver Co. v. Andrea Dumon, Inc., 466 F.2d 705, 175 U.S.P.Q. 194 (7th Cir.1972), the lower court had relied on this test to find that the face side of plaintiff's feminine hygiene spray container was copyrightable. Further, "on the back side, the colored art work and the connecting phrase 'is the most personal sort of deodorant' was copyrightable and is valid. The remaining language on the back side is purely descriptive or deals with directions and cautions. As this language has no separate value as composition or an extension of the original art work, it was not copyrightable and is not valid." 466 F.2d at 711.

The Seventh Circuit Court of Appeals agreed in all respects but one: "the phrase 'most personal sort of deodorant' is not subject to copyright protection." In the court's view, the phrase was "merely a 'short phrase or expression' which hardly qualifies as an 'appreciable amount of original text'" as is required for copyrightability. Further, "this phrase is just as descriptive as the rest of the text. The ingenuity and creativity reflected in the development of the product itself does not give appropriate descriptive language, such as 'personal sort of deodorant,' any separate value as a composition or as an extension of a work of art. We conclude that this ordinary phrase is not subject to copyright protection." 466 F.2d at 711.

4. *Unlawful Content.* Should copyright be withheld if a work is seditious, libelous, fraudulent or obscene? Courts early declined to protect such works on the ground that protection would contravene the constitutional purpose "to promote the progress of . . . science."

Mitchell Bros. Film Group v. Cinema Adult Theatre, 604 F.2d 852, 203 U.S.P.Q. 1041 (5th Cir.1979), cert. denied, 445 U.S. 917, 100 S.Ct. 1277, 63 L.Ed.2d 601 (1980), marks a turning point for decision in the area. In an action brought by the copyright owners of the motion picture, "Behind the Green Door," the district court had accepted the defense that because the movie was obscene the plaintiffs were barred from relief under the unclean hands doctrine. The court of appeals reversed. In an extensive and closely-reasoned opinion, the court held that neither the Copyright Act nor the Constitution's copyright clause required protection to be withheld because of obscene content.

The court of appeals looked first at the Copyright Act and found nothing to suggest a congressional intent to withhold copyright from obscene subject matter. Indeed, "the history of content-based restrictions on copyrights, trademarks and patents suggests that the absence of such limitations in the Copyright Act of 1909 is the result of an intentional policy choice and not simply an omission." 604 F.2d at 854. The court noted that on the few occasions that Congress had introduced content-based restrictions into the Copyright Act, it later removed them. By contrast, Congress has placed express content restrictions in the Trademark Act (prohibiting registration of "immoral, deceptive or scandalous matter," see page 250, above) and the Patent Act (requiring utility, see page 410, above). 604 F.2d at 855. The court was particularly concerned that to deny copyright "to works adjudged obscene by the standards of one era would frequently result in lack of copyright protection (and thus lack of financial incentive to create) for works that later generations might consider to be not only non-obscene but even of great literary merit." Among the works "held in high regard today," but "adjudged obscene in previous eras" are: Edmund Wilson's Memoirs of Hecate County, Henry Miller's Tropic of Cancer and Tropic of Capricorn, Erskine Caldwell's God's Little Acre, D.H. Lawrence's Lady Chatterley's Lover and Theodore Dreiser's An American Tragedy. 604 F.2d at 857.

To the argument that copyright protection for obscene works would violate the constitutional limit on Congress's copyright power "to promote the progress of science and useful arts," the court answered that, while Congress could indeed "require that each copyrighted work be shown to promote the useful arts (as it has with patents,) it need not do so." Instead, Congress could put "promotion of science and useful arts" in a larger frame, and "conclude that the best way to promote creativity is not to impose any governmental restrictions on the subject matter of copyrightable works." 604 F.2d at 860.

Mitchell relied in part on Belcher v. Tarbox, 486 F.2d 1087, 180 U.S.P.Q. 1 (9th Cir.1973), which had declined to withhold copyright protection from allegedly fraudulent subject matter. "There is nothing in the Copyright Act to suggest that the courts are to pass upon the truth or falsity, the soundness or unsoundness, of the views embodied in a copyrighted work. The gravity and immensity of the problems, theological, philosophical, economic and scientific, that would confront a court if this view were adopted are staggering to contemplate. It is surely not a task lightly to be assumed, and we decline the invitation to assume it." 486 F.2d at 1088.

If Mitchell and Belcher had reached contrary conclusions, would any problems be raised by the fact that obscenity and fraud are typically determined by reference to local community standards and state laws that vary across the country?

For an early study of the general issue, see Rogers, Copyright and Morals, 18 Mich.L.Rev. 390 (1920). See also, Phillips, Copyright in Obscene Works: Some British and American Problems, 6 Anglo–American L.Rev. 138 (1977); Note, The Obscenity Defense in Actions to Protect Copyright, 46 Fordham L.Rev. 1037 (1978); Note, 74 Colum.L. Rev. 1351 (1974); Note, 51 Denver L.J. 621 (1974).

5. *U.S. Government Works.* Section 105 of the 1976 Copyright Act provides that "[c]opyright protection under this title is not available for any work of the United States Government, but the United States Government is not precluded from receiving and holding copyrights transferred to it by assignment, bequest, or otherwise." Section 101 defines a "work of the United States Government" as "a work prepared by an officer or employee of the United States Government as part of that person's official duties."

When is a work by a government employee prepared as part of her "official duties?" According to the House Report on the 1976 Act, "a Government official or employee would not be prevented from securing copyright in a work written at that person's own volition and outside his or her duties, even though the subject matter involves the Government work or professional field of the official or employee." H.R.Rep. No. 1476, 94th Cong., 2d Sess. 58 (1976). Under this test, presidential testimony would constitute a United States government work while the President's reflections on events during his tenure, written after he left office, would not. See Harper & Row Publishers, Inc. v. Nation Enters., 723 F.2d 195, 220 U.S.P.Q. 321 (2d Cir.1983), rev'd on other grounds, 471 U.S. 539, 105 S.Ct. 2218, 85 L.Ed.2d 588 (1985).

6. The Copyright Office has listed several examples of "works not subject to copyright" for which it will not issue certificates of registration:

(a) Words and short phrases such as names, titles, and slogans; familiar symbols or designs; mere variations of typographic ornamentation, lettering or coloring; mere listing of ingredients or contents;

(b) Ideas, plans, methods, systems, or devices, as distinguished from the particular manner in which they are expressed or described in a writing;

(c) Blank forms, such as time cards, graph paper, account books, diaries, bank checks, scorecards, address books, report forms, order forms and the like, which are designed for recording information and do not in themselves convey information;

(d) Works consisting entirely of information that is common property containing no original authorship, such as, for example: Standard calendars, height and weight charts, tape measures and rulers, schedules of sporting events, and lists or tables taken from public documents or other common sources.

37 C.F.R. § 202.1 (1989). Why should the fact that a work is designed for recording information, and does not in itself "convey information,"

disqualify it from copyright protection? If the copyright registration application reproduced at page 549, above were not a U.S. Government work, would it qualify for copyright protection?

3. ORIGINAL EXPRESSION

a. THE ORIGINALITY STANDARD

SHELDON v. METRO–GOLDWYN PICTURES CORP., 81 F.2d 49, 28 U.S.P.Q. 330 (2d Cir.), cert. denied, 298 U.S. 669, 56 S.Ct. 835, 80 L.Ed. 1392 (1936), L. HAND, J.: We are to remember that it makes no difference how far the play was anticipated by works in the public demesne which the plaintiffs did not use. The defendants appear not to recognize this, for they have filled the record with earlier instances of the same dramatic incidents and devices, as though, like a patent, a copyrighted work must be not only original, but new. That is not however the law as is obvious in the case of maps or compendia, where later works will necessarily be anticipated. At times, in discussing how much of the substance of a play the copyright protects, courts have indeed used language which seems to give countenance to the notion that, if a plot were old, it could not be copyrighted. But we understand by this no more than that in its broader outline a plot is never copyrightable, for it is plain beyond peradventure that anticipation as such cannot invalidate a copyright. Borrowed the work must indeed not be, for a plagiarist is not himself pro tanto an "author"; but if by some magic a man who had never known it were to compose anew Keats's Ode on a Grecian Urn, he would be an "author," and, if he copyrighted it, others might not copy that poem, though they might of course copy Keats's. Bleistein v. Donaldson Lithographing Co., 188 U.S. 239, 249, 23 S.Ct. 298, 47 L.Ed. 460 (1903). But though a copyright is for this reason less vulnerable than a patent, the owner's protection is more limited, for just as he is no less an "author" because others have preceded him, so another who follows him, is not a tort-feasor unless he pirates his work. If the copyrighted work is therefore original, the public demesne is important only on the issue of infringement; that is, so far as it may break the force of the inference to be drawn from likenesses between the work and the putative piracy. If the defendant has had access to other material which would have served him as well, his disclaimer becomes more plausible.

BLEISTEIN v. DONALDSON LITHOGRAPHING CO.

Supreme Court of the United States, 1903.
188 U.S. 239, 23 S.Ct. 298, 47 L.Ed. 460.

Mr. Justice HOLMES delivered the opinion of the court.

This case comes here from the United States Circuit Court of Appeals for the Sixth Circuit by writ of error. It is an action brought by the plaintiffs in error to recover the penalties prescribed for infringements of copyrights. The alleged infringements consisted in the copying in reduced form of three chromolithographs prepared by employes of the plaintiffs for advertisements of a circus owned by one Wallace. Each of the three contained a portrait of Wallace in the corner and lettering bearing some slight relation to the scheme of decoration, indicating the subject of the design and the fact that the reality was to be seen at the circus. One of the designs was of an ordinary ballet, one of a number of men and women, described as the Stirk family, performing on bicycles, and one of groups of men and women whitened to represent statues. The Circuit Court directed a verdict for the defendant on the ground that the chromolithographs were not within the protection of the copyright law, and this ruling was sustained by the Circuit Court of Appeals. Courier Lithographing Co. v. Donaldson Lithographing Co., 104 Fed.Rep. 993.

There was evidence warranting the inference that the designs belonged to the plaintiffs, they having been produced by persons employed and paid by the plaintiffs in their establishment to make those very things. It fairly might be found also that the copyrights were taken out in the proper names. One of them was taken out in the name of the Courier Company and the other two in the names of the Courier Lithographing Company. The former was the name of an unincorporated joint stock association formed under the laws of New York, Laws of 1894, c. 235, and made up of the plaintiffs, the other a trade variant on that name.

Finally, there was evidence that the pictures were copyrighted before publication. There may be a question whether the use by the defendant for Wallace was not lawful within the terms of the contract with Wallace, or a more general one as to what rights the plaintiffs reserved. But we cannot pass upon these questions as matter of law; they will be for the jury when the case is tried again, and therefore we come at once to the ground of decision in the courts below. That ground was not found in any variance between pleading and proof, such as was put forward in argument, but in the nature and purpose of the designs.

We shall do no more than mention the suggestion that painting and engraving unless for a mechanical end are not among the useful arts, the progress of which Congress is empowered by the Constitution to promote. The Constitution does not limit the useful to that which satisfies immediate bodily needs. It is obvious also that the plaintiffs' case is not affected by the fact, if it be one, that the pictures represent actual groups—visible things. They seem from the testimony to have been composed from hints or description, not from sight of a performance. But even if they had been drawn from the life, that fact would not deprive them of protection. The opposite proposition would mean that a portrait by Velasquez or Whistler was common property because others might try their hand on the same face. Others are free to copy the original. They are not free to copy the copy. The copy is the personal reaction of an individual upon nature. Personality always contains something unique. It expresses its singularity even in handwriting, and a very modest grade of art has in it something irreducible,

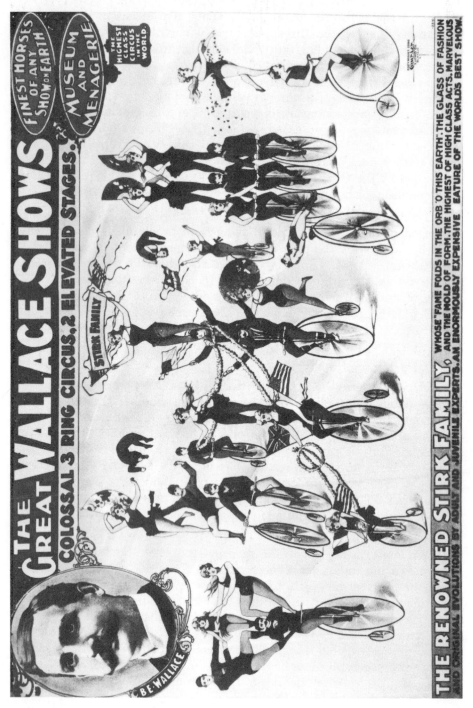

Poster in Bleistein v. Donaldson Lithographing Co.

which is one man's alone. That something he may copyright unless there is a restriction in the words of the act.

If there is a restriction it is not to be found in the limited pretensions of these particular works. The least pretentious picture has more originality in it than directories and the like, which may be copyrighted. The amount of training required for humbler efforts than those before us is well indicated by Ruskin. "If any young person, after being taught what is, in polite circles, called 'drawing,' will try to copy the commonest piece of real *work*,—suppose a lithograph on the title page of a new opera air, or a woodcut in the cheapest illustrated newspaper of the day—they will find themselves entirely beaten." Elements of Drawing, 1st ed. 3. There is no reason to doubt that these prints in their *ensemble* and in all their details, in their design and particular combinations of figures, lines and colors, are the original work of the plaintiffs' designer. If it be necessary, there is express testimony to that effect. It would be pressing the defendant's right to the verge, if not beyond, to leave the question of originality to the jury upon the evidence in this case, as was done in Hegeman v. Springer, 110 Fed.Rep. 374.

We assume that the construction of Rev.Stat. § 4952, allowing a copyright to the "author, inventor, designer, or proprietor . . . of any engraving, cut, print . . . [or] chromo" is affected by the act of 1874, c. 301, § 3, 18 Stat. 78, 79. That section provides that "in the construction of this act the words 'engraving,' 'cut' and 'print' shall be applied only to pictorial illustrations or works connected with the fine arts." We see no reason for taking the words "connected with the fine arts" as qualifying anything except the word "works," but it would not change our decision if we should assume further that they also qualified "pictorial illustrations," as the defendant contends.

These chromolithographs are "pictorial illustrations." The word "illustrations" does not mean that they must illustrate the text of a book, and that the etchings of Rembrandt or Steinla's engraving of the Madonna di San Sisto could not be protected today if any man were able to produce them. Again, the act however construed, does not mean that ordinary posters are not good enough to be considered within its scope. The antithesis to "illustrations or works connected with the fine arts" is not works of little merit or of humble degree, or illustrations addressed to the less educated classes; it is "prints or labels designed to be used for any other articles of manufacture." Certainly works are not the less connected with the fine arts because their pictorial quality attracts the crowd and therefore gives them a real use—if use means to increase trade and to help to make money. A picture is none the less a picture and none the less a subject of copyright that it is used for an advertisement. And if pictures may be used to advertise soap, or the theatre, or monthly magazines, as they are, they may be used to advertise a circus. Of course, the ballet is as legitimate a subject for illustration as any other. A rule cannot be laid down that would excommunicate the paintings of Degas.

Finally, the special adaptation of these pictures to the advertisement of the Wallace shows does not prevent a copyright. That may be a circumstance for the jury to consider in determining the extent of Mr. Wallace's rights, but it is not a bar. Moreover, on the evidence, such prints are used by less pretentious exhibitions when those for whom they were prepared have given them up.

It would be a dangerous undertaking for persons trained only to the law to constitute themselves final judges of the worth of pictorial illustrations, outside of the narrowest and most obvious limits. At the one extreme some works of genius would be sure to miss appreciation. Their very novelty would make them repulsive until the public had learned the new language in which their author spoke. It may be more than doubted, for instance, whether the etchings of Goya or the paintings of Manet would have been sure of protection when seen for the first time. At the other end, copyright would be denied to pictures which appealed to a public less educated than the judge. Yet if they command the interest of any public, they have a commercial value—it would be bold to say that they have not an aesthetic and educational value—and the taste of any public is not to be treated with contempt. It is an ultimate fact for the moment, whatever may be our hopes for a change. That these pictures had their worth and their success is sufficiently shown by the desire to reproduce them without regard to the plaintiffs' rights. We are of opinion that there was evidence that the plaintiffs have rights entitled to the protection of the law.

The judgment of the Circuit Court of Appeals is reversed; the judgment of the Circuit Court is also reversed and the cause remanded to that court with directions to set aside the verdict and grant a new trial.

Mr. Justice HARLAN, with whom concurred Mr. Justice McKENNA, dissenting.

Judges Lurton, Day and Severens, of the Circuit Court of Appeals, concurred in affirming the judgment of the District Court. Their views were thus expressed in an opinion delivered by Judge Lurton: "What we hold is this: That if a chromo, lithograph, or other print, engraving, or picture has no other use than that of a mere advertisement, and no value aside from this function, it would not be promotive of the useful arts, within the meaning of the constitutional provision, to protect the 'author' in the exclusive use thereof, and the copyright statute should not be construed as including such a publication, if any other construction is admissible. If a mere label simply designating or describing an article to which it is attached, and which has no value separated from the article, does not come within the constitutional clause upon the subject of copyright, it must follow that a pictorial illustration designed and useful only as an advertisement, and having no intrinsic value other than its function as an advertisement, must be equally without the obvious meaning of the Constitution. It must have some connection with the fine arts to give it intrinsic value, and that it shall have is the meaning which we attach to the act of June 18, 1874, amending the provisions of the copyright law. We are unable to discover anything useful or meritorious in the design copyrighted by the plaintiffs in error other than as an advertisement of acts to be done or exhibited to the public in Wallace's show. No evidence, aside from the deductions which are to be drawn from the prints themselves, was offered to show that these designs had any original artistic qualities. The jury could not reasonably have found merit or value aside from the purely business object of advertising a show, and the instruction to find for the defendant was not error. Many other points have been urged as justifying the result reached in the court below. We find it unnecessary to express any opinion upon them, in view of the conclusion already announced. The judgment must be affirmed." Courier Lithographing Co. v. Donaldson Lithographing Co., 104 Fed.Rep. 993, 996.

I entirely concur in these views, and therefore dissent from the opinion and judgment of this court. The clause of the Constitution giving Congress power to promote the progress of science and useful arts, by securing for limited terms to authors and inventors the exclusive right to their respective works and discoveries, does not, as I think, embrace a mere advertisement of a circus.

Mr. Justice McKENNA authorizes me to say that he also dissents.

NOTES

1. It is some measure of the originality test that Learned Hand propounded in *Sheldon* that, in a long career deciding copyright cases, Judge Hand never once found that a work was insufficiently original to qualify for copyright protection.* What are the "narrowest and most obvious limits," referred to in *Bleistein,* within which courts may judge a work's artistic worth? To put the question in the terms of Justice Holmes' reasoning, at what point do judgments on artistic worth rendered by persons trained only to the law—or by anyone, for that matter—cease to be "a dangerous undertaking"?

Consider the result that the *Sheldon* and *Bleistein* tests would produce in the following case. Plaintiff, who executed a scaled-down reproduction of Rodin's "Hand of God" that is identical to the Rodin piece in all respects other than size and configuration of base, seeks to enjoin defendant from producing and distributing exact copies of the reproduction. Defendant answers that, because plaintiff admittedly copied the public domain Rodin work, the reproduction necessarily fails the originality test. In Alva Studios, Inc. v. Winninger, 177 F.Supp. 265, 123 U.S.P.Q. 487 (S.D.N.Y. 1959), the court held plaintiff's reproduction to be original in light of the "great skill and originality" required to "produce a scale reduction of a great work with exactitude." 177 F.Supp. at 267.

Compare L. Batlin & Son, Inc. v. Snyder, 536 F.2d 486, 189 U.S.P.Q. 753 (2d Cir.1976), cert. denied, 429 U.S. 857, 97 S.Ct. 156, 50 L.Ed.2d 135, 191 U.S.P.Q. 588, in which the court held a plastic model of an

---

* I am grateful to Professor Douglas Baird, of the University of Chicago Law School, for this observation, made in his unpublished study, *The Copyright Decisions of Learned Hand.*

antique cast iron "Uncle Sam" bank to be unoriginal. The plastic model differed from the prototype in size and details. Among other differences, "the carpetbag shape of the plastic bank is smooth, the iron bank is rough; the metal bank bag is fatter at its base; the eagle on the front of the platform in the metal bank is holding arrows in his talons while in the plastic bank he clutches leaves." 536 F.2d at 489. In the court's judgment, the "complexity and exactitude . . . involved [in *Alva v. Winninger*] distinguishes that case amply from the one at bar." 536 F.2d at 491–492. From this, the court turned the proof of differences between the plastic model and the cast iron prototype *against* the copyright claimant: "[t]hus concededly the plastic version is not, and was scarcely meticulously produced to be, an exactly faithful reproduction." 536 F.2d 486, 492.

Are the results in *Alva* and *Batlin* just the opposite of what they should be? The copyright claimant in *Alva* presumably invested more painstaking effort than the copyright claimant in *Batlin*. Is the purpose of copyright to induce investment in the production of works that exactly copy public domain works, or production of works that embody expressive differences?

See generally, Olson, Copyright Originality, 48 Mo.L.Rev. 29 (1983).

2. *"Novelty" and "Originality."* Novelty has a limited use in determinations of originality. In Alfred Bell & Co. v. Catalda Fine Arts, Inc., 191 F.2d 99, 90 U.S.P.Q. 153 (2d Cir.1951), the court upheld the originality of plaintiff's mezzotint engravings of paintings by old masters on the ground that "[t]here is evidence that they were not intended to and did not, imitate the paintings they reproduced. But even if their substantial departures from the paintings were inadvertent, the copyrights would be valid. A copyist's bad eyesight or defective musculature, or a shock caused by a clap of thunder, may yield sufficiently distinguishable variations. Having hit upon such a variation unintentionally, the 'author' may adopt it as his and copyright it." 191 F.2d at 104–105. In cases like this, in which copying is either admitted or, as in Hand's Keats example, is irrebuttably self-evident, the court looks for new matter, for some variation from previous works, not to break the inference of copying, for copying is assumed, but rather to find some copyrightable—uncopied—component in claimant's work.

Should novelty enjoy even this limited role? Copyright law possesses none of the search mechanisms for determining novelty that have developed around patent law's novelty and nonobviousness requirements. The few recorded and largely vain efforts at introducing prior art on the issue of copyright novelty only dramatize copyright law's incapacity to measure novelty systematically. See for example Hollywood Jewelry Mfg. Co. v. Dushkin, 136 F.Supp. 738, 107 U.S.P.Q. 354 (S.D.N.Y.1955) (introduction of expired design patents to rebut the originality of plaintiff's copyrighted jewelry).

The point was apparently lost on Justice Douglas who, dissenting from the Court's denial of certiorari in Lee v. Runge, 404 U.S. 887, 92 S.Ct. 197, 30 L.Ed.2d 169, 171 U.S.P.Q. 322 (1971), suggested that the lower court had erred in holding that "[t]he standard of 'novelty' urged by appellants is applicable to patents, but not copyrights. The copyright standard is one of 'originality' . . . . Runge v. Lee, 441 F.2d 579, 169 U.S.P.Q. 388 (9th Cir.1971)." Giving a constitutional dimension to patent law's novelty requirement, Douglas argued that "no reason can be offered why we should depart from the plain import of this grant of congressional power and apply more lenient constitutional standards to copyrights than to patents. . . . To create a monopoly under the copyright power which would not be available under the patent power would be to betray the common birthright of all men at the altar of hollow formalisms." 404 U.S. at 890–91.

3. *The Idea–Expression Distinction.* Section 102(b) of the 1976 Copyright Act enshrines the longstanding rule that copyright does not protect ideas: "In no case does copyright protection for an original work of authorship extend to any idea, procedure, process, system, method of operation, concept, principle, or discovery, regardless of the form in which it is described, explained, illustrated, or embodied in such work."

Under the "merger" doctrine, courts will withhold protection from otherwise copyrightable expression if the idea embodied in the expression can effectively be expressed in only one or a limited number of ways. For example, in Herbert Rosenthal Jewelry Corp. v. Kalpakian, 446 F.2d 738, 170 U.S.P.Q. 557 (9th Cir.1971), the court held that the plaintiff's jewelled pin in the shape of a bee was not copyrightable because a jewelled bee pin was "an 'idea' that defendants were free to copy" and "the 'idea' and its 'expression' appear to be indistinguishable." In the court's view, when "the 'idea' and its 'expression' are thus inseparable, copying the 'expression' will not be barred, since protecting the 'expression' in such circumstances would confer a monopoly of the 'idea' upon the copyright owner free of the conditions and limitations imposed by the patent law." 446 F.2d at 742.

See generally Samuels, The Idea–Expression Dichotomy in Copyright Law, 56 Tenn.L.Rev. 321 (1989). See also Libott, Round the Prickly Pear: The Idea–Expression Fallacy in a Mass Communications World, 14 UCLA L.Rev. 735 (1967).

b. THE ORIGINALITY STANDARD APPLIED

P. GOLDSTEIN, COPYRIGHT § 2.2.1 (1989) *: Courts apply the originality requirement differently to different types of subject matter. In the case of fictional works, such as Keats' *Ode,* that filter reality through their creator's distinctive vision, courts will find originality in even the smallest variations. But originality becomes more problematic in fact works and functional works, such as maps and legal forms, that characteristically adhere to physical realities or to well worn formulae, and in photographs and other representational works of art that seek to mirror reality. Some courts have resolved the problem of

* Copyright © 1989 by Paul Goldstein.

originality in cases involving fact works, functional works, and works of visual art by engrafting one or more of three requirements onto the basic originality standard—a novelty threshold, a quantitative threshold, and an expenditure of labor threshold. These judicial additions may contradict Congress' apparent intent to confine the originality standard to its traditionally low level—that copyrightable elements be original only in the sense that they are not copied from another source. On the other hand, since these modifications of the traditional originality standard antedate the 1976 Act, Congress may have intended to incorporate them in the Act, at least to the extent that they conform to the overriding object of the originality requirement—encouraging the production of the widest possible variety of literary, musical and artistic expression.

MILLER v. UNIVERSAL CITY STUDIOS, INC.

United States Court of Appeals, Fifth Circuit, 1981.
65 F.2d 1365, 212 U.S.P.Q. 345.

RONEY, Circuit Judge:

A sensational kidnapping, committed over a decade ago, furnishes the factual backdrop for this copyright infringement suit. The issue is whether a made-for-television movie dramatizing the crime infringes upon a copyrighted book depicting the unsuccessful ransom attempt. After careful and lengthy study and consideration, we conclude that the verdict for plaintiff must be reversed and the cause remanded for a new trial because at the request of plaintiff and over defendants' objection, the case was presented and argued to the jury on a false premise: that the labor of research by an author is protected by copyright.

The decision to reverse is made more difficult because the record and the arguments to this Court reveal sufficient evidence to support a finding of infringement and a verdict for plaintiff under correct theories of copyright law. Plaintiff's presentation and argument to the jury, however, make it improper to conclude that the short erroneous instruction, imbedded in a field of proper instructions, was harmless error.

Facts

The facts are fully developed in the district court's opinion, Miller v. Universal City Studios, Inc., 460 F.Supp. 984 (S.D.Fla.1978). A synopsis will suffice for purposes of this appeal.

In December 1968 the college-aged daughter of a wealthy Florida land developer was abducted from an Atlanta motel room and buried alive in a plywood and fiberglass capsule. A crude life-support system kept her alive for the five days she was underground before her rescue. Gene Miller, a reporter for the *Miami Herald*, covered the story and subsequently collaborated with the victim to write a book about the crime. Published in 1971 under the title *83 Hours Till Dawn*, the book was copyrighted along with a condensed version in *Reader's Digest* and a serialization in the *Ladies Home Journal.* The co-author has assigned her interest in this litigation to Miller.

In January 1972 a Universal City Studios (Universal) producer read the condensed version of the book and thought the story would make a good television movie. He gave a copy of the book to a scriptwriter, who immediately began work on a screenplay. Although negotiations for purchase of the movie rights to *83 Hours Till Dawn* were undertaken by Universal, no agreement with Miller was ever reached. The scriptwriter was eventually advised that use of the book in completing the script was "verboten." The movie was completed, however, and aired as an ABC Movie of the Week, *The Longest Night.*

The evidence at trial was conflicting on whether the scriptwriter relied almost entirely on the book in writing the screenplay or whether he arrived at his version of the kidnapping story independently. Both plaintiff and his expert witness testified to numerous similarities between the works. The jury, which had copies of the book and viewed the movie twice during the trial, found the movie infringed Miller's copyright and awarded him over $200,000 in damages and profits.

The most substantial question presented on appeal is whether the district court erred in instructing the jury that "research is copyrightable." Because the Court finds reversible error in this regard, other issues raised on this appeal will be discussed only as necessary to avoid further confusion on retrial.

Is Research Copyrightable?

The district court instructed the jury that if an author engages in research on factual matters, "his research is copyrightable." This instruction, at best confusing, at worst wrong, was given with some reluctance by the trial court over the strenuous objection of defendants on the urging by plaintiff, "That's the heart of the case."

As it develops on appeal, plaintiff may have won without the instruction, but later explanation by the trial court and the brief on appeal convinces this Court that the idea conveyed to the jury by the court and trial counsel contained an erroneous view of the law. In context, the instruction is found in this portion of the extended jury charge:

> Copyrightability is best defined in terms of what can and cannot be copyrighted. Ideas can never be copyrighted. Only the particular expression of an idea can be copyrighted. A general theme cannot be copyrighted but its expression throughout the pattern of the work, the sequence of its events, the development of the interplay of its characters, and its choice of detail and dialogue can be copyrighted. If, however, the expression of the idea necessarily follows from the idea to such an extent that the idea is capable of expression only in a more or less stereotyped form, it is not copyrightable.

Similarly, in a case like the instant one, which deals with factual matters such as news events, the facts themselves are not copyrightable but the form of expression of the facts and their arrangement and selection are copyrightable. *Moreover, if an author, in writing a book concerning factual matters, engages in research on those matters, his research is copyrightable.* As was the case with ideas, if the expression arrangement and selection of the facts must necessarily, by the nature of the facts, be formulated in given ways then they are not copyrightable. (Challenged instruction underlined).

It is well settled that copyright protection extends only to an author's expression of facts and not to the facts themselves. This dichotomy between facts and their expression derives from the concept of originality which is the premise of copyright law. Under the Constitution, copyright protection may secure for a limited time to "Authors . . . the exclusive Right to their respective Writings." U.S. Const. Art. I, § 8, cl. 8. An "author" is one "to whom anything owes its origin; originator; maker; one who completes a work of science or literature." Burrow–Giles Lithographic Co. v. Sarony, 111 U.S. 53, 58, 4 S.Ct. 279, 281, 28 L.Ed. 349 (1884). Obviously, a fact does not originate with the author of a book describing the fact. Neither does it originate with one who "discovers" the fact. "The discoverer merely finds and records. He may not claim that the facts are 'original' with him although there may be originality and hence authorship in the manner of reporting, i.e., the 'expression,' of the facts." 1 M. Nimmer, *Nimmer on Copyright* § 2.03[E], at 2–34 (1980). Thus, since facts do not owe their origin to any individual, they may not be copyrighted and are part of the public domain available to every person.

The district court's charge to the jury correctly stated that facts cannot be copyrighted. Nevertheless, in its order denying defendants' motion for a new trial the court said it viewed "the labor and expense of the research involved in the obtaining of those uncopyrightable facts to be intellectually distinct from those facts and more similar to the expression of the facts than to the facts themselves." The court interpreted the copyright law to reward not only the effort and ingenuity involved in giving expression to facts, but also the efforts involved in discovering and exposing facts. In its view, an author could not be expected to expend his time and money in gathering facts if he knew those facts, and the profits to be derived therefrom, could be pirated by one who could then avoid the expense of obtaining the facts himself. Applying this reasoning to the case at bar, the court concluded "[i]n the age of television 'docudrama' to hold other than research is copyrightable is to violate the spirit of the copyright law and to provide to those persons and corporations lacking in requisite diligence and ingenuity a license to steal."

Thus the trial court's explanation of its understanding of its charge undercuts the argument to this Court that the word "research" was intended to mean the original expression by the author of the results of the research, rather than the labor of research.

The issue is not whether granting copyright protection to an author's research would be desirable or beneficial, but whether such protection is intended under the copyright law. In support of its instruction, the district court cited a number of cases, one of which involved the use of another's historical research in writing a literary work.

It is difficult to adequately distinguish some of the directory cases, and particularly the language of the opinions. A copyright in a directory, however, is properly viewed as resting on the originality of the selection and arrangement of the factual material, rather than on the industriousness of the efforts to develop the information. Copyright protection does not extend to the facts themselves, and the mere use of the information contained in a directory without a substantial copying of the format does not constitute infringement.

In any event, it may be better to recognize the directory cases as being in a category by themselves rather than to attempt to bring their result and rationale to bear on nondirectory cases. Under the 1909 Copyright Act, directories are specifically identified as copyrightable subject matter, 17 U.S.C. § 5(a) (1970), and the rule is now well settled that they can be copyrighted. However appropriate it may be to extend copyright protection to the selection and arrangement of factual material in a directory if it involves originality and hence authorship, and however difficult it may be to reconcile these cases with the principle that facts are not copyrightable, the special protection granted directories under the copyright law has generally not been applied to other factual endeavors. For example, the labor involved in news gathering and distribution is not protected by copyright although it may be protected under a misappropriation theory of unfair competition. International News Service v. The Associated Press, 248 U.S. 215, 39 S.Ct. 68, 63 L.Ed. 211 (1918). In the *International News* case, the Supreme Court commented in dicta that while a newspaper story, as a literary production, can be copyrighted,

> the news element—the information respecting current events contained in the literary production—is not the creation of the writer, but is a report of matters that ordinarily are *publici juris;* it is the history of the day. It is not to be supposed that the framers of the Constitution . . . intended to confer upon one who might happen to be the first to report a historic event the exclusive right for any period to spread the knowledge of it.

Id. at 234, 39 S.Ct. at 71.

Apart from the directory cases, the only decision cited to this Court which lends support for the challenged instruction is Toksvig v. Bruce Publishing Co., 181 F.2d 664 (7th Cir.1950). In *Toksvig,* plaintiff had written a biography of Hans Christian Anderson after extensive research of primary Danish sources. Defendant, who could not read Danish, copied twenty-four specific passages from plaintiff's book in writing her own biography. The Seventh Circuit held the copying of these passages, original translations from Danish separately copyrightable under 17 U.S.C. § 6 (1970), constituted copyright infringement. The court went on to reject defendant's fair use defense, primarily because defendant's use of the translations from Danish had allowed her to write her biography in one-third the time it took plaintiff. The court said the question was not whether defendant could have obtained the same information by going to the sources plaintiff had used, but whether she in fact had done her own independent research.

Although most circuits apparently have not addressed the question, the idea that historical research is copyrightable was expressly rejected by the Second Circuit in the more soundly reasoned case of Rosemont Enterprises, Inc. v. Random House, Inc., 366 F.2d 303 (2d Cir.1966), cert. denied, 385 U.S. 1009, 87 S.Ct. 714, 17 L.Ed.2d 546 (1967). In *Rosemont,* it was alleged that defendant's biography of Howard Hughes infringed the copyright on a series of *Look* articles about Hughes. The district court had asserted in sweeping language that an author is not entitled to utilize the fruits of another's labor in lieu of independent research, relying on *Toksvig.* The Second Circuit reversed. While not challenging the holding of *Toksvig* that substantial copying of specific passages amounted to copyright infringement, it rejected the language regarding independent research:

> We . . . cannot subscribe to the view that an author is absolutely precluded from saving time and effort by referring to and relying upon prior published material. . . . It is just such wasted effort that the proscription against the copyright of ideas and facts, and to a lesser extent the privilege of fair use, are designed to prevent.

366 F.2d at 310 (citations omitted).

The Second Circuit had adhered to its position in the most recent appellate case to address the question, Hoehling v. Universal City Studios, Inc., 618 F.2d 972 (2d Cir.), cert. denied, 449 U.S. 841, 101 S.Ct. 121, 66 L.Ed.2d 49 (1980). *Hoehling* involved various literary accounts of the last voyage and mysterious destruction of the German dirigible Hindenberg. Plaintiff A.A. Hoehling published a book in 1962 entitled, *Who Destroyed the Hindenberg?* Written as a factual account in an objective, reportorial style, the premise of his extensively researched book was that the Hindenberg had been deliberately sabotaged by a member of its crew to embarrass the Nazi regime. Ten years later, defendant Michael McDonald Mooney published his book, *The Hindenberg.* While a more literary than historical account, it also hypothesized sabotage. Universal City Studios purchased the movie rights to Mooney's book and produced a movie under the same title, although the movie differed somewhat from the book. During the litigation, Mooney acknowledged he had consulted Hoehling's book and relied on it for some details in writing his own, but he maintained he first discovered the sabotage theory in Dale Titler's *Wings of Mystery,* also released in 1962.

Hoehling sued Mooney and Universal for copyright infringement. The district court granted defendants' motion for summary judgment and the Second Circuit affirmed, holding that, assuming both copying and substantial similarity, all the similarities pertained to categories of noncopyrightable material. The court noted the sabotage hypothesis espoused in Hoehling's book was based entirely on interpretation of historical fact and was not copyrightable. The same reasoning applied to Hoehling's claim that a number of specific facts, ascertained through his personal research, were copied by defendants. Relying on the *Rosemont* case, the court stated that factual information is in the public domain and "each [defendant] had the right to 'avail himself of the facts contained' in Hoehling's book and to 'use such information, whether correct or incorrect, in his own literary work.'" 618 F.2d at 979 (quoting Greenbie v. Noble, 151 F.Supp. 45, 67 (S.D.N.Y.1957)).

We find the approach taken by the Second Circuit in *Hoehling* and *Rosemont* to be more consistent with the purpose and intended scope of protection under the copyright law than that implied by *Toksvig*. The line drawn between uncopyrightable facts and copyrightable expression of facts serves an important purpose in copyright law. It provides a means of balancing the public's interest in stimulating creative activity, as embodied in the Copyright Clause, against the public's need for unrestrained access to information. It allows a subsequent author to build upon and add to prior accomplishments without unnecessary duplication of effort. As expressed by the Second Circuit in *Hoehling*:

> The copyright provides a financial incentive to those who would add to the corpus of existing knowledge by creating original works. Nevertheless, the protection afforded the copyright holder has never extended to history, be it documented fact or explanatory hypothesis. The rationale for this doctrine is that the cause of knowledge is best served when history is the common property of all, and each generation remains free to draw upon the discoveries and insights of the past. Accordingly, the scope of copyright in historical accounts is narrow indeed, embracing no more than the author's original expression of particular facts and theories already in the public domain.

618 F.2d at 974.

The valuable distinction in copyright law between facts and the expression of facts cannot be maintained if research is held to be copyrightable. There is no rational basis for distinguishing between facts and the research involved in obtaining facts. To hold that research is copyrightable is no more or no less than to hold that the facts discovered as a result of research are entitled to copyright protection. Plaintiff argues that extending copyright protection to research would not upset the balance because it would not give the researcher/author a monopoly over the facts but would only ensure that later writers obtain the facts independently or follow the guidelines of fair use if the facts are no longer discoverable. But this is precisely the scope of protection given any copyrighted matter, and the law is clear that facts are not entitled to such protection. We conclude that the district court erred in instructing the jury that research is copyrightable.

Our inquiry does not end here, however. In reviewing a trial court's instructions to the jury an appellate court must consider the charge as a whole from the standpoint of the jury, in view of the allegations made, the evidence presented and the arguments of counsel. If the charge as a whole correctly instructs the jury, no reversible error may be committed even though a portion of the charge may be technically imperfect.

In this case the erroneous statement of law was one sentence in a charge of twelve pages correctly stating the distinction between facts and expression and that facts are not copyrightable. The idea that research is copyrightable was nevertheless impressed upon the jury throughout the liability phase of the trial. In opening argument, counsel for plaintiff stressed the amount of labor and research done by Miller in writing the book. Over defendants' objection, Miller was permitted to testify extensively regarding the amount of time spent researching the book. Although relevant to damages, such testimony was clearly irrelevant to the question of whether defendants' work had infringed plaintiff's book. In closing argument, plaintiff's counsel again stressed that everything Miller did in his research for eighteen to twenty months and put in his book was copyrightable. The fact that counsel considered the faulty instruction to be "the heart" and "the guts of the case," as he told the trial court, is further indication that the "research is copyrightable" theory permeated the entire liability phase of the trial.

Viewing the record as a whole, the Court is left with a substantial and ineradicable doubt as to whether the jury was properly guided in its deliberations. Because there is uncertainty as to whether the jury was actually misled, the erroneous instruction cannot be ruled harmless and a new trial is required. . . .

. . . Additional issues raised by defendants on appeal, including the correctness of the special verdict form, the propriety of certain comments made by plaintiff's counsel during closing arguments, and the reasonableness of the attorney's fee award to plaintiff, need not be decided in light of the remand for a new trial.

REVERSED AND REMANDED.

DONALD v. ZACK MEYER'S T.V. SALES AND SERV.

United States Court of Appeals, Fifth Circuit, 1970.
426 F.2d 1027, 165 U.S.P.Q. 751, cert. denied, 400 U.S. 992, 91 S.Ct. 459,
27 L.Ed.2d 441 (1971).

GOLDBERG, Circuit Judge.

In this infringement suit a maker of business forms seeks copyright protection for a common legal form. The characters in this drama are O.W. Donald, the copyright claimant; Moore Business Forms, Inc., the alleged infringer; and Zack Meyer's T.V. Sales and Service, the innocent bystander. Act I of this play ended when the trial court found for Donald. We rewrite the script and reverse.

In 1961 Donald registered with the copyright office the following paragraph:

"Agreement"

"For value received, the undersigned jointly and severally promise to pay to the Dealer, or order, the unpaid balance shown on this invoice according to the agreed terms. Title to said Chattel, described hereon by model, make and serial number, is hereby retained, or transferred to Dealer until Customer has paid in cash all amounts owing said Dealer. Customer shall not misuse, secrete, sell, encumber, remove or otherwise dispose of or lose possession of said Chattel. There is no outstanding lien, mortgage, or other encumbrance against said Chattel. Should Customer fail to pay its indebtedness when due, or breach this contract, the entire unpaid balance shall at once become due and payable, and Dealer may without notice or demand, by process of law, or otherwise, take possession of said Chattel wherever located and retain all monies paid thereon for use of said Chattel. This Agreement may be assigned."

This language, known as the "Agreement," was printed at the bottom of standard invoice forms which Donald printed and sold to television dealers and repairmen. Moore began using this language on its forms when one of its customers ordered a set of invoices and specifically requested that this language be included on the forms. The customer apparently had clipped the requested language from a form prepared by Donald. Subsequently, when Zack Meyer ordered invoice forms from Moore, Moore copied the language that its previous customer had requested.

Upon discovering Zack Meyer's forms, Donald brought suit against Moore and Zack Meyer, claiming that their use of the language contained in the "Agreement" infringed Donald's copyright. The trial court, while expressing doubt concerning the originality of the "Agreement," found that Donald had a valid copyright on the language used by Moore and that Moore had infringed Donald's copyright by printing and selling the offending forms. The court enjoined Moore from any future infringement and assessed the costs of suit against Moore as required by 17 U.S.C.A. § 116. Finding that Zack Meyer had nothing whatever to do with the selection of language in the forms supplied by Moore, the court held that Zack Meyer was not liable for any copyright infringement and had been unnecessarily joined as a party defendant by Donald. Zack Meyer's counsel fees were divided equally between Moore and Donald.

Moore has appealed from the decision of the trial court, claiming that Donald's copyright is invalid for lack of originality. We agree.

It is too plain to be denied that the "Agreement" is nothing more than an ordinary conditional sales contract or chattel mortgage agreement, an instrument familiar to even the most inexperienced legal practitioner. It is the type of contract which has been published in numerous form books, many of which are themselves copyrighted.

Plaintiff, a non-lawyer who stated that he studied law for approximately one year, has denied that he used these prior works in preparing the "Agreement." However, considering the technical difficulties involved in drafting such a form, plaintiff's limited legal education, and his obvious access to and knowledge of these forms from his uncompleted legal studies, we have no doubt that plaintiff either consciously or unconsciously availed himself of these prior works while drafting the "Agreement." Moreover, the striking similarity in arrangement, order, and wording between plaintiff's "Agreement" and the standard forms is sufficient to compel a finding that plaintiff used these earlier works.

Neither the existence of these earlier forms nor Donald's use of them, however, necessarily renders his paragraph ineligible for copyright protection. It is settled law that to obtain a valid copyright, as distinguished from a patent, the applicant need not show that the material in question is unique or novel; it need only be original. Thus a work may be protected by copyright even though it is based on a prior copyrighted work or something already in the public domain if the author, through his skill and effort, has contributed a distinguishable variation from the older works. In such a case, of course, only those parts which are new are protected by the new copyright.

In determining the amount of originality required it is frequently stated that the standards are minimal and that in copyright law "originality means little more than a prohibition against copying." Gelles–Widmer Co. v. Milton Bradley Co., [313 F.2d 143]. Nevertheless, something more than merely refraining from outright copying is required before a new variation on an old work has sufficient originality to be copyrightable. The author must add "some substantial not merely trivial originality." Chamberlin v. Uris Sales Corp., 2 Cir.1945, 150 F.2d 512, 513, 65 U.S.P.Q. 544, 545; the variation must be meaningful and must result from original creative work on the author's part. Amsterdam v. Triangle Publications, Inc., 3 Cir.1951, 189 F.2d 104, 89 U.S.P.Q. 468; Smith v. George E. Muehlebach Brewing Co., W.D.Mo. 1956, 140 F.Supp. 729, 110 U.S.P.Q. 177. As the court said in Smith,

> 'Originality' in the above context means that the material added to what is in the public domain, must have aspects of 'novelty' and be something more than a trivial addition or variation. If what is added does not itself give some value to a public domain composition, or serve some purpose other than to merely emphasize what is present and subsisting in the public domain, it is not entitled to copyright. 140 F.Supp. at 731, 110 U.S.P.Q. at 178.

In the case before us we search in vain for the requisite originality in plaintiff's "Agreement." The "Agreement" contains nothing of substance which resulted from Donald's creative work. The order and arrangement of the subject matter in the "Agreement" are identical with several forms suggested in prior works. The word arrangement used, while not identical, is at most only a paraphrase of various portions of earlier forms, and in copyright law paraphrasing is equivalent to outright copying. The plaintiff did no original legal research which resulted in a significant addition to the standard conditional sales contract or chattel mortgage forms; he merely made trivial word changes by combining various forms and servilely imitating the already stereotyped language found therein. In fact it may be fairly assumed that such variations in language as did occur in plaintiff's "Agreement" were deliberately insignificant, for he plainly wanted a valid conditional sales contract or chattel mortgage, and validity was an attribute which the earlier forms had been proved through use to have.

In Amsterdam v. Triangle Publications, Inc., supra, the Third Circuit faced a claim to copyright protection in a similar situation. The plaintiff in that case had used several existing maps but little independent original research of his own to prepare a map upon which he claimed a copyright. In denying his map copyright protection from a claimed infringement, the court, adopting the language of the trial court, said:

> To make his map, the plaintiff had to determine only what information he was going to use from other maps, the emphasis to be given to that information and the coloring scheme and symbols he was going to use. When he finished, his map by comparison was a new map that contained some information that was not on any one of his base maps but was collectively on all of these maps.

> Is this exercise of judgment and discretion by the plaintiff the type of original work that is intended to be protected by the Copyright Act? I think not.

>   .   .   .

> The presentation of ideas in the form of books, movies, music and other similar creative work is protected by the Copyright Act. However, the presentation of information available to everybody, such as is found on maps, is protected only when the publisher of the map in question obtains originally some of that information by the sweat of his own brow. Almost anybody could combine the information from several maps onto one map, but not everybody can go out and get that information originally and then transcribe it into a map.

> The plaintiff's reputation as a qualified map maker cannot make copyrightable maps for him. He, or his agents, must first do some original work, get more than an infinitesimal amount of original information. With no reflection whatsoever upon the plaintiff's ability as a map maker or upon other maps published and copyrighted by the plaintiff, it seems to me that the plaintiff's map entitled 'Map of Delaware County, Pa.' is, for lack or (sic) original work, not subject to copyright. 189 F.2d at 106, 89 U.S. P.Q. at 469.

In the case before us Donald has contributed nothing more than the map maker in Amsterdam. While the "Agreement" is not identical to any single existing form, the substance of each sentence can be found in an earlier form. Thus, like the map in Amsterdam, Donald's form is nothing more than a mosaic of the existing forms, with no original piece added. The Copyright Act was not designed to protect such neglible efforts. We reward creativity and originality with a copyright but we do not accord copyright protection to a mere copycat. As one noted authority has observed, "to make the copyright turnstile revolve, the author should have to deposit more than a penny in the box." B. Kaplan, An Unhurried View of Copyright 46 (1966). In our case not even the proverbial penny has been placed in the box. Indeed the box is virtually empty. We hold, therefore, that Donald's copyright is invalid for lack of originality. Having concluded that Donald's "Agreement" was not subject to copyright, we think it goes without saying that Moore's use of the form language was not an infringement.

The only remaining questions concern the assessment of costs and attorney's fees. The trial court assessed the costs of suit against the losing party, Moore, as required by 17 U.S.C.A. § 116. Since we have reversed the trial court's determination on the merits, Donald, the losing party, must pay the costs as required by statute. An award of attorneys' fees is discretionary under § 116, and the trial court exercised this discretion by directing that Donald and Moore pay their own counsel fees. We see no reason to disturb this determination. The counsel fees incurred by Zack Meyer were divided by the trial court equally between Donald and Moore. We think, however, that the entire amount of this expense must be assessed against Donald. Moore has already been put to the expense of defending an infringement suit against an invalid copyright claim. It was Donald who unnecessarily joined Zack Meyer as a party defendant, and it is Donald who should bear the expense for this error.

Reversed.

NOTES

1. *Fact Works.* Was *Miller* correct to conclude that "[t]here is no rational basis for distinguishing between facts and the research involved in obtaining facts?" Fact works will often be protected as compilations—works "formed by the collection and assembling of preexisting materials or of data that are selected, coordinated, or arranged in such a way that the resulting work as a whole constitutes an original work of authorship." 17 U.S.C.A. § 101. Why should copyright law treat the research involved in obtaining facts less generously than the selection, coordination or arrangement of facts?

On copyright protection for fact works, see Denicola, Copyright in Collections of Facts: A Theory for the Protection of Nonfiction Literary Works, 81 Colum.L.Rev. 516 (1981); Patry, Copyright in Collection of Facts: A Reply, 6 Comm. & Law 11 (1984); Shipley & Hay, Protecting Research: Copyright, Common Law Alternatives, and Federal Preemption, 63 N.C.L.Rev. 125 (1984). See also two articles by Professor Robert Gorman, Copyright Protection for the Collection and Representation of Facts, 76 Harv.L.Rev. 1569 (1963) and Fact or Fancy? The Implications for Copyright, 29 J. Copyright Soc'y U.S.A. 560 (1982).

2. *Maps.* Maps have long raised thorny issues for copyright protection. Amsterdam v. Triangle Publications, Inc., 189 F.2d 104, 89 U.S.P.Q. 468 (3d Cir.1951), typifies some of the doctrinal problems. Plaintiff contended that defendant's county map infringed the copyright in its map consisting of information compiled at the expense of "considerable time and effort," and obtained almost exclusively "from maps already in existence, although none of this information had been published previously on any one map." Acknowledging defendant's concession that it had copied, the court of appeals ruled that plaintiff's map was insufficiently original to qualify for copyright protection. First, "[t]he location of county lines, township lines and municipal lines is information within the public domain, and is not copyrightable." Second, "the presentation of information available to everybody, such as is found on maps, is protected only when the publisher of the map in question obtains originally some of that information by the sweat of his own brow. . . . He, or his agents, must first do some original work, get more than an infinitesimal amount of original information." 189 F.2d at 106.

United States v. Hamilton, 583 F.2d 448, 200 U.S.P.Q. 14 (9th Cir. 1978), is the leading case to reject *Amsterdam* 's direct observation rule. *Hamilton* upheld copyright in a map that, though based on a state highway department map, also contained elements compiled from other maps and information that had not previously appeared in map form. "[T]he elements of authorship embodied in a map consist not only of the depiction of a previously undiscovered landmark or the correction or improvement of scale or placement, but also in selection, design, and synthesis." The court observed that "[e]xpression in cartography is not so different from other artistic forms seeking to touch upon external realities that unique rules are needed to judge whether the authorship is original." Consequently, "elements of compilation which amount to more than a matter of trivial selection may, either alone or when taken into consideration with direct observation, support a finding that a map is sufficiently original to merit copyright protection." 583 F.2d at 451–52.

See generally, Whicher, Originality, Cartography, and Copyright, 38 N.Y.U. L.Rev. 280 (1963).

3. *Directories.* Two decisions of the Court of Appeals for the Second Circuit illuminate the boundaries of copyright protection for directories. In Eckes v. Card Prices Update, 736 F.2d 859, 222 U.S.P.Q. 762 (2d Cir.1984), the court held that plaintiff's comprehensive listing of 18,000 baseball cards with their market prices—divided into 5,000 premium cards and 13,000 common cards—was copyrightable: "We have no doubt that appellants exercised selection, creativity and judgment in choosing among the 18,000 or so different baseball cards in order to determine which were the 5,000 premium cards." 736 F.2d at 863.

By contrast, in Financial Information, Inc. v. Moody's Investors Service, Inc., 808 F.2d 204, 1 U.S.P.Q.2d 1279 (2d Cir.1986), cert. denied,

108 S.Ct. 79, 98 L.Ed.2d 42 (1987), the court held that plaintiff's "Daily Bond Cards," which reported all municipal bond redemptions across the country, and listed the issuing authority, the series of bonds being called, the date and price of the redemption, and the name of the trustee or paying agent, were not copyrightable. In the court's view, the Copyright Act "requires that copyrightability not be determined by the amount of effort the author expends, but rather by the nature of the final result." 808 F.2d at 207. The court distinguished *Eckes* on the ground that the selectivity, creativity and judgment present there were missing from the facts before it. "Relying in significant measure on its evaluation of the credibility of witnesses—which we are ill-disposed to disturb on appeal—the district court found that there was insufficient proof of 'independent creation' to render the Daily Bond Cards copyrightable. The researchers had five facts to fill in on each card—nothing more and nothing less. They sometimes did minor additional research in order to find these facts, but little 'independent creation' was involved. This conclusion is amply supported by the record and certainly not clearly erroneous." 808 F.2d at 208.

Would the court have found protectible selection if, instead of reporting all redeemed bonds, plaintiff reported only the redemption of bonds rated by a particular rating agency? Should the court have found protectible selection in plaintiff's initial choice of the five facts to be filled in on each card?

4. *Case Reports.* The leading decision on case reports, Callaghan v. Myers, 128 U.S. 617, 9 S.Ct. 177, 32 L.Ed. 547 (1888), held that copyright extends not only to a report's "title-page, table of cases, head-notes, statements of facts, arguments of counsel, and index," but also to "the order of arrangement of the cases, the division of the reports into volumes, the numbering and paging of the volumes, the table of cases cited in the opinions, (where such table is made,) and the subdivision of the index into appropriate, condensed titles, involving the distribution of the subjects of the various head-notes, and cross-references, where such exist." 128 U.S. at 649, 9 S.Ct. at 185.

West Publishing Co. v. Mead Data Central, Inc., 799 F.2d 1219, 230 U.S.P.Q. 801 (8th Cir.1986), cert. denied, 479 U.S. 1070, 107 S.Ct. 962, 93 L.Ed.2d 1010 (1987), may approach the high-water mark for copyright protection of case reports. The court there upheld the lower court's grant of preliminary relief to West on the ground that its arrangement of cases in its case reports was protectible because it was the "result of considerable labor, talent, and judgment." The court held that the pagination of West's reports, which reflected this arrangement, was also copyrightable, and that the insertion of plaintiff's page numbers in defendant's computer-based legal research system would infringe plaintiff's copyright. See generally, Locke, A Critical Analysis of West Publishing Company v. Mead Data Central, Inc., 36 J. Copyright Soc'y 182 (1989); Patterson & Joyce, Monopolizing the Law: The Scope of Copyright Protection for Law Reports and Statutory Compilations, 36 UCLA L.Rev. 719 (1989).

5. *Functional Works.* Functional works, such as the legal form in *Zack Meyer's,* differ from other types of copyright subject matter. Where most copyrighted works aim to please the senses, functional works aim mainly at efficiency. Consequently, the room for expression and originality in functional works will typically be cramped—and sometimes nonexistent. For example, in Morrissey v. Procter & Gamble Co., 379 F.2d 675, 678, 154 U.S.P.Q. 193 (1st Cir.1967), the court held that the plaintiff's statement of rules, though original and expressive, was uncopyrightable. "When the uncopyrightable subject matter is very narrow, so that 'the topic necessarily requires,' if not only one form of expression, at best only a limited number, to permit copyrighting would mean that a party or parties, by copyrighting a mere handful of forms, could exhaust all possibilities of future use of the substance."

B. RIGHTS AND REMEDIES

1. RIGHTS

See Statute Supplement 17 U.S.C.A. §§ 106–119, 201–205, 302–305, 602–603, 801–810.

a. THE NATURE OF COPYRIGHT

BAKER v. SELDEN

Supreme Court of the United States, 1879.
101 U.S. 99, 25 L.Ed. 841.

Mr. Justice BRADLEY delivered the opinion of the court.

Charles Selden, the testator of the complainant in this case, in the year 1859 took the requisite steps for obtaining the copyright of a book, entitled "Selden's Condensed Ledger, or Bookkeeping Simplified," the object of which was to exhibit and explain a peculiar system of book-keeping. In 1860 and 1861, he took the copyright of several other books, containing additions to and improvements upon the said system. The bill of complaint was filed against the defendant, Baker, for an alleged infringement of these copyrights. The latter, in his answer, denied that Selden was the author or designer of the books, and denied the infringement charged, and contends on the argument that the matter alleged to be infringed is not a lawful subject of copyright.

The parties went into proofs, and the various books of the complainant, as well as those sold and used by the defendant, were exhibited before the examiner, and witnesses were examined on both sides. A decree was rendered for the complainant, and the defendant appealed.

The book or series of books of which the complainant claims the copyright consists of an introductory essay explaining the system of book-keeping referred to, to which are annexed certain forms or blanks, consisting of ruled lines, and headings, illustrating the system and showing how it is to be used and carried out in practice. This system effects the same results as book-keeping by double entry; but, by a peculiar arrangement of columns and headings, presents the entire operation, of a day, a week, or a month, on a single page, or on two pages facing each other, in an account-book. The defendant uses a similar plan so far as results are concerned; but makes a different arrangement of the columns, and uses different headings. If the complainant's testator had the exclusive right to the use of the system explained in his book, it would be difficult to contend that the defendant does not infringe it, notwithstanding the difference in his form of arrangement; but if it be assumed that the system is open to the public use, it seems to be equally difficult to contend that the books made and sold by the defendant are a violation of the copyright of the complainant's book considered merely as a book explanatory of the system. Where the truths of a science or the methods of an art are the common property of the whole world, any author has the right to express the one, or explain and use the other, in his own way. As an author, Selden explained the system in a particular way. It may be conceded that Baker makes and uses account-books arranged on substantially the same system; but the proof fails to show that he has violated the copyright of Selden's book, regarding the latter merely as an explanatory work; or that he has infringed Selden's right in any way, unless the latter became entitled to an exclusive right in the system.

The evidence of the complainant is principally directed to the object of showing that Baker uses the same system as that which is explained and illustrated in Selden's books. It becomes important, therefore, to determine whether, in obtaining the copyright of his books, he secured the exclusive right to the use of the system or method of book-keeping which the said books are intended to illustrate and explain. It is contended that he has secured such exclusive right, because no one can use the system without using substantially the same ruled lines and headings which he has appended to his books in illustration of it. In other words, it is contended that the ruled lines and headings, given to illustrate the system, are a part of the book, and, as such, are secured by the copyright; and that no one can make or use similar ruled lines and headings, or ruled lines and headings made and arranged on substantially the same system, without violating the copyright. And this is really the question to be decided in this case. Stated in another form, the question is, whether the exclusive property in a system of book-keeping can be claimed, under the law of copyright, by means of a book in which that system is explained? The complainant's bill, and the case made under it, are based on the hypothesis that it can be.

It cannot be pretended, and indeed it is not seriously urged, that the ruled lines of the complainant's account-book can be claimed under any special class of objects, other than books, named in the law of copyright existing in 1859. The law then in force was that of 1831, and specified only books, maps, charts, musical compositions, prints, and engravings. An account-book, consisting of ruled lines and blank columns, cannot be called by any of these names unless by that of a book.

There is no doubt that a work on the subject of book-keeping, though only explanatory of well-known systems, may be the subject of a copyright; but, then, it is claimed only as a book. Such a book may be explanatory either of old systems, or of an entirely new system; and, considered as a book, as the work of an author, conveying information on the subject of book-keeping, and containing detailed explanations of the art, it may be a very valuable acquisition to the practical knowledge of the community. But there is a clear distinction between the book, as such, and the art which it is intended to illustrate. The mere statement of the proposition is so evident, that it requires hardly any argument to support it. The same distinction may be predicated of every other art as well as that of book-keeping. A treatise on the composition and use of medicines, be they old or new; on the construction and use of ploughs, or watches, or churns; or on the mixture and application of colors for painting or dyeing; or on the mode of drawing lines to produce the effect of perspective,—would be the subject of copyright; but no one would contend that the copyright of the treatise would give the exclusive right to the art or manufacture described therein. The copyright of the book, if not pirated from other works, would be valid without regard to the novelty, or want of novelty, of its subject-matter. The novelty of the art or thing described or explained has nothing to do with the validity of the copyright. To give to the author of the book an exclusive property in the art described therein, when no examination of its novelty has ever been officially made, would be a surprise and a fraud upon the public. That is the province of letters-patent, not of copyright. The claim to an invention or discovery of an art or manufacture must be subjected to the examination of the Patent Office before an exclusive right therein can be obtained; and it can only be secured by a patent from the government.

The difference between the two things, letters-patent and copyright, may be illustrated by reference to the subjects just enumerated. Take the case of medicines. Certain mixtures are found to be of great value in the healing art. If the discoverer writes and publishes a book on the subject (as regular physicians generally do), he gains no exclusive right to the manufacture and sale of the medicine; he gives that to the public. If he desires to acquire such exclusive right, he must obtain a patent for the mixture as a new art, manufacture, or composition of matter. He may copyright his book, if he pleases; but that only secures to him the exclusive right of printing and publishing his book. So of all other inventions or discoveries.

The copyright of a book on perspective, no matter how many drawings and illustrations it may contain, gives no exclusive right to the modes of drawing described, though they may never have been known or used before. By publishing the book, without getting a patent for the art, the latter is given to the public. The fact that the art described in the book by illustrations of lines and figures which are reproduced in practice in the application of the art, makes no difference. Those illustrations are the mere language employed by the author to convey his ideas more clearly. Had he used words of description instead of diagrams (which merely stand in the place of words), there could not be the slightest doubt that others, applying the art to practical use, might lawfully draw the lines and diagrams which were in the author's mind, and which he thus described by words in his book.

The copyright of a work on mathematical science cannot give to the author an exclusive right to the methods of operation which he propounds, or to the diagrams which he employs to explain them, so as to prevent an engineer from using them whenever occasion requires. The very object of publishing a book on science or the useful arts is to communicate to the world the useful knowledge which it contains. But this object would be frustrated if the knowledge could not be used without incurring the guilt of piracy of the book. And where the art it teaches cannot be used without employing the methods and diagrams used to illustrate the book, or such as are similar to them, such methods and diagrams are to be considered as necessary incidents to the art, and given therewith to the public; not given for the purpose of publication in other works explanatory of the art, but for the purpose of practical application.

Of course, these observations are not intended to apply to ornamental designs, or pictorial illustrations addressed to the taste. Of these it may be said, that their form is their essence, and their object, the production of pleasure in their contemplation. This is their final end. They are as much the product of genius and the result of composition, as are the lines of the poet or the historian's periods. On the other hand, the teachings of science and the rules and methods of useful art have their final end in application and use; and this application and use are what the public derive from the publication of a book which teaches them. But as embodied and taught in a literary composition or book, their essence consists only in their statement. This alone is what is secured by the copyright. The use by another of the same methods of statement, whether in words or illustrations, in a book published for teaching the art, would undoubtedly be an infringement of the copyright.

Recurring to the case before us, we observe that Charles Selden, by his books, explained and described a peculiar system of book-keeping, and illustrated his method by means of ruled lines and blank columns, with proper headings on a page, or on successive pages. Now, whilst no one has a right to print or publish his book, or any material part thereof, as a book intended to convey instruction in the art, any person may practice and use the art itself which he has described and illustrated therein. The use of the art is a totally different thing from a publication of the book explaining it. The copyright of a book on book-keeping cannot secure the exclusive right to make, sell, and use account-books prepared upon the plan set forth in such book. Whether the art might or might not have been patented, is a question which is not before us. It was not patented, and is open and free to the use of the public. And, of course, in using the art, the ruled lines and headings of accounts must necessarily be used as incident to it.

The plausibility of the claim put forward by the complainant in this case arises from a confusion of ideas produced by the peculiar nature of the art described in the books which have been made the subject of copyright. In describing the art, the illustrations and diagrams employed happen to correspond more closely than usual with the actual work performed by the operator who uses the art. Those illustrations and diagrams consist of ruled lines and headings of accounts; and it is similar ruled lines and headings of accounts which, in the application of the art, the book-keeper makes with his pen, or the stationer with his press; whilst in most other cases the diagrams and illustrations can only be represented in concrete forms of wood, metal, stone, or some other physical embodiment. But the principle is the same in all. The description of the art in a book, though entitled to the benefit of copyright, lays no foundation for an exclusive claim to the art itself. The object of the one is explanation; the object of the other is use. The former may be secured by copyright. The latter can only be secured, if it can be secured at all, by letters-patent. . . .

Another case, that of Page v. Wisden (20 L.T.N.S. 435), which came before Vice–Chancellor Malins in 1869, has some resemblance to the present. There a copyright was claimed in a cricket scoring-sheet, and the Vice–Chancellor held that it was not a fit subject for copyright, partly because it was not new, but also because "to say that a particular mode of ruling a book constituted an object for a copyright is absurd."

These cases, if not precisely in point, come near to the matter in hand, and, in our view, corroborate the general proposition which we have laid down. . . .

The conclusion to which we have come is, that blank account-books are not the subject of copyright; and that the mere copyright of Selden's book did not confer upon him the exclusive right to make and use account-books, ruled and arranged as designated by him and described and illustrated in said book.

The decree of the Circuit Court must be reversed, and the cause remanded with instructions to dismiss the complainant's bill; and it is so ordered.

RUSSELL v. PRICE

United States Court of Appeals, Ninth Circuit, 1979.
612 F.2d 1123, 205 U.S.P.Q. 206, cert. denied, 446 U.S. 952, 100 S.Ct. 2919,
64 L.Ed.2d 809 (1980).

GOODWIN, Circuit Judge:

Defendants distributed copies of the film "Pygmalion", the copyright for which had expired. They were sued by the owners of the renewal copyright in the George Bernard Shaw play upon which the film was based. Defendants appeal the resulting judgment for damages and attorney fees.

Plaintiffs cross appeal, claiming that the court erred in not award-ing them statutory "in lieu" damages. We affirm.

In 1913 Shaw registered a copyright on his stage play "Pygmalion". The renewal copyright on the play, obtained in 1941 and originally scheduled to expire in 1969, was extended by Congressional action to the year 1988. Shaw died in 1950 and the plaintiffs, except for Janus Films, are current proprietors of the copyright. Janus Films is a licensee.

In 1938 a derivative version of the play, a motion picture also entitled "Pygmalion", was produced under a license from Shaw; neither the terms nor the licensee's identity appear in the record. The film was produced by Gabriel Pascal, copyrighted by Loew's, and distributed by Metro–Goldwyn–Mayer ("MGM"). For undisclosed rea-sons, the film's copyright was allowed to expire in 1966. When and if the original film rights agreement expired is also not disclosed.

In 1971 the play's copyright proprietors licensed Janus Films to be the exclusive distributor of the film "Pygmalion". Shortly after discov-ering in 1972 that Budget Films was renting out copies of the 1938 film, Janus brought action against Budget in a California state court, alleg-ing state causes of action—in particular, unfair competition. That case ended in Budget's favor upon a determination that the action was essentially one for copyright infringement over which the state court lacked jurisdiction. The English copyright proprietors then executed a power of attorney in favor of their licensee Janus, and Janus promptly brought this action in federal district court in May 1975. . . .

Defendants' main contention on the primary issue in this litigation is simply stated: Because the film copyright on "Pygmalion" has expired, that film is in the public domain, and, consequently, prints of that film may be used freely by anyone. Thus, they argue that their renting out of the film does not infringe the statutory copyright on Shaw's play.

Defendants rely almost entirely on the recent opinion of Judge Friendly in Rohauer v. Killiam Shows, Inc., 551 F.2d 484 (2d Cir.), cert. denied, 431 U.S. 949, 97 S.Ct. 2666, 53 L.Ed.2d 266 (1977). However, in so relying, they ignore or fail to appreciate the significant differences between that case and this one.

In *Rohauer* the author of a novel which was statutorily copyrighted in 1925 assigned exclusive movie rights to one Moskowitz, specifically promising in the contract to reassign to him or his successor in interest all film rights for the novel's copyright renewal term. A successful silent film was made under that assignment and separately copyrighted in 1926 by an assignee of Moskowitz. Unfortunately, the novel's author died prior to the end of the novel's first copyright term. The author's daughter, as statutory beneficiary of the right to renew, inherited the renewal term free from the film license granted by her mother.[11] The daughter then granted exclusive movie and television

---

11. The optional renewal term under the Copyright Act of 1909, 17 U.S.C. § 24 (1976), was considered to be a "new estate", so that the proprietor of the renewal term

rights for the renewal term to Rohauer. Killiam Shows, Inc., successor in interest to the 1926 film's renewal copyright, allowed the film to be shown on educational television without Rohauer's or the daughter's authorization, whereupon the latter two brought a copyright infringement action against Killiam.

The Second Circuit held on those facts that the derivative film's independent copyright entitled the defendant to continue showing the film without infringing rights under the renewal copyright in the underlying novel. Defendants here understand by this that a derivative copyright covers more than the new matter which the producer of the derivative work added to the underlying work. Thus, they say that when the derivative copyright expires the whole product enters the public domain free of the monopoly protection of any subsisting copyright in the underlying work. The court's opinion in *Rohauer*, however, makes it clear that this is simply not the case.

First, the *Rohauer* court placed heavy emphasis on the nongratuitous intent of the nonsurviving author to convey film rights in the novel's renewal term, a promise which had been bargained for in the initial assignment. The defendants here have never bargained with Shaw or his successors for anything, nor do they enjoy any relationship with anyone who had so bargained.

A second important difference between the favored party in *Rohauer* and the defendants here is that the defendant Killiam there was the proprietor of the still valid copyright in the film. By virtue of that copyright, Killiam was held to have sufficient rights in the matter derived from the novel to continue showing it as part of the film. A prominent rationale in that case for awarding those limited rights in favor of the owner of the derivative copyright is the protection and encouragement of the "large and independently copyrightable" "literary, musical and economic" contributions of the "person who with the consent of the author has created an opera or a motion picture film" from a copyrighted novel. 551 F.2d at 493. However, whatever place sympathy for the position of creators of derivative works might properly have under the 1909 Copyright Act, the defendants here can take advantage of none, having contributed nothing to the production of the film "Pygmalion".

Nor is it apparent under *Rohauer* that such sympathy should have any place at all when the independent copyright on the derivative work has been allowed to expire. For then there is no longer a conflict between two copyrights, each apparently granting "their proprietors overlapping 'exclusive' rights to use whatever underlying material * * * had been incorporated into the derivative film." Comment, Derivative Copyright and the 1909 Act—New Clarity or Confusion?, 44 Brooklyn L.Rev. 905, 912 (1978) (footnote omitted). Thus, the persons who might have had standing to raise the *Rohauer* claim here could,

copyright could exploit it free of any rights, interests or licenses assigned or made during the copyright's initial term.

consistently with that case, be held to have forfeited it by their failure to renew the derivative copyright. Defendants here could never have laid claim to the right recognized in *Rohauer,* and we perceive no reason to award it to them at the expense of the holders of the renewal copyright which still covers the Shaw play.

Thus, we reaffirm, without finding it necessary to repeat the rationale, the well-established doctrine that a derivative copyright protects only the new material contained in the derivative work, not the matter derived from the underlying work. Thus, although the derivative work may enter the public domain, the matter contained therein which derives from a work still covered by statutory copyright is not dedicated to the public. The established doctrine prevents unauthorized copying or other infringing use of the underlying work or any part of that work contained in the derivative product so long as the underlying work itself remains copyrighted. Therefore, since exhibition of the film "Pygmalion" necessarily involves exhibition of parts of Shaw's play, which is still copyrighted, plaintiffs here may prevent defendants from renting the film for exhibition without their authorization. . . .

. . . The underlying statutory copyright in the instant case will expire in 1988. After that time Budget may freely distribute its copies of the 1938 film. The result we reach here does not conflict with the limited monopoly policy rooted in the Copyrights Clause of the constitution and advanced in the congressional acts.

For the foregoing reasons, we conclude that defendants' activities here infringed the subsisting copyright in Shaw's play and were properly enjoined.

. . . Affirmed.

NOTES

1. Did Baker v. Selden hold that plaintiff's subject matter was not copyrightable? That, though copyrightable, plaintiff had no rights in it against the use being made by defendant? That, although plaintiff had rights in the work, they were not infringed by defendant's work? The case has been cited as authority for each of these three propositions.

Baker's second proposition, if taken to hold that copyright secures no right to use, obviously goes too far. Although the Copyright Act, unlike the Patent Act, nowhere grants a blanket right to use, each of its specific rights implies some specific use. For example, in Scholz Homes, Inc. v. Maddox, 379 F.2d 84, 154 U.S.P.Q. 197 (6th Cir.1967), plaintiff accused defendant of copying his architectural plans and of building a house from them. The court distinguished two cases that had "considered and rejected the contention that copyrighted plans were infringed merely by constructing buildings according to those plans" and concluded that "even if the holder of a copyright of architectural plans cannot prevent others from building according to those plans, he might still retain the exclusive right to their duplication." 379 F.2d at 85. Noting that *Baker* would seem to go farther than the two distinguished cases and permit even the copying of plans, the court added:

> perhaps the most promising method of avoiding this difficulty is to argue that copyrighted architectural plans should be treated differently from copyrighted books, and that the principles enunciated in *Baker* should therefore be held inapplicable. . . . It is far less obvious that architectural plans are prepared for the purpose of instructing the general public as to how the depicted structure might be built. Rather, they are often prepared so that they may be used in the building of unique structures, or at least structures limited in number. If the copyright statute protected merely against the vending of plans instead of against their unauthorized use, it would therefore fail to afford a form of protection architects might strongly desire. This protection would most effectively be provided by holding the unauthorized construction of a building according to a copyrighted plan to be an infringement; if *Baker* is followed to the extent of holding that the possession of the copyright in the plans gives no exclusive right to construct the building, then protection could be provided by declaring the making of unauthorized copies of the plans to be an infringement.

379 F.2d at 86. For a more straightforward declaration that the copying of architectural plans constitutes infringement, see Imperial Homes Corp. v. Lamont, 458 F.2d 895, 173 U.S.P.Q. 519 (5th Cir.1972).

2. As a practical matter, what fell into the public domain when the motion picture copyright in Russell v. Price was not renewed? See generally, Nevins, The Doctrine of Copyright Ambush: Limitations on the Free Use of Public Domain Derivative Works, 25 St. Louis U.L.J. 58 (1981). See also Brown, The Widening Gyre: Are Derivative Works Getting Out of Hand?, 3 Cardozo Arts & Ent.L.J. 1 (1984); Goldstein, Derivative Rights and Derivative Works in Copyright, 30 J.Copyright Soc'y 209 (1983).

3. How would you decide the following cases:

Plaintiff, which compiled and published a booklet of forms, "Standard Documents of the American Institute of Architects," seeks damages from defendant who has made and used six copies of one form and delivered them to contractors. See American Institute of Architects v. Fenichel, 41 F.Supp. 146, 51 U.S.P.Q. 29 (S.D. N.Y.1941).

Plaintiff, who secured copyright in a work described as "Bridge Approach—The drawing shows a novel bridge approach to unsnarl traffic congestion," seeks damages from defendant which allegedly used the work in its "design, plan, construction and operation of the Approach to Cross Bay Parkway Bridge." See Muller v. Triborough Bridge Auth., 43 F.Supp. 298, 52 U.S.P.Q. 227 (S.D.N.Y. 1942).

Plaintiff, owner of copyright in a series of books that expound a system of shorthand, claims infringement by defendant's work which contains a substantial portion of the system together with plaintiff's "expression of the mode and manner of teaching it." See Brief English Systems, Inc. v. Owen, 48 F.2d 555, 9 U.S.P.Q. 20 (2d Cir.1931).

Plaintiff, owner of rights to "Rapid Contract Bridge," charges infringement by defendant's publication in its newspaper of a problem substantially similar to one appearing in plaintiff's book. See Russell v. Northeastern Pub. Co., 7 F.Supp. 571, 23 U.S.P.Q. 123 (D.Mass.1934).

Plaintiff, copyright owner of two college physics texts containing problems—without answers—based on the text material, seeks an injunction against defendant's publication of a book containing solutions to the problems. See Addison–Wesley Pub. Co. v. Brown, 223 F.Supp. 219, 139 U.S.P.Q. 47 (E.D.N.Y.1963).

What other facts would you want to know in formulating your answers to these questions?

b. STATUTORY RIGHTS

COPYRIGHT LAW REVISION, H.R. REP. NO. 94–1476
94th Cong., 2d Sess. 61–65 (1976).

Section 106. Exclusive Rights in Copyrighted Works

General Scope of Copyright

The five fundamental rights that the bill gives to copyright owners—the exclusive rights of reproduction, adaptation, publication, performance, and display—are stated generally in section 106. These exclusive rights, which comprise the so-called "bundle of rights" that is a copyright, are cumulative and may overlap in some cases. Each of the five enumerated rights may be subdivided indefinitely and, as discussed below in connection with section 201, each subdivision of an exclusive right may be owned and enforced separately.

The approach of the bill is to set forth the copyright owner's exclusive rights in broad terms in section 106, and then to provide various limitations, qualifications, or exemptions in the 12 sections that follow. Thus, everything in section 106 is made "subject to sections 107 through 118," * and must be read in conjunction with those provisions.

The exclusive rights accorded to a copyright owner under section 106 are "to do and to authorize" any of the activities specified in the five numbered clauses. Use of the phrase "to authorize" is intended to avoid any questions as to the liability of contributory infringers. For example, a person who lawfully acquires an authorized copy of a motion picture would be an infringer if he or she engages in the business of renting it to others for purposes of unauthorized public performance.

---

* The Satellite Home Viewer Act of 1988, Pub.L. No. 100–667, 102 Stat. 3949, added a new section 119 to the 1976 Act.

Rights of Reproduction, Adaptation, and Publication

The first three clauses of section 106, which cover all rights under a copyright except those of performance and display, extend to every kind of copyrighted work. The exclusive rights encompassed by these clauses, though closely related, are independent; they can generally be characterized as rights of copying, recording, adaptation, and publishing. A single act of infringement may violate all of these rights at once, as where a publisher reproduces, adapts, and sells copies of a person's copyrighted work as part of a publishing venture. Infringement takes place when any one of the rights is violated: where, for example, a printer reproduces copies without selling them or a retailer sells copies without having anything to do with their reproduction. The references to "copies or phonorecords," although in the plural, are intended here and throughout the bill to include the singular (1 U.S. C.A. § 1).

Reproduction.—Read together with the relevant definitions in section 101, the right "to reproduce the copyrighted work in copies or phonorecords" means the right to produce a material object in which the work is duplicated, transcribed, imitated, or simulated in a fixed form from which it can be "perceived, reproduced, or otherwise communicated, either directly or with the aid of a machine or device." As under the present law, a copyrighted work would be infringed by reproducing it in whole or in any substantial part, and by duplicating it exactly or by imitation or simulation. Wide departures or variations from the copyrighted work would still be an infringement as long as the author's "expression" rather than merely the author's "ideas" are taken. An exception to this general principle, applicable to the reproduction of copyrighted sound recordings, is specified in section 114.

"Reproduction" under clause (1) of section 106 is to be distinguished from "display" under clause (5). For a work to be "reproduced," its fixation in tangible form must be "sufficiently permanent or stable to permit it to be perceived, reproduced, or otherwise communicated for a period of more than transitory duration." Thus, the showing of images on a screen or tube would not be a violation of clause (1), although it might come within the scope of clause (5).

Preparation of Derivative Works.—The exclusive right to prepare derivative works, specified separately in clause (2) of section 106, overlaps the exclusive right of reproduction to some extent. It is broader than that right, however, in the sense that reproduction requires fixation in copies or phonorecords, whereas the preparation of a derivative work, such as a ballet, pantomime, or improvised performance, may be an infringement even though nothing is ever fixed in tangible form.

To be an infringement the "derivative work" must be "based upon the copyrighted work," and the definition in section 101 refers to "a translation, musical arrangement, dramatization, fictionalization, motion picture version, sound recording, art reproduction, abridgment, condensation, or any other form in which a work may be recast, transformed, or adapted." Thus, to constitute a violation of section 106(2), the infringing work must incorporate a portion of the copyrighted work in some form; for example, a detailed commentary on a work or a programmatic musical composition inspired by a novel would not normally constitute infringements under this clause. . . .

Public Distribution.—Clause (3) of section 106 establishes the exclusive right of publication: The right "to distribute copies or phonorecords of the copyrighted work to the public by sale or other transfer of ownership, or by rental, lease, or lending." Under this provision the copyright owner would have the right to control the first public distribution of an authorized copy or phonorecord of his work, whether by sale, gift, loan, or some rental or lease arrangement. Likewise, any unauthorized public distribution of copies or phonorecords that were unlawfully made would be an infringement. As section 109 makes clear, however, the copyright owner's rights under section 106(3) cease with respect to a particular copy or phonorecord once he has parted with ownership of it.

Rights of Public Performance and Display

Performing Rights and the "For Profit" Limitation.—The right of public performance under section 106(4) extends to "literary, musical, dramatic, and choreographic works, pantomimes, and motion pictures and other audiovisual works and sound recordings" and, unlike the equivalent provisions now in effect, is not limited by any "for profit" requirement. The approach of the bill, as in many foreign laws, is first to state the public performance right in broad terms, and then to provide specific exemptions for educational and other nonprofit uses.

This approach is more reasonable than the outright exemption of the 1909 statute. The line between commercial and "nonprofit" organizations is increasingly difficult to draw. Many "non-profit" organizations are highly subsidized and capable of paying royalties, and the widespread public exploitation of copyrighted works by public broadcasters and other noncommercial organizations is likely to grow. In addition to these trends, it is worth noting that performances and displays are continuing to supplant markets for printed copies and that in the future a broad "not for profit" exemption could not only hurt authors but could dry up their incentive to write.

The exclusive right of public performance is expanded to include not only motion pictures, including works recorded on film, video tape, and video disks, but also audiovisual works such as filmstrips and sets of slides. This provision of section 106(4), which is consistent with the assimilation of motion pictures to audiovisual works throughout the bill, is also related to amendments of the definitions of "display" and "perform" discussed below. The important issue of performing rights in sound recordings is discussed in connection with section 114.

Right of Public Display.—Clause (5) of section 106 represents the first explicit statutory recognition in American copyright law of an exclusive right to show a copyrighted work, or an image of it, to the public. The existence or extent of this right under the present statute is uncertain and subject to challenge. The bill would give the owners of copyright in "literary, musical, dramatic, and choreographic works, pantomimes, and pictorial, graphic, or sculptural works", including the individual images of a motion picture or other audiovisual work, the exclusive right "to display the copyrighted work publicly."

Definitions

Under the definitions of "perform," "display," "publicly," and "transmit" in section 101, the concepts of public performance and public display cover not only the initial rendition or showing, but also any further act by which that rendition or showing is transmitted or communicated to the public. Thus, for example: a singer is performing when he or she sings a song; a broadcasting network is performing when it transmits his or her performance (whether simultaneously or from records); a local broadcaster is performing when it transmits the network broadcast; a cable television system is performing when it retransmits the broadcast to its subscribers; and any individual is performing whenever he or she plays a phonorecord embodying the performance or communicates the performance by turning on a receiving set. Although any act by which the initial performance or display is transmitted, repeated, or made to recur would itself be a "performance" or "display" under the bill, it would not be actionable as an infringement unless it were done "publicly," as defined in section 101. Certain other performances and displays, in addition to those that are "private," are exempted or given qualified copyright control under sections 107 through 118.

To "perform" a work, under the definition in section 101, includes reading a literary work aloud, singing or playing music, dancing a ballet or other choreographic work, and acting out a dramatic work or pantomime. A performance may be accomplished "either directly or by means of any device or process," including all kinds of equipment for reproducing or amplifying sounds or visual images, any sort of transmitting apparatus, any type of electronic retrieval system, and any other techniques and systems not yet in use or even invented.

The definition of "perform" in relation to "a motion picture or other audio visual work" is "to show its images in any sequence or to make the sounds accompanying it audible." The showing of portions of a motion picture, filmstrip, or slide set must therefore be sequential to constitute a "performance" rather than a "display", but no particular order need be maintained. The purely aural performance of a motion picture sound track, or of the sound portions of an audiovisual work, would constitute a performance of the "motion picture or other audiovisual work"; but, where some of the sounds have been reproduced separately on phonorecords, a performance from the phonorecord would not constitute performance of the motion picture or audiovisual work.

The corresponding definition of "display" covers any showing of a "copy" of the work, "either directly or by means of a film, slide, television image, or any other device or process." Since "copies" are defined as including the material object "in which the work is first fixed," the right of public display applies to original works of art as well as to reproductions of them. With respect to motion pictures and other audiovisual works, it is a "display" (rather than a "performance") to show their "individual images nonsequentially." In addition to the direct showings of a copy of a work, "display" would include the projection of an image on a screen or other surface by any method, the transmission of an image by electronic or other means, and the showing of an image on a cathode ray tube, or similar viewing apparatus connected with any sort of information storage and retrieval system.

Under clause (1) of the definition of "publicly" in section 101, a performance or display is "public" if it takes place "at a place open to the public or at any place where a substantial number of persons outside of a normal circle of a family and its social acquaintances is gathered." One of the principal purposes of the definition was to make clear that, contrary to the decision in Metro–Goldwyn–Mayer Distributing Corp. v. Wyatt, 21 C.O.Bull. 203 (D.Md.1932), performances in "semipublic" places such as clubs, lodges, factories, summer camps, and schools are "public performances" subject to copyright control. The term "a family" in this context would include an individual living alone, so that a gathering confined to the individual's social acquaintances would normally be regarded as private. Routine meetings of businesses and governmental personnel would be excluded because they do not represent the gathering of a "substantial number of persons."

Clause (2) of the definition of "publicly" in section 101 makes clear that the concepts of public performance and public display include not only performances and displays that occur initially in a public place, but also acts that transmit or otherwise communicate a performance or display of the work to the public by means of any device or process. The definition of "transmit"—to communicate a performance or display "by any device or process whereby images or sound are received beyond the place from which they are sent"—is broad enough to include all conceivable forms and combinations of wired or wireless communications media, including but by no means limited to radio and television broadcasting as we know them. Each and every method by which the images or sounds comprising a performance or display are picked up and conveyed is a "transmission," and if the transmission reaches the public in any form, the case comes within the scope of clauses (4) or (5) of section 106.

Under the bill, as under the present law, a performance made available by transmission to the public at large is "public" even though the recipients are not gathered in a single place, and even if there is no proof that any of the potential recipients was operating his receiving apparatus at the time of the transmission. The same principles apply whenever the potential recipients of the transmission represent a limited segment of the public, such as the occupants of hotel rooms or the subscribers of a cable television service. Clause (2) of the definition of "publicly" is applicable "whether the members of the public capable of receiving the performance or display receive it in the same place or in separate places and at the same time or at different times."

GOLDSTEIN, PREEMPTED STATE DOCTRINES, INVOLUNTARY TRANSFERS AND COMPULSORY LICENSES: TESTING THE LIMITS OF COPYRIGHT *
24 U.C.L.A.L.Rev. 1107, 1127–1135 (1977).

Of the thirteen sections defining the new law's statutory rights, four impose compulsory licenses. Section 111 specifies the conditions and fees under which cable television operators may transmit copyrighted materials without the consent of the copyright proprietor. Sections 115 and 116 prescribe the conditions and fees for recording musical compositions or performing them on jukeboxes without consent. Section 118 introduces compulsory licensing into the context of public broadcasting. Chapter 8 creates a Copyright Royalty Tribunal to oversee the administration of these provisions and to review and adjust the compulsory fees.

Like other systems of private property, copyright law is founded on the notion that privately bargained prices are preferable to publicly administered rates. Why, then, did Congress so warmly embrace the questionable economics of compulsory licensing? The most likely reason is consensus politics, not market economics. Faced with a welter of contending industrial and regulatory interests, Congress sought compromise positions lying somewhere between exclusive rights and no rights at all.[83] In the circumstances, it is a hard question whether the decision for compulsory licensing was correct. A closer look at the new provisions and at their possible investment effects is needed.

A. *Compulsory Licenses in the New Act*

In a sense, compulsory licenses are as old as equity's discretion to withhold injunctions when issuance of the decree would harm the defendant disproportionately to the plaintiff's benefit. By allowing defendants in these cases to continue their invasion of property rights upon payment of damages, courts substitute their estimate of appropri-

---

* Copyright © 1977 Paul Goldstein.

83. The Register of Copyrights, Barbara Ringer, has perceptively traced a recurrent theme in the political evolution of contemporary copyright law. The process begins with the exploitation of a new technological development expanding the use of copyrighted works. Next comes the question whether the new use constitutes copyright infringement; the discovery that "the 1909 copyright statute and the cases interpreting it contain no answers, only analogies;" and then an action for copyright infringement. Because the allegedly infringing activities have become widespread, and be-cause the 1909 Act is considered inapposite, courts "reluctantly hold against the copyright owner and urgently call upon Congress to do its duty and reform an archaic and unjust statute." Caught between the traditionally protected interests of creators and the pressures exerted by representatives of the newly emergent user industries, Congress is politically compelled to compromise. "Now, and even more in the future, the compromises seem likely to consist of compulsory licensing." Ringer, Copyright and the Future of Authorship, 101 Lib.J. 229, 231 (1976).

ate compensation for the figure that the parties would have arrived at privately. This result has been reached in real property cases and in patent cases. Compulsory licensing of patents has also been specifically authorized by statute in narrowly defined sets of circumstances. In all these situations, the compelled license fees are set individually for the particular parcel or invention involved so that the owner's reward is proportioned to the perceived value of his real property or invention.

The compulsory license provisions of the new copyright statute depart from this individualized approach by pegging their compulsory fees to a fixed rate. As a consequence, the royalties to be paid are uniform regardless of the work's individual market value. Some room for differentiated compensation does exist under the new law. Section 115 multiplies its uniform rate by the number of records distributed by the compulsory licensees, connecting total license fees to market appeal. Sections 111, 116 and 118, though generally undiscriminating, do leave some room for differentiation at the point at which fees are distributed to the copyright proprietors.

1. Section 111: Cable Transmission

Section 111 resolves the question of cable television's liability for retransmitting copyrighted programs originated by broadcast stations. The question, twice considered by the Supreme Court, occupied an important place on the copyright revision agenda from the outset. Section 111 is the product of many compromises and, more explicitly than any other aspect of the new law, commits its operation to assumptions about industry structure and regulation. The provision can be understood only against its industrial and regulatory background.

The earliest cable television systems consisted of prominently placed antennae connected by coaxial cable to the homes of subscribers in the surrounding area. The sole purpose of these early facilities was to provide television signals to areas that had been physically cut off from television.

Under the prevailing business arrangements in the broadcast industry, television stations, networks and copyright proprietors all stood to gain, not lose, from this new service. Television stations and networks get their revenues from advertisers and, roughly speaking, advertisers will pay more as the size of the audience delivered by a station increases. The interests of copyright proprietors generally coincide with the interests of the television stations and networks they license to carry their programs. As broadcast markets, and advertising revenues, expand, so do the prices at which broadcasters bid for copyrighted programs.

Cable quickly outgrew its early role, and broadcasters and copyright proprietors soon perceived the new medium's larger implications. By the 1960's cable systems were importing the broadcast signals of distant independent stations into markets that were already served by the three networks and by independent stations. In some communities cable also served to improve the quality of local signals already being received or originated programming on its own. The new services moved cable well beyond its initial role of expanding television markets and increasing broadcasters' revenues. Cable now competed with local broadcasters, capturing portions of their markets with programs received at no cost to the cable systems. Broadcasters, and the copyright proprietors who supplied them with programming, began to complain.

The Federal Communications Commission responded erratically to the question of liability of cable systems for distant signal importation. In 1966, seven years after it refused to take jurisdiction on the ground that cable did not interfere with broadcast television, the Commission asserted jurisdiction and imposed stringent limits on cable's freedom to import distant signals into the one hundred largest television markets. However, these regulations were soon suspended and, after a series of abortive proposals, the Commission in 1972 settled on the regulatory approach that is followed today. Under this approach, cable systems are required to serve a public utility function in carrying local signals and are permitted to carry a prescribed complement of distant signals. It is this approach that forms the basis for section 111's compulsory license provisions.

The basic approach of the present FCC regulations, and of section 111's compulsory licensing provisions, is embodied in the regulations' division between signals that a cable system is required to carry and those that it may, but not must, carry. Essentially, local signals fall into the category of "must carry," and distant signals into the category of "may carry," with the precise number of signals in each category assigned to a cable system determined by a calculus of technical and economic factors. For example, the number of distant signals that a system may import will vary with the size of the television market in which it is situated. Distant signal carriage is further limited by exclusivity rules under which, for example, a system may not import a program if a local network station is carrying the same program at the same time.

Because, in part, the fortunes of copyright proprietors are tied to those of broadcasters, the FCC's compromise between broadcasters and cable operators is also a compromise between copyright proprietors and cable operators. Section 111 takes the logic of this compromise as its starting point. Section 111(c) provides that "secondary transmissions to the public by a cable system of a primary transmission made by a broadcast station licensed by the Federal Communications Commission" shall be subject to compulsory licensing "where the carriage of the signals comprising the secondary transmission is permissible under the rules, regulations, or authorizations of the Federal Communications Commission." In short, retransmission of "must carry" and "may carry" signals falls within the statute's compulsory license.

Section 111 refines the logic of the FCC regulations in its method for computing the fees to be paid by any cable system under the compulsory license. Under a formula prescribed in section 111(d), fees are tied to the number of distant signal "equivalents" carried and to the gross receipts derived by the system from providing secondary transmissions. As gross receipts and number of distant signal equivalents increase, so do the compulsory license fees levied. Once royalties are received by the Copyright Office, and administrative costs deducted, aggregate royalties for the period are to be distributed to copyright proprietors in proportions determined by the Copyright Royalty Tribunal. Michael Botein, a close observer of cable-copyright issues, has aptly observed that the "failure to relate copyright consumption to copyright compensation points up Section 111's highly regulatory aspects."

Outside this basic regulatory scheme, section 111 specifies the circumstances under which secondary transmissions will be completely exempted from copyright liability, and those under which there will be full liability. Full liability is imposed for willful or repeated transmissions where the carriage of signals is not permissible under FCC rules or where the cable operator fails to comply with the prescribed compulsory licensing procedures; for retransmission of nonbroadcast primary transmissions, such as programs originated by another cable system; for transmission of Canadian and Mexican signals outside prescribed zones; and for transmission of foreign signals generally. Cable systems are also subject to full copyright liability if they substitute other program materials for the advertised messages carried by the primary transmitter. And, with narrow exceptions, full liability exists by definition where the cable system's transmission is not simultaneous with the primary transmission.

2. Section 115: Phonorecords

Section 115 updates section 1(e) of the 1909 Act, the provision that introduced compulsory licensing into copyright. Under section 1(e), once a copyright owner permits his composition to be recorded, anyone else may, without his authority, record the composition upon payment of a statutorily prescribed royalty.

The new law differs from the old in several respects. Section 1(e)'s royalty rate, two cents for each record manufactured by the compulsory licensee, has been altered by the new law to 2.75 cents per work or .5 cents per minute of playing time, whichever is greater. The new royalty is to be figured on the basis of the number of phonorecords actually distributed by the compulsory licensee and not, as under the 1909 Act, on the basis of number of records manufactured. Section 115(a)(1) premises compulsory licensing on the first authorized distribution of phonorecords by the copyright owner, rather than on the making or licensing of the first recording, as under the 1909 law. Another part of section 115(a)(1) restricts the compulsory license to the making of phonorecords primarily for distribution to the public for private use. This presumably excludes compulsory licensing for specialized production for commercial uses such as background music systems and broadcast and jukebox operations.

3. Section 116: Jukeboxes

The 1909 Act exempted jukebox uses of musical compositions by providing that the "reproduction or rendition of a musical composition by or upon coin operated machines shall not be deemed a public performance for profit unless a fee is charged for admission to the place where such reproduction or rendition occurs." Almost as soon as it was enacted, the jukebox exemption became the target of proposals ranging from outright repeal and imposition of full copyright liability to variations on the compulsory licensing theme. The resolution reached by section 116 is imposition of an annual compulsory fee of eight dollars per unit on jukebox operators.

The mechanics of section 116's compulsory license are simple. Upon payment of the eight dollar royalty to the Copyright Office, the Register of Copyrights issues a certificate which the operator is then required to place on the jukebox. The fees collected are to be distributed annually upon claims submitted to the Copyright Royalty Tribunal. Section 116(c)(4) expressly provides for different means for allocating payments as between individual claimants and performing rights societies. Like the royalty rates fixed in the other compulsory licensing provisions, the eight dollar jukebox fee is open to review and adjustment by the Copyright Royalty Tribunal created by Chapter 8.

4. Section 118: Public Broadcasting

Section 118 authorizes the Copyright Royalty Tribunal to prescribe rates for the use by public broadcasters of published nondramatic musical works and pictorial, graphic and sculptural works. Within thirty days of the President's announcement of initial appointments to the Tribunal, the Tribunal is to initiate proceedings to determine the "reasonable terms and rates" on which these uses can be made. The Tribunal is to publish terms and rates within six months of the notice of initiation of proceedings. The Tribunal's adoption of fixed rates and terms will not bar broadcasters and copyright proprietors from entering into negotiated agreements although, of course, private negotiations will unavoidably be colored by the availability of the compelled alternative. Section 118 further limits private discretion by requiring that voluntarily negotiated agreements be filed with the Copyright Office in order to be given effect.

Section 118, as enacted, marks a retreat from the terms first proposed in a predecessor bill introduced by Senator Charles Mathias, Jr., in the ninety-third Congress. The Mathias Bill would have given public broadcasters a compulsory license to broadcast nondramatic literary works as well as nondramatic musical works and pictorial, graphic, or sculptural works. The bill would have authorized the Copyright Royalty Tribunal to establish reasonable fees "for public television and radio broadcasts by public broadcasting entities." The bill also provided for distribution of royalties deposited with the Register of Copyrights. Faced with sharp resistance from the Register of Copyrights and from organizations and individuals representing authors and publishers and producers of audiovisual works objecting to the inclusion of nondramatic literary works, the House Committee withdrew to the more limited coverage now embodied in section 118.

Congress' purpose in enacting section 118 was to encourage agreements, yet provide a mechanism ensuring the availability of copyrighted materials on terms satisfactory to the broadcasters. The provision reflects the judgment that public broadcasting is different from commercial enterprises "due to such factors as the special nature of programming, repeated use of programs, and, of course, limited financial resources." While the House Committee Report artfully states that copyright owners should not be required to subsidize public broadcasting, it cannot obscure the fact that, whatever the source, it is in fact a subsidy that section 118 confers on public broadcasters.

COLUMBIA PICTURES INDUSTRIES, INC. v. REDD HORNE, INC.

United States Court of Appeals, Third Circuit, 1984.
749 F.2d 154, 224 U.S.P.Q. 641.

RE, Chief Judge.

In this copyright infringement case, defendants appeal from an order of the United States District Court for the Western District of Pennsylvania which granted the plaintiffs' motion for summary judgment, and enjoined defendants from exhibiting plaintiffs' copyrighted motion pictures. The defendants, Redd Horne, Inc., Maxwell's Video Showcase, Ltd., Glenn W. Zeny and Robert Zeny, also appeal from the dismissal of their antitrust counterclaims, and from an award of damages against them in the amount of $44,750.00.

Defendant-appellants raise three questions on this appeal: (1) whether the activities of the defendant Maxwell's Video Showcase, Ltd. (Maxwell's) constitute an infringement of plaintiffs' copyright protections which would entitle the plaintiffs to injunctive relief and damages; (2) if so, whether the activities of the other defendants, Robert Zeny, the president and sole shareholder of Maxwell's, Redd Horne, Inc., Maxwell's advertising and public relations firm, and Glenn W. Zeny, the president of Redd Horne, Inc., and Robert Zeny's brother, are sufficient to hold each of them liable as co-infringers with Maxwell's; and (3) whether the antitrust counterclaims of the defendants were properly dismissed by the district court. Since we agree with the district court, we affirm.

The Facts

Maxwell's Video Showcase, Ltd., operates two stores in Erie, Pennsylvania. At these two facilities, Maxwell's sells and rents video cassette recorders and prerecorded video cassettes, and sells blank video cassette cartridges. These activities are not the subject of the plaintiffs' complaint. The copyright infringement issue in this case arises from defendants' *exhibition* of video cassettes of the plaintiffs' films, or what defendants euphemistically refer to as their "showcasing" or "in-store rental" concept.

Each store contains a small showroom area in the front of the store, and a "showcase" or exhibition area in the rear. The front showroom contains video equipment and materials for sale or rent, as well as dispensing machines for popcorn and carbonated beverages. Movie posters are also displayed in this front area. In the rear "showcase" area, patrons may view any of an assortment of video cassettes in small, private booths with space for two to four people. There are a total of eighty-five booths in the two stores. Each booth or room is approximately four feet by six feet and is carpeted on the floor and walls. In the front there is a nineteen inch color television and an upholstered bench in the back.

The procedure followed by a patron wishing to utilize one of the viewing booths or rooms is the same at both facilities. The customer selects a film from a catalogue which contains the titles of available films. The fee charged by Maxwell's depends on the number of people in the viewing room, and the time of day. The price is $5.00 for one or two people before 6 p.m., and $6.00 for two people after 6 p.m. There is at all times a $1.00 surcharge for the third and fourth person. The fee also entitles patrons to help themselves to popcorn and soft drinks before entering their assigned rooms. Closing the door of the viewing room activates a signal in the counter area at the front of the store. An employee of Maxwell's then places the cassette of the motion picture chosen by the viewer into one of the video cassette machines in the front of the store and the picture is transmitted to the patron's viewing room. The viewer may adjust the light in the room, as well as the volume, brightness, and color levels on the television set.

Access to each room is limited to the individuals who rent it as a group. Although no restriction is placed on the composition of a group, strangers are not grouped in order to fill a particular room to capacity. Maxwell's is open to any member of the public who wishes to utilize its facilities or services.

Maxwell's advertises on Erie radio stations and on the theatre pages of the local newspapers. Typically, each advertisement features one or more motion pictures, and emphasizes Maxwell's selection of films, low prices, and free refreshments. The advertisements do not state that these motion pictures are video cassette copies. At the entrance to the two Maxwell's facilities, there are also advertisements for individual films, which resemble movie posters.

Infringement of Plaintiffs' Copyright

It may be stated at the outset that this is not a case of unauthorized taping or video cassette piracy. The defendants obtained the video cassette copies of plaintiffs' copyrighted motion pictures by purchasing them from either the plaintiffs or their authorized distributors. The sale or rental of these cassettes to individuals for home viewing is also not an issue. Plaintiffs do not contend that in-home use infringes their copyright.

The plaintiffs' complaint is based on their contention that the exhibition or showing of the video cassettes in the private booths on defendants' premises constitutes an unauthorized public performance in violation of plaintiffs' exclusive rights under the federal copyright laws.

It is acknowledged that it is the role of the Congress, not the courts, to formulate new principles of copyright law when the legislature has determined that technological innovations have made them necessary. See, e.g., Sony Corp. v. Universal City Studios, Inc., 464 U.S. 417, 104 S.Ct. 774, 783, 78 L.Ed.2d 574 (1984); Teleprompter Corp. v. CBS, 415 U.S. 394, 414, 94 S.Ct. 1129, 1141, 39 L.Ed.2d 415 (1974). In the words of Justice Stevens, "Congress has the constitutional authority and the institutional ability to accommodate fully the varied permutations of competing interests that are inevitably implicated by such new technology." Sony Corp., supra, 104 S.Ct. at 783. A defendant, however, is not immune from liability for copyright infringement simply because the technologies are of recent origin or are being applied to innovative uses. Although this case involves a novel application of relatively recent technological developments, it can nonetheless be readily analyzed and resolved within the existing statutory framework.

Section 106 of the Copyright Act confers upon the copyright holder certain exclusive rights. This section provides:

> Subject to sections 107 through 118, the owner of copyright under this title has the exclusive rights to do and to authorize any of the following:
>
> (1) to reproduce the copyrighted work in copies or phonorecords;
>
> (2) to prepare derivative works based upon the copyrighted work;
>
> (3) to distribute copies or phonorecords of the copyrighted work to the public by sale or other transfer of ownership, or by rental, lease, or lending;
>
> (4) in the case of literary, musical, dramatic, and choreographic works, pantomimes, and *motion pictures and other audiovisual works, to perform the copyrighted work publicly;* and
>
> (5) in the case of literary, musical, dramatic, and choreographic works, pantomimes, and pictorial, graphic, or sculptural works, including the individual images of a motion picture or other audiovisual work, to display the copyrighted work publicly.

17 U.S.C. § 106 (1982) (emphasis supplied).

It is undisputed that the defendants were licensed to exercise the right of distribution. A copyright owner, however, may dispose of a copy of his work while retaining all underlying copyrights which are not expressly or impliedly disposed of with that copy. Thus, it is clear that the plaintiffs have retained their interest in the other four enumerated rights. Since the rights granted by section 106 are separate and distinct, and are severable from one another, the grant of one does not waive any of the other exclusive rights. Thus, plaintiffs' sales of video cassette copies of their copyrighted motion pictures did not result in a waiver of any of the other exclusive rights enumerated in section 106, such as the exclusive right to perform their motion pictures publicly. In essence, therefore, the fundamental question is whether the defendants' activities constitute a public performance of the plaintiffs' motion pictures. We agree with the conclusion of the district court that these activities constitute a public performance, and are an infringement.

"To perform a work means . . . in the case of a motion picture or other audiovisual work, to show its images in any sequence or to make the sounds accompanying it audible." 17 U.S.C. § 101 (1982). Clearly, playing a video cassette results in a sequential showing of a motion picture's images and in making the sounds accompanying it audible. Thus, Maxwell's activities constitute a performance under section 101.

The remaining question is whether these performances are public. Section 101 also states that to perform a work "publicly" means "[t]o perform . . . it at a place open to the public or at any place where a substantial number of persons outside of a normal circle of a family and its social acquaintances is gathered." The statute is written in the disjunctive, and thus two categories of places can satisfy the definition of "to perform a work publicly." The first category is self-evident; it is "a place open to the public." The second category, commonly referred to as a semi-public place, is determined by the size and composition of the audience.

The legislative history indicates that this second category was added to expand the concept of public performance by including those places that, although not open to the public at large, are accessible to a significant number of people. Clearly, if a place is public, the size and composition of the audience are irrelevant. However, if the place is not public, the size and composition of the audience will be determinative.

We find it unnecessary to examine the second part of the statutory definition because we agree with the district court's conclusion that Maxwell's was open to the public. On the composition of the audience, the district court noted that "the showcasing operation is not distinguishable in any significant manner from the exhibition of films at a conventional movie theater." 568 F.Supp. at 500. Any member of the public can view a motion picture by paying the appropriate fee. The services provided by Maxwell's are essentially the same as a movie theatre, with the additional feature of privacy. The relevant "place" within the meaning of section 101 is each of Maxwell's two stores, not each individual booth within each store. Simply because the cassettes can be viewed in private does not mitigate the essential fact that Maxwell's is unquestionably open to the public.

The conclusion that Maxwell's activities constitute public performances is fully supported by subsection (2) of the statutory definition of public performance:

(2) to transmit or otherwise communicate a performance . . . of the work to a place specified by clause (1) or to the public, by means of any device or process, whether the members of the public capable of receiving the performance . . . receive it in the same place or in separate places and at the same time or at different times.

17 U.S.C. § 101 (1982). As explained in the House Report which accompanies the Copyright Revision Act of 1976, "a performance made available by transmission to the public at large is 'public' even though the recipients are not gathered in a single place. . . . The same principles apply whenever the potential recipients of the transmission represent a limited segment of the public, such as the occupants of hotel rooms. . . ." *House Report,* supra, at 64–65, U.S.Code Cong. & Admin.News, p. 5678. Thus, the transmission of a performance to members of the public, even in private settings such as hotel rooms or Maxwell's viewing rooms, constitutes a public performance. As the statutory language and legislative history clearly indicate, the fact that members of the public view the performance at different times does not alter this legal consequence.

Professor Nimmer's examination of this definition is particularly pertinent: "*if the same copy* . . . of a given work is repeatedly played (i.e., 'performed') by different members of the public, albeit at different times, this constitutes a 'public' performance." 2 M. Nimmer, § 8.14[C][3], at 8–142 (emphasis in original). Indeed, Professor Nimmer would seem to have envisaged Maxwell's when he wrote:

one may anticipate the possibility of theaters in which patrons occupy separate screening rooms, for greater privacy, and in order not to have to await a given hour for commencement of a given film. These too should obviously be regarded as public perform-ances within the underlying rationale of the Copyright Act.

Id. at 8–142. Although Maxwell's has only one copy of each film, it shows each copy repeatedly to different members of the public. This constitutes a public performance.

The First Sale Doctrine

The defendants also contend that their activities are protected by the first sale doctrine. The first sale doctrine is codified in section 109(a) of Title 17. This section provides:

Notwithstanding the provisions of section 106(3), the owner of a particular copy or phonorecord lawfully made under this title, or any person authorized by such owner, is entitled, without the authority of the copyright owner, to sell or otherwise dispose of the possession of that copy or phonorecord.

17 U.S.C. § 109(a) (1982). Section 109(a) is an extension of the principle that ownership of the material object is distinct from ownership of the copyright in this material. See 17 U.S.C. § 202 (1982). The first sale doctrine prevents the copyright owner from controlling the future

transfer of a particular copy once its material ownership has been transferred. The transfer of the video cassettes to the defendants, however, did not result in the forfeiture or waiver of all of the exclusive rights found in section 106. The copyright owner's exclusive right "to perform the copyrighted work publicly" has not been affected; only its distribution right as to the transferred copy has been circumscribed.

In essence, the defendants' "first sale" argument is merely another aspect of their argument that their activities are not public performances. For the defendants' argument to succeed, we would have to adopt their characterization of the "showcasing" transaction or activity as an "in-store rental." The facts do not permit such a finding or conclusion. The record clearly demonstrates that showcasing a video cassette at Maxwell's is a significantly different transaction than leasing a tape for home use. Maxwell's never disposed of the tapes in its showcasing operations, nor did the tapes ever leave the store. At all times, Maxwell's maintained physical dominion and control over the tapes. Its employees actually played the cassettes on its machines. The charges or fees received for viewing the cassettes at Maxwell's facilities are analytically indistinguishable from admission fees paid by patrons to gain admission to any public theater. Plainly, in their showcasing operation, the appellants do not sell, rent, or otherwise dispose of the video cassette. On the facts presented, Maxwell's "showcasing" operation is a public performance, which, as a matter of law, constitutes a copyright infringement.

Liability of Co–Defendants

Defendant-appellants, Robert Zeny, Glenn W. Zeny, and Redd Horne, Inc., challenge that part of the district court's order which holds them liable as co-infringers. We agree with the district court and affirm.

It is well settled that "one who, with knowledge of the infringing activity, induces, causes or materially contributes to the infringing activity of another, may be held liable as a 'contributory' infringer." Gershwin Publishing Corp. v. Columbia Artists Management, Inc., 443 F.2d 1159, 1162 (2d Cir.1971). An officer or director of a corporation who knowingly participates in the infringement can be held personally liable, jointly and severally, with the corporate defendant.

Robert Zeny is the president and the sole shareholder of Maxwell's Video Showcase, Ltd. He knowingly initiated and participated in the infringing activity, and ignored repeated requests from the plaintiffs that he cease and desist the activity. He too, therefore, is clearly liable as a co-infringer.

Glenn W. Zeny, Robert's brother, is not a stockholder or officer, nor does he have a direct financial interest in Maxwell's Video Showcase, Ltd. Glenn W. Zeny, however, conducted negotiations and wrote letters, on Redd Horne, Inc., stationery, on behalf of Maxwell's and its predecessor corporation. Some of these letters on Redd Horne, Inc., stationery, refer to "our company" and "our concept" without mentioning Maxwell's. The impression conveyed by the letters is that Glenn Zeny and Redd Horne, Inc., are principals in the venture. Glenn W. Zeny, like his brother, participated knowingly and significantly in the infringing activity and ignored the plaintiffs' persistent requests that the activity cease.

Redd Horne, Inc., conducted all of the advertising and promotional work for Maxwell's. It also provided financial, accounting, and administrative services for Maxwell's. All of these services, and the advertising services in particular, contributed and, indeed, were essential to the copyright infringement. In addition, Glenn W. Zeny's knowledge of, and substantial participation in, the infringing activities may be imputed to his employer, Redd Horne, Inc. Thus, we hold that the substantial, knowing participation of Glenn W. Zeny and Redd Horne, Inc., was more than sufficient to hold them liable as co-infringers. . . .

Conclusion

In view of the foregoing, it is the holding of this Court that the defendants' activities constituted an unauthorized, and, therefore, an unlawful public performance of the plaintiffs' copyrighted motion pictures. We also conclude that the activities of each named defendant were sufficient to hold each jointly and severally liable for the copyright infringement. In addition, we hold that the defendants' counterclaims were properly dismissed.

The judgment of the district court, therefore, will be affirmed.

SPRINGSTEEN v. PLAZA ROLLER DOME, INC.

United States District Court, M.D. North Carolina, 1985.
602 F.Supp. 1113, 225 U.S.P.Q. 1008.

BULLOCK, District Judge.

Plaintiffs in this copyright infringement action are ten copyright owners and members of the American Society of Composers, Authors, and Publishers ("ASCAP"), seeking monetary damages and injunctive relief against Defendants Plaza Roller Dome, Inc., and Gerald E. Manuel for their allegedly unauthorized transmission via radio and speaker system of Plaintiffs' copyrighted compositions. The unlawful transmissions allegedly were made at the Plaza Putt–Putt golf course in Laurinburg, North Carolina, which is owned and controlled by Defendants. This action arises under the federal copyright laws. Defendants have filed an answer and counterclaim based on allegations arising from the same transaction. Pending before the court are the parties' cross-motions for summary judgment as to whether Defendants' Putt–Putt course falls within the 17 U.S.C. § 110(5) exemption to the copyright laws. For the reasons set forth below, Defendants' motion for summary judgment will be granted, Plaintiffs' cross-motion for summary judgment will be denied, and Plaintiffs' six causes of action will be dismissed.

Factual Background

The complex owned and controlled by Defendant Plaza Roller Dome, Inc., consists of an indoor roller rink and an adjacent outdoor miniature golf course and is located at the College Plaza Shopping Center in Laurinburg, North Carolina. Defendant Gerald E. Manuel is the president and principal shareholder of Plaza Roller Dome, Inc. The genesis of the present dispute between the two parties was the October 15, 1980, initialing of a licensing agreement between Defendants and ASCAP whereby Defendants would be entitled to perform musical compositions by ASCAP's members. The agreement was the result of a long, arduous, and often bitter negotiating process; it provided for ASCAP to settle any and all claims of copyright infringement against the Defendants through October 14, 1980, for the payment of $500.00, and Defendants agreed to pay $300.00 per year for the privilege of performing musical compositions by ASCAP's members thereafter. Defendants claim that they understood and were led to believe by ASCAP that the settlement covered both the roller rink and the Putt–Putt course. Plaintiffs disagree, claiming that the agreement does not cover the Putt–Putt course.

Shortly after the October 15, 1980, signing of the licensing agreement, ASCAP, as agent for Plaintiffs, approached Defendants and insisted that the Defendants pay an additional fee in order to license the Putt–Putt course. Defendants contend that Plaintiffs, through their agent ASCAP, were well aware of the scope of the initial agreement, and that ASCAP, on behalf of Plaintiffs, threatened suit and ultimately brought about the institution of this action in order to coerce the Defendants into paying for privileges to which they were already entitled under the 1980 agreement. This course of action was pursued by Plaintiffs and ASCAP, the Defendants contend, to punish them for being tough negotiators in the discussions leading up to the agreement. As a result, when Plaintiffs instituted this litigation, Defendants filed their counterclaim alleging state law causes of action sounding in fraud, deceit, intentional harassment, and unfair trade practices.

The specific infringements complained of by Plaintiffs are alleged to have arisen from the performance, via radio and speaker system, of copyrighted musical compositions at Defendants' Putt–Putt course on August 27, 1983. The radio and speaker system at the Putt–Putt course consists of a radio receiver wired to six separate speakers mounted on light poles interspersed over the 7,500 square foot area of the course. The Defendants contend (and are not controverted by Plaintiffs) that the speakers are very unsophisticated, do not project well, and can be heard without distortion only at a close proximity thereto. They argue that this lack of sophistication, inferior to many home systems, and the limited revenue generated by the Putt–Putt course ($24,308.00 over the six-year period ending July 31, 1983 or slightly over $4,000.00 per year—or less than 3% of the gross revenue of the Plaza Roller Dome) support their contention that the course is not of sufficient size to justify, as a practical matter, a subscription to a commercial background music system and thus is exempt under Section 110(5).

Discussion

Section 106(4) of Title 17 of the United States Code grants copyright owners the exclusive rights publicly to perform, or authorize the performance of, their copyrighted works. Pursuant to this provision of the copyright law, Plaintiffs, through ASCAP, received licensing fees from radio stations for the performance of their copyrighted works. Plaintiffs and ASCAP now claim that the "further transmission or performance" of its members' copyrighted works via a radio receiving apparatus "not of a kind commonly used in private homes" by the Plaza Roller Dome and Putt–Putt golf course constitutes copyright infringement. Defendants contend that their use of Plaintiffs' copyrighted materials falls within the 17 U.S.C. § 110(5) exemption to the copyright laws.

The Supreme Court, in Twentieth Century Music Corp. v. Aiken, 422 U.S. 151, 95 S.Ct. 2040, 45 L.Ed.2d 84 (1975), created an exemption to the copyright laws for small business establishments, noting that the absence of such an exemption "would result in a regime of copyright law that would be both wholly unenforceable and highly inequitable." Id. at 162, 95 S.Ct. at 2047. Specifically, the court held that the owner and operator of a chain of fast-food restaurants in the Pittsburgh area who kept a radio with outlets to four speakers in the ceiling turned on throughout the business day for the enjoyment of the customers and employees in his downtown restaurant was exempt from coverage of the 1909 copyright laws. The size of the particular restaurant in *Aiken* was 1,055 square feet, of which 620 square feet were open to the public; no mention of the revenues of the restaurant was included in the opinion.

In 1976, primarily as a result of this decision, Congress enacted Section 110(5) (17 U.S.C. § 110[5]) to limit the exemption from rights granted copyright owners under Section 106(4).

Section 110(5) exempts from liability:

[C]ommunication of a transmission embodying a performance or display of a work by the public reception of a transmission on a single receiving apparatus of a kind commonly used in private homes, unless—

(A) a direct charge is made to see or hear the transmission; or

(B) the transmission thus received is further transmitted to the public.

The meaning of this statutory language is far from clear, and its reach has scarcely been tested in the courts. Only two reported cases, each involving virtually identical factual situations, have interpreted Section 110(5) and both have relied very heavily on the legislative history in determining whether the exemption applies in a particular factual setting. In Sailor Music v. Gap Stores, Inc., 516 F.Supp. 923

(S.D.N.Y.1981), aff'd, 668 F.2d 84 (7th Cir.1981), cert. denied, 456 U.S. 945, 102 S.Ct. 2012, 72 L.Ed.2d 468 (1982), (hereinafter "the *Gap* case"), the defendant was a well-known chain of approximately 420 clothing stores with annual revenues of nearly $300 million. Plaintiffs, members of ASCAP, brought an infringement action against defendant seeking monetary damages and injunctive relief against every Gap Store in the country. It was Gap's policy to transmit for the enjoyment of its customers radio programs by means of radio receivers connected to recessed loudspeakers arranged so that the music was audible throughout their stores. The allegedly infringing acts occurred at two Gap Stores located in New York City—one on Sixth Avenue and the other on Thirty–Fourth Street. In each of the stores the speakers were recessed behind wire grids in the store's ceiling and were connected to the receiver by built-in wiring. There were four speakers at the Sixth Avenue store and seven speakers at the Thirty–Fourth Street store. The two stores had areas of 2,679 and 6,770 square feet, respectively, and the average size of all Gap stores was 3,500 square feet.

In his consideration of whether the Section 110(5) exemption applied to the Gap Stores, Judge Gagliardi quoted at length from the House Judiciary Committee report on the 1976 copyright act. The relevant discussion from the committee report provides:

> Under the particular fact situation in the *Aiken* case, assuming a small commercial establishment and the use of a home receiver with four ordinary loud-speakers grouped within a relatively narrow circumference from the set, it is intended that the performances would be exempt under clause (5). However, the Committee considers this fact situation to represent the outer limit of the exemption, and believes that the line should be drawn at that point. Thus, the clause would exempt small commercial establishments whose proprietors merely bring onto their premises standard radio or television equipment and turn it on for their customers' enjoyment, but it would impose liability where the proprietor has a commercial 'sound system' installed or converts a standard home receiving apparatus (by agumenting [sic] it with sophisticated or extensive amplification equipment) into the equivalent of a commercial sound system. Factors to consider in particular cases would include the size, physical arrangement, and noise level of the areas within the establishment where the transmissions are made audible or visible, and the extent to which the receiving apparatus is altered or augmented for the purpose of improving the oral or visual quality of the performance for individual members of the public using those areas.

U.S.Code Cong. & Admin.News 1976, pp. 5659, 5701 (*quoted* by Judge Gagliardi in the *Gap* case, 516 F.Supp. 923, 924–25).

Applying the standard set forth above for the Gap Stores, Judge Gagliardi held that Congress clearly did not intend for stores of that size to fall within the scope of the exemption. The court, noting that the Gap Stores, with an average size of 3,500 square feet, were much larger than the public area of 620 square feet in the fast-food store at issue in *Aiken* (which fact situation the Committee emphasized, was to be "the outer limit" of the Section 110[5] exemption), concluded, by virtue of the size of the Gap Stores, that the radio transmissions received on the radio receivers and played via recessed loudspeakers were "further transmitted to the public," thus placing the stores outside the scope of the exemption.

Judge Gagliardi found further support for his conclusion in the following statement of the Conference Committee Report:

> It is the intent of the conferees that a small commercial establishment of the type involved in Twentieth Century Music Corp. v. Aiken, 422 U.S. 151 [95 S.Ct. 2040, 45 L.Ed.2d 84] (1975), which merely augmented a home-type receiver and which was not of sufficient size to justify, as a practical matter, a subscription to a commercial background music service, would be exempt. H.Rep. No. 94–1733, 94th Cong., 2d Sess. 75 (1976), U.S.Code Cong. & Admin.News (1976), p. 5816.

516 F.Supp. at 925. Without specifying whether by size he meant the revenues of the Gap Stores, which totaled over $300 million in 1979, or the average size of each Gap store, which was nearly 3,500 square feet (indoors), Judge Gagliardi held that "[t]he Gap is 'of sufficient size to justify, as a practical matter, a subscription to a commercial background music service.'" The court thus held that Gap was not a small commercial establishment whose reception and performance of radio transmissions via commonly used stereo equipment Congress intended in Section 110(5) to exempt from the category of copyright infringing uses, granted plaintiff's motion for summary judgment, and entered an order enjoining defendant's infringing use of plaintiff's copyrighted works.

The only other reported case which has interpreted the Section 110(5) exemption is Broadcast Music, Inc. v. United States Shoe Corporation, 211 U.S.P.Q. 43 (C.D.Cal.1980), aff'd, 678 F.2d 816 (9th Cir.1982) (hereinafter "*BMI v. U.S. Shoe*"). *BMI v. U.S. Shoe*, as was mentioned supra, presented a factual situation virtually identical to that presented by the *Gap* case. Defendant United States Shoe Corporation owned and operated a chain of more than 600 women's retail apparel stores under the name "Casual Corner." In many of its stores, radio broadcasts were played to the public through the use of a single radio receiver connected to four or more speakers mounted on the store's ceiling. The radio broadcasts included many copyrighted songs. BMI was the licensee of the public performance rights of many of the songs which were played at the facilities without BMI's permission. BMI thus brought suit against United States Shoe Corporation seeking injunctive relief and damages for defendant's unauthorized use of plaintiff's copyrighted materials. Defendant in turn contended that it was eligible for the 17 U.S.C. § 110(5) exemption and both sides submitted cross-motions for summary judgment on that issue.

The Ninth Circuit Court of Appeals upheld the district court's order granting summary judgment in favor of Plaintiffs. The court relied heavily on the Section 110(5) legislative history quoted in the *Gap* case, as well as on Judge Gagliardi's opinion. The court held that the Casual Corner stores exceeded the "outer limit" of the exemption (specified by the House Judiciary Committee to approximate the facts in *Aiken*), because each store had a commercial monaural system, with widely separated speakers of a type not used in private homes, and the size and nature of the operation justified, in the eyes of the court, the use of a commercial background music system. 678 F.2d at 817.

Turning now to the case at bar, there are several significant distinctions between the facts presented in the *Gap* and *BMI v. U.S. Shoe* cases, where the exemption was held not to apply, and the instant litigation. Plaintiffs contend that since the *Aiken* case was intended, according to the House Judiciary Committee Report, to "represent the outer limit of the exemption," and since the Plaza Roller Dome Putt–Putt course is both larger in area and has a greater number of speakers than did the exempted restaurant in *Aiken,* that the exemption clearly should not apply to Defendants' Putt–Putt facility. However, an objective assessment of the facts is much more complex than Plaintiffs' open and shut analysis.

It is true, as Plaintiffs contend, that the public area of Defendants' Putt–Putt course is larger (by a factor of 12—7,500 square feet to 620) than that of the restaurant in *Aiken,* and that the Putt–Putt course employed more speakers (six) than did the *Aiken* facility (four). The size of the allegedly offending facility and the number of speakers are not, however, standing alone, the sole or even predominant factors to consider in determining the applicability of the exemption. According to the House Judiciary Committee Report, "size, physical arrangement, and noise level of the areas within the establishment where the transmissions are made audible or visible, and the extent to which the receiving apparatus is altered or augmented for the purpose of improving the oral or visual quality of the performance" are all factors to consider in determining whether the receiving apparatus has been converted into the equivalent of a "commercial sound system" so as to remove the establishment from the scope of the Section 110(5) exemption.

Applying these factors to Defendants' Putt–Putt course, the argument against applying the Section 110(5) exemption becomes much less persuasive. To begin with, ASCAP's own field representative described the sound system at Defendants' Putt–Putt facility as follows:

> [S]ix speakers, attached to white posts that also provide lighting for evening Putt–Putt are equidistantly spread throughout the course. *The speakers did not project very well and one needed to be in a close proximity to the speaker to hear without much distortion.*

Brief in Support of Defendants' Motion for Summary Judgment— Exhibit A (emphasis added).

Clearly, the noise level and audibility of songs transmitted over Defendants' loud-speakers, by Plaintiffs' own admission, is not comparable to the sound systems in the *Gap* case and *BMI v. U.S. Shoe,* and does not rise to the level or minimum quality requisite for a commercial sound system. Unlike the systems involved in those two cases, where the infringing performances were audible throughout the stores and the speakers improved the quality of the performance, the allegedly infringing performances at Defendants' Putt–Putt course were scarcely audible without distortion even at very close proximity to the speakers. Under such circumstances, the speakers could scarcely be said to have "improved the quality of the performance." Indeed, the poor quality of speakers and the outdoor nature of the course guaranteed that the quality of sound performed for customers at Defendants' course would be lower than that which was performed for customers in the Gap and Casual Corner stores. Moreover, with respect to audibility and lack of improvement in the quality of the performance via augmentation, the receiving apparatus and speakers at Defendants' Putt–Putt course are inferior to those involved in the *Aiken* case. Hence, when all relevant factors have been taken into account, including those set out in the House Judiciary Committee Report, Defendants' sound system does not exceed the outer limit of the exemption as specified by the fact situation in *Aiken* and should therefore be entitled to the exemption to the copyright laws pursuant to Section 110(5).

This conclusion is reinforced by the language of the Conference Committee Report, incorporated into the legislative history subsequent to the House Judiciary Committee Report, which stated that a small commercial establishment of the type involved in *Aiken* which was not of sufficient size to justify, as a practical matter, a subscription to a commercial background service, would be exempt. The courts in the *Gap* and *BMI v. U.S. Shoe* cases held that operations with 420 and 600 prosperous retail outlets, respectively, both of which did hundreds of millions of dollars of business annually, were not within the purview of the Section 110(5) exemption. This court does not contest the soundness of those opinions. However, if any operation is "not of sufficient size to justify, as a practical matter, a subscription to a commercial background music service," it is Defendants' Putt–Putt course.

The restaurant involved in the *Aiken* case was a fast-food restaurant in Pittsburgh which operated year-round, did a brisk business, and undoubtedly generated substantial revenues. It was one of a chain of restaurants in the area. Defendants' Putt–Putt course, by contrast, is open for only roughly six months per year and rarely if ever generates over $1,000.00 per month. Writing in the New York Law School Law Review, Mr. Bernard Korman, general counsel for ASCAP, correctly described the congressionally-mandated scope of the Section 110(5) exemption as follows: "it [is] a very limited exemption which . . . require[s] any establishment large enough to be a potential customer of a background music service to obtain a license if it chooses to perform music broadcast by any radio station." Korman, Performance Rights in Music under Sections 110 and 118 of the 1976 Copyright Act, 22 N.Y.L.Sch.L.Rev. 521, 534 (1977).

Based on all of the factors analyzed above, this court must conclude that the Plaza Roller Dome Putt–Putt course is not of sufficient size to justify a subscription to a commercial background music service and therefore is within the scope of the Section 110(5) exemption. When due weight is given to each of the factors mentioned by Congress in determining the applicability of the exemption, the size of the course and the slightly larger number of speakers involved in the instant case vis-a-vis *Aiken*, standing alone, do not alter this conclusion.

Consequently, Defendants' motion for summary judgment will be granted and Plaintiffs' motion for partial summary judgment will be denied.

A judgment will be entered in accordance with this Memorandum Opinion.

MIRAGE EDITIONS, INC. v. ALBUQUERQUE A.R.T. CO.

United States Court of Appeals, Ninth Circuit, 1988.
856 F.2d 1341, 8 U.S.P.Q.2d 1171, cert. denied, ___ U.S. ___, 109 S.Ct. 1135, 103 L.Ed.2d 196 (1989).

BRUNETTI, Circuit Judge:

Albuquerque A.R.T. (appellant or A.R.T.) appeals the district court's granting of summary judgment in favor of appellees Mirage, Dumas, and Van Der Marck (Mirage). The district court, in granting summary judgment, found that appellant had infringed Mirage's copyright and issued an order enjoining appellant from further infringing Mirage's copyright.

Patrick Nagel was an artist whose works appeared in many media including lithographs, posters, serigraphs, and as graphic art in many magazines, most notably Playboy. Nagel died in 1984. His widow Jennifer Dumas owns the copyrights to the Nagel art works which Nagel owned at the time of his death. Mirage is the exclusive publisher of Nagel's works and also owns the copyrights to many of those works. Dumas and Mirage own all of the copyrights to Nagel's works. No one else holds a copyright in any Nagel work. Appellee Alfred Van Der Marck Editions, Inc. is the licensee of Dumas and Mirage and the publisher of the commemorative book entitled *NAGEL: The Art of Patrick Nagel* ("the book"), which is a compilation of selected copyrighted individual art works and personal commentaries.

Since 1984, the primary business of appellant has consisted of: 1) purchasing artwork prints or books including good quality artwork page prints therein; 2) gluing each individual print or page print onto a rectangular sheet of black plastic material exposing a narrow black margin around the print; 3) gluing the black sheet with print onto a major surface of a rectangular white ceramic tile; 4) applying a transparent plastic film over the print, black sheet and ceramic tile surface; and 5) offering the tile with artwork mounted thereon for sale in the retail market.

It is undisputed, in this action, that appellant did the above process with the Nagel book. The appellant removed selected pages from the book, mounted them individually onto ceramic tiles and sold the tiles at retail.

Mirage, Dumas and Van Der Marck brought an action alleging infringement of registered copyrights in the artwork of Nagel and in the book. Mirage also alleged trademark infringement and unfair competition under the Lanham Act, 15 U.S.C. § 1051 et seq. and the state law of unfair competition, Cal.Bus. & Prof.Code §§ 17200 et seq.

Appellant moved for summary judgment on the Lanham Act and Copyright Act causes of action. The district court granted summary judgment as to the Lanham Act cause of action but denied summary judgment on the copyright cause of action. Mirage then moved for summary judgment on the copyright claim which was granted. The court also enjoined appellants from removing individual art images from the book, mounting each individual image onto a separate tile and advertising for sale and/or selling the tiles with the images mounted thereon.

The Copyright Act of 1976, 17 U.S.C. § 101 et seq., confers upon the copyright holder exclusive rights to make several uses of his copyright. Among those rights are: (1) the right to reproduce the copyrighted work in copies, 17 U.S.C. § 106(1); (2) the right to prepare derivative works based upon the copyrighted work, 17 U.S.C. § 106(2); (3) the right to distribute copies of the copyrighted work to the public by sale or other transfer of ownership, or by rental, lease or lending, 17 U.S.C. § 106(3); and (4) in the case of literary, pictorial, graphic and sculptural works, including individual images, the right to display the copyrighted work publicly.

The district court concluded appellant infringed the copyrights in the individual images through its tile-preparing process and also concluded that the resulting products comprised derivative works.

Appellant contends that there has been no copyright infringement because (1) its tiles are not derivative works, and (2) the "first sale" doctrine precludes a finding of infringement.

The Copyright Act of 1976, 17 U.S.C. § 101 defines a derivative work as:

[A] work based upon one or more preexisting works such as a translation, musical arrangement, dramatization, fictionalization, motion picture version, sound recording, art reproduction, abridgment, condensation or *any other form in which a work may be recast, transformed, or adapted.* A work consisting of editorial revisions, annotations, elaborations, or other modifications which, as a whole, represent an original work of authorship is a 'derivative work.'

(Emphasis added).

The protection of derivative rights extends beyond mere protection against unauthorized copying to include the right to make other versions of, perform, or exhibit the work. Lone Ranger Television v. Program Radio Corp., 740 F.2d 718, 722 (9th Cir.1984); Russell v. Price, 612 F.2d 1123, 1128 n. 16 (9th Cir.1979). . . .

What appellant has clearly done here is to make another version of Nagel's art works, *Lone Ranger,* supra, and that amounts to preparation of a derivative work. By borrowing and mounting the preexisting, copyrighted individual art images without the consent of the copyright proprietors—Mirage and Dumas as to the art works and Van Der Marck as to the book—appellant has prepared a derivative work and infringed the subject copyrights.

Appellant's contention that since it has not engaged in "art reproduction" and therefore its tiles are not derivative works is not fully dispositive of this issue. Appellant has ignored the disjunctive phrase "or any other form in which a work may be recast, transformed or adapted." The legislative history of the Copyright Act of 1976 indicates that Congress intended that for a violation of the right to prepare derivative works to occur "the infringing work must incorporate a portion of the copyrighted work in *some form.*" 1976 U.S.Code Cong. & Admin.News 5659, 5675. (emphasis added). The language "recast, transformed or adapted" seems to encompass other alternatives besides simple art reproduction. By removing the individual images from the book and placing them on the tiles, perhaps the appellant has not accomplished reproduction. We conclude, though, that appellant has certainly recast or transformed the individual images by incorporating them into its tile-preparing process.

The "first sale" doctrine, which appellant also relies on in its contention that no copyright infringement has occurred, appears at 17 U.S.C. § 109(a). That section provides:

> Notwithstanding the provisions of Section 106(3), the owner of a particular copy or phonorecord lawfully made under this title, or any person authorized by such owner, is entitled, without the authority of the copyright owner, to sell or otherwise dispose of the possession of that copy or phonorecord.

In United States v. Wise, 550 F.2d 1180 (9th Cir.1977), which concerned a criminal prosecution under the pre–1976 Copyright Act, this court held that:

> [T]he 'first sale' doctrine provides that where a copyright owner parts with title to a particular copy of his copyrighted work, he divests himself of his exclusive right to vend that particular copy. While the proprietor's other copyright rights (reprinting, copying, etc.) remain unimpaired, the exclusive right to vend the transferred copy rests with the vendee, who is not restricted by statute from further transfers of that copy.

550 F.2d at 1187.

We recognize that, under the "first sale" doctrine as enunciated at 17 U.S.C. § 109(a) and as discussed in *Wise,* appellant can purchase a copy of the Nagel book and subsequently alienate its ownership in that book. However, the right to transfer applies only to the particular copy of the book which appellant has purchased and nothing else. The mere sale of the book to the appellant without a specific transfer by the copyright holder of its exclusive right to prepare derivative works, does not transfer that right to appellant. The derivative works right, remains unimpaired and with the copyright proprietors—Mirage, Dumas and Van Der Marck. As we have previously concluded that appellant's tile-preparing process results in derivative works and as the exclusive right to prepare derivative works belongs to the copyright holder, the "first sale" doctrine does not bar the appellees' copyright infringement claims.

We AFFIRM.

NOTES

1. Does it constitute public performance for a hotel to rent video-discs of copyrighted motion pictures to guests for viewing on videodisc players in their individual rooms? Columbia Pictures Industries, Inc. v. Professional Real Estate Investors, Inc., 866 F.2d 278, 9 U.S.P.Q.2d 1653 (9th Cir.1989), held that it does not. The court rejected plaintiffs' argument that, because defendant's hotel rooms can be rented by members of the public, they are "open to the public" within the terms of section 101; "[w]hile the hotel may indeed be 'open to the public,' a guest's hotel room, once rented, is not." 866 F.2d at 281.

The court also rejected plaintiffs' argument that the effect of defendant's activities was to "otherwise communicate" the motion pictures to the public within the terms of section 101's "transmit or otherwise communicate" clause:

> A plain reading of the transmit clause indicates that its purpose is to prohibit transmissions and other forms of broadcasting from one place to another without the copyright owner's permission. The Act provides a definition of 'transmit.' 'To "transmit" a performance or display is to communicate it by any device or process whereby images and sounds are received beyond the place from which they are sent.' Section 101. According to the rule of *ejusdem generis,* the term 'otherwise communicate' should be construed consistently with the term 'transmit.' Consequently, the 'otherwise communicate' phrase must relate to a 'process whereby images or sounds are received beyond the place from which they are sent.'
>
> This reading is reinforced by the rest of the transmit clause which refers to the use of transmission devices or processes and the reception by the public of the performance. Devices must refer to transmission or communication devices, such as, perhaps, wires, radio towers, communication satellites, and coaxial cable, while reception of the performance by the public describes acts, such as listening to a radio, or watching—network, cable, or closed-circuit—television 'beyond the place' of origination.

In sum, when one adds up the various segments of clause (2), one must conclude that under the transmit clause a public performance at least involves sending out some sort of signal via a device or process to be received by the public at a place beyond the place from which it is sent.

866 F.2d at 282.

2. *The Compulsory Recording License.* Section 115 of the 1976 Act attempts to resolve the more troublesome questions that had arisen under its predecessor provision in the 1909 Act, 17 U.S.C.A. § 1(e). Section 115(a)(1) carries forward the 1909 Act's distinction between "musical works" and "sound recordings" and makes clear "that a person is not entitled to a compulsory license of copyrighted *musical works* for the purpose of making an unauthorized duplication of a musical *sound recording* originally developed and produced by another." H.R.Rep. No. 94–1476, 108 [Emphasis added]. Also, section 115(a)(2) was "intended to recognize the practical need for a limited privilege to make arrangements of music being used under a compulsory license, but without allowing the music to be perverted, distorted, or travestied." H.R.Rep. No. 94–1476, 109.

Section 115 does not shake the earlier commitment to compulsory licensing for phonorecords. In section 1(e) Congress had sought to mediate between contemporary demands for a mechanical reproduction right and fears that an exclusive right would permit one firm, the Aeolian Company, to monopolize recording rights to popular music, "and by controlling these copyrights monopolize the business of manufacturing and selling music producing machines, otherwise free to the world." H.R.Rep. No. 2222, 60th Cong.2d Sess. 4 (1909).

In the years after its passage, section 1(e) was the object of numerous proposals for modification or outright repeal, most significantly in the 1961 Report of the Register of Copyrights. The Register subsequently revised his opinion: "During the discussion following issuance of the [1961] Report, it became apparent that record producers, small and large alike, regard the compulsory license as too important to their industry to accept its outright elimination." Copyright Law Revision, Part 6, Supplementary Report of the Register of Copyrights, 1965 Revision Bill 53 (1965). Earlier proposals had called for removal of compulsory licensing from the Copyright Act and for its ad hoc administration by the Federal Trade Commission, H.R. 3456, 77th Cong. 1st Sess. (1941), or the Federal Communications Commission, H.R. 10633, 75th Cong.3d Sess. (1938).

The economic arguments advanced for and against the compulsory licensing provision are shaky at best. The one systematic appraisal of section 1(e)'s place in the economics of the record industry indicates that institutional divisions in the industry and the fugitive success that attends popular compositions, taken together, make it extremely unlikely that elimination of the compulsory license scheme would lead to new monopoly effects. Blaisdell, The Economic Aspects of the Compulsory License, Study No. 6, Subcommittee on Patents, Trademarks and

Copyrights, Senate Committee on the Judiciary, 86th Cong. 1st Sess. 91, 109 (1960).

3. *Library Photocopying.* Section 108 exempts a wide range of reproduction activities by libraries and archives—from copying for archival purposes, covered by subsections (b) and (c), to photocopying for users, covered by subsections (d) and (e). It was the permission to photocopy for users that produced the most intricate drafting and the greatest controversy, focused primarily on subsection (g). As originally proposed in the Senate, section 108(g) sought to quell publisher's fears that libraries would effectively compete with them through the "systematic reproduction" of copyrighted works. Librarians argued that the restriction went too far and would seriously jeopardize interlibrary loan activities. In response, the House added the proviso that now appears at the end of section 108(g)(2)—"nothing in this clause prevents a library or archives from participating in interlibrary arrangements that do not have, as their purpose or effect, that the library or archives receiving such copies or phonorecords for distribution does so in such aggregate quantities as to substitute for a subscription to or purchase of such work."

What constitutes "such aggregate quantities" for purposes of the proviso? The most authoritative answer can be found in guidelines that the principal library, publisher and author organizations agreed upon shortly before the law was enacted. The guidelines, embodied in the Conference Report, provide, for example, that "aggregate quantities" shall mean "(a) with respect to any given periodical (as opposed to any given issue of a periodical), filled requests of a library or archives . . . within any calendar year for a total of six or more copies of an article or articles published in such periodical within five years prior to the date of the request." House Conf.Rep. No. 94–1733, 94th Cong. 2d Sess. 72 (1976).

The National Commission on New Technological Uses of Copyright Works (CONTU) played a key role in bringing the parties together to frame the photocopying guidelines. It also contributed to the agenda for section 108's future, offering suggestions to aid the Register of Copyrights in designing the first five-year study of the section's operation, mandated by section 108(i). "The research effort should attempt to determine the impact of copying fees on the health of the publishing industry, with special emphasis on the publication of scientific, technical, and medical journals. In particular, the study should attempt to determine: (1) whether the imposition of copying fees contributes to the viability of individual journal titles; (2) what impact, if any, the imposition of copying fees has on journal subscriptions and library acquisitions; and (3) what information concerning the use of individual journal titles and their contents is provided by the numbers of photocopies for which payments are made." CONTU, Final Report 50 (1978).

CONTU's Final Report also provides a superb overview of the law and practice of photocopying in the United States and elsewhere. Circular R21, Reproduction of Copyrighted Works by Educators and

Librarians (1978), published by the Copyright Office, collects and analyzes many of the relevant documents. See also, Oman, The Register's Second Report: An Update on Library Photocopying, 13 Colum.—VLA J.L. & Arts 39 (1988); Treece, Library Photocopying, 24 UCLA L.Rev. 1025 (1977).

4. *The Distribution Right and the First Sale Doctrine.* Section 106(3) of the Copyright Act grants the exclusive right to distribute "copies or phonorecords of the copyrighted work to the public by sale or other transfer of ownership, or by rental, lease, or lending." The most important limitation on the distribution right is the first sale doctrine embodied in section 109(a): "the owner of a particular copy or phonorecord lawfully made under this title, or any person authorized by such owner, is entitled, without the authority of the copyright owner, to sell or otherwise dispose of the possession of that copy or phonorecord." See generally, Nolan, All Rights Not Reserved After the First Sale, 23 Bull. Copyright Soc'y 76 (1975).

Section 109(b), added by the Record Rental Amendment of 1984, Pub.L. No. 98–450, 98 Stat. 1727, creates a narrow exception to the first sale doctrine by providing that an owner of a phonorecord may not rent, lease or lend the phonorecord without the copyright owner's permission. The House Report explains:

> At present, according to industry estimates, there are approximately 200 commercial record rental establishments in the United States. Testimony before this Committee's Subcommittee had indicated that these establishments rent phonorecords for 24 to 72 hours for fees of $.99 to $2.50 per disc. Frequently, blank audio cassette tapes are sold in the same establishment. One such establishment advertised, 'Never, ever buy another record.'

> The direct link between the commercial rental of a phonorecord and the making of a copy of a record without the permission of or compensation to the copyright owners is the economic and policy concern behind this legislation. The Subcommittee has found that the nexus of commercial record rental and duplication may directly and adversely affect the ability of copyright holders to exercise their reproduction and distribution rights under the Copyright Act.

H.R.Rep. No. 987, 98th Cong., 2d Sess. 2 (1984). See generally, Horowitz, The Record Rental Amendment of 1984: A Case Study in the Effort to Adapt Copyright Law to New Technology, 12 Colum.—VLA J.L. & Arts 31 (1987).

5. *Jukebox Performances.* Congress has historically treated jukebox performances with special charity. The 1909 Act exempted jukebox performances from copyright control so long as the owner of the establishment where the jukebox was located did not charge for admission. Section 116 of the 1976 Act continued the exemption for establishment owners, but required payment of an annual license fee by jukebox operators. Acknowledging that the Berne Convention "apparently does not permit compulsory licensing of non-broadcast perform-

ances," Congress in the 1988 Berne Implementation Amendments added a new section 116A to the Act to "encourage the representatives of authors and jukebox operators to negotiate licenses or submit to arbitration. If negotiations fail, the compulsory license provisions in effect on the day before the amendment takes effect—that is, section 116—would operate." H.R.Rep. No. 609, 100th Cong., 2d Sess. 47 (1988).

6. *Rights in Sound Recordings.* The Copyright Act closely circumscribes rights in sound recordings. Under sections 106 and 114(a), rights in sound recordings include the reproduction right, the right to prepare derivative works and the distribution right, but not the performance right or the display right. Section 114(b) further confines the reproduction and derivative rights in sound recordings to exact replication or dubbing; imitations are exempted.

Section 114(d) required the Register of Copyrights to file a report on the desirability of performance rights in sound recordings. The Register's report, submitted to Congress on January 3, 1978, and supplemented on March 13, 1978, recommended that "section 114 be amended to provide performance rights, subject to compulsory licensing, in copyrighted sound recordings, and that the benefits of this right be extended both to performers (including employees for hire) and to record producers as joint authors of sound recordings." In part, the Register rested her recommendation on the view that the "lack of copyright protection for performers since the commercial development of records has had a drastic and destructive effect on both the performing and the recording arts." Performance Rights in Sound Recordings 43 Fed.Reg. 12765–66 (1978).

For another view on performance rights in sound recordings, see Bard & Kurlantzick, A Public Performance Right in Recordings: How to Alter the Copyright System Without Improving It, 43 Geo.Wash.L. Rev. 152 (1974).

7. *The Display Right.* The 1976 Copyright Act created a new statutory right—section 106(5)'s right, "in the case of literary, musical, dramatic, and choreographic works, pantomimes, and pictorial, graphic, or sculptural works, including the individual images of a motion picture or other audiovisual work, to display the copyrighted work publicly."

The display right responds to a concern over "the enormous potential importance of showing, rather than distributing, copies as a means of disseminating an author's work. . . . It is not inconceivable that, in certain areas at least, 'exhibition' may take over from 'reproduction' of 'copies' as the means of presenting authors' works to the public, and we are now convinced that a basic right of public exhibition should be expressly recognized in the statute." House Comm. on the Judiciary, 89th Cong., 1st Sess., Copyright Law Revision Part 6: Supplementary Report of the Register of Copyrights on the General Revision of the U.S. Copyright Law: 1965 Revision Bill 20 (Comm.Print 1965).

What limits are there to section 106(5)? Can an artist who has sold a painting prevent the buyer from displaying it publicly? Section 109(b) reflects the House Committee's intention "to preserve the traditional privilege of the owner of a copy to display it directly, but to place reasonable restrictions on the ability to display it indirectly in such a way that the copyright owner's market for reproduction and distribution of copies would be affected. Unless it constitutes a fair use under section 107, or unless one of the special provisions of section 110 or 111 is applicable, projection of more than one image at a time, or transmission of an image to the public over television or other communication channels, would be an infringement for the same reasons that reproduction in copies would be." H.R.Rep. No. 1476, 94th Cong., 2d Sess. 80 (1976).

8. *Contributory Infringement and Vicarious Liability.* As new technologies emerge for the dissemination of copyrighted works, so have the occasions for infringement. Generally these new technologies divert accountability from centralized institutions, such as publishers and television networks, and toward more dispersed users. In a world where everyone with access to a photocopy machine is her own publisher, and everyone with access to a home videotape recorder is his own movie exhibitor, copyright owners cannot hope to recover all of their works' value from centralized publishers and television networks.

Copyright owners can capture some of the value of dispersed uses, without incurring the enforcement and transaction costs of pursuing dispersed users, by obtaining relief against the institutions that facilitate these uses. Contributory infringement and vicarious liability are two sources of relief.

Contributory Infringement. "[O]ne who, with knowledge of the infringing activity, induces, causes or materially contributes to the infringing conduct of another, may be held liable as a 'contributory' infringer." Gershwin Publishing Corp. v. Columbia Artists Management, Inc., 443 F.2d 1159, 1162, 170 U.S.P.Q. 182 (2d Cir.1971). *Gershwin* gave as an example the decision in Screen Gems–Columbia Music, Inc. v. Mark–Fi Records, Inc., 256 F.Supp. 399, 150 U.S.P.Q. 523 (S.D. N.Y.1966), where "the district court held that an advertising agency which placed non-infringing advertisements for the sale of infringing records, a radio station which broadcast such advertisements and a packaging agent which shipped the infringing records could each be held liable as a 'contributory' infringer if it were shown to have had knowledge, or reason to know, of the infringing nature of the records. Their potential liability was predicated upon 'the common law doctrine that one who knowingly participates or furthers a tortious act is jointly and severally liable with the prime tort-feasor. . . .' 256 F.Supp. at 403." 443 F.2d at 1162.

The more difficult case for contributory infringement arises when the defendant has only provided material or equipment for use in the infringing activity. In Sony Corp. of America v. Universal City Studios, Inc., 464 U.S. 417, 104 S.Ct. 774, 78 L.Ed.2d 574, 220 U.S.P.Q. 665 (1984), the Court held that a manufacturer of home videotape machines was not contributorily liable for selling the machines to consumers who used them to copy plaintiffs' copyrighted motion pictures off the air from television broadcasts. The Court drew for its decision on section 271(c) of the Patent Act, page 484, above, which provides that the sale of a "staple article or commodity of commerce suitable for substantial noninfringing use" does not constitute contributory infringement. In the Court's view "the sale of copying equipment, like the sale of other articles of commerce, does not constitute contributory infringement if the product is widely used for legitimate, unobjectionable purposes. Indeed, it need merely be capable of substantial noninfringing uses." 464 U.S. at 442, 104 S.Ct. at 789. Because home videotape machines had a significant noninfringing use—"time-shifting" to enable home viewers to record programs for viewing at a later, more convenient time—the defendant was not liable for contributory infringement. Why is time-shifting a noninfringing use? See page 629, below.

Vicarious Liability. "When the right and ability to supervise coalesce with an obvious and direct financial interest in the exploitation of copyrighted materials—even in the absence of actual knowledge that the copyright monopoly is being impaired, the purposes of the copyright law may be best effectuated by the imposition of liability upon the beneficiary of that exploitation." Shapiro, Bernstein & Co. v. H.L. Green Co., 316 F.2d 304, 307, 137 U.S.P.Q. 275 (2d Cir.1963).

Defendant in *Green,* the H.L. Green Co., operated a chain of retail stores. In twenty-three of these stores, defendant Jalen operated a phonograph record concession and, without H.L. Green's knowledge, sold unlicensed recordings of plaintiffs' copyrighted compositions. The extent of Green's supervisory power and direct financial interest were obvious from the face of its license agreement with Jalen: "Jalen and its employees were to 'abide by, observe and obey all rules and regulations promulgated from time to time by H.L. Green Company, Inc. . . . .' Green, in its 'unreviewable discretion', had the authority to discharge any employee believed to be conducting himself improperly. Jalen, in turn, agreed to save Green harmless from any claims arising in connection with the conduct of the phonograph record concession. Significantly, the licenses provided that Green was to receive a percentage—in some cases 10%, in others 12%—of Jalen's gross receipts from the sale of records, as its full compensation as licensor." 316 F.2d at 306.

The court concluded that "the imposition of *vicarious* liability in the case before us cannot be deemed unduly harsh or unfair. Green has the power to police carefully the conduct of its concessionaire Jalen; our judgment will simply encourage it to do so, thus placing responsibility where it can and should be effectively exercised. Green's burden will not be unlike that quite commonly imposed upon publishers, printers, and vendors of copyrighted materials." 316 F.2d at 308 (emphasis in original).

NOTE: COLLECTING SOCIETIES

Musical Performance Rights. Institutional mechanisms, such as collecting societies, will often be more effective than legal mechanisms, such as contributory infringement lawsuits, in reducing the transaction costs of obtaining payment for dispersed uses of copyrighted works. The operations of the American Society of Composers, Authors and Publishers (ASCAP) are illustrative. In 1914, responding to the decline of sheet music sales and the rise of radio and other media for public performance, Victor Herbert led several composers, authors and music publishers to form ASCAP. They organized ASCAP as a nonprofit association to pool the nondramatic ("small") performance rights in members' musical compositions for licensing to anyone who wished to make a nondramatic public performance for profit. Under this arrangement, ASCAP would give blanket licenses to its repertory, and the royalties collected would be distributed among association members according to a schedule that accounted for the general character and standing of their works and for the number of times each work was performed. By 1980, ASCAP's membership consisted of approximately 6,000 music publishing companies and 16,000 composers, and the society held the small performance rights to approximately 3,000,000 compositions. Radio and television networks and stations are ASCAP's major licensees; restaurants, dance halls and hotels also take licenses.

ASCAP's success invited competition—and antitrust regulation. Competition came from broadcasters, who formed Broadcast Music, Inc. (BMI) in 1939. BMI has proved to be a strong rival. By 1980, BMI was affiliated with 10,000 publishers and 20,000 authors and composers, and had a repertory of about 1,000,000 compositions. Together with AS-CAP, it controls the small performance rights to virtually all domestic copyrighted musical compositions. On the operations of ASCAP, BMI and SESAC—a much smaller collecting society—see S. Shemel & M. Krasilovsky, This Business of Music 182–201 (5th ed. 1985).

A consent decree entered in March, 1941, terminating Justice Department charges filed earlier that year, significantly resolved AS-CAP's antitrust exposure. The 1941 decree was amended in 1950 and 1960 to relax the society's membership requirements, to adjust voting rights and put revenue distributions on a more objective basis, to broaden the choices available to licensees, and to impose reasonable royalties when ASCAP and an applicant are unable to reach agreement. Members received the unrestricted right to license their works to users who were unwilling to take a blanket license. BMI is also governed by an antitrust consent decree. The ASCAP consent decrees appear at 1940–43 Trade Cas, (CCH) ¶ 56,104 (1941); 1950–51 Trade Cas, (CCH) ¶ 62,595 (1950); 1960 Trade Cas, (CCH) ¶ 69,612. The BMI consent decrees appear at 1940–43 Trade Cas (CCH) ¶ 56,096 (1941); 1966 Trade Cas (CCH) ¶ 71,941. See generally, Timberg, The Antitrust Aspects of Merchandising Modern Music: The ASCAP Consent Judgment of 1950, 19 Law & Contemp.Probs. 294 (1954); Garner, *United States v. ASCAP:* The Licensing Provisions of the Amended Final Judgment of 1950, 23 Bull.Copyright Soc'y 119 (1975).

See generally, Korman & Koenigsberg, Performing Rights in Music and Performing Rights Societies, 33 J.Copyright Soc'y 332 (1986).

Reproduction Rights. The Senate Report on the bill that eventually became the 1976 Copyright Act recommended the development of workable clearance procedures for library photocopying. S.Rep. No. 473, 94th Cong., 1st Sess. 70–71 (1975). On January 1, 1978—the day the 1976 Act came into effect—the Copyright Clearance Center began operations. Organized by publishers, the CCC facilitates the collection of photocopying fees from users and the distribution of fees to member publishers.

The CCC employs two collecting mechanisms. Under the Transactional Reporting System, the first page of each work registered with the CCC will indicate a copying permission fee and instructions for remitting the fee to the CCC for each copy made; the CCC then distributes the fees collected for each work to the member who owns the copyright in the work. Under its Annual Authorization Service, the CCC audits a user's photocopying activity and uses this audit to derive a statistical model indicating the frequency with which the user photocopies works of particular publishers; this model becomes the basis for determining the user's annual license fee and each individual publisher's entitlement.

For an institutional and comparative overview of copyright collecting societies, see S. Besen & S. Kirby, Compensating Creators of Intellectual Property (1989).

c. FAIR USE

P. GOLDSTEIN, COPYRIGHT (1989) *

§ 10.1   The Fair Use Calculus

Courts have for more than a century excused certain otherwise infringing uses of copyrighted works as "fair" uses. Fair use is most commonly defined as "a privilege in others than the owner of a copyright to use the copyrighted material in a reasonable manner without his consent, notwithstanding the monopoly granted to the owner by the copyright."[1] Variations on the theme define fair use as "an equitable rule of reason,"[2] as a use "technically forbidden by the law, but allowed as reasonable and customary on the theory that the author must have foreseen it and tacitly consented to it,"[3] and as a version of the Golden Rule: "Take not from others to such an extent and in such a manner that you would be resentful if they so took from you."[4]

---

* Copyright © 1989 by Paul Goldstein.

1. H. Ball, The Law of Copyright and Literary Property 260 (1944).

2. Sony Corp. of Am. v. Universal City Studios, Inc., 464 U.S. 417, 448, 104 S.Ct. 774, 792, 78 L.Ed.2d 574, 220 U.S.P.Q. 665 (1984).

3. R. De Wolf, An Outline of Copyright Law 143 (1925). Under the logic of this

view, an express declaration appearing on the copyrighted work prohibiting certain customary or reasonable uses would defeat the fair use defense. The policies underlying fair use, discussed in this section, require that its salutary effects not be so easily circumvented.

4. McDonald, Non–Infringing Uses, 9 Bull. Copyright Soc'y 466, 467 (1962).

Section 107 of the 1976 Copyright Act represents the first statutory codification of fair use in United States copyright law. Section 107's first sentence identifies six exemplary purposes, any one of which will bring a use within the general scope of fair use—"criticism, comment, news reporting, teaching (including multiple copies for classroom use), scholarship or research." Section 107's second sentence lists four factors for courts to weigh in determining whether a use that falls within the general scope of fair use is in fact fair:

(1) the purpose and character of the use, including whether such use is of a commercial nature or is for non-profit educational purposes;

(2) the nature of the copyrighted work;

(3) the amount and substantiality of the portion used in relation to the copyrighted work as a whole; and

(4) the effect of the use upon the potential market for or value of the copyrighted work.

The House Report accompanying the 1976 Copyright Act illustrates section 107's reach with several examples: "quotation of excerpts in a review or criticism for purposes of illustration or comment; quotation of short passages in a scholarly or technical work, for illustration or clarification of the author's observations; use in a parody of some of the content of the work parodied; summary of an address or article, with brief quotations, in a news report; reproduction by a library of a portion of a work to replace part of a damaged copy; reproduction by a teacher or student of a small part of a work to illustrate a lesson; reproduction of a work in legislative or judicial proceedings or reports; incidental and fortuitous reproduction, in a newsreel or broadcast, of a work located in the scene of an event being reported." [6]

SONY CORP. OF AMERICA v. UNIVERSAL CITY STUDIOS, INC.

Supreme Court of the United States, 1984.
464 U.S. 417, 104 S.Ct. 774, 78 L.Ed.2d 574, 220 U.S.P.Q. 665.

Justice STEVENS delivered the opinion of the Court.

Petitioners manufacture and sell home video tape recorders. Respondents own the copyrights on some of the television programs that are broadcast on the public airwaves. Some members of the general public use video tape recorders sold by petitioners to record some of these broadcasts, as well as a large number of other broadcasts. The question presented is whether the sale of petitioners' copying equipment to the general public violates any of the rights conferred upon respondents by the Copyright Act.

Respondents commenced this copyright infringement action against petitioners in the United States District Court for the Central District of California in 1976. Respondents alleged that some individuals had used Betamax video tape recorders (VTR's) to record some of

6. House Report, 65.

respondents' copyrighted works which had been exhibited on commercially sponsored television and contended that these individuals had thereby infringed respondents' copyrights. Respondents further maintained that petitioners were liable for the copyright infringement allegedly committed by Betamax consumers because of petitioners' marketing of the Betamax VTR's. Respondents sought no relief against any Betamax consumer. Instead, they sought money damages and an equitable accounting of profits from petitioners, as well as an injunction against the manufacture and marketing of Betamax VTR's.

After a lengthy trial, the District Court denied respondents all the relief they sought and entered judgment for petitioners. The United States Court of Appeals for the Ninth Circuit reversed the District Court's judgment on respondent's copyright claim, holding petitioners liable for contributory infringement and ordering the District Court to fashion appropriate relief. We granted certiorari; since we had not completed our study of the case last Term, we ordered reargument. We now reverse.

An explanation of our rejection of respondents' unprecedented attempt to impose copyright liability upon the distributors of copying equipment requires a quite detailed recitation of the findings of the District Court. In summary, those findings reveal that the average member of the public uses a VTR principally to record a program he cannot view as it is being televised and then to watch it once at a later time. This practice, known as "time-shifting," enlarges the television viewing audience. For that reason, a significant amount of television programming may be used in this manner without objection from the owners of the copyrights on the programs. For the same reason, even the two respondents in this case, who do assert objections to time-shifting in this litigation, were unable to prove that the practice has impaired the commercial value of their copyrights or has created any likelihood of future harm. Given these findings, there is no basis in the Copyright Act upon which respondents can hold petitioners liable for distributing VTR's to the general public. The Court of Appeals' holding that respondents are entitled to enjoin the distribution of VTR's, to collect royalties on the sale of such equipment, or to obtain other relief, if affirmed, would enlarge the scope of respondents' statutory monopolies to encompass control over an article of commerce that is not the subject of copyright protection. Such an expansion of the copyright privilege is beyond the limits of the grants authorized by Congress. . . .

[The Court's analysis of contributory infringement doctrine, omitted here but discussed at page 625, above, led it to conclude that "the sale of copying equipment, like the sale of other articles of commerce, does not constitute contributory infringement if the product is widely used for legitimate, unobjectionable purposes. Indeed, it need merely be capable of substantial noninfringing uses."]

IV

The question is thus whether the Betamax is capable of commercially significant noninfringing uses. In order to resolve that question, we need not explore *all* the different potential uses of the machine and determine whether or not they would constitute infringement. Rather, we need only consider whether on the basis of the facts as found by the district court a significant number of them would be non-infringing. Moreover, in order to resolve this case we need not give precise content to the question of how much use is commercially significant. For one potential use of the Betamax plainly satisfies this standard, however it is understood: private, noncommercial time-shifting in the home. It does so both (A) because respondents have no right to prevent other copyright holders from authorizing it for their programs, and (B) because the District Court's factual findings reveal that even the unauthorized home time-shifting of respondents' programs is legitimate fair use.

A. *Authorized Time Shifting*

Each of the respondents owns a large inventory of valuable copyrights, but in the total spectrum of television programming their combined market share is small. The exact percentage is not specified, but it is well below 10%. If they were to prevail, the outcome of this litigation would have a significant impact on both the producers and the viewers of the remaining 90% of the programming in the Nation. No doubt, many other producers share respondents' concern about the possible consequences of unrestricted copying. Nevertheless the findings of the District Court make it clear that time-shifting may enlarge the total viewing audience and that many producers are willing to allow private time-shifting to continue, at least for an experimental time period.

The District Court found:

> Even if it were deemed that home-use recording of copyrighted material constituted infringement, the Betamax could still legally be used to record noncopyrighted material or material whose owners consented to the copying. An injunction would deprive the public of the ability to use the Betamax for this noninfringing off-the-air recording.

> Defendants introduced considerable testimony at trial about the potential for such copying of sports, religious, educational and other programming. This included testimony from representatives of the Offices of the Commissioners of the National Football, Basketball, Baseball and Hockey Leagues and Associations, the Executive Director of National Religious Broadcasters and various educational communications agencies. Plaintiffs attack the weight of the testimony offered and also contend that an injunction is warranted because infringing uses outweigh noninfringing uses.

Whatever the future percentage of legal versus illegal home-use recording might be, an injunction which seeks to deprive the public of the very tool or article of commerce capable of some noninfringing use would be an extremely harsh remedy, as well as one unprecedented in copyright law. 480 F.Supp., at 468.

Although the District Court made these statements in the context of considering the propriety of injunctive relief, the statements constitute a finding that the evidence concerning "sports, religious, educational, and other programming" was sufficient to establish a significant quantity of broadcasting whose copying is now authorized, and a significant potential for future authorized copying. That finding is amply supported by the record. In addition to the religious and sports officials identified explicitly by the District Court, two items in the record deserve specific mention.

First is the testimony of John Kenaston, the station manager of Channel 58, an educational station in Los Angeles affiliated with the Public Broadcasting Service. He explained and authenticated the station's published guide to its programs. For each program, the guide tells whether unlimited home taping is authorized, home taping is authorized subject to certain restrictions (such as erasure within seven days), or home taping is not authorized at all. The Spring 1978 edition of the guide described 107 programs. Sixty-two of those programs or 58% authorize some home taping. Twenty-one of them or almost 20% authorize unrestricted home taping.

Second is the testimony of Fred Rogers, president of the corporation that produces and owns the copyright on Mr. Rogers' Neighborhood. The program is carried by more public television stations than any other program. Its audience numbers over 3,000,000 families a day. He testified that he had absolutely no objection to home taping for non-commercial use and expressed the opinion that it is a real service to families to be able to record children's programs and to show them at appropriate times.

If there are millions of owners of VTR's who make copies of televised sports events, religious broadcasts, and educational programs such as Mister Rogers' Neighborhood, and if the proprietors of those programs welcome the practice, the business of supplying the equipment that makes such copying feasible should not be stifled simply because the equipment is used by some individuals to make unauthorized reproductions of respondents' works. The respondents do not represent a class composed of all copyright holders. Yet a finding of contributory infringement would inevitably frustrate the interests of broadcasters in reaching the portion of their audience that is available only through time-shifting.

Of course, the fact that other copyright holders may welcome the practice of time-shifting does not mean that respondents should be deemed to have granted a license to copy their programs. Third party conduct would be wholly irrelevant in an action for direct infringement of respondents' copyrights. But in an action for *contributory* infringement against the seller of copying equipment, the copyright holder may not prevail unless the relief that he seeks affects only his programs, or unless he speaks for virtually all copyright holders with an interest in the outcome. In this case, the record makes it perfectly clear that there are many important producers of national and local television programs who find nothing objectionable about the enlargement in the size of the television audience that results from the practice of time-shifting for private home use. The seller of the equipment that expands those producers' audiences cannot be a contributory infringer if, as is true in this case, it has had no direct involvement with any infringing activity.

B. *Unauthorized Time–Shifting*

Even unauthorized uses of a copyrighted work are not necessarily infringing. An unlicensed use of the copyright is not an infringement unless it conflicts with one of the specific exclusive rights conferred by the copyright statute. Moreover, the definition of exclusive rights in § 106 of the present Act is prefaced by the words "subject to sections 107 through 118." Those sections describe a variety of uses of copyrighted material that "are not infringements of copyright notwithstanding the provisions of § 106." The most pertinent in this case is § 107, the legislative endorsement of the doctrine of "fair use."

That section identifies various factors that enable a Court to apply an "equitable rule of reason" analysis to particular claims of infringement. Although not conclusive, the first factor requires that "the commercial or nonprofit character of an activity" be weighed in any fair use decision. If the Betamax were used to make copies for a commercial or profit-making purpose, such use would presumptively be unfair. The contrary presumption is appropriate here, however, because the District Court's findings plainly establish that time-shifting for private home use must be characterized as a noncommercial, nonprofit activity. Moreover, when one considers the nature of a televised copyrighted audiovisual work, and that timeshifting merely enables a viewer to see such a work which he had been invited to witness in its entirety free of charge, the fact that the entire work is reproduced, does not have its ordinary effect of militating against a finding of fair use.

This is not, however, the end of the inquiry because Congress has also directed us to consider "the effect of the use upon the potential market for or value of the copyrighted work." The purpose of copyright is to create incentives for creative effort. Even copying for noncommercial purposes may impair the copyright holder's ability to obtain the rewards that Congress intended him to have. But a use that has no demonstrable effect upon the potential market for, or the value of, the copyrighted work need not be prohibited in order to protect the author's incentive to create. The prohibition of such noncommercial uses would merely inhibit access to ideas without any countervailing benefit.

Thus, although every commercial use of copyrighted material is presumptively an unfair exploitation of the monopoly privilege that belongs to the owner of the copyright, noncommercial uses are a different matter. A challenge to a noncommercial use of a copyrighted work requires proof either that the particular use is harmful, or that if it should become widespread, it would adversely affect the potential market for the copyrighted work. Actual present harm need not be shown; such a requirement would leave the copyright holder with no defense against predictable damage. Nor is it necessary to show with certainty that future harm will result. What is necessary is a showing by a preponderance of the evidence that *some* meaningful likelihood of future harm exists. If the intended use is for commercial gain, that likelihood may be presumed. But if it is for a noncommercial purpose, the likelihood must be demonstrated.

In this case, respondents failed to carry their burden with regard to home time-shifting. The District Court described respondents' evidence as follows:

> Plaintiffs' experts admitted at several points in the trial that the time-shifting without librarying would result in 'not a great deal of harm.' Plaintiffs' greatest concern about time-shifting is with 'a point of important philosophy that transcends even commercial judgment.' They fear that with any Betamax usage, 'invisible boundaries' are passed: 'the copyright owner has lost control over his program.'

Later in its opinion, the District Court observed:

> Most of plaintiffs' predictions of harm hinge on speculation about audience viewing patterns and ratings, a measurement system which Sidney Sheinberg, MCA's president, calls a 'black art' because of the significant level of imprecision involved in the calculations.

There was no need for the District Court to say much about past harm. "Plaintiffs have admitted that no actual harm to their copyrights has occurred to date."

On the question of potential future harm from time-shifting, the District Court offered a more detailed analysis of the evidence. It rejected respondents' "fear that persons 'watching' the original telecast of a program will not be measured in the live audience and the ratings and revenues will decrease," by observing that current measurement technology allows the Betamax audience to be reflected. It rejected respondents' prediction "that live television or movie audiences will decrease as more people watch Betamax tapes as an alternative," with the observation that "[t]here is no factual basis for [the underlying] assumption." It rejected respondents' "fear that time-shifting will reduce audiences for telecast reruns," and concluded instead that "given current market practices, this should aid plaintiffs rather than harm them." And it declared that respondents' suggestion "that theater or film rental exhibition of a program will suffer because of time-shift recording of that program" "lacks merit."

After completing that review, the District Court restated its overall conclusion several times, in several different ways. "Harm from time-shifting is speculative and, at best, minimal." "The audience benefits from the time-shifting capability have already been discussed. It is not implausible that benefits could also accrue to plaintiffs, broadcasters, and advertisers, as the Betamax makes it possible for more persons to view their broadcasts." Ibid. "No likelihood of harm was shown at trial, and plaintiffs admitted that there had been no actual harm to date." "Testimony at trial suggested that Betamax may require adjustments in marketing strategy, but it did not establish even a likelihood of harm." "Television production by plaintiffs today is more profitable than it has ever been, and, in five weeks of trial, there was no concrete evidence to suggest that the Betamax will change the studios' financial picture."

The District Court's conclusions are buttressed by the fact that to the extent time-shifting expands public access to freely broadcast television programs, it yields societal benefits. Earlier this year, in Community Television of Southern California v. Gottfried, [459 U.S. 498, 508–12] n. 12, 103 S.Ct. 885, 891–892, 74 L.Ed.2d 705 (1983), we acknowledged the public interest in making television broadcasting more available. Concededly, that interest is not unlimited. But it supports an interpretation of the concept of "fair use" that requires the copyright holder to demonstrate some likelihood of harm before he may condemn a private act of time-shifting as a violation of federal law.

When these factors are all weighed in the "equitable rule of reason" balance, we must conclude that this record amply supports the District Court's conclusion that home time-shifting is fair use. In light of the findings of the District Court regarding the state of the empirical data, it is clear that the Court of Appeals erred in holding that the statute as presently written bars such conduct.

In summary, the record and findings of the District Court lead us to two conclusions. First, Sony demonstrated a significant likelihood that substantial numbers of copyright holders who license their works for broadcast on free television would not object to having their broadcasts time-shifted by private viewers. And second, respondents failed to demonstrate that time-shifting would cause any likelihood of non-minimal harm to the potential market for, or the value of, their copyrighted works. The Betamax is, therefore, capable of substantial noninfringing uses. Sony's sale of such equipment to the general public does not constitute contributory infringement of respondent's copyrights.

V

The direction of Art. I is that *Congress* shall have the power to promote the progress of science and the useful arts. When, as here, the Constitution is permissive, the sign of how far Congress has chosen to go can come only from Congress. Deepsouth Packing

Co. v. Laitram Corp., 406 U.S. 518, 530, 92 S.Ct. 1700, 1707, 32 L.Ed.2d 273 (1972).

One may search the Copyright Act in vain for any sign that the elected representatives of the millions of people who watch television every day have made it unlawful to copy a program for later viewing at home, or have enacted a flat prohibition against the sale of machines that make such copying possible.

It may well be that Congress will take a fresh look at this new technology, just as it so often has examined other innovations in the past. But it is not our job to apply laws that have not yet been written. Applying the copyright statute, as it now reads, to the facts as they have been developed in this case, the judgment of the Court of Appeals must be reversed.

It is so ordered.

[The opinion of Justice Blackmun, with whom Justices Marshall, Powell and Rehnquist joined, dissenting, is omitted.]

HARPER & ROW, PUBLISHERS, INC. v. NATION ENTERPRISES

Supreme Court of the United States, 1985.
471 U.S. 539, 105 S.Ct. 2218, 85 L.Ed.2d 588.

Justice O'CONNOR delivered the opinion of the Court.

This case requires us to consider to what extent the "fair use" provision of the Copyright Revision Act of 1976, 17 U.S.C. § 107 (hereinafter the Copyright Act), sanctions the unauthorized use of quotations from a public figure's unpublished manuscript. In March 1979, an undisclosed source provided The Nation magazine with the unpublished manuscript of "A Time to Heal: The Autobiography of Gerald R. Ford." Working directly from the purloined manuscript, an editor of The Nation produced a short piece entitled "The Ford Memoirs—Behind the Nixon Pardon." The piece was timed to "scoop" an article scheduled shortly to appear in Time magazine. Time had agreed to purchase the exclusive right to print prepublication excerpts from the copyright holders, Harper & Row Publishers, Inc. (hereinafter Harper & Row) and Reader's Digest Association, Inc. (hereinafter Reader's Digest). As a result of The Nation article, Time canceled its agreement. Petitioners brought a successful copyright action against The Nation. On appeal, the Second Circuit reversed the lower court's finding of infringement, holding that The Nation's act was sanctioned as a "fair use" of the copyrighted material. We granted certiorari and we now reverse.

I

In February 1977, shortly after leaving the White House, former President Gerald R. Ford contracted with petitioners Harper & Row and The Reader's Digest, to publish his as yet unwritten memoirs. The memoirs were to contain "significant hitherto unpublished material" concerning the Watergate crisis, Mr. Ford's pardon of former President Nixon and "Mr. Ford's reflections on this period of history, and the morality and personalities involved." In addition to the right to publish the Ford memoirs in book form, the agreement gave petitioners the exclusive right to license prepublication excerpts, known in the trade as "first serial rights." Two years later, as the memoirs were nearing completion, petitioners negotiated a prepublication licensing agreement with Time, a weekly news magazine. Time agreed to pay $25,000, $12,500 in advance and an additional $12,500 at publication, in exchange for the right to excerpt 7,500 words from Mr. Ford's account of the Nixon pardon. The issue featuring the excerpts was timed to appear approximately one week before shipment of the full length book version to bookstores. Exclusivity was an important consideration; Harper & Row instituted procedures designed to maintain the confidentiality of the manuscript, and Time retained the right to renegotiate the second payment should the material appear in print prior to its release of the excerpts.

Two to three weeks before the Time article's scheduled release, an unidentified person secretly brought a copy of the Ford manuscript to Victor Navasky, editor of The Nation, a political commentary magazine. Mr. Navasky knew that his possession of the manuscript was not authorized and that the manuscript must be returned quickly to his "source" to avoid discovery. He hastily put together what he believed was "a real hot news story" composed of quotes, paraphrases and facts drawn exclusively from the manuscript. Mr. Navasky attempted no independent commentary, research or criticism, in part because of the need for speed if he was to "make news" by "publish[ing] in advance of publication of the Ford book." The 2,250 word article, reprinted in the Appendix to this opinion, appeared on April 3, 1979. As a result of The Nation's article, Time canceled its piece and refused to pay the remaining $12,500.

Petitioners brought suit in the District Court for the Southern District of New York, alleging conversion, tortious interference with contract and violations of the Copyright Act. After a 6-day bench trial, the District Judge found that "A Time to Heal" was protected by copyright at the time of The Nation publication and that respondents' use of the copyrighted material constituted an infringement under the Copyright Act, § 106(1), (2), and (3), protecting respectively the right to reproduce the work, the right to license preparation of derivative works, and the right of first distribution of the copyrighted work to the public. The District Court rejected respondents' argument that The Nation's piece was a "fair use" sanctioned by § 107 of the Act. Though billed as "hot news," the article contained no new facts. The magazine had "published its article for profit," taking "the heart" of "a soon-to-be-published" work. This unauthorized use "caused the *Time* agreement to be aborted and thus diminished the value of the copyright." 557 F.Supp., at 1072. Although certain elements of the Ford memoir, such as historical facts and memoranda, were not *per se* copyrightable the District Court held that it was "the totality of these facts and memoranda collected together with Ford's reflections that made them of value to The Nation, [and] this . . . totality . . . is protected by the copyright laws." Id., at 1072–1073. The court awarded actual damages of $12,500.

A divided panel of the Court of Appeals for the Second Circuit reversed. The majority recognized that Mr. Ford's verbatim "reflections" were original "expression" protected by copyright. But it held that the District Court had erred in assuming the "coupling [of these reflections] with uncopyrightable fact transformed that information into a copyrighted 'totality.'" 723 F.2d 195, 205 (2d Cir.1983). The majority noted that copyright attaches to expression, not facts or ideas. It concluded that, to avoid granting a copyright monopoly over the facts underlying history and news, " 'expression' [in such works must be confined] to its barest elements—the ordering and choice of the words themselves." Id., at 204. Thus similarities between the original and the challenged work traceable to the copying or paraphrasing of uncopyrightable material, such as historical facts, memoranda and other public documents, and quoted remarks of third parties, must be disregarded in evaluating whether the second author's use was fair or infringing.

> When the uncopyrighted material is stripped away, the article in *The Nation* contains, at most, approximately 300 words that are copyrighted. These remaining paragraphs and scattered phrases are all verbatim quotations from the memoirs which had not appeared previously in other publications. They include a short segment of Ford's conversations with Henry Kissinger and several other individuals. Ford's impressionistic depictions of Nixon, ill with phlebitis after the resignation and pardon, and of Nixon's character, constitute the major portion of this material. It is these parts of the magazine piece on which [the court] must focus in [its] examination of the question whether there was a 'fair use' of copyrighted matter. Id., at 206.

Examining the four factors enumerated in § 107, the majority found the purpose of the article was "news reporting," the original work was essentially factual in nature, the 300 words appropriated were insubstantial in relation to the 2,250 word piece, and the impact on the market for the original was minimal as "the evidence [did] not support a finding that it was the very limited use of expression *per se* which led to Time's decision not to print the excerpt." The Nation's borrowing of verbatim quotations merely "len[t] authenticity to this politically significant material . . . complementing the reporting of the facts." 723 F.2d, at 208. The Court of Appeals was especially influenced by the "politically significant" nature of the subject matter and its conviction that it is not "the purpose of the Copyright Act to impede that harvest of knowledge so necessary to a democratic state" or "chill the activities of the press by forbidding a circumscribed use of copyrighted words." Id., at 197, 209.

II

We agree with the Court of Appeals that copyright is intended to increase and not to impede the harvest of knowledge. But we believe the Second Circuit gave insufficient deference to the scheme established by the Copyright Act for fostering the original works that provide the seed and substance of this harvest. The rights conferred by copyright are designed to assure contributors to the store of knowledge a fair return for their labors.

Article I, § 8, of the Constitution provides that:

> The Congress shall have Power . . . to Promote the Progress of Science and useful Arts, by securing for limited Times to Authors and Inventors the exclusive Right to their respective Writings and Discoveries.

As we noted last Term, "[this] limited grant is a means by which an important public purpose may be achieved. It is intended to motivate the creative activity of authors and inventors by the provision of a special reward, and to allow the public access to the products of their genius after the limited period of exclusive control has expired." Sony Corp. v. Universal City Studios, Inc., 464 U.S. 417, 429 (1984). "The monopoly created by copyright thus rewards the individual author in order to benefit the public." Id., at 477 (dissenting opinion). This principle applies equally to works of fiction and nonfiction. The book at issue here, for example, was two years in the making, and began with a contract giving the author's copyright to the publishers in exchange for their services in producing and marketing the work. In preparing the book, Mr. Ford drafted essays and word portraits of public figures and participated in hundreds of taped interviews that were later distilled to chronicle his personal viewpoint. It is evident that the monopoly granted by copyright actively served its intended purpose of inducing the creation of new material of potential historical value.

Section 106 of the Copyright Act confers a bundle of exclusive rights to the owner of the copyright. Under the Copyright Act, these rights—to publish, copy, and distribute the author's work—vest in the author of an original work from the time of its creation. In practice, the author commonly sells his rights to publishers who offer royalties in exchange for their services in producing and marketing the author's work. The copyright owner's rights, however, are subject to certain statutory exceptions. Among these is § 107 which codifies the traditional privilege of other authors to make "fair use" of an earlier writer's work. In addition, no author may copyright facts or ideas. The copyright is limited to those aspects of the work—termed "expression"—that display the stamp of the author's originality.

Creation of a nonfiction work, even a compilation of pure fact, entails originality. . . . The copyright holders of "A Time to Heal" complied with the relevant statutory notice and registration procedures. Thus there is no dispute that the unpublished manuscript of "A

Time to Heal," as a whole, was protected by § 106 from unauthorized reproduction. Nor do respondents dispute that verbatim copying of excerpts of the manuscript's original form of expression would constitute infringement unless excused as fair use. Yet copyright does not prevent subsequent users from copying from a prior author's work those constituent elements that are not original—for example, quotations borrowed under the rubric of fair use from other copyrighted works, facts, or materials in the public domain—as long as such use does not unfairly appropriate the author's original contributions. Perhaps the controversy between the lower courts in this case over copyrightability is more aptly styled a dispute over whether The Nation's appropriation of unoriginal and uncopyrightable elements encroached on the originality embodied in the work as a whole. Especially in the realm of factual narrative, the law is currently unsettled regarding the ways in which uncopyrightable elements combine with the author's original contributions to form protected expression. . . .

We need not reach these issues, however, as The Nation has admitted to lifting verbatim quotes of the author's original language totalling between 300 and 400 words and constituting some 13% of The Nation article. In using generous verbatim excerpts of Mr. Ford's unpublished manuscript to lend authenticity to its account of the forthcoming memoirs, The Nation effectively arrogated to itself the right of first publication, an important marketable subsidiary right. For the reasons set forth below, we find that this use of the copyrighted manuscript, even stripped to the verbatim quotes conceded by the Nation to be copyrightable expression, was not a fair use within the meaning of the Copyright Act.

III

A

Fair use was traditionally defined as "a privilege in others than the owner of the copyright to use the copyrighted material in a reasonable manner without his consent." H. Ball, Law of Copyright and Literary Property 260 (1944) (hereinafter Ball). The statutory formulation of the defense of fair use in the Copyright Act of 1976 reflects the intent of Congress to codify the common-law doctrine. Section 107 requires a case-by-case determination whether a particular use is fair, and the statute notes four nonexclusive factors to be considered. This approach was "intended to restate the [pre-existing] judicial doctrine of fair use, not to change, narrow, or enlarge it in any way." H.R.Rep. No. 94–1476, p. 66 (1976) (hereinafter House Report).

"[T]he author's consent to a reasonable use of his copyrighted works ha[d] always been implied by the courts as a necessary incident of the constitutional policy of promoting the progress of science and the useful arts, since a prohibition of such use would inhibit subsequent writers from attempting to improve upon prior works and thus . . . frustrate the very ends sought to be attained." Ball 260. Professor Latman, in a study of the doctrine of fair use commissioned by Congress for the revision effort, see Sony Corp. v. Universal City Studios, Inc., 464 U.S., at 462–463, n. 9 (dissenting opinion), summarized prior law as turning on the "importance of the material copied or performed from the point of view of the reasonable copyright owner. In other words, would the reasonable copyright owner have consented to the use?"

As early as 1841, Justice Story, gave judicial recognition to the doctrine in a case that concerned the letters of another former President, George Washington.

> [A] reviewer may fairly cite largely from the original work, if his design be really and truly to use the passages for the purposes of fair and reasonable criticism. On the other hand, it is as clear, that if he thus cites the most important parts of the work, with a view, not to criticise, but to supersede the use of the original work, and substitute the review for it, such a use will be deemed in law a piracy. Folsom v. Marsh, 9 F.Cas. 342, 344–345 (No. 4,901) (CC Mass.).

As Justice Story's hypothetical illustrates, the fair use doctrine has always precluded a use that "supersede[s] the use of the original." Ibid. Accord S.Rep. No. 94–473, p. 65 (1975) (hereinafter Senate Report).

Perhaps because the fair use doctrine was predicated on the author's implied consent to "reasonable and customary" use when he released his work for public consumption, fair use traditionally was not recognized as a defense to charges of copying from an author's as yet unpublished works. Under common-law copyright, "the property of the author . . . in his intellectual creation [was] absolute until he voluntarily part[ed] with the same." American Tobacco Co. v. Werckmeister, 207 U.S. 284, 299 (1907). This absolute rule, however, was tempered in practice by the equitable nature of the fair use doctrine. In a given case, factors such as implied consent through *de facto* publication or performance or dissemination of a work may tip the balance of equities in favor of prepublication use. But it has never been seriously disputed that "the fact that the plaintiff's work is unpublished . . . is a factor tending to negate the defense of fair use." Ibid. Publication of an author's expression before he has authorized its dissemination seriously infringes the author's right to decide when and whether it will be made public, a factor not present in fair use of published works. Respondents contend, however, that Congress, in including first publication among the rights enumerated in § 106, which are expressly subject to fair use under § 107, intended that fair use would apply *in pari materia* to published and unpublished works. The Copyright Revision Act does not support this proposition.

The Copyright Revision Act of 1976 represents the culmination of a major legislative reexamination of copyright doctrine. Among its other innovations, it eliminated publication "as a dividing line between common law and statutory protection," House Report, at 129, extending statutory protection to all works from the time of their creation. It also recognized for the first time a distinct statutory right of first publication, which had previously been an element of the common-law protections afforded unpublished works. The Report of the House Committee on the Judiciary confirms that "Clause (3) of section 106, establishes the exclusive right of publication. . . . Under this provision the copyright owner would have the right to control the first public distribution of an authorized copy . . . of his work." Id., at 62.

Though the right of first publication, like the other rights enumerated in § 106, is expressly made subject to the fair use provision of § 107, fair use analysis must always be tailored to the individual case. The nature of the interest at stake is highly relevant to whether a given use is fair. From the beginning, those entrusted with the task of revision recognized the "overbalancing reasons to preserve the common law protection of undisseminated works until the author or his successor chooses to disclose them." Copyright Law Revision, Report of the Register of Copyrights on the General Revision of the U.S. Copyright Law, 87th Cong., 1st Sess., 41 (Comm. Print 1961). The right of first publication implicates a threshold decision by the author whether and in what form to release his work. First publication is inherently different from other § 106 rights in that only one person can be the first publisher; as the contract with Time illustrates, the commercial value of the right lies primarily in exclusivity. Because the potential damage to the author from judicially enforced "sharing" of the first publication right with unauthorized users of his manuscript is substantial, the balance of equities in evaluating such a claim of fair use inevitably shifts.

The Senate Report confirms that Congress intended the unpublished nature of the work to figure prominently in fair use analysis. In discussing fair use of photocopied materials in the classroom the Committee Report states:

> A key, though not necessarily determinative, factor in fair use is whether or not the work is available to the potential user. If the work is 'out of print' and unavailable for purchase through normal channels, the user may have more justification for reproducing it. . . . The applicability of the fair use doctrine to unpublished works is narrowly limited since, although the work is unavailable, this is the result of a deliberate choice on the part of the copyright owner. Under ordinary circumstances, the copyright owner's 'right of first publication' would outweigh any needs of reproduction for classroom purposes. Senate Report, at 64.

Although the Committee selected photocopying of classroom materials to illustrate fair use, it emphasized that "the same general standards of fair use are applicable to all kinds of uses of copyrighted material." Id., at 65. We find unconvincing respondent's contention that the absence of the quoted passage from the House Report indicates an intent to abandon the traditional distinction between fair use of published and unpublished works. It appears instead that the fair use discussion of photocopying of classroom materials was omitted from the final report because educators and publishers in the interim had negotiated a set of guidelines that rendered the discussion obsolete.

House Report, at 67. The House Report nevertheless incorporates the discussion by reference, citing to the Senate Report and stating that "The Committee has reviewed this discussion, and considers it still has value as an analysis of various aspects of the [fair use] problem." Ibid.

Even if the legislative history were entirely silent, we would be bound to conclude from Congress' characterization of § 107 as a "restatement" that its effect was to preserve existing law concerning fair use of unpublished works as of other types of protected works and not to "change, narrow, or enlarge it." Id., at 66. We conclude that the unpublished nature of a work is "[a] key, though not necessarily determinative, factor" tending to negate a defense of fair use. Senate Report, at 64.

We also find unpersuasive respondents' argument that fair use may be made of a soon-to-be-published manuscript on the ground that the author has demonstrated he has no interest in nonpublication. This argument assumes that the unpublished nature of copyrighted material is only relevant to letters or other confidential writings not intended for dissemination. It is true that common-law copyright was often enlisted in the service of personal privacy. In its commercial guise, however, an author's right to choose when he will publish is no less deserving of protection. The period encompassing the work's initiation, its preparation, and its grooming for public dissemination is a crucial one for any literary endeavor. The Copyright Act, which accords the copyright owner the "right to control the first public distribution" of his work, House Report, at 62, echoes the common law's concern that the author or copyright owner retain control throughout this critical stage. The obvious benefit to author and public alike of assuring authors the leisure to develop their ideas free from fear of expropriation outweighs any short term "news value" to be gained from premature publication of the author's expression. The author's control of first public distribution implicates not only his personal interest in creative control but his property interest in exploitation of prepublication rights, which are valuable in themselves and serve as a valuable adjunct to publicity and marketing. Under ordinary circumstances, the author's right to control the first public appearance of his undisseminated expression will outweigh a claim of fair use. . . .

IV

Fair use is a mixed question of law and fact. Where the District Court has found facts sufficient to evaluate each of the statutory factors, an appellate court "need not remand for further factfinding . . . [but] may conclude as a matter of law that [the challenged use] do[es] not qualify as a fair use of the copyrighted work." Id., at 1495. Thus whether The Nation article constitutes fair use under § 107 must be reviewed in light of the principles discussed above. The factors enumerated in the section are not meant to be exclusive: "[S]ince the doctrine is an equitable rule of reason, no generally applicable definition is possible, and each case raising the question must be decided on its own facts." House Report, at 65. The four factors identified by Congress as especially relevant in determining whether the use was fair are: (1) the purpose and character of the use; (2) the nature of the copyrighted work; (3) the substantiality of the portion used in relation to the copyrighted work as a whole; (4) the effect on the potential market for or value of the copyrighted work. We address each one separately.

Purpose of the Use. The Second Circuit correctly identified news reporting as the general purpose of The Nation's use. News reporting is one of the examples enumerated in § 107 to "give some idea of the sort of activities the courts might regard as fair use under the circumstances." Senate Report, at 61. This listing was not intended to be exhaustive, see id.; § 101 (definition of "including" and "such as"), or to single out any particular use as presumptively a "fair" use. The drafters resisted pressures from special interest groups to create presumptive categories of fair use, but structured the provision as an affirmative defense requiring a case by case analysis. "[W]hether a use referred to in the first sentence of section 107 is a fair use in a particular case will depend upon the application of the determinative factors, including those mentioned in the second sentence." Senate Report, at 62. The fact that an article arguably is "news" and therefore a productive use is simply one factor in a fair use analysis.

We agree with the Second Circuit that the trial court erred in fixing on whether the information contained in the memoir was actually new to the public. As Judge Meskill wisely noted, "[c]ourts should be chary of deciding what is and what is not news." 723 F.2d, at 215 (Meskill, J., dissenting). "The issue is not what constitutes 'news,' but whether a claim of newsreporting is a valid fair use defense to an infringement of *copyrightable expression.*" Patry [The Fair Use Privilege in Copyright Law (1985)] 119. The Nation has every right to seek to be the first to publish information. But The Nation went beyond simply reporting uncopyrightable information and actively sought to exploit the headline value of its infringement, making a "news event" out of its unauthorized first publication of a noted figure's copyrighted expression.

The fact that a publication was commercial as opposed to non-profit is a separate factor that tends to weigh against a finding of fair use. "[E]very commercial use of copyrighted material is presumptively an unfair exploitation of the monopoly privilege that belongs to the owner of the copyright." Sony Corp. v. Universal City Studios, Inc., 464 U.S., at 451. In arguing that the purpose of news reporting is not purely commercial, The Nation misses the point entirely. The crux of the profit/nonprofit distinction is not whether the sole motive of the use is monetary gain but whether the user stands to profit from exploitation of the copyrighted material without paying the customary price.

In evaluating character and purpose we cannot ignore The Nation's stated purpose of scooping the forthcoming hardcover and Time abstracts. The Nation's use had not merely the incidental effect but the *intended purpose* of supplanting the copyright holder's commercially valuable right of first publication. Also relevant to the "character" of the use is "the propriety of the defendant's conduct." "Fair use presupposes 'good faith' and 'fair dealing.'" Time Inc. v. Bernard Geis Associates, 293 F.Supp. 130, 146 (SDNY 1968), quoting Schulman, Fair Use and the Revision of the Copyright Act, 53 Iowa L.Rev. 832 (1968). The trial court found that The Nation knowingly exploited a purloined manuscript. Unlike the typical claim of fair use, The Nation cannot offer up even the fiction of consent as justification. Like its competitor newsweekly, it was free to bid for the right of abstracting excerpts from "A Time to Heal." Fair use "distinguishes between 'a true scholar and a chiseler who infringes a work for personal profit.'" Wainwright Securities Inc. v. Wall Street Transcript Corp., 558 F.2d, at 94, quoting from Hearings on Bills for the General Revision of the Copyright Law before the House Committee on the Judiciary, 89th Cong., 1st Sess., ser. 8, pt. 3, p. 1706 (1966) (Statement of John Schulman).

Nature of the Copyrighted Work. Second, the Act directs attention to the nature of the copyrighted work. "A Time to Heal" may be characterized as an unpublished historical narrative or autobiography. The law generally recognizes a greater need to disseminate factual works than works of fiction or fantasy.

> [E]ven within the field of fact works, there are gradations as to the relative proportion of fact and fancy. One may move from sparsely embellished maps and directories to elegantly written biography. The extent to which one must permit expressive language to be copied, in order to assure dissemination of the underlying facts, will thus vary from case to case. Id., at 563.

Some of the briefer quotes from the memoir are arguably necessary adequately to convey the facts; for example, Mr. Ford's characterization of the White House tapes as the "smoking gun" is perhaps so integral to the idea expressed as to be inseparable from it. But The Nation did not stop at isolated phrases and instead excerpted subjective descriptions and portraits of public figures whose power lies in the author's individualized expression. Such use, focusing on the most expressive elements of the work, exceeds that necessary to disseminate the facts.

The fact that a work is unpublished is a critical element of its "nature." Our prior discussion establishes that the scope of fair use is narrower with respect to unpublished works. While even substantial quotations might qualify as fair use in a review of a published work or a news account of a speech that had been delivered to the public or disseminated to the press, the author's right to control the first public appearance of his expression weighs against such use of the work before its release. The right of first publication encompasses not only the choice whether to publish at all, but also the choices when, where and in what form first to publish a work.

In the case of Mr. Ford's manuscript, the copyright holder's interest in confidentiality is irrefutable; the copyrightholders had entered into a contractual undertaking to "keep the manuscript confidential" and required that all those to whom the manuscript was shown also "sign an agreement to keep the manuscript confidential." While the copyrightholders' contract with Time required Time to submit its proposed article seven days before publication, The Nation's clandestine publication afforded no such opportunity for creative or quality control. It was hastily patched together and contained "a number of inaccuracies." A use that so clearly infringes the copyright holder's interests in confidentiality and creative control is difficult to characterize as "fair."

Amount and Substantiality of the Portion Used. Next, the Act directs us to examine the amount and substantiality of the portion used in relation to the copyrighted work as a whole. In absolute terms, the words actually quoted were an insubstantial portion of "A Time to Heal." The district court, however, found that "[T]he Nation took what was essentially the heart of the book." 557 F.Supp., at 1072. We believe the Court of Appeals erred in overruling the district judge's evaluation of the qualitative nature of the taking. A Time editor described the chapters on the pardon as "the most interesting and moving parts of the entire manuscript." The portions actually quoted were selected by Mr. Navasky as among the most powerful passages in those chapters. He testified that he used verbatim excerpts because simply reciting the information could not adequately convey the "absolute certainty with which [Ford] expressed himself," or show that "this comes from President Ford," or carry the "definitive quality" of the original. In short, he quoted these passages precisely because they qualitatively embodied Ford's distinctive expression.

As the statutory language indicates, a taking may not be excused merely because it is insubstantial with respect to the *infringing* work. As Judge Learned Hand cogently remarked, "[N]o plagiarist can excuse the wrong by showing how much of his work he did not pirate." Sheldon v. Metro–Goldwyn Pictures Corp., 81 F.2d 49, 56 (CA2), cert. denied, 298 U.S. 669 (1936). Conversely, the fact that a substantial portion of the infringing work was copied verbatim is evidence of the qualitative value of the copied material, both to the originator and to the plagiarist who seeks to profit from marketing someone else's copyrighted expression.

Stripped to the verbatim quotes,[8] the direct takings from the unpublished manuscript constitute at least 13% of the infringing article. The Nation article is structured around the quoted excerpts which serve as its dramatic focal points. In view of the expressive value of

---

8. See Appendix to this opinion, *post*, p. 570. The Court of Appeals found that only "approximately 300 words" were copyrightable but did not specify which words. The court's discussion, however, indicates it excluded from consideration those portions of The Nation's piece that, although copied verbatim from Ford's manuscript, were quotes attributed by Ford to third persons and quotations from government documents. At oral argument, counsel for

The Nation did not dispute that verbatim quotes and very close paraphrase could constitute infringement. Thus the Appendix identifies as potentially infringing only verbatim quotes or very close paraphrase and excludes from consideration government documents and words attributed to third persons. The Appendix is not intended to endorse any particular rule of copyrightability but is intended merely as an aid to facilitate our discussion.

the excerpts and their key role in the infringing work, we cannot agree with the Second Circuit that the "magazine took a meager, indeed an infinitesimal amount of Ford's original language." 723 F.2d, at 209.

Effect on the Market. Finally, the Act focuses on "the effect of the use upon the potential market for or value of the copyrighted work." This last factor is undoubtedly the single most important element of fair use. "Fair use, when properly applied, is limited to copying by others which does not materially impair the marketability of the work which is copied." 1 Nimmer § 1.10[D], at 1–87. The trial court found not merely a potential but an actual effect on the market. Time's cancellation of its projected serialization and its refusal to pay the $12,500 were the direct effect of the infringement. The Court of Appeals rejected this fact finding as clearly erroneous, noting that the record did not establish a causal relation between Time's nonperformance and respondents' unauthorized publication of Mr. Ford's *expression* as opposed to the facts taken from the memoirs. We disagree. Rarely will a case of copyright infringement present such clear cut evidence of actual damage. Petitioners assured Time that there would be no other authorized publication of *any* portion of the unpublished manuscript prior to April 23, 1979. *Any* publication of material from chapters 1 and 3 would permit Time to renegotiate its final payment. Time cited The Nation's article, which contained verbatim quotes from the unpublished manuscript, as a reason for its nonperformance. With respect to apportionment of profits flowing from a copyright infringement, this Court has held that an infringer who commingles infringing and noninfringing elements "must abide the consequences, unless he can make a separation of the profits so as to assure to the injured party all that justly belongs to him." Sheldon v. Metro–Goldwyn Pictures Corp., 309 U.S. 390, 406 (1940). Cf. 17 U.S.C. § 504(b) (the infringer is required to prove elements of profits attributable to other than the infringed work). Similarly, once a copyright holder establishes with reasonable probability the existence of a causal connection between the infringement and a loss of revenue, the burden properly shifts to the infringer to show that this damage would have occurred had there been no taking of copyrighted expression. Petitioners established a prima facie case of actual damage that respondent failed to rebut. The trial court properly awarded actual damages and accounting of profits.

More important, to negate fair use one need only show that if the challenged use "should become widespread, it would adversely affect the *potential* market for the copyrighted work." Sony Corp. v. Universal City Studios, Inc., 464 U.S., at 451 (emphasis added); id., at 484, and n. 36 (collecting cases) (dissenting opinion). This inquiry must take account not only of harm to the original but also of harm to the market for derivative works. "If the defendant's work adversely affects the value of any of the rights in the copyrighted work (in this case the adaptation [and serialization] right) the use is not fair." 3 Nimmer § 13.05[B], at 13–77—13–78 (footnote omitted).

It is undisputed that the factual material in the balance of The Nation's article, besides the verbatim quotes at issue here, was drawn exclusively from the chapters on the pardon. The excerpts were employed as featured episodes in a story about the Nixon pardon—precisely the use petitioners had licensed to Time. The borrowing of these verbatim quotes from the unpublished manuscript lent The Nation's piece a special air of authenticity—as Navasky expressed it, the reader would know it was Ford speaking and not The Nation. Thus it directly competed for a share of the market for prepublication excerpts. The Senate Report states:

> With certain special exceptions . . . . a use that supplants any part of the normal market for a copyrighted work would ordinarily be considered an infringement. Senate Report, at 65.

Placed in a broader perspective, a fair use doctrine that permits extensive prepublication quotations from an unreleased manuscript without the copyright owner's consent poses substantial potential for damage to the marketability of first serialization rights in general. "Isolated instances of minor infringements, when multiplied many times, become in the aggregate a major inroad on copyright that must be prevented." Ibid.

V

The Court of Appeals erred in concluding that The Nation's use of the copyrighted material was excused by the public's interest in the subject matter. It erred, as well, in overlooking the unpublished nature of the work and the resulting impact on the potential market for first serial rights of permitting unauthorized prepublication excerpts under the rubric of fair use. Finally, in finding the taking "infinitesimal," the Court of Appeals accorded too little weight to the qualitative importance of the quoted passages of original expression. In sum, the traditional doctrine of fair use, as embodied in the Copyright Act, does not sanction the use made by The Nation of these copyrighted materials. Any copyright infringer may claim to benefit the public by increasing public access to the copyrighted work. But Congress has not designed, and we see no warrant for judicially imposing, a "compulsory license" permitting unfettered access to the unpublished copyrighted expression of public figures.

The Nation conceded that its verbatim copying of some 300 words of direct quotation from the Ford manuscript would constitute an infringement unless excused as a fair use. Because we find that The Nation's use of these verbatim excerpts from the unpublished manuscript was not a fair use, the judgment of the Court of Appeals is reversed and remanded for further proceedings consistent with this opinion.

It is so ordered.

APPENDIX TO OPINION OF THE COURT

The portions of The Nation article which were copied verbatim from "A Time to Heal," excepting quotes from government documents and quotes attributed by Ford to third persons, are identified in boldface in the text. The corresponding passages in the Ford manuscript are footnoted.

THE FORD MEMOIRS BEHIND THE NIXON PARDON

In his memoirs, *A Time to Heal,* which Harper & Row will publish in late May or early June, former President Gerald R. Ford says that the idea of giving a blanket pardon to Richard M. Nixon was raised before Nixon resigned from the Presidency by Gen. Alexander Haig, who was then the White House chief of staff.

Ford also writes that, but for a misunderstanding, he might have selected Ronald Reagan as his 1976 running mate, that Washington lawyer Edward Bennett Williams, a Democrat, was his choice for head of the Central Intelligence Agency, that Nixon was the one who first proposed Rockefeller for Vice President, and that he regretted his **"cowardice"** [1] in allowing Rockefeller to remove himself from Vice Presidential contention. Ford also describes his often prickly relations with Henry Kissinger.

The Nation obtained the 655–page typescript before publication. Advance excerpts from the book will appear in *Time* in mid-April and in *The Reader's Digest* thereafter. Although the initial print order has not been decided, the figure is tentatively set at 50,000; it could change, depending upon the public reaction to the serialization.

Ford's account of the Nixon pardon contains significant new detail on the negotiations and considerations that surrounded it. According to Ford's version, the subject was first broached to him by General Haig on August 1, 1974, a week before Nixon resigned. General Haig revealed that the newly transcribed White House tapes were the equivalent of the **"smoking gun"** [2] and that Ford should prepare himself to become President.

Ford was deeply hurt by Haig's revelation: **"Over the past several months Nixon had repeatedly assured me that he was not involved in Watergate, that the evidence would prove his innocence, that the matter would fade from view."** [3] Ford had believed him, but he let Haig explain the President's alternatives.

He could **"ride it out"** [4] or he could resign, Haig said. He then listed the different ways Nixon might resign and concluded by pointing out that **Nixon could agree to leave in return for an agreement that the new President, Ford, would pardon him.** [5] Although Ford

---

1. I was angry at myself for showing cowardice in not saying to the ultraconservatives, "It's going to be Ford and Rockefeller, whatever the consequences." p. 496.

2. [I]t contained the so-called smoking gun. p. 3.

3. [O]ver the past several months Nixon had repeatedly assured me that he was not involved in Watergate, that the evidence would prove his innocence, that the matter would fade from view. p. 7.

4. The first [option] was that he could try to "ride it out" by letting impeachment take its natural course through the House and the Senate trial, fighting against conviction all the way. p. 4.

5. Finally, Haig said that according to some on Nixon's White House staff, Nixon could agree to leave in return for an agreement that the new President—Gerald Ford—would pardon him. p. 5.

said it would be improper for him to make any recommendation, he basically agreed with Haig's assessment and adds, **"Because of his references to the pardon authority, I did ask Haig about the extent of a President's pardon power."** [6]

"It's my understanding from a White House lawyer," Haig replied, "that a President does have authority to grant a pardon even before criminal action has been taken against an individual."

But because Ford had neglected to tell Haig he thought the idea of a resignation conditioned on a pardon was improper, his press aide, Bob Hartmann, suggested that Haig might well have returned to the White House and told President Nixon that he had mentioned the idea and Ford seemed comfortable with it. "Silence implies assent."

Ford then consulted with White House special counsel James St. Clair, who had no advice one way or the other on the matter more than pointing out that he was not the lawyer who had given Haig the opinion on the pardon. Ford also discussed the matter with Jack Marsh, who felt that the mention of a pardon in this context was a "time bomb," and with Bryce Harlow, who had served six Presidents and who agreed that **the mere mention of a pardon "could cause a lot of trouble."** [7]

As a result of these various conversations, Vice President Ford called Haig and read him a written statement: "I want you to understand that I have no intention of recommending what the President should do about resigning or not resigning and that nothing we talked about yesterday afternoon should be given any consideration in whatever decision the President may wish to make."

Despite what Haig had told him about the "smoking gun" tapes, Ford told a Jackson, Mich., luncheon audience later in the day that **the President was not guilty of an impeachable offense. "Had I said otherwise at that moment,"** he writes, **"the whole house of cards might have collapsed."** [8]

In justifying the pardon, Ford goes out of his way to assure the reader that **"compassion for Nixon as an individual hadn't prompted my decision at all."** [9] Rather, he did it because he had **"to get the monkey off my back one way or the other."** [10]

The precipitating factor in his decision was a series of secret meetings his general counsel, Phil Buchen, held with Watergate Special Prosecutor Leon Jaworski in the Jefferson Hotel, where they were both

6. Because of his references to pardon authority, I did ask Haig about the extent of a President's pardon power. pp. 5–6.

7. Only after I had finished did [Bryce Harlow] let me know in no uncertain terms that he agreed with Bob and Jack, that the mere mention of the pardon option could cause a lot of trouble in the days ahead. p. 18.

8. During the luncheon I repeated my assertion that the President was not guilty

of an impeachable offense. Had I said otherwise at that moment, the whole house of cards might have collapsed. p. 21.

9. But compassion for Nixon as an individual hadn't prompted my decision at all. p. 266.

10. I had to get the monkey off my back one way or another. p. 236.

staying at the time. Ford attributes Jaworski with providing some "crucial" information[11]—i.e., that Nixon was under investigation in ten separate areas, and that **the court process could "take years."** [12] Ford cites a memorandum from Jaworski's assistant, Henry S. Ruth Jr., as being especially persuasive. Ruth had written:

"If you decide to recommend indictment I think it is fair and proper to notify Jack Miller and the White House sufficiently in advance so that pardon action could be taken before the indictment." He went on to say: "One can make a strong argument for leniency and if President Ford is so inclined, I think he ought to do it early rather than late."

Ford decided that court proceedings against Nixon might take six years, that **Nixon "would not spend time quietly in San Clemente,"** [13] and **"it would be virtually impossible for me to direct public attention on anything else."** [14]

Buchen, Haig and Henry Kissinger agreed with him. Hartmann was not so sure.

Buchen wanted to condition the pardon on Nixon agreeing to settle the question of who would retain custody and control over the tapes and Presidential papers that might be relevant to various Watergate proceedings, but Ford was reluctant to do that.

At one point a plan was considered whereby the Presidential materials would be kept in a vault at a Federal facility near San Clemente, but the vault would require two keys to open it. One would be retained by the General Services Administration, the other by Richard Nixon.

The White House did, however, want Nixon to make a full confession on the occasion of his pardon or, at a minimum, express true contrition. Ford tells of the negotiation with Jack Miller, Nixon's lawyer, over the wording of Nixon's statement. But as Ford reports Miller's response, Nixon was not likely to yield. **"His few meetings with his client had shown him that the former President's ability to discuss Watergate objectively was almost nonexistent."** [15]

The statement they really wanted was never forthcoming. As soon as Ford's emissary arrived in San Clemente, he was confronted with an ultimatum by Ron Zeigler, Nixon's former press secretary. "Let's get one thing straight immediately," Zeigler said, "President Nixon is not issuing any statement whatsoever regarding Watergate, whether Jerry Ford pardons him or not." Zeigler proposed a draft, which was turned down on the ground that **"no statement would be better than**

---

11. Jaworski gave Phil several crucial pieces of information. p. 246.

12. And if the verdict was Guilty, one had to assume that Nixon would appeal. That process would take years. p. 248.

13. The entire process would no doubt require years: a minimum of two, a maximum of six. And Nixon would not spend time quietly in San Clemente. p. 238.

14. It would be virtually impossible for me to direct public attention on anything else. p. 239.

15. But [Miller] wasn't optimistic about getting such a statement. His few meetings with his client had shown him that the former President's ability to discuss Watergate objectively was almost nonexistent. p. 246.

that." [16] They went through three more drafts before they agreed on the statement Nixon finally made, which stopped far short of a full confession.

When Ford aide Benton Becker tried to explain to Nixon that acceptance of a pardon was an admission of guilt, he felt the President wasn't really listening. Instead, Nixon wanted to talk about the Washington Redskins. And when Becker left, Nixon pressed on him some cuff links and a tiepin "out of my own jewelry box."

Ultimately, Ford sums up the philosophy underlying his decision as one he picked up as a student at Yale Law School many years before. **"I learned that public policy often took precedence over a rule of law. Although I respected the tenet that no man should be above the law, public policy demanded that I put Nixon—and Watergate—behind us as quickly as possible."** [17]

Later, when Ford learned that Nixon's phlebitis had acted up and his health was seriously impaired, he debated whether to pay the ailing former President a visit. **"If I made the trip it would remind everybody of Watergate and the pardon. If I didn't, people would say I lacked compassion."** [18] Ford went:

He was stretched out flat on his back. There were tubes in his nose and mouth, and wires led from his arms, chest and legs to machines with orange lights that blinked on and off. His face was ashen, and I thought I had never seen anyone closer to death.[19]

The manuscript made available to The Nation includes many references to Henry Kissinger and other personalities who played a major role during the Ford years.

On Kissinger. Immediately after being informed by Nixon of his intention to resign, Ford returned to the Executive Office Building and phoned Henry Kissinger to let him know how he felt. **"Henry,"** he said, **"I need you. The country needs you. I want you to stay. I'll do everything I can to work with you."** [20]

"Sir," Kissinger replied, "it is my job to get along with you and not yours to get along with me."

---

16. When Zeigler asked Becker what he thought of it, Becker replied that no statement would be better than that. p. 251.

17. Years before, at Yale Law School, I'd learned that public policy often took precedence over a rule of law. Although I respected the tenet that no man should be above the law, public policy demanded that I put Nixon—and Watergate—behind us as quickly as possible. p. 256.

18. My staff debated whether or not I ought to visit Nixon at the Long Beach Hospital, only half an hour away. If I made the trip, it would remind everyone of Watergate and the pardon. If I didn't,

people would say I lacked compassion. I ended their debate as soon as I found out it had begun. Of course I would go. p. 298.

19. He was stretched out flat on his back. There were tubes in his nose and mouth, and wires led from his arms, chest and legs to machines with orange lights that blinked on and off. His face was ashen, and I thought I had never seen anyone closer to death. p. 299.

20. "Henry," I said when he came on the line, "I need you. The country needs you. I want you to stay. I'll do everything I can to work with you." p. 46.

"We'll get along," Ford said. **"I know we'll get along."** Referring to Kissinger's joint jobs as Secretary of State and National Security Adviser to the President, Ford said, **"I don't want to make any change. I think it's worked out well, so let's keep it that way."** [21]

Later Ford did make the change and relieved Kissinger of his responsibilities as National Security Adviser at the same time that he fired James Schlesinger as Secretary of Defense. Shortly thereafter, he reports, Kissinger presented him with a "draft" letter of resignation, which he said Ford could call upon at will if he felt he needed it to quiet dissent from conservatives who objected to Kissinger's role in the firing of Schlesinger.

On John Connally. When Ford was informed that Nixon wanted him to replace Agnew, he told the President he had **"no ambition to hold office after January 1977."** [22] Nixon replied that that was good since his own choice for his running mate in 1976 was John Connally. "He'd be excellent," observed Nixon. Ford says he had "no problem with that."

On the Decision to Run Again. Ford was, he tells us, so sincere in his intention not to run again that he thought he would announce it and enhance his credibility in the country and the Congress, as well as keep the promise he had made to his wife, Betty.

Kissinger talked him out of it. "You can't do that. It would be disastrous from a foreign policy point of view. For the next two and a half years foreign governments would know that they were dealing with a lame-duck President. All our initiatives would be dead in the water, and I wouldn't be able to implement your foreign policy. It would probably have the same consequences in dealing with the Congress on domestic issues. You can't reassert the authority of the Presidency if you leave yourself hanging out on a dead limb. You've got to be an affirmative President."

On David Kennerly, the White House photographer. Schlesinger was arguing with Kissinger and Ford over the appropriate response to the seizure of the *Mayaguez.* At issue was whether airstrikes against the Cambodians were desirable; Schlesinger was opposed to bombings. Following a lull in the conversation, Ford reports, up spoke the 30–year–old White House photographer David Kennerly who had been taking pictures for the last hour.

"Has anyone considered," Kennerly asked, "that this might be the act of a local Cambodian commander who has just taken it into his own hands to stop any ship that comes by?" Nobody, apparently, had considered it, but following several seconds of silence, Ford tells us, the view carried the day. **"Massive airstrikes would constitute overkill,"** Ford decided. **"It would be far better to have Navy jets**

---

21. "We'll get along," I said. "I know we can get along." We talked about the two hats he wore, as Secretary of State and National Security Adviser to the President. "I don't want to make any change," I said, "I think it's worked out well, so let's keep it that way." p. 46.

22. I told him about my promise to Betty and said that I had no ambitions to hold office after January 1977. p. 155.

from the Coral Sea make surgical strikes against specific targets." [23]

On Nixon's Character. **Nixon's flaw,** according to Ford **was "pride." "A terribly proud man,"** writes Ford, **"he detested weakness in other people. I'd often heard him speak disparagingly of those whom he felt to be soft and expedient. (Curiously, he didn't feel that the press was weak. Reporters, he sensed, were his adversaries. He knew they didn't like him, and he responded with reciprocal disdain.)"** [24]

Nixon felt disdain for the Democratic leadership of the House, whom he also regarded as weak. According to Ford, **"His pride and personal contempt for weakness had overcome his ability to tell the difference between right and wrong,"** [25] all of which leads Ford to wonder whether Nixon had known in advance about Watergate.

On hearing Nixon's resignation speech, which Ford felt lacked an adequate plea for forgiveness, he was persuaded that **"Nixon was out of touch with reality."** [26]

In February of last year, when *The Washington Post* obtained and printed advance excerpts from H.R. Haldeman's memoir, *The Ends of Power,* on the eve of its publication by Times Books, *The New York Times* called *The Post's* feat "a second-rate burglary."

The Post disagreed, claiming that its coup represented "first-rate enterprise" and arguing that it had burglarized nothing, that publication of the Haldeman memoir came under the Fair Comment doctrine long recognized by the courts, and that "There is a fundamental journalistic principle here—a First Amendment principle that was central to the Pentagon Papers case."

In the issue of *The Nation* dated May 5, 1979, our special Spring Books number, we will discuss some of the ethical problems raised by the issue of disclosure.

[The opinion of Justice Brennan, with whom Justices White and Marshall joined, dissenting, is omitted.]

WALT DISNEY PRODUCTIONS v. AIR PIRATES, 581 F.2d 751, 753, 756–758, 199 U.S.P.Q. 769 (9th Cir.1978). CUMMINGS, J.: ["The individual defendants have participated in preparing and publishing two magazines of cartoons entitled 'Air Pirates Funnies.' The characters in defendants' magazines bear a marked similarity to those of

---

23. Subjectively, I felt that what Kennerly had said made a lot of sense. Massive airstrikes would constitute overkill. It would be far better to have Navy jets from the *Coral Sea* make surgical strikes against specific targets in the vicinity of Kompong Som. p. 416.

24. In Nixon's case, that flaw was pride. A terribly proud man, he detested weakness in other people. I'd often heard him speak disparagingly of those whom he felt to be soft and expedient. (Curiously,

he didn't feel that the press was weak. Reporters, he sensed, were his adversaries. He knew they didn't like him, and he responded with reciprocal disdain.) p. 53.

25. His pride and personal contempt for weakness had overcome his ability to tell the difference between right and wrong. p. 54.

26. The speech lasted fifteen minutes, and at the end I was convinced Nixon was out of touch with reality. p. 57.

plaintiff. The names given to defendants' characters are the same names used in plaintiff's copyrighted work. However, the themes of defendants' publications differ markedly from those of Disney. While Disney sought only to foster 'an image of innocent delightfulness,' defendants supposedly sought to convey an allegorical message of significance. Put politely by one commentator, the 'Air Pirates' was 'an "underground" comic book which had placed several well-known Disney cartoon characters in incongruous settings where they engaged in activities clearly antithetical to the accepted Mickey Mouse world of scrubbed faces, bright smiles and happy endings.' It centered around 'a rather bawdy depiction of the Disney characters as active members of a free thinking, promiscuous, drug ingesting counterculture.' Note, Parody, Copyrights and the First Amendment. 10 U.S.F.L.Rev. 564, 571, 582 (1976)."]

Defendants do not contend that their admitted copying was not substantial enough to constitute an infringement, and it is plain that copying a comic book character's graphic image constitutes copying to an extent sufficient to justify a finding of infringement. Defendants instead claim that this infringement should be excused through the application of the fair use defense, since it purportedly is a parody of Disney's cartoons.

At least since this Court's controversial ruling in Benny v. Loew's Inc., 239 F.2d 532, 112 U.S.P.Q. 11 (9th Cir.1956), affirmed by an equally divided Court, 356 U.S. 43, 78 S.Ct. 667, 2 L.Ed.2d 583, 116 U.S. P.Q. 479 (1958), the standards for applying the fair use defense in parody cases, like the standards for applying fair use in other contexts, have been a source of considerable attention and dispute. As a general matter, while some commentators have urged that the fair use defense depends only on whether the infringing work fills the demand for the original this Court and others have also consistently focused on the substantiality of the taking.

In inquiring into the substantiality of the taking, the district court read our Benny opinion to hold that any substantial copying by a defendant, combined with the fact that the portion copied constituted a substantial part of the defendant's work, automatically precluded the fair use defense. That such a strict reading of Benny was unjustified is indicated first by the fact that it would essentially make any fair use defense fruitless. If the substantiality of the taking necessary to satisfy the first half of that test is no different from the substantiality necessary to constitute an infringement, then the Benny test would be reduced to an absurdity, covering any infringement except those falling within the much-criticized and abandoned exception for cases in which the part copied was not a substantial part of the defendant's work.

The language in Benny concerning the substantiality of copying can be given a reading much more in keeping with the context of that case and the established principles at the time of that case if the opinion is understood as setting a threshold that eliminates from the fair use defense copying that is virtually complete or almost verbatim.

It was an established principle at the time of Benny that such verbatim copying precluded resort to the fair use defense. Moreover, the Benny facts presented a particularly appropriate instance to apply that settled principle. As the Benny district court found, Benny's "Autolight" tracked the parodied "Gas Light" in almost every respect: the locale and period, the setting, characters, story points, incidents, climax and much of the dialogue all were found to be identical. In this context, Benny should not be read as taking the drastic step of virtually turning the test for fair use into the test for infringement. To do otherwise would be to eliminate fair use as a defense except perhaps for those infringers who added an extra act at the end of their parody.

Thus Benny should stand only as a threshold test that eliminates near-verbatim copying. In the absence of near-verbatim copying, other courts have analyzed the substantiality of copying by a parodist by asking whether the parodist has appropriated a greater amount of the original work than is necessary to "recall or conjure up" the object of his satire. Berlin v. E.C. Publications, Inc., 329 F.2d 541, 141 U.S.P.Q. 1 (2d Cir.1964), cert. denied, 379 U.S. 822, 85 S.Ct. 46, 13 L.Ed.2d 33, 143 U.S.P.Q. 464.

In order to facilitate application of either the Benny threshold test or the Berlin test, it is important to determine what are the relevant parts of each work that are compared in analyzing similarity. Plaintiff assumes in its brief that the graphic depiction, or pictorial illustration, is separately copyrightable as a component part, so that a verbatim copy of the depiction alone would satisfy the Benny test. Defendants proceed on the assumption that comparing their characters with plaintiff's involves a comparison not only of the physical image but also of the character's personality, pattern of speech, abilities, and other traits. Apparently this issue has not been addressed previously, and neither position is without merit. On the one hand, since an illustration in a book or catalogue can be copyrighted separately it might follow that an illustration in a comic strip is entitled to the same protection by virtue of Section 3 of the former Copyright Act. On the other hand, to a different extent than in other illustrations, a cartoon character's image is intertwined with its personality and other traits, so that the "total concept and feel" (Roth Greeting Cards v. United Card Co., 429 F.2d 1106, 1110, 166 U.S.P.Q. 291, 294 (9th Cir.1970)) of even the component part cannot be limited to the image itself.

We need not decide which of these views is correct, or whether this copying was so substantial to satisfy the Benny test, because it is our view that defendants took more than is allowed even under the Berlin test as applied to both the conceptual and physical aspects of the characters. In evaluating how much of a taking was necessary to recall or conjure up the original, it is first important to recognize that given the widespread public recognition of the major characters involved here, such as Mickey Mouse and Donald Duck, in comparison with other characters very little would have been necessary to place Mickey Mouse and his image in the minds of the readers. Second, when the medium involved is a comic book, a recognizable caricature is not difficult to draw, so that an alternative that involves less copying is more likely to be available than if a speech, for instance, is parodied. Also significant is the fact that the essence of this parody did not focus on how the characters looked, but rather parodied their personalities, their wholesomeness and their innocence.[15] Thus arguably defendants' copying could have been justified as necessary more easily if they had paralleled closely (with a few significant twists) Disney characters and their actions in a manner that conjured up the particular elements of the innocence of the characters that were to be satirized. While greater license may be necessary under those circumstances, here the copying of the graphic image appears to have no other purpose than to track Disney's work as a whole as closely as possible.

Defendants' assertion that they copied no more than necessary appears to be based on an affidavit, which stated that "the humorous effect of parody is best achieved when at first glance the material appears convincingly to be the original, and upon closer examination is discovered to be quite something else." The short answer to this assertion, which would also justify substantially verbatim copying, is that when persons are parodying a copyrighted work, the constraints of the existing precedent do not permit them to take as much of a component part as they need to make the "best parody." Instead, their desire to make the "best parody" is balanced against the rights of the copyright owner in his original expressions. That balance has been struck at giving the parodist what is necessary to conjure up the original, and in the absence of a special need for accuracy that standard was exceeded here. By copying the images in their entirety, defendants took more than was necessary to place firmly in the reader's mind the parodied work and those specific attributes that are to be satirized.

Because the amount of defendant's copying exceeded permissible levels, summary judgment was proper. While other factors in the fair use calculus may not be sufficient by themselves to preclude the fair use defense, this and other courts have accepted the traditional American rule that excessive copying precludes fair use.

NOTES

1. "... *purposes such as criticism, comment, news reporting, teaching (including multiple copies for classroom use), scholarship, or research. ...*" To be excused, an otherwise infringing use must come within the scope of fair use as described in section 107's first sentence. *Sony* did not expressly address this threshold requirement; however, since the Court held that home videotaping for time-shifting purposes was fair, it evidently assumed that the activity came within

---

15. In making this distinction, we do not regard it as fatal, as some courts have done (see e.g., Walt Disney Productions v. Mature Pictures Corp., 389 F.Supp. 1397, 186 U.S.P.Q. 48 (S.D.N.Y.1975)), that the "Air Pirates" were parodying life and society in addition to parodying the Disney characters. Such an effect is almost an inherent aspect of any parody. To the extent that the Disney characters are not also an object of the parody, however, the need to conjure them up would be reduced if not eliminated.

the scope of fair use as defined in section 107's first sentence. Can you find a rational connection between home videotaping and "criticism, comment, news reporting, teaching . . . scholarship or research"?

Justice Blackmun, dissenting in *Sony*, read section 107's first sentence to encompass only "productive" uses—a scholar's use of the copyrighted work in writing her own work, for example—and not "ordinary" uses—uses of a work that add no value to it. "Section 107 establishes the fair use doctrine 'for purposes such as criticism, comment, news reporting, teaching, . . . scholarship, or research.' These are all productive uses. It is true that the legislative history states repeatedly that the doctrine must be applied flexibly on a case-by-case basis, but those references were only in the context of productive uses. Such a limitation on fair use comports with its purpose, which is to facilitate the creation of new works. There is no indication that the fair use doctrine has any application for purely personal consumption on the scale involved in this case, and the Court's application of it here deprives fair use of the major cohesive force that has guided evolution of the doctrine in the past." 464 U.S. at 495, 104 S.Ct. at 816.

Does section 107's first sentence support a distinction between "productive" uses and "ordinary" uses? In what ways, and to what extent, does a teacher who makes "multiple copies for classroom use" facilitate the creation of new works?

2. ". . . *purpose and character of the use. . . .*" If a defendant's activities have a commercial purpose, section 107's first factor weighs this purpose against fair use; nonprofit, educational purpose weighs in favor of fair use. The first factor will sometimes be a makeweight. For example, some courts have disfavored advertising on the ground that it is a commercial use while other courts have favored it on the ground that advertisements inform the public of important facts. Compare Consumers Union of the United States, Inc. v. New Regina Corp., 664 F.Supp. 753, 4 U.S.P.Q.2d 1257 (S.D.N.Y.1987) with Triangle Publications, Inc. v. Knight–Ridder Newspapers, Inc., 626 F.2d 1171 (5th Cir.1980).

Section 107's commercial purpose factor may have little predictive force. Justice Brennan, dissenting in the *Nation* case, observed, "[m]any uses § 107 lists as paradigmatic examples of fair use, including criticism, comment, and *news reporting,* are generally conducted for profit in this country, a fact of which Congress was obviously aware when it enacted § 107." 471 U.S. at 592, 105 S.Ct. at 2247 (emphasis in original). Justice Blackmun, dissenting in *Sony,* rejected the Court's characterization of time-shifting as a noncommercial activity. "As one commentator has observed, time-shifting is noncommercial in the same sense that stealing jewelry and wearing it—instead of reselling it—is noncommercial." 464 U.S. at 496, 104 S.Ct. at 816.

3. ". . . *nature of the copyrighted work. . . .*" Two questions about the nature of the copyrighted work recur: Is the work fictional or factual? Is it published or unpublished? Justice Blackmun, dissenting in *Sony,* weighed the fictional content of plaintiff's works against fair

use. "The rationale guiding application of this factor is that certain types of works, typically those involving 'more of diligence than of originality or inventiveness' require less copyright protection than other original works. Thus, for example, informational works, such as news reports, that readily lend themselves to productive use by others, are less protected than creative works of entertainment." 464 U.S. at 496–97, 104 S.Ct. at 816–17.

The *Nation* case was hard because President Ford's memoirs had qualities that both favored and disfavored the second factor. As an historical work, Ford's memoirs invited free use; as an unpublished work, they rejected it. In the view of the dissenters, "[t]he quotation of 300 words from the manuscript infringed no privacy interest of Mr. Ford. This author intended the words in the manuscript to be a public statement about his Presidency. . . . What the Court depicts as the copyright owner's 'confidentiality' interest is not a privacy interest at all. Rather, it is no more than an economic interest in capturing the full value of initial release of information to the public, and is properly analyzed as such. Lacking too is any suggestion that *The Nation's* use interfered with the copyright owner's interest in editorial control of the manuscript. The Nation made use of the Ford quotes on the eve of official publication." 471 U.S. at 597–98, 105 S.Ct. at 2249–50.

Compare Salinger v. Random House, Inc., 811 F.2d 90, 1 U.S.P.Q.2d 1673 (2d Cir.), cert. denied, 484 U.S. 890, 108 S.Ct. 213, 98 L.Ed.2d 177 (1987), directing that a preliminary injunction issue against defendant's publication of a biography of the reclusive writer, J.D. Salinger, that drew in part on several of Salinger's unpublished letters. The court relied on the special protection that the *Nation* Court gave to unpublished works. "[T]he tenor of the Court's entire discussion of unpublished works conveys the idea that such works normally enjoy complete protection against copying any protection expression." 811 F.2d at 97.

4. *". . . amount and substantiality of the portion used in relation to the copyrighted work as a whole. . . ."* Justice Blackmun, dissenting in *Sony,* objected that the Court had ignored section 107's third factor. "It is undisputed that virtually all VTR owners record entire works, thereby creating an exact substitute for the copyrighted original. Fair use is intended to allow individuals engaged in productive uses to copy small portions of original works that will facilitate their own productive endeavors. Time-shifting bears no resemblance to such activity, and the complete duplication that it involves might alone be sufficient to preclude a finding of fair use. It is little wonder that the Court has chosen to ignore this statutory factor." 464 U.S. at 497, 104 S.Ct. at 817.

Courts have used quantitative measures in weighing section 107's third factor, holding that it is not fair use to copy four notes and two words out of 100 musical measures and 45–words, or 2.5 minutes out of a 28–minute film. See Elsmere Music, Inc. v. National Broadcasting Co., 482 F.Supp. 741, 206 U.S.P.Q. 913 (S.D.N.Y.1980), aff'd per curiam, 623 F.2d 252, 207 U.S.P.Q. 277 (2d Cir.); Iowa State Univ. Research

Found., Inc. v. American Broadcasting Cos., 621 F.2d 57, 207 U.S.P.Q. 97 (2d Cir.1980). Courts have also employed qualitative measures, weighing the factor against fair use where the portions taken were particularly important to the copyrighted work as a whole. See Meredith Corp. v. Harper & Row, Publishers, Inc., 378 F.Supp. 686, 182 U.S. P.Q. 609 (S.D.N.Y.1974), aff'd, 500 F.2d 1221, 182 U.S.P.Q. 577 (2d Cir.).

The weight given to the third factor will vary with the context of the use. Justice Brennan, dissenting in the *Nation* case, observed that "[h]ad these quotations been used in the context of a critical book review of the Ford work, there is little question that such a use would be fair use within the meaning of § 107 of the Act. The amount and substantiality of the use—in both quantitative and qualitative terms—would have certainly been appropriate to the purpose of such a use. It is difficult to see how the use of these quoted words in a news report is less appropriate. The Court acknowledges as much: '[E]ven substantial quotations might qualify as a fair use in a review of a published work or a news account of a speech that had been delivered to the public.' With respect to the motivation for the pardon and the insights into the psyche of the fallen President, for example, Mr. Ford's reflections and perceptions are so laden with emotion and deeply personal value judgments that full understanding is immeasurably enhanced by reproducing a limited portion of Mr. Ford's own words. The importance of the work, after all, lies not only in revelation of previously unknown fact but also in revelation of the thoughts, ideas, motivations, and fears of two Presidents at a critical moment in our national history. Thus, while the question is not easily resolved, it is difficult to say that the use of the six quotations was gratuitous in relation to the news reporting purpose." 471 U.S. at 601, 105 S.Ct. at 2252.

5. "*. . . effect of the use upon the potential market for or value of the copyrighted work.*" It is comparatively easy to apply section 107's fourth factor when plaintiff and defendant occupy the same market. The fourth factor becomes more problematic when the copyright owner has neither made nor licensed the type of use made by the defendant. Consider Justice Blackmun's criticism of the Court's approach to the fourth factor in *Sony:*

[T]he statute requires a court to consider the effect of the use on the *potential* market for the copyrighted work. The Court has struggled mightily to show that VTR use has not *reduced* the value of the Studios' copyrighted works in their *present* markets. Even if true, that showing only begins the proper inquiry. The development of the VTR has created a new market for the works produced by the Studios. That market consists of those persons who desire to view television programs at times other than when they are broadcast, and who therefore purchase VTR recorders to enable them to time-shift. Because time-shifting of the Studios' copyrighted works involves the copying of them, however, the Studios are entitled to share in the benefits of that new market. Those benefits currently go to Sony through Betamax sales. Respondents therefore can show harm from VTR use simply by showing that the value of their copyrights would *increase* if they were compensated for copies that are used in the new market. The existence of this effect is self-evident.

464 U.S. at 497–98, 104 S.Ct. at 817–18.

Compare Williams & Wilkins Co. v. United States, 487 F.2d 1345, 180 U.S.P.Q. 49 (Ct.Cl.1973), aff'd by an equally divided Court, 420 U.S. 376, 95 S.Ct. 1344, 43 L.Ed.2d 264, 184 U.S.P.Q. 705 (1975), in which the Court of Claims held that it was fair use for the defendant to photocopy articles from plaintiff's medical journals for distribution to medical researchers. In the court's view, plaintiff had not shown "that it is being or will be harmed substantially" by defendants' practices. "It is wrong to measure the detriment to plaintiff by loss of presumed royalty income—a standard which necessarily assumes that plaintiff had a right to issue licenses. That would be true, of course, only if it were first decided that the defendant's practices did not constitute 'fair use.' In determining whether the company has been sufficiently hurt to cause these practices to become 'unfair,' one cannot assume at the start the merit of the plaintiff's position. . . ." 487 F.2d at 1357 n. 19.

What role should "harm" to the copyright owner play in application of the fourth factor? Is a copyright owner ever "harmed" by a decision that denies it exclusive rights to a particular market? Or is it the public that is harmed by the copyright owner's consequent decision to reduce its investment in producing works for these markets? See Goldstein, The Private Consumption of Public Goods: A Comment on *Williams & Wilkins Co. v. United States,* 21 Bull.Copyright Soc'y 204 (1973).

6. *Parody and Satire.* In Benny v. Loew's, discussed in the *Air Pirates* case, the copyrighted work in issue was "Gaslight," a motion picture produced by plaintiff and starring Charles Boyer, Ingrid Bergman and Joseph Cotton. The infringing work was "Autolight," a fifteen-minute segment of Jack Benny's half-hour television show, starring Benny and Barbara Stanwyck.

Comparison of the two works led Judge Carter to find:

(1) that the locale and period of the works are the same; (2) the main setting is the same; (3) the characters are generally the same; (4) the story points are practically identical; (5) the development of the story, the treatment (except that defendants' treatment is burlesque), the incidents, the sequences of events, the points of suspense, the climax are almost identical and finally, (6) there has been a detailed borrowing of much of the dialogue with some variation in wording. There has been a substantial taking by defendants from the plaintiffs' copyright property.

"If this was the ordinary plagiarism case," the court concluded, "without the defense of burlesque as a fair use, it would be crystal clear, under the controlling authorities, that there had been access, a substantial taking and therefore infringement." Loew's, Inc. v. Columbia Broadcasting System, Inc., 131 F.Supp. 165, 171–172 (S.D.Cal.1955).

Judge Carter rested his refusal to exempt defendant's burlesque on several grounds. He found that the attempted exemption "has been the subject of several decisions and has been disposed of, not by determining whether the alleged infringing use was parody or burlesque, but by ascertaining whether it amounted to a taking of substantial, copyrightable material. In other words, a parodized or burlesqued taking is treated no differently from any other appropriation." Carter compared a case involving a directory: "Defendants have transposed the work, from the serious to the comic vein. This is analogous to the situation in Leon v. Pacific Telephone & Telegraph Co., 9 Cir.1937, 91 F.2d 484, when defendant took plaintiff's copyrighted telephone book and inverted the list from an alphabetical one to a numerical one."

Judge Carter had the opportunity to refine his views on parody, burlesque and fair use in a case he decided later that same year, Columbia Pictures Corp. v. National Broadcasting Co., 137 F.Supp. 348, 107 U.S.P.Q. 344 (S.D.Cal.1955). Ruling that defendant's broadcast of a parody, "From Here to Obscurity," did not infringe plaintiff's rights in its motion picture, "From Here to Eternity," he noted that "this case tests the general principle and dictum in Loew's. . . . Unlike Loew's here there was a taking of only sufficient to cause the viewer to recall and conjure up the original. This is a necessary element of burlesque." If, as has been suggested, *Columbia Pictures* represents a withdrawal from the position staked out in *Loew's,* the change made little difference to the *Loew's* defendants who had by then taken their appeal to the Ninth Circuit Court of Appeals. Seventeen days after Judge Carter's decision in *Columbia,* the circuit court released its decision affirming his disposition of *Loew's,* 239 F.2d 532 (1956). The Ninth Circuit decision was affirmed by an evenly divided, 4–4, Supreme Court, 356 U.S. 43 (1958).

To be excused, must a use directly parody the copyrighted work, or may it use the copyrighted work merely as the vehicle for a satire of cultural, social or political institutions generally? Does the approach offered in footnote 15 of *Air Pirates* resolve the issue satisfactorily? Courts have generally declined to distinguish between parody and satire for purposes of fair use. See, e.g., Berlin v. E.C. Publications, Inc., 329 F.2d 541, 141 U.S.P.Q. 1 (2d Cir.), cert. denied, 379 U.S. 822, 85 S.Ct. 46, 13 L.Ed.2d 33, 143 U.S.P.Q. 1 (1964); Elsmere Music, Inc. v. National Broadcasting Co., 482 F.Supp. 741, 206 U.S.P.Q. 913 (S.D.N.Y. 1980), aff'd per curiam, 623 F.2d 252, 207 U.S.P.Q. 277 (2d Cir.). But see MCA, Inc. v. Wilson, 677 F.2d 180, 211 U.S.P.Q. 577 (2d Cir.1981).

See generally, Light, Parody, Burlesque, and the Economic Rationale for Copyright, 11 Conn.L.Rev. 615 (1979); Netterville, Copyright and Tort Aspects of Parody, Mimicry and Humorous Commentary, 35 S.Cal.L.Rev. 225 (1962); Selvin, Parody and Burlesque of Copyrighted Works as Infringement, 6 Bull.Copyright Soc'y 53 (1958); Rossett, Burlesque as Copyright Infringement, 9 ASCAP Copyright L.Symp. 1 (1958).

7. *Classroom Photocopying.* From the time that section 107 was first proposed, debate centered on the status of classroom copying, particularly photocopying, of copyrighted works. According to the House Report, the House Committee resisted educators' proposals for " a specific exemption freeing certain reproductions of copyrighted works for educational and scholarly purposes from copyright control." The Committee did, however, recognize "a need for greater certainty and protection for teachers." One step toward meeting this need was section 504(c), "to provide innocent teachers and other nonprofit users of copyrighted material with broad insulation against unwarranted liability for infringement." H.R.Rep. No. 94–1476, 66–67.

As another step in the direction of certainty, the House Committee encouraged education and trade groups to agree on joint guidelines for permissible classroom uses. The effort bore fruit. On March 19, 1976 educator groups, the Authors League, and the Association of American Publishers reached an Agreement on Guidelines for Classroom Copying in Not–For–Profit Educational Institutions with Respect to Books and Periodicals. The Guidelines cover unlicensed copying in the form both of single copies made by teachers for their own use, and multiple copies made for classroom use. Under the Guidelines a teacher may, for research or teaching purposes, make a single copy of a chapter from a book, an article from a periodical or newspaper, a short story, essay or poem, or a chart, graph, diagram, drawing, cartoon or picture. The Guidelines impose more rigorous and detailed standards of "brevity," "spontaneity" and "cumulative effect" for multiple copies for classroom use. H.R.Rep. No. 94–1476, 68–70.

The House Committee accepted these, and counterpart Guidelines for educational uses of music, as "a reasonable interpretation of the minimum standards of fair use. Teachers will know that copying within the Guidelines is fair use." H.R.Rep. No. 94–1476, 72. The House and Senate Conferees also accepted the Guidelines "as part of their understanding of fair use." House Conf.Rep. No. 94–1733, 94th Cong.2d Sess. 72 (1976). Six years later, the House Committee on the Judiciary endorsed negotiated guidelines for classroom videotaping of audiovisual works. The guidelines apply only to nonprofit educational institutions' off-air recording of programs "transmitted by television stations for reception by the general public without charge." See H.R. Rep. No. 495, 97th Cong., 2d Sess. 8–9 (1982).

8. How would you dispose of the fair use defense raised in each of the following cases:

(a) Plaintiff, *Hustler* Magazine, publishes a satire on the Reverend Jerry Falwell. Defendant makes hundreds of thousands of copies of the satire for distribution to its members as part of a solicitation to support Falwell's lawsuit against *Hustler* for libel, invasion of privacy and intentional infliction of emotional distress. See Hustler Magazine, Inc. v. Moral Majority, Inc., 796 F.2d 1148, 230 U.S.P.Q. 646 (9th Cir.1985).

(b) Plaintiff, an institutional research and brokerage firm, prepares in-depth analytical reports on approximately 275 industrial, financial, utility and railroad corporations. Defendant publishes abstracts of these copyrighted research reports in its newspaper. See Wainwright Securities, Inc. v. Wall Street Transcript Corp., 558 F.2d 91, 194 U.S. P.Q. 401 (2d Cir.1977), cert. denied, 434 U.S. 1014, 98 S.Ct. 730, 54 L.Ed. 2d 759 (1978).

(c) Plaintiff publishes the New York Times and the New York Times Index and operates a computer data bank consisting of a subject index to the New York Times. Access to data in the computer is obtained through key words, of which approximately 350,000 are personal names. Defendants are in the process of publishing a 22–volume personal name index to the annual New York Times Index. Defendants compile their index by culling all personal names that appear as headings in the New York Times Index; after each name, they cite the pages in the New York Times Index on which the name appears. See New York Times Co. v. Roxbury Data Interface, Inc., 434 F.Supp. 217, 194 U.S.P.Q. 371 (D.N.J.1977).

(d) Plaintiff publishes the periodical, *TV Guide*. Defendant publishes a television supplement to the Sunday edition of its newspaper. In one of defendant's television advertisements for its supplement, an actor displays the cover of an issue of *TV Guide* for a few seconds. Plaintiff charges that the use violates the exclusive right to display its copyrighted work. See Triangle Publications, Inc. v. Knight–Ridder Newspapers, Inc., 626 F.2d 1171, 207 U.S.P.Q. 977 (5th Cir.1980).

9. *Fair Use and the First Amendment.* What connections exist between the fair use defense and the first amendment's free speech and press guarantees? *Air Pirates* rejected defendants' arguments that the "First Amendment should bar any liability for their parody because otherwise protected criticism would be discouraged." Recognizing that there is "of course some tension between the First Amendment and the Copyright Act," the court concluded that because defendants "could have expressed their theme without copying Disney's protected expression," their first amendment challenge should be dismissed. 581 F.2d 751, 758–759.

The *Nation* case may have effectively ended any debate over the first amendment's role in copyright cases: "In our haste to disseminate news, it should not be forgotten that the Framers intended copyright itself to be the engine of free expression. By establishing a marketable right to the use of one's expression, copyright supplies the economic incentive to create and disseminate ideas. . . . In view of the First Amendment protections already embodied in the Copyright Act's distinction between copyrightable expression and uncopyrightable facts and ideas, and the latitude for scholarship and comment traditionally afforded by fair use, we see no warrant for expanding the doctrine of fair use to create what amounts to a public figure exception to copyright. Whether verbatim copying from a public figure's manuscript in a given case is or is not fair must be judged according to the traditional equities of fair use." 471 U.S. at 558, 560, 105 S.Ct. at 2230.

See generally, Denicola, Copyright and Free Speech: Constitutional Limitations on the Protection of Expression, 67 Calif.L.Rev. 283 (1979); Goldstein, Copyright and the First Amendment, 70 Colum.L.Rev. 983 (1970); Nimmer, Does Copyright Abridge the First Amendment Guarantees of Free Speech and Press?, 17 UCLA L.Rev. 1180 (1970); Patterson, Private Copyright and Public Communication: Free Speech Endangered, 28 Vand.L.Rev. 1161 (1975); Sobel, Copyright and the First Amendment: A Gathering Storm? 19 ASCAP Copyright L.Symp. 43 (1971).

10. The fair use defense has attracted extensive commentary, including two book-length works, W. Patry, The Fair Use Privilege in Copyright Law (1985) and L. Seltzer, Exemptions and Fair Use in Copyright (1978). Professor Wendy Gordon's pathbreaking article, Fair Use as Market Failure: A Structural and Economic Analysis of the *Betamax* Case and its Predecessors, 82 Colum.L.Rev. 1600 (1982), places the doctrine in its economic context. See also, Cirace, When Does Complete Copying of Copyrighted Works for Purposes Other Than for Profit or Sale Constitute Fair Use? An Economic Analysis of the *Sony Betamax* and *Williams & Wilkins* Cases, 28 St. Louis U.L.J. 647 (1984); Fisher, Reconstructing the Fair Use Doctrine, 101 Harv.L.Rev. 1659 (1988); Subcomm. on Patents, Trademarks, and Copyrights of the Senate Comm. on the Judiciary, 86th Cong., 2d Sess., Study No. 14, The Fair Use of Copyrighted Works (Latman) (Comm.Print 1960).

d. Duration, Ownership and Transfer

COPYRIGHT LAW REVISION, H.R. REP. NO. 1476
94th Cong., 2d Sess. 120–129 (1976).

Section 201. Ownership of Copyright

Initial Ownership

Two basic and well-established principles of copyright law are restated in section 201(a): that the source of copyright ownership is the author of the work, and that, in the case of a "joint work," the coauthors of the work are likewise coowners of the copyright. Under the definition of section 101, a work is "joint" if the authors collaborated with each other, or if each of the authors prepared his or her contribution with the knowledge and intention that it would be merged with the contributions of other authors as "inseparable or interdependent parts of a unitary whole." The touchstone here is the intention, at the time the writing is done, that the parts be absorbed or combined into an integrated unit, although the parts themselves may be either "inseparable" (as the case of a novel or painting) or "interdependent" (as in the case of a motion picture, opera, or the words and music of a song). The definition of "joint work" is to be contrasted with the definition of "collective work," also in section 101, in which the elements of merger and unity are lacking; there the key elements are assemblage or gathering of "separate and independent works . . . into a collective whole."

The definition of "joint works" has prompted some concern lest it be construed as converting the authors of previously written works, such as plays, novels, and music, into coauthors of a motion picture in which their work is incorporated. It is true that a motion picture would normally be a joint rather than a collective work with respect to those authors who actually work on the film, although their usual status as employees for hire would keep the question of coownership from coming up. On the other hand, although a novelist, playwright, or songwriter may write a work with the hope or expectation that it will be used in a motion picture, this is clearly a case of separate or independent authorship rather than one where the basic intention behind the writing of the work was for motion picture use. In this case, the motion picture is a derivative work within the definition of that term, and section 103 makes plain that copyright in a derivative work is independent of, and does not enlarge the scope of rights in, any pre-existing material incorporated in it. There is thus no need to spell this conclusion out in the definition of "joint work."

There is also no need for a specific statutory provision concerning the rights and duties of the coowners of a work; court-made law on this point is left undisturbed. Under the bill, as under the present law, coowners of a copyright would be treated generally as tenants in common, with each coowner having an independent right to use or license the use of a work, subject to a duty of accounting to the other coowners for any profits.

Works Made for Hire

Section 201(b) of the bill adopts one of the basic principles of the present law: that in the case of works made for hire the employer is considered the author of the work, and is regarded as the initial owner of copyright unless there has been an agreement otherwise. The subsection also requires that any agreement under which the employee is to own rights be in writing and signed by the parties.

The work-made-for-hire provisions of this bill represent a carefully balanced compromise, and as such they do not incorporate the amendments proposed by screenwriters and composers for motion pictures. Their proposal was for the recognition of something similar to the "shop right" doctrine of patent law: with some exceptions, the employer would acquire the right to use the employee's work to the extent needed for purposes of his regular business, but the employee would retain all other rights as long as he or she refrained from the authorizing of competing uses. However, while this change might theoretically improve the bargaining position of screenwriters and others as a group, the practical benefits that individual authors would receive are highly conjectural. The presumption that initial ownership rights vest in the employer for hire is well established in American copyright law, and to exchange that for the uncertainties of the shop right doctrine would not only be of dubious value to employers and employees alike, but might also reopen a number of other issues.

The status of works prepared on special order or commission was a major issue in the development of the definition of "works made for hire" in section 101, which has undergone extensive revision during the legislative process. The basic problem is how to draw a statutory line between those works written on special order or commission that should be considered as "works made for hire," and those that should not. The definition now provided by the bill represents a compromise which, in effect, spells out those specific categories of commissioned works that can be considered "works made for hire" under certain circumstances.

Of these, one of the most important categories is that of "instructional texts." This term is given its own definition in the bill: "a literary, pictorial, or graphic work prepared for publication with the purpose of use in systematic instructional activities." The concept is intended to include what might be loosely called "textbook material," whether or not in book form or prepared in the form of text matter. The basic characteristic of "instructional texts" is the purpose of their preparation for "use in systematic instructional activities," and they are to be distinguished from works prepared for use by a general readership.

Contributions to Collective Works

Subsection (c) of section 201 deals with the troublesome problem of ownership of copyright in contributions to collective works, and the relationship between copyright ownership in a contribution and in the collective work in which it appears. The first sentence establishes the basic principle that copyright in the individual contribution and copyright in the collective work as a whole are separate and distinct, and that the author of the contribution is, as in every other case, the first owner of copyright in it. Under the definitions in section 101, a "collective work" is a species of "compilation" and, by its nature, must involve the selection, assembly, and arrangement of "a number of contributions." Examples of "collective works" would ordinarily include periodical issues, anthologies, symposia, and collections of the discrete writings of the same authors, but not cases, such as a composition consisting of words and music, a work published with illustrations or front matter, or three one-act plays, where relatively few separate elements have been brought together. Unlike the contents of other types of "compilations," each of the contributions incorporated in a "collective work" must itself constitute a "separate and independent" work, therefore ruling out compilations of information or other uncopyrightable material and works published with editorial revisions or annotations. Moreover, as noted above, there is a basic distinction between a "joint work," where the separate elements merge into a unified whole, and a "collective work," where they remain unintegrated and disparate.

The bill does nothing to change the rights of the owner of copyright in a collective work under the present law. These exclusive rights extend to the elements of compilation and editing that went into the collective work as a whole, as well as the contributions that were written for hire by employees of the owner of the collective work, and those copyrighted contributions that have been transferred in writing to the owner by their authors. However, one of the most significant aims of the bill is to clarify and improve the present confused and frequently unfair legal situation with respect to rights in contributions.

The second sentence of section 201(c), in conjunction with the provisions of section 404 dealing with copyright notice, will preserve the author's copyright in a contribution even if the contribution does not bear a separate notice in the author's name, and without requiring any unqualified transfer of rights to the owner of the collective work. This is coupled with a presumption that, unless there has been an express transfer of more, the owner of the collective work acquires "only the privilege of reproducing and distributing the contribution as part of that particular collective work, any revision of that collective work, and any later collective work in the same series."

The basic presumption of section 201(c) is fully consistent with present law and practice, and represents a fair balancing of equities. At the same time, the last clause of the subsection, under which the privilege of republishing the contribution under certain limited circumstances would be presumed, is an essential counterpart of the basic presumption. Under the language of this clause a publishing company could reprint a contribution from one issue in a later issue of its magazine, and could reprint an article from a 1980 edition of an encyclopedia in a 1990 revision of it; the publisher could not revise the contribution itself or include it in a new anthology or an entirely different magazine or other collective work.

Transfer of Ownership

The principle of unlimited alienability of copyright is stated in clause (1) of section 201(d). Under that provision the ownership of a copyright, or of any part of it, may be transferred by any means of conveyance or by operation of law, and is to be treated as personal property upon the death of the owner. The term "transfer of copyright ownership" is defined in section 101 to cover any "conveyance, alienation, or hypothecation," including assignments, mortgages, and exclusive licenses, but not including nonexclusive licenses. Representatives of motion picture producers have argued that foreclosures of copyright mortgages should not be left to varying State laws, and that the statute should establish a Federal foreclosure system. However, the benefits of such a system would be of very limited application, and would not justify the complicated statutory and procedural requirements that would have to be established.

Clause (2) of subsection (d) contains the first explicit statutory recognition of the principle of divisibility of copyright in our law. This provision, which has long been sought by authors and their representatives, and which has attracted wide support from other groups, means that any of the exclusive rights that go to make up a copyright, including those enumerated in section 106 and any subdivision of them, can be transferred and owned separately. The definition of "transfer of copyright ownership" in section 101 makes clear that the principle of divisibility applies whether or not the transfer is "limited in time or place of effect," and another definition in the same section provides that the term "copyright owner," with respect to any one exclusive right, refers to the owner of that particular right. The last sentence of section 201(d)(2) adds that the owner, with respect to the particular exclusive right he or she owns, is entitled "to all of the protection and remedies accorded to the copyright owner by this title." It is thus clear, for example, that a local broadcasting station holding an exclusive license to transmit a particular work within a particular geographic area and for a particular period of time, could sue, in its own name as copyright owner, someone who infringed that particular exclusive right.

Subsection (e) provides that when an individual author's ownership of a copyright, or of any of the exclusive rights under a copyright, have not previously been voluntarily transferred, no action by any governmental body or other official or organization purporting to seize, expropriate, transfer, or exercise rights of ownership with respect to the copyright, or any of the exclusive rights under a copyright, shall be given effect under this title.

The purpose of this subsection is to reaffirm the basic principle that the United States copyright of an individual author shall be secured to that author, and cannot be taken away by any involuntary transfer. It is the intent of the subsection that the author be entitled, despite any purported expropriation or involuntary transfer, to continue exercising all rights under the United States statute, and that the governmental body or organization may not enforce or exercise any rights under this title in that situation.

It may sometimes be difficult to ascertain whether a transfer of copyright is voluntary or is coerced by covert pressure. But subsection (e) would protect foreign authors against laws and decrees purporting to divest them of their rights under the United States copyright statute, and would protect authors within the foreign country who choose to resist such covert pressures.

Traditional legal actions that may involve transfer of ownership, such as bankruptcy proceedings and mortgage foreclosures, are not within the scope of this subsection; the authors in such cases have voluntarily consented to these legal processes by their overt actions— for example, by filing in bankruptcy or by hypothecating a copyright.

Section 202. Distinction Between Ownership of Copyright and Material Object

The principle restated in section 202 is a fundamental and important one: that copyright ownership and ownership of a material object in which the copyrighted work is embodied are entirely separate things. Thus, transfer of a material object does not of itself carry any rights under the copyright, and this includes transfer of the copy or pho-norecord—the original manuscript, the photographic negative, the unique painting or statute, the master tape recording, etc.—in which the work was first fixed. Conversely, transfer of a copyright does not necessarily require the conveyance of any material object.

As a result of the interaction of this section and the provisions of sections 204(a) and 301, the bill would change a common law doctrine exemplified by the decision in Pushman v. New York Graphic Society, Inc., 287 N.Y. 302, 39 N.E.2d 249 (1942). Under that doctrine, authors or artists are generally presumed to transfer common law literary property rights when they sell their manuscript or work of art, unless those rights are specifically reserved. This presumption would be reversed under the bill, since a specific written conveyance of rights would be required in order for a sale of any material object to carry with it a transfer of copyright.

Section 203.   Termination of Transfers and Licenses

The Problem in General

The provisions of section 203 are based on the premise that the reversionary provisions of the present section on copyright renewal (17 U.S.C.A. § 24) should be eliminated, and that the proposed law should substitute for them a provision safeguarding authors against unremu-nerative transfers. A provision of this sort is needed because of the unequal bargaining position of authors, resulting in part from the impossibility of determining a work's value until it has been exploited. Section 203 reflects a practical compromise that will further the objec-tives of the copyright law while recognizing the problems and legiti-mate needs of all interests involved.

Scope of the Provision

Instead of being automatic, as is theoretically the case under the present renewal provision, the termination of a transfer or license under section 203 would require the serving of an advance notice within specified time limits and under specified conditions. However, although affirmative action is needed to effect a termination, the right to take this action cannot be waived in advance or contracted away. Under section 203(a) the right of termination would apply only to transfers and licenses executed after the effective date of the new statute, and would have no retroactive effect.

The right of termination would be confined to inter vivos transfers or licenses executed by the author, and would not apply to transfers by the author's successors in interest or to the author's own bequests. The scope of the right would extend not only to any "transfer of copyright ownership," as defined in section 101, but also to nonexclusive licenses. The right of termination would not apply to "works made for hire," which is one of the principal reasons the definition of that term assumed importance in the development of the bill.

Who Can Terminate a Grant

Two issues emerged from the disputes over section 203 as to the persons empowered to terminate a grant: (1) the specific classes of beneficiaries in the case of joint works; and (2) whether anything less than unanimous consent of all those entitled to terminate should be required to make a termination effective. The bill to some extent reflects a compromise on these points, including a recognition of the dangers of one or more beneficiaries being induced to "hold out" and of unknown children or grandchildren being discovered later. The provision can be summarized as follows:

1. In the case of a work of joint authorship, where the grant was signed by two or more of the authors, majority action by those who signed the grant, or by their interests, would be required to terminate it.

2. There are three different situations in which the shares of joint authors, or of a dead author's widow or widower, children, and grandchildren, must be divided under the statute: (1) The right to effect a termination; (2) the ownership of the terminated rights; and (3) the right to make further grants of reverted rights. The respective shares of the authors, and of a dead author's widow or widower, children, and grandchildren, would be divided in exactly the same way in each of these situations. The terms "widow," "widower," and "children" are defined in section 101 in an effort to avoid problems and uncertainties that have arisen under the present renewal section.

3. The principle of per stirpes representation would also be applied in exactly the same way in all three situations. Take for example, a case where a dead author left a widow, two living children, and three grandchildren by a third child who is dead. The widow will own half of the reverted interests, the two children will each own 16⅔ percent, and the three grandchildren will each own a share of roughly 5½ percent. But who can exercise the right of termination? Obviously, since she owns 50 percent, the widow is an essential party, but suppose neither of the two surviving children is willing to join her in the termination; is it enough that she gets one of the children of the dead child to join, or can the dead child's interest be exercised only by the action of a majority of his children? Consistent with the per stirpes principle, the interest of a dead child can be exercised only as a unit by majority action of his surviving children. Thus, even though the widow and one grandchild would own 55½ percent of the reverted copyright, they would have to be joined by another child or grandchild in order to effect a termination or a further transfer of reverted rights. This principle also applies where, for example, two joint authors executed a grant and one of them is dead; in order to effect a termination, the living author must be joined by a per stirpes majority of the dead author's beneficiaries. The notice of termination may be

signed by the specified owners of termination interests or by "their duly authorized agents," which would include the legally appointed guardians or committees of persons incompetent to sign because of age or mental disability.

When a Grant Can Be Terminated

Section 203 draws a distinction between the date when a termination becomes effective and the earlier date when the advance notice of termination is served. With respect to the ultimate effective date, section 203(a)(3) provides, as a general rule, that a grant may be terminated during the 5 years following the expiration of a period of 35 years from the execution of the grant. As an exception to this basic 35–year rule, the bill also provides that "if the grant covers the right of publication of the work, the period begins at the end of 35 years from the date of publication of the work under the grant or at the end of 40 years from the date of execution of the grant, whichever term ends earlier." This alternative method of computation is intended to cover cases where years elapse between the signing of a publication contract and the eventual publication of the work.

The effective date of termination, which must be stated in the advance notice, is required to fall within the 5 years following the end of the applicable 35– or 40–year period, but the advance notice itself must be served earlier. Under section 203(a)(4)(A), the notice must be served "not less than two or more than ten years" before the effective date stated in it.

As an example of how these time-limit requirements would operate in practice, we suggest two typical contract situations:

Case 1: Contract for theatrical production signed on September 2, 1987. Termination of grant can be made to take effect between September 2, 2022 (35 years from execution) and September 1, 2027 (end of 5 year termination period). Assuming that the author decides to terminate on September 1, 2022 (the earliest possible date) the advance notice must be filed between September 1, 2012 and September 1, 2020.

Case 2: Contract for book publication executed on April 10, 1980; book finally published on August 23, 1987. Since contract covers the right of publication, the 5–year termination period would begin on April 10, 2020 (40 years from execution) rather than April 10, 2015 (35 years from execution) or August 23, 2022 (35 years from publication). Assuming that the author decides to make the termination effective on January 1, 2024, the advance notice would have to be served between January 1, 2014, and January 1, 2022.

Effect of Termination

Section 203(b) makes clear that, unless effectively terminated within the applicable 5–year period, all rights covered by an existing grant will continue unchanged, and that rights under other Federal, State, or foreign laws are unaffected. However, assuming that a copyright transfer or license is terminated under section 203, who are bound by the termination and how are they affected?

Under the bill, termination means that ownership of the rights covered by the terminated grant reverts to everyone who owns termination interests on the date the notice of termination was served, whether they joined in signing the notice or not. In other words, if a person could have signed the notice, that person is bound by the action of the majority who did; the termination of the grant will be effective as to that person, and a proportionate share of the reverted rights automatically vests in that person. Ownership is divided proportionately on the same per stirpes basis as that provided for the right to effect termination under section 203(a) and, since the reverted rights vest on the date notice is served, the heirs of a dead beneficiary would inherit his or her share.

Under clause (3) of subsection (b), majority action is required to make a further grant of reverted rights. A problem here, of course, is that years may have passed between the time the reverted rights vested and the time the new owners want to make a further transfer; people may have died and children may have been born in the interim. To deal with this problem, the bill looks back to the date of vesting; out of the group in whom rights vested on that date, it requires the further transfer or license to be signed by "the same number and proportion of the owners" (though not necessarily the same individuals) as were then required to terminate the grant under subsection (a). If some of those in whom the rights originally vested have died, their "legal representatives, legatees, or heirs at law" may represent them for this purpose and, as in the case of the termination itself, any one of the minority who does not join in the further grant is nevertheless bound by it.

An important limitation on the rights of a copyright owner under a terminated grant is specified in section 203(b)(1). This clause provides that, notwithstanding a termination, a derivative work prepared earlier may "continue to be utilized" under the conditions of the terminated grant; the clause adds, however, that this privilege is not broad enough to permit the preparation of other derivative works. In other words, a film made from a play could continue to be licensed for performance after the motion picture contract had been terminated but any remake rights covered by the contract would be cut off. For this purpose, a motion picture would be considered as a "derivative work" with respect to every "preexisting work" incorporated in it, whether the preexisting work was created independently or was prepared expressly for the motion picture.

Section 203 would not prevent the parties to a transfer or license from voluntarily agreeing at any time to terminate an existing grant and negotiating a new one, thereby causing another 35-year period to start running. However, the bill seeks to avoid the situation that has arisen under the present renewal provision, in which third parties have brought up contingent future interests as a form of speculation. Section 203(b)(4) would make a further grant of rights that revert under a terminated grant valid "only if it is made after the effective date of the termination." An exception, in the nature of a right of "first refusal," would permit the original grantee or a successor of such grantee to negotiate a new agreement with the persons effecting the termination at any time after the notice of termination has been served.

Nothing contained in this section or elsewhere in this legislation is intended to extend the duration of any license, transfer or assignment made for a period of less than thirty-five years. If, for example, an agreement provides an earlier termination date or lesser duration, or if it allows the author the right of cancelling or terminating the agreement under certain circumstances, the duration is governed by the agreement. Likewise, nothing in this section or legislation is intended to change the existing state of the law of contracts concerning the circumstances in which an author may cancel or terminate a license, transfer, or assignment.

Section 203(b)(6) provides that, unless and until termination is effected under this section, the grant, "if it does not provide otherwise," continues for the term of copyright. This section means that, if the agreement does not contain provisions specifying its term or duration, and the author has not terminated the agreement under this section, the agreement continues for the term of the copyright, subject to any right of termination under circumstances which may be specified therein. If, however, an agreement does contain provisions governing its duration—for example, a term of fifty years—and the author has not exercised his or her right of termination under the statute, the agreement will continue according to its terms—in this example, for only fifty years. The quoted language is not to be construed as requiring agreements to reserve the right of termination.

Sections 204, 205. Execution and Recordation of Transfers

Section 204 is a somewhat broadened and liberalized counterpart of sections 28 and 29 of the present statute. Under subsection (a), a transfer of copyright ownership (other than one brought about by operation of law) is valid only if there exists an instrument of conveyance, or alternatively a "note or memorandum of the transfer," which is in writing and signed by the copyright owner "or such owner's duly authorized agent." Subsection (b) makes clear that a notarial or consular acknowledgment is not essential to the validity of any transfer, whether executed in the United States or abroad. However, the subsection would liberalize the conditions under which certificates of acknowledgment of documents executed abroad are to be accorded prima facie weight, and would give the same weight to domestic acknowledgments under appropriate circumstances.

The recording and priority provisions of section 205 are intended to clear up a number of uncertainties arising from sections 30 and 31 of the present law and to make them more effective and practical in operation. Any "document pertaining to a copyright" may be recorded under subsection (a) if it "bears that actual signature of the person who executed it," or if it is appropriately certified as a true copy. However, subsection (c) makes clear that the recorded document will give constructive notice of its contents only if two conditions are met: (1) the document or attached material specifically identifies the work to which it pertains so that a reasonable search under the title or registration number would reveal it, and (2) registration has been made for the work. Moreover, even though the Register of Copyrights may be compelled to accept for recordation documents that on their face appear self-serving or colorable, the Register should take care that their nature is not concealed from the public in the Copyright Office's indexing and search reports.

The provisions of subsection (d), requiring recordation of transfers as a prerequisite to the institution of an infringement suit, represent a desirable change in the law. The one- and three-month grace periods provided in subsection (e) are a reasonable compromise between those who want a longer hiatus and those who argue that any grace period makes it impossible for a bona fide transferee to rely on the record at any particular time.

Under subsection (f) of section 205, a nonexclusive license in writing and signed, whether recorded or not, would be valid against a later transfer, and would also prevail as against a prior unrecorded transfer if taken in good faith and without notice. Objections were raised by motion picture producers, particularly to the provision allowing unrecorded nonexclusive licenses to prevail over subsequent transfers, on the ground that a nonexclusive license can have drastic effects on the value of a copyright. On the other hand, the impracticalities and burdens that would accompany any requirement of recordation of nonexclusive licenses outweigh the limited advantages of a statutory recordation system for them.

COMMUNITY FOR CREATIVE NON–VIOLENCE v. REID

Supreme Court of the United States, 1989.
___ U.S. ___, 109 S.Ct. 2166, 104 L.Ed.2d 811, 10 U.S.P.Q.2d 1985.

Justice MARSHALL delivered the opinion of the Court.

In this case, an artist and the organization that hired him to produce a sculpture contest the ownership of the copyright in that work. To resolve this dispute, we must construe the "work made for hire" provisions of the Copyright Act of 1976 (Act or 1976 Act), 17 U.S.C. §§ 101 and 201(b), and in particular, the provision in § 101, which defines as a "work made for hire" a "work prepared by an employee within the scope of his or her employment" (hereinafter § 101(1)).

I

Petitioners are the Community for Creative Non–Violence (CCNV), a nonprofit unincorporated association dedicated to eliminating homelessness in America, and Mitch Snyder, a member and trustee of

CCNV. In the fall of 1985, CCNV decided to participate in the annual Christmastime Pageant of Peace in Washington, D.C., by sponsoring a display to dramatize the plight of the homeless. As the District Court recounted:

> Snyder and fellow CCNV members conceived the idea for the nature of the display: a sculpture of a modern Nativity scene in which, in lieu of the traditional Holy Family, the two adult figures and the infant would appear as contemporary homeless people huddled on a streetside steam grate. The family was to be black (most of the homeless in Washington being black); the figures were to be life-sized, and the steam grate would be positioned atop a platform 'pedestal,' or base, within which special-effects equipment would be enclosed to emit simulated 'steam' through the grid to swirl about the figures. They also settled upon a title for the work—'Third World America'—and a legend for the pedestal: 'and still there is no room at the inn.' 652 F.Supp. 1453, 1454 (D.D.C. 1987).

Snyder made inquiries to locate an artist to produce the sculpture. He was referred to respondent James Earl Reid, a Baltimore, Maryland, sculptor. In the course of two telephone calls, Reid agreed to sculpt the three human figures. CCNV agreed to make the steam grate and pedestal for the statue. Reid proposed that the work be cast in bronze, at a total cost of approximately $100,000 and taking six to eight months to complete. Snyder rejected that proposal because CCNV did not have sufficient funds, and because the statue had to be completed by December 12 to be included in the pageant. Reid then suggested, and Snyder agreed, that the sculpture would be made of a material known as "Design Cast 62," a synthetic substance that could meet CCNV's monetary and time constraints, could be tinted to resemble bronze, and could withstand the elements. The parties agreed that the project would cost no more than $15,000, not including Reid's services, which he offered to donate. The parties did not sign a written agreement. Neither party mentioned copyright.

After Reid received an advance of $3,000, he made several sketches of figures in various poses. At Snyder's request, Reid sent CCNV a sketch of a proposed sculpture showing the family in a creche-like setting: the mother seated, cradling a baby in her lap; the father standing behind her, bending over her shoulder to touch the baby's foot. Reid testified that Snyder asked for the sketch to use in raising funds for the sculpture. Snyder testified that it was also for his approval. Reid sought a black family to serve as a model for the sculpture. Upon Snyder's suggestion, Reid visited a family living at CCNV's Washington shelter but decided that only their newly born child was a suitable model. While Reid was in Washington, Snyder took him to see homeless people living on the streets. Snyder pointed out that they tended to recline on steam grates, rather than sit or stand, in order to warm their bodies. From that time on, Reid's sketches contained only reclining figures.

Throughout November and the first two weeks of December 1985, Reid worked exclusively on the statue, assisted at various times by a dozen different people who were paid with funds provided in installments by CCNV. On a number of occasions, CCNV members visited Reid to check on his progress and to coordinate CCNV's construction of the base. CCNV rejected Reid's proposal to use suitcases or shopping bags to hold the family's personal belongings, insisting instead on a shopping cart. Reid and CCNV members did not discuss copyright ownership on any of these visits.

On December 24, 1985, 12 days after the agreed upon date, Reid delivered the completed statue to Washington. There it was joined to the steam grate and pedestal prepared by CCNV and placed on display near the site of the pageant. Snyder paid Reid the final installment of the $15,000. The statue remained on display for a month. In late January 1986, CCNV members returned it to Reid's studio in Baltimore for minor repairs. Several weeks later, Snyder began making plans to take the statue on a tour of several cities to raise money for the homeless. Reid objected, contending that the Design Cast 62 material was not strong enough to withstand the ambitious itinerary. He urged CCNV to cast the statue in bronze at a cost of $35,000, or to create a master mold at a cost of $5,000. Snyder declined to spend more of CCNV's money on the project.

In March 1986, Snyder asked Reid to return the sculpture. Reid refused. He then filed a certificate of copyright registration for "Third World America" in his name and announced plans to take the sculpture on a more modest tour than the one CCNV had proposed. Snyder, acting in his capacity as CCNV's trustee, immediately filed a competing certificate of copyright registration.

Snyder and CCNV then commenced this action against Reid and his photographer, Ronald Purtee, seeking return of the sculpture and a determination of copyright ownership. The District Court granted a preliminary injunction, ordering the sculpture's return. After a 2–day bench trial, the District Court declared that "Third World America" was a "work made for hire" under § 101 of the Copyright Act and that Snyder, as trustee for CCNV, was the exclusive owner of the copyright in the sculpture. The court reasoned that Reid had been an "employee" of CCNV within the meaning of § 101(1) because CCNV was the motivating force in the statue's production. Snyder and other CCNV members, the court explained, "conceived the idea of a contemporary Nativity scene to contrast with the national celebration of the season," and "directed enough of [Reid's] effort to assure that, in the end, he had produced what they, not he, wanted." Id., at 1456.

The Court of Appeals for the District of Columbia reversed and remanded, holding that Reid owned the copyright because "Third World America" was not a work for hire. Adopting what it termed the "literal interpretation" of the Act as articulated by the Fifth Circuit in Easter Seal Society for Crippled Children and Adults of Louisiana, Inc. v. Playboy Enterprises, 815 F.2d 323, 329 (1987), cert. denied, 485 U.S.

981, 108 S.Ct. 1280, 99 L.Ed.2d 491 (1988), the court read § 101 as creating "a simple dichotomy in fact between employees and independent contractors." 270 U.S.App.D.C., at 33, 846 F.2d, at 1492. Because, under agency law, Reid was an independent contractor, the court concluded that the work was not "prepared by an employee" under § 101(1). Id., at 35, 846 F.2d, at 1494. Nor was the sculpture a "work made for hire" under the second subsection of § 101 (hereinafter § 101(2)): sculpture is not one of the nine categories of works enumerated in that subsection, and the parties had not agreed in writing that the sculpture would be a work for hire. The court suggested that the sculpture nevertheless may have been jointly authored by CCNV and Reid, and remanded for a determination whether the sculpture is indeed a joint work under the Act.

We granted certiorari to resolve a conflict among the Courts of Appeals over the proper construction of the "work made for hire" provisions of the Act. We now affirm.

II

A

The Copyright Act of 1976 provides that copyright ownership "vests initially in the author or authors of the work." 17 U.S.C. § 201(a). As a general rule, the author is the party who actually creates the work, that is, the person who translates an idea into a fixed, tangible expression entitled to copyright protection. The Act carves out an important exception, however, for "works made for hire." If the work is for hire, "the employer or other person for whom the work was prepared is considered the author" and owns the copyright, unless there is a written agreement to the contrary. § 201(b). Classifying a work as "made for hire" determines not only the initial ownership of its copyright, but also the copyright's duration, § 302(c), and the owners' renewal rights, § 304(a), termination rights, § 203(a), and right to import certain goods bearing the copyright, § 601(b)(1). The contours of the work for hire doctrine therefore carry profound significance for freelance creators—including artists, writers, photographers, designers, composers, and computer programmers—and for the publishing, advertising, music, and other industries which commission their works.[4]

Section 101 of the 1976 Act provides that a work is "for hire" under two sets of circumstances:

(1) a work prepared by an employee within the scope of his or her employment; or

---

4. As of 1955, approximately 40 percent of all copyright registrations were for works for hire, according to a Copyright Office study. See Varmer, Works Made for Hire and On Commission, in Studies Prepared for the Subcommittee on Patents, Trademarks, and Copyrights of the Senate Committee on the Judiciary, Study No. 13, 86th Cong., 2d Sess. 139, n. 49 (Comm. Print, 1960) (hereinafter Varmer, Works Made for Hire). The Copyright Office does not keep more recent statistics on the number of work for hire registrations.

(2) a work specially ordered or commissioned for use as a contribution to a collective work, as a part of a motion picture or other audiovisual work, as a translation, as a supplementary work, as a compilation, as an instructional text, as a test, as answer material for a test, or as an atlas, if the parties expressly agree in a written instrument signed by them that the work shall be considered a work made for hire.

The petitioners do not claim that the statue satisfies the terms of § 101(2). Quite clearly, it does not. Sculpture does not fit within any of the nine categories of "specially ordered or commissioned" works enumerated in that subsection, and no written agreement between the parties establishes "Third World America" as a work for hire.

The dispositive inquiry in this case therefore is whether "Third World America" is "a work prepared by an employee within the scope of his or her employment" under § 101(1). The Act does not define these terms. In the absence of such guidance, four interpretations have emerged. The first holds that a work is prepared by an employee whenever the hiring party retains the right to control the product. See Peregrine v. Lauren Corp., 601 F.Supp. 828, 829 (Colo.1985); Clarkstown v. Reeder, 566 F.Supp. 137, 142 (SDNY 1983). Petitioners take this view. A second, and closely related, view is that a work is prepared by an employee under § 101(1) when the hiring party has actually wielded control with respect to the creation of a particular work. This approach was formulated by the Court of Appeals for the Second Circuit, Aldon Accessories Ltd. v. Spiegel, Inc., 738 F.2d 548, cert. denied, 469 U.S. 982, 105 S.Ct. 387, 83 L.Ed.2d 321 (1984), and adopted by the Fourth Circuit, Brunswick Beacon, Inc. v. Schock–Hopchas Publishing Co., 810 F.2d 410 (1987), the Seventh Circuit, Evans Newton, Inc. v. Chicago Systems Software, 793 F.2d 889, cert. denied, 479 U.S. 949, 107 S.Ct. 434, 93 L.Ed.2d 383 (1986), and, at times, by petitioners. A third view is that the term "employee" within § 101(1) carries its common law agency law meaning. This view was endorsed by the Fifth Circuit in Easter Seal Society for Crippled Children and Adults of Louisiana, Inc. v. Playboy Enterprises, 815 F.2d 323 (1987), and by the Court of Appeals below. Finally, respondent and numerous amici curiae contend that the term "employee" only refers to "formal, salaried" employees. The Court of Appeals for the Ninth Circuit recently adopted this view. See Dumas v. Gommerman, 865 F.2d 1093 (1989).

The starting point for our interpretation of a statute is always its language. The Act nowhere defines the terms "employee" or "scope of employment." It is, however, well established that "[w]here Congress uses terms that have accumulated settled meaning under . . . the common law, a court must infer, unless the statute otherwise dictates, that Congress means to incorporate the established meaning of these terms." NLRB v. Amax Coal Co., 453 U.S. 322, 329, 101 S.Ct. 2789, 2794, 69 L.Ed.2d 672 (1981). In the past, when Congress has used the term "employee" without defining it, we have concluded that Congress intended to describe the conventional master-servant relationship as understood by common law agency doctrine. Nothing in the text of the work for hire provisions indicates that Congress used the words "employee" and "employment" to describe anything other than " 'the conventional relation of employer and employeé.' " On the contrary, Congress' intent to incorporate the agency law definition is suggested by § 101(1)'s use of the term, "scope of employment," a widely used term of art in agency law. See Restatement (Second) of Agency § 228 (1958) (hereinafter Restatement).

In past cases of statutory interpretation, when we have concluded that Congress intended terms such as "employee," "employer," and "scope of employment" to be understood in light of agency law, we have relied on the general common law of agency, rather than on the law of any particular State, to give meaning to these terms. This practice reflects the fact that "federal statutes are generally intended to have uniform nationwide application." Mississippi Band of Choctaw Indians v. Holyfield, 109 S.Ct. 1597, 1605, 104 L.Ed.2d 29 (1989). Establishment of a federal rule of agency, rather than reliance on state agency law, is particularly appropriate here given the Act's express objective of creating national uniform copyright law by broadly pre-empting state statutory and common-law copyright regulation. We thus agree with the Court of Appeals that the term "employee" should be understood in light of the general common law of agency.

In contrast, neither test proposed by petitioners is consistent with the text of the Act. The exclusive focus of the right to control the product test on the relationship between the hiring party and the product clashes with the language of § 101(1), which focuses on the relationship between the hired and hiring parties. The right to control the product test also would distort the meaning of the ensuing subsection, § 101(2). Section 101 plainly creates two distinct ways in which a work can be deemed for hire: one for works prepared by employees, the other for those specially ordered or commissioned works which fall within one of the nine enumerated categories and are the subject of a written agreement. The right to control the product test ignores this dichotomy by transforming into a work for hire under § 101(1) any "specially ordered or commissioned" work that is subject to the supervision and control of the hiring party. Because a party who hires a "specially ordered or commissioned" work by definition has a right to specify the characteristics of the product desired, at the time the commission is accepted, and frequently until it is completed, the right to control the product test would mean that many works that could satisfy § 101(2) would already have been deemed works for hire under § 101(1). Petitioners' interpretation is particularly hard to square with § 101(2)'s enumeration of the nine specific categories of specially ordered or commissioned works eligible to be works for hire, e.g., "a contribution to a collective work," "a part of a motion picture," and "answer material for a test." The unifying feature of these works is that they are usually prepared at the instance, direction, and risk of a publisher or producer. By their very nature, therefore, these types of works would be works by an employee under petitioners' right to control the product test.

The actual control test, articulated by the Second Circuit in *Aldon Accessories,* fares only marginally better when measured against the language and structure of § 101. Under this test, independent contractors who are so controlled and supervised in the creation of a particular work are deemed "employees" under § 101(1). Thus work for hire status under § 101(1) depends on a hiring party's *actual* control, rather than *right* to control, of the product. Under the actual control test, a work for hire could arise under § 101(2), but not under § 101(1), where a party commissions, but does not actually control, a product which falls into one of the nine enumerated categories. Nonetheless, we agree with the Fifth Circuit Court of Appeals that "[t]here is simply no way to milk the 'actual control' test of *Aldon Accessories* from the language of the statute." *Easter Seal Society,* 815 F.2d, at 334. Section 101 clearly delineates between works prepared by an employee and commissioned works. Sound though other distinctions might be as a matter of copyright policy, there is no statutory support for an additional dichotomy between commissioned works that are actually controlled and supervised by the hiring party and those that are not.

We therefore conclude that the language and structure of § 101 of the Act do not support either the right to control the product or the actual control approaches.[8] The structure of § 101 indicates that a work for hire can arise through one of two mutually exclusive means, one for employees and one for independent contractors, and ordinary canons of statutory interpretation indicate that the classification of a particular hired party should be made with reference to agency law.

This reading of the undefined statutory terms finds considerable support in the Act's legislative history. The Act, which almost completely revised existing copyright law, was the product of two decades of negotiation by representatives of creators and copyright-using industries, supervised by the Copyright Office and, to a lesser extent, by Congress. Despite the lengthy history of negotiation and compromise which ultimately produced the Act, two things remained constant. First, interested parties and Congress at all times viewed works by employees and commissioned works by independent contractors as separate entities. Second, in using the term "employee," the parties

---

8. We also reject the suggestion of respondent and *amici* that the § 101(1) term "employee" refers only to formal, salaried employees. While there is some support for such a definition in the legislative history, the language of § 101(1) cannot support it. The Act does not say "formal" or "salaried" employee, but simply "employee." Moreover, the respondent and those *amici* who endorse a formal, salaried employee test do not agree upon the content of this test. Compare, e.g., Brief for Respondent 37 (hired party who is on payroll is an employee within § 101(1)) with Tr. of Oral Arg. 31 (hired party who receives a salary or commissions regularly is an employee within § 101(1)); and Brief for Volunteer Lawyers for the Arts Inc. *et al.* as *Amici Curiae* 4 (hired party who receives a salary *and* is treated as an employee for Social Security and tax purposes is an employee within § 101(1)). Even the one Court of Appeals to adopt what it termed a formal, salaried employee test in fact embraced an approach incorporating numerous factors drawn from the agency law definition of employee which we endorse. See *Dumas,* 865 F.2d, at 1104.

and Congress meant to refer to a hired party in a conventional employment relationship. These factors militate in favor of the reading we have found appropriate.

In 1955, when Congress decided to overhaul copyright law, the existing work for hire provision was § 62 of the 1909 Copyright Act, 17 U.S.C. § 26 (1976 ed.) (1909 Act). It provided that "the word 'author' shall include an employer in the case of works made for hire." Because the 1909 Act did not define "employer" or "works made for hire," the task of shaping these terms fell to the courts. They concluded that the work for hire doctrine codified in § 62 referred only to works made by employees in the regular course of their employment. As for commissioned works, the courts generally presumed that the commissioned party had impliedly agreed to convey the copyright, along with the work itself, to the hiring party.

In 1961, the Copyright Office's first legislative proposal retained the distinction between works by employees and works by independent contractors. After numerous meetings with representatives of the affected parties, the Copyright Office issued a preliminary draft bill in 1963. Adopting the Register's recommendation, it defined "work made for hire" as "a work prepared by an employee within the scope of the duties of his employment, but not including a work made on special order or commission." Preliminary Draft for Revised U.S. Copyright Law and Discussions and Comments on the Draft, 88th Cong., 2d Sess., Copyright Law Revision, Part 3, p. 15, n. 11 (H.Judiciary Comm.Print 1964) (hereinafter Preliminary Draft).

In response to objections by book publishers that the preliminary draft bill limited the work for hire doctrine to "employees," the 1964 revision bill expanded the scope of the work for hire classification to reach, for the first time, commissioned works. The bill's language, proposed initially by representatives of the publishing industry, retained the definition of work for hire insofar as it referred to "employees," but added a separate clause covering commissioned works, without regard to the subject matter, "if the parties so agree in writing." S. 3008, H.R. 11947, H.R. 1254, 88th Cong., 2d Sess., § 54 (1964) reproduced in 1964 Revision Bill with Discussions and Comments, 89th Cong., 1st Sess., Copyright Law Revision, Part 5, p. 31 (H.Judiciary Comm.Print 1965). Those representing authors objected that the added provision would allow publishers to use their superior bargaining position to force authors to sign work for hire agreements, thereby relinquishing all copyright rights as a condition of getting their books published.

In 1965, the competing interests reached an historic compromise which was embodied in a joint memorandum submitted to Congress and the Copyright Office, incorporated into the 1965 revision bill, and ultimately enacted in the same form and nearly the same terms 11 years later, as § 101 of the 1976 Act. The compromise retained as subsection (1) the language referring to "a work prepared by an employee within the scope of his employment." However, in exchange for concessions from publishers on provisions relating to the termination of transfer rights, the authors consented to a second subsection which classified four categories of commissioned works as works for hire if the parties expressly so agreed in writing: works for use "as a contribution to a collective work, as a part of a motion picture, as a translation, or as supplementary work." S. 1006, H.R. 4347, H.R. 5680, H.R. 6835, 89th Cong., 1st Sess., § 101 (1965). The interested parties selected these categories because they concluded that these commissioned works, although not prepared by employees and thus not covered by the first subsection, nevertheless should be treated as works for hire because they were ordinarily prepared "at the instance, direction, and risk of a publisher or producer." Supplementary Report, at 67. The Supplementary Report emphasized that only the "four special cases specifically mentioned" could qualify as works made for hire; "[o]ther works made on special order or commission would not come within the definition." Id., at 67–68.

In 1966, the House Committee on the Judiciary endorsed this compromise in the first legislative report on the revision bills. See H.R.Rep. No. 2237, 89th Cong., 2d Sess., 114, 116 (1966). Retaining the distinction between works by employees and commissioned works, the House Committee focused instead on "how to draw a statutory line between those works written on special order or commission that should be considered as works made for hire, and those that should not." Id., at 115. The House Committee added four other enumerated categories of commissioned works that could be treated as works for hire: compilations, instructional texts, tests, and atlases. With the single addition of "answer material for a test," the 1976 Act, as enacted, contained the same definition of works made for hire as did the 1966 revision bill, and had the same structure and nearly the same terms as the 1966 bill. Indeed, much of the language of the 1976 House and Senate Reports was borrowed from the Reports accompanying the earlier drafts.

Thus, the legislative history of the Act is significant for several reasons. First, the enactment of the 1965 compromise with only minor modifications demonstrates that Congress intended to provide two mutually exclusive ways for works to acquire work for hire status: one for employees and the other for independent contractors. Second, the legislative history underscores the clear import of the statutory language: only enumerated categories of commissioned works may be accorded work for hire status. The hiring party's right to control the product simply is not determinative. Indeed, importing a test based on a hiring party's right to control or actual control of a product would unravel the " 'carefully worked out compromise aimed at balancing legitimate interests on both sides.' " H.R.Rep. No. 2237, supra, at 114, quoting Supplemental Report, at 66.

We do not find convincing petitioners' contrary interpretation of the history of the Act. They contend that Congress, in enacting the Act, meant to incorporate a line of cases decided under the 1909 Act holding that an employment relationship exists sufficient to give the hiring party copyright ownership whenever that party has the right to control or supervise the artist's work. In support of this position, petitioners note: "[n]owhere in the 1976 Act or in the Act's legislative history does Congress state that it intended to jettison the control standard or otherwise to reject the pre-Act judicial approach to identifying a work for hire employment relationship."

We are unpersuaded. Ordinarily, "Congress' silence is just that—silence." Alaska Airlines, Inc. v. Brock, 480 U.S. 678, 686, 107 S.Ct. 1476, 1481, 94 L.Ed.2d 661 (1987). Petitioners' reliance on legislative silence is particularly misplaced here because the text and structure of § 101 counsel otherwise. Furthermore, the structure of the work for hire provisions was fully developed in 1965 and the text was agreed upon in essentially final form by 1966. At that time, however, the courts had applied the work for hire doctrine under the 1909 Act exclusively to traditional employees. Indeed, it was not until after the 1965 compromise was forged and adopted by Congress that a federal court for the first time applied the work for hire doctrine to commissioned works. Congress certainly could not have "jettisoned" a line of cases that had not yet been decided.

Finally, petitioners' construction of the work for hire provisions would impede Congress' paramount goal in revising the 1976 Act of enhancing predictability and certainty of copyright ownership. In a "copyright marketplace," the parties negotiate with an expectation that one of them will own the copyright in the completed work. With that expectation, the parties at the outset can settle on relevant contractual terms, such as the price for the work and the ownership of reproduction rights.

To the extent that petitioners endorse an actual control test, CCNV's construction of the work for hire provisions prevents such planning. Because that test turns on whether the hiring party has closely monitored the production process, the parties would not know until late in the process, if not until the work is completed, whether a work will ultimately fall within § 101(1). Under petitioners' approach, therefore, parties would have to predict in advance whether the hiring party will sufficiently control a given work to make it the author. "If they guess incorrectly, their reliance on 'work for hire' or an assignment may give them a copyright interest that they did not bargain for." *Easter Seal Society,* 815 F.2d, at 333. This understanding of the work for hire provisions clearly thwarts Congress' goal of ensuring predictability through advance planning. Moreover, petitioners' interpretation "leaves the door open for hiring parties, who have failed to get a full assignment of copyright rights from independent contractors falling outside the subdivision (2) guidelines, to unilaterally obtain work-made-for-hire rights years after the work has been completed as long as they directed or supervised the work, a standard that is hard not to meet when one is a hiring party." Hamilton, Commissioned Works as Works Made for Hire Under the 1976 Copyright Act: Misinterpretation and Injustice, 135 U.Pa.L.Rev. 1281, 1304 (1987).

In sum, we must reject petitioners' argument. Transforming a commissioned work into a work by an employee on the basis of the hiring party's right to control, or actual control of, the work is inconsistent with the language, structure, and legislative history of the work for hire provisions. To determine whether a work is for hire under the Act, a court first should ascertain, using principles of general common law of agency, whether the work was prepared by an employee or an independent contractor. After making this determination, the court can apply the appropriate subsection of § 101.

B

We turn, finally, to an application of § 101 to Reid's production of "Third World America." In determining whether a hired party is an employee under the general common law of agency, we consider the hiring party's right to control the manner and means by which the product is accomplished. Among the other factors relevant to this inquiry are the skill required; the source of the instrumentalities and tools; the location of the work; the duration of the relationship between the parties; whether the hiring party has the right to assign additional projects to the hired party; the extent of the hired party's discretion over when and how long to work; the method of payment; the hired party's role in hiring and paying assistants; whether the work is part of the regular business of the hiring party; whether the hiring party is in business; the provision of employee benefits; and the tax treatment of the hired party. See Restatement § 220(2) (setting forth a nonexhaustive list of factors relevant to determining whether a hired party is an employee). No one of these factors is determinative.

Examining the circumstances of this case in light of these factors, we agree with the Court of Appeals that Reid was not an employee of CCNV but an independent contractor. True, CCNV members directed enough of Reid's work to ensure that he produced a sculpture that met their specifications. But the extent of control the hiring party exercises over the details of the product is not dispositive. Indeed, all the other circumstances weigh heavily against finding an employment relationship. Reid is a sculptor, a skilled occupation. Reid supplied his own tools. He worked in his own studio in Baltimore, making daily supervision of his activities from Washington practicably impossible. Reid was retained for less than two months, a relatively short period of time. During and after this time, CCNV had no right to assign additional projects to Reid. Apart from the deadline for completing the sculpture, Reid had absolute freedom to decide when and how long to work. CCNV paid Reid $15,000, a sum dependent on "completion of a specific job, a method by which independent contractors are often compensated." Holt v. Winpisinger, 258 U.S.App.D.C. 343, 351, 811 F.2d 1532, 1540 (1987). Reid had total discretion in hiring and paying assistants. "Creating sculptures was hardly 'regular business' for CCNV." 270 U.S.App.D.C., at 35, n. 11, 846 F.2d, at 1494, n. 11. Indeed, CCNV is not a business at all. Finally, CCNV did not pay payroll or social security taxes, provide any employee benefits, or contribute to unemployment insurance or workers' compensation funds.

Because Reid was an independent contractor, whether "Third World America" is a work for hire depends on whether it satisfies the terms of § 101(2). This petitioners concede it cannot do. Thus, CCNV is not the author of "Third World America" by virtue of the work for hire provisions of the Act. However, as the Court of Appeals made clear, CCNV nevertheless may be a joint author of the sculpture if, on remand, the District Court so determines that CCNV and Reid prepared the work "with the intention that their contributions be merged into inseparable or interdependent parts of a unitary whole." 17 U.S.C. § 101. In that case, CCNV and Reid would be co-owners of the copyright in the work. See § 201(a).

For the aforestated reasons, we affirm the judgment of the Court of Appeals for the District of Columbia.

It is so ordered.

ODDO v. RIES

United States Court of Appeals, Ninth Circuit, 1984.
743 F.2d 630, 222 U.S.P.Q. 799.

GOODWIN, Circuit Judge.

In the guise of a copyright infringement suit, this case presents an accounting problem between two partners. Ries and his codefendants appeal from a judgment awarding Oddo $10,000 statutory damages for infringement, $20,000 attorneys' fees, general damages of $1,000, and costs of suit.

Oddo and Ries entered into a partnership in March 1978 to create and publish a book describing how to restore Ford F–100 pickup trucks. According to the partnership agreement, Ries was to provide capital and supervise the business end of the venture; Oddo was to write and edit the book. By January 1980, Oddo had delivered to Ries a manuscript that contained much but not all of the material the partners planned to include in the book. This manuscript consisted partly of a reworking of previously published magazine articles that Oddo had written and partly of new material, also written by Oddo, that had never before been published.

At about the same time, Ries became dissatisfied with the progress Oddo had made on the manuscript. Ries hired another writer to complete Oddo's manuscript, and then published the finished product. The book that Ries eventually published contained substantial quantities of Oddo's manuscript but also contained material added by the new writer.

I. Infringement

Three copyrighted works are at issue in this case. The first, actually a set of copyrighted works, consists of the magazine articles that Oddo reworked into the manuscript that he delivered to Ries. The second work is Oddo's manuscript, and the third is the book that Ries published. We will refer to these works as the articles, the manuscript, and the book. The district court did not specify which copyright Ries had infringed; it simply held "[t]hat the copyright of Plaintiff Oddo was infringed by Defendant Ries when he caused the Guide [i.e., the Book] to be published. . . ."

A. Book and Manuscript

The district court erred if it meant that Ries infringed the copyright in the manuscript or the book. The district court concluded that the Oddo/Ries partnership owns the copyrights in the book and the manuscript. As a partner, Ries is a co-owner of the partnership's assets, including the copyrights. A co-owner of a copyright cannot be liable to another co-owner for infringement of the copyright. Rather, each co-owner has an independent right to use or license the use of the copyright. A co-owner of a copyright must account to other co-owners for any profits he earns from licensing or use of the copyright, but the duty to account does not derive from the copyright law's proscription of infringement. Rather, it comes from "equitable doctrines relating to unjust enrichment and general principles of law governing the rights of co-owners." Harrington v. Mure, 186 F.Supp. 655, 657–58 (S.D.N.Y. 1960) (footnote omitted).

We have not found any cases dealing with the rights of partners in copyrights held by their partnership, but we see no reason why partners should be excluded from the general rules governing copyright co-ownership. Many of the copyright co-ownership cases might be distinguished from ours on the grounds that co-ownership in those cases arose from joint authorship of the work subject to copyright, and Oddo and Ries are not joint authors. However, nothing in those cases suggests that the rules they set out are restricted to cases of joint authorship. Moreover, the general rule of copyright co-ownership has been applied to co-owners who are not joint authors.

Accordingly, Ries could not infringe the partnership's copyrights in the manuscript or the book, but he can be required to account to Oddo for any profits he has made from use of those copyrights. Ries may also be liable to Oddo under California partnership law for misuse of the partnership copyrights. A violation of state partnership law, however, would not transform Ries' use of the copyrights into infringement under federal law.

B. Articles

In finding infringement, the district court may have meant that Ries infringed Oddo's copyrights in his magazine articles. If so, we must first consider Ries' contention that the publisher of the magazines, not Oddo, owns the copyrights to the articles.

The articles were contributions to collective works. Copyright to such a contribution vests initially in the author of the contribution; in this case, Oddo. The owner of the copyright in the collective work (here, the magazine publisher) is presumed to have acquired only the privilege of publishing the contribution in that particular collective work unless he has received greater rights by an "express transfer." 17 U.S.C. § 201(c) (1982). Ries has not pointed to any evidence of such an "express transfer." Nor can Ries claim that the magazine publisher acquired ownership of the copyrights in the articles as "works made for hire" pursuant to § 201(b), because a contribution to a collective work will be considered a work made for hire only if the parties expressly so agree in a written instrument, § 101, and Ries has not pointed to any such instrument. Oddo owns the copyrights to the articles.

We now turn to infringement of the copyrights in the articles. The manuscript and the book are both derivative works based on the articles. See § 101. As derivative works they necessarily infringe the copyrights in the articles unless Oddo granted permission to use the articles.

The district court made no findings on whether Oddo gave Ries or the partnership permission to use his articles in the manuscript or the book. We conclude that Oddo, by preparing a manuscript based on his preexisting articles as part of his partnership duties, impliedly gave the partnership a license to use the articles insofar as they were incorporated in the manuscript, for without such a license, Oddo's contribution to the partnership venture would have been of minimal value. However, the implied license to use the articles in the manuscript does not give Ries or the partnership the right to use the articles in any work other than the manuscript itself. Because the book is a work distinct from the manuscript, Ries exceeded the scope of the partnership's license when he used the articles in the book. Ries has not shown that he was otherwise licensed to use the articles in the book, so his publication of the book infringed Oddo's copyright in the articles. . . .

The judgment of the district court is vacated insofar as it awards Oddo statutory damages and attorneys' fees. The cause is remanded for an award of the actual damages that Oddo suffered from infringement of his copyrights in the articles. On remand the district court may also consider whether, in its discretion, it should exercise jurisdiction pendent to the infringement claim to compel Ries to account to Oddo for any profits earned from use of the co-owned copyrights.

AFFIRMED IN PART; VACATED IN PART; AND REMANDED.

NOTES

1. Is *Reid* likely to promote "Congress' paramount goal in revising the 1976 Act of enhancing predictability and certainty of copyright ownership?" Does the Agency Restatement's "nonexhaustive" list of common law factors—relied upon by the *Reid* Court—offer greater predictability than the supervision and control test previously employed in work for hire cases? Note that "control" is an essential element of the Restatement's definition of "servant": "A servant is a person employed to perform services in the affairs of another and who with respect to the physical conduct in the performance of the services

is subject to the other's control or right to control." Restatement (Second) of Agency § 220(1) (1957).

A copyright owner can always transfer ownership consensually through a written instrument. As a practical matter, is *Reid* likely to have any effect on prospective allocations of ownership?

2. *Joint Works.* As indicated by the remand in *Reid* to determine whether CCNV and Reid were joint owners, the same facts that underlie a claim that a work was made for hire may support a claim that the work is a joint work. For a contributor to be a coauthor—and joint owner—of a work, she must contribute original expression that can stand on its own as copyrightable subject matter. For example, a client who contributed only design concepts would not be a coauthor of the resulting architectural plans. Aitken, Hazen, Hoffman, Miller, P.C. v. Empire Constr. Co., 542 F.Supp. 252, 218 U.S.P.Q. 409 (D.Neb.1982). The practical consequence of a finding that two or more individuals are co-authors is that each is free to exploit the copyright, subject only to a duty to account.

Will an interviewer and his interviewee be joint authors of the resulting interview? The scant case law on the question suggests a negative answer. See Suid v. Newsweek Magazine, 503 F.Supp. 146, 211 U.S.P.Q. 898 (D.D.C.1980).

3. *Does the 1909 Copyright Act or the 1976 Copyright Act Govern Ownership?* Some works that would be considered to have been made for hire under the 1909 Act would not be considered to have been made for hire under the 1976 Act. Some works that would be considered to have been created as joint works under the 1909 Act would not be considered joint works under the 1976 Act. The 1909 Act's ownership rules govern works created—and legal relationships formed—before the effective date of the 1976 Act, and the 1976 Act governs works and relationships created since. See, Roth v. Pritikin, 710 F.2d 934, 937–39, 219 U.S.P.Q. 204 (2d Cir.), cert. denied, 464 U.S. 961, 104 S.Ct. 394, 78 L.Ed.2d 337, 220 U.S.P.Q. 385 (1983), aff'd in part, rev'd in part on remand, 787 F.2d 54, 229 U.S.P.Q. 388 (2d Cir.1986).

4. *Copyright Term.* One of the 1976 Act's main innovations was to alter the duration of copyright from a term measured by 28 years from the date of publication, with a renewal period of 28 years, to a term measured by the life of the author plus 50 years. The change brings United States law into line with the copyright terms of most other nations.

(a) *If the copyright term is measured by the "life of the author," how is the term measured when a work has more than one author?* Section 302(b) provides that where two or more authors prepare a joint work, the copyright will last for a term measured by the life of the last surviving author plus 50 years. The rule obviously requires careful attention to the Act's definition of "joint work."

(b) *How is the term measured for anonymous or pseudonymous works, or works made for hire, whose author is not known or, as a corporation, enjoys an indeterminate life?* Section 302(c)'s response to these situations is to approximate an author's life plus 50 years with a term of 75 years from the year of a work's first publication or 100 years from the year of its creation, whichever expires first. If, before the end of this term, the identity of the anonymous or pseudonymous author is revealed in Copyright Office records, the copyright will last for the standard life plus 50 term.

(c) *How, as a practical matter, will prospective users be able to determine the life and death facts that will tell them whether a work is in or out of copyright?* Section 302(d) gives the copyright owner, or anyone having an interest in the copyright, the opportunity to record in the Copyright Office a statement of the date of the author's death, or a statement that the author is still living. Why should the owner record? Section 302(e) provides that if, after 75 years from first publication or 100 years from a work's creation, whichever expires first, a prospective user obtains a certified report from the Copyright Office that its records disclose nothing to indicate that the author of the work is living or died less than 50 years before, the prospective user becomes entitled to the benefit of a presumption that the author has been dead for at least 50 years. Good faith reliance on the report constitutes a complete defense to any action for infringement.

(d) *What of works created and copyrighted before the Act's effective date, January 1, 1978?* Section 304 divides its treatment of these works between those that were in their first copyright term on January 1, 1978 and those that were in their renewal term, or registered for renewal, before January 1, 1978. For copyrights in their first term on January 1, 1978, section 304(a) retains the previous 28–year copyright term, allows renewal, but extends the renewal term from the previous 28–year term to 47 years. Effectively, this creates a total term of 75 years from publication, establishing parity between works protected under the old Act and works created after January 1, 1978 and protected under the new Act. Section 304(b) creates parity for works already in their renewal term on January 1, 1978 by automatically extending the renewal term to 75 years from the date copyright was originally secured.

(e) *What of works created, but not under statutory copyright, before January 1, 1978?* Congress recognized that there may be many unpublished works that have been in existence for a long time—centuries even—and whose authors are long since dead. It provided in section 303 that these works are to enjoy the same term as works created after January 1, 1978, but added that copyright in this class of works will in any event not expire before December 31, 2002, thus assuring at least 25 years of protection. As an inducement to publication, section 303 also provides that if the work is published on or before December 31, 2002, the term will be extended through December 31, 2027. See generally, Cohen, Duration, 24 UCLA L.Rev. 1180 (1977).

5. *Copyright Renewal.* Section 24's renewal provisions were among the more problematic parts of the old Act. These provisions promise to create problems for many years to come, for section 304(a)

perpetuates the renewal scheme for works in their first copyright term before January 1, 1978. The House Report explains: "A great many of the present expectancies in these cases are the subject of existing contracts, and it would be unfair and immensely confusing to cut off or alter these interests." H.R.Rep. No. 94–1476, 94th Cong.2d Sess. 139 (1976).

The opacity of the renewal provisions may explain the attention that the Supreme Court lavished on them in a trio of decisions, Fred Fisher Music Co., Inc. v. M. Witmark & Sons, 318 U.S. 643, 63 S.Ct. 773, 87 L.Ed. 1055, 57 U.S.P.Q. 50 (1943); De Sylva v. Ballentine, 351 U.S. 570, 76 S.Ct. 974, 100 L.Ed. 1415, 109 U.S.P.Q. 431 (1956); and Miller Music Corp. v. Charles N. Daniels, Inc., 362 U.S. 373, 80 S.Ct. 792, 4 L.Ed.2d 804, 125 U.S.P.Q. 147 (1960).

The question for decision in Fisher v. Witmark was, "Does the Copyright Act nullify an agreement by an author, made during the original copyright term, to assign his renewal?" 318 U.S. 643, 647, 63 S.Ct. 773, 774, 775. Justice Frankfurter rested a negative answer upon an extensive review of the pre–1909 legislation, which did not restrict assignability, and the legislative history of the 1909 Act, which indicated an intent to continue the earlier position. "Neither the language nor the history of the Copyright Act of 1909 lend support to the conclusion that the 'existing law' prior to 1909, under which authors were free to assign their renewal interests if they were so disposed, was intended to be altered." 318 U.S. at 656.

Another tenet of existing law incorporated in the 1909 Act was that, before expiration of the initial 28–year term, the author's interest in the renewal term is contingent and will vest in him or his assignee only if the author is alive at the time prescribed for vesting. If the author is not alive, rights to the renewal term vest in the "widow, widower, or children of the author" or, if they are not alive, in the other individuals designated by section 24. De Sylva v. Ballentine considered whether for these purposes, "the widow and children take as a class, or in order of enumeration." 351 U.S. at 572. Acknowledging that "the matter is far from clear," it held for the first proposition. The Court left open, however, "the question of what are the respective rights of the widow and child in the copyright renewals, once it is accepted that they both succeed to the renewals as members of the same class." 351 U.S. at 582. For the assumption that the widow and children are to share equally, see Bartok v. Boosey & Hawkes, Inc., 523 F.2d 941, 942 n. 2, 187 U.S.P.Q. 529, 530 n. 2 (2d Cir.1975).

Miller v. Daniels involved a mix of the issues raised in *Witmark* and *De Sylva* and found Justice Frankfurter, who wrote the *Witmark* opinion, and Justice Harlan, who wrote the *De Sylva* opinion, in dissent, and Justice Douglas, who dissented in *Witmark* and concurred in *De Sylva*, delivering the majority opinion. The question in *Miller* differed from the question in *Witmark* in one detail: "The question for decision is whether by statute the renewal rights accrue to the executor in spite of a prior assignment by his testator." 362 U.S. at 374.

Taking the *Witmark* assumption—that if the author expires before the initial term, the widow or widower and children take regardless of the *inter vivos* transfer—together with petitioner's concession—"that where the author dies intestate prior to the renewal period leaving no widow, widower, or children, the next of kin obtain the renewal copyright free of any claim founded upon an assignment made by the author in his lifetime"—the Court concluded: "We fail to see the difference in this statutory scheme between widows, widowers, children, or next of kin on the one hand and executors on the other. . . . Section 24 reflects, it seems to us, a consistent policy to treat renewal rights as expectancies until the renewal period arrives. When that time arrives, the renewal rights pass to one of the four classes listed in § 24 according to the then-existing circumstances." 362 U.S. at 375–78.

The rule that an author's renewal interest is contingent, and will vest in her transferee only if the author is alive at the time prescribed for vesting, can create problems if the author dies before the renewal term vests. In Rohauer v. Killiam Shows, Inc., 551 F.2d 484, 192 U.S. P.Q. 545 (2d Cir.), cert. denied, 431 U.S. 949, 97 S.Ct. 2666, 53 L.Ed.2d 266 (1977), a licensee had produced a derivative work, relying on a license—for both the initial and renewal terms—obtained from a grantor who had died before the renewal term vested; the court held that the licensee could nonetheless continue exploiting the derivative work during the renewal term. But in Abend v. MCA, Inc., 863 F.2d 1465, 9 U.S.P.Q.2d 1337 (9th Cir.1988), cert. granted, 110 S.Ct. 47, 107 L.Ed.2d 16 (1989), the Ninth Circuit Court of Appeals held that, in comparable circumstances, an initial term licensee could not continue exploiting the work during the renewal term without the consent of the renewal term copyright owner.

See generally, Mimms, Reversion and Derivative Works Under the Copyright Acts of 1909 and 1976, 25 N.Y.L.Sch.L.Rev. 595 (1980); Note, *Rohauer v. Killiam Shows, Inc.* and the Derivative Work Exception to the Termination Right: Inequitable Anomalies Under Copyright Law, 52 S.Cal.L.Rev. 635 (1979).

6. *Termination of Transfers.* The 1909 Copyright Act did not expressly address the question raised in *Rohauer* and *Abend*. The 1976 Act sought to protect producers of derivative works in the comparable situation created by the 1976 Act's termination of transfer provisions. Section 203(b)(1) provides that "[a] derivative work prepared under authority of the grant before its termination may continue to be utilized under the terms of the grant after its termination, but this privilege does not extend to the preparation after the termination of other derivative works based upon the copyrighted work covered by the termination grant." See generally, Curtis, Caveat Emptor in Copyright: A Practical Guide to the Termination–of–Transfers Provisions of the New Copyright Code, 25 Bull. Copyright Soc'y 19 (1977); Curtis, Protecting Authors in Copyright Transfers: Revision Bill § 203 and the Alternatives, 72 Colum.L.Rev. 799 (1972); Stein, Termination of Transfers and Licenses Under the New Copyright Act: Thorny Problems for the Copyright Bar, 24 UCLA L.Rev. 1141 (1977). See also See, Copy-

right Ownership of Joint Works and Terminations of Transfers, 30 U.Kan.L.Rev. 517 (1982).

An author will often assign his copyright to an intermediary—typically a publisher—and the intermediary will then license derivative rights to one or more third parties. If the author later terminates his grant to the intermediary, must the third-party licensee—who can continue to use the derivative work under section 203(b)(1)—pay its royalties to the intermediary or to the author? In Mills Music, Inc. v. Snyder, 469 U.S. 153, 105 S.Ct. 638, 83 L.Ed.2d 556, 224 U.S.P.Q. 313 (1985), reh'g denied, 470 U.S. 1065, 105 S.Ct. 1782, 84 L.Ed.2d 841 (1985), the United States Supreme Court held that, in these circumstances, the intermediary, not the author, is entitled to the royalties paid by the licensee for continued use of the derivative work. Although the case involved section 304(c) rather than section 203, the Court left no doubt that it intended its decision to govern terminations of transfers under section 203 as well as under section 304(c). 469 U.S. at 159 n. 17, 105 S.Ct. at 643 n. 17. See generally, Abrams, Who's Sorry Now? Termination Rights and the Derivative Works Exception, 62 U.Det.L. Rev. 181 (1985).

7. *Involuntary Transfers.* The origins of section 201(e), voiding involuntary governmental transfers of copyright, can be traced to the Soviet Union's announced adherence to the Universal Copyright Convention in February, 1973. The Soviet move, initially hailed as a long overdue acceptance of "responsibility toward the authors and other creators of works distributed and performed in the Soviet Union," was soon perceived as a possible device for tightening control over the circulation abroad "of literature which does not meet with Communist approval." 119 Cong.Rec. 9387 (Mar. 26, 1973). In March 1973, prodded by the Author's League of America, Senator McClellan introduced S. 1359, the predecessor to section 201(e). S. 1359 provided that any copyright would "remain the property of the author . . . regardless of any law, decree or other act of a foreign state or nation which purports to divest the author or said other persons of the United States copyright in his work." S. 1359, 93d Cong., 1st Sess. (1973).

By invalidating domestic as well as foreign involuntary transfers, section 201(e) offers a symmetry that is missing from S. 1359. Does section 201(e) threaten to interfere with common practice in domestic copyright industries? An involuntary transfer occurs any time a mortgage on a copyright interest is foreclosed. Involuntary transfers are also implicit in the power of federal and state governments to condemn individual copyrights.

Section 201(e) may also unintentionally disrupt techniques employed by other nations to mediate between the interests of citizen and state. For example, in the interest of broad public access to copyrighted works, Brazil's Civil Code art. 660 (1968), provides that "If the owner of a published work refuses to authorize new editions thereof, the Union and any of its States may, after indemnification, expropriate the work for reasons of public utility." Would expropriation on the ground that the author has suppressed publication constitute a voluntary or an involuntary transfer? To call it a voluntary transfer would offend the clear language of section 201(e). To call it an involuntary transfer would reinforce suppression, something that section 201(e) intended to eliminate.

Was section 201(e) really needed to combat repressive practices? How effective is copyright as a tool for suppressing political views? Can copyright be enlisted to enjoin news reports and commentary describing a work's dissident themes? What of the idea-expression distinction? The fair use defense? See generally, Goldstein, Preempted State Doctrines, Involuntary Transfers and Compulsory Licenses: Testing the Limits of Copyright, 24 UCLA L.Rev. 1107, 1123–1127 (1977).

2. REMEDIES

See Statute Supplement 17 U.S.C.A. §§ 412, 502–510.

COPYRIGHT LAW REVISION, H.R. REP. NO. 1476
94th Cong., 2d Sess. 160–164 (1976).

Section 502. Injunctions

Section 502(a) reasserts the discretionary power of courts to grant injunctions and restraining orders, whether "preliminary," "temporary," "interlocutory," "permanent," or "final," to prevent or stop infringements of copyright. This power is made subject to the provisions of section 1498 of title 28, dealing with infringement actions against the United States. The latter reference in section 502(a) makes it clear that the bill would not permit the granting of an injunction against an infringement for which the Federal Government is liable under section 1498.

Under subsection (b), which is the counterpart of provisions in sections 112 and 113 of the present statute, a copyright owner who has obtained an injunction in one State will be able to enforce it against a defendant located anywhere else in the United States.

Section 503. Impounding and Disposition of Infringing Articles

The two subsections of section 503 deal respectively with the courts' power to impound allegedly infringing articles during the time an action is pending, and to order the destruction or other disposition of articles found to be infringing. In both cases the articles affected include "all copies or phonorecords" which are claimed or found "to have been made or used in violation of the copyright owner's exclusive rights," and also "all plates, molds, matrices, masters, tapes, film negatives, or other articles by means of which such copies of phonorecords may be reproduced." The alternative phrase "made or used" in both subsections enables a court to deal as it sees fit with articles which, though reproduced and acquired lawfully, have been used for infringing purposes such as rentals, performances, and displays.

Articles may be impounded under subsection (a) "at any time while an action under this title is pending," thus permitting seizures of articles alleged to be infringing as soon as suit has been filed and without waiting for an injunction. The same subsection empowers the court to order impounding "on such terms as it may deem reasonable." The present Supreme Court rules with respect to seizure and impounding were issued even though there is no specific provision authorizing them in the copyright statute, and there appears no need for including a special provision on the point in the bill.

Under section 101(d) of the present statute, articles found to be infringing may be ordered to be delivered up for destruction. Section 503(b) of the bill would make this provision more flexible by giving the court discretion to order "destruction or other reasonable disposition" of the articles found to be infringing. Thus, as part of its final judgment or decree, the court could order the infringing articles sold, delivered to the plaintiff, or disposed of in some other way that would avoid needless waste and best serve the ends of justice.

Section 504. Damages and Profits

In General

A cornerstone of the remedies sections and of the bill as a whole is section 504, the provision dealing with recovery of actual damages, profits, and statutory damages. The two basic aims of this section are reciprocal and correlative: (1) to give the courts specific unambiguous directions concerning monetary awards, thus avoiding the confusion and uncertainty that have marked the present law on the subject, and, at the same time, (2) to provide the courts with reasonable latitude to adjust recovery to the circumstances of the case, thus avoiding some of the artificial or overly technical awards resulting from the language of the existing statute.

Subsection (a) lays the groundwork for the more detailed provisions of the section by establishing the liability of a copyright infringer for either "the copyright owner's actual damages and any additional profits of the infringer," or statutory damages. Recovery of actual damages and profits under section 504(b) or of statutory damages under section 504(c) is alternative and for the copyright owner to elect; as under the present law, the plaintiff in an infringement suit is not obliged to submit proof of damages and profits and may choose to rely on the provision for minimum statutory damages. However, there is nothing in section 504 to prevent a court from taking account of evidence concerning actual damages and profits in making an award of statutory damages within the range set out in subsection (c).

Actual Damages and Profits

In allowing the plaintiff to recover "the actual damages suffered by him or her as a result of the infringement," plus any of the infringer's profits "that are attributable to the infringement and are not taken into account in computing the actual damages," section 504(b) recognizes the different purposes served by awards of damages and profits. Damages are awarded to compensate the copyright owner for losses from the infringement, and profits are awarded to prevent the infringer from unfairly benefiting from a wrongful act. Where the defendant's profits are nothing more than a measure of the damages suffered by the copyright owner, it would be inappropriate to award damages and profits cumulatively, since in effect they amount to the same thing. However, in cases where the copyright owner has suffered damages not reflected in the infringer's profits, or where there have been profits attributable to the copyrighted work but not used as a measure of damages, subsection (b) authorizes the award of both.

The language of the subsection makes clear that only those profits "attributable to the infringement" are recoverable; where some of the defendant's profits result from the infringement and other profits are caused by different factors, it will be necessary for the court to make an apportionment. However, the burden of proof is on the defendant in these cases; in establishing profits the plaintiff need prove only "the infringer's gross revenue," and the defendant must prove not only "his or her deductible expenses" but also "the element of profit attributable to factors other than the copyrighted work."

Statutory Damages

Subsection (c) of section 504 makes clear that the plaintiff's election to recover statutory damages may take place at any time during the trial before the court has rendered its final judgment. The remainder of clause (1) of the subsection represents a statement of the general rates applicable to awards of statutory damages. Its principal provisions may be summarized as follows:

1. As a general rule, where the plaintiff elects to recover statutory damages, the court is obliged to award between $250 and $10,000. It can exercise discretion in awarding an amount within that range but, unless one of the exceptions provided by clause (2) is applicable, it cannot make an award of less than $250 or of more than $10,000 if the copyright owner has chosen recovery under section 504(c).

2. Although, as explained below, an award of minimum statutory damages may be multiplied if separate works and separately liable infringers are involved in the suit, a single award in the $250 to $10,000 range is to be made "for all infringements involved in the action." A single infringer of a single work is liable for a single amount between $250 and $10,000, no matter how many acts of infringement are involved in the action and regardless of whether the acts were separate, isolated, or occurred in a related series.

3. Where the suit involves infringement of more than one separate and independent work, minimum statutory damages for each work must be awarded. For example, if one defendant has

infringed three copyrighted works, the copyright owner is entitled to statutory damages of at least $750 and may be awarded up to $30,000. Subsection (c)(1) makes clear, however, that, although they are regarded as independent works for other purposes, "all the parts of a compilation or derivative work constitute one work" for this purpose. Moreover, although the minimum and maximum amounts are to be multiplied where multiple "works" are involved in the suit, the same is not true with respect to multiple copyrights, multiple owners, multiple exclusive rights, or multiple registrations. This point is especially important since, under a scheme of divisible copyright, it is possible to have the rights of a number of owners of separate "copyrights" in a single "work" infringed by one act of a defendant.

4. Where the infringements of one work were committed by a single infringer acting individually, a single award of statutory damages would be made. Similarly, where the work was infringed by two or more joint tort feasors, the bill would make them jointly and severally liable for an amount in the $250 to $10,000 range. However, where separate infringements for which two or more defendants are not jointly liable are joined in the same action, separate awards of statutory damages would be appropriate.

Clause (2) of section 504(c) provides for exceptional cases in which the maximum award of statutory damages could be raised from $10,000 to $50,000, and in which the minimum recovery could be reduced from $250 to $100. The basic principle underlying this provision is that the courts should be given discretion to increase statutory damages in cases of willful infringement and to lower the minimum where the infringer is innocent. The language of the clause makes clear that in these situations the burden of proving willfulness rests on the copyright owner and that of proving innocence rests on the infringer, and that the court must make a finding of either willfulness or innocence in order to award the exceptional amounts.

The "innocent infringer" provision of section 504(c)(2) has been the subject of extensive discussion. The exception, which would allow reduction of minimum statutory damages to $100 where the infringer "was not aware and had no reason to believe that his or her acts constituted an infringement of copyright," is sufficient to protect against unwarranted liability in cases of occasional or isolated innocent infringement, and it offers adequate insulation to users, such as broadcasters and newspaper publishers, who are particularly vulnerable to this type of infringement suit. On the other hand, by establishing a realistic floor for liability, the provision preserves its intended deterrent effect; and it would not allow an infringer to escape simply because the plaintiff failed to disprove the defendant's claim of innocence.

In addition to the general "innocent infringer" provision clause (2) deals with the special situation of teachers, librarians, archivists, and public broadcasters, and the nonprofit institutions of which they are a part. Section 504(c)(2) provides that, where such a person or institution infringed copyrighted material in the honest belief that what they were doing constituted fair use, the court is precluded from awarding any statutory damages. It is intended that, in cases involving this provision, the burden of proof with respect to the defendant's good faith should rest on the plaintiff.

Sections 505 Through 509. Miscellaneous Provisions on Infringement and Remedies

The remaining sections of chapter 5 of the bill deal with costs and attorneys' fees, criminal offenses, the statute of limitations, notification of copyright actions, and remedies for alteration of programming by cable systems.

Under section 505 the awarding of costs and attorney's fees are left to the court's discretion, and the section also makes clear that neither costs nor attorney's fees can be awarded to or against "the United States or an officer thereof."

Four types of criminal offenses actionable under the bill are listed in section 506: willful infringement for profit, fraudulent use of a copyright notice, fraudulent removal of notice, and false representation in connection with a copyright application. The maximum fine on conviction has been increased to $10,000 and, in conformity with the general pattern of the Criminal Code (18 U.S.C.A.), no minimum fines have been provided. In addition to or instead of a fine, conviction for criminal infringement under section 506(a) can carry with it a sentence of imprisonment of up to one year. Section 506(b) deals with seizure, forfeiture, and destruction of material involved in cases of criminal infringement.

Section 506(a) contains a special provision applying to any person who infringes willfully and for purposes of commercial advantage the copyright in a sound recording or a motion picture. For the first such offense a person shall be fined not more than $25,000 or imprisoned for not more than one year, or both. For any subsequent offense a person shall be fined not more than $50,000 or imprisoned not more than two years, or both.

Section 507, which is substantially identical with section 115 of the present law, establishes a three-year statute of limitations for both criminal proceedings and civil actions. The language of this section, which was adopted by the act of September 7, 1957 (71 Stat. 633), represents a reconciliation of views, and has therefore been left unaltered. Section 508, which corresponds to some extent with a provision in the patent law (35 U.S.C.A. § 290), is intended to establish a method for notifying the Copyright Office and the public of the filing and disposition of copyright cases. The clerks of the Federal courts are to notify the Copyright Office of the filing of any copyright actions and of their final disposition, and the Copyright Office is to make these notifications a part of its public records.

Section 509(b) specifies a new discretionary remedy for alteration of programming by cable systems in violation of section 111(c)(3): the court in such cases may decree that, "for a period not to exceed thirty days, the cable system shall be deprived of the benefit of a compulsory license for one or more distant signals carried by such cable system." The term "distant signals" in this provision is intended to have a meaning consistent with the definition of "distant signal equivalent" in section 111.

Under section 509(a), four types of plaintiffs are entitled to bring an action in cases of alteration of programming by cable systems in violation of section 111(c)(3). For regular copyright owners and local broadcaster-licensees, the full battery of remedies for infringement would be available. The two new classes of potential plaintiffs under section 501(d)—the distant-signal transmitter and other local stations—would be limited to the following remedies: (i) discretionary injunctions; (ii) discretionary costs and attorney's fees; (iii) any actual damages the plaintiff can prove were attributable to the act of altering program content; and (iv) the new discretionary remedy of suspension of compulsory licensing.

STEVENS LINEN ASSOCIATES v. MASTERCRAFT CORP.

United States Court of Appeals, Second Circuit, 1981.
656 F.2d 11, 210 U.S.P.Q. 865.

LUMBARD, Circuit Judge:

Plaintiff Stevens Linen Co. appeals from that part of an order entered in the Southern District of New York, Motley, J., denying plaintiff compensatory damages resulting from the copyright infringement of plaintiff's upholstery fabric entitled "Chestertown." The district court held that defendant's fabrics "Rio Grande" and "Grand Canyon" infringed plaintiff's copyright for its Chestertown fabric, granted a permanent injunction barring future sales of the infringing fabrics, and awarded plaintiff reasonable attorney's fees. The district court denied an award of compensatory damages, however, because it believed any damages suffered by plaintiff to be too speculative to be determined. We now modify the order and remand it for computation of damages.

I.

Stevens Linen Co. and defendant Mastercraft Corp. are direct competitors in the manufacture and marketing of woven upholstery fabrics. In the summer of 1976, a Stevens Linen employee created a new fabric design, known as Chestertown. The fabric was first shown publicly in July of 1976 and first sold in September of that year. A copyright registration was then obtained. Stevens Linen displayed the fabric in North Carolina at a national furniture market called the "High Point Market." After attending that market, a Mastercraft designer created the two infringing fabrics: Rio Grande and Grand Canyon.

Stevens commenced this suit on April 19, 1979, alleging that Mastercraft's two fabrics infringed Steven's copyright for the Chestertown fabric. The district court found the Mastercraft fabrics to be substantially similar in appearance to Steven's copyrighted fabric and therefore entered an order of preliminary injunction, temporarily enjoining the sale of the infringing fabrics, on February 15, 1980. The order was affirmed by this court in an unpublished ruling on April 21, 1980.

A non-jury trial of the merits ensued. At trial, the parties again contested the issue of infringement. In addition, Stevens presented evidence to support several possible theories as to its damages from infringement. First, Mastercraft admitted having sold 253,867 yards of its Rio Grande and Grand Canyon fabrics. Therefore, Stevens claimed that it suffered damages of lost profits on the entire amount of Mastercraft's sales, since it could have sold this amount of Chestertown had there been no infringement. Stevens offered testimony that it had excess production capacity during the time of Mastercraft's sales.

Second, Stevens offered evidence that twenty-two of its Chestertown customers had also purchased Mastercraft's Rio Grande and Grand Canyon fabrics. These twenty-two customers purchased a total of 95,422⅝ yards of Mastercraft's two fabrics. Thus, Stevens argued that it was damaged at the minimum in the amount of lost profits on these sales. Stevens also placed into evidence the 14,234⅛ yards of sales by Mastercraft of its two fabrics to purchasers to whom Stevens had distributed samples of its Chestertown fabrics, and the 97,258 yards of Mastercraft sales to customers who had been solicited to purchase Chestertown.

Third, Stevens offered testimony by its Vice President and Director of Design as to Steven's original projections for Chestertown sales. Based upon the fact that Chestertown had tripled in sales from 1977 to 1978, Stevens had projected that sales would again triple in 1979 (to about 270,000 yards), would increase by about 12% in 1980, would begin tapering off in 1981, and would have a total sales life of about ten years. Stevens also introduced evidence of Chestertown's actual performance: in 1979, the year in which Mastercraft's fabrics were first sold in competition with Chestertown, sales increased only 4%, instead of the tripling projected, and in the first six months of 1980, sales of Chestertown declined by 64%.

Finally, Stevens compared the sales of Chestertown with its overall sales during the times in question. During 1978, before Mastercraft began sales of its two fabrics, Chestertown's sales had increased by 216%, while Stevens's overall sales increased by 37% and its sales not including Chestertown increased 30%. In 1979, when Mastercraft began its sales of Rio Grande and Grand Canyon, and when sales of Chestertown increased only 4%, Stevens's overall sales increased 28%, and sales without including Chestertown increased 30%. In the six months ending July 31, 1980, when Chestertown sales declined 64%, overall sales declined only 16% and sales not including Chestertown declined only 12%.

Stevens also introduced into evidence certain Mastercraft invoices for sales of Rio Grande and Grand Canyon. Twenty-four of the invoices, totalling 4,329⅜ yards with a total sales price of $15,362.91, carried dates subsequent to entry of the preliminary injunction. Stevens argued that it should be awarded that sum in addition to any compensatory damages for losses of sales prior to the granting of the preliminary injunction.

With respect to damages, Mastercraft pointed out that Stevens's Chestertown fabric was priced at $5.40 per yard, while Mastercraft's fabrics sold for approximately $3.50 per yard. Mastercraft's President testified that, because of the difference in price, he did not believe Stevens would have obtained all of Mastercraft's sales in the period in question. He also pointed to the existence of similar, cheaper fabrics on the market. Finally, Mastercraft offered evidence suggesting that the dates on the invoices in question did not reflect dates of shipping, but merely dates of billing.

The district court held that the two Mastercraft fabrics infringed Stevens's copyright for its Chestertown fabric. As for damages, the court noted that the applicable statute, 17 U.S.C. § 504 (1976 & Supp. III 1979), provides for an award of either the copyright owner's damages plus the infringer's profits or, at the election of the copyright owner, specified statutory damages, and that Stevens had elected to pursue actual damages and any of the infringer's profits. The court found that Mastercraft had indeed lost money on its infringing fabrics, and therefore no profits could be awarded. As to actual damages to Stevens, although finding that "it is reasonable to assume that the infringement affected plaintiff's sales," the court refused to award any compensatory damages, finding them too speculative.

The court specifically rejected the theory that Stevens would have sold additional amounts of its Chestertown fabric in the total amounts of the infringing fabrics sold by Mastercraft. It also rejected the theory that Stevens would have sold additional amounts of Chestertown to those of its customers who purchased both Chestertown and Mastercraft's fabrics. Finally, it dismissed the projections testified to by a Stevens employee as even more speculative than the other theories of lost sales. The court made no mention of either the comparison to sales of Stevens's other fabrics or the evidence as to post-injunction sales of Mastercraft's fabrics. The court did award Stevens its attorney's fees.

II.

We believe the district court erred in failing to award Stevens compensatory damages. In establishing lost sales due to sales of an infringing product, courts must necessarily engage in some degree of speculation. Although, as Mastercraft argues on appeal, there is a distinction between proof of causation—meaning proof that defendant's acts caused any harm to plaintiff at all—and proof of the amount of damage, in this case the district court found that Stevens's copyright had been infringed and that this infringement necessarily caused some loss of sales by Stevens. Therefore the only issue was the extent of that damage.

Given the difference in price between the infringed and infringing products, the district court was correct in refusing to grant to Stevens damages based upon the assumption that it would have sold the entire amount of fabric sold by Mastercraft. Moreover, it was also proper for the district court to reject the projections of Chestertown sales offered by Stevens's Vice President and Director of Design. While under other circumstances, such testimony might support an award of damages, here the testimony was completely devoid of documentary support, and the witness furnished the court with no basis for the projections and hence no basis on which the court could evaluate the validity of the projections.

Nevertheless, the district court should have awarded damages measured either (1) by lost profits which Stevens would have realized from sales to customers who bought both Stevens and Mastercraft fabrics, or (2) by lost profits based upon the difference between sales of Chestertown and the average sales of all of Stevens's other fabrics, whichever sum proves to be larger. As to the first theory, admittedly we cannot be certain that all of the purchases of these twenty-two customers would have been made from Stevens rather than Mastercraft had no infringing products been offered. Nevertheless, we can reasonably believe that these customers of Stevens had a demand for this type of fabric and were shifting their purchasing to the cheaper infringing fabrics and away from Chestertown. Although Stevens might not have made every one of Mastercraft's sales, we believe that once Stevens established that it had been damaged, and that its customers purchased both the infringed and the infringing products, the burden shifted to the infringer, Mastercraft, to prove that the customers of Chestertown to whom it sold would not have acquired from Stevens alone all of the yardage they purchased had there been no infringement.

Regarding the second plausible theory, we believe that, at the least, Stevens should be able to recover lost profits based upon the difference between its actual sales of Chestertown during the period in which it was forced to compete with the infringing fabrics and Stevens's average sales figures for its remaining fabric products. This approach was recently taken in a copyright infringement suit involving competing sales of infringing record albums. See Big Seven Music Corp. v. Lennon, 554 F.2d 504 (2d Cir.1977) (comparing sales of infringed album with sales of contemporary albums by same performer). We believe it more appropriate to compare sales of Chestertown to Stevens's sales for all of its fabrics *not including* Chestertown, since the Chestertown figures were clearly affected by competition with the infringing items, and since the object of the damages inquiry is to determine what sales probably would have been made without the infringement. Therefore, under this theory, the district court could award Stevens lost profits based upon the difference between the 4% increase in Chestertown sales in 1979 and the 30% sales increase in Stevens's other fabric lines, and the difference between the 64% decline in Chestertown sales in the first six months of 1980 and the 12% decline in Stevens's other products during that period.

Thus we must remand to the district court to determine the amount of damages. Under the first of the two foregoing measures, damages would be awarded in the amount of Stevens's lost profits for additional sales of Chestertown to those of its customers who also purchased the infringing fabrics, less profits on sales which Mastercraft proves that Stevens would not have made. The measure under the alternative theory would be lost profits based upon the difference between Chestertown sales in the period in question and Stevens's average sales of its other fabric products. Having calculated damages according to these two alternative measures, the court should award to Stevens whatever sum proves to be greater.

Finally, upon remand, the court should consider an additional award of damages based upon the Mastercraft invoices introduced by Stevens which bear dates subsequent to the entry of the injunction. Mastercraft argues on appeal that Stevens did not ask the district court to award these damages, but the trial record clearly refutes this position. Stevens entered these invoices into evidence and asked questions of Mastercraft employees concerning them. Mastercraft obviously saw the potentially damaging nature of these invoices for it responded by eliciting testimony suggesting that the dates on the invoices were billing dates rather than dates of delivery. The district court, however, made no findings as to these sales. With respect to any sales referred to in these invoices which Mastercraft cannot establish as having been made prior to the preliminary injunction, the total amount of the revenues received by Mastercraft from these sales should be awarded to Stevens.

Order modified and remanded for further proceedings consistent with this opinion.

CREAM RECORDS, INC. v. JOS. SCHLITZ BREWING CO.

United States Court of Appeals, Ninth Circuit, 1985.
754 F.2d 826, 225 U.S.P.Q. 896.

PER CURIAM:

Appellant Cream sued appellees alleging that music in a TV commercial prepared by Benton and Bowles to advertise Schlitz beer infringed appellant's copyright on a popular rhythm and blues composition, "The Theme from Shaft."

The jury found infringement. By agreement of the parties the issue of damages was submitted to the court which awarded Cream a total of $17,000. Cream appealed.

DAMAGES

Schlitz applied to Cream for a one-year license to use the Shaft theme music in its commercial. Cream quoted a fee of $100,000. (Cream conceded at trial, and the district court found, that the market value of such a license was $80,000.) After Schlitz failed to take a license, another manufacturer approached Cream for a license but withdrew when the Schlitz commercial was aired. There was testimony that use of a well-known popular song in a commercial destroys its value to other advertisers for that purpose.

The district court awarded Cream $12,000 in damages for loss of the license fee. The court reasoned that the value of a license for use of the entire song for a year was $80,000, that only a small portion of the song was actually used in the Schlitz commercial, and the reasonable value of a license for use of that portion was 15% of the value of a license to use the entire song.

The only evidence before the court was that unauthorized use of the Shaft theme music in Schlitz's commercial ended Cream's opportunity to license the music for this purpose. There was no evidence that Schlitz sought, or Cream was willing to grant, a license for use of less than the entire copyrighted work, that a license limited to the portion used in the commercial would have had less value, or that use limited to this portion would have had a less devastating effect upon Cream's opportunity to license to another. Since defendants' unauthorized use destroyed the value of the copyrighted work for this purpose, plaintiff was entitled to recover that value as damages.

PROFITS

17 U.S.C. § 504(b) (1982) provides that, in addition to actual damages suffered as a result of the infringement, the copyright owner is entitled to recover "any profits of the infringer that are attributable to the infringement and are not taken into account in computing the actual damages." The statute also defines and allocates the burden of proof, providing, "[i]n establishing the infringer's profits, the copyright owner is required to present proof only of the infringer's gross revenue, and the infringer is required to prove his or her deductible expenses and the elements of profit attributable to factors other than the copyrighted work."

Schlitz. Cream offered proof that Schlitz's profit on malt liquor for the period during which the infringing commercial was broadcast was $4.876 million. Cream sought to recover $66,800 as the portion of Schlitz's profit attributable to the infringement, arguing that the expenditure for the infringing commercial constituted 13.7% of Schlitz's advertising budget for the year, the infringing music was responsible for 10% of the commercial's advertising power, and, therefore, 1.37% of the profit on malt liquor were attributable to the infringement.

The district court concluded that the infringement "was minimal," consisting principally of a ten-note ostinato, and that the infringing material did not add substantially to the value of the commercial. The court also concluded, however, that the commercial was successful, that "it sold some beer," and "that the music had a portion of that." The court continued, "So I have to find some profit of the defendants which is allocable to the infringement, but, as I say, I think it's miniscule. I have interpolated as best I can. They made a profit of $5 million. One-tenth of 1 percent is $5,000, so I will add that. . . ."

Cream argues that since it established Schlitz's total profits from the sale of malt liquor, the burden was placed on Schlitz to prove any portion of the profits not attributable to the infringement, and since the defendants put on no evidence, Cream was entitled to recover the part of Schlitz's profits it sought. The court's lesser award, Cream argues, was wholly arbitrary, and supported by no evidence in the record.

Defendants respond that Cream failed to establish that any part of the profits from the sale of malt liquor were attributable to the commercial, much less to its infringing portion, and was therefore entitled to no share of the profits at all. One of the court's formal findings, prepared by defendants, might be read as stating that no causal connection had been shown between the infringement and defendants' profits. It is clear from the court's statements, including those quoted above, however, that the court concluded from the jury's verdict and from the evidence that some of the profits from malt liquor sales were in fact attributable to the use of plaintiff's copyrighted music in the commercial. The court determined the share of the profits attributable to the infringing material as best it could and awarded Cream 1/10th of 1% of those profits. Defendants have not cross-appealed the judgment, and may not challenge the determination of causation upon which it rests.

We also reject Cream's contention. Although the statute imposes upon the infringer the burden of showing "the elements of profit attributable to factors other than the copyrighted work," 17 U.S.C. § 504(b), nonetheless where it is clear, as it is in this case, that not all of the profits are attributable to the infringing material, the copyright owner is not entitled to recover all of those profits merely because the infringer fails to establish with certainty the portion attributable to the non-infringing elements. "In cases such as this where an infringer's profits are not entirely due to the infringement, and the evidence suggests some division which may rationally be used as a springboard it is the duty of the court to make some apportionment." Orgel v. Clark Boardman Co., 301 F.2d 119, 121 (2d Cir.1962). As Learned Hand said in Sheldon v. Metro–Goldwyn Pictures Corp., 106 F.2d 45, 51 (2d Cir. 1939), aff'd, 309 U.S. 390, 60 S.Ct. 681, 84 L.Ed. 825 (1940):

> But we are resolved to avoid the one certainly unjust course of giving the plaintiffs everything, because the defendants cannot with certainty compute their own share. In cases where plaintiffs fail to prove their damages exactly, we often make the best estimate we can, even though it is really no more than a guess and

under the guise of resolving all doubts against the defendants we will not deny the one fact that stands undoubted.

By claiming only 1.37% of Schlitz's malt liquor profits, Cream recognizes the impropriety of awarding Cream all of Schlitz's profits on a record that reflects beyond argument that most of these profits were attributable to elements other than the infringement. As to the amount of profits attributable to the infringing material, "what is required is . . . only a reasonable approximation," Sheldon v. Metro–Goldwyn Pictures Corp., 309 U.S. at 408, 60 S.Ct. at 688 and Cream's calculation is in the end no less speculative than that of the court. The disparity between the amount sought by Cream and the amount awarded by the court appears to rest not so much upon a difference in methods of calculation as upon a disagreement as to the extent to which the commercial infringed upon the copyright and the importance of the copyrighted material to the effectiveness of the commercial. These were determinations for the district court to make.

The parties agreed that the issue of damages and profits would be tried to the court. The jury's verdict did not expressly determine the degree to which the commercial infringed upon Cream's copyright. The court's factual findings, though perhaps unfavorable to Cream, do not conflict with the general verdict.

Benton. Cream claimed all of Benton's profit from the TV commercial; the district court awarded none at all. In announcing its judgment the court initially overlooked the claim against Benton. When alerted to the omission the court said, "I will somehow incorporate that into the profit that I awarded with respect to the company. I can't conceive of an award of more than the amount I gave. You can find Benton and Bowles' profit in there by reducing the amount of profit of the beer company."

Obviously it would be improper to assume the profits of the advertising company would be subsumed in the profits of the firm hiring it, if that was the court's intention. Indeed, the profits of the advertising firm were necessarily excluded from the award against the hiring company, since, under § 504(b), Schlitz must be allowed to deduct the monies paid to the advertising firm in calculating its profits.

To avoid unjust enrichment of Benton as a result of its unlawful use of Cream's copyrighted music, the district court must assess a separate award of damages against Benton by making a reasonable approximation of the portion of Benton's profits due to the use of the infringing music.

Plaintiff is awarded costs on appeal including reasonable attorney's fees in an amount to be determined by the district court.

Reversed and remanded for proceedings not inconsistent with this opinion.

NOTES

1. In a handful of short, bold strokes, section 504 of the 1976 Act resolved several questions that had vexed the 1909 Act's provisions for monetary awards. One question, whether the 1909 Act intended awards for damages and profits to be cumulative or alternative, had found the two major copyright circuits sharply divided. Compare Thomas Wilson & Co. v. Irving J. Dorfman Co., 433 F.2d 409, 167 U.S. P.Q. 417 (2d Cir.1970), cert. denied, 401 U.S. 977, 91 S.Ct. 1200, 28 L.Ed. 2d 326, 169 U.S.P.Q. 65 (1971) (cumulative) with Sid & Marty Krofft Television Productions, Inc. v. McDonald's Corp., 562 F.2d 1157, 196 U.S.P.Q. 97 (9th Cir.1977) (alternative). Section 504(b) strikes a balance between the Second Circuit's deterrent approach and the Ninth Circuit's compensatory approach by allowing the copyright owner to recover actual damages and any of the infringer's profits "not taken into account in computing the damages." Thus if, as one element of damages, the copyright owner recovers the profits it would have made on sales lost to the infringer, it can only recover the infringer's profits to the extent that they exceed the owner's lost profits.

Section 504(c), allowing the copyright owner to elect statutory damages, resolves earlier questions about the circumstances in which statutory damage awards were discretionary and the circumstances in which they were mandatory.

2. *Damages.* There are two basic measures of copyright damages. Where the infringer directly competes with the copyright owner, courts commonly use a lost sales measure of damages on the theory that defendant's sales displaced plaintiff's. If the infringer does not directly compete with the copyright owner, courts will typically measure damages by a reasonable royalty or market value. Courts will use the reasonable royalty measure where the copyright owner has previously given licenses; the license fees charged become the "reasonable royalty." If there are no preexisting licenses, courts will measure damages by market value—"what a willing buyer would have been reasonably required to pay to a willing seller for plaintiff['s] work." Sid & Marty Krofft Television Prods., Inc. v. McDonald's Corp., 562 F.2d 1157, 1174, 196 U.S.P.Q. 97 (9th Cir.1977).

3. *Profits.* Sheldon v. Metro–Goldwyn Pictures Corp., 309 U.S. 390, 60 S.Ct. 681, 84 L.Ed. 825, 44 U.S.P.Q. 607 (1940), presaged section 504(b)'s provision for apportioning defendant's profits between those allocable to use of the copyrighted work and those allocable to other elements in the infringing work. The defendant in *Sheldon* had copied plaintiff's play, *Dishonored Lady,* in producing its motion picture, *Letty Lynton.* Defendant had also obtained a license to use another copyrighted work as the basis for its production and had made a substantial investment in producing and promoting the motion picture. Recognizing that a large part of defendant's profits traced to these expenditures, and to the reputation and effort of the movie stars involved, the Court affirmed the lower court's decree apportioning plaintiff's recovery to

twenty percent of the profits earned by the motion picture—"only that part of the profits found to be attributable to the use of the copyrighted material as distinguished from what the infringer himself has supplied. . . ." 309 U.S. at 396, 60 S.Ct. at 682.

Awards of indirect profits, as in *Cream,* are particularly appropriate where the infringing use generates no profits of its own, as is typically the case with advertising. Consider the abuses that might result in these cases from section 504(b)'s allocation of the burden of proof to the infringer: "If General Motors were to steal your copyright and put it in a sales brochure, you could not just put a copy of General Motors' corporate income tax return in the record and rest your case for an award of infringer's profits." Taylor v. Meirick, 712 F.2d 1112, 1122, 219 U.S.P.Q. 420 (7th Cir.1983).

4. *Statutory Damages.* Section 412 of the 1976 Copyright Act provides as a general rule that a copyright owner will not be entitled to statutory damages or attorney's fees for "any infringement of copyright in an unpublished work commenced before the effective date of its registration" or for "any infringement of copyright commenced after first publication of the work and before the effective date of its registration, unless such registration is made within three months after the first publication of the work." Section 412 makes an exception for actions instituted under section 411(b) governing works consisting "of sounds, images, or both, the first fixation of which is made simultaneously with its transmission."

The Berne Convention Implementation Act of 1988 doubled the statutory awards previously available under the 1976 Act—from a $250 minimum and a $10,000 maximum to $500 and $20,000, respectively; from $50,000 to $100,000 for willful infringements; and from $100 to $200 for innocent infringements. Pub.L. No. 100–568, § 10.102 Stat. 2853, 2860 (1988). One reason for the increases was to strengthen the incentive to register claims to copyright.

5. *Attorney's Fees.* Most courts will award attorney's fees where the losing party—plaintiff or defendant—acted in bad faith. A defendant acts in bad faith if it proceeds without any reasonable defense or refuses a reasonable settlement offer. See, e.g., Transgo, Inc. v. Ajac Transmission Parts Corp., 768 F.2d 1001, 227 U.S.P.Q. 598 (9th Cir. 1985), cert. denied, 474 U.S. 1059, 106 S.Ct. 802, 88 L.Ed.2d 778 (1986). A plaintiff acts in bad faith if its "real motive" is "to vex and harass the defendant" or if its "claim is so lacking in merit as to present no arguable question of law or genuine issue of fact." Cloth v. Hyman, 146 F.Supp. 185, 193, 112 U.S.P.Q. 254 (S.D.N.Y.1956).

Courts divide on whether a party must prove bad faith to recover attorney's fees. Some courts require both plaintiffs and defendants to prove bad faith. Other courts apply a double standard: a prevailing defendant must demonstrate the plaintiff's bad faith, but a prevailing plaintiff need not demonstrate the defendant's bad faith. Still other courts have rejected a double standard in favor of an "evenhanded approach" and will award attorney's fees to any prevailing party—

plaintiff or defendant—even absent any showing of bad faith. See P. Goldstein, Copyright § 12.3.2.2 (1989).

6. *Temporary (Preliminary) Injunctions.* Temporary injunctions are more freely available to copyright owners than to patent or trademark owners. Generally, a copyright owner can obtain preliminary relief upon making a prima facie case of the copyright's validity and infringement. Demonstration of irreparable harm, though helpful, is usually not necessary. Compare Rushton Co. v. Vitale, 218 F.2d 434, 436, 104 U.S.P.Q. 158 (2d Cir.1955) ("When a prima facie case for copyright infringement has been made, plaintiffs are entitled to a preliminary injunction without a detailed showing of danger of irreparable harm"), with American Metropolitan Enterprises of New York, Inc. v. Warner Brothers Records, Inc., 389 F.2d 903, 905, 157 U.S.P.Q. 69 (2d Cir.1968) ("A copyright holder in the ordinary case may be presumed to suffer irreparable harm when his right to the exclusive use of the copyrighted material is invaded."). See generally Latman, Preliminary Injunctions in Patent, Trademark and Copyright Cases, 60 Trademark Rep. 506 (1970).

What considerations weigh for and against such liberality in giving threshold relief? Is it a matter for concern that the injunction is directed against conduct that in other contexts might be protected under the first amendment's free speech and press guarantees? If the underlying concern is that the eventual monetary award, coupled with a permanent injunction, will not make the copyright owner whole, would it be better to increase the statutory damage schedule or, possibly, introduce treble damages? Is there anything about the behavior of copyright industries or the solvency of copyright infringers that distinguishes them for these purposes from patent and trademark infringers?

Should the tests for preliminary relief be more closely attuned to the equities and hardships of particular copyright industries? Compare, for example, the situation of fabric designers, whose designs go out of fashion quickly and are even more quickly appropriated by competitors, with the situation of the writer who claims that her story or script outline is being appropriated by defendant motion picture producer in the course of a multimillion dollar production. What are the relative costs of delay to the parties in these two situations? Does it matter that, while the ultimate award of defendant's profits will be apportioned to the benefits gained from use of plaintiff's work, a preliminary injunction will not cut nearly so fine and will effectively halt *all* of defendant's production activities?

On the coercive remedies of seizure and destruction, see Alexander, Discretionary Power to Impound and Destroy Infringing Articles: An Historical Perspective, 29 J. Copyright Soc'y 479 (1982).

7. *Final (Permanent) Injunctions.* On principle, if an infringing work takes only part of a copyrighted work a court will frame its injunction to require only that the infringing matter be deleted. But in cases involving derivative works such as translations and motion pictures, where the infringing and noninfringing material are inextricably

intertwined, courts will enjoin dissemination of the entire infringing work, even though this will prevent the defendant from exploiting its independent contribution.

In cases where the infringing and noninfringing elements cannot be separated, and where the copyrighted elements form only a small part of the defendant's work, would it be preferable to withhold injunctive relief and award only damages or profits? The United States Supreme Court took this approach in Dun v. Lumbermen's Credit Ass'n, 209 U.S. 20, 28 S.Ct. 335, 52 L.Ed. 663 (1908). Noting that the defendant had copied only a small amount of copyrighted material from plaintiff's work, the Court affirmed the lower court's ruling that "the proportion is so insignificant compared with the injury from stopping appellees' use of their enormous volume of independently acquired information, that an injunction would be unconscionable. In such cases, the copyright owner should be remitted to his remedy at law." Specifically, "we think the discretion of the court was wisely exercised in refusing an injunction and remitting the appellants to a court of law to recover such damage as they might there prove that they had sustained." 209 U.S. at 23–24, 28 S.Ct. at 337.

Justice Blackmun, dissenting in Sony Corp. v. Universal City Studios, 464 U.S. 417, 104 S.Ct. 774, 78 L.Ed.2d 574 (1984), concurred in the lower court's "suggestion that an award of damages, or continuing royalties, or even some form of limited injunction, may well be an appropriate means of balancing the equities in this case." 464 U.S. at 499, 104 S.Ct. at 817. Compare Calabresi & Melamed, Property Rules, Liability Rules, and Inalienability: One View of the Cathedral, 85 Harv.L.Rev. 1089 (1972).

8. *Criminal Sanctions.* Section 506(a) of the Copyright Act makes it a crime to infringe a copyright willfully and for purposes of commercial advantage or private financial gain. Willfulness means that the infringer knew not only that she was copying a copyrighted work without the copyright owner's permission, but also that her acts constituted copyright infringement. See, e.g., United States v. Whetzel, 589 F.2d 707, 200 U.S.P.Q. 193 (D.C.Cir.1978). Sections 506(c)–(e) of the Act outlaw fraudulent placement of copyright notice, fraudulent removal of copyright notice, and knowingly false representations of a material fact in a copyright registration application.

9. *Copyright Royalty Tribunal.* The 1976 Copyright Act created the Copyright Royalty Tribunal to administer the Act's compulsory license provisions. As created, the Tribunal consists of five commissioners appointed by the President, with advice and consent of the Senate, for a term of seven years each. Section 801 of the Act directs the Tribunal periodically to adjust the statutorily prescribed license rates for cable transmissions, mechanical reproductions, jukebox performances and public broadcasting. Section 119(c) authorizes the Tribunal to initiate arbitration proceedings to determine the license fees payable under section 119's statutory license for satellite retransmissions. Section 801 directs the Tribunal "to distribute royalty fees

deposited with the Register of Copyrights under sections 111, 116 and 119(b), and to determine, in cases where controversy exists, the distribution of such fees."

See generally, Greenman & Deutsch, The Copyright Royalty Tribunal and the Statutory Mechanical Royalty: History and Prospect, 1 Cardozo Arts & Ent.L.J. 1 (1982). For a comparison of copyright royalty tribunals in several countries, see Copyright Royalty Tribunals: Experiences in Various Countries, 34 J. Copyright Soc'y 147 (1987).

C. INFRINGEMENT

See Statute Supplement 17 U.S.C.A. § 501.

ARNSTEIN v. PORTER, 154 F.2d 464, 68 U.S.P.Q. 288 (2d Cir. 1946). FRANK, J.: The principal question on this appeal is whether the lower court, under Rule 56, properly deprived plaintiff of a trial of his copyright infringement action. The answer depends on whether "there is the slightest doubt as to the facts."

In applying that standard here, it is important to avoid confusing two separate elements essential to a plaintiff's case in such a suit: (a) that defendant copied from plaintiff's copyrighted work and (b) that the copying (assuming it to be proved) went so far as to constitute improper appropriation.

As to the first—copying—the evidence may consist (a) of defendant's admission that he copied or (b) of circumstantial evidence—usually evidence of access—from which the trier of the facts may reasonably infer copying. Of course, if there are no similarities, no amount of evidence of access will suffice to prove copying. If there is evidence of access and similarities exist, then the trier of the facts must determine whether the similarities are sufficient to prove copying. On this issue, analysis ("dissection") is relevant, and the testimony of experts may be received to aid the trier of the facts. If evidence of access is absent, the similarities must be so striking as to preclude the possibility that plaintiff and defendant independently arrived at the same result.

If copying is established, then only does there arise the second issue, that of illicit copying (unlawful appropriation). On that issue . . . the test is the response of the ordinary lay hearer; accordingly, on that issue, "dissection" and expert testimony are irrelevant.

In some cases, the similarities between the plaintiff's and defendant's work are so extensive and striking as, without more, both to justify an inference of copying and to prove improper appropriation. But such double-purpose evidence is not required; that is, if copying is otherwise shown, proof of improper appropriation need not consist of similarities which, standing alone, would support an inference of copying.

SEE v. DURANG

United States Court of Appeals, Ninth Circuit, 1983.
711 F.2d 141, 219 U.S.P.Q. 771.

PER CURIAM

The district court granted summary judgment for defendants-appellees on the ground that no reasonable person could find any substantial similarity of expression between plaintiff's "Fear of Acting" and defendant's "The Actor's Nightmare." We affirm.

I.

Summary judgment was appropriate. Plaintiff has cited no authority for the contention that the court must always view a production of the play, rather than relying solely on the script. That course might be desirable where the question of substantial similarity is close, but here it is not. In any event, it was not alleged that defendant copied his play from the revised version of plaintiff's play, which plaintiff wished to have performed for comparison, but instead from plaintiff's first draft, which was before the court.

The court properly concluded that judgment should not be deferred to afford plaintiff an opportunity to present evidence at trial that defendant had previously copied another author's play, which defendant denied. Had the case been tried, the court could have excluded such evidence as minimally relevant and presenting serious problems of delay and confusion.

Summary judgment did not preclude reasonable discovery. The only discovery plaintiff suggests is the production of early drafts of defendant's play on the theory they might reflect copying from plaintiff's play that was disguised or deleted in later drafts. Copying deleted or so disguised as to be unrecognizable is not copying.

II.

No special standard is applied in determining whether summary judgment is appropriate on the issue of substantial similarity of expression in a copyright case. Contrary to plaintiff's contention, Sid & Marty Krofft Television Productions v. McDonald's Corp., 562 F.2d 1157, 196 USPQ 97 (9th Cir.1977), does not hold that summary judgment is always inappropriate on the issue of substantial similarity of expression if there is a substantial similarity of ideas. Plaintiff offers neither authority nor reason supporting such a per se rule. Summary judgment is proper if reasonable minds could not differ as to the presence or absence of substantial similarity of expression. Twentieth Century–Fox Film Corp. v. MCA, Inc., 696 F.2d 689, 691, 217 USPQ 611, 613 (9th Cir.1983). Sid & Marty Krofft, 562 F.2d at 1165, 196 USPQ at 103 (9th Cir.1977), rejected the suggestion in Arnstein v. Porter, 154 F.2d 464, 473, 68 USPQ 288, 297 (2d Cir.1946), that summary judgment can be granted for the defendant only if the similarities are "trifling."

Twentieth Century–Fox cites Arnstein with approval, but not on this point. 696 F.2d at 691, 217 USPQ at 613.

We also disagree with plaintiff's contention that the district court improperly applied the "scenes a faire" doctrine. The court's characterization of the doctrine as relating to unprotected *"ideas"* may have been technically inaccurate, but the court properly applied the doctrine to hold unprotectable forms of expression that were either stock scenes or scenes that flowed necessarily from common unprotectable ideas. "Common" in this context means common to the works at issue, not necessarily, as plaintiff suggests, commonly found in other artistic works. Nor has the doctrine "fallen into disuse in this circuit" as plaintiff suggests.

The district court correctly concluded that no reasonable trier of fact could find the two plays to be substantially similar in their form of expressing common ideas.

Although our reasons differ from those of the district court with respect to a few of the alleged similarities relied upon by plaintiff, we have no difficulty joining in the district court's conclusion as to each of these alleged similarities.

Alleged similarities one, two, four, five, six, seven, eight, nine, twelve, and nineteen follow obviously from the unprotected idea of a surprised understudy, and are therefore unprotected "scenes a faire."

Alleged similarities ten, thirteen, fourteen, fifteen, sixteen, seventeen, and twenty are not in fact similarities. There is no similarity between the life-size cut-outs on stage and flash bulbs going off in the audience; Potter does not try to explain to the audience what is going on as the accountant does; the references to Jane Fonda are entirely different; in plaintiff's play, Potter must fill three roles at once, while in defendant's play additional understudies are introduced, none of whom shares the accountant's confusion; completely different types of characters are shown reading lines from a script; and the death scene and the clue to the audience that a dream may be involved are not related in the time or logic in plaintiff's play in the same way they are in defendant's play.

The remaining five similarities are not sufficient to convince any reasonable trier of fact that the plays are substantially similar. The two plays differ substantially in their treatment of the surprised understudy. In plaintiff's play, Potter's predicament is one of many illustrations of actors' fears, not the focus of the play, and the dominant emotion during her performance is the humiliation of performing incompetently. In defendant's play, the accountant is not one of several examples, but the central figure with whom the audience identifies, and the dominant emotion is not humiliation but an Alice in Wonderland-like bewilderment about what is going on and why no one else seems to think it strange.

Plaintiff argues the district court erred by comparing the plays "as a whole" in addition to considering the alleged similarities individually, because copying of only a portion of another's work constitutes infringement. The cases plaintiff cites establish only that where substantial similarity in protected expression does exist, it is not excused by the presence of additional, dissimilar material. Here the district court correctly found no substantial similarities in the manner in which protected ideas were expressed. In arriving at this conclusion, it was entirely appropriate to view the individual similarities together and in context since, as plaintiff himself insists, substantial similarity in the expression of an idea may appear from the mood evoked by the work as a whole. The district court's analysis excluded neither the possibility of substantial similarity that was partial, nor substantial similarity that arose from the cumulation of individually trivial similarities.

III.

We deny defendant's request for an award for attorney's fees pursuant to 17 U.S.C. § 505. Although plaintiff's argument on substantial similarity was weak, we do not consider the appeal frivolous in light of the relatively strict approach this court has taken to summary judgment in copyright cases.

The judgment is *Affirmed*.

NOTES

1. *Unlawful Appropriation.* In Sid & Marty Krofft Television Prods., Inc. v. McDonald's Corp., 562 F.2d 1157, 196 U.S.P.Q. 97 (9th Cir.1977), the Ninth Circuit Court of Appeals applied a somewhat cloudy gloss to Arnstein v. Porter's two-part test for unlawful appropriation. *Krofft* characterized the first part of the test as an "extrinsic" test and the second part as an "intrinsic" test. The first part requires analysis of plaintiff's and defendant's works to separate their expression from their underlying ideas; it "is extrinsic because it depends not on the responses of the trier of fact, but on specific criteria which can be listed and analyzed. Such criteria include the type of artwork involved, the materials used, the subject matter, and the setting for the subject. Since it is an extrinsic test, analytic dissection and expert testimony are appropriate." By contrast, the second, "intrinsic" measure depends on "the response of the ordinary reasonable person. . . . It is intrinsic because it does not depend on the type of external criteria and analysis which marks the extrinsic test. . . . Because this is an intrinsic test, analytic dissection and expert testimony are not appropriate." 562 F.2d at 1164.

Krofft said that the aim of the extrinsic test is to determine "whether there is substantial similarity of ideas." 652 F.2d at 1164. Can you imagine a copyright infringement case in which the ideas underlying the two works will not be similar? Presumably *Krofft* intended only to require an initial separation of unprotected ideas from protected expression and, at the second stage, to subject protected expression to the "intrinsic" test. The court might have made the point more clearly if it had retained the phrasing it reportedly employed in an earlier draft of its opinion—using the term "objective" in place of the term "extrinsic" and "subjective" in place of "intrinsic." See Knowles & Palmieri, Dissecting Krofft: An Expression of New Ideas in Copyright?, 8 San Fern. V.L.Rev. 109, 133 n. 81 (1980).

2. *Audience Test.* The audience test—the second part of Arnstein v. Porter's test of unlawful appropriation—traces to a dictum in Daly v. Palmer, 6 F.Cas. 1132 (C.C.S.D.N.Y.1868) (No. 3552), that a copyright is infringed if the plaintiff's and defendant's works are "recognized by the spectator, through any of the senses to which the representation is addressed, as conveying substantially the same impressions to, and exciting the same emotions in, the mind, in the same sequence or order." Id. at 1138. What differences separate copyright law's audience test from trademark law's consumer confusion measure, page 341, above? See generally, Kegan, Survey Evidence in Copyright Litigation, 32 J. Copyright Soc'y 283 (1984).

3. *Common Errors.* The presence of common errors in plaintiff's and defendant's works provides virtually irrefutable proof that the defendant copied from the plaintiff. Coincidence can rarely if ever explain the fact that defendant's map, like plaintiff's, contains sixteen misspellings and locates a river on the wrong side of a main highway, or that defendant's doll has the same misplaced right thumbnail as does plaintiff's. See General Drafting Co. v. Andrews, 37 F.2d 54, 4 U.S.P.Q. 72 (2d Cir.1930); Hassenfeld Bros., Inc. v. Mego Corp., 150 U.S.P.Q. 786 (S.D.N.Y.1966). Defendant's only excuse in these cases may be that the error appeared in a common source from which both the plaintiff and defendant copied.

A study of fifty-two cases involving common errors revealed that in at least eight cases the plaintiff had inserted the error to trap unwary copyists; seven of these cases involved directories and one involved a catalogue. In American Travel & Hotel Directory Co. v. Gehring Publishing Co., 4 F.2d 415 (S.D.N.Y.1925), for example, the plaintiff listed several nonexistent hotels in its hotel directory. The study's author observed, "My sympathies, however, are with the weary traveler who late at night tries to locate one of the trap hotels." Taylor, Common Errors as Evidence of Copying, 22 Bull. Copyright Soc'y 444, 448 (1975).

4. *The Role of Similarity in Proof of Infringement.* As noted in Arnstein v. Porter, similarities between two works may be used to prove one or more of three facts. First, similarities between plaintiff's and defendant's works—taken together with evidence of defendant's access to plaintiff's work—may support the inference that the defendant copied from the plaintiff's work. Second, similarities between the two works may substitute for direct proof of access. Third, similarities may support a finding of unlawful appropriation.

Should courts require a more extensive showing of similarity when there is no direct proof of access than when there is? At least one court has espoused an "inverse ratio" rule: "[W]hen access is established a lesser degree of similarity is required." Morse v. Fields, 127 F.Supp. 63, 66, 104 U.S.P.Q. 54 (S.D.N.Y.1954). Judge Clark rejected this rule in Arc Music Corp. v. Lee, 296 F.2d 186, 187, 131 U.S.P.Q. 338 (2d Cir.1961): "We fear that counsel with that semantic proclivity natural to our profession have allowed themselves to be seduced by a superficially attractive apophthegm which upon examination confuses more than it clarifies. The logical outcome of the claimed principle is obviously that proof of actual access will render a showing of similarities entirely unnecessary." Is it?

5. *Expert Testimony.* Courts today generally admit expert testimony on the question of copying. Just as surface similarities may lead a lay factfinder to conclude that the defendant copied from plaintiff's work, so dissimilarities may lead to the opposite conclusion. The expert eye or ear can discern more subtle, structural clues. Courts also allow experts to dissect the competing works to identify the protectible elements they have in common. However, courts generally reject expert testimony on the question of audience reaction.

See generally, Orth, The Use of Expert Witness in Musical Infringement Cases, 16 U.Pitt.L.Rev. 232 (1955); Sorensen & Sorensen, Re–Examining the Traditional Legal Test of Literary Similarity: A Proposal for Content Analysis, 37 Cornell L.Q. 638 (1952).

6. *Strict Liability.* Although a plaintiff must, to prevail, prove that the defendant copied his work, he need not prove that the copying was intentional. One who copies an overheard tune or another's copy of a copyrighted work is liable even if he had no knowledge that the work was covered by copyright. The reason for the rule, given in De Acosta v. Brown, 146 F.2d 408, 63 U.S.P.Q. 311 (2d Cir.1944), cert. denied, 325 U.S. 862, 65 S.Ct. 1197, 89 L.Ed.1983 (1945), is that "the protection accorded literary property would be of little value if it did not go against third persons, or if, it might be added, insulation from payment of damages could be secured by a publisher by merely refraining from making inquiry." 146 F.2d at 412. Learned Hand dissented in *De Acosta.* "If my brothers are right, a publisher must be prepared to respond in damages to any author who can prove that the publisher has incorporated, however innocently, and at whatever remove, any part of the author's work. If that possibility were to hover over all publication, it would, I believe, be a not negligible depressant upon the dissemination of knowledge." 146 F.2d at 413.

The Copyright Act meliorates the strict liability principle through an adjustment of remedies. Section 504(c)(2) reduces the floor for statutory damages if the "infringer was not aware and had no reason to believe that his or her acts constituted an infringement of copyright," and remits statutory damages entirely in certain circumstances if the infringer believed that its use was fair under the terms of section 107. Do these remedial limitations sufficiently answer Judge Hand's concerns?

Should the rule of strict liability be made to depend upon the innocent infringer's ability to insure against errors and omissions, or to contract for an indemnity from the knowing infringer? One form of agreement used in the book publishing trade provides:

The Author represents and warrants that he has full power to enter into this agreement; that he will use all reasonable care to ensure that the work as submitted is innocent and without matter that is libelous or injurious or otherwise actionable or that will infringe any copyright, proprietary right at common law, or any right of privacy; that if it should be necessary for him to incorporate in the work any material, illustrations, or text that has been published or is the property of others, he will incorporate such material only with the knowledge and consent of the Publisher and will furnish to the Publisher such releases as the Publisher may deem necessary. The Author agrees that he and his legal representatives will indemnify and hold the Publisher harmless from any claim, suit, proceeding, or prosecution, including the reasonable costs of defense (or any resulting liability, loss, expense, or damage), asserted or instituted by reason of publication or sale of the work and arising from the lack of reasonable care or intentional act of the Author. The Author hereby authorizes the Publisher to defend any and all suits and proceedings that may be brought against it arising out of the publication of the work; provided, however, that the Author will not be liable for any amount which the Publisher has agreed to pay in settlement of any such suit or proceeding unless the Author shall consent to such settlement.

What changes to this language would you advise Author to propose? How would you advise Publisher?

See Radin, The Significance of Intent to Copy in a Civil Action for Copyright Infringement, 54 Temple L.Q. 1 (1981).

7. Courts apply the tests for copyright infringement differently to different kinds of subject matter. For example, because the elements available for musical composition—rhythm, melody, harmony—are more limited than the elements of literary composition, courts dealing with musical compositions apply the infringement tests more exactingly.

Consider the following description of the differences posed by literary works, visual works and characters:

A story has a linear dimension: it begins, continues, and ends. If a defendant copies substantial portions of a plaintiff's sequence of events, he does not escape infringement by adding original episodes somewhere along the line. A graphic or three-dimensional work is created to be perceived as an entirety. Significant dissimilarities between two works of this sort inevitably lessen the similarity that would otherwise exist between the total perceptions of the two works. The graphic rendering of a character has aspects of both the linear, literary mode and the multi-dimensional total perception. What the character thinks, feels, says, and does and the descriptions conveyed by the author through the comments of other characters in the work episodically fill out a viewer's understanding of the character. At the same time, the visual perception of the character tends to create a dominant impression against which the similarity of a defendant's character may be readily compared, and significant differences readily noted.

Ultimately, care must be taken to draw the elusive distinction between a substantially similar character that infringes a copyrighted character despite slight differences in appearance, behavior, or traits, and a somewhat similar though non-infringing character whose appearance, behavior, or traits, and especially their combination, significantly differ from those of a copyrighted character, even though the second character is reminiscent of the first one. Stirring one's memory of a copyrighted character is not the same as appearing to be substantially similar to that character, and only the latter is infringement.

Warner Bros., Inc. v. American Broadcasting Cos., 720 F.2d 231, 241–42, 222 U.S.P.Q. 101 (2d Cir.1983).

1. LITERATURE

NICHOLS v. UNIVERSAL PICTURES CORP.

United States Circuit Court of Appeals, Second Circuit, 1930.
45 F.2d 119, 7 U.S.P.Q. 84.

L. HAND, Circuit Judge.

The plaintiff is the author of a play, "Abie's Irish Rose," which it may be assumed was properly copyrighted under section five, subdivision (d), of the Copyright Act, 17 U.S.C.A. § 5(d). The defendant produced publicly a motion picture play, "The Cohens and The Kellys," which the plaintiff alleges was taken from it. As we think the defendant's play too unlike the plaintiff's to be an infringement, we may assume, arguendo, that in some details the defendant used the plaintiff's play, as will subsequently appear, though we do not so decide. It therefore becomes necessary to give an outline of the two plays.

"Abie's Irish Rose" presents a Jewish family living in prosperous circumstances in New York. The father, a widower, is in business as a merchant, in which his son and only child helps him. The boy has philandered with young women, who to his father's great disgust have always been Gentiles, for he is obsessed with a passion that his daughter-in-law shall be an orthodox Jewess. When the play opens the son, who has been courting a young Irish Catholic girl, has already married her secretly before a Protestant minister, and is concerned to soften the blow for his father, by securing a favorable impression of his bride, while concealing her faith and race. To accomplish this he introduces her to his father at his home as a Jewess, and lets it appear that he is interested in her, though he conceals the marriage. The girl somewhat reluctantly falls in with the plan; the father takes the bait, becomes infatuated with the girl, concludes that they must marry, and assumes that of course they will, if he so decides. He calls in a rabbi, and prepares for the wedding according to the Jewish rite.

Meanwhile the girl's father, also a widower, who lives in California, and is as intense in his own religious antagonism as the Jew, has been called to New York, supposing that his daughter is to marry an Irishman and a Catholic. Accompanied by a priest, he arrives at the house at the moment when the marriage is being celebrated, but too late to prevent it, and the two fathers, each infuriated by the proposed union of his child to a heretic, fall into unseemly and grotesque antics. The priest and the rabbi become friendly, exchange trite sentiments about religion, and agree that the match is good. Apparently out of abundant caution, the priest celebrates the marriage for a third time, while the girl's father is inveigled away. The second act closes with each father, still outraged, seeking to find some way by which the union, thus trebly insured, may be dissolved.

The last act takes place about a year later, the young couple having meanwhile been abjured by each father, and left to their own resources. They have had twins, a boy and a girl, but their fathers know no more than that a child has been born. At Christmas each, led by his craving to see his grandchild, goes separately to the young folks' home, where they encounter each other, each laden with gifts, one for a boy, the other for a girl. After some slapstick comedy, depending upon the insistence of each that he is right about the sex of the grandchild, they become reconciled when they learn the truth, and that each child is to bear the given name of a grandparent. The curtain falls as the fathers are exchanging amenities, and the Jew giving evidence of an abatement in the strictness of his orthodoxy.

"The Cohens and The Kellys" presents two families, Jewish and Irish, living side by side in the poorer quarters of New York in a state of perpetual enmity. The wives in both cases are still living, and share in the mutual animosity, as do two small sons, and even the respective dogs. The Jews have a daughter, the Irish a son; the Jewish father is in the clothing business; the Irishman is a policeman. The children are in love with each other, and secretly marry, apparently after the play opens. The Jew, being in great financial straits, learns from a lawyer that he has fallen heir to a large fortune from a great-aunt, and moves into a great house, fitted luxuriously. Here he and his family live in vulgar ostentation, and here the Irish boy seeks out his Jewish bride, and is chased away by the angry father. The Jew then abuses the Irishman over the telephone, and both become hysterically excited. The extremity of his feelings makes the Jew sick, so that he must go to Florida for a rest, just before which the daughter discloses her marriage to her mother.

On his return the Jew finds that his daughter has borne a child; at first he suspects the lawyer, but eventually learns the truth and is overcome with anger at such a low alliance. Meanwhile, the Irish family who have been forbidden to see the grandchild, go to the Jew's house, and after a violent scene between the two fathers in which the Jew disowns his daughter, who decides to go back with her husband, the Irishman takes her back with her baby to his own poor lodgings. The lawyer, who had hoped to marry the Jew's daughter, seeing his plan foiled, tells the Jew that his fortune really belongs to the Irishman, who was also related to the dead woman, but offers to conceal his knowledge, if the Jew will share the loot. This the Jew repudiates, and, leaving the astonished lawyer, walks through the rain to his enemy's house to surrender the property. He arrives in great dejection, tells the truth, and abjectly turns to leave. A reconciliation ensues, the Irishman agreeing to share with him equally. The Jew shows some interest in his grandchild, though this is at most a minor motive in the reconciliation, and the curtain falls while the two are in their cups, the Jew insisting that in the firm name for the business, which they are to carry on jointly, his name shall stand first.

It is of course essential to any protection of literary property, whether at common-law or under the statute, that the right cannot be limited literally to the text, else a plagiarist would escape by immaterial variations. That has never been the law, but, as soon as literal appropriation ceases to be the test, the whole matter is necessarily at large, so that, as was recently well said by a distinguished judge, the decisions cannot help much in a new case. Fendler v. Morosco, 253 N.Y. 281, 292, 171 N.E. 56. When plays are concerned, the plagiarist may excise a separate scene, or he may appropriate part of the dialogue. Then the question is whether the part so taken is "substantial," and therefore not a "fair use" of the copyrighted work; it is the same question as arises in the case of any other copyrighted work. But when the plagiarist does not take out a block in situ, but an abstract of the whole, decision is more troublesome. Upon any work, and especially upon a play, a great number of patterns of increasing generality will fit equally well, as more and more of the incident is left out. The last may perhaps be no more than the most general statement of what the play is about, and at times might consist only of its title; but there is a point in this series of abstractions where they are no longer protected, since otherwise the playwright could prevent the use of his "ideas," to which, apart from their expression, his property is never extended. Nobody has ever been able to fix that boundary, and nobody ever can. In some cases the question has been treated as though it were analogous to lifting a portion out of the copyrighted work, but the analogy is not a good one, because, though the skeleton is a part of the body, it pervades and supports the whole. In such cases we are rather concerned with the line between expression and what is expressed. As respects plays, the controversy chiefly centers upon the characters and sequence of incident, these being the substance.

We did not in Dymow v. Bolton, 11 F. (2d) 690, hold that a plagiarist was never liable for stealing a plot; that would have been flatly against our rulings in Dam v. Kirk La Shelle Co., 175 F. 902, 41 L.R.A.(N.S.) 1002, 20 Ann.Cas. 1173, and Stodart v. Mutual Film Co., 249 F. 513, affirming my decision in (D.C.) 249 F. 507; neither of which we meant to overrule. We found the plot of the second play was too different to infringe, because the most detailed pattern, common to both, eliminated so much from each that its content went into the public domain; and for this reason we said, "this mere subsection of a plot was not susceptible of copyright." But we do not doubt that two plays may correspond in plot closely enough for infringement. How far that correspondence must go is another matter. Nor need we hold that the same may not be true as to the characters, quite independently of the "plot" proper, though, as far as we know, such a case has never arisen. If Twelfth Night were copyrighted, it is quite possible that a second comer might so closely imitate Sir Toby Belch or Malvolio as to infringe, but it would not be enough that for one of his characters he cast a riotous knight who kept wassail to the discomfort of the household, or a vain and foppish steward who became amorous of his mistress. These would be no more than Shakespeare's "ideas" in the play, as little capable of monopoly as Einstein's Doctrine of Relativity, or Darwin's theory of the Origin of Species. It follows that the less developed the characters, the less they can be copyrighted; that is the penalty an author must bear for marking them too indistinctly.

In the two plays at bar we think both as to incident and character, the defendant took no more—assuming that it took anything at all—than the law allowed. The stories are quite different. One is of a religious zealot who insists upon his child's marrying no one outside his faith; opposed by another who is in this respect just like him, and is his foil. Their difference in race is merely an obbligato to the main theme, religion. They sink their differences through grandparental pride and affection. In the other, zealotry is wholly absent; religion does not even appear. It is true that the parents are hostile to each other in part because they differ in race; but the marriage of their son to a Jew does not apparently offend the Irish family at all, and it exacerbates the existing animosity of the Jew, principally because he has become rich, when he learns it. They are reconciled through the honesty of the Jew and the generosity of the Irishman; the grandchild has nothing whatever to do with it. The only matter common to the two is a quarrel between a Jewish and an Irish father, the marriage of their children, the birth of grandchildren and a reconciliation.

If the defendant took so much from the plaintiff, it may well have been because her amazing success seemed to prove that this was a subject of enduring popularity. Even so, granting that the plaintiff's play was wholly original, and assuming that novelty is not essential to a copyright, there is no monopoly in such a background. Though the plaintiff discovered the vein, she could not keep it to herself; so defined, the theme was too generalized an abstraction from what she wrote. It was only a part of her "ideas."

Nor does she fare better as to her characters. It is indeed scarcely credible that she should not have been aware of those stock figures, the low comedy Jew and Irishman. The defendant has not taken from her more than their prototypes have contained for many decades. If so, obviously so to generalize her copyright, would allow her to cover what was not original with her. But we need not hold this as matter of fact, much as we might be justified. Even though we take it that she devised her figures out of her brain de novo, still the defendant was within its rights.

There are but four characters common to both plays, the lovers and the fathers. The lovers are so faintly indicated as to be no more than stage properties. They are loving and fertile; that is really all that can be said of them, and anyone else is quite within his rights if he puts loving and fertile lovers in a play of his own, wherever he gets the cue. The plaintiff's Jew is quite unlike the defendant's. His obsession is his religion, on which depends such racial animosity as he has. He is affectionate, warm and patriarchal. None of these fit the defendant's Jew, who shows affection for his daughter only once, and who has none but the most superficial interest in his grandchild. He is tricky, ostentatious and vulgar, only by misfortune redeemed into honesty. Both are grotesque, extravagant and quarrelsome; both are fond of display; but these common qualities make up only a small part of their simple pictures, no more than any one might lift if he chose. The Irish fathers are even more unlike; the plaintiff's a mere symbol for religious fanaticism and patriarchal pride, scarcely a character at all. Neither quality appears in the defendant's, for while he goes to get his grandchild, it is rather out of a truculent determination not to be forbidden, than from pride in his progeny. For the rest he is only a grotesque hobbledehoy, used for low comedy of the most conventional sort, which any one might borrow, if he chanced not to know the exemplar.

The defendant argues that the case is controlled by my decision in Fisher v. Dillingham (D.C.) 298 F. 145. Neither my brothers nor I wish to throw doubt upon the doctrine of that case, but it is not applicable here. We assume that the plaintiff's play is altogether original, even to an extent that in fact it is hard to believe. We assume further that, so far as it has been anticipated by earlier plays of which she knew nothing, that fact is immaterial. Still, as we have already said, her copyright did not cover everything that might be drawn from her play; its content went to some extent into the public domain. We have to decide how much, and while we are as aware as any one that the line, wherever it is drawn, will seem arbitrary, that is no excuse for not drawing it; it is a question such as courts must answer in nearly all cases. Whatever may be the difficulties a priori, we have no question on which side of the line this case falls. A comedy based upon conflicts between Irish and Jews, into which the marriage of their children enters, is no more susceptible of copyright than the outline of Romeo and Juliet.

The plaintiff has prepared an elaborate analysis of the two plays, showing a "quadrangle" of the common characters, in which each is represented by the emotions which he discovers. She presents the resulting parallelism as proof of infringement, but the adjectives employed are so general as to be quite useless. Take for example the attribute of "love" ascribed to both Jews. The plaintiff has depicted her father as deeply attached to his son, who is his hope and joy; not so, the defendant, whose father's conduct is throughout not actuated by any affection for his daughter, and who is merely once overcome for the moment by her distress when he has violently dismissed her lover.

"Anger" covers emotions aroused by quite different occasions in each case; so do "anxiety," "despondency" and "disgust." It is unnecessary to go through the catalogue for emotions are too much colored by their causes to be a test when used so broadly. This is not the proper approach to a solution; it must be more ingenuous, more like that of a spectator, who would rely upon the complex of his impressions of each character.

We cannot approve the length of the record, which was due chiefly to the use of expert witnesses. Argument is argument whether in the box or at the bar, and its proper place is the last. The testimony of an expert upon such issues, especially his cross-examination, greatly extends the trial and contributes nothing which cannot be better heard after the evidence is all submitted. It ought not to be allowed at all; and while its admission is not a ground for reversal, it cumbers the case and tends to confusion, for the more the court is led into the intricacies of dramatic craftsmanship, the less likely it is to stand upon the firmer, if more naive, ground of its considered impressions upon its own perusal. We hope that in this class of cases such evidence may in the future be entirely excluded, and the case confined to the actual issues; that is, whether the copyrighted work was original, and whether the defendant copied it, so far as the supposed infringement is identical.

The defendant, "the prevailing party," was entitled to a reasonable attorney's fee (section 40 of the Copyright Act [17 U.S.C.A. § 40]).

Decree affirmed.

NOTE

Just as, for purposes of copyright infringement, literary works differ from musical works and from works of visual art, so pertinent differences may exist between different forms of literary works. Should novels be treated differently from plays? From textbooks? From directories?

In Kepner–Tregoe, Inc. v. Carabio, 203 U.S.P.Q. 124 (E.D.Mich. 1979), the court took care to distinguish between conventional literary works and instructional materials. One distinction is that "in teaching, a noticeable style is a hindrance. Two simple and straightforward explanations of an economic law or principle must bear a close resemblance, so greater similarity must be allowed." 203 U.S.P.Q. at 132. Another distinction is that in a literary work, plot, theme and character are important. "There is an unlimited variety which may be invented. Authors are not confined. In addition, there is no societal interest in many variants on a single theme or plot, nor is there the likelihood that by extending broad protection, entry to the market for literary works will be foreclosed. But with respect to the useful arts, there is a societal interest in having many offer the art in the marketplace. Our economy functions best under competition. And, if many can present variants on the copyrighted material, we hope that advances in its teaching will result. As a consequence, more similarity between two works of a commercial and useful character is required to

find infringement than between two literary works." 203 U.S.P.Q. at
131. The court concluded that although plaintiff had a "thin" copyright, defendant had infringed it "in certain minor respects." 203 U.S.
P.Q. at 132.

What if the copyrighted work is a scientific paper from which the
accused work—a novel—borrows literary elements? See Musto v. Meyer, 434 F.Supp. 32, 196 U.S.P.Q. 820 (S.D.N.Y.1977), aff'd without
opinion, 598 F.2d 609 (2d Cir.1979).

2. MUSIC

SELLE v. GIBB

United States Court of Appeals, Seventh Circuit, 1984.
741 F.2d 896, 223 U.S.P.Q. 195.

CUDAHY, Circuit Judge.

The plaintiff, Ronald H. Selle, brought a suit against three brothers, Maurice, Robin and Barry Gibb, known collectively as the popular
singing group, the Bee Gees, alleging that the Bee Gees, in their hit
tune, "How Deep Is Your Love," had infringed the copyright of his
song, "Let It End." The jury returned a verdict in plaintiff's favor on
the issue of liability in a bifurcated trial. The district court, Judge
George N. Leighton, granted the defendants' motion for judgment
notwithstanding the verdict and, in the alternative, for a new trial.
Selle v. Gibb, 567 F.Supp. 1173 (N.D.Ill.1983). We affirm the grant of
the motion for judgment notwithstanding the verdict.

I

Selle composed his song, "Let It End," in one day in the fall of 1975
and obtained a copyright for it on November 17, 1975. He played his
song with his small band two or three times in the Chicago area and
sent a tape and lead sheet of the music to eleven music recording and
publishing companies. Eight of the companies returned the materials
to Selle; three did not respond. This was the extent of the public
dissemination of Selle's song. Selle first became aware of the Bee Gees'
song, "How Deep Is Your Love," in May 1978 and thought that he
recognized the music as his own, although the lyrics were different. He
also saw the movie, "Saturday Night Fever," the sound track of which
features the song "How Deep Is Your Love," and again recognized the
music. He subsequently sued the three Gibb brothers; Paramount
Pictures Corporation, which made and distributed the movie; and
Phonodisc, Inc., now known as Polygram Distribution, Inc., which made
and distributed the cassette tape of "How Deep Is Your Love."

The Bee Gees are internationally known performers and creators of
popular music. They have composed more than 160 songs; their sheet
music, records and tapes have been distributed worldwide, some of the
albums selling more than 30 million copies. The Bee Gees, however, do
not themselves read or write music. In composing a song, their
practice was to tape a tune, which members of their staff would later

transcribe and reduce to a form suitable for copyrighting, sale and performance by both the Bee Gees and others.

In addition to their own testimony at trial, the Bee Gees presented testimony by their manager, Dick Ashby, and two musicians, Albhy Galuten and Blue Weaver, who were on the Bee Gees' staff at the time "How Deep Is Your Love" was composed. These witnesses described in detail how, in January 1977, the Bee Gees and several members of their staff went to a recording studio in the Chateau d'Herouville about 25 miles northwest of Paris. There the group composed at least six new songs and mixed a live album. Barry Gibb's testimony included a detailed explanation of a work tape which was introduced into evidence and played in court. This tape preserves the actual process of creation during which the brothers, and particularly Barry, created the tune of the accused song while Weaver, a keyboard player, played the tune which was hummed or sung by the brothers. Although the tape does not seem to preserve the very beginning of the process of creation, it does depict the process by which ideas, notes, lyrics and bits of the tune were gradually put together.

Following completion of this work tape, a demo tape was made. The work tape, demo tape and a vocal-piano version taken from the demo tape are all in the key of E flat. Lead sheet music, dated March 6, 1977, is in the key of E. On March 7, 1977, a lead sheet of "How Deep Is Your Love" was filed for issuance of a United States copyright, and in November 1977, a piano-vocal arrangement was filed in the Copyright Office.

The only expert witness to testify at trial was Arrand Parsons, a professor of music at Northwestern University who has had extensive professional experience primarily in classical music. He has been a program annotator for the Chicago Symphony Orchestra and the New Orleans Symphony Orchestra and has authored works about musical theory. Prior to this case, however, he had never made a comparative analysis of two popular songs. Dr. Parsons testified on the basis of several charts comparing the musical notes of each song and a comparative recording prepared under his direction.

According to Dr. Parsons' testimony, the first eight bars of each song (Theme A) have twenty-four of thirty-four notes in plaintiff's composition and twenty-four of forty notes in defendants' composition which are identical in pitch and symmetrical position. Of thirty-five rhythmic impulses in plaintiff's composition and forty in defendants', thirty are identical. In the last four bars of both songs (Theme B), fourteen notes in each are identical in pitch, and eleven of the fourteen rhythmic impulses are identical. Both Theme A and Theme B appear in the same position in each song but with different intervening material.

Dr. Parsons testified that, in his opinion, "the two songs had such striking similarities that they could not have been written independent of one another." Tr. 202. He also testified that he did not know of two songs by different composers "that contain as many striking similarities" as do the two songs at issue here. However, on several occasions, he declined to say that the similarities could only have resulted from copying.

Following presentation of the case, the jury returned a verdict for the plaintiff on the issue of liability, the only question presented to the jury. Judge Leighton, however, granted the defendants' motion for judgment notwithstanding the verdict and, in the alternative, for a new trial. He relied primarily on the plaintiff's inability to demonstrate that the defendants had access to the plaintiff's song, without which a claim of copyright infringement could not prevail regardless how similar the two compositions are. Further, the plaintiff failed to contradict or refute the testimony of the defendants and their witnesses describing the independent creation process of "How Deep Is Your Love." Finally, Judge Leighton concluded that "the inferences on which plaintiff relies is not a logical, permissible deduction from proof of 'striking similarity' or substantial similarity; it is 'at war with the undisputed facts,' and it is inconsistent with the proof of nonaccess to plaintiff's song by the Bee Gees at the time in question.". . . .

III

Selle's primary contention on this appeal is that the district court misunderstood the theory of proof of copyright infringement on which he based his claim. Under this theory, copyright infringement can be demonstrated when, even in the absence of any direct evidence of access, the two pieces in question are so strikingly similar that access can be inferred from such similarity alone. Selle argues that the testimony of his expert witness, Dr. Parsons, was sufficient evidence of such striking similarity that it was permissible for the jury, even in the absence of any other evidence concerning access, to infer that the Bee Gees had access to plaintiff's song and indeed copied it.

In establishing a claim of copyright infringement of a musical composition, the plaintiff must prove (1) ownership of the copyright in the complaining work; (2) originality of the work; (3) copying of the work by the defendant, and (4) a substantial degree of similarity between the two works. See Sherman, *Musical Copyright Infringement: The Requirement of Substantial Similarity.* Copyright Law Symposium, Number 92, American Society of Composers, Authors and Publishers 81–82. Columbia University Press (1977) [hereinafter "Sherman, *Musical Copyright Infringement* "]. The only element which is at issue in this appeal is proof of copying; the first two elements are essentially conceded, while the fourth (substantial similarity) is, at least in these circumstances, closely related to the third element under plaintiff's theory of the case.

Proof of copying is crucial to any claim of copyright infringement because no matter how similar the two works may be (even to the point of identity), if the defendant did not copy the accused work, there is no infringement. However, because direct evidence of copying is rarely available, the plaintiff can rely upon circumstantial evidence to prove this essential element, and the most important component of this sort of circumstantial evidence is proof of access. The plaintiff may be able to introduce direct evidence of access when, for example, the work was sent directly to the defendant (whether a musician or a publishing company) or a close associate of the defendant. On the other hand, the plaintiff may be able to establish a reasonable possibility of access when, for example, the complaining work has been widely disseminated to the public.

If, however, the plaintiff does not have direct evidence of access, then an inference of access may still be established circumstantially by proof of similarity which is so striking that the possibilities of independent creation, coincidence and prior common source are, as a practical matter, precluded. If the plaintiff presents evidence of striking similarity sufficient to raise an inference of access, then copying is presumably proved simultaneously, although the fourth element (substantial similarity) still requires proof that the defendant copied a substantial amount of the complaining work. The theory which Selle attempts to apply to this case is based on proof of copying by circumstantial proof of access established by striking similarity between the two works.

One difficulty with plaintiff's theory is that no matter how great the similarity between the two works, it is not their similarity *per se* which establishes access; rather, their similarity tends to prove access in light of the nature of the works, the particular musical genre involved and other circumstantial evidence of access. In other words, striking similarity is just one piece of circumstantial evidence tending to show access and must not be considered in isolation; it must be considered together with other types of circumstantial evidence relating to access.

As a threshold matter, therefore, it would appear that there must be at least some other evidence which would establish a reasonable possibility that the complaining work was *available* to the alleged infringer. As noted, two works may be identical in every detail, but, if the alleged infringer created the accused work independently or both works were copied from a common source in the public domain, then there is no infringement. Therefore, if the plaintiff admits to having kept his or her creation under lock and key, it would seem logically impossible to infer access through striking similarity. Thus, although it has frequently been written that striking similarity *alone* can establish access, the decided cases suggest that this circumstance would be most unusual. The plaintiff must always present sufficient evidence to support a reasonable possibility of access because the jury cannot draw an inference of access based upon speculation and conjecture alone.

For example, in Twentieth Century–Fox Film Corp. v. Dieckhaus, 153 F.2d 893 (8th Cir.), cert. denied, 329 U.S. 716, 67 S.Ct. 46, 91 L.Ed. 621 (1946), the court reversed a finding of infringement based solely on the similarities between plaintiff's book and defendant's film. The court stated that the plaintiff herself presented no evidence that the defendant had had access to her book, and the only people to whom the plaintiff had given a copy of her book testified that they had not given it to the defendant. While the court also concluded that the similarities between the book and the film were not that significant, the result turned on the fact that "[t]he oral and documentary evidence in the record . . . establishes the fact that the defendant had no access to plaintiff's book unless the law of plagiarism permits the court to draw an inference contrary to such proof from its finding of similarities on comparison of the book with the picture." Id. at 897. Thus, although proof of striking similarity may permit an inference of access, the plaintiff must still meet some minimum threshold of proof which demonstrates that the inference of access is reasonable.

The greatest difficulty perhaps arises when the plaintiff cannot demonstrate any direct link between the complaining work and the defendant but the work has been so widely disseminated that it is not unreasonable to infer that the defendant might have had access to it. In Cholvin v. B. & F. Music Co., 253 F.2d 102 (7th Cir.1958), the plaintiffs' work had been distributed in 2000 professional copies of sheet music and four recordings, of which 200,000 records were sold, and it had been performed on several nationwide broadcasts. The court held that, in light of this circumstantial evidence, it was reasonable to infer, in combination with similarities between the two pieces, that there had been an infringement. In Abkco Music, Inc. v. Harrisongs Music, Ltd., 722 F.2d 988, 997–99 (2d Cir.1983), the court found that there had been a copyright infringement based on a theory of subconscious copying. The complaining work, "He's So Fine," had been the most popular song in the United States for five weeks and among the thirty top hits in England for seven weeks during the year in which George Harrison composed "My Sweet Lord," the infringing song. This evidence, in addition to Harrison's own admission that the two songs were "strikingly similar," supported the finding of infringement. On the other hand, in Jewel Music Publishing Co. v. Leo Feist, Inc., 62 F.Supp. 596, 598 (S.D.N.Y.1945), almost 10,000 copies of the complaining song had been distributed or sold and the music had also been broadcast on national performances. The court still concluded that the showing of access was insufficient, in combination with the other evidence, to support a reasonable inference of access.

The possibility of access in the present case is not as remote as that in *Dieckhaus* because neither side elicited testimony from the individuals (primarily employees of the publishing companies) to whom the plaintiff had distributed copies of his song. Such evidence might have conclusively disproved access. On the other hand, Selle's song certainly did not achieve the extent of public dissemination existing in *Cholvin, Jewel Music Publishing Co.,* or *Harrisongs Music,* and there was also no evidence that any of the defendants or their associates were in Chicago on the two or three occasions when the plaintiff played his song publicly. It is not necessary for us, given the facts of this case, to determine the number of copies which must be publicly distributed to raise a reasonable inference of access. Nevertheless, in this case, the availability of Selle's song, as shown by the evidence, was virtually *de minimis*.

In granting the defendants' motion for judgment notwithstanding the verdict, Judge Leighton relied primarily on the plaintiff's failure to adduce any evidence of access and stated that an inference of access may not be based on mere conjecture, speculation or a bare possibility of access. Thus, in Testa v. Janssen, 492 F.Supp. 198, 202–03 (W.D.Pa. 1980), the court stated that "[t]o support a finding of access, plaintiffs' evidence must extend beyond mere speculation or conjecture. And, while circumstantial evidence is sufficient to establish access, a defendant's opportunity to view the copyrighted work must exist by a reasonable possibility—not a bare possibility."

Judge Leighton thus based his decision on what he characterized as the plaintiff's inability to raise more than speculation that the Bee Gees had access to his song. The extensive testimony of the defendants and their witnesses describing the creation process went essentially uncontradicted, and there was no attempt even to impeach their credibility. Judge Leighton further relied on the principle that the testimony of credible witnesses concerning a matter within their knowledge cannot be rejected without some impeachment, contradiction or inconsistency with other evidence on the particular point at issue. Judge Leighton's conclusions that there was no more than a bare possibility that the defendants could have had access to Selle's song and that this was an insufficient basis from which the jury could have reasonably inferred the existence of access seem correct. The plaintiff has failed to meet even the minimum threshold of proof of the possibility of access and, as Judge Leighton has stated, an inference of access would thus seem to be "at war with the undisputed facts."

IV

The grant of the motion for judgment notwithstanding the verdict might, if we were so minded, be affirmed on the basis of the preceding analysis of the plaintiff's inability to establish a reasonable inference of access. This decision is also supported by a more traditional analysis of proof of access based only on the proof of "striking similarity" between the two compositions. The plaintiff relies almost exclusively on the testimony of his expert witness, Dr. Parsons, that the two pieces were, in fact, "strikingly similar." [3] Yet formulating a meaningful definition of "striking similarity" is no simple task, and the term is often used in a conclusory or circular fashion.

Sherman defines "striking similarity" as a term of art signifying "that degree of similarity as will permit an inference of copying even in the absence of proof of access. . . ." Sherman, *Musical Copyright Infringement*, at 84 n. 15. Nimmer states that, absent proof of access,

---

3. Plaintiff also relies on the fact that both songs were played on numerous occasions in open court for the jury to hear and on the deposition testimony of one of the Bee Gees, Maurice, who incorrectly identified Theme B of Selle's song as the Bee Gees' composition, "How Deep Is Your Love."

"the similarities must be so striking as to preclude the possibility that the defendant independently arrived at the same result." Nimmer, *Copyright*, at 13–14.[4]

"Striking similarity" is not merely a function of the number of identical notes that appear in both compositions. An important factor in analyzing the degree of similarity of two compositions is the uniqueness of the sections which are asserted to be similar.

If the complaining work contains an unexpected departure from the normal metric structure or if the complaining work includes what appears to be an error and the accused work repeats the unexpected element or the error, then it is more likely that there is some connection between the pieces. If the similar sections are particularly intricate, then again it would seem more likely that the compositions are related. Finally, some dissimilarities may be particularly suspicious. While some of these concepts are borrowed from literary copyright analysis, they would seem equally applicable to an analysis of music.

The judicially formulated definition of "striking similarity" states that "plaintiffs must demonstrate that 'such similarities are of a kind that can only be explained by copying, rather than by coincidence, independent creation, or prior common source.'" Testa v. Janssen, 492 F.Supp. 198, 203 (W.D.Pa.1980) (quoting Stratchborneo v. Arc Music Corp., 357 F.Supp. 1393, 1403 (S.D.N.Y.1973)). Sherman adds:

> To prove that certain similarities are "striking," plaintiff must show that they are the sort of similarities that cannot satisfactorily be accounted for by a theory of coincidence, independent creation, prior common source, or any theory other than that of copying. Striking similarity is an extremely technical issue—one with which, understandably, experts are best equipped to deal.

Sherman, *Musical Copyright Infringement*, at 96.

Finally, the similarities should appear in a sufficiently unique or complex context as to make it unlikely that both pieces were copied from a prior common source, or that the defendant was able to compose the accused work as a matter of independent creation. With these principles in mind, we turn now to an analysis of the evidence of "striking similarity" presented by the plaintiff.

As noted, the plaintiff relies almost entirely on the testimony of his expert witness, Dr. Arrand Parsons. The defendants did not introduce any expert testimony, apparently because they did not think Parsons' testimony needed to be refuted. Defendants are perhaps to some degree correct in asserting that Parsons, although eminently qualified in the field of classical music theory, was not equally qualified to analyze popular music tunes. More significantly, however, although

---

4. At oral argument, plaintiff's attorney analyzed the degree of similarity required to establish an inference of access as being in an inverse ratio to the quantum of direct evidence adduced to establish access. While we have found no authoritative support for this analysis, it seems appropriate. In this case, it would therefore appear that, because the plaintiff has introduced virtually no direct evidence of access, the degree of similarity required to establish copying in this case is considerable.

Parsons used the magic formula, "striking similarity," he only ruled out the possibility of independent creation; he did not state that the similarities could only be the result of copying. In order for proof of "striking similarity" to establish a reasonable inference of access, especially in a case such as this one in which the direct proof of access is so minimal, the plaintiff must show that the similarity is of a type which will preclude any explanation other than that of copying.

In addition, to bolster the expert's conclusion that independent creation was not possible, there should be some testimony or other evidence of the relative complexity or uniqueness of the two compositions. Dr. Parsons' testimony did not refer to this aspect of the compositions and, in a field such as that of popular music in which all songs are relatively short and tend to build on or repeat a basic theme, such testimony would seem to be particularly necessary. We agree with the Sixth Circuit which explained that "we do not think the affidavit of [the expert witness], stating in conclusory terms that 'it is extremely unlikely that one set [of architectural plans] could have been prepared without access to the other set,' can fill the gap which is created by the absence of any direct evidence of access." Scholz Homes, Inc. v. Maddox, 379 F.2d 84, 86 (6th Cir.1967).

To illustrate this deficiency more concretely, we refer to a cassette tape, Plaintiff's Exhibit 27, and the accompanying chart, Plaintiff's Exhibit 26. These exhibits were prepared by the defendants but introduced into evidence by the plaintiff. The tape has recorded on it segments of both themes from both the Selle and the Gibb songs interspersed with segments of other compositions as diverse as "Footsteps," "From Me To You" (a Lennon–McCartney piece), Beethoven's 5th Symphony, "Funny Talk," "Play Down," and "I'd Like To Leave If I May" (the last two being earlier compositions by Barry Gibb).[5] There are at least superficial similarities among these segments, when played on the same musical instrument, and the plaintiff failed to elicit any testimony from his expert witness about this exhibit which compared the Selle and the Gibb songs to other pieces of contemporary, popular music. These circumstances indicate that the plaintiff failed to sustain his burden of proof on the issue of "striking similarity" in its legal sense—that is, similarity which reasonably precludes the possibility of any explanation other than that of copying.

The plaintiff's expert witness does not seem to have addressed any issues relating to the possibility of prior common source in both widely disseminated popular songs and the defendants' own compositions. At oral argument, plaintiff's attorney stated that the burden of proving common source should be on the defendant; however, the burden of proving "striking similarity," which, by definition, includes taking steps to minimize the possibility of common source, is on the plaintiff. In essence, the plaintiff failed to prove to the requisite degree that the similarities identified by the expert witness—although perhaps "strik-

---

5. The plaintiff, on cross-examination, admitted that there were some similarities, primarily in melody rather than rhythm, between his song and various other popular tunes, including "From Me To You" and several earlier Bee Gee compositions.

ing" in a non-legal sense—were of a type which would eliminate any explanation of coincidence, independent creation or common source, including, in this case, the possibility of common source in earlier compositions created by the Bee Gees themselves or by others. In sum, the evidence of striking similarity is not sufficiently compelling to make the case when the proof of access must otherwise depend largely upon speculation and conjecture.

Therefore, because the plaintiff failed both to establish a basis from which the jury could reasonably infer that the Bee Gees had access to his song and to meet his burden of proving "striking similarity" between the two compositions, the grant by the district court of the defendants' motion for judgment notwithstanding the verdict is affirmed. Because of our doubts concerning the defendants' cross-appeal on the denial of the summary judgment, we order that, under Fed.R. App.P. 38, each party shall bear its own costs.

3. VISUAL ARTS

STEINBERG v. COLUMBIA PICTURES INDUSTRIES, INC.

United States District Court, S.D. New York 1987.
663 F.Supp. 706, 3 U.S.P.Q.2d 1593.

STANTON, District Judge.

In these actions for copyright infringement, plaintiff Saul Steinberg is suing the producers, promoters, distributors and advertisers of the movie "Moscow on the Hudson" ("Moscow"). Steinberg is an artist whose fame derives in part from cartoons and illustrations he has drawn for *The New Yorker* magazine. Defendant Columbia Pictures Industries, Inc. (Columbia) is in the business of producing, promoting and distributing motion pictures, including "Moscow." . . . .

Plaintiff alleges that defendants' promotional poster for "Moscow" infringes his copyright on an illustration that he drew for *The New Yorker* and that appeared on the cover of the March 29, 1976 issue of the magazine, in violation of 17 U.S.C. §§ 101–810. Defendants deny this allegation and assert the affirmative defenses of fair use as a parody, estoppel and laches.

Defendants have moved, and plaintiff has cross-moved, for summary judgment. For the reasons set forth below, this court rejects defendants' asserted defenses and grants summary judgment on the issue of copying to plaintiff. . . .

II

The essential facts are not disputed by the parties despite their disagreements on nonessential matters. On March 29, 1976, *The New Yorker* published as a cover illustration the work at issue in this suit, widely known as a parochial New Yorker's view of the world. The magazine registered this illustration with the United States Copyright Office and subsequently assigned the copyright to Steinberg. Approximately three months later, plaintiff and *The New Yorker* entered into

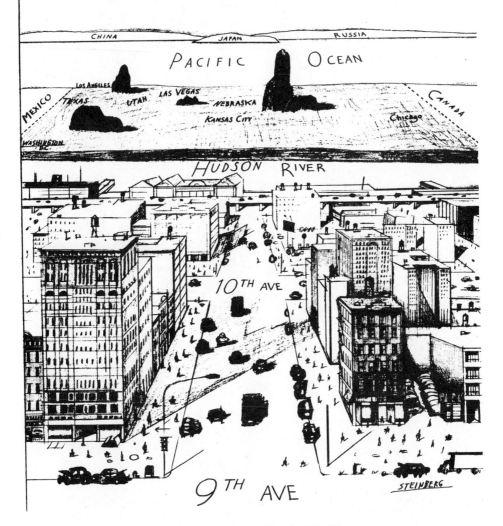

Columbia Pictures' poster
Reproduced with permission of Columbia Pictures

an agreement to print and sell a certain number of posters of the cover illustration.

It is undisputed that unauthorized duplications of the poster were made and distributed by unknown persons, although the parties disagree on the extent to which plaintiff attempted to prevent the distribution of those counterfeits. Plaintiff has also conceded that numerous posters have been created and published depicting other localities in the same manner that he depicted New York in his illustration. These facts, however, are irrelevant to the merits of this case, which concerns only the relationship between plaintiff's and defendants' illustrations.

Defendants' illustration was created to advertise the movie "Moscow on the Hudson," which recounts the adventures of a Muscovite who defects in New York. In designing this illustration, Columbia's executive art director, Kevin Nolan, has admitted that he specifically referred to Steinberg's poster, and indeed, that he purchased it and hung it, among others, in his office. Furthermore, Nolan explicitly directed the outside artist whom he retained to execute his design, Craig Nelson, to use Steinberg's poster to achieve a more recognizably New York look. Indeed, Nelson acknowledged having used the facade of one particular edifice, at Nolan's suggestion that it would render his drawing more "New York-ish." While the two buildings are not identical, they are so similar that it is impossible, especially in view of the artist's testimony, not to find that defendants' impermissibly copied plaintiff's.[1]

To decide the issue of infringement, it is necessary to consider the posters themselves. Steinberg's illustration presents a bird's eye view across a portion of the western edge of Manhattan, past the Hudson River and a telescoped version of the rest of the United States and the Pacific Ocean, to a red strip of horizon, beneath which are three flat land masses labeled China, Japan and Russia. The name of the magazine, in *The New Yorker*'s usual typeface, occupies the top fifth of the poster, beneath a thin band of blue wash representing a stylized sky.

The parts of the poster beyond New York are minimalized, to symbolize a New Yorker's myopic view of the centrality of his city to the world. The entire United States west of the Hudson River, for example, is reduced to a brown strip labeled "Jersey," together with a light green trapezoid with a few rudimentary rock outcroppings and the names of only seven cities and two states scattered across it. The few blocks of Manhattan, by contrast, are depicted and colored in detail. The four square blocks of the city, which occupy the whole lower half of the poster, include numerous buildings, pedestrians and cars, as well as parking lots and lamp posts, with water towers atop a few of the buildings. The whimsical, sketchy style and spiky lettering are recognizable as Steinberg's.

1. Nolan claimed also to have been inspired by some of the posters that were inspired by Steinberg's; such secondary inspiration, however, is irrelevant to whether or not the "Moscow" poster infringes plaintiff's copyright by having impermissibly copied it.

The "Moscow" illustration depicts the three main characters of the film on the lower third of their poster, superimposed on a bird's eye view of New York City, and continues eastward across Manhattan and the Atlantic Ocean, past a rudimentary evocation of Europe, to a clump of recognizably Russian-styled buildings on the horizon, labeled "Moscow." The movie credits appear over the lower portion of the characters. The central part of the poster depicts approximately four New York city blocks, with fairly detailed buildings, pedestrians and vehicles, a parking lot, and some water towers and lamp posts. Columbia's artist added a few New York landmarks at apparently random places in his illustration, apparently to render the locale more easily recognizable. Beyond the blue strip labeled "Atlantic Ocean," Europe is represented by London, Paris and Rome, each anchored by a single landmark (although the landmark used for Rome is the Leaning Tower of Pisa).

The horizon behind Moscow is delineated by a red crayoned strip, above which are the title of the movie and a brief textual introduction to the plot. The poster is crowned by a thin strip of blue wash, apparently a stylization of the sky. This poster is executed in a blend of styles: the three characters, whose likenesses were copied from a photograph, have realistic faces and somewhat sketchy clothing, and the city blocks are drawn in a fairly detailed but sketchy style. The lettering on the drawing is spiky, in block-printed handwritten capital letters substantially identical to plaintiff's, while the printed texts at the top and bottom of the poster are in the typeface commonly associated with *The New Yorker* magazine.[2]

III

To succeed in a copyright infringement action, a plaintiff must prove ownership of the copyright and copying by the defendant. There is no substantial dispute concerning plaintiff's ownership of a valid copyright in his illustration. Therefore, in order to prevail on liability, plaintiff need establish only the second element of the cause of action.

"Because of the inherent difficulty in obtaining direct evidence of copying, it is usually proved by circumstantial evidence of access to the copyrighted work and substantial similarities as to protectible material in the two works." *Reyher,* 533 F.2d at 90, citing Arnstein v. Porter, 154 F.2d 464, 468 (2d Cir.1946). "Of course, if there are no similarities, no amount of evidence of access will suffice to prove copying." Arnstein v. Porter, 154 F.2d at 468.

Defendants' access to plaintiff's illustration is established beyond peradventure. Therefore, the sole issue remaining with respect to liability is whether there is such substantial similarity between the copyrighted and accused works as to establish a violation of plaintiff's copyright. The central issue of "substantial similarity," which can be considered a close question of fact, may also validly be decided as a question of law.

---

2. The typeface is not a subject of copyright, but the similarity reinforces the impression that defendants copied plaintiff's illustration.

"Substantial similarity" is an elusive concept. This circuit has recently recognized that

> [t]he 'substantial similarity' that supports an inference of copying sufficient to establish infringement of a copyright is not a concept familiar to the public at large. It is a term to be used in a courtroom to strike a delicate balance between the protection to which authors are entitled under an act of Congress and the freedom that exists for all others to create their works outside the area protected by infringement.

Warner Bros., 720 F.2d at 245.

The definition of "substantial similarity" in this circuit is "whether an average lay observer would recognize the alleged copy as having been appropriated from the copyrighted work." Ideal Toy Corp. v. Fab–Lu Ltd., 360 F.2d 1021, 1022 (2d Cir.1966); Silverman v. CBS, Inc., 632 F.Supp. at 1351–52. A plaintiff need no longer meet the severe "ordinary observer" test established by Judge Learned Hand in Peter Pan Fabrics, Inc. v. Martin Weiner Corp., 274 F.2d 487 (2d Cir.1960). Under Judge Hand's formulation, there would be substantial similarity only where "the ordinary observer, unless he set out to detect the disparities, would be disposed to overlook them, and regard their aesthetic appeal as the same." 274 F.2d at 489.

Moreover, it is now recognized that "[t]he copying need not be of every detail so long as the copy is substantially similar to the copyrighted work." Comptone Co. v. Rayex Corp., 251 F.2d 487, 488 (2d Cir. 1958).

In determining whether there is substantial similarity between two works, it is crucial to distinguish between an idea and its expression. It is an axiom of copyright law, established in the case law and since codified at 17 U.S.C. § 102(b), that only the particular expression of an idea is protectible, while the idea itself is not.

"The idea/expression distinction, although an imprecise tool, has not been abandoned because we have as yet discovered no better way to reconcile the two competing societal interests that provide the rationale for the granting of and restrictions on copyright protection," namely, both rewarding individual ingenuity, and nevertheless allowing progress and improvements based on the same subject matter by others than the original author. *Durham Industries*, 630 F.2d at 912, *quoting Reyher*, 533 F.2d at 90.

There is no dispute that defendants cannot be held liable for using the *idea* of a map of the world from an egocentrically myopic perspective. No rigid principle has been developed, however, to ascertain when one has gone beyond the idea to the expression, and "[d]ecisions must therefore inevitably be ad hoc." Peter Pan Fabrics, Inc. v. Martin Weiner Corp., 274 F.2d 487, 489 (2d Cir.1960) (L. Hand, J.). As Judge Frankel once observed, "Good eyes and common sense may be as useful as deep study of reported and unreported cases, which themselves are tied to highly particularized facts." Couleur International Ltd. v. Opulent Fabrics, Inc., 330 F.Supp. 152, 153 (S.D.N.Y.1971).

Even at first glance, one can see the striking stylistic relationship between the posters, and since style is one ingredient of "expression," this relationship is significant. Defendants' illustration was executed in the sketchy, whimsical style that has become one of Steinberg's hallmarks. Both illustrations represent a bird's eye view across the edge of Manhattan and a river bordering New York City to the world beyond. Both depict approximately four city blocks in detail and become increasingly minimalist as the design recedes into the background. Both use the device of a narrow band of blue wash across the top of the poster to represent the sky, and both delineate the horizon with a band of primary red.[3]

The strongest similarity is evident in the rendering of the New York City blocks. Both artists chose a vantage point that looks directly down a wide two-way cross street that intersects two avenues before reaching a river. Despite defendants' protestations, this is not an inevitable way of depicting blocks in a city with a grid-like street system, particularly since most New York City cross streets are one-way. Since even a photograph may be copyrighted because "no photograph, however simple, can be unaffected by the personal influence of the author," Time Inc. v. Bernard Geis Assoc., 293 F.Supp. 130, 141 (S.D.N.Y.1968), *quoting Bleistein,* supra, one can hardly gainsay the right of an artist to protect his choice of perspective and layout in a drawing, especially in conjunction with the overall concept and individual details. Indeed, the fact that defendants changed the names of the streets while retaining the same graphic depiction weakens their case: had they intended their illustration realistically to depict the streets labeled on the poster, their four city blocks would not so closely resemble plaintiff's four city blocks. Moreover, their argument that they intended the jumble of streets and landmarks and buildings to symbolize their Muscovite protagonist's confusion in a new city does not detract from the strong similarity between their poster and Steinberg's.

While not all of the details are identical, many of them could be mistaken for one another; for example, the depiction of the water towers, and the cars, and the red sign above a parking lot, and even many of the individual buildings. The shapes, windows, and configurations of various edifices are substantially similar. The ornaments, facades and details of Steinberg's buildings appear in defendants', although occasionally at other locations. In this context, it is significant that Steinberg did not depict any buildings actually erected in New York; rather, he was inspired by the general appearance of the structures on the West Side of Manhattan to create his own New York-ish structures. Thus, the similarity between the buildings depicted in

---

3. Defendants claim that since this use of thin bands of primary colors is a traditional Japanese technique, their adoption of it cannot infringe Steinberg's copyright. This argument ignores the principle that while "[o]thers are free to copy the original . . . [t]hey are not free to copy the copy." Bleistein v. Donaldson Lithographing Co.,

188 U.S. 239, 250, 23 S.Ct. 298, 300, 47 L.Ed. 460 (1903) (Holmes, J.). Cf. Dave Grossman Designs, Inc. v. Bortin, 347 F.Supp. 1150, 1156–57 (N.D.Ill.1972) (an artist may use the same subject and style as another "so long as the second artist does not *substantially copy* [the first artist's] specific expression of his idea.")

the "Moscow" and Steinberg posters cannot be explained by an assertion that the artists happened to choose the same buildings to draw. The close similarity can be explained only by the defendants' artist having copied the plaintiff's work. Similarly, the locations and size, the errors and anomalies of Steinberg's shadows and streetlight, are meticulously imitated.

In addition, the Columbia artist's use of the childlike, spiky block print that has become one of Steinberg's hallmarks to letter the names of the streets in the "Moscow" poster can be explained only as copying. There is no inherent justification for using this style of lettering to label New York City streets as it is associated with New York only through Steinberg's poster.

While defendants' poster shows the city of Moscow on the horizon in far greater detail than anything is depicted in the background of plaintiff's illustration, this fact alone cannot alter the conclusion. "Substantial similarity" does not require identity, and "duplication or near identity is not necessary to establish infringement." *Krofft,* 562 F.2d at 1167. Neither the depiction of Moscow, nor the eastward perspective, nor the presence of randomly scattered New York City landmarks in defendants' poster suffices to eliminate the substantial similarity between the posters. As Judge Learned Hand wrote, "no plagiarist can excuse the wrong by showing how much of his work he did not pirate." Sheldon v. Metro–Goldwyn Pictures Corp., 81 F.2d 49, 56 (2d Cir.), cert. denied, 298 U.S. 669, 56 S.Ct. 835, 80 L.Ed. 1392 (1936).

Defendants argue that their poster could not infringe plaintiff's copyright because only a small proportion of its design could possibly be considered similar. This argument is both factually and legally without merit. "[A] copyright infringement may occur by reason of a substantial similarity that involves only a small portion of each work." Burroughs v. Metro–Goldwyn–Mayer, Inc., 683 F.2d 610, 624 n. 14 (2d Cir.1982). Moreover, this case involves the entire protected work and an iconographically, as well as proportionately, significant portion of the allegedly infringing work.

The process by which defendants' poster was created also undermines this argument. The "map," that is, the portion about which plaintiff is complaining, was designed separately from the rest of the poster. The likenesses of the three main characters, which were copied from a photograph, and the blocks of text were superimposed on the completed map.

I also reject defendants' argument that any similarities between the works are unprotectible *scenes a faire,* or "incidents, characters or settings which, as a practical matter, are indispensable or standard in the treatment of a given topic." *Walker,* 615 F.Supp. at 436. It is undeniable that a drawing of New York City blocks could be expected to include buildings, pedestrians, vehicles, lampposts and water towers. Plaintiff, however, does not complain of defendants' mere use of these elements in their poster; rather, his complaint is that defendants copied his *expression* of those elements of a street scene.

While evidence of independent creation by the defendants would rebut plaintiff's prima facie case, "the absence of any countervailing evidence of creation independent of the copyrighted source may well render clearly erroneous a finding that there was not copying." Roth Greeting Cards v. United Card Co., 429 F.2d 1106, 1110 (9th Cir.1970).

Moreover, it is generally recognized that ". . . since a very high degree of similarity is required in order to dispense with proof of access, it must logically follow that where proof of access is offered, the required degree of similarity may be somewhat less than would be necessary in the absence of such proof." 2 Nimmer § 143.4 at 634, *quoted in Krofft,* 562 F.2d at 1172. As defendants have conceded access to plaintiff's copyrighted illustration, a somewhat lesser degree of similarity suffices to establish a copyright infringement than might otherwise be required. Here, however, the demonstrable similarities are such that proof of access, although in fact conceded, is almost unnecessary. . . .

VI

For the reasons set out above, summary judgment is granted to plaintiffs as to copying.

GROSS v. SELIGMAN
United States Circuit Court of Appeals, Second Circuit, 1914.
212 F. 930.

Appeal from the District Court of the United States for the Southern District of New York.

This cause comes here upon appeal from an order of the District Court, Southern District of New York, enjoining defendant from publishing a photograph. The suit is brought under the provisions of the Copyright Act. One Rochlitz, an artist, posed a model in the nude, and therefrom produced a photograph, which he named the 'Grace of Youth.' A copyright was obtained therefor; all the artist's rights being sold and assigned to complainants. Two years later the same artist placed the same model in the identical pose, with the single exception that the young woman now wears a smile and holds a cherry stem between her teeth. He took a photograph of this pose, which he called 'Cherry Ripe'; this second photograph is published by defendants, and has been enjoined as an infringement of complainant's copyright.

LACOMBE, Circuit Judge (after stating the facts as above). This is not simply the case of taking two separate photographs of the same young woman.

When the Grace of Youth was produced a distinctly artistic conception was formed, and was made permanent as a picture in the very method which the Supreme Court indicated in the Oscar Wilde Case (Burrow–Giles Company v. Sarony, 111 U.S. 53, 4 Sup.Ct. 279, 28 L.Ed. 349) would entitle the person producing such a picture to a copyright to protect it. It was there held that the artist who used the camera to produce his picture was entitled to copyright just as he would have been had he produced it with a brush on canvas. If the copyrighted picture were produced with colors on canvas, and were then copyrighted and sold by the artist, he would infringe the purchaser's rights if thereafter the same artist, using the same model, repainted the same picture with only trivial variations of detail and offered it for sale.

Of course when the first picture has been produced and copyrighted every other artist is entirely free to form his own conception of the Grace of Youth, or anything else, and to avail of the same young woman's services in making it permanent, whether he works with pigments or a camera. If, by chance, the pose, background, light, and shade, etc., of this new picture were strikingly similar, and if, by reason of the circumstance that the same young woman was the prominent feature in both compositions, it might be very difficult to distinguish the new picture from the old one, the new would still not be an infringement of the old because it is in no true sense a *copy* of the old. This is a risk which the original artist takes when he merely produces a likeness of an existing face and figure, instead of supplementing its features by the exercise of his own imagination.

It seems to us, however, that we have no such new photograph of the same model. The identity of the artist and the many close identities of pose, light, and shade, etc., indicate very strongly that the first picture was used to produce the second. Whether the model in the second case was posed, and light and shade, etc., arranged with a copy of the first photograph physically present before the artist's eyes, or whether his mental reproduction of the exact combination he had already once effected was so clear and vivid that he did not need the physical reproduction of it, seems to us immaterial. The one thing, viz., the exercise of artistic talent, which made the first photographic picture a subject of copyright, has been used not to produce another picture, but to duplicate the original.

The case is quite similar to those where indirect copying, through the use of living pictures, was held to be an infringement of copyright.

The eye of an artist or a connoisseur will, no doubt, find differences between these two photographs. The backgrounds are not identical, the model in one case is sedate, in the other smiling; moreover the young woman was two years older when the later photograph was taken, and some slight changes in the contours of her figure are discoverable. But the identities are much greater than the differences, and it seems to us that the artist was careful to introduce only enough differences to argue about, while undertaking to make what would seem to be a copy to the ordinary purchaser who did not have both photographs before him at the same time. In this undertaking we think he succeeded.

The order is affirmed.

NOTE

Compare with *Steinberg* and *Gross,* Franklin Mint Corp. v. National Wildlife Art Exchange, Inc., 575 F.2d 62, 197 U.S.P.Q. 721 (3d Cir. 1978), cert. denied, 439 U.S. 880, 99 S.Ct. 217, 58 L.Ed.2d 193, 199 U.S. P.Q. 576, where the court observed that "in the world of fine art, the ease with which a copyright may be delineated may depend on the artist's style. A painter like Monet when dwelling upon impressions created by light on the facade of the Rouen Cathedral is apt to create a work which can make infringement attempts difficult. On the other hand, an artist who produces a rendition with photograph-like clarity and accuracy may be hard-pressed to prove unlawful copying by another who uses the same subject matter and the same technique. A copyright in that circumstance may be termed 'weak,' since the expression and the subject matter converge. In contrast, in the impressionist's work, the lay observer will be able to differentiate more readily between the reality of subject matter and subjective effect of the artist's work." 575 F.2d at 65.

D. RIGHTS BEYOND COPYRIGHT: MORAL RIGHT

SARRAUTE, CURRENT THEORY ON THE MORAL RIGHT OF AUTHORS AND ARTISTS UNDER FRENCH LAW, 16 AM.J.COMP.L. 465–67, 480–81 (1968).* In French law the concept of literary and artistic rights involves two elements.

The first is analogous to the English-speaking countries' copyright. It is a property right, and consists of a temporary monopoly over the exploitation of protected works. It assures the author of the exclusive right to control the reproduction and the performance or exhibition of his creation.

The second element is the "moral" right. It includes non-property attributes of an intellectual and moral character which give legal expression to the intimate bond which exists between a literary or artistic work and its author's personality; it is intended to protect his personality as well as his work. . . .

Until this moment of disengagement, the work is an expression of the artist's personality and remains strictly his own. No one can claim any right to it whatsoever. It is a rough draft, a design which the artist may modify or destroy at will. He alone can determine from the moment when his plan has been realized, when his work is completed, when he feels that he can, without injuring his reputation, reveal it to the public and surrender his rights over it to a third party.

Once this decision is made, the work is separated from the artist; it falls into commerce, becomes the subject of transactions. It is published, exhibited, performed. But the artist still retains certain rights over the work. In some cases he retains the right to suppress it if he is no longer satisfied with it; in all instances he retains the right to demand that he be recognized as its author, that his name be associated with it, and, above all, that the work be neither abridged nor distorted.

Thus the moral right is generally composed of four aspects:

(1) The right of disclosure (*divulgation*);

Then, after the work has been made public and the author's rights to it have been transferred:

(2) The right to withdraw or disavow;

(3) The right of paternity—i.e., the right to have one's name and authorship recognized;

(4) The right of integrity of the work of art. . . .

As we have seen, Article 6 of the law of March 11, 1957 recognizes the author's right to insist that the integrity of his work be respected. This right has always been acknowledged by the courts. It does not arise until, after completion, the work has been put on the market by the author, has been sold, or has been made the subject of contracts of publication or performance. From that time on the author has the right to insist that its integrity must not be violated by measures which could alter or distort it.

This principle is unquestioned and its practical application presents few theoretical difficulties. A case in point is the recent decision of the Court of Cassation on July 6, 1965, which affirmed a decision rendered by the Paris Court of Appeals of May 30, 1962. Both Courts found in favor of the painter Bernard Buffet, who maintained that the refrigerator he had decorated was an indivisible artistic unit, and opposed the sale of any of the elements of the ornamentation separately from the others.

An extremely delicate problem does, however, arise in one situation. This is the problem of protecting the integrity of a work when the author has authorized its adaptation to a different medium, as in the case of the adaptation of an opera or a ballet for the theatre or the cinema. The problem here is to ascertain to what extent the right of the author of the original work can insist on its integrity, when this claim conflicts with creative freedom of the adapter, as the author of a work which purports to be equally original. How may a conflict between two equally valid moral rights be resolved?

GILLIAM v. AMERICAN BROADCASTING COMPANIES, INC.

United States Court of Appeals, Second Circuit, 1976.
538 F.2d 14, 192 U.S.P.Q. 1.

LUMBARD, Circuit Judge.

Plaintiffs, a group of British writers and performers known as "Monty Python," appeal from a denial by Judge Lasker in the Southern

District of a preliminary injunction to restrain the American Broadcasting Company (ABC) from broadcasting edited versions of three separate programs originally written and performed by Monty Python for broadcast by the British Broadcasting Corporation (BBC). We agree with Judge Lasker that the appellants have demonstrated that the excising done for ABC impairs the integrity of the original work. We further find that the countervailing injuries that Judge Lasker found might have accrued to ABC as a result of an injunction at a prior date no longer exist. We therefore direct the issuance of a preliminary injunction by the district court.

Since its formation in 1969, the Monty Python group has gained popularity primarily through its thirty-minute television programs created for BBC as part of a comedy series entitled "Monty Python's Flying Circus." In accordance with an agreement between Monty Python and BBC, the group writes and delivers to BBC scripts for use in the television series. This scriptwriters' agreement recites in great detail the procedure to be followed when any alterations are to be made in the script prior to recording of the program.[2] The essence of this section of the agreement is that, while BBC retains final authority to make changes, appellants or their representatives exercise optimum control over the scripts consistent with BBC's authority and only minor changes may be made without prior consultation with the writers. Nothing in the scriptwriters' agreement entitles BBC to alter a program once it has been recorded. The agreement further provides that, subject to the terms therein, the group retains all rights in the script.

Under the agreement, BBC may license the transmission of recordings of the television programs in any overseas territory. The series has been broadcast in this country primarily on non-commercial public broadcasting television stations, although several of the programs have

---

2. The Agreement provides:

V. When script alterations are necessary it is the intention of the BBC to make every effort to inform and to reach agreement with the Writer. Whenever practicable any necessary alterations (other than minor alterations) shall be made by the Writer. Nevertheless the BBC shall at all times have the right to make (a) minor alterations and (b) such other alterations as in its opinion are necessary in order to avoid involving the BBC in legal action or bringing the BBC into disrepute. Any decision under (b) shall be made at a level not below that of Head of Department. It is however agreed that after a script has been accepted by the BBC alterations will not be made by the BBC under (b) above unless (i) the Writer, if available when the BBC requires the alterations to be made, has been asked to agree to them but is not willing to do so and (ii) the Writer has had, if he so requests and if the BBC agrees that time permits if rehearsals and recording are to proceed as planned, an opportunity to be represented by the Writers' Guild of Great Britain (or if he is not a member of the Guild by his agent) at a meeting with the BBC to be held within at most 48 hours of the request (excluding weekends). If in such circumstances there is no agreement about the alterations then the final decision shall rest with the BBC. Apart from the right to make alterations under (a) and (b) above the BBC shall not without the consent of the Writer or his agent (which consent shall not be unreasonably withheld) make any structural alterations as opposed to minor alterations to the script, provided that such consent shall not be necessary in any case where the Writer is for any reason not immediately available for consultation at the time which in the BBC's opinion is the deadline from the production point of view for such alterations to be made if rehearsals and recording are to proceed as planned.

been broadcast on commercial stations in Texas and Nevada. In each instance, the thirty-minute programs have been broadcast as originally recorded and broadcast in England in their entirety and without commercial interruption.

In October 1973, Time–Life Films acquired the right to distribute in the United States certain BBC television programs, including the Monty Python series. Time–Life was permitted to edit the programs only "for insertion of commercials, applicable censorship or governmental . . . rules and regulations, and National Association of Broadcasters and time segment requirements." No similar clause was included in the scriptwriters' agreement between appellants and BBC. Prior to this time, ABC had sought to acquire the right to broadcast excerpts from various Monty Python programs in the spring of 1975, but the group rejected the proposal for such a disjoined format. Thereafter, in July 1975, ABC agreed with Time–Life to broadcast two ninety-minute specials each comprising three thirty-minute Monty Python programs that had not previously been shown in this country.

Correspondence between representatives of BBC and Monty Python reveals that these parties assumed that ABC would broadcast each of the Monty Python programs "in its entirety." On September 5, 1975, however, the group's British representative inquired of BBC how ABC planned to show the programs in their entirety if approximately 24 minutes of each 90 minute program were to be devoted to commercials. BBC replied on September 12, "we can only reassure you that ABC have [sic] decided to run the programmes 'back to back,' and that there is a firm undertaking not to segment them."

ABC broadcast the first of the specials on October 3, 1975. Appellants did not see a tape of the program until late November and were allegedly "appalled" at the discontinuity and "mutilation" that had resulted from the editing done by Time–Life for ABC. Twenty-four minutes of the original 90 minutes of recording had been omitted. Some of the editing had been done in order to make time for commercials; other material had been edited, according to ABC, because the original programs contained offensive or obscene matter.

In early December, Monty Python learned that ABC planned to broadcast the second special on December 26, 1975. The parties began negotiations concerning editing of that program and a delay of the broadcast until Monty Python could view it. These negotiations were futile, however, and on December 15 the group filed this action to enjoin the broadcast and for damages. Following an evidentiary hearing, Judge Lasker found that "the plaintiffs have established an impairment of the integrity of their work" which "caused the film or program . . . to lose its iconoclastic verve." According to Judge Lasker, "the damage that has been caused to the plaintiffs is irreparable by its nature." Nevertheless, the judge denied the motion for the preliminary injunction on the grounds that it was unclear who owned the copyright in the programs produced by BBC from the scripts written by Monty Python; that there was a question of whether Time–Life and

BBC were indispensable parties to the litigation; that ABC would suffer significant financial loss if it were enjoined a week before the scheduled broadcast; and that Monty Python had displayed a "somewhat disturbing casualness" in their pursuance of the matter.

Judge Lasker granted Monty Python's request for more limited relief by requiring ABC to broadcast a disclaimer during the December 26 special to the effect that the group dissociated itself from the program because of the editing. A panel of this court, however, granted a stay of that order until this appeal could be heard and permitted ABC to broadcast, at the beginning of the special, only the legend that the program had been edited by ABC. We heard argument on April 13 and, at that time, enjoined ABC from any further broadcast of edited Monty Python programs pending the decision of the court.

I

In determining the availability of injunctive relief at this early stage of the proceedings, Judge Lasker properly considered the harm that would inure to the plaintiffs if the injunction were denied, the harm that defendant would suffer if the injunction were granted, and the likelihood that plaintiffs would ultimately succeed on the merits. We direct the issuance of a preliminary injunction because we find that all these factors weigh in favor of appellants.

There is nothing clearly erroneous in Judge Lasker's conclusion that any injury suffered by appellants as a result of the broadcast of edited versions of their programs was irreparable by its nature. ABC presented the appellants with their first opportunity for broadcast to a nationwide network audience in this country. If ABC adversely misrepresented the quality of Monty Python's work, it is likely that many members of the audience, many of whom, by defendant's admission, were previously unfamiliar with appellants, would not become loyal followers of Monty Python productions. The subsequent injury to appellants' theatrical reputation would imperil their ability to attract the large audience necessary to the success of their venture. Such an injury to professional reputation cannot be measured in monetary terms or recompensed by other relief.

In contrast to the harm that Monty Python would suffer by a denial of the preliminary injunction, Judge Lasker found that ABC's relationship with its affiliates would be impaired by a grant of an injunction within a week of the scheduled December 26 broadcast. The court also found that ABC and its affiliates had advertised the program and had included it in listings of forthcoming television programs that were distributed to the public. Thus a last minute cancellation of the December 26 program, Judge Lasker concluded, would injure defendant financially and in its reputation with the public and its advertisers.

However valid these considerations may have been when the issue before the court was whether a preliminary injunction should immediately precede the broadcast, any injury to ABC is presently more speculative. No rebroadcast of the edited specials has been scheduled and no advertising costs have been incurred for the immediate future. Thus there is no danger that defendant's relations with affiliates or the public will suffer irreparably if subsequent broadcasts of the programs are enjoined pending a disposition of the issues.

We then reach the question whether there is a likelihood that appellants will succeed on the merits. In concluding that there is a likelihood of infringement here, we rely especially on the fact that the editing was substantial, i.e., approximately 27 percent of the original program was omitted, and the editing contravened contractual provisions that limited the right to edit Monty Python material. It should be emphasized that our discussion of these matters refers only to such facts as have been developed upon the hearing for a preliminary injunction. Modified or contrary findings may become appropriate after a plenary trial.

Judge Lasker denied the preliminary injunction in part because he was unsure of the ownership of the copyright in the recorded program. Appellants first contend that the question of ownership is irrelevant because the recorded program was merely a derivative work taken from the script in which they hold the uncontested copyright. Thus, even if BBC owned the copyright in the recorded program, its use of that work would be limited by the license granted to BBC by Monty Python for use of the underlying script. We agree.

Section 7 of the Copyright Law, 17 U.S.C.A. § 7, provides in part that "adaptations, arrangements, dramatizations . . . or other versions of . . . copyrighted works when produced with the consent of the proprietor of the copyright in such works . . . shall be regarded as new works subject to copyright. . . ." Manifestly, the recorded program falls into this category as a dramatization of the script, and thus the program was itself entitled to copyright protection. However, section 7 limits the copyright protection of the derivative work, as works adapted from previously existing scripts have become known, to the novel additions made to the underlying work, and the derivative work does not affect the "force or validity" of the copyright in the matter from which it is derived. Thus, any ownership by BBC of the copyright in the recorded program would not affect the scope or ownership of the copyright in the underlying script.

Since the copyright in the underlying script survives intact despite the incorporation of that work into a derivative work, one who uses the script, even with the permission of the proprietor of the derivative work, may infringe the underlying copyright. See Davis v. E.I. duPont deNemours & Co., 240 F.Supp. 612, 145 U.S.P.Q. 258 (S.D.N.Y.1965) (defendants held to have infringed when they obtained permission to use a screenplay in preparing a television script but did not obtain permission of the author of the play upon which the screenplay was based).

If the proprietor of the derivative work is licensed by the proprietor of the copyright in the underlying work to vend or distribute the derivative work to third parties, those parties will, of course, suffer no liability for their use of the underlying work consistent with the license to the proprietor of the derivative work. Obviously, it was just this type of arrangement that was contemplated in this instance. The scriptwriters' agreement between Monty Python and BBC specifically permitted the latter to license the transmission of the recordings made by BBC to distributors such as Time–Life for broadcast in overseas territories.

One who obtains permission to use a copyrighted script in the production of a derivative work, however, may not exceed the specific purpose for which permission was granted. Most of the decisions that have reached this conclusion have dealt with the improper extension of the underlying work into media or time, i.e., duration of the license, not covered by the grant of permission to the derivative work proprietor. Appellants herein do not claim that the broadcast by ABC violated media or time restrictions contained in the license of the script to BBC. Rather, they claim that revisions in the script, and ultimately in the program, could be made only after consultation with Monty Python, and that ABC's broadcast of a program edited after recording and without consultation with Monty Python exceeded the scope of any license that BBC was entitled to grant.

The rationale for finding infringement when a licensee exceeds time or media restrictions on his license—the need to allow the proprietor of the underlying copyright to control the method in which his work is presented to the public—applies equally to the situation in which a licensee makes an unauthorized use of the underlying work by publishing it in a truncated version. Whether intended to allow greater economic exploitation of the work, as in the media and time cases, or to ensure that the copyright proprietor retains a veto power over revisions desired for the derivative work, the ability of the copyright holder to control his work remains paramount in our copyright law. We find, therefore, that unauthorized editing of the underlying work, if proven, would constitute an infringement of the copyright in that work similar to any other use of a work that exceeded the license granted by the proprietor of the copyright.

If the broadcast of an edited version of the Monty Python program infringed the group's copyright in the script, ABC may obtain no solace from the fact that editing was permitted in the agreements between BBC and Time–Life or Time–Life and ABC. BBC was not entitled to make unilateral changes in the script and was not specifically empowered to alter the recordings once made; Monty Python, moreover, had reserved to itself any rights not granted to BBC. Since a grantor may not convey greater rights than it owns, BBC's permission to allow Time–Life, and hence ABC, to edit, appears to have been a nullity.

ABC answers appellants' infringement argument with a series of contentions, none of which seems meritorious at this stage of the litigation. The network asserts that Monty Python's British representative, Jill Foster, knew that ABC planned to exclude much of the original BBC program in the October 3 broadcast. ABC thus contends that by not previously objecting to this procedure, Monty Python ratified BBC's authority to license others to edit the underlying script.

Although the case of Ilyin v. Avon Publications, Inc., 144 F.Supp. 368, 373, 110 U.S.P.Q. 356, 359 (S.D.N.Y.1956), may be broadly read for the proposition that a holder of a derivative copyright may obtain rights in the underlying work through ratification, the conduct necessary to that conclusion has yet to be demonstrated in this case. It is undisputed that appellants did not have actual notice of the cuts in the October 3 broadcast until late November. Even if they are chargeable with the knowledge of their British representative, it is not clear that she had prior notice of the cuts or ratified the omissions, nor did Judge Lasker make any finding on the question. While Foster, on September 5, did question how ABC was to broadcast the entire program if it was going to interpose 24 minutes of commericals, she received assurances from BBC that the programs would not be "segmented." The fact that she knew precisely the length of material that would have to be omitted to allow for commercials does not prove that she ratified the deletions. This is especially true in light of previous assurances that the program would contain the original shows in their entirety. On the present record, it cannot be said that there was any ratification of BBC's grant of editing rights. ABC, of course, is entitled to attempt to prove otherwise during the trial on the merits.

ABC next argues that under the "joint work" theory adopted in Shapiro, Bernstein & Co. v. Jerry Vogel Music, Inc., 221 F.2d 569, 105 U.S.P.Q. 178 (2d Cir.1955), the script produced by Monty Python and the program recorded by BBC are symbiotic elements of a single production. Therefore, according to ABC, each contributor possesses an undivided ownership of all copyrightable elements in the final work and BBC could thus have licensed use of the script, including editing, written by appellants.

The joint work theory as extended in Shapiro has been criticized as inequitable unless "at the time of creation by the first author, the second author's contribution [is envisaged] as an integrated part of a single work," and the first author intends that the final product be a joint work. Furthermore, this court appears to have receded from a broad application of the joint work doctrine where the contract which leads to collaboration between authors indicates that one will retain a superior interest. In the present case, the screenwriters' agreement between Monty Python and BBC provides that the group is to retain all rights in the script not granted in the agreement and that at some future point the group may license the scripts for use on television to parties other than BBC. These provisions suggest that the parties did not consider themselves joint authors of a single work. This matter is subject to further exploration at the trial, but in the present state of the record, it presents no bar to issuance of a preliminary injunction.

Aside from the question of who owns the relevant copyrights, ABC asserts that the contracts between appellants and BBC permit editing of the programs for commercial television in the United States. ABC argues that the scriptwriters' agreement allows appellants the right to participate in revisions of the script only prior to the recording of the programs, and thus infers that BBC had unrestricted authority to revise after that point. This argument, however, proves too much. A reading of the contract seems to indicate that Monty Python obtained control over editing the script only to ensure control over the program recorded from that script. Since the scriptwriters' agreement explicitly retains for the group all rights not granted by the contract, omission of any terms concerning alterations in the program after recording must be read as reserving to appellants exclusive authority for such revisions.

Finally, ABC contends that appellants must have expected that deletions would be made in the recordings to conform them for use on commercial television in the United States. ABC argues that licensing in the United States implicitly grants a license to insert commercials in a program and to remove offensive or obscene material prior to broadcast. According to the network, appellants should have anticipated that most of the excised material contained scatological references inappropriate for American television and that these scenes would be replaced with commercials, which presumably are more palatable to the American public.

The proof adduced up to this point, however, provides no basis for finding any implied consent to edit. Prior to the ABC broadcasts, Monty Python programs had been broadcast on a regular basis by both commercial and public television stations in this country without interruption or deletion. Indeed, there is no evidence of any prior broadcast of edited Monty Python material in the United States. These facts, combined with the persistent requests for assurances by the group and its representatives that the programs would be shown intact belie the argument that the group knew or should have known that deletions and commercial interruptions were inevitable.

Several of the deletions made for ABC, such as elimination of the words "hell" and "damn," seem inexplicable given today's standard television fare. If, however, ABC honestly determined that the programs were obscene in substantial part, it could have decided not to broadcast the specials at all, or it could have attempted to reconcile its differences with appellants. The network could not, however, free from a claim of infringement, broadcast in a substantially altered form a program incorporating the script over which the group had retained control.

Our resolution of these technical arguments serves to reinforce our initial inclination that the copyright law should be used to recognize the important role of the artist in our society and the need to encourage production and dissemination of artistic works by providing adequate legal protection for one who submits his work to the public. We therefore conclude that there is a substantial likelihood that, after a full trial, appellants will succeed in proving infringement of their copyright by ABC's broadcast of edited versions of Monty Python programs. In reaching this conclusion, however, we need not accept appellants' assertion that any editing whatsoever would constitute infringement. Courts have recognized that licensees are entitled to some small degree of latitude in arranging the licensed work for presentation to the public in a manner consistent with the licensee's style or standards. That privilege, however, does not extend to the degree of editing that occurred here especially in light of contractual provisions that limited the right to edit Monty Python material.

II

It also seems likely that appellants will succeed on the theory that, regardless of the right ABC had to broadcast an edited program, the cuts made constituted an actionable mutilation of Monty Python's work. This cause of action, which seeks redress for deformation of an artist's work, finds its roots in the continental concept of droit moral, or moral right, which may generally be summarized as including the right of the artist to have his work attributed to him in the form in which he created it.

American copyright law, as presently written, does not recognize moral rights or provide a cause of action for their violation, since the law seeks to vindicate the economic, rather than the personal, rights of authors. Nevertheless, the economic incentive for artistic and intellectual creation that serves as the foundation for American copyright law, cannot be reconciled with the inability of artists to obtain relief for mutilation or misrepresentation of their work to the public on which the artists are financially dependent. Thus courts have long granted relief for misrepresentation of an artist's work by relying on theories outside the statutory law of copyright, such as contract law, Granz v. Harris, 198 F.2d 585 (2d Cir.1952) (substantial cutting of original work constitutes misrepresentation), or the tort of unfair competition, Prouty v. National Broadcasting Co., 26 F.Supp. 265, 40 U.S.P.Q. 331 (D.C. Mass.1939). Although such decisions are clothed in terms of proprietary right in one's creation, they also properly vindicate the author's personal right to prevent the presentation of his work to the public in a distorted form. See Gardella v. Log Cabin Products Co., 89 F.2d 891, 895–96, 34 U.S.P.Q. 145, 148–150 (2d Cir.1937); Roeder, The Doctrine of Moral Right, 53 Harv.L.Rev. 554, 568 (1940).

Here, the appellants claim that the editing done for ABC mutilated the original work and that consequently the broadcast of those programs as the creation of Monty Python violated the Lanham Act § 43(a), 15 U.S.C.A. § 1125(a). This statute, the federal counterpart to state unfair competition laws, has been invoked to prevent misrepresentations that may injure plaintiff's business or personal reputation, even where no registered trademark is concerned. It is sufficient to violate the Act that a representation of a product, although technically true, creates a false impression of the product's origin. See Rich v. RCA Corp., 390 F.Supp. 530, 185 U.S.P.Q. 508 (S.D.N.Y.1975) (recent picture of plaintiff on cover of album containing songs recorded in distant past held to be a false representation that the songs were new).

These cases cannot be distinguished from the situation in which a television network broadcasts a program properly designated as having been written and performed by a group, but which has been edited, without the writer's consent, into a form that departs substantially from the original work. "To deform his work is to present him to the public as the creator of a work not his own, and thus makes him subject to criticism for work he has not done." Roeder, supra, at 569. In such a case, it is the writer or performer, rather than the network, who suffers the consequences of the mutilation, for the public will have only the final product by which to evaluate the work. Thus, an allegation that a defendant has presented to the public a "garbled," distorted version of plaintiff's work seeks to redress the very rights sought to be protected by the Lanham Act, 15 U.S.C.A. § 1125(a), and should be recognized as stating a cause of action under that statute. See Autry v. Republic Productions, Inc., 213 F.2d 667, 101 U.S.P.Q. 478 (9th Cir. 1954); Jaeger v. American Int'l Pictures, Inc., 330 F.Supp. 274, 169 U.S. P.Q. 668 (S.D.N.Y.1971), which suggests the violation of such a right if mutilation could be proven.

During the hearing on the preliminary injunction, Judge Lasker viewed the edited version of the Monty Python program broadcast on December 26 and the original, unedited version. After hearing argument of this appeal, this panel also viewed and compared the two versions. We find that the truncated version at times omitted the climax of the skits to which appellants' rare brand of humor was leading and at other times deleted essential elements in the schematic development of a story line.[12] We therefore agree with Judge Lasker's conclusion that the edited version broadcast by ABC impaired the integrity of appellants' work and represented to the public as the product of appellants what was actually a mere caricature of their talents. We believe that a valid cause of action for such distortion exists and that therefore a preliminary injunction may issue to prevent repetition of the broadcast prior to final determination of the issues.[13]

12. A single example will illustrate the extent of distortion engendered by the editing. In one skit, an upper class English family is engaged in a discussion of the tonal quality of certain words as "woody" or "tinny." The father soon begins to suggest certain words with sexual connotations as either "woody" or "tinny," whereupon the mother fetches a bucket of water and pours it over his head. The skit continues from this point. The ABC edit eliminates this middle sequence so that the father is comfortably dressed at one moment and, in the next moment, is shown in a soaken condition without any explanation for the change in his appearance.

13. Judge Gurfein's concurring opinion suggests that since the gravamen of a complaint under the Lanham Act is that the origin of goods has been falsely described, a legend disclaiming Monty Python's approval of the edited version would preclude violation of that Act. We are doubtful that a few words could erase the indelible impression that is made by a television broadcast, especially since the viewer has no means of comparing the truncated version with the complete work in order to determine for himself the talents of plaintiffs. Furthermore, a disclaimer such as the one originally suggested by Judge Lasker in the exigencies of an impending broadcast last December, would go unnoticed by viewers who tuned into the broadcast a few minutes after it began.

We therefore conclude that Judge Gurfein's proposal that the district court could find some form of disclaimer would

III

We do not share Judge Lasker's concern about the procedures by which the appellants have pursued this action. The district court indicated agreement with ABC that appellants were guilty of laches in not requesting a preliminary injunction until 11 days prior to the broadcast. Our discussion above, however, suggests that the group did not know and had no reason to believe until late November that editing would take place. Several letters between BBC and Monty Python's representative indicate that appellants believed that the programs would be shown in their entirety. Furthermore, the group did act to prevent offensive editing of the second program immediately after viewing the tape of the first edited program. Thus we find no undue delay in the group's failure to institute this action until they were sufficiently advised regarding the facts necessary to support the action. In any event, ABC has not demonstrated how it was prejudiced by any delay.

Finally, Judge Lasker denied a preliminary injunction because Monty Python had failed to join BBC and Time–Life as indispensable parties. We do not believe that either is an indispensable party. ABC argues that joinder of both was required because it acted in good faith pursuant to its contractual rights with Time–Life in broadcasting edited versions of the programs, and Time–Life, in turn, relied upon its contract with BBC. Furthermore, ABC argues, BBC must be joined since it owns the copyright in the recorded programs.

Even if BBC owns a copyright relevant to determination of the issues in this case, the formalistic rule that once required all owners of a copyright to be parties to an action for its infringement has given way to equitable considerations. In this case, the equities to be considered under Fed.R.Civ.P. 19(a) strongly favor appellants. Monty Python is relying solely on its copyright in the script and on its rights as an author. No claim is being made that Monty Python has rights derived from the copyright held by another. One of the parties is an English corporation, and any action that appellants, a group of English writers and performers, might have against that potential defendant would be better considered under English law in an English court.

Complete relief for the alleged infringement and mutilation complained of may be accorded between Monty Python and ABC, which alone broadcast the programs in dispute. If ABC is ultimately found liable to appellants, a permanent injunction against future broadcasts and a damage award would satisfy all of appellants' claims. ABC's assertion that failure to join BBC and Time–Life may leave it subject to inconsistent verdicts in a later action against its licensors may be resolved through the process of impleader, which ABC has thus far avoided despite a suggestion from the district court to use that procedure. Finally, neither of the parties considered by ABC to be indispens-

be sufficient might not provide appropriate relief.

able has claimed any interest in the subject matter of this litigation. See Fed.R.Civ.P. 19(a)(2).

For these reasons we direct that the district court issue the preliminary injunction sought by the appellants.

GURFEIN, Circuit Judge, concurring.

I concur in my brother Lumbard's scholarly opinion, but I wish to comment on the application of Section 43(a) of the Lanham Act, 15 U.S. C.A. § 1125(a).

I believe that this is the first case in which a federal appellate court has held that there may be a violation of Section 43(a) of the Lanham Act with respect to a common-law copyright. The Lanham Act is a trademark statute, not a copyright statute. Nevertheless, we must recognize that the language of Section 43(a) is broad. It speaks of the affixation or use of false designations of origin or false descriptions or representations, but proscribes such use "in connection with any goods or services." It is easy enough to incorporate trade names as well as trademarks into Section 43(a) and the statute specifically applies to common law trademarks, as well as registered trademarks. Lanham Act § 45, 15 U.S.C.A. § 1127.

In the present case, we are holding that the deletion of portions of the recorded tape constitutes a breach of contract, as well as an infringement of a common-law copyright of the original work. There is literally no need to discuss whether plaintiffs also have a claim for relief under the Lanham Act or for unfair competition under New York law. I agree with Judge Lumbard, however, that it may be an exercise of judicial economy to express our view on the Lanham Act claim, and I do not dissent therefrom. I simply wish to leave it open for the District Court to fashion the remedy.

The Copyright Act provides no recognition of the so-called droit moral, or moral rights of authors. Nor are such rights recognized in the field of copyright law in the United States. If a distortion or truncation in connection with a use constitutes an infringement of copyright, there is no need for an additional cause of action beyond copyright infringement. An obligation to mention the name of the author carries the implied duty, however, as a matter of contract, not to make such changes in the work as would render the credit line a false attribution of authorship.

So far as the Lanham Act is concerned, it is not a substitute for droit moral which authors in Europe enjoy. If the licensee may, by contract, distort the recorded work, the Lanham Act does not come into play. If the licensee has no such right by contract, there will be a violation in breach of contract. The Lanham Act can hardly apply literally when the credit line correctly states the work to be that of the plaintiffs which, indeed it is, so far as it goes. The vice complained of is that the truncated version is not what the plaintiffs wrote. But the Lanham Act does not deal with artistic integrity. It only goes to misdescription of origin and the like.

The misdescription of origin can be dealt with, as Judge Lasker did below, by devising an appropriate legend to indicate that the plaintiffs had not approved the editing of the ABC version. With such a legend, there is no conceivable violation of the Lanham Act. If plaintiffs complain that their artistic integrity is still compromised by the distorted version, their claim does not lie under the Lanham Act, which does not protect the copyrighted work itself but protects only against the misdescription or mislabelling.

So long as it is made clear that the ABC version is not approved by the Monty Python group, there is no misdescription of origin. So far as the content of the broadcast itself is concerned, that is not within the proscription of the Lanham Act when there is no misdescription of the authorship.

I add this brief explanation because I do not believe that the Lanham Act claim necessarily requires the drastic remedy of permanent injunction. That form of ultimate relief must be found in some other fountainhead of equity jurisprudence.

NOTES

1. *Moral Right and the Berne Convention.* Article 6*bis* of the Berne Convention for the Protection of Literary and Artistic Works requires member states to recognize the rights of integrity and paternity. Noting that "Article 6*bis* of Berne has generated one of the biggest controversies surrounding United States adherence to Berne," the House Report on the Berne Implementation amendments concluded that existing state and federal law satisfied the Convention's requirements:

> According to this view, there is a composite of laws in this country that provides the kind of protection envisioned by Article 6*bis*. Federal laws include 17 U.S.C. § 106, relating to derivative works; 17 U.S.C. § 115(a)(2), relating to distortions of musical works used under the compulsory license respecting sound recordings; 17 U.S.C. § 203, relating to termination of transfers and licenses, and section 43(a) of the Lanham Act, relating to false designations of origin and false descriptions. State and local laws include those relating to publicity, contractual violations, fraud and misrepresentation, unfair competition, defamation, and invasion of privacy. In addition, eight states have recently enacted specific statutes protecting the rights of integrity and paternity in certain works of art. Finally, some courts have recognized the equivalent of such rights.

H.R.Rep. No. 609, 100th Cong., 2d Sess. 32–34 (1988).

The Berne Implementation Act provides that "[t]he obligations of the United States under the Berne Convention may be performed only pursuant to appropriate domestic law," and that "[t]he amendments made by this Act, together with the law as it exists on the date of the enactment of this Act, satisfy the obligations of the United States in adhering to the Berne Convention and no further rights or interests shall be recognized or created for that purpose." Pub.L. No. 100–568, § 2(2), (3) 102 Stat. 2853 (1988).

2. *Derivative Rights and the Right of Integrity.* Does *Gilliam* imply that the exclusive right to make an edited version of a work is part of copyright's adaptation right, today secured by section 106(2) of the Copyright Act? The paradox of relying on section 106(2)'s derivative right to secure the integrity of a copyrighted work is that the more completely an unauthorized work distorts the original, the less substantially similar to the original it will be—and the less likely it will be to infringe. See Goldstein, Adaptation Rights and Moral Rights in the United Kingdom, the United States and the Federal Republic of Germany, 1 Int. Rev. Indust. Prop. & Copyright L. 43 (1983).

3. *Section 43(a) and the Right of Paternity.* Section 43(a) of the Lanham Act secures more than a right against distortion; it may also secure an author's interest in attribution of authorship. In Lamothe v. Atlantic Recording Corp., 847 F.2d 1403, 7 U.S.P.Q.2d 1249 (9th Cir. 1988), the court ruled that defendants' failure to identify all of the authors of two musical compositions would violate section 43(a). Relying on its earlier decision in Smith v. Montoro, 648 F.2d 602, 211 U.S. P.Q. 775 (9th Cir.1981), the court held that defendant's conduct would constitute "express reverse palming off"—"when the wrongdoer removes the name or trademark on another party's product and sells that product under a name chosen by the wrongdoer." 847 F.2d at 1406.

4. *State Fine Arts Statutes.* Several state legislatures have passed laws to secure artists' interests in works of fine art. See, e.g., Cal.Civ. Code § 987 (West Supp.1988); N.Y.Arts & Cult.Aff.Law § 14.03 (McKinney Supp.1988). California's statute, for example, protects works of fine art—an "original painting, sculpture, or drawing, or an original work of art in glass, of recognized quality"—against any intentional "physical defacement, mutilation, alteration, or destruction." New York's statute protects "works of fine art or limited edition multiples of not more than three hundred copies knowingly displayed in a place accessible to the public, published or reproduced in this state" against publication or display of a mutilated version if the publication or display represents the work as the work of the artist and is reasonably likely to damage the artist's reputation. Both laws give the artist the right to disclaim authorship of a work.

See also La.Rev.Stat.Ann. tit. 51, §§ 2151–2156 (West 1987); Me. Rev.Stat.Ann. tit. 27, § 303 (West Supp.1986); Mass.Ann.Laws ch. 231, § 85S(d) (Law Co-op.1986).

5. *Federal Fine Arts Bills.* Similar, but not identical, bills to amend the Copyright Act to give rights of integrity and paternity to visual artists have been introduced in the Senate and the House. S. 1198, 101st Cong. 1st Sess. (1989); H.R. 2690, 101st Cong. 1st Sess. (1989). The bills, which would exclude works made for hire from their ambit, define a "work of visual art" as "a painting, drawing, print, sculpture, or still photographic image produced for exhibition purposes

only, existing in a single copy, in a limited edition of 200 copies or fewer, or, in the case of a sculpture, in multiple cast sculptures of 200 or fewer." § 2.

The bills would add a new section 106A to the 1976 Copyright Act. The Senate version, S.1198, § 3, would provide:

(a) RIGHTS OF ATTRIBUTION AND INTEGRITY.—Subject to section 107 and independent of the exclusive rights provided in section 106, the author of a work of visual art—

(1) shall have the right—

(A) to claim authorship of that work, and

(B) to prevent the use of his or her name as the author of any work of visual art which he or she did not create;

(2) shall have the right to prevent the use of his or her name as the author of the work of visual art in the event of a distortion, mutilation, or other modification of the work as described in paragraph (3); and

(3) subject to the limitations set forth in section 113(d), shall have the right—

(A) to prevent any distortion, mutilation, or other modification of that work which would be prejudicial to his or her honor or reputation, and any intentional or grossly negligent distortion, mutilation, or modification of that work is a violation of that right, and

(B) to prevent any destruction of a work of recognized stature, and any intentional or grossly negligent destruction of that work is a violation of that right.

In determining whether a work is of recognized stature, a court or other trier of fact may take into account the opinions of artists, art dealers, collectors of fine art, curators of art museums, conservators of recognized stature, and other persons involved with the creation, appreciation, history, or marketing of works of recognized stature. Evidence of commercial exploitation of a work as a whole, or of particular copies, does not preclude a finding that the work is a work of recognized stature.

(b) SCOPE AND EXERCISE OF RIGHTS.—The author of a work of visual art has the rights conferred by subsection (a), whether or not the author is the copyright owner, and whether or not the work qualifies for protection under section 104. Where the author is not the copyright owner, only the author shall have the right during his or her lifetime to exercise the rights set forth in subsection (a).

(c) EXCEPTIONS.—(1) The modification of a work of visual art which is a result of the passage of time or the inherent nature of the materials is not a destruction, distortion, mutilation, or other modification described in subsection (a)(3) unless the modification was the result of gross negligence in maintaining or protecting the work.

(2) The modification of a work of visual art which is the result of conservation is not a destruction, distortion, mutilation, or other modification described in subsection (a)(3) unless the modification is caused by gross negligence.

(d) DURATION OF RIGHTS.—(1) With respect to works of visual art created on or after the effective date set forth in section 10(a) of the Visual Artists Rights Act of 1989, the rights conferred by subsection (a) shall endure for a term consisting of the life of the author and fifty years after the author's death.

(2) With respect to works of visual art created before the effective date set forth in section 10(a) of the Visual Artists Rights Act of 1989, but not published before such effective date, the rights conferred by subsection (a) shall be coextensive with, and shall expire at the same time as, the rights conferred by section 106.

(3) All terms of the rights conferred by subsection (a) run to the end of the calendar year in which they would otherwise expire.

(e) TRANSFER AND WAIVER.—(1) Except as provided in paragraph (2), the rights conferred by subsection (a) may not be waived or otherwise transferred.

(2) After the death of an author, the rights conferred by subsection (a) on the author may be exercised by the person to whom such rights pass by bequest of the author or by the applicable laws of intestate succession.

(3) Ownership of the rights conferred by subsection (a) with respect to a work of visual art is distinct from ownership of any fixation of that work, or of a copyright or any exclusive right under a copyright in that work.

6. *Resale Royalty Legislation.* S.1198 § 9 and H.R.2690 § 9 would direct the Register of Copyrights, in consultation with the Chair of the National Endowment for the Arts, to "conduct a study on the feasibility of implementing— . . . a requirement that, after the first sale of a work of art, a royalty on any resale of the work, consisting of a percentage of the price, be paid to the author of the work; and . . . other possible requirements that would achieve the objective of allowing an author of a work of art to share monetarily in the enhanced value of that work." The concept of resale royalties comes from the continental doctrine of *droit de suite* entitling an artist to receive a royalty each time her work is resold. California's Artist's Resale Royalty Act, Cal.Civ.Code § 986 (West Supp.1988), approximates the *droit de suite.*

See generally, Camp, Art Resale Rights and the Art Resale Market: An Empirical Study, 28 J. Copyright Soc'y 146 (1980); Price, Government Policy and Economic Security for Artists: The Case of the *Droit de Suite,* 77 Yale L.J. 1333 (1968). See also, Note, Artists' Resale Royalties Legislation: Ohio House Bill 808 and a Proposed Alternative,

9 U.Tol.L.Rev. 366 (1978); Note, A Proposal for National Uniform Art–Proceeds Legislation, 53 Ind.L.J. 129 (1977).

7. *Bibliographic Note.* On moral right generally, see Damich, The Right of Personality: A Common–Law Basis for the Protection of the Moral Rights of Authors, 23 Ga.L.Rev. 1 (1988); DaSilva, Droit Moral and the Amoral Copyright: A Comparison of Artists' Rights in France and the United States, 28 Bull.Copyright Soc'y 1 (1980); Subcomm. on Patents, Trademarks & Copyrights of the Sen.Comm. on the Judiciary, 86th Cong., 1st Sess., Study No. 4, The Moral Right of the Author (Strauss) (Comm.Print 1960); Merryman, The Refrigerator of Bernard Buffet, 27 Hastings L.J. 1023 (1976); Roeder, The Doctrine of Moral Right: A Study in the Law of Artists, Authors and Creators, 53 Harv.L. Rev. 554 (1940); Treece, American Law Analogues of the Author's "Moral Right," 16 Am.J.Comp.L. 487 (1968).

E. PREEMPTION OF STATE LAW

P. GOLDSTEIN, COPYRIGHT (1989) *

§ 15.2 Statutory Preemption: Section 301

Section 301(a) of the 1976 Copyright Act prescribes three conditions, all of which must be met, for a state law to be preempted. First, the state right in question must be "equivalent to any of the exclusive rights within the general scope of copyright as specified by section 106." Second, the right must be in a work of authorship that is fixed in a tangible medium of expression. Third, the work of authorship must come within "the subject matter of copyright as specified by sections 102 and 103."

Section 301(a)'s preemptive formula is easily applied to the garden variety common law copyright case. If, before the 1976 Act, an author distributed the manuscript for her novel to a small circle of friends and later discovered that one recipient had published the novel without her permission, the author would have had an action for common law copyright infringement. After the 1976 Act no common law copyright action would lie. The novel is a work of authorship fixed in a tangible medium of expression and the work comes within the subject matter of copyright under section 102(a)(1). Further, the rights sought to be vindicated are rights against reproduction and distribution that are clearly equivalent to the rights prescribed by sections 106(1) and 106(3). Consequently, section 301(a) would bar the state law action and the author would have to rely on federal law for relief. Yet preemption would deprive the author of little since, in this case at least, the Copyright Act would give her the rough equivalent of the protection that she previously enjoyed at common law.

Section 301's application to state law doctrines other than common law copyright may be more problematic. The roots of common law copyright extend deep and wide into state jurisprudence, and related state doctrines are sometimes too entangled in common law copyright to be neatly severed for purposes of preemption. The common law right of privacy, for example, stems in part from common law copyright's right of first publication. If the author in the example just given had written not a novel but a diary, she would, before the 1976 Act, have had an action for common law copyright infringement or for invasion of privacy against a scandal sheet that purloined and published the diary. Section 301 might today bar not only the common law copyright action against the diary's publication, but also the privacy action. Since the diary is fixed in a tangible medium of expression and comes within the subject matter of copyright as a literary work under section 102(a)(1), section 301 would preempt the privacy action if a court held that the right of privacy is equivalent to section 106(1)'s reproduction right. A privacy-minded author would in this case lose something in the exchange of state protection for federal protection since, as a condition to bringing a copyright infringement action, she must register and deposit—and thus publicly expose—the diary.

The House Report on the 1976 Act observes that the declaration of section 301's preemptive principle "is intended to be stated in the clearest and most unequivocal language possible, so as to foreclose any conceivable misinterpretation of its unqualified intention that Congress shall act preemptively, and to avoid the development of any vague borderline areas between State and Federal protection." Although Congress' preemptive purpose is clear, the language that section 301 employs to effectuate this purpose is not. Courts have divided over the precise meaning of two of section 301(a)'s three conditions for preemption—that the state right be equivalent to copyright and that the subject matter of the state right come within the subject matter of copyright. Some confusion also surrounds section 301(b)'s exclusion of certain rights from preemption.

§ 15.2.1 "Equivalent" Rights

As its first condition for preemption, section 301(a) requires that the state right in issue be a "legal or equitable" right that is "equivalent to any of the exclusive rights within the general scope of copyright as specified by section 106." This means that on and after January 1, 1978, a state right will be preempted if it attaches to a tangibly fixed work of authorship coming within the subject matter of copyright and is equivalent to the right to reproduce the work in copies or phonorecords, to prepare derivative works based upon the work, to distribute copies or phonorecords of the work publicly, to perform the work publicly or to display the work publicly.

Congress evidently recognized that the test of equivalence could not be painted with such broad brush-strokes as the "purpose" or "effect" of the state law in issue. To preempt state doctrines because their purpose is equivalent to the purpose of copyright would cut too narrowly, for it is easy to find an independent, noncopyright purpose behind any state law. Common law copyright, for example, may seek to protect personal interests in privacy as well as strictly reputational interests. On the other hand, to preempt state doctrines because their effects are equivalent to copyright would cut too broadly into state doctrines that Congress surely would have wanted to survive preemption. Privacy, trade secret and unfair competition law are only a few of the many state doctrines that, like section 106 of the Copyright Act, prohibit the reproduction, distribution, performance or display of protected subject matter and consequently produce effects equivalent to copyright.

The language and legislative history of section 301, as well as most of the judicial decisions applying the section, support a more discriminating test for equivalence. The mainstream test of equivalence under section 301 focuses on the nature of the state right involved and on the elements required to make out a prima facie case for violation of the right. Courts generally hold that a state law right is equivalent to copyright for the purposes of section 301 if (1) the right encompasses conduct coming within the scope of one or more of section 106's exclusive rights, and (2) if applicable state law requires the plaintiff to prove no more than the elements that the Copyright Act requires for proof of infringement of one or more of section 106's five exclusive rights. The first part of this test would preempt state doctrines that are broader, as well as those that are narrower, than the counterpart statutory right. The second part of the test would exempt state doctrines that require proof of an extra substantive element—beyond the elements required for infringement of a right under the Copyright Act—to make out a prima facie case.

§ 15.2.1.1   State Rights Whose Scope Is Broader Than Statutory Rights

Section 301(a) measures the equivalence of state laws not against section 106's specific exclusive rights, but against "the exclusive rights *within the general scope of copyright* as specified by section 106." The House Report on the 1976 Act explains, "The preemption of rights under State law is complete with respect to any work coming within the scope of the bill, even though the scope of exclusive rights given the work under the bill is narrower than the scope of common law rights in the work might have been." [17]

The "general scope of copyright" means the full scope that Congress could have described for any particular right. For example, the general scope of copyright includes section 106(4)'s exclusive right to perform a work, and any state right that prohibits performance will be considered an equivalent right. Although section 106(4) limits its right to public performances, a state law that prohibited private performances would nonetheless come within the general scope of the right. While the state law right would be broader than the statutory right, it would fall within the general ambit of the performance right and thus be subject to preemption. Similarly, state laws against the private display or private distribution of works would come within the general

17. House Report, 131.

scope of section 106(3)'s right of public distribution or section 106(5)'s right of public display respectively.

It is less clear that section 301 would treat a state law as coming within the general scope of copyright if instead of filling a gap in the scope of a statutory right—prohibiting private rather than public performances for example—it grants a right that section 106 entirely withholds. For example, section 106(4) gives no performance rights to sound recordings. Does a state law against performance of sound recordings come within the general scope of section 106(4)'s performance right? On the one hand, this might be considered an instance of the federal law being "narrower" than the state law, thus subjecting the state law to preemption. On the other hand, the fact that the Act omits a right against performance of sound recordings may mean that state laws against performance of sound recordings are immune from preemption since a right that does not exist—a performance right in sound recordings—cannot be said to have a "general scope."

Section 301 can be read to save state laws that grant a right to subject matter from which section 106 entirely withholds the same right. Nonetheless, the purposes behind section 301 and Congress' "unqualified intention" to act preemptively [18] suggest that Congress may have intended to treat these state rights as equivalent to copyright. Although Congress could have outlawed the unauthorized performance of sound recordings, it withheld the right in an effort to strike a balance between the need for copyright incentives and competing economic and political pressures for free use in a specific circumstance. Section 301 arguably reflects Congress' belief that this balance should govern not only rights under the Copyright Act but under state law as well. Even if section 301 does exempt state rights from preemption in situations where the Copyright Act withholds particular rights, these state laws may nonetheless be subject to preemption under the Constitution's supremacy clause.

§ 15.2.1.2   State Rights Containing No "Extra Element"

Courts generally hold that a state right is not equivalent to copyright, and thus is not subject to preemption, if the state cause of action contains an operative element that is absent from the cause of action for copyright infringement. To save a state right from preemption, the extra element must relate to the economic scope of the right and not to the state of mind of the defendant. Because an extra element circumscribes the scope of the property right granted by state law, the extra element test directly serves section 301's central purpose: to bar states from extending property rights that are equivalent to the property rights conferred by the Copyright Act.

Contract law is a good example of a state law that will be immune from preemption under the extra element test. Contract law may be employed to prohibit the unauthorized reproduction, distribution, performance or display of a work. But, in addition to these acts, contract

---

18.   House Report, 130.

law requires the plaintiff to prove the existence of a bargained-for exchange—something she need not prove in a cause of action for copyright infringement. Similarly, section 301 will not preempt the traditional cause of action for unjust enrichment because to recover under this theory a plaintiff must prove the extra element that the defendant used plaintiff's work under circumstances giving the defendant notice of plaintiff's expectation of payment. An action for unfair competition will not be preempted if the plaintiff can prove the extra element of consumer confusion as to source. An action for trade secret appropriation, and actions based on a confidential relationship generally, will not be preempted if the plaintiff can prove the extra element of breach of confidence. A state law action for conversion will not be preempted if the plaintiff can prove the extra element that the defendant unlawfully retained the physical object embodying plaintiff's work.

Courts applying the extra element test have consistently looked to the substance rather than the form of the state law claim in issue. Simply casting a claim as one for contract breach will not save it from preemption. Courts have held that if a state law claim for tortious interference with contractual relations or prospective business advantage or for unjust enrichment alleges none of the elements that distinguish those causes of action from copyright infringement, the claim will be subject to preemption under section 301. Courts have held that section 301(a) encompasses state unfair competition claims that allege misappropriation, but not the extra element of consumer confusion as to source, and trade secret claims that allege unlawful appropriation, but not breach of confidence. Courts have also held that section 301(a) encompasses claims for conversion in cases where the plaintiff alleges only the unlawful retention of its intellectual property rights and not the unlawful retention of the tangible object embodying its work.

§ 15.2.1.3 State Regulatory Programs

Parties have relied on both section 301(a) of the Copyright Act and the supremacy clause of the Constitution to challenge state laws regulating the use of copyrighted works. Motion picture producers have challenged state laws that prohibit the imposition of blind bidding requirements on theater owners, the Association of American Medical Colleges has attacked a state law requiring it to reproduce and distribute copies of its standardized admission test, and criminal defendants have challenged state laws proscribing the unauthorized reproduction and distribution of sound recordings. The results in the cases have differed. In the blind bidding cases, the courts held that section 301 did not preempt a state law requiring distributors to give potential exhibitors an opportunity to view motion pictures before bidding on them. In the *American Medical Colleges* case, the court held that the plaintiff's preemption claim under section 301 had merit. Courts have invalidated state theft laws on the ground that they are preempted by section 301.

State regulatory programs do not fit comfortably within the design of section 301. To varying degrees these programs do affect copyright subject matter. But none creates a right equivalent to copyright. For example, the plaintiff's argument in the blind bidding case that the state law interfered with its distribution and performance rights fell far short of the equivalence that section 301 requires. At most, the state law undercut the value of plaintiff's copyrights and thus may have affected its incentives to produce motion pictures. Such claims are better resolved under the Constitution's supremacy clause. Criminal laws grant no private right or remedy and thus fall outside section 301's express language. To be sure, the fact that enforcement of criminal laws may produce the same economic effects as private enforcement of copyright arguably brings them within the purpose of section 301. But section 301's limited scope suggests that these laws, too, are better tested under the supremacy clause.

§ 15.2.1.4 Other Guidelines for Determining Whether Rights Are "Equivalent"

The drafters of the 1976 Copyright Act recognized the difficulty of defining equivalence for purposes of preemption and originally listed several examples of state laws that would not be preempted by section 301. Section 301(b)(3), as submitted to Congress in 1965, exempted "activities violating rights that are not equivalent to any of the exclusive rights within the general scope of copyright as specified by section 106, including breaches of contract, breaches of trust, invasion of privacy, defamation, and deceptive trade practices such as passing off and false representation." [41] In the version that went to the floor of the House in 1976, section 301(b)(3) included three more examples of exempted state doctrines—trespass, conversion and, most significantly, "rights against misappropriation not equivalent to any of such exclusive rights [within the general scope of copyright as specified by section 106]." [42] According to the 1976 House Report, " 'Misappropriation' is not necessarily synonymous with copyright infringement, and thus a cause of action labeled as 'misappropriation' is not preempted if it is in fact based neither on a right within the general scope of copyright as specified by section 106 nor a right equivalent thereto." [43]

A last-minute amendment offered on the floor of the House removed all of the state law examples listed in section 301(b)(3)'s savings provision. The amendment was evidently prompted by a letter from the Justice Department: "While 'misappropriation' is almost certain to nullify preemption, any of the causes of action listed in paragraph (3) following the phrase 'as specified by section 106' may be construed to

---

41. H.R. 4347, 89th Cong., 1st Sess. (1965).

42. S. 22, 94th Cong., 2d Sess., 122 Cong.Rec. 31988–32006 (1976).

43. House Report, 132. This change represents a departure from the position that the House Report took on misappropriation in the 1965 bill. According to

that report, "where the cause of action involves the form of unfair competition commonly referred to as 'misappropriation,' which is nothing more than copyright protection under another name, section 301 is intended to have preemptive effect." H.R.Rep. No. 2237, 89th Cong., 2d Sess. 129 (1966).

have the same effect. For example, a court could construe the copyright of an uncopyrighted published book to be an invasion of the author's right to privacy, i.e., the right to keep the control of the publication of his book privately to himself." [44] Discussion of the amendment on the House floor only clouded the amendment's meaning. In introducing the amendment, its sponsor suggested that the amendment merely intended to subject misappropriation doctrine to preemption.[45] A question from a subcommittee member reflected his understanding that the amendment would leave misappropriation and the other cited examples of state law untouched.[46] The amendment's sponsor subsequently acceded to this understanding.[47] A concluding comment from the subcommittee chair reflected the belief that the amendment would in fact preempt misappropriation doctrine and possibly the other cited state doctrines as well.[48]

The amendment striking the state law examples from section 301(b)(3)'s savings provision leaves some doubt about the continued relevance of these examples in construing section 301's reference to "equivalent" state doctrines. History suggests that, with the possible exception of misappropriation, courts should refer to these doctrines as examples of unpreempted state laws since in one form or another the examples had been associated with section 301 from the beginning, forming a benchmark by which the section's thrust was understood and measured. Some courts have expressly adopted this position. The many courts that have adopted the "extra element" test of equivalence may view the deleted examples in the same light since the extra elements test apparently underlay the drafters' selection of these examples.

The status of state law misappropriation doctrine after its deletion as an example of a nonequivalent state law is more problematic. Of all the state doctrines listed as examples, misappropriation represents the

44. Quoted in Appendix IV to Fetter, Copyright Revision and the Preemption of State "Misappropriation" Law: A Study in Judicial and Congressional Interaction, 25 Bull. Copyright Socy. USA 367, 423 (1978). This excellent article also reprints, in Appendices II and III, the preemption provisions of successive copyright bills beginning with section 19 of the Preliminary Draft Revision Bill of 1963.

45. 122 Cong.Rec. 32015 (1976) (statement of Rep. Seiberling).

46. 122 Cong.Rec. 32015 (1976) (statement of Rep. Railsback: "Mr. Chairman, may I ask the gentleman from Ohio, for the purpose of clarifying the amendment that by striking the word 'misappropriation,' the gentleman in no way is attempting to change the existing state of the law, that is as it may exist in certain States that have recognized the right of recovery relating to 'misappropriation'; is that correct?").

47. 122 Cong.Rec. 32015 (1976) (Rep. Seiberling: "That is correct. All I am trying to do is prevent the citing of them as examples in the statute. We are, in effect, adopting a rather amorphous body of State law and codifying it, in effect. Rather I am trying to have this bill leave the State law alone and make it clear we are merely dealing with copyright laws, laws applicable to copyrights.").

48. 122 Cong.Rec. 32015 (1976) (statement of Rep. Kastenmeier: "Mr. Chairman, I too have examined the gentleman's amendment and was familiar with the position of the Department of Justice. Unfortunately, the Justice Department did not make its position known to the committee until the last day of markup. . . . However, Mr. Chairman, I think that the amendment the gentleman is offering is consistent with the position of the Justice Department and accept it on this side as well.").

most effective surrogate for statutory copyright and, indeed, probably motivated the amendment. This suggests that in applying section 301 to misappropriation doctrine courts might properly bring a presumption of equivalence that they do not bring to other state doctrines. Further, even if misappropriation is not preempted under the terms of section 301, it may be subject to preemption under the supremacy clause.

§ 15.2.2 "Fixed in a Tangible Medium of Expression"

Section 301's second requirement for preemption of state law is that the state right be in "works of authorship that are fixed in a tangible medium of expression." Statutory copyright does not extend to works that have not been fixed in a tangible medium of expression. As a consequence, section 301 leaves regulation of unfixed works to the states. The House Report gives several examples of unfixed works that may be protected by state law: "choreography that has never been filmed or notated, an extemporaneous speech, 'original works of authorship' communicated solely through conversations or live broadcasts, and a dramatic sketch or musical composition improvised or developed from memory and without being recorded or written down." [55] State rights in a work will be subject to preemption if the work, though originally unfixed, becomes fixed in a larger copyrightable work with the author's permission. For example, one court held that baseball players' rights of publicity arising from their appearances in ball games were subject to preemption because the ball games were videotaped as they were televised.

§ 15.2.3 "Works of Authorship That . . . Come Within the Subject Matter of Copyright"

Section 301's third requirement for preemption is that the work of authorship that is subject to the state right must "come within the subject matter of copyright as specified by sections 102 and 103." The principal ambiguity in the requirement stems from the fact that neither section 102 nor section 103 defines the "subject matter of copyright." At most, section 102(a) defines copyright subject matter obliquely by stating that copyright protection subsists "in original works of authorship fixed in any tangible medium of expression" and by listing seven categories of "works of authorship." Section 102(b) provides that "copyright protection for an original work of authorship does not extend to any idea, procedure, process, system, method of operation, concept, principle, or discovery, regardless of the form in which it is described, explained, illustrated, or embodied in such work." Section 103 adds only that the subject matter of copyright specified by section 102 includes compilations and derivative works.

The thorniest interpretational problem posed by section 301's subject matter test lies in the interplay between sections 301(a) and 102(b). Does section 102(b) say that procedures, processes and similar ideas are

---

55. House Report, 131.

not the subject matter of copyright? Or does section 102(b) say that these elements come within the scope of copyright subject matter but that the Act withholds protection from them? The first interpretation would allow states to protect procedures, processes and similar ideas. The second interpretation would prohibit states from protecting these elements, if fixed, through rights equivalent to copyright.

The soundest reading of section 102, supported by the legislative history and case law, is that only works of authorship constitute copyright subject matter and that the ideas, procedures, processes and other elements listed in section 102(b) are not copyrightable subject matter because they are not works of authorship. Just as section 102(b) denies copyright to ideas that appear in otherwise copyrightable works, it implicitly denies copyright to ideas that appear separately, outside the context of an otherwise copyrightable work. As a consequence, section 301 allows states to protect ideas, procedures, processes and methods, whether or not they appear in the context of otherwise copyrightable works. To be sure, states will often decline to protect ideas for the very same reasons that underlay Congress' decision to withhold copyright from ideas. Further, although state idea protection is exempt from preemption under section 301, it is subject to review under the supremacy clause of the Constitution and the first amendment as incorporated in the fourteenth amendment to the Constitution.

Facts, like ideas, are not copyrightable subject matter. As a consequence, section 301 allows states to protect facts appearing in such forms as "hot news" and uncopyrightable compilations of data, including data compiled in computer databases. The House Report on the 1976 Act observed that "state law should have the flexibility to afford a remedy (under traditional principles of equity) against a consistent pattern of unauthorized appropriation by a competitor of the facts (i.e., not the literary expression) constituting 'hot' news, whether in the traditional mold of International News Service v. Associated Press, 248 U.S. 215 (1918), or in the newer form of data updates from scientific, business, or financial data bases." [64] Courts have indicated that section 301 does not preempt state law protection for facts.

Section 301 will preempt a state law granting a right equivalent to copyright to a tangibly fixed work coming within the scope of copyrightable subject matter if the work is in the public domain because it is not original, because the term of copyright has expired or because publicly distributed copies or phonorecords of the work did not bear the copyright notice required before March 1, 1989, the effective date of the Berne Implementation Amendments. According to the House Report on the 1976 Act, "As long as a work fits within one of the general subject matter categories of sections 102 and 103, the bill prevents the States from protecting it even if it fails to achieve Federal statutory

---

64. House Report, 132. The observation in the House Report is less than definitive, however, since it was evidently addressed to examples of state law, including misappropriation, that section 301(b)(3) had originally declared to be exempt from preemption but that were deleted at the last moment by an amendment introduced on the floor of the House. See § 15.2.1.4, above.

copyright because it is too minimal or lacking in originality to qualify, or because it has fallen into the public domain." [69] One court rejected the argument that section 301 did not preempt the state law right of publicity of baseball players in their on-field performances because the performances lacked sufficient creativity to qualify for copyright.[70] In the court's view, section 301(a) "preempts all equivalent state-law rights claimed in any work within the subject matter of copyright whether or not the work embodies any creativity." [71]

Courts deciding copyright infringement cases do not always distinguish between elements that fall outside the scope of copyright subject matter because they are unprotectible ideas and elements that come within the scope of copyright subject matter but nonetheless fail to meet the copyright law's originality standard. Plots, for example, may be unprotectible because they are akin to ideas or because, though they are akin to expression, they are so common that they probably did not originate with their putative author. Such line-drawing is unnecessary in the usual infringement case where the fact, and not the rationale, of unprotectibility is the only question in issue. But it is necessary to identify the rationale for withholding protection from plots and similar elements where the question in issue is whether section 301 preempts state law protection for the element. If the element is uncopyrightable because it is an idea, it may be protected under state law. If, however, the element is uncopyrightable only because it is not original—and if section 301's other two conditions are met—the element may not be protected under state law because it comes within the subject matter of copyright.

NOTES

1. Section 301 casts its preemptive net far wider than state common law copyright. No state intellectual property law is beyond its potential reach.

Contract Law. Idea submitters have a hard time recovering under express or implied contract theories—not because of preemption, but because idea recipients will rarely expose themselves to liability under either of these theories. See page 41, above. The submitter who has elaborated her idea in detailed, concrete form has a greater chance of recovery under state law, but she also faces a greater likelihood of preemption under section 301 since her elaborated submission may constitute the "subject matter of copyright" as described in section 102(a), and a right against noncontracting parties may be equivalent to copyright.

Trade Secrets. Does section 301 preempt a state law action against the misappropriation of secret drawings and specifications? Avco Corp. v. Precision Air Parts, Inc., 210 U.S.P.Q. 894 (M.D.Ala.1980), aff'd on

69. House Report, 131.

70. Baltimore Orioles, Inc. v. Major League Baseball Players Assn., 805 F.2d 663, 676, 231 U.S.P.Q. 673 (7th Cir.1986),

cert. denied, 480 U.S. 941, 107 S.Ct. 1593, 94 L.Ed.2d 782 (1987).

71. 805 F.2d at 676.

other grounds, 676 F.2d 494, 216 U.S.P.Q. 1086 (11th Cir.1982) held that it does: "The essence of plaintiff's complaint is that Defendant has copied its drawings and specifications and prepared derivative works based upon those drawings and specifications. Thus, the complaint fits squarely into § 106(1) and (2). It is undisputed that the drawings and specifications are 'fixed in a tangible medium of expression.' Finally, the drawings and specifications in issue could certainly be characterized as pictorial or graphic works. Thus, this court is of the opinion that the requirements of 17 U.S.C.A. § 301(a) are satisfied by the facts in this case." The court added that Congress did not intend to preempt trade secret actions involving elements "such as an invasion of personal rights or a breach of trust or confidentiality, that are different in kind from copyright infringement." But plaintiff had not alleged that defendant "has committed any of the elements that allow the common law rights of 'trade secrets' to avoid preemption." 210 U.S.P.Q. at 897–98, 898 n. 9.

Unfair Competition. According to the House Report on the 1976 Copyright Act, "[s]ection 301 is not intended to preempt common law protection in cases involving activities such as false labeling, fraudulent representation, and passing off even where the subject matter involved comes within the scope of the copyright statute." H.R.Rep. No. 1476, 94th Cong., 2d Sess. 132 (1976).

Courts have generally held that section 301 does not preempt state law passing off actions because the required proof of consumer confusion represents an "extra element" that distinguishes the right from the exclusive rights granted by section 106 of the 1976 Act. See, e.g., Donald Frederick Evans & Assocs. v. Continental Homes, Inc., 785 F.2d 897, 229 U.S.P.Q. 321 (11th Cir.1986). What of misappropriation doctrine, which does not require deception? What of state trademark statutes that protect emblems and insignia apart from any requirement of consumer deception?

Right of Publicity. Names and likenesses—the usual objects of state rights of publicity—fall outside the subject matter of copyright and consequently lie beyond the reach of section 301. What of more original and expressive subject matter, such as the circus act in *Zacchini,* page 186, above and the voice and singing style in *Midler,* page 185, above? See Shipley, Three Strikes and They're Out at the Old Ball Game: Preemption of Performers' Rights of Publicity Under the Copyright Act of 1976, 20 Ariz.St.L.J. 369 (1988).

Moral Right. To what extent does section 301 preempt state law protection of an author's moral right? Would a state law that prohibited distortion of a work be equivalent to section 106(2)'s provision for derivative rights? Would a state law that permitted authors to recall their copyrighted works be equivalent to section 106(3)'s distribution right as limited by section 109's first sale doctrine?

The Berne Implementation Act of 1988 introduced no aspects of moral right into the Copyright Act. Consequently, it had no effect on the preemption of state laws that approximate these rights. Section

301(e), added by the Berne Implementation Act, makes this point explicit: "The scope of Federal preemption under this section is not affected by the adherence of the United States to the Berne Convention or the satisfaction of obligations of the United States thereunder."

2. *History.* Copyright preemption battles were fought in the courts for more than two decades before passage of the 1976 Act. Tape piracy was the principal battleground. Because the 1909 Copyright Act did not protect sound recordings, record producers turned for relief to state law, mainly unfair competition law's misappropriation doctrine. The Supreme Court's landmark preemption decisions in *Sears* and *Compo,* pages 103 and 107, above, did little to curb the use of misappropriation doctrine in the fight against record pirates. Because tape piracy involved the "appropriation" of a work and not its mere "copying," courts reasoned, *Sears* and *Compo* did not apply. See, e.g., Columbia Broadcasting Sys. v. Documentaries Unlimited, Inc., 42 Misc.2d 723, 248 N.Y.S.2d 809, 140 U.S.P.Q. 686 (Sup.Ct.1964). Goldstein v. California, 412 U.S. 546, 93 S.Ct. 2303, 37 L.Ed.2d 163, 178 U.S.P.Q. 129 (1973), discussed in note 3 below, sanctioned these state decisions.

The 1971 Sound Recording Act, P.L. 92–140, 85 Stat. 391, and successor provisions in the 1976 Copyright Act giving federal copyright protection to sound recordings, marked the end of state protection for recordings fixed on or after February 15, 1972. Section 301(c) of the 1976 Act exempts pre-February 15, 1972 recordings from preemption until February 15, 2047.

For more on these issues, see Brown, Publication and Preemption in Copyright Law: Elegiac Reflections on *Goldstein v. California,* 22 UCLA L.Rev. 1022 (1975); Goldstein, Federal System Ordering of the Copyright Interest, 69 Colum.L.Rev. 49 (1969); Kaplan, Performer's Right and Copyright: The Capitol Records Case, 69 Harv.L.Rev. 409 (1956).

3. *Constitutional Preemption.* Petitioners in Goldstein v. California, 412 U.S. 546, 93 S.Ct. 2303, 37 L.Ed.2d 163, 178 U.S.P.Q. 129 (1973), had been successfully prosecuted for record piracy under California Penal Code § 653. Appealing their conviction, they argued that "Congress intended to allow individuals to copy any work which was not protected by a federal copyright." Since, at the time, the Copyright Act did not protect sound recordings, and since section 653 prohibited "the copying of works which are not entitled to federal protection . . . it conflicts directly with congressional policy and must fall under the Supremacy Clause of the Constitution." Petitioners also argued that "the statute establishes a state copyright of unlimited duration and thus conflicts with Art. I, § 8, cl. 8 of the Constitution" restricting the congressional power to grants of protection for "limited times." 412 U.S. at 551, 93 S.Ct. at 2307.

The Court's answer to the petitioners' first argument reads like a primer on the federal system. The Court began with Federalist No. 32, defining those areas in which states are considered to have given up their reserved powers:

> [T]his alienation, of State sovereignty, would only exist in three cases: where the Constitution in express terms granted an exclusive authority to the Union; where it granted in one instance an authority to the Union, and in another prohibited the States from exercising the like authority; and where it granted an authority to the Union to which a similar authority in the States would be absolutely and totally *contradictory* and *repugnant.*

412 U.S. at 553, 93 S.Ct. at 2308. The "first two instances," the Court observed, "present no barrier to a State's enactment of copyright statutes": the Constitution nowhere makes the grant of copyright authority exclusive, and it nowhere withholds the power from the states. Id.

The Court then turned to the formula's third prong. Conceding that the "objective of the Copyright Clause was clearly to facilitate the granting of rights national in scope," the Court concluded that, although "the Copyright Clause thus recognizes the potential benefits of a national system, it does not indicate that all writings are of national interest or that state legislation is, in all cases, unnecessary or precluded." The Court went on: "Since the subject matter to which the Copyright Clause is addressed may thus be of purely local importance and not worthy of national attention or protection, we cannot discern such an unyielding national interest as to require an inference that state power to grant copyrights has been relinquished to *exclusive* federal control." 412 U.S. at 555–558 (emphasis in original). Since Congress had not expressly withdrawn state power over sound recordings, the California statute was valid.

To petitioners' second argument, that the California statute violated the Constitution's "limited times" restriction, the Court answered that "Section 8 enumerates those powers which have been granted *to Congress;* whatever limitations have been appended to such powers can only be understood as a limit on congressional, and not state, action." It added that, in any event, "it is not clear that the dangers to which this limitation was addressed apply with equal force to both the Federal Government and the States. When Congress grants an exclusive right or monopoly, its effects are pervasive; no citizen or State may escape its reach. As we have noted, however, the exclusive right granted by a State is confined to its borders. Consequently, even when the right is unlimited in duration, any tendency to inhibit further progress in science or the arts is narrowly circumscribed." 412 U.S. at 560–61, 93 S.Ct. at 2311 (emphasis in original).

5. *Interplay of Statutory and Constitutional Preemption.* Does section 301 leave any room for constitutional preemption of state laws bordering on copyright? Several courts have treated section 301 and the supremacy clause as discrete sources of preemption. See, e.g., Associated Film Distrib. Corp. v. Thornburgh, 614 F.Supp. 1100, 227 U.S.P.Q. 184 (E.D.Pa.1985), aff'd, 800 F.2d 369, 231 U.S.P.Q. 143 (3d Cir.

1986), cert. denied, 480 U.S. 933, 107 S.Ct. 1573, 94 L.Ed.2d 765 (1987). If the Copyright Act—including section 301—is part of the "supreme law of the land," how can any state law that passes muster under section 301 not also pass muster under the supremacy clause? Do the First Amendment's free speech and press guarantees provide an independent basis for preemption?

Part Four

INTELLECTUAL PROPERTIES IN CONCERT: COMPUTER PROGRAMS AND INDUSTRIAL DESIGN

I. COMPUTER PROGRAMS

Copyright law, patent law and trade secret law protect computer programs. C. Sherman, H. Sandison & M. Guren, Computer Software Protection Law (1989), examines the applicable laws in useful detail. Several books explore intellectual property protection for computer programs within the larger frame of "computer law." Among them are D. Bender, Computer Law (1989); R. Bernacchi, P. Frank & N. Statland, Bernacchi on Computer Law (1989); G. Davis, Software Protection (1985); L.J. Kutten, Computer Software (1989); R. Nimmer, The Law of Computer Technology (1985); M. Scott, Computer Law (1989).

A. COPYRIGHT LAW

---

1. SCOPE OF PROTECTION

a. OPERATING SYSTEMS AND APPLICATION PROGRAMS

WHELAN ASSOCIATES, INC. v. JASLOW DENTAL LABORATORY, INC.

United States Court of Appeals, Third Circuit, 1986.
797 F.2d 1222, cert. denied, 479 U.S. 1031, 107 S.Ct. 877, 93 L.Ed.2d 831 (1987).

BECKER, Circuit Judge.

This appeal involves a computer program for the operation of a dental laboratory, and calls upon us to apply the principles underlying our venerable copyright laws to the relatively new field of computer technology to determine the scope of copyright protection of a computer program. More particularly, in this case of first impression in the courts of appeals, we must determine whether the structure (or sequence and organization)[1] of a computer program is protectible by copyright, or whether the protection of the copyright law extends only as far as the literal computer code. The district court found that the copyright law covered these non-literal elements of the program, and

---

1. We use the terms "structure," "sequence," and "organization" interchangeably when referring to computer programs, and we intend them to be synonymous in this opinion.

773

we agree. This conclusion in turn requires us to consider whether there was sufficient evidence of substantial similarity between the structures of the two programs at issue in this case to uphold the district court's finding of copyright infringement. Because we find that there was enough evidence, we affirm.

I. *FACTUAL BACKGROUND*

Appellant Jaslow Dental Laboratory, Inc. ("Jaslow Lab") is a Pennsylvania corporation in the business of manufacturing dental prosthetics and devices. Appellant Dentcom, Inc. ("Dentcom") is a Pennsylvania corporation in the business of developing and marketing computer programs for use by dental laboratories. Dentcom was formed out of the events that gave rise to this suit, and its history will be recounted below. Individual appellants Edward Jaslow and his son Rand Jaslow are officers and shareholders in both Jaslow Lab and Dentcom. Appellants were defendants in the district court. Plaintiff-appellee Whelan Associates, Inc. ("Whelan Associates") is also a Pennsylvania corporation, engaged in the business of developing and marketing custom computer programs.

Jaslow Lab, like any other small- or medium-sized business of moderate complexity, has significant bookkeeping and administrative tasks. Each order for equipment must be registered and processed; inventory must be maintained; customer lists must be continually updated; invoicing, billing, and accounts receivable, must be dealt with. While many of these functions are common to all businesses, the nature of the dental prosthetics business apparently requires some variations on the basic theme.

Although Rand Jaslow had not had extensive experience with computers, he believed that the business operations of Jaslow Lab could be made more efficient if they were computerized. In early 1978, he therefore bought a small personal computer and tried to teach himself how to program it so that it would be of use to Jaslow Lab. Although he wrote a program for the computer, he was ultimately not successful, limited by both his lack of expertise and the relatively small capacity of his particular computer.

A few months later, stymied by his own lack of success but still confident that Jaslow Lab would profit from computerization, Rand Jaslow hired the Strohl Systems Group, Inc. ("Strohl"), a small corporation that developed custom-made software to develop a program that would run on Jaslow Lab's new IBM Series One computer and take care of the Lab's business needs. Jaslow Lab and Strohl entered into an agreement providing that Strohl would design a system for Jaslow Lab's needs and that after Strohl had installed the system Strohl could market it to other dental laboratories. Jaslow Lab would receive a 10% royalty on all such sales. The person at Strohl responsible for the Jaslow Lab account was Elaine Whelan, an experienced programmer who was an officer and half-owner of Strohl.

Ms. Whelan's first step was to visit Jaslow Lab and interview Rand Jaslow and others to learn how the laboratory worked and what its needs were. She also visited other dental laboratories and interviewed people there, so that she would better understand the layout, workflow, and administration of dental laboratories generally. After this education into the ways of dental laboratories, and Jaslow Lab, in particular, Ms. Whelan wrote a program called Dentalab for Jaslow Lab. Dentalab was written in a computer language known as EDL (Event Driven Language), so that it would work with IBM Series One machines. The program was completed and was operative at Jaslow Lab around March 1979.

Presumably with an eye towards exploiting the economic potential of the Dentalab program, Ms. Whelan left Strohl in November, 1979, to form her own business, Whelan Associates, Inc., which acquired Strohl's interest in the Dentalab program. Shortly thereafter, Whelan Associates entered into negotiations with Jaslow Lab for Jaslow Lab to be Whelan Associates' sales representative for the Dentalab program. Whelan Associates and Jaslow Lab entered into an agreement on July 30, 1980, according to which Jaslow Lab agreed to use its "best efforts and to act diligently in the marketing of the Dentalab package," and Whelan Associates agreed to "use its best efforts and to act diligently to improve and augment the previously successfully designed Dentalab package." The agreements stated that Jaslow Lab would receive 35% of the gross price of any programs sold and 5% of the price of any modifications to the programs. The agreement was for one year and was then terminable by either party on thirty days' notice.

The parties' business relationship worked successfully for two years. During this time, as Rand Jaslow became more familiar with computer programming, he realized that because Dentalab was written in EDL it could not be used on computers that many of the smaller dental prosthetics firms were using, for which EDL had not been implemented. Sensing that there might be a market for a program that served essentially the same function as Dentalab but that could be used more widely, Rand Jaslow began in May or June of 1982 to develop in his spare time a program in the BASIC language for such computers. That program, when completed, became the alleged copyright infringer in this suit; it was called the Dentcom PC program ("Dentcom program").

It appears that Rand Jaslow was sanguine about the prospects of his program for smaller computers. After approximately a year of work, on May 31, 1983, his attorney sent a letter to Whelan Associates giving one month notice of termination of the agreement between Whelan Associates and Jaslow Lab. The letter stated that Jaslow Lab considered itself to be the exclusive marketer of the Dentalab program which, the letter stated, "contains valuable trade secrets of Jaslow Dental Laboratory." The letter concluded with a thinly veiled threat to Whelan Associates: "I . . . look for your immediate response confirming that you will respect the rights of Jaslow and not use or disclose to others the trade secrets of Jaslow."

Approximately two months later, on about August 1, Edward and Rand Jaslow, Paul Mohr, and Joseph Cerra formed defendant-appellant Dentcom to sell the Dentcom program. At about the same time, Rand Jaslow and Jaslow Lab employed a professional computer programmer, Jonathan Novak, to complete the Dentcom program. The program was soon finished, and Dentcom proceeded to sell it to dental prosthetics companies that had personal computers. Dentcom sold both the Dentalab and Dentcom programs, and advertised the Dentcom program as "a new version of the Dentlab computer system."

Despite Jaslow Lab's May 31 letter warning Whelan Associates not to sell the Dentalab program, Whelan Associates continued to market Dentalab. This precipitated the present litigation. . . .

The district court ruled for Whelan Associates on all grounds. It found that Elaine Whelan was the sole author of the Dentalab system (and, hence, that Rand Jaslow was not a co-author) and that the contract between Strohl and Rand Jaslow made clear that Strohl would retain full ownership over the software. The court thus concluded that Whelan Associates' copyright in the Dentalab System was valid, and that Dentcom's sales of the Dentalab program were violations of that copyright.

The court also found that Rand Jaslow had not created the Dentcom system independently, and that the Dentcom system, although written in a different computer language from the Dentalab system, and although not a direct transliteration of Dentalab, was substantially similar to Dentalab because its structure and overall organization were substantially similar. This substantial similarity, in conjunction with Rand Jaslow's acknowledged access to the Dentalab system, led the district court to conclude that each sale of the Dentcom program by Dentcom violated Whelan Associates' copyright on the Dentalab system. The court therefore awarded Whelan Associates damages for these copyright infringements, and enjoined Dentcom from selling any more copies of the Dentalab or Dentcom programs. The court also held that plaintiffs had exclusive use of the term "Dentalab," and enjoined defendants from using either "Dentalab" or "Dentlab" in their business.

The parties filed a series of post-trial motions, primarily concerned with damage calculations and attorneys fees. Upon the district court's disposition of these motions, the defendants filed their notices of appeal. On appeal, they raise a single issue: whether the district court erred in its finding that the Dentcom program infringes the copyright of plaintiffs' Dentalab system.

III. *TECHNOLOGICAL BACKGROUND*

We begin with a brief description of computer programs and an explanation of how they are written. This introduction is necessary to our analysis of the issue in this case.

A computer program is a set of instructions to the computer. Most programs accept and process user-supplied data. The fundamental processes utilized by a program are called algorithms (mechanical computational procedures) and are at the heart of the program. These algorithms must be developed by the human creativity of the programmer, and the program therefore cannot contain any algorithms not already considered by humans. Although a computer cannot think or develop algorithms, it can execute them faster and more accurately than any human possibly could.

The creation of a program often takes place in several steps, moving from the general to the specific. Because programs are intended to accomplish particular tasks, the first step in creating the program is identifying the problem that the computer programmer is trying to solve. In this case, Rand Jaslow went to Strohl and stated that his problem was recordkeeping for his business. Although this was an accurate statement of the problem, it was not specific enough to guide Elaine Whelan. Before she could write the Dentalab program, she needed to know more about Jaslow Lab's business—how orders were processed, what special billing problems might arise, how inventory might be correlated to orders, and other characteristics of the dental prosthetics trade.

As the programmer learns more about the problem, she or he may begin to outline a solution. The outline can take the form of a flowchart, which will break down the solution into a series of smaller units called "subroutines" or "modules," each of which deals with elements of the larger problem. A program's efficiency depends in large part on the arrangements of its modules and subroutines; although two programs could produce the same result, one might be more efficient because of different internal arrangements of modules and subroutines. Because efficiency is a prime concern in computer programs (an efficient program being obviously more valuable than a comparatively inefficient one), the arrangement of modules and subroutines is a critical factor for any programmer. In the present case, the Dentalab program had numerous modules pertaining to inventory, accounts receivable, various dentist-patient matters, and payroll, among others. Some of the modules were simple; others were quite complex and involved elaborate logical development.

As the program structure is refined, the programmer must make decisions about what data are needed, where along the program's operations the data should be introduced, how the data should be inputted, and how it should be combined with other data. The arrangement of the data is accomplished by means of data files, and is affected by the details of the program's subroutines and modules, for different arrangements of subroutines and modules may require data in different forms. Once again, there are numerous ways the programmer can solve the data-organization problems she or he faces. Each solution may have particular characteristics—efficiencies or inefficiencies, conveniences or quirks—that differentiate it from other solutions and make the overall program more or less desirable. Because the Dentalab program was intended to handle all of the business-related aspects of a dental laboratory, it had to accommodate and interrelate many different pieces and types of data including patients' names, dentists' names, inventory, accounts receivable, accounts payable, and payroll.

Once the detailed design of the program is completed, the coding begins. Each of the steps identified in the design must be turned into a language that the computer can understand. This translation process in itself requires two steps. The programmer first writes in a "source code," which may be in one of several languages, such as COBOL, BASIC, FORTRAN, or EDL. The choice of language depends upon which computers the programmer intends the program to be used by, for some computers can read only certain languages. Once the program is written in source code, it is translated into "object code," which is a binary code, simply a concatenation of "0"s and "1"s. In every program, it is the object code, not the source code, that directs the computer to perform functions. The object code is therefore the final instruction to the computer.

As this brief summary demonstrates, the coding process is a comparatively small part of programming. By far the larger portion of the expense and difficulty in creating computer programs is attributable to the development of the structure and logic of the program, and to debugging, documentation and maintenance, rather than to the coding. The evidence in this case shows that Ms. Whelan spent a tremendous amount of time studying Jaslow Labs, organizing the modules and subroutines for the Dentalab program, and working out the data arrangements, and a comparatively small amount of time actually coding the Dentalab program.

IV.   *LEGAL BACKGROUND*

A. *The elements of a copyright infringement action* —To prove that its copyright has been infringed, Whelan Associates must show two things: that it owned the copyright on Dentalab, and that Rand Jaslow copied Dentalab in making the Dentcom program. Although it was disputed below, the district court determined, and it is not challenged here, that Whelan Associates owned the copyright to the Dentalab program. We are thus concerned only with whether it has been shown that Rand Jaslow copied the Dentalab program.

As it is rarely possible to prove copying through direct evidence, copying may be proved inferentially by showing that the defendant had access to the allegedly infringed copyrighted work and that the allegedly infringing work is substantially similar to the copyrighted work. The district court found, and here it is uncontested, that Rand Jaslow had access to the Dentalab program, both because Dentalab was the program used in Jaslow Labs and because Rand Jaslow acted as a sales representative for Whelan Associates. Thus, the sole question is whether there was substantial similarity between the Dentcom and Dentalab programs.

B. *The appropriate test for substantial similarity in computer program cases* —The leading case of Arnstein v. Porter, 154 F.2d 464, 468–69 (2d Cir.1946), suggested a bifurcated substantial similarity test whereby a finder of fact makes two findings of substantial similarity to support a copyright violation. First, the fact-finder must decide whether there is sufficient similarity between the two works in question to conclude that the alleged infringer used the copyrighted work in making his own. On this issue, expert testimony may be received to aid the trier of fact. (This has been referred to as the "extrinsic" test of substantial similarity. Sid & Marty Krofft Television Prods., Inc. v. McDonald's Corp., 562 F.2d at 1164–65.) Second, if the answer to the first question is in the affirmative, the fact-finder must decide without the aid of expert testimony, but with the perspective of the "lay observer," whether the copying was "illicit," or "an unlawful appropriation" of the copyrighted work. (This has been termed an "intrinsic" test of substantial similarity. Id.) The *Arnstein* test has been adopted in this circuit.

The district court heard expert testimony. It did not bifurcate its analysis, however, but made only a single finding of substantial similarity. It would thus appear to have contravened the law of this circuit. Nevertheless, for the reasons that follow, we believe that the district court applied an appropriate standard.

The ordinary observer test, which was developed in cases involving novels, plays, and paintings, and which does not permit expert testimony, is of doubtful value in cases involving computer programs on account of the programs' complexity and unfamiliarity to most members of the public. Moreover, the distinction between the two parts of the *Arnstein* test may be of doubtful value when the finder of fact is the same person for each step: that person has been exposed to expert evidence in the first step, yet she or he is supposed to ignore or "forget" that evidence in analyzing the problem under the second step. Especially in complex cases, we doubt that the "forgetting" can be effective when the expert testimony is essential to even the most fundamental understanding of the objects in question.

On account of these problems with the standard, we believe that the ordinary observer test is not useful and is potentially misleading when the subjects of the copyright are particularly complex, such as computer programs. We therefore join the growing number of courts which do not apply the ordinary observer test in copyright cases involving exceptionally difficult materials, like computer programs, but instead adopt a single substantial similarity inquiry according to which both lay and expert testimony would be admissible. That was the test applied by the district court in this case.

C. *The arguments on appeal* —On appeal, the defendants attack on two grounds the district court's holding that there was sufficient evidence of substantial similarity. First, the defendants argue that because the district court did not find any similarity between the "literal" elements (source and object code) of the programs, but only similarity in their overall structures, its finding of substantial similarity was incorrect, for the copyright covers only the literal elements of computer programs, not their overall structures. Defendants' second argument is that even if the protection of copyright law extends to "non-literal" elements such as the structure of computer programs, there was not sufficient evidence of substantial similarity to sustain the district court's holding in this case. We consider these arguments in turn.

V. *THE SCOPE OF COPYRIGHT PROTECTION OF COMPUTER PROGRAMS*

It is well, though recently, established that copyright protection extends to a program's source and object codes. In this case, however, the district court did not find any copying of the source or object codes, nor did the plaintiff allege such copying. Rather, the district court held that the Dentalab copyright was infringed because the *overall structure* of Dentcom was substantially similar to the overall structure of Dentalab. The question therefore arises whether mere similarity in the overall structure of programs can be the basis for a copyright infringement, or, put differently, whether a program's copyright protection covers the structure of the program or only the program's literal elements, i.e., its source and object codes.

Title 17 U.S.C. § 102(a)(1) extends copyright protection to "literary works," and computer programs are classified as literary works for the purposes of copyright. The copyrights of other literary works can be infringed even when there is no substantial similarity between the works' literal elements. One can violate the copyright of a play or book by copying its plot or plot devices. By analogy to other literary works, it would thus appear that the copyrights of computer programs can be infringed even absent copying of the literal elements of the program. Defendants contend, however, that what is true of other literary works is not true of computer programs. They assert two principal reasons, which we consider in turn.

A. *Section 102(b) and the dichotomy between idea and expression* —It is axiomatic that copyright does not protect ideas, but only expressions of ideas. This rule, first enunciated in Baker v. Selden, 101 U.S. (11 Otto) 99, 25 L.Ed. 841 (1879), has been repeated in numerous cases. The rule has also been embodied in statute. Title 17 U.S.C. § 102(b) (1982) states:

> In no case does copyright protection for an original work of authorship extend to any idea, procedure, process, system, method of operation, concept, principle, or discovery, regardless of the form in which it is described, explained, illustrated, or embodied in such work.

The legislative history of this section, adopted in 1976, makes clear that § 102(b) was intended to express the idea-expression dichotomy.

Defendants argue that the structure of a computer program is, by definition, the idea and not the expression of the idea, and therefore that the structure cannot be protected by the program copyright. Under the defendants' approach, any other decision would be contrary to § 102(b). We divide our consideration of this argument into two parts. First, we examine the case law concerning the distinction between idea and expression, and derive from it a rule for distinguishing idea from expression in the context of computer programs. We then apply that rule to the facts of this case.

1. *A rule for distinguishing idea from expression in computer programs* —It is frequently difficult to distinguish the idea from the expression thereof. No less an authority than Learned Hand, after a career that included writing some of the leading copyright opinions, concluded that the distinction will "inevitably be *ad hoc.*" Peter Pan Fabrics, Inc. v. Martin Weiner Corp., 274 F.2d 487, 489 (2d Cir.1960). Although we acknowledge the wisdom of Judge Hand's remark, we feel that a review of relevant copyright precedent will enable us to formulate a rule applicable in this case. In addition, precisely because the line between idea and expression is elusive, we must pay particular attention to the pragmatic considerations that underlie the distinction and copyright law generally. In this regard, we must remember that the purpose of the copyright law is to create the most efficient and productive balance between protection (incentive) and dissemination of information, to promote learning, culture and development.

We begin our analysis with the case of Baker v. Selden, which, in addition to being a seminal case in the law of copyright generally, is particularly relevant here because, like the instant case, it involved a utilitarian work, rather than an artistic or fictional one. In Baker v. Selden, the plaintiff Selden obtained a copyright on his book, "Selden's Condensed Ledger, or Bookkeeping Simplified," which described a new, simplified system of accounting. Included in the book were certain "blank forms," pages with ruled lines and headings, for use in Selden's accounting system. Selden alleged that Baker had infringed Selden's copyright by making and selling accounting books that used substantially the same system as Selden's and that reproduced Selden's blank forms. No one disputed that Baker had the right to use and promulgate Selden's system of accounting, for all parties agreed that the system could not be copyrighted, although the Court opined that it might be patentable. Nor did the parties dispute that the text of Baker's book on accounting did not infringe Selden's copyright. The dispute centered on whether Selden's blank forms were part of the method (idea) of Selden's book, and hence non-copyrightable, or part of the copyrightable text (expression).

In deciding this point, the Court distinguished what was protectible from what was not protectible as follows:

> [W]here the art [i.e., the method of accounting] it teaches cannot be used without employing the methods and diagrams used to illustrate the book, or such as are similar to them, such methods and diagrams are to be considered as necessary incidents to the art, and given to the public.

Id. at 103. Applying this test, the Court held that the blank forms were necessary incidents to Selden's method of accounting, and hence were not entitled to any copyright protection.

The Court's test in Baker v. Selden suggests a way to distinguish idea from expression. Just as Baker v. Selden focused on the end sought to be achieved by Selden's book, the line between idea and expression may be drawn with reference to the end sought to be achieved by the work in question. In other words, *the purpose or function of a utilitarian work would be the work's idea, and everything that is not necessary to that purpose or function would be part of the expression of the idea.* Where there are various means of achieving the desired purpose, then the particular means chosen is not necessary to the purpose; hence, there is expression, not idea. . . .[28]

2. *Application of the general rule to this case*—The rule proposed here is certainly not problem-free. The rule has its greatest force in the analysis of utilitarian or "functional" works, for the purpose of such works is easily stated and identified. By contrast, in cases involving works of literature or "non-functional" visual representations, defining the purpose of the work may be difficult. Since it may be impossible to discuss the purpose or function of a novel, poem, sculpture or painting, the rule may have little or no application to cases involving such works. The present case presents no such difficulties, for it is clear that the purpose of the utilitarian Dentalab program was to aid in the business operations of a dental laboratory. It is equally clear that the structure of the program was not essential to that task: there are other programs on the market, competitors of Dentalab and Dentcom, that perform the same functions but have different structures and designs.

This fact seems to have been dispositive for the district court:

> The mere idea or concept of a computerized program for operating a dental laboratory would not in and of itself be subject to copyright. Copyright law protects the manner in which the author expresses an idea or concept, but not the idea itself. Copyrights do not protect ideas—only expressions of ideas. There are many ways that the same data may be organized, assembled, held, retrieved and utilized by a computer. *Different computer systems may functionally serve similar purposes without being copies of each other. There is evidence in the record that there are other software programs for the business management of dental laboratories in competition with plaintiff's program. There is no contention that any of them infringe although they may incorporate many of the same ideas and functions.* The 'expression of the idea' in a software computer program is the manner in which the program operates, controls and regulates the computer in receiving, assembling, calculating, retaining, correlating, and producing useful information either on a screen, print-out or by audio communication.

28. This test is necessarily difficult to state, and it may be difficult to understand in the abstract. It will become more clear as we discuss and explain it in the textual discussion that follows this footnote. As will be seen, the idea of the Dentalab program was the efficient management of a dental laboratory (which presumably has significantly different requirements from those of other businesses). Because that idea could be accomplished in a number of different ways with a number of different structures, the structure of the Dentalab program is part of the program's expression, not its idea.

Whelan Associates v. Jaslow Laboratory, 609 F.Supp. at 1320 (emphasis added). We agree. The conclusion is thus inescapable that the detailed structure of the Dentalab program is part of the expression, not the idea, of that program.

Our conclusion is supported by SAS Institute, Inc. v. S & H Computer Systems, Inc., 605 F.Supp. 816 (M.D.Tenn.1985), the only other case that has addressed this issue specifically, in which the court found that a program's copyright could extend beyond its literal elements to its structure and organization. In *SAS*, plaintiffs supported their allegation of copyright infringement of their computer program with evidence of both literal and organizational similarities between its program and the alleged infringer. The court found a copyright infringement, and although it did not discuss in detail its evaluation of the evidence, it is apparent that the organizational similarities of the programs were relevant to its decision. After a brief discussion of the programs' literal similarities, the court said:

> In addition, the copying proven at trial does not affect only the specific lines of code cited by Dr. Peterson in his testimony. Rather, to the extent that it represents copying of the organization and structural details of SAS, such copying pervades the entire S & H product.

Id. at 830. Although the *SAS* court did not analyze the point in great depth, we are encouraged by its conclusion.

The Copyright Act of 1976 provides further support, for it indicates that Congress intended that the structure and organization of a literary work could be part of its expression protectible by copyright. Title 17 U.S.C. § 103 (1982) specifically extends copyright protection to compilations and derivative works. Title 17 U.S.C. § 101, defines "compilation" as "a work formed by the collection and *assembling* of preexisting materials or of data that are selected, *coordinated, or arranged* in such a way that the resulting work as a whole constitutes an original work of authorship," and it defines "derivative work," as one "based upon one or more preexisting works, such as . . . *abridgement, condensation,* or any other form in which a work may be *recast,* transformed, or adapted." (Emphasis added). Although the Code does not use the terms "sequence," "order" or "structure," it is clear from the definition of compilations and derivative works, and the protection afforded them, that Congress was aware of the fact that the sequencing and ordering of materials could be copyrighted, i.e., that the sequence and order could be parts of the expression, not the idea, of a work.

Our solution may put us at odds with Judge Patrick Higginbotham's scholarly opinion in Synercom Technology, Inc. v. University Computing Co., 462 F.Supp. 1003 (N.D.Tex.1978), which dealt with the question whether the "input formats" of a computer program—the configurations and collations of the information entered into the program—were idea or expression. The court held that the input formats were ideas, not expressions, and thus not protectible. *Synercom* did not deal with precisely the materials at issue here—input formats are structurally simple as compared to full programs—and it may therefore be distinguishable. However, insofar as the input formats are devices for the organization of data into forms useful for computers, they are *similar* to programs; thus, *Synercom* is relevant and we must come to grips with it.

Central to Judge Higginbotham's analysis was his conviction that the organization and structure of the input formats was inseparable from the idea underlying the formats. Although the court acknowledged that in some cases structure and sequence might be part of expression, not idea, see id. at 1014, it stated that in the case of input formats, structure and organization were inherently part of the idea. The court put its position in the form of a powerful rhetorical question: "if sequencing and ordering [are] expression, what separable idea is being expressed?" Id. at 1013.

To the extent that *Synercom* rested on the premise that there was a difference between the copyrightability of sequence and form in the computer context and in any other context, we think that it is incorrect. As just noted, the Copyright Act of 1976 demonstrates that Congress intended sequencing and ordering to be protectible in the appropriate circumstances, and the computer field is not an exception to this general rule. Although Congress was aware that computer programs posed a novel set of issues and problems for the copyright law, Congress did not then make, and has not since made, any special provision for ordering and sequencing in the context of computer programs. There is thus no statutory basis for treating computer programs differently from other literary works in this regard.

Despite the fact that copyright protection extends to sequence and form in the computer context, unless we are able to answer Judge Higginbotham's powerful rhetorical question—"if sequencing and ordering [are] expression, what separable idea is being expressed?"—in our own case, we would have to hold that the structure of the Dentalab program is part of its idea and is thus not protectible by copyright. Our answer has already been given, however: the idea is the efficient organization of a dental laboratory (presumably, this poses different problems from the efficient organization of some other kinds of laboratories or businesses). Because there are a variety of program structures through which that idea can be expressed, the structure is not a necessary incident to that idea. . . .

VI. *EVIDENCE OF SUBSTANTIAL SIMILARITY*

Defendants' second argument is that even if copyright protection is not limited to computer programs' literal elements as a matter of law, there is insufficient evidence of substantial similarity presented in this case to support a finding of copyright infringement. The defendants claim that all three parts of Dr. Moore's expert testimony as to the similarity of the programs were flawed, and also that the district court erred in evaluating the relative weight of Dr. Moore's and Mr. Ness' testimony. We consider these arguments in turn.

A. *File structures*—Defendants claim that Dr. Moore's examination and conclusions with respect to file structures are irrelevant to the question whether there was a copyright violation. Defendants analogize files to blank forms, which contain no information but merely collect and organize information that is entered from another source. They argue, relying on Baker v. Selden, that, as a matter of law, blank forms cannot be copyrighted. Thus, they conclude, neither can file structures be part of the copyright of a program.

Defendants' description of the file structures is indeed correct. Dr. Moore himself described a computer's file as "a storage place for data, and it's really no different in a computer than it is in a file drawer, it's like a manila folder that contains all the data on a particular subject category in a computer." (Another analogy, particularly accessible to lawyers, is to a very complex cataloguing structure like the structure of Lexis or Westlaw without any entries yet made.) Defendants' legal conclusion is not correct, however. Although some courts have stated that the meaning of Baker v. Selden is that blank forms cannot be copyrighted, this circuit, like the majority of courts that have considered the issue, has rejected this position and instead has held that blank forms may be copyrighted if they are sufficiently innovative that their arrangement of information is itself informative.

This is not to say that *all* blank forms or computer files are copyrightable. Only those that by their arrangement and organization convey some information can be copyrighted. Cf. 1 Nimmer at 2–201: "Thus books intended to record the events of baby's first year, or a record of a European trip, or any one of a number of other subjects, may evince considerable originality in suggestions of specific items of information which are to be recorded, and in the arrangement of such items." (footnote omitted). Defendants do not contend, however, that the file structures convey no information, and it appears to us that the structures are sufficiently complex and detailed that such an argument would not succeed. As we have noted, there are many ways in which the same goal—the organization of the business aspects of a dental laboratory—might be accomplished, and several of these approaches might use significantly different file structures. The file structures in the Dentalab and Dentcom systems require certain information and order that information in a particular fashion. Other programs might require different information or might use the same information differently. When we compare the comprehensiveness and complexity of the file structures at issue here with the "blank forms" at issue in the cases mentioned above, we have no doubt that these file structures are sufficiently informative to deserve copyright protection.

B. *Screen outputs*—Defendants' second line of argument is slightly confusing. Defendants appear to argue that to the extent that the district court relied upon the similarity of the screen outputs of Dentalab and Dentcom its finding of substantial similarity was erroneous because (1) the screen outputs are covered by a different copyright from the program's, and/or (2) the screen outputs bear no relation to the programs that produce them. Although these arguments are not always clearly distinguished, the distinction is important because whereas the first argument is weak, we feel that the second is more persuasive.

It is true that screen outputs are considered audio-visual works under the copyright code, and are thus covered by a different copyright than are programs, which are literary works. It is also true that Whelan Associates asserts no claim of copyright infringement with respect to the screen outputs. But the conclusion to be drawn from this is not, as defendants would have it, that screen outputs are completely irrelevant to the question whether the copyright in the program has been infringed. Rather, the only conclusion to be drawn from the fact of the different copyrights is that the screen output cannot be *direct* evidence of copyright infringement. There is no reason, however, why material falling under one copyright category could not be indirect, inferential evidence of the nature of material covered by another copyright.

Thus, the question is whether the screen outputs have probative value concerning the nature of the programs that render them sufficient to clear the hurdles of Fed.R.Evid. 401 and 403. The defendants argue that the screen outputs have *no* probative value with respect to the programs because many different programs can create the same screen output. Defendants rely on Stern Electronics Inc. v. Kaufman, 669 F.2d at 855 ("many different computer programs can produce the same 'results,' whether those results are an analysis of financial records or a sequence of images and sounds."), and *Midway Manufacturing Co.*, 564 F.Supp. at 749 ("it is quite possible to design a game that would infringe Midway's audiovisual copyright but would use an entirely different computer program."). Neither court, however, was presented with the question that faces us today, the evidentiary value of screen outputs in a suit for infringement of the underlying program.

Insofar as everything that a computer does, including its screen outputs, is related to the program that operates it, there is necessarily a causal relationship between the program and the screen outputs. The screen outputs must bear *some* relation to the underlying programs, and therefore they have some probative value. The evidence about the screen outputs therefore passes the low admissibility threshold of Fed. R.Evid. 401. . . .

C. *The five subroutines* —With respect to the final piece of evidence, Dr. Moore's testimony about the five subroutines found in Dentalab and Dentcom, defendants state that they "fail to understand how a substantial similarity in *structure* can be established by a comparison of only a small fraction of the two works." The premise underlying this declaration is that one cannot prove substantial similarity of two works without comparing the entirety, or at least the greater part, of the works. We take this premise to be the defendants' argument.

The premise does not apply in other areas of copyright infringement. There is no general requirement that most of each of two works be compared before a court can conclude that they are substantially similar. In the cases of literary works—novels, movies, or plays, for example—it is often impossible to speak of "most" of the work. The substantial similarity inquiry cannot be simply quantified in such instances. Instead, the court must make a qualitative, not quantitative, judgment about the character of the work as a whole and the importance of the substantially similar portions of the work.

Computer programs are no different. Because all steps of a computer program are not of equal importance, the relevant inquiry cannot therefore be the purely mechanical one of whether most of the programs' steps are similar. Rather, because we are concerned with the overall similarities between the programs, we must ask whether the most significant steps of the programs are similar. This is precisely what Dr. Moore did. He testified as follows:

> What I decided to do was to look at the programs that had the primary, or let's say most important, tasks of the system, and also ones which manipulate files, because there are a lot of programs that simply print lists, or answer a question when you ask him it, but I thought that the programs which actually showed the flow of information, through the system, would be the ones that would illustrate the system back.

Dr. Moore's testimony was thus in accord with general principles of copyright law. As we hold today that these principles apply as well to computer programs, we therefore reject the defendants' argument on this point.

D. *Sufficiency of the evidence*—Defendants' final argument is that the district court erred in evaluating the testimony of Dr. Moore and Mr. Ness. They contend that, properly evaluated, Mr. Ness' testimony was sufficiently strong and Dr. Moore's sufficiently weak, that there was not sufficient evidence of substantial similarity for plaintiff to prevail.

We have described the testimony of Dr. Moore and Mr. Ness, and it is recounted in the district court opinion. The district court explained its evaluation of the evidence as follows:

> I conclude . . . that Dr. Moore, plaintiffs' expert, had greater knowledge as to the particular programs at issue. Dr. Hess [*sic*], the defendants' expert witness, reviewed only the source and object codes of the IBM–Series 1 [Dentalab program], the IBM Datamaster and the IBM–PC Dentcom system. He never observed the computer in operation nor viewed the various screens or the user's manual. He stated he was not familiar with EDL coding. More basically, however, his comparison as to dissimilarities was between the IBM Datamaster and the IBM–PC Dentcom systems. Plaintiff contends that the IBM–PC Dentcom is a copy of the IBM Series 1 System—not the IBM–Datamaster system. Dr. Hess's [*sic*] conclusions were that although the overall structures of those systems is similar, the code in the IBM–PC Dentcom is not 'directly derived' from either plaintiff's IBM Series–1 or its IBM–

Datamaster system. To the extent that Dr. Moore's testimony supports plaintiff's contentions of copying, I find his testimony more credible and helpful because of his detailed and thorough analysis of the many similarities.

Determinations of credibility and the relative weight to be given expert witnesses are, of course, left primarily to the discretion of the district court. Our review of the record convinces us that the district court's analysis of the two experts' opinions was far from being erroneous. As the district court pointed out, Mr. Ness had studied the programs, but he had never observed them at work in computers. The district court also pointed out that Mr. Ness was unfamiliar with EDL coding. These factors suffice to support the court's conclusion.

In addition, we believe, on re-reading the trial transcript, that although Mr. Ness' testimony was quite competent, Dr. Moore's was more persuasive on the issues relevant to this appeal. Whereas the greater part of Mr. Ness' testimony was concerned with the dissimilarities between the two programs' source and object codes, Dr. Moore discussed the crucial issue in this case, the similarities and differences in the programs' *structures*. For example, when he discussed the programs' invoicing subroutine, Dr. Moore testified as follows:

> In the Dentalab system, the same kind of thing again, same information is up there, description, unit price, extension, items and program reads all those things in from te [*sic*] number of files actually, and displays them and then gives the operator a number of options to change the order as it appears on the screen to skip this one, to cancel it, or to accept it.

> The same choices are given in Dentalab systems, change, skip, cancel.

> Assuming that the order is accepted, both systems then calculate the money, calculate the amount of money that will be billed, and at this point they use the price code to find which of the four prices are to be charged for this particular customer. Both systems do that. They pick that one of the four prices and calculate the total amount, write [*sic*] then the record of this invoice that has been formed to show the invoice's file, sets the flag in the order's file to show that this order has now been invoiced so that it doesn't get reinvoiced.

> Q. What is a flag?

> A. Well, a flag would be, in this case, a certain location is marked I for invoices, just an indicator that invoicing has been done on this record.

> Q. Both used it?

> A. Both used a flag. I don't remember whether Dentcom uses a letter I or some other symbol, but there is a flag there that it's a field number 12, in which it's indicated that this file has been invoiced or this order has been invoiced.

*   *   *

Q. Do you have any comment about the invoicing?

A. *Well, I think it should be clear, it was clear to me from going through these programs that there is a very marke[d] similarity between the two, that they, item by item, are doing pretty much the same thing with the same fields in the same files, and accomplishing roughly the same results.*

So there was quite a match, line by line, between these two, flow in these two.

Q. What do you conclude from that?

A. Well, back together with the file's structure, sort of set up with the—how the programs have to proceed. I would think that the person who designed or constructed the Dentalab system must have been thoroughly familiar with the Dentcom system.

The person who constructed the Dentcom system must have been familiar with the series 1 system, because the same file structure and same program steps are followed, same overall flow takes place in both systems.

(Emphasis added.) Dr. Moore's testimony about Dentcom's and Dentalab's month-end subroutines also demonstrates the structural comparisons in which he engaged:

Q. What did you find in month-end?

A. Okay. Month-end, the calling program in Dentcom, this obviously is done at the end of each month.

In the Dentcom system there is a program called MOEND, which chains all these other programs, that is, MOEND calls MOPRDL, and after that program runs, goes back to MOEND, calls the print sale and so on.

In the Dentalab system there is a supervisory program also called MOEND, and that system calls or runs a series of programs doing various functions.

Now *if we look at the functions done by the programs in order, we find that they are the same except for a flipping of the order in the first two things.*

The Dentcom system, it first prints product group report, and then prints the monthly customer sales analysis.

In Dentalab, just reverses, prints sales analysis first, product group report second.

After that, both systems do the same thing in the same order.

They now do accounts receivable aging, since a month has gone by they have to update all the 30 days, 60 days, et cetera, calculate service charges. Then they print the monthly AR reports that had to do with service charges, only those that involve service charges, they both do that. Then they both print the age file balance, balance report, and following that they print the month and accounts receivable report. That's the total accounts receivable rport [*sic*].

Then they both go through and look for accounts that are not active that month, and print a list of these accounts, accounts not serviced, an account that doesn't have any access.

The final thing that the Dentcom system does is to calculate the new AR total for the entire lab, which I mentioned is contained in the company file.

Dentalab doesn't keep that total, so that's the last item, that is not as far as I can tell, done by Dentalab. I may have said—did I say Dentcom keeps that total? Dentalab does not. That's the only difference.

(Emphasis added.) Dr. Moore testified in similar detail and to similar effect about the other three subroutines that he felt were particularly important, order entry, accounts receivable, and day's end. This testimony, in addition to Dr. Moore's exhaustive comparison of the two programs' file structures and his testimony about the screen outputs demonstrates the marked similarity between the programs. Defendants' argument as to sufficiency of the evidence therefore fails.

VII. *CONCLUSION*

We hold that (1) copyright protection of computer programs may extend beyond the programs' literal code to their structure, sequence, and organization, and (2) the district court's finding of substantial similarity between the Dentalab and Dentcom programs was not clearly erroneous. The judgment of the district court will therefore be affirmed.

PLAINS COTTON COOPERATIVE ASSOCIATION OF LUBBOCK, TEXAS v. GOODPASTURE COMPUTER SERVICE, INC.

United States Court of Appeals, Fifth Circuit, 1987.
807 F.2d 1256, cert. denied, 484 U.S. 821, 108 S.Ct. 80, 98 L.Ed.2d 42 (1987).

JERRE S. WILLIAMS, Circuit Judge:

Appellant Plains Cotton Cooperative Association of Lubbock, Texas, appeals the denial of its application for a preliminary injunction against appellees Goodpasture Computer Service, Inc., Peter H. Cushman, Richard R. Fisher, William James Godlove, and Clarence Michael Smith, to prevent them from marketing, distributing, or otherwise using software allegedly stolen or copied from appellant. Because we agree with the district court that appellant has not satisfied its burden of demonstrating irreparable harm or substantial likelihood of success on the merits, we affirm the denial of the application for a preliminary injunction.

I.

Plains Cotton Cooperative Association of Lubbock, Texas ("Plains") is a non-profit agricultural cooperative comprised of approximately twenty thousand cotton farmers residing in Texas and Oklahoma. Its purpose is to assist its members in the growing and marketing of cotton. Toward that end, Plains developed a computer software system, Telcot, designed to provide its members with information regarding cotton prices and availability, with accounting services, and with the capability to consummate actual sales electronically.

The Telcot "system" comprises functional specifications outlining what the software can accomplish, design specifications determining how the software accomplishes those functions, programs implementing the design specifications, and documentation detailing the programming and specifications so that future programmers can understand and modify the software. The programs, written in human-readable computer language, are called "source code;" translated into a computer-readable language, they are called "object code." The Telcot system is used by cotton farmers, ginners, and buyers through terminals connected to Plains' large central computer by telephone lines. These terminals allow the system's users to retrieve the desired cotton market information from Plains, but they provide no access to the documentation, programming, design or functional specifications of the Telcot system.

Telcot was first marketed in 1975, and improvements and refinements in the software have been made continuously since that date. The system was developed at Plains by a team of programmers that included appellees Cushman, Fisher, Godlove, and Smith ("employee/appellees"). None of these employees was required to sign confidentiality agreements as a condition of his employment with Plains.

In 1979, Plains' general manager Dan Davis left the company in order to start a new venture called Commodity Exchange Service Company ("CXS"). Davis had been heavily involved with the creation of Telcot, and he wanted to expand its capabilities by adapting Telcot for use on personal computers. CXS and Plains entered into an agreement, on July 5, 1979, for the development, refinement, and marketing of a personal-computer version of Telcot. Under the agreement, any modifications, developments or enhancements of Telcot would be owned jointly by Plains and CXS.

On April 13, 1984, CXS hired Cushman, Fisher, Godlove and Smith away from Plains, and put all four of them to work on the Telcot personal-computer project. When Godlove left Plains, he copied and took possession of a complete tape record of the Telcot source code detailing Telcot's programming. Five days later, Plains gave CXS written notice that it intended to terminate their contract. Subsequently, the parties agreed that their contract would terminate on April 18, 1985, and that Plains would have an irrevocable option through April 18, 1986 to purchase CXS's interest in various programs. Plains never exercised that option.

After working at CXS for approximately one year, the four employees/appellees succeeded in designing a personal-computer version of Telcot, and they produced a document setting out design specifications for the new software. The preliminary nature of the design and the comprehensiveness of the design document are disputed by the parties in this appeal. No programming was actually written for the new software.

In March, 1985, CXS filed for bankruptcy, and the four employee/appellees began to search for other employment opportunities. At that same time, appellee Goodpasture Computer Service, Inc. ("Goodpasture"), a computer service company located in Brownfield, Texas, began discussions with CXS and its employees concerning various possible joint ventures or working relationships. Goodpasture knew that former Plains employees were working at CXS to create a personal-computer version of Telcot. No agreement was made between Goodpasture and CXS, but Goodpasture did succeed in hiring away from CXS appellees Cushman, Fisher, Godlove, and Smith.

The four employee/appellees signed employment agreements with Goodpasture in which they agreed not to breach any confidences of their former employers, Plains and CXS, while working for Goodpasture. In violation of this employment agreement, however, Fisher brought to his new job a computer diskette containing Telcot programming designs. Twenty days after arriving at Goodpasture, the four former Plains employees had completed a design of a personal-computer version of a cotton exchange program, designated "GEMS" by Goodpasture. By November, 1985 Goodpasture began to market GEMS in a rough, incomplete form. At the time of the preliminary injunction hearing, the software was still not fully operational.

GEMS is very similar to Telcot on the functional specification, programming, and documentation levels. In fact, several pages of the GEMS design manual appear to be direct copies of pages from the design manual appellees created at CXS. The main difference between the two systems is that Telcot is designed to work on a mainframe computer, whereas GEMS is designed for a personal-computer. Appellees allege that, with one exception, they did not copy programs used for Telcot, but instead "drew on their knowledge of the cotton industry and expertise in computer programming and design gained over a number of years." The exception is appellee Fisher's admission that he did copy one Telcot subroutine in programming GEMS. When Goodpasture discovered the copying on February 7, 1986, the subroutine was replaced, and Fisher was discharged.

On January 15, 1986, Plains filed suit against Goodpasture and its employees Cushman, Fisher, Godlove, and Smith, seeking damages and injunctive relief for misappropriation of trade secrets, unfair competition, conversion, breach of confidential relationship, and trade dress infringement. After registering its copyright in the Telcot computer programs and associated manuals, Plains amended its complaint to include claims for copyright infringement.

Plains made a motion for a preliminary injunction based on its copyright and trade secret claims, and a hearing was held on February 7 and 10, 1986. Both sides presented expert testimony on the issue of whether GEMS was copied from Telcot. On February 17, the district court denied the motion, and Plains subsequently instituted this appeal.

II.

In order to secure a preliminary injunction, the movant has the burden of proving four elements: (1) a substantial likelihood of success on the merits; (2) a substantial threat of irreparable injury if the injunction is not issued; (3) that the threatened injury to the movant outweighs any damage the injunction might cause to the opponent; and (4) that the injunction will not disserve the public interest. These four elements are mixed questions of fact and law. . . .

In denying the motion for a preliminary injunction, the district court concluded that appellant had failed to satisfy two of the four prerequisites for injunctive relief: a showing of irreparable harm and a showing of a substantial likelihood of success on the merits. Appellant contends that the district court abused its discretion (1) by using the wrong legal standard in analyzing the copyright infringement claim, and (2) by not addressing the misappropriation of trade secrets claim.

III.

Appellant argues that the district court applied the wrong legal standard in determining that appellant had not demonstrated a sufficient likelihood of success on the merits of its copyright infringement claim. Copyright infringement is shown by proof that the injured party owned copyrighted material and that the infringer copied that material. Copyright ownership, in turn, is shown by proof of originality, copyrightability, and compliance with applicable statutory formalities. Since direct evidence of copying is often difficult to find, copying can be shown by proof of both access to the copyrighted material and substantial similarity between the two works.

Appellant asserts that the district court failed to consider evidence of substantial similarity between GEMS and Telcot. This argument is based on the district court's apparent reliance on the testimony of two expert witnesses, which testimony, according to appellant, conflicts only on the issue of direct copying. But direct copying is not the central issue in the case, appellant argues; it is "organizational copying": the reproduction of the organizational structure of a software system, outlined generally in the software's design specifications. Appellant asserts that because the expert testimony concerning organizational copying does not conflict, and because the court decided the preliminary injunction motion based on the conflict in testimony of the experts, then the court must have made its decision solely on the basis of whether direct copying occurred. The decision, therefore, ignored the allegedly uncontroverted evidence of substantial similarity resulting from organizational copying.

We do not accept the contention that the district court ignored the evidence of organizational copying and focused exclusively on evidence of direct copying. While the opinion by the district court is admittedly lean, it is open to interpretations other than the one profferred by appellant. The district court specifically based its finding "upon the hearing and the part's [sic] post-hearing briefs," not just on the testimony of the experts. A complete review of the record reveals testimony by several witnesses for appellees that the similarity between the two programs exists on a level not protected by appellant's copyright. Appellees' expert witness, James Bruce Walker, testified that appellees did not copy Telcot. In his opinion, appellant's programs were too large to have been copied and modified in the amount of time appellees took to create GEMS. Walker testified that appellees must have created the software based on their personal skills as computer programmers: "I believe they can take their knowledge of the cotton industry and repeatedly recreate a similar vehicle."

Appellant argues that Mr. Walker was not competent to testify as to whether "copying" occurred because he did not look for organizational copying. The record reveals, however, that Mr. Walker simply was not familiar with the term "organizational" to describe copying on a level broader than verbatim, line-by-line copying. However, Mr. Walker did testify on direct examination that he compared the "overall structure of these programs," and on cross-examination that he "expanded his study" of the programs from the narrow search for verbatim copying. The district court was entitled to rely on both of these statements in interpreting Mr. Walker's expert opinion that GEMS was not "copied" from Telcot.

Further support can be found in appellee William James Godlove's testimony that he did not rely on any material belonging to Plains or CXS during his employment at Goodpasture, that a mainframe program such as Telcot could be altered to run on a personal computer only with enormous changes so that rewriting the programs would be faster than modifying them, and that the residual familiarity with Telcot on which he relied when designing GEMS was "just experience and industry knowledge." Finally, witness Stinson Stokes Smith testified that the subroutines he wrote for Goodpasture were written without reference to any material relating to any of Plains' or CXS's software systems. This testimony is sufficient to support a tentative finding that appellees did not copy appellant's software. The district court's conclusion that appellant did not demonstrate a sufficient likelihood of success on the merits is not clearly erroneous. . . .

The legal finding by the district court ultimately rests on a judgment about the extent of the protection offered by appellant's copyright. On that issue, we look to our colleague Judge Higginbotham's opinion in Synercom Technology, Inc. v. University Computing Co., 462 F.Supp. 1003 (N.D.Tex.1978). In that case, Judge Higginbotham held that "input formats" of a computer program—the organization and configuration of the information fed to the computer—were ideas, not expressions, and thus were not protected by copyright.

To the extent that input formats represent a level of computer software design more specific than functional design and more general than line-by-line program design, the issue of their copyrightability is relevant to the issue of whether GEMS infringes on protected Telcot designs. Appellant urges that we adopt the reasoning of Whelan Associates, Inc. v. Jaslow Dental Laboratory, Inc., 797 F.2d 1222 (3rd Cir.1986), which is admittedly "at odds with Judge Higginbotham's scholarly opinion." Id. at 1239. *Whelan* rejects the premise developed in *Synercom* that "there [is] a difference between the copyrightability of sequence and form in the computer context and in any other context," id. at 1240, holding that the structure, sequence, and organization of computer programs are copyrightable.

We decline to embrace *Whelan* for two reasons. First, the issue is presented to us on review of a denial of a motion for preliminary injunction. Thus, the record is only partially developed, and our review is one step removed from the actual merits of the case. Second, appellees presented evidence that many of the similarities between the GEMS and Telcot programs are dictated by the externalities of the cotton market. To that extent, the facts of this case fit squarely within *Synercom's* powerful analogy to the hypothetical development of gear stick patterns. The record supports the inference that market factors play a significant role in determining the sequence and organization of cotton marketing software, and we decline to hold that those patterns cannot constitute "ideas" in a computer context.

Appellant has thus failed to demonstrate that the factual findings of the district court regarding the copyright infringement claim are clearly erroneous or that the findings of law are incorrect. We affirm the denial of the motion for a preliminary injunction on the copyright claim. . . .

CONCLUSION

Appellant failed to demonstrate a sufficient likelihood of success on the merits of its claims, and failed to present sufficient proof of irreparable harm to justify a preliminary injunction. The judgment of the district court denying the motion for a preliminary injunction is

Affirmed.

SYNERCOM TECHNOLOGY, INC. v. UNIVERSITY COMPUTING CO., 462 F.Supp. 1003, 199 U.S.P.Q. 537 (N.D.Tex.1978), P. HIGGINBOTHAM, J.: The difficult question is whether EDI plagiarized Synercom's idea or its expression. If the idea is the sequence and ordering of data, there was no infringement. If sequencing and ordering of data was, however, expression, it follows that EDI's preprocessor program infringed. As earlier suggested and as will be demonstrated, Synercom's argument is double-edged. If sequencing and ordering is expression, what separable idea is expressed?

A hypothetical, oversimplified, may serve to illuminate the idea versus expression controversy. The familiar "figure-H" pattern of an automobile stick is chosen arbitrarily by an auto manufacturer. Several different patterns may be imagined, some more convenient for the driver or easier to manufacture than others, but all representing possible configurations. The pattern chosen is arbitrary, but once chosen, it is the only pattern which will work in a particular model. The pattern (analogous to the computer "format") may be expressed in several different ways: by a prose description in a driver's manual, through a diagram, photograph, or driver training film, or otherwise. Each of these expressions may presumably be protected through copyright. But the copyright protects copying of the particular expressions of the pattern, and does not prohibit another manufacturer from marketing a car using the same pattern. Use of the same pattern might be socially desirable, as it would reduce the retraining of drivers. Likewise, the second manufacturer is free to use its own prose descriptions, photographs, diagrams, or the like, so long as these materials take the form of original expressions of the copied idea (however similar they may be to the first manufacturer's materials) rather than copies of the expressions themselves. Admittedly, there are many more possible choices of computer formats, and the decision among them more arbitrary, but this does not detract from the force of the analogy.

NOTES

1. *Computer Programs as Copyright Subject Matter.* The United States Copyright Office has accepted computer programs as copyrightable subject matter since 1964. See Cary, Copyright Registration and Computer Programs, 11 Bull. Copyright Soc'y 362 (1964).

In 1978 the National Commission on New Technological Uses of Copyrighted Works issued its final report recommending that the Copyright Act be amended "to make it explicit that computer programs, to the extent that they embody an author's original creation, are proper subject matter of copyright." National Comm'n on New Technological Uses of Copyrighted Works, Final Report 1 (1978). Congress relied on the Report in amending the 1976 Copyright Act to add a definition of "computer program" to section 101: "A 'computer program' is a set of statements or instructions to be used directly or indirectly in a computer in order to bring about a certain result." Act of Dec. 12, 1980, Pub.L. No. 96–517, § 10, 94 Stat. 3015, 3028. See generally, Samuelson, CONTU Revisited: The Case Against Copyright Protection for Computer Programs in Machine–Readable Form, 1984 Duke L.J. 663.

So long as it is original and sufficiently expressive, a computer program will be copyrightable whether it is expressed in words, in a flow chart, in source code or object code, and whether it is embodied in paper, magnetic disk, tape or semiconductor chip. See Apple Computer, Inc. v. Franklin Computer Corp., 714 F.2d 1240, 1249, 219 U.S.P.Q. 113 (3d Cir.1983), cert. dismissed, 464 U.S. 1033, 104 S.Ct. 690, 79 L.Ed. 2d 158 (1984).

Computer programs exist today that can, without an author's intervention, create such finished works as crossword puzzles and daily weather maps. The day may not be far off when computer programs can create fully realized literary and artistic productions. Should copyright extend to such productions? Who would be the "author" of such a production? Does copyright law's originality standard presuppose a human author? See generally, Samuelson, Allocating Ownership Rights in Computer–Generated Works, 47 U.Pitt.L.Rev. 1185 (1986).

2. *Infringement: Copying.* Proof of copying through inferences drawn from access and similarity is much the same in computer program cases as in copyright infringement cases generally. See page 715, above. For example, striking similarities may support an inference of copying. In Midway Mfg. Co. v. Strohon, 564 F.Supp. 741, 753, 219 U.S.P.Q. 42 (N.D.Ill.1983), the court found copying where defendant's program embodied 89% of the 16,000 bytes in plaintiff's program and there was "virtually an infinite number of ways to write a set of program instructions." Also, copyists sometimes fall into traps laid by the copyright owner and fail to excise such telltale clues as the programmer's name embedded in object code. See, e.g., Apple Computer Inc. v. Franklin Computer Corp., 714 F.2d 1240, 219 U.S.P.Q. 113 (3d Cir.1983), cert. dismissed, 464 U.S. 1033, 104 S.Ct. 690, 79 L.Ed.2d 158 (1984).

3. *Infringement: Unlawful Appropriation.* Cases like Apple v. Franklin, note 1, above, establishing the copyrightability of computer programs, represent the first generation of copyright decisions on computer programs. Cases like *Whelan* and *Goodpasture* represent the second generation of computer copyright cases, testing the scope of rights in admittedly protectible subject matter against nonliteral copying. Can you reconcile *Whelan* and *Goodpasture?* Which approach to scope of protection strikes the better balance between protection for, and access to, computer programs? Which decision better conforms to general principles of copyright law? If the *Whelan* court had *Romeo and Juliet* before it, would it have held that the play's unprotectible idea was the theme of two star-crossed lovers and that all of the play's other elements—plot, incident and basic character types—were copyrightable?

For several views on the second generation of copyright infringement cases involving computer programs, see LaST Frontier Conference Report, Computer Software and Copyright Protection, 30 Jurimetrics J. 15 (1989); Clapes, Lynch & Steinberg, Silicon Epics and Binary Bards: Determining the Proper Scope of Copyright Protection for Computer Programs, 34 UCLA L.Rev. 1493 (1987); Goldstein, Infringement of Copyright in Computer Programs, 47 U.Pitt.L.Rev. 1119 (1986); Menell, An Analysis of the Scope of Copyright Protection for Application Programs, 41 Stan.L.Rev. 1045 (1989); Reichman, Computer Programs as Applied Scientific Know–How: Implications of Copyright Protection for Commercialized University Research, 42 Vand.L.Rev. 639 (1989).

4. *Merger.* Under copyright law's merger doctrine, courts will withhold protection from an otherwise protectible expression of an idea if there is only a limited number of ways to express the idea. See page 571, above. The level at which a court draws the line between idea and

expression will substantially influence its decision on merger. Could a court ever find merger under the *Whelan* approach to the idea-expression distinction? Consider the following passage in Apple Computer, Inc. v. Franklin Computer Corp., 714 F.2d 1240, 1253, 219 U.S.P.Q. 113, cert. dismissed, 464 U.S. 1033, 104 S.Ct. 690, 79 L.Ed.2d 158 (1984):

> Franklin claims that whether or not the programs can be rewritten, there are a limited 'number of ways to arrange operating systems to enable a computer to run the vast body of Apple-compatible software,' Brief of Appellee at 20. This claim has no pertinence to either the idea/expression dichotomy or merger. The idea which may merge with the expression, thus making the copyright unavailable, is the idea which is the subject of expression. The idea of one of the operating system programs is, for example, how to translate source code into object code. If other methods of expressing that idea are not foreclosed as a practical matter, then there is no merger. Franklin may wish to achieve total compatibility with independently developed application programs written for the Apple II, but that is a commercial and competitive objective which does not enter into the somewhat metaphysical issue of whether particular ideas and expressions have merged.

Compare Secure Services Technology, Inc. v. Time & Space Processing, Inc., 722 F.Supp. 1354 (E.D.Va.1989).

If a program's underlying idea does not sufficiently constrain expression to compel a finding of merger, a court may nonetheless hold that the constraints should limit infringement to literal or close to literal copying. In NEC Corp. v. Intel Corp., 10 U.S.P.Q.2d 1177 (N.D. Cal.1989), a declaratory judgment action, Intel had licensed NEC to duplicate its patented 8086/88 microprocessor hardware; experts for both sides testified that this hardware substantially limited NEC's choices in writing microcode for its competing product. Finding that some of NEC's shorter, simpler microcode subroutines resembled Intel's, the court concluded that "the expression of the ideas underlying the shorter, simpler microroutines (including those identified earlier as substantially similar) may be protected only against virtually identical copying, that NEC properly used the underlying ideas, without virtually identically copying their limited expression." 10 U.S.P.Q.2d at 1189.

5. *Databases.* Anyone who has used a legal research database like LEXIS or WESTLAW knows that the computer offers fast and powerful access to compilations of data. Data in a computerized database are typically arranged in ways that, though unintelligible to the user, make the stored data most readily accessible through the computer. Should the fact that the arrangement of a computer database is not perceptible by the user deprive it of protection as a copyrightable compilation? In National Business Lists, Inc. v. Dun & Bradstreet, Inc., 552 F.Supp. 89, 97, 215 U.S.P.Q. 595 (N.D.Ill.1982), the court observed that "[t]he information is stored without arrangement and form, capable of being called forth as sheets of stickers at the touch

of a button. In those circumstances an emphasis upon arrangement and form in compilation protection becomes even more meaningless than in the past."

6. *International Protection.* Many industrialized countries have followed the lead of the United States in bringing computer programs within copyright. See Keplinger, Authorship in the Information Age: Protection for Computer Programs Under the Berne and Universal Copyright Conventions, 21 Copyright 119 (1985). However, few countries have extended copyright to computer programs on the same terms as the United States, and many have conformed protection to national traditions. For example, the West German Federal Supreme Court has held that, to be protectible, a computer program must exhibit a degree of creativity that is much higher than the originality standard imposed in the United States—a measure that will exclude all but the most inventive programs from copyright protection. See Lehmann, The Legal Protection of Computer Programs in Germany: A Summary of the Present Situation, 19 I.I.C. 473 (1988). See also Professor Dennis Karjala's valuable study, Lessons from the Computer Software Protection Debate in Japan, 1984 Ariz.St.L.J. 53.

b. PICTORIAL, GRAPHIC AND AUDIOVISUAL WORKS

BRODERBUND SOFTWARE, INC. v. UNISON WORLD, INC.

United States District Court, N.D. California, 1986.
648 F.Supp. 1127, 231 U.S.P.Q. 700.

ORRICK, District Judge.

In this action for audiovisual copyright infringement, textual copyright infringement, trademark infringement, and unfair competition, the Court severed the case, and tried only the liability portion of the audiovisual copyright infringement claim. For the reasons set forth in this Opinion, which constitute the Court's findings of fact and conclusions of law required by Federal Rule of Civil Procedure 52(a), the Court finds the defendant has infringed the copyright of plaintiff Pixellite Software on the audiovisual displays of the computer program known as The Print Shop.

I

Plaintiffs, Broderbund Software, Inc. ("Broderbund"), and Pixellite Software ("Pixellite"), are the exclusive licensee and the copyright holder, respectively, of a computer software printing program called "The Print Shop" ("Print Shop"). Defendant, Unison World, Inc. ("Unison"), markets a computer software printing program called "The Printmaster" ("Printmaster"). Both "Print Shop" and "Printmaster" are menu-driven programs that enable their users to create customized greeting cards, signs, banners, and posters. Plaintiffs claim that the overall appearance, structure, and sequence of the audiovisual displays in "Printmaster" infringe plaintiffs' copyright on "Print Shop."

David Balsam and Martin Kahn, the principals of plaintiff Pixellite Software, began developing "Print Shop" in the spring of 1983. At the time, the program was known as "Perfect Occasion" and was not a printing program. Rather, it was a program that would allow its users to create custom greeting cards out of the software disks themselves. "Perfect Occasion" would have allowed users to type their greetings, surrounded by graphics and borders, onto the disks. The disks would then be mailed or otherwise delivered to the recipient, who would need access to a compatible personal computer to view the "greeting card." Balsam and Kahn spent two or three months developing "Perfect Occasion" and showed it to Broderbund in the summer of 1983.

Concerned about the salability of a program that created greetings cards legible only on computers, Broderbund encouraged Balsam and Kahn to convert "Perfect Occasion" into a printing program. Balsam and Kahn, with the help of Broderbund artists, spent almost an entire year developing what was to become "Print Shop." Broderbund obtained from Pixellite an exclusive license to distribute "Print Shop" worldwide and began marketing the product in May 1984. At the time of its introduction onto the market, "Print Shop" could be operated only on Apple computers. The product was a success, selling approximately 500,000 copies (to date of trial) at a manufacturer's suggested retail price of $49.95.

Defendant, Unison, is primarily engaged in the business of converting other publishers' software to make it adaptable with different computers. Unison rarely, if ever, develops entirely original programs. As of April 15, 1986, Unison had developed software for Epson, Sharp, and Panasonic. In May 1984, the president of Unison, Hong Lu, approached the president of Broderbund, Douglas Carlston. At the time, Unison was programming a video game called "Flappy," which was a conversion of a game created by DB Soft, a Japanese company. Lu wanted to know if Broderbund would consider publishing "Flappy."

From their dealings concerning "Flappy," Broderbund and Unison also began discussing the possibility of converting the just-released "Print Shop" to make it adaptable with other computers, mostly Japanese. Lu had excellent contacts with Japanese software producers. When Broderbund personnel went to tour Unison's facilities, Lu told them he was also interested in the conversion rights to an IBM version of "Print Shop." Lu told Edward Bernstein, Broderbund's director of product development, that Unison could create a "Print Shop" version for IBM computers in three months. Bernstein was skeptical about whether Unison could actually produce a quality conversion within three months. Broderbund had already made several unsuccessful attempts to produce an IBM version of "Print Shop."

Although Broderbund originally informed Lu that the IBM rights to "Print Shop" were unavailable, at some point Broderbund developed a need for an IBM conversion. Unison personnel met with Balsam and Kahn to discuss whether it was really possible in three months to create an IBM version that was faithful to the original. Broderbund made it clear that if Unison were to receive the IBM rights to "Print Shop," it had to produce an exact reproduction of the original. Balsam very briefly showed the source code (the text that is translated into an "object code" and then directs the computer to perform its functions) to one of Unison's programmers, MacDuff Hughes, to give Hughes a feel for the depth and complexity of "Print Shop." Balsam also gave Unison personnel some commercially-available copies of "Print Shop" to show Japanese producers.

For the next four to six weeks, programmer Hughes was under orders from both Lu and David Lodge, Unison's products manager, to develop a program as identical to "Print Shop" as possible—to "imitate" it. Balsam and Kahn would meet periodically with Hughes to discuss Hughes' progress in developing the IBM version. Kahn, who handled the programming duties for Pixellite, told Hughes that the aspect ratios (governing the proportioning of dots), hollowing (placing white borders on individual letters to make them stand out) and kerning (closing spaces between letters) would be difficult. Hughes set out to recreate "Print Shop" as closely as possible.

After Hughes had made considerable progress toward a faithful reproduction of "Print Shop," however, negotiations for the IBM rights broke down. Lu felt Broderbund was offering an insufficient advance payment on Unison's percentage of the royalties. Lu now told Hughes to stop copying "Print Shop" because the negotiations had failed. Instead, Lu instructed Hughes to finish developing their *enhanced* version of "Print Shop" as soon as possible. Hughes was no longer to feel "constrained" by the actual structure or appearance of "Print Shop"—he was now free to improve on it. This enhanced version would then be released by Unison as its own creation. By releasing its own enhanced version of "Print Shop," Unison was simply following what had been Lu's game plan all along. Lu wished to obtain the "Print Shop" or Broderbund name, but he always intended to release some enhanced version of "Print Shop," whether or not he could reach a licensing agreement with Broderbund.

Lu's order to stop any further copying of "Print Shop" did not include copying that had already been incorporated into Hughes' work in progress. Hughes had already finished the menu screens, so he kept them. He had also finished about ten screens in the "greeting card" and "sign" functions, which he kept. And, despite the fact that he had a totally different idea for the user interface in the "picture editor" function, Hughes used the "Print Shop" user interface because it was "much further along." Hughes thought it would be a waste of time to go back and redesign the screens, and he was in a hurry to finish the project so he could get back to Stanford, where he was a mathematics major.

After Hughes finished his part of the project, other programmers at Unison added a "calendar" function to the IBM version, streamlined the method by which the user could select ready-made designs, and provided for the memorization of designs. The Unison–IBM version otherwise remained the same as Hughes had designed it.

In March 1985, Unison released its program under the name "Printmaster." On May 28, 1985, plaintiffs brought this action for copyright infringement, trademark infringement, and unfair competition. In November 1985, Broderbund released its IBM version of "Print Shop." It is to these facts that the Court now applies the law applicable to audiovisual copyrights.

II

A. *Are the Audiovisual Displays Protected under the Copyright Laws?*

First and foremost, the Court must deal with the threshold issue, the protection *vel non* of audiovisual displays under the copyright laws.

1. *The dichotomy between ideas and expression.*

It is axiomatic that copyright protects only the expression of ideas and not the ideas themselves. . . .

Defendant herein argues that the idea underlying the menu screens, input formats, and sequencing of screens in "Print Shop" is indistinguishable from its expression. Any menu-driven computer program that allows its users to print greeting cards, signs, banners, and posters will have a user interface substantially similar to that in "Print Shop," defendant contends, because there is no other conceivable way to structure such a program. The evidence at trial disproved defendant's contention. Plaintiffs introduced a program titled "Stickybear Printer," marketed by Weekly Reader Family Software, that allows its users to print greeting cards, signs, banners, and posters with variable combinations of user-dictated text, graphics, and borders. The functions of "Stickybear Printer" are substantially the same as the functions of "Print Shop"; thus, it can be said that the ideas underlying "Stickybear Printer" and "Print Shop" are the same. Yet the expressions of those ideas are very different. The menu screens and sequence of screens in the two programs are different. The entire structure and organization of the user interfaces are different. In short, the existence of "Stickybear Printer" proves that there do exist other, quite different ways of expressing the ideas embodied in "Print Shop." The Court rejects defendant's contention that the idea and expression of "Print Shop" are indistinguishable from one another.

2. *Case authority regarding computer software.*

Two reported cases involving the alleged infringement of computer software offer valuable guidance in the present case. Specifically, defendant cites Synercom Technology, Inc. v. University Computer Co., 462 F.Supp. 1003 (N.D.Tex.1978), for the proposition that only the literal aspects of a computer program (the source and object codes) are protected under the copyright laws, and that nonliteral aspects, such as the user interface, are not protected. At the same time, plaintiffs argue that Whelan Associates, Inc. v. Jaslow Dental Laboratory, Inc., 797 F.2d 1222 (3d Cir.1986), requires the opposite conclusion—that the user interface of a computer program *can* be protected. A brief examination of these two cases is in order.

In *Synercom*, the plaintiff contended that the defendant had copied the "input formats" used in plaintiff's computer program, which was designed to solve engineering problems incident to structural analysis. The input formats in *Synercom* appear to have served essentially the same function as the menu screens in "Print Shop" and "Printmaster," i.e., through the placement of lines, shaded art, and text, these formats told the user what type of data to enter, where to place them and how to do it. The plaintiff in *Synercom* argued that the sequencing and organization of data inherent in the input formats constituted an expression of the idea underlying the formats and, therefore, that the formats were protected. Judge Higginbotham was not persuaded; he responded with the question, "If sequencing and ordering is expression, what separable idea is expressed?" *Id.* at 1013. Finding no such separable idea, he went on to hold that the idea underlying the input formats and the expression of that idea were indistinguishable, thus disqualifying the formats for copyright protection.

In *Whelan*, the Third Circuit was faced with a similar situation. There, the plaintiff held the copyright to a computer program designed to aid the administration of dental prosthetics laboratories. The plaintiff in *Whelan* argued that the overall structure and organization of the copyrighted program, and not just the source and object codes, were protected. After thoroughly canvassing the case authority and the legislative history of the Copyright Act of 1976, the Court of Appeals held that the overall structure, sequencing, and organization of the program could be distinguished from the idea underlying the program, and that the former constituted expression of the latter. *Whelan* thus stands for the proposition that copyright protection is not limited to the literal aspects of a computer program, but rather that it extends to the overall structure of a program, including its audiovisual displays. . . .

As for Judge Higginbotham's question implying the need for some "separable idea," the *Whelan* court answered it by stating that the separable idea of the dental lab program was the efficient organization of a dental laboratory, which could be expressed in a variety of ways through a variety of computer program structures. Likewise, in the present case, the separable idea of "Print Shop" is the creation of greeting cards, banners, posters and signs that contain infinitely variable combinations of text, graphics, and borders. A rival software publisher is completely free to market a program with the same underlying idea, but it must express the idea through a substantially different structure. That "Stickybear Printer" shares the basic idea of "Print Shop" and yet expresses it through a different structure disproves defendant's contention that it was incapable of conceiving another form of expression.

Notwithstanding Judge Higginbotham's excellent opinion in *Synercom*, this Court is persuaded by the reasoning of *Whelan*. Applied to the facts of the present case, *Whelan* compels the rejection of defendant's argument that the overall structure, sequencing, and arrangement of screens in "Print Shop" fall outside the ambit of copyright protection.

3. *Mechanical or utilitarian constraints.*

Defendant also argues that the audiovisual displays of "Print Shop" are ineligible for copyright protection because they do not fall within the definition of "pictorial" or "graphic" works in 17 U.S.C. § 101 (1977), which states in pertinent part:

> [T]he design of a useful article . . . shall be considered a pictorial, graphic, or sculptural work only if, and only to the extent that, such design incorporates pictorial, graphic, or sculptural features that can be identified separately from, and are capable of existing independently of, the utilitarian aspects of the article.

Put another way, copyright protection extends only to the artistic aspects, and not the mechanical or utilitarian features, of a protected work. . . .

In the present case, it is clear that the structure, sequence, and layout of the audiovisual displays in "Print Shop" were dictated primarily by artistic and aesthetic considerations, and not by utilitarian or mechanical ones. Repeatedly, the testimony of David Balsam showed that, in creating the screens of "Print Shop," he based textual and graphic decisions on the basis of aesthetic and artistic preferences. On the "Now Type Your Message" screen of "Print Shop," for instance, no mechanical or practical constraint forced Balsam to make the "Stencil" typeface smaller on the display than the "Alexia" typeface. The choice was purely arbitrary. On the "Choose a Font" screen, no mechanical or practical factor compelled Balsam to use those exact words ("Choose a Font"). He could have written, "Select a Font," or "Indicate a Typeface Preference," or "Which Type Style Do You Prefer," or any combination of these terms. Another example is the "Screen Magic" function—Balsam considered calling this "See Animation." He could have called it "Kaleidoscope." The bottom line is that the designer of any program that performed the same functions as "Print Shop" had available a wide range of expression governed predominantly by artistic and not utilitarian considerations. Thus, the Court cannot accept defendant's argument that the audiovisual displays of "Print Shop" fall outside the scope of "pictorial" or "graphic" works as set forth in § 101.

4. *The "rules and instructions" doctrine.*

Defendant's next argument is that courts have established a separate doctrine under which rules and instructions for unprotected games or processes cannot themselves be protected under the copyright laws. Defendant further argues that this "rules and instructions" doctrine applies to the menu screens of "Print Shop," requiring the conclusion that such screens are ineligible for copyright protection. In support of this argument, defendant cites Affiliated Hospital Products, Inc. v. Merdel Game Manufacturing Co., 513 F.2d 1183 (2d Cir.1975), and Decorative Aides Corp. v. Staple Sewing Aides Corp., 497 F.Supp. 154 (S.D.N.Y.1980).

The rationale that underlies *Affiliated Hospital* and *Decorative Aides* is that, in cases where an idea can be expressed in only a very limited number of ways, affording copyright protection to the rules or instructions would be tantamount to affording copyright protection to the games or processes themselves. Id. In the present case, the Court has already noted that the existence of "Stickybear Printer" disproves defendant's argument that there are a very limited number of ways to express the idea underlying "Print Shop." Thus, there is no danger in the present case that affording copyright protection to the "instructions" of "Print Shop" will amount to awarding plaintiff a monopoly over the idea of a menu-driven program that prints greeting cards, banners, signs and posters.

Defendant's argument is unavailing for another important reason. The menu screens in "Print Shop" contain much more than just instructions on how to operate the program. Their artwork is aesthetically pleasing. Their layout and sequence, viewed as part of a total user interface, provides a significant element of entertainment for the user (often a child). Because the menu screens contain "stylistic creativity above and beyond the bare expression" of rules or instructions, they do not fall within the holdings of *Affiliated Hospital* and *Decorative Aides.*

B. *Did defendant copy plaintiffs' work?*

Having determined that the overall structure, sequence and arrangement of the screens, text, and artwork (i.e., the audiovisual displays in general) are protected under the copyright laws, the Court now turns to the question of whether defendant in fact copied protected portions of "Print Shop." . . . .

Plaintiffs produced sufficient direct evidence of copying to establish infringement.

The uncontradicted testimony at trial was that both Hong Lu and David Lodge ordered Unison's programmers, MacDuff Hughes in particular, to copy "Print Shop." The programmers evidently executed these orders to the best of their ability. Some of the copying was done so carelessly that it left unmistakable traces. For example, in the "Custom Layout" screen of "Print Shop," the user is instructed to press the "Return" key on the Apple keyboard. Similarly, in the "Custom Layout" screen of "Printmaster," the user is instructed to press the "Return" key on the IBM keyboard. Actually, the IBM keyboard contains no "Return" key, only an "Enter" key. Lodge admitted that Unison's failure to change "Return" to "Enter" was a result of its programmers' intense concentration on copying "Print Shop."

The testimony of Hughes also provided probative direct evidence of copying. Even after negotiations with Broderbund had collapsed and Lu had told Hughes not to feel as if he any longer had to produce an exact copy of "Print Shop," Hughes finished the portions that he had been copying and kept them. He was hurrying to finish the project so that he could get back to school on time. In particular, Hughes copied the screens in the "Greeting Card," "Sign," and "Picture Editor" functions. Hughes even had an idea for a totally different user interface in the "Picture Editor" function, but he copied the "Print Shop" interface because his copied version of the interface was "much further along."

Based on the foregoing, the Court finds that plaintiffs have adduced sufficient direct evidence of copying to prove infringement of the protected portions of "Print Shop."

3. *Access.*

In the interest of creating a comprehensive record, the Court deems it desirable also to undertake a circumstantial analysis of copying, i.e., a determination of whether defendant had access to the copyrighted work and whether there exists "substantial similarity" between the copyrighted work and defendant's work. See Sid & Marty Krofft Television Productions, Inc. v. McDonald's Corp., 562 F.2d 1157, 1162 (9th Cir.1977).

There is no question but that defendant had access to the copyrighted work. David Balsam gave Hong Lu several commercially-available copies of "Print Shop" for the purpose of representing to Japanese firms that Unison could do conversions of "Print Shop" for them. Hughes, the Unison programmer, used a copy of "Print Shop" as a model for the IBM version that he was ordered to create. Although the Court finds that Unison did not have access to the source or object code to "Print Shop," the uncontradicted testimony was that access to the literal aspects of the program were not necessary to copy "Print Shop." Plaintiff has proven that defendant had access to the protected work.

4. *Substantial similarity.*

The leading case in this area is Arnstein v. Porter, 154 F.2d 464 (2d Cir.1946), cert. denied, 330 U.S. 851, 67 S.Ct. 1096, 91 L.Ed. 1294 (1947). There, the court established a two-step test for determining substantial similarity. In *Krofft*, 562 F.2d at 1164–65, the Ninth Circuit, albeit with some modification, adopted the *Arnstein* test and interpreted it to require the application of (1) an "extrinsic" test aimed at determining whether there exists a substantial similarity in underlying ideas; and (2) an "intrinsic" test to ascertain whether there exists a substantial similarity in the expression of the underlying idea. "Analytic dissection" and expert testimony are admissible to prove similarity under the extrinsic test, but the intrinsic test consists solely of the response of the "ordinary reasonable person." *Id.* at 1164. Thus, under *Krofft*, neither analytic dissection nor expert testimony is appropriate in applying the intrinsic test.

In *Whelan,* 797 F.2d at 1233–35, the Third Circuit joined the "growing number of courts" that have abandoned the bifurcated test of substantial similarity in complex copyright actions, such as those involving computer programs. In its place, the *Whelan* court adopted an integrated substantial similarity test pursuant to which both lay and expert testimony would be admissible. Id. The *Whelan* court did not say whether analytical dissection (the side-by-side comparison of each element of the copyrighted and allegedly infringing works) would be appropriate under its integrated test. Although this Court is of the opinion that an integrated test involving expert testimony and analytic dissection may well be the wave of the future in this area, the Ninth Circuit's position is clearly marked out in *Krofft,* and controls the analysis herein.

(a) *Application of the extrinsic test.*

As stated above, the extrinsic test is aimed at determining whether there exists a substantial similarity between the underlying ideas of the copyrighted and allegedly infringing works. There is no question but that "Print Shop" and "Printmaster" share the same underlying idea. Plaintiffs' expert, Lawrence Tesler, who is Acting Manager of the Advanced Development Group at Apple Computer, stated that the idea behind "Printmaster" was exactly the same as the idea behind "Print Shop." One of defendant's experts, Peter Antoniak, who is a software consultant, stated that "Printmaster" and "Print Shop" do almost the same thing—they provide the user with an output. Expert opinion notwithstanding, it is obvious that the purpose and uses of "Printmaster" and "Print Shop" are virtually identical. Both programs allow their users to create greeting cards, signs, banners and posters with various, user-selected combinations of text, graphics, and borders. Both operate in conjunction with dot-matrix printers. The application of the extrinsic test enunciated in *Krofft* to the programs at issue in this case clearly compels a finding of substantial similarity of ideas.

(b) *Application of the intrinsic test.*

In applying the intrinsic test, the finder of fact (in this case the Court) is to determine whether an "ordinary reasonable person" would find the expression of the subject works to be substantially similar. *Krofft,* 562 F.2d at 1164. The question is whether the infringing work captures the "total concept and feel" of the protected work. Id. at 1167, quoting *Roth Greeting Cards,* 429 F.2d at 1110. Having viewed both programs at trial, the Court finds that an ordinary reasonable person would think the expression of "Print Shop" and "Printmaster" substantially similar.

The ordinary observer could hardly avoid being struck by the eerie resemblance between the screens of the two programs. In general, the sequence of the screens and the choices presented, the layout of the screens, and the method of feedback to the user are all substantially similar. Specifically, the following similarities exist, *inter alia:* the structures of the "Main Menu" screens; the "staggered" layout of 3-2-3-2-3, totaling thirteen graphics; the "tiled" layout of 5×7 in both programs; the second screen in the "Custom Layout" function, in which the word "place" is highlighted and the word "remove" is inversely highlighted in both programs; the fact that the "tiled" option disappears in both programs in the medium-size graphic mode; the use of only left and right arrow keys on both keyboards, despite the fact that the IBM keyboard has up and down arrow capability; the offering in both programs of only three types of lines (solid, outline, and three-dimensional); and the fact that both programs require the user to create the front of the printed product before creating the inside of it. Other similarities are too numerous to list.

Mere lists of similarities cannot adequately convey the impression of overall similarity between "Print Shop" and "Printmaster." No ordinary observer could reasonably conclude that the expression of the ideas underlying these two programs were not substantially similar. Put simply, "Printmaster" looks like a copy of "Print Shop," with a few embellishments scattered about in no particular order. The "total concept and feel" of these programs, *Krofft,* 562 F.2d at 1167, is virtually identical. The application of the intrinsic test in the present case compels the finding that their expression is substantially similar. . . .

III

For the foregoing reasons, and good cause appearing therefor, IT IS HEREBY ORDERED that:

1. Defendant, Unison World, Inc., is adjudged to have infringed the copyright of plaintiff, Pixellite Software, on the audiovisual displays of the computer program known as "Print Shop". . . .

NOTES

1. Computer programs are considered to be "literary works" under the Copyright Act. Did *Broderbund* effectively hold that the audiovisual display in issue was part of a "computer program," so that it was a "literary work" rather than a "pictorial" or "graphic" work? Classification of a screen display as a computer program, and thus as a literary work rather than an audiovisual, pictorial or graphic work, has legal consequence. Rights in literary works are subject to statutory exemptions that differ in several respects from the exemptions for rights in audiovisual, pictorial and graphic works.

The United States Copyright Office has taken the position that "all copyrightable expression owned by the same claimant and embodied in a computer program, or first published as a unit with a computer program, including computer screen displays, is considered a single work and should be registered on a single application form." Registration and Deposit of Computer Screen Displays, 53 Fed.Reg. 21,817 (1988). "Ordinarily, where computer program authorship is part of the work, literary authorship will predominate, and one registration should be made on application Form TX. Where, however, audiovisual authorship predominates, the registration should be made on Form PA." 53 Fed.Reg. at 21818.

Was *Broderbund* adequately sensitive to the factors that may constrain the design of screen displays? Screen displays are "user interfaces," mediating between the programmed computer and the computer user. Some user interfaces—the QWERTY typewriter keyboard is the most common example—have become industry standards. Even if an interface has not become an industry standard, its configuration may uniquely conform to users' habits and predilections. For copyright to protect such interfaces could seriously hobble second comers to the industry. On the role that such constraints should play in copyright infringement determinations, see LaST Frontier Conference Report, Computer Software and Copyright Protection, 30 Jurimetrics J. 15 (1989); Menell, An Analysis of the Scope of Copyright Protection for Application Programs, 41 Stan.L.Rev. 1045 (1989).

2. *Subject Matter.* The question of copyright for computer-driven visual displays first arose in the context of videogames. In Stern Electronics, Inc. v. Kaufman, 669 F.2d 852, 213 U.S.P.Q. 443 (2d Cir. 1982), the court rejected the argument that copyright could protect only the computer program that predetermined the game's audiovisual display. "While that approach would have afforded some degree of protection, it would not have prevented a determined competitor from manufacturing a 'knock-off' of [plaintiff's] 'Scramble' that replicates precisely the sights and sounds of the game's audiovisual display. This could be done by writing a new computer program that would interact with the hardware components of a video game to produce on the screen the same images seen in 'Scramble,' accompanied by the same sounds." 669 F.2d at 855.

The defendants also argued that plaintiff's display was uncopyrightable because it was neither fixed nor original. The court answered the fixation argument by observing that, while "the entire sequence of all the sights and sounds of the game are different each time the game is played, depending upon the route and speed the player selects for his spaceship and the timing and accuracy of his release of his craft's bombs and lasers . . . many aspects of the sights and the sequence of their appearance remain constant during each play of the game." 669 F.2d at 856.

To the contention that "the audiovisual display contains no originality because all of its reappearing features are determined by the previously created computer program," the court answered that the "visual and aural features of the audiovisual display are plainly original variations sufficient to render the display copyrightable even though the underlying written program has an independent existence and is itself eligible for copyright. . . . Moreover, the argument overlooks the sequence of the creative process. Someone first conceived what the audiovisual display would look like and sound like. Originality occurred at that point. Then the program was written. Finally, the program was imprinted into the memory devices so that, in operation with the components of the game, the sights and sounds could be seen and heard. The resulting display satisfies the requirement of an original work." 669 F.2d at 856–57.

See generally, Grabowski, Copyright Protection for Video Game Programs and Audiovisual Displays; And—Substantial Similarity and the Scope of Audiovisual Copyrights for Video Games, 3 Loy.Ent.L.J. 139 (1983); Hemnes, The Adaptation of Copyright Law to Video Games, 131 U.Pa.L.Rev. 171 (1982); Patry, Electronic Audiovisual Games: Navigating the Maze of Copyright, 31 J.Copyright Soc'y 1 (1983).

3. *Infringement.* Courts have generally applied the same infringement measure to video games as they have to other audiovisual media such as motion pictures. In Atari, Inc. v. North American Philips Consumer Elecs. Corp., 672 F.2d 607, 214 U.S.P.Q. 33 (7th Cir. 1982), cert. denied, 459 U.S. 880, 103 S.Ct. 176, 74 L.Ed.2d 145, the court reversed the lower court's denial of a preliminary injunction to copyright owner, Atari. In the appellate court's view, "North American not only adopted the same basic characters but also portrayed them in a manner which made K.C. Munchkin appear substantially similar to PAC–MAN. The K.C. Munchkin gobbler has several blatantly similar features including the relative size and shape of the 'body,' the V-shaped 'mouth,' its distinctive gobbling action (with appropriate sounds), and especially the way in which it disappears upon being captured. An examination of the K.C. Munchkin ghost monsters reveals even more significant visual similarities. In size, shape, and manner of movement, they are virtually identical to their PAC–MAN counterparts. K.C. Munchkin's monsters, for example, exhibit the same peculiar 'eye' and 'leg' movement. Both games, moreover, express the role reversal and 'regeneration' process with such great similarity that an ordinary observer could conclude only that North American copied plaintiffs' PAC–MAN." 672 F.2d at 618.

Should courts apply a more stringent infringement measure to computer screen displays that provide a functional interface between the computer and its user? See Manufacturers Technologies, Inc. v. Cams, Inc., 706 F.Supp. 984, 10 U.S.P.Q.2d 1321 (D.Conn.1989).

2. LIMITS OF PROTECTION

VAULT CORPORATION v. QUAID SOFTWARE LIMITED

United States Court of Appeals, Fifth Circuit, 1988.
847 F.2d 255, 7 U.S.P.Q.2d 1281.

REAVLEY, Circuit Judge:

Vault brought this copyright infringement action against Quaid seeking damages and preliminary and permanent injunctions. The district court denied Vault's motion for a preliminary injunction, holding that Vault did not have a reasonable probability of success on the merits. By stipulation of the parties, this ruling was made final and judgment was entered accordingly. We affirm.

I

Vault produces computer diskettes under the registered trademark "PROLOK" which are designed to prevent the unauthorized duplication of programs placed on them by software computer companies, Vault's customers. Floppy diskettes serve as a medium upon which computer companies place their software programs. To use a program, a purchaser loads the diskette into the disk drive of a computer, thereby allowing the computer to read the program into its memory. The purchaser can then remove the diskette from the disk drive and operate the program from the computer's memory. This process is repeated each time a program is used.

The protective device placed on a PROLOK diskette by Vault is comprised of two parts: a "fingerprint" and a software program ("Vault's program").[1] The "fingerprint" is a small mark physically placed on the magnetic surface of each PROLOK diskette which contains certain information that cannot be altered or erased. Vault's program is a set of instructions to the computer which interact with the "fingerprint" to prevent the computer from operating the program recorded on a PROLOK diskette (by one of Vault's customers) unless the computer verifies that the *original* PROLOK diskette, as identified by the "fingerprint," is in the computer's disk drive. While a purchaser can copy a PROLOK protected program onto another diskette, the computer will not read the program into its memory from the copy unless the original PROLOK diskette is also in one of the computer's disk drives. The fact that a fully functional copy of a program cannot be made from a PROLOK diskette prevents purchasers from buying a single program and making unauthorized copies for distribution to others.

Vault produced PROLOK in three stages. The original commercial versions, designated as versions 1.01, 1.02, 1.03, 1.04 and 1.06 ("version 1.0") were produced in 1983. Vault then incorporated improvements into the system and produced version 1.07 in 1984. The third major revision occurred in August and September of 1985 and was designated as versions 2.0 and 2.01 ("version 2.0"). Each version of PROLOK has been copyrighted and Vault includes a license agreement with every PROLOK package that specifically prohibits the copying, modification, translation, decompilation or disassembly of Vault's program. Begin-

---

1. A PROLOK diskette contains two programs, the program placed on the diskette by a software company (e.g., word processing) and the program placed on the diskette by Vault which interacts with the "fingerprint" to prevent the unauthorized duplication of the software company's program. We use the term "software pro-gram" or "program" to refer to the program placed on the diskette by one of Vault's customers (a computer company) and "Vault's program" to refer to the program placed on the diskette by Vault as part of the protective device. We collectively refer to the "fingerprint" and Vault's program as the "protective device."

ning with version 2.0 in September 1985, Vault's license agreement contained a choice of law clause adopting Louisiana law.

Quaid's product, a diskette called "CopyWrite," contains a feature called "RAMKEY" which unlocks the PROLOK protective device and facilitates the creation of a fully functional copy of a program placed on a PROLOK diskette. The process is performed simply by copying the contents of the PROLOK diskette onto the CopyWrite diskette which can then be used to run the software program *without* the original PROLOK diskette in a computer disk drive. RAMKEY interacts with Vault's program to make it appear to the computer that the CopyWrite diskette contains the "fingerprint," thereby making the computer function as if the original PROLOK diskette is in its disk drive. A copy of a program placed on a CopyWrite diskette can be used without the original, and an unlimited number of fully functional copies can be made in this manner from the program originally placed on the PROLOK diskette.

Quaid first developed RAMKEY in September 1983 in response to PROLOK version 1.0. In order to develop this version of RAMKEY, Quaid copied Vault's program into the memory of its computer and analyzed the manner in which the program operated. When Vault developed version 1.07, Quaid adapted RAMKEY in 1984 to defeat this new version. The adapted version of RAMKEY contained a sequence of approximately 30 characters found in Vault's program and was discontinued in July 1984. Quaid then developed the current version of RAMKEY which also operates to defeat PROLOK version 1.07, but does not contain the sequence of characters used in the discontinued version. Quaid has not yet modified RAMKEY to defeat PROLOK version 2.0, and has agreed not to modify RAMKEY pending the outcome of this suit. Robert McQuaid, the sole owner of Quaid, testified in his deposition that while a CopyWrite diskette can be used to duplicate programs placed on all diskettes, whether copy-protected or not, the only purpose served by RAMKEY is to facilitate the duplication of programs placed on copy-protected diskettes. He also stated that without the RAMKEY feature, CopyWrite would have no commercial value.

II

Vault brought this action against Quaid seeking preliminary and permanent injunctions to prevent Quaid from advertising and selling RAMKEY, an order impounding all of Quaid's copies of CopyWrite which contain the RAMKEY feature, and monetary damages in the amount of $100,000,000. Vault asserted three copyright infringement claims cognizable under federal law, 17 U.S.C. § 101 et seq. (1977 & Supp.1988) (the "Copyright Act"), which included: (1) that Quaid violated 17 U.S.C. §§ 501(a) & 106(1) by copying Vault's program into its computer's memory for the purpose of developing a program (RAMKEY) designed to defeat the function of Vault's program; (2) that Quaid, through RAMKEY, contributes to the infringement of Vault's copyright and the copyrights of its customers in violation of the Copyright Act as interpreted by the Supreme Court in Sony Corp. of Am. v. Universal City Studios, 464 U.S. 417, 104 S.Ct. 774, 78 L.Ed.2d 574 (1984); and (3) that the second version of RAMKEY, which contained approximately thirty characters from PROLOK version 1.07, and the latest version of RAMKEY, constitute "derivative works" of Vault's program in violation of 17 U.S.C. §§ 501(a) & 106(2). Vault also asserted two claims based on Louisiana law, contending that Quaid breached its license agreement by decompiling or disassembling Vault's program in violation of the Louisiana Software License Enforcement Act, La.Rev.Stat.Ann. § 51:1961 *et seq.* (West 1987), and that Quaid misappropriated Vault's program in violation of the Louisiana Uniform Trade Secrets Act, La.Rev.Stat.Ann. § 51:1431 *et seq.* (West 1987).

The district court originally dismissed Vault's complaint for lack of in personam jurisdiction. This court reversed the district court's order of dismissal and remanded the case for further proceedings. On remand, the district court, after a three-day bench trial, denied Vault's motion for a preliminary injunction holding that Vault had not established a reasonable probability of success on the merits. Subsequently, the parties agreed to submit the case for final decision based on the evidence adduced at the preliminary injunction trial. On July 31, 1987 the district court entered final judgment in accordance with its decision on the preliminary injunction.

Vault now contends that the district court improperly disposed of each of its claims.

III Vault's Federal Claims

An owner of a copyrighted work has the exclusive right to reproduce the work in copies, to prepare derivative works based on the copyrighted work, to distribute copies of the work to the public, and, in the case of certain types of works, to perform and display the work publicly. 17 U.S.C. § 106. Sections 107 through 118 of the Copyright Act limit an owner's exclusive rights, and section 501(a) provides that "[a]nyone who violates any of the exclusive rights of the copyright owner as provided by sections 106 through 118 . . . is an infringer of the copyright."

It is not disputed that Vault owns the copyright to the program it places on PROLOK diskettes and is thus an "owner of copyright" under § 106. Therefore, Vault has, subject to the exceptions contained in sections 107 through 118, the exclusive right to reproduce its program in copies and to prepare derivative works based on its program. Vault claims that Quaid infringed its copyright under § 501(a) by: (1) directly copying Vault's program into the memory of Quaid's computer; (2) contributing to the unauthorized copying of Vault's program and the programs Vault's customers place on PROLOK diskettes; and (3) preparing derivative works of Vault's program.

Section 117 of the Copyright Act limits a copyright owner's exclusive rights under § 106 by permitting an owner of a computer program to make certain copies of that program without obtaining permission from the program's copyright owner. With respect to Vault's first two claims of copyright infringement, Quaid contends that its activities fall within the § 117 exceptions and that it has, therefore, not infringed Vault's exclusive rights under § 501(a). To appreciate the arguments of the parties, we examine the legislative history of § 117.

A. Background

In 1974 Congress established the National Commission on New Technological Uses of Copyrighted Works (the "CONTU") to perform research and make recommendations concerning copyright protection for computer programs. Before receiving the CONTU's recommendations, Congress amended the Copyright Act in 1976 to include computer programs in the definition of protectable literary works and to establish that a program copied into a computer's memory constitutes a reproduction. Congress delayed further action and enacted an interim provision to maintain the status quo until the CONTU completed its study and made specific recommendations.

In 1978 the CONTU issued its final report in which it recognized that "[t]he cost of developing computer programs is far greater than the cost of their duplication," CONTU Report at 26, and concluded that "some form of protection is necessary to encourage the creation and broad distribution of computer programs in a competitive market," id. at 27. After acknowledging the importance of balancing the interest of proprietors in obtaining "reasonable protection" against the risks of "unduly burdening users of programs and the general public," id. at 29, the Report recommended the repeal of section 117 (the interim provision) and the enactment of a new section 117 which would proscribe the unauthorized copying of computer programs but permit a "rightful possessor" of a program

> to make or authorize the making of another copy or adaptation of that computer program *provided:*
>
> > (1) that such a new copy or adaptation is created as an essential step in the utilization of the computer program in conjunction with a machine and that it is used in no other manner, or
> >
> > (2) that such new copy or adaptation is for archival purposes only and that all archival copies are destroyed in the event that continued possession of the computer program should cease to be rightful.

Id. at 29–30 (emphasis in original).

Because the act of loading a program from a medium of storage into a computer's memory creates a copy of the program, the CONTU reasoned that "[o]ne who rightfully possesses a copy of a program . . . should be provided with a legal right to copy it to that extent which will permit its use by the possessor," and drafted proposed § 117(1) to "provide that persons in rightful possession of copies of programs be able to use them freely without fear of exposure to copyright liability." Id. at 31. With respect to proposed section 117(2), the "archival exception," the Report explained that a person in rightful possession of a program should have the right "to prepare archival copies of it to guard against destruction or damage by mechanical or electrical failure. But this permission would not extend to other copies of the program. Thus one could not, for example, make archival copies of a program and later sell some to another while retaining some for use." Id.

In 1980, Congress enacted the Computer Software Copyright Act which adopted the recommendations contained in the CONTU Report. Section 117 was repealed, proposed section 117 was enacted, and the proposed definition of "computer program" was added to section 101. The Act's legislative history, contained in a short paragraph in a committee report, merely states that the Act, "embodies the recommendations of [the CONTU] with respect to clarifying the law of copyright of computer software." H.R.Rep. No. 1307, 96th Cong., 2d Sess., pt. 1, at 23, *reprinted in* 1980 U.S.Code Cong. & Admin.News 6460, 6482. The absence of an extensive legislative history and the fact that Congress enacted proposed section 117 with only one change have prompted courts to rely on the CONTU Report as an expression of legislative intent. See Micro–Sparc, Inc. v. Amtype Corp., 592 F.Supp. 33, 35 (D.Mass.1984); Atari, Inc. v. JS & A Group, Inc., 597 F.Supp. 5, 9 (N.D.Ill.1983); Midway Mfg. Co. v. Strohon, 564 F.Supp. 741, 750 n. 6 (N.D.Ill.1983).

B. Direct Copying

In order to develop RAMKEY, Quaid analyzed Vault's program by copying it into its computer's memory. Vault contends that, by making this unauthorized copy, Quaid directly infringed upon Vault's copyright. The district court held that "Quaid's actions clearly fall within [the § 117(1)] exemption. The loading of [Vault's] program into the [memory] of a computer is an 'essential step in the utilization' of [Vault's] program. Therefore, Quaid has not infringed Vault's copyright by loading [Vault's program] into [its computer's memory]." *Vault*, 655 F.Supp. at 758.

Section 117(1) permits an owner of a program to make a copy of that program provided that the copy "is created as an essential step in the utilization of the computer program in conjunction with a machine and that it is used in no other manner." Congress recognized that a computer program cannot be used unless it is first copied into a computer's memory, and thus provided the § 117(1) exception to permit copying for this essential purpose. *See* CONTU Report at 31. Vault contends that, due to the inclusion of the phrase "and that it is used in no other manner," this exception should be interpreted to permit only the copying of a computer program for the purpose of using it for *its intended purpose*. Because Quaid copied Vault's program into its computer's memory for the express purpose of devising a means of defeating its protective function, Vault contends that § 117(1) is not applicable.

We decline to construe § 117(1) in this manner. Even though the copy of Vault's program made by Quaid was *not* used to prevent the copying of the program placed on the PROLOK diskette by one of Vault's customers (which is the purpose of Vault's program), and was, indeed, made for the express purpose of devising a means of defeating its protective function, the copy made by Quaid *was* "created as an essential step in the utilization" of Vault's program. Section 117(1) contains no language to suggest that the copy it permits must be employed for a use intended by the copyright owner, and, absent clear congressional guidance to the contrary, we refuse to read such limiting language into this exception. We therefore hold that Quaid did not infringe Vault's exclusive right to reproduce its program in copies under § 106(1).

C. Contributory Infringement

Vault contends that, because purchasers of programs placed on PROLOK diskettes use the RAMKEY feature of CopyWrite to make unauthorized copies, Quaid's advertisement and sale of CopyWrite diskettes with the RAMKEY feature violate the Copyright Act by contributing to the infringement of Vault's copyright and the copyrights owned by Vault's customers. Vault asserts that it lost customers and substantial revenue as a result of Quaid's contributory infringement because software companies which previously relied on PROLOK diskettes to protect their programs from unauthorized copying have discontinued their use.

While a purchaser of a program on a PROLOK diskette violates sections 106(1) and 501(a) by making and distributing unauthorized copies of the program, the Copyright Act "does not expressly render anyone liable for the infringement committed by another." *Sony,* 464 U.S. at 434, 104 S.Ct. at 785. The Supreme Court in *Sony,* after examining the express provision in the Patent Act which imposes liability on an individual who "actively induces infringement of a patent," 35 U.S.C. § 271(b) & (c), and noting the similarity between the Patent and Copyright Acts, recognized the availability, under the Copyright Act, of vicarious liability against one who sells a product that is used to make unauthorized copies of copyrighted material. The Court held that liability based on contributory infringement could be imposed only where the seller had constructive knowledge of the fact that its product was used to make unauthorized copies of copyrighted material, and that the sale of a product "does not constitute contributory infringement if the product is widely used for legitimate, unobjectionable purposes. Indeed, it need merely be capable of substantial noninfringing uses." Id. at 442, 104 S.Ct. at 789.

While Quaid concedes that it has actual knowledge that its product is used to make unauthorized copies of copyrighted material, it contends that the RAMKEY portion of its CopyWrite diskettes serves a substantial noninfringing use by allowing purchasers of programs on PROLOK diskettes to make archival copies as permitted under 17

U.S.C. § 117(2), and thus that it is not liable for contributory infringement. The district court held that Vault lacked standing to raise a contributory infringement claim because "it is not Vault, but the customers of Vault who place their programs on PROLOK disks, who may assert such claims. Clearly the copyright rights to these underlying programs belong to their publishers, not Vault." *Vault,* 655 F.Supp. at 759. Alternatively the court held that CopyWrite is capable of "commercially significant noninfringing uses" because the RAMKEY feature permits the making of archival copies of copy-protected software, and CopyWrite diskettes (without the RAMKEY feature) are used to make copies of unprotected software and as a diagnostic tool to analyze the quality of new computer programs. Id. Therefore, the court held that the sale of CopyWrite did not constitute contributory infringement.

While we hold that Vault has standing to assert its contributory infringement claim, we find that RAMKEY is capable of substantial noninfringing uses and thus reject Vault's contention that the advertisement and sale of CopyWrite diskettes with RAMKEY constitute contributory infringement. . . .

2. *Substantial Noninfringing Uses of RAMKEY*

Vault's allegation of contributory infringement focuses on the RAMKEY feature of CopyWrite diskettes, not on the non-RAMKEY portions of these diskettes. Vault has no objection to the advertising and marketing of CopyWrite diskettes without the RAMKEY feature, and this feature is separable from the underlying diskette upon which it is placed. Therefore, in determining whether Quaid engaged in contributory infringement, we do not focus on the substantial noninfringing uses of CopyWrite, as opposed to the RAMKEY feature itself. The issue properly presented is whether the RAMKEY feature has substantial noninfringing uses.

The starting point for our analysis is with *Sony.* The plaintiffs in *Sony,* owners of copyrighted television programs, sought to enjoin the manufacture and marketing of Betamax video tape recorders ("VTR's"), contending that VTR's contributed to the infringement of their copyrights by permitting the unauthorized copying of their programs. After noting that plaintiffs' market share of television programming was less than 10%, and that copyright holders of a significant quantity of television broadcasting authorized the copying of their programs, the Court held that VTR's serve the legitimate and substantially noninfringing purpose of recording these programs, as well as plaintiffs' programs, for future viewing (authorized and unauthorized time-shifting respectively), and therefore rejected plaintiffs' contributory infringement claim.

Quaid asserts that RAMKEY serves the legitimate purpose of permitting purchasers of programs recorded on PROLOK diskettes to make archival copies under § 117(2) and that this purpose constitutes a substantial noninfringing use. At trial, witnesses for Quaid testified that software programs placed on floppy diskettes are subject to damage by *physical and human mishap* and that RAMKEY protects a purchaser's investment by providing a fully functional archival copy that can be used if the original program on the PROLOK protected diskette, or the diskette itself, is destroyed. Quaid contends that an archival copy of a PROLOK protected program, made without RAMKEY, does not serve to protect against these forms of damage because a computer will not read the program into its memory from the copy unless the PROLOK diskette containing the original undamaged program is also in one of its disk drives, which is impossible if the PROLOK diskette, or the program placed thereon, has been destroyed due to physical or human mishap.

Computer programs can be stored on a variety of mediums, including floppy diskettes, hard disks, non-erasable read only memory ("ROM") chips, and a computer's random access memory, and may appear only as printed instructions on a sheet of paper. Vault contends that the archival exception was designed to permit *only* the copying of programs which are subject to "destruction or damage by *mechanical or electrical failure.*" CONTU Report at 31 (emphasis added). While programs stored on all mediums may be subject to damage due to physical abuse or human error, programs stored on certain mediums are not subject to damage by mechanical or electrical failure. Therefore, Vault argues, the medium of storage determines whether the archival exception applies, thus providing only owners of programs, placed on mediums of storage which subject them to damage by mechanical or electrical failure, the right to make back-up copies. To support its construction of § 117(2), Vault notes that one court has held that the archival exception does not apply to the copying of programs stored on ROM chips where there was no evidence that programs stored on this medium were subject to damage by mechanical or electrical failure, *Atari,* 597 F.Supp. at 9–10, and another court has likewise held that the archival exception does not apply to the copying of programs which appear only in the form of printed instructions in a magazine, *Micro–Sparc,* 592 F.Supp. at 35–36.

Vault contends that the district court's finding that programs stored on floppy diskettes are subject to damage by mechanical or electrical failure is erroneous because there was insufficient evidence presented at trial to support it, and, based on this contention, Vault asserts that the archival exception does not apply to permit the unauthorized copying of these programs. Vault performed a trial demonstration to prove that even if a program on an original PROLOK diskette, and Vault's protective program, were completely erased from this diskette, these programs could be restored on the original diskette using a copy made *without* RAMKEY. Therefore, Vault argues that even if a program recorded on a PROLOK diskette is subject to damage by mechanical or electrical failure, the non-operational copy of a PROLOK protected program made without RAMKEY is sufficient to protect against this type of damage. Vault concludes that, in light of the fact that RAMKEY facilitates the making of unauthorized copies and owners of PROLOK protected programs can make copies to protect against damage by mechanical and electrical failure without RAMKEY, the RAMKEY feature is not capable of substantial noninfringing uses.

The narrow construction of the archival exception, advanced by Vault and accepted in the *Atari* and *Micro–Sparc* decisions, has undeniable appeal. This construction would leave the owner of a protected software program free to make back-up copies of the software to guard against erasures, which is probably the primary concern of owners as well as the drafters of the CONTU Report. Software producers should perhaps be entitled to protect their product from improper duplication, and Vault's PROLOK may satisfy producers and most purchasers on this score—*if* PROLOK cannot be copied by the purchaser onto a CopyWrite diskette without infringing the PROLOK copyright. That result does have appeal, but we believe it is an appeal that must be made to Congress. "[I]t is not our job to apply laws that have not yet been written." *Sony,* 464 U.S. at 456, 104 S.Ct. at 796. We read the statute as it is now written to authorize the owner of the PROLOK diskette to copy both the PROLOK program and the software program for any reason so long as the owner uses the copy for archival purposes only and not for an unauthorized transfer. . . .

A copy of a PROLOK protected program made with RAMKEY protects an owner from all types of damage to the original program, while a copy made without RAMKEY only serves the limited function of protecting against damage to the original program by mechanical and electrical failure. Because § 117(2) permits the making of fully functional archival copies, it follows that RAMKEY is capable of substantial noninfringing uses. Quaid's advertisement and sale of CopyWrite diskettes with the RAMKEY feature does not constitute contributory infringement.

D. Derivative Work

Section 106(2) of the Copyright Act provides the copyright owner exclusive rights "to prepare derivative works based on the copyrighted work." Section 101 defines a derivative work as:

> a work based on one or more preexisting works, such as a translation, musical arrangement, dramatization, fictionalization, motion picture version, sound recording, art reproduction, abridgment, condensation, or any other form in which a work may be recast, transformed, or adapted. A work consisting of editorial revisions, annotations, elaborations or other modifications which, as a whole, represent an original work of authorship is a 'derivative work.'

To constitute a derivative work, "the infringing work must incorporate in some form a portion of the copyrighted work." *Litchfield v. Spielberg,* 736 F.2d 1352, 1357 (9th Cir.1984), cert. denied, 470 U.S. 1052, 105 S.Ct. 1753, 84 L.Ed.2d 817 (1985). In addition, the infringing work must be substantially similar to the copyrighted work. *Id.*

The 1984 version of RAMKEY contained approximately 30 characters of source code copied from Vault's program. Vault's program contained the equivalent of approximately 50 pages of source code, and the 1984 version of RAMKEY contained the equivalent of approximately 80 pages of source code. By all accounts, the 30 character sequence shared by RAMKEY and Vault's program constituted a quantitatively minor amount of source code. In response to Vault's contention that RAMKEY constitutes a derivative work, the district court found that "the copying in 1984 was not significant" and that "there has been no evidence . . . that there has been any further duplication." Holding that "RAMKEY is not a substantially similar copy of PROLOK," the court concluded that "RAMKEY is not a derivative work." *Vault,* 655 F.Supp. at 759.

Vault now contends that the district court, in evaluating the 1984 version of RAMKEY, incorrectly emphasized the *quantity* of copying instead of the *qualitative* significance of the copied material, and cites Whelan Assoc's., Inc. v. Jaslow Dental Laboratory, Inc., 797 F.2d 1222 (3d Cir.1986), cert. denied, 479 U.S. 1031, 107 S.Ct. 877, 93 L.Ed.2d 831 (1987), for the proposition that a "court must make a qualitative, not quantitative, judgment about the character of the work as a whole and the importance of the substantially similar portions of the work." Id. at 1245. See Midway Mfg. Co. v. Artic Int'l, Inc., 704 F.2d 1009, 1013–14 (7th Cir.), cert. denied, 464 U.S. 823, 104 S.Ct. 90, 78 L.Ed.2d 98 (1983). The sequence copied, Vault asserts, constituted the identifying portion of Vault's program which interacts with the "fingerprint" to confirm that the original PROLOK diskette is in the computer's disk drive. Vault contends that, because this sequence was crucial to the operation of Vault's program and RAMKEY's ability to defeat its protective function, the copying was qualitatively significant.

The cases upon which Vault relies, *Whelan* and *Midway,* both involved situations where the derivative work performed essentially the same function as the copyrighted work. In this case, Vault's program and RAMKEY serve opposing functions; while Vault's program is designed to prevent the duplication of its customers' programs, RAMKEY is designed to facilitate the creation of copies of Vault's customers' programs. Under these circumstances, we agree with the district court that the 1984 copying was not significant and that this version of RAMKEY was not a substantially similar copy of Vault's program.

While Vault acknowledges that the latest version of RAMKEY does not contain a sequence of characters from Vault's program, Vault contends that this version is also a derivative work because it "alters" Vault's program. Vault cites *Midway* for the proposition that a product can be a derivative work where it alters, rather than copies, the copyrighted work. The court in *Midway,* however, held that the sale of a product which speeded-up plaintiff's programs constituted contributory infringement because the speeded-up programs were derivative works. The court did not hold, as Vault asserts, that defendant's product itself was a derivative work. We therefore reject Vault's contention that the latest version of RAMKEY constitutes a derivative work.

IV   Vault's Louisiana Claims

Seeking preliminary and permanent injunctions and damages, Vault's original complaint alleged that Quaid breached its license agreement by decompiling or disassembling Vault's program in violation of the Louisiana Software License Enforcement Act (the "License Act"), La.Rev.Stat.Ann. § 51:1961 et seq. (West 1987), and that Quaid misappropriated Vault's program in violation of the Louisiana Uniform Trade Secrets Act, La.Rev.Stat.Ann. § 51:1431 et seq. (West 1987). On appeal, Vault abandons its misappropriation claim, and, with respect to its breach of license claim, Vault only seeks an injunction to prevent Quaid from decompiling or disassembling PROLOK version 2.0.

Louisiana's License Act permits a software producer to impose a number of contractual terms upon software purchasers provided that the terms are set forth in a license agreement which comports with La. Rev.Stat.Ann. §§ 51:1963 & 1965, and that this license agreement accompanies the producer's software. Enforceable terms include the prohibition of: (1) any copying of the program for any purpose; and (2) modifying and/or adapting the program in any way, including adaptation by reverse engineering, decompilation or disassembly. La.Rev. Stat.Ann. § 51:1964. The terms "reverse engineering, decompiling or disassembling" are defined as "any process by which computer software is converted from one form to another form which is more readily understandable to human beings, including without limitation any decoding or decrypting of any computer program which has been encoded or encrypted in any manner." La.Rev.Stat.Ann. § 51:1962(3).

Vault's license agreement, which accompanies PROLOK version 2.0 and comports with the requirements of La.Rev.Stat.Ann. §§ 51:1963 & 1965, provides that "[y]ou may not . . . copy, modify, translate, convert to another programming language, decompile or disassemble" Vault's program. Vault asserts that these prohibitions are enforceable under Louisiana's License Act, and specifically seeks an injunction to prevent Quaid from decompiling or disassembling Vault's program.

The district court held that Vault's license agreement was "a contract of adhesion which could only be enforceable if the [Louisiana License Act] is a valid and enforceable statute." *Vault*, 655 F.Supp. at 761. The court noted numerous conflicts between Louisiana's License Act and the Copyright Act, including: (1) while the License Act authorizes a total prohibition on copying, the Copyright Act allows archival copies and copies made as an essential step in the utilization of a computer program; (2) while the License Act authorizes a perpetual bar against copying, the Copyright Act grants protection against unauthorized copying only for the life of the author plus fifty years; and (3) while the License Act places no restrictions on programs which may be protected, under the Copyright Act, only "original works of authorship" can be protected. The court concluded that, because Louisiana's License Act "touched upon the area" of federal copyright law, its provisions were preempted and Vault's license agreement was unenforceable. Id. at 763.

In Sears, Roebuck & Co. v. Stiffel Co., 376 U.S. 225, 84 S.Ct. 784, 11 L.Ed.2d 661 (1964), the Supreme Court held that "[w]hen state law touches upon the area of [patent or copyright statutes], it is 'familiar doctrine' that the federal policy 'may not be set at naught, or its benefits denied' by the state law." Id. at 229, 84 S.Ct. at 787 (quoting Sola Elec. Co. v. Jefferson Elec. Co., 317 U.S. 173, 176, 63 S.Ct. 172, 173, 87 L.Ed. 165 (1942)). See Compco Corp. v. Day–Brite Lighting, Inc., 376 U.S. 234, 84 S.Ct. 779, 11 L.Ed.2d 669 (1964). Section 117 of the Copyright Act permits an owner of a computer program to make an adaptation of that program provided that the adaptation is either "created as an essential step in the utilization of the computer program in conjunction with a machine," § 117(1), or "is for archival purpose only," § 117(2). The provision in Louisiana's License Act, which permits a software producer to prohibit the adaptation of its licensed computer program by decompilation or disassembly, conflicts with the rights of computer program owners under § 117 and clearly "touches upon an area" of federal copyright law. For this reason, and the reasons set forth by the district court, we hold that at least this provision of Louisiana's License Act is preempted by federal law, and thus that the restriction in Vault's license agreement against decompilation or disassembly is unenforceable.

V Conclusion

We hold that: (1) Quaid did not infringe Vault's exclusive right to reproduce its program in copies under § 106(1); (2) Quaid's advertisement and sale of RAMKEY does not constitute contributory infringement; (3) RAMKEY does not constitute a derivative work of Vault's program under § 106(2); and (4) the provision in Vault's license agreement, which prohibits the decompilation or disassembly of its program, is unenforceable.

The judgment of the district court is AFFIRMED.

NOTES

1. *The "Essential Step" and "Archival Copy" Exemptions.* The key difference between section 117 as passed by Congress and as proposed by CONTU lies in the statute's requirement that the otherwise infringing copy be made or authorized by "the owner of a copy of the computer program." CONTU had used the term "rightful possessor" rather than "owner." National Comm'n on New Technological Uses of Copyrighted Works, Final Report 12 (1978). This departure complicates the statute since section 117 does adopt CONTU's proposal that archival copies be destroyed "in the event that continued possession of the computer program should cease to be rightful." For example, if the owner of a copy of a computer program makes an archival copy and leases the original copy to a third party, section 117 requires him to destroy the archival copy since he is no longer entitled

to possess the original. At the same time, the third party may not make an archival copy because, though entitled to possess the original, she does not own it.

See generally, Stern, Section 117 of the Copyright Act: Charter of Software Users' Rights or an Illusory Promise?, 7 W.New Eng.L.Rev. 459 (1985).

2. *Reverse Engineering.* Software producers commonly disseminate their programs only in the form of object code—a form that is usable in computers but incomprehensible to humans. Source code—the form in which computer programs are initially written—is humanly comprehensible. But, for that reason, and because source code would reveal the logical techniques embodied in the program, producers typically withhold source code, guarding it as a trade secret.

Object code can be decompiled to reveal its underlying source code. Will decompilation infringe section 106(1)'s reproduction right if it entails making a copy of the object code? At least one court looked to industry custom to conclude that decompilation does not infringe copyright: "The mere fact that defendant's engineers dumped, flow charted, and analyzed plaintiff's code does not, in and of itself, establish pirating. As both parties' witnesses admitted, dumping and analyzing competitors' code is a standard practice in the industry. Had Uniden contented itself with surveying the general outline of the EFJ Program, thereafter converting the scheme into detailed code through its own imagination, creativity, and independent thought, a claim of infringement would not have arisen." E.F. Johnson Co. v. Uniden Corp. of America, 623 F.Supp. 1485, 1501 n.17, 228 U.S.P.Q. 891 (D.Minn.1985).

Does decompilation for research purposes constitute fair use under section 107 of the 1976 Copyright Act? In a report, Reverse Engineering and Intellectual Property Law, 44 The Record 132 (1989), the Committee on Computer Law of the Association of the Bar of the City of New York examined several examples of reverse engineering against the background of section 107's four factors. Two examples are illustrative: reverse engineering to learn about a program's structure, organization or algorithms as part of a classroom exercise, and reverse engineering in a commercial setting to "develop a directly competing functionally interchangeable program which uses only unprotected features of the first [program], that is, ideas which are not subject to copyright and have not been patented." Id at 135.

The Report concluded that section 107's first factor—purpose and character of the use—weighs in favor of the classroom use and against the commercial use. The second factor—the nature of the copyrighted work—"strongly" favors a fair use finding in both cases; "[u]nlike a book whose ideas can be discovered by reading it, the nature of a computer program distributed only in object code is such that the ideas embodied in it largely cannot be studied and understood by humans without decompilation. Therefore, prohibiting decompilation could defeat an important societal interest in learning from and improving on the ideas contained in computer programs, by effectively giving the copyright owner a monopoly over the ideas, as well as the expression, in the copyrighted work." Id. at 140.

Since both examples involve the copying of the entire program, the third factor—amount and substantiality of the portion used in relation to the copyrighted work as a whole—weighs against fair use; "[h]owever, even complete verbatim copies may be noninfringing." In the Report's view, the fourth factor—effect of the use upon the potential market for, or value of the copyrighted work—favors the first use, but not the second, "since the effect of the use would be the creation of a competing program." Id at 140–41. In the usual fair use case, the defendant's work will embody protectible expression appearing in the copyrighted work. Is it relevant that the competing program in the second example embodies no protectible expression drawn from the copyrighted work?

3. *Software Rental.* Since 1984, bills have been introduced in Congress to exempt computer programs from section 109's first sale doctrine to enable copyright owners to prohibit rentals of their programs. See, e.g., S. 2727, 100th Cong., 2d Sess. (1988). These bills parallel the Record Rental Amendment of 1984, page 623, above, in object and method. "As in the case of sound recordings, the overwhelming rationale for renting a computer program is to make an unauthorized copy. Computer software cannot be enjoyed for an evening's entertainment and then returned. To have meaning to a user, the software packages require mastery of complex user manuals, often running hundreds of pages in length. Even after a user has mastered the use of a program, it has little value until he or she adds his or her own data base to the program. The functions of learning how to use a program and utilizing it in connection with one's own data base cannot be accomplished in a few hours or days available under a rental arrangement without copying the program and displacing a legitimate sale of that particular program.

"In the recording industry a typical compact disk sells for $16.95 and costs hundreds of thousands of dollars in developmental costs to bring to the marketplace. Some say millions of dollars under circumstances. A typical mass market computer package costs several hundred dollars at retail and requires millions of dollars to develop. Were computer programs to be rented for a few dollars a day, the multimillion dollar investments necessary to bring new software to the market could no longer be amortized, and one of the brightest stars of the modern U.S. economy would be extinguished in its very infancy." The Computer Software Rental Amendments Act of 1988: Hearing on S. 2727 Before the Subcomm. on Patents, Copyrights and Trademarks of the Senate Comm. on the Judiciary, 100th Cong., 2d Sess. 2 (1988) (statement of Senator Orrin G. Hatch).

4. *Preemption.* Vault v. Quaid rested its preemption holding on constitutional principle rather than on section 301 of the Copyright Act. Why?

On "shrink-wrap" licenses, see Einhorn, The Enforceability of "Tear–Me–Open" Software License Agreements, 67 J.Pat. & Trademark Off. Soc'y 509 (1985).

NOTE: THE SEMICONDUCTOR CHIP PROTECTION ACT OF 1984

Semiconductor chips are collections of transistors combined into a single structure to process and record information. Semiconductor masks are the intricate stencils used in manufacturing semiconductor chips. Concluding that neither patent nor copyright law offered adequate incentives for investment in chip design, Congress passed the Semiconductor Chip Protection Act of 1984 to protect "mask works" fixed in "semiconductor chip products." For definition of these terms, see 17 U.S.C.A. § 901(a)(1), (2).

Subject Matter. A mask work becomes eligible for protection under the Act when it is fixed in a semiconductor chip product. Under section 901(a)(3), "a mask work is 'fixed' in a semiconductor chip product when its embodiment in the product is sufficiently permanent or stable to permit the mask work to be perceived or reproduced from the product for a period of more than transitory duration. . . ." Section 902(b) withholds protection from any mask work that "(1) is not original; or (2) consists of designs that are staple, commonplace, or familiar in the semiconductor industry, or variations of such designs, combined in a way that, considered as a whole, is not original." Section 902(c) denies protection to "any idea, procedure, process, system, method of operation, concept, principle, or discovery, regardless of the form in which it is described, explained, illustrated, or embodied in such work."

To be protected under the Act, a mask work must meet one of three conditions: (1) it must have been first commercially exploited in the United States; (2) on the date of the work's registration or initial commercial exploitation—whichever occurs first—the work's owner must have been (a) a United States national or domiciliary, (b) a national, domiciliary or sovereign authority of a foreign nation that is party to a mask work treaty to which the United States is also a party, or (c) a stateless person; or (3) the work must come within the scope of a presidential proclamation under the Act. 17 U.S.C.A. § 902(a)(1)(A), (B), (C). Section 902(a)(2) empowers the President to extend mask work protection to foreign works upon finding that the foreign nation protects United States works on substantially the same basis as the Act or "on substantially the same basis as that on which the foreign nation extends protection to mask works of its own nationals and domiciliaries and mask works first exploited in that nation. . . ."

Registration and Notice. Affixation of notice "is not a condition of protection." However, section 909(a) provides that registration is a condition of continued protection under the Act. If a registration application is not made within two years after the date of a mask work's first commercial exploitation, protection for the work will terminate and the work will fall into the public domain. § 908(a). Section 910(b)(1) makes registration a prerequisite to the commencement of an infringement action and section 908(f) makes the certificate of registration prima facie evidence of the facts stated in the certificate and of compliance with the Act's requirements. Section 908(b) vests administrative responsibility in the Register of Copyrights.

Ownership and Rights. Protection under the Act lasts for ten years from the date on which protection began. § 904(b). Section 905 gives a mask work owner "the exclusive rights to do and to authorize any of the following: (1) to reproduce the mask work by optical, electronic, or any other means; (2) to import or distribute a semiconductor chip product in which the mask work is embodied; and (3) to induce or knowingly to cause another person to do any of the acts described in paragraphs (1) and (2)." The Act carves out three limitations from its exclusive rights. Section 906(a) creates a privilege to "reverse engineer" mask works; section 906(b) introduces a first sale defense; and section 907 protects innocent infringers under certain conditions.

The exemption for reverse engineering was one of the Act's most hotly debated provisions. Section 906(a) exempts two forms of reverse engineering. Under section 906(a)(1), it is not an infringement for "a person to reproduce the mask work solely for the purpose of teaching, analyzing, or evaluating the concepts or techniques embodied in the mask work or the circuitry, logic flow, or organization of components used in the mask work." Section 906(a)(2) provides that it is not an infringement for "a person who performs the analysis or evaluation described in paragraph (1) [of section 906(a)] to incorporate the results of such conduct in an original mask work which is made to be distributed." Effectively, this provision permits competitors to imitate protected mask works, and to obtain mask work protection for their "original" imitations, so long as the imitation is not "substantially identical" to the first mask work. According to the House Report, the provision permits "the 'unauthorized' creation of a second mask work whose layout, in substantial part, is similar to the layout of the protected mask work—if the second mask work was the product of substantial study and analysis, and not the mere result of plagiarism accomplished without such study or analysis." H.R.Rep. No. 781, 98th Cong., 2d Sess. 22 (1984).

On the legislative history of the Semiconductor Chip Act, see Kastenmeier & Remington, The Semiconductor Chip Protection Act of 1984: A Swamp or Firm Ground?, 70 Minn.L.Rev. 417 (1985). The Act generally is examined in Symposium, The Semiconductor Chip Protection Act of 1984 and Its Lessons, 70 Minn.L.Rev. 263 (1985); R. Stern, Semiconductor Chip Protection (1986); D. Ladd, D. Leibowitz & B. Joseph, Protection for Semiconductor Chip Masks in the United States (1986). See also, Dreier, Development of the Protection of Semiconductor Integrated Circuits, 19 Int.Rev.Indust.Prop. & Copyright L. 427 (1988); McManis, International Protection for Semiconductor Chip Designs and the Standard of Judicial Review of Presidential Proclamations Issued Pursuant to the Semiconductor Chip Protection Act of 1984, 22 Geo.Wash.Int'l J.L. & Econ. 331 (1988).

B. PATENT LAW

DIAMOND v. DIEHR

Supreme Court of the United States, 1981.
450 U.S. 175, 101 S.Ct. 1048, 67 L.Ed.2d 155, 209 U.S.P.Q. 1.

Mr. Justice REHNQUIST delivered the opinion of the Court.

We granted certiorari to determine whether a process for curing synthetic rubber which includes in several of its steps the use of a mathematical formula and a programmed digital computer is patentable subject matter under 35 U.S.C.A. § 101.

I

The patent application at issue was filed by the respondents on August 6, 1975. The claimed invention is a process for molding raw, uncured synthetic rubber into cured precision products. The process uses a mold for precisely shaping the uncured material under heat and pressure and then curing the synthetic rubber in the mold so that the product will retain its shape and be functionally operative after the molding is completed.[1]

Respondents claim that their process ensures the production of molded articles which are properly cured. Achieving the perfect cure depends upon several factors including the thickness of the article to be molded, the temperature of the molding process, and the amount of time that the article is allowed to remain in the press. It is possible using well-known time, temperature, and cure relationships to calculate by means of the Arrhenius equation[2] when to open the press and remove the cured product. Nonetheless, according to the respondents, the industry has not been able to obtain uniformly accurate cures because the temperature of the molding press could not be precisely measured thus making it difficult to do the necessary computations to determine cure time. Because the temperature *inside* the press has heretofore been viewed as an uncontrollable variable, the conventional industry practice has been to calculate the cure time as the shortest time in which all parts of the product will definitely be cured, assuming a reasonable amount of mold-opening time during loading and unload-

---

1. A "cure" is obtained by mixing curing agents into the uncured polymer in advance of molding, and then applying heat over a period of time. If the synthetic rubber is cured for the right length of time at the right temperature, it becomes a useable product.

2. The equation is named after its discoverer Svante Arrhenius and has long been used to calculate the cure time in rubber molding presses. The equation can be expressed as follows:

$$\ln v = CZ + x$$

wherein $\ln v$ is the natural logarithm of v, the total required cure time; C is the activation constant, a unique figure for each batch of each compound being molded, determined in accordance with rheometer measurements of each batch; Z is the temperature in the mold; and x is a constant dependent on the geometry of the particular mold in the press. A rheometer is an instrument to measure flow of viscous substances.

ing. But the shortcoming of this practice is that operating with an uncontrollable variable inevitably led in some instances to overestimating the mold-opening time and overcuring the rubber, and in other instances to underestimating that time and undercuring the product.

Respondents characterize their contribution to the art to reside in the process of constantly measuring the actual temperature inside the mold. These temperature measurements are then automatically fed into a computer which repeatedly recalculates the cure time by use of the Arrhenius equation. When the recalculated time equals the actual time that has elapsed since the press was closed, the computer signals a device to open the press. According to the respondents, the continuous measuring of the temperature inside the mold cavity, the feeding of this information to a digital computer which constantly recalculates the cure time, and the signaling by the computer to open the press, are all new in the art.

The patent examiner rejected the respondents' claims on the sole ground that they were drawn to nonstatutory subject matter under 35 U.S.C.A. § 101.[5] He determined that those steps in respondents' claims

5. Respondents' application contained 11 different claims. Three examples are claims 1, 2, and 11 which provide:

"1. A method of operating a rubber-molding press for precision molded compounds with the aid of a digital computer, comprising:

"providing said computer with a data base for said press including at least,

"natural logarithm conversion data (ln),

"the activation energy constant (C) unique to each batch of said compound being molded, and

"a constant (x) dependent upon the geometry of the particular mold of the press,

"initiating an interval timer in said computer upon the closure of the press for monitoring the elapsed time of said closure,

"constantly determining the temperature (Z) of the mold at a location closely adjacent to the mold cavity in the press during molding,

"constantly providing the computer with the temperature (Z),

"repetitively calculating in the computer, at frequent intervals during each cure, the Arrhenius equation for reaction time during the cure, which is

"$\ln\ v = CZ + x$

"where v is the total required cure time,

"repetitively comparing in the computer at said frequent intervals during the

cure each said calculation of the total required cure time calculated with the Arrhenius equation and said elapsed time, and

"opening the press automatically when a said comparison indicates equivalence.

"2. The method of claim 1 including measuring the activation energy constant for the compound being molded in the press with a rheometer and automatically updating said data base within the computer in the event of changes in the compound being molded in said press as measured by said rheometer.

"11. A method of manufacturing precision molded articles from selected synthetic rubber compounds in an openable rubber molding press having at least one heated precision mold, comprising:

"(a) heating said mold to a temperature range approximating a predetermined rubber curing temperature,

"(b) installing prepared unmolded synthetic rubber of a known compound in a molding cavity of a predetermined geometry as defined by said mold,

"(c) closing said press to mold said rubber to occupy said cavity in conformance with the contour of said mold and to cure said rubber by transfer of heat thereto from said mold,

"(d) initiating an interval timer upon the closure of said press for monitoring the elapsed time of said closure,

"(e) heating said mold during said closure to maintain the temperature there-that are carried out by a computer under control of a stored program constituted nonstatutory subject matter under this Court's decision in Gottschalk v. Benson, 409 U.S. 63 (1972). The remaining steps— installing rubber in the press and the subsequent closing of the press— were "conventional in nature and cannot be the basis of patentability." The examiner concluded that respondents' claims defined and sought protection of a computer program for operating a rubber molding press.

The Patent and Trademark Office Board of Appeals agreed with the examiner, but the Court of Customs and Patent Appeals reversed. The court noted that a claim drawn to subject matter otherwise statutory does not become nonstatutory because a computer is involved. The respondents' claims were not directed to a mathematical algorithm or an improved method of calculation but rather recited an improved process for molding rubber articles by solving a practical problem which had arisen in the molding of rubber products.

The Government sought certiorari arguing that the decision of the Court of Customs and Patent Appeals was inconsistent with prior decisions of this Court. Because of the importance of the question presented, we granted the writ.

II

Last Term in Diamond v. Chakrabarty, 447 U.S. 303, 100 S.Ct. 2204, 65 L.Ed.2d 144 (1980), this Court discussed the historical purposes of the patent laws and in particular 35 U.S.C.A. § 101. As in *Chakrabarty*, we must here construe 35 U.S.C.A. § 101 which provides:

> Whoever invents or discovers any new or useful process, machine, manufacture, or composition of matter, or any new and useful improvement thereof, may obtain a patent therefor, subject to the conditions and requirements of this Title.

In cases of statutory construction, we begin with the language of the statute. Unless otherwise defined, "words will be interpreted as taking their ordinary, contemporary, common meaning," Perrin v. United States, 444 U.S. 37, 42, 100 S.Ct. 311, 314, 62 L.Ed.2d 199 (1979),

of within said range approximating said rubber curing temperature,

"(f) constantly determining the temperature of said mold at a location closely adjacent said cavity thereof throughout closure of said press,

"(g) repetitively calculating at frequent periodic intervals throughout closure of said press the Arrhenius equation for reaction time of said rubber to determine total required cure time v as follows:

"$\ln v = cz + x$

"wherein c is an activation energy constant determined for said rubber being molded and cured in said press, z is the temperature of said mold at the time of each calculation of said Arrhenius equation, and x is a constant which is a function of said predetermined geometry of said mold,

"(h) for each repetition of calculation of said Arrhenius equation herein, comparing the resultant calculated total required cure time with the monitored elapsed time measured by said interval timer,

"(i) opening said press when a said comparison of calculated total required cure time and monitored elapsed time indicates equivalence, and

"(j) removing from said mold the resultant precision molded and cured rubber article."

and, in dealing with the patent laws, we have more than once cautioned that "courts 'should not read into the patent laws limitations and conditions which a legislature has not expressed.'" Diamond v. Chakrabarty, supra, at 308, 100 S.Ct., at 2207, quoting United States v. Dubilier Condenser Corp., 289 U.S. 178, 199 (1933).

The Patent Act of 1793 defined statutory subject matter as "any new and useful art, machine, manufacture or composition of matter, or any new or useful improvement [thereof]." Act of Feb. 21, 1793, ch. 11, § 1, 1 Stat. 318. Not until the patent laws were recodified in 1952 did Congress replace the word "art" with the word "process." It is that latter word which we confront today, and in order to determine its meaning we may not be unmindful of the Committee Reports accompanying the 1952 Act which inform us that Congress intended statutory subject matter to "include anything under the sun that is made by man." S.Rep. No. 1979, 82d Cong., 2d Sess. 5 (1952); H.R.Rep. No. 1923, 82d Cong., 2d Sess. 6 (1952).

Although the term "process" was not added to 35 U.S.C.A. § 101 until 1952, a process has historically enjoyed patent protection because it was considered a form of "art" as that term was used in the 1793 Act. In defining the nature of a patentable process, the Court stated:

> That a process may be patentable, irrespective of the particular form of the instrumentalities used, cannot be disputed. . . . A process is a mode of treatment of certain materials to produce a given result. It is an act, or a series of acts, performed upon the subject matter to be transformed and reduced to a different state or thing. If new and useful, it is just as patentable as is a piece of machinery. In the language of the patent law, it is an art. The machinery pointed out as suitable to perform the process may or may not be new or patentable; whilst the process itself may be altogether new, and produce an entirely new result. The process requires that certain things should be done with certain substances, and in a certain order; but the tools to be used in doing this may be of secondary consequence. Cochrane v. Deener, 94 U.S. 780, 787–788 (1876).

Analysis of the eligibility of a claim of patent protection for a "process" did not change with the addition of that term to § 101. Recently, in Gottschalk v. Benson, 409 U.S. 663 (1972), we repeated the above definition recited in Cochrane v. Deener, adding "Transformation and reduction of an article 'to a different state or thing' is the clue to the patentability of a process claim that does not include particular machines." Id., at 70.

Analyzing respondents' claims according to the above statements from our cases, we think that a physical and chemical process for molding precision synthetic rubber products falls within the § 101 categories of possibly patentable subject matter. That respondents' claims involve the transformation of an article, in this case raw uncured synthetic rubber, into a different state or thing cannot be disputed. The respondents' claims describe in detail a step-by-step method for accomplishing such beginning with the loading of a mold with raw uncured rubber and ending with the eventual opening of the press at the conclusion of the cure. Industrial processes such as this are the type which have historically been eligible to receive the protection of our patent laws.

III

Our conclusion regarding respondents' claims is not altered by the fact that in several steps of the process a mathematical equation and a programmed digital computer are used. This Court has undoubtedly recognized limits to § 101 and every discovery is not embraced within the statutory terms. Excluded from such patent protection are laws of nature, physical phenomena and abstract ideas. See Parker v. Flook, 437 U.S. 584 (1978); Gottschalk v. Benson, 409 U.S. 63, 67 (1973); Funk Bros. Seed Co. v. Kalo Co., 333 U.S. 127, 130 (1948). "An idea of itself is not patentable," Rubber–Tip Pencil Co. v. Howard, 20 Wall. 498, 507 (1874). "A principle, in the abstract, is a fundamental truth; an original cause; a motive; these cannot be patented, as no one can claim in either of them an exclusive right." Le Roy v. Tatham, 14 How. 156, 175 (1852). Only last Term, we explained:

> [A] new mineral discovered in the earth or a new plant found in the wild is not patentable subject matter. Likewise, Einstein could not patent his celebrated law that $E = mc^2$; nor could Newton have patented the law of gravity. Such discoveries are 'manifestations of . . . nature, free to all men and reserved exclusively to none.' Diamond v. Chakrabarty, 447 U.S. 309, 100 S.Ct., at 2208, quoting Funk Bros. Seed Co. v. Kalo Co., 333 U.S. 127, 130 (1948).

Our recent holdings in *Gottschalk v. Benson,* supra, and *Parker v. Flook,* supra, both of which are computer-related, stand for no more than these long established principles. In *Benson,* we held unpatentable claims for an algorithm used to convert binary code decimal numbers to equivalent pure binary numbers. The sole practical application of the algorithm was in connection with the programming of a general purpose digital computer. We defined "algorithm" as a "procedure for solving a given type of mathematical problem," and we concluded that such an algorithm, or mathematical formula, is like a law of nature, which cannot be the subject of a patent.

Parker v. Flook, supra, presented a similar situation. The claims were drawn to a method for computing an "alarm limit." An "alarm limit" is simply a number and the Court concluded that the application sought to protect a formula for computing this number. Using this formula, the updated alarm limit could be calculated if several other variables were known. The application, however, did not purport to explain how these other variables were to be determined, nor did it purport "to contain any disclosure relating to the chemical processes at work, the monitoring of process variables, or the means of setting off an alarm system. All that is provided is a formula for computing an updated alarm limit." 437 U.S. at 586.

In contrast, the respondents here do not seek to patent a mathematical formula. Instead, they seek patent protection for a process of curing synthetic rubber. Their process admittedly employs a well known mathematical equation, but they do not seek to pre-empt the use of that equation. Rather, they seek only to foreclose from others the use of that equation in conjunction with all of the other steps in their claimed process. These include installing rubber in a press, closing the mold, constantly determining the temperature of the mold, constantly recalculating the appropriate cure time through the use of the formula and a digital computer and, automatically opening the press at the proper time. Obviously, one does not need a "computer" to cure natural or synthetic rubber, but if the computer use incorporated in the process patent significantly lessens the possibility of "overcuring" or "undercuring," the process as a whole does not thereby become unpatentable subject matter.

Our earlier opinions lend support to our present conclusion that a claim drawn to subject matter otherwise statutory does not become nonstatutory simply because it uses a mathematical formula, computer program or digital computer. In *Gottschalk v. Benson,* supra, we noted "It is said that the decision precludes a patent for any program servicing a computer. We do not so hold." 409 U.S., at 71. Similarly, in *Parker v. Flook,* supra, we stated, "A process is not unpatentable simply because it contains a law of nature or a mathematical algorithm." 437 U.S., at 590. It is now commonplace that an *application* of a law of nature or mathematical formula to a known structure or process may well be deserving of patent protection. As Mr. Justice Stone explained four decades ago:

> While a scientific truth, or the mathematical expression of it, is not a patentable invention, a novel and useful structure created with the aid of knowledge of scientific truth may be. Mackay Radio Corp. & Telegraph Co. v. Radio Corp. of America, 306 U.S. 86, 94 (1939).

We think this statement in *Mackay* takes us a long way toward the correct answer in this case. Arrhenius' equation is not patentable in isolation, but when a process for curing rubber is devised which incorporates in it a more efficient solution of the equation, that process is at the very least not barred at the threshold by § 101.

In determining the eligibility of respondents' claimed process for patent protection under § 101, their claims must be considered as a whole. It is inappropriate to dissect the claims into old and new elements and then to ignore the presence of the old elements in the analysis. This is particularly true in a process claim because a new combination of steps in a process may be patentable even though all the constituents of the combination were well known and in common use before the combination was made. The "novelty" of any element or steps in a process, or even of the process itself, is of no relevance in determining whether the subject matter of a claim falls within the § 101 categories of possibly patentable subject matter.[12]

It has been urged that novelty is an appropriate consideration under § 101. Presumably, this argument results from the language in § 101 referring to any "new and useful" process, machine, etc. Section 101, however, is a general statement of the type of subject matter that is eligible for patent protection "subject to the conditions and requirements of this title." Specific conditions for patentability follow and § 102 covers in detail the conditions relating to novelty. The question therefore of whether a particular invention is novel is "fully apart from whether the invention falls into a category of statutory subject matter." In re Bergy, 596 F.2d 952, 961 (CCPA 1979). The legislative history of the 1952 Patent Act is in accord with this reasoning. The Senate Report provided:

> Section 101 sets forth the subject matter that can be patented, 'subject to the conditions and requirement of this title.' The conditions under which a patent may be obtained follow, and *Section 102 covers the conditions relating to novelty.* S.Rep.No. 1979, 82d Cong., 2d Sess. 5 (1952) (emphasis supplied).

It is later stated in the same report:

> Section 102, in general, may be said to describe the statutory novelty required for patentability, and includes, in effect, the amplification and definition of 'new' in Section 101. Id., at 6.

Finally, it is stated in the "Revision Notes":

> The corresponding section of [the] existing statute is split into two sections, Section 101 relating to the subject matter for which patents may be obtained, and Section 102 defining statutory novelty and stating other conditions for patentability. Id., at 17.

In this case, it may later be determined that the respondents' process is not deserving of patent protection because it fails to satisfy the statutory conditions of novelty under § 102 or nonobviousness under § 103. A rejection on either of these grounds does not affect the determination that respondents' claims recited subject matter which was eligible for patent protection under § 101.

12. It is argued that the procedure of dissecting a claim into old and new elements is mandated by our decision in *Flook* which noted that a mathematical algorithm must be assumed to be within the "prior art." It is from this language that the Government premises its argument that if everything other than the algorithm is determined to be old in the art, then the claim cannot recite statutory subject matter. The fallacy in this argument is that we did not hold in *Flook* that the mathematical algorithm could not be considered at all when making the § 101 determination. To accept the analysis proffered by the Government would, if carried to its extreme, make all inventions unpatentable because all inventions can be reduced to underlying principles of nature which, once known, make their implementation obvious. The analysis suggested by the Government would also undermine our earlier decisions regarding the criteria to consider in determining the eligibility of a process for patent protection.

IV

We have before us today only the question of whether respondents' claims fall within the § 101 categories of possibly patentable subject matter. We view respondents' claims as nothing more than a process for molding rubber products and not as an attempt to patent a mathematical formula. We recognize, of course, that when a claim recites a mathematical formula (or scientific principle or phenomenon of nature), an inquiry must be made into whether the claim is seeking patent protection for that formula in the abstract. A mathematical formula as such is not accorded the protection of our patent laws and this principle cannot be circumvented by attempting to limit the use of the formula to a particular technological environment. Similarly, insignificant post-solution activity will not transform an unpatentable principle into a patentable process. To hold otherwise would allow a competent draftsman to evade the recognized limitations on the type of subject matter eligible for patent protection. On the other hand, when a claim containing a mathematical formula implements or applies that formula in a structure or process which, when considered as a whole, is performing a function which the patent laws were designed to protect (e.g., transforming or reducing an article to a different state or thing), then the claim satisfies the requirements of § 101. Because we do not view respondents' claims as an attempt to patent a mathematical formula, but rather to be drawn to an industrial process for the molding of rubber products, we affirm the judgment of the Court of Customs and Patent Appeals.

Justice STEVENS, with whom Justice BRENNAN, Justice MARSHALL, and Justice BLACKMUN join, dissenting.

The starting point in the proper adjudication of patent litigation is an understanding of what the inventor claims to have discovered. The Court's decision in this case rests on a misreading of the Diehr and Lutton patent application. Moreover, the Court has compounded its error by ignoring the critical distinction between the character of the subject matter that the inventor claims to be novel—the § 101 issue—and the question whether that subject matter is in fact novel—the § 102 issue.

I

Before discussing the major flaws in the Court's opinion, a word of history may be helpful. As the Court recognized in Parker v. Flook, 437 U.S. 584, 595 (1978), the computer industry is relatively young. Although computer technology seems commonplace today, the first digital computer capable of utilizing stored programs was developed less than 30 years ago. Patent law developments in response to this new technology are of even more recent vintage. The subject of legal protection for computer programs did not begin to receive serious consideration until over a decade after completion of the first programmable digital computer. It was 1968 before the federal courts squarely addressed the subject, and 1972 before this Court announced its first decision in the area.

Prior to 1968, well-established principles of patent law probably would have prevented the issuance of a valid patent on almost any conceivable computer program. Under the "mental steps" doctrine, processes involving mental operations were considered unpatentable. The mental steps doctrine was based upon the familiar principle that a scientific concept or mere idea cannot be the subject of a valid patent. The doctrine was regularly invoked to deny patents to inventions consisting primarily of mathematical formulae or methods of computation. It was also applied against patent claims in which a mental operation or mathematical computation was the sole novel element or inventive contribution; it was clear that patentability could not be predicated upon a mental step. Under the "function of a machine" doctrine, a process which amounted to nothing more than a description of the function of a machine was unpatentable. This doctrine had its origin in several 19th–century decisions of this Court, and it had been consistently followed thereafter by the lower federal courts. Finally, the definition of "process" announced by this Court in Cochrane v. Deener, 94 U.S. 780, 787–788 (1876), seemed to indicate that a patentable process must cause a physical transformation in the materials to which the process is applied.

Concern with the patent system's ability to deal with rapidly changing technology in the computer and other fields led to the formation in 1965 of the President's Commission on the Patent System. After studying the question of computer program patentability, the Commission recommended that computer programs be expressly excluded from the coverage of the patent laws; this recommendation was based primarily upon the Patent Office's inability to deal with the administrative burden of examining program applications. At approximately the time that the Commission issued its report, the Patent Office published notice of its intention to prescribe guidelines for the examination of applications for patents on computer programs. Under the proposed guidelines, a computer program, whether claimed as an apparatus or as a process, was unpatentable. The Patent Office indicated, however, that a programmed computer could be a component of a patentable process if combined with unobvious elements to produce a physical result. The Patent Office formally adopted the guidelines in 1968.

The new guidelines were to have a short life. Beginning with two decisions in 1968, a dramatic change in the law as understood by the Court of Customs and Patent Appeals took place. By repudiating the well-settled "function of a machine" and "mental steps" doctrines, that court reinterpreted § 101 of the Patent Code to enlarge drastically the categories of patentable subject matter. This reinterpretation would lead to the conclusion that computer programs were within the categories of inventions to which Congress intended to extend patent protection.

In In re Tarczy–Hornoch, 397 F.2d 856 (CCPA 1968), a divided Court of Customs and Patent Appeals overruled the line of cases developing and applying the "function of a machine" doctrine. The majority acknowledged that the doctrine had originated with decisions of this Court and that the lower federal courts, including the Court of Customs and Patent Appeals, had consistently adhered to it during the preceding 70 years. Nonetheless, the court concluded that the doctrine rested on a misinterpretation of the precedents and that it was contrary to "the basic purposes of the patent system and productive of a range of undesirable results from the harshly inequitable to the silly." Id., at 867. Shortly thereafter, a similar fate befell the "mental steps" doctrine. In In re Prater, 415 F.2d 1378 (1968), modified on rehearing, 415 F.2d 1393 (CCPA 1969), the court found that the precedents on which that doctrine was based either were poorly reasoned or had been misinterpreted over the years. The court concluded that the fact that a process may be performed mentally should not foreclose patentability if the claims reveal that the process also may be performed without mental operations. This aspect of the original *Prater* opinion was substantially undisturbed by the opinion issued after rehearing. However, the second *Prater* opinion clearly indicated that patent claims broad enough to encompass the operation of a programmed computer would not be rejected for lack of patentable subject matter.

The Court of Customs and Patent Appeals soon replaced the overruled doctrines with more expansive principles formulated with computer technology in mind. In In re Bernhart, 417 F.2d 1395 (CCPA 1969), the court reaffirmed *Prater,* and indicated that all that remained of the mental steps doctrine was a prohibition on the granting of a patent that would confer a monoply on all uses of a scientific principle or mathematical equation. The court also announced that a computer programmed with a new and unobvious program was physically different from the same computer without that program; the programmed computer was a new machine or at least a new improvement over the unprogrammed computer. Therefore, patent protection could be obtained for new computer programs if the patent claims were drafted in apparatus form.

The Court of Customs and Patent Appeals turned its attention to process claims encompassing computer programs in In re Musgrave, 431 F.2d 882 (CCPA 1970). In that case, the court emphasized the fact that *Prater* had done away with the mental steps doctrine; in particular, the court rejected the Patent Office's continued reliance upon the "point of novelty" approach to claim analysis.[15] The court also announced a new standard for evaluating process claims under § 101: any sequence of operational steps was a patentable process under § 101 as long as it was within the "technological arts." This standard effectively disposed of any vestiges of the mental steps doctrine remain-

---

15. Under the "point of novelty" approach, if the novelty or advancement in the art claimed by the inventor resided solely in a step of the process embodying a mental operation or other unpatentable element, the claim was rejected under § 101 as being directed to nonstatutory subject matter.

ing after *Prater* and *Bernhart*. The "technological arts" standard was refined in In re Benson, 441 F.2d 682 (CCPA 1971), in which the court held that computers, regardless of the uses to which they are put, are within the technological arts for purposes of § 101.

In re Benson, of course, was reversed by this Court in Gottschalk v. Benson, 409 U.S. 63 (1972). Justice Douglas' opinion for a unanimous Court made no reference to the lower court's rejection of the mental steps doctrine or to the new technological arts standard. Rather, the Court clearly held that new mathematical procedures that can be conducted in old computers, like mental processes and abstract intellectual concepts, are not patentable processes within the meaning of § 101.

The Court of Customs and Patent Appeals had its first opportunity to interpret *Benson* in In re Christensen, 478 F.2d 1392 (CCPA 1973). In *Christensen*, the claimed invention was a method in which the only novel element was a mathematical formula. The court resurrected the point of novelty approach abandoned in *Musgrave* and held that a process claim in which the point of novelty was a mathematical equation to be solved as the final step of the process did not define patentable subject matter after *Benson*. Accordingly, the court affirmed the Board of Patent Appeals' rejection of the claims under § 101.

The Court of Customs and Patent Appeals in subsequent cases began to narrow its interpretation of *Benson*. In In re Johnston, 502 F.2d 765 (CCPA 1974), the court held that a record-keeping machine system which comprised a programmed digital computer was patentable subject matter under § 101. The majority dismissed *Benson* with the observation that *Benson* involved only process, not apparatus, claims. Judge Rich dissented, arguing that to limit *Benson* only to process claims would make patentability turn upon the form in which a program invention was claimed. The court again construed *Benson* as limited only to process claims in In re Noll, 545 F.2d 141 (CCPA 1976), cert. denied, 434 U.S. 875 (1977); apparatus claims were governed by the court's pre-*Benson* conclusion that a programmed computer was structurally different from the same computer without that particular program. In dissent, Judge Lane, joined by Judge Rich, argued that *Benson* should be read as a general proscription of the patenting of computer programs regardless of the form of the claims. Judge Lane's interpretation of *Benson* was rejected by the majority in In re Chatfield, 545 F.2d 152 (CCPA 1976), cert. denied, 434 U.S. 875 (1977), decided on the same day as *Noll*. In that case, the court construed *Benson* to preclude the patenting of program inventions claimed as processes only where the claims would pre-empt all uses of an algorithm or mathematical formula. The dissenting judges argued, as they had in *Noll*, that *Benson* held that programs for general-purpose digital computers are not patentable subject matter.

Following *Noll* and *Chatfield*, the Court of Customs and Patent Appeals consistently interpreted *Benson* to preclude the patenting of a program-related process invention only when the claims, if allowed, would wholly pre-empt the algorithm itself. One of the cases adopting this view was In re Flook, 559 F.2d 21 (CCPA 1977), which was reversed in Parker v. Flook, 437 U.S. 584 (1978). Before this Court decided *Flook*, however, the lower court developed a two-step procedure for analyzing program-related inventions in light of *Benson*. In In re Freeman, 573 F.2d 1237 (CCPA 1978), the court held that such inventions must first be examined to determine whether a mathematical algorithm is directly or indirectly claimed; if an algorithm is recited, the court must then determine whether the claim would wholly pre-empt that algorithm. Only if a claim satisfied both inquiries was *Benson* considered applicable.

In *Flook*, this Court clarified *Benson* in three significant respects. First, *Flook* held that the *Benson* rule of unpatentable subject matter was not limited, as the lower court believed, to claims which wholly pre-empted an algorithm or amounted to a patent on the algorithm itself. Second, the Court made it clear that an improved method of calculation, even when employed as part of a physical process, is not patentable subject matter under § 101. Finally, the Court explained the correct procedure for analyzing a patent claim employing a mathematical algorithm. Under this procedure, the algorithm is treated for § 101 purposes as though it were a familiar part of the prior art; the claim is then examined to determine whether it discloses "some other inventive concept."

Although the Court of Customs and Patent Appeals in several post-*Flook* decisions held that program-related inventions were not patentable subject matter under § 101, in general *Flook* was not enthusiastically received by that court. In In re Bergy, 596 F.2d 952 (CCPA 1979), the majority engaged in an extensive critique of *Flook*, concluding that this Court had erroneously commingled "distinct statutory provisions which are conceptually unrelated." In subsequent cases, the court construed *Flook* as resting on nothing more than the way in which the patent claims had been drafted, and it expressly declined to use the method of claim analysis spelled out in that decision. The Court of Customs and Patent Appeals has taken the position that, if an application is drafted in a way that discloses an entire process as novel, it defines patentable subject matter even if the only novel element that the inventor claims to have discovered is a new computer program. The court interpreted *Flook* in this manner in its opinion in this case. In my judgment, this reading of *Flook* —although entirely consistent with the lower court's expansive approach to § 101 during the past 12 years—trivializes the holding in *Flook*, the principle that underlies *Benson*, and the settled line of authority reviewed in those opinions.

II

As I stated at the outset, the starting point in the proper adjudication of patent litigation is an understanding of what the inventor claims to have discovered. Indeed, the outcome of such litigation is often determined by the judge's understanding of the patent application. This is such a case.

In the first sentence of its opinion, the Court states the question presented as "whether a process for curing synthetic rubber . . . is patentable subject matter." Of course, that question was effectively answered many years ago when Charles Goodyear obtained his patent on the vulcanization process. The patent application filed by Diehr and Lutton, however, teaches nothing about the chemistry of the synthetic rubber-curing process, nothing about the raw materials to be used in curing synthetic rubber, nothing about the equipment to be used in the process, and nothing about the significance or effect of any process variable such as temperature, curing time, particular compositions of material, or mold configurations. In short, Diehr and Lutton do not claim to have discovered anything new about the process for curing synthetic rubber.

As the Court reads the claims in the Diehr and Lutton patent application, the inventors' discovery is a method of constantly measuring the actual temperature inside a rubber molding press. As I read the claims, their discovery is an improved method of calculating the time that the mold should remain closed during the curing process. If the Court's reading of the claims were correct, I would agree that they disclose patentable subject matter. On the other hand, if the Court accepted my reading, I feel confident that the case would be decided differently.

There are three reasons why I cannot accept the Court's conclusion that Diehr and Lutton claim to have discovered a new method of constantly measuring the temperature inside a mold. First, there is not a word in the patent application that suggests that there is anything unusual about the temperature-reading devices used in this process—or indeed that any particular species of temperature-reading device should be used in it. Second, since devices for constantly measuring actual temperatures—on a back porch, for example—have been familiar articles for quite some time, I find it difficult to believe that a patent application filed in 1975 was premised on the notion that a "process of constantly measuring the actual temperature" had just been discovered. Finally, the Board of Patent Appeals expressly found that "the only difference between the conventional methods of operating a molding press and that claimed in [the] application rests in those steps of the claims which relate to the calculation incident to the solution of the mathematical problem or formula used to control the mold heater and the automatic opening of the press." This finding was not disturbed by the Court of Customs and Patent Appeals and is clearly correct.

A fair reading of the entire patent application, as well as the specific claims, makes it perfectly clear that what Diehr and Lutton claim to have discovered is a method of using a digital computer to determine the amount of time that a rubber molding press should remain closed during the synthetic rubber curing process. There is no suggestion that there is anything novel in the instrumentation of the mold, in actuating a timer when the press is closed, or in automatically opening the press when the computed time expires. Nor does the application suggest that Diehr and Lutton have discovered anything about the temperatures in the mold or the amount of curing time that will produce the best cure. What they claim to have discovered, in essence, is a method of updating the original estimated curing time by repetitively recalculating that time pursuant to a well-known mathematical formula in response to variations in temperature within the mold. Their method of updating the curing time calculation is strikingly reminiscent of the method of updating alarm limits that Dale Flook sought to patent.

Parker v. Flook, 437 U.S. 584 (1978), involved the use of a digital computer in connection with a catalytic conversion process. During the conversion process, variables such as temperature, pressure, and flow rates were constantly monitored and fed into the computer; in this case, temperature in the mold is the variable that is monitored and fed into the computer. In *Flook,* the digital computer repetitively recalculated the "alarm limit"—a number that might signal the need to terminate or modify the catalytic conversion process; in this case, the digital computer repetitively recalculates the correct curing time—a number that signals the time when the synthetic rubber molding press should open.

The essence of the claimed discovery in both cases was an algorithm that could be programmed on a digital computer. In *Flook,* the algorithm made use of multiple process variables; in this case, it makes use of only one. In *Flook,* the algorithm was expressed in a newly-developed mathematical formula; in this case, the algorithm makes use of a well-known mathematical formula. Manifestly, neither of these differences can explain today's holding.[32] What I believe does

32. Indeed, the most significant distinction between the invention at issue in *Flook* and that at issue in this case lies not in the characteristics of the inventions themselves, but rather in the drafting of the claims. After noting that "[t]he Diehr claims are reminiscent of the claims in *Flook,*" Blumenthal & Riter, 62 J.Pat.Off. Soc'y, at 502–503, the authors of a recent article on the subject observe that the Court of Customs and Patent Appeals' analysis in this case "lends itself to an interesting exercise in claim drafting." Id., at 505. To illustrate their point, the authors redrafted the Diehr and Lutton claims into the format employed in the *Flook* application:

"An improved method of calculating the cure time of a rubber molding process utilizing a digital computer comprising the steps of:

"a. inputting into said computer input values including

"1. natural logarithm conversion data (ln),

"2. an activation energy constant (C) unique to each batch of rubber being molded,

"3. a constant (X) dependent upon the geometry of the particular mold of the press, and

"4. continuous temperature values (Z) of the mold during molding;

"b. operating said computer for

"1. counting the elapsed cure time,

"2. calculating the cure time from the input values using the Arrhenius equation $\ln v = CZ + X$, where v is the total cure time, and

"c. providing output signals from said computer when said calculated cure time is equal to said elapsed cure time." Id., at 505.

explain today's holding is a misunderstanding of the applicants' claimed invention and a failure to recognize the critical difference between the "discovery" requirement in § 101 and the "novelty" requirement in § 102.

III

The Court misapplies *Parker v. Flook* because, like the Court of Customs and Patent Appeals, it fails to understand or completely disregards the distinction between the subject matter of what the inventor *claims* to have discovered—the § 101 issue—and the question whether that claimed discovery is in fact novel—the § 102 issue. If there is not even a claim that anything constituting patentable subject matter has been discovered, there is no occasion to address the novelty issue. Or, as was true in *Flook,* if the only concept that the inventor claims to have discovered is not patentable subject matter, § 101 requires that the application be rejected without reaching any issue under § 102; for it is irrelevant that unpatentable subject matter—in that case a formula for updating alarm limits—may in fact be novel.

Proper analysis, therefore, must start with an understanding of what the inventor claims to have discovered—or phrased somewhat differently—what he considers his inventive concept to be. It seems clear to me that Diehr and Lutton claim to have developed a new method of programming a digital computer in order to calculate—promptly and repeatedly—the correct curing time in a familiar process. In the § 101 analysis, we must assume that the sequence of steps in this programming method is novel, unobvious, and useful. The threshold question of whether such a method is patentable subject matter remains.

If that method is regarded as an "algorithm" as that term was used in Gottschalk v. Benson, supra, and in Parker v. Flook, supra, and if no other inventive concept is disclosed in the patent application, the question must be answered in the negative. In both *Benson* and *Flook,* the parties apparently agreed that the inventor's discovery was properly regarded as an algorithm; the holding that an algorithm was a "law of nature" that could not be patented therefore determined that those discoveries were not patentable processes within the meaning of § 101.

As the Court recognizes today, *Flook* also rejected the argument that patent protection was available if the inventor did not claim a monopoly on every conceivable use of the algorithm but instead limited his claims by describing a specific post-solution activity—in that case setting off an alarm in a catalytic conversion process. In its effort to distinguish *Flook* from the instant case, the Court characterizes that post-solution activity as "insignificant," or as merely "token" activity. As a practical matter, however, the post-solution activity described in the *Flook* application was no less significant than the automatic opening of the curing mold involved in this case. For setting off an alarm

The authors correctly conclude that even the lower court probably would have found that this claim was drawn to unpatentable subject matter under § 101.

limit at the appropriate time is surely as important to the safe and efficient operation of a catalytic conversion process as is actuating the mold-opening device in a synthetic rubber curing process. In both cases, the post-solution activity is a significant part of the industrial process. But in neither case should that activity have any *legal* significance because it does not constitute a part of the inventive concept that the applicants claimed to have discovered.

In Gottschalk v. Benson, we held that a program for the solution by a digital computer of a mathematical problem was not a patentable process within the meaning of § 101. In Parker v. Flook, we further held that such a computer program could not be transformed into a patentable process by the addition of post-solution activity that was not claimed to be novel. That holding plainly requires the rejection of Claims 1 and 2 of the Diehr and Lutton application quoted in the Court's opinion. In my opinion, it equally requires rejection of Claim 11 because the presolution activity described in that claim is admittedly a familiar part of the prior art.

Even the Court does not suggest that the computer program developed by Diehr and Lutton is a patentable discovery. Accordingly, if we treat the program as though it were a familiar part of the prior art—as well-established precedent requires—it is absolutely clear that their application contains no claim of patentable invention. Their application was therefore properly rejected under § 101 by the Patent Office and the Board of Patent Appeals.

IV

The broad question whether computer programs should be given patent protection involves policy considerations that this Court is not authorized to address. As the numerous briefs *amicus curiae* filed in Gottschalk v. Benson, supra, Dann v. Johnston, supra, Parker v. Flook, supra, and this case demonstrate, that question is not only difficult and important, but apparently also one that may be affected by institutional bias. In each of those cases, the spokesmen for the organized patent bar have uniformly favored patentability and industry representatives have taken positions properly motivated by their economic self-interest. Notwithstanding fervent argument that patent protection is essential for the growth of the software industry, commentators have noted that "this industry is growing by leaps and bounds without it." [43] In addition, even some commentators who believe that legal protection for computer programs is desirable have expressed doubts that the present patent system can provide the needed protection.

Within the Federal Government, patterns of decision have also emerged. Gottschalk, Dann, Parker, and Diamond were not ordinary litigants—each was serving as Commissioner of Patents and Trademarks when he opposed the availability of patent protection for a program-related invention. No doubt each may have been motivated

---

43. Gemignani, supra, 7 Rut.J.Comp., Tech. & L., at 309.

by a concern about the ability of the Patent Office to process effectively the flood of applications that would inevitably flow from a decision that computer programs are patentable. The consistent concern evidenced by the Commissioner of Patents and Trademarks and by the Board of Patent Appeals of the Patent and Trademark Office has not been shared by the Court of Customs and Patent Appeals, which reversed the Board in *Benson, Johnston,* and *Flook,* and was in turn reversed by this Court in each of those cases.

Scholars have been critical of the work of both tribunals. Some of that criticism may stem from a conviction about the merits of the broad underlying policy question; such criticism may be put to one side. Other criticism, however, identifies two concerns to which federal judges have a duty to respond. First, the cases considering the patentability of program-related inventions do not establish rules that enable a conscientious patent lawyer to determine with a fair degree of accuracy which, if any, program-related inventions will be patentable. Second, the inclusion of the ambiguous concept of an "algorithm" within the "law of nature" category of unpatentable subject matter has given rise to the concern that almost any process might be so described and therefore held unpatentable.

In my judgment, today's decision will aggravate the first concern and will not adequately allay the second. I believe both concerns would be better addressed by (1) an unequivocal holding that no program-related invention is a patentable process under § 101 unless it makes a contribution to the art that is not dependent entirely on the utilization of a computer, and (2) an unequivocal explanation that the term "algorithm" as used in this case, as in *Benson* and *Flook,* is synonymous with the term "computer program." Because the invention claimed in the patent application at issue in this case makes no contribution to the art that is not entirely dependent upon the utilization of a computer in a familiar process, I would reverse the decision of the Court of Customs and Patent Appeals.

NOTES

1. *"Mathematical Algorithms."* What is left of *Benson* after *Diehr*? Of *Flook*? Does *Diehr* give patent applicants an incentive to claim their inventions without disclosing the invention's underlying mathematical principles, even if the principles are entirely new? Is such an incentive desirable? What if the inventor arrived at the invention accidentally, with no knowledge of the underlying principle? The Court of Customs and Patent Appeals held that "mathematical algorithms"—procedures "for solving a given type of mathematical problem"—are not statutory subject matter under section 101 of the Patent Act. See In re Abele, 684 F.2d 902, 907, 214 U.S.P.Q. 682, 687 (C.C.P.A.1982) ("The goal is to answer the question 'What did applicants invent?' If the claimed invention is a mathematical algorithm, it is improper subject matter for patent protection, whereas if the claimed invention is an application of the algorithm, § 101 will not bar the

grant of a patent.") Can you think of a useful "mathematical algorithm" that cannot, through artful drafting, be expressed as patentable subject matter within *Diehr's* requirements? The Court of Appeals for the Federal Circuit has construed "mathematical algorithm" narrowly. See, e.g., In re Iwahashi, 888 F.2d 1370, 12 U.S.P.Q.2d 1908 (Fed.Cir.1989). For an exhaustive study of the question see Chisum, The Patentability of Algorithms, 47 U.Pitt.L.Rev. 959 (1986).

For a superb review of the interplay between the Court of Customs and Patent Appeals and the Supreme Court in the years before *Diehr,* see Comment, Computer Program Patentability—the C.C.P.A. Refuses to Follow the Lead of the Supreme Court in *Parker v. Flook,* 58 N.C.L. Rev. 319 (1980). See also Milde, Life after *Diamond v. Diehr:* The CCPA Speaks Out on the Patentability of Computer–Related Subject Matter, 64 J.Pat.Off.Soc'y 434 (1982); Sheridan, Patent Protection of Computer Software—Practical Insights, 23 Santa Clara L.Rev. 989 (1983).

2. *International Developments.* Just as other countries followed the United States' lead in bringing computer programs within copyright, see page ___, above, several countries—at least on the European continent—appear to be tracing the steps taken in the United States to bring computer programs under patent protection. Article 52(2)(c) of the European Patent Convention excludes "programs for computers" from its definition of patentable subject matter. However, Article 52(3) provides that this exclusion applies "only to the extent to which a European patent application or European patent relates to such subject matter or activities as such." Courts in several member states have seized on this qualification to uphold patents on computers programmed to achieve a particular result and on processes comparable to the process involved in *Diehr.* See Wilder, Computer Software in Europe and the United States: Is it Patentable Subject Matter?, 25 IDEA 51 (1984).

C. TRADE SECRET LAW

JOSTENS, INC. v. NATIONAL COMPUTER SYSTEMS, INC.

Minnesota Supreme Court, 1982.
318 N.W.2d 691, 214 U.S.P.Q. 918.

SIMONETT, Justice.

Appellant, Jostens, Inc., sued several of its former employees and a computer firm for misappropriation of trade secrets and proprietary data in Jostens' computer system used for the design and manufacture of its class ring molds. The trial court found no misappropriation. Because the trial court's findings have support in the evidence, we affirm.

This appeal involves application of the trade secret doctrine to the rapidly expanding and highly complex field of computer technology. The appellant-plaintiff is Jostens, Inc., a Minnesota corporation, which manufactures and markets school products, including student class rings. Jostens sued National Computer Systems, Inc. (NCS), a Minnesota corporation which designs and makes computer systems; John S. Titus Jr., once an employee of Jostens and now an officer of NCS; and Robert J. Henderson and Allan Hoagberg, also former employees of Jostens who joined NCS.

For many years Jostens had used skilled artisans to engrave designs into the molds for the shanks of its rings. John Titus, an engineer at Jostens, became interested in developing a computer system to be used in making ring molds. In 1972 and 1973, Titus began putting such a system in Jostens' plant at Burnsville. By early 1974 the system was in operation and operating successfully, giving Jostens a competitive advantage over other ring manufacturers still using traditional manual methods of producing ring shank molds. In about January 1978, Jostens lost its position as the sole class ring manufacturer with a computerized mold-making system, when respondent National Computer Systems, Inc., designed and sold a similar computer system to L.C. Balfour Company, a competing ring manufacturer. That sale triggered this lawsuit.

The computer system before us is called a CAD/CAM system, which stands for a computer-aided design and computer-aided manufacturing system. Jostens' CAD/CAM system consisted of three subsystems: (1) a digitizer or scanner subsystem, which translates positional data from artwork and three-dimensional models into computer-readable magnetic tape, which is then fed into, (2) the interactive computer graphics subsystem, in which an image is displayed in three dimensions on a screen where it can be manipulated and corrected by an operator; and (3) the engraving subsystem, where the computer, instructed by data from a magnetic tape, in a process called numeric control, guides a machine which engraves the design on the mold for the ring shanks.

Titus purchased each subsystem from a different vendor. The scanner subsystem was purchased from Potter Instrument Company; the graphics subsystem was purchased from Adage, Inc., of Boston; and the hardware components of the engraving subsystem, such as the engraving machine and the controller, were purchased from different vendors and then connected at the Burnsville plant by Titus and the vendors.

Most of the focus at the trial was on the graphics subsystem purchased from Adage. It consisted of both hardware and software. The hardware was a standard item; the software, i.e., the instructions to the computer, was of two kinds—operations systems software and application software. Of these two types, the application software was written by Adage pursuant to Jostens' functional specifications and sold to Jostens for $49,500. Jostens claims the overall cost to put in its CAD/CAM system was the largest authorization for capital expenditure in the company's history. When Jostens placed its order with Adage for the graphics system, it added the following clause: "Propriety—All materials propared [sic] for Jostens' specific requirements shall become the property of Jostens."

In the midseventies, after Jostens' system was successfully in use, Titus urged his employer to consider merchandising the CAD/CAM system by selling either service or equipment to other manufacturers. Some interested persons were invited to tour the Burnsville plant, but in May 1975, Jostens decided against any further efforts to commercialize the system and ordered the Burnsville facility closed to outsiders. Also at that time, Titus, with Jostens' permission, spoke at a conference of the Numerical Control Society in Washington, D.C., about Jostens' CAD/CAM system, giving a multimedia presentation followed by publication of an article in a technical journal, also authorized by Jostens, which included a description of the major components of Jostens' system and the system's role in the production of ring molds.

In August of 1975, Titus left Jostens and soon thereafter began working full time for NCS, whose chief executive was Charles Oswald, a former president of Jostens. Apparently Titus' departure was amicable. Jostens knew that, in his new job at NCS, Titus would be working on the development of CAD/CAM technology for the general market. As Jostens' president put it, "Exactly how much that was exactly like Jostens' system, specialized tooling, I was not aware and was not concerned because I think we wanted John to go ahead and work in this area. It was fine with us." On the other hand, Titus had signed an agreement in 1969, 4 years after he was hired by Jostens, acknowledging that all papers prepared by him were Jostens' property and that he would not reveal to others any information concerning Jostens' business "including its inventions, shop practices, processes and methods of manufacturing and merchandising."

Soon after Titus began work at NCS, his new firm proposed a technical cooperation agreement to Jostens under which the hardware and software developed by NCS would be kept compatible with Jostens' Burnsville system in order to provide for current backup and future improvements. To ensure compatibility, the proposal provided that Jostens would furnish NCS with a current copy of its application software package and NCS would promise to refrain from marketing CAD/CAM systems to any of Jostens' competitors. During the same period that NCS and Jostens were considering the cooperation agreement, NCS was also negotiating with Adage, the vendor that had furnished Jostens with its graphics subsystem. NCS wanted Adage to supply it with a software package for its own CAD/CAM system, and it appears that NCS was hoping to get a copy of the software package of Jostens' graphics subsystem for Adage to use in this new project, at least as a reference point for the broader, basic system that NCS wished to develop. In February 1976, Jostens rejected the proposed technical cooperation agreement.

Although collapse of the proposed agreement meant that NCS was unable to get a copy of Jostens' software package, NCS continued plans for the development of a CAD/CAM system, still working with Adage. Titus says that he was told by Adage that NCS' proposed system would be "considerably more difficult" than Jostens' and that there would be "very little, if any, usability of Jostens' software per se." Oswald says he was told by Adage that they had checked with their own attorneys about whether they could produce the software for NCS notwithstanding their earlier work on Jostens' software and that counsel had said, "[I]t's no problem."

A central issue at trial was what and how much of the Adage material used to write Jostens' original package was also used to write NCS' programs. Specifically, this involved not the operating systems software, a standard component sold to all Adage customers, but the application software, used to adapt a system to a particular user's needs. Adage's programmers testified many of the routines they used in writing NCS' package were "utility routines," simply taken off their library shelf, and that in assembling new application packages, programmers usually wrote only about 10% new material, while in this case about half of the final NCS package was original work. Before Adage had completed the NCS software, Adage decided to discontinue its application software business. NCS then continued development of the software on its own and argued at trial that the version it eventually sold had been significantly changed and improved from that which NCS had received from Adage.

In the summer of 1977, NCS approached Balfour, a class ring manufacturer and competitor of Jostens, about the sale of a CAD/CAM system; by late September 1977, Balfour had tentatively decided to purchase NCS' model. One of the sale terms discussed was Balfour's request that NCS indemnify Balfour against any possible trade secret claim, specifically a trade secret challenge Jostens might make. Balfour says it was not aware of any facts to support such a claim but it was wary since it knew NCS' president, Oswald, had once been Jostens' president. Ultimately, the two parties agreed that NCS would repurchase the system from Balfour on a depreciated basis in the event of a suit by Jostens against Balfour within 5 years. Also in late 1977, while NCS and Balfour were negotiating a sale, NCS sent a letter to Jostens urging it to reconsider a decision it had made not to buy equipment from NCS. In the letter NCS said there was a large market for its new CAD/CAM system and "[w]e plan these installations to be made in the jewelry, class ring and toy industries." Jostens neither responded nor objected to NCS' apparent intent to sell its system on the market.

The sale and delivery of NCS' CAD/CAM system to Balfour took place in the period of December 1977 to February 1978. It appears that earlier, sometime between March and September 1976, Jostens' vice president of manufacturing had become aware that NCS might be using software programs developed by Adage for Jostens, and voiced concern over this to Jostens' vice president and general manager of the scholastic division. Defendants also contend Jostens should have understood as early as February 1976, when Jostens rejected the technical cooperation proposal which included an explicit noncompete agreement, that NCS might eventually market a system to other ring manufacturers. Jostens, however, did not start its lawsuit until July 1978. Thus defendants also raised issues of estoppel and laches, both of which the trial court found to be present.

As damages for misappropriation of its trade secrets, Jostens claimed all of NCS' gross profits on its CAD/CAM system and, from the three individual defendants, sums totaling salaries, stock option benefits, and commissions. Jostens also claimed a royalty of NCS revenues, punitive damages, and a permanent injunction prohibiting the defendants, among other things, from using, selling or leasing any part of any CAD/CAM system. The trial court denied all of these requests. For their part, defendants requested an award of their disbursements, a request also denied by the trial court, for which defendants petition for review here.

Issues

The case presents these broad issues: (1) Did Jostens possess a trade secret and, if so, of what did it consist; (2) as a corollary, was there any misappropriation of a trade secret by the defendants; (3) did Titus or Henderson breach their employment agreements with Jostens by revealing and using Jostens' business data; (4) is Jostens estopped or barred by laches from asserting its claims; and (5) is NCS entitled to its disbursements?

Since the trial court found no trade secret, no misappropriation and no breach and also found estoppel and laches, these issues are reviewed here in the form of whether the trial court's findings of fact are clearly erroneous. The trial was long and complex. The parties supplemented their testimony (including the live testimony of seven experts) with film, slide and videotape presentations; in addition, the trial judge visited both Jostens' and NCS' plants. The trial judge's decision includes detailed findings and an extensive memo. Here, we can give space only to some of the salient facts.

I. The existence of a trade secret

It is not always easy to follow Jostens' contentions because its claim of a trade secret is rather elastic. At times, the claim appears to include the entire CAD/CAM system; at other times, something less.

Plainly, Jostens is claiming secret status for the computer graphics subsystem, purchased from Adage, and for the customizing work done at Jostens' own plant to connect the subsystem and make the adjustments needed for the manufacture of ring molds. This seems to be the clearest and most plausible of Jostens' claims, but even here clarity is not always present. Does the trade secret encompass all three parts of Adage's graphics subsystem? For there is the hardware (a standard feature of Adage packages), the operating system software (also standard), and the application software (a more particularized feature, using some standard or utility routines). Or does the claim include only those programs and routines within the application software segment specifically written for Jostens? Or does the claim lie in the distinct combination of all these parts, standard and original, in Jostens' system?

A. Before reaching these questions, we must first consider a preliminary issue: What is the effect of the proprietary clause in Jostens' purchase order to Adage, where it is said, "all material prepared for Jostens specific requirements shall become the property of Jostens"? The trial court held this clause was never accepted by Adage and did not become a contract provision. We agree.

1. Adage's own quotation stated that the contract did not include research or development work by Adage and, in addition, expressly provided that no variation from the terms of the quotation would become a part of the contract unless specifically approved in writing by Adage. It is clear Adage never specifically approved Jostens' proposed proprietary clause. Mere performance and delivery of the items ordered, together with silence concerning the proposed additional clause, did not constitute an acceptance of that term where acceptance was expressly conditioned on the seller's assent to additional terms.

2. The trial court found, however, that the parties, nevertheless, did have an understanding that Adage would not sell to any other party a duplicate of Jostens' application software package and that, in the light of industry custom and practice, "Jostens' sole proprietary interest was in the application software package as a whole, and not in the individual routines or lines of code." There was evidence to support this finding and we cannot say it is clearly erroneous.

To say, however, that Jostens had a proprietary interest in the Adage application software package "as a whole," does not advance Jostens' claim very far. No one claims Adage sold a duplicate package to anyone else, not even to NCS. No one is suing Adage. On the other hand, Jostens' proprietary interest in the "whole" package may have a bearing on defendant Titus' conduct, reflecting on what he believed to be his employer Jostens' property.

B. This brings us, then, to the main issue, whether Jostens had a trade secret in the CAD/CAM system or any of its parts or any combination of the parts. The trial court held Jostens did not, and we agree.

1. In Cherne Industrial, Inc. v. Grounds & Associates, Inc., 278 N.W.2d 81, 90, 205 USPQ 854, 860–861, (Minn.1979), we held that a trade secret has four characteristics: (1) the matter involved is not generally known or readily ascertainable, (2) it provides a demonstrable competitive advantage, (3) it was gained at expense to the plaintiff-owner, and (4) the plaintiff-owner intended to keep it confidential. This characterization has been given statutory recognition under our state's Uniform Trade Secrets Act, enacted in 1980, after the events of this lawsuit.

Here, however, the trial court found that Jostens failed to establish any of the four Cherne requirements. Although it appears that appellant's proof fell short on the second and third Cherne requirements, we need not decide this, as we find only the first and fourth need to be discussed.

2. The first requirement is that the information be not generally known or readily ascertainable. Courts agree that trade secrets lie somewhere on a continuum from what is generally known in a field to what has some degree of uniqueness, although there need not be the degree of novelty or originality required for patent or copyright protection. Within these limits, courts have suggested a variety of further limitations. Some measure of discovery is required. Mere variations in general processes known in the field which embody no superior advances are not protected. But unique principles, engineering, logic and coherence in computer software may be accorded trade secret status. And a trade secret may modify and improve standard models to a point at which the newer version is unique in the industry.

Further, generally known computer elements may gain trade secret protection from the nature of their combination. Thus a combination of elements produced a unique and valuable computer software program in Structural Dynamics Research Corp. v. Engineering Mechanics Research Corp., 401 F.Supp. 1102 (E.D.Mich.1975).

3. Jostens starts with the fact it had the first and only CAD/CAM system in the jewelry ring industry. In that sense, perhaps, it can be said this system was not generally known; but, as the trial court found, the technology involved in CAD/CAM systems was both generally known and readily ascertainable. There was evidence that computer aided graphics systems were used for machine tooling in industries other than ring manufacture before Jostens ordered its CAD/CAM system and that the concept was known to the industry by the early sixties and is still developing. A defense witness and computer graphics expert involved in the design of similar hardware and software for Bell Telephone testified that within his company design teams had worked on interactive graphics programs performing functions similar to those performed by the Jostens system. Both the scanner subsystem and the engraving subsystem as well as the hardware and operating systems software for the graphics subsystem were all standard vendor products.

4. Although Jostens had purchased the hardware from outside vendors, it argues what is important is that it "built a system by combining components from a number of vendors because no complete system was commercially available." It argues substantial "customization" was needed to make the commercially available components into a productive system, and it points to such instances as Titus' work in constructing a three-axis capability for the engraving table.

The trial court found, however, "that the assembly of Jostens' CAD/CAM system did not require substantial research or experimentation" and that the system came about "through Titus' application of his general skill and knowledge to the integration of commonly available components to perform the desired function." We cannot say, after reviewing the evidence, that the trial court's findings are clearly erroneous. Clearly, the CAD/CAM system as such, as the combination of three generally known subsystems, does not achieve the degree of novelty or "unknownness" needed for a trade secret. As to a combination of lower levels within the system or within a subsystem, the likelihood of novelty increases, but even here we do not find plaintiff's burden of proof has been sustained. Again, we are plagued with the elasticity of plaintiff's claim. Simply to assert a trade secret resides in some combination of otherwise known data is not sufficient, as the combination itself must be delineated with some particularity in establishing its trade secret status.

5. Beyond a trade secret claim based on combination of parts or customization, Jostens spends the most time urging that the application software portion of the graphics subsystem, prepared for it by Adage, was not generally known or reasonably ascertainable. Jostens points out that when it placed its order with Adage, Adage at that time had never done an industrial numerical control application. On the other hand, there was evidence that Jostens' application software package was assembled by Adage's modified use of two application software systems (ORTHO and Cubic) that it already had in hand, having been written for other prior customers. Adage had used a modular or structured program practice, putting together small, self-contained routines and using them as building blocks for new application packages. Like others in the industry, Adage maintained a library of previously written routines and programs to use in building new programs. Experts for the defendants testified Jostens' application software did not involve any new or innovative advances in algorithmic technique. On the conflicting evidence the trial court could find, as it did, "that Jostens' CAD/CAM systems did not represent an 'invention', a discovery of any kind, or a novel technological contribution which differed materially from methods already well known in the field of manufacturing engineering, and that * * * Jostens system was no different in concept from other systems already in the public domain."

6. Even if a trade secret were not generally known or readily ascertainable, it might become so if its possessor disclosed it to the public. Here, especially, Jostens' proof fails to persuade. The trial court found that Jostens failed to meet the fourth requirement of the Cherne test, namely, that it intended to keep the relevant information secret. We agree.

Secrecy need not be total; depending on the circumstances, only partial or qualified secrecy will do. The information must be, as Minn. Stat. § 325C.01, subd. 5 (1980), now puts it, "the subject of efforts that are reasonable under the circumstances to maintain secrecy." These efforts may extend both to internal secrecy, keeping the information in-house, and to external secrecy, keeping the information from those outside in the general trade or industry. Thus, in Com–Share, Inc. v. Computer Complex, Inc., 338 F.Supp. 1229 (E.D.Mich.1971), computer software was protected both by plaintiff marking each page of the listings to emphasize its system as "confidential" and by building passwords into the system to prevent unauthorized access. Employees need to understand that information which is not readily available to the trade is not to be made so by them. The plaintiff employer in

Structural Dynamics Research Corp. v. Engineering Mechanics Research Corp., 401 F.Supp. 1102 (E.D.Mich.1975), specifically called the confidential nature of the work to each employee's attention in an individual confidential disclosure agreement each signed. On the other hand, in Pressure Science, Inc. v. Kramer, 413 F.Supp. 618 (D.Conn. 1976), the court found that a plaintiff's failure to require all employees working in a supposedly confidential area to sign a nondisclosure agreement evidenced a fatal lack of concern for confidentiality.

Here there was evidence that when Jostens installed its CAD/CAM system, no consideration was given or policy established to keep the development secret or confidential. Not until May 1975 did Jostens bar potential customers for its system from the Burnsville plant; until then, prospects were allowed in, although it is disputed what they might have learned. Particularly damaging, we think, is the presentation made and the article written by Titus, with Jostens' approval, explaining Jostens' CAD/CAM system to other experts in the field. The parties disagree on whether the information revealed was sufficient to make the purported trade secret accessible to other technologically sophisticated persons. NCS' expert testified that from Titus' article alone he could have duplicated the functions of Jostens' system, while an expert called by Jostens said it would be "very, very difficult" to translate into practical application the theoretical concepts described in the article. The trial court found that the information given in Titus' authorized disclosure was sufficient to enable an experienced engineer to duplicate both the hardware and the software of Jostens' system "without too much difficulty."

There was also evidence that none of the software tapes or documents at Jostens was marked "secret" or "confidential" until after this litigation began. Some of the employees working with the system were never asked to sign a confidentiality agreement even though Jostens had employed such a form elsewhere.

We hold the trial court's finding that "Jostens did not take reasonable steps to protect its alleged trade secrets" is not clearly erroneous.

II. The claim of misappropriation

This case may also be viewed from the standpoint of whether there was a misappropriation of a trade secret. This analysis centers on the misappropriation, the gist of which is breach of a confidential relationship, rather than on whether a property interest is involved, i.e., whether a trade secret exists. The protection afforded trade secrets is not intended to reward or promote the development of secret processes (although it does, of course, benefit the enterprising developer), but rather is to protect against breaches of faith and the use of improper methods to obtain information. Trade secret law seeks to maintain standards of loyalty and trust in the business community.

A. These two approaches overlap, since one of the requirements of a misappropriation cause of action is to first prove the existence of a trade secret. Plaintiff must then further prove that defendant acquired the trade secret as a result of a confidential relationship and that the defendant has used and disclosed the trade secret. These three elements are set out in Eutectic Welding Alloys Corp. v. West, 281 Minn. 13, 18, 160 N.W.2d 566, 570 (1968). What needs to be kept in mind, however, is that the various elements "should not be artificially separated for purposes of analysis since, in a significant sense, they are interdependent." 1 Milgrim, Trade Secrets § 7.07(1) at 95.

Here, Jostens contends that defendants Titus, Henderson and Hoagberg acquired knowledge of Jostens' trade secrets while in its employ, and they then used this information to produce a similar CAD/CAM system for their new employer, defendant NCS. As to Henderson, for example, the claim is that he used his experience gained at Jostens to train personnel at Balfour in the operation of the CAD/CAM system sold it by NCS. As to Titus, the claim is that he took his knowledge, experience and skills to NCS and used them to build a similar system for NCS. Defendants' defense to the claim of misappropriation was that there were no trade secrets, nothing to misappropriate, and in this connection that (1) NCS developed its system using only generally known computer concepts which are not protectable, and (2) if any of the concepts might be protectable, the protection was lost by Jostens' failure to take reasonable precautions against disclosure and use, and (3) the defendants developed their product independently from other sources.

B. First of all, even without the employment agreements signed by Titus and Henderson, employees have a common-law duty not to wrongfully use confidential information or trade secrets obtained from an employer. We do not find this common-law duty to have been breached.

1. Titus took with him (how could he not?) his experience and skills acquired while working for Jostens. These abilities, to the extent derived from generally known sources, are not considered confidential; a computer programmer, like a real estate salesperson, should be able to ply his trade. But knowledge gained at an employer's expense, which takes on the characteristics of a trade secret and which would be unfair for the employee to use elsewhere, is deemed confidential and is not to be disclosed or used. Cherne Industrial, Inc. v. Grounds & Associates, Inc., 278 N.W.2d 81, 205 USPQ 854 (Minn.1979). Even if this knowledge is only in the employee's memory, it may be protectable. Confidential information is that which an employee knew or should have known was confidential. Or as Minn.Stat. § 325C.01, subd. 2 (1980), now puts it, a person, such as an employee here, is not to disclose or use a trade secret that he knows or has reason to know was acquired by him under circumstances giving rise to a duty to maintain its secrecy or limit its use. On the other hand, the employee is entitled to fair notice of the confidential nature of the relationship and what material is to be kept confidential.

2. Jostens' failure to take reasonable precautions to protect the confidentiality of what it now claims to be secret was such that the

defendant employees could not be expected to have known what was confidential and what was not, what was unfair to disclose and what was not. The trial court found, and there is evidence to support the finding, that Jostens did not really know what it was about its Burnsville system that it intended to protect. Perhaps this difficulty existed because of all people at Jostens, Titus, the person against whom protection is now sought, was the most knowledgeable about what information should be protected. It appears Titus was not unaware of his position. Titus recognized Jostens' "proprietary interest" in his project. Thus he sought and obtained his employer's permission to disclose aspects of the CAD/CAM to the trade in his seminar presentation and journal article. Still, it can hardly be said that Jostens had an understanding with Titus not to disclose any particular information when, in lieu of any "exit interview," Jostens' president, on Titus' departure, said the company wanted Titus to go ahead and work in the area of CAD/CAM development and this "was fine with us."

Thus the trial court was not in error in finding that at the time Titus left Jostens, his knowledge of the operation of the Burnsville system was "part of his own general skill and experience." If some of Titus' knowledge might nevertheless be a likely subject for a trade secret, here, we think, Jostens failed to make it so by failing to insist on its secrecy. This is true also for the other defendant employees.

3. A misappropriation claim also requires proof under Eutectic that the defendants disclosed or used the trade secret. Much evidence was received on this issue. Jostens tried to show that the application software package used in the NCS graphics subsystem contained significant parts of the same software package in Jostens' system. Jostens showed, for example, through a comparison study made by two of its experts, that some 29 names of routines were identical and, within routines bearing the same names, a high percentage of the lines were syntactically identical. Jostens showed that copies of some of the source code furnished NCS by Adage were labeled "Jostens Application Software." On the other hand, Adage's programmer testified that only a small percentage of NCS' software routines, at most 10%, had been written from Jostens' package and that while a somewhat higher percentage had begun as routines for the Jostens package, they were substantially revised before being used in the NCS package. Then, too, some of the so-called Jostens routines were identical as standard utility routines, kept in Adage's library and used as building blocks as needed.

The fact that only a small percentage of Jostens' routines may have been used does not especially help the defendants; it may take only that small percentage, depending on what it entails, to make a program unique. Nevertheless, Jostens did not convince the trial court that NCS' system itself evidenced use of any of Jostens' alleged trade secrets. The court made extensive findings of specific ways in which the NCS system had functional capabilities totally nonexistent in or substantially different from Jostens' software package. There was testimony by an Adage programmer that at the time the technical cooperation agreement was still a possibility, he had already determined that NCS' proposed program would require such enormous modification of Jostens' package that Adage could as well start all over anyway. In light of such evidence, we cannot say that the trial court's findings that Jostens failed to prove disclosure or use of its claimed trade secret were clearly erroneous.

C. A confidence may be imposed contractually as well as by employment status, so Jostens also asserts a separate claim that defendants Titus and Henderson are liable for breach of their employment agreements. The trial court found the agreements unenforceable on the grounds neither was supported by consideration. We agree.

1. Four years after Titus began his employment with Jostens and two years after Henderson began his, they each signed the following agreement:

> All papers and apparatus relating to Jostens' business, including those prepared or made by me, shall be the property of Jostens and except as required by my work, I will not reveal them to others nor will I reveal any information concerning Jostens' business including its inventions, shop practices, processes and methods of manufacturing and merchandising.

There was no evidence that, by signing this agreement, either Titus or Henderson gained greater wages or a promotion or access to technical or operational parts of the Burnsville system that nonsigning employees did not have. According to Titus, he and the others asked to sign the agreement did so under the impression that they would lose their jobs if they did not. Jostens argues that the promise of future or continued employment is adequate consideration.

2. We have held that the adequacy of consideration for a non-competition contract in an ongoing employment relationship depends on the particular facts of each case. In Davies we observed that the contract provided the employee with real advantages. That does not appear to be the case here. The agreements obtained by Jostens did not increase Jostens' commitment to the employees for future benefits, as in Modern Controls, Inc. v. Andreadakis, 578 F.2d 1264 (8th Cir.1978) (applying Minnesota law). Nor do the agreements memorialize a prior oral agreement made between the employer and prospective employee, as in Cybertek Computer Products, Inc. v. Whitfield, 203 USPQ 1020 (1972).

Davies contains dicta that "[m]ere continuation of employment as consideration *could* be used to uphold coercive agreements." Id., 298 N.W.2d at 130–31 (emphasis added). In this instance, however, where no raises or promotions resulted, where other employees with similar access were not asked to sign, the mere continuation of employment for Titus and Henderson is not enough. To the extent the agreements encompassed the employees' common-law duty to their employer not to disclose, our disposition of that common-law duty makes any contractual duty moot. Since we find the employment agreements not enforceable, we need not decide the issue of whether their purported reach of "all" papers and information is overbroad or lacking in fair notice of what is not to be disclosed.

III. Other claims

Since we uphold the trial court's findings that there has been no misappropriation of any trade secret, we need not reach the issues of whether the trial court's findings of estoppel and laches are sustainable. . . .

Affirmed, but with respondents to be allowed their disbursements.

NOTE

Computer programs present special problems for trade secret protection. One problem is that a program's innovative elements may embody no more than general, unprotectible concepts. Another problem is that computer programs are easily reverse-engineered, giving competitors commodious shelter under the reverse engineering privilege. See p. 823, above. Professor Jerome Reichman has observed, a computer program tends to bear its know-how "on its face" so that "like an artistic work," it is "exposed to instant predation when successful and is likely to enjoy zero lead time after being launched on the market." Reichman, Computer Programs as Applied Scientific Know-How: Implications of Copyright Protection for Commercialized University Research, 42 Vand.L.Rev. 639, 660 (1989).

II. INDUSTRIAL DESIGN

Works of industrial design may be protected by design patent law, copyright law and trademark and unfair competition law. Much of the literature in the field has a strong comparative orientation. See A.L. A.I., The Protection of Designs and Models (1985); Design Protection (H. Cohen Jehoram, ed. 1976); C. Fellner, The Future of Legal Protection for Industrial Design (1985). Two pathbreaking articles by Professor Jerome Reichman compare different legal traditions of design protection in their historical setting: Design Protection in Domestic and Foreign Copyright Law: From the Berne Revision of 1948 to the Copyright Act of 1976, 1983 Duke L.J. 1143; Design Protection After The Copyright Act of 1976: A Comparative View of the Emerging Interim Models, 31 J. Copyright Soc'y 267 (1984).

A. Greene, Designs and Utility Models Throughout the World (1989) compiles digests of design laws in countries from Abu Dhabi to Zimbabwe. A valuable bibliography appears in U.S. Copyright Office, Bibliography of Design Protection (1955 & Supp.1976).

A. DESIGN PATENT LAW

IN RE NALBANDIAN
United States Court of Customs and Patent Appeals, 1981.
661 F.2d 1214, 211 U.S.P.Q. 782.

NIES, Judge.

This appeal is from the decision of the Patent and Trademark Office (PTO) Board of Appeals (board) affirming the rejection under 35 U.S.C. § 103 by the examiner of appellant's application, serial No. 792,482, filed April 29, 1977, for "Combined Tweezer and Spotlight." We affirm.

Background

The claimed ornamental design is for an implement referred to as an illuminable tweezer. The primary reference on which the examiner and the board relied is U.S. Patent Des. 175,259, issued to Johnson et al. (Johnson) on August 2, 1955, also for an illuminable tweezer. The respective designs are reproduced below:

Appellant's

Johnson's

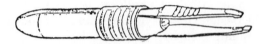

As can be seen from these drawings, appellant's design resembles Johnson's in overall form. The only readily noticeable difference is in the fluting on the cylindrical sleeve which surrounds the body of the implement near the end housing the spotlight. The board agreed with the examiner that secondary references disclosed fluting similar to that in appellant's design, as well as the slight differences in the pincers. However, as we consider it unnecessary to rely on these references, they are not reproduced herein.

The board, in affirming the examiner, stated:

It appears to us that the references are all from reasonably pertinent arts and the claimed design would have been obvious in view of such designs in the prior art. We arrive at this conclusion under Graham et al. v. John Deere Company, 383 U.S. 1, 86 S.Ct. 684, [15 L.Ed.2d 545] 825 OG 24, 148 USPQ 459 (1966), whether the test employs a 'worker of ordinary skill in the art' or an 'ordinary intelligent man.'

OPINION

The sole issue on appeal is whether appellant's design would have been obvious within the meaning of 35 U.S.C. § 103. In the words of the statute, are

. . . the differences between the subject matter sought to be patented and the prior art . . . such that the subject matter as a whole would have been obvious at the time the invention was made to a person having ordinary skill in the art to which said subject matter pertains[?]

In In re Laverne, 53 CCPA 1158, 356 F.2d 1003, 148 USPQ 674 (1966), this court specifically rejected the interpretation generally given to the statutory language "one of ordinary skill in the art" as referring to a designer. The court concluded that this interpretation would not effectuate the intent of Congress to promote progress in designs since it would result in the denial of patent protection for the work of competent designers. Accordingly, it was held that the obviousness of designs over the prior art must be tested by the eyes of the "ordinary intelligent man," who was also referred to as the "ordinary observer."

Since the *Laverne* decision, the Second, Third, Tenth and District of Columbia circuits have specifically considered the "ordinary observer" test set forth therein and rejected it. These circuits continue to interpret "one of ordinary skill" as requiring obviousness to be tested from the viewpoint of the "ordinary designer." Since board decisions may be reviewed by the District of Columbia Circuit as well as this court, the PTO has been faced with two standards in design cases.

We believe it is appropriate to close this schism. Accordingly, with this case we hold that the test of *Laverne* will no longer be followed. In design cases we will consider the fictitious person identified in § 103 as "one of ordinary skill in the art" to be the designer of ordinary capability who designs articles of the type presented in the application. This approach is consistent with Graham v. John Deere Co., 383 U.S. 1, 86 S.Ct. 684, 15 L.Ed.2d 545 (1966), which requires that the level of ordinary skill *in the pertinent art be determined.*

In *Laverne,* this court recognized that the statute does not specifically create a test for nonobviousness of a design which is different from that for inventions defined in 35 U.S.C. § 101. That § 103 applies to designs follows from 35 U.S.C. § 171, which states: "The provisions of this title relating to patents for inventions shall apply to patents for designs. . . ." An ordinary intelligent man was, nevertheless, held to be the person skilled in the art within the meaning of § 103, rather than a designer working in the art, on the following rationale:

> In the mechanical, chemical, and electrical 'arts' we have distinguished, since Hotchkiss v. Greenwood, 52 U.S. 248 [11 How 248, 13 L.Ed. 683] (1850), between 'an ordinary mechanic acquainted with the business' and the 'inventor'; between the craftsman or routineer on the one hand and the innovator on the other, now, by statute, the innovator who makes *unobvious* innovations. With respect to such inventions, these two categories of persons are workers in the same 'art.'

> In the field of design the analysis is not so easy. Design inventing or originating is done by designers. The examiner here has referred to 'the expected skill of a competent designer' as the basis of comparison. However, if we equate him with the class of mechanics, as the examiner did, and refuse design patent protection to his usual work product, are we not ruling out, as a practical matter, all patent protection for ornamental designs for articles of manufacture? Yet the clear purpose of the design patent law is to promote progress in the 'art' of industrial design and who is going to produce that progress if it is not the class of 'competent designers'?

> We cannot equate them with the mechanics in the mechanic vs. inventor test for patentability. Correspondingly, we cannot solve the problem here, obviousness, by using for our basis of comparison the inventor class in the field of industrial design. [Id. at 1162, 356 F.2d at 1006, 148 USPQ at 676–77. Emphasis in original.]

If an 'ordinary designer' test for designs were necessarily equivalent to applying an 'ordinary inventor' test for inventions, we would not return to it here. However, the problem thus stated can be viewed as one created by semantics. The 'ordinary designer' means one who brings certain background and training to the problems of developing designs in a particular field, comparable to the 'mechanic' or 'routineer' in non-design arts. We do not have a name for that person in the design field other than 'designer' which is also the name we must use for the person who creates a patentable design.

In any event, we do not believe the determination of the level of ordinary skill in the art, as required under *Graham v. John Deere Co.,* supra, cannot be made with respect to designs. Thus, in view of the statutory requirement that patents for designs must be evaluated on the same basis as other patents, the test of *Graham* must be followed.

It is apparent the "ordinary designer" standard has been found helpful to courts in infringement litigation because of the objective evidence which can be brought to bear on the question of obviousness under the tests of *Graham.* We believe it also can be more effectively dealt with by an applicant during patent prosecution than can the "ordinary observer" test. For example, where an examiner selects features from various designs, or relies on common knowledge in the art, the possibility is present of submitting an affidavit from an expert in whose opinion, subjective though it may be, it would not have been obvious to an ordinary designer, despite knowledge (or imputed knowledge) of the prior art to combine features or make modifications as shown in an applicant's design. This possibility is not present using the "ordinary observer" test. No affiant can be qualified as an expert ordinary observer who might, thereby, persuade the person who is deciding the matter that the latter's judgment of the reaction of an ordinary observer is in error.

Rejection of the "ordinary observer" test under 35 U.S.C. § 103 does not preclude its application in other contexts. The "ordinary observer" test was applied in determining whether a claim to a design had been infringed as long ago as Gorham Co. v. White, 81 U.S. (14 Wall.) 511, 20 L.Ed. 731 (1871). Further, the "ordinary observer" test has been applied when determining anticipation under § 102 by courts which apply the "ordinary designer" test under § 103.

Conclusion

Applying the "ordinary designer" test of § 103 to the case at bar, the question is whether the changes made by appellant in the Johnson design for an illuminated tweezer would have been obvious to an ordinary designer of such implements. As noted, the claimed design is substantially identical in overall configuration to the design shown in Johnson for the same type of article. The differences in the finger grips of a slightly different shape and the straight, rather than slightly curved pincers, are de minimis. We also agree that it is well within the skill of an ordinary designer in the art to make the modification of the fluting and that it would have been obvious to do so. Such changes do not achieve a patentably distinct design. We agree, therefore, that the PTO has shown a prima facie case of obviousness.

Once the prima facie case of obviousness was established, the burden shifted to appellant to rebut it, if he could, with objective evidence of nonobviousness. In response, appellant filed a declaration regarding alleged commercial success of his illuminable tweezer. Both the examiner and the board found, and we agree, that the declaration was not persuasive because the alleged commercial success was not shown to be attributable to the design.

In view of the unrebutted prima facie case of obviousness, the rejection of the claimed ornamental design must stand. Accordingly, the decision of the board is *affirmed.*

AFFIRMED.

RICH, Judge, concurring.

A majority of my colleagues choose to swing the court into alignment with the three circuits which have affirmatively rejected the reasoning of our fifteen-year old *In re Laverne* opinion which, until now, this court has always unanimously accepted without question.

Laverne thus being dead, I deem it appropriate, as the father of the so-called "ordinary observer" test (as applied to 35 U.S.C. § 103), to say a few kind words over the corpse.

From the passages quoted from my opinion by the majority, it will be seen that what was written in 1966 was a response to the examiner's reliance on what would be produced by "the expected skill of a competent designer," perhaps an imaginary person of somewhat greater skill than the imaginary "ordinary designer" now enthroned by the majority. I was interested in retaining within the ambit of the patent system the made-for-hire products of "competent designers" so businessmen or corporations would find it economically advantageous to employ them, thus carrying out the objective of 35 U.S.C. § 171, to promote the ornamental design of articles of manufacture.

The majority is not now talking of "competent designers" but of "ordinary designers" from which it follows that there may be extraordinary designers who will produce unobvious designs which ordinary designers will not routinely produce. It is probably true, as the majority says, that all this is just semantics and courts will, with phraseology of their own choosing, continue to find designs patentable or unpatentable according to their judicial "hunches."

The real problem, however, is not whether the § 103 fictitious "person" is an ordinary observer or an ordinary designer but with the necessity under Title 35 of finding unobviousness in a design. The problem long antedates 1952 and its Patent Act and existed from the beginning, the pre–1952 test being the presence of "invention" in a design. The problem was well known to the drafters of the 1952 Act (of which I was one) and it was also known that many prior legislative efforts had been made to solve it. When work on revision of the patent statutes began in 1950, a deliberate decision was made not to attempt any solution of the "controversial design problem" but simply to retain the substance of the existing design patent statute and attack the design problem at a later date, after the new Title 35 had been enacted.

Thus it was that the patentability of designs came to be subject to the new § 103 which was written with an eye to the kinds of inventions encompassed by § 101 with no thought at all of how it might affect designs. Therefore, the design protection problem was in no way made better; perhaps it was made worse.

The intention of the drafters of the 1952 Patent Act to tackle the design protection problem was carried out, by both the private and public sectors, commencing in 1954, by a new "Coordinating Committee" of which I was chairman, and by 1957 new legislation was introduced in the 85th Congress, 1st Session in the form of Willis Bill H.R. 8873. In the 86th Congress, 1st Session, S. 2075 was introduced by Senators O'Mahoney, Wiley, and Hart, being the same bill in substance. From that time on, the legislative effort was continuous until the bill became Title III of the Copyright Revision Bills, later became Title II, and finally was jettisoned to facilitate passage of the main bill, the Act of October 19, 1976, Pub.L. No. 94–553, now 17 U.S.C. § 101 et seq. (1977). Congressmen said they would deal with designs later.

The point of this review is to call attention to the resulting presently pending legislation, H.R. 20, 97th Congress, 1st Session, introduced January 5, 1981, by Mr. Railsback, a bill "To amend the copyright law, title 17 of the United States Code, to provide for protection of ornamental designs of useful articles." The present case and its companion, In re Spreter, 661 F.2d 1220 (Cust. & Pat.App.), concurrently decided, are but the latest examples of the need for a law tailored to the problems of designers, of their employers and clients in the business world, and of the government agencies now concerned. The now-pending legislation is substantially the same bill introduced in 1957, after the refining process of *24 years of legislative consideration. It is time to pass it* and get the impossible issue of obviousness in design patentability cases off the backs of the courts and the Patent and Trademark Office, giving some sense of certainty to the business world of what designs can be protected and how.

Commissioner of Patents and Trademarks Gerald Mossinghoff in his maiden speech to the ABA Patent, Trademark and Copyright Law Section in New Orleans on August 8, 1981, said,

> . . . we are *again* urging enactment of an inexpensive and effective form of registration protection for designs and, specifically, we are supporting H.R. 20 introduced by Congressman Railsback last January . . . largely because *the concept of unobviousness is not well suited to ornamental designs.* We believe a registration system, such as that contemplated in H.R. 20, would serve industry better at lower cost. [My emphasis.]

The bar would do well to devote its energies to backing this effort of the PTO rather than pursuing appeals such as these which may sometimes result in patents to "extraordinary" designers whose patents, as the Commissioner also pointed out, may then suffer a 70% mortality rate in the courts at the hands of judges reviewing the § 103 unobviousness of the designs.

I have one further comment on the majority opinion, which says that a "determination of the level of ordinary skill in the art" is "required under *Graham v. John Deere Co.*" It is not the Supreme Court that requires such a determination, but the statutory patent law which the Court was simply applying. The *statute* makes that requirement of the courts, all of them, from the highest on down. The Supreme Court said as much. 383 U.S. at 19, 86 S.Ct. at 694.

BALDWIN, Judge, dissenting.

While agreeing with the majority opinion that the "ordinary designer" test of § 103 should be applied, I would reach a different conclusion.

The major difference between the appealed design and the design shown in Johnson is in the fluting on the cylindrical sleeve. This difference is not de minimis but rather creates quite a difference in appearance between the two designs. I cannot agree with the majority that it would have been obvious to the ordinary designer to make the modification of the fluting.

Nor can I agree with the board's conclusion that "the references are all from reasonably pertinent arts and the claimed design would have been obvious in view of such designs in the prior art."

Appellant has taken issue with that board conclusion basically by arguing that the Deibel reference and the Mantelet reference are non-analogous art and that it is improper to use the two references to remedy a deficiency in the Johnson design in order to show a design similar to appellant's illuminable tweezer having a sleeve with longitudinal fluting over a portion of its length.

Even assuming, *arguendo,* that the board did not err by sanctioning utilization of bits and pieces of designs from five references to establish a prima facie case of obviousness of a claimed design, I agree with appellant that the board erred in concluding that all the references are from reasonably pertinent arts. Deibel and Mantelet are not analogous art and should not have been utilized to support the § 103 rejection.

Accordingly, I would reverse the decision of the board.

AVIA GROUP INTERNATIONAL, INC. v. L.A. GEAR CALIFORNIA, INC.

United States Court of Appeals, Federal Circuit, 1988.
853 F.2d 1557, 7 U.S.P.Q.2d 1548.

NIES, Circuit Judge.

L.A. Gear California, Inc. (LAG) appeals the decision of the United States District Court for the Central District of California, Pensa, Inc. v. L.A. Gear of California, Inc., 4 USPQ2d 1016 (C.D.Cal.1987), granting the motion of Avia Group International, Inc. (formerly Pensa, Inc.) for summary judgment holding United States Design Patent Nos. 284,420 ('420) and 287,301 ('301) valid as between the parties and willfully infringed, and the case exceptional under 35 U.S.C. § 285 (1982). We affirm.

I

BACKGROUND

Avia owns the '420 patent, claiming an ornamental design for an athletic shoe outer sole, and the '301 patent, claiming an ornamental design for an athletic shoe upper, by assignment from the inventor, James Tong. LAG ordered and sold shoes, Model No. 584 "Boy's Thrasher" ("Thrasher") and Model No. 588 "Boy's Thrasher Hi–Top" ("Hi–Top"), designed and manufactured for it by Sheng Chun Chemical Ind. Corp. in Taiwan. Avia filed suit against LAG alleging, *inter alia,* that both of LAG's models infringed its '420 design patent and that LAG's Hi–Top model also infringed the '301 design. LAG counter-claimed for a declaratory judgment that the two patents were not infringed and were invalid because the designs were both obvious and functional. Avia moved for partial summary judgment on the patent validity and infringement issues and for attorney fees.

Finding no bona fide dispute as to any material fact and that Avia had shown entitlement to judgment as a matter of law, the court granted Avia's motion after a hearing. It determined that the infringe-ment was willful and that the case was exceptional within the meaning of 35 U.S.C. § 285 (1982), thus providing the basis for an award of attorney fees. The court also issued a permanent injunction enjoining further infringement by LAG. Because the court reserved decision on the amounts to be awarded as damages and as attorney fees, these matters are not involved in this appeal. . . .

III

VALIDITY OF '420 AND '301 DESIGN PATENTS

A patent is presumed valid. 35 U.S.C. § 282 (1982). In an in-fringement action, it is not part of a patent owner's initial burden of going forward with proof of its case to submit evidence supporting validity. Rather, the burden is first on a challenger to introduce evidence which raises the issue of invalidity. Further, a challenger must establish facts, by clear and convincing evidence, which persua-sively lead to the conclusion of invalidity. Thus, "[a challenger's] silence leaves untouched at this stage what the statute presumes, namely, that [the] patent is valid." Roper Corp. v. Litton Sys., Inc., 757 F.2d 1266, 1270, 225 USPQ 345, 347 (Fed.Cir.1985) (footnote omitted).

With this understanding of the parties' obligations, LAG's argu-ment that Avia unfairly waited for rebuttal to present its evidence regarding validity clearly fails. Avia had no obligation to introduce any evidence initially on validity. Such evidence was required only in response to LAG's evidence.

Where a challenger does put in evidence disputing validity, the presumption of validity is neither eliminated nor undermined by the challenger's evidence, as LAG argues. This is so because the presumption is a procedural device, which assigns the burden of going forward as well as the burden of proof of facts to the challenger. Moreover, the presumption is one of law, not fact, and does not constitute "evidence" to be weighed against a challenger's evidence. Nevertheless, a patent having issued, the challenger bears the burden of persuasion that the established facts lead to a conclusion of invalidity.

The patents in suit are design patents. Under 35 U.S.C. § 171 (1982), a patent may be obtained on the design of an article of manufacture which is "new, original and ornamental" and "nonobvious" within the meaning of section 103, which is incorporated by reference into section 171. LAG attacks the validity of the patents for the subject designs covering parts of shoes on the grounds (1) that the designs are primarily functional rather than ornamental and (2) that the designs would have been obvious from the prior art.

A. *Ornamental versus Functional Designs*

We dispose first of LAG's argument that the record shows genuine issues of material fact with respect to whether the subject designs are ornamental within the meaning of section 171. LAG points only to conclusory, conflicting statements in affidavits, which create no genuine issue for trial, and to evidence of prior art references, none of which is in dispute. LAG's arguments are, thus, misfocused. Rather than arguing that there is a genuine issue of fact, in substance its arguments are that Avia was not entitled to judgment on the basis of the facts established by the record evidence.

LAG correctly asserts that if a patented design is "primarily functional," rather than primarily ornamental, the patent is invalid. When function dictates a design, protection would not promote the decorative arts, a purpose of the design patent statute. There is no dispute that shoes are functional and that certain features of the shoe designs in issue perform functions. However, a distinction exists between the functionality of an article or features thereof and the functionality of the particular design of such article or features thereof that perform a function. Were that not true, it would not be possible to obtain a design patent on a utilitarian article of manufacture, or to obtain both design and utility patents on the same article.

With respect to functionality of the design of the '301 patent, the court stated:

> [LAG] has taken each little aspect of the upper and pointed out that many of the aspects or features of the upper have a function. Even if, arguendo, true that would not make the design primarily functional. If the functional aspect or purpose could be accomplished in many other ways that [sic] is involved in this very design, that fact is enough to destroy the claim that this design is primarily functional. There are many things in the ['301] patent on the upper which are clearly ornamental and nonfunctional such as the location of perforations and how they are arranged, and the

stitching and how it's arranged, and the coloration of elements between black and white colors.

> The overall aesthetics of the various components and the way they are combined are quite important and are not functional. They are purely aesthetic. . . .

Pensa, Inc., 4 USPQ2d at 1019.

On the design of the '420 patent, the court made a similar analysis of various features and concluded:

> But every function which [LAG] says is achieved by one of the component aspects of the sole in this case could be and has been achieved by different components. And that is a very persuasive rationale for the holding that the design overall is not primarily functional. Moreover, there is no function which even defendant assigns to the swirl effect around the pivot point, which swirl effect is a very important aspect of the design.
>
>   . . . . . .
>
>   . . . [T]his is a unique and pleasing design and it's [sic] patentability in my view is not offset or destroyed by the fact that the utility patent is utilized and incorporated in this aesthetically pleasing design.
>
> Plaintiff has given us evidence of other shoes that incorporate the utility patent and its concavity—others of its own shoes—but with a totally different design, and has thus established that the utility patent does not make the design patent invalid in this case.

Pensa, Inc., 4 USPQ2d at 1019–20. We agree that the designs in suit have not persuasively been shown to be functional and that no genuine issue of material fact is present with respect to this issue.

B. *Obviousness*

Design patents must meet a nonobvious requirement identical to that applicable to utility patents. Accordingly, 35 U.S.C. § 103 (1982) applies to determine whether the designs of the '420 and '301 patents would have been obvious to one of ordinary skill in the art. The court found no genuine issue of material fact was raised with respect to the four factors to be considered in determining obviousness: the scope and content of the prior art, the differences between the prior art and claims at issue, the level of ordinary skill in the art when the invention was made, and secondary indicia, such as commercial success and copying.

LAG attempts to create a dispute as to the content of the prior art through the court's statement that "all of the shoes referred to as prior art in the record below had come out after the Model 750 [commercial embodiment of the '420 patent] was on the market." LAG mischaracterizes the court's statement. The court restricted that statement to shoes *mentioned by inventor Tong* in deposition answers. The court also noted that LAG's deposition questions were "so generally worded as to be almost meaningless." Neither LAG's failure to ask specific questions during discovery nor its mischaracterization of the court's decision can create a genuine issue of fact.

With respect to a design, obviousness is determined from the vantage of "the designer of ordinary capability who designs articles of the type presented in the application." *In re Nalbandian*, 661 F.2d at 1216, 211 USPQ at 784. LAG acknowledges that standard, but asserts that the court is required to defer to its expert testimony. As we have stated, however, an expert's opinion on the legal conclusion of obviousness is neither necessary nor controlling.

Further, a conflict in the legal opinions of experts creates no dispute of fact. LAG argues that the designs would have been obvious because they are "traditional ones consisting of features old in the art." That some components of Avia's designs exist in prior art references is not determinative. "[I]f the combined teachings suggest only components of the claimed design but not its overall appearance, a rejection under section 103 is inappropriate." *In re Cho*, 813 F.2d 378, 382, 1 USPQ2d 1662, 1663 (Fed.Cir.1987). There is no evidence that the overall appearances of the '420 and '301 designs would have been suggested to ordinary shoe designers by the references.

LAG does not contest the commercial success of Avia's shoes manufactured according to the patented designs, but argues the success is attributable to factors other than the designs themselves, such as advertising. Although commercial success is relevant only if a nexus is proven between the success of the patented product and the merits of the claimed invention, Avia did present evidence tending to prove nexus and LAG's conclusory statements to the contrary fail to create a genuine factual dispute. In addition, the trial court referred to the accused products as "copies" of the patented designs. Copying is additional evidence of nonobviousness. LAG's conclusory characterization of the evidence as "speculative" is insufficient to create a genuine factual dispute.

On the basis of its evaluation of the four factors outlined above, the court held that the ordinary designer would not have found the '420 or '301 designs, considered as whole designs, obvious in light of the differences between the prior art and the claimed designs. We agree. No genuine issue of material fact or error of law has been shown in the district court's ruling.

IV

PATENT INFRINGEMENT

The Supreme Court established the test for determining infringement of a design patent in Gorham Co. v. White, 81 U.S. (14 Wall.) 511, 20 L.Ed. 731 (1871):

> if, in the eye of an ordinary observer, giving such attention as a purchaser usually gives, two designs are substantially the same, if the resemblance is such as to deceive such an observer, inducing

him to purchase one supposing it to be the other, the first one
patented is infringed by the other.

Id. at 528. In addition to overall similarity of designs, "the accused
device must appropriate the novelty in the patented device which
distinguishes it from the prior art." Shelcore, Inc. v. Durham Indus.,
Inc., 745 F.2d 621, 628 n. 16, 223 USPQ 584, 590 n. 17 (Fed.Cir.1984);
Litton Sys., 728 F.2d at 1444, 221 USPQ at 109. Absent the presence of
the novel features in the accused products, a patented design has not
been appropriated.

The district court correctly applied the above test for infringement
of the subject patented designs, stating:

> I find them as to the ['420] sole virtually identical. In each
> instance [LAG has] appropriated the novelty of the patented arti-
> cle. One needs only to look at the two soles to see that the
> infringement exists. But if it is necessary to particularize it we
> have in the incriminated or accused sole copying of the swirl effect,
> copying of the separate coloration and configuration of the pivot
> point, though without the red dot. And we have in the accused
> sole the whole general appearance, which is almost a direct copy of
> the patented sole.
>
> As to the ['301] upper, in my view the same language could be
> used. It is almost a direct copy. It is much more than the
> substantially-the-same standard.

Pensa, Inc., 4 USPQ2d at 1021. Thus, the court found that LAG's shoes
had overall similarity to the patented designs and incorporated the
novel features thereof as well. For the '420 patent, those features
included the swirl effect and the pivot point; for the '301 patent, the
novelty consists, in light of the court's analysis of validity, of the
combination of saddle, eyestay, and perforations.

LAG asserts that a patent owner has the burden to prove infringement by preponderant evidence, and that Avia failed to meet that
burden. On a motion for summary judgment, however, the question is
not the "weight" of the evidence but the presence of a genuine issue of
material fact. A patent owner must, of course, present sufficient
evidence to make a prima facie case. Here, besides its patents and the
accused shoes, Avia presented evidence in the form of an expert's
declaration analyzing infringement and deposition testimony of LAG's
president, in which he confused LAG's Thrasher and Avia's Model 750.
In addition, the court performed its own comparison of LAG's shoes to
the patented designs. LAG merely challenges the "weight" accorded
the expert's declaration and the ultimate finding of infringement.
Neither argument raises a genuine issue of material fact which requires a trial.

Finally, LAG points to undisputed evidence that Avia's Model 750
shoe, made in accordance with the patent, and LAG's accused Models
584 and 588, are intended for different customers. The former are for
tennis players; the latter are for children. That fact, per LAG, renders
the products not "substantially the same," as necessary under Gorham.

LAG's understanding of *Gorham* is grossly in error. To find infringement, the accused shoes need only appropriate a patentee's protected design, not a patentee's market as well. The products of the parties need not be directly competitive; indeed, an infringer is liable even when the patent owner puts out no product. *A fortiori,* infringement is not avoided by selling to a different class of purchasers than the patentee.

Having considered the above and all other arguments of appellant, LAG, we are unpersuaded of error in the district court's judgment of infringement. . . .

VII

CONCLUSION

For the foregoing reasons, we affirm the grant of summary judgment to Avia in all respects.

AFFIRMED.

NOTES

1. The incorporation of the design patent provisions, 35 U.S.C. §§ 171–173, in the basic utility patent statute was dictated mainly by expedience. One reason the design provisions appear in the Patent Act, rather than in the Copyright Act or in a tailor-made statute, is that it was the Commissioner of Patents who first communicated the need for their enactment to Congress. Congress gave little systematic attention to the substantial differences between utility and design subject matter, such as the fact that the Patent Office's lengthy examination procedures may have been out of keeping with the needs of the many designs that enjoy only a short commercial season. Apart from the few specifically stated exceptions from the Act's general application, the Act leaves courts at large in determining the extent to which utility patent principles should govern design patent cases.

On design patents generally, see Hudson, A Brief History of the Development of Design Patent Protection in the United States, 30 J.Pat.Off. Soc'y 380 (1948); Michaelson, The Nature of the Protection of Artistic and Industrial Design, 37 J.Pat.Off. Soc'y 543 (1955). Contemporary efforts to enact a tailor-made industrial design statute along the lines described in Judge Rich's *Nalbandian* concurrence are described at page 908, below.

2. *Ornamentality.* Courts generally treat "ornamentality" as the opposite of "functionality" and construe section 171's requirement that design patent subject matter be "ornamental" to imply the absence of functional elements from the patent claims. Does "ornamentality" also require the claimed elements to be aesthetically attractive? Blisscraft of Hollywood v. United Plastics Co., 294 F.2d 694, 696, 131 U.S.P.Q. 55 (2d Cir.1961), read the ornamentality requirement to mean that the design "must be the product of aesthetic skill and artistic conception. Plaintiff's pitcher has no particularly aesthetic appeal in line, form,

color, or otherwise. It contains no dominant artistic motif either in detail or in its overall conception. Its lid, body, handle and base retain merely their individual characteristics when used in conjunction with each other without producing any combined artistic effect. The reaction which the pitcher inspires is simply that of the usual, useful and not unattractive piece of kitchenware. The design fails to meet the ornamental prerequisite of the statute."

Consider whether a requirement of aesthetic appeal contradicts the notion, expressed in a leading copyright case, that "[i]t would be a dangerous undertaking for persons trained only to the law to constitute themselves final judges of the worth of pictorial illustrations, outside of the narrowest and most obvious limits." Bleistein v. Donaldson Lithographing Co., page 564, above. Compare *Blisscraft* with the more recent rejection of an argument that a patented dolly for garbage cans was not ornamental: the argument "overlooks the important point that design patents are concerned with the *industrial* arts, not the fine arts. The statute refers to 'any . . . ornamental design for an *article of manufacture.*' 35 U.S.C. § 171. Perhaps it is too much to expect that a trash-can dolly be beautiful. It is enough for present purposes that it is not ugly, especially when compared to prior designs." Contico Int'l, Inc. v. Rubbermaid Commercial Products, Inc., 665 F.2d 820, 825, 212 U.S.P.Q. 741 (8th Cir.1981) (emphasis in original).

See generally, Mott, The Standard of Ornamentality in the United States Design Patent Law, 48 A.B.A. J. 548, 643 (1962).

3. During the period 1964–1983, courts held more than 70% of all litigated design patents invalid in cases where validity was in issue. See Lindgren, The Sanctity of the Design Patent: Illusion or Reality? Twenty Years of Design Patent Litigation Since *Compco v. Day–Brite Lighting, Inc.,* and *Sears, Roebuck & Co. v. Stiffel Co.,* 10 Okla. City U.L.Rev. 195 app. II (1985). The Court of Appeals for the Federal Circuit, which has generally loosened the standards for utility patents, see pages 371 to 377, above, may have relaxed the standards for design patents as well. See Reichman, Computer Programs as Applied Scientific Know–How: Implications of Copyright Protection for Commercialized Research, 42 Vand.L.Rev. 639, 664 (1989).

B. COPYRIGHT LAW

MAZER v. STEIN

Supreme Court of the United States, 1954.
347 U.S. 201, 74 S.Ct. 460, 98 L.Ed. 630, 100 U.S.P.Q. 325.

Mr. Justice REED delivered the opinion of the Court.

This case involves the validity of copyrights obtained by respondents for statuettes of male and female dancing figures made of semivitreous china. The controversy centers around the fact that although copyrighted as "works of art," the statuettes were intended for use and used as bases for table lamps, with electric wiring, sockets and lamp shades attached.

Statuette in Mazer v. Stein.

Respondents are partners in the manufacture and sale of electric lamps. One of the respondents created original works of sculpture in the form of human figures by traditional clay-model technique. From this model, a production mold for casting copies was made. The resulting statuettes, without any lamp components added, were submitted by the respondents to the Copyright Office for registration as "works of art" or reproductions thereof under § 5(g) or § 5(h) of the copyright law, and certificates of registration issued. Sales (publication in accordance with the statute) as fully equipped lamps preceded the applications for copyright registration of the statuettes. Thereafter, the statuettes were sold in quantity throughout the country both as lamp bases and as statuettes. The sales in lamp form accounted for all but an insignificant portion of respondents' sales.

Petitioners are partners and, like respondents, make and sell lamps. Without authorization, they copied the statuettes, embodied them in lamps and sold them.

The instant case is one in a series of reported suits brought by respondents against various alleged infringers of the copyrights, all presenting the same or a similar question. Because of conflicting decisions, we granted certiorari.

Petitioners, charged by the present complaint with infringement of respondents' copyrights of reproductions of their works of art, seek here a reversal of the Court of Appeals decree upholding the copyrights. Petitioners in their petition for certiorari present a single question:

> Can statuettes be protected in the United States by copyright when the copyright applicant intended primarily to use the statuettes in the form of lamp bases to be made and sold in quantity and carried the intentions into effect?

> Stripped down to its essentials, the question presented is: Can a lamp manufacturer copyright his lamp bases?

The first paragraph accurately summarizes the issue. The last gives it a quirk that unjustifiably, we think, broadens the controversy. The case requires an answer, not as to a manufacturer's right to register a lamp base but as to an artist's right to copyright a work of art intended to be reproduced for lamp bases. As petitioners say in their brief, their contention "questions the validity of the copyright based upon the actions of respondents." Petitioners question the validity of a copyright of a work of art for "mass" production. "Reproduction of a work of art" does not mean to them unlimited reproduction. Their position is that a copyright does not cover industrial reproduction of the protected article. Thus their reply brief states:

> When an artist becomes a manufacturer or a designer for a manufacturer he is subject to the limitations of design patents and deserves no more consideration than any other manufacturer or designer.

It is not the right to copyright an article that could have utility under § 5(g) and (h) that petitioners oppose. Their brief accepts the copyrightability of the great carved golden salt-cellar of Cellini but adds:

If, however, Cellini designed and manufactured this item in quantity so that the general public could have salt cellars, then an entirely different conclusion would be reached. In such case, the salt cellar becomes an article of manufacture having utility in addition to its ornamental value and would therefore have to be protected by design patent.

It is publication as a lamp and registration as a statute to gain a monopoly in manufacture that they assert is such a misuse of copyright as to make the registration invalid.

No unfair competition question is presented. The constitutional power of Congress to confer copyright protection on works of art or their reproductions is not questioned. Petitioners assume, as Congress has in its enactments and as do we, that the constitutional clause empowering legislation "To promote the Progress of Science and useful Arts, by securing for limited Times to Authors and Inventors the exclusive Right to their respective Writings and Discoveries", Art. I, § 8, cl. 8, includes within the term "Authors" the creator of a picture or a statue. The Court's consideration will be limited to the question presented by the petition for the writ of certiorari. In recent years the question as to utilitarian use of copyrighted articles has been much discussed.

In answering that issue, a review of the development of copyright coverage will make clear the purpose of the Congress in its copyright legislation. In 1790 the First Congress conferred a copyright on "authors of any map, chart, book or books already printed". Later, designing, engraving and etching were included; in 1831 musical composition; dramatic compositions in 1856; and photographs and negatives thereof in 1865.

The Act of 1870 defined copyrightable subject matter as:

> . . . any book, map, chart, dramatic or musical composition, engraving, cut, print, or photograph or negative thereof, or of a painting, drawing, chromo, *statue, statuary, and of models or designs intended to be perfected as works of the fine arts.* (Emphasis supplied.)

The italicized part added three-dimensional work of art to what had been protected previously. In 1909 Congress again enlarged the scope of the copyright statute. The new Act provided in § 4:

> That the works for which copyright may be secured under this Act shall include all the writings of an author.

Some writers interpret this section as being coextensive with the constitutional grant, but the House Report, while inconclusive, indicates that it was "declaratory of existing law" only. Section 5 relating to classes of writings in 1909 read as shown in the margin with subsequent additions not material to this decision.

Significant for our purposes was the deletion of the fine-arts clause of the 1870 Act. Verbal distinctions between purely aesthetic articles and useful works of art ended insofar as the statutory copyright language is concerned.

The practice of the Copyright Office, under the 1870 and 1874 Acts and before the 1909 Act, was to allow registration "as works of the fine arts" of articles of the same character as those of respondents now under challenge. Seven examples appear in the Government's brief *amicus curiae.* In 1910, interpreting the 1909 Act, the pertinent Copyright Regulations read as shown in the margin.[23] Because, as explained by the Government, this regulation "made no reference to articles which might fairly be considered works of art although they might also serve a useful purpose," it was reworded in 1917 as shown below.[24] The *amicus* brief gives sixty examples selected at five-year intervals, 1912–1952, said to be typical of registrations of works of art possessing utilitarian aspects. The current pertinent regulation, published in 37 CFR, 1949, § 202.8, reads thus:

> Works of art (Class G)—(a)—In General. This class includes works of artistic craftsmanship, in so far as their form but not their mechanical or utilitarian aspects are concerned, such as artistic jewelry, enamels, glassware, and tapestries, as well as all works belonging to the fine arts, such as paintings, drawings and sculpture.

So we have a contemporaneous and long-continued construction of the statutes by the agency charged to administer them that would allow the registration of such a statuette as is in question here.

This Court once essayed to fix the limits of the fine arts. That effort need not be appraised in relation to this copyright issue. It is clear Congress intended the scope of the copyright statute to include more than the traditional fine arts. Herbert Putnam, Esq., then Librarian of Congress and active in the movement to amend the copyright laws, told the joint meeting of the House and Senate Committees:

> The term 'works of art' is deliberately intended as a broader specification than 'works of the fine arts' in the present statute with the idea that there is subject-matter (for instance, of applied design, not yet within the province of design patents), which may properly be entitled to protection under the copyright law.

23. "Works of art.—This term includes all works belonging fairly to the so-called fine arts. (Paintings, drawings, and sculpture.)

"Productions of the industrial arts utilitarian in purpose and character are not subject to copyright registration, even if artistically made or ornamented." Rules and Regulations for the Registration of Claims to Copyright, Bulletin No. 15 (1910), 8.

24. "Works of art and models or designs for works of art.—This term includes all works belonging fairly to the so-called fine arts. (Paintings, drawings, and sculpture.)

"The protection of productions of the industrial arts, utilitarian in purpose and character, even if artistically made or ornamented depends upon action under the patent law; but registration in the Copyright Office has been made to protect artistic drawings notwithstanding they may afterwards be utilized for articles of manufacture." 37 CFR, 1939, § 201.4(7).

The successive acts, the legislative history of the 1909 Act and the practice of the Copyright Office unite to show that "works of art" and "reproductions of works of art" are terms that were intended by Congress to include the authority to copyright these statuettes. Individual perception of the beautiful is too varied a power to permit a narrow or rigid concept of art. As a standard we can hardly do better than the words of the present Regulation, § 202.8, naming the things that appertain to the arts. They must be original, that is, the author's tangible expression of his ideas. Such expression, whether meticulously delineating the model or mental image or conveying the meaning by modernistic form or color, is copyrightable. What cases there are confirm this coverage of the statute.

The conclusion that the statues here in issue may be copyrighted goes far to solve the question whether their intended reproduction as lamp stands bars or invalidates their registration. This depends solely on statutory interpretation. Congress may after publication protect by copyright any writing of an author. Its statute creates the copyright. It did not exist at common law even though he had a property right in his unpublished work.

But petitioners assert that congressional enactment of the design patent laws should be interpreted as denying protection to artistic articles embodied or reproduced in manufactured articles. They say:

> Fundamentally and historically, the Copyright Office is the repository of what each claimant considers to be a cultural treasure, whereas the Patent Office is the repository of what each applicant considers to be evidence of the advance in industrial and technological fields.

Their argument is that design patents require the critical examination given patents to protect the public against monopoly. Attention is called to Gorham Mfg. Co. v. White, 14 Wall. 511, 20 L.Ed. 731, interpreting the design patent law of 1842, 5 Stat. 544, granting a patent to anyone who by "their own industry, genius, efforts, and expense, may have invented or produced any new and original design for a manufacture . . . .." A pattern for flat silver was there upheld. The intermediate and present law differs little. "Whoever invents any new, original and ornamental design for an article of manufacture may obtain a patent therefor, ..." subject generally to the provisions concerning patents for invention. § 171, 66 Stat. 805, 35 U.S.C.A. § 171. As petitioner sees the effect of the design patent law:

> If an industrial designer can not satisfy the novelty requirements of the design patent laws, then his design as used on articles of manufacture can be copied by anyone.

Petitioner has furnished the Court a booklet of numerous design patents for statuettes, bases for table lamps and similar articles for manufacture, quite indistinguishable in type from the copyrighted statuettes here in issue. Petitioner urges that overlapping of patent and copyright legislation so as to give an author or inventor a choice between patents and copyrights should not be permitted. We assume petitioner takes the position that protection for a statuette for industrial use can only be obtained by patent, if any protection can be given.

As we have held the statuettes here involved copyrightable, we need not decide the question of their patentability. Though other courts have passed upon the issue as to whether allowance by the election of the author or patentee of one bars a grant of the other, we do not. We do hold that the patentability of the statuettes, fitted as lamps or unfitted, does not bar copyright as works of art. Neither the Copyright Statute nor any other says that because a thing is patentable it may not be copyrighted. We should not so hold.

Unlike a patent, a copyright gives no exclusive right to the art disclosed; protection is given only to the expression of the idea—not the idea itself. Thus, in Baker v. Selden, 101 U.S. 99, 25 L.Ed. 841, the Court held that a copyrighted book on a peculiar system of bookkeeping was not infringed by a similar book using a similar plan which achieved similar results where the alleged infringer made a different arrangement of the columns and used different headings. The distinction is illustrated in Fred Fisher, Inc. v. Dillingham, D.C., 298 F. 145, 151, when the court speaks of two men, each a perfectionist, independently making maps of the same territory. Though the maps are identical each may obtain the exclusive right to make copies of his own particular map, and yet neither will infringe the other's copyright. Likewise a copyrighted directory is not infringed by a similar directory which is the product of independent work. The copyright protects originality rather than novelty or invention—conferring only "the sole right of multiplying copies." Absent copying there can be no infringement of copyright. Thus, respondents may not exclude others from using statuettes of human figures in table lamps; they may only prevent use of copies of their statuettes as such or as incorporated in some other article. Regulation § 202.8 makes clear that artistic articles are protected in "form but not their mechanical or utilitarian aspects." The dichotomy of protection for the aesthetic is not beauty and utility but art for the copyright and the invention of original and ornamental design for design patents. We find nothing in the copyright statute to support the argument that the intended use or use in industry of an article eligible for copyright bars or invalidates its registration. We do not read such a limitation into the copyright law.

Nor do we think the subsequent registration of a work of art published as an element in a manufactured article, is a misuse of the copyright. This is not different from the registration of a statuette and its later embodiment in an industrial article.

"The copyright law, like the patent statutes, makes reward to the owner a secondary consideration." United States v. Paramount Pictures, 334 U.S. 131, 158, 68 S.Ct. 915, 929, 92 L.Ed. 1260. However, it is "intended definitely to grant valuable, enforceable rights to authors, publishers, etc., without burdensome requirements; 'to afford greater encouragement to the production of literary [or artistic] works of lasting benefit to the world.'" Washingtonian Pub. Co. v. Pearson, 306 U.S. 30, 36, 59 S.Ct. 397, 400, 83 L.Ed. 470.

The economic philosophy behind the clause empowering Congress to grant patents and copyrights is the conviction that encouragement of individual effort by personal gain is the best way to advance public welfare through the talents of authors and inventors in "Science and useful Arts." Sacrificial days devoted to such creative activities deserve rewards commensurate with the services rendered.

Affirmed.

Opinion of Mr. Justice DOUGLAS, in which Mr. Justice BLACK concurs.

An important constitutional question underlies this case—a question which was stirred on oral argument but not treated in the briefs. It is whether these statuettes of dancing figures may be copyrighted. Congress has provided that "works of art", "models or designs for works of art", and "reproductions of a work of art" may be copyrighted, 17 U.S.C. § 5, 17 U.S.C.A. § 5; and the Court holds that these statuettes are included in the words "works of art". But may statuettes be granted the monopoly of the copyright?

Article I, § 8 of the Constitution grants Congress the power "To promote the Progress of Science and useful Arts, by securing for limited Times to Authors . . . the exclusive Right to their respective Writings. . . ." The power is thus circumscribed: it allows a monopoly to be granted only to "authors" for their "writings." Is a sculptor an "author" and is his statue a "writing" within the meaning of the Constitution? We have never decided the question.

Burrow–Giles Lithographic Co. v. Sarony, 111 U.S. 53, 4 S.Ct. 279, 28 L.Ed. 349, held that a photograph could be copyrighted.

Bleistein v. Donaldson Lithographing Co., 188 U.S. 239, 23 S.Ct. 298, 47 L.Ed. 460, held that chromolithographs to be used as advertisements for a circus were "pictorial illustrations" within the meaning of the copyright laws. Broad language was used in the latter case, ". . . a very modest grade of art has in it something irreducible, which is one man's alone. That something he may copyright unless there is a restriction in the words of the act." 188 U.S., at page 250, 23 S.Ct. at page 300. But the constitutional range of the meaning of "writings" in the field of art was not in issue either in the Bleistein case nor in F.W. Woolworth Co. v. Contemporary Arts, 344 U.S. 228, 73 S.Ct. 222, 97 L.Ed. 276, recently here on a writ for certiorari limited to a question of damages.

At times the Court has on its own initiative considered and decided constitutional issues not raised, argued, or briefed by the parties. . . . We could do the same here and decide the question here and now. This case, however, is not a pressing one, there being no urgency for a decision. Moreover, the constitutional materials are quite meager and much research is needed.

The interests involved in the category of "works of art," as used in the copyright law, are considerable. The Copyright Office has supplied us with a long list of such articles which have been copyrighted— statuettes, book ends, clocks, lamps, door knockers, candlesticks, inkstands, chandeliers, piggy banks, sundials, salt and pepper shakers, fish bowls, casseroles, and ash trays. Perhaps these are all "writings" in the constitutional sense. But to me, at least, they are not obviously so. It is time that we came to the problem full face. I would accordingly put the case down for reargument.

CAROL BARNHART INC. v. ECONOMY COVER CORP.
United States Court of Appeals, Second Circuit, 1985.
773 F.2d 411, 228 U.S.P.Q. 385.

MANSFIELD, Circuit Judge:

Carol Barnhart Inc. ("Barnhart"), which sells display forms to department stores, distributors, and small retail stores, appeals from a judgment of the Eastern District of New York, Leonard D. Wexler, Judge, granting a motion for summary judgment made by defendant Economy Cover Corporation ("Economy"), which sells a wide variety of display products primarily to jobbers and distributors. Barnhart's complaint alleges that Economy has infringed its copyright and engaged in unfair competition by offering for sale display forms copied from four original "sculptural forms" to which Barnhart holds the copyright. Judge Wexler granted Economy's motion for summary judgment on the ground that plaintiff's mannequins of partial human torsos used to display articles of clothing are utilitarian articles not containing separable works of art, and thus are not copyrightable. We affirm.

The bones of contention are four human torso forms designed by Barnhart, each of which is life-size, without neck, arms, or a back, and made of expandable white styrene. Plaintiff's president created the forms in 1982 by using clay, buttons, and fabric to develop an initial mold, which she then used to build an aluminum mold into which the polystyrene is poured to manufacture the sculptural display form. There are two male and two female upper torsos. One each of the male and female torsos is unclad for the purpose of displaying shirts and sweaters, while the other two are sculpted with shirts for displaying sweaters and jackets. All the forms, which are otherwise life-like and anatomically accurate, have hollow backs designed to hold excess fabric when the garment is fitted onto the form. Barnhart's advertising stresses the forms' uses to display items such as sweaters, blouses, and dress shirts, and states that they come "[p]ackaged in UPS-size boxes for easy shipping and [are] sold in multiples of twelve."

Plaintiff created the first of the forms, Men's Shirt, shortly after its founding in March, 1982, and by the end of July it had attracted $18,000 worth of orders. By December 1982, plaintiff had designed all four forms, and during the first morning of the twice-yearly trade show sponsored by the National Association of the Display Industry

("NADI"), customers had placed $35,000 in orders for the forms. Plaintiff's president maintains that the favorable response from visual merchandisers, Barnhart's primary customers, "convinced me that my forms were being purchased not only for their function but for their artistically sculptured features."

Economy, which sells its wide range of products primarily to jobbers, distributors, and national chain stores, not to retail stores, first learned in early 1983 that Barnhart was selling its display forms directly to retailers. After observing that no copyright notice appeared either on Barnhart's forms or in its promotional literature, Economy contracted to have produced for it four forms which it has conceded, for purposes of its summary judgment motion, were "copied from Barnhart's display forms" and are "substantially similar to Barnhart's display forms." Economy began marketing its product, "Easy Pin Shell Forms," in September 1983. Later in the same month, Barnhart wrote to NADI to complain that Economy was selling exact duplicates of Barnhart's sculptural forms at a lower price and asked it to stop the duplication and underselling. Economy responded with a letter from its counsel dated October 17, 1983 to the Chairman of NADI's Ethics Committee stating that Economy was not guilty of any "underhanded" business practices since Barnhart's forms were not protected by "patent, copyright, trademark, or otherwise."

On the same date (October 17, 1983) Barnhart applied for copyright registration for a number of products, including the four forms at issue here. It identified each of the forms as "sculpture" and sought expedited examination of its applications because of the possibility of litigation over copyright infringement. Copyright registration was granted the same day. Then, on October 18, Barnhart informed Economy that its Easy Pin Shell Forms violated Barnhart's rights and demanded that it discontinue its advertising and sale of the forms. In November 1983, more than 18 months after selling its first form, Barnhart advised its customers that copyright notice had "inadvertently [been] omitted" from the display forms previously distributed and enclosed adhesive stickers bearing a copyright notice, which it asked the customers to affix to unmarked products in inventory.

Barnhart filed this suit in December 1983. Count I charges Economy with violating Barnhart's rights under the Copyright Act, 17 U.S.C. §§ 101–810 (1982), by copying and selling Barnhart's four display forms. Count II alleges that Economy has engaged in unfair competition under the common law of the State of New York. The complaint seeks an adjudication that Economy has infringed Barnhart's copyrights, a preliminary and permanent injunction against Economy's producing, advertising, or selling its forms, damages (consequential, statutory, and punitive), and attorney's fees. Economy moved for summary judgment on the issue of the copyrightability of Barnhart's display forms (and the issue of statutory damages and attorney's fees).

After a hearing on February 3, 1984, Judge Wexler issued an order and opinion on September 12, 1984 granting defendant's motion for summary judgment on the issue of copyrightability. The district court rejected plaintiff's arguments that the issue of copyrightability was an improper subject for summary judgment and that the Copyright Office's issuance of certificates of registration for Barnhart's four forms created an insurmountable presumption of the validity of the copyrights. On the central issue of copyrightability, it reviewed the statutory language, legislative history, and recent case authority, concluding that they all speak with "a single voice," i.e., that a useful article may be copyrighted only to the extent that "there is a physically or conceptually separable work of art embellishing it. . . ." Id. at 370. Applying this test, the district court determined that since the Barnhart forms possessed no aesthetic features that could exist, either physically or conceptually, separate from the forms as utilitarian articles, they were not copyrightable.

On March 6, 1985, 603 F.Supp. 432, Judge Wexler denied Barnhart's motion for reargument. The present appeal followed.

Discussion

Appellant's threshold argument, that the district court erred in ignoring the statutory presumption of validity accorded to a certificate of copyright registration and to the line-drawing expertise of the Copyright Office, can be disposed of briefly. With respect to the prima facie validity of Copyright Office determinations, 17 U.S.C. § 410(c) states:

> In any judicial proceedings the certificate of a registration made before or within five years after first publication of the work shall constitute prima facie evidence of the validity of the copyright and of the facts stated in the certificate. The evidentiary weight to be accorded the certificate of a registration made thereafter shall be within the discretion of the court.

However, "a certificate of registration creates no irrebuttable presumption of copyright validity." Durham Industries, Inc. v. Tomy Corp., 630 F.2d 905, 908 (2d Cir.1980). Extending a presumption of validity to a certificate of copyright registration

> merely orders the burdens of proof. The plaintiff should not ordinarily be forced in the first instance to prove all of the multitude of facts that underline the validity of the copyright unless the defendant, by effectively challenging them, shifts the burden of doing so to the plaintiff.

H.Rep. No. 1476, 94th Cong., 2d Sess. 157, *reprinted in* 1976 U.S.Code Cong. & Ad.News 5659, 5773.

Judge Wexler properly exercised the discretion conferred on him by 17 U.S.C. § 410(c). Once defendant's response to plaintiff's claim put in issue whether the four Barnhart forms were copyrightable, he correctly reasoned that the "mute testimony" of the forms put him in as good a position as the Copyright Office to decide the issue. While the expertise of the Copyright Office is in "interpretation of the law and its application to the facts presented by the copyright application," Norris Industries, Inc. v. I.T. & T., 696 F.2d 918, 922 (11th Cir.), cert. denied, 464 U.S. 818, 104 S.Ct. 78, 78 L.Ed.2d 89 (1983), it is permissible for the district court itself to consider how the copyright law applies to the articles under consideration.

Since the four Barnhart forms are concededly useful articles, the crucial issue in determining their copyrightability is whether they possess artistic or aesthetic features that are physically or conceptually separable from their utilitarian dimension. A "useful article" is defined in 17 U.S.C. § 101 as "an article having an intrinsic utilitarian function that is not merely to portray the appearance of the article or to convey information." Although 17 U.S.C. § 102(a)(5) extends copyright protection to "pictorial, graphic, and sculptural works," the definition of "pictorial, graphic, and sculptural works," at 17 U.S.C. § 101, provides that the design of a useful article

> shall be considered a pictorial, graphic, or sculptural work only if, and only to the extent that, such design incorporates pictorial, graphic, or sculptural features that can be identified separately from, and are capable of existing independently of, the utilitarian aspects of the article.

To interpret the scope and applicability of this language, and the extent to which it may protect useful articles such as the four Barnhart forms, we must turn to the legislative history of the 1976 Copyright Act, which is informative.

Congress, acting under the authority of Art. I, § 8, cl. 8 of the Constitution, extended copyright protection to three-dimensional works of art in the Copyright Act of 1870, which defined copyrightable subject matter as:

> any book, map, chart, dramatic or musical composition, engraving, cut, print, or photograph or negative thereof, or of a painting, drawing, chromo, statue, statuary, and of models or designs intended to be perfected as works of the fine arts. . . . Act of July 8, 1870, ch. 230, § 86, 16 Stat. 198, 212 (repealed 1916).

The Supreme Court upheld an expansive reading of "authors" and "writings" in Burrow–Giles Lithographic Co. v. Sarony, 111 U.S. 53, 60, 4 S.Ct. 279, 282, 28 L.Ed. 349 (1884), rejecting the claim that Congress lacked the constitutional authority to extend copyright protection to photographs and negatives thereof. The Court further contributed to the liberalization of copyright law in Bleistein v. Donaldson Lithographing Co., 188 U.S. 239, 23 S.Ct. 298, 47 L.Ed. 460 (1903) (Holmes, J.), in which it held that chromo-lithographs used on a circus poster were not barred from protection under the copyright laws. In *Bleistein,* Justice Holmes stated his famous "anti-discrimination" principle:

> It would be a dangerous undertaking for persons trained only to the law to constitute themselves final judges of the worth of pictorial illustrations, outside of the narrowest and most obvious limits. At the one extreme some works of genius would be sure to miss appreciation. Their very novelty would make them repulsive

until the public had learned the new language in which their author spoke. It may be more than doubted, for instance, whether the etchings of Goya or the paintings of Manet would have been sure of protection when seen for the first time. At the other end, copyright would be denied to pictures which appealed to a public less educated than the judge. Id. at 251–52, 23 S.Ct. at 300–01.

The Copyright Act of 1909 expanded the scope of the copyright statute to protect not only traditional fine arts, but also "[w]orks of art; models or designs for works of art." However, this language was narrowly interpreted by Copyright Office regulations issued in 1910, which stated in part:

> *Works of art.*—This term includes all works belonging fairly to the so-called fine arts. (Paintings, drawings and sculpture).
>
> Productions of the industrial arts utilitarian in purpose and character are not subject to copyright registration, even if artistically made or ornamented. Copyright Office, Rules and Regulations for the Registration of Claims to Copyright, Bulletin No. 15 (1910), 8.

The prospects for a work of applied art obtaining a copyright were enhanced in December 1948, when the Copyright Office changed the definition of a "work of art" in its Regulation § 202.8:

> *Works of art (Class G)—(a) In General.* This class includes works of artistic craftsmanship, in so far as their form but not their mechanical or utilitarian aspects are concerned, such as artistic jewelry, enamels, glassware, and tapestries, as well as all works belonging to the fine arts, such as paintings, drawings and sculpture. 37 C.F.R. § 202.8 (1949).

While this regulation seemed to expand coverage for works of applied art, it did not explicitly extend copyright protection to industrial design objects.

The next significant historical step was taken not by Congress but by the Supreme Court in its 1954 decision in *Mazer v. Stein,* where it upheld § 202.8 as a proper standard for determining when a work of applied art is entitled to copyright protection, in the context of deciding whether lamps which used statuettes of male and female dancing figures made of semivitreous china as bases were copyrightable.. . .

The Copyright Office implemented *Mazer v. Stein* by promulgating new regulations interpreting § 5(g) of the 1909 Act, which stated in part:

> (c) If the sole intrinsic function of an article is its utility, the fact that the article is unique and attractively shaped will not qualify it as a work of art. However, if the shape of a utilitarian article incorporates features, such as artistic sculpture, carving, or pictorial representation, which can be identified separately and are capable of existing independently as a work of art, such features will be eligible for registration. 37 C.F.R. § 202.10(c) ((1959), as amended June 18, 1959) (revoked 1978).

In an effort to provide some form of protection to "three-dimensional designs of utilitarian articles as such," a number of separate design bills were introduced into Congress. Finally, Title II of a bill passed by the Senate in 1975, S. 22 (The Design Protection Act of 1975), proposed to offer legal protection to the creators of ornamental designs of useful articles. It defined "pictorial, graphic, and sculptural works" to "include two-dimensional and three-dimensional works of fine, graphic, and applied art, photographs, prints and art reproductions, maps, globes, charts, plans, diagrams, and models."

The House, however, responded by passing a strikingly different version. To the text passed by the Senate it added the following:

> Such works shall include works of artistic craftsmanship insofar as their form but not their mechanical or utilitarian aspects are concerned; the design of a useful article, as defined in this section, shall be considered a pictorial, graphic, or sculptural work only if, and only to the extent that such design incorporates pictorial, graphic, or sculptural features that can be identified separately from, and are capable of existing independently of, the utilitarian aspects of the article.

Both of the added clauses were from work of the Copyright Office: the first from its 1948 Regulation § 202.8, approved by the Supreme Court in *Mazer v. Stein;* the second from its post-*Mazer* § 202.10(c). The bill as finally enacted omitted entirely the proposed Title II.

The legislative history thus confirms that, while copyright protection has increasingly been extended to cover articles having a utilitarian dimension, Congress has explicitly refused copyright protection for works of applied art or industrial design which have aesthetic or artistic features that cannot be identified separately from the useful article. Such works are not copyrightable regardless of the fact that they may be "aesthetically satisfying and valuable." H.R.Rep. No. 1476, supra, at 55, 1976 U.S.Code Cong. & Ad.News at 5668.

Applying these principles, we are persuaded that since the aesthetic and artistic features of the Barnhart forms are inseparable from the forms' use as utilitarian articles the forms are not copyrightable. Appellant emphasizes that clay sculpting, often used in traditional sculpture, was used in making the molds for the forms. It also stresses that the forms have been responded to as sculptural forms, and have been used for purposes other than modeling clothes, e.g., as decorating props and signs without any clothing or accessories. While this may indicate that the forms are "aesthetically satisfying and valuable," it is insufficient to show that the forms possess aesthetic or artistic features that are physically or conceptually separable from the forms' use as utilitarian objects to display clothes. On the contrary, to the extent the forms possess aesthetically pleasing features, even when these features are considered in the aggregate, they cannot be conceptualized as existing independently of their utilitarian function.

Appellant seeks to rebut this conclusion by arguing that the four forms represent a concrete expression of a particular idea, e.g., the idea of a woman's blouse, and that the form involved, a human torso, is traditionally copyrightable. Appellant suggests that since the Barnhart forms fall within the traditional category of sculpture of the human body, they should be subjected to a lower level of scrutiny in determining its copyrightability. We disagree. We find no support in the statutory language or legislative history for the claim that merely because a utilitarian article falls within a traditional art form it is entitled to a lower level of scrutiny in determining its copyrightability. Recognition of such a claim would in any event conflict with the anti-discrimination principle Justice Holmes enunciated in Bleistein v. Donaldson Lithographing Co., supra, 188 U.S. at 251–52, 23 S.Ct. at 300.

Nor do we agree that copyrightability here is dictated by our decision in Kieselstein–Cord v. Accessories by Pearl, Inc., 632 F.2d 989 (2d Cir.1980), a case we described as being "on a razor's edge of copyright law." There we were called on to determine whether two belt buckles bearing sculptured designs cast in precious metals and principally used for decoration were copyrightable. Various versions of these buckles in silver and gold sold wholesale at prices ranging from $147.50 to $6,000 and were offered by high fashion and jewelry stores. Some had also been accepted by the Metropolitan Museum of Art for its permanent collection.

In concluding that the two buckles were copyrightable we relied on the fact that "[t]he primary ornamental aspect of the Vaquero and Winchester buckles is conceptually separable from their subsidiary utilitarian function." Id. at 993. A glance at the pictures of the two buckles, coupled with the description in the text, confirms their highly ornamental dimensions and separability. What distinguishes those buckles from the Barnhart forms is that the ornamented surfaces of the buckles were not in any respect required by their utilitarian functions; the artistic and aesthetic features could thus be conceived of as having been added to, or superimposed upon, an otherwise utilitarian article. The unique artistic design was wholly unnecessary to performance of the utilitarian function. In the case of the Barnhart forms, on the other hand, the features claimed to be aesthetic or artistic, e.g., the life-size configuration of the breasts and the width of the shoulders, are inextricably intertwined with the utilitarian feature, the display of clothes. Whereas a model of a human torso, in order to serve its utilitarian function, must have some configuration of the chest and some width of shoulders, a belt buckle can serve its function satisfactorily without any ornamentation of the type that renders the *Kieselstein–Cord* buckles distinctive.

The judgment of the district court is affirmed.

JON O. NEWMAN, Circuit Judge, dissenting:

This case concerns the interesting though esoteric issue of "conceptual separability" under the Copyright Act of 1976. Because I believe the majority has either misunderstood the nature of this issue or applied an incorrect standard in resolving the issue in this case, I respectfully dissent from the judgment affirming the District Court's grant of summary judgment for the defendant. I would grant summary judgment to the plaintiff as to two of the objects in question and remand for trial of disputed issues of fact as to the other two objects in question.

The ultimate issue in this case is whether four objects are eligible for copyright protection. The objects are molded forms of styrene. Each is a life-size, three-dimensional representation of the front of the human chest. Two are chests of males, and two are chests of females. For each gender, one form represents a nude chest, and one form represents a chest clad with a shirt or a blouse.

Section 102(a)(5) of the Act extends copyright protection to "sculptural works," which are defined to include "three-dimensional works of fine, graphic, and applied art" and "works of artistic craftsmanship insofar as their form but not their mechanical or utilitarian aspects are concerned." 17 U.S.C. § 101 (1982). The definition of "sculptural works" contains a special limiting provision for "useful articles":

> the design of a useful article, as defined in this section, shall be considered a . . . sculptural work only if, and only to the extent that, such design incorporates . . . sculptural features that can be identified separately from, and are capable of existing independently of, the utilitarian aspects of the article.

Id. Each of the four forms in this case is indisputably a "useful article" as that term is defined in section 101 of the Act, 17 U.S.C. § 101 (1982), since each has the "intrinsic utilitarian function" of serving as a means of displaying clothing and accessories to customers of retail stores. Thus, the issue becomes whether the designs of these useful articles have "sculptural features that can be identified separately from, and are capable of existing independently of, the utilitarian aspects" of the forms.

This elusive standard was somewhat clarified by the House Report accompanying the bill that became the 1976 Act. The Report states that the article must contain "some element that, *physically or conceptually,* can be identified as separable from the utilitarian aspects of that article." H.R.Rep. No. 1476, 94th Cong., 2d Sess. 55, *reprinted in* 1976 U.S.Code Cong. & Ad.News 5668 (emphasis added). In this Circuit it is settled, and the majority does not dispute, that "conceptual separability" is distinct from "physical separability" and, when present, entitles the creator of a useful article to a copyright on its design. . . .

There are several possible ways in which "conceptual separability" might be understood. One concerns usage. An article used primarily to serve its utilitarian function might be regarded as lacking "conceptually separable" design elements even though those design elements rendered it usable secondarily solely as an artistic work. There is danger in this approach in that it would deny copyright protection to designs of works of art displayed by a minority because they are also used by a majority as useful articles. The copyrightable design of a life-size sculpture of the human body should not lose its copyright protection simply because mannequin manufacturers copy it, replicate it in cheap materials, and sell it in large quantities to department stores to display clothing.

A somewhat related approach, suggested by a sentence in Judge Oakes' opinion in *Kieselstein–Cord,* is to uphold the copyright whenever the decorative or aesthetically pleasing aspect of the article can be said to be "primary" and the utilitarian function can be said to be "subsidiary." 632 F.2d at 993. This approach apparently does not focus on frequency of utilitarian and non-utilitarian usage since the belt buckles in that case were frequently used to fasten belts and less frequently used as pieces of ornamental jewelry displayed at various locations other than the waist. The difficulty with this approach is that it offers little guidance to the trier of fact, or the judge endeavoring to determine whether a triable issue of fact exists, as to what is being measured by the classifications "primary" and "subsidiary."

Another approach, also related to the first, is suggested by Professor Nimmer, who argues that "conceptual separability exists where there is any substantial likelihood that even if the article had no utilitarian use it would still be marketable to some significant segment of the community simply because of its aesthetic qualities." 1 *Nimmer,* supra, § 2.08[B] at 2–96.2. This "market" approach risks allowing a copyright only to designs of forms within the domain of popular art, a hazard Professor Nimmer acknowledges. However, various sculpted forms would be recognized as works of art by many, even though those willing to purchase them for display in their homes might be few in number and not a "significant segment of the community."

Some might suggest that "conceptual separability" exists whenever the design of a form has sufficient aesthetic appeal to be appreciated for its artistic qualities. That approach has plainly been rejected by Congress. The House Report makes clear that, if the artistic features cannot be identified separately, the work is not copyrightable even though such features are "aesthetically satisfying and valuable." H.R. Rep. No. 1476, supra, at 55, 1976 U.S.Code Cong. & Ad.News at 5668. A chair may be so artistically designed as to merit display in a museum, but that fact alone cannot satisfy the test of "conceptual separateness." The viewer in the museum sees and apprehends a well-designed chair, not a work of art with a design that is conceptually separate from the functional purposes of an object on which people sit.

How, then, is "conceptual separateness" to be determined? In my view, the answer derives from the word "conceptual." For the design features to be "conceptually separate" from the utilitarian aspects of the useful article that embodies the design, the article must stimulate in the mind of the beholder a concept that is separate from the concept evoked by its utilitarian function. The test turns on what may reasonably be understood to be occurring in the mind of the beholder or, as some might say, in the "mind's eye" of the beholder. This formulation requires consideration of who the beholder is and when a concept may be considered "separate."

I think the relevant beholder must be that most useful legal personage—the ordinary, reasonable observer. This is the same person the law enlists to decide other conceptual issues in copyright law, such as whether an allegedly infringing work bears a substantial similarity to a copyrighted work. Of course, the ordinary observer does not actually decide the issue; the trier of fact determines the issue in light of the impressions reasonably expected to be made upon the hypothetical ordinary observer. And, as with other issues decided by reference to the reactions of an ordinary observer, a particular case may present undisputed facts from which a reasonable trier could reach only one conclusion, in which event the side favored by that conclusion is entitled to prevail as a matter of law and have summary judgment entered in its favor.

The "separateness" of the utilitarian and non-utilitarian concepts engendered by an article's design is itself a perplexing concept. I think the requisite "separateness" exists whenever the design creates in the mind of the ordinary observer two different concepts that are not inevitably entertained simultaneously. Again, the example of the artistically designed chair displayed in a museum may be helpful. The ordinary observer can be expected to apprehend the design of a chair whenever the object is viewed. He may, in addition, entertain the concept of a work of art, but, if this second concept is engendered in the observer's mind simultaneously with the concept of the article's utilitarian function, the requisite "separateness" does not exist. The test is not whether the observer fails to recognize the object as a chair but only whether the concept of the utilitarian function can be displaced in the mind by some other concept. That does not occur, at least for the ordinary observer, when viewing even the most artistically designed chair. It may occur, however, when viewing some other object if the utilitarian function of the object is not perceived at all; it may also occur, even when the utilitarian function is perceived by observation, perhaps aided by explanation, if the concept of the utilitarian function can be displaced in the observer's mind while he entertains the separate concept of some non-utilitarian function. The separate concept will normally be that of a work of art.

Some might think that the requisite separability of concepts exists whenever the design of a form engenders in the mind of the ordinary observer any concept that is distinct from the concept of the form's utilitarian function. Under this approach, the design of an artistically designed chair would receive copyright protection if the ordinary observer viewing it would entertain the concept of a work of art in addition to the concept of a chair. That approach, I fear, would subvert the Congressional effort to deny copyright protection to designs of useful articles that are aesthetically pleasing. The impression of an aesthetically pleasing design would be characterized by many as the impression of a work of art, thereby blurring the line Congress has sought to maintain. I believe we would be more faithful to the Congressional scheme if we insisted that a concept, such as that of a work of art, is "separate" from the concept of an article's utilitarian function only when the non-utilitarian concept can be entertained in the mind of the ordinary observer without at the same time contemplating the utilitarian function. This temporal sense of separateness permits the designs of some useful articles to enjoy copyright protection, as provided by the 1976 Act, but avoids according protection to every design that can be appreciated as a work of art, a result Congress rejected. The utilitarian function is not truly a separate concept for purposes of "conceptual separateness" unless the design engenders a non-utilitarian concept without at the same time engendering the concept of a utilitarian function.

In endeavoring to draw the line between the design of an aesthetically pleasing useful article, which is not copyrightable, and the copyrightable design of a useful article that engenders a concept separate from the concept of its utilitarian function, courts will inevitably be drawn into some minimal inquiry as to the nature of art. The need for the inquiry is regrettable, since courts must not become the arbiters of taste in art or any other aspect of aesthetics. However, as long as "conceptual separability" determines whether the design of a useful article is copyrightable, some threshold assessment of art is inevitable since the separate concept that will satisfy the test of "conceptual separability" will often be the concept of a work of art. Of course, courts must not assess the *quality* of art, but a determination of whether a design engenders the concept of a work of art, separate from the concept of an article's utilitarian function, necessarily requires some consideration of whether the object *is* a work of art.

Both the trier determining the factual issue of "conceptual separability" and the judge deciding whether the undisputed facts permit a reasonable trier to reach only one conclusion on the issue are entitled to consider whatever evidence might be helpful on the issue, in addition to the visual impressions gained from the article in question. Thus, the fact that an object has been displayed or used apart from its utilitarian function, the extent of such display or use, and whether such display or use resulted from purchases would all be relevant in determining whether the design of the object engenders a separable concept of a work of art. In addition, expert opinion and survey evidence ought generally to be received. The issue need not turn on the immediate reaction of the ordinary observer but on whether visual inspection of the article and consideration of all pertinent evidence would engender in the observer's mind a separate non-utilitarian concept that can displace, at least temporarily, the utilitarian concept.

This approach seems consistent with and may even explain the few cases to have considered the issue, although the language in all of the decisions may not be entirely reconcilable. In *Kieselstein–Cord*, we upheld the copyrightability of the artistic design of two belt buckles. This holding was based upon a conclusion that the design of the buckles was conceptually separate from the utilitarian function of fastening a belt. That view, in turn, was based in part on the undisputed fact that consumers with some frequency wore the buckles as ornamental jewelry at locations other than the waist. The Court apparently concluded that the buckles had created in the minds of those consumers a conception of the design as ornamental jewelry separate from the functional aspect of a belt buckle. Expert testimony supported the view that the buckles "rise to the level of creative art." 632 F.2d at 994. The case was characterized by Judge Oakes as "on a razor's edge of copyright law," id. at 990, as indeed it was; some might have thought that even though some consumers wore the buckle as ornamental jewelry, they still thought of the article as a belt buckle, albeit one so artistically designed as to be appropriate for wearing elsewhere than at the waist. Whether the concept in the mind of the ordinary observer was of a piece of ornamental jewelry separate from the concept of a belt buckle, or only the concept of a belt buckle that could be used either to fasten a belt or decorate clothing at any location was undoubtedly a close question.

In *Trans–World Manufacturing Corp.,* supra, the interesting design of a display case for eyeglasses was deemed to create for the trier of fact a fair question as to whether a concept separable from the utilitarian function existed. By contrast, the designs of the wheel cover in Norris Industries v. I.T. & T., 696 F.2d 918 (11th Cir.), cert. denied, 464 U.S. 818, 104 S.Ct. 78, 78 L.Ed.2d 89 (1983), and the outdoor lighting fixture in *Esquire, Inc. v. Ringer,* supra, were each deemed, as a matter of law, to engender no concept that was separable from the utilitarian function of each article. It evidently was thought that an ordinary observer viewing the articles would have in mind no conception separate from that of a wheel cover (*Norris*) or a lighting fixture (*Esquire*).

Our case involving the four styrene chest forms seems to me a much easier case than *Kieselstein–Cord.* An ordinary observer, indeed, an ordinary reader of this opinion who views the two unclothed forms depicted in figures 1 and 2 below, would be most unlikely even to entertain, from visual inspection alone, the concept of a mannequin with the utilitarian function of displaying a shirt or a blouse. The initial concept in the observer's mind, I believe, would be of an art object, an entirely understandable mental impression based on previous viewing of unclad torsos displayed as artistic sculptures. Even after learning that these two forms are used to display clothing in retail stores, the only reasonable conclusion that an ordinary viewer would reach is that the forms have both a utilitarian function and an entirely separate function of serving as a work of art. I am confident that the ordinary observer could reasonably conclude only that these two forms are not simply mannequins that happen to have sufficient aesthetic appeal to qualify as works of art, but that the conception in the mind is that of a work of art *in addition to and capable of being entertained separately from* the concept of a mannequin, if the latter concept is entertained at all. As appellant contends, with pardonable hyperbole, the design of Michelangelo's "David" would not cease to be copyrightable simply because cheap copies of it were used by a retail store to display clothing.

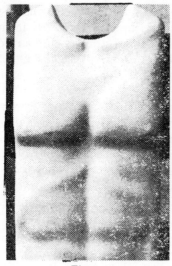

Figure 1   Figure 2

This is not to suggest that the design of every form intended for use as a mannequin automatically qualifies for copyright protection whenever it is deemed to have artistic merit. Many mannequins, perhaps most, by virtue of the combination of the material used, the angular configuration of the limbs, the facial features, and the representation of hair create the visual impression that they are mannequins and not anything else. The fact that in some instances a mannequin of that sort is displayed in a store as an eye-catching item apart from its function of enhancing the appearance of clothes, in a living room as a conversation piece, or even in a museum as an interesting example of contemporary industrial design does not mean that it engenders a concept separate from the concept of a mannequin. The two forms depicted in figures 1 and 2, however, if perceived as mannequins at all, clearly engender an entirely separable concept of an art object, one that can be entertained in the mind without simultaneously perceiving the forms as mannequins at all.

The majority appears to resist this conclusion for two reasons. First, the majority asserts that the appellant is seeking application of a lower level of scrutiny on the issue of copyrightability because the forms depict a portion of the human body. I do not find this argument anywhere in the appellant's briefs. In any event, I agree with the majority that no lower level of scrutiny is appropriate. But to reject a lower level is not to explain why appellant does not prevail under the normal level. Second, the majority contends that the design features of the forms are "inextricably intertwined" with their utilitarian function. This intertwining is said to result from the fact that a form must have "some configuration of the chest and some width of shoulders" in order to serve its utilitarian function. With deference, I believe this approach misapplies, if it does not ignore, the principle of "conceptual separability." Of course, the design features of these forms render them suitable for their utilitarian function. But that fact only creates the issue of "conceptual separability"; it does not resolve it. The question to be decided is whether the design features of these forms create in the mind of an ordinary viewer a concept that is entirely separable from the utilitarian function. Unlike a form that always creates in the observer's mind the concept of a mannequin, each of these unclothed forms creates the separate concept of an object of art— not just an aesthetically pleasing mannequin, but an object of art that in the mind's eye can be appreciated as something other than a mannequin.

Of course, appellant's entitlement to a copyright on the design of the unclothed forms would give it only limited, though apparently valuable, protection. The copyright would not bar imitators from designing human chests. It would only bar them from copying the precise design embodied in appellant's forms.

As for the two forms, depicted in figures 3 and 4 below, of chests clothed with a shirt or a blouse, I am uncertain what concept or concepts would be engendered in the mind of an ordinary observer.

Figure 3 Figure 4

I think it is likely that these forms too would engender the separately entertained concept of an art object whether or not they also engendered the concept of a mannequin. But this is not the only conclusion a reasonable trier could reach as to the perception of an ordinary observer. That observer might always perceive them as mannequins or perhaps as devices advertising for sale the particular style of shirt or blouse sculpted on each form. I think a reasonable trier could conclude either way on the issue of "conceptual separability" as to the clothed forms. That issue is therefore not amenable to summary judgment and should, in my view, be remanded for trial. In any event, I do not agree that the only reasonable conclusion a trier of fact could reach is that the clothed forms create no concept separable from the concept of their utilitarian function.

I would grant summary judgment to the copyright proprietor as to the design of the two nude forms and remand for trial with respect to the two clothed forms.

NOTES

1. Can you reconcile *Barnhart* with Mazer v. Stein? Say that plaintiff had first displayed its works as sculptures in an art gallery and only later marketed them as display forms. What difference, if any, would the court have found between these "sculptures" and the statuettes later used as lamp bases in *Mazer?*

Should the *Barnhart* court have rested its decision on the less troubled ground that the works in issue may have been insufficiently original or expressive to qualify for copyright? In Esquire v. Ringer, 591 F.2d 796, 199 U.S.P.Q. 1 (D.C.Cir.1978), cert. denied, 440 U.S. 908, 99 S.Ct. 1217, 59 L.Ed.2d 456 (1979)—where plaintiff unsuccessfully sought copyright registration for the configuration of an outdoor lighting fixture—the Register of Copyrights, Barbara Ringer argued:

> There are several economic considerations that Congress must weigh before deciding whether, for utilitarian articles, shape alone, no matter how aesthetically pleasing, is enough to warrant copyright protection. First, in the case of some utilitarian objects, like scissors or paper clips, shape is mandated by function. If one manufacturer were given the copyright to the design of such an article, it could completely prevent others from producing the same article. Second, consumer preference sometimes demands uniformity of shape for certain utilitarian articles, like stoves for instance. People simply expect and desire certain everyday useful articles to look the same particular way. Thus, to give one manufacturer the monopoly on such a shape would also be anticompetitive. Third, insofar as geometric shapes are concerned, there are only a limited amount of basic shapes, such as circles, squares, rectangles and ellipses. These shapes are obviously in the public domain and accordingly it would be unfair to grant a monopoly on the use of any particular such shape, no matter how aesthetically well it was integrated into a utilitarian article.

591 F.2d at 801 n.15. Would these concerns be better resolved under copyright law's tests of originality and expressive content than under its tests of physical and conceptual separability?

Does the rule denying copyright to utilitarian features of industrial design make sense? Copyright law embraces such patently utilitarian subject matter as computer programs and instruction manuals. What reason is there to distinguish between two-dimensional verbal works and three-dimensional visual works? If the concern is that copyright for industrial designs will create a monopoly over their functions, would it be better to allow registration—as is done with computer programs and instruction manuals—but to limit rights so that function is not protected?

2. *Separability.* Some courts have required that, to be protected, a design must be "physically separable" from the utilitarian article to which it is attached. See, e.g., Esquire, Inc. v. Ringer, 591 F.2d 796 (D.C.Cir.1978), cert. denied, 440 U.S. 908, 99 S.Ct. 1217, 59 L.Ed.2d 456, reh'g denied, 441 U.S. 917, 99 S.Ct. 2019, 60 L.Ed.2d 389 (1979). Other courts, most notably the Second Circuit Court of Appeals, have followed the suggestion made in the House Report on the 1976 Copyright Act that "conceptually separable" features are also copyrightable. Neither measure is free from difficulty.

Physical Separability. Courts hold that a feature of a useful article is physically separable if the feature can stand alone as a work of art and if separation of the feature will not impair the article's utility. In Ted Arnold Ltd. v. Silvercraft Co., 259 F.Supp. 733 (S.D.N.Y.1966), the court held that a simulated antique telephone that plaintiff used to house a pencil sharpener was copyrightable since the telephone configuration could be physically separated from the pencil sharpener and exist as an independent work of art.

The physical separability test may produce arbitrary distinctions. For example, in Esquire, Inc. v. Ringer, the court held that the configuration of plaintiff's outdoor lighting fixture was not copyrightable because it was not physically separable from the lighting fixture itself. Is the only difference between *Ted Arnold* and *Esquire* that in *Ted Arnold* the copyright claimant had attached its design to a preexisting article, while in *Esquire* it had merged the design into the article itself? If so, could the claimant in *Esquire* have obtained registration for its housing by designing the housing separately, as a work of sculpture, and then welding it to a preexisting lighting fixture?

Conceptual Separability. In Brandir Int'l, Inc. v. Cascade Pacific Lumber Co., 834 F.2d 1142, 5 U.S.P.Q.2d 1089 (2d Cir.1987), a different Second Circuit panel added a new test of conceptual separability to the array explored in *Barnhart's* majority and dissenting opinions. Drawing on an article by Professor Robert Denicola, Applied Art and Industrial Design: A Suggested Approach to Copyright in Useful Articles, 67 Minn.L.Rev. 707 (1983), the court held that "if design elements reflect a merger of aesthetic and functional considerations, the artistic aspects of a work cannot be said to be conceptually separable from the utilitarian elements. Conversely, where design elements can be identified as reflecting the designer's artistic judgment exercised independently of functional influences, conceptual separability exists." 834 F.2d at 1145. Does this test advance analysis of conceptual separability?

Consider whether the following test accurately—or helpfully—synthesizes the prevailing views on conceptual separability: "[A] pictorial, graphic or sculptural feature incorporated in the design of a useful article is conceptually separable if it can stand on its own as a work of art traditionally conceived, and if the useful article in which it is embodied would be equally useful without it." P. Goldstein, Copyright § 2.5.3.1 (1989). Under this formulation, the ornamental belt buckle in

Kieselstein–Cord, discussed in *Barnhart,* would be conceptually separable because the ornamental design could stand on its own as a work of art and the belt buckle would be equally useful without the design; anyone who pays hundreds or even thousands of dollars for an ornamental belt buckle clearly wants something that will do more than hold up his pants. What result would this formulation have produced in *Barnhart?*

3. *"Useful Articles."* Section 101 of the Copyright Act defines "useful article" as "an article having an intrinsic utilitarian function that is not merely to portray the appearance of the article or to convey information. An article that is normally a part of a useful article is considered a 'useful article.'" Is it clear—as the *Barnhart* majority and dissent evidently assumed—that the works in issue there were useful articles? The Venus de Milo could be used as a mannequin for sleeveless blouses, yet few would claim that it is a useful article. Does section 101's use of the adjective "intrinsic" to modify the term "utilitarian function" exclude such marginally useful works from the scope of "useful articles"?

Courts have generally characterized as useful only those articles that have utility as their primary purpose and whose utility lies in their capacity to achieve material ends. One district court held that a toy airplane was a useful article because it possessed "utilitarian and functional characteristics in that it permits a child to dream and to let his or her imagination soar." Gay Toys, Inc. v. Buddy L Corp., 522 F.Supp. 622, 625 (E.D.Mich.1981). The court of appeals reversed: "[A] toy airplane is to be played with and enjoyed, but a painting of an airplane, which is copyrightable, is to be looked at and enjoyed. Other than the portrayal of a real airplane, a toy airplane, like a painting, has no intrinsic utilitarian function." 703 F.2d 970, 973 (6th Cir.1983).

4. *Two–Dimensional Works.* Designs for useful articles appearing in two-dimensional form encounter few hurdles to copyright protection. For example, an architect may obtain copyright for blueprints for a building. Since the intrinsic function of the blueprints is to convey information, they are not useful articles within the terms of section 101.

Does the owner of copyright in a two-dimensional work—architectural plans, for example—have rights against the unauthorized construction of a three-dimensional work—a building—that embodies the plans? Courts have generally held that, so long as the competitor does not reproduce the plans themselves, the copyright owner will have no cause of action. What is the extent of a defendant's liability if it first makes a copy of the plans—itself an infringement—and then builds from the copied plans? In Robert R. Jones Assocs. v. Nino Homes, 858 F.2d 274, 8 U.S.P.Q.2d 1224 (6th Cir.1988), the court held that "one may construct a house which is identical to a house depicted in copyrighted architectural plans, but one may not directly copy those plans and then use the infringing copy to construct the house. As a logical extension of this rule, we hold that, where someone makes infringing copies of another's copyrighted architectural plans, the damages recoverable by the copyright owner include the losses suffered as a result of the infringer's subsequent use of the infringing copies." 858 F.2d at 280.

See generally, Shipley, Copyright Protection for Architectural Works, 37 S.C.L.Rev. 393 (1986).

C. TRADEMARK AND UNFAIR COMPETITION LAW

IN RE MORTON–NORWICH PRODUCTS, INC.

United States Court of Customs and Patent Appeals, 1982.
671 F.2d 1332, 213 U.S.P.Q. 9.

RICH, Judge.

This appeal is from the ex parte decision of the United States Patent and Trademark Office (PTO) Trademark Trial and Appeal Board (board), in application serial No. 123,548, filed April 21, 1977, sustaining the examiner's refusal to register appellant's container configuration on the principal register. We reverse the holding on "functionality" and remand for a determination of distinctiveness.

Background

Appellant's application seeks to register the following container configuration as a trademark for spray starch, soil and stain removers, spray cleaners for household use, liquid household cleaners and general grease removers, and insecticides:

Appellant owns U.S. Design Patent 238,655, issued Feb. 3, 1976, on the above configuration, and U.S. Patent 3,749,290, issued July 31, 1973, directed to the mechanism in the spray top.

The above-named goods constitute a family of products which appellant sells under the word-marks FANTASTIK, GLASS PLUS, SPRAY 'N WASH, GREASE RELIEF, WOOD PLUS, and MIRAKILL. Each of these items is marketed in a container of the same configuration but appellant varies the color of the body of the container according to the product. Appellant manufactures its own containers and stated in its application (amendment of April 25, 1979) that:

Since such first use [March 31, 1974] the applicant has enjoyed substantially exclusive and continuous use of the trademark [i.e., the container] which has become distinctive of the applicant's goods in commerce.

The PTO Trademark Attorney (examiner), through a series of four office actions, maintained an unshakable position that the design sought to be registered as a trademark is not distinctive, that there is no evidence that it has become distinctive or has acquired a secondary meaning, that it is "merely functional," "essentially utilitarian," and non-arbitrary, wherefore it cannot function as a trademark. In the second action she requested applicant to "amplify the description of the mark with such particularity that *any portion* of the alleged mark considered to be non functional [sic] is incorporated in the description." (Emphasis ours.) She said, "The Examiner sees none." Having already furnished two affidavits to the effect that consumers spontaneously associate the package design with appellant's products, which had been sold in the container to the number of 132,502,000 by 1978, appellant responded to the examiner's request by pointing out, in effect, that it is the overall configuration of the container rather than any particular feature of it which is distinctive and that it was intentionally designed to be so, supplying several pieces of evidence showing several other containers of different appearance which perform the same functions. Appellant also produced the results of a survey conducted by an independent market research firm which had been made in response to the examiner's demand for evidence of distinctiveness. The examiner dismissed all of the evidence as "not persuasive" and commented that there had "still not been one iota of evidence offered that the subject matter of this application has been promoted as a trademark," which she seemed to consider a necessary element of proof. She adhered to her view that the design "is no more than a non-distinctive purely functional container for the goods plus a purely functional spray trigger controlled closure . . . essentially utilitarian and non-arbitrary. . .."

Appellant responded to the final rejection with a simultaneously filed notice of appeal to the board and a request for reconsideration, submitting more exhibits in support of its position that its container design was not "purely functional." The examiner held fast to all of her views and forwarded the appeal, repeating the substance of her rejections in her Answer to appellant's appeal brief. An oral hearing was held before the board.

Board Opinion

The board, citing three cases, stated it to be "well-settled" that the configuration of a container "may be registrable for the particular contents thereof if the shape is nonfunctional in character, and is, in fact, inherently distinctive, or has acquired secondary meaning as an indication of origin for such goods." In discussing the "utilitarian nature" of the alleged trademark, the board took note of photographs of appellant's containers for FANTASTIK spray cleaner and GREASE RELIEF degreaser, the labels of which bore the words, respectively, "adjustable easy sprayer," and "NEW! Trigger Control Top," commenting that "the advertising pertaining to applicant's goods promotes the word marks of the various products and the desirable functional features of the containers."

In light of the above, and after detailed review of appellant's survey evidence without any specific comment on it, the board concluded its opinion as follows:

After a careful review of the evidence in the case before us, we cannot escape the conclusion that the container for applicant's products, *the configuration* of which it seeks to register, *is dictated primarily by functional (utilitarian) considerations,* and is therefore unregistrable despite any de facto secondary meaning which applicant's survey and other evidence of record might indicate. As stated in the case of In re Deister Concentrator Company, Inc., 48 CCPA 952, 289 F.2d 496, 129 USPQ 314 (1961), "not every word or configuration that has a de facto secondary meaning is protected as a trademark." [Emphasis ours.]. . . .

II. Determining "Functionality"

A. In general

Keeping in mind, as shown by the foregoing review, that "functionality" is determined in light of "utility," which is determined in light of "superiority of design," and rests upon the foundation "essential to effective competition," Ives Laboratories, Inc. v. Darby Drug Co., 601 F.2d 631, 643, 202 USPQ 548, 558 (2d Cir.1979), and cases cited supra, there exist a number of factors, both positive and negative, which aid in that determination.

Previous opinions of this court have discussed what evidence is useful to demonstrate that a particular design is "superior." In In re Shenango Ceramics, Inc., 53 CCPA 1268, 1273, 362 F.2d 287, 291, 150 USPQ 115, 119 (1966), the court noted that the existence of an expired utility patent which disclosed the *utilitarian advantage of the design* sought to be registered as a trademark was *evidence* that it was "functional." It may also be significant that the originator of the design touts its utilitarian advantages through advertising.

Since the effect upon competition "is really the crux of the matter," it is, of course, significant that there are other alternatives available.

It is also significant that a particular design results from a comparatively simple or cheap method of manufacturing the article. In Schwinn Bicycle Co. v. Murray Ohio Mfg. Co., 339 F.Supp. 973, 980, 172 USPQ 14, 19 (M.D.Tenn.1971), *aff'd,* 470 F.2d 975, 176 USPQ 161 (6th Cir.1972), the court stated its reason for refusing to recognize the plaintiff's bicycle rim surface design as a trademark:

The evidence is uncontradicted that the various manufacturers of bicycle rims in the United States consider it commercially necessary to mask, hide or camouflage the roughened and charred appearance resulting from welding the tubular rim sections together. The evidence represented indicates that the only other process used by bicycle rim manufacturers in the United States is the more complex and more expensive process of grinding and polishing.

B. *The case at bar*

1. *The evidence of functionality*

We come now to the task of applying to the facts of this case the distilled essence of the body of law on "functionality" above discussed. The question is whether appellant's plastic spray bottle is de jure functional; is it the best or one of a few superior designs available? We hold, on the basis of the evidence before the board, that it is not.

The board thought otherwise but did not state a single supporting reason. In spite of her strong convictions about it, neither did the examiner. Each expressed mere opinions and it is not clear to us what either had in mind in using the terms "functional" and "utilitarian." Of course, the spray bottle is highly useful and performs its intended functions in an admirable way, but that is not enough to render the *design* of the spray bottle—which is all that matters here—functional.

As the examiner appreciated, the spray bottle consists of two major parts, a bottle and a trigger-operated, spray-producing pump mechanism which also serves as a closure. We shall call the latter the spray top. In the first place, a molded plastic bottle can have an infinite variety of forms or designs and still *function* to hold liquid. No one form is *necessary* or appears to be "superior." Many bottles have necks, to be grasped for pouring or holding, and the necks likewise can be in a variety of forms. The PTO has not produced one iota of evidence to show that the shape of appellant's bottle was *required* to be as it is for any de facto functional reason, which might lead to an affirmative determination of de jure functionality. The evidence, consisting of competitor's molded plastic bottles for similar products, demonstrates that the same functions can be performed by a variety of other shapes with no sacrifice of any functional advantage. There is no necessity to copy appellant's trade dress to enjoy any of the functions of a spray-top container.

As to the appearance of the spray top, the evidence of record shows that it too can take a number of diverse forms, all of which are equally suitable as housings for the pump and spray mechanisms. Appellant acquired a patent on the pump mechanism (No. 3,749,290) the drawings of which show it embodied in a structure which bears not the slightest resemblance to the appearance of appellant's spray top. The pictures of the competition's spray bottles further illustrate that no particular housing *design* is necessary to have a pump-type sprayer. Appellant's spray top, seen from the side, is rhomboidal, roughly speaking, a design which bears no relation to the shape of the pump mechanism housed within it and is an arbitrary decoration—no more de jure functional than is the grille of an automobile with respect to its under-the-hood power plant. The evidence shows that even the shapes of pump triggers can and do vary while performing the same function.

What is sought to be registered, however, is no single design feature or component but the overall composite design comprising both bottle and spray top. While that design must be *accommodated* to the functions performed, we see no evidence that it was *dictated* by them and resulted in a functionally or economically superior design of such a container.

Applying the legal principles discussed above, we do not see that allowing appellant to exclude others (upon proof of distinctiveness) from using this trade dress will hinder competition or impinge upon the rights of others to compete effectively in the sale of the goods named in the application, even to the extent of marketing them in *functionally* identical spray containers. The fact is that many others are doing so. Competitors have apparently had no need to simulate appellant's trade dress, in whole or in part, in order to enjoy all of the *functional* aspects of a spray top container. Upon expiration of any patent protection appellant may now be enjoying on its spray and pump mechanism, competitors may even copy and enjoy all of its functions without copying the external appearance of appellant's spray top.[3] . . . .

The decision of the board is *reversed* and the case is *remanded* for further proceedings consistent with this opinion.

REVERSED AND REMANDED.

KEENE CORP. v. PARAFLEX INDUSTRIES, INC.

United States Court of Appeals, Third Circuit, 1981.
653 F.2d 822, 211 U.S.P.Q. 201.

SLOVITER, Circuit Judge.

I.

We must in this case consider the scope and meaning of the doctrine of aesthetic functionality pursuant to which the manufacturer of a product is deprived of the right to enjoin imitations of the product's design or configuration.

II.

The facts are relatively straightforward. Keene Corporation (Keene), appellant, manufactures and markets a non-residential lighting fixture, the "Wall Cube", an outdoor wall-mounted luminaire. Luminaires of this type are intended to be mounted (typically 15 to 20 feet in the air) on the outside walls of commercial buildings, such as factories and apartment buildings, to illuminate the adjacent area. The design of the exterior housing of Keene's Wall Cube consists of two oblong right triangular solids, one being a bronze colored metal housing

---

3. It is interesting to note that appellant also owns design patent 238,655 for the design in issue, which, at least pre-sumptively, indicates that the design is *not de jure* functional.

and the other being a slightly smaller glass lens. The two parts are joined along the plane opposite the right angle of each triangular solid to form an object approximating a rectangular solid. When mounted, the glass lens forms the bottom and front of the luminaire, while the metal housing forms the top and back. The design of the Wall Cube is not patented.

In 1979 appellee, Paraflex Industries, Inc. (Paraflex), began to market the housing of an outdoor wall-mounted luminaire which is nearly identical to and was admittedly copied from the exterior of the Keene Wall Cube. Paraflex imports the glass lens and metal housing manufactured for it in Taiwan and sells these parts to electrical manufacturers such as appellee Sim–Kar Lighting Fixture Co., Inc. who supply the electrical parts, and assemble and market the finished product under their own names. For convenience, the look-alike unit will be referred to as the Paraflex unit.

In this action Keene seeks to enjoin marketing of the Paraflex luminaire, alleging false representation of goods, common law trademark infringement and unfair competition under section 43(a) of the Lanham Trade–Mark Act, 15 U.S.C. § 1125(a) (1976) and New Jersey state law. It is conceded that Paraflex copied Keene's Wall Cube, that the exteriors of the two products are virtually identical, and that the Keene unit had acquired a secondary meaning in that it had come to be recognized in the industry as a Keene product. To avoid confusion of source and to prevent palming off, the district court preliminarily and then permanently ordered Paraflex to affix to its luminaire a metal plate containing the statement that the fixture was "Made in Taiwan" for one of Paraflex's customers and that it was "Not a Product of Keene Corporation." The court refused to enter an order either preliminarily or permanently enjoining Paraflex from copying the design of the Keene unit, because the court concluded that there was a functional aspect to the design of the Keene luminaire and therefore its exclusive appropriation by Keene was precluded by the doctrine of aesthetic functionality.

III.

Before turning to the specific findings in this case, it will be useful to review the rationale for and application of the doctrine of aesthetic functionality. One of the essential elements of the law of trademarks, even at common law where it was part of the law of unfair competition, was the principle that no legal protection would be available for products or features that were functional. The purpose of the rule precluding trademark significance for functional features is to prevent the grant of a perpetual monopoly to features which cannot be patented. Sylvania Electric Products v. Dura Electric Lamp Co., 247 F.2d 730, 732 (3d Cir.1957). If this area of the law were to be compartmentalized, one could ascribe to the patent laws protection of those utilitarian features which Congress has chosen to protect, and to the trademark law protection of fanciful or arbitrary features which have achieved recognition as indicia of origin. Products or features which have not qualified for patent protection but which are functional are in the public domain, and are fair game for imitation and copying. Our natural inclination to disapprove of such conduct must give way to the public policy favoring competition, even by slavish copying, of products not entitled to federal patent protection.

The focal question is whether certain features or products are functional, and hence not susceptible of exclusive appropriation. Where the feature is essential to the utility of the item, as was the blue dot on the *Sylvania* photographic flashbulbs which served to indicate in the course of manufacture those bulbs which were defective and to indicate to the consumer those bulbs which later developed air leakage and were unsuitable for use, it is now well-established that the functionality prevents the acquisition of a trademark in that feature. See *Sylvania Electric Products v. Dura Electric Lamp Co.,* supra. The concept of functionality has not been limited, however, to those features that are strictly utilitarian. A more expansive approach was taken in the Restatement (First) of Torts:

> § 742. Functional and Non–Functional Features.
>
> A feature of goods is functional . . . if it affects their purpose, action or performance, or the facility or economy of processing, handling or using them; it is non-functional if it does not have any of such effects.

Restatement of Torts § 742 (1938). This expansive view of functionality is further reflected in the comment to that Restatement section where there is a reference to aesthetic functionality.

The doctrine of aesthetic functionality has been variously articulated and applied by those courts which have had occasion to consider it. The broadest scope to aesthetic functionality, which in turn permits the widest imitation, is illustrated by the Ninth Circuit's decision in Pagliero v. Wallace China Co., 198 F.2d 339 (9th Cir.1952), where the court refused to enjoin copying of hotel china with distinctive designs. The court concluded that even though plaintiff may show that the china acquired a secondary meaning, the designs had become "functional". It stated, "If the particular feature is an important ingredient in the commercial success of the product, the interest in free competition permits its imitation in the absence of a patent or copyright." Id. at 343.[3] Some support for this view, which defines aesthetic functionality in terms of consumer acceptance, may be gleaned from the comment to the Restatement section.[4]

---

3. In Vuitton et Fils S.A. v. J. Young Enterprises, Inc., 644 F.2d 769 (9th Cir. 1981), the Ninth Circuit may have retreated somewhat from its *Pagliero* language since it expressly disapproved the district court's holding that any feature of a product which contributes to consumer appeal and saleability of the product is, as a matter of law, a functional element of that product. Id. at 773.

4. "When goods are bought largely for their aesthetic value, their features may be functional because they definitely contribute to that value and thus aid the performance of an object for which the goods are intended." Restatement of Torts § 742, Comment a (1938).

The difficulty with accepting such a broad view of aesthetic functionality, which relates the doctrine to the commercial desirability of the feature at issue without consideration of its utilitarian function, is that it provides a disincentive for development of imaginative and attractive design. The more appealing the design, the less protection it would receive. As our ambience becomes more mechanized and banal, it would be unfortunate were we to discourage use of a spark of originality which could transform an ordinary product into one of grace. The doctrine of aesthetic functionality need not be construed in such a manner for it to fulfill its important public policy function of protecting free competition.

Instead, the inquiry should focus on the extent to which the design feature is related to the utilitarian function of the product or feature. When the design itself is not significantly related to the utilitarian function of the product, but is merely arbitrary, then it is entitled to protection as a design trademark if it has acquired the distinctiveness necessary to achieve a secondary meaning. Despite the language used in some of the opinions in this area which suggest a broader scope for the doctrine of aesthetic functionality, in fact the holding of many of those cases is consistent with this view of the doctrine.

In the oft-cited concurrence of Judge Rich to the decision of the Court of Customs and Patent Appeals which held that a distinctive wine decanter could function as a trademark, he concluded that the design of the wine bottle was "of such an *arbitrary* nature that depriving the public of the right to copy it is insignificant. . . ." Application of Mogen David Wine Corp., 328 F.2d 925, 933 (C.C.P.A.1964) (emphasis in original). Similarly, the stylized key design featured on the trademark applicant's jewelry was held to be entitled to registration because the key configuration was not dictated by "functional considerations." The court stated:

> The stylized key design in the present case may have the function of attracting purchasers, but the shape of the jewelry, like the mark, is arbitrary and nonessential to a functioning piece of jewelry.

Application of Penthouse Int'l Ltd., 565 F.2d 679, 682 (C.C.P.A.1977). The unique exterior design of a bulk commodity semitrailer which featured a twin hopper design was held to be subject to protection against imitation because its distinctive features were only "incidentally functional." Truck Equipment Service Co. v. Fruehauf Corp., 536 F.2d 1210, 1218 (8th Cir.), cert. denied, 429 U.S. 861, 97 S.Ct. 164, 50 L.Ed.2d 139 (1976). As the Second Circuit stated recently, in upholding the trademark for the uniforms worn by the Dallas Cowboys Cheerleaders, when a feature of the construction of the item is arbitrary, the feature may become a trademark even though it serves a useful purpose. Dallas Cowboys Cheerleaders, Inc. v. Pussycat Cinema, Ltd., 604 F.2d 200, 204 (2d Cir.1979).

On the other hand, where the design is in essence utilitarian, such as the outline shape of the deck of a shaking table held functional in

Application of Deister Concentrator Co., 289 F.2d 496, 505 (C.C.P.A. 1961), the courts have precluded plaintiffs from obtaining a potentially perpetual monopoly. Even mere color, such as the pink color of tablets designed for an upset stomach, may have functional value. In considering this issue recently, Judge Gibbons summarized for this court the distinction between functionality and non-functionality as follows: "Proof of nonfunctionality generally requires a showing that the element of the product serves no purpose other than identification." SK & F, Co. v. Premo Pharmaceutical Laboratories, Inc., 625 F.2d 1055, 1063 (3d Cir.1980).

IV.

The facts in this case present a unique situation. The luminaire itself is essentially a utilitarian product, used to light exterior area. However, because it is a wall-mounted luminaire, as distinguished from a free-standing street lamp, part of its function includes its architectural compatibility with the structure or building on which it is mounted. Thus its design configuration, rather than serving merely as an arbitrary expression of aesthetics, is intricately related to its function.

We believe this was the basis for Judge Meanor's finding of aesthetic functionality and his refusal to enjoin copying of the design of the Keene Wall Cube. His pivotal finding was that "architectural compatibility between the luminaire selected and the configuration or the design of the building on which it is to be placed is often a significant criteria of selection." Although he recognized that architectural compatibility was not the only consideration nor was it always a consideration in the selection process, he found that it was "a sufficiently significant criterion in a sufficiently number [sic] of elections so that the design of a particular wall mounted luminaire has aesthetic or architectural functionality."

Keene argues that the district court's finding that the Wall Cube design was functional is clearly erroneous. It points to evidence in the record to support its position that outdoor wall-mounted luminaires are intended for use in areas where aesthetics are not important. Appellees for their part, stress the following evidence: (1) advertising brochures of numerous manufacturers of outdoor luminaires, including Keene, which depict luminaires being used where aesthetics are important; (2) Keene's advertising brochure, which refers to the Wall Cube as an "architectural luminaire" and boasts that the product's "crisp clean lines match contemporary architectural styling;" (3) testimony of two electrical engineers, the individuals who generally specify the fixtures for a construction project, that aesthetics play a part in their selection of lighting fixtures; (4) testimony of an architect that architects may reject a fixture chosen by an electrical engineer if it is incompatible with the design of the building; and (5) testimony of Paraflex's Vice President that the design of contemporary buildings is characterized by straight lines and basic geometric shapes and that architects therefore demand lighting fixtures which are characterized by straight lines and basic geometric shapes. From our review of the record, we cannot denominate as clearly erroneous the district court's finding that the design of the Wall Cube was functional to a sufficient extent so that on balance the interest in free competition in the luminaire market outweighed Keene's interest in having the exclusive right to the design of the Wall Cube.

Keene argues that the court's finding that its product had acquired a secondary meaning is inherently inconsistent with the court's finding of aesthetic functionality. However, we see nothing inconsistent between a finding that a distinctive design has become sufficiently identified with its original producer to serve as an indication of its source and a finding that the design is nonetheless not insignificantly related to its utilitarian function. This is amply supported by case law. In SK & F, Co. v. Premo Pharmaceutical Laboratories, Inc. the court referred to the "*conjunctive* requirements of secondary meaning and nonfunctionality." 625 F.2d at 1063 (emphasis added). The courts have generally treated the issue of functionality, including aesthetic functionality, as a separate consideration from secondary meaning.

Keene also contends that the court failed to consider whether competition would be substantially hindered by restricting the copying of the Wall Cube, and that this consideration is the test of functionality. As we previously noted, the policy predicate for the entire functionality doctrine stems from the public interest in enhancing competition. Thus both the Restatement and courts considering this issue have referred to the question "whether prohibition of imitation by others will deprive the others of something which will substantially hinder them in competition." Restatement of Torts § 742, Comment a (1938).

Judge Meanor gave ample consideration to this factor. He found that there is "a limited number of designs" possible for an outdoor wall-mounted luminaire. He noted that presently there are around twelve or fifteen wall-mounted luminaires from which to choose, and perceived a danger to competition in the luminaire market if manufacturers were given the exclusive right to a design. Although Keene would have us adopt a standard inquiring whether the specific design features of the product "were competitively essential," we believe that is an unnecessarily narrow view of functionality. This court has previously indicated that merely because there are other shapes and designs "which defendant could use and still produce a workable" product, the design used is not thereby non-functional. The same approach was followed by the Court of Customs and Patent Appeals in Application of Honeywell, 532 F.2d 180, 182 (C.C.P.A.1976), when, in affirming a refusal to register as a mark a round thermostat covering with a transparent center "button" through which the temperature setting could be viewed, the court quoted with approval the opinion of the Patent Appeal Board:

> The fact that both the cover and the thermostat are round does not detract from the functional characteristics thereof. In fact, it may add to the utilitarian aspects. There are only so many basic shapes in which a thermostat or its cover can be made. . . . The fact

that thermostat covers may be produced in other forms or shapes does not and cannot detract from the functional character of the configuration here involved.

Because there are only a limited number of configurations or designs for a luminaire which are architecturally compatible with the type of structures on which they are placed, the selection of a luminaire design does not have the unlimited boundaries as does the selection of a wine bottle or ashtray design, and the court's finding that competition will be stifled is again not clearly erroneous.

Keene's final argument is that the remedy to which it has been relegated, *i.e.,* the injunction requiring labeling imposed by the district court to prevent confusion and palming off, is inadequate to insure against the possibility of confusion of source. Again it urges that it is therefore entitled to an injunction against manufacture and sale of the imitative product. The most direct response to this contention is afforded by the Supreme Court's treatment of a similar claim in the Sears, Roebuck & Co. v. Stiffel Co., 376 U.S. 225, 231–32, 84 S.Ct. 784, 788–89, 11 L.Ed.2d 661 (1964), where it said:

> In the present case the 'pole lamp' sold by Stiffel has been held not to be entitled to the protection of either a mechanical or a design patent. An unpatentable article, like an article on which the patent has expired, is in the public domain and may be made and sold by whoever chooses to do so. What Sears did was to copy Stiffel's design and to sell lamps almost identical to those sold by Stiffel. This it had every right to do under the federal patent laws. That Stiffel originated the pole lamp and made it popular is immaterial. 'Sharing in the goodwill of an article unprotected by patent or trade-mark is the exercise of a right possessed by all— and in the free exercise of which the consuming public is deeply interested.' Kellogg Co. v. National Biscuit Co., supra, 305 U.S., at 122, [59 S.Ct. at 115].

> . . . .

> Sears has been held liable here for unfair competition because of a finding of likelihood of confusion based only on the fact that Sears' lamp was copied from Stiffel's unpatented lamp and that consequently the two looked exactly alike. Of course there could be 'confusion' as to who had manufactured these nearly identical articles. *But mere inability of the public to tell two identical articles apart is not enough to support an injunction against copying or an award of damages for copying that which the federal patent laws permit to be copied.* (Emphasis added.)

For the foregoing reasons, the order of the district court will be affirmed.

W.T. ROGERS CO. v. KEENE, 778 F.2d 334, 339, 228 U.S.P.Q. 145 (7th Cir.1985), POSNER, J.: If the feature is ornamental, fanciful, decorative, like the patterns on a piece of china or of silverware, then the manufacturer can use it as his name, his symbol, his identifying mark. Ornamental, fanciful shapes and patterns are not in short supply, so appropriating one of them to serve as an identifying mark does not take away from any competitor something that he needs in order to make a competing brand. But if the feature is not ornamental or fanciful or whimsical or arbitrary, but is somehow intrinsic to the entire product consisting of this manufacturer's brand and his rivals' brands, trademark production will be denied. The name of this principle is "functionality," on which see, e.g., In re Morton–Norwich Products, Inc., 671 F.2d 1332, 1338–41 (C.C.P.A.1982). Thus the first company to make an airplane cannot use the characteristic shape of an airplane as its trademark, thereby condemning its rivals to build airplanes that won't fly. A firm that makes footballs could not use as its trademark the characteristic oval shape of the football, thereby forcing its rivals to find another shape for their footballs; since they wouldn't be able to sell any round or oblong or hexagonal footballs, that firm would have, not an identifying mark, but a product monopoly, and a product monopoly not for a term of years as under the patent laws but forever.

The football's oval shape is "functional" in the following practical sense: it would be found in all or most brands of the product even if no producer had any desire to have his brand mistaken for that of another producer. A feature functional in this sense—a feature that different brands share rather than a feature designed to differentiate the brands—is unlike those dispensable features of the particular brand that, like an arbitrary identifying name, rivals do not need in order to compete effectively.

NOTES

1. *Functionality.* Consider whether the following definition of functionality is helpful: "In general terms, a product feature is functional if it is essential to the use or purpose of the article or if it affects the cost or quality of the article." Inwood Laboratories, Inc. v. Ives Laboratories, Inc., 456 U.S. 844, 850 n. 10, 102 S.Ct. 2182, 2186 n. 10, 72 L.Ed.2d 606, 214 U.S.P.Q. 1 (1982). What feature that results from investment in artistic design will not affect an article's "cost"? What feature that enhances an article's attractiveness to consumers will not affect its "quality"? Is it any more helpful to hold that a feature is functional if rivals need to employ it to compete effectively? Compete effectively with respect to what? Would it be relevant that, because of plaintiff's success in the marketplace, its configuration has become a standard that competitors must employ if they wish to make products that are interchangeable with plaintiff's? Is genericness rather than functionality the proper touchstone for decision in such cases? See page 224, above.

2. *Aesthetic Functionality.* The doctrine of utilitarian functionality guards against giving perpetual monopolies to works that do not meet the standards for a utility patent or on which a utility patent has expired. Does the doctrine of aesthetic functionality provide a comparable safeguard against perpetual protection of works that do not

qualify for a design patent or copyright or on which the design patent or copyright has expired? The doctrine of aesthetic functionality applied in Pagliero v. Wallace China, discussed in *Paraflex,* is now in retreat among the circuits. See Brunswick Corp. v. Spinit Reel Co., 832 F.2d 513 (10th Cir.1987).

See generally Duft, "Aesthetic" Functionality, 73 Trademark Rep. 151 (1983).

3. *Subject Matter of Expired Design Patents.* Application of Mogen David Wine Corp., 54 C.C.P.A. 1086, 372 F.2d 539, 152 U.S.P.Q. 593 (1967), raised the question whether *Sears* and *Compco,* the Supreme Court's seminal preemption decisions, pp. 103 and 107 above, require that registration be denied to subject matter that has once been covered by a design patent. On an earlier appeal, Application of Mogen David Wine Corp., 51 C.C.P.A. 1260, 328 F.2d 925, 140 U.S.P.Q. 575 (1964), decided before *Sears* and *Compco* were released, the court held that the design patent had no bearing on trademark registrability and remanded for decision on the factual issue, whether applicant's bottle for wines functioned distinctively as a trademark. On the second appeal, the court rebuffed the Commissioner's argument that *Sears* and *Compco* required the court to withdraw from the rule of law announced in the first appeal. The court did, however, affirm the Board's refusal to register on the ground that applicant had not shown that the bottle in fact served to indicate origin.

Because the "prior decision did not expressly consider *Sears* and *Compco,*" Judge Smith concurred for the purpose of more closely examining the implications of the two cases for federal trademark law. Smith started from the Supreme Court's affirmative answer to the question, "whether the use of a state unfair competition law to give relief against the copying of an unpatented industrial design conflicts with the federal patent laws," and concluded that "the Supreme Court did not purport to consider or to decide the boundaries between federal patent law and trademark law." Smith acknowledged that "the heart of the controversy here is the *duration* of these interests"—patent law providing for a limited term, trademark law for an indefinite term—but brushed aside the Commissioner's argument that applicant was seeking a "perpetual patent." Since the objectives of the two laws are discrete, Smith reasoned, each law is to be judged independently of the other. "The solicitor's brief portrays appellant as attempting to extract something from the 'public domain,' contrary to federal law. If the public recognizes and accepts appellant's container shape in a trademark sense, appellant seeks only federal recognition of that public interest. It is the public that is protected. . . . Perhaps the solicitor's argument is that the public has the 'right' to be confused, mistaken or deceived, or that recognizing the narrow interest of trademark owners in preventing confusion, mistake and deception is so great an 'evil' that sacrificing the public interest is a small price to pay. It seems to me that confusion in commerce would be an unnecessary and great price to pay." 372 F.2d at 542-45.

Seven years later, in Application of Honeywell, Inc., 497 F.2d 1344, 181 U.S.P.Q. 821 (C.C.P.A.1974), cert. denied, 419 U.S. 1080, 95 S.Ct. 669, 42 L.Ed.2d 674, 184 U.S.P.Q. 129, the court endorsed Judge Smith's rationale and rejected the argument that the subject matter of expired design patents should be treated on the same footing as the subject matter of expired utility patents. "We believe the solicitor has failed to draw a crucial distinction between functional subject matter disclosed in utility patents and subject matter disclosed in design patents, which may or may not be functional, in the context of their relationship with trademarks." 497 F.2d at 1347.

4. *Design Patent, Copyright, Trademark and Unfair Competition Compared.* Design patent, copyright, trademark and unfair competition law reveal several parallels, divergences and overlaps in their protection of industrial design. The most striking parallel between these four bodies of law is their denial of protection to functional subject matter. The CAFC has relied on a determination that subject matter was functional for purposes of the design patent law to conclude that it was also functional—and unprotectible—under state and federal unfair competition law. Power Controls Corp. v. Hybrinetics, Inc., 806 F.2d 234, 231 U.S.P.Q. 774 (Fed.Cir.1986).

An important difference between design patent, copyright, trademark and unfair competition law lies in the conduct that they proscribe. Like patents generally, a design patent is infringed any time the invention is made, used or sold without the patent owner's permission. See page 506, above. Copyright law requires the copyright owner to prove copying and unlawful appropriation. See page 714, above. Trademark and unfair competition law do not require proof of copying, but do require proof that consumers are likely to be confused. See page 341, above. See also Unette Corp. v. Unit Pack Co., 785 F.2d 1026, 1029, 228 U.S.P.Q. 933 (Fed.Cir.1986) ("Likelihood of confusion as to the source of the goods is not a necessary or appropriate factor for determining infringement of a design patent.")

The Court of Customs and Patent Appeals—the CAFC's predecessor—held that a design patent can issue on a copyrighted work. In re Yardley, 493 F.2d 1389, 181 U.S.P.Q. 331 (C.C.P.A.1974). The Copyright Office, by contrast, will not register a claim to copyright for subject matter on which a design patent has issued. 37 C.F.R. § 202.10(a) (1989). Can a creator desiring dual protection circumvent the Copyright Office rule by obtaining a copyright registration before her design patent issues?

NOTE: PROPOSED INDUSTRIAL DESIGN LEGISLATION

No intellectual property topic has been on the legislative agenda longer than the question of protection for industrial design. Proposals date to H.R. 11321, 63d Cong., 2d Sess. (1914). The constituencies proposing and opposing industrial design bills have shifted over the years. In the early years, dress designers backed the legislation and were opposed by retailers and manufacturers. More recently, industrial and typeface designers have been the principal supporters of design legislation; they have been opposed by automobile insurers worried about the increased cost of replacement parts. See generally, The Industrial Innovation and Technology Act: Hearing on S. 791 Before the Subcomm. on Patents, Copyrights and Trademarks of the Senate Comm. on the Judiciary, 100th Cong., 1st Sess. 213 (1987) (Statement of Ralph Oman, Register of Copyrights.)

H.R. 3499, 101st Cong., 1st Sess. (1989), typifies contemporary legislative proposals. The bill would entitle the "designer or other proprietor of an original design of a useful article which makes the article attractive or distinct in appearance to the purchasing or using public" to ten years of protection beginning on the date of publication of registration for the design, or the date the design is first made public, whichever occurs first. The bill contains three definitions:

(1) A 'useful article' is an article which in normal use has an intrinsic utilitarian function that is not merely to portray the appearance of the article or to convey information. An article which normally is a part of a useful article shall be deemed to be a useful article.

(2) The 'design of a useful article', hereinafter referred to as a 'design', consists of those aspects or elements of the article, including its two-dimensional or three-dimensional features of shape and surface, which make up the appearance of the article. The design must be fixed in a useful article to be protectable under this Act.

(3) A design is 'original' if it is the independent creation of a designer who did not copy it from another source.

H.R. 3499 would exclude protection for designs that are "not original;" that are "staple or commonplace, such as standard geometric figures, familiar symbols, emblems, or motifs; or other shapes, patterns, or configurations which have become common, prevalent, or ordinary;" that are "dictated solely by a utilitarian function of the article that embodies it;" or that are "composed of three-demensional [sic] features of shape and surface with respect to men's, women's, and children's apparel, including undergarments and outerwear."

The bill conditions the recovery of damages or profits on the affixation of a design notice "except on proof that the infringer was notified of the design protection and continued to infringe thereafter, in which event damages or profits may be recovered only for infringement occurring after such notice." Omission of notice would not otherwise affect protection under the bill. But failure to apply for registration within one year after the design was first made public would forfeit protection.

H.R. 3499 defines infringement to include the unauthorized manufacture, importation, sale or distribution of any "infringing article"—defined as "any article, the design of which has been copied from the protected design, without the consent of the proprietor." The bill authorizes injunctive relief, awards of damages—including increased damages—profits and costs, including attorney's fees. The bill would vest responsibility for administering the Act in the Register of Copy-rights.

D. FEDERAL PREEMPTION

BONITO BOATS, INC. v. THUNDER CRAFT BOATS, INC.

Supreme Court of the United States, 1989.
—— U.S. ——, 109 S.Ct. 971, 103 L.Ed.2d 118, 9 U.S.P.Q.2d 1847.

Justice O'CONNOR delivered the opinion of the Court.

We must decide today what limits the operation of the federal patent system places on the States' ability to offer substantial protection to utilitarian and design ideas which the patent laws leave otherwise unprotected. In Interpart Corp. v. Italia, 777 F.2d 678 (1985), the Court of Appeals for the Federal Circuit concluded that a California law prohibiting the use of the "direct molding process" to duplicate unpatented articles posed no threat to the policies behind the federal patent laws. In this case, the Florida Supreme Court came to a contrary conclusion. It struck down a Florida statute which prohibits the use of the direct molding process to duplicate unpatented boat hulls, finding that the protection offered by the Florida law conflicted with the balance struck by Congress in the federal patent statute between the encouragement of invention and free competition in unpatented ideas. We granted certiorari to resolve the conflict, and we now affirm the judgment of the Florida Supreme Court.

I

In September 1976, Petitioner Bonito Boats, Inc. (Bonito), a Florida Corporation, developed a hull design for a fiberglass recreational boat which it marketed under the trade name Bonito Boat Model 5VBR. App. 5. Designing the boat hull required substantial effort on the part of Bonito. A set of engineering drawings was prepared, from which a hardwood model was created. The hardwood model was then sprayed with fiberglass to create a mold, which then served to produce the finished fiberglass boats for sale. The 5VBR was placed on the market sometime in September 1976. There is no indication in the record that a patent application was ever filed for protection of the utilitarian or design aspects of the hull, or for the process by which the hull was manufactured. The 5VBR was favorably received by the boating public, and "a broad interstate market" developed for its sale.

In May 1983, after the Bonito 5VBR had been available to the public for over six years, the Florida Legislature enacted Fla.Stat. § 559.94 (1987). The statute makes "[i]t . . . unlawful for any person to use the direct molding process to duplicate for the purpose of sale any manufactured vessel hull or component part of a vessel made by another without the written permission of that other person." § 559.94(2). The statute also makes it unlawful for a person to "knowingly sell a vessel hull or component part of a vessel duplicated in violation of subsection (2)." Damages, injunctive relief, and attorney's fees are made available to "[a]ny person who suffers injury or damage as the result of a violation" of the statute. The statute was made applicable to vessel hulls or component parts duplicated through the use of direct molding after July 1, 1983. § 559.94(5).

On December 21, 1984, Bonito filed this action in the Circuit Court of Orange County, Florida. The complaint alleged that respondent here, Thunder Craft Boats, Inc. (Thunder Craft), a Tennessee corporation, had violated the Florida statute by using the direct molding process to duplicate the Bonito 5VBR fiberglass hull, and had knowingly sold such duplicates in violation of the Florida statute. Bonito sought "a temporary and permanent injunction prohibiting [Thunder Craft] from continuing to unlawfully duplicate and sell Bonito Boat hulls or components," as well as an accounting of profits, treble damages, punitive damages, and attorney's fees. Respondent filed a motion to dismiss the complaint, arguing that under this Court's decisions in Sears, Roebuck & Co. v. Stiffel Co., 376 U.S. 225, 84 S.Ct. 784, 11 L.Ed. 2d 661 (1964), and Compco Corp. v. Day–Brite Lighting, Inc., 376 U.S. 234, 84 S.Ct. 779, 11 L.Ed.2d 669 (1964), the Florida statute conflicted with federal patent law and was therefore invalid under the Supremacy Clause of the Federal Constitution. The trial court granted respondent's motion, and a divided Court of Appeals affirmed the dismissal of petitioner's complaint.

On discretionary review, a sharply divided Florida Supreme Court agreed with the lower courts' conclusion that the Florida law impermissibly interfered with the scheme established by the federal patent laws. The majority read our decisions in *Sears* and *Compco* for the proposition that "when an article is introduced into the public domain, only a patent can eliminate the inherent risk of competition and then but for a limited time." 515 So.2d, at 222. Relying on the Federal Circuit's decision in the *Interpart* case, the three dissenting judges argued that the Florida anti-direct molding provision "does not prohibit the copying of an unpatented item. It prohibits one method of copying; the item remains in the public domain." 515 So.2d, at 223 (Shaw, J., dissenting).

II

Article I, § 8, cl. 8, of the Constitution gives Congress the power "[t]o promote the Progress of Science and the useful Arts, by securing for limited Times to Authors and Inventors the exclusive Right to their respective Writings and Discoveries." The Patent Clause itself reflects a balance between the need to encourage innovation and the avoidance of monopolies which stifle competition without any concomitant advance in the "Progress of Science and the useful Arts." As we have noted in the past, the clause contains both a grant of power and certain limitations upon the exercise of that power. Congress may not create patent monopolies of unlimited duration, nor may it "authorize the issuance of patents whose effects are to remove existent knowledge from the public domain, or to restrict free access to materials already available." Graham v. John Deere Co. of Kansas City, 383 U.S. 1, 6, 86 S.Ct. 684, 688, 15 L.Ed.2d 545 (1966).

From their inception, the federal patent laws have embodied a careful balance between the need to promote innovation and the recognition that imitation and refinement through imitation are both necessary to invention itself and the very lifeblood of a competitive economy. . . .

The applicant whose invention satisfies the requirements of novelty, nonobviousness, and utility, and who is willing to reveal to the public the substance of his discovery and "the best mode . . . of carrying out his invention," 35 U.S.C. § 112, is granted "the right to exclude others from making, using, or selling the invention throughout the United States," for a period of 17 years. 35 U.S.C. § 154. The federal patent system thus embodies a carefully crafted bargain for encouraging the creation and disclosure of new, useful, and nonobvious advances in technology and design in return for the exclusive right to practice the invention for a period of years. "[The inventor] may keep his invention secret and reap its fruits indefinitely. In consideration of its disclosure and the consequent benefit to the community, the patent is granted. An exclusive enjoyment is guaranteed him for seventeen years, but upon expiration of that period, the knowledge of the invention inures to the people, who are thus enabled without restriction to practice it and profit by its use." United States v. Dubilier Condenser Corp., 289 U.S. 178, 186–187, 53 S.Ct. 554, 557, 77 L.Ed. 1114 (1933).

The attractiveness of such a bargain, and its effectiveness in inducing creative effort and disclosure of the results of that effort, depend almost entirely on a backdrop of free competition in the exploitation of unpatented designs and innovations. The novelty and nonobviousness requirements of patentability embody a congressional understanding, implicit in the Patent Clause itself, that free exploitation of ideas will be the rule, to which the protection of a federal patent is the exception. Moreover, the ultimate goal of the patent system is to bring new designs and technologies into the public domain through disclosure. State law protection for techniques and designs whose disclosure has already been induced by market rewards may conflict with the very purpose of the patent laws by decreasing the range of ideas available as the building blocks of further innovation. The offer of federal protection from competitive exploitation of intellectual property would be rendered meaningless in a world where substantially similar state law protections were readily available. To a limited extent, the federal patent laws must determine not only what is protected, but also what is free for all to use.

Thus our past decisions have made clear that state regulation of intellectual property must yield to the extent that it clashes with the balance struck by Congress in our patent laws. The tension between the desire to freely exploit the full potential of our inventive resources and the need to create an incentive to deploy those resources is constant. Where it is clear how the patent laws strike that balance in a particular circumstance, that is not a judgment the States may second guess. We have long held that after the expiration of a federal patent, the subject matter of the patent passes to the free use of the public as a matter of federal law. Where the public has paid the congressionally mandated price for disclosure, the States may not render the exchange fruitless by offering patent-like protection to the subject matter of the expired patent. . . .

At the heart of *Sears* and *Compco* is the conclusion that the efficient operation of the federal patent system depends upon substantially free trade in publicly known, unpatented design and utilitarian conceptions. In *Sears,* the state law offered "the equivalent of a patent monopoly," 376 U.S., at 233, 84 S.Ct., at 789, in the functional aspects of a product which had been placed in public commerce absent the protection of a valid patent. While, as noted above, our decisions since *Sears* have taken a decidedly less rigid view of the scope of federal pre-emption under the patent laws, e.g., *Kewanee,* supra, 416 U.S., at 479–480, 94 S.Ct., at 1885–1886, we believe that the *Sears* Court correctly concluded that the States may not offer patent-like protection to intellectual creations which would otherwise remain unprotected as a matter of federal law. Both the novelty and the nonobviousness requirements of federal patent law are grounded in the notion that concepts within the public grasp, or those so obvious that they readily could be, are the tools of creation available to all. They provide the baseline of free competition upon which the patent system's incentive to creative effort depends. A state law that substantially interferes with the enjoyment of an unpatented utilitarian or design conception which has been freely disclosed by its author to the public at large impermissibly contravenes the ultimate goal of public disclosure and use which is the centerpiece of federal patent policy. Moreover, through the creation of patent-like rights, the States could essentially redirect inventive efforts away from the careful criteria of patentability developed by Congress over the last 200 years. We understand this to be the reasoning at the core of our decisions in *Sears* and *Compco* and we reaffirm that reasoning today.

III

We believe that the Florida statute at issue in this case so substantially impedes the public use of the otherwise unprotected design and utilitarian ideas embodied in unpatented boat hulls as to run afoul of the teaching of our decisions in *Sears* and *Compco*. It is readily apparent that the Florida statute does not operate to prohibit "unfair competition" in the usual sense that the term is understood. The law of unfair competition has its roots in the common-law tort of deceit: its general concern is with protecting *consumers* from confusion as to source. While that concern may result in the creation of "quasi-property rights" in communicative symbols, the focus is on the protection of consumers, not the protection of producers as an incentive to product innovation. Judge Hand captured the distinction well in

Crescent Tool Co. v. Kilborn & Bishop Co., 247 F. 299, 301 (CA2 1917), where he wrote:

> [T]he plaintiff has the right not to lose his customers through false representations that those are his wares which in fact are not, but he may not monopolize any design or pattern, however trifling. The defendant, on the other hand, may copy plaintiff's goods slavishly down to the minutest detail: but he may not represent himself as the plaintiff in their sale.

With some notable exceptions, including the interpretation of the Illinois law of unfair competition at issue in *Sears* and *Compco,* see *Sears,* supra, 376 U.S., at 227–228, n. 2, 84 S.Ct., at 786–787, n. 2, the common-law tort of unfair competition has been limited to protection against copying of nonfunctional aspects of consumer products which have acquired secondary meaning such that they operate as a designation of source. The "protection" granted a particular design under the law of unfair competition is thus limited to one context where consumer confusion is likely to result; the design "idea" itself may be freely exploited in all other contexts.

In contrast to the operation of unfair competition law, the Florida statute is aimed directly at preventing the exploitation of the design and utilitarian conceptions embodied in the product itself. The sparse legislative history surrounding its enactment indicates that it was intended to create an inducement for the improvement of boat hull designs. See Transcript of Meeting of Transportation Committee, Florida House of Representatives, May 3, 1983, reprinted at App. 22. ("[T]here is no inducement for [a] quality boat manufacturer to improve these designs and secondly, if he does, it is immediately copied. This would prevent that and allow him recourse in circuit court"). To accomplish this goal, the Florida statute endows the original boat hull manufacturer with rights against the world, similar in scope and operation to the rights accorded a federal patentee. Like the patentee, the beneficiary of the Florida statute may prevent a competitor from "making" the product in what is evidently the most efficient manner available and from "selling" the product when it is produced in that fashion. The Florida scheme offers this protection for an unlimited number of years to all boat hulls and their component parts, without regard to their ornamental or technological merit. Protection is available for subject matter for which patent protection has been denied or has expired, as well as for designs which have been freely revealed to the consuming public by their creators.

In this case, the Bonito 5VBR fiberglass hull has been freely exposed to the public for a period in excess of six years. For purposes of federal law, it stands in the same stead as an item for which a patent has expired or been denied: it is unpatented and unpatentable. Whether because of a determination of unpatentability or other commercial concerns, petitioner chose to expose its hull design to the public in the marketplace, eschewing the bargain held out by the federal patent system of disclosure in exchange for exclusive use. Yet, the

Florida statute allows petitioner to reassert a substantial property right in the idea, thereby constricting the spectrum of useful public knowledge. Moreover, it does so without the careful protections of high standards of innovation and limited monopoly contained in the federal scheme. We think it clear that such protection conflicts with the federal policy "that all ideas in general circulation be dedicated to the common good unless they are protected by a valid patent." Lear, Inc. v. Adkins, 395 U.S., at 668, 89 S.Ct., at 1910.

That the Florida statute does not remove all means of reproduction and sale does not eliminate the conflict with the federal scheme. In essence, the Florida law prohibits the entire public from engaging in a form of reverse engineering of a product in the public domain. This is clearly one of the rights vested in the federal patent holder, but has never been a part of state protection under the law of unfair competition or trade secrets. The duplication of boat hulls and their component parts may be an essential part of innovation in the field of aquadynamic design. Variations as to size and combination of various elements may lead to significant advances in the field. Reverse engineering of chemical and mechanical articles in the public domain often leads to significant advances in technology. If Florida may prohibit this particular method of study and recomposition of an unpatented article, we fail to see the principle that would prohibit a State from banning the use of chromatography in the reconstitution of unpatented chemical compounds, or the use of robotics in the duplication of machinery in the public domain.

Moreover, as we noted in *Kewanee,* the competitive reality of reverse engineering may act as a spur to the inventor, creating an incentive to develop inventions which meet the rigorous requirements of patentability. The Florida statute substantially reduces this competitive incentive, thus eroding the general rule of free competition upon which the attractiveness of the federal patent bargain depends. The protections of state trade secret law are most effective at the developmental stage, before a product has been marketed and threat of reverse engineering becomes real. During this period, patentability will often be an uncertain prospect, and to a certain extent, the protection offered by trade secret law may "dovetail" with the incentives created by the federal patent monopoly. In contrast, under the Florida scheme, the would-be inventor is aware from the outset of his efforts that rights against the public are available regardless of his ability to satisfy the rigorous standards of patentability. Indeed, it appears that even the most mundane and obvious changes in the design of a boat hull will trigger the protections of the statute. See Fla.Stat. § 559.94(2) (1987) (protecting "any manufactured vessel hull or component part"). Given the substantial protection offered by the Florida scheme, we cannot dismiss as hypothetical the possibility that it will become a significant competitor to the federal patent laws, offering investors similar protection without the *quid pro quo* of substantial creative effort required by the federal statute. The prospect of all 50 States establishing similar protections for preferred industries without the rigorous requirements of patentability prescribed by Congress could pose a substantial threat to the patent system's ability to accomplish its mission of promoting progress in the useful arts.

Finally, allowing the States to create patent-like rights in various products in public circulation would lead to administrative problems of no small dimension. The federal patent scheme provides a basis for the public to ascertain the status of the intellectual property embodied in any article in general circulation. Through the application process, detailed information concerning the claims of the patent holder is compiled in a central location. The availability of damages in an infringement action is made contingent upon affixing a notice of patent to the protected article. The notice requirement is designed "for the information of the public," Wine Railway Appliance Co. v. Enterprise Railway Equipment Co., 297 U.S. 387, 397, 56 S.Ct. 528, 531, 80 L.Ed. 736 (1936), and provides a ready means of discerning the status of the intellectual property embodied in an article of manufacture or design. The public may rely upon the lack of notice in exploiting shapes and designs accessible to all.

The Florida scheme blurs this clear federal demarcation between public and private property. One of the fundamental purposes behind the Patent and Copyright Clauses of the Constitution was to promote national uniformity in the realm of intellectual property. Since the Patent Act of 1800, Congress has lodged exclusive jurisdiction of actions "arising under" the patent laws in the federal courts, thus allowing for the development of a uniform body of law in resolving the constant tension between private right and public access. Recently, Congress conferred exclusive jurisdiction of all patent appeals on the Court of Appeals for the Federal Circuit, in order to "provide nationwide uniformity in patent law." H.R.Rep. No. 97–312, p. 20 (1981). This purpose is frustrated by the Florida scheme, which renders the status of the design and utilitarian "ideas" embodied in the boat hulls it protects uncertain. Given the inherently ephemeral nature of property in ideas, and the great power such property has to cause harm to the competitive policies which underlay the federal patent laws, the demarcation of broad zones of public and private right is "the type of regulation that demands a uniform national rule." Ray v. Atlantic Richfield Co., 435 U.S. 151, 179, 98 S.Ct. 988, 1005, 55 L.Ed.2d 179 (1978). Absent such a federal rule, each State could afford patent-like protection to particularly favored home industries, effectively insulating them from competition from outside the State.

Petitioner and its supporting *amici* place great weight on the contrary decision of the Court of Appeals for the Federal Circuit in *Interpart Corp. v. Italia.* In upholding the application of the California "antidirect molding" statute to the duplication of unpatented automobile mirrors, the Federal Circuit stated: "The statute prevents unscrupulous competitors from obtaining a product and using it as the 'plug' for making a mold. The statute does not prohibit copying the design of the product in any other way; the latter if in the public domain, is free for anyone to make, use or sell." 777 F.2d, at 685. The court went on to indicate that "the patent laws 'say nothing about the right to copy or the right to use, they speak only in terms of the right to exclude.' " Ibid., quoting Mine Safety Appliances Co. v. Electric Storage Battery Co., 56 C.C.P.A. (Pat.) 863, 864, n. 2, 405 F.2d 901, 902, n. 2 (1969).

We find this reasoning defective in several respects. The Federal Circuit apparently viewed the direct molding statute at issue in *Interpart* as a mere regulation of the use of chattels. Yet, the very purpose of antidirect molding statutes is to "reward" the "inventor" by offering substantial protection against public exploitation of his or her idea embodied in the product. Such statutes would be an exercise in futility if they did not have precisely the effect of substantially limiting the ability of the public to exploit an otherwise unprotected idea. As *amicus* points out, the direct molding process itself has been in use since the early 1950's. Indeed, U.S. Patent No. 3,419,646, issued to Robert L. Smith in 1968, explicitly discloses and claims a method for the direct molding of boat hulls. The specifications of the Smith Patent indicate that "[i]t is a major object of the present invention to provide a method for making large molded boat hull molds at very low cost, once a protype hull has been provided." Id., at 15a. In fact, it appears that Bonito employed a similar process in the creation of its own production mold. It is difficult to conceive of a more effective method of creating substantial property rights in an intellectual creation than to eliminate the most efficient method for its exploitation. *Sears* and *Compco* protect more than the right of the public to contemplate the abstract beauty of an otherwise unprotected intellectual creation—they assure its efficient reduction to practice and sale in the marketplace. . . .

Our decisions since *Sears* and *Compco* have made it clear that the Patent and Copyright Clauses do not, by their own force or by negative implication, deprive the States of the power to adopt rules for the promotion of intellectual creation within their own jurisdictions. See *Aronson*, 440 U.S., at 262, 99 S.Ct., at 1099; Goldstein v. California, 412 U.S. 546, 552–561, 93 S.Ct. 2303, 2307–2312, 37 L.Ed.2d 163 (1973); *Kewanee*, 416 U.S., at 478–479, 94 S.Ct., at 1884–1885. Thus, where "Congress determines that neither federal protection nor freedom from restraint is required by the national interest," *Goldstein*, supra, 412 U.S., at 559, 93 S.Ct., at 2311, the States remain free to promote originality and creativity in their own domains.

Nor does the fact that a particular item lies within the subject matter of the federal patent laws necessarily preclude the States from offering limited protection which does not impermissibly interfere with the federal patent scheme. As *Sears* itself makes clear, States may place limited regulations on the use of unpatented designs in order to prevent consumer confusion as to source. In *Kewanee*, we found that state protection of trade secrets, as applied to both patentable and unpatentable subject matter, did not conflict with the federal patent laws. In both situations, state protection was not aimed exclusively at the promotion of invention itself, and the state restrictions on the use of unpatented ideas were limited to those necessary to promote goals outside the contemplation of the federal patent scheme. Both the law of unfair competition and state trade secret law have co-existed harmoniously with federal patent protection for almost 200 years, and Congress has given no indication that their operation is inconsistent with the operation of the federal patent laws.

Indeed, there are affirmative indications from Congress that both the law of unfair competition and trade secret protection are consistent with the balance struck by the patent laws. Section 43(a) of the Lanham Act, 60 Stat. 441, 15 U.S.C. § 1125(a), creates a federal remedy for making "a false designation of origin, or any false description or representation, including words or other symbols tending falsely to describe or represent the same. . . ." Congress has thus given federal recognition to many of the concerns which underlie the state tort of unfair competition and the application of *Sears* and *Compco* to nonfunctional aspects of a product which have been shown to identify source must take account of competing federal policies in this regard. Similarly, as Justice MARSHALL noted in his concurring opinion in *Kewanee*, "[s]tate trade secret laws and the federal patent laws have co-existed for many, many, years. During this time, Congress has repeatedly demonstrated its full awareness of the existence of the trade secret system, without any indication of disapproval. Indeed, Congress has in a number of instances given explicit federal protection to trade secret information provided to federal agencies." *Kewanee,* supra, 416 U.S., at 494, 94 S.Ct., at 1892 (concurring in result) (citation omitted). The case for federal pre-emption is particularly weak where Congress has indicated its awareness of the operation of state law in a field of federal interest, and has nonetheless decided to "stand by both concepts and to tolerate whatever tension there [is] between them." Silkwood v. Kerr–McGee Corp., 464 U.S. 238, 256, 104 S.Ct. 615, 625, 78 L.Ed.2d 443 (1984). The same cannot be said of the Florida statute at issue here, which offers protection beyond that available under the law of unfair competition or trade secret, without any showing of consumer confusion, or breach of trust or secrecy.

The Florida statute is aimed directly at the promotion of intellectual creation by substantially restricting the public's ability to exploit ideas which the patent system mandates shall be free for all to use. Like the interpretation of Illinois unfair competition law in *Sears* and *Compco,* the Florida statute represents a break with the tradition of peaceful co-existence between state market regulation and federal patent policy. The Florida law substantially restricts the public's ability to exploit an unpatented design in general circulation, raising the specter of state-created monopolies in a host of useful shapes and processes for which patent protection has been denied or is otherwise unobtainable. It thus enters a field of regulation which the patent laws have reserved to Congress. The patent statute's careful balance between public right and private monopoly to promote certain creative activity is a "scheme of federal regulation . . . so pervasive as to make reasonable the inference that Congress left no room for the States to supplement it." Rice v. Sante Fe Elevator Corp., 331 U.S. 218, 230, 67 S.Ct. 1146, 1152, 91 L.Ed. 1447 (1947).

Congress has considered extending various forms of limited protection to industrial design either through the copyright laws or by relaxing the restrictions on the availability of design patents. Congress explicitly refused to take this step in the copyright laws, and despite sustained criticism for a number of years, it has declined to alter the patent protections presently available for industrial design. It is for Congress to determine if the present system of design and utility patents is ineffectual in promoting the useful arts in the context of industrial design. By offering patent-like protection for ideas deemed unprotected under the present federal scheme, the Florida statute conflicts with the "strong federal policy favoring free competition in ideas which do not merit patent protection." *Lear, Inc.,* 395 U.S., at 656, 89 S.Ct., at 1903. We therefore agree with the majority of the Florida Supreme Court that the Florida statute is preempted by the Supremacy Clause and the judgment of that court is hereby affirmed.

It is so ordered.

QUESTIONS

Was *Bonito Boats* a foregone conclusion after *Sears* and *Compco,* pages 103, 107, above? Did the Court in *Bonito Boats* adequately reconcile the decision with its decision in Kewanee v. Bicron, page 152, above? Aronson v. Quick Point, page 48, above? Goldstein v. California, page 770 above, which *Bonito Boats* nowhere addressed directly, held that states could prohibit copying of sound recordings even though the Copyright Act at the time excluded sound recordings from federal copyright protection. How do the facts in *Bonito Boats* differ from the facts in *Goldstein?*

Could the *Bonito Boats* Court have rested its decision on the nonconstitutional ground that section 301 of the 1976 Copyright Act preempted the Florida statute?

Early in its opinion, the Court observed that under Article I, § 8, cl. 8, "Congress may not create patent monopolies of unlimited duration. . . ." The duration of protection given by section 43(a) of the Lanham Act is indeterminate. Does this mean that a constitutional question arises any time a court must determine whether a product feature is functional or nonfunctional? See generally, Dratler, Trademark Protection for Industrial Design, 1988 U.Ill.L.Rev. 887, 923 *et seq.*

Part Five

INTERNATIONAL PROTECTION OF INTELLECTUAL PROPERTY

Three multilateral treaties represent the primary sources of international private law protection for intellectual property—the Berne Convention for the Protection of Literary and Artistic Works and the Universal Copyright Convention in the case of copyright, and the Paris Convention for the Protection of Industrial Property in the case of patent and trademark. Bilateral and regional treaties also play an important role.

United States trade initiatives have increasingly focussed on intellectual property protection. Section 301 of the 1974 Trade Act, as amended by the 1988 Omnibus Trade Act, directs the United States Trade Representative to identify countries that fail to give adequate and effective intellectual property protection to United States nationals; the Trade Representative may impose sanctions against offending countries. 19 U.S.C.A. §§ 2242, 2411 (Supp.1989). The 1974 Trade Act also established the Generalized System of Preferences. In determining whether to designate a country as a "beneficiary developing country" entitled to relief from the imposition of duties, the Act, as amended, provides that the President "shall take into account . . . the extent to which such country is providing adequate and effective means under its laws for foreign nationals to secure, to exercise, and to enforce exclusive rights in intellectual property, including patents, trademarks, and copyrights." 19 U.S.C.A. § 2462(c)(5) (Supp.1989).

Section 337 of the Tariff Act of 1930, as amended, 19 U.S.C.A. § 1337 (Supp.1989), outlaws the "importation into the United States, the sale for importation, or the sale within the United States after importation by the owner, importer, or consignee" of articles that infringe a copyright, patent, or trademark, or rights under the Semiconductor Chip Protection Act, if an industry in the United States relating to the articles "exists or is in the process of being established." The United States International Trade Commission has jurisdiction to investigate and determine violations of section 337, and to issue exclusion orders barring further imports and cease and desist orders barring the sale of articles already inside the country.

See generally, Kaye & Plaia, Unfair Trade Practices in International Trade Competition: A Review of Developments Under Section 337, 64 J.Pat.Off.Soc'y 360 (1982); Katz & Cohen, Effective Remedies Against the Importation of Knock–Offs: A Comparison of Remedies Available from the International Trade Commission, Customs and Federal Courts, 66 J.Pat.Off.Soc'y 660 (1984); Lupo, International Trade Commission Section 337 Proceedings and Their Applicability to Copyright Ownership, 32 J. Copyright Soc'y 193 (1985); Wineburg,

Litigating Intellectual Property Disputes at the International Trade Commission, 68 J.Pat. & Trademark Off.Soc'y 473 (1986); Wilson & Hovanec, The Growing Importance of Trademark Litigation Before the International Trade Commission Under Section 337, 76 Trademark Rep. 1 (1986).

Intellectual property protection has been on the agenda of the Uruguay Round of the General Agreement on Tariffs and Trade. See Contracting Parties to the General Agreement on Tariffs and Trade, GATT Activities 1987, 40–42, 130–31 (1988). See also Symposium, Trade–Related Aspects of Intellectual Property, 22 Vand.J.Transnat'l L. 223, 689 (1989); Damschroder, Intellectual Property Rights and the GATT: United States Goals in the Uruguay Round, 21 Vand.J.Transnat'l L. 367 (1988); Knight, Section 337 and the GATT: A Necessary Protection or an Unfair Trade Practice?, 18 Ga.J.Int'l & Comp.L. 47 (1988).

I. COPYRIGHT

RINGER, THE ROLE OF THE UNITED STATES IN INTERNATIONAL COPYRIGHT—PAST, PRESENT, AND FUTURE

56 Georgetown L.J. 1050, 1051–64 (1968).*

Historical Background

The Origins of International Copyright

Copyright as a legal concept originated in the form of direct sovereign grants of monopolies during the Renaissance as a response to the needs created by the invention of movable type. During the Age of Reason, copyright in the form of national statutory protection developed as part of the growth of organized publishing industries. Similarly, international copyright appears to have been a response to the Industrial Revolution; the expanding technology in communications necessitated reciprocal protection of works between countries.

At first, international copyright protection was the exception rather than the rule. National copyright laws usually denied protection to works originating in other countries, and such exceptions as existed were derived from bilateral treaties negotiated between particular countries on the basis of strict reciprocity. Domestic printers and publishers were unwilling to give up their ready markets for unauthorized reprints, but the local "piratical" copies were cheap in quality as well as price. Foreign authors had ample reason to complain of the mutilation of their works and the loss of royalties in other countries. National authors "found that their interests were prejudiced by the abundant publication and sale of unauthorized foreign works at cheap prices."

European attitudes toward this situation first began to change around the middle of the 19th century. In 1852 France extended copyright protection to all works, foreign and domestic alike, and while this generous gesture did not set a pattern, it accelerated the movement toward a multilateral copyright system. The Association Litteraire et Artistique Internationale (ALAI) was formed in Paris and took the lead in seeking ways to establish an international union of countries pledged to the protection of authors' rights.

Development of The Berne Convention

A conference held under ALAI auspices in Berne in 1883 marked the end of the discussion phase and the beginning of actual work on what became the Berne Convention of 1886. The goals of the conference were: "(1) The study of the legislative enactments affecting literary property in all civilized countries; (2) the study of important points of these enactments with a view to unification and the foundation of a union for the protection of literary property; (3) the drawing up of certain articles, clear and concise, setting forth the principles that are most likely to be accepted by the various powers and which should constitute the text of a universal convention."

A draft convention prepared by the ALAI was discussed at the 1883 conference, and the government of Switzerland agreed to circulate it to "all civilized countries." The Swiss president's letter of transmittal emphasized the "imperative necessity" of protecting the rights of writers and artists in international relations. He stated that previous agreements were "far from protecting the author's rights in a uniform, efficacious, and complete manner" and that the problem was "connected with the divergency of national laws, which the conventional regime ha[d] necessarily been obliged to take into account."

Intergovernmental conferences considering the draft convention were held at Berne in 1884, 1885, and 1886, the last comprising a full diplomatic conference at which the final instrument was signed. The original Berne Convention of September 9, 1886, was a modest beginning; nevertheless, it was the first truly multilateral copyright treaty in history, and it established some important basic principles. Rather than reciprocity ("I'll protect your works, but only to the extent you protect my works"), the Berne Convention adopted the principle of national treatment ("I'll protect your works to the same extent I protect my own works, if you promise to do the same"). The convention set up a "Union for the protection of authors over their literary and artistic works" consisting of the contracting states, and established a requirement that among Union members the right of translation had to be protected for a minimum of ten years.

The original Berne Convention provided that rights enjoyed under it "shall be subject to the accomplishment of the conditions and formalities prescribed by law in the country of origin of the work, and must not exceed in the other countries the term of protection granted in the said country of origin." In the successive revisions of the Convention, the minimum requirements governing protection have been substantially expanded. A Berne Union member accepting the Brussels text of 1948, which is the latest revision now in effect, must, with some exceptions, accord protection to the works of other member countries without requiring compliance with any formalities, during the life of the author and fifty years after his death. The Convention provides specific minimum requirements with respect to the protection of certain exclusive rights, most notably the so-called "moral rights" of the author. Any country that now wants to join the Berne Union must obligate itself to grant a very high level of copyright protection.

The original Berne Union consisted of 14 countries. The present membership comprises 58 countries that have adhered to one or more of the Berne revisions; one country is still bound by the Berlin revision of 1908, 14 countries are bound by the Rome text of 1928, and 43 countries are bound by the Brussels revision of 1948. On July 14, 1967, a new revision of the Berne Convention was signed at Stockholm, but as yet it has not been ratified or acceded to by any country. The Stockholm revisions, notably the new "Protocol Regarding Developing Countries," mark a substantial departure from the high level of copyright protection that hitherto has been characteristic of the Berne Convention. The implications of the Stockholm Act for international copyright in general and the United States in particular will be examined more closely below.

International Copyright in the United States Before World War II

For a century after enactment of the first United States copyright statute in 1790, only published works by citizens and residents of the United States could secure statutory copyright protection. For a century, the United States was exceptionally parochial in copyright matters, not only denying any protection to the published works of nonresident foreign authors, but actually appearing to encourage piracy. Common law protection for unpublished works regardless of the nationality of their authors was cold comfort at a time when publication was the only profitable way to disseminate a work. "Under such circumstances, other nations were understandably reluctant to protect American works."

Literary piracy, particularly of British works, became common in the 19th century, and efforts began in the United States in the 1830's to secure an "international copyright law." In 1837 Henry Clay, as chairman of a Senate select committee, submitted a report strongly recommending enactment of international copyright legislation. "In principle," he said, "the committee perceives no objection to considering the republic of letters as one great community, and adopting a system of protection for literary property which should be common to all parts of it." Clay's report was accompanied by a bill intended to extend U.S. copyright protection to British and French authors under rigorous conditions. The Clay bill was reintroduced several times between 1837 and 1842, but never reached a vote.

There followed more than a half-century of agitation for international copyright protection in the United States. Efforts to conclude a bilateral copyright treaty with Great Britain failed, and legislation to extend U.S. copyright protection to foreign authors attracted strong opposition, principally by American printing and publishing interests who believed that their livelihood depended upon cheap reprints of English books. They demanded that the extension of U.S. copyright to foreign works be conditioned on compliance with a requirement of manufacture in this country.

The legislative phase of the international copyright movement in the United States began shortly after the Civil War and finally achieved success in the International Copyright Act of March 3, 1891. During much of this same period the Berne Convention of 1886 was under gestation, and its development was well known to those interested in international copyright in the United States. Yet U.S. government representatives refrained from participating directly in the development of the Convention, under circumstances that leave many questions unanswered.

The prevailing official attitude was summarized in a letter sent by Secretary of State Bayard on June 29, 1886, in response to a Swiss note inviting U.S. participation in the final diplomatic conference. Secretary Bayard stated that the question of international copyright pending before Congress had not advanced far enough in the legislative channel to enable the Executive to act with the assurance of congressional approval, and that the pendency of measures in Congress made it impracticable for the United States to appoint a plenipotentiary to attend the conference at Berne for the purpose of signing the proposed convention. The American government's attitude toward the project was "merely one of expectancy and reserve," favoring the plan in principle but without determinate views as to the shape it should assume. It was "unprepared to suggest modifications which might conform the convention to the legislation which Congress may hereafter deem appropriate." Secretary Bayard specifically held out the possibility of future accession to the convention "should it become expedient and practicable to do so," thus echoing President Cleveland's message to Congress on December 8, 1885. This possibility was also reflected in the language of the International Copyright Act of 1891:

> That this act shall apply to a citizen or subject of a foreign state or nation when such foreign state or nation permits to citizens of the United States of America the benefit of copyright on substantially the same basis as its own citizens; or when such foreign state or nation is a party to an international agreement which provides for reciprocity in the granting of copyright, by the terms of which agreement the United States may, at its pleasure, become a party to such agreement.

The compromise that made the Act of 1891 possible was the introduction of a requirement of domestic manufacture for "a book, photograph, chromo, or lithograph." Under section 4956 of the Act, copyright could be secured only by making registration before publication and by depositing two copies of the work on or before the date of publication anywhere. Moreover, in the case of books and certain graphic works, the two copies had to be manufactured in the United States.

The requirements of the 1891 "manufacturing clause" were so rigid that they made the extension of copyright protection to foreigners illusory. Acts were passed in 1904 and 1905 in an effort to liberalize the clause by giving foreigners extra time to comply with the manufacturing requirement, and finally, in 1906, Congress undertook work on a general revision of the U.S. copyright laws. This revision effort was at its peak when, on October 14, 1908, a major conference for revision of the Berne Convention was held in Berlin. The United States was invited to attend with "full freedom of action," but the delegate, Thorvald Solberg, the Register of Copyrights, was sent as an observer only. Mr. Solberg explained to the Conference that the United States found it impracticable to send a delegate authorized to commit it to actual adhesion to the Berne Convention since some of the questions to be discussed there were pending before the Congress and premature action at the Convention might embarrass the legislative branch of the Government.

The original Berne Convention of 1886 had allowed member countries to impose certain formalities, such as notice, registration, and domestic manufacture, as conditions of copyright. This was changed by article 4 of the Berlin revision of 1908, which provided without qualification that "the enjoyment and exercise of these rights shall not be subject to the performance of any formality." This made it impossible for the United States to join the Berne Union without substantial changes in its domestic law.

In 1909, the year after the Berlin revision abolished formalities in international copyright, Congress passed a complete revision of the United States copyright law. The Act of March 3, 1909, which was essentially the same as the present American copyright law, retained rather rigid notice formalities, and, while further liberalizing the manufacturing provisions, retained the basic requirement of domestic manufacture as a condition of copyright in English-language books and periodicals. American adherence to the Berne Convention thus became impossible unless Congress could be persuaded to change the law again, but this obviously was unfeasible in the immediate future. Active U.S. participation in the development and revision of the Berne Convention in its nascent stages might not have avoided this result, but it might have prevented the paths from diverging so sharply.

The 1909 Act continued the provision of the 1891 statute under which the President is empowered to proclaim the existence of bilateral copyright relations between the United States and particular foreign countries. This system has proved cumbersome and ineffective in comparison with the simplicity, certainty, and other advantages offered by multilateral arrangements. In fact, efforts to achieve adherence to the Berne Convention began less than 15 years after the enactment of the 1909 statute; following the First World War, the increasing use of American works in other countries brought with it a demand that the United States adhere to the Berne Convention. Beginning in 1922, a series of bills for this purpose was introduced in Congress.

The history during the 1920's and 1930's of the combined legislative programs to obtain general revision of the copyright law and U.S. adherence to the Berne Convention makes painful reading. One commentator attributed the total failure of both these programs to the effort to link them together, pointing out that "the development of radio and motion picture technology during the 1920's introduced new interests into the orbit of intellectual properties, and made more difficult the task of securing agreement on proposals to effect a general revision of the copyright law." On the other hand, a motion picture attorney felt that the United States never adhered to Berne "primarily because it contains concepts which are foreign to our concepts of copyright, such as copyright without formalities, protection of moral rights, retroactivity and also because of the requirement of our manufacturing clause."

Whatever the reason for the failure of these legislative programs, the United States had become an exporter in the copyright trade, and something had to be done. It did not take American copyright owners long to discover an attractive loophole that has come to be known as the "backdoor to Berne." By the simple device of simultaneous publication of an American work in the United States and in a country which was a Berne Union member, such as Canada, a work became entitled to protection throughout the Berne Union without any corresponding obligations on the United States to protect Berne works. This practice of simultaneous publication became extremely widespread, and provoked resentment that is surprising only in its relative mildness. In 1914 the Berne Union adopted a retaliatory protocol under which member countries could, if they chose, limit the protection of nonmember authors under certain conditions, and there were cases in which the existence of true simultaneous publication was decided on narrow grounds.

In 1928 the Berne Convention was revised at Rome, and the level of protection was again raised. In an effort to induce the United States to join the Union, however, the Rome Convention permitted nonmembers to adhere to the Berlin text of 1908 until August 1, 1931. Strenuous efforts in Congress to meet this deadline were unsuccessful; although Senate approval of the Rome version was prematurely obtained in 1935, it was immediately withdrawn. Another major effort sponsored by a committee formed under the auspices of an American organization related to the League of Nations resulted in the introduction of a bill in 1940, but it died in committee.

Inter–American Conventions

Efforts to develop multilateral copyright arrangements in the Americas began in the 1880's, at about the same time the Berne Convention and the United States International Copyright Act were being formed. These efforts produced a series of Pan–American copyright conventions, but for all practical purposes the United States is a member of only one of them, the Buenos Aires Convention of 1910. It has failed to accept the later revisions adopted at Havana in 1928 and at Washington in 1946, which are more closely analogous to the principles of the Berne Convention.

Under the Buenos Aires Convention a work is protected in a member country if it has been copyrighted in another member country and bears a form of copyright notice. Since no legislation implementing it has ever been enacted, the conditions and extent of protection under this convention remain somewhat unclear in the United States.

Furthermore, during the past twenty years there has been an unmistakable trend away from regional conventions and in favor of worldwide copyright arrangements, and the Universal Copyright Convention has superseded the Pan–American conventions in many cases.

The Universal Copyright Convention

After the Second World War it became even more imperative for the Berne Union and the United States to reach an accommodation. The failure of the United States to offer foreign works the level of copyright protection generally available throughout the Berne Union gave rise to indignation, which was intensified by the practice of American copyright owners' taking full advantage of Berne protection in other countries. The situation grew worse with the emergence of the United States as the leading exporter of copyrighted works in the world. As one commentator has said, "Consideration was given to attracting the Americas into Berne, but member countries refused to tolerate their own retrogression for the simple expediency of attracting the American countries." The postwar situation was urgent, but it seemed clear at that time that the Berne countries would refuse to lower protection sufficiently to attract American adherence and that further efforts by the United States to join the Berne Union would be futile. The approach that was adopted represented a compromise: a new "common denominator" convention that was intended to establish a minimum level of international copyright relations throughout the world, without weakening or supplanting the Berne Convention. The Universal Copyright Convention, as it came to be called, was sponsored by UNESCO, and one of the leaders in its development was the United States.

Advocates of international copyright protection began once again to lay the groundwork for altering the domestic law in the United States while concomitantly devising universal agreement that would appeal to all countries committed to the promotion of cultural interchange. Furthermore, "vigorous leaders appeared in the United States among the champions of international copyright, and organizations of creators, producers, and consumers of literary works became alerted to the[se] questions."

The landmark Universal Copyright Convention was signed at Geneva on September 6, 1952, and, following the required 12 ratifications, took effect on September 16, 1955. The United States was one of the first signatories to ratify it. The most significant provisions of the Convention can be summarized as follows:

1. Adequate and Effective Protection. Under article I, the contracting states are obliged to "provide for the adequate and effective protection of the rights of authors and other copyright proprietors. . . ."

2. National Treatment. Article II provides that the "published works of nationals of any Contracting State and works first published in that State shall enjoy in each other Contracting State the same protection as that other State accords to works of its nationals first published in its own territory." There is a similar provision for unpublished works.

3. *Formalities.* Article III, which represents the great compromise of the U.C.C., provides that the formal requirements, such as notice, registration, and manufacture, of a contracting state's copyright law are satisfied with respect to foreign U.C.C. works "if from the time of first publication all of the copies of the work . . . bear the symbol © accompanied by the name of the copyright proprietor and the year of first publication placed in such manner and location as to give reasonable notice of claim of copyright."

4. *Duration of Protection.* Another major compromise is embodied in article IV of the U.C.C. The minimum term, subject to various detailed qualifications and exceptions, is to be either 25 years from the death of the author or from the date of first publication.

5. *Translation Rights.* The U.C.C., in article V, requires contracting states to give exclusive translation rights to foreign U.C.C. authors for at least seven years; thereafter a rather cumbersome compulsory licensing system can be established.

6. *Nonretroactivity.* Under article VII a contracting state is not obliged to protect works that are permanently in its public domain on the date the Convention becomes effective in that state.

7. *Berne Safeguard Clause.* An enormously important provision of the U.C.C. is found in article XVII and the "Appendix Declaration" attached to it. These provide, in effect, that no Berne country can denounce the Berne Convention and rely on the U.C.C. in its copyright relations with Berne Union members.

Thus, at least in comparison with the 1948 Brussels revision of the Berne Convention, the Universal Copyright Convention represents a rather low-level copyright arrangement, resembling in many ways the original 1886 Berne text.

The minimum requirements as to exclusive rights are extremely modest, being limited to providing "adequate and effective protection" and translation rights which can be subject to compulsory licensing. The requirements as to minimum duration of protection are also very permissive, and a system of copyright notice is actually sanctioned as a substitute for other formalities. It is therefore understandable that Berne Union members regarded the U.C.C. as a retrogressive step, and insisted on safeguarding the Berne Convention from the danger of being undermined by the defection of Berne members to the U.C.C.

Developments, 1952–1967

U.S. Ratification of the Universal Copyright Convention

Getting the United States to ratify the Universal Copyright Convention and to enact the statutory revisions necessary to implement it was more of an accomplishment than the development of the U.C.C. itself. That there was opposition goes without saying, but it was neutralized or overcome in a remarkably short time. On August 31, 1954, President Eisenhower signed Public Law 743 which conformed the indigenous copyright law to the Convention, and on November 5, 1954, he signed the instrument of ratification of the U.C.C. itself.

Since the Universal Copyright Convention was to a considerable extent tailored to meet the requirements of existing United States law, the changes necessary to implement it were, for the most part, technical. The most important alteration involved a complete waiver of all formalities as to deposit, registration, manufacture, and importation for foreign U.C.C. works, as long as the copies of the work bore the notice of copyright prescribed by the Convention. As a practical matter, this has removed the manufacturing requirement for the majority of English language works of foreign authorship and has induced a much greater use of copyright notices on foreign works.

Current Status of the U.C.C.

In general, the Universal Copyright Convention has been a genuine success. It has been ratified or acceded to by 55 countries, nearly as many as belong to the Berne Union. It has vastly simplified the international copyright relations of the United States with other countries and of other countries with the United States, and it has brought some newly independent or developing countries into the international copyright community on terms that they found acceptable.

For some time after the U.C.C. came into effect, it appeared to have achieved a reasonably harmonious coexistence with the Berne Union. There was some acrimony between the two secretariats, but the governing bodies of the two conventions began holding their meetings together, and there was some talk of working toward a merger that would raise the level of U.C.C. protection. However, the emergence of newly independent countries seeking to import foreign educational materials on favorable terms began to impair this accord in the late 1950's and the problem reached crisis proportions by 1967.

HADL, TOWARD INTERNATIONAL COPYRIGHT REVISION, REPORT ON THE MEETINGS IN PARIS AND GENEVA, SEPTEMBER 1970

18 Bull. Copyright Soc'y 183–189, 207–208 (1971).*

International copyright was plunged into crisis in 1967 at the Stockholm Intellectual Property Conference. One of the objectives of this Conference was the revision of the Berne Convention including special provisions for the benefit of developing countries. These provisions were annexed to the draft text of the Convention as a Protocol Regarding Developing Countries (hereafter, "Protocol", or "Stockholm Protocol"). During the Conference, however, it became apparent that the developing countries were not satisfied with the concessions proposed in the draft text. Led by India, they were able to orchestrate a chorus of protest which sought much wider gains. The developed countries, unprepared for this onslaught and without strong leadership, found themselves in disarray and unable to silence the developing countries. As a result, the final text of the Protocol adopted by the Conference gave developing countries very broad and uncontrolled privileges with respect to works copyrighted in Berne Union countries. For the most part, these privileges were considered unacceptable by the developed countries.

The Stockholm victory won by the developing countries proved, however, to be a hollow one. They had left one loophole, namely, the provision that unless a developed country agreed to accept the Stockholm Protocol, it could not be bound by it. To this day, no major developed country has ratified or acceded to the Stockholm Protocol, and none is expected to do so in the future. In the aftermath of Stockholm what became apparent was that the developing countries had won the opening battle, but they had not won the war.

For their part, the developing countries were not without recourse against the refusal of the developed countries to accept the Stockholm Protocol. They had two substantial weapons in their arsenal. First, they could renounce their international copyright obligations completely by withdrawing from the UCC and Berne Convention. Second, they could alter their membership in the two major multilateral copyright conventions by resigning from one but maintaining membership in the other. At this point, the existence of two different copyright conventions with different levels of protection and a large overlap in membership created added complexities to the crisis produced by the Stockholm Protocol.

The UCC, to which the United States is a party, is characterized chiefly by the principle of national treatment: even if a country's domestic legislation provides for relatively low-level protection, it can still belong to the UCC. The Berne Convention requires its parties to provide a specified minimum of copyright protection for other Berne works in their domestic legislation, and that minimum establishes a standard providing for a high level of copyright protection.

The situation is further complicated by the fact that the original Berne Convention of 1886 has been revised a number of times and there are, as a result, several different "Berne texts," each providing for different standards of protection. Protection in Berne Convention countries will vary depending upon which text the particular country has accepted. Moreover, some of the texts permit reservations on particular points, and others do not. In addition, the UCC contains the so-called "Berne safeguard clause"—Article XVII and its Appendix Declaration—a provision prohibiting a Berne Convention country from denouncing Berne and relying on the UCC for protection of its works in Berne Union countries. Thus, under this clause, a country resigning from the Berne Union but remaining in the UCC would continue to have obligations under the UCC, but would have no protection for its own works under either convention.

Under these circumstances, the developing countries wishing to leave the Berne Convention for the lower level UCC were frustrated by the existence of the "Berne safeguard clause." To remove this difficulty, they launched a counter-offensive designed to suspend the effectiveness of the "Berne safeguard clause." They argued that without such a suspension their only practical alternative was denunciation of both major copyright conventions. The latter prospect was not appealing to the developed countries, despite their displeasure with the Stockholm Protocol.

It was with this background that the Register of Copyrights announced to a meeting of the IGCC and Berne Permanent Committee in December, 1967, that it would be impossible for the United States to join the Berne Convention if it had to accept the Stockholm Protocol, and that he viewed with very great concern the confusion and erosion in standards of international copyright protection resulting from the Stockholm Conference. He urged that the representatives of both developed and developing countries join together to restudy the whole international copyright situation, including practical ways of meeting the needs of developing countries.

Underlying the Register's remarks were two policy goals. The first was to renegotiate the concessions for developing countries contained in the Stockholm Protocol. The second was to maintain the structure of international copyright and the balance between the two major multilateral copyright conventions. In both of these he had to overcome the opposition of the developing countries. In the second, he also had to persuade some of the developed countries, members of the Berne Union, that Stockholm did not justify a reorganization of the international copyright system. In their view, Stockholm proved the danger to the developed countries of keeping the developing countries in the Berne Convention. The clear answer was to pave the way for the renunciation of Berne in favor of the UCC by suspension of the "Berne safeguard clause."

Time was needed, however, to review the ramifications of Stockholm and to consider new policies. Thus, it was early 1969 before the curtain rose on the next act of the diplomatic melodrama. At this point the representatives were ready to accept the suggestion made by the Register in December, 1967. The IGCC and Berne Permanent Committee adopted resolutions establishing an International Copyright Joint Study Group, and upon the invitation of the United States, agreed that the Joint Study Group would meet in Washington in September, 1969.

At that meeting, attended by representatives from twenty-five countries, a proposal to end the international copyright crisis was presented and adopted. Dubbed the "Washington Recommendation," this proposal called for the simultaneous revision of both the UCC and Berne Convention to achieve the following objectives:

(1) In the UCC the level of protection would be improved by the adoption of certain minimum rights. These would include the rights of

reproduction, public performance, and broadcasting. At the same time, special provisions would be included in the UCC for the benefit of developing countries. Finally, the "Berne safeguard clause" would be suspended to permit developing countries to leave the Berne Convention without penalty under the UCC.

(2) In the Berne Convention, the Protocol would be separated from the Stockholm Act and, in turn, the developing countries would be able to substitute the special provisions included for their benefit in the UCC. This would mean that the developing countries could remain in the Berne Convention and would not be forced to exercise the option provided by the suspension of the "Berne safeguard clause." As a protective measure, it was provided that the Stockholm Protocol could not be separated from the Stockholm text until such time as France, Spain, the United Kingdom and the United States had ratified the revised text of the UCC. Furthermore, developing countries would be relieved of the obligation to pay assessments to the Berne Union if they continued their membership after the new revision.

The Washington Recommendation won the general support of all the countries that attended the meeting. While it was a sound proposal on paper, the unresolved question was whether it could be implemented successfully. The meetings that have taken place since then have all addressed themselves to this problem.

In December, 1969, the IGCC and Berne Permanent Committee met to consider the results of the Washington meeting. With the exception of France, they agreed that the preparations for revision of each Convention should be made "in accordance with the considerations stated in the preamble to the Washington Recommendation and the specific recommendations contained therein, including, in particular, the recommendation that the Universal Copyright Convention and the Berne Convention be revised in revision conferences to be held at the same time and place. . . ." In addition they scheduled several preparatory meetings to consider draft texts.

Pursuant to these arrangements, two Ad Hoc Preparatory Committees met in Paris and Geneva in May, 1970. Based largely upon a proposal for revision of the UCC submitted by the United States, draft texts were prepared for the two conventions. As contrasted with the trend represented by the Stockholm Protocol, several important demands of the developing countries were abandoned at this meeting. These included the concessions respecting the term of copyright, the exclusive right of broadcasting, and the broad right to restrict the protection of literary and artistic works for "teaching, study and research in all fields of education." Accordingly, the concessions for developing countries were limited to restricting the rights of translation and reproduction. The major negotiations in May concerned these points.

The draft texts produced in May were then circulated to governments and interested international non-governmental organizations. As recommended by the resolutions adopted in December, 1969, the

IGCC and Berne Permanent Committee met in extraordinary sessions in September, 1970, to consider the draft texts and to make final preparations for the revision conferences. . . .

Conclusion

The international copyright crisis started by the Stockholm Protocol seems headed for a successful resolution. At Stockholm, the developing countries had won concessions relating to the term of copyright, the rights of broadcasting, translation and reproduction. They had also gained broad power to restrict the protection of literary and artistic works for "teaching, study and research in all fields of education." The possible economic benefits from all of these concessions were further enhanced by exceptionally loose provisions concerning the export of copies made under compulsory licenses and royalty payments.

In the final texts of the draft Conventions adopted by the two Committees, the concessions relating to the term of copyright and the right of broadcasting have been eliminated. The broad power to restrict the protection of literary and artistic works for "teaching, study and research in all fields of education" has also disappeared. The export of copies made under compulsory licenses has been prohibited and the payment provisions and standards for determining royalties have been improved considerably. Furthermore, the translation and reproduction provisions are now more realistic and generally represent the kind of concessions which the copyright owners in the developed countries are ready and willing to make.

Moreover, the level of protection in the UCC has been improved by the introduction of certain minimum rights. This will guarantee a minimum level of protection in the UCC which had previously been subject, under the national treatment standard, to any level the particular country wished to set.

With respect to maintaining the equilibrium between the two Conventions, the final texts carry out the thrust of the Washington Recommendation by duplicating the concessions for developing countries in each Convention. While some substantive differences exist because of differences in structure, they should not lead to a wholesale defection by developing countries from the Berne Convention to the UCC. Thus, the Berne Convention will continue to maintain its historic role of improving the level of copyright protection throughout the world, and the United States can continue to look with hope upon the day when it may become a member.

Given the results of the September, 1970 meetings, it would seem that the chances are good for successful diplomatic conferences next July. As contrasted with the Stockholm situation, the developing countries have moderated their demands, the developed countries have had an affirmative program, there have been careful preparations beforehand, firm leadership, and the discussions have taken place in a more rational and less emotionally charged atmosphere. All of these are the ingredients for success, and the United States has contributed substantially to each of them.*

NOTES

1. *U.S. Adherence to the Berne Convention.* On October 31, 1988, more than a century after the Berne Convention for the Protection of Literary and Artistic Works came into force, President Ronald Reagan signed the Berne Convention Implementation Act of 1988, Pub.L. No. 100–568, 102 Stat. 2853 (1988), conforming the 1976 Copyright Act to the Convention's requirements and enabling the United States to join the Convention. The treaty was ratified, and came into force in the United States on March 1, 1989.

Even before the United States adhered to the Berne Convention, United States nationals could obtain Berne-level protection in other countries. One way was the so-called "back door to Berne:" a United States national could obtain protection in Berne member countries through the expedient of publishing its work in a Berne member country at the same time it published the work in the United States. Even apart from the Berne back door, United States nationals effectively received Berne-level protection in UCC member states that also belonged to the Berne Convention and conformed their copyright laws to Berne standards.

Obtaining Berne protection through the back door entailed private costs: arranging for simultaneous publication was not cheap. It also carried social costs, diminishing the United States' stature in bilateral and multilateral trade negotiations over intellectual property. Combined, these costs led virtually all major industry forces to unite for the first time behind proposals for adherence to the Berne Convention.

On the Berne Convention generally, the authoritative work is S. Ricketson, The Berne Convention for the Protection of Literary and Artistic Works: 1886–1986 (1987). See also C. Masouyé, Guide to the Berne Convention (1978); Ginsberg & Kernochan, One Hundred and Two Years Later: The U.S. Joins the Berne Convention, 13 Colum.VLA J.L. & Arts 1 (1988); Preliminary Report of the Ad Hoc Working Group on U.S. Adherence to the Berne Convention, 33 J. Copyright Soc'y 183 (1986); Conference Celebrating the Centenary of the Berne Convention, 1886–1986, 11 Colum.VLA J.L. & Arts 1 (1986).

2. *Protection of U.S. Works Abroad.* "To obtain relief against the unauthorized use of its work in another country, a United States copyright owner must show that its work is entitled to copyright protection in that country and that it owns the copyright in that country. A work's eligibility for protection under the copyright law of a foreign country will commonly turn on compliance with one of four

---

* With amendments, the 1970 draft texts of the UCC and Berne Convention were adopted at the Paris conferences. The revised UCC was signed at Paris on July 24, 1971 by the United States and twenty-five other member countries. The United States ratified the Paris revision in September, 1972. The UCC and Berne revisions came into force on July 10, 1974. Ed.

conditions: (1) the author of the work is a national or domiciliary of the foreign country; (2) the author of the work is a national or domiciliary of a country with which the foreign country has established copyright relations through a multilateral or bilateral treaty or through proclamation; (3) the work was first published in the foreign country; or (4) the work was first published in a country with which the foreign country has established copyright relations. The most common basis today for protecting the works of United States nationals abroad is the United States' adherence to two multilateral copyright treaties—the Universal Copyright Convention and the Berne Convention for the Protection of Literary and Artistic Works." P. Goldstein, Copyright § 16.0 (1989).*

3. *Prohibitions on Importation.* Section 602 of the 1976 Copyright Act governs the importation of copies and phonorecords of copyrighted works into the United States. The provision differentiates between piratical goods—copies or phonorecords made without permission from the copyright owner—and gray market goods—copies or phonorecords that, though lawfully manufactured and marketed abroad, cannot be imported into the United States without violating the terms of a territorial licensing agreement with the copyright owner. Section 602(a) encompasses both piratical and gray market goods and makes their unauthorized importation an infringement of section 106(3)'s distribution right. Section 602(b) prohibits—and authorizes the United States Customs Service to bar—only the importation of piratical goods.

4. *Liability Under U.S. Law for Acts Committed Abroad.* Although copyright law is territorial, cases may arise in which a defendant will be liable under United States law for acts committed abroad. For example, in Peter Starr Production Co. v. Twin Continental Films, Inc., 783 F.2d 1440, 1442–43, 229 U.S.P.Q. 127 (9th Cir.1986), the court held that, because the defendant had executed a contract in the United States authorizing a direct infringer to distribute plaintiff's copyrighted motion picture outside the United States, the defendant could be held liable for contributory infringement even though the direct infringement occurred outside the United States.

5. *Neighboring Rights.* Two traditions dominate intellectual property protection for literary, musical and artistic works. The "copyright" tradition, which prevails in the United States, the United Kingdom and other countries associated with the common law system, emphasizes a utilitarian balance between incentives to investment and consumer interests in access. The "author's right" tradition, which prevails in European and Latin American countries and other countries that adhere to the civil law system, posits that authors deserve protection for their works as an inherent natural right.

Differences between the copyright and author's right traditions are evident in the way the two traditions have dealt with the question of protection for new media, such as motion pictures, sound recordings and broadcasting, that typically involve corporate creators and minimal creative contributions. The challenge of protection for these new media was particularly severe for author's rights systems which typically presuppose an individual author and a high level of artistic creativity. By contrast, copyright, which has long accepted the principle of corporate authorship and traditionally sets a low standard for protection, easily absorbed these new media into its fabric of protection.

Author's right countries met the challenge of the new media by diverting them to an alternate system of protection—"neighboring rights." The most important categories of neighboring rights are: "the right of performers to prevent fixation and direct broadcasting or communication to the public of their performances without their consent; the right of producers of phonograms to authorize or prohibit reproduction of their phonograms and the import and distribution of unauthorized duplicates thereof; the right of broadcasting organizations to authorize or prohibit rebroadcasting, fixation and reproduction of their broadcasts." World Intellectual Property Organization, Glossary of Terms of the Law of Copyright and Neighboring Rights 164 (1980).

The United States has not adhered to the principal multilateral treaty governing neighboring rights, the International Convention for the Protection of Performers, Producers of Phonograms and Broadcasting Organizations (Rome Convention). The United States has, however, adhered to two other neighboring rights conventions—the Convention for the Protection of Producers of Phonograms Against Unauthorized Duplication of Their Phonograms (Geneva Convention) and the Convention Relating to the Distribution of Programme–Carrying Signals Transmitted by Satellite (Brussels Satellite Convention).

6. *Bibliography.* On international copyright generally, see M. Nimmer & P. Geller, eds., International Copyright Law and Practice (1989); W. Nordemann, K. Vinck, P. Hertin & G. Meyer, International Copyright and Neighboring Rights Law (1990); S. Ladas, The International Protection of Literary and Artistic Property (1938); S. Stewart, International Copyright and Neighbouring Rights (1983); U.S. Copyright Office, To Secure Intellectual Property Rights in World Commerce, Report to the Subcomm. on Patents, Copyrights & Trademarks of the Senate Comm. on the Judiciary and to the Subcomm. on Western Hemisphere Affairs of House Comm. on Foreign Affairs, printed in Oversight on International Copyrights: Hearing Before the Subcomm. on Patents, Trademarks & Copyrights of the Senate Comm. on the Judiciary, 98th Cong., 2d Sess. 8 (1984).

On the Universal Copyright Convention, see A. Bogsch, The Law of Copyright Under the Universal Convention (3d rev. ed. 1968); Universal Copyright Convention Analyzed (Kupferman & Foner eds. 1955). For background on the Paris revisions and the relationships between UCC and Berne, see Olian, International Copyright and the Needs of Developing Countries: The Awakening at Stockholm and Paris, 7 Cornell Int'l L.J. 81 (1974); Ulmer, International Copyright After the Paris Revisions, 19 Bull. Copyright Soc'y 263 (1972); Johnson, The Origins of the Stockholm Protocol, 18 Bull. Copyright Soc'y 91 (1970);

Schrader, Analysis of the Protocol Regarding Developing Countries, 17 Bull. Copyright Soc'y 160 (1970).

On copyright in the European Economic Community, see G. Davies & H. von Rauscher auf Weeg, Challenges to Copyright and Related Rights in the European Community (1983); A. Dietz, Copyright Law in the European Community (1978); Dietz, Copyright Issues in the E.E.C., 30 J. Copyright Soc'y 517 (1983).

On the questions posed by economically developing countries, see Terán, International Copyright Developments—A Third World Perspective, 30 Bull. Copyright Soc'y 129 (1982); Tocups, The Development of Special Provisions in International Copyright Law for the Benefit of Developing Countries, 29 Bull. Copyright Soc'y 402 (1982).

On copyright relations with the Soviet Union, see J. Baumgarten, US–USSR Copyright Relations Under the Universal Copyright Convention (1973); M. Boguslavsky, Copyright in International Relations: International Protection of Literary and Scientific Works (N. Poulet trans., D. Catterns ed. 1979); Maggs, New Directions in US–USSR Copyright Relations, 68 Am.J.Int'l L. 391 (1974). See also M. Newcity, Copyright Law in the Soviet Union (1978).

II. PATENT

VERNON, THE INTERNATIONAL PATENT SYSTEM AND FOREIGN POLICY

Study No. 5, Subcommittee on Patents, Trademarks and Copyrights, Senate Committee on the Judiciary, 85th Cong., 1st Sess. 1–4 (1957).

A. The Nature of the System

In November 1957, the 45 signatories of the International Convention for the Protection of Industrial Property will assemble in Lisbon to consider whether the convention should be amended. This will be the first such meeting since 1934. Since the convention represents the principal agreement defining the rights of inventors who patent in foreign countries, the meeting will afford the first opportunity in nearly a quarter of a century for a full-dress review of international patent relations.

The international convention is 1 of 3 elements which go to make up what we have called the "international patent system." The other 2 elements are the national patent laws of the sovereign States, and the practices which involve the use of foreign patents in international trade and investment.

The national patent laws of the various sovereign governments of the world, to the extent that they have a common theme, grant patentees the right to prevent others in the grantor government's jurisdiction from making and selling the object or from using the process which is the subject of the patent. But the right is circumscribed in a variety of ways from one jurisdiction to the next. To begin with, the duration of the patent grant varies from country to country; in the United States, the patent's life is 17 years, while in other countries it may be as little as 5 years for "little patents" or as long as 20. In addition, different countries exclude different types of product from the patent grant. Finally, national concepts of patent "abuse" and penalties for misuse, such as compulsory licensing, revocation, and dedication, are also varied.

These different national patent laws have been ingeniously linked together by the International Convention for the Protection of Industrial Property. The treaty, now in its 74th year, includes among its 45 signatory nations every major industrialized nation of the free world and a few in the Soviet orbit. In substance, the convention deals essentially with the rights to which patentees in any signatory country may be entitled under the national patent laws of the other signatories. Only 3 or 4 of its main provisions, however, need be considered here.

The great achievement of the treaty, from the point of view of inventors and investors, is the fact that its signatories have agreed to grant patent treatment to nationals or residents of other signatory countries equal to the treatment they grant their own nationals.

939

Adopted in 1883, this was an extraordinary provision for its time. It eliminated the possibility of discrimination against foreigners and excluded a pattern of international patent relations based on reciprocity, that is, on the principle that foreigners were entitled to get in other countries only as much as their governments gave to foreigners at home. Instead, this unusual convention represented the "open" form of international agreement, extending its provisions to any nation which was willing to give nondiscriminatory patent rights to foreigners.

The practice of granting national treatment to foreigners is sensible on many counts, for reasons whose applicability extend beyond the confines of this paper. The practice has proved particularly appropriate as regards patents. For one thing, a considerable proportion of the world's patentholders are corporations; and the "nationality" of a corporation—the question whether or not it is a "foreigner" for purposes of domestic law—revolves largely around certain fictions and ordinarily depends not upon the identity of the natural persons who created the corporation but upon the nation under whose corporate statutes such persons have chosen to place their enterprise. Thus a Swedish corporation organized by United States nationals would be regarded as an entity of Swedish nationality for the purposes of Swedish patent law.

The convention goes further in securing foreigners' rights. It provides that a prospective patentee who has filed his application in any signatory country and who is entitled to the convention's protection has a period of 1 year in which to apply for patent protection in any other convention jurisdiction. This provision has extensive implications. For in the absence of some such provision, the inventor of a product or a process in country A, having duly made a patent application in his own country, might well find that country B was unwilling to consider him entitled to claim a patent in that country; country B might insist, for instance, that the first introducer of the invention in its territory was the eligible patentee, or it might even insist that no patent was issuable at all if the invention was already being publicly used in country A. This 1–year priority provision, therefore, greatly increases the probability that an applicant will acquire a legal monopoly not only in his own nation but also in other signatory countries.

The international convention grants still another right to the patentee. The convention provides that once a patent has been granted on the basis of the priority provisions of the convention, the subsequent invalidation of the patent by the original granting nation will not of itself affect the validity of patents granted elsewhere on the same invention. This means that even if it were later determined that the patent in the first country of application should never have been granted—either because the invention had been developed previously or because the subject matter of the patent was eventually determined to be lacking in inventiveness or on any other grounds on which the courts may invalidate patents—the patents proliferated in other countries on the basis of the convention's priority rights remain unaffected by their invalidation in the original country of issue. To be sure, the facts which led to invalidation in the first country, when adduced by the proper party in the proper courts of other nations, might eventually invalidate these counterpart patents. But in the absence of some such action, these patents must be allowed to continue to stand.

Another feature of the convention which has a direct bearing on this review is its provisions with respect to the compulsory licensing of patents. The institution of the patent grant was originally devised partly as a means by which the sovereign might reward his favorites and partly as a device for stimulating domestic industry. This latter philosophy—this emphasis on the development of domestic industry—had pervaded many early patent laws and had led quite logically to provisions which required the patentee to "work" his patent in the jurisdiction where the patent was granted. To this end, for example, some patent laws had automatically withdrawn the grant whenever the patentee imported his product into the country; other laws obliged the patentee, on pain of losing his grant, to "work" the patent in some stated period, either by actually producing the product or using the process within the jurisdiction, or by some other statutory test.

The international convention has put various restraints on the scope of these "working" provisions. It prohibits the cancellation of a patent when the action is based simply on the fact that the relevant product had been imported into the jurisdiction. Moreover the convention prevents its signatories from taking any steps to compel "working" in the first 3 years after a patent is issued; thereafter, the convention binds its signatories to resort initially to compulsory *licensing* at reasonable royalties, rather than to cancellation of the patent grant, as a remedy under the "working" provisions or indeed for any other patent "abuse" under their respective laws. Cancellation is permitted only as a final remedy, after the compulsory licensing technique has been tried for at least 2 years and has failed. These compulsory licensing provisions of the convention, it is evident, have altered the complexion of the patent grant from one designed primarily to stimulate domestic industry to one in which the foreign patentee has an increased chance of producing where he chooses and retaining his patent monopoly.

A third element of the international patent system is the body of practices by which patentees use their foreign patent rights in international trade and investment. There are few generalizations about the practices of foreign patentees which are not subject to major qualifications. Yet it is fair to say that a foreign patentee is usually subject to different forces and motivations in the strategy of patent use from those of his domestic counterpart. A foreign patentee, by hypothesis, is the recipient of a monopoly grant covering an area which is not his principal locus of operation. This means that a license granted by him for the use of the patent is less likely to create direct and immediate competition for his own production than would be the case for patent licenses in his home territory. The fact that the patent applies to a foreign market means also that there are frequently limitations on the value of the patent grant to its owner arising out of the inaccessibility of the foreign market in which he has the patent monopoly.

BENSON, THE IMPACT OF THE PATENT COOPERATION TREATY (PCT) AND THE EUROPEAN PATENT CONVENTION (EPC) ON U.S. PRACTITIONERS

60 Journal of the Patent Office Society 118–126 (1978).

Back in the mid-1960s President Johnson appointed a special commission to study the United States patent system. One of the recommendations of this commission was that "the United States promote direct interim steps towards the ultimate goal—a universal patent including harmonization of patent practices." As a direct result of this recommendation, the United States Government, along with some other countries, asked the United International Bureau for the Protection of Intellectual Property (BIRPI) to develop a proposal that would meet the recommendation of the Presidential Commission. Specifically, they were asked to draft a proposal that would (a) simplify the procedures in filing foreign patent applications corresponding to the basic initially filed patent application, (b) reduce the cost of obtaining patents in foreign countries, (c) promote more uniform national laws relating to procurement and enforcement of patents and (d) improve the patent systems in countries that did not have a patent examination system.

The first proposal from BIRPI came out in February of 1967 and called for a system of international cooperation that included a uniform format for patent applications, a centralized searching system and a preliminary examination which could result in the issuance of what was then called "a certificate of patentability." This proposal then became the basic document from which the various drafts of the proposed Patent Cooperation Treaty were drawn. The negotiations for the Patent Cooperation Treaty culminated in a diplomatic conference in June of 1970 at which conference the Patent Cooperation Treaty was signed by some 26 countries.

A lot has been written about the various provisions of the Patent Cooperation Treaty and I will not go into them in detail except to outline the principal provisions. First the form and content of the international applications would be accepted by all countries who participate in the Patent Cooperation Treaty. Secondly, the PCT called for searching authorities which would have to have minimum prior art documentation for their searches. The PCT defined minimum standards of patentability against which the applications would be examined. In the first phase, or Chapter I, of the Patent Cooperation Treaty a prior art search would be conducted and a search report issued to the applicant. In the second phase of the Patent Cooperation Treaty, referred to as Chapter II, a preliminary examination would be conducted with the prior art actually being applied to the claimed invention. The PCT applicant has the right to amend his application, including the claims, to distinguish from the art cited by the searching authority and as applied during the examination phase. At the end of this procedure, copies of the application together with the search report would be forwarded to the national offices of the countries the applicant had designated. The national patent offices of the designated countries are responsible for finally issuing a patent. After the patent is issued, it is to be enforced in each country strictly in accordance with the national laws of that country.

Immediately after the Patent Cooperation Treaty was signed, the common market countries reopened negotiations relative to a European patent and a common market patent. The Common Market Patent Convention providing for a single patent for all of the EEC countries has been signed but now must be ratified by all the member countries before coming into force. The negotiations leading to the European Patent Convention continued through 1973 at which time a number of European countries signed what is now known as the "European Patent Convention." The European Patent Convention contains a large number of clauses which were extracted almost verbatim from the Patent Cooperation Treaty and are completely compatible with that Treaty. In accordance with the European Patent Convention, initial proceedings take place in the European Patent Office in Munich, but the prior art searches are conducted in the branch of the European Patent Office at The Hague. The proceedings in the European Patent Convention include not only a preliminary search but a complete examination against a specific standard of invention for all applications filed in the European Patent Office. Upon completion of the examination stage and a determination of patentability, a copy of the patent application is transferred to the Patent Office in each of the individual countries that were designated in the original application. The application is then translated (if required) and issued as a patent. In effect, then, although you file a single patent application in the European Patent Office and prosecute it through to completion in that office, the result is that you have as many separate and distinct patents as the countries that were designated in the original application. As in the Patent Cooperation Treaty, patents in the European Patent Convention are enforced in each individual country strictly in accordance with the national laws of that country. A number of countries in the European community have amended or are planning to amend their patent laws to bring them into conformity with specific provisions set forth in the European Patent Convention.

Both the European Patent Convention and the Patent Cooperation Treaty become operational in June of 1978. As we look at it today, we will soon have two additional systems that we can utilize for obtaining patent protection for our clients' inventions. It will be interesting to measure the results from these treaties against the goal that was set forth in the mid–1960s. Have we really developed systems that will simplify the filing and obtaining of patents in various foreign countries at less cost? Will the new systems promote or encourage more uniform laws in various countries? Have we set up a system in which the less developed countries can participate and thereby significantly upgrade the patent systems in those countries? I think that we have met at least some of these goals, although only time will tell if there is sufficient use of the new system to achieve the goals. Furthermore, there is a good bit of controversy over whether or not the cost of obtaining patents through the new systems will be less than going the conventional country-by-country route.

A U.S. practitioner, especially those representing multinational companies who market their products or license their technology world-wide, must take a hard look at these systems to determine whether or not they are applicable to the inventions of his clients. Like any other new system which becomes available, there will be a period of experimentation during which we will become familiar with the system and we cannot expect perfect results immediately. However, I think both the PCT and European Patent Convention will be suitable vehicles that can be used for protecting inventions for those who plan to obtain patents in more than a few countries. As of now, Belgium, West Germany, France, Luxembourg, the Netherlands, Switzerland and Great Britain have adhered to the European Patent Convention. However, 7 more countries are expected to ratify the Convention in 1978, including Italy, Norway and Sweden. About 20 countries are expected to be party to the Patent Cooperation Treaty by June 1, 1978, including the United States, Great Britain, West Germany, France, Switzerland, Brazil and Russia. Japan and Austria are expected to join by the end of 1978.

Most American corporations, I believe, will look upon the European Patent Convention as the most significant of the two treaties at this time because the European Patent Convention procedures provide a full examination system. Furthermore, almost all of the significant industrialized countries of Europe either have already ratified the European Patent Convention or are expected to do so by the end of this year.

On the other hand, the U.S. has reserved under Chapter II of the PCT. Hence, U.S. applicants can only take advantage of the search phase of PCT. Therefore, even though such significant non-European countries as Russia, Brazil and Japan have or are expected to ratify the PCT, it will have less appeal to U.S. citizens and corporations, at least initially, than the European Patent Convention. The PCT does have the flexibility of permitting a U.S. applicant to file an international application in the U.S. Patent and Trademark Office under PCT and designate filing in national offices of European countries either directly via PCT or through the European Patent Convention.

Now let's look at some of the potential advantages of using the new systems.

The most significant advantage is the additional time provided before a final decision has to be made on the filing of individual applications in the different countries. In accordance with PCT, the applicant has eight additional months beyond the year provided by the Paris Convention, plus a preliminary search report on which to base the decision on whether to complete the filings in the designated countries. Under Article 27(7) and Rule 4.7, an applicant does not need to appoint a national attorney or agent until processing of the application has started in the designated national Patent Office. In practice, appointment of the associate attorney or agent can be delayed until the 20th month following the filing date of the international application. Under the European Patent Convention, you will not only have the preliminary search, but you will have a complete examination of the claimed invention against the prior art and the application will be prosecuted through to the point of allowance. In both PCT and the European Patent Convention, the applicant has the opportunity to amend the claims and the specification of the application.

If, under either system, the applicant decides that his invention is not patentable or that the protection he is likely to obtain is not valuable, he can withdraw his designations of countries and does not have to complete the filing of the applications in individually designated countries. Of course, if he has not yet appointed agents, he saves the initial "opening the file" type of charge that agents usually make. The possibility of changing the decision of filing additional applications has a very significant bearing on the potential cost of using either PCT or the European Patent Convention. For example, if in one case out of ten the applicant is able to make a better decision which results in not filing applications in initially designated countries, he could save more money than the additional costs he has incurred in using either the PCT or the European Patent Convention.

Another significant advantage is that the applications in the United States, the Patent Cooperation Treaty and the European Patent Convention can all be prepared in exactly the same format. The form and content of an application, if it meets the standards of the Patent Cooperation Treaty, must be accepted in the European Patent Convention and in all of the countries which have adhered to either the European Patent Convention or the Patent Cooperation Treaty. The format includes the drawings, the description of the invention, the claims and the typing which, in accordance with the new system, is 1½ spaced typing. As you know, under the present system many countries have different requirements for drawings, formalities in the application, paper size and type spacing. Although this may appear to be trivia, it all takes time which increases costs.

The fact that PCT and European Patent Convention applications, in the initial stages, can all be prepared and prosecuted in the English language is an advantage for those of us who do not have good command of a second and third language. This avoids at least some of the problems encountered in translations.

Another significant advantage, at least from our point of view, is the savings in valuable attorney time by using the international system. Simply being able to prosecute a single patent application through to issuance, such as in the European Patent Convention, before having to embark on the prosecution of patent applications in other countries, is a significant advantage. For example, an amendment in a patent application in the European Patent Convention automatically applies to all of the patent applications that will be filed based on that international application thus eliminating the need to make duplicate amendments. Furthermore, the arguments made to distinguish the invention from the prior art will automatically be part of the file in all applications filed in the designated countries. Thus, instead of attempting to prosecute patent applications on the same invention in four or five or more countries simultaneously, the attorney will have the opportunity to go through one complete prosecution before he has to spend any time on the applications filed in other countries. Furthermore, assuming that the European Patent Convention operates as expected, there will be no requirement for further prosecution of a patent application when it is filed in the other countries. However, some countries may require a translation of the entire application into their native language. The present rules require that the claims in each patent be translated into the other official languages of the treaty.

Another advantage of both the PCT and the European Patent Convention which will be available to all of us, even those that do not use the system, is the periodic publication of an Official Journal containing an abstract of all patents issued through either the European Patent Convention or the Patent Cooperation Treaty.

Let's now consider some of the possible disadvantages of using either one of the international patent systems. First and foremost, of course, is the question of cost. There is no question, but the cost of filing and prosecuting a patent application in either the PCT or the European Patent Convention is going to be considerably more than in any individual country. At one time, it was projected that filing through the PCT would be a cost savings if the applicant intended to file patent applications in three or more countries. Later studies seem to indicate that the break even point is higher than that. Furthermore, some of the quotations of costs coming in from associates abroad indicate that the overall cost in the European Patent Office is going to be substantially more than we originally anticipated. However, the costs that are being quoted are primarily the Patent Office and associate fees and do not take into account the savings in attorney time or the potential savings due to the applicant being in a position to make a better judgment as to whether or not to finally file the applications in the designated countries. Therefore, any such study should be carefully scrutinized and the quoted costs of filing through either of the international systems should be measured against some of the other potential cost-saving features of the treaties before a final decision is made that the system is prohibitively expensive.

Other potential disadvantages of using the system is the argument that you are placing all of your eggs in a single basket. It is pointed out that if you go the individual country route in Europe, you are certain to get patents issued in some countries even if you can't get them in the difficult examination countries such as Switzerland and Germany. While this may be true, I think that you have to consider the potential value of such patents to your client. I am sure that when it comes to enforcing patents in the European community, the courts are going to inquire as to whether or not the patent was prosecuted through the European Patent Office or whether or not it went directly through the national offices. Thus, even if the national standard of patentability is not harmonized with the European Patent Convention standard by national legislative action, the national courts of the European Patent Convention member countries are likely to achieve some harmonization. This will be especially true in countries that do not maintain an examination system.

NOTES

1. *Patent Cooperation Treaty.* On October 9, 1986, the Senate gave its advice and consent to United States withdrawal of the reservation respecting Chapter II of the Patent Cooperation Treaty. Less than a month later Congress passed legislation implementing the country's participation in Chapter II, Pub.L. No. 99–616, 100 Stat. 3485 (1986), and, effective July 1, 1987, the United States became bound by Chapter II. See generally 35 U.S.C.A. §§ 351–376 (1984 & Supp.1989).

On the PCT generally, see Bartels, The Advantages of the Patent Cooperation Treaty (PCT) for American Applicants, 65 J. Pat. Off. Soc'y 387 (1983); Gruszow, Raue, Thompson & Tsuji, The Patent Cooperation Treaty (PCT): Using it More Through Knowing it Better, 24 Industrial Property 195 (1985).

2. *The Paris Convention and Economically Developing Countries.* Treaty obligations have influenced the transfer of technology from economically developed to economically developing nations. Since the late 1970's, the developing countries (called the "Group of 77") have pressed for changes in the Paris Convention to accommodate their special economic position. Demands for such concessions as compulsory exclusive licenses and automatic forfeiture of unexploited patents have dominated diplomatic conferences aimed at ironing out substantive disagreements between the two sides. More recent efforts have centered on a Draft Treaty for the Harmonization of Patent Laws.

On the general issues raised by the conflict between developed and developing nations, see Boros, Industrial Property in the New International Economic Order, 11 Eur.Intell.Prop.Rev. 301 (1982); Everson, Intellectual Property Rights in the Third World, 12 Eur.Intell.Prop.Rev. 330 (1983); Oddi, The International Patent System and Third World Development: Reality or Myth?, 1987 Duke L.J. 831.

3. *Bibliographic Note.* See generally S. Ladas, Patents, Trademarks, and Related Rights: National and International Protection (1975); G. Bodenhausen, Guide to the Application of the Paris Convention for the Protection of Industrial Property as Revised at Stockholm in 1967 (1968); J. Baxter, World Patent Law and Practice (2d ed. 1973); Lang, Foreign Patent Laws, with Comparative Analysis (Wade ed. 1968); Lignac, Foreign Patent Applications (1969).

On the European Patent Convention, see Allen, Cannon, Petersen & Senior, The E.P.C. System: Eight Years of Progress, 1 Intell.Prop.L.

27 (1987); Beier, The European Patent System, 14 Vand.J.Transnat'l L. 1 (1981); Meller, Patenting on the Isar—The Central Procurement of Patents in Europe, 67 J. Pat. & Trademark Off. Soc'y 179 (1985); Richards, 10 Years of Substantive Law Development in the European Patent Office, 71 J. Pat. & Trademark Off. Soc'y 320 (1989).

III. TRADEMARK

FRAYNE, HISTORY AND ANALYSIS OF TRT

63 Trademark Reporter 422–437 (1973).*

Background

The problem for which the Trademark Registration Treaty (TRT) is an intended solution is one which has beset the manufacturer or trader engaged in international commerce since trademarks began to assume importance in such commerce, a period of approximately the last one hundred fifty years, beginning some time after the first flowering of the Industrial Revolution. That problem has its roots in the territoriality of trademark law (in which respect, of course, trademark law does not differ from nearly every other field of law). Businessmen find trademarks to be commercially valuable, and desire to preserve to themselves the exclusive use of their trademarks in every country in which they trade or might trade. To accomplish this end, they find it necessary to seek protection in each country separately, complying with the law of each country. National law varies greatly but, in general, it is necessary or highly advisable to register trademarks with a public body, usually the Registry of Trademarks administered by the Patent Office. To register, the international businessman is forced to meet different procedural and substantive requirements in every country, to complete a bewildering variety of different forms in different languages, to cope with different and sometimes unintelligible systems of classifications of goods, to submit electro-types and prints differing in size and number, and to pay disparate official fees in a plethora of currencies. After registration has been obtained, its assignment, licensing or renewal is again subject to differences in national treatment. Perhaps most painful of all, the international businessman's inability to cope directly with all of these differences compels him to retain, in each country in which he desires protection, trademark attorneys or agents to do the necessary, against payment, of course, of a reasonable professional fee for the unravelling of the mysteries of national law.

All of this entails a good deal of bother and expenditure of money, neither of which is very attractive to the international business community.

The seed of subsequent attempts to solve the problem may be found in the Paris Convention for the Protection of Industrial Property (1883), usually called simply the International Convention. The basic principle of the International Convention was "national treatment" in each country for the nationals of all other member countries. There was, however, an Article 6 (now Article 6 quinquies), the famous "telle-quelle" provision, which required each member country to register the trademark of a national of another member country "just as" it was registered in the home country. The immediate purpose of the "telle-quelle" provision was to overcome national differences in the form of the matter deemed registrable as a trademark; for example, one of the obstacles which this provision sought to overcome was the requirement of Russian law at the time that all word trademarks be spelt in the Cyrillic alphabet. Beyond the desire to deal with this kind of problem, however, the "telle-quelle" provision embodied a certain philosophy which was relevant to the more general problem described above. It was the thought that, save for certain specific exceptions touching upon the fundamentals of national trademark law, and stated explicitly in Article 6, a national of a member country of the International Convention should have the right to "extend" his national protection to other member countries. This principle was rooted in a sentiment akin to the "full-faith-and-credit" clause of our Constitution: whatever any member country had done to protect a trademark officially by way of registration, would be recognized by all of the others if at all possible under national law. Hence, Article 6 of the International Convention made the first breach in the hermetically sealed compartments of national law, but premised that breach upon the principle of respect by all member countries for the official acts of any; or, put more crudely, upon the principle of the mutual solidarity of all national bureaucracies.

The seed planted by the "telle-quelle" provision of the International Convention grew into the first full-fledged effort at a solution of the problem, the Madrid Arrangement for the International Registration of Trademarks (1891), usually known as the "Madrid Arrangement." The Madrid Arrangement institutionalized and systematized the underlying philosophy of the "telle-quelle" provision. Under the Madrid Arrangement, a national of a member country having obtained a registration in that country could request his national Patent Office to forward such national registration to the International Bureau created by the International Convention, with a request that the same form the basis for an International Registration; and that International Registration would have the force of a national registration in every member country for as long, if properly renewed, as the home registration subsisted. This system took two important steps forward as compared with the "telle-quelle" provision of the International Convention. First, the trademark owner's home registration could be extended to other member countries without a multiplicity of national filings. Second, a sort of procedural presumption in favor of protection was created: whereas in the ordinary situation, a national filing does not result in a registration unless specifically granted, under the Madrid Arrangement an International Registration automatically had the force of a national registration unless specifically refused by the national administration within a term of twelve months.

Naturally, the underlying philosophy of the Madrid Arrangement dictated that the International Registration would be strictly co-extensive and co-existent with the home registration, a concept which is now called "dependency" upon the home registration. The International Registration could not be obtained until the home registration had issued, covered exactly the same mark and goods, and died with the home registration. This opened the possibility for a third party to destroy the International Registration in all member countries through a successful attack on the basic home registration, a device later dubbed "Central Attack." This system provided a powerful but erratic weapon: powerful, because if available it destroyed the International Registration everywhere regardless of the merits of the cases of the litigants in all countries but the home country; erratic, because it was available only if the attacker had superior rights in the registrant's home country.

From fairly early in the life of the Madrid Arrangement, it became evident that it created a great deal of "deadwood" on the International Register, marks neither in use nor likely to be used, and that this "deadwood" formed a substantial obstacle to the ever more difficult search for new trademarks. This phenomenon, called in more recent years "proliferation," resulted from the absence of restraints at the two points where these might have been applied: at the national registration level (where the dependency mechanism of the Madrid Arrangement would have made restraints automatically effective internationally), and at the International Registration level. Nationally, most countries party to the Madrid Arrangement did not, until recent years, practice examination, have an opposition procedure, have user requirements before or after registration, or limit the number of goods or classes that might be covered by one registration; thus, the national registration basis for an International Registration was easily and broadly established and maintained. At the International Registration level, the Madrid Arrangement, until the 1957 Nice Revision came into force in December 1965, automatically extended protection to all member countries, and did not impose any limitation upon, or demand extra payment for, the inclusion of any number of goods or classes.

The United States never adhered to the Madrid Arrangement. Our reluctance to join sprang from two causes. First, our domestic legislation would, under the dependency rule of the Madrid Arrangement, place our nationals at a considerable disadvantage, since they could not establish the necessary United States registration basis until after actual use of the trademark in commerce subject to the regulation of Congress, and successful traverse through the examination and opposition process, and then only for a narrowly defined specification of goods. Second, there was considerable apprehension of the proliferation problem, the possible flooding of our Register with marks of no or little real commercial importance. For similar reasons, other Western Hemisphere countries have been reluctant to join; Brazil, Cuba and Mexico, which had actually joined, subsequently withdrew. Thus, the Madrid Arrangement remained essentially a European agreement, although even there it did not include the United Kingdom and the Scandinavian countries.

The members of the Madrid Arrangement, although generally satisfied with its workings, were not unaware of these defects, and did wish to make it more attractive to non-members. The 1957 Nice Revision took certain important steps. While dependency upon a basic home registration was left intact as a condition precedent to the International Registration, it was moderated as a condition subsequent for its maintenance: five years after the grant of an International Registration, it would become entirely independent of the home registration. Further, member countries were given the option (which nearly all have since exercised) of stating that they would not be covered by an International Registration unless the registrant specifically named them, and paid an additional fee. Finally, additional fees were imposed for all classes covered by an International Registration beyond the first three.

These changes did not seem to non-member countries to go far enough, and suggestions were made in 1969, particularly by the United States, for a more drastic revision. As a result, in December 1969 the World Intellectual Property Organization (WIPO) circulated a statement containing a list of possible further changes that might be made in the Madrid Arrangement.

There ensued in April 1970 the first of a series of WIPO-sponsored Conferences of (Government) Experts in Geneva. At that first conference, where the United States delegation was led by former Commissioner of Patents, William E. Schuyler, Jr., a deadlock quickly developed between non-member countries, and particularly the United States, on the one hand, and member countries of the Madrid Arrangement on the other. The United States wished to have complete abolition of dependency. Member countries, with the exception of Germany, wished to retain dependency at least as a condition precedent: in part, probably because it belonged to the traditional philosophy of the Madrid Arrangement; in part, because dependency provided one of the few restraints upon proliferation and constituted a sort of preliminary "sieve" which might preserve non-examining member countries from a flood of International Registrations emanating, for example, from the United States, whose examining system would thus do the work of that lacking in most member countries; and in part because of the member countries' attachment to a system of central attack, which seemed most difficult to provide for excepting in conjunction with dependency upon a home registration.

There were differences on other points also. Non-member countries wished separate fees to be payable for each country named and for each class named, both as a restraint on proliferation, and to meet the financial burden which would be imposed upon examining countries. Member countries preferred the simpler and cheaper system of the Madrid Arrangement. Non-member countries were generally favorable to international filings directly with WIPO; several member countries preferred retention of a requirement for filing through the home Patent Office. Non-member countries were skeptical, at best, of the possibility of a central attack system; most member countries were insistent upon its necessity. Some non-members, like the United States, were pleased by a WIPO proposal that international filings provide for the possibility of meeting the special requirements of certain countries (specifically, that a declaration alleging use in commerce must be filed with every international application naming the United States). Member countries were highly critical of any provision incorporating into the Madrid Arrangement recognition of the specific requirements of certain countries and, in particular, clearly indicated their opposition to the United States requirement for use in commerce as a precondition to registration; in their eyes, this requirement, to which the United States and Canada alone among the major countries of the world still adhere, would place their nationals at a comparative disadvantage in relation to American and Canadian nationals who would be confronted with no such difficulty when naming member countries in international applications.

At the end of the April 7, 1970 Conference, Commissioner Schuyler suggested that to break the impasse, the United States would consider submitting to the Executive Committee of the Paris Union a proposal for an agreement for the International Registration of Trademarks, capable of meeting the needs of all Paris Union members, in other words, a suggestion of an entirely new agreement, distinct from the Madrid Arrangement.

A recital of developments at the ensuing six further conferences in Geneva, and of their arguments, discussions, confrontations, etc., would fill volumes, and delight the heart of none but a professional historian. Suffice it to say that, by the time the Diplomatic Conference opened in Vienna on May 17, 1973, the following results had been achieved:

A new Treaty would be drafted, containing basically the provisions desired by non-member countries of the Madrid Arrangement but designed to co-exist with the Madrid Arrangement and to detract as little as possible from the viability of the continued existence of the Madrid Arrangement among its present members.

The new Treaty, in one of its rare substantive provisions, would require member countries not to refuse, nor to cancel for a number of years, International Registrations, on the ground that the marks covered thereby had not been used.

The latter provision, concerning which more is said below, is clearly aimed at the United States and at the elimination of that part of our law which foreigners find most obnoxious. Since that part of our law happens also to be at the very root of our entire Common Law of trademarks, the provision obviously presents us with a certain challenge. There is no doubt, however, that in the history of the negotiations leading to TRT, this provision was the essential consideration for the agreement of the members of the Madrid Arrangement countries to participate in the drafting of a new Treaty for which, with the major exception of Germany, they do not care, and which they fear would imperil the survival of their much-loved Madrid Arrangement.

The great fights having been fought in the preparatory conferences in Geneva, the May–June 1973 Vienna Diplomatic Conference produced few major changes in the text of TRT, but a host of lesser amendments, not unimportant but not basic to the TRT scheme. From the standpoint of the United States, there were two major debates.

The first dealt with the critical provision requiring member states to suspend their user requirements for a given term of years. A stalemate had developed on whether that term should be three years or five years. A compromise had been reached at one of the last Geneva Conferences, whereby that term would be three years, but extendible to five under certain circumstances. In Vienna, the United States delegation deemed it necessary to insist upon three years without possibility of an extension. This produced great opposition on the part of a number of other delegations, who thought that we had, in the vernacular, "welshed" on a deal. Nevertheless, the United States stood firm and indicated that the chances of ratification of the Treaty by the Senate would be poor unless the term were strictly limited to three years. On that argument, our position won the day.

Second, there was an unforeseen proposal by Brazil on behalf of the "developing countries," insisting upon special benefits to these countries in view of their economic inferiority vis-a-vis the developed countries. Specifically, Brazil proposed that the nationals of developing countries be entitled, for a number of years, to obtain International Registrations, without requiring such developing countries to adhere to TRT and thus be capable of designation in an International Registration by nationals of member countries. The United States delegation thought this proposal devoid of merit and quite unrelated to the needs of developing countries. To our surprise, however, we found that other developed countries such as Great Britain and Germany were ready to agree on some compromise language. Accordingly, the final text of TRT contains a complicated Article 40, under which for certain (extendible) terms, nationals of non-member developing countries will be entitled to obtain International Registrations.

There was also, somewhat unexpectedly, a great "non-fight" at Vienna. Throughout all of the conferences leading up to the Vienna Diplomatic Conference, the question of Central Attack had been the subject of prolonged and sometimes acidulous debate. Complex proposals had been submitted by WIPO, Switzerland, the Netherlands and Belgium. In the absence of the simple mechanism of dependency upon a home registration, none of these substitute proposals was found workable or acceptable to a majority. At no time, however, did any of the proponents of Central Attack formally abandon their quest, or indicate their willingness, however reluctant, to do without a Central Attack system if necessary. There was some expectation, therefore, that new proposals, or renewed efforts to gain acceptance of earlier proposals, would be made at the Vienna Diplomatic Conference. That this did not happen may indicate that the proponents of Central Attack have bowed to reality; or it may indicate that they have written off

TRT as an instrument to which they can adhere, and will make do with the Madrid Arrangement. Time will tell.

Thus was the Trademark Registration Treaty born: conceived in the clash of sharply differing opinions, and characterized by radical mutations from the properties of its ancestor, the Madrid Arrangement, mutations which are certain to put to the test the adaptability of the intended adoptive parents.

The Provisions of TRT

Before noting in detail the provisions of TRT, it is important to be clear in one's mind as to the essential nature of the Treaty. Despite its name, which can easily be misunderstood, TRT does not create a true International Registration. Such a legal creature, which indeed has been proposed in a number of responsible quarters, would have required one substantive law of trademarks, applicable in all member countries; supra-national administrative and juridical institutions capable of administering and interpreting such law, and adjudicating under it; and an International Registration having the same force and the same significance in every member country. This, a true supra-national trademark, would supersede national law and national institutions and represent, in the field of trademarks, a large surrender of national sovereignty. There is much to commend such a concept as an ultimate goal, at least for nations whose economies are sufficiently unified to constitute one market. Indeed, the supra-national mark is not merely a dream, but is already a reality for some countries: the Benelux mark is a true International Registration for the three countries involved, and the European trademark, if and when it comes to pass, will be a true International Registration for the nine countries of the European Common Market. The concept, however, does not yet seem warranted for the seventy-nine member countries of the Paris Union to whom adherence to TRT will be open (TRT being a special arrangement under Article 19 of the International Convention).

Thus TRT, like the Madrid Arrangement, is essentially a filing treaty. The supra-national character of TRT is exhausted at the filing stage (although, it will be seen, "filing" should be understood to include not merely filing for International Registrations, but also filing for later designations, assignments, changes of name, restrictions of specifications of goods, and renewals). A formally correct filing results in recordal on the International Register, and thereafter national law takes over, with the single major exception, mentioned above, of the suspension of national user requirements for a certain term of years. The International Registration when granted is but a bundle of national rights. The form of TRT is substance, but its substance is form: or, to speak in less Delphically oracular terms, while the language of TRT is frequently that of substantive trademark law, in fact it is concerned, with one major and a few minor exceptions, with the formalities of filing.

The principal provisions of TRT may be set forth as follows:

(1) International Registrations may be obtained by nationals or residents of member countries independent of any home registration (but member states have the option of requiring persons who are both nationals and residents of that state to file nationally before filing internationally).

(2) Applications may be filed directly with the International Bureau of WIPO in Geneva, in either English or French.

(3) International Applications may claim the priority date of an earlier national application within the six-month term established by the International Convention.

(4) International Applications must identify goods with reasonable precision, and according to the International Classification of Goods.

(5) International Applications must specifically name each TRT member state to be covered ("Designated State"). An interesting feature of TRT is "self-designation"; that is, an international applicant may designate his own home country, and indeed only his home country. Thus, depending upon his circumstances, an American trademark owner may well choose to obtain the equivalent of a United States registration by filing in Geneva rather than in Washington.

(6) Each International Application is subject to an international filing fee, presently set at 400 Swiss francs. In addition, there is payable a fee for each Designated State which, at the option of the Designated State, may be 100% of the national fees payable; this State Designation fee may vary according to the number of classes covered.

(7) After examination of the International Application for formalities, the International Bureau grants an International Registration, whose date is the filing date of the International Application.

(8) The International Bureau publishes the International Registration, and notifies the National Patent Office of each Designated State. At this point, TRT mostly leaves the stage, and national law takes over.

(9) The International Registration immediately has the effect, in each Designated State, of a national application and in due course thereafter, unless refused, has also the effect of a national registration in that State.

(10) After publication of the International Registration, each Designated State carries out its internal examination, and/or opens its opposition procedure, pursuant to national law. Each such State is granted a period of fifteen months (eighteen months in the case of certification marks) within which to notify the International Bureau of a refusal, or possible refusal, of the International Registration. The notification must include all grounds, including oppositions, for the refusal or possible refusal. Unless such notification is made within the fifteen (eighteen) months from the date of publication, the International Registration automatically gains national registration effect in the Designated State.

(11) Each Designated State may refuse on any ground established by national law, provided that such ground not be inconsistent with any provision of TRT, the International Convention, and in particular Article 6 quinquies (telle-quelle provision). As previously noted, TRT provides that the International Registration may not be refused on the ground that the mark has not been used anywhere. The "telle-quelle" provision also limits, but within generous boundaries, the grounds for refusal.

(12) Unless refused, an International Registration has in each Designated State an independent life as a national registration, and subject in almost all respects to national law. But it cannot be canceled for nonuse during at least the first three years and its renewable life span is ten years. The text leaves entirely to national law the legal rights flowing from a registration, although it is obvious that the expectation of TRT is that some substantive rights are created by registration.

(13) After the grant of an International Registration, the registrant may at any time during its life apply to designate additional States; these "later designations" are treated, mutatis mutandis, in the same fashion as the original International Application.

(14) The International Registration may be assigned, and the assignment recorded at the International Bureau. Recordal at the International Bureau has the effect of recordal with the Patent Office of each Designated State, but each such State may refuse the said effect on any ground provided by national law. Similarly, changes of name may be recorded with the International Bureau with national effect, but the Patent Office of each Designated State may require proof satisfactory to it of the change of name.

(15) Another provision relating to assignments permits the international registrant to assign the International Registration for some of the goods only, and/or for some of the Designated States only. This raises the interesting possibility of the virtual atomization of an International Registration. As to the separate alienability of rights in Designated States, it must be remembered that this is entirely consistent with the "bundle of national rights" nature of an International Registration; as to the divisibility of the goods, it remains open to Designated States to reject an assignment when the same would result in ownership of the International Registration by different parties in respect of goods which that State deems similar for trademark purposes.

(16) Renewal of an International Registration for ten-year periods is automatic in all Designated States, upon filing of the proper form with, and payment of the correct fee to, the International Bureau.

(17) An International Registration may be canceled, in each Designated State, on any ground established by national law, save for the limitation imposed by the normal three-year suspension of user requirements.

(18) An important provision, inserted at the insistence of the United States delegation, permits national law to state that no infringement action may be brought on the registration of an unused trademark; the action lies in a Designated State only after continuing use has commenced in that State, and damages are limited to the period subsequent to the commencement of such continuing use. Several things may be said concerning this provision. First, this provision is normally significant during only the first three years (or five in some States) of the life of an International Registration, which thereafter may be canceled for nonuse. Second, it does not touch upon other rights, such as oppositions and cancellation actions, which may be grounded upon an International Registration. Third, it may well prove to be a booby-trap for the unwary subsequent user, as the rights of the registrant, after continuing use has commenced, go back to the International Registration date. On the whole, the utility and wisdom in purely practical terms of this provision may be questioned, but there is no doubt that it represents a psychologically important gesture of respect to the Common Law concept that exclusionary rights to a trademark may be exercised only as an incident of its use.

(19) Provision is made for the absorption by an International Registration of the rights deriving from an earlier Madrid Arrangement or national registration in a given Designated State; and, conversely, provision is made for the possibility of a national application claiming the rights deriving from an earlier International Registration.

Prospects and Problems

. . .

Is Proliferation a Real Danger?

Proliferation had been a problem under the old Madrid Arrangement. TRT does contain just about all of the built-in "anti-proliferation" measures that could be devised, and which are absent from the original Madrid Arrangement: the obligation to name each country and class separately, and to pay corresponding fees for each. This will be some deterrent against proliferation, but hardly a decisive one.

Further, the danger of proliferation, if defined as the increase in the number of filings and registrations, cannot be evaluated on the same basis for every country. The United States, alone among the major countries, at present is the possessor of a powerful "anti-proliferation" weapon, the requirement for use of a trademark in commerce prior to filing. This requirement has a double inhibitory effect. First, and most obviously, a prospective United States resident applicant must go to the trouble and expense of making interstate use (genuine and commercial, if he hopes for a valid registration) before he can even file. Second, and more subtle, is the fact that a person who has made use of a trademark in the United States by that fact acquires Common Law rights; a federal registration, despite its very considerable advantages, is not necessary to establish ownership. Ironically, the small regional manufacturer or merchant who might most benefit from a federal registration is probably less aware of such benefits and less prone to go to the trouble and expense of a federal application than his larger competitors; while great corporations who market nationally build up such extensive Common Law rights that a federal registration is frequently deemed unnecessary.

Statistics disclose the anti-proliferative effect of our law both upon domestic business enterprises and foreign ones. The United States, as the largest market and most productive economy in the world, may reasonably be thought to offer a correspondingly favorable climate to trademarks. And yet, this fact is not reflected in the filing figures. In the year 1970, the United States Patent Office received a total of 33,326 trademark applications. This is about the same as the number filed in Brazil, 1½ times that filed in France, slightly more than 1½ times the number filed in West Germany, about twice the number filed in the United Kingdom, and—surprisingly—only about 15% more than the 26,968 filed in Spain. One almost hesitates to mention the statistics for Japan, all of whose economic figures in recent years seem to have been made in the Land of Oz: 139,367 in 1970, or more than four times the total filed in the United States.

The 1970 figures for filing by foreigners are equally striking. There were 3,053 such applications in the United States. That same year, that number was exceeded by the non-national filings in the following countries: Argentina, Belgium, Brazil, Canada, Chile, China (Taiwan), Denmark, France, West Germany, Italy, Japan, Mexico, South Africa, Sweden, Great Britain and Venezuela.

It is unimaginable that the huge and wealthy United States market is less attractive to trademark owners, both domestic and foreign, than those of the countries named in the preceding two paragraphs. Only a few of the named countries are party to the Madrid Arrangement. The explanation for the disparity of the figures must, therefore, lie in the inhibitory effect of our requirement for use as a condition to filing.

The conclusion, therefore, must be that TRT will bring about a great increase in the number of filings, and of registrations, in the United States: in part (for both United States nationals and non-nationals), because of the facility of filing under TRT, but in greater part, for United States nationals, because of the elimination of use as a pre-condition to filing and, for the first three years, as a condition to the maintenance of the registration. Under TRT, therefore, we must reconcile ourselves to a considerably greater number of registrations on our Register than at present, registrations which, moreover, do not reflect Common Law rights.

Thus the internal TRT safeguards against proliferation, while good in themselves, cannot be relied upon by the United States to prevent a large increase in the number of filings and registrations in this country. Our reliance must be upon our own domestic law, and while we cannot under TRT remove unused trademarks from the Register for at least the first three years, it is to be hoped that among the many other changes in our legislation which would ensue from our ratification of TRT, there would be included much more stringent procedures for the removal from the Register of trademarks unused after three years from the date of registration.

Still, TRT cannot be simultaneously criticized for providing negligible benefits to nationals of member countries, and for leading to proliferation. If the benefits are negligible, there will be no proliferation. If there is proliferation, it can only be because TRT is attractive to many trademark owners.

NOTES

1. In addition to the Paris Convention, the United States is a party to the Inter–American Convention for Trademark and Commercial Protection with nine Latin American nations and to several bilateral treaties.

2. *Trademark Registration Treaty.* Although the United States signed the Trademark Registration Treaty in 1973—and although the treaty entered into force in 1980—the United States has not yet ratified the TRT. Two stumbling blocks in the way of ratification have been the Lanham Act's use requirement and delays in Patent and Trademark Office examinations exceeding the TRT's fifteen-month period. See J.T. McCarthy, Trademarks and Unfair Competition § 19:56 (2d ed. 1984). To what extent do the intent to use provisions introduced by the Trademark Law Revision Act of 1988, p. 204, above, move the United States toward a position in which it can ratify the TRT?

On the TRT generally, see Symposium, The Trademark Registration Treaty (TRT), 63 Trademark Rep. 421 (1973); Allen, The Trademark Registration Treaty: Its Implementing Legislation, 21 Idea 161 (1980); Pattishall, The Proposed Trademark Registration Treaty and its Domestic Import, 62 Trademark Rep. 125 (1972).

3. *Importation of Infringing Goods.* Section 42 of the Lanham Act, 15 U.S.C. § 1124 (1988), provides in part that "no article of imported merchandise which shall copy or simulate the name of . . . any domestic manufacture, or manufacturer, or trader, or of any manufacturer or trader located in any foreign country which, by treaty, convention, or law affords similar privileges to citizens of the United States, or which shall copy or simulate a trademark registered in accordance with the provisions of this chapter or shall bear a name or mark calculated to induce the public to believe that the article is manufactured in the United States, or that it is manufactured in any foreign country or locality other than the country or locality in which it is in fact manufactured, shall be admitted to entry at any customhouse of the United States. . . ."

To prevent importation of infringing articles, the trademark or trade name owner must record the mark or name with the United States Customs Service. The Customs Service will then exclude any goods bearing a confusingly similar mark or name. See 19 C.F.R. 133.21 (1989). The strategic advantage of Customs exclusion is that it saves the trademark owner the effort of tracking down, and bringing infringement actions against, distributors who have purchased the imported goods for resale in the United States. See also section 526 of the Tariff Act of 1930, 19 U.S.C. § 1526 (1988). See generally, Kuhn, Remedies Available at Customs for Infringement of a Registered Trademark, 70 Trademark Rep. 387 (1980).

Does a trademark owner have any remedy under the Trademark Act or the Tariff Act against "gray market" goods? Gray market goods are genuine goods, lawfully manufactured abroad under the identical trademark, and imported into the United States without the consent of the United States trademark owner. See Weil Ceramics & Glass, Inc. v. Dash, below.

3. *Bibliographic Note.* See generally, S. Ladas, Patents, Trademarks, and Related Rights: National and International Protection (1975); E. Offner, International Trademark Protection (1965); European Trademark Law and Practice (P.L.I. ed. 1970).

WEIL CERAMICS AND GLASS, INC. v. DASH

United States Court of Appeals, Third Circuit, 1989.
878 F.2d 659, 11 U.S.P.Q.2d 1001.

A. LEON HIGGINBOTHAM, Jr., Circuit Judge.

On this appeal we are asked to determine the availability of trademark and tariff act protections to an American company—which is owned by the same entity that owns the foreign manufacturer of a good, but which holds a valid American trademark for the foreign manufactured good—against parallel imports or so-called "gray-market" goods. Specifically, we are asked to determine whether § 32 of the Lanham Act, 15 U.S.C. § 1114 (1982), makes damages available to the American trademark holder for trademark infringement and if § 42 of that act, 15 U.S.C. § 1124 (1982), may be employed on behalf of the American company to prohibit the importation of gray-market goods.

This appeal also raised the question of whether § 526 of the Tariff Act, 19 U.S.C. § 1526 (1982), could be employed to preclude the importation of gray-market goods. That section has been construed by the Customs agency in its regulations as allowing the importation of gray-market goods in those cases where the American trademark holder is owned by, or owns, the foreign manufacturer of the good. See 19 C.F.R. § 133.21 (1987). Appellee/Cross–Appellant contended, and the district court found, that the Customs agency's regulation was inapplicable. Since the filing of this appeal, however, the agency's regulation was construed in a decision of the Supreme Court—unrelated to the present appeal—which raised the same issue. See K Mart Corp. v. Cartier, Inc., 486 U.S. 281, 108 S.Ct. 1811, 100 L.Ed.2d 313 (1988). That decision controls the claim raised by the Appellee/Cross–Appellant regarding § 526 in this case, and directs that the decision entered by the district court on its behalf be reversed. K Mart is also instructive to the disposition of the Appellee/Cross–Appellant's contentions regarding §§ 42 and 32. We conclude that neither of these sections provides the relief sought and, accordingly, we will reverse the decision of the district court.

Finally, we conclude that the district court erred by dismissing the contention raised by Appellee/Cross–Appellant under § 33(b) of Lanham Act, 15 U.S.C. § 1115(b) (1982), on the grounds that that section does not expressly or implicitly provide a right for private action. We conclude that § 33(b) may be used by a private litigant in an infringement action and, therefore, we will reverse the judgment of the district court. Notwithstanding that conclusion, however, we will remand with instructions that judgment be entered in favor of the Appellant/Cross–Appellee. We review, *de novo,* the appropriate scope of the statute and conclude that § 33(b) does not provide the remedy sought by the Appellee/Cross–Appellant in this case.

I. *Background*

This is an appeal about gray-market goods. Appellee/Cross–Appellant, Weil Ceramics & Glass, Inc., ("Weil"), is the wholly owned subsidiary of Lladro Exportadora, S.A., a Spanish corporation that is a sister corporation to Lladro, S.A., which manufactures fine porcelain in Spain. The porcelain is handmade and each piece bears the trademark "LLADRO," accompanied by a flower logo.

In February 1966, Weil, a New York corporation in the business of importing and selling fine porcelain and glassware, became the exclusive distributor in the United States of Lladro porcelain. The following year Weil obtained a valid United States registration for the LLADRO trademark and continued as the exclusive distributor of the porcelain.

In 1973, Lladro, S.A. acquired 50% of Weil's stock. At that time, Weil assigned all of its rights in its United States LLADRO trademark to Lladro, S.A. In 1977, Lladro Exportadora obtained Lladro, S.A.'s shares of Weil stock, as well as the remaining 50% of Weil stock, and became the sole owner of Weil. In 1983, Lladro Exportadora assigned the United States LLADRO trademark back to Weil.

In 1982, Appellants/Cross–Appellees Jalyn Corporation and its president, Bernard Dash, (together "Jalyn"), began importing LLADRO porcelain. Jalyn legally obtained the porcelain in Spain from distributors of Lladro, S.A. and sold it in the United States without the consent of Weil. In 1984, Weil filed a complaint in the federal district court for the district of New Jersey seeking declaratory and injunctive relief against Jalyn's continued import of Lladro porcelain and money damages for trademark infringement.

The District Court's Decision

In its complaint, Weil contended that Jalyn's import and sale of Lladro porcelain violated Weil's exclusive right to use the trademark pursuant to § 33(b) of the Lanham Act. 15 U.S.C. § 1115(b) (1982). Weil further contended that Jalyn's actions constituted an infringement on its trademark in violation of §§ 32(1)(a) and 42 of the Lanham Act, and a violation of § 526 of the Tariff Act. 19 U.S.C. § 1526 (1982).

After the completion of discovery, Weil and Jalyn filed cross motions for summary judgment.

The district court dismissed Weil's contention under § 33(b) because it concluded that that section does not provide for private enforcement. It held that the language of § 33(b) "does not establish any intent by Congress to create a cause of action." *Weil Ceramics & Glass, Inc. v. Dash,* 618 F.Supp. 700, 703 (D.N.J.1985). The district court determined that § 33(b) "merely states the evidentiary status of an incontestable mark," id., and noted that "§ 32 [of the Lanham Act] provides an effective remedy for the owner of a mark which has been improperly used by another. . . . [and] since § 32 expressly provides a remedy, the statutory scheme effectively negates any congressional intent to create a cause of action under § 33(b)." *Id.* at 704.

In light of its conclusion regarding § 33(b), the district court stated its view that Weil's infringement action turned upon § 32. On the claim based on that section, however, the district court granted Weil's motion for summary judgment. It held, in pertinent part, that "[i]n order to prevail on its claim under § 32(1)(a), Weil must show that . . . [Jalyn's] use [of the LLADRO trademark] is likely to cause 'confusion.'" *Weil Ceramics,* 618 F.Supp. at 704. Jalyn had argued, as it does on this appeal, that because the porcelain that it sold was genuine—i.e., the trademark was affixed by the manufacturer and was no different in character from the porcelain sold by Weil—the goods did not cause the "confusion" to which § 32(1)(a) refers. The district court rejected that argument. It found that the porcelain goods imported by Jalyn "are not a copy or imitation," *Id.* at 703, but nonetheless concluded that the trademark act proscriptions applied. Noting that "relatively few cases have confronted this issue and the courts have split, . . . [the district court] conclude[d] . . . that genuine goods may cause confusion." *Id.* at 706.

As support for its holding, the district court relied principally upon the Supreme Court's decision in A. Bourjois & Co. v. Katzel, 260 U.S. 689, 43 S.Ct. 244, 67 L.Ed. 464 (1923). The district court read that decision as having established the "territoriality principle" of trademark law which views trademarks as having separate legal existences in each country in which they are registered, and as symbolic of "the goodwill of the domestic markholder whose reputation backs the particular product in that territory." *Weil Ceramics,* 618 F.Supp. at 705. In that light, the district court concluded that "even if a trademark correctly identified the manufacturer of the goods, it would still be an infringing product if it deceived the public into believing that the domestic markholder's goodwill stood behind the product." Id. The district court then analyzed the factual evidence of Weil's independent goodwill in the LLADRO trademarked porcelain, and concluded that Weil had demonstrated that no issue of material fact existed concerning Weil's claim that Jalyn's distribution of the porcelain in the United States had infringed Weil's trademark.

Finally, the district court reviewed Weil's contention that § 42 of the Lanham Act and § 526 of the Tariff Act precluded Jalyn's continued importation of the LLADRO porcelain. Jalyn sought summary judgment on this contention on two bases: first, Jalyn contended that § 42, like § 32, does not provide that genuine goods are subject to claims raised under the trademark act. The district court rejected that argument and cited the Supreme Court's decision in A. Bourjois & Co. v. Aldridge, 263 U.S. 675, 44 S.Ct. 4, 66 L.Ed. 501 (1923) for the proposition that "genuine goods may infringe under the trademark laws and further that such infringing goods would be excludable under both the trademark and customs laws." *Weil Ceramics,* 618 F.Supp. at 715. It noted that a separate federal statute provides that § 42 and § 526 are not applicable to importations into the Virgin Islands of "genuine foreign merchandise bearing a genuine foreign trademark." Id. at 715. In light of that specific preclusion, the district court concluded that "[i]f Congress did not believe that genuine goods were excludable under § 42 and § 526, then it would not have had to create a special exception for imports into the Virgin Islands." Id. It held, therefore, that Jalyn's importation of the LLADRO porcelain infringed Weil's trademark pursuant to § 42 and was excludable under § 526.

Alternatively, Jalyn argued that neither § 526 nor § 42 could be employed to bar importation of the porcelain because of the federal regulation that explicitly excludes from § 526's prohibition against parallel imports those goods that are distributed by a United States trademarkholder that has a corporate relationship with the foreign manufacturer. See 19 C.F.R. § 133.21(c)(2) (1987). The district court also rejected that argument. It concluded that "Weil has established a separate and independent goodwill for the Lladro mark," *Weil Ceramics,* 618 F.Supp. at 715, and therefore had demonstrated that it was the "owner" of the trademark. In the district court's view, "whether the domestic markholder is independent does not depend on its relation to a foreign entity, but rather upon whether there is a distinct goodwill for the product in the United States." Id. at 716. The district court held that the "common control" exclusion from the prohibition of parallel imports was inapplicable because that exclusion did not define or limit the scope of § 526 or § 42, but rather only defined the Customs agency's role administering the statute. Id. at 717. It held that the exclusions in §§ 133.21(c)(1) and (2) provided only that the goods imported by Jalyn were not subject to "*automatic exclusion* by Customs under the regulations." Id. at 718. (emphasis in original). Accordingly, the district court held that the regulation did not proscribe a judicial determination that the goods "cause[d] confusion under § 42 and may be excluded under § 526." Id. It found that such confusion existed and, therefore, that both § 42 and § 526 were available to preclude Jalyn's continued import of the porcelain.

Jalyn filed this appeal from the decision of the district court granting summary judgment to Weil on its claims regarding §§ 32 and 42 of the Lanham Act and § 526 of the Tariff Act. Weil cross-appealed the dismissal of its claim based upon § 33(b) of the Lanham Act.

Subsequent to the filing of appeals in this case, the Supreme Court granted certiorari review of a consolidation of cases, decided by the Court of Appeals for the District of Columbia, in which that Court of Appeals had determined that the Customs Agency's promulgation of § 133.21 was inconsistent with § 526. We held disposition of this appeal in abeyance *curia advisari vult*, pending the decision of the Supreme Court. In *K Mart*, the Supreme Court resolved explicitly one of the principal issues raised in the present appeal, and gave important guidance for the resolution of the remaining issues.

II. *K Mart v. Cartier, Inc.*

K Mart, similar to the present case, concerned the import of parallel goods without the consent of the American trademark holder. The focus of the Court's opinion was the Customs Agency's construction of § 526 of the Tariff Act as reflected by its promulgation of § 133.21. Section 526 prohibits the importation

> into the United States [of] any merchandise of foreign manufacture if such merchandise . . . bears a trademark owned by a citizen of, or by a corporation or association created or organized within, the United States, and registered in the Patent and Trademark Office by a person domiciled in the United States . . . unless written consent of the owner of such trademark is produced at the time of making entry.

19 U.S.C. § 1526(a) (1982). By its promulgation of § 133.21, however, the Customs Agency construed § 526 to except goods for which the United States trademark is not solely "owned by" a domestic entity. Accordingly, that regulation permits the entry of goods manufactured abroad by the "same person" who holds the United States trademark or by a person who is "subject to common control" with the United States trademark holder. 19 C.F.R. §§ 133.21(c)(1), (2) (1987).[4]

In *K Mart*, the Court addressed claims that these two exceptions for "common control" and "authorized use" to § 526's prohibition against parallel imports are inconsistent with § 526. The Court determined that §§ 133.21(c)(1) & (2) were reasonable constructions of ambiguity in the language of § 526 and concluded that those sections were consistent with the intent of § 526.

In its analysis, the Court identified three general case scenarios in which the gray-market goods issue is presented, and evaluated the reasonableness of the application of § 133.21 to each of those scenarios.

---

4. Section 133.21 implements the "[r]estrictions on importations of articles bearing recorded trademarks and tradenames." 19 C.F.R. § 133.21 (1987). Significantly, however, the section delineates specific circumstances in which the restrictions do not apply. In pertinent part, the regulation provides that

[t]he restrictions set forth in [this section] do not apply to imported articles when:

(1) Both the foreign and the U.S. trademark or trade name are owned by the same person or business entity; [or]

(2) *The foreign and domestic trademark or trade name owners are parent and subsidiary companies or are otherwise subject to common ownership or control*

19 C.F.R. §§ 133.21(c)(1), (2) (1987) (emphasis added).

The case 1 scenario, which the Court described as prototypical, involves a domestic company—that is independent of the foreign manufacturer—which purchases the right from the foreign company to register and use that company's trademark in the United States. The case 2 scenario involves a domestic company that registers a trademark for a good produced by a foreign manufacturer with which the domestic company shares a corporate affiliation. This scenario has three variations: a foreign company that has an incorporated subsidiary in the United States which distributes its product domestically (case 2a); a domestic company that incorporates a subsidiary manufacturing company abroad and then imports its goods (case 2b); or a domestic company that establishes an unincorporated manufacturing division abroad and then imports the foreign manufactured product into the United States (case 2c). The case 3 scenario involves a domestic trademark holder that authorizes an independent foreign manufacturer to use its trademark.

The opinion of the Court, written by Justice Kennedy, was founded upon different majorities for each of the holdings announced in its separate parts.[5] Significantly, however, that opinion stated the unanimous judgment of the Court regarding application of § 133.21 to the scenario in which a domestic subsidiary is the trademark holder for foreign manufactured goods that are produced by its foreign parent. The Court concluded that the term "owned by," as it appears in § 526, "is sufficiently ambiguous, in the context of the statute, that it applies to situations involving a foreign parent, which is case 2a." The Court noted further that "[t]his ambiguity arises from the inability to discern, from the statutory language, which of the two entities involved in case 2a can be said to 'own' the U.S. trademark if, as in some instances, the domestic subsidiary is wholly owned by its foreign parent."

The case before us most closely resembles the case 2(a) scenario. Weil is the wholly owned subsidiary of the foreign manufacturer and, consistent with the Supreme Court's decision regarding that scenario, we are persuaded that § 133.21 excludes the goods imported by Jalyn from § 526's prohibition of parallel imports.

---

5. In part I of Justice Kennedy's opinion, in which Chief Justice Rehnquist and Justices White, Blackmun, O'Connor and Scalia joined, the Court held that "the common-control exception of the Customs Service Regulation, 19 C.F.R. § 133.21(c)(1)–(2) (1987), is consistent with § 526." *K Mart,* 108 S.Ct. at 1817. That holding was concurred with in an opinion by Justice Brennan in which Justices Marshall and Stevens joined.

Significantly, a separate majority of the Court concluded that subsection (c)(3) of the regulation, which precluded the domestic trademark holder from prohibiting the importation of goods made by an *independent* foreign manufacturer whom the do-

mestic markholder has authorized to use the trademark, could not stand. As to that scenario (case 3), the Court concluded that

> [u]nder no reasonable construction of the statutory language can goods made in a foreign country by an *independent* foreign manufacturer be removed from the purview of the statute.

K Mart, 108 S.Ct. at 1818–19 (emphasis added). In this holding, as in the Court's holding as to the case 1 and case 2 scenarios (and, in our view, *Katzel*) the court relied upon the corporate relationship between the domestic markholder and the foreign manufacturer in the determination of the appropriate trademark protection.

Weil argues that *K Mart* does not preclude it from protection against parallel importation by § 526 because Weil has demonstrated factually that it is the *independent* owner of the United States LLADRO trademark even though Weil is not independent of the foreign manufacturer, Lladro, S.A. It reads *K Mart* as affirming only the application of § 133.21 to instances of sham incorporation, in which a foreign manufacturer incorporates a shell domestic corporation so that it can control the distribution of its product in the United States without competition. Weil contends, essentially, that § 133.21 is properly viewed as a presumption against the extension of § 526 to goods imported in the 2(a) circumstance, but that that presumption should not be irrebuttable. Accordingly, it asserts that since it can demonstrate factually that it was not a sham incorporation by Lladro, S.A., and that it independently owns the LLADRO trademark, § 133.21 should not operate to preclude the application of § 526.

Although Weil is not a subsidiary that was incorporated by its parent, its affiliation with Lladro, S.A. enables it nonetheless to enjoy every benefit that inheres in the corporate relationship that the Supreme Court described in the case 2(a) scenario. More significantly, that relationship also provides the opportunity for the foreign manufacturer's control of the United States market—under the auspices of the trademark act—that § 133.21 intended to preclude. Thus, although Weil was not a "sham" incorporated by Lladro with the specific intent to benefit from the protections of the trademark act, its present relationship with Lladro nonetheless presents the potential for undesired monopoly of the domestic market and warrants application of § 133.21. Moreover, we note that the Court did not limit its holding in *K Mart* to the decision that § 133.21 is a reasonable construction of § 526 only so far as that regulation provides a "presumption" of ownership in the trademark. We read § 133.21 as providing an *absolute* exception from § 526 for the import of parallel goods in the case 2a scenario and we read *K Mart* as upholding that construction.

III. *Sections 42 and 32*

Weil argues that even if § 526 does not bar importation by Jalyn of the LLADRO porcelain, § 42—which was not specifically addressed in *K Mart*—does. Moreover, Weil contends that nothing in *K Mart* precludes its recovery of damages for infringement under § 32 for Jalyn's distribution of the LLADRO porcelain in the United States. We are persuaded, however, because of the relationship that Weil has with Lladro, S.A., that the protections afforded by §§ 42 and 32 of the Lanham Act are also inapplicable.

Weil's argument on this point has two components: first, it asserts that it owns the United States LLADRO trademark independently of its foreign parent and, pursuant to the territoriality theory attributed to *Katzel*, it is entitled to the full measure of trademark protection provided by the Lanham Act. In that light, Weil contends that § 42's preclusion of goods that "copy or simulate" a trademark and that § 32's preclusion of marks that "imitate" a registered trademark are applicable—notwithstanding the fact that the goods are genuine and bear the trademark of the manufacturer—because Jalyn's importation of LLADRO porcelain into the United States, without Weil's permission, represents a "copying" of the registered United States trademark.

a. The "territoriality" theory

Weil's argument relies in large measure upon a theoretical concept of trademark law, attributed to the Supreme Court's decision in *Katzel,* that is the subject of significant debate in the courts. That theory is also the subject of significant discussion among the commentators. As we discussed above, that theory recognizes the separate existence of a trademark in each territory in which it has been registered. In the present case, the district court was persuaded that the theory should be available to Weil in the circumstances of this case. We do not agree.

In reaching its decision, the district court relied significantly upon the rationale of the Supreme Court's decision in *Katzel.* That case also concerned the import of genuine goods without the consent of the holder of a valid United States trademark. It involved a United States company, Bourjois, that purchased all of the United States business, the goodwill and rights to the United States trademark in "Java" face powder from the French manufacturer. Bourjois was completely independent of the French company, and its purchase of the rights to the United States trademark in the face powder was made at significant expense. A competitor of Bourjois was able to purchase the face powder abroad, import it into the United States and market it here under the French trademark in competition with Bourjois. The Supreme Court, reversing the decision of the Court of Appeals for the Second Circuit, held that the import of the competing goods infringed the domestic trademark holder's rights.

The Court noted that the French manufacturer would violate its assignment agreement if it marketed the product in the United States itself and similarly, it could not usurp that agreement by benefitting from the sale abroad to Bourjois's United States competitor.

That case, however, does not present the same scenario as the present case. First, and perhaps most significantly, Bourjois was completely independent from the foreign manufacturer. It entered into an arms-length exchange to acquire the rights to the trademark with the clear intent that the foreign manufacturer would not market the trademarked good in the United States. Moreover, Bourjois obtained control over the quality of the product and, presumably, could have improved the quality of the product that it marketed in the United States while retaining use of the trademark. It had no control over the goods that the foreign manufacturer sold abroad which were imported into the United States and sold with the same trademark.

In the present case, no such compelling circumstances exist. Weil is not independent of the foreign manufacturer. Although it was not incorporated by Lladro, S.A., it nonetheless benefits from the corporate relationship that exists. Thus, even if Weil loses some share of its United States market to Jalyn, it nonetheless benefits from the profits it received as part of the corporate entity from which Jalyn purchased the goods abroad. Moreover, if that corporate entity decides that the profit margin from the sale of the goods to Jalyn abroad is not as significant as would be the profit margin from a United States market in which Jalyn did not compete, it has an obvious self-help mechanism: it can cease the sale to Jalyn abroad and thereby eliminate effectively its United States competition with Weil. We do not read the Lanham Act, however, to protect a foreign manufacturer—that either owns or is owned by a domestic trademark holder—from competition in the sale of its product in the United States by a domestic importer that it has supplied. Moreover, the LLADRO porcelain that Jalyn imports is *identical* to the porcelain that Weil distributes. Weil has made no contention that, pursuant to its agreement with Lladro, S.A., Weil is entitled to, and does in fact, alter the quality of the porcelain that it distributes in the United States.

In our view, the Court's conclusion in *Katzel* does not represent the establishment of a broad "territoriality theory" applicable to every instance in which a domestic company acquires the United States trademark for a foreign manufactured good. We read that decision as creating an exception to the general application of trademark law in order to protect adequately the interests of domestic trademark holders such as Bourjois.

Our conclusion is consonant with both *K Mart* and *Katzel*, and illustrates the synthesis between those Supreme Court decisions. If placed within the context of the scenarios identified by the Court in *K Mart*, *Katzel* would be described as case 1. *K Mart* clearly held that § 526 was intended to protect domestic trademark holders in that type of case and, indeed, § 526 was enacted specifically to counter the decision of the Court of Appeals for the Second Circuit in *Katzel* which had reached the opposite result. In our view, *Katzel* was intended specifically to reach the case 1 scenario and extend trademark act protection to domestic trademark holders that are truly independent of the foreign manufacturer. We do not read *Katzel* to extend beyond that circumstance. Indeed, in his explication of *Katzel* in *K Mart*, Justice Brennan noted that Bourjois, the domestic trademark holder in *Katzel*, was "the prototypical (case 1) gray-market victim, [that had] purchased its trademark rights, at arms length and at a substantial cost, from an unaffiliated foreign producer." *K Mart*, 108 S.Ct. at 1822 (Brennan, J. concurring). Justice Brennan stated that it was on the basis of those facts that the Supreme Court extended the trademark act protections to Bourjois. He noted, however, that

> the gray-market encroachment on the Java market *would have been considerably less troubling had Bourjois had control over the foreign manufacturer's import conduct or over its sales abroad to third parties who might import;* it would essentially have been seeking to protect itself from its own competition.

Id. (emphasis added). Justice Brennan concluded that the reasons that compelled application of § 526 to the case 1 instance (i.e. that the independent domestic trademark holder, unlike the affiliated holder, stands to lose the full benefit of its investment as the result of gray-market interference and it has no control over the importation of the competing goods *or* the sale to third parties abroad), do not apply to the case 2 instance. See *id.* at 1823. In his view,

> [t]hese differences furnish perfectly rational reasons that Congress might have intended to distinguish between a domestic firm that purchases trademark rights from an independent foreign firm and one that either acquires identical rights from an affiliated foreign firm or develops identical rights and permits a manufacturing subsidiary or division to use them abroad.

Id. In that light, Justice Brennan perceived no basis for the conclusion that § 526 was intended to reach the case 2 circumstance. In our view, Justice Brennan's opinion also demonstrates that *Katzel* was not intended to extend the provisions of § 42 or § 32 to the case 2 instance.

The view that we express today is shared by the Court of Appeals for the Ninth Circuit, which noted in *NEC Electronics* that the rationales supporting the Supreme Court's decision in *Katzel* "presuppose the American owner's real independence from the foreign manufacturer, and courts interpreting *Katzel* have repeatedly emphasized this factor." *NEC Electronics,* 810 F.2d at 1509. The appellate court noted further that "[w]here the American trademark owner is a wholly-owned and controlled subsidiary of the foreign manufacturer, neither of the *Katzel* rationales applies." *Id.* at 1510.

b. Goods that "copy," "simulate," "counterfeit," or "imitate"

Having concluded that *Katzel* did not create a broad territoriality principle that is applicable to every instance of parallel imports, we can more easily resolve the remainder of Weil's argument regarding § 42 and § 32. Essentially, Weil argues that our reading of § 42's prohibition of goods that "copy or simulate" a United States trademark, and of § 32's similar proscription of the commercial distribution of goods that "counterfeit" or "imitate" a valid United States trademark, should be informed by the principle attributed to *Katzel.* Accordingly, it argues, Weil's registration of the LLADRO trademark in the United States should be viewed as having created a trademark in the United States that is distinct from any other mark (even the identical mark placed by the same manufacturer) and that that mark should be accorded the full measure of United States trademark law. Weil contends, therefore, that its trademark is "copied" by *any* unauthorized use. In that light, Weil argues that, notwithstanding the fact that the porcelain imported by Jalyn is genuine and that the marks affixed to the porcelain are placed by the manufacturer just as the marks affixed to the porcelain sold by Weil, the porcelain that Jalyn imports "copies" Weil's trademark.

Because of our conclusion that nothing in *Katzel* extends the trademark act protections to the circumstances of this case, we need not attempt the strained interpretation of the language of § 42 or § 32 that Weil advocates. Our inquiry is only to discern the plain meaning of the language of those sections and, on that review, we do not reach the conclusion urged by Weil.

As the starting point for our analysis, we must ascertain the appropriate definition to be given to the terms employed by § 42 and § 32 of the Lanham Act. In pertinent part § 42 provides that

> no article of imported merchandise . . . which shall copy or simulate a trademark registered in accordance with the provisions of this chapter . . . shall be admitted to entry at any custom house of the United States.

15 U.S.C. § 1124 (1982). Section 32(1)(a) provides that

> (1) [a]ny person who shall, without the consent of the registrant—
>
> (a) use in commerce any reproduction, counterfeit, copy, or colorable imitation of a registered mark in connection with the sale, offering for sale, distribution, or advertising of any goods or services on or in connection with which such use is likely to cause confusion, or to cause a mistake or to deceive; . . . shall be liable in a civil action by the registrant for the remedies hereinafter provided

15 U.S.C. § 1114(1)(a) (1982). Weil urges that § 42 is applicable to provide injunctive relief against importation even if § 526 does not and that § 32 is applicable to make damages available, and to provide injunctive relief against distribution, even if neither § 526 or § 42 bar importation. It contends that "the words 'copy or simulate' are neutral terms and are only directed to the physical and visual similarity between the registered mark and the mark on the imported product." Supplemental Brief of Appellee (Dec. 5, 1988) at 2. Consequently, it argues, "[w]hether or not the act of importation is a violation of § 42 depends on whether the importation is *with* or *without* the consent of the registrant." Id. We can perceive of no basis, either in the specific language of the statute or in its underlying intent that supports such a reading.

In this inquiry of statutory construction, we are assisted again by the Supreme Court's decision in *K Mart* which noted that "[i]n ascertaining the plain meaning of [a] statute, the court must look to the particular statutory language at issue, as well as [to] the language and design of the statute as a whole." *K Mart*, 108 S.Ct. at 1817. In the light of these precedents, we look first to the plain language of the statute, which do we do not find to be ambiguous. In our view, the language of these sections reflects Congress' intent to provide a remedy only to the domestic trademark holder who is injured by the distribution of *like* goods, which bear facsimile marks, that result in confusion to consumers or detriment to the goodwill developed by the trademark holder in the trademarked goods. "Trademark law generally does not reach the sale of *genuine* goods bearing a true mark even though such sale is without the owner's consent." *NEC Electronics,* 810 F.2d at 1509.

The terms "copy," "simulate," "counterfeit" and "imitate" have readily comprehensible ordinary meanings. They are used commonly to refer to items that resemble, but are not themselves, the original or genuine artifacts. We are convinced that the Congress understood this commonly held meaning of these terms and intended to apply them literally in §§ 42 and 32. We are, therefore, unpersuaded that those sections are properly applied to the present case.

Our analysis of the "design of the statute as a whole" compels us even more to the conclusion that we have reached. The stated intent of the trademark act is

> to regulate commerce within the control of Congress by making actionable the deceptive and misleading use of marks in such commerce; to protect registered marks used in such commerce from interference by State, or territorial legislation; to protect persons engaged in such commerce against unfair competition; to prevent fraud and deception in such commerce by the use of reproductions, copies, counterfeits, or colorable imitations of registered marks; and to provide rights and remedies stipulated by treaties and conventions respecting trademarks, trade names, and unfair competition entered into between the United States and foreign nations.

15 U.S.C. § 1127 (1982). From this statement of purpose, we discern two broad policy goals that Congress sought to foster by this legislation: (1) protection against consumer deception (i.e. purchase of a good that is not what the consumer intended to purchase, but because of packaging or other deceptive imitation of the trademark appears to be the genuine trademarked good); (2) protection of the trademark holder's investment in goodwill and noteworthiness that has been generated by the holder's advertisements and quality from imitative goods over which the trademark holder has no control of quality. Sections 42 and 32 advance these policy goals but neither of the goals is undermined by the importation of genuine goods as in this case. Consumers who purchase Jalyn imported LLADRO porcelain get precisely what they believed that they were purchasing. For that same reason, Weil's investment in and sponsorship of its trademark is not adversely affected because the goodwill that stands behind its product is not diminished by an association with goods of a lesser quality.

The only "injury" that we perceive Weil endures is the uncompensated for benefit that its advertisement and promotion of the trademark confers upon Jalyn. That loss to Weil is not inconsequential or insignificant. The remedy for it, however, is not properly found in the trademark law, particularly not in this case. Moreover, as we noted earlier, that "injury" is not completely uncompensated because Weil's parent corporation profits by the sale of Jalyn abroad.

It is more than likely that the framers of the trademark act did not contemplate the instance in which the "source" of a trademarked good would be different from its place of manufacture. The primary concern was to protect consumers and trademark holders from spurious imitations. In *Katzel,* the Court recognized that a broader measure of protection was necessary because of the difference in "source" between the trademark holder and the manufacturer in instances in which a foreign manufacturer sells its rights in the United States trademark to a domestic company. The Court, therefore, reasonably extended the trademark protections to that circumstance. In this case, however, for all intents and purposes, the trademark holder and the manufacturer are the same and there is no reason that compels us to read anything in the language of the act and extend further the protections of the trademark act to this circumstance. . . .

V. *Conclusion*

In light of the foregoing, we will reverse the decision of the district court granting summary judgment in favor of Weil on its claims that § 42 and § 526 are correctly employed to enjoin Jalyn's importation of LLADRO porcelain. We will also reverse the decision of the district court granting summary judgment on behalf of Weil on its claim that § 32 provides damages for infringement for Jalyn's distribution of the porcelain. Finally, we conclude that the district court erred by its dismissal of Weil's claim on § 33(b), but notwithstanding that error, summary judgment in favor of Jalyn is appropriate. Accordingly, we will vacate the district court's judgment as to that claim, and remand with instructions that the district court enter summary judgment on behalf of Jalyn.

All parties to this appeal will bear their own costs.

[The opinion of BECKER, J. concurring is omitted.]

BIBLIOGRAPHIC NOTE

See generally, Davis, Applying Grecian Formula to International Trade: *K–Mart Corp. v. Cartier, Inc.* and the Legality of Gray Market Imports, 75 Va.L.Rev. 1397 (1989); Liebeler, Trademark Law, Economics and Grey–Market Policy, 62 Ind.L.J. 753 (1987); Palladino, Gray Market Goods: The United States Trademark Owners' View, 79 Trademark Rep. 158 (1989); Smart, Squaring the Gray Goods Circle, 10 Cardozo L.Rev. 1963 (1989); Steiner & Sabath, Intellectual Property and Trade Law Approaches to Gray Market Importation, And the Restructuring of Transnational Entities to Permit Blockage of Gray Goods in the United States, 15 Wm. Mitchell L.Rev. 433 (1989).

INDEX

References are to pages